CHI•98

HUMAN FACTORS IN COMPUTING SYSTEMS

CHI 98 CONFERENCE PROCEEDINGS

EDITORS

Clare-Marie Karat, Conference and Technical Program Co-Chair

Arnold Lund, Conference and Technical Program Co-Chair

Joëlle Coutaz, Papers Co-Chair

John Karat, Papers Co-Chair

ASSOCIATE EDITOR

Steven Pemberton

CONFERENCE ON HUMAN FACTORS IN COMPUTING SYSTEMS

Sponsored by ACM's Special Interest Group on Computer-Human Interaction

(ACM SIGCHI)

The Association for Computing Machinery, Inc.
1515 Broadway
New York, NY 10036

...In proceedings of the CHI 98, ACM, New York, 1997 pp. 23-35.
1998 (Los Angeles, CA, USA, April 18-23)

Ordering Information
Nonmembers
Nonmember orders placed within the U.S. should be directed to:

Addison-Wesley Publishing Company
Order Department
Jacob Way
Reading, MA 01867
Tel: +1 800 447 2226

Addison-Wesley will pay postage and handling on orders accompanied by check. Credit card orders may be placed by mail or by calling the Addison-Wesley Order Department at the number above. Follow-up inquiries should be directed to the Customer Service Department at the same number. Please include the Addison-Wesley ISBN number with your order:

A-W ISBN 0-201-30987-4

Nonmember orders from outside the U.S. should be addressed as noted below:

Europe/Middle East

Addison-Wesley Publishing Group
Concertgebouwplein 25
1071 LM Amsterdam
The Netherlands
Tel: +31 20 6717296
Fax: +31 20 6645334

Germany/Austria/Switzerland

Addison-Wesley Verlag Deutschland GmbH
Hildachstrasse 15d
Wachsbleiche 7-12
53111 Bonn
Germany
Tel: +49 228 98 515 0
Fax: +49 228 98 515 99

UK/Ireland/Africa

Addison Wesley Longman Ltd.
Edinburgh Gate
Harlow, Essex CM20 2JE
United Kingdom
Tel: +44 1279 623623
Fax: +44 1279 431059

Asia

Addison-Wesley Singapore Pte. Ltd.
No. 11 Cantonment Road
Singapore 089736
Tel: +65 223 8155
Fax: +65 223 7155

Japan

Addison-Wesley Publishers Japan Ltd.
Nichibo Building
1-2-2 Sarugakucho
Chiyoda-ku, Tokyo 101
Japan
Tel: +81 33 291 4581
Fax: +81 33 291 4592

Australia

Addison Wesley Longman Australia Pty. Ltd.
95 Coventry Street
South Melbourne, VIC 3205
Australia
Tel: +61 3 9697 0666
Fax: +61 3 9699 2041

New Zealand

Additon Wesley Longman
New Zealand Ltd.
46 Hillside Road
Glenfield
Auckland 10
New Zealand
Tel: +64 9 444 4069
Fax: +64 9 444 4957

Latin America

Addison-Wesley Iberoamericana S.A.
Boulevard de las Cataratas #3
Colonia Jardines del Pedregal
Delegacion Alvaro Obregon
01900 Mexico D. F.
Tel: +52 5 660 2695
Fax: +52 5 660 4930

Canada

Addison-Wesley Publishing (Canada) Ltd.
26 Prince Andrew Place
Don Mills, Ontario M3C 2T8
Canada
Tel: +416 447 5101
Fax: +416 443 0948

ACM Members
A limited number of copies are available at the ACM member discount. Send order with payment in US dollars

ACM Order Department
P.O. Box 12114
Church Street Station
New York, N.Y. 10257

OR

ACM European Service Center
108 Cowley Rd. Oxford
OX4/JF, UK
Tel: +44 1865 382338
Fax: +44 1865 381338
email:acm_europe@acm.org

Credit card orders from U.S.A. and Canada:
+1 800 342 6626

New York Metropolitan Area and outside of the U.S.:
+1 212 626 0500
Fax +1 212 944 1318

Email:orders@acm.org

Please include your ACM member number and the ACM Order number with your order.

ACM Order Number: 608981
ACM ISBN: 0-89791-975-0

welcome

FROM THE ACM SIGCHI CHAIR AND EXECUTIVE VICE-CHAIR

Welcome to CHI 98! CHI is the premier event for the people in the field of HCI. Many notable events have taken place at past CHI conferences and this year is no exception.

The CHI conference, sponsored by ACM's Special Interest Group on Computer-Human Interaction (SIGCHI), is an ideal forum for people to meet, both formally and informally, to exchange views, to share experiences and to learn. This conference is also an excellent opportunity to explore taking a more active role in SIGCHI activities. You can do this by stopping by the ACM Booth or by attending the SIGCHI Business Meeting at the conference.

SIGCHI is comprised of an international group of researchers, practitioners and others in industry who share an interest in the many facets of HCI. SIGCHI is committed both to advancing the field of HCI and to exchanging information within the SIGCHI community.

While the CHI conference is the most visible activity of SIGCHI, we also support conferences in computer-supported cooperative work (CSCW), virtual reality software and technology (VRST), user interface software and technology (UIST), design of interactive systems (DIS) and intelligent user interfaces (IUI).

SIGCHI also distributes the highly-respected quarterly *SIGCHI Bulletin* to members and others interested in the discipline of human-computer interaction. In addition, SIGCHI supports two new publications—*Transactions on Computer-Human Interactions* (*TOCHI*), a member of the ACM Transactions series, and *interactions*, ACM's first magazine devoted to HCI practitioners.

The SIGCHI Development Fund supports many activities proposed by our members and Calls for Proposals appear frequently in the *SIGCHI Bulletin* and on the SIGCHI Web site.

Finally, on behalf of ACM SIGCHI, we thank and congratulate the conference committee and all of the volunteers who make this conference possible and who ensure a valuable experience for each of us.

Thanks to the entire CHI 98 committee for a job well done!

MIKE ATWOOD, SIGCHI CHAIR • GUY BOY, SIGCHI EXECUTIVE VICE-CHAIR

welcome

FROM THE CONFERENCE CO-CHAIRS

MAKING THE IMPOSSIBLE POSSIBLE

At CHI 98, we offer a multifaceted forum for the advancement, transfer and sharing of human-computer interaction (HCI) knowledge that can be used to improve the quality of life. We welcome you to a multidisciplinary group of people exploring advances in HCI, tackling current real-world challenges and creating the foundation for a promising future. Let's clarify where HCI has evolved, understand more about the context of HCI work and solutions and provide a forum for theory and processes that may be applied to solve real-world challenges. Let's focus on the seemingly impossible challenges facing our communities, and create breakthroughs by channeling the expertise of the people working in these domain areas with the HCI and technology expertise from the SIGCHI community.

The CHI conferences are known for leading-edge programs of Demonstrations, Exhibits, Late-Breaking Results, Panels, Papers, SIGs, Tutorials, Videos, Workshops and much more! This year is no exception, and the conference will build on the strength of the past and explore new innovations as well. All this occurs in the midst of the most important part of the conference, the great group of people who come to hear and discuss current issues with each other!

There are many application domains and solutions that CHI 98 is highlighting; the education, entertainment and health care application domains have been selected for special focus. Since these areas touch all of our lives, they are expected to generate significant general interest for the HCI community. We are providing the opportunity to enhance the growth of core multidisciplinary groups of individuals communicating and collaborating with each other on new projects and application solutions in a wide variety of domain areas.

At CHI 98 researchers, practitioners and educators, students and professionals; from academia, industry, government, health care and the arts; people who have never attended CHI before, and returning CHI attendees; from all over the world, will come and meet each other, participate in the variety of events at CHI, and begin new collaborations.

Welcome to CHI 98!

CLARE-MARIE KARAT AND ARNOLD LUND, CONFERENCE CO-CHAIRS

Special Thanks

CHI depends heavily on the efforts of volunteers, and would not be possible without the contribution made by the conference committee. We would like to thank them, and the following organizations whose support has made their participation possible:

AT&T Consumer Lab

Belgacom

Carnegie Mellon University

CLIPC - IMAG

DePaul University

Dray and Associates

Florida International University

Fraunhofer IAO

George Mason University

GMD

Hawthorne Elementary School

IBM T. J. Watson Research Center

KPN Research

Loughborough University of Technology

LSUMC

Microsoft Research

National Physical Laboratory

New Media Centers

Pacific Bell

Shizuoka University

Sun Microsystems

Swedish Institute of Computer Science

Université de Paris-Sud

University of Colorado

University of Maryland

University of Sunderland

University of Technology - UTS

University of Twente

U S WEST Advanced Technologies

Vrije Universiteit

Washington University School of Medicine

Sponsor Program

CHI 98 would like to gratefully acknowledge its sponsor program participants. It is the generosity of those organizations that enable the conference to provide technical content and operational services that otherwise might not have been possible.

CHI 98 Champion Sponsors

NOKIA
CONNECTING PEOPLE

CHI 98 Contributing Sponsors

Bellcore

ORACLE

Rent-a-Computer

TRILOGY

CHI 98 thanks Adobe, Hewlett Packard, Intel, KiddieCorp, Microsoft, Morgan Kaufmann, Rent-a-Computer and User Interface Engineering for their support of CHIkids.

CHI 98 is sponsored by the ACM Special Interest Group on Computer-Human Interaction (ACM SIGCHI).

Cooperating Societies

ACM/SIGDOC

ACM/SIGGRAPH

ACM/SIGGROUP

ACM/SIGLINK

Austrian Computer Society (OCG)

British HCI Group, B-HCI-G(BCS)

CHISIG New Zealand

Dutch Computer Society (NGI), HCI Special Interest Group

Eurographics

European Association of Cognitive Ergonomics (EACE)

German Society for Informatics (GI), Fachausschuss 2.3

Hong Kong Chapter of ACM

Human Communication Group [HCG] of the IEICE of Japan

Human Factors and Ergonomics Society

IPSJ (Information Processing Society of Japan), SIGGroupware

International Artificial Intelligence in Education Society (AIED)

Italian Association for Artificial Intelligence (AIIA)

Italian Computer Society (AICA)

Italian Ergonomics Society (SIE)

Swedish Interdisciplinary Interest Group for Human-Computer Interaction (STIMDI)

Swiss Society for Informatics (SGI), Fachgruppe Software Ergonomie

With changing technology we have made every effort to include special characters in volunteer listings. We apologize in advance for any omission and we will work to correct this for future CHI proceedings.

Management Team

Conference and Technical Program Co-Chairs
Clare-Marie Karat
IBM T. J. Watson Research Center
Arnold Lund
U S WEST Advanced Technologies

SIGCHI CMC Liaison
Gerrit C. van der Veer
Vrije Universiteit

ACM Liaison
David S. Riederman, CAE
ACM SIGCHI Program Director

Conference Management
Paul Henning
Conference & Logistics Consultants, Inc.

Technical Program

CHIkids Co-Chairs
Angela Boltman
Hawthorne Elementary School
Allison Druin
University of Maryland, College Park
Mark Platt
LSUMC

Demonstrations Co-Chairs
Eric Bergman
Sun Microsystems
Nancy Frishberg
New Media Centers

Design Briefings Co-Chairs
Mary Czerwinski
Microsoft Research
Bob Schumacher
Belgacom

Development Consortium Co-Chairs
Allison Druin
University of Maryland, College Park
Angela Boltman
Hawthorne Elementary School
Jürgen Koenenmann
GMD

Doctoral Consortium Co-Chairs
Deborah Boehm-Davis
George Mason University
Clayton Lewis
University of Colorado

Education Application Domain Chair
Allison Druin
University of Maryland, College Park

Entertainment Application Domain Chair
Francine Arble
AT&T Labs

Health Care Application Domain Chair
Janette Coble
Washington University School of Medicine

Late-Breaking Results and Student Posters Co-Chairs
Nigel Bevan
National Physical Laboratory
Gilbert Cockton
University of Sunderland

Mentoring Liaison
Robin Jeffries
Sun Microsystems

Panels Co-Chairs
Michel Beaudouin-Lafon
Université de Paris-Sud
Catherine Wolf
IBM Research

Technical Papers Co-Chairs
Joëlle Coutaz
CLIPS - IMAG
John Karat
IBM T. J. Watson Research Center

Tutorials Co-Chairs
Julie Jacko
Florida International University
Andrew Sears
DePaul University

Videos Co-Chairs
Benjamin B. Bederson
University of Maryland, College Park
Kristian T. Simsarian
Swedish Institute of Computer Science

Workshops and SIGs Co-Chairs
Susan Dumais
Microsoft Research
Jürgen Ziegler
Fraunhofer IAO

Operations

Americas Regional Liaison
Susan Dray
Dray and Associates

Asia Regional Liaison
Masaaki Kurosu
Shizuoka University

Australia Regional Liaison
Robert Rist
University of Technology

Europe Regional Liaison
Susan Harker
Loughborough University of Technology

Local Lab Tour/Arrangements Liaison
Leila Johannesen
Pacific Bell

Sponsorship Liaison
Jakob Nielsen
Sun Microsystems

Student Volunteers Co-Chairs
Mike Byrne
Carnegie Mellon University
Hans de Graaff
KPN Research

Technical Liaisons
David Hamilton
IBM Santa Teresa Laboratory
Marilyn Salzman
George Mason University

Professional Staff

Conference Administration/ Conference Logistics
Borysa O. Struk
Mike Yancy
Conference & Logistics Consultants, Inc.

Graphic Design
Mo Viele
Mo Viele, Inc.

Online Communications
Keith Instone
Usable Web

Publications Coordination & Exhibit Promotion
Debbie Hall
Meeting Hall, Inc.

Publicity
Rosemary Wick Stevens
Ace Public Relations

Registration
Carole Mann
Registration Systems Lab

Sponsorship Support
Carol Klyver
Foundations of Excellence

Papers Committees

Executive Associate Chair
Wendy A. Kellogg
IBM T. J. Watson Research Center

Associate Chairs for Papers
Francine Arble
AT&T Labs
Rachel Bellamy
Apple Computer
Victoria Bellotti
Apple Computer
Sara A. Bly
Consultant
Tom Carey
University of Waterloo
John M. Carroll
Virginia Polytechnic Institute and State University
Janette Coble
Washington University School of Medicine
Mary Czerwinski
Microsoft Research
Allison Druin
University of Maryland, College Park
D. A. Duce
Rutherford Appleton Laboratory
Tom Erickson
IBM T. J. Watson Research Center
Steven Feiner
Columbia University
Saul Greenberg
University of Calgary
Marti Hearst
University of California, Berkeley
Robert J.K. Jacob
Tufts University
Robin Jeffries
Sun Microsystems
Rick Kazman
Carnegie Mellon University
Wendy A. Kellogg
IBM T.J. Watson Research Center
Allan MacLean
Xerox Research Centre Europe
Wendy Mackay
Université de Paris-Sud
Dan R. Olsen Jr.
Carnegie Mellon University
Gary M. Olson
University of Michigan
Sharon Oviatt
Oregon Graduate Institute of Science & Technology
Fabio Paterno'
CNUCE - C.N.R.
Peter G. Polson
University of Colorado
Angel Puerta
Stanford University
George G. Robertson
Microsoft Research
Teresa L. Roberts
Sun Microsystems
Bob Schumacher
Belgacom
John C. Thomas
Bell Atlantic Science and Technology
Steve Whittaker
AT&T Labs—Research
Jürgen E. Ziegler
Fraunhofer Institute IAO

Paper Review Support

Mark Day
Lotus Development
Irene Greif
Lotus Development
Anna Long
IBM T. J. Watson Research
Kenneth Pang
MIT

Application Domain Teams

Education Domain Team

Angela Boltman
Hawthorne Elementary School

Tom Carey
University of Waterloo

Jürgen Koenemann
GMD - German National Research Center for Information Technology

Debra Lieberman
Media Research Consultant

Mark Schlager
SRI International

Elliot Soloway
University of Michigan

Michael Tauber
University of Paderborn

Entertainment Domain Team

William Buxton
University of Toronto

Lynn Cherny
AT&T Labs—Research

Chuck Clanton
Aratar

Bruce Damer
Digital Space

Abbe Don
Abbe Don Interactive

Mary Flanagan
State University of New York, Buffalo

Kevin Keeker
Microsoft

Merryanna Swartz
Magnet Interactive Communications

Anna Wichansky
Oracle

Health Care Domain Team

Richard J. Appleyard
Oregon Health Sciences University

Susan Dray
Dray and Associates

John Gosbee
Michigan State University Kalamazoo Center for Medical Studies

Angel Puerta
Stanford University

Reviewers for Papers

Gregory Abowd
Georgia Institute of Technology

Johnny Accot
Centre d'Études de la Navigation Aérienne

Beth Adelson
Rutgers University

Bengt Ahlstrom
UI Design AB

Motoyuki Akamatsu
National Institute of Bioscience and Human-Technology

Michael Albers
Sun Microsystems - JavaSoft

Robert (Bob) B. Allen
Bellcore

Carl Martin Allwood
Dept of Psychology, Gothenburg University

James Lenton Alty
Loughborough University of Technology

Ben Anderson
BT Laboratories

Kenneth M. Anderson
University of California, Irvine

Keith Andrews
IICM, Graz University of Technology

Mark Apperley
University of Waikato

Albert G. Arnold
Delft University of Technology

Jonathan Arnowitz
Informaat, BV

Michael Atyeo
Nortel

Brent Auernheimer
California State University, Fresno

Flavio Azevedo
UC Berkeley School of Education (EMST)

Maribeth Back
Xerox PARC

Ravin Balakrishnan
University of Toronto & Alias|Wavefront

Sandrine Balbo
CSIRO Mathematical and Information Sciences

J. M. Christian Bastien
Institut National de Recherche en Informatique et en Automatique

Thomas Baudel
Alias|Wavefront

Michel Beaudouin-Lafon
Université de Paris-Sud

Doug Beck
Hewlett-Packard

Karen Bedard
TeleWorld

Mathilde M. Bekker
Queen Mary & Westfield College, University of London

Steve Benford
The University of Nottingham

Olav W Bertelsen
Aarhus University

Ann Blandford
Middlesex University

Jeanette Blomberg
Xerox PARC

Sarah Bloomer
The Hiser Group

Susanne Bodker
Aarhus University

Heinz-Dieter Boecker
German National Research Center for Information Technology

Peter Boersma
General Design

Richard A. Bolt
MIT Media Laboratory

Linda Borghesani
MITRE

James Boritz
University of British Columbia

James H Bradford
Western Illinois University

Jeff Brandenburg
Persimmon IT

Charles Brennan
BT Laboratories

Stephen Brewster
University of Glasgow

Lauren Bricker
University of Washington

Tom Brinck
Diamond Bullet Design

John Brooke
Redhatch Consulting

Barry Brown
University of Surrey

Arnout Bruins
Kenniscentrum CIBIT

Kathy Buckner
Queen Margaret College

Elizabeth Buie
Computer Sciences Corporation

Margaret Burnett
Oregon State University

Catherine Burns
University of Toronto

Robert Burns
Boeing

Mike Byrne
Carnegie Mellon University

Licia Calvi
University of Antwerp (UIA)

Andy Cargile
Personal Health Connections

David A. Carr
Lulea University

George Casaday
IRI Software

Rhona Charron
ISM-BC Telecom Solutions

Chaomei Chen
Brunel University

Lynn Cherny
AT&T Labs—Research

Joan M. Cherry
University of Toronto

Ed H. Chi
University of Minnesota & Xerox PARC

Yee-Yin Choong
GE Information Services

Michael Christel
Carnegie Mellon University

Elizabeth Churchill
FXPAL

William Cockayne
Daimler-Benz Research and Technology

Tom Cocklin
Hewlett-Packard

Gilbert Cockton
University of Sunderland

Maxine Cohen
Nova Southeastern University

Martin Colbert
University College London

Penny Collings
University of Canberra

Alex Conn
Digital Equipment Corporation

Matt Conway
Microsoft

Albert Corbett
CMU

Mauricio Cortes
Bell Labs

Steve Cousins
Xerox PARC

Lynne Coventry
NCR Financial Systems

Lisa Covi
University of Michigan/CREW

Allen Cypher
Stagecast Software

David Darvill
ISM-BC Telecom Solutions

Duco Das
Philips Research/USIT

Jim Davis
Xerox PARC

Donald Day
The University of New South Wales

Nadja De Carolis Berardina
Dipartimento di Informatica - Universita'di Bari

Boris De Ruyter
Philips Research

Michel C. Desmarais
Computer Research Institute of Montreal (CRIM)

Andreas Dieberger
Emory University

Stephanie Doane
University of Illinois

Mike Dooner
University of Hull

Claire Dormann
Center for Tele-Information

Paul Dourish
Xerox Palo Alto Research Center

Laurie Dringus
Nova Southeastern University

Tim Dudley
Nortel Technology

Susan T. Dumais
Microsoft Research

Elizabeth Dykstra-Erickson
Apple Computer

Wolfgang Dzida
GMD

Alistair D N Edwards
University of York

Berry Eggen
Philips Research

Kate Ehrlich
Lotus Development

Paul Eisen
CIBC

Kerstin S. Eklundh
Royal Institute of Technology

Don Elman
Microsoft

George Engelbeck
Boeing

Kathryn Engholm
Tektronix

Stefania Errore
CORINTO - COnsorzio RIcerca Nazionale Tecnologia Oggetti

Stephanie Everett
US Naval Research Laboratory

Michael Ewins
Panasonic OWL

Robert Fein
Intel

Sidney Fels
ATR Media Integration & Communications Research Laboratories

Bob Fields
University of York

Ken Fishkin
Xerox PARC

Robert S. Fish
Panasonic Information and Networking Technologies Laboratory

George Fitzmaurice
Alias/Wavefront

BJ Fogg
Stanford University

James Foley
MERL- A Mitsubishi Electric Research Lab

Peter W. Foltz
New Mexico State University

Peter Forbrig
Universitaet Rostock

William K. Foster
Synopsys

Ian Franklin
Employment Service

Bjorn N. Freeman-Benson
Object Technology International

George W. Furnas
University of Michigan

Deb Galdes
Silicon Graphics

Cyndy Gal

Bjoern Gambaeck
Royal Institute of Technology

Jörg Geißler
GMD-IPSI

Nektarios Georgalas
UMIST

Douglas Gillan
New Mexico State University

Andreas Girgensohn
FX Palo Alto Laboratory

Gene Golovchinsky
FX Palo Alto Laboratory

Louis M. Gomez
Northwestern University

Cleotilde Gonzalez
CMU/UDLA

Narciso Gonzalez

Michael D. Good
SAP Labs

Peter Gorny
University of Oldenburg

Nicholas Graham
Queen's University

Simon Grant
University of Liverpool

Stephan Greene
University of Maryland

Irene Greif
Lotus Development

Doug Griffith
ERIM International

Chris Grounds
Schafer

Steve Guest
Groupworks

Ashok Gupta
Philips Research Labs (U.K.)

Nils-Erik Gustafsson
Ericsson Utvecklings AB

Eben Haber
Silicon Graphics

Hirohide Haga
Doshisha University

Judy Hammond
University of Technology, Sydney

Libby Hanna
Microsoft

Morten Borup Harning
Copenhagen Business School

Beverly Harrison
Xerox PARC

Bradley Hartfield
Hartfield Design Group/Stanford University

H. Rex Hartson
Virginia Tech

Bill Hefley
Carnegie Mellon University

Austin Henderson
Rivendel Consulting

Richard Henneman
NCR Human Interface Technology Center

Scott Henninger
University of Nebraska-Lincoln

James D. Herbsleb
Bell Labs

Harry M. Hersh
Fidelity Investments

William C. Hill
AT&T Labs—Research

Debby Hindus
Interval Research

Stephen Hirtle
University of Pittsburgh

Hans-Jürgen Hoffmann
Darmstadt University of Technology

James D. Hollan
UCSD

Karen Holtzblatt
InContext Enterprises

Seung Hong
Brown University

H. Ulrich Hoppe
University of Duisburg

Steve Howard
Swinburne University of Technology

Teresa Hubscher-Younger
Georgia Institute of Technology

William Hunt
University of Toronto

Kori Inkpen
Simon Fraser University

Hiroshi Ishii
MIT Media Laboratory

Ismail Aras Ismail
University College London

Maddy D. Janse
Philips Research Laboratories - USIT

Pamela Jennings
IBM

Andrew Johnson
Electronic Visualization Laboratory

Jeff Johnson
UI Wizards

Lorraine Johnston
University of Melbourne

Steve Jones
University of Waikato

Anker Helms Jørgensen
Copenhagen University

Joaquim Armando Pires Jorge
INESC

Susanne Jul
University of Michigan

Hussein Kanji
Sun/Stanford

Klaus Kansy
GMD-FIT

Clare-Marie Karat
IBM T. J. Watson Research Center

Demetrios Karis
GTE Laboratories

Cecilia Katzeff
WM-data & SITI/SISU

Judy Kay
University of Sydney

Alan Keahey
Indiana University

Rudolf K. Keller
University of Montreal

Lisa Kimball
Metasystems Design Group

Arthur (Ted) Kirkpatrick
University of Oregon

Muneo Kitajima
National Institute of Bioscience and Human-Technology

Jonathan Klein
MIT Media Laboratory

Jayne Klenner-Moore
King's College & Pennsylvania State University

Jente Klok
KPN Research

Shinichi Konomi
GMD-IPSI

Joseph A. Konstan
University of Minnesota

Panu Korhonen
Nokia Research Center

Philip Kortum
Southwestern Bell Technology Resources

Peter Koss-Nobel
Microsoft

Christopher Koster
Bellcore

Christopher 'Blade' Kotelly
Applied Language Technologies

Larry Koved
IBM T. J. Watson Research Center

Werner Kuhn
University of Muenster

Hideaki Kuzuoka
University of Tsukuba

Mary LaLomia
Intel

Ericca Lahti
Lotus

James Landay
UC Berkeley

Jim Larson
Intel

Sharon Laskowski
NIST

Darryn Lavery
University of Glasgow

David Lees
University of the West of England

Alfred Lee
Beta Research

Adrienne Lee
New Mexico State University

Mark Lee
NCR

John J. Leggett
Texas A&M University

Ying K Leung
Swinburne University of Technology

Laura Leventhal
Bowling Green State University

Vicki Levett
Microsoft

Henry Lieberman
MIT Media Lab

Mark Linton
Vitria Technology

Steven Liu
Hauser

Jerry Lohse
The Wharton School of the University of Pennsylvania

Ben Loh
Northwestern University

Chris Long
UC Berkeley

April Luehmann
University of Michigan

Paul Luff
University of Nottingham

Jay Lundell
Intel

Kipp Lynch
Cambridge Technology Partners

Blair MacIntyre
Columbia University

Jock Mackinlay
Xerox PARC

Robert Mack
IBM Research

Scott D. Mainwaring
Interval Research

David Maltz
Carnegie Mellon University

Andrea Mankoski
Sun Microsystems

Marilyn Mantei-Tremaine
private consultant

Joe Marks
MERL - A Mitsubishi Electric Research Laboratory

Gloria Mark
German National Research Center for Information Technology

Catherine R Marshall
CollabTech

Kevin Martin
Hughes Research Labs

Toshiyuki Masui
Sony Computer Science Laboratory

Kevin A. Mayo
Thomson Technology Consulting Group (TTCG), Online Practice

Marshall R. McClintock
Microsoft

Richard McDaniel
Carnegie Mellon University

Susan McDaniel
University of Michigan

Jean McKendree
University of Edinburgh

William W. McMillan
Eastern Michigan University

Jon Meads
Usability Architects

Hans van der Meij
University of Twente

Shane Melton
Kazan Software

Douglas Merrill
Price Waterhouse

Beth Meyer
Georgia Institute of Technology

Spyros Michaelides
SPIMITECH-ICR & National Technology University of Athens

Allen Milewski
AT&T Labs

Jim Miller
Independent Consultant

Mark L. Miller
Consultant

Anant Kartik Mithal
Sun Microsystems

Tom Moher
University of Illinois at Chicago

Gregor Molan

Jay Moonah
Ryerson Polytechnic University

Youngme Moon
MIT

Thomas P. Moran
Xerox PARC

Anders Mørch
University of Bergen

Paula Moreland
Kazan Software

Osamu Morikawa
National Institute of Bioscience and Human Technology (AIST in M.I.T.I.)

Hirohiko Mori
Musashi Institute of Technology

Sougata Mukherjea
NEC USA

Judie Mulholland
Florida State University

Michael Muller
Microsoft

Robert M. Mulligan
AT&T Labs

Alice Mulvehill
BBN Technologies

Kazunori Muraki
NEC

Dianne Murray
Consultant

Maya Murthy
SUNY at Buffalo

Pardo Mustillo
Nortel

Brad A. Myers
Carnegie Mellon University

Beth Mynatt
Xerox PARC

Manfred Nagl
Aachen University of Technology

Yasushi Nakauchi
National Defense Academy

Frieder Nake
University of Bremen

Jocelyne Nanard
Université de Montpellier

Marc Nanard
Université de Montpellier

Clifford Nass
Stanford University

Alan F. Newell
University of Dundee

William Newman
Xerox Research Centre Europe

Laurence Nigay
CLIPS-IMAG

Alexander Nikov

Erik Nilsen
Lewis & Clark College

Lorraine F. Normore
OCLC

David G. Novick
EURISCO

Kimberly O'Brien
Sun Microsystems

Horst Oberquelle
Hamburg University

Reinhard Oppermann
GMD

Ran Osnat
Enigma Information Systems

Scott P. Overmyer
Drexel University

Nadine Ozkan
CSIRO - CMIS

Philippe Palanque
University of Toulouse

Susan Palmiter
Design Technologies

Tanya Payne
Kazan Software

Elin Ronby Pedersen
FX Palo Alto Laboratory

Rob Pedlow
Telstra Research Laboratories

Kara Pernice Coyne
Lotus Development

Tom Perry
Xerox

Daniela Petrelli
IRST

Helen Petrie
University of Hertfordshire

Richard W. Pew
BBN Technologies

Catherine Plaisant
University of Maryland

Andrea Polli
University of Illinois, Chicago

Steve Portigal
GVO

Kathy Potosnak
Interface Concepts

Manuel A. Pérez-Quiñones
Universidad de Puerto Rico-Mayaguez

Chris Quintana
University of Michigan

Kari-Jouko Räihä
University of Tampere

Roope Raisamo
University of Tampere

Ramana Rao
Inxight Software & Xerox PARC

Elaine M. Raybourn
University of New Mexico

Michael J Rees
Bond University

Mary Beth Rettger
The MathWorks

John T. Richards
IBM T. J. Watson Research Center

Doug Riecken
Bell Labs-Lucent Technologies

Kirsten Risden
Microsoft

Robert Rist
University of Technology

Frank E. Ritter
University of Nottingham

Chris R. Roast
Sheffield Hallam University

Daniel Robbins
Microsoft

Scott Robertson
U S WEST

Penelope Roberts
Telstra Research Laboratories

Elizabeth Rosenzweig
Eastman Kodak

Laurie Roshak
Sun Microsystems (SunSoft)

Peter Rowley
MediaLinx Interactive

Richard Rubinstein
Human Factors International

Daniel Salber
Georgia Institute of Technology & INRIA

Marilyn Coleman Salzman
George Mason University

Alfredo Sanchez
Universidad de las Americas-Puebla

Martina Angela Sasse
University College London

Anthony Savidis
Foundation for Research and Technology - Hellas

Dominique L. Scapin
INRIA

Mark Schlager
SRI International

Egbert Schlungbaum
University Rostock

Franz Schmalhofer
DFKI GmbH

Kevin Schofield
Microsoft

Eric Schuh
Microsoft

Dore'e Duncan Seligmann
Bell Labs

Abigail J. Sellen
Rank Xerox Research Centre

Brian Shackel
HUSAT Research Institute
Loughborough University

Chris Shaw
University of Regina

Donald P. Sheridan
Auckland University

Frank M. Shipman III
Texas A&M University

John L. Sibert
The George Washington University

Linda Sibert
Naval Research Laboratory

Ms Charanjit K. Sidhu
BT Human Factors

Brian Smith
MIT Media Laboratory

Phil Smythe
BT Laboratories

Michael Smyth
Napier University

Jeff Sokolov
GTE Laboratories

Liz Sonenberg
The University of Melbourne

Jared M. Spool
User Interface Engineering

Robert St. Amant
North Carolina State University

Tim Stamper
Sprint

Karl Steiner
Ariel Performance Centered Systems

Constantine Stephanidis
Foundation for Research and Technology-Hellas

Markus Stolze
IBM, Zurich Research Lab

Carol Strohecker
MERL - A Mitsubishi Electric Research Laboratory

Piyawadee Sukaviriya
IBM T. J. Watson Research Center

Joseph W. Sullivan
FX Palo Alto Laboratory

Kent Sullivan
Microsoft

Tamara Sumner
The Open University

Alistair Sutcliffe
City University

Dan Suthers
University of Pittsburgh

Gerd Szwillus
Universitaet - GH Paderborn

Haruo Takemura
Nara Institute of Science and Technology

Yuzuru Tanaka
Hokkaido University

John C. Tang
Sun Microsystems

Masayuki Tani
Hitachi

Ross Teague
Intel

Barbee Teasley
Ameritech

Loren Terveen
AT&T Labs—Research

Linda Tetzlaff
IBM T. J. Watson Research Center

Bruce Thomas
University of South Australia

Jennifer Thomas
Pace University

Richard Thomas
The University of Western Australia

David Thurman
Georgia Institute of Technology

Yoshinobu Tonomura
NTT Human Interface Laboratories

Michael D. Travers
IBM T. J. Watson Research Center

Susan Trickett
George Mason University

Randall Trigg
Xerox PARC

Manfred Tscheligi
University of Vienna

Susan Turner
University of Northumbria at Newcastle

Lisa Tweedie
Imperial College

Claus Unger
University of Hagen

Brian Utesch
Nortel

Bradley T. Vander Zanden
University of Tennessee

Jean Vanderdonckt
Université of Namur

Steven Verjans
Odense Steel Shipyard - Odense University

Robert A. Virzi
GTE Laboratories

Willemien Visser
INRIA

Carl Vogel
University of Dublin

Pawan Vora
U S WEST Communications

Josef Voss
University of Hagen

Colin Ware
University of New Brunswick

Clive P. Warren
British Aerospace, Sowerby Research Centre

Terry L. Webb
DSTO

Anette Weisbecker
Fraunhofer Institute IAO

Louis Weitzman
IBM

Alan Wexelblat
MIT Media Lab

Cathleen Wharton
U S WEST Advanced Technologies

Jackie Wheeler
IBM

Susan Wiedenbeck
University of Nebraska

Mark C. Wilkes
IBM

Marian G. Williams
University of Massachusetts Lowell

Eve Wilson
University of Kent at Canterbury

Michael Wilson
Rutherford Appleton Laboratory

Stephanie Wilson
Queen Mary and Westfield College

Terry Winograd
Stanford University

G. Bowden Wise
Rensselaer Polytechnic Institute

Patricia Wright
Cardiff University of Wales

Volker Wulf
University of Bonn

Ming-Hsuan Yang
University of Illinois at Urbana-Champaign

Nicole Yankelovich
Sun Microsystems Laboratories

Massimo Zancanaro
Istituto per la Ricerca Scientifica e Tecnologica (IRST)

Polle Zellweger
Xerox PARC

Ronald J. Zeno
Zeno and Associates

Shumin Zhai
IBM Almaden Research Center

J. W. van Aalst
Interaction Designer

Gerrit C. van der Veer
Vrije Universiteit

Videos Review Committee

Mark Apperley
University of Waikato

Michel Beaudouin-Lafon
Université de Paris-Sud

Karen Bedard
TeleWorld

Andy Cargile
Personal Health Connections

Ed H. Chi
University of Minnesota and Xerox PARC

William Cockayne
Daimler-Benz Research and Technology

Matt Conway
Microsoft

Elizabeth Dykstra-Erickson
Apple Computer

George Fitzmaurice
Alias|Wavefront

Jörg Geißler
GMD-IPSI

Peter Gorny
University of Oldenburg

Saul Greenberg
University of Calgary

Beverly Harrison
Xerox PARC

Wendy A. Kellogg
IBM T. J. Watson Research Center

Larry Koved
IBM T. J. Watson Research Center

Sharon Laskowski
NIST

Kari-Jouko Räihä
University of Tampere

Linda Tetzlaff
IBM T. J. Watson Research Center

John C. Thomas
Bell Atlantic Science and Technology

Terry Winograd
Stanford University

CHI 98 IS ABOUT MAKING THE IMPOSSIBLE POSSIBLE

We have a particularly exciting technical program this year. Records were set for submissions in almost every program category, and the response from reviewers was almost overwhelming! The result is that the quality of the program is higher than ever. One of our goals is to continue to try new venues for presenting content. In order to make room for new areas, we used your feedback from the last two years to decide which program areas would benefit from a sabbatical. Another goal is to infuse new perspectives about HCI into the program, and we will be very interested in your feedback on how well this works. A third goal is to provide more opportunities for developing the skills that will be needed as the industries supported by our community continue to evolve. Overall, the diversity of the program provides something for everyone. There are opportunities for learning and contributing whether you are a practitioner or a researcher, whether you are in industry or academia, whether you are just entering the field or whether you have been in it for awhile.

The major area of innovation this year is the introduction of an increased emphasis on application domains. For CHI 98, efforts were made to bring in experts in the areas of education, health care and entertainment. You will have the opportunity to hear special speakers over lunch, take tutorials, attend panels and listen to papers in each of these areas. You will hear about the challenges faced in each of these areas that the HCI community can help to address; you will find new ways of thinking about our discipline. As a result, we hope conversations throughout the conference will be stimulating and informative.

The Tutorial Program draws on lessons and requests from the past. For example, there will be several opportunities to develop skills in Web design, and breakthrough courses in developing drawing skills. Many of the tutorials are organized into groups and scheduled such that a set of interrelated skills can be developed over the tutorial program. A great deal of work has gone into continuing to enrich the Demonstrations, Late-Breaking Results, Papers, Panels, Workshops and Video areas of the program. This year, the posters program focuses on Student Posters and opportunities to talk with students about their work. The SIGs provide another wonderful opportunity for meeting with other professionals to exchange ideas about topics of common interest.

The CHIkids program is back for its third exciting year at CHI 98! The CHIkids "computer camp" is an ideal way for children and parents to share in the evolving HCI adventure! The Development Consortium will draw on the CHIkids program to provide unique opportunities for a group of teachers to participate in CHI and exchange ideas about how to introduce and work with technology in the classroom. Students participating as part of the Doctoral Consortium and Student Volunteers at the conference will have a chance to meet speakers informally, share ideas and build upon their knowledge of the field.

A technical program such as CHI 98's would not be possible without the tireless efforts of many volunteers. In particular, we would like to acknowledge the creativity, time, energy and spirit of our Technical Program Area Chairs. We would especially like to recognize their deep commitment to the future of our field. They are wonderful examples of "making the impossible possible!"

CLARE-MARIE KARAT AND ARNOLD LUND, TECHNICAL PROGRAM CO-CHAIRS

NaviPoint: An Input Device for Mobile Information Browsing

Kiyokuni KAWACHIYA and Hiroshi ISHIKAWA
IBM Research, Tokyo Research Laboratory
1623-14, Shimotsuruma,
Yamato, Kanagawa 242-8502, Japan
+81 462 73 4938
kawatiya@trl.ibm.co.jp

ABSTRACT
A mobile computing environment imposes various restrictions on users. For example, most mobile devices have a limited screen size, and it may be difficult to watch the screen closely. While the user is walking or standing in a bus or train, he or she may have only one hand free to manipulate the device. Therefore, some new operation method must be developed for comfortable information browsing in the mobile environment. In this paper, several existing methods are first introduced and compared from the viewpoint of their applicability in a mobile environment. A new input device for such an environment, named "NaviPoint," is then introduced. NaviPoint is a specialized device for mobile information browsing. By using this device, a user can perform three types of input — "analog input," "digital input," and "click input" — with just one finger. After an explanation of the conceptual structure and a qualitative analysis of NaviPoint, the structure of a prototype is described. Experiments using the prototype show that information browsing is possible with an overhead of less than 50% on the usual "mouse and scroll bar" method.

Keywords
Input device, information browsing, user interface, PDAs, hand-held devices, mobile computing

INTRODUCTION
With the evolution of compactization technology and the consolidation of the wireless communication infrastructure, it has become possible to access information through a network even while one is in transit from one place to another. In such an environment, it is considered that simple "information browsing" with no input of characters will become one of the major uses of mobile information devices. One typical example is access to hypermedia information such as the WWW. However, a mobile computing environment imposes various restrictions on users, and some new method of operation must be developed for comfortable information browsing. For example, a mouse cannot be used without a desk, and a pen, while of course indispensable for inputting characters, requires both hands even for simple browsing.

CHI 98 Los Angeles CA USA
Copyright 1998 0-89791-975-0/98/ 4..$5.00

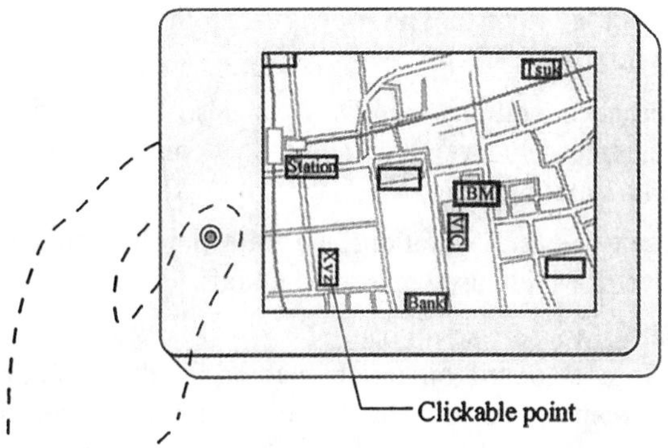

Figure 1. Example of mobile information browsing

This paper reports a new input device named "NaviPoint" that solves these problems and allows mobile information browsing with just one finger. The next section first introduces several existing operation methods for information browsing and describes the problems involved in applying them to a mobile environment. A new input device called NaviPoint that solves the problems is then introduced, and its basic mechanism is described. Next, the structure of a prototype is explained and its performance is evaluated. After a discussion of related work, the last section offers some conclusions and outlines future work.

INFORMATION BROWSING IN A MOBILE ENVIRONMENT
"Mobile information browsing" is becoming a major use of small mobile information devices such as PDAs [5]. One of the most general types of accessed information is "hypermedia information," which contains "clickable (selectable) points" that link it to other information. Figure 1 shows an example of such hypermedia browsing in a mobile environment. Part of a large map containing several clickable points is displayed. When one of these points is clicked, corresponding new information is displayed.

In recent years, as a result of the spread of the WWW, hypermedia browsing has become very popular in a desktop environment. However in a mobile environment, there are several restrictions. For example, most mobile devices have a limited screen size, and it may be difficult to watch the screen closely. The user may have only one hand free to manipulate the device. Comfortable information browsing requires some new operation method that includes an input device.[1]

Existing Operation Methods

Two fundamental operations for information browsing (hypermedia browsing) are "scrolling" and "pointing" [21]. The scrolling operation is necessary to browse information that lies outside the screen, and the pointing operation is necessary to select a clickable point on the screen. In most information browsing, the following two operations are performed repeatedly:

1. Browse the document by using the "scrolling" operation.
2. Select a clickable point by using the "pointing" operation.

Menu-based operations on PDAs can also be classified into the same category as scrolling and pointing if they require no input operation.

For these two basic operations, the following list summarizes several widely used existing methods.[2]

Method A. Mouse + scroll bars

This is a standard operation method in the desktop environment. An arrow-shaped pointer (mouse pointer) is displayed on the screen. A scrolling operation is performed by dragging the slider of a scroll bar at the side of the screen (or window). A pointing operation is performed by moving the pointer to a clickable point and clicking.

Method A'. Trackball + scroll bars

This operation method is generally used on notebook PCs. The basic scrolling and pointing methods are the same as in method A, except that a trackball (with an attached switch) is used instead of a mouse as an input device. There is another variation in which an analog input stick at the center of a keyboard is used instead of a trackball.

Method B. Pen + sheet-picking

This operation method is used with most PDAs. A scrolling operation is performed by "picking" the document itself with a pen and dragging. A pointing operation is performed by directly pointing to (tapping) a clickable point in the screen.

Method C. Cursor keys + highlighting

This operation method is mainly used with smaller mobile devices that are not equipped with a pen. One of the clickable points in the screen is "highlighted." A pointing operation is performed by moving the highlight to the target item by using up/down/left/right keys and pushing an execute key. Scrolling is performed implicitly according to this highlight movement, or by using a specially provided operation mode or keys.

[1] Of course, there are also various system-level problems such as how to utilize low network bandwidth or small memory capacity efficiently [12, 13], but these are beyond the scope of this paper.

[2] The four listed operation methods are typical examples. In addition, there are some combined methods and completely different methods.

Table 1. Comparison of existing operation methods

Methods \ Reqs.	1. Arbitrary scrolling	2. Quick pointing	3. One-handed operation
A. Mouse + scroll bars	*Fair* (no angled scrolling)	Poor (close watching needed)	Poor (desk needed)
A'. Trackball + scroll bars	*Fair* (no angled scrolling)	Poor (close watching needed)	*Fair* (separate switch)
B. Pen + sheet-picking	*Fair* (1 screen in 1 op.)	**Good** (can be done directly)	Poor (two hands needed)
C. Cursor keys + highlighting	Poor (implicit scrolling)	**Good** (no slipping)	*Fair* (multiple keys)

The next subsection compares and examines these operation methods from the viewpoint of their applicability in a mobile environment.

Applicability to a Mobile Environment

Compared with a desktop environment, a mobile environment imposes various restrictions on user operations. Therefore, a specially designed operation method is necessary for comfortable information browsing. The following requirements should be satisfied:

Requirement 1. Arbitrary scrolling

The scrolling operation is particularly important in a mobile environment, because the screen size is limited. For efficient operation, it should be possible to scroll in an arbitrary direction at an arbitrary speed.

Requirement 2. Quick pointing

In a mobile environment, it may be difficult to watch the screen closely or continuously. Therefore, the pointing operation should move directly to a clickable point and select it.

Requirement 3. One-handed operation

It should be possible to browse information even while walking or standing in a bus or train. It should therefore be possible to perform the above two types of operation with one hand.

Now let us evaluate the four operation methods described in the previous subsection on the basis of these requirements.

In methods A (mouse + scroll bars) and A' (trackball + scroll bars), the pointer itself can be moved in any direction. However, scrolling at an angle is impossible because these methods use scroll bars. In methods that display a pointer on the screen, continuous feedback from the screen is needed to move the pointer to a target item. Therefore, the pointing operation becomes very hard in an environment where the screen cannot be watched closely. First of all, an ordinary mouse cannot be used without a surface to press on, and is not suitable as an input device in a mobile environment. A trackball can be used in a mobile environment, but one-handed operation is somewhat difficult because it requires a separate switch.

In method B (pen + sheet-picking), the sheet-pick scrolling method allows scrolling in any direction. However, the length of one scrolling operation is limited by the screen size. The method allows the user to point to an item on the screen directly, but it always require two hands for operation in a mobile environment.

In method C (cursor keys + highlighting), comfortable scrolling is difficult, because it is performed implicitly. Even if some specialized operation mode is provided, it is still limited to at most eight directions and a fixed speed. On the other hand, pointing can be performed quickly and accurately because one clickable point is always highlighted. However, one-handed operation is difficult without special care, because the method requires multiple keys.

As we have seen, existing operation methods do not completely satisfy the three requirements for mobile information browsing. Table 1 summarizes the results of our analysis.

NAVIPOINT: A NEW INPUT DEVICE

Taking account of these requirements and problems, we have developed a new input device that allows comfortable one-handed mobile information browsing [6, 7, 8]. It is named "NaviPoint," because information navigation is facilitated by this pointing device.[3]

Basic Structure

NaviPoint is based on the "TrackPoint" analog input device [16] fitted to the center of the keyboard in IBM ThinkPads. A TrackPoint device can be used as a substitute for a mouse, and consists of a stick for two-dimensional analog input and several switches that correspond to mouse buttons. The stick senses horizontal forces but does not move physically.

As mentioned in the previous section, it is better for one-handed operation if the stick and switches are integrated. However, simply adding a switch at the bottom of the stick often causes unintentional pointer movement upon clicking. In NaviPoint, a physical "insensitive zone" is provided around the stick, allowing *click input* operation without any sensing of unintentional horizontal forces.

Figure 2 shows the conceptual structure of NaviPoint. NaviPoint consists of a stick with a micro-switch and a ring-shaped two-dimensional stress sensor around the stick (the left part of Figure 2). The stick can be depressed by applying a certain pressure, and can also be tilted in an arbitrary direction inside the ring. When the stick is tilted and presses against the ring, the direction and magnitude of the pressure are detected by the stress sensor. The hardware of this sensor is similar to that of the TrackPoint.

The right part of Figure 2 shows a state in which the stick is tilted. The ring-shaped part does not move physically. Therefore, the user knows when the stick touches the ring from the physical feedback of "contact feeling." At the same time, the pressure on the ring is sensed. If the user returns the stick right away, a *digital input* operation is executed in that direction, like when a cursor key is pushed. But unlike with cursor keys, NaviPoint's digital input can specify an arbitrary direction. The software classifies the input into several directions (4 directions, 8 directions, etc.) according to the environment.

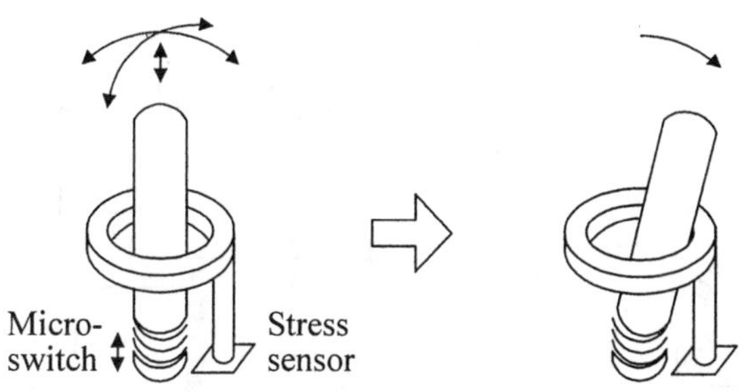

Figure 2. Conceptual structure of NaviPoint

Table 2. Qualitative analysis of NaviPoint

Methods \ Reqs.	1. Arbitrary scrolling	2. Quick pointing	3. One-handed operation
D. NaviPoint	**Good** (by analog input)	**Good** (by digital & click input)	**Very Good** (just one finger)

On the other hand, when the stick is tilted and pushes the ring continuously or firmly, an *analog input* operation corresponding to the force is performed, as in the original TrackPoint.

In a word, by using NaviPoint a user can perform three types of input — "analog input," "digital input," and "click input" — with just one finger. Because of the physical feedback from the micro-switch or the feeling of contact with the ring, a user can perform these input operations accurately without looking at the device or screen.

Information Browsing

To browse information with NaviPoint, use

- "Analog inputs" for scrolling,
- "Digital inputs" for changing the highlighted item, and
- "Click inputs" for selecting the highlighted item.

The basic method is similar to method C (cursor keys + highlighting) in the previous section, and one of the clickable points in the screen is highlighted. When the highlighted item goes off the screen as a result of a scrolling operation, the highlight is automatically moved to a clickable point on the screen. A typical information browsing procedure using NaviPoint is as follows:

1. Tilt the stick continuously (or firmly) to scroll the document.
2. Tilt and return the stick several times to move the highlight to the target item.
3. Depress the stick to select the highlighted item.

[3] The name has been changed from "ScrollPoint," which was used in [7, 8].

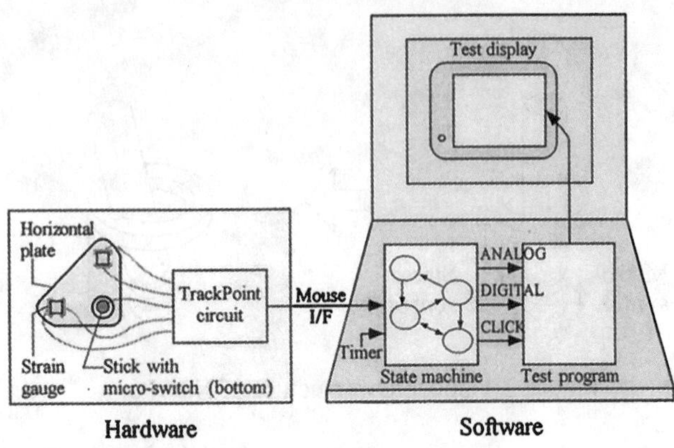

Figure 3. Structure of NaviPoint prototype

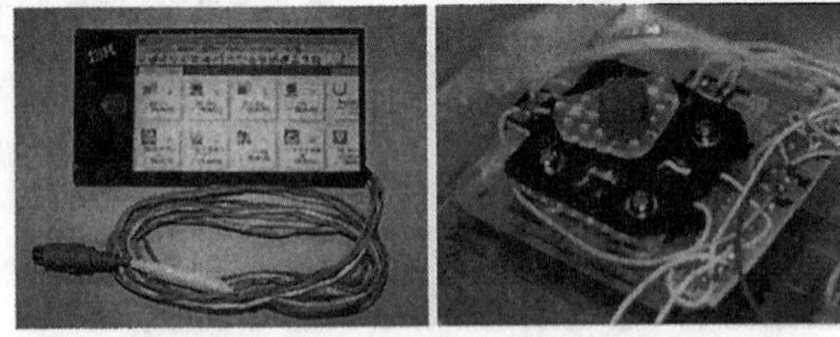

Figure 4. Prototype hardware (external and internal views)

Table 2 shows a qualitative analysis of NaviPoint based on the three requirements described in the previous section. The results show that NaviPoint is suitable for mobile information browsing. Especially as regards requirement 3, it has a big advantage in that it can be controlled *with just one finger*.

With isometric joystick-type input devices like TrackPoint, it is said, fine control is difficult and it takes time to point to a small target [11]. With NaviPoint, however, this is not a problem, because analog input is used only for rough scrolling of a document, and digital inputs are used to select a final target precisely.

THE NAVIPOINT PROTOTYPE

To show the efficiency of NaviPoint as an input device in a mobile environment, we made a prototype using TrackPoint parts. Figure 3 shows the structure of the prototype. The prototype consists of a hardware part (on the left), which implements the basic structure shown in Figure 2, and a software part (on the right), which analyzes the bare input from the hardware and categorizes it as "analog," "digital," or "click" input.

Hardware

The first prototype was developed to verify the feasibility of the NaviPoint concept. Therefore, the hardware was developed as a stand-alone device and is not compactized or built into an actual mobile device. Figure 4 shows external and internal photographs of the prototype hardware. The internal photograph is viewed from the lower-right corner of the hardware part of Figure 3.

The prototype hardware consists of the following three components, as shown in Figure 5:

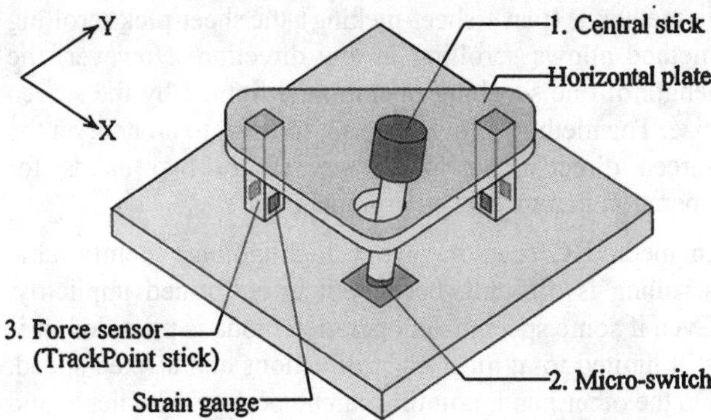

Figure 5. Structure of the prototype hardware

1. A central stick and a suspension mechanism[4] that moves the stick back to its neutral position
2. A micro-switch, located under the central stick, that is used for the click operation
3. Force sensors that detect a two-dimensional force exerted in the horizontal plane by the central stick

For this prototype, we used the force-sensing mechanism of the TrackPoint, which is composed of a stick and a special processing circuit.

At the bottom end of the TrackPoint stick, there are four strain gauges to detect a two-dimensional force exerted on the stick. The values of the force are amplified and converted into digital signals by A/D. They are then translated into corresponding velocity values and output as a standard mouse interface signal by the special processing circuit.

We use two TrackPoint sticks and one special processing circuit, as shown in the left part of Figure 3. The central stick goes through the center of a horizontal plate, and two TrackPoint sticks parallel to the central stick are fixed to the plate at their top ends so that the lines connecting each of them to the central stick are orthogonal to each other in the plate. This horizontal plate corresponds to the ring in Figure 2. When the central stick is tilted and pushes against the horizontal plate, the exerted force is transferred to the TrackPoint sticks. Each of the sticks detects one element of a 2D orthogonal force. For example, when the central stick is tilted along the X-axis, a bending moment is generated at the bottom of one TrackPoint stick, while a torsional moment is generated at the bottom of the other stick. In this prototype, only the bending moment is used for force detection.

The central stick and the horizontal plate are loosely coupled with a considerable area of slack. This creates a force-insensitive zone around the neutral position of the stick, which avoids undesired detection of force when the stick is depressed for click input. It also provides the user with a sense of contact when the central stick is tilted from the neutral position and presses against the horizontal plate.

[4] The suspension mechanism is omitted in Figure 5.

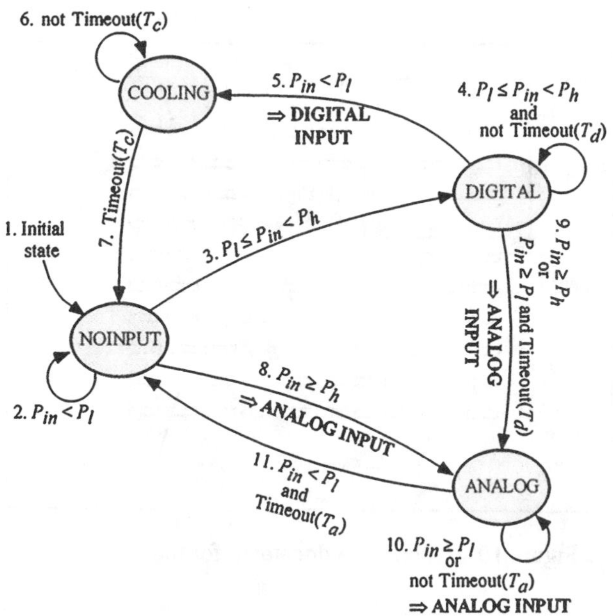

Figure 6. Software state machine

Software

In the prototype, the software discriminates digital and analog parts of the mouse-signal input from the hardware. This software is constructed as a state machine whose inputs are the velocity of the mouse (P_{in}) and timer information for timeout processing. It has the following four states:

NOINPUT — Initial state, represents no input

DIGITAL — State preparing a "digital input"

ANALOG — State processing "analog inputs"

COOLING — State to avoid chattering

Figure 6 shows transitions among states. In the figure, P_l, P_h, T_d, T_c, and T_a are threshold parameters for controlling the transition. Expressions shown along the transition arrows are conditions for the corresponding transitions, and statements after " ⇒ " indicate the handled (discriminated) inputs (digital or analog input). As for click input, input from the micro-switch, which corresponds to the left mouse button signal, is directly used.

Calibration

As explained in the previous subsection, the prototype software uses five constants, P_l, P_h, T_d, T_c, and T_a, as threshold parameters for state transition. These parameters can be calibrated by simple experiments.

The first experiment decides P_l, P_h, and T_d, which are parameters for discriminating the digital input. In this experiment, a user tilts the central stick until it touches the horizontal plate and returns the stick repeatedly. This operation corresponds to digital input. Figure 7 gives the results for one subject, K, and shows the temporal variation of the input P_{in} with 19 digital-input operations at intervals of about 0.5 seconds. Because of the implementation of the prototype hardware, the input P_{in} does not directly represent the force exerted on the plate, but rather the "velocity

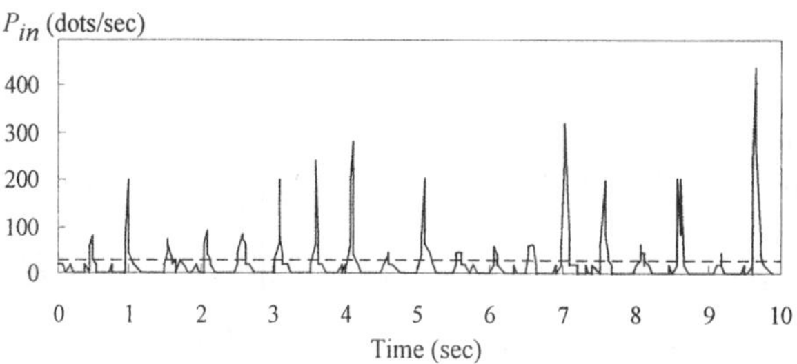

Figure 7. Results of the parameter-tuning experiment

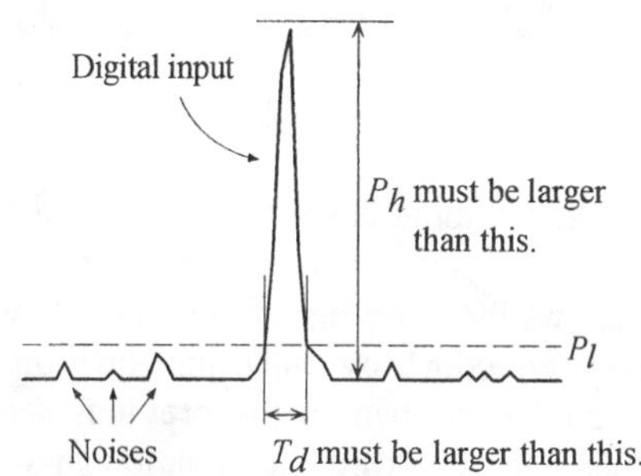

Figure 8. Parameters for discriminating a digital input

of the mouse" translated from the force information by the TrackPoint circuit. Therefore, the unit of the vertical axis of this graph is "number of mouse-pointer movements normalized to the value in 1 second (dots/sec)."

P_l is a parameter for canceling minute noises contained in the input P_{in}. In Figure 7, noises that are not intentional inputs by the subject exist at around 0, 0.8, and 6.3 seconds, etc. In the prototype, P_l is set to 30 dots/sec to cancel these noises. In the figure, the horizontal dotted line represents the threshold, and inputs smaller than this are ignored by the software.

P_h and T_d are central parameters for discriminating the digital input. A sequence of input that is smaller than P_h and continues no longer than T_d is handled as a digital input. In other words, P_h and T_d must be large enough to include all input sequences for which the user intends to perform digital inputs, as shown in Figure 8. From the results shown in Figure 7, P_h must be larger than about 500 dots/sec and T_d must be larger than about 200 msec for this subject. These parameters should essentially be adjustable according to the user. However, in the current implementation, fixed values P_h = 800 dots/sec and T_d = 300 msec are set as maximum-common values, on the basis of experiments with multiple subjects.

T_c is a parameter to avoid chattering just after a digital input has been processed, and inputs during this period are ignored. T_a is a parameter to prevent analog input from being cut into pieces by a momentary non-input status, and the analog-input state continues during this period even if the input is zero. These two parameters are introduced for comfortable operation. If they are too large, however, a user's intentional series of operations will be ignored. In the current implementation, both T_c and T_a are set to 100 msec.

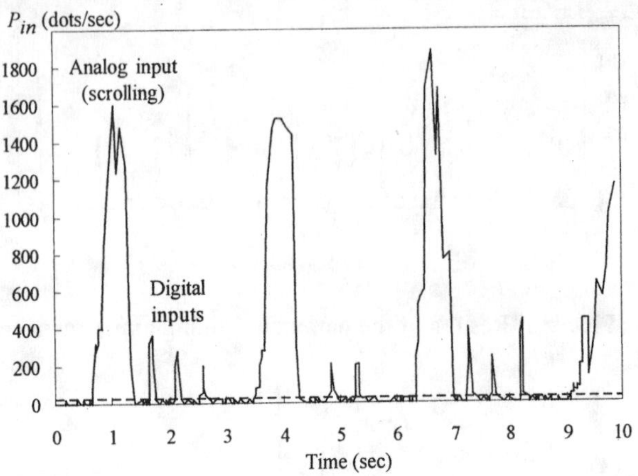

Figure 9. Actual input pattern for hypermedia browsing

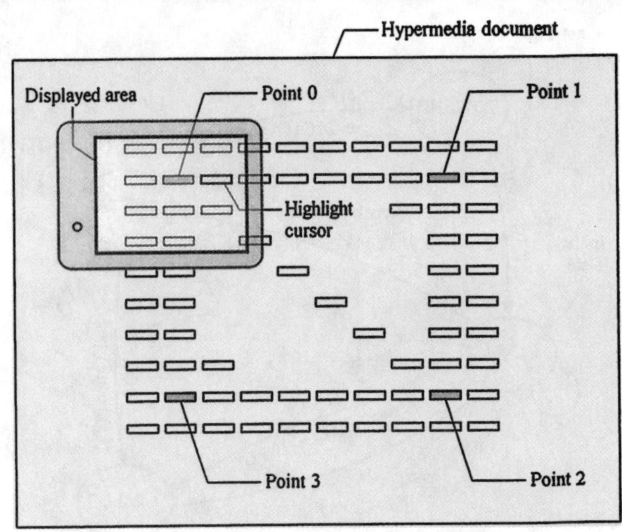

Figure 10. Hypermedia document for the evaluation

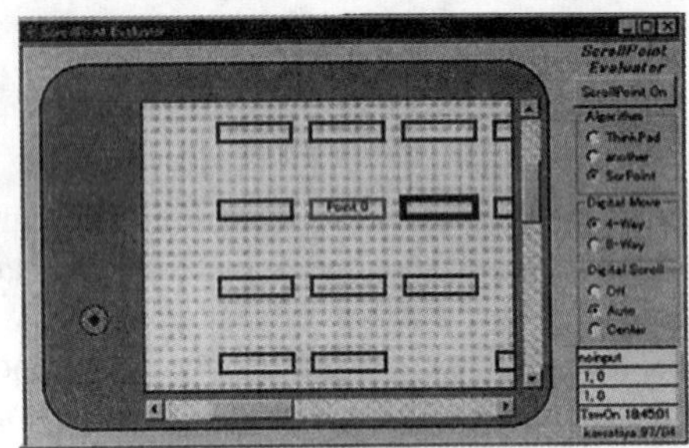

Figure 11. Screen of the evaluation program

Figure 9 shows the variation of the input P_{in} while a user performs hypermedia browsing using NaviPoint according to the method described in the previous section.[5] This graph illustrates very well the situation in which a user roughly scrolls a document by means of an analog input and then changes the highlighted item by means of several digital inputs. In this result, the intervals between input operations are at least 200 msec. Therefore, the value of 100 msec for T_c and T_a is considered to be reasonable.

EVALUATION EXPERIMENTS

Next, to verify the efficiency of NaviPoint in mobile information browsing, we carried out evaluation experiments. As a basis for comparison, we chose the "mouse and scroll bar" method (method A) which is the most widely used operation method. The time taken with NaviPoint was compared with the "mouse time" in several cases where both scrolling and pointing are used.

Experimental Procedure

The experimental procedure was as follows. Figure 10 shows an imaginary hypermedia document used in the experiments. Rectangles in the document represent clickable points (hyperlinks). The document is larger than the screen (16 times the screen size), and a user cannot view the whole of the document at one time. In such an environment, the following operation:

Exp. 1: Click point 0 → Scroll → Click point 1

Exp. 2: Click point 0 → Scroll → Click point 2

was performed repeatedly by subjects with a mouse or NaviPoint, and the elapsed times were measured.[6]

When a mouse was used, the scrolling operation was performed by dragging the slider of a scroll bar with the mouse pointer. Because scrolling at an angle is impossible with a scroll bar, two scroll bars must be operated successively in Exp. 2. When NaviPoint was used, the user had to first roughly scroll to the neighbor of the target item by means of an analog input, then adjust the highlight to the target item with several digital inputs, and select the item with a click input.

The subjects in the experiments were nine computer users who had mastered mouse operation. They received about 10 to 20 minutes advance explanation and training in operating NaviPoint. The NaviPoint prototype is held with two hands and its stick is manipulated with the left thumb.

The experiments were carried out on an IBM ThinkPad 755C (9545-L, Intel DX4-75MHz). The operating system was Windows 95, and the speed of the mouse pointer was set to medium. Figure 11 shows the display of the evaluation program. The screen size of the imitated mobile device is 320 x 240 dots (105 x 79 mm in absolute size) and the size of each clickable item is 64 x 16 dots (21 x 5 mm in absolute size).

Results and Discussion

Figure 12 shows the results of the experiments. These graphs show the elapsed times for nine subjects with a mouse and NaviPoint. Each bar shows the average elapsed time of ten examinations, and the supplementary vertical line shows the 95% confidence interval. The number over the initial of each subject represents the ratio of the NaviPoint time to the mouse time.

[5] More precisely speaking, an evaluation program that will be described in the next section is used.

[6] The main object of the experiments was to measure the performance of scrolling and pointing. Therefore, when a clickable point was selected, only a beep sound was processed, and the document was not replaced.

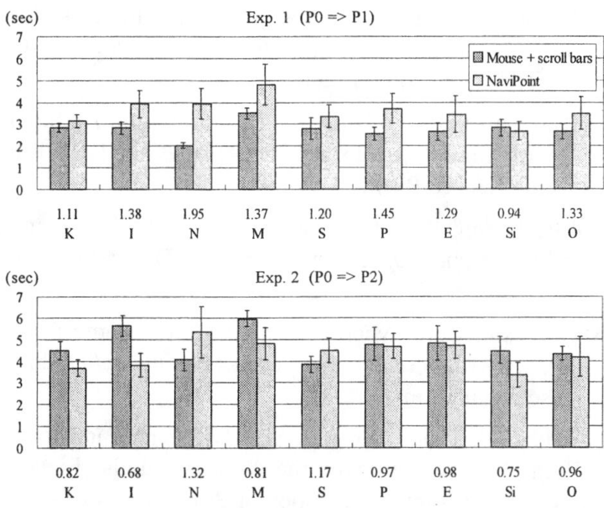

Figure 12. Evaluation result (comparing mouse and NaviPoint)

From the result of Exp. 1, it can be said that NaviPoint can be manipulated with an overhead of less than 50% on the usual mouse operation.[7] Considering the advantages of NaviPoint in a mobile environment, this overhead is acceptable for practical use. However, the deviation with NaviPoint tends to become larger than with a mouse. Possible reasons for this phenomenon are as follows:

- The number of digital inputs affects the elapsed time.
- Faulty execution of digital and analog input causes unintentional movement and increases the elapsed time.

The latter is thought to be the major reason, since the difference is very small for subjects K and Si, who mastered NaviPoint very well. In this regard, several improvements are being planned for more accurate operation, such as calibrating the parameters dynamically for each user, as explained in the previous section, and redesigning the physical hardware.

In Exp. 2, many subjects achieved better results with NaviPoint, because of its advantage of allowing the user to scroll in any direction. The number at the bottom of Figure 12 shows the ratio of the result in Exp. 2 to Exp. 1 for each subject and operation method. Compared to the 1.4–2 times increase in mouse operation, NaviPoint shows an increase of less than 1.4 times for all subjects. Considering the larger scrolling distance in Exp. 2, it can be said that with NaviPoint a user can operate with the same performance and feeling in any direction.

To summarize the results, NaviPoint is suitable for browsing hypermedia documents with arbitrary scrolling on a small screen in a mobile environment.

[7] As an exception, subject N showed a 95% overhead. However, this can be considered as a special case in which the user had mastered mouse operation extremely well.

RELATED WORK

As a result of the spread of the WWW, the importance of the scrolling operation has received greater attention recently. For example, Microsoft's IntelliMouse [10] can perform scrolling (or zooming) by rotating a wheel installed between two mouse buttons. Zhai et al. have proposed several methods that combine scrolling with pointing — such as using a mouse with a TrackPoint device, and using multiple pointing devices — and compared and examined them [21]. These devices and ideas are mainly concerned with the desktop environment, and try to add a direct scrolling operation by adding new parts without losing the feel of the original operation.

As input devices for mobile information devices, pens and keypads (cursor keys) are currently popular. The problems associated with these devices in information browsing have already been discussed in the early section of this paper. Other devices for a mobile environment include a depressable digital dial [18, 20]. The functions of this device are almost the same as those of cursor keys, but it has the advantage of being manipulatable with one hand. However, arbitrary scrolling is difficult, because it allows input in only one dimension.

Among the new scrolling methods for mobile information devices is the "Scroll Display" proposed by Siio [19]. This is a display device, with a built-in mouse on the back, in which the movement of the display itself is treated as a scrolling operation. This idea may be effective as a metaphor for intuitive scrolling operation, but the device is difficult to use while moving. As a method for improving scrolling efficiency, "Alphaslider" has been proposed by Ahlberg et al. [1]. It is effective for selecting an item from a text-based list or menu, but its performance in scrolling of general graphics is considered to be the same as that of a normal scroll bar.

Other interesting input devices include "Rockin'Mouse" [2] and Rekimoto's tilting display [14]. These devices utilize "tilting" operation as an additional input method, and are very useful for controlling 3D objects interactively. However, they are not always suitable for mobile information browsing, because the first needs a flat surface to operate on and the second requires the display itself to be moved.

Many input devices that can be used with one hand or without any hands have also been proposed [4, 9, 17], but most of them need special dexterity for operation and/or are difficult to integrate into a mobile information device such as a PDA.

The most notable characteristic of NaviPoint in relation to the above devices and methods is that it is a specialized device for mobile information browsing. By sacrificing the generality of mouse pointer display and character input, NaviPoint gains an important advantage for mobile information browsing in that it can be manipulated with just one finger without watching.

CONCLUSION

This paper has reported a new input device, NaviPoint, that allows hypermedia information to be browsed comfortably on mobile information devices such as PDAs. With this device, three types of input — "analog input," "digital input," and "click input" — can be performed by using just one finger. Experiments using the prototype have shown that user's performance in hypermedia browsing with NaviPoint was comparable with their performance when they used existing operation methods.

Although they are not mentioned in this paper, NaviPoint has other advantageous features for the mobile environment, such as easy waterproofing [6]. It can also be used to control other devices such as a television set [15]. However, NaviPoint is a specialized device for information browsing, and is not suited for inputting information such as characters. Therefore, to build up a real mobile information device, it must be combined with another input device such as a pen.

One future task will be to build and evaluate such a mobile information device that incorporates NaviPoint. Another theme at the software level is the construction of an operation scheme suitable for information browsing that incorporates menu handling. As another idea, we are currently planning to apply a software part that implements input discrimination in existing hardware such as TrackPoint. Investigation of the microstructure of the movement [11] and evaluation on the basis of Fitts' law [3] are also planned.

REFERENCES

1. Ahlberg, C. and Shneiderman, B. The Alphaslider: A Compact and Rapid Selector, in *Proceedings of ACM CHI '94 Conference*, 365–371, 1994.
2. Balakrishnan, R. et al. The Rockin'Mouse: Integral 3D Manipulation on a Plane, in *Proceedings of ACM CHI '97 Conference*, 311–318, 1997.
3. Fitts, P.M. The Information Capacity of the Human Motor System in Controlling the Amplitude of Movement. *Journal of Experimental Psychology 47*, 6, 381–391, 1954.
4. Fukumoto, M. and Tonomura, Y. "Body Coupled FingeRing": Wireless Wearable Keyboard, in *Proceedings of ACM CHI '97 Conference*, 147–154, 1997.
5. Kawachiya, K. and Siio, I. A Framework for Mobile Information Cache, in *Proceedings of 53rd Annual Convention IPS Japan*, 1B-9, 1-17–1-18, in Japanese, 1996.
6. Kawachiya, K. and Ishikawa, H. A Single-Finger Controller for Mobile Devices, in *Proceedings of 54th Annual Convention IPS Japan*, 4R-3, 4-111–4-112, in Japanese, 1997.
7. Kawachiya, K. and Ishikawa, H. A Useful Input Device for Hypermedia Browsing. *IPSJ SIG Notes 97*, 43 (97-HI-72), 55–60, in Japanese, 1997.
8. Kawachiya, K. and Ishikawa, H. ScrollPoint: An Input Device for Mobile Information Browsing. IBM Research Report, RT0211, 1997.
9. McAlindon, P.J. et al. The Keybowl: An Ergonomically Designed Document Processing Device, in *Proceedings of ACM ASSETS '96*, 86–93, 1996.
10. Microsoft Corp. Microsoft IntelliMouse Home Page. http://www.microsoft.com/products/hardware/intellimouse/default.htm.
11. Mithal, A.K. and Douglas, S.A. Differences in Movement Microstructure of the Mouse and the Finger-Controlled Isometric Joystick, in *Proceedings of ACM CHI '96 Conference*, 300–307, 1996.
12. Narayanaswamy, S. et al. Application and Network Support for InfoPad. *IEEE Personal Communications 3*, 2, 4–17, 1996.
13. Negishi, Y. et al. Tuplink: A System Structure for Mobile Micro Clients. IBM Research Report, RT5123, 1997.
14. Rekimoto, J. Tilting Operations for Small Screen Interfaces, in *Proceedings of ACM UIST '96*, 167–168, 1996.
15. Robertson, S. et al. Dual Device User Interface Design: PDAs and Interactive Television, in *Proceedings of ACM CHI '96 Conference*, 79–86, 1996.
16. Rutledge, J.D. and Selker, T. Force-to-Motion Functions for Pointing, in *Proceedings of INTERACT '90: The IFIP Conference on Human-Computer Interaction*, 701–705, 1990.
17. Salem, C. and Zhai, S. An Isometric Tongue Pointing Device, in *Proceedings of ACM CHI '97 Conference*, 538–539, 1997.
18. Siio, I. and Murata, H. A palmtop computer equipping a dial switch, in *Proceedings of. 54th Annual Convention IPS Japan*, 4R-1, 4-109–4-110, in Japanese, 1997.
19. Siio, I. Scroll Display: Pointing Device for Palmtop Computers. *IPSJ SIG Notes 97*, 24 (97-HI-71), 91–98, in Japanese, 1997.
20. Sony Electronics Inc. Sony Simplifies Wireless Communications With Unique Jog Dial Control. http://www.sel.sony.com/SEL/corpcomm/news/wtc/6.html.
21. Zhai, S., Smith, B.A., and Selker, T. Improving Browsing Performance: A Study of Four Input Devices for Scrolling and Pointing Tasks, in *Proceedings of INTERACT '97: The 6th IFIP Conference on Human-Computer Interaction*, 286–292, 1997.

The PadMouse: Facilitating Selection and Spatial Positioning for the Non-Dominant Hand

Ravin Balakrishnan[1,2] and Pranay Patel[2]

[1]Dept. of Computer Science
University of Toronto
Toronto, Ontario
Canada M5S 3G4
ravin@dgp.toronto.edu

[2]Alias|wavefront
210 King Street East
Toronto, Ontario
Canada M5A 1J7
{ravin | ppatel}@aw.sgi.com

ABSTRACT

A new input device called the PadMouse is described and evaluated. The PadMouse consists of a two degree-of-freedom touchpad mounted on a regular mouse base. Like the regular mouse, the PadMouse allows for spatial positioning tasks to be performed by moving the device on a planar surface. In addition, when coupled with an interaction technique we call Marking Keys, users can use the touchpad to activate modifiers and commands. An experiment shows that up to 32 modifiers/commands can be quickly and accurately activated using this technique, making it a viable device for the non-dominant hand in two-handed user interfaces. Other uses for the PadMouse and design alternatives are also discussed.

Keywords

Input devices, marking-menus, bimanual input, touchpad, mouse, interaction techniques, gestures, hot-keys, toolglass.

INTRODUCTION

Several user interface researchers over the past decade, having recognized that in the physical world people often use both hands to cooperatively perform many tasks, have explored the possibility of using both hands simultaneously in the computer interface. In an early study, Buxton and Myers [3] showed that in a compound task, a one-handed interface (i.e. the status-quo) was inferior to a two-handed interface which split the compound task into subtasks that could be performed in parallel by both hands. Kabbash, Buxton, and Sellen [10] came to a similar conclusion, however, they also showed that two hands could be worse than one if an inappropriate interaction technique is employed, particularly when cognitive load is increased.

Building partly on this empirical work, Bier et al. [1, 2] developed the click-through Toolglass and Magic Lenses interface which utilized both hands for its operation. More recently, Kurtenbach et al. [13] described an interface called "T3" which effectively integrated the Toolglass and Magic Lenses concepts with other two-handed techniques for performing direct manipulation operations in a 2D drawing program. Zeleznik, Forsberg, and Strauss [15] incorporated and extended some of these techniques into their "Sketch" 3D modeling system, demonstrating the use of two cursors controlled by two hands to enhance 3D interaction.

While the existing body of research has investigated a variety of two-handed interaction techniques, the issue of what constitutes an appropriate input device for the non-dominant hand remains unexplored. Furthermore, these systems have limited the non-dominant hand to coarse positioning tasks, relying on the dominant hand for almost everything else including selection of tools, commands, and modes.

In this paper, we first explore the various tasks that could (or should) be performed using the non-dominant hand within a two-handed user-interface. We then describe a new device, the PadMouse (Figure 1), coupled with an interaction technique called Marking Keys. Together, these enhance the role of the non-dominant hand by allowing it to activate modifiers and commands in addition to performing spatial positioning. Finally, we present the results of an experiment to investigate the performance of Marking Keys on the PadMouse.

Figure 1. The PadMouse

TWO-HANDED INTERACTION

Much recent work in two-handed user interfaces [1, 2, 5, 7, 10, 13, 15] has been guided by the theoretical work of Guiard [6]. In his Kinematic Chain model of skilled bimanual action, the two hands are thought to be two abstract motors assembled in a serial linkage, thus forming a cooperative kinematic chain. Three general principles emerge from this model:

1. *Dominant-to-Non-Dominant Spatial Reference:* The non-dominant hand sets the frame of reference relative to which the dominant hand performs its motions.

2. *Asymmetric Scales of Motion:* The two hands operate in asymmetric spatial-temporal scales of motion. For instance, when writing on a piece of paper, the motion of the non-dominant hand controlling the position of the paper is of lower temporal and spatial frequency than the writing movements of the dominant hand which nonetheless depends on the non-dominant hand's movement for spatial reference.

3. *Precedence of the Non-Dominant Hand:* Contribution of the non-dominant hand to a cooperative bimanual task starts earlier than the dominant hand. In the handwriting example, the dominant hand starts writing *after* the paper has been oriented and positioned by the non-dominant hand.

The two-handed interfaces developed to date have by and large adhered to these principles, although perhaps not exploiting them to maximum advantage. In the Toolglass and Magic Lenses interface [1, 2] the non-dominant hand controls the spatial position of the Toolglass sheet, setting up a context for the dominant hand which performs precise positioning and drawing tasks in their 2D drawing application. In their "T3" concept application, Kurtenbach et al. [13] use the non-dominant hand for a greater variety of tasks: positioning and orienting the artwork, positioning a Toolglass, and cooperating with the dominant hand to scale, orient, and position graphical objects. Zeleznik et al. [15] rely on the non-dominant hand cooperating with the dominant hand to translate and rotate 3D objects, control the virtual camera, and perform a variety of other editing tasks.

I've got two hands, but lost my hot-keys!

A characteristic feature of today's ubiquitous WIMP (windows, icons, menus, and pointer) user interface is the use of the non-dominant hand to activate commands and modifiers using the keyboard (sometimes referred to as 'hot-keys' or 'keyboard shortcuts') while the dominant hand operates the mouse. We use the term "commands" to mean operations that are performed once when a key or combination of keys is pressed (e.g., Control-C for Copy, Control-V for Paste in many applications); and "modifiers" to mean operations that put the application into a particular mode only for the duration of the keypress (e.g., on a Mac, holding down the Shift key allows for multiple selections to be made with the pointer. Releasing the key returns the system to its default single selection mode).

In high-end 2D and 3D graphics applications, there are in the order of five hundred available commands and modifiers: the most frequently used ones are usually rapidly accessible via hot-keys. Ironically, the speed and functionality of this albeit limited form of two-handed interaction has not been incorporated in the more recent two-handed interfaces discussed in the previous sections. For example, the Toolglass and Magic lenses interface [1, 2] uses the non-dominant hand only to control the spatial position of the Toolglass sheet via a trackball or touchpad, while the dominant hand selected tools from this sheet. Also, the *contents* of the sheet were selected from a master sheet using the dominant hand. Similarly, Kurtenbach et al.'s "T3" application [13] relied on the dominant hand to select the contents of the Toolglass via a Marking Menu [11]. Thus, the dominant hand is required to serially select the tool and then perform the operation with the tool. The non-dominant hand merely keeps the tools within easy reach of the dominant hand. We believe that a system in which the non-dominant hand selects the tool or mode which is then used by the dominant hand would be more in line with Guiard's Kinematic Chain model [6] where the actions of the non-dominant hand naturally precedes and sets the stage for the actions of the dominant hand. One way to achieve this while retaining the favourable aspects of the Toolglass and T3 style two-handed interfaces would be to provide the non-dominant hand with an input device that allowed for rapid activation of commands and modifiers *in addition* to performing spatial positioning.

THE PADMOUSE

The PadMouse (Figure 1) is a new input device that integrates a two degree-of-freedom touchpad with the ubiquitous two degree-of-freedom mouse. This allows for the input of gestures by the user's middle or index finger on the touchpad, while the user's hand controls the 2D spatial position of the device on the work surface (like a regular mouse).

In our prototype implementation, we mounted a Synaptics T1002D touchpad on a generic serial/PS2 mouse base. Two serial ports (or one serial port and one PS2 mouse port) are required to interface it to a host computer. This is sufficient for evaluating our design and interaction techniques. A product would require the integration of the mouse and touchpad firmware.

While the PadMouse can foreseeably be incorporated into a variety of user interface techniques, in this paper we focus on its use as an enhanced device for the non-dominant hand. In addition to using the PadMouse for spatial positioning in Toolglass and T3 style interfaces, the touchpad on the PadMouse can be used to activate commands and modifiers using a technique we call Marking Keys.

MARKING KEYS

Marking Keys is an adaptation of Marking Menus [11]: a mark based interaction technique that allows a user to select items from a menu which may be single level or hierarchical. As Kurtenbach [11] describes, selections using Marking Menus can be made in two ways (Figure 2):

1. *menu mode:* The user enters this mode by pressing a button on a stylus or mouse and pausing for a short time (less than 1 second). A radial menu then appears on the display,

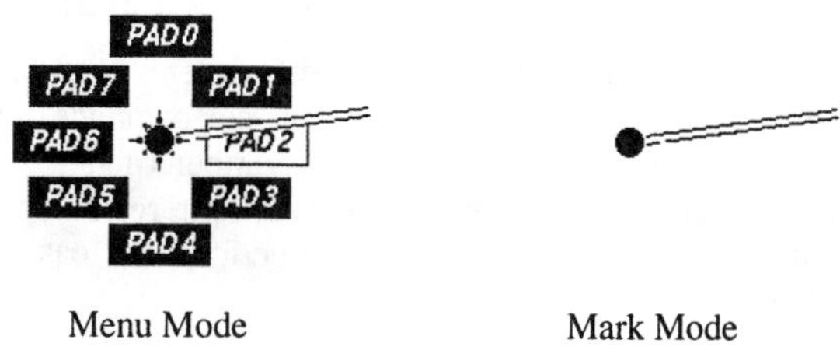

Figure 2a. Selecting from a single level marking menu. In menu mode, the menu is displayed and the user moves to the desired item. Users who are familiar with the menu layout select items in mark mode where no menu is displayed.

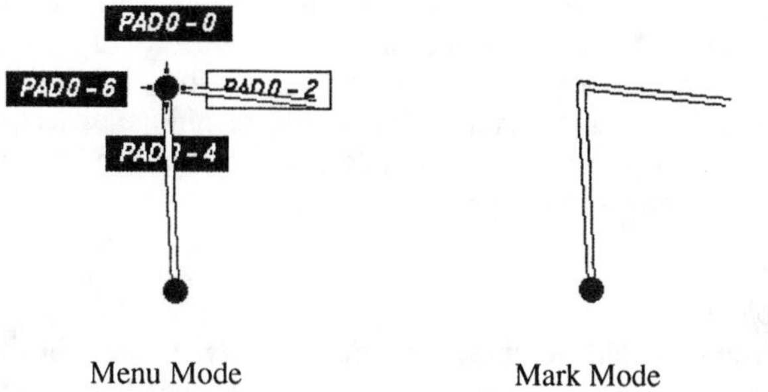

Figure 2b. Selecting from a hierarchical marking menu. The first segment of the mark selects a submenu and the second segment selects the desired menu item. In menu mode, the current (sub)menu is displayed and the user moves to the desired item. Users who are familiar with the menu layout select items in mark mode by making a compound mark.

centered around the cursor position. The user selects a menu item by moving the cursor into the desired sector of the radial menu, the selected item is highlighted, and selection confirmed when the mouse/stylus button is released.

2. *mark mode:* The user enters this mode by pressing a button on a stylus or mouse and *immediately* moving the cursor in the direction of the desired menu item. Instead of displaying the radial menu, the system displays an ink-trail following the cursor. When the button is released, the menu item that corresponds to the direction of movement is selected. If the user stops moving but does not release the button, the system assumes that the user is unsure of the menu layout and displays the menu, effectively providing guidance by self-revelation only when required. Studies have shown that making selections in mark mode can be 3.5 times faster than when the menu is displayed [11].

The beauty of Marking Menus is that a user who is unfamiliar with the menu layout only has to wait a split second before the menu is displayed. The mark made to select an item from this menu is similar to the mark required to make a selection when in mark mode. Each time a user makes a selection in menu mode, they are rehearsing the mark that would be required when in mark mode. This helps the user learn the markings. Once the user is familiar with the menu layout, selection is achieved very quickly by simply making a mark without waiting for the menu to be displayed. Thus, Marking Menus effectively utilizes self-revelation, guidance, and rehearsal to aid the user in making a smooth transition from novice to expert behaviour.

Our Marking Keys interaction technique, whose behaviour is illustrated in Figure 3, retains the favourable characteristics of Marking Menus while introducing several changes which result in a gesture based alternative to hot-keys:

- Instead of using a stylus or mouse to drive a cursor which then makes the required mark, users simply use their index finger to create the mark on the PadMouse's touchpad.
- No button presses are required. Rather, the menuing system is activated when the user's finger first touches the touchpad. If the user pauses for 0.4 seconds, a radial menu of options is displayed and the system is in menu mode. If the user starts moving immediately after touching the pad, the system is in mark mode and no menu is displayed.
- Recognition of the mark is achieved by pausing for 0.2 seconds after the mark is made. If a valid mark results in the selection of a command, that command is performed and the system returns to an idle state. If the mark results in the selection of a modifier, that modifier is activated and remains active as long as the finger remains on the touchpad. When the finger is lifted off the pad, the modi-

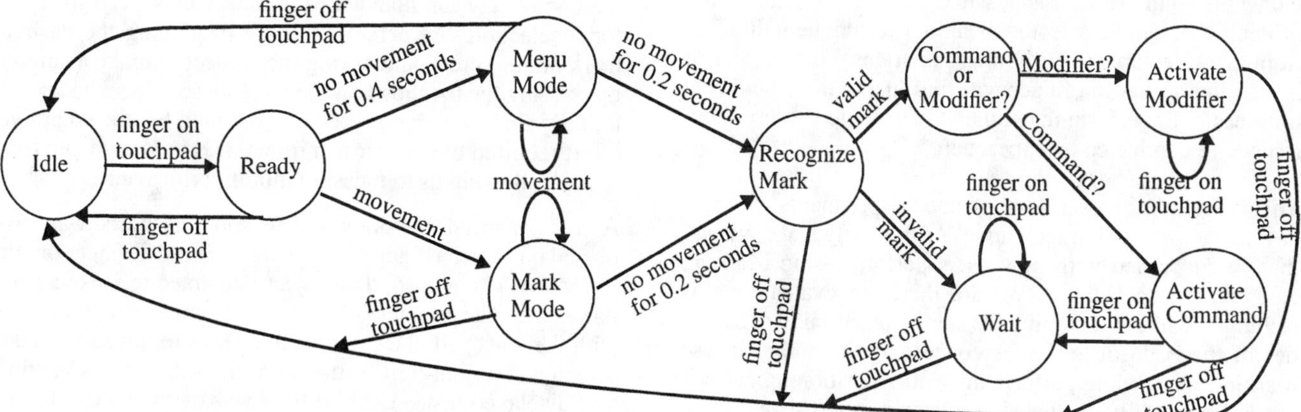

Figure 3. State transition diagram illustrating the behaviour of Marking Keys on the PadMouse. In Menu Mode the menu is displayed; in Mark Mode only the ink-trail of the mark is displayed. Once in the "Recognize Mark" state, no menu or marks are displayed.

fier is inactivated and the system returns to its default mode. This is where Marking Keys differs from traditional Marking Menus: in Marking Menus there is no mechanism for activating modifiers; only commands can be selected. Thus, Marking Keys mimic the action of hot-keys, using gestures to select a command or modifier from a menu instead of pressing a key on a keyboard.

With hot-keys, there is no built-in mechanism for revealing the assignment of keys to functions. Users have to rely on on-line help pages or other documentation to discover the key mappings. This can be frustrating, particularly for novice users. Users of the PadMouse with Marking Keys get all the functionality of hot-keys with the added benefit of self-revelation, as well as a built-in spatial positioning device. Also, the actions required of the user when activating Marking Keys are conceptually and physically distinct from the actions required to control the spatial position of the PadMouse. As Jacob et al. [9] have shown, tasks which are conceptually independent benefit from input devices that allow the tasks to be performed separately. Users of the PadMouse and Marking Keys should likewise benefit from the separation of the two tasks it is designed to perform.

Our implementation of Marking Keys on the PadMouse allows users to activate commands and modifiers using simple marks (i.e., using a single level menu – Figure 2a) as well as compound marks (i.e., using a two level hierarchical menu – Figure 2b). A question of interest, therefore, is the bounds on how many items can be in each level, before the use of a mark for item selection becomes too slow or error prone. Kurtenbach and Buxton [12] explored this question in the context of using a stylus or mouse to select from a Marking Menu. They found that users could select from menus with up to two levels and eight items per level with an error rate under 10%. With menus more than two levels deep and greater than eight items, selection became error prone. Other research [8] also indicates that menus with up to eight items result in acceptable performance. Unfortunately, since Marking Keys on the PadMouse relies on the index finger for performing the marks rather than a mouse or stylus, this previous body of research can only serve as a guideline to us. The range and type of movement afforded by the index finger is very different from that afforded by the whole hand. Thus, it is possible that the optimal number of items that can be selected using our technique will differ from that selectable using a mouse or stylus. Furthermore, it is also likely that the finger will find marks in some directions easier to perform than others. In order to explore these issues, we conducted an experiment.

This is the first of a series of planned experiments with this device and interaction technique. At this early stage, we are mainly concerned with how users perform using Marking Keys on the PadMouse. We are therefore evaluating this technique without including the spatial positioning capabilities of the PadMouse. Issues concerning the ability to use Marking Keys while performing spatial positioning tasks is left to be formally evaluated at a later date; however, a discussion and informal observations are presented later in this paper.

EXPERIMENT

Goal

We had two primary goals for this experiment. Firstly, we wanted to determine the differences in performance when selecting using Marking Keys as the number of items and levels are increased. Secondly, we were interested in the issue of whether marks in certain directions are easier to perform than others.

In order to determine the limits of performance, we needed to measure expert behaviour. Like Kurtenbach and Buxton [12], we defined expert behaviour to occur when the user is completely familiar with the layout of the menu and knew the exact mark required to select a particular item. Research on Marking Menus [11, 12] has shown that users eventually reach this level of expertise, selecting using marks alone (i.e., without displaying the menu) over 90% of the time. The cognitive aspects of this previous work is directly applicable to our technique. Where our technique differs is in the motor skills required to perform the mark, and this is what we sought to measure.

Method

Subjects

12 right-handed volunteers participated as subjects in the experiment. All used their non-dominant hand to perform the experiment.

Apparatus

The experiment was conducted on a Silicon Graphics Indy workstation with a 19 inch colour display. The PadMouse was used as the input device. The mark recognition software was identical to that of a commercial implementation of Marking Menus and has been extensively tested in both experimental and real world settings. The workstation ran in single-user mode, disconnected from all network traffic. Subjects were seated approximately 60 cm in front of the display with their non-dominant hand manipulating the PadMouse with the index finger used to activate Marking Keys on the PadMouse's touchpad. As discussed earlier, the spatial positioning feature of the PadMouse was not used in this experiment.

Task and Stimuli

In this experiment we simulate the situation where subjects are completely familiar with the marks they need to make for a selection. We achieve this by displaying the desired mark on the screen and asking the subject to make a similar mark using the touchpad on the PadMouse. Since the user is told *a priori* what the desired mark should be, the cognitive effort required of the user is minimal and constant from trial to trial, allowing us to measure motor performance.

A trial occurred as follows. The stimulus mark was displayed on screen (Figure 4a). Using their index finger on the PadMouse's touchpad, the subject attempted to make a similar mark. The moment the subject's finger made contact with the touchpad, the stimulus mark was removed from the screen and an ink-trail of the mark the subject was making was displayed instead. At no time was the menu displayed. Identical to our implementation of Marking Keys (Figure 3), the mark was recognized and the trial ended when the

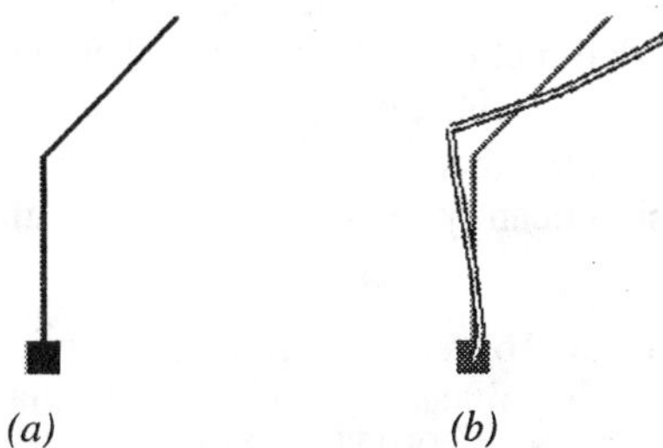

Figure 4. Stimulus and response for one experimental condition. (a) shows the desired mark presented to the subject at the start of a trial. (b) shows the subject's mark overlaid on the desired mark on completion of the trial.

subject's finger was stationary on the touchpad for 0.2 seconds. Once the mark was recognized, the stimulus mark was displayed overlaid with the ink-trail of the mark the subject made (Figure 4b). This served to reinforce learning and aid in correcting errors for future trials. If the subject's mark did not result in the same command or modifier selection as the stimulus mark, the system would beep to indicate an error.

Design

Guided by the results of previous work [8, 11, 12] as well as our informal use of the device and technique, we decided to limit our study to menus up to two levels deep and up to eight items per level as we felt that this would be the upper limit beyond which performance would definitely degrade. We chose three menu layouts (Figure 5):

1 level, 8 items: this was the simplest layout studied. The eight items are laid out in a circle, each occupying a 45 degree sector. Only simple straight marks are required to select from this menu.

2 levels, 16 items: Four possible first level marks lead to a second level menu which in turn has four items, resulting in 4x4=16 items in total. All the required marks are aligned to the horizontal or vertical axes (often referred to as on-axis layout). Compound marks are required for selection.

2 levels, 64 items: Eight possible first level marks lead to a second level menu which in turn has eight items, resulting in 8x8=64 items in total. Compound marks are required for selection. Both on-axis and off-axis marks are required. This layout exhausts all possible combinations for menus up to two levels deep and up to eight items per level. The simpler layouts above were included because they allow for higher spatial variability in the required marks.

A within subjects completely counterbalanced repeated measures design was used. All subjects performed the experiment using all three menu layouts. The presentation order of the three layouts was completely counterbalanced across the subjects. For each menu layout, subjects performed 10 blocks of trials. Each block consisted of 1 trial for each of the possible marks for that menu layout, presented in random order within the block. Subjects were told in advance the menu layout for the upcoming 10 blocks and were also given several practise trials to familiarize themselves with the task, They were allowed breaks after every

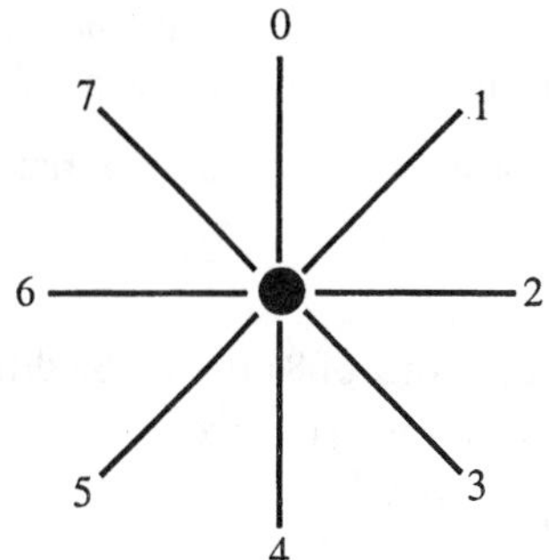

Figure 5(a). 1 level, 8 item layout

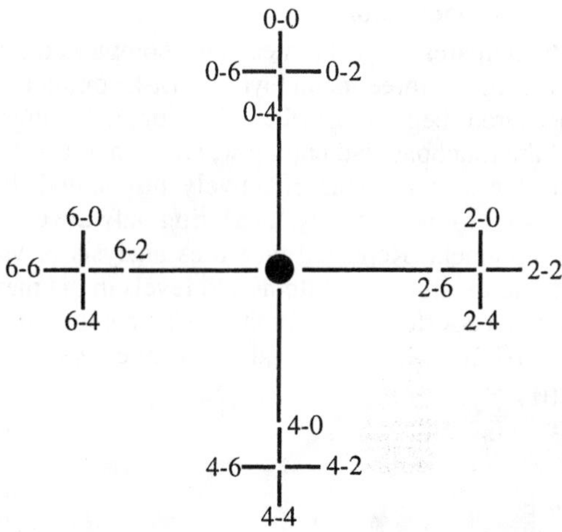

Figure 5(b). 2 level, 16 item layout. The first segment of the mark selects the submenu and the second segment selects the item from that submenu. All the marks are aligned to the horizontal or vertical axes (on-axis layout).

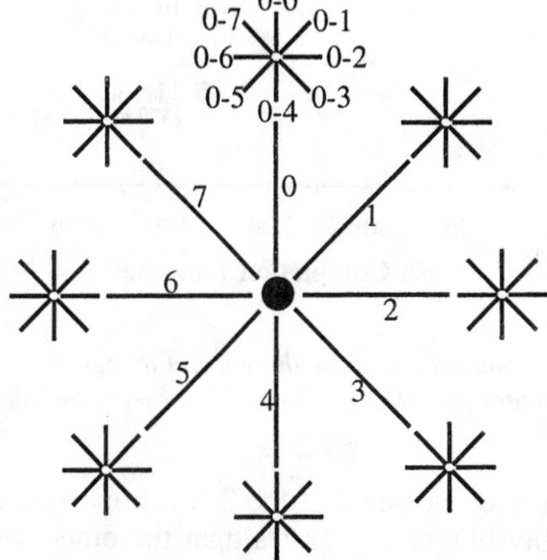

Figure 5(c). 2 level, 64 item layout. The first segment of the mark selects the submenu and the second segment selects the item from that submenu. Both on-axis and off-axis marks are included. To avoid clutter, we have only labeled one submenu. The others are labeled in a similar fashion: first segment number followed by second segment number

eight trials. After the completion of one trial within this group of eight, the next trial began after a 0.5 second pause.

The experiment consisted of 10560 total trials, computed as follows:

12 subjects x

3 menu layouts consisting of 8+16+64=88 different marks x

10 blocks of trials for each layout x

1 trial per mark per block

= 10560 total trials.

The experiment was conducted in one sitting and lasted about an hour per subject.

Results and Discussion

Figure 6 compares subjects' mean task completion time and error rates for the three menu layouts. Task completion time was measured beginning when the subject's finger first touched the touchpad and ending when the mark was recognized by the system. This effectively discounted the time taken to react to the stimulus, measuring only the cost of the motor component. Repeated measures analysis of variance showed that the number of items and levels in the menu had a significant effect on both task completion time ($F_{2,11} = 110.91$, $p < .0001$) and error rate ($F_{2,11} = 47.75$, $p < .0001$).

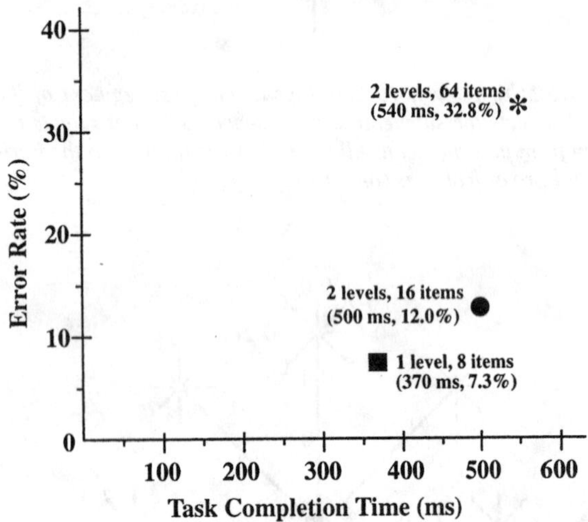

Figure 6. Comparison of the three menu layouts for error rates and movement time. Data from all 12 subjects and all trials.

From Figure 6, we see that the 2 level, 64 item menu had considerably higher error rates than the other two layouts. However, task completion time was not as drastically affected although the difference was statistically significant.

One possible cause of the drastic increase in errors could be that marks in some directions are particularly hard to perform and data from these trials is skewing our results. We therefore took a closer look at the performance differences between the various marks.

For the 1 level, 8 item layout, analysis of variance showed that the mark direction had a significant effect on error rates ($F_{7,77} = 2.08$, $p < .05$). A Ryan-Einot-Gabriel-Welsch post-hoc test revealed that the mark for item 7 (refer to Figure 5a) was significantly harder to perform than the other marks.

For the 2 level, 16 item layout, analysis of variance again showed a significant effect for mark direction ($F_{15,165} = 3.31$, $p < .0001$). As expected, the easiest items were the four where both segments of the compound mark were in the same direction (items 0-0, 2-2, 4-4, and 6-6 in Figure 5b). The most error prone marks were those whose first segment was a left or right mark followed by a second segment that was an up or down mark (items 2-0, 2-4, 6-0, 6-4 in Figure 5b).

For the 2 level, 64 item layout, the situation gets more complex. Like the 2 level, 16 item layout, the marks where both segments of the compound mark were in the same direction (items 0-0, 1-1, 2-2, 3-3, 4-4, 5-5, 6-6, 7-7 in Figure 5c) performed best, with error rates under 10%. Previous research on Marking Menus with large numbers of items and levels [12] have found that when the mark segments are confined to the horizontal or vertical axes (on-axis marks), performance is better than for off-axis marks. An analysis of variance on our data grouped according to whether the mark segments were on-axis or off-axis showed a significant effect for axis ($p < .05$). Marks where both segments were on-axis performed best, followed by those where both segments were off-axis. When one segment was off-axis and the other segment on-axis, performance degraded. A possible explanation is that these "on-off" and "off-on" axis marks account for all the cases with the smallest angle between the two segments of the mark (i.e., a 45 degree turn) which are generally difficult marks to make accurately. If we consider only the 32 marks where both segments were either on-axis or off-axis, the error rate goes down to under 20%.

What constitutes an acceptable error rate for tasks like this? As Kurtenbach & Buxton [12] point out, "the answer depends on the consequences of an error, the cost of undoing an error or redoing the command, and the attitude of the user." Like Marking Menus, Marking Keys present us with the typical trade-off between speed and accuracy. A redeeming feature of Marking Keys is that if the error rate when in mark mode is too high, users can always resort to the slower but more accurate fallback technique of displaying the menu and making a selection.

Comparing our results to the prior art, we find that Marking Keys fares well. Kurtenbach [11] reports that users with 10 to 30 hours of practice are able to select from a six-item Marking Menu using a mouse at a rate between 200 and 400 ms. Nilsen [14] reports that a selection from a six-item linear menu using a mouse required on average 790 ms. Card, Moran, & Newell's [4] Keystroke-Level model indicates that a "good typist" takes 120 ms to execute a key-press on a keyboard, and 400 ms to home in on the desired key. This results in an approximate figure of 520 ms for selection using keyboard hot-keys. Our subjects, with only an hour of practice, averaged 370 ms for an eight-item menu.

This experiment has demonstrated that users of Marking Keys can quickly activate up to 32 commands and modifiers with an error rate of under 20%. This is probably more than the number of hot-keys required in a typical application. If we restrict ourselves to single level menus with a small number of items, much better performance (speed faster than hot-keys, and errors under 8%) is possible.

As mentioned earlier, this is the first of a series of planned experiments to evaluate this device and interaction technique. At this stage, we sought to determine the limits of user performance with Marking Keys and did not confound the issue by utilizing the spatial positioning capabilities of the PadMouse. An obvious question, therefore, is the extent to which spatial positioning of the mouse interferes with the ability to make correct marks on the touchpad and vice versa. Informal observations of users of the device in prototype applications (see section below) do not show evidence of interference between the finger movements on the toucpad and wrist/arm movements controlling the mouse. Indeed, experienced users (including the authors of this paper) are able to activate modifiers and commands with Marking Keys while simultaneously using the spatial positioning capabilities of the device. While it appears that interference between the two parts of the device is minimal, a formal experimental evaluation is required for confirmation and this will be conducted in the near future.

APPLICATIONS

We have prototyped the use of the PadMouse with Marking Keys within one of Alias|wavefront's new 3D modeling/animation applications, Maya. We use the spatial positioning capability of the PadMouse to control the virtual camera in the non-dominant hand (Zeleznik et al. [15] describe similar use of a non-dominant hand input device) while Marking Keys is used to activate frequently used commands (e.g. "undo", "redo last command", "copy"), and modifiers (e.g., activation of graphical manipulator widgets for object translation, rotation, scaling, etc.). The dominant hand uses a regular mouse to perform operations in the 3D scene using those graphical manipulator widgets. In the default unimanual interface, the dominant hand has to constantly switch between camera manipulation and object manipulation. Our bimanual interface has the advantage of having the non-dominant hand control the camera so that users can now tumble/track/dolly around the 3D scene to get the best view of their work while changing parts of the scene with their dominant hand. Preliminary feedback from those who have tried this implementation is encouraging.

We have also incorporated the PadMouse and Marking Keys in a prototype 2D drawing application with a Toolglass and Magic Lenses interface similar to the "T3" concept application of Kurtenbach et al. [13]. Here, the spatial positioning capability of the PadMouse replaces the digitizing tablet puck used in the "T3" application, while Marking Keys are used to select the contents of the Toolglass sheet (the previous implementation [13] uses the dominant hand to make this selection using a Marking Menu).

FUTURE DIRECTIONS

In this paper, we have focused on the use of the PadMouse as a non-dominant hand device in a two-handed user interface. Clearly, this is not the only application for this device. Other possible uses include using the touchpad to perform scrolling and other tasks. Zhai, Smith, and Selker [15] recently performed a comparison of various input devices in scrolling tasks. It would be interesting to see how the PadMouse fares in such a comparison.

We are also exploring alternative designs to the PadMouse for providing command/modifier selection and spatial positioning in an integrated device. One design we have prototyped (Figure 7) is a mouse with 10 keys in an arrangement designed to facilitate comfortable key activation without much finger movement. This design is an evolution of the obvious solution of placing a keypad on the back of the mouse – a design where it is impossible to move the mouse spatially while pressing buttons on the keypad. Preliminary use of our prototype indicates that some users find it difficult to activate buttons with the fourth and fifth fingers, but this could perhaps be overcome with improved button designs. Performance differences between this device and the PadMouse with Marking Keys will have to be evaluated.

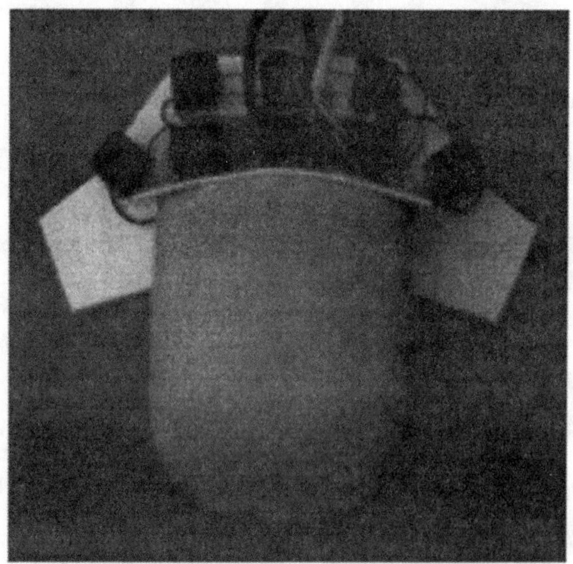

Figure 7. Prototype Ten-key mouse.

CONCLUSIONS

We have presented a new input device, the PadMouse, and an associated interaction technique called Marking Keys. This allows users to perform both spatial positioning tasks as well as activate commands and modifier using the non-dominant hand. Our experiment showed that subjects were able to effectively activate up to 32 commands/modifiers using this device and interaction technique. We believe that incorporating a device like this in two-handed interfaces can lead to more facile and efficient human-computer interaction.

ACKNOWLEDGMENTS

We thank Thomas Baudel, Bill Buxton, George Fitzmaurice, Gordon Kurtenbach, Scott MacKenzie, and Russell Owen for valuable discussions and assistance during the course of this work. We'd also like to thank the other members of the Input Research Group at the University of Toronto and all the volunteers who participated in our experiment. The support of Aliaslwavefront is gratefully acknowledged.

REFERENCES

[1] Bier, E. A., Stone, M. C., Pier, K., Buxton, W., & DeRose, T.D. (1993). Toolglass and magic lenses: The see-through interface. *Computer Graphics Proceedings, Annual Conference Series,* 73-80, New York: ACM SIGGRAPH.

[2] Bier, E. A., Stone, M. C., Fishkin, K., Buxton, W., & Baudel, T. (1994). A taxonomy of see-through tools. *Proceedings of the CHI'94 Conference on Human Factors in Computing Systems,* 358-364, New York: ACM.

[3] Buxton, W., & Myers, B. A. (1986). A study in two-handed input. *Proceedings of the CHI'86 Conference in Human Factors in Computing Systems,* 321-326, New York: ACM.

[4] Card, S. K., Moran, T.P., & Newell, A. (1980). The Keystroke-Level model for user performance time with interactive systems. *Communications of the ACM, 23, 7,* 396-410, New York: ACM.

[5] Fitzmaurice, G. W., & Buxton, W. (1997). An empirical evaluation of graspable user interfaces: towards specialized, space-multiplexed input. *Proceedings of CHI'97 Conference on Human Factors in Computing Systems,* 43-50, New York: ACM.

[6] Guiard, Y. (1987). Asymmetric division of labour in human skilled bimanual action: The kinematic chain as a model. *Journal of Motor Behaviour, 19,* 486-517.

[7] Hinckley, K., Pausch, R., Proffitt, D., Patten, J., & Kassell, N. (1997). Cooperative Bimanual Action. *Proceedings of the CHI'97 Conference on Human Factors in Computing Systems,* 27-34, New York: ACM.

[8] Hopkins, D. (1991). The design and implementation of pie menus. *Dr. Dobbs' Journal,* December 1991, 16-26.

[9] Jacob, R. J. K., Sibert, L. E., McFarlane, D. C., & Mullen, M. P. (1994). Integrality and separability of input devices. *ACM Transactions on Computer-Human Interaction, 1, 1,* 3-26.

[10] Kabbash, P., Buxton, W., & Sellen, A. (1994). Two-handed input in a compound task. *Proceedings of the CHI'94 Conference on Human Factors in Computing Systems,* 417-423, New York: ACM.

[11] Kurtenbach, G. (1993). *The Design and Evaluation of Marking Menus.* Ph.D. Thesis, Department of Computer Science, University of Toronto, Toronto, Canada.

[12] Kurtenbach, G., & Buxton, W. (1993). The limits of expert performance using hierarchical marking menus. *Proceedings of InterCHI'93 Conference on Human Factors in Computing Systems,* 482-487, New York: ACM.

[13] Kurtenbach, G., Fitzmaurice, G., Baudel, T., & Buxton, W. (1997). The design of a GUI paradigm based on tablets, two-hands, and transparency. *Proceedings of the CHI'97 Conference on Human Factors in Computing Systems,* 35-42, New York: ACM.

[14] Nilsen, E. L. (1991). Perceptual-motor control in human-computer interaction. Technical Report NO. 37, Cognitive Science and Machine Intelligence Laboratory, University of Michigan.

[15] Zeleznik, R. C., Forsberg, A. S., & Strauss, P. S. (1997). Two pointer input for 3D interaction. *Proceedings of 1997 Symposium on Interactive 3D Graphics,* Providence, Rhode Island.

[16] Zhai, S., Smith, B. A., & Selker, T. (1997). Improving browsing performance: A study of four input devices for scrolling and pointing. *Proceedings of INTERACT'97: The Sixth IFIP Conference on Human-Computer Interaction*, Sydney, Australia.

Squeeze Me, Hold Me, Tilt Me! An Exploration of Manipulative User Interfaces

Beverly L. Harrison, Kenneth P. Fishkin, Anuj Gujar, Carlos Mochon*, Roy Want

Xerox Palo Alto Research Center
3333 Coyote Hill Road, Palo Alto, California, USA 94304
{beverly, fishkin, agujar, want}@parc.xerox.com, carlosm@mit.edu

ABSTRACT

This paper reports on the design and use of tactile user interfaces embedded within or wrapped around the devices that they control. We discuss three different interaction prototypes that we built. These interfaces were embedded onto two handheld devices of dramatically different form factors. We describe the design and implementation challenges, and user feedback and reactions to these prototypes. Implications for future design in the area of manipulative or haptic user interfaces are highlighted.

KEYWORDS: Physical, tactile, and haptic UIs, pressure and tilt sensors, UI design, interaction technology.

INTRODUCTION

Over the past 5 years there has been increasing interest in augmented reality and physically–based user interfaces [4, 6, 7, 8, 10, 12, 15, 16, 17]. A goal of these emerging projects is to seamlessly blend the affordances and strengths of physically manipulatable objects with virtual environments or artifacts, thereby leveraging the particular strengths of each. Typically, this integration exists in the form of physical input devices (e.g., "phicons" [7], "bricks" [4]) virtually linked to electronic graphical objects. Manipulation of the physical objects signals a related operation on the associated electronic objects. This mapping is further reinforced by tightly coupling the placement of the physical objects relative to the electronic objects on a flat table-like display surface.

Another approach has been to use standard monitors or even stereoscopic monitors with more realistic input devices [6, 8]. In these cases, unique physical input devices are cleverly matched to the requirements of the specific application domain (e.g., MRIs, remote telerobotic control). The affordances of the input devices are well matched to the virtual representation of the object that they represent. Designers of commercial video games have been taking such an approach to user interface manipulation since the invention of the Data Glove™ and, more recently with such games as flight simulators and car racing, where the UI is controlled by steering throttles or steering wheels. Again, in these examples a specialized input device controls a separate electronic display.

CHI 98 Los Angeles CA USA

These extensions to graphical user interfaces seem logical in view of the widespread support and acceptance of direct manipulation interfaces [11] and of real-world metaphors, such as trash cans and file folders [12]. We believe that such physical user interface manipulators are a natural step towards making the next UI metaphor the real world itself: real objects having real properties that are linked to or embedded in the virtual artifacts that they control. Furthermore, we conjecture that this metaphor reflects a powerful, largely unexplored user interface paradigm.

We set out to further explore this new area. We have been influenced by several previous research prototypes that reflect elements of an "embedded physicality" approach. Fitzmaurice [3], Rekimoto [9], and Small & Ishii [12] attached sensors to small handheld displays and subsequently used these displays to "scroll" through or view a larger virtual space. Movement of the display is mapped to corresponding movements in the virtual space, such as changing the view perspective [9] or to the degree of magnification [12]. These prototypes demonstrated the intuitiveness of this embedded physicality approach. The work we report here incorporates manipulations different from these previous examples to further improve our understanding of the breadth and potential of these new kinds of interactions.

Our work differs from the previous work on "physical handles" in one particularly interesting way. We are investigating situations in which the physical manipulations are directly integrated with the device or artifact, such as a small PDA, that is being controlled. We are not exploring separate input devices, but rather making the physical artifact itself become the input device by means of embedded sensor technologies.

The goal of this paper is to share our experiences in designing, building, and using several prototypes of such user interface techniques and devices and in reflecting on new ways for thinking about this new class of user interface.

* Intern at Xerox PARC from the MIT Department of Physics.

CHOOSING TASKS

We chose three diverse and previously unexamined user tasks. This allows us to explore alternative kinds of manipulations, test different sensing technologies, and more thoroughly probe the research space. Additionally, we selected tasks that represented two different types of interaction: active user interaction via explicit physical manipulations or via passive user interaction, sensed implicitly. Finally, we selected tasks that were relevant for other PARC research groups who were implementing applications for portable document devices [10]. For this reason, we focused on portable pen-based systems.

By implementing new user tasks, we hope to contribute to the general body of knowledge about physically manipulatable interfaces. We believe that this experience will assist us in formulating a more general framework, design principles, and theoretical foundations for physically afforded interfaces [2].

We chose several simple tasks: navigation within a book or document, navigation through long sequential lists, and document annotation. In the next section, we describe manipulation of real world, traditional artifacts and outline the task representation, user actions, and feedback for each of our selected tasks. Following this, we describe our three task UI designs in terms of how these real world manipulations were mapped to the devices we selected. Again we discuss our designs in terms of task representation, user actions required, and feedback. We then highlight some of the implementation decisions and tradeoffs that impacted the interaction design. Finally, we discuss feedback from the informal evaluations and interviews conducted thus far and the implications for future work.

Navigation within a Book or Document

The task representation assumes that the book or document has a number of predictable properties. These include physically manipulatable page units, a sequential organization, a thickness or "extent", and obvious start/end points. These properties afford page-by-page manipulation and movement through blocks of pages relative to the start/end points of the whole book or document. The user actions we looked at were flicking corners of pages (for page-by-page navigation) and thumbing into a location of the book/document by moving blocks of pages relative to the beginning or ending. Manipulation of these traditional artifacts provides feedback in the form of visual cues (pages move or "animate", new destination page shows, new relative location shows), auditory cues (the sound of pages turning), and kinesthetic cues (tactile pressure on finger or thumb, tactile feedback of pages moving or sliding).

Navigation through Sequential Lists

Generally, users conceptualize lists in different ways than books or documents (though similar navigation techniques could be used). We decided to use a Rolodex listing of index cards for this list navigation task. In this case, the task representation assumes physically manipulatable items or cards, a circular sequential organization, and a knob that controls the Rolodex. User actions are manipulation via turning the knob (with a rate parameter) and stopping at a desired location. Visual feedback includes the flipping of items or cards, the rate of flipping, and a new destination item or card. Auditory feedback is the sound of the cards flipping. Kinesthetic cues include finger pressure, extent of rotational movement, and direction of rotation.

Annotation and Handedness Detection

We defined this task as hand written annotation on a page-by-page basis (i.e., one page at a time), where the original page contains margins and white space within which the annotations are made. User actions are typically bimanual: the non-dominant hand anchors the page while the dominant hand writes the annotations wherever there is room. Visual feedback is the appearance of the annotations. There is minimal auditory feedback. Kinesthetic cues are the pen pressure in the hand, anchoring pressure in the non-dominant hand, and the pen/writing movement and friction.

This task is of particular interest to us in that we introduced new capabilities not available in the real world annotation task. As such, it represents an opportunity for computationally enhanced interaction. In traditional page annotation users must fit the annotations into existing, limited white space based on the static layout of the page. During annotation, their writing hand also often obstructs the text that they are commenting on. We decided to optimize annotation by maximizing the amount of white space and its position within the page. We detect the handedness of the user and then dynamically shift the text "away" from the writing hand thereby maximizing white space directly under that hand (see Figure 4 bottom). We describe this design and the implementation of it in subsequent sections.

SELECTION OF DEVICES

Our design criteria were that the devices chosen would be handheld, support pen-based input, allow serial port input (for sensor communication), have a development environment for custom applications, and be cost effective (since we anticipated embedded hardware). Ideally, we wanted several devices with different form factors.

We decided to use two different portable devices to test our manipulations. We chose to use a handheld computer for the page turning and handedness detection manipulations (a Casio Cassiopeia™). For the list navigation manipulations, we chose a Palm Pilot™. Clearly, a number of other devices could have been selected – these two were chosen for their ubiquity.

DESIGNING THE INTERACTION

Navigation within a Book or Document

This task was divided into several simple, common subtasks: turning to the next page, turning to the previous page, and moving forward or backwards in large "chunks" relative to the beginning and ending of the document.

Page-by-page navigation

We now had to decide on how these tasks would be accomplished by a user – we tried for manipulations similar to those used in traditional artifacts. As the Cassio™ displayed individual pages with a sequential ordering, we decided to use a flick on the upper right corner from right to left to indicate "forward one page". A flick on the upper left corner from left to right would indicate "back one page". These actions were highly similar to the real world actions. Visual feedback was similar; pages changed (without animation), and the new destination page and page number became visible after the user action. After a page turning manipulation, both the page number and the contents change to reflect either the preceding or next page, depending upon the direction of the stroke. However, we did not implement sound effects in this iteration and some kinesthetic feedback was lost (notably the friction of pages sliding). Figure 1 shows a "real-world" page-turning gesture (top), and the implemented interface to the page-turning command (bottom) on the Cassio™.

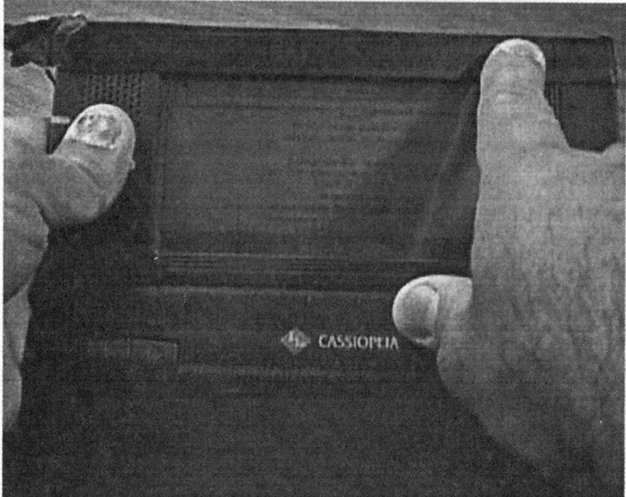

Figure 1. Page-by-page navigation, real-world (top) and with the prototype (bottom)

This interaction requires that the left and right upper corner detect a finger press, the direction of a stroke, and a release of pressure. Several implementation options are possible. Within each application where document reading occurs, a touch sensitive display can detect pressure points and their origin, determine if this aligns with a document upper corner, track the path of pressure to determine the stroke direction, and execute the appropriate page turn. Alternatively, the surface of the device can have pressure sensors attached to it, which detect when they are pressed, detect the direction of pressure from a stroke, and have the active application respond appropriately. We decided to try this approach since this allowed us to "retro-fit" pressure-sensing technology onto a normally pressure-insensitive device. Also, we did not need to use valuable screen real estate for the large area graphics needed to display a finger operated button. Finally, this would provide us with opportunities to later use the sensor technology in other application contexts and across applications.

Navigation by relative position

The extent and start/end points were not obviously represented (the thickness of the Cassio™ was invariant and too narrow for relative positioning). Hence moving forward or backward by chunks relative to the beginning or ending of a document was more difficult to represent for virtual documents. We decided to use a grasping manipulation at the top of the device, where the relative position of the grasp determined the relative position within the document. Far left corresponded to page 1 and far right corresponded to the last page. While this was not tightly analogous to known real world metaphors, it appealed to the well-known GUI metaphor of the scroll bar. A grasp gesture will move to a new location in the document and display the new location's page number and contents.

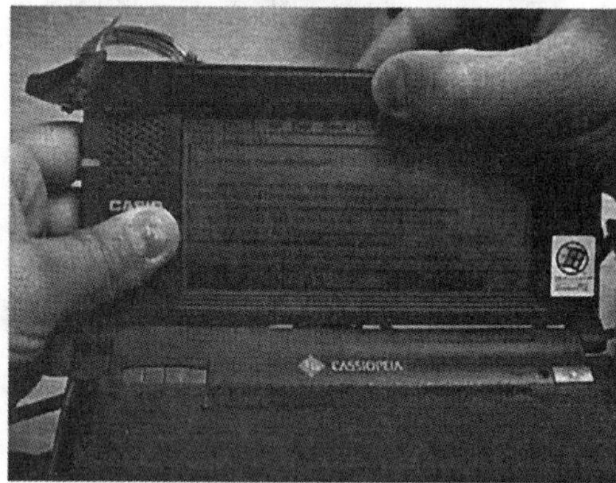

Figure 2. Navigation by relative position

Based on our chosen representation for moving by "chunks" and the corresponding user action, we again decided to use pressure sensors. To detect a grasp with the thumb and a finger, pressure strips were attached along the front top edge of the device. Grasping any portion of the strip moves to a document position relative to the beginning or ending of the document, where the beginning maps to the far left of the strip and the end maps to the far right of the strip. For example, Figure 2 shows a "grasp" gesture moving the display to roughly 2/3 of the way through of the document.

Navigation through Sequential Lists

We used a Rolodex metaphor-based technique for list navigation (see Figure 3, top). The circular list is manipulated by turning the Rolodex, while the direction of the turn determines whether the cards flip from A to Z or from Z to A. Our device-embodied representation was similar to the real world artifact in that we used items with visual tabs arranged in a sequence. Turning the circular list towards the user would begin flipping through from A towards Z (assuming an alphabetized list) and vice-versa. On a physical Rolodex, users turn the knob rotationally (at some rate of speed) (Figure 3, top). On the Palm Pilot™, the user action was in fact a tilt movement away from a neutral resting position and not a rotational turn of a knob (this would be more akin to rotation of the entire Rolodex). Instead of having a rate or speed of turning we used the extent or degree of tilt (Figure 3, bottom). Turning "harder" (i.e., to a larger extreme) moves faster through the list, similar to Rekimoto [9]. To stop at or select a particular item, the user either ceases to tilt (i.e., maintains the list container in a neutral or vertical position relative to that item), or squeezes the device, mimicking a grasping gesture (akin to grasping the Rolodex card).

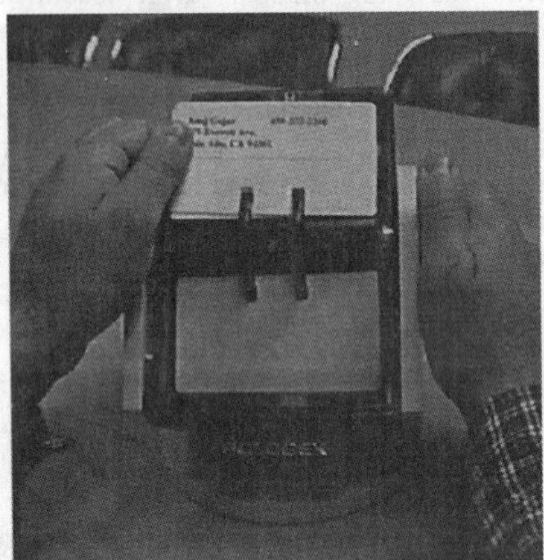

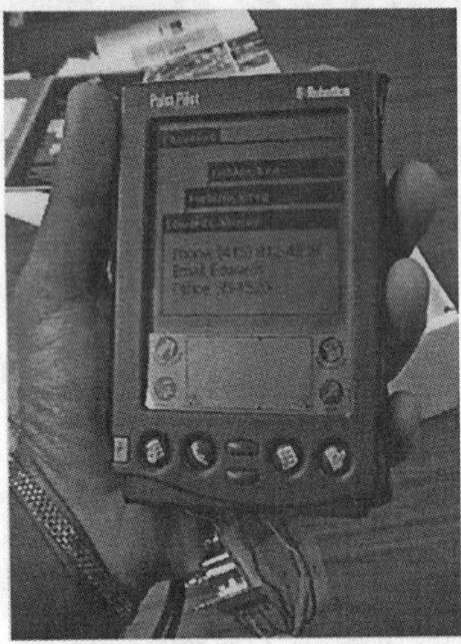

Figure 3. list navigation, real-world, knob rotation (top), and with the prototype, device tilt (bottom)

Annotation and Handedness Detection

Finally, we consider the task of optimizing annotation through maximizing "appropriate" white space and maximizing text visibility by detecting handedness. Sensing handedness means that text or graphics would be moved towards the non-dominant hand while screen space would be maximized on the opposite side (next to the hand holding the stylus). This strategy is appropriate for maximizing legibility of the text while holding the stylus and annotating adjacent to the text (Figure 4, top). In general, we were also interested in exploring different unobtrusive mechanisms for determining handedness.

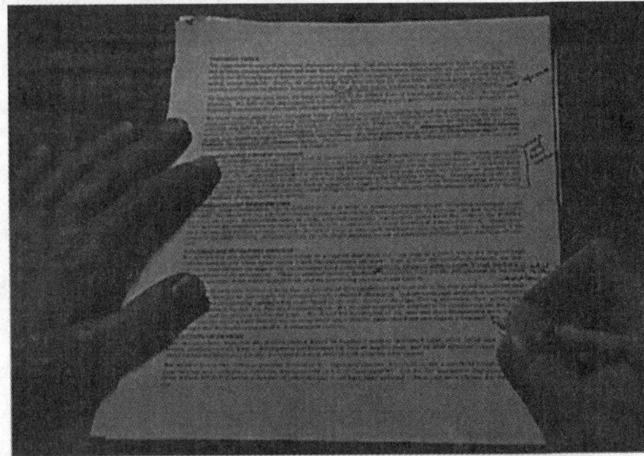

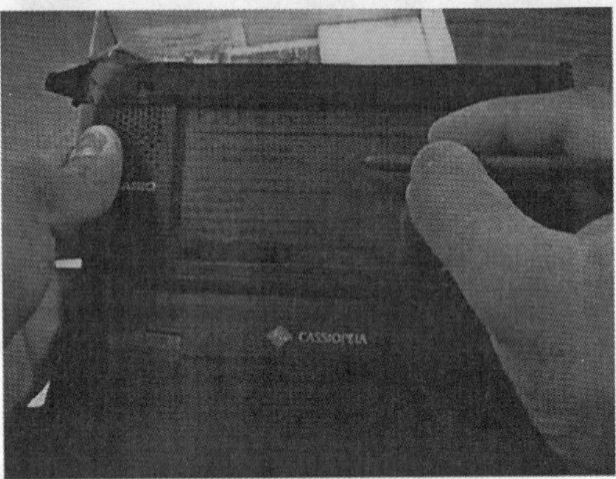

Figure 4. Annotation, real-world (top) and with the prototype (bottom)

For the handedness detection task we needed to understand something about how users hold and operate the intended device. We designed this such that no special manipulation was needed other than picking up the device and/or stylus. (i.e., "passive user interaction"). The handedness detection is immediately visible when the user invokes any application that wants to be "handedness-aware". In the specific task we implemented, for a right-handed user, text is immediately left justified and annotation space remains at the right side of the text (Figure 4, bottom). The reverse is true for left handed users. When both hands are used or the device is set down (i.e., no hands), the text appears centered. Feedback from the annotation remains consistent with the real world case; ink trails appear as the pen writes.

Finally, we examined sensor options for unobtrusively determining handedness. Several implementation paths were considered. Heat sensors on either side of the device could potentially detect whether contact with a hand occurred on the right or left side of the device (based on heat from the user's hand). However, this detection would be complex since physical extremities such as hands and feet generate heat levels comparable to many other environmental factors, including that of the device itself. Another alternative was to detect properties of the writing which are unique to left handed or right handed writing styles. This is somewhat problematic since these algorithms are complex and the system can only take effect after the user has started writing. We decided to use pressure sensors again, this time to determine the points of contact and detect how the device was being held (if at all). Pressure sensing pads were attached to the back of the device, on the left and right sides, in alignment with positions used for holding the device.

IMPLEMENTATION

We now focus on the implementation details and issues that directly impacted the user interface and interaction design.

Navigation within a Book or Document

The Casio device was augmented with a network of pressure sensors. Two overlaid strips on the top edge detect the page turning manipulations (Figures 1 and 2). The pressure sensor network reports its current values through an interface connected to the RS232 port on the device. A simple communications protocol was devised, where each packet indicates the ID of the reporting sensor, and the current value of the sensor. Packets are only sent when the value changes. Absolute values, rather than deltas, are reported, so that we can recover from dropped/damaged packets. The document reading application runs as a multi-threaded application under Windows CE: one thread performs user I/O, while the other monitors the sensor stream.

To implement the page turning manipulations, two pressure sensors are overlaid at the top edge of the device. One type of sensor strip reports pressure, but not spatial location. The second type reports spatial location, but not pressure. Unfortunately, the spatial sensor tended to have a great deal of jitter. In order to compensate for this, two measurements were made from the spatial sensor: the first measuring the distance from the left end, the second measuring the distance from the right end. The sum of these two values should be a constant - if they differ too much from this constant, the values are rejected. Otherwise, the average of the two values is used. The {location, pressure} values are stored from the moment of pressure-down to pressure-up. If the sum of the inter-location differences is negative, the user is deemed to be stroking from right-to-left. If the sum is positive, the user is deemed to be stroking from left-to-right. If, regardless of this sum, the range of spatial locations is in a narrow range, the user is deemed to be pressing at a certain spot (i.e., the "grasp" gesture).

Navigation through Sequential Lists

In order to implement a tilt detection mechanism for continuous list scrolling on a handheld computer, we investigated a number of sensors. The commercially available tilt-sensor design we chose is based on an electrolyte bordered on two sides by a pair of conductive plates. As the device is angled towards or away from either plate, the amount of electrolyte in contact with the plate varies. The area of fluid in contact with each plate will affect the impedance presented by the contacts of the sensor. By monitoring this impedance and converting its change into a voltage, a simple ADC interface to a microcontroller can capture the data and then process it. In our system the tilt angle is converted into a 4-bit value and transmitted to the Palm Pilot™ across an RS232 link after being prefixed with the 4-bit sensor-ID, a total of 8 bits for each tilt sample.

By mounting a tilt sensor of this type to the case of a Palm Pilot™, with the sensor plates parallel to the plane of the display, we were able to use the sensor readings as a crude measure of the computer's orientation relative to gravity. We arranged it so that the Pilot generated a neutral reading at the 45 degree point and produced 8 readings forward and backwards from that position: 45 degrees being close to the angle that most people use to read from the display of the Pilot. Even though the range of angles detectable is thus very coarsely defined, we found that it has been adequate to implement and support the Rolodex–like metaphor.

In addition to sensing tilt, the system must differentiate between inadvertent tilting, such as when walking with it, and intentional tilting, when the user wishes to navigate. There are two possible ways of addressing this issue. The first method is to apply higher threshold values to the tilt sensing itself, thereby removing manipulations which are not of extremes and hence presumably retaining only deliberate user requests. This was infeasible in our desired application since we wished to use ranges of tilt to indicate the rate of list movement. Another possible solution is to create a second specific manipulation that indicates user intention. In our case, we decided to use an initial squeeze of the device to indicate the desire to navigate through the list, followed by a second squeeze to "grasp" the desired item, thereby ending the navigation task. To avoid muscle stress, users did not have to maintain the squeezing pressure during navigation. The device was padded with foam to further suggest squeezing capability.

To achieve the squeeze feature, we attached pressure sensors along both sides of the Palm Pilot™ in positions that aligned with the users' fingers and thumb (independent of which hand was holding the device). To differentiate squeezing from holding the device, we tested 10 users and derived an appropriate threshold value for the pressure sensors. (In this case, using higher pressure threshold values to differentiate inadvertent from intentional action was appropriate). The "squeezing" gesture has several advantages for users of a hand-held device. It doesn't require that the user reposition either hand, or that the users alter their viewing angle or viewing distance to the device, requiring only a momentary increase in the pressure used to hold the device. While the sensors report which finger(s) are exerting this pressure, at present our algorithms make no use of this additional information.

The list navigation task provides two levels of user feedback. Since the device is often moved about, the "tilt feature" is initially disabled. When users wish to navigate through lists they commence movement by squeezing the device. At this point the device is tilt-enabled. At present we have a message displayed indicating this to the users (it says "Go Tilt!"). Clearly, a different message and a different means of conveying tilt-enabled would be better. Independent of this or any message, it is visually obvious when tilt-based navigation is enabled. Tilting works as described and users can see the list flipping through entries at varying rates of speed in the appropriate direction, depending upon the direction and magnitude of the tilt. The display ceases moving when the user either holds the device in the neutral position or again squeezes the device, thereby disabling tilt. (This is akin to grabbing the currently displayed item).

Annotation and Handedness Detection

Since these handheld devices are typically gripped by the edge with one hand, while they are used with the other hand, we detected handedness by mounting two pressure-sensitive pads on the back surface. If the pressure pad on the back left is pressed, the sensor thread of the program concludes that the user is holding the device with (at least) the left hand. If the pad on the back right is pressed, the program concludes that the user is holding the device with (at least) the right hand.

USAGE

A number of design issues arose as we iterated through the design and development of the prototypes. We did a number of in-laboratory, informal user tests to estimate threshold values for sensors. Typically this was done with our immediate research project group and a few other interested people (n=7). Once the sensor values were initially determined, we then carried out informal user testing and interviews on 15 different people outside our research project group. These users were fellow research staff who had little experience with physically manipulatable interfaces. Users were not instructed on how to hold the devices. They were given only brief descriptions of what the sensors would do (e.g., turns pages like you would in a paper document, tilting this moves through the Rolodex list). Following this, we observed them and recorded their comments. We asked them specific questions about what they expected to occur, what problems they encountered, and what they liked most and least.

General Comments and Impressions

In general, our test users found the manipulations "intuitive", "cool", and "pretty obvious in terms of what was going on." Some users needed quick demonstrations to understand that their manipulations would actually be interpreted. Our users had little or no exposure to physically embedded user interfaces and therefore often did not expect interaction with the device to be understood. Undoubtedly, conveying the basic paradigm will be necessary in the same way that users needed to understand the conceptual foundation for direct manipulation interfaces and mice. Once users understood the basic paradigm, they immediately began to explore the range of interaction. Just as GUIs users try to find out what is "clickable" by moving around the screen with the cursor and clicking, our test users tried a variety of manipulations on the prototypes to see what the range of detectable manipulations was. For example, to turn pages they tried long and short strokes, fast and slow strokes, light and hard strokes, and starting the stroke at different points on the device surface.

While the user explicit actions were quickly understood, the passive interaction (handedness) was perceived as "magical." Since no explicit commands or manipulations were needed, users seemed amazed that the device recognized and optimized for handedness. They were unable to tell how this was accomplished without us explaining it. This suggests not only that passive manipulations can be powerful, but that they greatly impact a user's interaction experience when well integrated with the form factor of the device. We clearly need to explore more passive manipulations to see if this is a general property. Additionally, this illustrates an opportunity for computationally augmented task representations that provide more than the real world analogy (in experientially positive ways).

Navigation within a Book or Document

Several interesting usage observations were made in these tasks. Because of our need to overlay pressure sensors, users now had to exert greater pressure than they expected for the page-turning manipulations. Users try out manipulations based on their expectations from the real world. A page turn in a paperback book, for example, takes very little pressure. All of our users initially attempted exactly the same manipulation on the device, which was too light to be sensed. However, they were able to quickly adjust with practice.

In general, we believe that users will attempt to exactly replicate the analogous real–world manipulation, when those metaphors are used; and they will expect them to work. If we are striving for enriched interaction experiences, the more exactly we can support or match these expectations the better. Making our sensors more sensitive to detect lighter page turning strokes would clearly be an improvement.

Users had no problem in discovering the manipulation needed for "previous page" once they had tried the "next page" manipulation. Despite slight differences in the pressure required over that of real–world interaction, users relied on extending their understanding of the real–world metaphor to guide their further assumptions about what was possible with the device–embodied interface. As in GUI design, small inconsistencies in metaphor seem to be forgiven.

Users needed to have the "navigation by chunks" mechanism described to them. Almost certainly this was because the device did not resemble a book, nor did the manipulation map directly to the manipulation in the real world. Grasping along a strip to indicate relative position is unique to this interaction. Once described or briefly demonstrated, users had no trouble remembering this manipulation or applying it.

One difficulty arose as a consequence of our implementation strategy. Since page turning strokes and grasping are both done on the same region and using the same pressure sensors, it was sometimes difficult to differentiate between a very short "stroke" and a wide "grasp." Our disambiguating algorithm would sometimes compute this incorrectly, which would surprise the users. Since users' finger widths vary and we also want to support short strokes, this problem is not easily solved. We need to re-examine (a) whether there are better sensing technologies available or a different sensor configuration that would solve this, (b) whether minor alterations to the manipulations used would help differentiate the two, or (c) whether there is a better metaphor for navigation by chunks. (We have already implemented another version of page-by-page navigation on a tablet computer using 2 independent but adjacent small pressure sensors in the corners of the device. This seems highly reliable but makes integration with a stroke gesture (relative positioning) less seamless since pressure strips are not extended over these pressure pads to the edges of the device).

In general, the "navigation by chunks" task illustrates the tradeoff between intuitive real–world mappings which try to stay true to the real–world (and hence may be difficult to implement) versus learned mappings (which may be more easily integrated into the device). At this point, it is unclear how much learning is reasonable given that the overall goal is enriched interaction experience and intuitive interfaces.

Navigation through Sequential Lists

The list navigation task revealed some additional design issues (thus supporting our strategy of prototyping different device form factors, different manipulations, and different sensing technologies).

One issue was determining the range of angles for the tilt operation and the value for the neutral angle where the device remains in a resting state. We determined the initial neutral angle by in-laboratory testing. The range of tilt angles was partly based on just noticeable differences, both in terms of discernable tilt angles and in terms of discernable list scrolling speeds. The range of perceptible tilt is clearly an important determinant in setting and assigning values for the tilt manipulation's parameters. At present the 16 sensed tilt angles map to 6 different rates of scrolling.

One result of broader user testing identified the difficulty in stopping at a particular item within a list. Users would scroll quickly to the correct general area, then attempt to scroll slowly to the desired item. We now believe that our slow scrolling speed is still set too fast, as users tend to overshoot the target item. We believe that it is generally necessary to fine tune continuously issued gestural commands that control rate and/or direction of a corresponding action. We are investigating this issue further to determine how much individual difference amongst users effects their ability to precisely control list manipulation. This suggests that some "layered manipulations" may be useful, with one type of manipulation for coarsely specified actions, followed by a second manipulation for finely specified actions (as Guiard's bi-manual research suggests for handedness [5]). Trained parameterization or user-customized settings may also help alleviate this problem.

Finally, as a consequence of using tilt to control list navigation, display visibility was an issue. In particular, we avoided use of extreme angles of tilt, since the Palm Pilot™ display was not readable at these angles. Different devices and/or displays have different viewing angle restrictions with must be taken into account if the display is the primary feedback mechanism or if the display plays a central role in the task.

Annotation and Handedness Detection

The passive sensing used in the detection of handedness worked amazingly well. It detected and responded correctly, and users did not need to alter their usage of the device in any way from what seemed natural. All users remarked on the "magical" nature of this feature. We believe that the success of this feature is partly due to the in-laboratory, pre-testing we carried out. We tested 15 different users to fine-tune the placement of the pressure pads to accommodate different sized hands, slight differences in method for holding the device, and whether the left and right hand were used in exactly the same positions.

A possibility for the strong positive reactions to the seamingly "magical" feature was the augmentation of real-world capabilities. By optimizing annotation space, we have created a function that does not exist in the corresponding real-world scenario. In order to create computational *enhancements* (as opposed to unexpected and bizarre system performance), the system must accurately "know" what the user wants to do. These underlying assumptions and the subsequent matching of systems responses to user expectation are crucial. In this case, annotation optimization worked well because our assumptions accurately predicted user goals.

One aspect of this interaction that still requires adjustment is the changeover from one hand to another. If users momentarily shift the device from one hand to the other, the contents of the screen immediately move as well. Some users commented that seeing the screen contents jump around was disconcerting. However, it is unclear how often this scenario would arise in actual day-to-day usage. One improvement would be to briefly delay the screen change to determine that the user is not merely rapidly shifting the device to be more comfortable. Determining this time duration for detecting a "resting state" versus a "transient and temporary change" might improve the current interface.

FUTURE DIRECTIONS

In this paper we have explored the design, implementation and testing of three specific cases of physical manipulation prototypes. We discussed issues raised in designing and implementing these prototypes. And we have briefly outlined some of the results of user testing of these prototypes. Much interesting research remains to be done.

Our strategy is to implement other novel manipulations, new device-embodied task representations, and test new sensor technologies. We are interested in further exploring explicit manipulations as well as seamlessly sensed passive manipulations, with a goal of better understanding how this new paradigm can enrich the user's interaction experience.

This new type of interaction can be very dependent on the form factor of the device being augmented. We are interested in incorporating new manipulations into a number of different devices including tablet computers, conventional scanners, copiers, and monitors.

User expectation is often based on real–world experience and feedback, particularly if strongly analogous situations are represented. We would like to augment the simple visual feedback of the current prototypes to also include auditory feedback, animation, and potentially increased tactile feedback (though not necessarily forced-feedback).

We would also like to prototype some devices without displays and determine what kinds of manipulations and status indicators are possible and what types of computational power can be enhanced by such devices.

These all represent interesting research avenues for further systematic investigation. These should lead us to a better understanding of physically embedded user interfaces as a new paradigm, its limitations and strengths, and design principles to guide others exploring this area.

ACKNOWLEDGMENTS

We wish to particularly thank Tom Moran of Xerox PARC for his many substantive suggestions on the structure of this paper and for his extensive collaborative efforts in defining possible theoretical frameworks for this work [2]. We also thank the CHI reviewers for their helpful comments and suggestions. Our research additionally benefited from input given by members of the Portable Document Reader group at Xerox PARC, DpiX, and FXPAL. Finally, thanks to Rob Burtzlaff, patent attorney extraordinaire, without whom this paper might not have been released for publication.

REFERENCES

1. Card, S. K., Mackinlay, J. D., and Robertson, G. A. A Morphological Analysis of the Design Space of Input Devices. *ACM Transactions on Information Systems*, (2), April 1991, pp. 99-122.
2. Fishkin, K. P., Moran, T., and Harrison, B. L. Design Principles for Manipulative User Interfaces. Working Paper, December 1997. Xerox Palo Alto Research Center. Palo Alto, CA.
3. Fitzmaurice, G. Situated Information Spaces and Spatially Aware Palmtop Computers, *CACM*, *36*(7), July 1993, pp.38-49.
4. Fitzmaurice, G., Ishii, H., and Buxton, W. A. S. Laying the Foundations for Graspable User Interfaces. *Proceedings of CHI'95*, pp. 422-449.
5. Guiard, Y. and Ferrand, T. Asymmetry in Bimannual Skills. In *Manual Asymmetries in Motor Performance*, Elliot & Roy (eds), 1995, pp. 176-195. CRC Press, Boca Raton FL.
6. Hinckley, K., Pausch, R., Goble, J. and Kassel, N. Passive Real-World Interface Props for Neurosurgical Visualization, *Proceedings of CHI'94*, pp. 452-458.
7. Ishii, H. and Ullmer, B. Tangible Bits: Towards Seamless Interfaces between People, Bits, and Atoms. *Proceedings of CHI'97*, pp. 234-241.
8. Milgram, P. Rastogi, A., and Grodski, J. J. Telerobotic Control Using Augmented Reality. *IEEE Robot and Human Communication (RO-MAN)'95*, Japan, July 1995.
9. Rekimoto, J. Tilting Operations for Small Screen Interfaces. *Proceedings of UIST '96*, pp.167-168.
10. Schilit B. N., Golovchinsky, G and Price M. Beyond Paper: Supporting Active Reading with free-form digital ink annotations. *Proceedings of CHI'98.*
11. Schneiderman, B. The Future of Interactive Systems and the Emergence of Direct Manipulation. *Behaviour and Information Technology*, *1*, 1982, pp. 237-256.
12. Small, D., and Ishii, H. Design of Spatially Aware Graspable Displays. *Extended Abstracts of CHI'97*, pp. 367-368.
13. Smith, D. C., Irby, C. H., Kimball, R., Verplank, W., and Harslem, E. Deisgning the Star User Interface. *Byte* 7(4), April 1982, pp. 242-282.
14. Taylor, A. R., Nonverbal Communications Systems in Native North America. *Semiotica*, *13*(4), 1975, pp. 329-374.
15. Want, R., Schilit, B. N., Adams, N. I., Gold, R., Petersen, K., Goldberg, D., Ellis, J. R., and Weiser, M. An Overview of the ParcTab Ubiquitous Computing Experiment. *IEEE Personal Communications*, December 1995, pp. 28-43.
16. Weiser, M. The Computer for the 21st Century. *Scientific America*, *265*(3), 1991, pp. 94-104.
17. Wellner, P. Mackay, W., and Gold, R. Computer Augmented Environments: Back to the Real World. *CACM*, *36*(7), July 1993.

Web Page Design: Implications of Memory, Structure and Scent for Information Retrieval

Kevin Larson and Mary Czerwinski
Microsoft Research
One Microsoft Way
Redmond, WA 98052, USA
+1-425-936-8259, +1-425-703-4882
a-kevlar@microsoft.com, marycz@microsoft.com

ABSTRACT
Much is known about depth and breadth tradeoff issues in graphical user interface menu design. We describe an experiment to see if large breadth and decreased depth is preferable, both subjectively and via performance data, while attempting to design for optimal scent throughout different structures of a website. A study is reported which modified previous procedures for investigating depth/breadth tradeoffs in content design for the web. Results showed that, while increased depth did harm search performance on the web, a medium condition of depth and breadth outperformed the broadest, shallow web structure overall.

Keywords
Information retrieval, memory, depth and breadth in information design, web page design, hypertext, searching.

INTRODUCTION
The goal of this study was to discover principles for the design of multiple hyperlinks on a web page for information retrieval tasks. Of particular interest was the optimal depth versus breadth of the hyperlinks' distribution across expertly categorized web content, with an emphasis on the importance of structure. In addtion, an effort was made to tie the findings both to current research in information retrieval and web design for large information spaces. The differential effects of short-term memory and visual scanning were examined as cognitive covariates in the experiment.

Optimal Number of Menu Items
There has been a vast amount of work exploring the optimal number of items in a menu design [8, 2, 15, 6, 5]. Most studies concluded that breadth was better than depth when it came to organizing menu contents, although the breadth of the menus examined has varied from study to study.

D. Miller [8] tested four structures with 64 bottom level nodes: 2^6 (six levels of depth each with two items of breadth), 4^3 (three levels of depth each with four items of breadth), 8^2 (two levels of depth each with eight items of breadth), & 64^1 (64 top-level items). The 8^2 condition allowed the fastest acquisition and fewest errors of the four structures. D. Miller suggested that depth of a hierarchy should be minimized, but not at the expense of display crowding. He also mentioned that the level of breadth that tested well (8^2), fit well within the range of G. Miller's [9] 7+/-2 finding on the limits of short-term memory.

Snowberry, Parkinson & Sisson [15] replicated and extended D. Miller's [8] study by examining the same for depth/breadth tradeoff conditions (2^6, 4^3, 8^2, and 64^1). They included an initial screening session during which subjects were administered memory span and visual scanning tests in an effort to tease out their contributions in subjects' performance data. They found that memory span was not predictive of performance in any of the conditions, but that visual scanning was predictive of performance, especially in the deepest hierarchies.

Kiger [6] tested five structures with 64 bottom level nodes (2^6, 4^3, 8^2, 16x4, 4x16) and collected both performance and preference data. The 4x16 structure (four top level items each containing 16 items) had the fastest reaction times, followed closely, and not reliably different from 16x4 and 8^2. The 4x16 structure also had the fewest errors, followed closely, and again not reliably different from the 8^2 and 16x4 conditions. Subjectively, subjects favored the 8^2 structure when asked about both ease of use and preference. For both ease of use and preference, the 4^3 and 4x16 conditions followed behind by a non-reliable difference.

Jacko & Salvendy [5] tested six structures varying both depth and breadth without controlling for the size of lowest-level search area. The structures (2^2, 2^3, 2^6, 8^2, 8^3, and $8^{6)}$ were measured for reaction time, error rates, and subjective preference. Jacko & Salvendy found reliable differences in reaction time for depth, breadth, subjects, and the depth by breadth interaction. There were reliable differences in accuracy and perceived complexity only for depth. Relating these findings back to complexity theory [1], they concluded that as you increase breadth and/or depth, reaction time, error rates, and perceived complexity will all increase. The cognitive substrate governing this complexity was assumed to be short-term memory (although neither short-term memory nor attentional contributions were uniquely factored out in this study). This stands in contrast to Snowberry et al.'s conclusions that found visual scanning to be more predictive of performance, especially in deep structures.

The Importance of Category Structure

D. Miller [8] and Kiger [6] created categories that had identical bottom level nodes in each of their structures. While on the surface this was a sound experimental control, it had the side effect of creating somewhat unwieldy category structures. For instance, "Science News: Psychology", "Science News: Biology", "Science News: Physics", and "Science News: Chemistry" all existed together on a level of one structure where the four sciences were all under the category "Science News" in another structure. In effect the same category structure existed in both hierarchy levels, but counted as one level of depth in the first instance, and two levels of depth in the second instance. Note that this experimental control could be related to the theoretical notion of "scent" [12], where scent has been described as conveying distal target information via category labeling. According to Information Foraging Theory [13], scent is the amount of remote indication a user can derive from an information structure's design and labeling about the relative location of a target. Therefore, in these studies, some structures may have performed better than others because they had stronger scent for the target at the top levels of the hierarchy (i.e., their category labels were more distinctive at the top level). Couched in these theoretical terms, the views of the information structures were examined, but not their navigability [4]. Snowberry, Parkinson, and Sisson [15] showed the strong advantage for structurally grouping like objects. As mentioned earlier they re-ran the D. Miller [8] study, but they did so with one additional structure. In addition to the 2^6, 4^3, & 8^2 structures, they ran 2 forms of the 64^1 structure. One form of the 64^1 structure was similar to D. Miller's, with items randomly grouped on screen. The other 64^1 structure included items grouped into coherent categories. Snowberry et al. found that when categorical grouping was utilized, there was an advantage for the broad 64^1 structure in both accuracy and speed, and these advantages were not eliminated with practice. This was not true for the randomly organized 64^1 structure.

Landauer & Nachbar [7] presented a predictive equation for amount of time to make a decision given X number of extremely grouped alternatives. They created 4 different structures (2^{12}, 4^6, 8^4, and 16^3) with 4096 bottom level nodes each. The bottom level nodes were the numbers 1 through 4096, and at higher levels the numbers were grouped into equal categories, such as 1-2048 and 2049-4096 at the top level of the structure with 2 items of breadth. Landauer and Nachbar found that the reaction time for any given screen would increase linearly with number of alternatives, but that total search time decreased with higher numbers of alternatives per screen because there were fewer levels of depth. They also found the same results with 4096 alphabetized words, and came out in favor of designing broad, shallow displays based on these results.

Training

An important issue in both D. Miller's and Snowberry et al.'s studies was that subjects were given the hierarchies to study for rather long periods of time, and given extensive feedback during testing when correct or incorrect categorical choices had been made during searches. This could have contributed to subjects' relying much more heavily upon a learned structure than they normally would or could when traversing the World Wide Web. Since most of the studies reviewed showed significant effects of training on performance, these studies were clearly examining best case performance. Given that the World Wide Web is constantly being altered and extended, how generalizable are these findings to web design? Will broad, shallow web pages really provide a performance advantage when searching through unfamiliar or loosely related constructs?

The Magic Number 7

Four decades ago, G. Miller [9] offered a general rule of thumb that the span of immediate memory is about 7 +/- 2 items. When people are asked to distinguish between different tones, if the number of tones presented is over about 5, their accuracy at this task decreases rapidly. When asked to recall a series of unrelated words or numbers, people fail when the size of the series increases to 6 or 7. In other words, the span of immediate memory imposes severe limitations on the number of items we are able to receive, process and remember. Although there has been much controversy over the "magic number 7", as it is often referred to, G. Miller recognized that by organizing items into categorical units or chunks, we can at least stretch an apparent short-term memory bottleneck.

A commonality with the D. Miller, Kiger, and Jacko & Salvendy papers is that the breadth of the structures with superior performance falls in the range of 7 +/- 2. Kiger [6] says, "...the data seem to indicate both preference and performance advantage for broad, shallow trees. Interestingly, the tree structure resulting in best user performance used a menu breadth that falls within G.A. Miller's [9] 'seven plus or minus two' estimation of short-term memory capacity... As a general principle, the depth of a tree structure should be minimized by providing broad menus of up to eight or nine items each." In essence, G. Miller's findings that people are only able to make quick, accurate decisions with a small handful of objects at a time has had wide support across studies, and may provide useful guidance in the design of web hyperlinks across pages.

Breadth on the Web

While limiting the breadth of items in menu design has been standard practice, the same is certainly not true of information design on the web, or with some of the newer information visualization techniques. There are numerous examples of structures with enormous breadth. One need not travel far to see structures with breadths wider than what were covered in the studies mentioned above. For example:

http://www.cnet.com/ – technology magazine
http://www.yahoo.com/ – indexed content
http://www.cnn.com – newspaper
http://www.lycos.com – search engine
http://www.cs.uh.edu/~clifton/index.html – encyclopedia
http://www.slate.com/ – political magazine

Zaphiris & Mtei [17] examined the depth/breadth tradeoff on the web. In their study they attempted to replicate Kiger's structures, but using web hyperlinks. They found that of the 5 structures tested (2^6, 4^3, 8^2, 16x4, 4x16) the 8^2 structure was the fastest to search, followed by the 4x16 structure (with non-reliable differences). Subjects ranked the structures in order of ease of use from easiest to hardest: 16x4, 4x16, 4^3, 8^2, and 2^6, though there were no reliable differences among the top 4. Zaphiris & Mtei state, "...overall our results are in agreement with those of Kiger [6] where it has been proven that access time is proportional to depth in menu selection".

While there is overwhelming evidence that structures with a breadth less than G. Miller's magical number are not optimal (when depth is high), there is less evidence that structures with greater breadth are to be recommended (if depth is reasonable). Snowberry et al. and Landauer and Nachbar provided the first evidence in the literature that suggests a broad, shallow structure that does not fall within Miller's magic number of seven might be optimal for menu design. It remains unclear which of these design principles (memory-constrained or depth-constrained design) holds more weight, and how tightly they are coupled to the category structure of the information space.

In addition, there has been the aforementioned movement in the information retrieval literature to provide the user interface artifacts of "scent" [12] optimally for the end user in web design. According to these theoretical perspectives, the design challenge is to distribute "scent" optimally throughout a well-partitioned information structure. We describe an experiment to see if large breadth and decreased depth is preferable, both subjectively and via performance data, while attempting to design for optimal scent throughout different structures of a website. In the discussion section, we will attempt to link our findings to the theoretical notions of scent and any corresponding design issues.

METHODS

Subjects

19 subjects were taken from the Microsoft database of people who identify themselves as willing participants in computer related studies. The subjects were all experienced computer and web users: users who had used windows computers for at least two years, had used the web for at least one year, and were using the web at least twice per week. Subjects were rewarded with Microsoft software for participating in the study.

Materials

The visual scanning and memory span pre-tests were chosen from the Kit of Factor-Referenced Cognitive Tests [3]. The Memory Span pre-test chosen was the Auditory Number Span Test (MS-1); the visual scanning pre-test presented to subjects was the Finding A's Test (P-1) from the Perceptual Speed sub-tests. Due to time constraints, only one fifth of each sub-test was included in this study. The visual scanning sub-test took 30 seconds to complete, while the memory span test was verbally presented to subjects, at the rate of one digit per second. The test administration took approximately 3 minutes.

Both the content and the categorization scheme that subjects searched were pulled from the Encarta® encyclopedia. There were three different categorization structures, each with 512 bottom level nodes. The three different structures were 8x8x8 (8 top-level categories, each with 8 sub-levels, and 8 content level categories under each sub-level), 16x32 (16 top-level categories, each with 32 content level categories), and 32x16 (32 top-level categories, each with 16 content level categories). One problem with previous studies on this topic is that category "soundness" or naturalness was confounded across depth and breadth conditions. In order to create natural categories, therefore, it was not optimal to use identical content level categories for each structure. The emphasis was to create category labels that would be sensible to users, or to maintain good scent throughout the structures. Instead of choosing 512 bottom level nodes, then fitting different structures to those items, three sensible structures were created and populated with items that naturally belonged to the structures. Because of this, only a quarter of the total 512 items in each structure (128 items) appeared in all three structures. These 128 overlapping items therefore became the set of possible search targets for the study. A nagging problem for us was that these structures were not user tested to control for category soundness, which would have been optimal. Instead, due to time constraints, we invited an editor to establish the category contents for each structure, which resulted in categories that appeared natural to us. This therefore resulted in at least an initial effort to tease apart the effects of structure, scent and category soundness. A portion of each of the three category structures is included in Appendix A.

Since the same 128 targets appeared in each of the hierarchies, subjects' semantic knowledge of the target as well as the target word's length and frequency was controlled. Because items outside of the target search set varied from hierarchy to hierarchy, subject's semantic knowledge, as well as word frequency and length, were not controlled among those non-target items. Instead, we relied on the fact that the Encarta encyclopedia has gone through five generations of content refinement to create understandable category structures. As stated above, the items used in each structure were picked from Encarta by an editor with the instructions to pick items that are representative of each category.

Each web page was marked with title information indicating where this page was located in the hierarchy. The top page of each hierarchy was marked either 'hierarchy 1:', 'hierarchy 2:', or 'hierarchy 3:'. Second level pages were marked 'hierarchy X: appropriate page title:' where X was replaced with the appropriate hierarchy number and the appropriate category title was filled in. On second level pages 'hierarchy X' was a link back to the top-level page of the hierarchy. If there were three levels, the third level was titled 'hierarchy X: appropriate sub-level category name: appropriate bottom level category name:' and the appropriate sub-level category name and hierarchy X were both backwards links. Under the category name on each page was a vertical list(s) of all the items in a randomized order. The items were formatted on the web page following conventional web style guidelines for optimal scanning [10] and for more efficient view traversability [4]. If the page had 8 or 16 items, they were arranged in a single column. If the page had 32 items, they were arranged in two columns, so that scrolling was never necessary. Example pages from each hierarchy are included in Appendix B.

Procedures

Each subject performed 8 searches in each structure for a total of 24 searches. The search target was always one of the 128 bottom level nodes that overlapped with all three hierarchies. Target items for each hierarchy were chosen at random from the 128 possible targets with two restrictions: each subject would search for a target only once regardless of hierarchy, and, within a hierarchy, no more than one target was chosen per category. The 24 trials were not blocked by hierarchy, but presented in a random order. Subjects were given both the search target and the hierarchy to search in directly preceding each trial, and were not told about future targets. Each trial's target and hierarchy information was presented to the subject on paper next to the computer so it was constantly available as a reference material, with one target and hierarchy presented per page. At the start of each trial, the subject was asked to turn the page in order to see the new target and hierarchy to be used for the next trial.

Subjects were told the purpose of the experiment ahead of time. They were told that we were interested in determining the optimal number of links on a page and that we were having them perform searches in three different hierarchies to explore this issue. They were asked to perform all searches as quickly as possible while making as few mouse clicks as possible. Subjects were not told about the experimenters' expectations of the results. Subjects were warned that the hierarchies did not contain cross-referenced material, so they may choose a logical pathway to a target and find that an alternative path to the target is not provided there. They were told that when this happens, they should try to find another route to the target.

Data for three kinds of analysis was collected: lostness measures, reaction times, and subjective ratings. Smith [14] defined lostness in hyperspace as distance on the hypotenuse of a right triangle where one side of the triangle is the number of different nodes accessed over the number of total nodes accessed (minus 1), and the other side is number of nodes required to complete the task over the number of different nodes accessed (minus 1). Lostness scores can be helpful in identifying when subjects are effectively "going around in circles". In addition, reaction time was measured. There was a start screen for each trial with links to 'hierarchy 1', 'hierarchy 2', and 'hierarchy 3'. The reaction time measure was initiated when the subject pressed the link to the appropriate structure and stopped when the link for the target item was selected. The web server was located on the subjects' computer, in an effort to control for any problems with differential web download and lag times.After the subjects finished all 24 trials, subjective preference and rank order responses were collected for the three hierarchies. Finally, subjects answered the following five subjective questions on a 5 point Likert scale about each hierarchy: "I liked this structure", "Right when I started I knew what information was available", "It was easy to get where I wanted in this structure", "This structure is easy to use", and "This structure feels familiar". Subjects were allowed to go back and review the hierarchies while answering all but the first subjective question.

RESULTS

Reaction Times

Figure 1 shows that on average, subjects completed search tasks fastest in the 16x32 hierarchy (Avg. RT=36 seconds, SD=16), second fastest in the 32x16 hierarchy (Avg. RT = 46 seconds, SD = 26), and slowest in the 8x8x8 hierarchy (Avg. RT = 58 seconds, SD = 23).

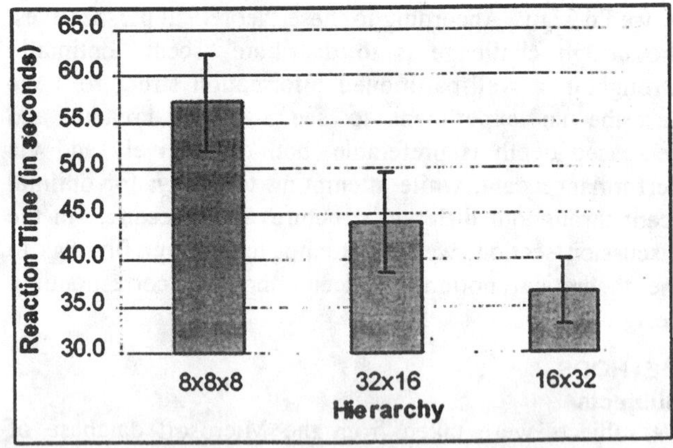

Figure 1: Average reaction time for each hierarchy.

A one-way Analysis of Variance (ANOVA) of the reaction time data revealed a significant main effect of hierarchy [$F(2, 36) = 6.34$, $p<.01$]. A post-hoc analysis using the Bonferroni method showed that the 8x8x8 hierarchy was significantly slower than both of the broader, shallower, hierarchies. However, there was no significant difference between the 16x32 and the 32x16 hierarchies for reaction time. No meaningful pattern in the error data was observed in this study, as subjects were for the most part required to continue searching until the target item was found. However, if the subject took longer than five minutes to find a target, the experimenter asked the subject to abandon the search. In the fourteen cases when this happened, the reaction time was recorded as five minutes. The 8x8x8 hierarchy, which had the longest reaction times, had the most time-outs (9 timeouts for 8x8x8, 2 for 16x32 and 3 for 32x16).

Lostness

An analysis of the number of unique and total links visited in comparison to the "optimal" path was performed. Smith [13] defined lostness as any score greater than 0.5 and any score less than 0.4 as not lost. On average, subjects were not lost in the 16x32 hierarchy (Lostness score = 0.38, SD = 0.19), were somewhat lost in the 32x16 hierarchy (Lostness score = 0.49, SD = 0.25), and were very lost in the 8x8x8 hierarchy (Lostness score = 0.63, SD = 0.20).

An ANOVA showed that there was a significant main effect of lostness, $F(2,36)=9.22$, $p<.001$. Post-hoc analyses (Bonferroni method) showed that the 8x8x8 hierarchy contributed to significantly more users being lost than did the other two hierarchies. The 32x16 hierarchy was marginally more likely to contribute to lostness than was the 16x32 hierarchy (p=. 067).

Memory and Visual Scanning Ability

The pre-test scores for visual scanning and memory span tasks were correlated with reaction times across the different hierarchies. Although the relationships were non-significant, the memory span scores were slightly more correlated with subjects' reaction time overall, $r = -0.27$, than were the visual scanning scores, $r = -0.12$. A negative correlation means that better memory span and visual scanning scores were predictive of faster search times.

Further analyses were carried out checking for whether or not memory or scanning pretest scores were more likely to be predictive of one of the three hierarchies. Table 1 shows the correlation between the cognitive tests and reaction time in each hierarchy. Greater memory and scanning ability was most highly correlated with faster reaction times in the 16x32 hierarchy. Memory span scores had no correlation with reaction time in the 8x8x8 hierarchy, and poorer scanning ability correlated with faster performance in that hierarchy. None of these correlations were statistically reliable.

	8x8x8	*32x16*	*16x32*
Memory	0.02	-0.31	-0.35
Scanning	0.16	-0.18	-0.32

Table 1: Correlations between visual scanning and memory span and reaction time in each of the hierarchies

Subjective Ratings and Preference Measures

Subjects filled out subjective ratings for each hierarchy, as well as a forced-choice preference after completing their searches in all of the hierarchies. In the forced choice preference data, Table 2 shows that the 32x16 hierarchy was ranked as most preferred more often than the other two hierarchies.

	8x8x8	*32x16*	*16x32*
Best	6	11	2
Second Best	2	3	14
Worst	11	5	3

Table 2: Rank ordered votes for the three hierarchies

The average score on a 5 point Likert scale and standard deviation for each subjective questionnaire item are provided in Table 3. Although the 32x16 hierarchy had the highest average ratings overall, there were no significant differences across any of the questionnaire items for the three hierarchies.

	8x8x8	*32x16*	*16x32*
Liked Hierarchy	3.0 (1.5)	3.4 (1.4)	3.1 (1.1)
Availability	3.2 (1.5)	3.4 (1.3)	3.4 (0.8)
Easy to navigate	3.2 (1.5)	3.5 (1.3)	3.1 (1.0)
Easy to use	3.4 (1.6)	3.5 (1.2)	3.1 (1.1)
Familiar	3.4 (1.5)	3.5 (1.1)	3.3 (1.1)

Table 3: Average subjective measures for the three hierarchies on a five point Likert scale (S.D. in parenthesis)

DISCUSSION

The reaction time and lostness data together paint a clear picture that subjects performed best with the 16x32 hierarchy and worst with the 8x8x8 hierarchy. This corroborates previous findings that demonstrated that increasing the levels of depth hurt user performance during search. Both of the hierarchies with two levels of depth resulted in better user performance than did the hierarchy with three levels of depth. But the findings stand in contrast to recent web design and information visualization techniques that herald increased breadth of items to extremely large sizes on the top page of a website. Although not statistically reliable, the hierarchy with 32 top-level items resulted in not only slower search times, on the average, but also more subjects feeling "lost in hyperspace".

Our findings that memory span was a slightly better performance predictor than visual scanning differed from Snowberry et al.'s [15] findings (although these cognitive pretests were not found to be reliably predictive of performance in either study). Snowberry et al. found that visual scanning was more predictive of performance than memory span. They also found a slightly better correlation between memory span and accuracy in the deepest structure. In fact, detailed error analyses in Snowberry et al.'s [15] study determined that subjects performed less well in the deep structures due to forgetting the target, or because the category labels at the top levels of the deep structures were too general for subjects to remember the correct traversal paths to a target. We found that memory span was more predictive of performance in the two hierarchies with less depth/greater breadth. The differences between the findings in the two studies are likely the product of different methodologies. In Snowberry et al., subjects were required to remember the target item (taxing short-term memory), as well as index the target, retain that index in short-term memory, and map the index to a response. Under these high cognitive load conditions, only people with large memory spans may have correctly retained the target through deep structures. In our experiment, subjects were given paper instructions presenting them with the target item, and this paper remained with the subject throughout the trial. Therefore, in the present study, both memory span and visual scanning may have been taxed more in the large breadth hierarchies, explaining why people with higher scores on these tests exhibited accelerated performance.

As Snowberry et al. found, the subjective ratings of the three hierarchies did not always match the performance data. In a forced choice preference question, most subjects preferred the 32x16 hierarchy over the other two hierarchies (though there was a cluster of five subjects who selected the 8x8x8 hierarchy as their favorite and 32x16 as their least favorite). While the 32x16 hierarchy scored slightly better on average for the five Likert scale questions on appeal, there were no large differences between the three hierarchies.

The magic number 7 +/- 2

At the onset of this study the authors were convinced that short-term memory limitations would play an important role in users' ability to learn and remember the structure of a website, to aid information retrieval. Instead we have shown that memory is only one variable in this debate, at least over the short course of time that users searched through the web pages used in this study. The present results demonstrated that depth, or the number of levels inherent to a web structure, was a stronger determinant of performance, and that three levels of depth resulted in significantly more problems during searching than two, regardless of breadth. So, our findings are consistent with those reviewed earlier that favored breadth over depth, even with our structures that were expertly organized to deliver optimal scent.

We did find stronger correlations between memory span and the two hierarchies with greater breadth. Subjects with better memory abilities were able to perform better in these hierarchies. There was no correlation between memory span and performance for the 8x8x8 hierarchy. Apparently the breadth of the 8x8x8 hierarchy was small enough that it did not tax users' memory, so subjects with better or worse than average memory performed equally well.

Implications for design

This study was an investigation of the effects of memory, response mapping, structure, and scent on designing web sites for efficient information retrieval. We have tried to couch the last twenty years of research on depth and breadth in menu design in a current theoretical framework for information design on the web. The danger of generalizing from earlier research to web design is that there may be a tendency to assume that broader, shallower web site designs are always preferable. The current study has demonstrated that, for one well-organized, large information space, our moderate level of breadth (the 16x32 structure) may actually afford optimal user performance. The results of this study map nicely into the information foraging and effective view navigation lines of research. As has been demonstrated in previous work on that topic, it is extremely difficult to distribute residue, or scent, throughout an information structure effectively [4]. For this study and its expertly organized content, the 16x32 and 32x16 information structures most likely afforded optimal performance because their category labels were more distinct at the top levels (better scent) than those of the 8x8x8 hierarchy. The 8x8x8 structure suffered from the fact that subjects had to make another categorical decision at the second level of the hierarchy. It seems reasonable that the 16x32 hierarchy performed better than the 32x16 hierarchy (though non-reliable in this study) because there were fewer categorical judgments to be made at the top level. As justification for this claim, researchers in cognitive science have long modeled decision making behavior as a more time-intensive cognitive process than simple visual search [16].

In summary, one implication for design based on the current set of results is that web designers need to balance the number of categorical decisions made for their information structure against the number of items needing to be visually searched on the web page. To help designers with understanding this tradeoff, the authors wish to emphasize the need to consider the layout as well as the semantics and labeling of web content. More research on matching category soundness and labeling to a user's understanding of the information space should augment our understanding of how to best design for large-scale information spaces, such as the World Wide Web.

ACKNOWLEDGEMENTS

The authors would like to acknowledge Ben Shniederman, Andrew Sears and Julie Jacko for their guidance in the early stages of this research. Early comments from George Robertson and Sue Dumais were very helpful in refining rough drafts of this paper. We would also like to offer special thanks to Linda Loba for her help with developing the web hierarchies.

REFERENCES

1. Campbell, D. J. (1988). Task complexity: a review and analysis. Academy of Management Review, 13, 40-52.
2. Card, S. (1984). Visual search of computer command menus. In Bouma, H. & Bouwhis, D. (Eds.) *Attention and Performance X, Control of Language Processes*: Hillsdale, N.J.
3. Eckstrom, R. B., French, J.W., Harman, H.H. & Derman, D. (1976). *Kit of factor-referenced cognitive tests.* Educational Testing Service, Princeton, N.J.
4. Furnas, G. W. (1997). Effective view navigation. In Proceedings of *CHI '97 Human Factors in Computing Systems* (Atlanta, GA, April, 1997), ACM press, pp. 367-374.
5. Jacko, J. A. & Salvendy, G. (1996). Hierarchical menu design: Breadth, depth, and task complexity. Perceptual and Motor Skills, 82, 1187-1201.
6. Kiger, J. I. (1984). The depth/breadth tradeoff in the design of menu-driven interfaces. International Journal of Man-Machine Studies, 20, 201-213.
7. Landauer, T. K. & Nachbar, D. W. (1985). Selection from alphabetic and numeric menu trees using a touch screen: Breadth, depth, and width. In Proceedings *of CHI '85 Human Factors in Computing Systems*, ACM press, pp. 73-78.
8. Miller, D. P. (1981). The depth/breadth tradeoff in hierarchical computer menus. Proceedings of the *Human Factors Society*, 296-300.
9. Miller, G. A. (1956). The magical number seven plus or minus two: Some limits on our capacity for processing information. Psychological Review, 63, 81-97.
10. Nygren, E. & Allard, A. (1996). Between the clicks: Skilled users' scanning of web pages. Paper presented at *Designing for the Web: Empirical Studies*, Redmond, WA.
11. Parkinson, S. R., Sisson, N., & Snowberry, K. (1985). Organization of broad computer menu displays. International Journal of Man-Machine Studies, 23, 6, 689-697.
12. Pirolli, P. (1997). Computational models of information scent-following in a very large browsable text collection. In Proceedings *of CHI '97 Human Factors in Computing Systems* (Atlanta, GA, April, 1997), ACM press, pp. 3-10.
13. Pirolli, P. & Card, S. (1995). Information foraging in information access environments. In Proceedings of the Conference on Human Factors in Computing Systems, CHI '95 (pp. 51-58), Denver, CO: ACM Press.
14. Smith, P. A. (1986). Towards a practical measure of hypertext usability. Interacting with Computers, 8, 4, 365-381.
15. Snowberry, K., Parkinson, S. R., & Sisson N. (1983). Computer display menus. Ergonomics, 26, 7, 699-712.
16. Sternberg, S. (1966). High-speed scanning in human memory. Science, 153, 652-654.
17. Zaphiris, P. & Mtei, L. (1997). Depth vs Breadth in the Arrangement Web Links. Available at http://otal.umd.edu/SHORE/bs04/.

Appendix A

Comparison of semantic content in the 3 hierarchies. 64 (of 512) bottom level categories are shown from each structure. The 16 (of 128) items that appear in each of the three hierarchies are bolded.

32x16 Hierarchy. Four of the top 32 levels are shown. Items that match items in other hierarchies are bolded.

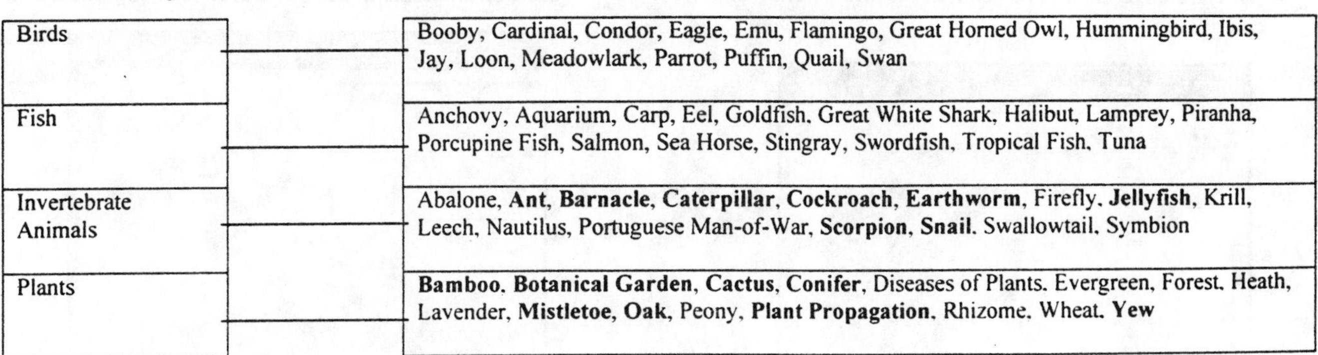

Top level	Bottom level categories
Birds	Booby, Cardinal, Condor, Eagle, Emu, Flamingo, Great Horned Owl, Hummingbird, Ibis, Jay, Loon, Meadowlark, Parrot, Puffin, Quail, Swan
Fish	Anchovy, Aquarium, Carp, Eel, Goldfish, Great White Shark, Halibut, Lamprey, Piranha, Porcupine Fish, Salmon, Sea Horse, Stingray, Swordfish, Tropical Fish, Tuna
Invertebrate Animals	Abalone, **Ant**, **Barnacle**, **Caterpillar**, **Cockroach**, **Earthworm**, Firefly, **Jellyfish**, Krill, Leech, Nautilus, Portuguese Man-of-War, **Scorpion**, **Snail**, Swallowtail, Symbion
Plants	**Bamboo**, **Botanical Garden**, **Cactus**, **Conifer**, Diseases of Plants, Evergreen, Forest, Heath, Lavender, **Mistletoe**, **Oak**, Peony, **Plant Propagation**, Rhizome, Wheat, **Yew**

16x32 Hierarchy. Two of the top 16 levels are shown. Items that match items in other hierarchies are bolded.

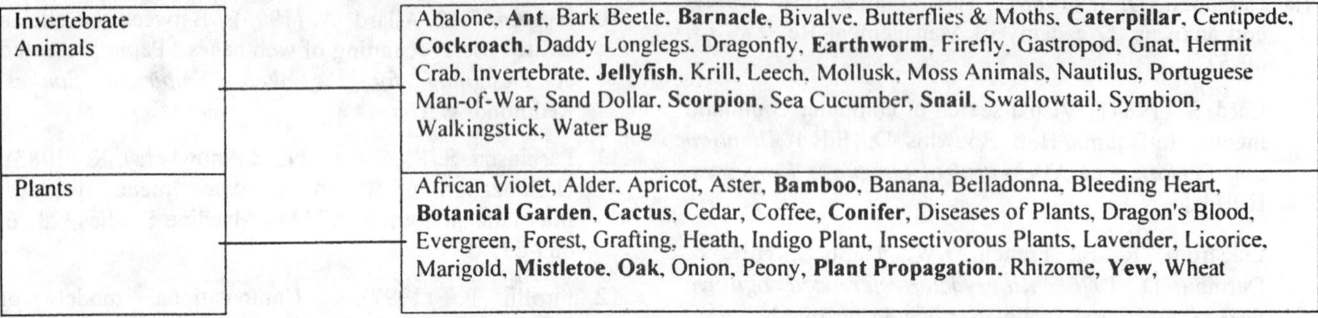

8x8x8 Hierarchy. One of the top 8 levels are shown. All 8 items under the top level are shows, as are all the bottom level items under each. Items that match items in other hierarchies are bolded.

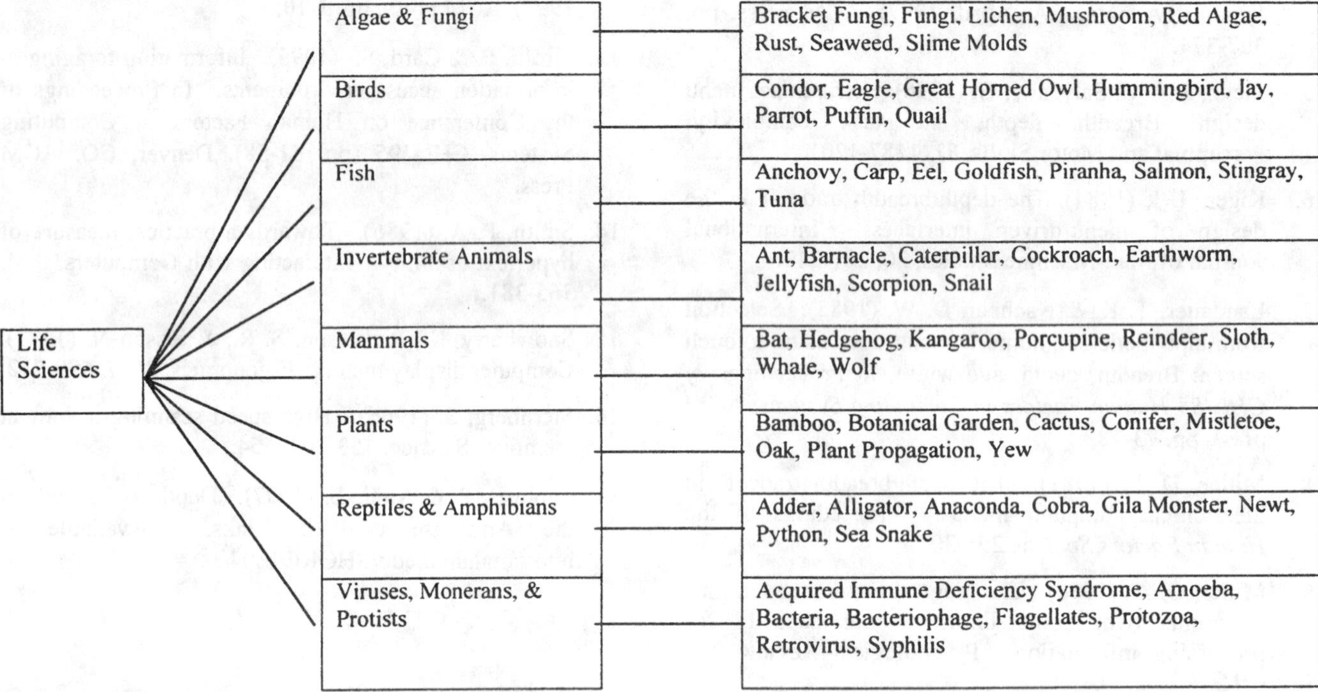

Appendix B: Screen Shots.

1) A bottom level page from the 8x8x8 structure. 'Hierarchy 1' is a link back to the top level page, and 'Life Science' is a link back to the life science sub-category.

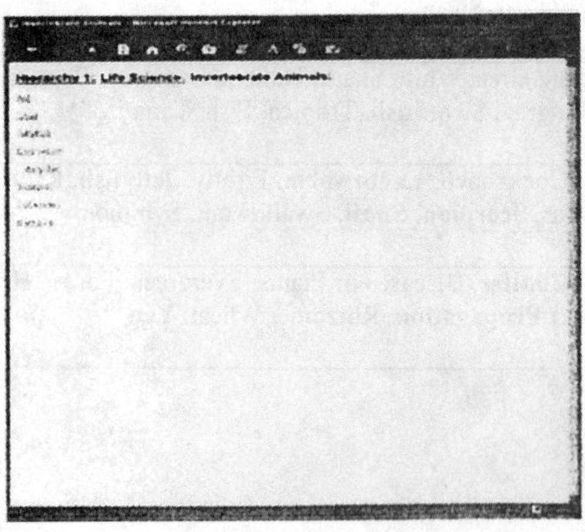

2) A bottom level page in the 16x32 hierarchy. 'Hierarchy 3' links back to the top level node, and each of the items in the column link to content.

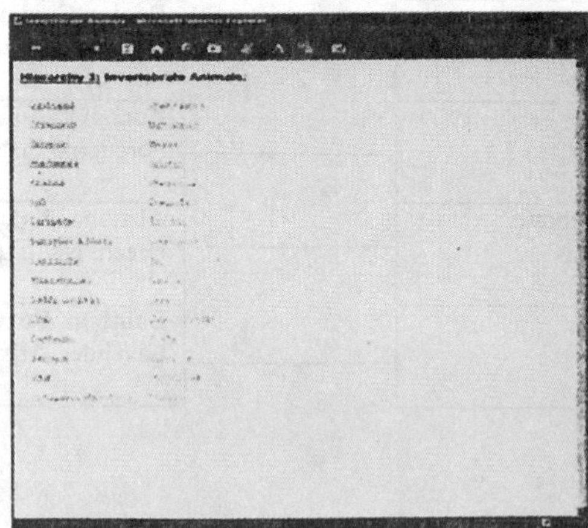

Exploring Browser Design Trade-offs Using a Dynamical Model of Optimal Information Foraging

Peter Pirolli
Xerox PARC
3333 Coyote Hill Road
Palo Alto, CA 94304
pirolli@parc.xerox.com

ABSTRACT

Designers and researchers of human-computer interaction need tools that permit the rapid exploration and management of hypotheses about complex interactions of designs, task conditions, and user strategies. Dynamic programming is introduced as a such a tool for the analysis of information foraging technologies. The technique is illustrated in the context of the Scatter/Gather text clustering browser. Hypothetical improvements in browser speed and text clustering are examined in the context of variations in task deadlines and the quality of the document repository. A complex and non-intuitive set of tradeoffs emerge from even this simple space of factors, illustrating the general utility of the approach.

Keywords

Dynamic programming, information foraging, Scatter/Gather, user models.

INTRODUCTION

Surveys of users of the World Wide Web (WWW) find that the two most frequently reported problems are poor speed of access and failure to find information that is known to be available (e.g., Pitkow & Kehoe, 1996). Designers of browsers for such large and rapidly-growing hypermedia repositories will naturally be concerned with alleviating those problems. Like all complex design problems, however, there will be many interacting constraints and trade-offs in the space of potential designs. These design trade-offs may also vary according to the space of conditions that will be faced by potential users. Furthermore, one may want to predict some of the effects of these designs on user strategies.

For designers of user interfaces, such as browsers, it might be helpful to have techniques that allow one to explore various complex "what-if" design scenarios. For instance, what if system algorithms are made faster as opposed to more accurate? What if presentations are made more informative but slower to read? What if the user has unlimited time as opposed to a hard deadline? What if the user is faced with a repository rich with relevant information vs a poor one? This paper presents a modeling technique for exploring a space of human-computer interaction designs. It is a dynamical modeling technique that was initially suggested in the context of Information Foraging Theory (Pirolli & Card, 1995). Here I present a more elaborate description of the technique and its application to exploring the design space for a browser for very large text repositories. It seems likely that these techniques could be extended to other browsers, such as those for the World Wide Web.

Basically, the approach requires that the analyst find an abstract representation of the different states of interaction, such as the state of a browser display, and the different changes that can be made from state to state, such as the changes that result from user actions. This defines an abstract *state space* representing the possible paths that human-computer interaction may take. One also must have some method for assigning costs and values to different states and moves. In the example I describe below, the values are the expected number of relevant documents that will be encountered while browsing, and the costs are just the amounts of user time involved. Different state spaces, with different costs and values, are used to represent alternative interfaces. I then use a technique called *dynamic programming* (Bertsekas, 1995) to perform an evaluation of the different interfaces. Conceptually, it does this by searching through the different possible paths of human-computer interaction, evaluating the costs and values of different paths, and finding the best paths. In this manner, one can find the best-case performance of a user interface. This is the *fitness* of the interface.

One goal of this paper is to provide a more thorough introduction to the dynamic programming analysis of information foraging by application to a concrete example. For the engineer/designer this technique is proposed as a sorely needed tool for the rapid exploration of "what-if" variations in complex designs. For the researcher, it is a technique for exploring and generating hypothesis about the interaction of design trade-offs, task conditions, and user strategies. It should be viewed as a technique for making well-informed hypothesis about complex design trade-offs. The validity of the technique will depend on many factors that the designer may wish to check empirically.

A dynamic programming analysis of information foraging is presented for a browser that clusters large-scale text collections, called Scatter/Gather (Cutting, Karger, & Pedersen, 1993; Cutting, Karger, Pedersen, & Tukey, 1992; Pirolli, Schank, Hearst, & Diehl, 1996) The

CHI 98 Los Angeles CA USA
Copyright 1998 0-89791-975-0/98/ 4..$5.00

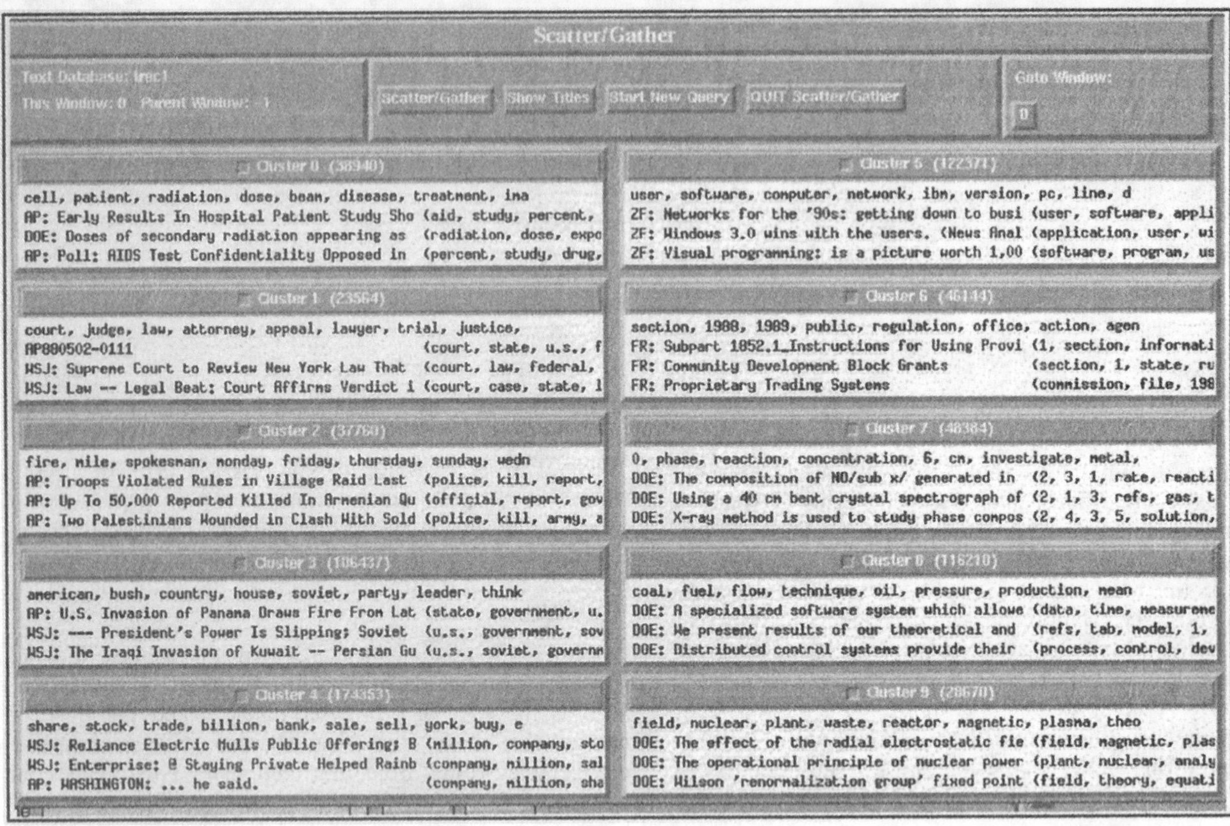

Figure 1. The Scatter/Gather cluster display window.

interaction space of the baseline model is based on empirical data (Pirolli & Card, 1995; Pirolli et al., 1996). Variations on this model consider the simulated effects of, and interactions among, (a) different deadlines, (b) different amounts of available relevant information, (c) possible improvements in interaction time costs, and (d) possible improvements clustering of relevant information.

THE SCATTER/GATHER BROWSER

The Scatter/Gather browser (Cutting et al., 1993; Cutting et al., 1992; Pirolli et al., 1996) uses the clustering of documents as the basis of a browser suitable for large numbers of documents (Figure 1). Each of the ten subwindows in Figure 1 represents a cluster of documents. Each subwindow presents a cluster digest, which contains topical words and the titles of the most typical documents in that cluster. The clustering and cluster digests are computed by automatic means based on the texts themselves. The user may *gather* clusters of interest by pointing and selecting buttons above each cluster. On command, the system will pool together the documents in those clusters, then automatically *scatter* that subcollection into another set of clusters. The user may repeatedly scatter then gather clusters, moving from very large cluster collections to very small cluster collections. Eventually the user may display all the titles of documents in one or more clusters, then select individual documents to read.

In studies (Pirolli & Card, 1995; Pirolli et al., 1996) Scatter/Gather was applied to the Tipster collection of about 750,000 documents created for the TREC text retrieval conference (Harman, 1993). Standard information retrieval tasks (queries) have been defined on it together with lists of known relevant and non-relevant Tipster documents, as judged by experts. We studied this version of Scatter/Gather under experimental conditions (Pirolli & Card, 1995; Pirolli et al., 1996) in which the general objective for users was to find as many bibliographic references as possible relevant to a set of the TREC queries. This forms the basic starting point for our dynamic programming model.

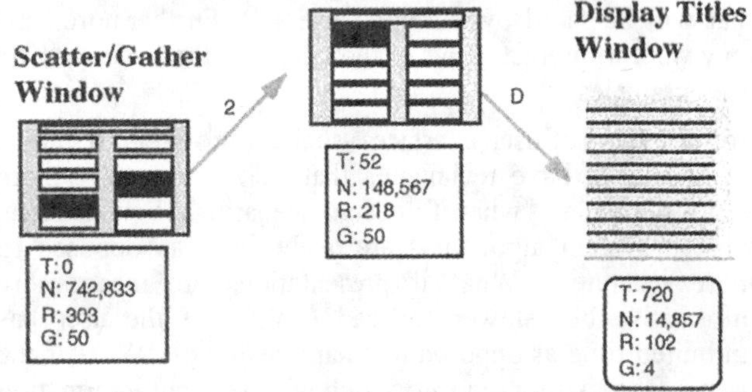

Figure 2. A schematic of a simple path of Scatter/Gather interaction.

DYNAMIC INFORMATION FORAGING MODELS

The dynamic modeling approach to information foraging taken here was inspired by similar approaches in the study of the ecology of animal behavior (Mangel & Clark, 1988).

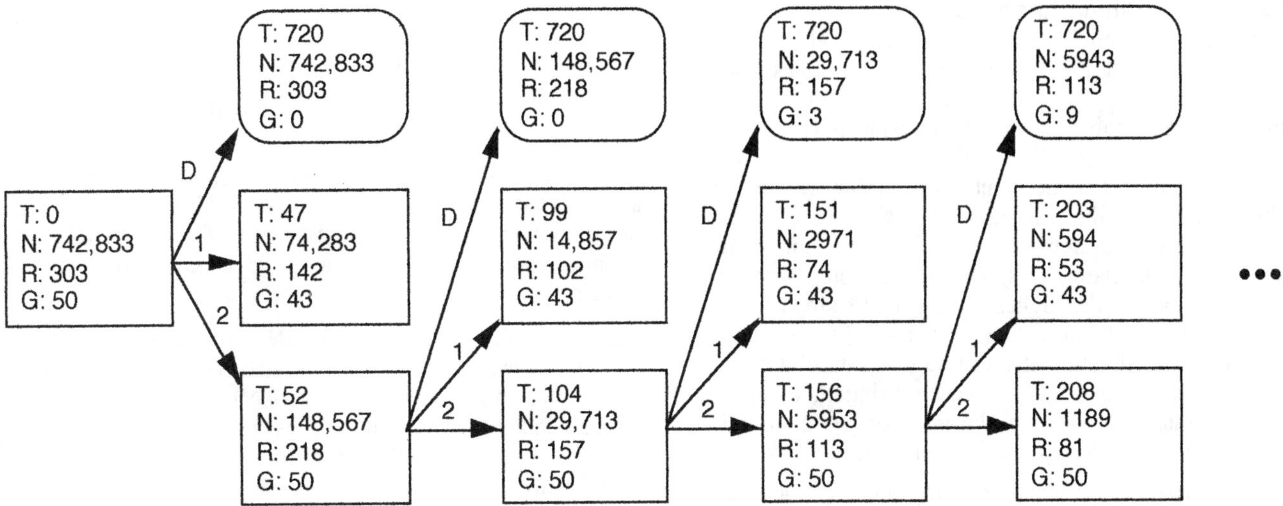

Figure 3. A portion of the Scatter/Gather state space.

A more technical and mathematical treatment of the current model is provided in Pirolli and Card (1997). The dynamic optimization techniques used here are just a small example of an extensive set of such models (Bertsekas, 1995).

State Space of Interaction

Figure 2 gives a schematic overview of a path of human-computer interaction using the Scatter/Gather browser. Each icon in Figure 2 represents an interaction state involving one of the two main kinds of display windows. The Scatter/Gather display window presents clusters that the user may gather. Eventually, a Display Titles window is used to display the titles of documents in clusters chosen by the user, and the user scans these seeking relevant ones. The boxes beneath the icons schematically represent information about the interaction states. The sharp-cornered boxes represent Scatter/Gather states and the round-edged boxes represent Display Titles states. The boxes in Figure 2 contain a the following subset of state information used in the models:

- Time (T) in seconds from the start of the simulated foraging task. For the Scatter/Gather states, these times record the point at which the window is displayed and the next user action begins. For the Display Titles states these times record the point at which the window has been displayed and the user has completed scanning and selecting titles. If this display scanning would go beyond the task deadline (720 seconds in the Figure 2 example), then the state's time is set to the deadline.
- Total number of documents (N) in the part of the collection displayed in the current window.
- The estimated number of relevant documents (R) in the collection displayed in the current window
- The best-case (optimal) number of relevant documents (G) that can be gained from the current state.

The number label on the arrow between the icons in Figure 2 indicates the number of clusters gathered at a state along the path (the model assumes that the best clusters are chosen), or a "D" label indicates that the chosen clusters were displayed in a Display Titles window.

The path in Figure 1 models a user who starts out by gathering two clusters at time $T = 0$ seconds, and scattering these into a new Scatter/Gather state that appears at time $T = 52$ seconds. One cluster from this state is gathered and displayed in a Display Title window, and scanned and selected until the deadline time $T = 720$ seconds. One can note in Figure 2 that the total number of documents as well as the number of relevant documents are reduced as one moves from state to state. However, one can also see that the proportion of relevant documents R/N is increasing. The manner in which the expected G is computed is at the core of the dynamic programming algorithm and is discussed below.

The collection of all the states achievable along all the paths of interaction from some given start state define a state space. Rather than the single path shown in Figure 2, a subset of the paths are shown in Figure 3 (the icons are now omitted). Only a small portion of the full state space is displayed in Figure 3 for the purposes of illustration. Only the first few steps in the interaction space are shown, only alternative moves along the best paths are displayed, and only three of the alternatives are shown. The full space gets explosively large as more alternatives are added,[1] and this is often the main computational drawback to using dynamic state-space models.

---

[1] From this conception of the search process, the state space grows exponentially with each additional step of interaction analyzed. If one considers all interaction paths of length L, with b alternative branches from every state, then there will be L^b states in that state space. See Bertsekas (1995) for discussion of how dynamic programming problems generally grow exponentially with the number of dimensions used to represent states (e.g., T, N, and R in this example).

Dynamic Programming Approach

Imagine that one could, however, generate all possible paths and isolate all the possible interaction states that a user could get to by the task deadline (this may be an infinite set of end states). One could evaluate these states to determine their value. This value might be any resource, but in our example it is the number of relevant articles that can be collected by the task deadline. Now imagine that one could take one step backward from the end states. From these penultimate states, the optimum step would be the one that goes to the highest valued end state, which is known from the evaluation of end states. So, the optimum value of the penultimate states can be calculated by tracing backward from the end states. Generalizing this process, one may iterate the process backwards from states to prior states until one gets back to the starting state.

To summarize, the dynamic programming approach involves defining a state space and an optimization criterion. In the current example, the state space is defined by the representation of states, a particular starting state, a set of feasible strategies and actions, and the state dynamics produced by those state-changing actions. If the optimization problem is formulated in an appropriate and tractable way (Bertsekas, 1995), then dynamic programming finds the sequence of states and action choices that optimizes the specified criterion. Conceptually, the dynamic programming optimization technique finds the value of end states (at a task deadline) and works backward along the interaction paths to label states with their optimal gains. In practice, there are many ways to implement dynamic programming (Bertsekas, 1995).

Technical Summary of Dynamic Programming[2]

Let $X(t) = x$ be a state variable representing the state of interaction at time t. As described in Pirolli and Card (1997) we use a multi-dimensional vector to represent the Scatter/Gather states. The components of the $X(t)$ vector in this example would include N, R, T, G, as well as other state attributes.

There will also be a set of state-change operators $\delta_i(X(t))$, that produce some new state, $X(t + C) = \delta_i(X(t))$. For instance, the user actions of gathering and scattering clusters in Scatter/Gather are examples of such state-change operators. The time cost of the operator will be C, and its value may be state-dependent. For instance, the time cost of displaying titles in Scatter/Gather depends on the total documents, N, and relevant documents, R.

For our current definition, let time t be indexed in seconds remaining to deadline. For a task with a deadline of 720 seconds: at the beginning of the task, $t = 720$ and at deadline $t = 0$ seconds. Using the foraging terminology of Mangel and Clark (1988), we construct a *fitness* evaluation function $\phi(X(t))$ for the final end states. For the current Scatter/Gather example, *final fitness values* can be defined recursively as,

$$F(x,t) = \begin{cases} \phi(x), \text{ if } t = 0 \\ \max_i[F(\delta_i(x), t - C_i(x))], \text{ if } t > 0, \end{cases} \quad (1)$$

where $C_i(x)$ is a cost evaluation function of operator δ_i applied to state x. This is the kind of dynamic programming specification used in the Scatter/Gather example, and applicable to a broad class of information foraging problems.

ALTERNATIVE INTERACTION SPACES

The dynamical models of the alternative interface designs were defined on the basis of data collected in two studies of Scatter/Gather (Pirolli & Card, 1995; Pirolli et al., 1996), by variations in task conditions, and by "what-if" specifications of system improvements.

Task Conditions

The "what-if" simulations here explored two factors affecting task conditions: (1) deadlines and (2) quality of the repository relative to given queries; that is the number of items in the repository relevant to a given query. The deadline conditions were:

- *Soft deadline* of 720 seconds, which is the mean time taken by Scatter/Gather users studied in Pirolli and Card (1995) who had no time pressure in their task specifications.
- *Hard deadline* of 360 seconds.

The repository quality conditions were:

- *Sparse repository* in which there were $R = 303$ relevant documents among the $N = 742{,}833$ total documents for a given query. This corresponds the TREC queries in the medium range of difficulty (Pirolli et al., 1996).
- *Rich repository* in which there were $R = 865$ relevant documents among the $N = 742{,}833$ total documents. This corresponds the TREC queries in the easy range of difficulty(Pirolli et al., 1996).

Table 1. Empirical cost estimates from Pirolli and Card (1995)

Operation	Cost
Scanning a cluster and judging relevance	$t_{sc} = 3$ s
Adding a cluster to gather list	$t_{gc} = 5$ s
Scanning a document title and judging relevance	$t_s = 1$ s
Selecting, cutting, and pasting title to record window	$t_h = 5$ s
System time to scatter new clusters	$t_{cl} = 23$ s
System time to display titles in a cluster	$t_d = 20$ s

[2] This section may be skipped. It is provided for the mathematically inclined reader.

Baseline System Specifications

Table 1 contains time cost estimates for various events involving the baseline Scatter/Gather system (Pirolli & Card, 1995). Using these estimates, Table 2 presents relevant state changes and costs incurred by various user actions.

To model the effects of gathering clusters and scattering them in Table 2 we use a function *D(k)*. It models the proportion of relevant documents contained in the best *k* clusters presented in the Scatter/Gather state. That is if, *R* is the total number of relevant documents in all the clusters on a Scatter/Gather display, then *D(k)* is the proportion of *R* that is in the *k* best clusters. This function is based on the analyses of Pirolli and Card (Pirolli & Card, 1997), is described in the Appendix, and plotted in Figure 4.

Table 2. Effects and time costs of state-change operators. *N* is the total documents and *R* the number of relevant documents in the current state. Time costs are described in Table 1 and *D(k)* in the Appendix.

Operator	New state	Time Cost (sec)
Scan Display Titles window until end of display	Collected relevant titles= R	$N\ t_s + R\ t_h$
Scan Display Titles window until deadline hit after t sec	Collected relevant titles = $(R\ t)/(N\ t_s + R\ t_h)$	t
Gather k clusters and scatter	New $N = N\ k/10$ New $R = D(k)\ R$	$10\ t_{sc} + k\ t_{gc} + t_{cl}$

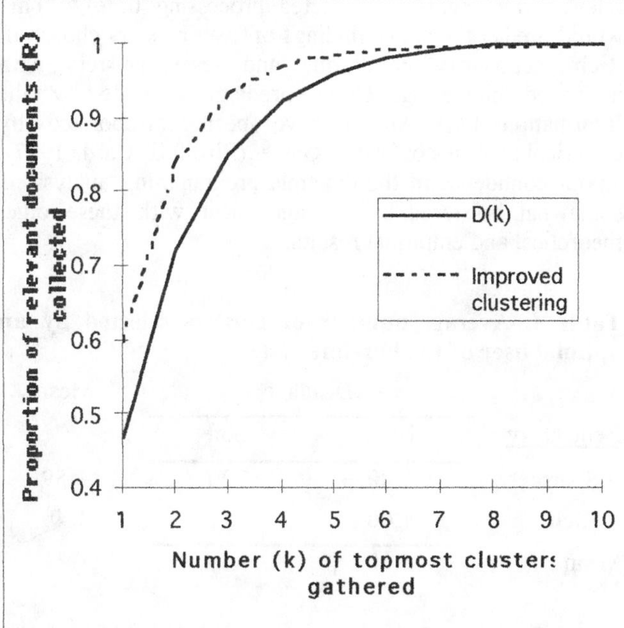

Figure 4. Proportion of relevant documents collected by gathering the *k* best clusters.

Alternative System Specifications

Two system improvements were explored:

- *Faster interaction*, in which the time cost of computing a new Scatter/Gather cluster display was cut by 1/2.
- *Improved clustering*, in which the clustering algorithm was improved so that it placed 25% more relevant documents in the best cluster (see Figure 4 and Appendix).

RESULTS

The dynamic programming results show that substantial and non-intuitive trade-offs emerge regarding the performance of system improvements across task conditions. The simulated best-case gains of relevant documents for the baseline Scatter/Gather system are presented in Table 3. Against these baseline data we can examine the effects of system improvements. Overall, the best-case gains for improved clustering simulations were, on average 23% better than the baseline system, whereas the faster interaction simulations were, on average, 18% better than baseline. However, improved clustering was not always predicted to be better than faster interaction; there were, in fact, many subtle System × Task interactions, as I show next.

Table 3. Simulated optimal number of relevant documents gained in the baseline Scatter/Gather system (numbers rounded to integers).

	Deadline		Mean
Repository	Hard	Soft	
Sparse	11	49	30
Rich	16	65	40
Mean	13	57	

System × Repository Effects

Figure 5 shows the improvements predicted for a faster interaction system and a system with improved clustering, under different repository conditions. With a repository rich with relevant information, the simulations suggest there will be no major difference between two particular improvements that were examined. However, when the repository is relatively sparse with relevant information, the simulations predict that a system with improved clustering will be superior.

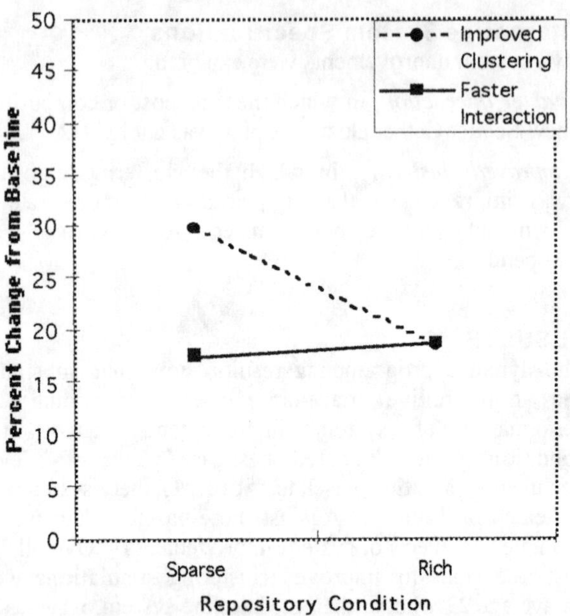

Figure 5. Simulated improvements in expected number of relevant documents collected by task deadline as a function of repository condition.

System × Deadline Effects

Figure 6 shows simulated improvements under different deadline conditions. The simulations suggest that improved clustering will be superior when the deadlines are soft. On the other hand, when there is a hard deadline, with less time available, a system with faster interaction time will have better pay-offs.

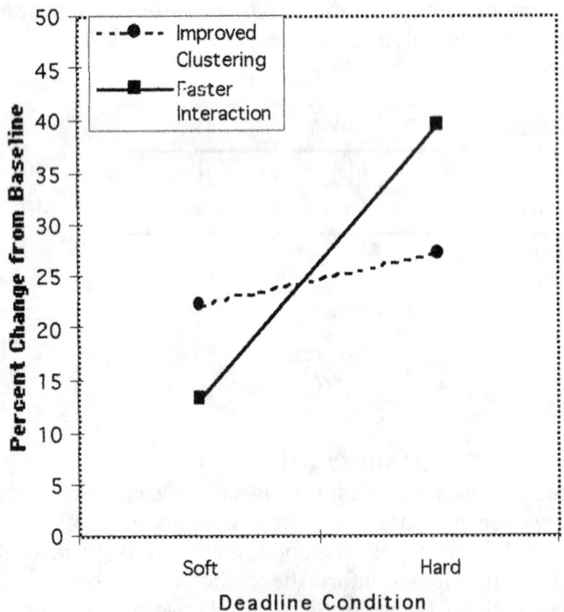

Figure 6. Simulated improvements in expected number of relevant documents collected by task deadline as a function of deadline condition.

Effects on Strategy

The dynamic programming simulations can also afford some exploration of the optimal user strategies for the different Scatter/Gather system configurations. The optimal strategies are the action choices made along the optimal interaction path, as determined by dynamic programming. For instance, in the simple state space of Figure 3, the optimal path can be traced by following the bottommost arrows from state to state. That path is optimal because each move goes to the highest gain (G) next state. The action choice along the portion of the optimal path depicted in Figure 3 is to choose two clusters at each stage.

The optimal user strategies may vary across the different system improvements and task conditions. Here I examine the average number of clusters the ideal user would have to chose on each Scatter/Gather display, and the amount of time the ideal user would spend scanning titles for relevant results. It turns out that the dynamic programming analyses shows strategy shifts that are consistent with models developed in Information Foraging Theory (Pirolli & Card, 1997).

Table 4 shows the average number of clusters chosen from Scatter/Gather displays in the simulation of an optimal user on the baseline system. The simulations for the faster interaction system and the improved clustering system only showed differences from Table 4 in the soft deadline conditions. Under soft deadlines, the faster interaction simulations showed the same or more clusters being chosen than baseline, whereas the improved clustering simulations showed less clusters being chosen.

These results are consistent with Information Foraging Theory. The Information Diet Model (Pirolli & Card, 1997) predicts that fewer clusters should be chosen with increases in profitability of clusters (the ratio of expected relevant documents to expected processing time). This would predict the above findings of fewer clusters chosen in Rich Repository conditions and fewer clusters with improved clustering. Other predictions made by the Information Diet Model have been corroborated by empirical analyses of Scatter/Gather (Pirolli & Card, 1997), so our confidence in the dynamic programming analysis is somewhat bolstered by its agreement with these other theoretical and empirical results.

Table 4. Average number of clusters selected by an optimal user of the baseline system.

	Deadline		Mean
Repository	Hard	Soft	
Sparse	1.00	2.17	1.59
Rich	1.00	1.80	1.40
Mean	1.00	1.99	

Table 5 shows the time spent scanning the Display Titles window by an ideal user on the baseline system. Figures 7 and 8 and show the reduction in these scanning times expected for the two system improvements across the task conditions. Under optimal use, a faster interaction system would require the least scanning time in sparse repositories or hard deadline conditions, whereas an improved clustering systems would require least scanning time in rich repositories or under soft deadline conditions.

Table 5. Time spent scanning the Display Titles window by an optimal user in the baseline condition (sec).

	Deadline		Mean
Repository	Hard	Soft	
Sparse	232.0	383.0	307.5
Rich	232.0	310.0	271.0
Mean	232.0	346.5	

Again, these results are consistent with the predictions of Information Foraging Theory (Pirolli & Card, 1997). The Information Patch Model would treat the Display Titles window as an *information patch*. That model predicts that the time spent in information patches should (a) decrease as one goes from Sparse to Rich Repository conditions, (b) decrease from baseline to improved clustering systems, and (c) decrease from baseline to faster interaction systems. Again, other predictions of the Information Patch Model are corroborated by empirical analyses (Pirolli & Card, 1997), and this provides another set of consistency checks on the dynamic programming model.

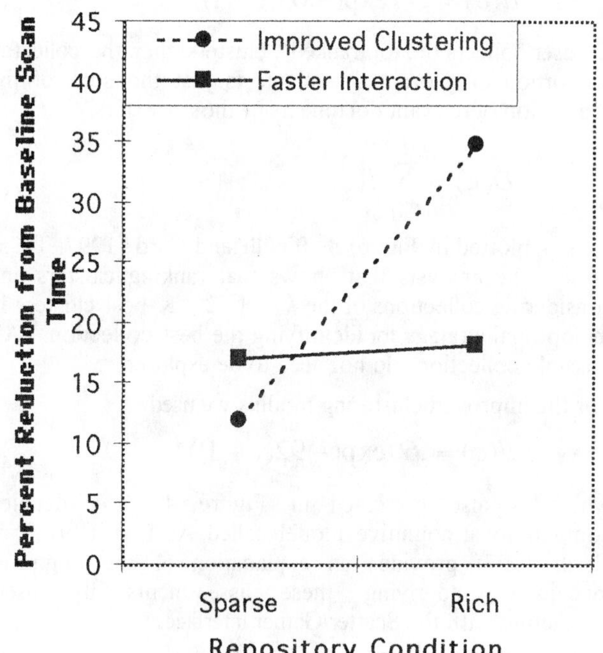

Figure 7. Simulated reductions in Display Titles scanning times as a function of repository conditions.

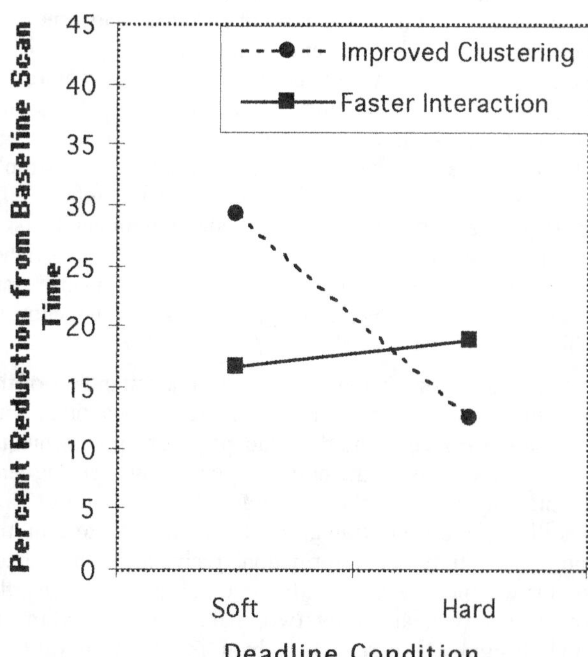

Figure 8. Simulated reductions in Display Titles scanning times as a function of deadline conditions.

GENERAL DISCUSSION

Dynamic programming was used to explore some trade-offs in a browser design. Specifically, the analysis explored making the browser system faster (faster interaction) and making the relevant information easier to find (improved clustering). These improvements directly address the two most common problems reported by WWW users (Pitkow & Kehoe, 1996). Dynamic programming analysis permitted the exploration of "what-if" scenarios testing these hypothetical design improvements against variations in task conditions involving repository quality and deadline conditions. Finally, the dynamic programming analysis permitted the exploration of changes in ideal user strategies across system and task conditions.

The main aim of this paper was to describe and illustrate the dynamic programming technique applied to an information foraging technology. The illustration showed how—even for this relatively simple space of designs and usage conditions—that complex and non-intuitive trade-offs emerge from the analysis. This sort of complexity faces virtually every interface designer. Tools such dynamic programming are needed to explore and manage such design complexity.

Without doubt, the extension of this analysis to other browsers—for the World Wide Web, for instance—will not be simple. The aim here was to illustrate the technique using a tractable example, as a beachhead for more complex analyses. The analysis here assumed a very simple assessment of value: the number of relevant documents found while searching. As discussed elsewhere (Pirolli & Card, 1997; Pirolli & Card, 1995), characterizing the value of information is usually more complex, since it typically varies (at least) with tasks, individual needs, and time. In addition, the unidimensional value assessment here is overly simplistic because real-world tasks often require the assessment of information along many dimensions. Similarly, costs often involve more than just time (e.g., money) . The analysis here also assumed a very simple range of user strategies and actions. This reflects the Scatter/Gather browser as used in our experimental tasks, but other tasks and browsers will undoubtedly have richer interaction spaces. None of these extensions are problematic in principle, although they may require effort to achieve in practice.

For the researcher aiming at scientific understanding of the principles underlying human-computer interaction with information systems, the dynamic programming technique can be viewed as a method for generating strong and complex hypotheses about interactions of designs, task conditions, and user strategies. It is unfortunate that the traditional study of information technology has been dominated since the Cranfield studies of the 1960's by the notion that two, and only two, factors are important to good design: (1) *precision,* which is the proportion of relevant items in a retrieved set of items, and (2) *recall,* which is the proportion of all items in the corpus that are retrieved (Harter & Cheng, in press; vanRijsbergen, 1979). The model presented here can be taken as a rational analysis that illustrates the myopia of such a view with respect the broader complexity and trade-offs of information foraging.

ACKNOWLEDGMENT

This research was supported in part by an Office of Naval Research grant No. N00014-96-C-0097 to Peter Pirolli and Stuart Card.

REFERENCES

Bertsekas, D. P. (1995). *Dynamic programming and optimal control theory.* Belmont, MA: Athena Scientific.

Cutting, D. R., Karger, D. R., & Pedersen, J. O. (1993). Constant interaction-time Scatter/Gather browsing of very large document collections. *Proceedings of the SIGIR '93*

Cutting, D. R., Karger, D. R., Pedersen, J. O., & Tukey, J. W. (1992). Scatter/gather: A cluster-based approach to browsing large document collections. *Proceedings of the SIGIR '92* (pp. 318-329).

Harman, D. (1993). Overview of the first text retrieval conference. *Proceedings of the 16th Annuam International ACM/SIGIR Conference* (pp. 36-38), Pittsburgh, PA.

Harter, S. & Cheng, Y. (in press). Evaluation of information retrieval systems: A review article. *Annual Review of Information Science and Technology.*

Mangel, M. & Clark, C. W. (1988). *Dynamic modeling in behavioral ecology.* Princeton, NJ: Princeton University Press.

Pirolli, P. & Card, S. (1997). *The evolutionary ecology of information foraging* (Tech. Rep. UIR-R97-01). Palo Alto, CA: Xerox PARC.

Pirolli, P. & Card, S. K. (1995). Information foraging in information access environments. *Proceedings of the CHI '95, ACM Conference on Human Factors in Software* (pp. 51–58), New York.

Pirolli, P., Schank, P., Hearst, M., & Diehl, C. (1996). Scatter/Gather browsing communicates the topic structure of a very large text collection. *Proceedings of the Conference on Human Factors in Computing Systems, CHI '96* Vancouver, BC.

Pitkow, J. E. & Kehoe, C. M. (1996). GVU's Sxth WWW User Survey. *Online Publication: http://www.gvu.gatech.edu/user_surveys.*

vanRijsbergen, C. J. (1979). *Information retrieval*(2nd ed.). Boston, MA: Butterworth & Co.

APPENDIX

If there are R relevant documents in a Scatter/Gather state, then those documents will be distributed somehow across the 10 clusters in the state. Analyses (Pirolli & Card, 1997) show that when clusters are ranked $c = 1, 2, \ldots 10$ in decreasing order by how many relevant documents they contain, then they are distributed in an exponentially decreasing fashion according to,

$$d(c) = .47\exp(-.63(c-1)) \quad (2)$$

If a user collects the top ranked k clusters, then the collected proportion of relevant documents is just the sum of the proportion of relevant documents in those clusters:

$$D(k) = \sum_{c=1}^{k} d(c) \quad (3)$$

This is plotted in Figure 4. Pirolli and Card (1997; 1995) present the analysis that shows that ranking clusters and considering collections of the $k = 1, 2, \ldots K$ best clusters is the optimal strategy for identifying the best collection. All possible collections do not need to be explored.

For the improved clustering models we used

$$d(c) = .60\exp(-.92(c-1)), \quad (4)$$

which is also presented in Figure 4. A detailed computational cognitive model called ACT-IF (Pirolli & Card, 1997) provides an explanation of the cognitive machinery underlying these assessments by users interacting with the Scatter/Gather interface.

Information Archiving with Bookmarks: Personal Web Space Construction and Organization

David Abrams
Perceptual Robotics, Inc.
1840 Oak Ave
Evanston, IL 60201
abrams@perceptualrobotics.com

Ron Baecker
Knowledge Media Design Institute
University of Toronto
Toronto, ON M5S 1A4
rmb@dgp.toronto.edu

Mark Chignell
Interactive Media Laboratory
University of Toronto
Toronto, ON M5S 1A4
chignell@mie.toronto.edu

ABSTRACT
Bookmarks are used as "personal Web information spaces" to help people remember and retrieve interesting Web pages. A study of personal Web information spaces surveyed 322 Web users and analyzed the bookmark archives of 50 Web users. The results of this study are used to address why people make bookmarks, and how they create, use, and organize them. Recommendations for improving the organization, visualization, representation, and integration of bookmarks are provided. The recommendations include simple mechanisms for filing bookmarks at creation time, the use of time-based visualizations with automated filters, the use of contextual information in representing bookmarks, and the combination of hierarchy formation and Web page authoring to aid in organizing and viewing bookmarks.

Keywords
WWW, bookmark, information space, survey, empirical study, design.

1. INTRODUCTION
The millions of documents on the rapidly expanding World Wide Web (WWW) further exacerbates the information overload problem documented by [8], [17] and others. The Web as we know it today has no classification system for Web sites, no formal indexing policy or controlled vocabulary, and no systematic system for naming Web pages or assigning authorship in a particular catalogue (except for domain names). Consequently, searching for specific information on the Web is a challenging and often frustrating task.

One strategy for dealing with information overload is to develop personal information systems consisting of focused subsets of information highly relevant to a particular user. Bookmarks are a simple tool for building these personalized subsets of information where interesting or useful Web pages (URLs) can be stored for later use. Users keep track of the resulting pointers to Web pages by creating a bookmark archive — a *personal Web information space*.

Bookmarks are very popular among users. In a 1996 survey of 6619 Web users [12], over 80% of respondents cited bookmarks as a strategy for locating information. Bookmarks were used slightly more than other navigation strategies: querying a search engine, referencing an index page, entering a known URL, and traversing links to a specific page. Over 92% of users had a bookmark archive and over 37% had more than 50 bookmarks.

Bookmarks serve as convenient shortcuts to frequently used Web pages as well historical pointers to useful information that may otherwise be forgotten. Bookmarks are file surrogates (aliases) pointing to original files in "tertiary storage," the massive distributed file system located in Web servers distributed around the world. Users create their own personal information space for the Web by making bookmarks, structuring the resulting collection, and managing its growth.

Personal information spaces have been studied in a variety of contexts (e.g., [6], [2], and [7]). Yet very little empirical research on Web users has been done and this research is the first in-depth empirical study of personal Web information spaces. Our goal was to uncover basic aspects of bookmarking behavior as a prelude to modeling large scale information archiving, thereby providing a scientific basis for the design of future bookmark management systems.

2. METHODOLOGY
Bookmark usage was studied using survey questionnaires, and through analyses of Web users' bookmark archives.

2.1 Survey of Bookmark Usage
The survey instrument was developed based on a pilot study of 12 university students with WWW experience done with informal interviews and pilot questionnaires. We used the results in the design of a formal survey questionnaire. More details on this questionnaire and its development (including the questions asked) appear in [1].

Approximately 450 of the questionnaires were distributed at The Internet Beyond the Year 2000 Conference (held in Toronto in early 1996). During the conference, registrants were asked to fill out a copy of the questionnaire. Respondents were instructed to identify themselves by their conference registration number, and were told that their data would be confidential and reported in the form of aggregations with questionnaire data from other participants.

The respondents consisted of University of Toronto faculty, staff, and students, and individuals from industry, government, and other universities. Most participants had an expressed interest in the Internet and the WWW.

322 completed survey forms were collected from the 450 distributed. 200 (62%) of the completed surveys were correctly filled in on every question. 76.5% of the 322 survey respondents were male and 23.5% were female; these proportions were roughly consistent across all sizes of bookmark archives. Age distribution was approximately normal with a mean of about 35 years. We estimate that approximately 80% of respondents were Netscape 1.x or 2.0 users, and there were very few Internet Explorer users at the time of the survey (we did not explicitly ask for browser type and version in the survey).

We stratified users by the number of bookmarks in our analysis. 6% of respondents had no bookmarks, 10% had 1-10, 24% had 11-25, 44% had 26-100, 14% had 101-300, and 2% had 300+ bookmarks. We selected these groups based on our pilot study which suggested distinct characteristics for each user segment. Respondents were asked to choose from this list of groups.

2.2. Bookmark Files of 50 Users

56 bookmark files were collected through electronic mail in late summer of 1996. 70% of the people volunteering bookmark files were from the Knowledge Media Design Institute (KMDI), a multi-disciplinary group of faculty and students in Toronto interested in new media. 20% of the bookmark files were from Computer Science students. The remaining 10% were from industry professionals. 95% of the sample consisted of Netscape users (identified by the file meta-tags). Six files were missing data. 50 bookmark files were then analyzed using the date/time that each bookmark URL was (i) created, (ii) last visited, (iii) last modified, and its location in the folder hierarchy.

3. THE PROCESS OF SELECTING BOOKMARKS

Users judiciously select useful Web sites to add to their bookmark archives. The comments made in the questionnaire illustrate why bookmarks are created and how they are used. Our analysis of the bookmark files identified patterns in the types of sites which users bookmark.

3.1 Why Bookmarks are Created

Bookmarks take very little physical interaction to create and they are "*easy to make.*" The survey respondents employed five criteria to determine whether to bookmark a Web page: (i) general usefulness, (ii) quality, (iii) personal interest, (iv) frequency of use, and (v) potential future use.

Usefulness is an important factor in bookmark creation and in organizing and pruning a personal archive ("*I typically only organize useful information.*"). Another user complained that "*weeding ones [which are] no longer useful*" takes too much time and cognitive effort. Since criteria for the usefulness of information changes over time [13], the usefulness of pages stored in a personal archive will tend to be re-evaluated from time to time.

Bookmarks also provide "*quick access to key sites*" and make it "*easy to return to key pages.*" Users like being "*able to return to useful/interesting sites*" and "*the ability to quickly get to the URL of a site of personal interest.*" One respondent described his bookmarks as a "*customized interest list.*" Thus bookmarking a set of Web pages results in a *personal Web information space.*

Since bookmark invocation is fast and easy, users bookmark pages they frequently return to. "*I constantly use them — it's the best way to get back to frequently used sites. I'd be lost without them.*" Bookmarks provide "*speedy access to 4-5 very frequently used sites.*"

Bookmarks are also created when people want to defer reading an interesting page until a future session, possibly because they are too busy dealing with a current problem. For example, one respondent uses bookmarks to "*store all the useful sites that I would use for future use.*"

3.2 How Bookmarks are Used

Bookmarks (i) reduce the cognitive and physical load of managing URL addresses, (ii) facilitate the return to groups of related pages, and (iii) enable users to create a personal information space for themselves and others. Below is a summary of a taxonomy from [1]:

Reducing user load
- Avoiding managing URL addresses
- Aiding memory and keeping history

Facilitating navigation/access
- Speeding information access
- Finding Web information

Collaborating/publishing/archiving
- Creating a personal Web information space
- Authoring and publishing Web pages
- Collaboratively using Web information

Bookmarks reduce the cognitive and physical load of browsing hypertext [16]. They insulate users from the tedious task of typing, managing, storing and interpreting URL addresses (the "*convenience of not having to retype a long Web site address.*") The result is more fluid movement from one page to the next. Bookmarks let users "*easily store an address without having to write it down.*" Representing Web pages by titles rather than by URLs reduces cognitive load and enables users to focus on the contents of the page. URLs are "*cumbersome*" and "*tedious.*" Bookmarks serve as a "*mnemonic device*" for users, reminding them of important information they have found on the Web. One user wrote "*they [bookmarks] free me from the exhaustive task of remembering everything.*" Bookmarks are a "*memory replacement,*" external artifacts that mediate cognition [10].

Respondents associated bookmarks with the temporal sequence of browsing sessions. One user wrote, "*I can keep track of what I was doing lately and a few weeks earlier*" with bookmarks. A single bookmark may represent an individual (or discrete group of) browsing sessions. When reviewing a list of bookmarks, the user sees a time-ordered view of separate information foraging tasks (one respondent viewed bookmarked "*pages as a history of using the Web.*"). However, when users organize their bookmarks they tend to lose this temporal sequencing. One user wrote that bookmarks "*take me to the last site where I was not finished during the last session."* This user associated tasks with individual browsing sessions, and also used bookmarks as an inter-session history mechanism, writing, *"bookmarks are essential to finding good sites again and remembering previous sessions."*

The temporal and task association of bookmarks is illustrated by users' suggestions for better Web browsers. One user wants to be able to find Web pages based on the *"last time I visited a site or used a bookmark."* Associating tasks with discrete browsing sessions is a key element defining the relationship between bookmarks and history mechanisms. *"I want a way to see and understand the history of my Web browsing for the last few weeks or more."* For example, *"I want to find a page I looked at two weeks ago but didn't think to bookmark. "* Users do not always think to bookmark a page *"for future use,"* but require a means of accessing inter-session history. In the absence of such functionality, users are bookmarking pages to enable access to previous browsing sessions.

Bookmarks are also used to jump between Web localities [1]. Users create bookmarks to help them quickly find Web pages, reduce time spent foraging, and mark serendipitous sites found along the way.

Bookmarks provide *"fast access to information"* because the time to select a bookmark is very short compared to browsing for a page, entering the URL or using a search engine. They provide a *"most spontaneous response"* to users because of the *"direct access to important pages."*

Users collect bookmarks so that they can create their own personal information space and share it with others. This personal Web information space represents their most critical information resources on the Web. For example, *"I like being able to create my own classification system."* Creating a personal Web information space means users *"can create an organized, logical format for getting fast and easy access to a site."*

Users create Web pages out of bookmarks by authoring an HTML file with the bookmarks as hypertext links. They can thereby easily add annotations and create customized views.

Bookmarks are used to share Web resources with third parties. A group of users working on the same project will mail each other bookmarks in order to collaborate. Users share bookmarks based on individual expertise. A user that regularly manages a set of bookmarks in one domain is a precious resource to other members of the group. One respondent uses bookmarks *"in my course to provide students with initial navigational markers."* A librarian wrote that she *"collects [bookmarks] for clients."*

Bookmarks are used in presentations. One user wrote *"I mostly use them while giving lectures,"* using them to move quickly from one site to the next.

3.3. Bookmarking Metaphors

Survey respondents mentioned a number of different metaphors for describing how they used bookmarks. We observed four major metaphors: *identification*, *collection*, *movement*, and *episodes*.

The identification metaphor conceptualizes bookmarks as small tags or distinctive labels that are placed on information. For example, one user wrote that bookmarks are an *"extremely easy method to mark information."* Another respondent uses bookmarks to mark a spot and come back to it later.

The collection metaphor is based on the notion that the user is stationary and he/she is pulling specific information out of the vast information space of the WWW. One respondent likes *"the ability to quickly retrieve sites"* with bookmarks.

Many users employ notions of location and movement in describing the process of browsing. They perceive themselves to be traveling through a vast space of information. The traveling metaphor implies destinations, landmarks and paths. For example, bookmarks tell *"where I was."* They are an *"easy way to find places I've been."* Bookmarked pages standout as landmarks, and as temporal and navigational guides. A subset of the traveling metaphor is information foraging which encompasses an active process of finding or searching for a piece of information [11] (e.g., [3] is an information foraging tool).

Bookmarks also represent a chronological list of episodes. One user wrote that bookmarks tell *"what I was doing over a period of many browsing sessions. I can keep track of what I was doing lately and a few weeks earlier"* and they describe *"my history"* of navigating the Web.

3.4. What is Bookmarked

The users that we studied tended to create only one bookmark for each distinct Web site. On average, 86% of the bookmarks in a user's archive pointed to distinct domain names. The proportion of bookmarks that pointed to distinct domain names dropped off only slightly with larger archives, ranging from a high of 93% distinct domain names for small archives (1-25 bookmarks) to 81% distinct domain names for the largest archives (over 300).

Over 95% of users with 20 or more bookmarks had at least one search engine or index site in their archive. When bookmarking a query engine (e.g., Lycos) users bookmarked the page for entering queries. In contrast, they tended to bookmark selected parts of the hierarchy when bookmarking a meta-index (e.g., Yahoo). They rarely bookmarked search results pages.

When bookmarking on-line news sites (e.g. CNN, NY Times), users tend to bookmark the newspaper-like front page with headlines and links to articles. Most publishers regularly update this page with fresh content. Users rarely bookmark Web pages of individual news articles. [1] presents a taxonomy and details on what users bookmark.

3.5. Rate of Growth of Bookmark Archives

Time-series analyses of the bookmark files of 50 users showed that archives grow incrementally in spurts and that many bookmarks go unused for months.

To examine the rate of growth in bookmarks over time, the bookmark files of 50 participants were combined in an aggregate file tracing one year's growth. For each bookmark file, we calculated the creation date of every bookmark relative to date that the archive began. The average number of bookmarks was highly correlated with time (R = .996, P < 0.001). The best fitting linear regression equation is:

$$N = 7.45 + 0.18*T$$

where N is the number of bookmarks and T is number of days. Bookmarks in our aggregated sample were added at a fairly constant rate of about one every five days.

Over 94% of users surveyed created an average of five or fewer bookmarks during each browsing session. We analyzed bookmark files from individual users to identify patterns in their growth. Figure 1 illustrates this, showing the time course of bookmarking for a particular user by plotting the elapsed number of days each bookmark was added to the archive relative to the date when the first bookmark was created. Vertical segments in the figure show clusters of bookmarks added on the same day.

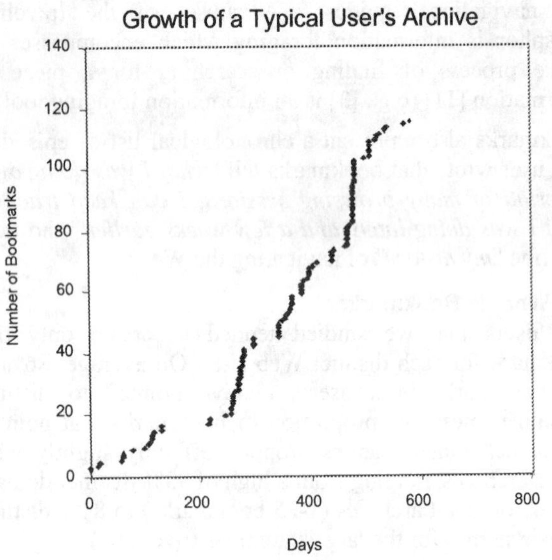

Figure 1. Growth rate of a typical user's bookmark archive.

It can be seen that the user adds bookmarks sporadically with periods of intense bookmarking separated by periods where few if any bookmarks are added.

4. ORGANIZATION OF A BOOKMARK ARCHIVE

Users organize their bookmark archive to fight entropy and add structure [1]. This helps reduce retrieval time, and enables the user to collaborate with other users by sharing the structured archive. Large bookmark archives become unwieldy when they are not organized. Organizing bookmarks is one of the top three Web usability problems reported by 6619 survey respondents in [12].

Users must continually tradeoff the cost of organizing their bookmarks and remembering which bookmarks are in which folders versus the cost of having to deal with a disorganized set of bookmarks. They optimize the cost structure of their information environment to make a small amount of information available at very low cost, and larger amounts available at higher costs [11]. Many users cost-tune their archives by expending the least amount of effort needed to build up enough structure to support fast retrieval of their most useful bookmarks.

4.1. Methods of Organizing Bookmarks

Our 322 users employed seven methods for organizing bookmarks (Table 1, Figure 2).

Approximately 37% of respondents checked "*I don't organize bookmarks — they stay in the order in which I created them.*" Organizing bookmarks is labor intensive, requires extensive time, and is difficult to do. One respondent noted "*I'm just getting started. I didn't even consider this [organizing bookmarks] yet.*" Users with fewer than 35 bookmarks tended not to organize them.

Table 1. Methods for Organizing Bookmarks
No Organization: bookmarks stay in the order created.
Ordered List: users manually re-arrange a list.
Set: users create folders to categorize bookmarks.
Hierarchy: users create folders within folders.
External: users export bookmarks to a separate program.
Web Page: users create Web pages out of their bookmarks.
Other: users search, sort and use unusual methods.

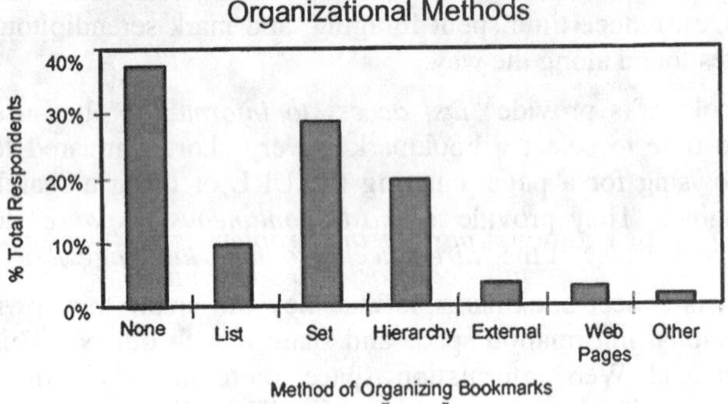

Figure 2. Percentage of survey respondents who reported using each of the seven methods to organize bookmarks,

Relatively few users managed a list without also using folders. The strategy of using an ordered list was most likely to occur for users who had relatively few (less than 25) bookmarks.

Many users organized bookmarks within a single-tiered set of folders. An analysis of variance indicated that the self-reported frequency of creating folders depended on the reported total number of bookmarks the user had, ($F[4,257] = 6.24$, $P < 0.001$). The use of a set of folders peaked with the 101-300 bookmark group and dropped considerably when users had 300 or more bookmarks. The 300+ bookmark users reported that they preferred to use a multi-level hierarchy to manage their bookmarks.

Users with 26-100 bookmarks and with 101-300 bookmarks created folders within folders 28.7% and 24.1% of the time, respectively, in contrast to a corresponding figure of 44.4% of users with 300+ bookmarks. The reported frequency of use of sub-folders (i.e., a hierarchy) differed significantly with the reported total number of bookmarks ($F[4,249] = 3.63$, $P < 0.01$). More hierarchies were used by the group with the largest number of bookmarks (300+) as indicated by a post hoc comparison ($P < 0.05$).

Relatively few (2.2%) of the survey respondents reported using Web pages for archiving bookmarks. Users wrote "*I put links on my bookmarks page.*" and "*I create Web pages once I get more than 10 bookmarks.*" This provides an expressive medium for managing bookmarks, which can include the use of comments and embedded hierarchies: "*I organize certain categories into home pages.*" I organize "*by section in sub-pages of my home page.*"

2.9% of users in our survey created bookmarks and then off-loaded them to a separate application. This was in spite of the fact that such tools as were available at the time of the survey were difficult to use, were not powerful enough to manage a large number of bookmarks, and possessed a steep learning curve. Offloading to a separate application was generally done by respondents who had a large number of bookmarks (e.g., 44.4% of users with 300+ bookmarks offloaded them to separate programs). Users stored bookmarks in simple text files or databases, or used bookmark management tools.

Poor scalability makes visualization, retrieval, and browsing difficult. For example, it is "*hard to get an 'overall' view of bookmarks in long lists.*", "*I can't see them all at once.*" The multi-tier pull-down menu is difficult to use. "*The menu system is awkward and folders are in the way when browsing.*" Semantic hierarchies break down easily, as one user wrote "*bookmarks are unstable if they are not kept in meaningful categories, which takes a lot of time.*" In addition, "*part of the problem is software the other is creating stable categories in one's mind.*"

4.2. Organizational Methods and Experience

The sophistication of the organizational method used increased with the experience level of the user (Figure 3).

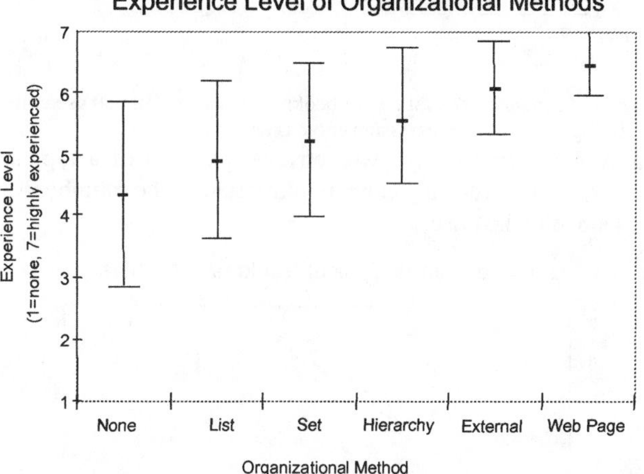

Figure 3. Self-reported experience level from 291 respondents, showing means and error bars (plus or minus the standard error).

There was a significant correlation (Spearman's rho) between level of experience and organization method used ($r[291] = 0.3333$, $P < 0.001$). Users who authored Web pages with bookmarks had a mean experience level of 6.50 (on a scale with 7 as the maximum), while those who do not organize their bookmarks had a mean self-reported experience level of 4.36.

4.3. Organizational Habits of Bookmark Users

Users file bookmarks at different times and rates. The filing habits we observed in bookmark users (Table 2, Figure 4) and are similar to the way users manage electronic mail archives [15].

Table 2. Bookmark Filing Strategies
No Filers: users who never organize bookmarks. The bookmarks stay in the order in which they were created.
Creation-time Filers: users who store a new bookmark in the appropriate category when it is first created.
End-of-session Filers: users who organize all their new bookmarks at the end of the session.
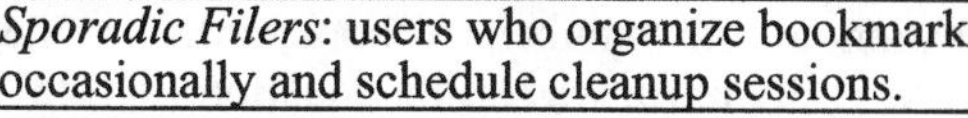 *Sporadic Filers*: users who organize bookmarks occasionally and schedule cleanup sessions.

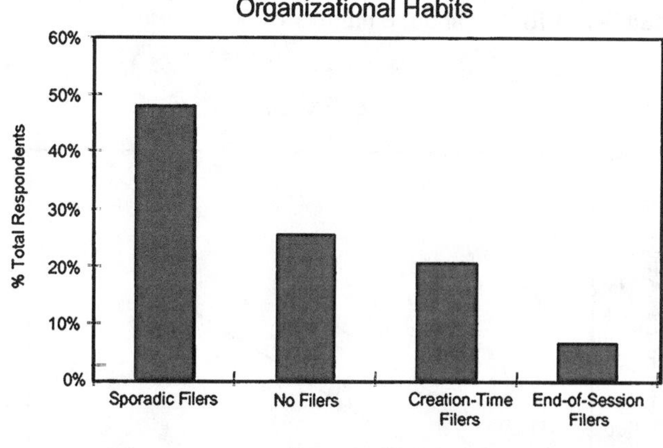

Figure 4. Bookmark filing habits of 299 respondents, showing the percentage of total users in each category

Roughly half of the respondents organized their bookmarks sporadically. 26% or respondents never organized their bookmarks, and 23% of them stored each new bookmark in its proper place at the time it is created. Only 7% of users organized bookmarks at the end of every session.

Sporadic filers chose when to optimize their work environment. They started a special "*spring-cleaning*" session to organize their bookmarks. As a result of these decisions to clean up their bookmarks, they tended to "*organize 2-3 times/week*" or "*organize once a week.*"

Creation-time filers categorized a new bookmark and stored it in a folder at the time when the bookmark was created. These users avoided a pile-up of unorganized bookmarks because they "*organize often at the time of creation.*" Overall, 23% of users surveyed reported filing at creation time; however, a much higher proportion (67%) of users with over 300 bookmarks reported filing at creation time.

Very few users (7%) organized bookmarks at the end of every browsing session. End-of-session filers must set aside a special period of time to organize after each session. Most users, 94% of all respondents, create relatively few (at most five) bookmarks per WWW browsing session. There is therefore no large accumulation of unorganized bookmarks at the end of each session which forces them to file.

An analysis of variance indicated that the average time spent per session varied significantly with when bookmarks were organized ($F[3,278] = 3.5237$, $P < 0.05$). Post hoc analysis indicated that subjects who organized their bookmarks at the end of the session spent significantly more time per session than did subjects who either sporadically organized or never organized ($P < 0.05$). They also used folders extensively, with 80% of end-of-session filers using folders in some manner to organize bookmarks.

One user said that he organizes bookmarks "*when they no longer fit in my drop down menu.*" Beyond the 35 bookmark threshold for easy visibility, users created folders in direct relation to the number of bookmarks in their archive (Figure 5). A linear regression equation ($F[1,26] = 38.52$, $p < .001$) describes the relationship between the number of folders and the number of bookmarks:

$$Folders = 1.14 + 0.14*N$$

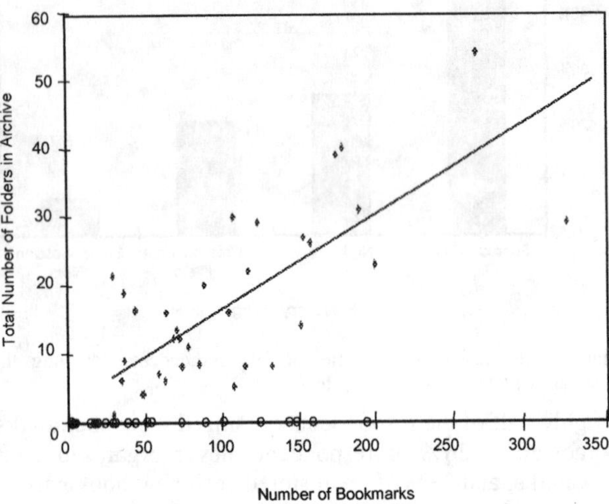

Figure 5. Use of folders in 50 users' bookmark archives, showing the number of folders in each archive as a function of the its size.

As shown in Figure 5, users with less than 35 bookmarks have no folders. Above 35 bookmarks, folders grow linearly with bookmarks.

5. RETRIEVAL OF BOOKMARKS

Users create many bookmarks that they subsequently do not use. When bookmarks are used, they may be stored temporarily (for short term use) or archivally (for use over the long term); they may be published or used collaboratively. One of the survey items asked respondents to rate the importance of these four different types of bookmark usage (temporary, archival, publishing, collaborative) on a seven-point scale (1=not important, 7=very important). There was a significant difference in the degree of importance assigned to the four different types of bookmark use ($F[3,1064] = 2.61$, $P<=0.05$). Respondents reported using bookmarks as archives (for long-term storage) rather than as caches for frequently used information. Respondents assigned the archival use of bookmarks a mean importance rating of about 6, as compared with mean ratings of about 3 for each of the other types of use (temporary, publishing, and collaborative).

Tauscher [14] found that users employ history to revisit pages they have just visited. They access only a few pages frequently and browse in very small clusters of related pages. [1] includes a detailed analysis of the navigation patterns which emerge after bookmark use. Bookmarks are usually a launching point for exploring clusters and a means of jumping between different clusters.

Our analysis of bookmark files substantiates the archival use of bookmarks. The cumulative plot (aggregated over users) for the number of days since the last time each user visited each bookmark is shown in Figure 6.

There is a median time of about 100 days since the last visit to a bookmark. Roughly half of bookmarks in the study had been visited in the preceding three months; 67% of the bookmarks had been visited in the last 6 months; and 96% of the bookmarks had been visited in the past year. Bookmarks were used infrequently, but almost all of them had been used at least once in the previous year.

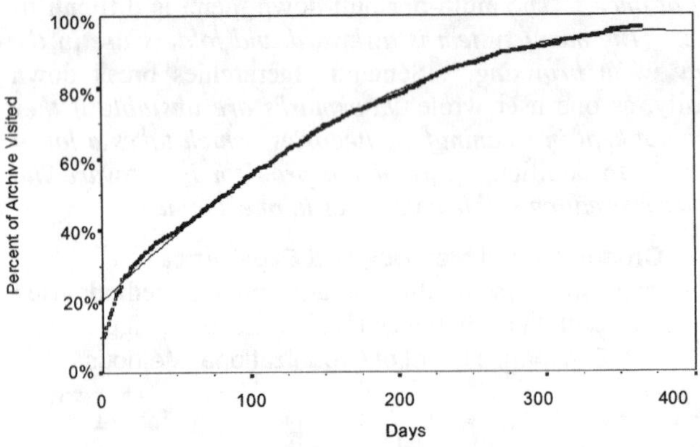

Figure 6. Aggregate retrieval rate of bookmarks pooled from 50 users (the best fitting second order regression curve is also shown).

Figure 7 shows the archival retrieval patterns of a typical user by rank ordering each bookmark by the number of days since its last use.

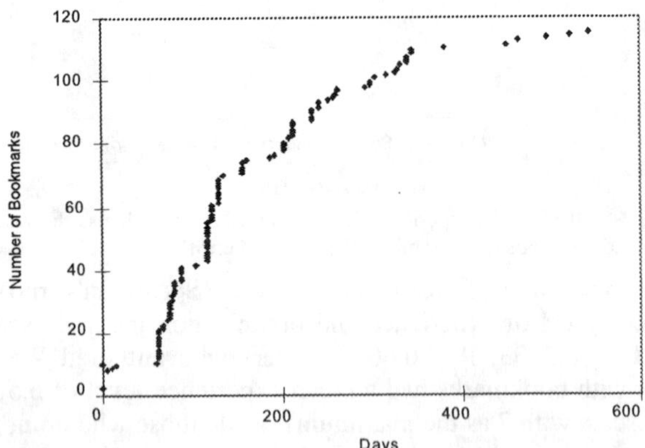

Figure 7. Typical user's retrieval pattern from an archive of 115 bookmarks.

Only 6% of this user's bookmarks had been visited in the previous month, and only 30% were visited in the previous 3 months.

5.1. Retrieval from a Hierarchy of Bookmarks

The comments from survey respondents showed that bookmark users find it difficult to manage a large number of bookmarks. The bookmark hierarchy is created incrementally and somewhat informally over time, but once in place it enforces a rigid structure. Users must then remember where bookmarks are stored within this structure. Finding an item in a deeply nested hierarchy is often challenging for users [5].

Labeling of bookmarks also tended to be a problem, because "*bookmarks are not descriptive enough*" and they "*aren't great describers of the actual content*" of the Web page. 276 respondents reported on a scale of 1 (not a problem) to 7 (very significant problem) that descriptiveness of titles is a problem (mean=4.2, std.-2.1). Yet very few users reported that they actually change the name of bookmarks. This may be due to lack of good tools and traditional difficulties of naming items [4].

Since a bookmark is a pointer to a Web page which can be modified at any time, the content can change without warning and URLs can become invalid. One user wrote, "*I cannot easily tell when a bookmark has become obsolete because the URL has changed or the page has disappeared (I would like a link checker).*"

6. DESIGN IMPLICATIONS

Our interpretation of the results is that bookmarking is a rational process that transfers knowledge in the head to knowledge in the world [9]. Users have to deal with a number of tradeoffs and concerns in bookmarking, including:

A. Is it worth making a bookmark when it will probably be used infrequently?
B. Is the time taken to organize bookmarks (a current cost) worth the future benefit?

Bookmarking behavior seems to change as the number of bookmarks increase. The use of folders begins at about 35 bookmarks, while use of multi-level hierarchies becomes prevalent in archives of over 100 bookmarks. 44% of users with over 300 bookmarks offload to a database and many invent their own creative organizational schemes. Users with archives of over 300 bookmarks tend to be motivated to organize because they share the resulting index of URLs with others.

For many users who cannot expend the significant effort required to maintain a growing archive the value of the user's personal information space breaks down. Entropy creates disorder until the archive finally becomes a *complex information space* [1]. As the WWW becomes the dominant global information resource and new compelling Web sites emerge, users will need bookmark management systems that scale-up to manage their growing archives. Consideration of these results leads us to design recommendations in four fundamental areas: organization, visualization, representation and integration.

Organization

Users need scalable tools because "*bookmarks pile up too fast and become unmanageable.*" They should minimize the effort needed to organize bookmarks and build hierarchies. "*I cannot place it in the prescribed folder easily at the mouse click.*" Systems should provide users with an immediate filing mechanism so that bookmarks can be filed at creation-time, thereby avoiding the buildup of disordered bookmarks. Since many users "*hate having to sort them [bookmarks] into folders,*" systems should provide automated sorting capabilities and let hierarchies be organized within the context of the browsing session. "*I'd like to have another metaphor for managing bookmarks than folders.*" Bookmarks could be organized based on usage patterns so users can easily cost-tune their archives. For example, users could order bookmarks based on frequency of use. The most commonly used bookmarks could be stored within the pull-down menu for navigation, and archival bookmarks could be stored separately for long-term retrieval.

Visualization

Poor visualization hampers users with large archives. "*My problem is that I cannot get all the bookmarks on the screen.*" Bookmark management systems must provide ways of visualizing large numbers of bookmarks to aid retrieval. Our research showed that visualization directly affects organizational habits (i.e. they create folders once the pull-down fills the screen limit of approximately 35 items). For example, one user wrote "*folders are in the way when browsing.*" Visual clutter results from pollution of a growing archive. "*I end up with many bookmarks that I don't use; it clutters my list.*" Designers should investigate time-based visualization with automated filters to display large numbers of bookmarks [18].

Representation

Bookmarks are represented by texts which defaults to the title of the respective Web site. Consequently, "*bookmarks aren't great describers of the actual content [of the Web page].*" Systems should allow users to easily rename a bookmark when it is created because it is "*difficult to change the name to something more descriptive.*" Multiple representations would help users visualize a large archive. Currently, the "*limited information in the top level listing of bookmarks*" makes it difficult to find bookmarks. One user suggested to "*make a short descriptive title available at the top level.*" Designers should also investigate the use of contextual information in representing bookmarks (e.g. based on the bookmark's surrounding hypertext cluster).

Integration

"*There is no really good bookmark organizer that doesn't demand that you exit the browser.*" An integrated bookmark management system should fit naturally into the Web browser. One user suggested a tight coupling between bookmarks and search engines: "*I tend to collect and organize resources in batches. An interface between the search queries and my bookmarks would be nice.*" Since bookmarks are used to collaborate with other users and publish information, tools should combine hierarchy formation and Web page authoring to aid organizing and viewing bookmarks. Users with more than one computer need ways of integrating multiple lists. For example, "*I cannot reference a single bookmark file across multiple platforms. I need NFS-like networkable bookmarks.*"

7. CONCLUSION

Bookmarks serve as starting points for hypertext exploration. They are created and stored for archival purposes, and often not visited for months. Users must weigh the costs of organizing bookmarks against the expected gains. Thus bookmarking takes place within the context of the users' ongoing information requirements and their assessment of how important current bookmarks will be to them in the future.

The advantage for users who maintain a few bookmarks in a single list is that they can see all of their bookmarks on the screen at the same time. This strategy also minimizes current effort. However, as the number of bookmarks increases, users typically employ more sophisticated organizational strategies such as hierarchies of folders. Our results indicate that a sizable proportion of users organize their bookmarks only when they have to, i.e., when a backlog of unorganized bookmarks is accumulated.

Proactive organization of bookmarks tends to occur when people have large numbers of bookmarks. Many users with 300+ bookmarks tend to file at the time of creation because they must keep an up-to-date archive in order to manage so many bookmarks. For these users the benefits of an up-to-date organizational structure outweigh the distraction from the browsing that is required to file a bookmark.

Our study used a questionnaire and an analysis of bookmark files to obtain an initial assessment of how bookmarks are archived and why. Many questions remain to be answered: What happens when people try to manage many hundreds or even thousands of bookmarks? How do these results depend upon the bookmark management capabilities of the browser? Do our results hold with larger samples of users taken from broader populations of users? What other functions do bookmarks serve? For example, a mental maps study of 27 users in [1] suggests that users may create bookmarks to personalize the Web and structure the "*cloud of unmapped resources*" in terms of familiar landmarks, but further study is needed.

Given the ever increasing importance of the Web and its role as a general repository of information, understanding the bookmarking process and developing appropriate tools for organizing large numbers of bookmarks are likely to become pressing issues. This research [1] lays an empirical foundation for further study of Web user behavior and the design of bookmark management systems.

ACKNOWLEDGMENTS

Bruce Homer was instrumental in analyzing the data set. We are also grateful to Colin Furness and Jade Rubick for assistance, and to the Information Technology Research Centre of Ontario and the Natural Sciences and Engineering Research Council of Canada for financial support.

REFERENCES

1. Abrams, D. *Human Factors of Personal Web Information Spaces*. MS Thesis, Department of Computer Science, University of Toronto, 1997. Also available as http://www.dgp.toronto.edu/~abrams.
2. Burton, H.D. (1987). FAMULUS revisited: Ten years of Personal Information Systems. *Journal American Society for Information Science* 32, 440-443.
3. Card, S.K., Robertson, G.G., and York., W.M. (1996). The WebBook and the Web Forager: An Information Workspace for the WWW. *Proc. CHI'96,* 111-117.
4. Carroll, J.M. (1982). Creating Names for Personal Files in an Interactive Computing Environment. *Int. Journal of Man-Machine Studies* 16, 405-438.
5. Lansdale, M. (1983). The Psychology of Personal Information Management. *Applied Ergonomics*19,55-66.
6. Malone, T.W. (1983) How Do People Organize their Desks? Implications for the Design of Office Information Systems. *ACM Transactions on Office Information Systems* 1, 99-112.
7. Nardi, B., Barreau, D. (1995) Finding and Reminding: File organization from the Desktop. *ACM SIGCHI Bulletin*, 27(3), 39-43.
8. Nielsen, J. (1990). *Hypertext and Hypermedia.* Academic Press.
9. Norman, D.A. (1988). *The Design of Everyday Things.* N.Y.: Basic Books.
10. Norman, D. (1993). *Things That Make Us Smart.* Addison-Wesley
11. Pirolli, P. and Card, S. (1995). Information Foraging in Information Access Environments, *Proc.CHI'95,*118-25.
12. Pitkow, J. (1996). GVU's 5th WWW User Survey. http://www.cc.gatech.edu/gvu/user_surveys/survey-04-1996.
13. Schamber, L., Eisenberg, M.B., and Nilan, M.S. (1990). A Re-examination of Relevance: Towards a Dynamic Situational Definition. *Information Processing and Management* 26, 755-776.
14. Tauscher, L. and Greenberg, S. (1997). How People Revisit Web Pages: Empirical Findings and Implications for the Design of History Systems. *Int. Journal of Human Computer Studies*, 47(1), 97-138.
15. Whittaker, S., and Sidner, C. (1996). Email Overload: Exploring Personal Information Management of Email, *Proc. CHI '96,* 276-283.
16. Wright, P. (1991). Cognitive Overheads and Prostheses: Some Issues in Evaluating Hypertexts. *Proc. ACM Hypertext '91 Conference*, 1-12.
17. Wurman, Richard. (1989). *Information Anxiety.* Doubleday, New York, NY.
18. Yiu, K., Baecker, R.M., Silver, N., and Long, B., A Time-based Interface for Electronic Mail and Task Management, *Proc. HCI International '97*, 1997.

Triangles: Tangible Interface for Manipulation and Exploration of Digital Information Topography

Matthew G. Gorbet
Tangible Media Group
MIT Media Laboratory
20 Ames Street
Cambridge, MA 02139 USA
+1 617 253 0128
mgorbet@media.mit.edu

Maggie Orth
Hyperinstruments Group
MIT Media Laboratory
20 Ames Street
Cambridge, MA 02139 USA
+1 617 253 0804
morth@media.mit.edu

Hiroshi Ishii
Tangible Media Group
MIT Media Laboratory
20 Ames Street
Cambridge, MA 02139 USA
+1 617 253 7514
ishii@media.mit.edu

ABSTRACT

This paper presents a system for interacting with digital information, called Triangles. The Triangles system is a physical/digital construction kit, which allows users to use two hands to grasp and manipulate complex digital information. The kit consists of a set of identical flat, plastic triangles, each with a microprocessor inside and magnetic edge connectors. The connectors enable the Triangles to be physically connected to each other and provide tactile feedback of these connections. The connectors also pass electricity, allowing the Triangles to communicate digital information to each other and to a desktop computer. When the pieces contact one another, specific connection information is sent back to a computer that keeps track of the configuration of the system. Specific two and three-dimensional configurations of the pieces can trigger application events.

The Triangles system provides a physical embodiment of digital information topography. The individual tiles have a simple geometric form which does not inherit the semantics of everyday physical objects. Their shape, size, and connectors encourage rapid rearrangement and exploration of groups of Triangles. The infinitely reconfigurable 2D and 3D topographies of the Triangles system create a new language for tangible interface.

Keywords

Interface design, tangible interface, physical interface, graspable interface, digital connector, physical connector, magnetic connector, tangible bits.

INTRODUCTION

Physical building blocks are powerful tools for thought and play. They allow quick construction and manipulation of structures through two-handed tactile interaction. This enables an easy exploration and understanding of the blocks' interactions with one another, and also of physical properties like balance, gravity, composition, and form (Fig. 1).

However, these blocks are usually passive objects, and computers can not recognize or interpret the composite structures of blocks.

Fig. 1: physical world

In comparison, personal computers allow users to create, edit, and store complicated digital information structures. Manipulating these digital objects is heavily graphical-display-oriented, with the information relationships represented visually on a screen. Although computers support malleable information manipulation, current interactions are largely constrained by the mouse and keyboard (Fig. 2). Shifting focus between the 'controls' of the computer (keyboard and mouse) and the 'data' (as represented by visual images on the screen) can be a source of confusion and delay in working with digital information [7]. The affordances of physical building blocks are inherently richer than what current GUI affords through conventional "direct manipulation" techniques. How can we get the best of both the digital and physical worlds?

Fig. 2: looking into the digital world

Increasingly, we have seen an interest in physical systems for interacting with information [2, 3, 6, 11, 12, 13]. The Triangles system was designed to address this issue by physically embodying the *topography* of digital information – the relationships and connections between data elements – so that users can directly feel and manipulate the digital information with their two hands (Fig. 3). In the same way that building blocks help explore physical properties like balance and composition, Triangles were designed to provide easier interaction with and understanding of data space.

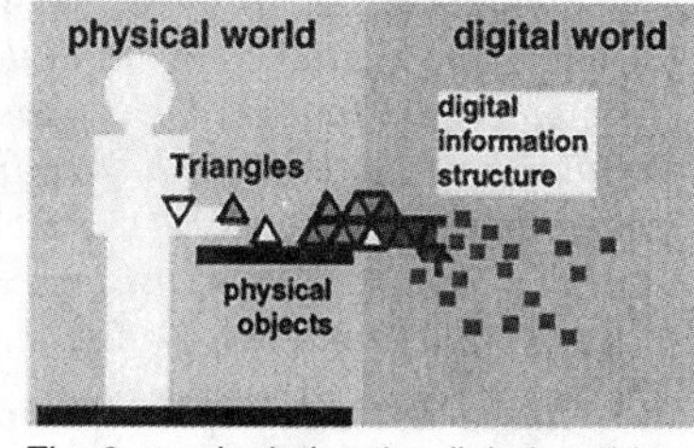

Fig. 3: manipulating the digital world

Unique contributions of the Triangles system are the following:

- The introduction of a concept of joint digital/physical objects which, by design, embody information and provide a general physical means to make a computer aware of their topography
- A user interface that
  - takes advantage of the human ability to easily manipulate physical objects with both hands,
  - provides a persistent physical indicator of state, and
  - allows many people to use it simultaneously.
- A new design for an electrical and magnetic connection mechanism that provides
  - a low-bandwidth, computationally inexpensive means for sensing the manipulation of complex physical structures, and
  - tactile feedback to users in attach and detach operations.

In this paper, we introduce the Triangles system, along with four Triangles applications. We discuss salient features of these applications and lessons learned from developing them. We also describe the iterative design and development of the Triangles system itself, including hardware, software and conceptual design. We begin with a brief scenario from one of our current Triangles applications.

CINDERELLA

Two children are sitting on the floor, with a set of ten triangular tiles in between them. On the tiles are images from the popular fairy-tale Cinderella. One child spreads the tiles out on the floor, looking through them. She picks one up, with an image of Cinderella's evil stepmother on it. The other child hands her a tile with Cinderella's house on it, and she brings them together. They snap together magnetically with an audible click, and instantly the step-mother's voice is heard (emanating from a set of nearby speakers) echoing through the halls of the house: "Cinderella! Cinderella?! Oh, where is that girl?..."

The stepmother's voice continues, calling out for Cinderella, until one of the children picks up the image of Cinderella sweeping, and snaps it onto another edge of the stepmother triangle.

"Ah, there you are! I need you to clean up this messy room. And when you're done with that, there's laundry to fold downstairs," says the stepmother. Cinderella obeys, and sounds of sweeping and humming are heard. Next, the children remove the stepmother. As soon as she is gone, Cinderella explains how she longs to be free from her stepmother's tyrannical rule. Just then, the children attach an image of the stepsisters, and we hear them burst into the room, teasing Cinderella...

This scenario is an example of an interaction with one of the storytelling applications that was developed for the Triangles system. These applications will be discussed in detail later in this paper.

THE TRIANGLES SYSTEM

Overview

The Triangles system consists of a set of identical flat, plastic equilateral triangles, each with a microprocessor inside and a unique digital ID. The Triangles each have different images or markings on them, which can be changed depending on the intended application. They have magnetic connectors on their edges which allow easy physical interconnection, as shown in Figure 4. The connectors also pass electricity, and the Triangles use them to communicate digital information to each other and to a desktop computer. Thus, when the pieces contact one another, specific information about that connection is sent back to the computer, which keeps track of the history of connections and current topography of the system.

Fig. 4: The Triangles

The triangles can be used to make two- and three-dimensional objects whose exact configuration is known to the computer. Changes in this configuration can trigger specific computer-controlled events. For example, connecting or disconnecting two specific Triangles could provide access to a specific web page, or cause a digitized audio sample to play. Events can also be associated with specific groupings of Triangles, rather than simple connection or disconnection of individual triangles. The actual output event that results from a given interaction depends on the application being used, but can be practically anything that a computer can control. The roles played by each part of the Triangles system are illustrated in Figure 5.

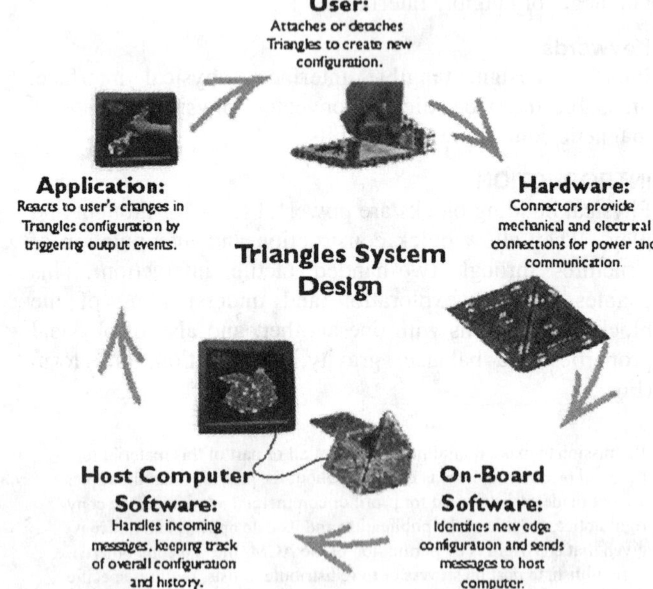

Fig. 5: Elements of the Triangles system and their roles.

The triangular tiles that make up the Triangles system have many affordances that help them to create a new language for interacting with digital information:

- They are easily handled and sorted with two hands.
- They can tile or make branching structures in two dimensions or create three-dimensional polyhedra.
- They can be manipulated by more than one person at a time.
- Their connections remain physically persistent, as a physical reminder of the state of the system.
- They provide tactile feedback when connections are made or broken, through their magnetic connectors.
- Their very general shape allows them to represent any type of digital information without carrying the semantic weight often associated with everyday physical objects.

Why Triangles?

The aim is to create a generic object that can represent the topographical relationships of information elements. Keeping the form of the objects generic enables them to be all about connections and relationships -- a simple geometric shape has less semantic loading [1] than familiar objects such as a digitally augmented set of dolls or books. Pieces that can be tiled are appropriate to physically embody the idea of connection or association, and the flat faces of tiles enable them to carry a pictorial representation of the information which they represent.

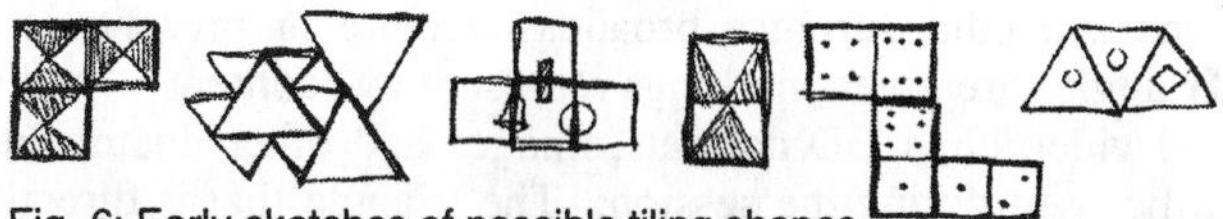

Fig. 6: Early sketches of possible tiling shapes

With these concerns in mind, many shapes were considered for the individual tiles (Fig. 6). Equilateral triangles are the simplest shape that can tile in two dimensions, so triangular tiles have the minimum number of sides required to physically reflect the complex possibilities of branching structures and relations in computer information. The three sides of a Triangle suggest junctions with one input and two outputs, or vice-versa. In contrast, objects with only two points of connection, like stacking blocks, suggest structurally linear data relationships, with only one input and one output. Another advantage to Triangles over other shapes like squares is that the triangular pieces allow robust three-dimensional (polyhedral) forms to be built.

Even though the interaction with Triangles is fairly simple, allowing users to quickly create and manipulate associations between the elements, the configurations that can be created are quite complex, due to the combinatorics of equilateral triangles. Since any edge of each tile can create a uniquely identifiable physical connection with any edge of another triangle, the number of unique configuration possibilities for a set of tiles is given by:

$$x \geq \frac{3^n (n+1)!}{6}$$

where n is the number of triangles and x is the number of possible unique configurations.

This means that for a set of just four triangles there are 1,620 possible 2D configurations. As the number of triangles increases, this number of configurations quickly grows to millions. Such a potentially vast world of information combined with the simplicity of interaction on the part of the user makes Triangles flexible and powerful, while creating interesting design issues for applications.

APPLICATIONS

The Triangles system presents a very specific means for interaction, lending itself to certain types of applications over others. For example, while it might be very well suited to exploring a non-linear narrative or configuring an audio/visual system, it would not be appropriate for applications which require a rich input vocabulary, like text editing or technical illustration.

The Triangles system has been seen and used by hundreds of people during the first year of its development. These include researchers from a wide variety of fields, artists, children visiting our laboratory, and representatives of many diverse industries. Our observations of these users' interactions with the system have contributed a great deal to its development. Following, we discuss four applications that we developed for the Triangles system, and what we learned from each.

Non-Linear Storytelling

The first applications that were developed for the Triangles system (March/April 1997) were storytelling systems.

Galapagos! – A World-Wide Web Story

In *Galapagos!*, partial illustrations of characters, places and events are placed on the faces of the Triangles in such a way that one or more users connecting two edges together can complete these images. As the two halves of a character or event are connected, web pages containing the content of the story appear on the user's screen. Which triangles are chosen and the order in which they are connected to one another determine aspects of the progression of the story. The result is a non-linear narrative that is told partially by a comic book-like arrangement of physical tiles, and partially by animated images and text on a computer screen (Fig. 7).

One problem with *Galapagos!* is that its content is entirely visual, requiring the user to split their visual focus between the images and text on the computer screen and the Triangles themselves. Children who played with the application did not always know where they should be looking, and expected audio feedback. This issue was addressed in the next storytelling application that we created, *Cinderella 2000*.

Fig. 7: Interacting with *Galapagos!*, a user connects Triangles to access web content.

Cinderella 2000 -- An Audio Comic Book

Cinderella 2000 presents a modern version of the Cinderella fairy tale. Interactively arranging seven triangles that depict various aspects of the story, user can trigger audio samples stored on a desktop computer, creating a soundtrack of sound effects, narration and dialogue in the voices of the characters. These sounds are synchronized with the progression of the story, because they are triggered by specific connection events and Triangle configurations. Using audio for the output avoided the split-focus experienced with *Galapagos!*, creating a more compelling and complete storytelling experience. One interaction scenario for Cinderella 2000 is described at the beginning of this paper.

The images for *Cinderella 2000* were more varied in their arrangement and design than those in *Galapagos!* The design of the visuals was greatly influenced by the techniques and visual language of comics [9], making use of framing, scale, implied action and composition to create a narrative progression through still frames (Fig 8).

Fig. 8: The *Cinderella 2000* Triangles

Also, two specific Triangles were created as interaction devices:

- *Event Triangles*, symbolizing specific events in the story, for example the arrival of the invitation to the ball. Attaching an event triangle changes the context of the story, and thus the behavior of the characters.
- An *Info Triangle*, depicting three comic-book 'voice bubbles'. Attaching a specific edge of this triangle to a character would cause that character to reveal certain information about themselves.

Lessons Learned from Storytelling Applications

With *Galapagos!* and *Cinderella 2000*, we showed the potential of the Triangles system as a general interface for non-linear storytelling. In creating these applications, we also explored techniques and developed general authoring tools that would be useful for others creating nonlinear Triangles content.

However, one thing that became clear from implementing these two applications was the difficulty inherent in authoring unique content for the astonishing number of configurations possible with the Triangles system. The *Galapagos!* and *Cinderella 2000* applications each used seven triangles, offering literally millions of possible unique configurations. It was clear that limiting the number of 'appropriate' connections was necessary, in order to avoid having to create a huge number of unique content events. This was addressed in *Galapagos!* by using the partial illustrations to suggest which connections would be appropriate. Still, interaction issues arose around what would happen if 'incorrect' connections were made. For example, connecting half of a turtle to half of a bird might seem reasonable in a fantasy story about mythical animals.

If the application could respond appropriately to any of hundreds of thousands of possible connections, some extremely compelling and interesting storytelling applications might be possible. Advanced artificial intelligence and emergent behavior research [8] suggests that such applications could actually be written, generating or modifying content on the fly and thus making full use of the Triangles system's potential. In the future, we hope to collaborate with experts in this field to further investigate this possibility.

Another critical lesson learned from the storytelling applications was the importance of providing a single focus for the user's attention. The use of audio feedback was much more effective with children than pure visual content, as discussed above.

Triangles provide a very simple means for interacting with a potentially very complicated set of character relationships and storytelling situations. This ease of manipulation can also be applied to other sorts of information relationships. The next applications we developed use Triangles as an interface for configuring complicated media systems.

Media Configuration

TriMediaManager

Triangles' potential as a control system for information was further explored in *TriMediaManager*, an application in which the Triangles system is used to select and configure various media during a broadcast lecture or presentation. Triangles are given markings representing 'content' – audio and video clips, 3D datasets, images and other documents to be used during the session. The triangle that is directly attached to the computer is labeled as the *display*. During the session, the presenter can interactively decide which media is being shown by physically rearranging the positions of the triangles in relation to each other and to the *display* Triangle.

For example, if a presenter has access to a live video feed of herself, an audio clip, two video clips and a variety of images (presentation slides, for example), these can each be selected at any time by simply attaching the appropriate tile to the *display* triangle. If the presenter wishes to present several of these media in parallel, this can be achieved by joining the content triangles with one another. When this occurs, *TriMediaManager* attempts to simultaneously display as much of the total content as possible, giving precedence according to the proximity of each tile to the *display* triangle. In our example, if the tile representing the live feed of the presenter were directly connected to the *display* triangle, it would be broadcast as a full-screen image with audio. If an *image* tile were then connected to another edge of the *live video* triangle, it would appear as a smaller image, inset into the video feed (Fig. 9). Connecting a *video clip* triangle on the remaining edge of the *live video* tile would inset the appropriate video clip in another corner of the screen (the audio streams from the live feed and the clip would be mixed).

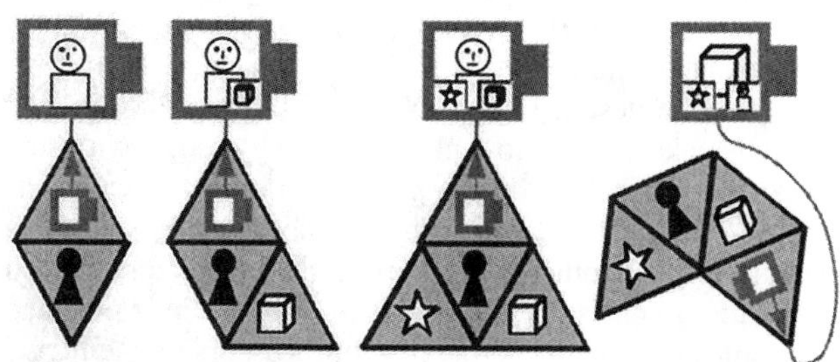
Fig. 9: *TriMediaManager*

At any point in the presentation, the presenter could easily change the display priorities of the various media: Moving the *display* triangle so that it was connected directly to the *video clip* tile would cause the hierarchy to shift, and the output to respond accordingly: the clip would take over the full screen, with the image and the live video feed each inset as smaller windows.

The presenter might attach still more triangles to the configuration, which might or might not be immediately displayed, depending on available output resources and proximity to the *display* triangle. The *TriMediaManager* application keeps track of what display resources are available (inset windows, audio channels, volume control, etc) and how each type of information is being displayed (i.e. moving video, still image, audio, or rendered object) and allocates resources for as much of the data as possible.

The human ability to intuitively manipulate, sort and arrange physical objects is exploited in *TriMediaManager*, creating a physical interface for accessing and arranging the display of a great deal of presentation information in realtime. Using the Triangles to represent high-level content selection like 'vacation clip' or 'earnings slide' as opposed to using traditional patching controls like 'VCR1→MON2' or 'carousel advance' allows the presenter to focus on content and dynamically rearrange their presentation if the need arises.

Artistic Expression

In creating *Galapagos!*, *Cinderella 2000*, and *TriMediaManager*, we explored many of the benefits of the Triangles system, including the exploratory nature of rearranging Triangles, the combinatorial potential of Triangles configurations, and the narrative potential of spatial tile arrangements.

One drawback common to all of these applications is their use of pre-defined mappings of information to Triangles. This requires extensive content authoring before each application can be used. *The Digital Veil*, the next Triangles project that was undertaken, allows users to control not only the output generated by specific Triangles interactions, but to assign and reassign meaning to groupings of Triangles during the course of an interaction. *The Digital Veil* was created as an art installation for the 1997 *Ars Electronica* festival in Linz, Austria.[4]

The piece consists of a table on which are laid out 35 Triangles. Each tile has a photograph, illustration, graphic symbol or physical texture applied to its surface(Fig. 10). These elements were designed to be beautiful, evocative and meaningful, both individually and in combination with each other. The public is invited to interact with the tiles in two locations on the table (Fig. 11), creating arrangements of Triangles and connecting them to the 'input station' or the 'output station' – two small boxes on the table with exposed triangle-edge connectors. The 'input station' has a light-up button and a microphone on it. When a user connects up to four triangles together and attaches this arrangement to the input station, the button lights up, and the user can push it and speak into the microphone. Their voice is sampled and linked with the specific arrangement of Triangles that they created. In this way, participants can 'assign meaning' to their configurations, creating illustrated phrases and small narratives that hold personal meaning.

Photo: rubra

Fig. 10: Images used in *The Digital Veil*, designed to be beautiful and evocative.

At the 'output station,' participants can create large configurations of triangles, building a visual and tactile texture on the table in front of them. As they do so, each individual triangle that they add triggers its own evocative audio sample, building an aural texture to accompany the configuration that they create. In creating the large configuration, if the user arranges any of the tiles to form one of the 'phrases' that had been recorded by a previous participant, that audio recording is also played back. In this way, the piece grows and changes over the course of its presentation, keeping a memory of the meanings and associations that users have created.

Fig. 11: Members of the Public interacting with *The Digital Veil*.

The Digital Veil was created to address the reconfigurability of meaning that is inherent in digital information systems. Its use of Triangles allows participants to explore this in an interactive and creative way without needing to learn the particulars of a new user interface. The Triangles provide the feeling that users are actually holding and rearranging the information itself.

Audience members greatly enjoyed being able to quickly make new groupings of Triangles that they could personalize with their voice. They found their own uses for the application, sometimes leaving 'secret messages' in the system to be retrieved later, or even singing 'rounds' that could be controlled by adding new Triangles at the right time.

DESIGN AND DEVELOPMENT OF THE SYSTEM

The development of the system brought together skills from a variety of fields to give the Triangles functionality in the physical and digital worlds. Software architecture, electrical engineering, mechanical and industrial design converged to make the Triangles balanced physical/digital objects. One example of this balance is the physical form of the tiles, which suggest association and rearrangement (key elements of data manipulation). Another is the use of the physical properties of magnets to ensure good mechanical and digital connections while reducing ambiguity and providing tactile feedback to the user.

The design process was an iterative undertaking by two researchers, each with extensive prior interaction-design experience. One was well-versed in the physical and mechanical design of interactive objects, and the other had experience in software systems and traditional (GUI) user interface design. Close collaboration and a good understanding of each other's field of expertise enabled us to find innovative solutions to design challenges at many levels. A tight design loop was established, with new hardware, software and conceptual design maturing simultaneously. Following is a discussion of key conceptual, mechanical and software design issues faced in the development of the Triangles system.

Entropy and Physical Delimiters

When designing physical interfaces, it is important to consider the number of degrees of freedom and possible scenarios that can occur. This is sometimes called the *entropy* of the system. It is impossible to anticipate all of the potential interactions that people can have with real-world objects; for example, a user might pick up the interface and wave it around in the air, juggle it, or otherwise use it in unpredictable ways. Some interface systems, such as speech recognition systems or vision systems, continuously track of all of the user's interactions. These systems must determine *action delimiters* to differentiate between continuous action events in order for those actions to be correctly interpreted. Although powerful in certain situations, this kind of continuous physical sensing can be complicated and computationally expensive [10].

In the design of the Triangles, we sought to address the issues of entropy and action delimiters through the physical design of the objects themselves. Limiting the types of interaction that are suggested by the form of the object reduces the entropy of the system. The equilateral triangle shapes suggest tiling and edge-to-edge connections as appropriate ways of manipulating the objects, and the magnetic edge connectors reinforce this with tactile feedback when appropriate connections are made. Action delimiters are provided by the physical connection mechanism itself, which reports only *significant* changes to the system (connections and disconnections), as discrete events. These physical design decisions helped create a low-bandwidth and computationally inexpensive means for accurately interpreting a user's interaction with the Triangles system.

Physical Connectors

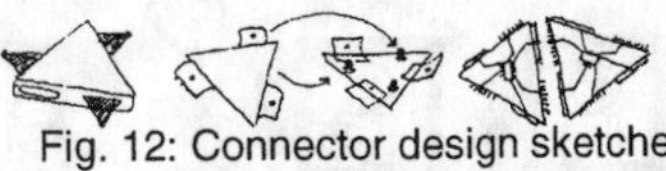

Fig. 12: Connector design sketches

The physical connectors had to be designed so as to make it easy to link any Triangle edge with any other edge in a robust, hinging configuration. Disconnecting the Triangles also had to be as simple as pulling them apart from one another. In addition, the connectors needed to provide a consistent supply of power and uninterrupted data connections between the microprocessors on the tiles.

Several designs for the physical connectors were examined, including slotted edges, snaps, zippers and conductive Velcro® fasteners (Fig. 12). Since equilateral triangles are radially symmetrical, connections such as magnets, snaps or Velcro, which have 'male' and 'female' components (or polarity, in the case of magnets) needed to be arranged so that 'male' would always meet 'female' and vice-versa (Fig. 13). Depending on the design of the electronic circuit, issues of symmetry arose in ensuring that each transmit pin would meet a receive pin, and that shared pins, such as power and ground, would always find the correct mate when connected.

Fig. 13

Fig. 14: Many prototypes of Triangles were built.

Many prototypes were built (Fig. 14), and eventually it was decided that the feel of the magnetic connectors was important to reinforcing the sensation of connection and disconnection. They make the triangles easy to attach and remove, and because they require no lateral motion, as do zippers or slots, connecting complex forms such as hexagons is easy. In addition, clever arrangement of the polarity of the magnets on the individual connectors can help force the edges into proper alignment with one another when making connections, and enables them to physically resist being wrongly connected. This avoids false connections and further reduces the entropy of the system.

Microprocessor Code

One of the Triangles in a given set acts as the *mother triangle*. It differs from the others in that it has a cable that provides power to itself and to the other triangles, as well as serial communication to a *host* computer. As soon as any Triangle is connected to this *mother triangle*, the new Triangle's microprocessor receives power through its edge connectors, and it can communicate with its neighbors and the host computer. The new Triangle then provides power and a communication pathway to subsequent Triangles as they are connected to it, and so on.

The microprocessor inside each Triangle is responsible for managing that Triangle's identity and information about its connections. When a Triangle receives power, its microprocessor begins alternately polling and transmitting its ID to each of its edges. If any other Triangles are connected to it, they will be able to identify it and also the edge to which they are connected. Whenever such an event occurs, each Triangle involved generates a message containing the new configuration information, which it passes to the host computer. Disconnections between Triangles result in a similar message being passed by the Triangle that is still connected to the system.

The host computer receives these messages, and the Triangles system software layer interprets them. It reconciles connection messages that were generated simultaneously by two Triangles into *connection events* and keeps track of *disconnection events*. The system keeps a time-stamped history of all such events, and provides functionality, through an Application Programming Interface (API), for independent software applications to access and react to specific interactions with the Triangles.

Communication Structure

In order for the host computer (to which the Triangles are attached) to know the exact configuration of the system, a distributed network routing system was implemented. Each Triangle is responsible for determining when local events occur (connections and disconnections) and relaying information about these events back to the host computer, as discrete messages. The host computer then consolidates and reconciles these messages with one another in order to determine the configuration of the entire system.

To help develop and test the host software and various message-passing schemes in parallel with the development of the hardware, computer simulations (Fig. 15) of several routing algorithms were built, including:

- Probabilistic 'broadcasting' and regeneration of messages to every triangle with the expectation that the host would eventually receive the message;
- 'Maze-walking' which attempts to find the host connection by exploring all the possible connections;
- 'Topography maps' stored within each microprocessor to route the message at each step of its journey;
- 'Perimeter hugging' which attempts to find the edge of the configuration, and from there to trace a path back to the host;
- 'Gradient descent' which establishes gradients between each triangle and the host, and pass messages 'downhill' to ensure that they reach their goal.

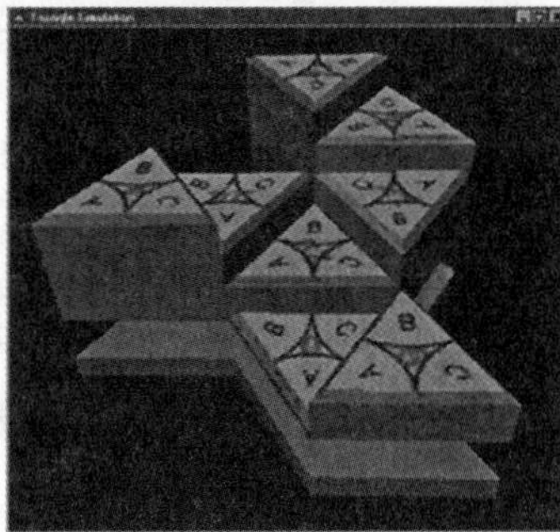

Fig. 15: Software Simulation of 'Gradient Descent'

Each of these algorithms had flaws, especially when implemented in a distributed system of low-memory microprocessors. For the initial implementation of the Triangles system, the 'gradient descent' algorithm [5] was used. This ensured that connection and disconnection messages would always be reported, but was unforgiving of errors caused by noisy connections, and introduced an undesirable amount of latency into the system.

Eventually, message-passing was simplified by making a hardware modification to the Triangles: A common serial bus was added to the architecture of the system, so that in addition to communicating with one another locally, any Triangle could pass messages directly to the host computer or to any other Triangle. This greatly improved the speed of the system and simplified the software design.

This illustrates a recurring theme in the design and development of the Triangles system. Almost every design challenge that was encountered could be solved in microprocessor software, electronics, mechanical hardware, or host software. Understanding the relationships between these elements and the trade-offs and balances between them was crucial to developing this system.

The Triangles API

A comprehensive API layer was developed for creating applications which use the Triangles system. The API layer consists of a C++ library of function calls and data structures that manage information about a user's interactions with the system.

The simplest way for developers to use the API is to specify certain Triangle *events* which the system should watch for, and provide functions in their application that should be called when these events occur. An *event* is either a connection or a disconnection between two Triangles. The event structure contains the following information:

- *Event type:* was this a connection or a disconnection?
- *Event time*: at what time did the event occur?
- *Triangle IDs:* what were the IDs of each triangle?
- *Triangle edges:* which edge of each triangle was involved in the event?

The event registration functionality is flexible, so that an application may specify some, all or none of these fields to monitor, allowing very general or very specific interactions to be specified. For example, an application might specify an action to be triggered when Triangle 4, side 2 is connected to Triangle 12, side 0, or simply any time Triangle 3 is connected or disconnected from anything else. (If none of the fields are specified, the application will be notified whenever *any* event occurs.) When a registered event does occur, the specified application function is called, and the details of the event that occurred are passed as parameters to the function. This enables the application to know exactly how the user interacted with the system.

The API also provides more comprehensive functionality. Using a simple command structure and a set of linked lists, an application can retrieve a complete description of which Triangles are present in the system and their connections. Once this list is provided, the application can query the API for information about any individual Triangles, including a complete history of that Triangles' interactions with its neighbors. In this way, an application can act not only on events that are occurring in real-time, but also on past changes in the system. For example, if a Triangle is connected to another Triangle for the first time, it might trigger a different event than if the same Triangle is connected again later. If two Triangles are connected and another, specific Triangle is present in the system, this might have a different meaning than if the two Triangles were connected alone.

Using the API, developers need not be concerned with the message-passing protocols or internal functionality of the Triangles themselves. This creates a useful abstraction that allows Triangles applications to be developed by competent programmers from a variety of backgrounds. One of the aims of the Triangles project is to allow researchers in other fields such as computer science, design, education or physics to experiment with this tangible interface system.

FUTURE WORK

The Triangles system was conceived of as a foundation for exploring tangible interface in a broad variety of fields. Future work on this project will focus on providing the complete Triangles system to other researchers who are interested in developing interactive applications using the tangible interfaces.

Research areas that we have targeted at present include:

- Nonlinear narrative

  Further development of the storytelling potential of 'comic-book' Triangles with audio feedback.

- Groupwork Coordination

  Exploration of scheduling, group dynamics modeling and workflow systems using Triangles.

- Emergent behavior/AI models for content generation

  Using semantic webs and intelligent agent technology to interpret the meanings of various Triangles associations.

Continued refinement of the API is planned, along with the development of GUI and tangible authoring tools to support Triangles application development. Software ports of the API from its current Windows® platform to Silicon Graphics™, MacOS™, and general UNIX platforms will enable a broader variety of applications to be accessed with the Triangles.

CONCLUSIONS

We have presented a new tangible interface for the manipulation and exploration of digital information topography. Bridging the gap between the physical and digital worlds is not trivial. Rather than attempting to give computers a complete understanding of human language (voice, gesture) and the real world, our approach provides a new language which both people and computers can understand. Synchronization of what users have in their hands with the digital connections that computers can perceive occurs when the Triangle pieces are attached and detached from each other. Although this language (connect/disconnect) is quite simple, the power of expression enabled by a topography of multiple triangles is tremendous and very rich.

The concept of Triangles was born in October 1996. Many physical mockups of the Triangles and scenarios were created along with software models and simulations. This iterative development process led to the first working prototype in March 1997, which was demonstrated internally, with the sample application *Galapagos!* The benefits and limitations of Triangles became apparent through the development of several other applications and refinement of the system itself. Although we have not yet undertaken extensive usability testing with the Triangles system, our internal development has led us to be confident about this new language for tangible interface.

Acknowledgments

We would like to express our sincere thanks to the following people and organizations for their contributions to this project: Wendy Chien, Emily Cooper, James Hsiao, Chris Lopes, Betty Lou McClanahan, Gong Ke Shen, Paul Yarin, and the MIT Media Laboratory's Things That Think consortium.

REFERENCES

1. Csikszentmihaly, M. and Rochberg-Halton, E. (1981). "The Meaning of Things: Domestic Symbols and the Self", Cambridge University Press, 1981.
2. Feiner, S., MacIntyre, B. and Seligmann, D. (1993). Knowledge-based augmented reality. *Communications of the ACM.* 36, 7 (1993), 52-62.
3. Fitzmaurice, G. W., Ishii, H. and Buxton, W. (1995). Bricks: Laying the Foundations for Graspable User Interfaces. *Proceedings of Conference on Human Factors in Computing Systems (CHI '95)*, Denver, Colorado, ACM Press, 442-449.
4. Gorbet, M, and Orth, M. (1997). Triangles and The Digital Veil, *FleshFactor: Informationsmacschine mensch (1997 Ars Electronica Festival Catalog)*, Linz, Austria, SpringerWein-NewYork, 280-283.
5. Gorbet, M. and Orth, M. (1997). Triangles: Design of a Physical/Digital Construction Kit. *Proceedings of Designing Interactive Systems: Processes, Practices, Methods, and Techniques (ACM DIS '97)*, Amsterdam, ACM, 125-128.
6. Ishii, H. and Ullmer, B. (1997). Tangible Bits: Towards Seamless Interfaces between People, Bits and Atoms. *Proceedings of Conference on Human Factors in Computing Systems (CHI '97)*, Atlanta, Georgia, ACM Press, 234-241.
7. Kurtenback, G., Fitzmaurice, G., Baudel, T., and Buxton, W. (1997). The Design of a GUI Paradigm based on Tablets, Two-hands, and Transparency. *Proceedings of the ACM CHI '97 Conference on Human Factors in Computing Systems (CHI '97)*, Atlanta, Georgia, ACM Press, 35-42.
8. Maes, P. and Brooks, R. (1990). Learning to Coordinate Behaviors. *Proceedings of AAAI-90: The American Conference on Artificial Intelligence*, Boston, MA, AAAI Press/MIT Press, 796-802.
9. McCloud, Scott. "Understanding Comics." Kitchen Sink Press, 1994.
10. Pentland, A. P. (1996). Smart Rooms. *Scientific American.* 274, 4 (1996), 54-62.
11. Resnick, M. (1993). Behavior Construction Kits. *Communications of the ACM.* 36, 7 (1993), 64-71.
12. Suzuki, H., Kato, H. (1993). AlgoBlock: a Tangible Programming Language, a Tool for Collaborative Learning. *Proceedings of 4th European Logo Conference*, Aug. 1993, Athens Greece, 297-303.
13. Wellner, P. (1993). Interacting with Paper on the DigitalDesk. *Communications of the ACM.* 36, 7 (1993), 87-96.

HandJive:

A Device for Interpersonal Haptic Entertainment

BJ Fogg
Stanford University
P.O. Box 8338
Stanford, CA 94309
USA
bjfogg@stanford.edu

Lawrence D. Cutler
Pixar Animation Studios
1001 W. Cutting
Richmond, CA 94804
USA
larryc@pixar.com

Perry Arnold
Trilogy Dev. Group
6034 W. Courtyard Dr.
Austin, TX 78730
USA
perry_arnold@trilogy.com

Chris Eisbach
IBM
User Systems
Ergonomic Research
USA
chrisbac@almaden.ibm.com

ABSTRACT
The paper describes how we designed and prototyped HandJive, a haptic device for interpersonal entertainment. HandJive is notable because it relies entirely on haptic input and output. The design process included typical steps such as analyzing user needs and performing iterative prototyping and testing. However, developing a haptic interface like HandJive also presented special challenges, such as creating rapid physical prototypes that could withstand abuse, developing a preliminary system of haptic interaction, and testing haptic interfaces through low-tech prototypes.

KEYWORDS
Entertainment, interaction design, haptics, product design, rapid prototyping, user testing, ubiquitous computing, tactile feedback, interpersonal communication

INTRODUCTION
For the 1996 University Workshop at Interval Research, we developing a system based on the workshop theme "remote play." The challenge in the design brief was to "prototype ways in which people could use computer-mediated objects/interfaces together for enjoyment." Our four-person team combined a variety of academic pursuits including communication, psychology, drama, product design, mechanical engineering, computer science, computer graphics, and human-computer interaction. We worked on this project for approximately three months.

Although we began without biases towards any user group or resulting technology, our eventual goal became to create a haptic-only, "ubiquitous computing" device for entertainment and interpersonal communication. We hoped to push the computerized aspects of our device into the periphery, making the computer more transparent to the user. This briefing explains the incremental steps in our design process, as well as the resulting system which we call "HandJive."

WHAT IS HANDJIVE?
HandJive is a handheld object that allows remote play through haptic input and output. Specifically, HandJive is a device that:

- fits in one hand
- moves in interesting ways (so you can fidget with it)
- can communicate wirelessly with similar devices
- has only haptic input and output (no visuals, no sound)
- sends movements to another HandJive device
- receives movements from another HandJive device

RELATED WORK ON HAPTICS
Haptic research in the Computer Graphics and HCI communities has blossomed during the past few years, in part due to the development of high-fidelity force feedback devices such as the PHANToM [9]. Much work has focused on simulating our physical environment [8, 14, 16] and on augmenting GUI interfaces with haptic technology [7, 11, 12]. As an alternative form of haptic feedback, other systems [3, 4, 10, 15] use physical, everyday objects as input devices to provide users with crucial affordances and constraints. Tangible Bits [6] extends this approach by seamlessly integrating these physical objects with the virtual world. However, our project scope differs from all the above systems in that none of these technologies focus on interpersonal communication or on entertainment.

At the same time we were developing HandJive, other research projects also began incorporating haptics into interpersonal communication devices. The Bed environment [2] connects two people remotely to allow for intimate and non-verbal communication. Billow [13] enables children isolated in hospitals to play with one another. Both of these interfaces combine tactile input with auditory, visual, and/or ambient media. In contrast, HandJive has no audio-visual component: the interaction is completely haptic. Also developed during this timeframe, inTouch [1] gives the illusion that two people in separate locations are interacting with one shared object through a haptic-only interface. Our work differs in that HandJive allows orthogonal or indirect manipulations coupled with discrete articulation positions (as opposed to a continuous range of motion). We feel this distinction leads to a significantly different design space.

EARLY DESIGN STEPS

The initial stages of design can often be the most difficult to quantify and describe. Although our process for HandJive was iterative and recursive, we outline below the beginning phases of our design, some of which took place simultaneously.

Defining Our User Group: Friends isolated in silence

The first step in our research and design process was to put aside all ideas about interfaces and technologies; instead, we wanted to focus on a user group that had unmet needs. After considerable brainstorming and lightweight investigations, we found that our team was generally interested in designing for people who were "captive in silence." In other words, we wanted to create entertaining activities for people who were isolated in a public context (see Figure 1). We then began "people watching"; we observed individuals on buses and subways, at airports, in elevators, at cafes, at classes, in church services, and so on. We eventually discarded situations involving complete strangers, primarily because we feared that the interactions could be creepy and/or awkward.

After much observation, we decided that our key user group was friends isolated in classrooms and meetings. For purposes of research, design, and evaluation, we narrowed our user group further, focusing on freshmen and sophomores in college classes. We accepted the special challenge of this user population: On one hand, we wanted to create a device which allowed students to interact playfully with each other, but on the other hand we did not want to create something so immersive that it would distract students from the class content or interactions. This was an important objective throughout the project. However, in a broader sense, we hoped to develop a system that would allow people to interact playfully with each other in any context in which they were isolated in silence.

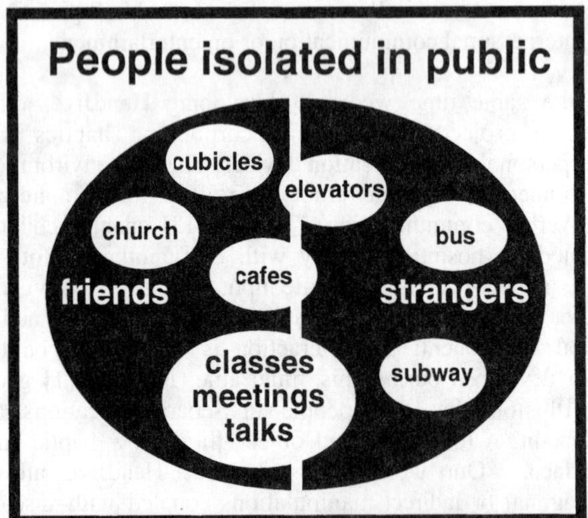

Figure 1: Our broad user group: people isolated in public contexts. As we observed this user population, we became most interested in designing for friends isolated in silence.

Studying Our User Group

We then began to study our user group so we could understand their needs, behaviors, attitudes, and contexts. Both at Stanford and at Foothill Community College, we attended classes with a high percentage of freshmen and sophomores. We also observed listeners in other related contexts, including a BayCHI meeting. We soon realized that almost everyone seems to fidget in these situations. As one user later commented, "Fidgeting is a national pastime." Some of the behaviors we observed included:

whispering	playing with jewelry
stretching	doodling
playing with hair	reading
taking notes	looking around
eating	sleeping

In addition to making observations, we questioned students about their classroom behaviors. Through these informal interviews, we learned that some students come to class prepared to play games with others (e.g., bringing dice or a squirt gun). So at a later stage of research, we provided our users with some simple games, such as "Hangman," to play in class. We wanted to see how different types of activities fit into the classroom context. We discovered that interactive games which allowed students to stop and restart were most amenable to a classroom setting. Other games were simply too immersive, either in pacing or in mental effort.

From our observations and interviews we created six user profiles of fictional characters who represented key users. These profiles were intended to run the gamut of our user population. Creating these profiles helped us gain a clearer picture of the attitudes and behaviors exhibited by our typical users.

Narrowing our Design Space

Our investigations and insights into college students in classroom settings led us to narrow our design space in important ways. At this point we had not decided on any device or technology, but we realized that whatever system we built for "remote play" would have to:

- be unobtrusive and possibly concealable
- allow stops and restarts
- allow remote interaction with other people
- scale to various levels of cognitive load

These constraints played a pivotal role throughout the rest of our design process.

Scenario Building: Leading us to key issues

Once we defined our users and narrowed our design space, we began exploring ways to fill our users' needs. We created various narrative scenarios that described how our target users could overcome their isolation in classes by using technology. Some of these scenarios we visually scripted with storyboards (see Figure 2). Others we enacted verbally using improvisational techniques.

Figure 2: Storyboards brought up key design issues.

The storyboards and improvisations helped us face key design issues. For example, the following questions emerged repeatedly as we discussed our scenarios:

Should we design a gaming device OR a communication device?
We decided to develop a gaming device because the task seemed to be a more constrained and challenging problem. Also, the gaming device pushed our scenarios in more interesting directions.

Should our device be exclusively haptic OR multi-modal?
We hypothesized that a tactile-only device might be better suited for the classroom context in comparison to a multi-modal system. Ultimately, we chose the exclusively haptic route because the possibilities intrigued us more.

ITERATIVE DESIGNS AND USER TESTS

At this point we built physical prototypes for some of the sketches in our design notebooks, and we began to test the prototypes with users. The next sections describe the five basic iterations on our design.

1. Proof of Concept Prototype

We built the first prototype as a proof of concept for interpersonal haptic interaction. The prototype was simply two balloons filled with liquid and connected by a tube (see Figure 3).

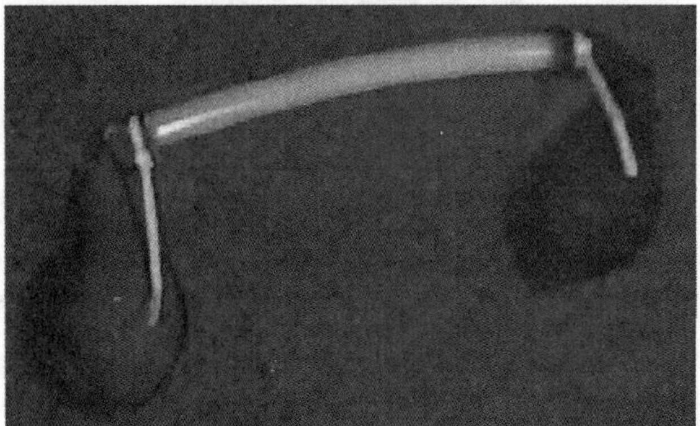

Figure 3: This rapid physical prototype, made from balloons and a tube, helped us investigate haptic interactions.

Each user holds one of the balloons in hand, and squeezing the balloons moves the liquid back and forth. In this simple manner, users could interact with each other. For this user test, we got responses from a convenience sample of people we found in public places. On later investigations, we tested people who were members of the target user population.

Testing this prototype led to key findings and design implications:

Balloon Prototype	
Finding	**Design Implication**
Users found the simple haptic device compelling	Explore more complex haptic designs
Direct hydraulic resistance inspired users to fight for control	Explore indirect interactions to reduce the impulse to fight

We found that most users were intrigued by this type of interaction, although a few also felt the interaction was too "one-dimensional," which did not surprise us. What did surprise us, however, was that during the tests many users would squeeze their balloons very hard to force the liquid into their partner's balloon. In other words, the direct resistance of liquid moving back and forth seemed to make people want to fight for control. One user commented that she wanted to see if she could make the balloon pop on the other side. Of course, this type of reaction put considerable stress on our prototypes (so we had to create various versions of the model).

More important, discovering users' inclination to fight started us thinking about indirect haptic interactions. We hypothesized that an indirect interaction—one that did not allow direct resistance—would likely produce a more cooperative environment than a direct interaction could provide. (In addition, we knew it would be difficult to build a device that could withstand this kind of stress.)

Toward the end of these user tests, we asked people to imagine themselves with a similar device in a classroom setting. Many volunteered that they would use the device to communicate. A few suggested the possibility of playing games. We learned that although this balloon device may not compete with video games for entertainment value, users thought it would be fun in a classroom setting. In other words, "fun" is a relative concept, depending heavily on context. Even a simple device could be fun in a situation where people are isolated in silence.

The next step was to have users play "Three's Company," a game much like "Follow the Leader," with the balloon prototype. Users liked "Three's Company," but it seemed to require too much concentration to be useful in a classroom setting. Students would not be able to play the game and listen at the same time.

2. Prototypomania Alpha

With some confidence in our idea for an exclusively haptic device, we began to rapid prototype many possible solutions, keeping in mind that an indirect haptic interaction would likely be better than a direct one. We used Play-Doh, clay, and styrofoam to quickly mock up potential devices. By building these 3-D prototypes, we were able to communicate our ideas better than by just using the drawings in our design notebooks. Our ideas for a handheld haptic device included finger rings, a joystick, spinning disks, and a squeeze ball. We explored different kinds of playful activities that each of the various devices would allow. And we prototyped some of these ideas with more robust materials, giving them some limited movement. Figure 4 shows a variety of these prototypes:

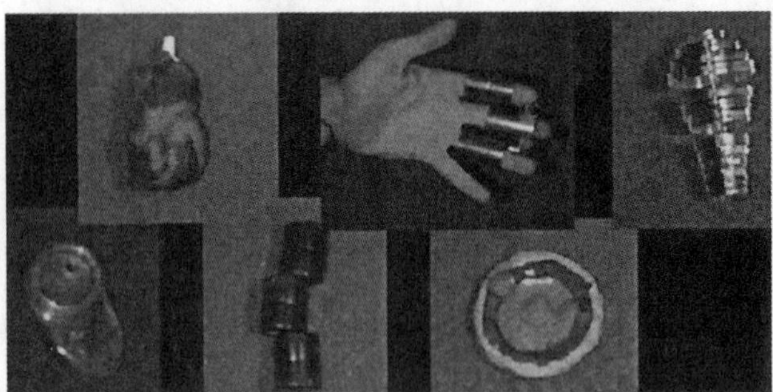

Figure 4: Some of the rapid prototypes we tested.

We then tested our rapid prototypes with target users. At the beginning of each evaluation, we simply handed the devices to users to get their reactions. Later, we specifically asked them to compare and contrast different devices, hoping to gain insight into what people did and did not like. The tests on these rapid prototypes provided us with many insights, including the following:

Multiple Haptic Prototypes	
Finding	**Design Implication**
Users liked devices that clicked into discrete positions	Explore different types of discrete motion
Three stacked cylinders felt good in their hands	Explore designs with hand-fitting objects

One important finding was that most users preferred the devices that could be manipulated into discrete positions (i.e. parts that snapped into place) more than the devices that had a continuous range of motion (such as a disk they could spin). Although we are still not certain why users preferred discrete over continuous manipulations, we suspect it has something to do with the greater certainty and feedback a discrete movement provides. In contrast, perhaps our continuous-motion prototypes offered too many degrees of freedom, creating a less compelling interaction.

In this round of testing, as in others, we found that users exerted a surprising amount of force in manipulating and handling the devices. In one extreme case, a woman used both hands to rip a neoprene cover off a device, destroying the prototype! In general, it seemed that users took great liberties in squeezing, bending, and generally manhandling these creations. We suspect that two factors caused this reaction: (1) these were handheld devices, and (2) they looked playful.

We also found that some users were suspicious of our purposes. Users sometimes perceived these haptic devices to have sensual undertones, causing them to question our motives. Although we never intended to design a sensual device, Hofmeester et. al. confirms our experiences: products which fit comfortably in the hand as well as ones which are soft and flexible tend to induce a sensual feeling [5].

3. Prototypomania Beta

For our next iteration, we developed a range of new prototypes based on the design implications from the previous step. During this phase we specifically explored two types of motion: sliding (moving in a straight path) and rocking (articulating like a hinge). We also compared various form factors such as rings (like brass knuckles) and within-hand devices (like a grip from a ski pole).

Not only did these user tests confirm our previous finding that users prefer discrete manipulations over continuous ones, but the tests also clearly showed that people preferred devices that fit inside the hand with parts that articulated in a rocking motion. Figure 5 shows an example of one such device.

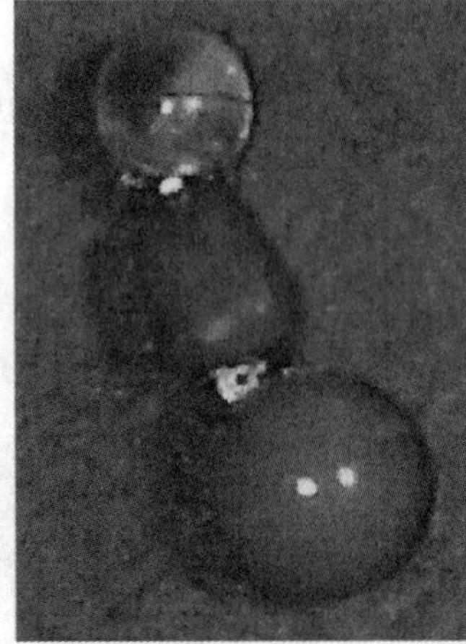

Figure 5: Users liked this haptic prototype for various reasons. This became our basic form factor for HandJive.

Although other types of form factors and articulations were possible within our design space, because of time constraints we settled on the above prototype for further refinements and testing. We made these basic devices with superballs, two electrical switches (rocker switches with three positions), and various kinds of putty. This kludge of material had a strong appeal for our users. In fact, reactions to this simple toy hinted at how much adults like to play, though they often hide that fact.

We refined this basic three-part device with further user-testing, learning that most people liked a squishy center with a combination of one large and one small ball at each end. We also found that one size did not fit all; users were sensitive to moderate variation in the size of these devices.

4. Developing Interactions for HandJive

As we went through the previous steps, we simultaneously explored the interactions users could have with the various prototypes.

A. Creating an indirect, orthogonal interaction

One important challenge was to develop an indirect way of interacting through the devices. Our first prototype test had shown that direct resistance would likely inspire fighting for control, so we discussed a number of alternatives.

The interaction scheme that seemed most viable was to give each user control over a separate and orthogonal plane of movement. More specifically, a user could manipulate each ball on their device forward and backward into three discrete positions, like articulating a hinge forward and backward. The balls on the device could also lean from side to side in three discrete positions; however, this side-to-side movement would be a result of the forward and back motion on the partner's device. Figure 6 attempts to show how this orthogonal interaction works.

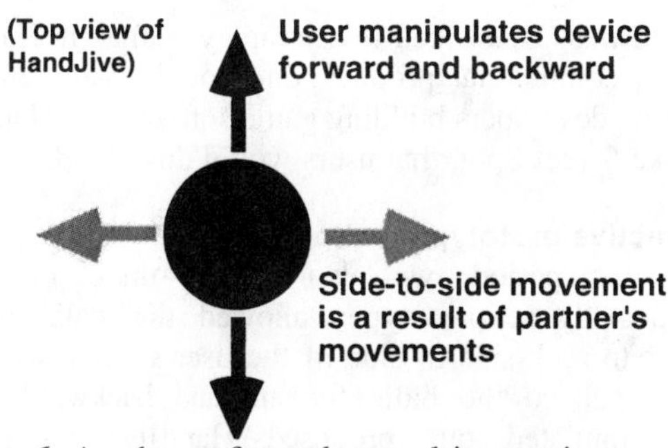

Figure 6: A scheme for orthogonal interactions.

Using words and pictures to explain this scheme of orthogonal and indirect interaction was a considerable challenge throughout the project. In contrast, whenever we had the opportunity to demonstrate the interaction with a physical prototype, people readily understood the interaction scheme. This difficulty illustrates how words and pictures are often insufficient to communicate ideas about movement, and it shows the value of quick physical prototypes, especially for haptic-only devices.

B. Developing patterns and routines

With our orthogonal interaction scheme in place, we then began developing our first iteration of a haptic language for HandJive. We hypothesized that HandJive would allow a new type of interaction not found anywhere else. The HandJive interaction could be something like social dance, jazz improv, and conversation. We examined these three activities to gain some insight into how to create interactions for HandJive, noting interesting similarities among them:

	jazz improv	conversation	social dance
small units	notes	words	positions
ordered combinations of units	riffs	utterances	patterns
guiding principles for how units fit together	scales	grammars	routines

Because these three types of interactions were built of smaller units, we suspected that a haptic interaction language for HandJive should rely on putting smaller units together to create a larger possibility of interactions. At first we called these sets of movements "grammars." Although this term worked well for us, we later realized that "grammar" was not a word our users associated with fun, so we changed the terminology to "patterns" and "routines."

After various attempts at defining and user testing "Tactilese," our haptic language, we eventually settled on the following: Tactilese consists of single units called "positions," simple movements called "patterns," and more complex movements called "routines" (see Figures 7 and 8). A user can move the HandJive into one of nine discrete positions. Patterns combine these positions and are the building blocks for the routines. For example, the Two-Step Pattern is embedded in the Mambo Routine below.

We hypothesized that these patterns and routines could be the building blocks for both collaborative activities (much like dances) and competitive activities (perhaps like thumb wrestling or a shared Rubik's cube). To become a competent HandJive player, one would need to learn a certain number of patterns and routines. Both types of interaction would involve computer mediation.

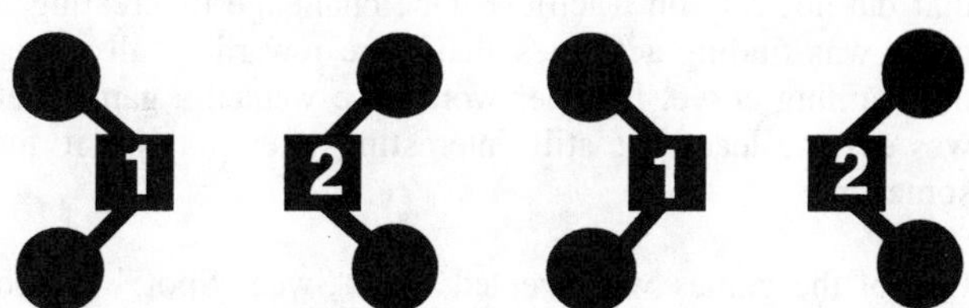

Figure 7: An example of a HandJive "pattern" which consists of two positions, repeated twice. We called this simple movement the "Two-Step Pattern."

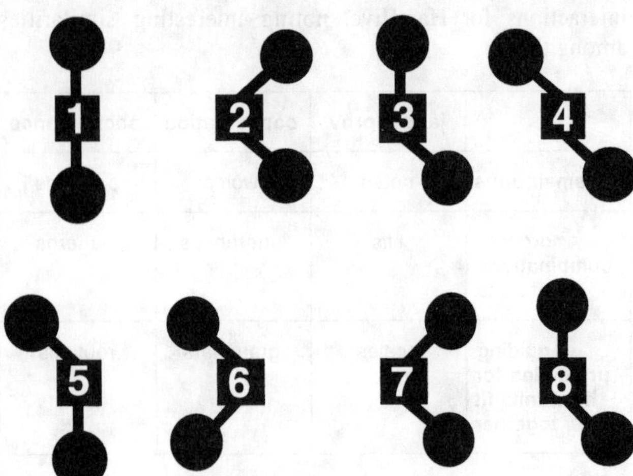

Figure 8: An example of a HandJive "routine." We called this series of movements the "Mambo Routine." Notice that the Two-Step Pattern is embedded in steps 6 and 7.

In conducting user tests, we found that people could easily perform the patterns. However, these users could not master the routines during the timeframe of a testing session, giving us little helpful feedback. As a result, we asked five users to practice these more complicated movements. We found that after two hours of practice, our experienced users

- could perform our most complex routines
- enjoyed manipulating the device
- could manipulate the top ball more easily than the bottom one
- preferred the complex routines over the simple ones
- preferred routines that offered variety: both small and dramatic moves
- improvised their own routines

Of course, we realize that Tactilese is an artificial language. If HandJive were an actual product, users would likely evolve their own interaction patterns. We were curious how this haptic language might evolve but did not have the time or resources to answer this question.

C. Developing potential games

In addition to developing a tactile language, we also explored different games people could play with HandJive that did not rely on Tactilese. One challenge in creating a game was finding activities that were rewarding all along the learning curve. In other words, we wanted a game that was easy to learn but still interesting after playing it for some time.

One of the games we invented was "Sweet Spot," which somewhat resembles the childhood favorite "Battleship." Initially, the computer secretly assigns each player two sweet spots. The two players take turns moving their own HandJive, which in turn affects the position of the opponent's HandJive. The objective is to position the top ball into one of the sweet spots and the bottom ball into the other. The device might send a victory signal to the winning player (perhaps a vibration) while the losing opponent might receive a small electric shock. Alternatively, a user can compete in single-player mode against the computer.

Since Sweet Spot requires significant computing and micro-electronic technology, we could not user test this tactile game with the mechanical prototypes we built. Instead, we developed a software version with Hypercard and tested the game in a visual manner (see Figure 9).

Figure 9: We tested a tactile game idea using a laptop computer with a divider that separated the screen.

We found that users liked this strategy game. If HandJive became a commercial product, one could easily envision application developers building game software for HandJive, much like Sweet Spot, that users would download.

5. Interactive prototype testing

During this period, we also created three interactive prototypes. These prototypes allowed the balls on the HandJive to rock side to side in the user's hand, while the user manipulated the balls forward and backward. These devices simulated our proposed HandJive movements almost exactly and would allow for "Wizard of Oz" testing. We built our prototypes using bike cables that ran to a control board (see Figure 10).

We tested the interactive prototype with our five experienced users. We had two key questions going into these interactive user tests: (1) Would users be able to sense the side-to-side position of the balls? and (2) Would users have difficulty manipulating the balls as they moved from side to side?

We took each user into a classroom and allowed him or her to interact via the HandJive with our wizard at the control board. These tests showed that users:

- found the movement in their hand compelling but difficult to describe
- could sense the orthogonal movement of the balls fairly well

- found that manipulating the moving balls was simpler than they expected.

These user tests dispelled our main fears. Users could indeed sense the position of the moving balls, with the top ball being easier to sense than the bottom. Furthermore, users could manipulate the balls while they were moving orthogonally.

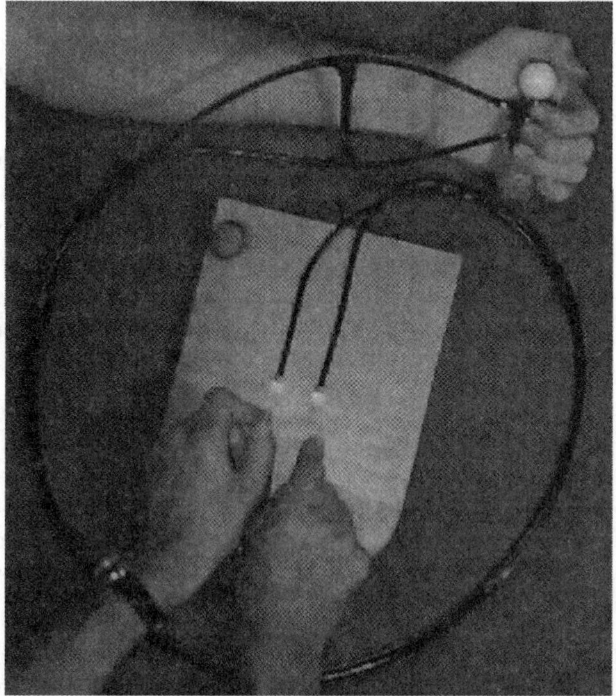

Figure 10: A low-tech interactive prototype for testing HandJive interactions. The user can manipulate the HandJive, while the wizard interacts via bicycle cables.

We also tested the interactive prototype on five novice users—people who had never used HandJive before. Although these users had not practiced any of the patterns or routines, they seemed fairly adept in manipulating the interactive device and enjoyed the moving sensation in their hands. Even novice users could manipulate the balls forward and backward, despite the fact that the balls were simultaneously moving side to side.

FUTURE DIRECTIONS FOR DESIGN

Although HandJive presents a new type of computer-mediated technology and pushes forward the possibilities for haptic interactions, the design process is not yet complete. The future steps for developing and understanding this device include:

- testing fully functional devices in a classroom setting
- having users spend extensive time with the device and noting how the interactions evolve
- exploring other user groups, such as the blind or those in corporate cubicles

One unanswered question is whether users would adopt the patterns and routines we created. We think not; users would likely invent their own language and games. Another question is whether HandJive would be used as we have intended. We cannot be sure, though we suspect that people would use HandJive in unanticipated ways. Because this device does not rely on visuals or sound, it could be a significant communication or entertainment medium for the deaf or blind.

KEY LEARNINGS FROM THIS PROJECT

While creating this new interface, we gained insights that are common to many design problems, such as the benefits of rapid prototyping, user tests, and iterative design. However, the nature of our device also led to less-common insights. They are as follows:

Designing devices for play

- Fun is a relative term: What is fun in one context may not be fun in another.
- A major challenge for a play device is providing rewards all along the learning curve.
- Meeting in locations like toy stores and parks inspires design. Having toys at design meetings is also helpful.
- Play is never free-form; it relies on some form of imposed structure.

Designing handheld devices

- People exert considerable force on handheld objects.
- Fidgeting is surprisingly pervasive.
- Handheld objects easily become "objects of desire" and can often be charged with sensual undertones.
- The technical aspects of handheld devices (battery life, mechanical functioning, etc.) are challenging.
- Handheld objects are not "one size fits all."

Designing haptic devices

- It is difficult to communicate haptic events in words or pictures.
- Rapid prototyping is more effective than language in conveying haptic ideas.
- People can learn haptic skills fairly quickly.
- A simple haptic device can support complex interactions.
- Our users liked discrete manipulations over continuous ones.
- Haptic interactions can be compelling and powerful, making this an exciting area for research and design.

ACKNOWLEDGMENTS

We would like to thank the following people for their many insights and contributions to our project: Al Cho, David Kelley, Chris Rohrer, Ellen Tauber, and Terry Winograd. This work was supported by Interval Research and Stanford University.

REFERENCES

[1] Brave, S. and Dahley, A. inTouch: a medium for haptic interpersonal communication. *Extended Abstracts of CHI'97*, Atlanta, 1997. 363-364.

[2] Dodge, C. The bed: a medium for intimate communication. *Extended Abstracts of CHI'97*, Atlanta, 1997. 371-372.

[3] Fitzmaurice, G., Ishii, H., Buxton, W. Bricks: laying the foundations for graspable user interfaces. *Proceedings of CHI'95*, Denver, 1995. 442-449.

[4] Hinckley, K., Pausch, R., Goble, J., Kassell, N. Passive real-world interface props for neurosurgical visualization. *Proceedings of CHI'94*. Boston, 1994. 452-458.

[5] Hofmeester, G., Kemp, J., Blankendaal, A. Sensuality in product design: a structured approach. *Proceedings of CHI'96*, Vancouver, 1996. 428-435.

[6] Ishii, H. and Ullmer, B. Tangible bits: towards seamless interfaces between people, bits and atoms. *Proceedings of CHI'97*, Atlanta, 1997. 234-241.

[7] MacKenzie, I. and Oniszczak, A. The tactile touchpad. *Extended Abstracts of CHI'97*, Atlanta, 1997. 309-310.

[8] Mark, W., Randolph, S., Finch, M., Van Verth, J., Taylor, R. Adding force feedback to graphics systems: isues and solutions. *Proceedings of SIGGRAPH'96*, New Orleans, 1996. 447-452.

[9] Massie, T. and Salisbury, J. The PHANToM haptic interface: a device for probing virtual objects. *Dynamic Systems and Control*, Chicago, 1994. 295-301.

[10] Pausch, R., Burnette, T., Brockway, D., Weiblen, M. Navigation and locomotion in virtual worlds via flight into hand-held miniatures. *Proceedings of SIGGRAPH'95*, LA, 1995. 399-400.

[11] Ramstein, C., Arcand, J., Deveault, M. Adaptive user interfaces with force feedback. *Video Proceedings of CHI'96*, Vancouver, 1996.

[12] Rosenberg, L. and Brave, S. Using force feedback to enhance human performance in graphical user interfaces. *Extended Abstracts of CHI'96*, Vancouver, 1996. 291-292.

[13] Rueb, T., Wardzala, J., Millstone, J. Billow: networked hospital playspace for children. Extended *Abstracts of CHI'97*, Atlanta, 1997. 357-358.

[14] Ruspini, D., Krasimir, K., Khatib, O. The haptic display of complex graphical environments. *Proceedings of SIGGRAPH'97*, LA, 1997. 345-352.

[15] Sachs, E., Roberts, A., Stoops, D. 3-draw: a tool for designing 3D shapes. *IEEE Computer Graphics and Applications*, 11(6), 1991. 18-26.

[16] Salisbury, K., Brock, D., Massie, T., Swarup, N., Zilles, C. Haptic rendering: programming touch interaction with virtual objects. *Proceedings 1995 Symposium on Interactive 3D Graphics*, Monterey, 1995. 123-130.

Simplifying the Controls of an Interactive Movie Game

Jeff Johnson
UI Wizards, Inc.
231 Moscow St.
San Francisco, CA USA
+1 415 586 5285
jjohnson@uiwizards.com

ABSTRACT

Eight months before an interactive movie game was due to be shipped, its developers and funders decided that its user interface had to be radically simplified. The author was given the task of designing a new, simpler control scheme. This paper describes the redesign process, the design issues that arose and how they were resolved, the tests that were conducted to evaluate new design ideas, and concludes with an evaluation of the resulting design, lessons learned, and thoughts on user-interface design *vs.* game design.

Keywords

User interface, design, games, usability testing, interactive movies

INTRODUCTION

In July 1996, Advance Reality, a game software developer, hired me as a consultant to solve a user-interface design problem in a game they were developing. I was referred to them by AnyRiver Entertainment, the game's "producer"[1]. AnyRiver was responsible for testing the game on computer-game enthusiasts (referred to as *play-testing*), and their tests indicated that players were having difficulty operating the game's controls.

The Game

The game is called *A Fork in the Tale*, abbreviated *Fork*. The developers had shot a full-length feature film viewed through the eyes of the protagonist. In contrast to a normal movie, each scene was filmed with many outcomes. The developers were editing the footage together to create an interactive game. Such games are known in the game software industry as "full motion video" (FMV) games.

Every few seconds while the movie is playing on an individual's computer screen, mouse-sensitive control symbols appear over the movie action providing opportunities for the player to affect what the protagonist does or says, e.g., leave, enter door, ask question, make comment, don magic cloak, dodge punch. The software selects the sequence of clips to show based on the player's choices and various state-variables.

CHI 98 Los Angeles CA USA
Copyright 1998 0-89791-975-0/98/ 4..$5.00

The high frequency of choices provided in *Fork* represents an advance over previous interactive movies, which offer players a choice only every several minutes. The frequency of choices also makes the game much more complex (i.e., branchy) than most FMV games: five CD-ROMs are required to hold all of the footage a player might encounter. To keep the game's complexity manageable, at most three control symbols are presented at a time.

Another difference between *Fork* and most other FMV games is that it is real-time: the movie does not stop while a player considers which action to choose. If a player fails to make a choice within a few seconds, the opportunity passes and a choice is made by default.

The game's premise is that you, the player and movie protagonist, innocently walk into the midst of a shoot-out, get wounded, black out, and wake up washed ashore on an island. The goal is to figure out where you are, who the other people on the island are, and how to get back home. Your character (the protagonist) is an average guy who has an active sense of humor (his voice is that of comedian Rob Schneider). He is basically non-violent, but will defend himself if attacked. Others on the island range from friendly and helpful to hostile and dangerous.

The Design Problem

The problem facing the developers was that the symbols for controlling the movie-action were much too complicated for players to master: they were non-intuitive, unsystematic, and too numerous. Players could not make meaningful choices between control symbols quickly enough.

Simplifying the controls was regarded as critical to the success of the game. The game developers of course wanted the game's mysteries and puzzles to be challenging, but they didn't want operating the game to be difficult.

The developers had tried three times to design action controls for the game, but none of the resulting control schemes had proved satisfactory. They were therefore open to the game producer's suggestion to hire a consultant.

The Assignment

My task was to devise a new control scheme: a way of organizing and representing protagonist actions that was easier to understand than the previous schemes had been.

The game developers first wanted to be sure that they could work with me and that I would design a control scheme that they liked, so they structured my assignment such that they could decide quickly if they wanted me to continue. In three days, I was to produce a document describing a new control scheme. It didn't have to have the final action categories or control art, but it did have to explain, abstractly, how actions would be categorized and approximately how many categories would be needed.

ANALYSIS

I started by playing *Fork* and asking questions about it. I played it not as a normal player would, but rather using special production software that allowed me to jump around, replay clips, etc. I focused on a few game scenes that the designers said contained intensive action or conversation. My goal was to understand the expressive requirements of the game.

Previous Action Controls

I also examined the most recent control scheme. Though it had been designed with care and thought, rather than in an *ad hoc* fashion as many game designers do, it had several flaws that contributed to its poor usability:

1. *Too many symbols.* Action-symbols were organized in a three-dimensional set, with color, shape, and bitmap image as independent axes of meaning. With five colors, about 10 shapes, and dozens of images, the old scheme used hundreds of symbols. Furthermore, the meanings assigned to shapes and colors were arbitrary, e.g., *color*: yellow = helpful, green = curious; *shape*: spiked = aggressive, rounded = passive. It was nearly impossible for players to learn all of the symbols.
2. *More semantic resolution than necessary.* The old control scheme distinguished each action-situation in the game from every other. This would make sense if players were in control of the time, subject, object, and mood of their actions, but in this case the *game* is in full control of the timing and effect of actions, only a few of which are available at a time. Therefore, the action-resolution required is much lower.
3. *Similar representation of very different actions.* In the old control scheme, most symbols were stationary opaque plates that appeared at the bottom of the screen. Whether a displayed symbol depicted, e.g., a physical movement or a speech act, was indicated only by the shape of the plate. This hindered recognition of even what general *type* of action a symbol represented.
4. *Flawed implementation.* The game editors (who, along with their other editing duties, added action-symbols to movie clips) didn't understand the old scheme, so they implemented it haphazardly. Each editor tended to use a subset of symbols s/he understood or liked the appearance of. Furthermore, editors made up new symbols occasionally, not all of which fit the scheme. The result was an *ad hoc* implementation of a principled (albeit flawed as described in points 1-3) design.

Expressive Requirements

Although the old control scheme was to be replaced, it was clear that an important feature of it should be retained: clickable action-symbols that appear at choice-points in the movie. The real-time (i.e., non-stop) nature of the game required that all available protagonist actions at choice-points be simultaneously visible, ruling out a control scheme such as that used in slower-paced games, where the cursor changes shape as it is moved around the screen to indicate what action is available there.

The main re-design task was therefore to design a simpler but sufficient categorization of actions, and symbols to represent the categories. Initial analysis of the game suggested that protagonist-actions fell into six categories: *navigate* in a direction, *look* in a direction, *interact* physically with objects or people, *speak*, *think* silently, and *memorize* events or faces.

Experience with iconic user interfaces [2] suggested to me that choosing among available actions would be easier if these six classes were grouped into two superordinate action-classes -- physical movements (navigate, look, and interact) *vs.* speech acts and thoughts -- with gross differences in how the two classes would be presented.

Opportunities for physical actions would be represented by black and white, semi-transparent, animated "hotspots". They would usually float over the action and pan with it (e.g., enter door, block punch), but might appear at the edges of the screen if they had no clear direct object (e.g., turn right, jump). A few such "hotspots" had already been introduced into the game by editors dissatisfied with the existing controls, and seemed successful.

In contrast, opportunities for speech and thought would be represented by cartoon speech balloons containing a symbol representing the specific speech or thought sub-category. They would appear at the bottom edge of the screen (to appear to come from the protagonist's own mouth) in one of three fixed positions.

Memorizing events and faces posed a dilemma: which main symbol class should it be in? Memorizing is a mental act, but has a definite target in the movie-action, like looking closely at something. The game editors had already used hotspots to represent opportunities to memorize things, and play-testing indicated that it worked well. Following the principle "if it isn't broken, don't fix it," I left this aspect of the game as it was.

An important goal was to reduce the number of action sub-categories (and symbols). The recognizability and discriminability of graphical symbols in a set does not depend *exclusively* on set size: people can discriminate fairly large sets if the symbols in the set are different enough from each other and if the mappings from symbols to meaning are intuitive [3]. Nevertheless, other things being equal, smaller symbol sets are preferable. Whatever the optimal number might be, hundreds of action sub-categories was clearly too many. It was also clear, however, that the game's expressive requirements ruled out having ten or fewer sub-categories *per* main action-class. Somewhat arbitrarily, I set myself the goal of having at most 30 symbols in each of the two main classes.

After playing critical game-scenes, I devised preliminary categorizations of movement and speech actions that seemed to cover the expressive requirements while not exceeding this limit (details below). Although the final control symbols would be drawn by graphic artists (one artist per set to assure consistent appearance within each set and clear differences between the two sets), I made rough sketches for each of the speech and movement sub-categories.

Having satisfied myself that a simplified control scheme that met the game's expressive needs was feasible, I presented it to the developers. They liked the simplified control scheme and asked me to continue refining it and to work with the graphic artists, game editors, and programmers to get it implemented.

Additional Requirements

Over time, I learned that, in addition to the game's expressive requirements, there were requirements and constraints arising from Advance Reality's schedule and resources, and from the wishes of the game designer.

An important constraint on the re-design effort was that the only funded usability testing was the play-testing being conducted by AnyRiver. Their support for *Fork* was based, in part, on positive results from testing early prototypes of the game on computer-game enthusiasts. They continued play-testing throughout the development period, reporting player enjoyment, usability problems, and bugs to Advance Reality. Any other usability testing had to be done very quickly and at essentially no cost. However, we sometimes needed to test specific design ideas before adding them to the game. In such cases, we had to devise quick, cheap tests.

A final set of requirements were based on the game designer's wishes and goals. Before describing them, it is important to clarify my role in the project.

In the computer game industry, the game designer is usually also the user-interface designer (supported by art directors and graphic artists). Because the roles were separate in this case, it was possible to observe how our concerns overlapped and interacted. The game designer was concerned mainly with how entertaining and aesthetically pleasing the game was and how well it embodied his overall vision. I was concerned mainly with usability. Our different concerns often led us to differences of opinion. As a consultant, I had to accept the game designer's judgment if he insisted. He respected my judgment and yielded to it more often than he overruled it, but, naturally, he was difficult to convince if a proposal ran counter to his vision of the game. His ideas about the game that affected the re-design included the following:

- Although he realized that the new control-scheme had to have far fewer action sub-categories than the old scheme, the game designer tended to favor having more categories than I did. To him, each protagonist-action had a meaning, and he preferred to represent actions in terms of the intended meaning, rather than in terms of just what was necessary to distinguish them at choice points. This issue arose repeatedly during the re-design effort.
- The game designer had strong feelings about the appearance of the control symbols. He wanted them to have three-dimensional depth, i.e., not appear flat in the plane of the screen. They had to "lead players' eyes into the movie action". The controls also had to fit with the game's woodsy, old-world fantasy theme: they had to look "antique and classy". While these graphic style requirements did enhance the aesthetic appeal of the game, they also biased the symbol art towards more-detailed styles, rather than toward the abstract, minimalist styles that graphic designers agree are easier to recognize [3].
- The game designer wanted to minimize the use of text throughout the game. The game software can display a text label under any action symbol, but the game designer felt that labeling every control symbol would slow players down and divert their attention from the movie-action, as well as hinder translating the game into other languages. I agreed, so my initial design used text labels: 1) only on speech symbols, not on physical action symbols, 2) mainly in early game scenes to help players learn the symbols, and 3) thereafter, only where necessary to distinguish choices (e.g., when multiple speech acts of the same type were offered). However, as is described later, the game producer disagreed with us on this issue.

RE-DESIGN: PHYSICAL ACTIONS

As described above, my initial analysis of the requirements for controlling the protagonist's physical actions yielded four action categories that were to be represented by hotspots: navigating in a direction, looking in a direction, interacting physically with objects or people, and memorizing events or faces. From playing the game, it seemed that the following sub-categories of each of these categories were needed:

- *Navigate*: forward, 45° right, 45° left, right, left, backward, turn around right, turn around left, turn right, turn left, turn 45° right, turn 45° left, stop/stand-still.
- *Look*: up, down, left, right, here.
- *Interact*: hit/knock, kick, push, block, grab/catch, duck, dodge left, dodge right, spin left, spin right, break free.
- *Memorize*: this.

Each action sub-category would be represented by its own symbol. Figure 1 shows early sketches of some of these symbols.

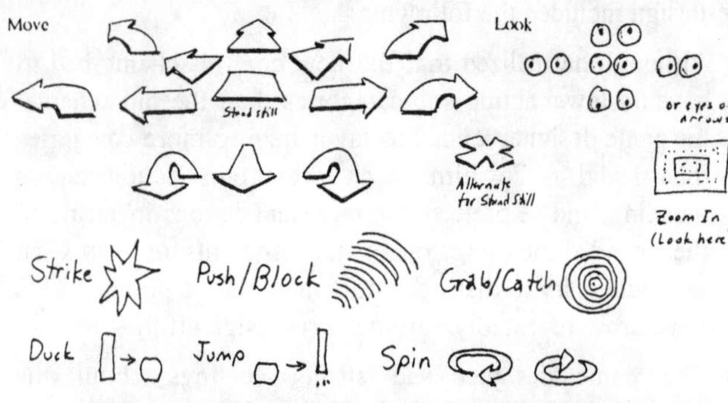

Figure 1: Sketches of physical-action symbols.

The total number of sub-categories (and therefore symbols) in this initial version of the physical-action controls was 30. This was worrisome, because it seemed likely that additional experience with the game would expose the need for physical actions not covered by these sub-categories. For example, I soon realized that we needed a sub-category and symbol for Jump.

Fortunately, further analysis also indicated that some of the initial sub-categories were not needed. For example, it became clear that many Look opportunities in the game could be represented by navigate symbols such as Turn Left, and the rest could be represented by a single Look Here symbol placed in the relevant screen-location. It also became clear that because users were choosing between available actions, not generating actions, it was not necessary to distinguish Hit from Kick: both could be represented by a single Strike symbol. Similarly, it was not necessary to distinguish Push from Block, or Dodge Right and Left from Navigate Right and Left. Finally, the need for some sub-categories disappeared as the game evolved: Break Free and Turn 45° right and left.

The final set of action sub-categories to be represented by hotspots numbered 21. It contained:

- *Navigate*: forward, right, left, 45° right, 45° left, backward, turn around right, turn around left, turn right, turn left, stop/stand-still.
- *Look*: here.
- *Interact*: strike, push/block left, push/block right, grab/catch, duck, jump, spin left, spin right.
- *Memorize*: this.

Once these sub-categories had been finalized, we instructed the game editors to use them throughout the game. It didn't matter that the symbols for the sub-categories did not yet exist, because each use of an action symbol in the game is just an index into a table of symbol bitmaps. We filled the table with placeholder images initially, and replaced them one by one as the symbols were finalized.

Even as the physical-action sub-categories were being refined, symbols to represent them were designed. My sketches served as input for a graphic artist, who produced successive iterations of the symbol set with feedback from me and the game designer.

Some of the sub-categories were easy to represent graphically. It was obvious that symbols for navigation actions should be arrows such as those painted on roads and road-signs. The only difficulty in designing the symbols for these was in achieving the animated three-dimensional perspective appearance that the game designer wanted. Other physical actions that proved easy to design symbols for were: strike (a jagged starburst borrowed from comic books), grab/catch (a target), spin (an animated arrow chasing its tail), and memorize (a small pulsating cloud). Once these symbols were in the game, AnyRiver's play-testing indicated that game players easily understood them.

In contrast, some physical action sub-categories were hard to represent graphically. I initially sketched Stop/Stand-Still as a stop sign, but it proved impossible to create a recognizable black and white stop-sign bitmap within the size and perspective constraints. We eventually settled on a perspective X. To represent Look Here, I initially sketched a pair of eyes, but the game designer was rightly concerned that symbolic eyes would not be recognizable, and that realistic eyes would look like something peering out of the movie rather than a symbol. We chose a zooming rectangle. Other action sub-categories that were difficult to find suitable symbols for were: Jump, Duck, and Block.

With each of the hard-to-depict sub-categories, the game designer and I worked with the graphic artist until we had a hotspot we considered worth trying in the game, then put it into the image table, and judged its effectiveness for ourselves as well as awaiting feedback from AnyRiver's play-testing. If it didn't work, we sent the artist back to the drawing board (or more precisely, the paint program).

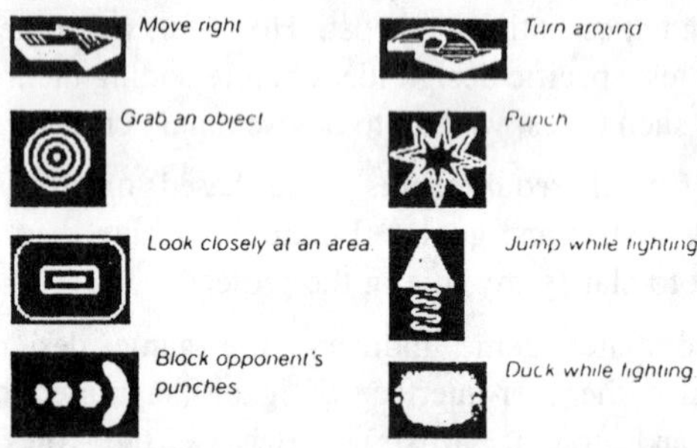

Figure 2: Final images for some physical-action symbols.

Play-testing yielded many complaints about early versions of the hotspots, but with revisions, the complaints ceased. In fact, it eventually seemed that players were using the physical action symbols without being fully conscious of them. When AnyRiver was preparing the game's instruction manual, they asked for a list of the hotspots. When we sent them the list, they were surprised that there were so many distinct images. We pointed out that, with the exception of the Stop/Stand-Still symbol, people don't perceive the navigation symbols as distinct symbols, but rather as the same arrow pointing in different directions. AnyRiver made use of this in the manual to simplify the explanation of the hotspots.

RE-DESIGN: SPEECH AND THOUGHT

The speech/thought controls were designed in parallel with the physical-action controls. Opportunities to speak were to be depicted by a cartoon speech balloon enclosing a symbol representing the type of speech-act. Opportunities to think internal thoughts would be represented by a thought balloon enclosing a subset of the speech-act symbols. As with the physical-action controls, we had to develop both the sub-categories and symbols.

My initial analysis of conversation-intensive game scenes suggested a need for 12 sub-categories of speech: statement, question, accept, refuse, offer help, aggressive/ /insult, sarcastic, humorous, need help/frustrated, flatter/praise/thank, grovel/beg/plead, and recall memory. An additional "speech" type was to represent keeping silent (although see discussion below). The sub-categories for thought were to be a subset of those for speech.

After defining the initial speech sub-categories, I began sketching symbols for them. I suggested using letters for some speech types (e.g., "?" for Question), faces for some (e.g., a comedy mask for Humorous), and hand gestures for others (e.g., a shaking fist for Aggressive). The game-designer preferred a scheme having a common visual theme for all speech symbols (in addition to their being inside the speech balloon), and decided that we would use human figures making mime-gestures.

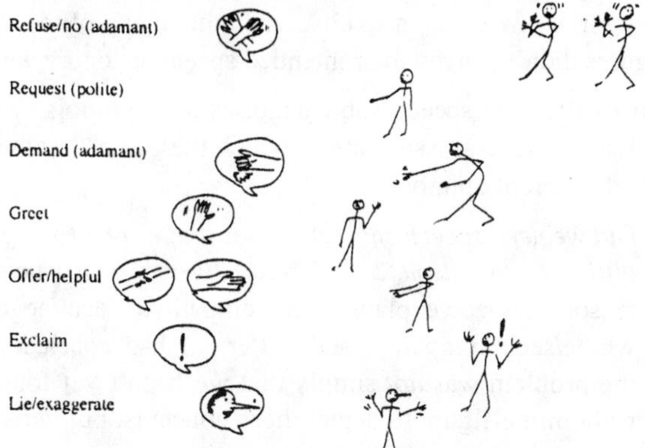

Figure 3: Initial sketches of speech figures.

Based on my initial sketches (see Fig. 3) and input from the game designer, an artist (not the one who created the hotspots) drew human figures miming the current set of speech sub-categories. Each mime-figure consisted of two frames, which would alternate rapidly on the display to produce a simple animation (see Fig. 4). Initially, the game designer and I met with the artist almost weekly over a two-month period to critique the latest mime-figures and inform the artist of changes in the speech sub-categories.

By this time, based on further experience with the game and pressure from the game designer (who tended to favor more specific speech sub-categories), the number of speech sub-categories had expanded to 27. They were: statement, question, accept/yes, decline/no (polite), refuse/no (adamant), request (polite), demand (adamant), greet, offer/helpful, exclaim, lie/exaggerate, whine/seek-sympathy, accuse, gratitude/thank, flatter, humorous/witty, sarcastic/snide, aggressive/insult/defiant, grovel/beg/plead, flirt, manipulate, reason/persuade/explain, care/empathy, deal/negotiate, get-real/get-a-grip, and recall memory.

Figure 4: Artist drawings of animating mime-figures.

Unlike the hotspots, which had been drawn using painting software, the new speech symbols and the speech balloon were drawn on paper. Digitizing them and combining the mime-figures with the speech balloon would be very expensive and time-consuming, so we wanted to wait until we were more confident that the speech sub-categories were stabile and the symbols were adequate. But this meant that the speech controls weren't being play-tested.

Speech Symbol	Participant Responses
Lie/Exaggerate	1. Exaggerating or lying. 2. Lie. Telling a tall tale. 3. Telling a lie. 4. Bigger. 5. He told a big lie. 6. Telling a fish story. 7. Lie. 8. The Pinocchio syndrome. 9. Telling a big lie. 10. Lying -- Exaggerate.
Sarcastic/Snide	1. Nudging. Getting their attention. 2. Bravado, brag. 3. Let me tell you. 4. Hey, big guy. 5. Don't you get it? Heh, heh. 6. D'ya get it? Huh? 7. ??? 8. Anger. 9. I'm the man. 10. Coughing.

Table 1: Example responses to paper speech symbol test. The upper symbol conveyed its intended meaning; the lower didn't.

To get empirical data on how well the mime-gestures conveyed their intended meanings, I conducted informal paper tests: I recruited ten volunteers who were not associated with Advance Reality or AnyRiver and knew nothing about the game, showed them the figure-pairs, told them that each pair was an animation of a man trying to express something silently, and asked them to write on an answer sheet, in a few words, what the man was trying to say. I then assigned each response a subjective score between 1 (missed intended meaning) and 10 (got it).

The results of the first such test were discouraging: a few symbols were conveying their intended meaning to most subjects, but most were not (see Table 1). I reported the poor test results to the artist and game designer, and we changed the basic miming figure, revised some of the symbols (see Fig. 5), and repeated the test with different participants. Some symbols did better in the second round of testing; others didn't. Based on the results of the second test, we revised some of the figures again.

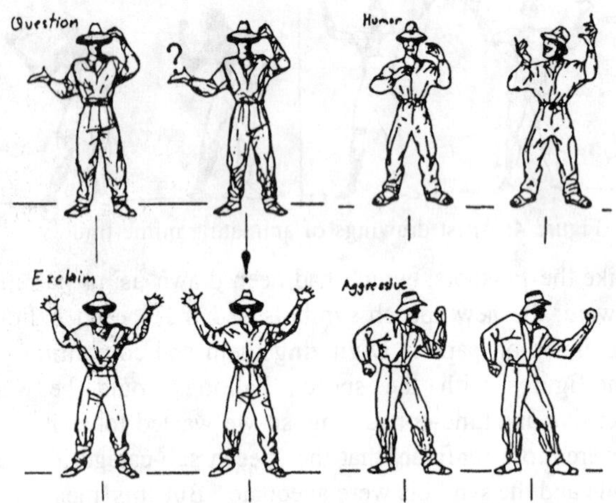

Figure 5: Examples of revised mime-figures.

We briefly considered adding color to the mime-figures as a *redundant* indicator of mood (in contrast to the old scheme's use of color as an *independent* dimension). To be helpful, the color scheme had to be obvious to players, rather than something additional to learn. Further analysis revealed that such a plan required finding not only a universal mapping of emotion-level to color, but also a universal mapping of our speech sub-categories to emotion-level. To check the latter, I conducted a quick informal test: I asked eight employees of Advance Reality who weren't involved in developing the speech symbols to rate each speech sub-category for "amount of emotion" on a 0-5 scale (0=low; 5=high). Some sub-categories received uniformly high emotion-ratings (e.g., accuse, exclaim, refuse), while others received uniformly low ones (e.g., statement, keep silent), but most received a wide range of ratings (e.g., accept, fear, manipulate, humorous). Comments from test participants suggested that variability for certain items was due to some people separating *amount* of emotion from *type* of emotion while others did not. Since finding the required two universal mappings seemed unachievable, we abandoned the idea of augmenting speech symbols with color.

The speech symbols still weren't satisfactory, and time was getting short. We decided to put some of them into selected game-scenes and use our own reactions and play-testing to guide further design. This exposed two new issues:

1. On-screen, the mime-figures were too small to be easily recognized. Enlarging both the figures and the enclosing speech balloon would obscure too much movie action. Our solution was twofold. First, we enlarged the figures but repositioned them in the speech balloons so that their legs were clipped off. All the information was in the upper bodies anyway. Second, we exaggerated whichever features carried the meaning (e.g., hands, mouth). This is a common practice of cartoonists and graphic artists [3].
2. Although the two-frame animation of the mime-figures worked well, it proved distracting and disorienting to have several speech symbols displayed at once, all animating in synchrony over the movie action. Simply assigning different animation rates to different mime-figures broke up this effect, reducing the visual impact of multiple speech symbols to acceptable levels.

Once these graphic-design issues were resolved, the main issues returned to the fore: determining the final speech sub-categories and symbols to convey them. The deadline was looming and we had to allow time for the editors to add the new speech sub-categories throughout the game. We were worried that we had too many speech sub-categories for players to remember: 27, not including the thought sub-categories. We were also concerned that many of the mime-figures didn't convey their intended speech-category well.

To finalize the speech sub-categories and symbols, we had to resolve several issues about which the game designer and I had different opinions:

- *Did we need speech sub-categories that were proving very difficult to depict?* These were: sarcastic/snide, reason/persuade/explain, care/empathy, deal/negotiate, whine/seek sympathy, and flatter. I had concluded that the problem was *not* simply that we hadn't yet found the right mime-figure to depict these concepts, but rather that they were too abstract to represent graphically. I convinced the game designer that we should drop them and "bend" other sub-categories to cover those situations.
- *Did we really need multiple symbols for thoughts?* The game designer preferred having a variety of thought-symbols to depict the different types of "silent" remarks the protagonist could make. I argued that thoughts can't be heard by other characters and don't affect the outcome of the game (most are just opportunities to hear one of Rob Schneider's funny wisecracks), so there was no need to distinguish one from another. We ended up with only one Thought symbol (an empty thought balloon).

- *Did we really need a symbol for* not *speaking?* I favored eliminating the symbol and having players keep silent by not selecting any speech symbol. The game designer wanted keeping silent to be an explicit choice because there are situations in the game where remaining silent is a strategic move. We compromised: eliminate Keep Silent, use no symbol wherever keeping silent isn't strategic, and use the Thought symbol wherever keeping silent is strategic (although this meant finding and adding a suitable recorded protagonist "thought" line).
- *Did we really need symbols that were hardly used?* Two speech symbols were needed only once or twice in the entire game: manipulate, get-real/get-a-grip. They seemed to me to be good candidates for elimination, but the game designer wanted to keep them because he felt that the attitudes they represented were critical for the scenes in which they appeared. We kept them. We also added a symbol for "Shhh!" (i.e., telling someone else to be quiet), even though it was only used once.

With these decisions behind us, the set of speech/thought sub-categories numbered 22. We felt comfortable with this number and with how the remaining mime-symbols were working, so we began instructing the game-editors on how to install the new speech sub-categories throughout the game. Assigning speech sub-categories required much more care and judgment than did adding physical-action sub-categories. I developed guidelines for editors to follow.

Unfortunately, installing the new speech controls was as difficult for editors to do correctly as the old ones had been. After the editors had made one pass through the game assigning speech symbols, I did some checking and estimated that about half of the thousands of assignments were incorrect. I revised my guidelines to be more explicit, and explained them verbally to most of the editors, to no avail. The game designer asked the editors to be more careful, to no avail.

The editors had a complex job, which included editing together video sequences, voice-tracks, and sound effects as well as placing the control symbols in space and time. Furthermore, they were working under intense time-pressure. One finally told me that she didn't have time to determine the correct speech sub-categories; she simply made everything a Statement, and assumed that someone else would fix it later. In response to this, I learned to use the editing software well enough to allow me to go through the entire game, listen to all the protagonist's lines, and assign speech sub-categories.

Once the speech controls were in the game, feedback from AnyRiver (based in part on their play-testing) was swift in coming. They wanted two further changes:

1. They wanted all speech symbols to include text labels. Although the game designer and I had decided to use text very sparingly, AnyRiver convinced us that the advantages of text labels outweighed the disadvantages. I went back through the game, composing and adding terse labels for each speech opportunity.
2. They wanted the set of speech symbols reduced further. They were preparing the user manual and were worried that the list of speech symbols would seem daunting. The game designer and I felt that the set was as small as it could be. A compromise was reached, based on the recognition that in most of the game, only a few speech sub-categories were needed (seven), but some scenes were "conversation games" requiring more expressiveness and hence more speech sub-categories. AnyRiver wrote the manual so as to list the seven frequently-used speech symbols separately from the rest.

Figure 6: Examples of final speech-figures.

RE-DESIGN: EVALUATION AND DISCUSSION

One goal of the re-design effort was to reduce drastically the number of control symbols game players had to distinguish and choose between without compromising the expressive choice that was needed to make the game entertaining and rewarding. We ended with 21 physical-action symbols and 22 speech/thought symbols: a total of 43. Obviously, this was a drastic reduction from the several hundred symbols of the old control scheme. The game designer also felt that we had done so without compromising expressive choice.

In critiquing the old control-scheme, I treated the lack of compliance by game editors with it as an indictment of it. However, the editors also had trouble assigning the *new* speech sub-categories. It is tempting to conclude that this has more to do with their heavy work-load than with the control scheme, but that conclusion won't withstand the observation that editors did not have much trouble installing the new physical-action controls. Perhaps work-load contributes to the problem, perhaps deciding the appropriate sub-category for a speech act is as hard as is devising a good categorization of speech acts, and perhaps our speech categorization was still not intuitive enough.

We can also ask how well the final control symbols depicted their intended meanings. My feeling is that the symbols for physical actions and memorizing were highly successful: so good that players hardly notice them even while using them heavily.

Whether the speech/thought controls were successful is debatable. In the end, we had to augment them with text labels. Play-testing indicated that, thus augmented, they were usable. With more time, I might have suggested revising the mime-figures yet again or trying other ways to represent speech acts.

OTHER ASPECTS OF THE USER INTERFACE

Although I had been hired to redesign the action-controls, the game developers expanded my charter to include other aspects of the game's user interface that needed refinement or redesign. These included: the cursor's various shapes, which indicate whether or not the movie is at a choice point and how much time remains to choose; the visual feedback when control symbols are hit or missed; the score counters that appear in certain scenes; the user interface for making use of saved magical objects; and the control panel for starting, saving, and loading games and setting game options. Play testing indicated that these aspects of the user interface were successful, but the processes by which they were designed are beyond the scope of this paper.

LESSONS AND CONCLUDING THOUGHTS

Working on *Fork* taught me the following lessons:

- A picture may be worth a thousand words, but finding the right picture to convey a verbal concept can be very hard. The best way to convey some verbal concepts is verbally.
- If symbols in a set depict their meanings well, people can discriminate and recognize them even if the set is large. Users may not even realize that the set is large.
- Universally recognized mappings between color and emotion depend on a universal emotion scale, which may not exist. Designs that map color to emotion are risky.
- Game developers understand the need to test on real users (better than do most software developers), but they could use help from user-interface specialists in understanding the distinction between play-testing and more focused usability testing, and the importance of the latter.
- User-interface designers have different concerns and skills than game designers and graphic designers. User-interface skills are as important for designing games as for productivity software, but the reverse is also true: the skills of game designers could be useful in making productivity software more engaging and fun.

Earlier, I stated that the game designer often yielded to my judgment on user interface issues. But what is a user-interface issue, especially in contrast to a game-design issue? The game's plot and dialogue and the challenge of solving its mysteries and puzzles clearly fall under game design. Users' ability to navigate successfully in the game-world and keep track of how they are doing clearly falls under user-interface design.

But consider the issue of deciding who the intended users are and designing a suitable product for them. That is often cited as an important, though neglected, concern of user-interface designers [4]. After I had played *Fork*, I had concerns about who it was for and whether it would appeal to them.

As someone who rarely plays computer games, I felt that the interactive-movie aspects of *Fork* were great, i.e., it was easy to become engrossed in the mystery and wanting to solve it. However, I was put off by some embedded puzzles that were not integral to the story: points at which the movie disappears and the player (not the protagonist) negotiates a maze or manipulates objects to find a combination. These were included to make *Fork* appealing to "hard-core gamers". I worried that they might make it unappealing to light-gamers and non-gamers, and that we ought to think more about the question of who *Fork* was for rather than glibly answering "everyone!" but *even I* didn't consider this a user-interface issue at the time.

Similarly, AnyRiver, *Fork*'s producer, prepared cover art for the package and manual that included sophomoric drawings of near-naked women, even though there is nothing so racy in the game. Again, this was done to appeal to gamers, but I felt that it would turn off non-gamers, light-gamers, parents (who often control purchases), and female gamers.

As it turns out, the game is selling rather poorly. I frankly don't think that this is due to poor controls: play-testing indicated that they were adequate. I think it is due to insufficient consideration of the target market. Maybe that should be treated as part of user interface after all.

ACKNOWLEDGMENTS

The author is grateful for the opportunity to work with the creative designers and developers at Advance Reality, especially film director and game designer Rob Lay and lead programmer Ken Carson. Thanks also to the graphic artists at 415 Productions and McMacken Graphics, to staff members at AnyRiver who contributed ideas to the user interface, especially Chuck Clanton and Stewart Bonn, and to several anonymous CHI'98 reviewers.

NOTES AND REFERENCES

1. It is common for three companies to be involved in the preparation and marketing of a computer game: the designer/developer, the producer/funder, and the distributor. The distributor of *Fork* is Electronic Arts.

2. Johnson, J., Roberts, T., Verplank, W., Smith, D.C., Irby, C., Beard, M., and Mackey, K. (1989) "The Xerox Star: A Retrospective," *IEEE Computer*, September, 22(9), pages 11-29.
3. Mullet, K. and Sano, (1995) D. *Designing Visual Interfaces*, Mountain View, CA: SunSoft Press.
4. Landauer, T.K. (1995) *The Trouble with Computers*, Cambridge, MA: MIT Press.

Patterns of Change in Design Metaphor
A Case Study

William A. Stubblefield
Sandia National Laboratories
P. O. Box 5800
Albuquerque, New Mexico 87185
505-284-2856
wastubb@sandia.gov

ABSTRACT

Although design metaphors play an important role in many software projects, their influence on system functionality, project methodology and the interactions among members of the development team is not well understood. This paper seeks insights into these issues by examining the development of a computer program under the influence of a particularly strong design metaphor.

Keywords

Metaphor, software design, user-oriented design.

INTRODUCTION

Metaphor has long been recognized to play an important role in user interface design, with developers exploiting *desktop metaphors*, *agent metaphors* and similar figures to enhance the usability of computer interfaces. Recently, there has been an increased recognition of metaphor's larger role in the design process, including its influence on program functionality, system architecture and knowledge representation [1-5].

The *Design for Machinability Advisor* [DFM] was built to assist mechanical engineers in improving the manufacturability of machined parts. From the beginning, the project was conceived to be a "spelling checker" for machinability problems. This paper examines the influence of the "spelling checker" metaphor on DFM's design, as well as the changes that occurred in our understanding of the metaphor itself as the design matured. It also considers the metaphor's social context, particularly differences in the way team members interpreted it, and the effects of these differences on their interactions.

THE USE OF METAPHOR IN DESIGN

The use of metaphor in design reflects its function in such areas as the development of language [6-8] and scientific discovery [9-11]. Metaphors are figures of the form: "A is B," where B is said to be the *source* of the metaphor, and A is the *target*. Interpretation of a metaphor is a process of discovering which properties of the source may be valid and useful to understanding the target [12]. For example, cognitive science's use of an *information processing* metaphor can be regarded as a process of finding which properties of computers can effectively be used to explain human thought. The metaphor provides a restricted set of hypotheses about human cognition. By focusing our attention on the significant properties of relatively well understood concepts (the source), metaphors impose an essential structure on the enormous problem spaces found in such target areas as scientific discovery, language development, or, as examined in this paper, design.

Hesse [9] has examined the use of analogies in science, providing a foundation for understanding design metaphors. She describes three components of analogies: the *positive* analogy consists of those properties of the source that are known to apply to the target, the *negative* analogy includes source properties that are either untrue or irrelevant for the target, and the *neutral* analogy contains those that have not yet been classified as positive or negative. Developing a metaphor or analogy requires evaluating the unclassified components of the neutral analogy.

Design and the Interaction Theory of Metaphor

This initial model must be refined if we are to understand the role of metaphor in design. Aspects of a design metaphor can seldom be classified as simply positive or negative: in transferring properties from the source to the target, both designers and users generally will re-interpret them. For example, direct manipulation interfaces are not so much an instantiation of the ways we manipulate objects in space, as they are a rethinking of those operations. Instead of grasping an object, we select it. Placing one object on top of another (such as a document on a printer icon) is not an act of physical stacking, but of invoking some operation (such as printing).

Similarly, properties that might initially seem to be part of the negative metaphor are often modified during design to maintain the metaphor's consistency. An example of this is in the use of a "trash can" icon to invoke file deletion. Unlike real trash cans, trash can icons never become full. This negative aspect of the metaphor can cause problems: users who only empty their physical trash cans when they overflow may neglect to empty their computer trash, eventually causing disk storage to fill up with deleted files. Some interfaces (e.g. the Macintosh) ignore this problem, while others attempt to repair the metaphor through such techniques as prompting the user to empty the trash when logging off of the system.

Black's *interaction theory of metaphor* [6] provides a framework for understanding these processes of adapting the positive and repairing the negative components of a design metaphor. Black argues that metaphor is not simply a process of transferring properties from the source to the target, but a complex interaction between them in which our knowledge of the target is equally capable of changing our understanding of the source. Metaphor induces complex shifts of meaning across both the target and the source. To paraphrase Black,[1] if implementing file deletion with a trash can icon improves usability, we must not forget that this will also change our understanding of "real" trash cans. As an informal example, colleagues have told me that they depend on the ability to retrieve things from their computer trash, treating it as an intermediate stage between long term storage and deletion. This has made them wish for more control over the schedule for emptying their office trash.

The interaction theory's view of metaphor as inducing shifts of meaning in both target and source is important to understanding design metaphors. During DFM's design, we encountered many situations that required modification of the "spelling checker" metaphor. One of the most notable resulted from the complexity involved in detecting machinability problems. Unlike a word processor's spelling checker, which simply looks for words that fail to appear in its dictionary, determining the machinability of a feature in a metal part requires an understanding of the feature's intended use, as well as its interactions with other features. Consequently, DFM required much richer evaluation criteria and user interactions than conventional spelling checkers. This, in turn, broadened our understanding of spelling checkers in general.

The Social Function of Metaphors

An important function of linguistic metaphors is in defining the structure and boundaries of social groups, with societies or segments of a society often defined by shared metaphors. Teenagers seek new figures of speech that adults will not share, just as hipsters have always used dense and rapidly changing metaphors to lock out "square" society. Cognitive science's use of an information processing metaphor virtually defines the field, and distinguishes it from other psychological and biological approaches to understanding thought.

As the development of the DFM advisor showed, this social function is one of the most important aspects of design metaphors. The "spelling checker" metaphor provided a common frame of reference that enhanced communication among members of the design team. This was particularly important in enabling us rapidly to outline an initial system design and development plan. It remained important as the project grew in complexity and different team members experienced potentially conflicting pressures from users, customers, technology, schedules, budget and organizational demands. The shared metaphor helped us to maintain a common understanding of the project and made it easier for us to negotiate compromises as the pressures of these competing demands increased.

These benefits were not without cost. Because the "spelling checker" metaphor enabled such rapid early progress, we made many decisions before we had a complete understanding of the user's needs and assumptions. These early commitments and the power of the metaphor often made it difficult to correct these problems.

Do Metaphors Ever Die?

A commonly accepted view of the use of metaphor holds that, as a metaphor develops and becomes better understood, its interpretation becomes conventionalized, reducing its ability to convey new ideas about the target. According to some views, the metaphor eventually becomes so conventionalized that it loses whatever suggestive power it had as a metaphor and effectively "dies." Linguistic idioms are common examples of *dead metaphors*. For example, "clawing his way to the top" is no longer seen as a metaphor for corporate success, but is simply a common, if not trite, idiom of everyday language. Similarly, as cognitive science has matured, the information processing metaphor has been conventionalized into the accepted problems of representation, search and cognitive architecture.

In general, design metaphors follow this life cycle, shifting from the broadly suggestive to the more conventionalized as they become reified in an artifact. As DFM neared completion, at least certain aspects of our interpretation of the "spelling checker" metaphor became effectively fixed in the design. However, the details of this process are far from straightforward. Rather than a process of steadily refining the metaphor, development alternates between periods of gradual refinement of a stable design, and radical shifts in the design and the underlying interpretation of the metaphor. This reflects Kuhn's classic model of scientific discovery [13]. The DFM Advisor went through at least three such radical interpretive shifts.

Many theorists [7] argue that metaphors never completely die, but retain both the structural properties of metaphor and at least some potential for revealing new meanings. This is also true of design metaphors, in spite of the reifying effect of the design artifact. As the development of DFM reveals, the eventual success of the project's initial stages further stimulated the "spelling checker" metaphor, and led to its expanded use in both talking about DFM and in proposing future projects.

PATTERNS OF CHANGE

The remainder of this paper uses the development of the Design for Machinability Advisor as a case study in the evolution of a strong central metaphor across the design process. It considers both the influence of the metaphor on the design, and the ways in which the design process changed our understanding of the metaphor in turn. Our experience supports the following observations:

- Although design metaphors do tend to move from being richly suggestive to more fixed as the design matures, the patterns of change are far from steady, but

---

1 "If to call a man a wolf is to put him in a special light, we must not forget that the metaphor makes the wolf seem more human than he otherwise would." [2] (page 44)

involve radical shifts in the interpretation and use of the metaphor. Periods of relatively stable interpretation alternate with more dynamic periods where the meaning of the metaphor once again becomes highly plastic and suggestive of multiple design options, including radical changes in the design. Finally, the metaphor never really "dies" but retains its metaphoric foundations and suggestive power even after the system has been completed.

- Strong design metaphors can be both a benefit and an obstacle [2, 14]. Where the metaphor is appropriate, it can quickly lead to a powerful solution; where it is not, it may make it harder to solve design problems.
- Design metaphors do not work only at a semantic level, i.e. in terms of system functionality and user interface. The metaphor also influences system architecture, complexity and algorithm design. These, in turn, can change the interpretation of the metaphor.
- A central function of design metaphors is social, supporting communication and cooperation among members of the design team. This process is far from simple. Different team members arrive at different interpretations of the metaphor, with often surprising results.

THE DESIGN FOR MACHINABILITY ADVISOR

The DFM Advisor was intended to help mechanical designers improve the manufacturability of machined metal parts. Typical problems that add to the difficulty of machining a part include unnecessarily tight tolerance requirements, features that require specialized machine tools, failure to standardize features across different parts, and use of hard to machine materials. Traditionally, mechanical designers have focused primarily on the functionality of parts, leaving manufacturability concerns until later in the design process. This delay in addressing manufacturability increases the cost and difficulty of making needed changes. DFM's goal is to help mechanical designers consider manufacturability early in the process, when designs are still flexible and easy to change.

When launching the project, our customer (a mechanical designer) proposed the metaphor of a "spelling checker" for mechanical designs. The initial specification called for a system that used a feature recognizer to find machined features (holes, slots, pockets, etc.) in a solid model of a part. Once found, these features were to be passed on to a knowledge-based system for evaluation.

The design team was composed of:

- A feature recognition team, consisting of two software engineers, who were to refine and adapt existing feature recognition software to the needs of the DFM Advisor. One member of this team was also experienced in artificial intelligence, and was extensively involved with the knowledge engineering team.
- A knowledge engineering team consisting of a knowledge engineer (myself) and an experienced manufacturing engineer who was initially intended to serve as a domain expert, but who also contributed significantly and actively to design decisions.
- A project management team consisting of two people, one who took primary responsibility for planning, budget and organizational concerns. This person also participated in the early phases of design, and helped the design team remain synchronized with more global requirements, such as organizational standards for network interactions, and the need for our system to eventually interact with other software also under development. The other member of the management team was primarily concerned with funding and project development, and did not participate actively in design after the early stages.
- The customer for the system was a mechanical engineer and functioned as our primary source of user input. We also sought out other engineers and machinists for their evaluation of prototype systems.

It is important to note that a central implication of the "spelling checker" metaphor, that the DFM advisor should be driven by feature recognition, was effectively set very early in the project by our choice of the design team.

Interactions among the design team were complicated by the fact that it was spread over four different organizations and buildings at Sandia National Laboratories. The feature recognition team was at one site, the primary project manager and I were at a second, the domain expert at a third, and the customer and sample users at several other organizations. Although we met regularly (at least once or twice per week during the early phases of the project), and communicated by phone and e-mail as needed, this organizational scattering did complicate our interactions. One of the benefits of the unusually strong design metaphor was in providing a common focus, one that allowed us to work independently while maintaining a shared but flexible understanding of our common goals.

Because of the ambitious nature of the project, we made an early decision to use an iterative, prototype-based methodology that would allow us to explore the design space more freely. Selecting this exploratory approach in place of a more structured, top-down approach was clearly the right decision, as many of our early assumptions eventually proved mistaken. Three prototypes were implemented and evaluated in the process of refining the design.

A final important aspect of the development milieu is Sandia National Laboratories' commitment to both research and the development of practical, immediately useful tools. As the project developed, these twin goals both supported the exploratory methodology we had selected, and also provided an additional set of design constraints that influenced our development of the advisor.

PROTOTYPE 1: A PURE SPELLING CHECKER

The first prototype system we constructed was an attempt at a direct realization of the "spelling checker" metaphor. The feature recognizer acquired features from a solid model of a part, and sent them to the design advisor for evaluation. This prototype was only concerned with holes.

The advisor applied a list of *critics* to each feature, and displayed those critics that detected potential problems. A critic was essentially a rule for detecting a specific type of machinability problem. The advisor displayed these "fired" critics one at a time, just as a word processor's spelling checker displays misspelled words. A "Next" button allowed the user to step through the applicable critics, while additional buttons allowed the user to skip a feature, redo a feature or start over with the first feature.

Figure 1 shows the main screen of this prototype. In order to let the user know which feature was being checked, the feature recognizer displayed the part with the current feature highlighted (not shown). The screen also displays the feature in profile (upper right), surrounded by information about its dimensions and tolerances. The box below displays the text of critics (in the figure, it shows a "dummy" test critic). The buttons at the bottom allow the user to move through both features and the critics of a given feature. This order is determined by the feature recognition algorithms.

The Order of Feature Evaluation

Implementing such a direct translation of the "spelling checker" metaphor required that we repair several potential breakdowns in its interpretation. The first of these was lack of any obvious sequence in feature recognition. A conventional spelling checker scans a document from start to finish, highlighting potentially misspelled words as it checks. In contrast, feature recognition exhibited no obvious sequence, although we did highlight the current feature in the feature recognizer's display. In initial evaluations, neither the domain expert nor potential users saw any difficulty in the essentially unpredictable order with which features were evaluated.

On reflection, the design team decided that there was no reason to be bound to an arbitrary order of evaluation and, in prototype 2, developed a "feature browser" that allowed the user to check features in any desired order. This browser displayed a list of features; clicking on a feature caused it to be highlighted in the display of the part drawing and sent to the advisor to be evaluated. The users appreciated this improved flexibility, although it is interesting to note that no one complained about the original, more rigid order of evaluation. I believe this results from the power of the original metaphor, and illustrates the way a strong design metaphor can lead a user to accept a less than optimal solution.

The Problem of Missing Information

A more difficult problem was in the lack of complete information from the feature recognizer. Due to limitations of the solid modeling software the feature recognizer was built upon, it was unable to recover information about tolerances from the original engineering drawing. This was a severe limitation, since nearly all machinability problems involve tolerances at some level: if you don't care about tolerances, practically anything can be machined. Although a related project was exploring the possibility of adding this capability to the feature recognizer, it was not available to us for use in the Design for Machinability Advisor.

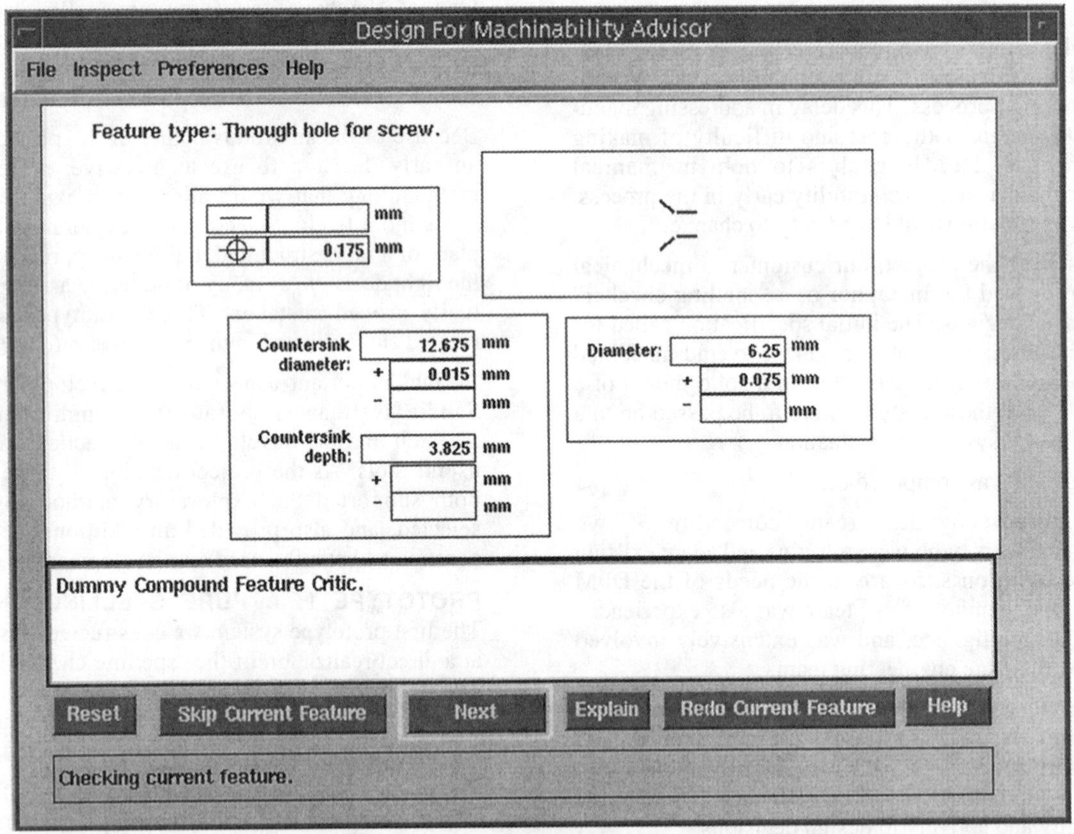

Figure 1

In order to minimize data entry requirements on the user, we felt it important to provide useful default values for tolerances on feature dimensions. This proved difficult, since "reasonable" tolerances depend upon the feature's intended function. Our solution to this problem was to construct a database of common features that could be matched with recognized features to obtain reasonable default tolerances. For example, a countersunk hole for a standard screw could be recognized with reasonable reliability, providing the user with recommended tolerance values for that feature.

This solution never proved fully satisfactory. Although we were able to classify many simple features, such as holes, in a reasonable manner, it was clear that we would have difficulty in extending the approach to more complex, novel features. Also, by providing recommended tolerances rather than those the user had initially entered into the design drawing, we were introducing an unacceptable possibility for confusion and error into their interaction with the system. These problems were among the main reasons for changing the approach taken in this early prototype.

Breakdowns Caused by Complexity Mismatch

A deeper problem was in the complexity of recognizing machinability problems. Spell checking a textual document is a relatively straightforward process of matching words in the document against those in a dictionary and indicating words that failed to match. Formally, this is a process of matching text strings, and algorithms exist for doing this efficiently. As we worked with our domain experts in acquiring knowledge of machinability problems it became clear that evaluating machinability problems was significantly more complex than finding a word in a spelling checker's dictionary. For example, determining whether a 0.002" diameter tolerance on a 0.25" hole is excessive or not depends entirely on the intended use of the hole. This, in turn, required asking extensive questions of the user, a further violation of the "spelling checker" metaphor. Although we did not formally characterize the complexity of evaluating features, it clearly cannot be done by simple matching algorithms, and is most likely context sensitive.

Further evidence of the interaction between metaphor and computational complexity can be found in the customer's initial suggestion that we not consider the intended use of features in our evaluations, as this was too difficult. On subsequent conversations with the customer, our domain expert and other engineers and machinists, everyone acknowledged the importance of this information. Although I can only speculate, it seems reasonable that the "spelling checker" metaphor may have led the customer to add this limitation to our initial requirements in an effort to fit the problem to the metaphor.

This impact of complexity on a design metaphor is both unexpected and significant. None of the literature I have encountered on the use of metaphor in discovery or design mentions the impact of complexity issues on metaphor interpretation. Generally, metaphors are assumed to fail if they make predictions that prove to be false. But, as we discovered, it is possible to implement a semantically valid interpretation of a metaphor, only to see the it break down because of differences in complexity between the source and target situations.

Finding vs. Preventing Mistakes

The final difficulty encountered in prototype 1 was in its emphasis on error detection, rather than error prevention. As a "spelling checker" for designs, it was natural to apply the advisor to existing engineering drawings. It was only as we made progress in knowledge acquisition that we recognized that machinability knowledge could be more easily and more effectively applied if we offered it to the engineer as he or she was creating a design, rather than after the design already existed. It is interesting to note that although the maxim, "it is better to prevent errors than to detect them," is part of every designer's knowledge, the influence of the "spelling checker" metaphor led us to ignore this valuable rule of thumb until relatively late in the development of the first prototype. Similarly, although our customer clearly specified that the advisor would be used to check finished designs, on seeing the prototype, he asked if it couldn't "detect errors as he was working."

PROTOTYPE 2: THE DUAL-USE APPROACH

The second prototype addressed many of these difficulties, but did not abandon the metaphor entirely. Although the domain expert and I had doubts about the metaphor by this time, the feature recognition team and the customer still found it to be useful. Our discussions revealed a number of effective arguments for the benefits of a feature driven approach. Among these was the ability of the advisor to serve as a final check before manufacture, the learnability and usability gains provided by the metaphor, the ease of fitting a "spelling checker" into the engineering development process, and the technical benefits of providing the feature recognition team with a challenging test of their capabilities. Consequently, we chose to implement a "dual-use" strategy, retaining the feature-driven approach as one mode of use for the advisor, while also allowing the advisor's machinability knowledge to be used without feature recognition.

When used as a checker for existing models, prototype 2 took an approach that was similar to prototype 1. The only real difference was in replacing the one-at-a-time approach to checking features with a more flexible feature browser that allowed the user to select features from the solid model and check them in any desired order. In providing a second, non-feature-driven interface, we made the database of typical features directly available to the user. They could browse this list, selecting, for example, recommended configurations for common features such as countersunk holes or holes for a rotating pin or shaft. The user could then edit these recommended configurations, changing either dimensions or tolerances. Where these changes violated any of the machinability checks, appropriate critics would fire to alert the user.

In evaluating this "dual-use" approach, it was clear that we had moved in the right direction. Although everyone agreed on the merits of a dual-use strategy, the team remained divided over the relative value of the "front end design tool" vs. the "spelling checker" modes of use.

PROTOTYPE 3: TOOLS AND CRITICS

The final prototype built on its predecessor's dual-use approach, but made two notable additions to it. The first of these was in recognizing that certain types of knowledge could be useful for either front-end design or feature checking, but not both. We supported this by dividing our knowledge base into "tools" and "critics." Critics were used exclusively to evaluate existing features, whereas tools could be used for either evaluation of existing features, or to design features from scratch. A key difference between tools and critics was that tools involved more extensive user interaction, while critics simply detected potential problems without requiring additional user input. This allowed critics to function more like "pure" textual spelling checkers, while letting the "tools" provide richer forms of advice to the user.

An example of a tool was the PIN FIT ADVISOR (Figure 2) which advised the user on dimensions and tolerances of holes that were to fit a pin or moving shaft. Even when initialized with the diameter of a recognized hole, the Pin Fit Advisor still asked the user a number of questions about the use of a hole (e.g. "is the hole intended to allow a shaft to rotate, or is it intended to fit tightly over a pin to accurately position a part?"), and recommended the tolerances for the pin and hole. This more extensive interaction with the user moves considerably beyond the "spelling checker" metaphor.

In contrast, critics were simple if/then tests and required no user input. A typical critic detected holes whose diameter failed to match any standard size drill bit, and called this problem to the user's attention. Because of their simplicity, critics were able to fit the "spelling checker" metaphor more directly than tools like the Pin Fit Advisor. In effect, prototype #3's critic facility returned to an almost pure implementation of a "spelling checker" for designs, although in doing so, it became only one component of a larger machinability tool kit.

Evaluating Solid Models

When checking an existing mechanical design, the user browsed the features, and selected those to be checked. Each tool or critic included a condition test to determine its applicability to a given feature. When the user requested a feature be checked, DFM displayed both critics that detected problems with the feature and tools that might be useful in its refinement. Selecting an entry either displayed a description of a problem (for the critics), or initialized the tool with the feature's dimensions and launched it as a separate application.

An Initial Design Tool Kit

When the tool kit was used during initial design (i.e. without a solid model or feature recognizer), the user selected tools from a browser. Critics were not available

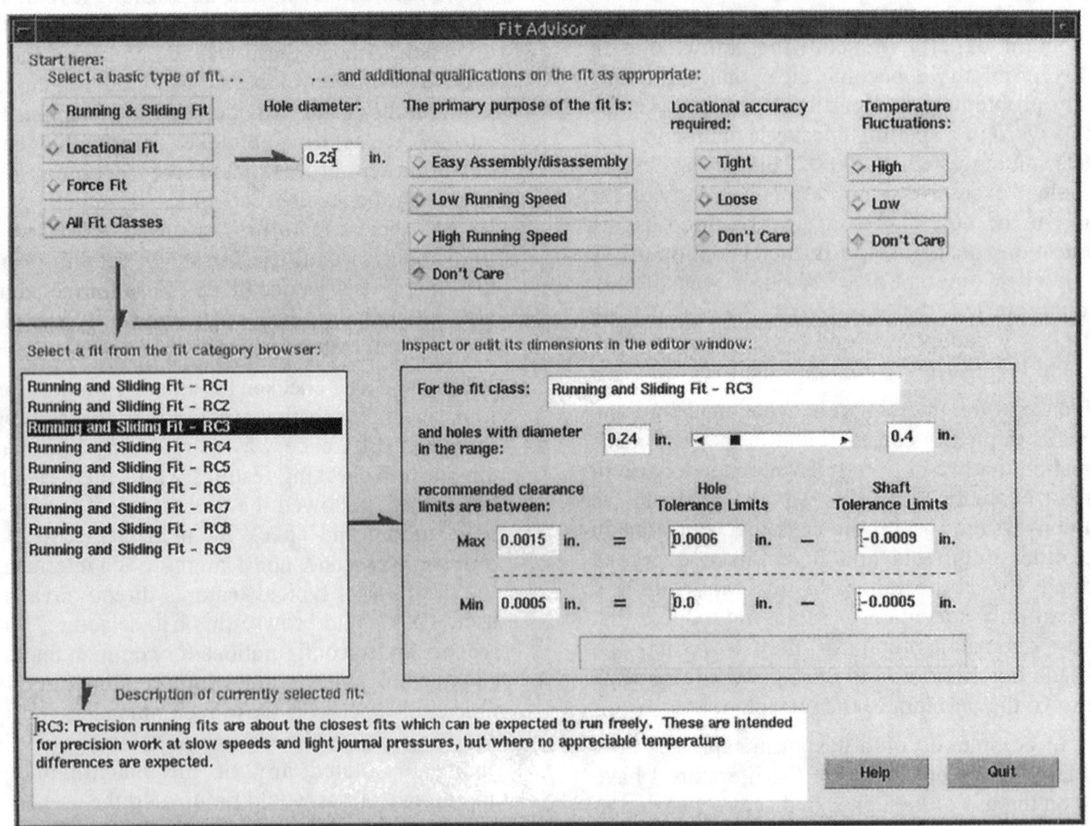

Figure 2

in this mode of use. Because the advisor did not use the feature recognizer to initialize tools with feature dimensions, the user entered the required dimensions and tolerance information directly.

Freed from this tight coupling with the feature recognizer, we had more freedom in designing tools that were not feature oriented. One of these tools, the SURFACE FINISH EVALUATOR, determined which machining processes would be needed to achieve a specified surface finish, and evaluated the relative cost of these processes. This tool bore no direct relationship to particular geometric features.

Architectural Implications

A significant change in the third prototype was architectural. The advisor was decomposed into much more specialized, independent objects than the earlier versions. For example, we recognized that the feature browser was a potentially valuable addition to the feature recognizer that could stand alone from the Design for Machinability Advisor. Consequently, it was separated from DFM, and implemented as a pure feature browser that communicated with clients (such as DFM) through message passing. Similarly, each feature analysis tool, such as the Pin Fit Advisor could be either invoked as an independent application, or initialized with data from the feature recognizer. These were deliberately designed as independent objects to enable later migration to a distributed object environment, as is consistent with broader corporate software strategy. As we came to understand the design (and the "spelling checker" metaphor) better, we were able to focus more clearly on these architectural issues.

CONCLUSION

The development of the Design for Machinability Advisor was a valuable lesson in the use of design metaphors. Lessons learned from the project include:

Design Metaphors have Complex Life Cycles

The development of design metaphors closely follows the interaction theory, being characterized by shifts in the interpretation of both the design (the metaphoric target) and the source metaphor. As the DFM Advisor developed, it extended our understanding of "spelling checkers" to include more complex interactions with the user and greater user control over the order with which items are checked.

Although design metaphors do tend to move from the broadly suggestive to a more static interpretation as the design becomes fixed, this is far from a steady process, but alternates between periods where the interpretation of the metaphor remains relatively stable, and times of radical shift in the understanding of the metaphor. In the development of DFM, there were three such shifts:

1. Recognizing the implications of the feature recognizer's lack of obvious order, and the rejection of a fixed order of analysis in favor of a more flexible feature browser.
2. The adoption of a dual-use strategy that allowed the user to access system knowledge either to check features, or independently of the feature recognizer.
3. Prototype 3's division of machinability knowledge into distinct "tools" and "critics", where only critics were required to be applicable to geometric features. This allowed us to create tools that had no direct link to the feature recognizer. Essentially, this step pushed the "spelling checker" metaphor back into part of the DFM Advisor (the feature recognizer/critic combination), both returning to a "purer" instantiation of the metaphor and allowing other parts of the tool to function in a less constrained manner.

In addition to exhibiting the shifts of meaning predicted by the interaction theory, the development of the "spelling checker" metaphor also supports Lakoff and Johnson's [7] contention that metaphors never really die. Although the third prototype of the advisor both reduces the metaphor's importance and fixes its interpretation in an artifact, both the customer and the project managers continue to use the metaphor for marketing DFM and planning future projects. The Design for Machinability Advisor has become one instance of a larger metaphor that will continue to be explored through future projects.

Metaphors are a Benefit and an Obstacle

Because the "spelling checker" metaphor was so strong, it enabled us to quickly agree on a basic design and rapidly develop the first prototype. Prototype 1 was completed in about 4 months, which was fairly impressive given the fact that it involved a separate feature recognizer and knowledge based system interacting over a computer network. However, as the design matured, the metaphor also interfered with our ability to respond to an emerging understanding of the user's needs and abilities. In particular, the "spelling checker" metaphor made it difficult to move into a fully dual-use approach that allowed both evaluation of existing designs and the provision of front-end design tools.

Metaphors and Computational Complexity

Although my understanding of metaphors in language and science had prepared me for the likelihood that certain implications of the "spelling checker" metaphor would prove wrong for the design advisor, I had assumed that these would be strictly semantic in nature; that is, I assumed that the metaphor would fail if it led to the wrong functionality or a confusing interface. Experience with the Design for Machinability Advisor demonstrated that a metaphor could also break down if the underlying computational complexity of the resulting design was drastically different from that of the source.

The Social Function of Design Metaphors

The most unexpected lesson learned was the importance of the design metaphor's social role. Because the design team was separated both geographically and organizationally, and because of the short development times required for a prototyping methodology, we often had to make decisions without adequately consulting other members of the team. This was particularly true of the feature recognition and the knowledge engineering groups. Although these often resulted in minor inconsistencies, none of these involved deeper semantic problems and all were easily repaired. I believe that this was due to the common understanding engendered by the shared metaphor.

Another surprising discovery was that different interpretations of the design metaphor coexisted harmoniously within the design team. As the project progressed, the interpretations of the metaphor developed along multiple lines: the machining expert and I came to reduce the importance of the "spelling checker" metaphor, while the customer and one of the management team retained a more direct interpretation. We were concerned that this might cause misunderstanding or rejection of the system. Surprisingly, they were quite happy to continue characterizing the advisor as a spelling checker, and accepted the final prototype as a faithful rendering of the metaphor. Although reliance on the "spelling checker" metaphor initially caused some confusion for the customer in using the final system, they quickly adapted, and did so without feeling a need to abandon the metaphor. Finalization of the design did not detract from the flexibility with which different team members interpreted the metaphor.

Similarly, the feature recognition team continued to regard the advisor as a "spelling checker" for designs, which is not surprising, since the use of the feature recognizer was closely tied to this metaphor. However, they were quick to accept such changes in the metaphor's interpretation as the shift to a feature browser driven approach. It is also interesting to mention that as the feature recognition team has started to explore other applications for their software, they have largely ignored the "spelling checker" metaphor. Although they continue to use it in discussing DFM, the metaphor plays little role in their continuing work. Because it serves no useful function, it is essentially dead for this portion of our team.

Design Metaphor as a Necessary Fiction

As our experience with the Design for Machinability Advisor indicates, the use of metaphor in design is far from a simple affair. It is characterized by radical shifts in interpretation of the metaphor and resulting changes in the design. In spite of the metaphor's ability to bring the design team to a common focus in a rapid manner, it often hindered our understanding of user reactions and a flexible response to problems in the developing design.

On balance, I believe that these are not so much problems that need to be fixed as they are essential features of an inherently complex process. I do not believe that we could have started, let alone completed, this project without the contributions of this strong central design metaphor. By leading us to develop an initial prototype quickly, we were able to impose a structure on what would have otherwise been an enormous and ill-defined design space. Although the system has largely moved beyond it, the "spelling checker" metaphor was, and remains an essential component of our understanding of the DFM Advisor.

The lessons to be learned are not that we should avoid metaphor in design, but that we should be prepared for the shifts in meaning that accompany their development, and their tendency to blind us to possibilities that do not fit the metaphor's obvious interpretations. I hope that the observations made in this paper will help designers use metaphors with the flexibility and insight they require.

ACKNOWLEDGMENTS

I would like to thank Sandia National Laboratories for their generous support of the Design for Machinability Project, and Ken Washington, Steve Kleban, Dwight Miller and John Linebarger for comments on early drafts of this paper. I also thank the members of the Design for Machinability team: John Mitchiner, Kim Mahin, Jill Rivera, Lothar Bieg, Robert LaFarge, David Plummer and Marcus Craig. Their knowledge, design sophistication and friendship made this project unusually rewarding.

REFERENCES

1. Carroll, J., R. Mack, and W. Kellogg, *Interface metaphors and user interface design*, in *Handbook of Human Computer Interaction*, Hellander, Editor. 1988, Elsevier: Amsterdam.
2. Erickson, T., *Working with interface metaphors*, in *The Art of Human-Computer Interface Design*, B. Laurel, Editor. 1990, Addison-Wesley: Reading, Mass.
3. Maclean, A., *et al. Reaching through analogy: A design rationale perspective on roles of analogy*. in *CHI-91*. 1991. New Orleans: Addison Wesley.
4. Madsen, K.H., *A Guide to Metaphorical Design*. Communications of the ACM, 1994. **37**(12): p. 57-62.
5. Coyne, R., *Designing Information Technology in the Postmodern Age: From Method to Metaphor*. 1995, Cambridge, Mass.: The MIT Press.
6. Black, M., *Models and Metaphors*. 1962, Ithaca, NY: Cornell University Press.
7. Lakoff, G. and M. Johnson, *Metaphors We Live By*. 1980, Chicago: University of Chicago Press.
8. Gibbs, R.W.J., *The Poetics of Mind*. 1994, Cambridge: Cambridge University Press.
9. Hesse, M., *Models and Analogies in Science*. 1966, Notre Dame, Indiana: University of Notre Dame Press.
10. Gentner, D., *Flowing waters or teaming crowds: Mental models of electricity*, in *Mental Models*, D. Gentner and A.L. Stevens, Editor. 1983, Lawrence Elbaum Associates: Hillsdale, N. J.
11. Stubblefield, W.A., *Source Selection for Analogical Reasoning: An Interactionist Approach*. 1995, University of New Mexico:
12. Gentner, D., *Structure mapping: A theoretical framework for analogy*. Cognitive Science, 1983. (7): p. 155-170.
13. Kuhn, T.S., *The Structure of Scientific Revolutions*. 1962, Chicago: University of Chicago Press.
14. Laurel, B., *Computers as Theater*. 1991, Reading, MA: Addison-Wesley.

Netscape Communicator's Collapsible Toolbars

Irene Au
Client User Experience Group
Netscape Communications Corp.
501 E. Middlefield Rd. MV-054
Mountain View, CA 94043
(650) 937-3967
irene@netscape.com

Shuang Li
Client Visual Design Group
Netscape Communications Corp.
501 E. Middlefield Rd. MV-054
Mountain View, CA 94043
(650) 937-3617
shuang@netscape.com

ABSTRACT

This paper describes the design process used for Netscape Communicator's collapsible toolbars. To meet our design goals, we designed a new widget whose roots came from objects in the "real world" instead of the "software world". The design of this widget illustrates how rapid prototyping and tight coupling between the visual design and interaction design are imperative to a widget's success.

Keywords

visual design, interaction design, collapsing widgets, toolbars

INTRODUCTION

Designers are often faced with the challenge of providing functionality within certain constraints and requirements. When standard interface widgets do not meet the design criteria, we must seek solutions unique to the problem at hand. Such solutions may involve inventing new widgets for interacting with the software. This paper describes such a design and the lessons learned from the process.

The Problem

Netscape Communicator is a suite of applications used to view information exchanged across the internet. Its target users are the corporate users, many of whom use laptops or 14" monitors running at 640 x 480 resolution (Figure 1). With this limited screen size, we felt it was important to increase the real estate as much as possible for viewing content in the browser.

The toolbars occupy a significant amount of real estate that is not always needed by the user when browsing the web. Thus, they were obvious candidates for helping us alleviate the real estate problem. Completely removing the toolbars was not an option. Although all items in the toolbar were accessible through Netscape Navigator's menus, they were instrumental in making the product easy to use and features more discoverable. The Directory buttons on the third toolbar were key entry points into Netscape's web site and would reduce our revenue potential if they were removed. The only option for us was to modify the toolbar system so that it would be readily available to users but could be hidden easily and quickly to provide more real estate for browsing content. Given this problem to solve, we formulated our design goals.

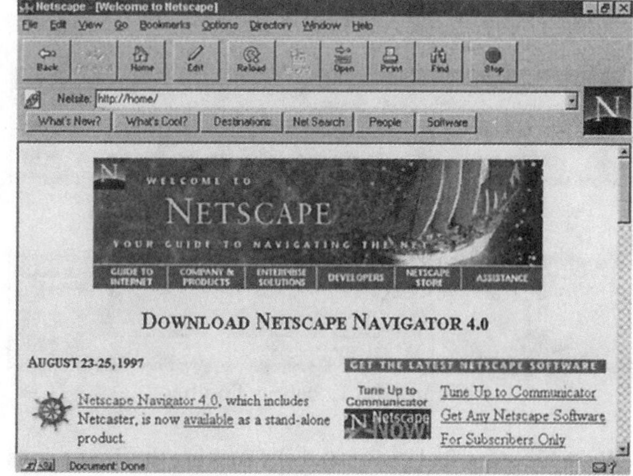

Figure 1: Netscape Navigator 3.0, maximized in 640x480 resolution

The Design Goals

- The primary design objective was to allow users to show and hide toolbars quickly and easily to increase viewing area for content. Users should be able to readily access the toolbars needed for navigation, bookmarks, and important links.

- The design had to work in the browser, mail and news client, and editor gracefully. Because the product is "more than just a browser", we had to ensure that our design was scalable to the other components in Communicator.
- The toolbar system should be one that novice users find accessible and that advanced users can leverage for their more advanced tasks.
- The design should be simple and easy to use, preferably by incorporating direct manipulation into the design.
- The toolbar system should be visually appealing and not distract the user from the content of the browser.
- Users should be able to understand and easily learn how to interact with the toolbars.

Given these design goals, we began designing the new Netscape Communicator toolbars.

INITIAL DESIGN: TABBED TOOLBARS

The preliminary design involved having tabs on the side of each toolbar so that users could directly control the toolbar order. The tab design would also allow users to stack the toolbars "on top" of each other and browse through the toolbars, making the "active" toolbar the frontmost toolbar (Figures 2a, 2b). Tooltips and tab placement were cues to the user to denote which toolbar corresponded to a particular tab. To bring a particular toolbar to the front, users would click on the tab corresponding to the toolbar to be viewed.

Figure 2a: Main Toolbar

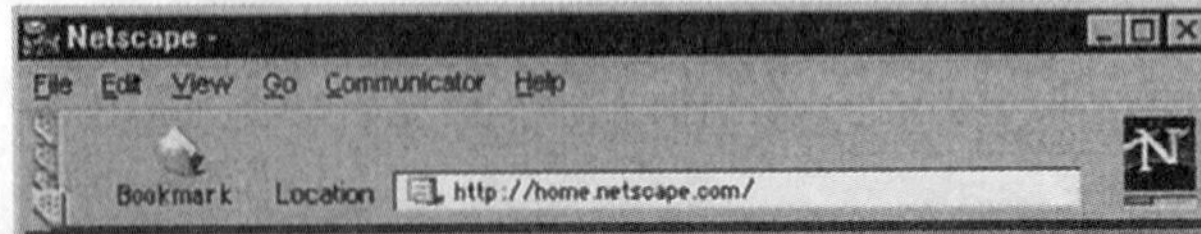

Figure 2b: Location Toolbar

We achieved visual consistency by making the dimensions of each toolbar the same. This design constraint resulted in a lot of wasted space, particularly in the Location toolbar. However, we felt it was necessary in order to make the tabbed toolbar design work visually. Users could also tile the toolbars by dragging a toolbar tab and moving it so that more than one toolbar could be seen at once (Figure 3).

This design allowed users to directly manipulate the toolbar ordering and allowed users to conserve vertical screen real estate. It was a model users already understood, although the visual controls were slightly different. The design was extensible to all windows in Communicator.

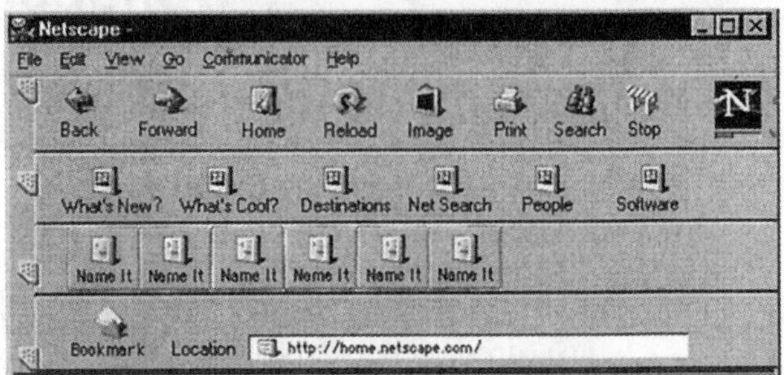

Figure 3: Tabbed Toolbars, tiled

However, this design had its drawbacks. It occupied considerable horizontal real estate on the toolbar, potentially eliminating room for toolbar buttons. For this reason, the tabs for the toolbars were limited in size. Consequently, the tabs were difficult to use because of their small target area.

Lack of resources in usability engineering prevented us from performing a formal usability study on this design. However, the implementation on the Windows platform was used by many of the engineers who were developing Communicator as the changes were "checked in" to the source code tree. Thus, we were able to collect informal usability feedback from many engineers at Netscape. Most users felt the tabs were visually too "heavy" and not pleasing or engaging. With this feedback, we worked toward the next iteration of the toolbar design.

ROTATING TOOLBARS

We believed that conceptually stacking the toolbars on top of each other worked well. For this reason, this aspect of the design persisted through the next design iteration. The second design addressed the small target area issue by staggering the toolbars horizontally rather than stacking the toolbars directly on top of each other.

We tried to make the tabs less visually "heavy" by simplifying their shape. Vertical tabs that occupied less horizontal space were placed on the left side of each toolbar. Users thus had the entire edge of the toolbar as a target area as opposed to the previous design, where the target area was a quarter of the height of the toolbar (Figures 4a, 4b).

The tabs were color coded to correspond to a particular toolbar. Tooltips were also used to help distinguish one toolbar from another. Users could drag toolbars by clicking on the tab and moving the mouse while the mouse button was still depressed. Users could also switch between toolbars by clicking on the tab; the toolbar corresponding to the tab would appear as the frontmost toolbar.

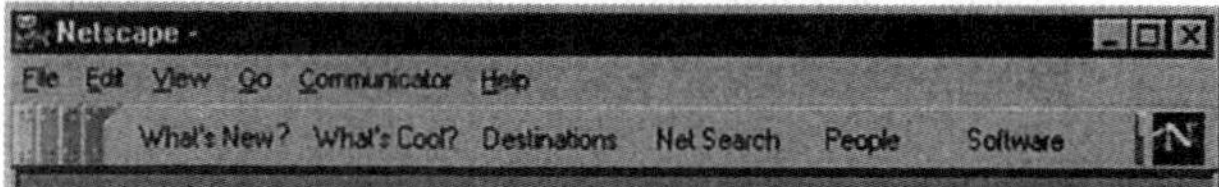

Figure 4a: Rotating Toolbars, stacked

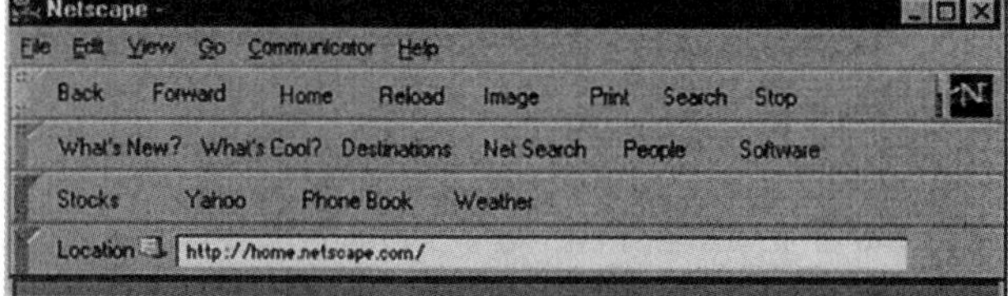

Figure 4b: Rotating Toolbars, tiled

Again, this design allowed users to directly manipulate the toolbar ordering and allowed users to conserve vertical screen real estate in a similar fashion to the earlier design. It was an improvement over the preliminary design because each toolbar had a larger target area for direct manipulation.

The interaction with the toolbar tabs was greatly improved by enlarging the target area with this visual design. Unfortunately, this improvement came at the expense of being able to bring the desired toolbar to the front easily. It was not clear what the user's expectation would be if, for example, the third tab were selected and brought to the front. We considered two possible behaviors. One solution would have the fourth tab obscured completely. We ruled out this behavior because it was not clear how to bring the obscured toolbar back to the front. Another solution would have the tabs rotate so that the frontmost tab would be the rightmost tab. In the initial implementation, the toolbar tabs rotated.

Like the first design, formal usability testing was not done on the design. Because of the pressure to produce a viable design quickly to accommodate the short development cycle, we resorted to informally showing colleagues an implementation of this design to get their feedback. This design proved to be problematic for many reasons. First, users did not like our use of color as visual cues to correspond to toolbars, despite our use of tooltips. Using color to distinguish between the toolbars was not an acceptable design for those users who are color-blind or run Communicator on black-and-white monitors. Second, users who wished to rely more heavily on positional memory could not do so in this design; making the translation between color and toolbar content was an extra cognitive step that was too cumbersome for users.

Visually, this design was an improvement despite the use of color on the tabs. User reaction to it was so favorable that we revisited this visual design in the final iteration. However, the interaction design did not work well. For this reason, we sought alternative solutions.

HORIZONTAL TABS

We learned from the second design that visually simplifying the tabs worked well. Placing the tabs along the edge of the toolbar was not only visually more pleasing than the first design, but also gave the users a larger target area for selecting toolbars. We had not surrendered the concept of stacking toolbars on top of each other, as it is a model users understand. Thus we struggled to find some way to allow users to select toolbars by giving them a reasonably sized target area. Our next design tried placing the tabs horizontally on the lower side of the toolbars (Figure 5). Users would click on the tabs to bring a toolbar to the front.

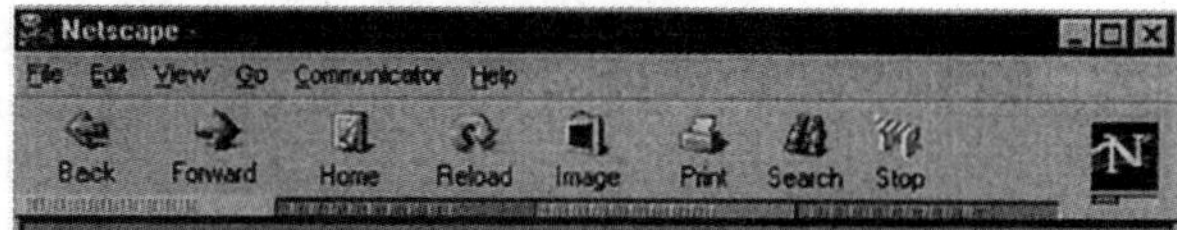

Figure 5: Horizontal Tabbed Toolbar Design

The problems presented in previous designs were somewhat addressed in this iteration. Users could show and hide toolbars quickly and easily. The horizontal tabs provided a large target area for direct manipulation. The biggest problem with the second design was how the various tabs interacted with each other when a toolbar was selected. In this iteration, we were able to keep the position of the toolbar tabs static, addressing a significant problem with the previous design.

However, visually, the design did not work well. We could not stray from using colors for the tabs; text in the tabs would have required so much more vertical real estate that it would not have justified using the tabs to save vertical space in the first place. The large colored tabs were distracting, visually conflicting with the content of the window. Moreover, we intended to show all toolbars in the default shipping state. The tiled toolbars would have required more vertical real estate than if there were no tabs at all. This design would have left the users with less space for viewing content than in Navigator 3.0.

Because the design did not work well visually or meet our design goal of decreasing the amount of vertical screen real estate required by the toolbars, our consideration of this design was short-lived. Consequently, this design was never implemented, and we did not gather user feedback on this design. However, this design is worth mentioning as it illustrates our endeavors to solve this design problem. It was becoming increasingly difficult to design a solution that addressed all the secondary design criteria we were gathering based on feedback from the first three designs:

- The target area should be reasonably large for selecting the toolbar.
- The visual design of the toolbar system should be simple and not distract users from the content of the window.
- The interaction model should be one that users understand. We believed that conceptually stacking the toolbars was one that worked well for users.

At this point we realized that in our efforts to allow users to conceptually stack toolbars on top of each other, we were placing an unnecessary constraint on the design. We tried to consider alternate ways of allowing users to show and hide toolbars easily.

RETHINKING THE DESIGN: ARROW-BUTTONS

In this iteration, we adopted arrow widgets that users could click on to show and hide toolbars. To the left of the toolbar system was a pair of arrows, one pointing up, the other pointing down (Figure 6a).

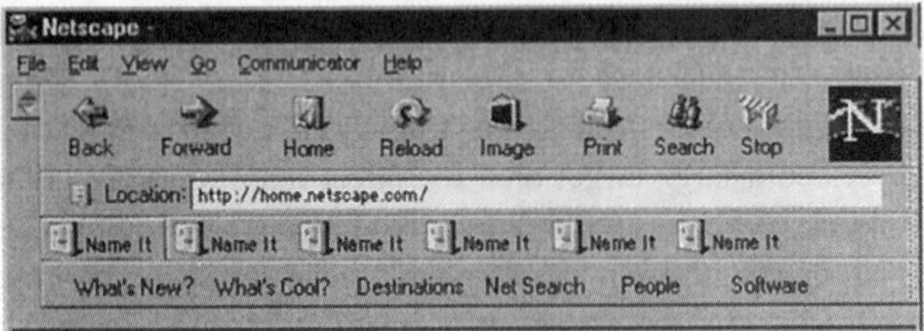

Figure 6a: Arrow-buttons to show and hide toolbars

Clicking on the top arrow would move the bottommost toolbar up "underneath" the other toolbars, effectively hiding the toolbar (Figure 6b). When all but one toolbar is left visible, the top arrow would be disabled. Similarly, clicking on the bottom arrow would make the most recently hidden toolbar visible.

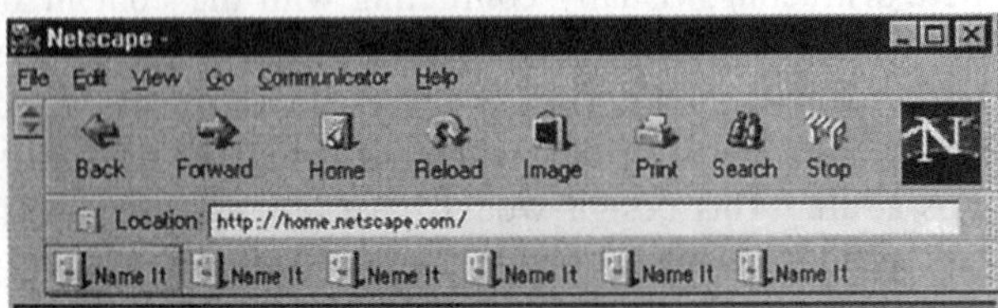

Figure 6b: Bottommost toolbar hidden

A review of the drawings for this design by peer designers and engineers working on the project exposed many problems with this design. Users would still be able to reorder toolbars through direct manipulation. However, because tabs were not used, there would be no conceptual "grabbing area" for users. Furthermore, because we had adopted a borderless button design, it would be more difficult for users to find a non-button background area on the toolbar to drag the toolbar. Finally, some reviewers felt that this design did not make it easy enough to allow users to show and hide toolbars easily and quickly. To hide a particular toolbar, users would have to reorder it to being the bottommost toolbar, and then click on the up arrow to hide it. This design did not sufficiently meet our goal of allowing users to show and hide toolbars quickly and easily.

Although this design was not revolutionary, it is considered a breakthrough in our design process because it is a significant departure from the previous designs. This was the first design that did not conceptually "stack" the toolbars. We changed the criteria for the interaction with the toolbars, which liberated us from the tab-as-toolbar-selector idea. By freeing our thinking from this unnecessary constraint, we were able to achieve a more workable and desirable solution.

FINAL DESIGN: COLLAPSIBLE TOOLBARS

We returned to the toolbar tab idea in previous iterations and considered ways in which the user could interact with the toolbars without conceptually stacking the toolbars. We were inspired by an ordinary object to use as our metaphor: the Swiss Army Knife. The Swiss Army Knife has several tools, but only one tool is used at a time. The unused tools are "collapsed". From this object, our final design was born. Each toolbar tab was considered a "tool". When users didn't want to use a particular tool, it could be "collapsed", changing its orientation in the same fashion as a Swiss Army Knife. As a result, users could show and hide toolbars quickly and easily by clicking on the tab (Figures 7a, 7b). Users could reorder toolbars through direct manipulation, because we returned to the toolbar a visible textured area that afforded dragging.

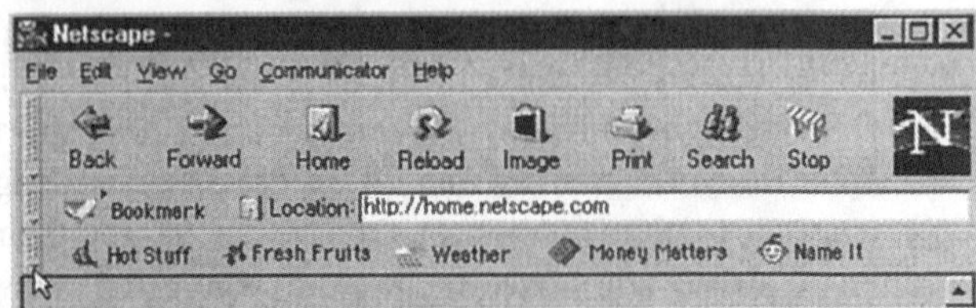

Figure 7a: Collapsible Toolbar Design

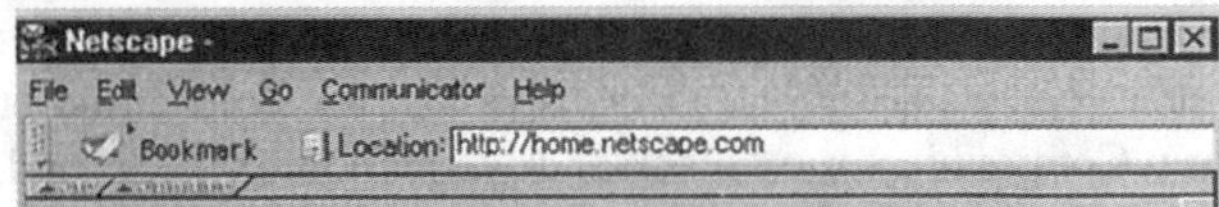

Figure 7b: Main Toolbar and Personal Toolbar collapsed

As opposed to earlier designs, this design did not rely on correspondence between tab color and toolbar content. We felt this design was strong enough to be implemented so we could assess the design, first informally with peer interaction designers and engineers, then formally with participants external to Netscape. In our informal observations of users working with the toolbar system, users could quickly identify toolbars when collapsed because of the size of the tab, with the larger tab corresponding to the taller command toolbar. This functionality proved to be discoverable in further usability tests; users understood that by clicking on the tab and seeing it replaced with a horizontal tab with no toolbar, they were conceptually collapsing the toolbar.

USABILITY TESTING THE "FINAL" DESIGN

Because of the rapid development cycle at Netscape, only informal user testing was done on the early designs. When we arrived at a design that we believed met the design goals and would be accepted by users, we conducted two usability studies of the collapsible toolbar design early in the development of Netscape Communicator 4.0 to assess the quality of the design.

The first study was conducted October 31 and November 1 with six users. All participants were corporate users and had previous experience with Netscape products. Participants spanned a range of expertise: computer usage ranged from ten hours a week to forty hours a week. Each two-hour study was performed in the usability lab at Netscape by a usability engineer. We collected data on the toolbar design by observing users' exploration of the software, as well as prompting them to find ways to increase the viewing space for content.

In the studies, though users found the collapsible toolbars useful, the discoverability of the tabs' function was a major problem. We observed that the grey tab texture was too subtle to be discovered. Users were not sure that the grey tabs with the texture was intended as an affordance for clicking and grabbing. We did not feel that giving the tabs a different color than the chrome would be a good solution, because it would be a visual distraction from the content. Our solution was to change the tab's color when the user moused over the toolbar tab (Figure 8). This solution also worked well because it was consistent with the mouse over feedback given on the borderless buttons on the toolbar. We also changed the cursor to a hand cursor when the user moused over the tabs.

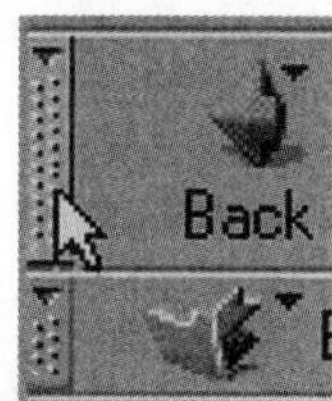

Figure 8: Mouse over feedback on toolbar tab

The second study was conducted on December 13 after the changes were made. Six different users participated in the study: four were corporate users; two were home users. Like the users in the first study, all had previous experience with Netscape products, and their computer usage ranged from ten hours a week to forty hours a week. The tasks and structure of the study mirrored that of the first study.

In this study, we observed that when users were asked to show and hide the toolbars with a method other than using the menu items, all users immediately went to the toolbar tabs. It was clear that the discoverability was improved by the changes we made. When the users collapsed all the toolbars, they were asked to identify the toolbar with which the collapsed tab corresponded. The users understood the large collapsed tab corresponded to the main toolbar, but they were unsure of the other two. Based on this feedback, we provided tooltips in the final version to help users identify toolbars when they are collapsed.

We also observed that the cursor feedback over the tabs proved to be a problem. We were compelled to change the cursor from an arrow to a hand to provide more mouse over feedback, but we found that users were inclined to drag the toolbar with the hand cursor instead of click on it. Although users were able to move the toolbars by dragging the toolbar tabs, it was not the primary objective of this design. Given the choice between a hand cursor and an arrow cursor, we felt it was more important to discover the show-hide functionality than the ability to reorder toolbars through direct manipulation. Thus, we followed the model used in Navigator, where an object that can be selected by a click or moved by dragging shows an arrow cursor when the user mouses over it.

CONCLUSIONS

Our design goals were met with a new widget that was considered a success. With the collapsible toolbar widget, users could show and hide toolbars easily and quickly to increase the content viewing area while keeping the toolbars needed for web browsing readily accessible. Users could gain as much as 95 pixels vertically for viewing content (Figure 9), compared to the 105 pixels occupied by the toolbars in Netscape Navigator 3.0. The design worked gracefully in all components of Communicator, as evidenced by its proliferation throughout the product. The interaction design of the widget was simple and easily understood by users. Visually, the widget was discoverable yet subtle enough so that it did not distract users from the content of the window.

The collapsible toolbar widget borrows not only the visual design from a real world object but also its functionality. Because its interaction principles come from a model that users are familiar with, the toolbars

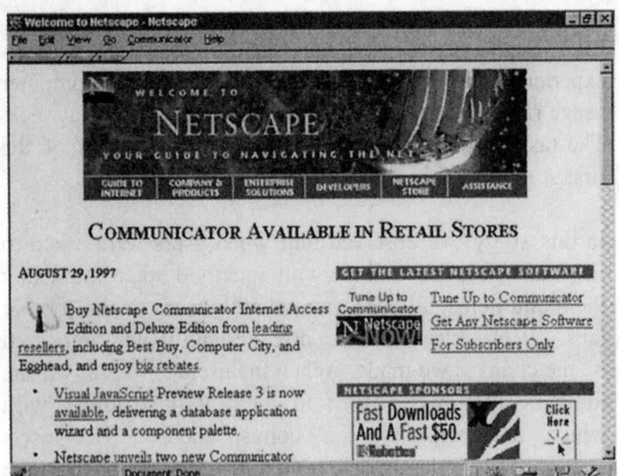

Figure 9: Netscape Communicator 4.0, toolbars collapsed

were quickly accepted and learned by users. We attribute its success to its roots in the real world, as well as the tight integration between visual design and interaction design. There were several lessons in design that we learned from this exercise:

1. When designing widgets, visual and interaction design must be tightly coupled. The collapsible toolbar design taught us how the visual design and interaction design greatly influence each other. Without strength in one area or the other, the design would not have been as successful. A widget's visual design influences how one interacts with it as much as the interaction design affects its visual design.

2. Look for directions in the real world when designing new widgets for software. Although an object may be completely unrelated to the software, its interaction design can be applied to the widget. It is a model with which users are familiar and understand.

3. Be aware of artificial constraints on the design problem. In the early iterations of our toolbar design, we were limited by the notion that the toolbars had to be conceptually stacked on top of each other in order for the design to achieve its goals. Such constraints proved to make the design a very difficult problem. Once we reassessed the goals, however, it was much easier to open our minds to other metaphors that would have otherwise not worked.

MORE INFORMATION

Netscape Communicator with its collapsible toolbars can be downloaded from the Netscape home page at http://home.netscape.com/

ACKNOWLEDGMENTS

The collapsible toolbar could not have been developed without the help of many key people. We thank Hagan Rivers for her initial thoughts on the toolbar system. Scott Putterman implemented many design iterations, which significantly contributed to the design process. Feedback from usability studies conducted by Tracy Halgren helped us refine our design.

A Study of Fonts Designed for Screen Display

Dan Boyarski
School of Design
Carnegie Mellon University

Christine Neuwirth
Department of English
Carnegie Mellon University

Jodi Forlizzi
ELab LLC
Chicago, IL

Susan Harkness Regli
Department of English
Carnegie Mellon University

Pittsburgh, PA 15232 USA +1 412-268-2828

ABSTRACT
This study examined the readability and subjective preferences of a set of fonts designed for screen display. Two new binary bitmap fonts performed well, suggesting that designers should consider incorporating similar attributes into default fonts for on-line type.

KEYWORDS
On-line typography, reading performance assessment, legibility, readability, CRT display, font design, anti-aliased, on-line help, World Wide Web

INTRODUCTION
This study examines reading for comprehension and users' preferences of fonts designed specifically for computer screens. Since the introduction of the personal computer and the more recent increase in the use of on-line sources of information (on-line help, database searching, and especially hypertext resources on the World Wide Web), the option of reading from paper rather than from computer screens has been drastically reduced and in some cases eliminated.

A substantial literature on the legibility, readability, and users' preferences for fonts exists (see [2] for a relatively recent comprehensive review). Recent work has studied users' performance on high resolution bit-mapped displays for a range of reading tasks such as proof-reading [3, 4, 5], reading for comprehension and skimming [8]. These studies indicate that there is no difference, at least under some circumstances, between paper and high quality screen displays. Nevertheless, reading from screens remains anecdotally problematic. In part, this situation may be due to differences between the conditions of the experiments and conditions of typical on-line presentation (e.g., [4, 5] studied anti-aliased text whereas actual practice for many long passages of on-line information is binary bitmap text; [8] studied text set in boldface whereas actual practice is regular face — strokes may appear thinner on a screen than on paper — with boldface reserved for cueing of highlights).

The current study was designed to look at users' performance with text as it is typically presented on-line — using fonts that were not designed specifically for screen display — with text that is likely to be presented on computer screens in the near future — using fonts designed specifically for screen display. The goal of the study was not to determine whether the newly designed screen fonts are better than those appearing on paper, but rather whether the newly designed screen fonts are better than currently used screen fonts and the relationship of the newly designed fonts to each other.

Part I of the study examined binary bitmap fonts. These fonts are used primarily for presenting long passages of text. Part II of the study examined grayscale (anti-aliased) fonts that are used primarily for headers and display purposes.

PART I: BINARY BITMAP FONTS
METHODS
PARTICIPANTS
There were forty-eight participants in the study, drawn from the faculty, staff, and graduate students at Carnegie Mellon University. They ranged in age from 20 to 53 with a mean age of 30.1 (S.D. = 7.8). Each subject was paid $10.00 for participation. Sixteen subjects participated in one of three tests.

MATERIALS
We compared the following fonts in three tests:

Designed for Screen Display		Designed for Print
Georgia (serif)	vs.	Times Roman (serif)
Georgia (serif)	vs.	Verdana (sans serif)
Verdana (sans serif)	vs.	Verdana Italic (sans serif)

Times Roman is a serif font commonly used to display on-line text, but which was not designed for screen display. It is the default text face on the majority of Web browsers.

Georgia and Verdana were both designed for screen display. They were commissioned by Microsoft, designed by Matthew Carter (Carter and Coyne, Boston) and hinted by Tom Rickner. Georgia is a serif font, while Verdana is a sans serif font. Both have a relatively large x-height, when compared to Times (see Figure 1). The x-height of a font greatly affects legibility [18]. Verdana also has extra space between characters so they don't touch, since touching letters can be especially problematic on-line. On both fonts, special care was taken with characters like 1, I, l, i and J so that they are legible, and aren't confused with each other. Microsoft's Web site states, "Curves are reduced to a minimum in the counters. Lowercase characters are a pixel taller than their uppercase counterparts at key screen sizes, to aid the distinguishing of particular characters." The comparison between Georgia and Times Roman is intended to determine whether a font designed specifically for the screen is, in fact, discernably better. The comparison between Georgia, a serif font, with Verdana, a sans serif font, is to determine whether Verdana succeeds at being as readable as Georgia, since the research suggests that serif fonts may be easier to read in contin-

The ability to read The ability to read The ability to read

Figure 1. Times Roman (left), Georgia (center), and Verdana (right) set at the same point size.

uous text than san serif faces. Finally, the comparison between Verdana and Verdana Italic is to determine whether an italic text font succeeds at being legible and readable, considering italic fonts are especially difficult to represent on-screen.

MEASURES

Reading task. In choosing a task for the study, we looked for one that was both ecologically valid (studies of typography have been much criticized for their use of tasks that bear little resemblance to the act of reading, cf. Dillon) and that had a track record for being able to detect differences (numerous studies that report "no difference" used passages that the experimenters devised, with no attention to the difficulties involved in creating a set of passages that can discriminate comprehension). Thus, we used established tests for reading comprehension and speed. In Part I of the study, we used the *Nelson-Denny Reading Test* [9], designed to assess college-level reading comprehension skills.

The *Nelson-Denny Test* has two Forms, E (9-83151) and F (9-83154). The level of difficulty and discourse structure of the passages are similar, so that an individual will score approximately the same on either form. By using a test like the *Nelson-Denny* that has comparable forms, we hoped to minimize form effects in a counterbalanced, within subjects design.

For each font (Georgia, Times, Verdana, Verdana Italic), we prepared eight passages drawn from the *Nelson-Denny Test,* four passages from Form E and four passages from Form F. Each passage consisted of three to seven paragraphs of text and four comprehension questions associated with each passage. All text was set in 10 point size, 13 point leading, with an average line length of 10 words.

The *Nelson-Denny* test was scored for the time needed to read all the passages and answer the questions and the number of comprehension questions answered correctly. Since participants can trade accuracy in answering questions for time (i.e., someone can be very accurate at the expense of speed or very speedy at the expense of accuracy), we also computed Effective Reading Speed (Score/Time).

Subjective Preference. In addition to the time and number of questions answered correctly, we developed two Subjective Perception Questionnaires (A & B) to measure participants' subjective impressions of the font. The literature suggests that readers do prefer some fonts over others. Although such preferences are associated with legibility and often agree with reading speed, measures of preference do not always agree with speed [21]. We adapted Shneiderman et al. QUIS, since the items on that questionnaire have been tested for validity and reliability [10, 19]. The first questionnaire asked participants to rate a font's characters (hard to read/easy to read), the image of the characters (fuzzy/sharp) and the shape of the characters (barely legible/very legible) on 9-point scales. The second questionnaire was used to assess whether subjects could discriminate fonts when they viewed them side-by-side, and asked participants to rate which of two fonts was easiest to read, most pleasing to read, and most fuzzy/least sharp on 9-point scales.

DESIGN

The study employed a within subjects design: for each of the three font contrasts (Test 1, 2, and 3 for Font A vs. Font B), sixteen participants saw both fonts. The order in which they saw the font and the order of the form of the test were counter-balanced across participants, with 4 participants in each of the following conditions:

Font A on Form E / Font B on Form F
Font A on Form F / Font B on Form E
Font B on Form E / Font A on Form F
Font B on Form F / Font A on Form E

PROCEDURE

Screens were presented using Microsoft Word 6.0 and viewed on a PC Gateway 2000 model P5-133 running Windows 95 with a 17" Sony Trinitron multiscan 17seII monitor. The window was set to display 640 x 480 pixels. Participants navigated from screen to screen by pressing the down-arrow key.

Training. At the beginning of the session, participants were shown the parts of the interface required for the study (a press of the down-arrow key) and practiced using the key to navigate from one screen to the next on a series of screens. In addition, participants did the practice items accompanying the *Nelson-Denny* test.

The following outlines the remainder of the session:

1.a. One minute timed test for speed of reading.

1.b. Nelson-Denny Test of reading comprehension. Participants read and answered questions on four passages, either from Font A/Form E, Font A/Form F, Font B/Form E, or Font B/Form F, depending on condition. Participants were instructed as follows: "Work for both speed and accuracy; that is, work rapidly but try not to make mistakes."

1.c. Subjective Perception Questionnaire A.

2.a. One minute timed test for speed of reading

2.b. Nelson-Denny Test of reading comprehension.

2.c. Subjective Perception Questionnaire A.

3. Direct comparison of fonts. After completing both tests and questionnaires, participants were shown both fonts on two monitors side-by-side, and were given Subjective Perception Questionnaire B and asked to directly compare the fonts. The screen (left or right) on which the fonts appeared was counterbalanced across conditions.

4. After completing the questionnaire, they were asked to talk about their reactions to the fonts on the screen. Their reactions were tape-recorded.

ANALYSIS

Since participants were counter-balanced across conditions, we used paired-samples t-tests to look at the effect of fonts; when n1=n2, the t-test is robust with respect to violation of the homogeneity-of-variance assumption. For the direct comparison of fonts, we tested the hypothesis that the mean was equal to 5, the neutral point on the scale.

RESULTS AND DISCUSSION

TEST 1
A serif font designed for screen (Georgia) vs. A serif font designed for print (Times Roman)

Score, Time, Effective Reading Speed

Table 1.1 shows the means and standard deviations for Score (the number of comprehension questions participants answered correctly; the maximum Score was 12).

	Georgia (serif)		Times Roman (serif)	
Score	9.6	(1.8)	10.2	(1.9)
Time (secs.)	376.4	(101.1)	377.4	(116.1)
Effective Reading Speed	.027	(.01)	.030	(.01)

Table 1.1. Means (S.D.s) Score, Time, and Effective Reading Speed by Font (N=16)

Subjective Perceptions of Fonts

Indirect Comparison. Participants rated Georgia, the serif font designed for screen display, as easier to read and the characters sharper and more legible than Times Roman, the font not designed for screen display ($p < .05$). Table 1.2 shows the means and standard deviations for these dimensions.[1]

Direct Comparison. In the direct comparison of the two fonts, participants expressed a preference for Georgia ($p < .05$) on the dimensions of easiest to read (7.3, S.D.=2.1), most pleasing to read (6.9, S.D.=2.6) and most sharp (7.3, S.D.=2.0.).

Although no differences were detected in the objective measures, the subjective measures of preference suggest that Georgia's design is succeeding over Times.

	Georgia (serif)	Times Roman (serif)
Hard/Easy to Read*	6.1 (2.1)	4.8 (2.3)
Fuzzy/Sharp*	6.3 (2.1)	5.1 (2.4)
Illegible/Legible*	6.7 (1.7)	5.6 (2.2)

*p < .05

Table 1.2. Means (S.D.s) for Subjective Perceptions by Font (N=16)

TEST 2
A serif font designed for screen display (Georgia) vs. A sans serif font designed for screen display (Verdana)

Score, Time, Effective Reading Speed

Participants answered more questions correctly (9.8 vs. 9.0) when viewing the test in Georgia than they did when viewing the test in Verdana ($p < .05$). The difference in mean scores expressed as a percentage of the mean score for Verdana is a difference of 8.9%. Table 2.1 shows the means and standard deviations for Score (the number of comprehension questions participants answered correctly; the maximum Score was 12).

	Georgia (serif)		Verdana (sans serif)	
Score*	9.8	(1.4)	9.0	(1.3)
Time (secs.)	362.9	(103.5)	377.4	(102.8)
Effective Reading Speed	.029	(.01)	.026	(.01)

*p < .05

Table 2.1. Means (S.D.s) Score, Time, and Effective Reading Speed by Font (N=16)

Indirect Comparison. Table 2.2 shows the means and standard deviations for these dimensions. No differences were detected for participants' rating of the fonts.

	Georgia (serif)	Verdana (sans serif)
Hard/Easy to Read	6.6 (1.8)	7.3 (1.7)
Fuzzy/Sharp	7.2 (2.6)	7.3 (1.5)
Illegible/Legible	7.1 (1.6)	7.5 (1.4)

Table 2.2. Means (S.D.s) for Subjective Perceptions for Georgia and Verdana (N=16)

Direct Comparison. In the direct comparison of the two fonts, however, participants expressed a slight preference for Verdana on the dimension of easiest to read (6.3, S.D.=2.3, $p < .05$). Scores for most pleasing to read (6.0, S.D.=2.6) and most sharp (5.4, S.D.=2.3) did not differ significantly from 5, the neutral point.

TEST 3
A sans serif font designed for screen display (Verdana) vs. A sans serif italic font designed for screen display (Verdana Italic)

Score, Time, Effective Reading Speed

There were no overall differences between the Sans Serif font (Verdana) and the Sans Serif Italic font (Verdana Italic) for comprehension and speed of reading (see Table 3.1).

[1]Note that the higher score indicates easier to read, sharper, and more legible.

	Verdana (sans serif)		Verdana Italic (sans serif italic)	
Score	10.1	(1.6)	10.1	(1.2)
Time (secs.)	356.2	(112.1)	353.8	(88.1)
Effective Reading Speed	.030	(.007)	.030	(.008)

Table 3.1. Mean (S.D.) for Score, Time, and Effective Reading Rate for A Sans Serif font (Verdana) and a Sans Serif Italic (Verdana Italic) (N=16)

Subjective Perceptions of Fonts

Indirect Comparison. Participants rated the sans serif font (Verdana) as easier to read and the characters as sharper and more legible than the Sans Serif Italic font (Verdana Italic). Table 1.4 shows the means and standard deviations for these dimensions.

	Verdana (sans serif)	Verdana Italic (sans serif italic)
Hard/Easy to Read*	6.4 (1.6)	5.4 (2.2)
Fuzzy/Sharp***	6.8 (1.1)	5.3 (1.7)
Illegible/Legible**	7.1 (1.2)	6.1 (1.5)

*p < .05; **p < .01; ***p < .001

Table 3.2. Means (S.D.s) for Subjective Perceptions by Font (N=16)

Direct Comparison. Moreover, in the direct side-by-side comparison of the two fonts, participants expressed a strong preference ($p < .001$) for Verdana over Verdana Italic on the dimension of easy to read (7.1, S.D. = 2.0) and how sharp the characters appeared (7.4, S.D.=1.6). No difference between the fonts was detected on the dimension of most pleasing to read (6.1, S.D. = 3.0). Note that the variance was unusually large, with participants diverging substantially in their opinions. A post-hoc k-means cluster analysis with k=2 indicated that ten of the participants had a strong preference for Verdana (8.2, S.D. = 0.9) and six of the participants a preference for Verdana Italic (7.5, S.D.=1.0) on the question of which of the two fonts is most pleasing to read.

This pattern of results suggests that, while failing to detect a difference on comprehension and time it takes to read, participants have a strong preference for the sans serif over the sans serif italic font, with subjects divided about which font is most pleasing.

OVERALL DISCUSSION OF PART I

On the Data. Overall, there were few differences detected on the objective comprehension measures. This situation raises the issue of the power of the test. For time to read, the smallest mean difference observed was 1 second and largest was 14 1/2 seconds over a period of approximately 6 min. With n=16 and the large variances (ranging from 88.1 to 116.1), the probability of detecting a significant effect ($\alpha = 0.05$) for even the largest mean difference observed is close to 0. To increase the probability to 90% would require hundreds of subjects (When n is large, even a very small difference may be large enough to be highly statistically significant.) On the other hand, if subjects had read for an hour, if the mean difference were linear (i.e., the mean difference observed over an hour turned out to be 1 minute to 2 1/2 minutes), and if the variance remained about the same, the probability would be approximately .7 for the smallest difference and greater than .9 for the largest that a significant effect ($\alpha = 0.05$) would be detected with n=16. It may be the case, then, that differences would show up between the fonts studied here with longer duration reading periods. Indeed, other researchers have speculated that studies reporting differences used much longer reading periods than studies reporting no differences [11]. For example, [8], which reported differences between fonts read on-line and on paper, required subjects to read for 2 hours.

This analysis raises the issue of what size differences are important. Would it matter if people read 1 minute or 2 1/2 minutes faster in an hour period when reading on-line text set in one font vs. another? Compared to other performance differences associated with on-line information (e.g., searching for the information), such differences seem quite small (cf. [29]).

The number of comprehension questions participants answered correctly seems more interesting. Here a modest increase in number of subjects (roughly double, or thirty-eight) could result in mean differences of 1 (assuming the largest standard deviation of 1.9) being detectable ($\alpha = 0.05$) with probability of 90%.

For the subjective perception measures, the test had a > 90% probability of detecting a mean difference of 2.0 on the scale ($\alpha = 0.05$), assuming a standard deviation of 2.0.

On the Fonts. It is worth noting that in test 3, where Verdana was tested against Verdana Italic, there were no marked differences in score, time, and effective reading speed. However, given that the subjective preferences clearly favored Verdana over Verdana Italic, caution should still be exercised in setting lengthy text passages in italic.

In our tests, line spacing was held constant. But it is likely that increasing the line spacing for the new fonts will make them easier to read in lengthy text settings (cf. Tinker, 1963, who suggested guidelines based on extensive studies of the relationship among type size, leading and line length). Carter's new fonts for Microsoft have larger x-heights — when compared with fonts like Times — which make them appear larger (cf. Figure 1), even though the point-size is identical, and, following guidelines based on Tinker's research, should probably be given greater line spacing, more than is currently the default.

PART II: GRAYSCALE (ANTI-ALIASED) FONTS

Anti-aliased fonts are fonts in which levels of gray are used in selected pixels in order to eliminate jagged edges — "jaggies" or "staircases" (see Figure 2). The levels of gray are usually computed in relation to the background of the font (e.g., on a white background, the levels of gray that make a black diagonal line look smooth range from black to white; on a gray background, the levels of gray range from black to gray).

Abyss Abyss

Figure 2. Binary bitmap font (left) and an anti-aliased font (right).

METHODS

PARTICIPANTS

The same participants as in Part I participated in Part II, with 16 participants in each test.

MATERIALS

We created materials to compare the following:

Anti-aliased fonts		Binary Bitmap Fonts
Adobe anti-aliased	vs.	Microsoft bitmap
Microsoft anti-aliased	vs.	Microsoft bitmap
Adobe anti-aliased	vs.	Microsoft anti-aliased

MEASURES

Because anti-aliased fonts require extra bits for the levels of gray, there are limits to the size of font that can be anti-aliased. The limit tends to be 14 pt and larger. This is a rule of thumb, which is sometimes broken or challenged, but anti-aliased fonts are typically used in headlines and subheads, rather than in long passages of text. Hence, for Part II of the study, we used the *Tinker Speed of Reading Test* [20]. *The Tinker Speed of Reading Test* is the test used by Tinker and Paterson in their ground-breaking studies of print typography reported in the *Journal of Applied Psychology* beginning in 1928 [12-17; 21-26] and summarized in Tinker's 1963 book, *The Legibility of Print.* Each test item consists of a thirty-word sentence. Participants read the item and indicate the word in the latter half of the item that spoils the meaning of the text. For example, in the item

"We wanted very much to get some good pictures of the baby, so in order to take some snapshots at the picnic grounds, we packed the stove into the car."[2]

the word "stove" spoils the meaning. The participant must read the entire item to figure out the correct answer, but the vocabulary is simple enough that errors are rare. Thus, the test minimizes effects of domain knowledge or poor problem-solving abilities.

For each font, we prepared 30 screens of items from the Tinker test, with five items per screen. Half the screens were from Tinker Form I and half from Tinker Form II. All text was displayed at 16 point size, 19 point leading, with an average line length of 10 words.

For the Microsoft binary bitmap conditions and the Microsoft anti-aliased conditions, screens were composed using Microsoft Word 6.0 for Windows. To switch from the binary bitmap condition to the anti-aliased condition, smoothing was turned off in the Microsoft Plus Control Panels. The Adobe anti-aliased conditions were created in Adobe Photoshop 3.0 for Windows.

DESIGN

This part of the study also employed a within subjects design: all participants saw both fonts. The order in which they saw the font and the order of the form of the test were counter-balanced across participants, with 4 participants in each of the following conditions:

Font A on Form I / Font B on Form II
Font A on Form II / Font B on Form I
Font B on Form I / Font A on Form II
Font B on Form II / Font A on Form I

PROCEDURE

Screens were presented using Microsoft Word 6.0 or Adobe Photoshop and viewed on a PC Gateway 2000 model P5-133 running Windows 95 with a 17" Sony Trinitron multiscan 17seII monitor. The window was set to display 640 x 480 pixels. Participants navigated from screen to screen by pressing the down-arrow key.

Participants took a 4-minute break between Part I and Part II. During this time, they left the experiment room.

At the beginning of Part II, participants were read the standard directions for the test, except they were asked to speak aloud the word that spoils the meaning for each item, rather than marking it. Participants completed the standard set of practice items.

Participants were instructed as follows: "Work for both speed and accuracy; that is, work rapidly but try not to make mistakes." They were told they had seven minutes in which to complete as many items as they could.

The following outlines the remainder of the session:

1.a. Tinker test. Participants read from either Font A/Form 1, Font A/Form 2, Font B/Form 1, or Font B/Form 2, depending on condition.

1.b. Subjective Perception Questionnaire A. Participants left the room briefly while the experimenter set up the machine for the next Font/Form comparison.

2.a. Tinker test.

2.b. Subjective Perception Questionnaire A.

Participants left the room briefly while the experimenter set up the monitors for a direct comparison of fonts.

3. Direct comparison of fonts. After completing both tests and questionnaires, participants were shown both fonts and were given the Subjective Perception Questionnaire B which asked them to directly compare the fonts.

4. After completing the questionnaire, they were asked to talk about their reactions to the fonts on the screen. Their reactions were tape-recorded.

5. At the end, participants were debriefed about the purpose of the study and the conditions.

[2]The Tinker Speed of Reading Test provided courtesy of the University of Minnesota Press: Copyright © 1947, 1955 (renewed 1983) by Miles A. Tinker. All rights reserved. Published by the University of Minnesota Press, Minneapolis.

ANALYSIS

The following score for the test was calculated:

Score = the number of items attempted – the number of incorrect items.

Incorrect items were rare. The accuracy on Form 1 was 100% and on Form 2 was 98%. This difference did not reach statistical significance.

RESULTS AND DISCUSSION

TEST 4

An anti-aliased font (Adobe) vs.
A binary bitmap font (Microsoft)

Table 4 shows the means and standard deviations for the number of anomalous items participants correctly identified in the given time as well as their subjective ratings of the ease of reading, sharpness and legibility of the two fonts. There were no significant differences.

	Binary Bitmap (Microsoft)	Anti-Aliased (Adobe)
Number of Anomalies Correctly Identified	50.7 (18.1)	50.8 (18.1)
Hard/Easy to Read	7.9 (1.6)	8.1 (1.3)
Fuzzy/Sharp	8.0 (1.7)	7.4 (1.8)
Illegible/Legible	7.9 (1.2)	8.0 (1.0)

Table 4. Means (S.D.s) for Score and Subjective Perceptions by Font (N=16)

In a direct comparison of the two fonts on the screen, participants indicated a small preference for the Anti-aliased font ($p < .01$) for ease of reading (6.3, S.D.=2.2) and most pleasing (6.6, S.D.=2.2), with no difference for most sharp (5.6, S.D.=2.0).

TEST 5

An anti-aliased font (Microsoft) vs.
A binary bitmap font (Microsoft)

Table 5 shows the means and standard deviations for the number of anomalous items participants correctly identified in the given time as well as their subjective ratings of the ease of reading, sharpness and legibility of the two fonts.

	Anti-Aliased (Microsoft)	Binary Bitmap (Microsoft)
Number of Anomalies Correctly Identified	51.7 (9.6)	51.0 (12.8)
Hard/Easy to Read	8.2 (1.3)	7.1 (2.6)
Fuzzy/Sharp	7.2 (2.2)	7.7 (1.5)
Illegible/Legible*	8.4 (0.8)	7.4 (1.5)

*$p < .05$

Table 5. Means (S.D.s) for Score and Subjective Perceptions by Font (N=16)

Participants rated Microsoft's anti-aliased font as more legible than a Microsoft binary bitmap font.

In a direct comparison of the two fonts on the screen, variation was large, with no significant difference emerging for which font was easiest to read (4.4, S.D. = 3.0), most pleasing to read (5.1 S.D. =3.0) and most sharp (4.9, S.D.=2.6). A post-hoc cluster analysis did not indicate any clear patterns among the participants.

TEST 6

An anti-aliased font (Adobe) vs.
An anti-aliased font (Microsoft)

Table 6 shows the means and standard deviations for the number of anomalous items participants correctly identified in the given time as well as their subjective ratings of the ease of reading, sharpness and legibility of the two fonts. There were no significant differences.

	Anti-Aliased (Microsoft)	Anti-Aliased (Adobe)
Number of Anomalies Correctly Identified	52.5 (18.5)	52.4 (17.3)
Hard/Easy to Read	8.0 (1.0)	8.1 (1.3)
Fuzzy/Sharp	7.8 (1.2)	7.4 (1.7)
Illegible/Legible	8.1 (1.0)	7.9 (1.2)

Table 6. Means (S.D.s) for Score and Subjective Perceptions by Font (N=16)

In a direct comparison of the two fonts on the screen, participants indicated a small preference for the Adobe anti-aliased font for ease of reading (6.2, S.D.=1.8, $p < .01$) and most sharp (5.8, S.D. = 1.3); no difference was detected for most pleasing to read (4.3, S.D.=2.0).

OVERALL DISCUSSION OF PART II

On the Data. As Tinker [20] observed, retarding effects which are marginal during short periods of reading may show up as significant when the reading lasts longer. But most headings are very short, so the relatively short test still seems appropriate, despite the failure to find differences.

The mean differences in subjective ratings was, on the whole, much smaller than those in Part I.

On the Fonts. While the subjective preferences favor anti-aliased fonts over bitmapped fonts, the majority of the subjects — as observed by the experimenters — had difficulty telling the difference. In other words, this was not a major issue for them. Still, the visual clarity and grace afforded by anti-aliased display fonts cannot be overlooked and, therefore, should be encouraged when available. Anti-aliasing will certainly not decrease the preference for a font, at least for the larger point sizes tested here.

OVERALL RESULTS AND DISCUSSION

This study focused on reading for comprehension and subjective preference of on-line fonts. Georgia, the new serif font designed by Matthew Carter, performed well compared to Times Roman, indicating that this font, designed for computer screen display, is perceived by readers to facilitate ease of reading on-line. A comparison of Verdana, Carter's new sans serif font designed for screen display, with Georgia, produced mixed results. Future research might test Verdana more directly against a sans serif font designed for print. Verdana was preferred over Verdana Italic.

These are, however, results based on initial studies, which should be further explored with attention to the following issues:

While this study focused on typeface, other factors must be considered when discussing typography, whether on paper or on-line. These factors include type size, line length, and line spacing (cf. [21]). Together with typeface, these three factors must considered together when designing typography for any presentation format, and, therefore, are issues that need to be tested concurrently. Both Georgia and Verdana rely on larger x-heights than the ubiquitous Times Roman and, as argued above, should probably be given more vertical breathing room with extra linespacing. It would be a great help if systems could build this into the default linespacing for each new font.

Finally, a much-needed step in typographic research is a more sophisticated framework to identify critical features that contribute to the differences that we observed. In the absence of such a framework, we don't know what the key factors are — larger x-heights, rounder letterforms, or more generous letter spacing — and, therefore, designers will find it difficult to generalize from the results obtained from studies such as the one reported here when producing other fonts.

ACKNOWLEDGMENTS

The authors thank the Riverside Publishing Company for permission to use *The Nelson-Denny Reading Test,* Forms E (9-83151) and F (9-83154) and The University of Minnesota Press for permission to use *The Tinker Speed of Reading Test.*

This research was supported by a grant from Microsoft Corporation. The authors also thank Virginia Howlett and Simon Earnshaw of Microsoft's Typography Group for their support, encouragement, and patience throughout this project.

REFERENCES

1. Anderson, R. C. (1972). How to construct achievement tests to assess comprehension. *Review of Educational Research,* 42(2), 145-170.

2. Dillon, A. (1992). Reading from paper vs. screens: A critical review of the empirical literature. *Ergonomics,* 35 (10), 1297-1326.

3. Gould, J. D. & Grischkowsky, N., (1984). Doing the same work with hard copy and with cathode-ray tube (CRT) computer terminals. Human Factors, 26(3), 323-337.

4. Gould, J. D., Alfaro, L., Barnes, V., Finn, R., Grischkowsky, N., & Minuto, A. (1987a). Reading is slower from CRT displays than from paper: Attempts to isolate a single-variable explanation. *Human Factors,* 29(3), 269-299.

5. Gould, J. D., Alfaro, L., Finn, R., Haupt, B., & Minuto, A. (1987b). Reading from CRT displays can be as fast as reading from paper. *Human Factors,* 29(5), 497-517.

6. Johnston, P. H. (1984). Assessment in reading. In P. D. Pearson (Ed.), *Handbook of Reading Research* (Vol I, pp. 147-182). NY: Longman.

7. Mills, C. B. & Weldon, L. J. (1987). Reading text from computer screens. *ACM Computing Surveys,* 19(4), 329-358.

8. Muter, P., Latrémouille, S. A., Treurniet, W. C. & Beam, P. (1982). Extended reading of continuous text on television screens. *Human Factors,* 24, 501-508.

9. *The Nelson-Denny Reading Test* (1981). Chicago, IL: The Riverside Publishing Company.

10. Norman, K.L. (1991). The psychology of menu selection: *Designing cognitive control at the human-computer interface.* New Jersey: Ablex.

11. Oborne, D. J. & Holton, D. (1988). Reading from screen vs. paper: there is no difference. *Int. J. Man-Machine Studies,* 28, 1-9.

12. Paterson, D. G. & Tinker, M. A. (1932a). Studies of typographical factors influencing speed of reading: X. Style of type face. *Journal of Applied Psychology,* 16(6), 605-613.

13. Paterson, D. G. & Tinker, M. A. (1932b). Studies of typographical factors influencing speed of reading: VIII. Space between lines or leading. *Journal of Applied Psychology,* 16(4), 388-397.

14. Paterson, D. G. & Tinker, M. A. (1931). Studies of typographical factors influencing speed of reading: VI. Black type versus white type. *Journal of Applied Psychology,* 15(2), 241-247.

15. Paterson, D. G. & Tinker, M. A. (1930). Studies of typographical factors influencing speed of reading: IV. Effect of practice on equivalence of test forms. *Journal of Applied Psychology,* 14(3), 211-217.

16. Paterson, D. G. & Tinker, M. A. (1929a). Studies of typographical factors influencing speed of reading: III. Length of line. *Journal of Applied Psychology,* 13(3), 205-219.

17. Paterson, D. G. & Tinker, M. A. (1929b). Studies of typographical factors influencing speed of reading: II. Size of type. *Journal of Applied Psychology,* 13(2), 120-130.

18. Poulton, E.C. (1955). Letter differentiation and rate of comprehension of reading. *Journal of Applied Psychology,* 49, 358-362.

19. Schneiderman, B. (1987). *Designing the user interface: Effective strategies for human-computer interaction.* Reading, MA: Addison-Wesley.

20. Tinker, M. A. (1947). *The Tinker speed of reading test.* Minneapolis, MN: The University of Minnesota Press.

21. Tinker, M. A. & Paterson, D. G. (1936). Studies of typographical factors influencing speed of reading: XIII. Methodological considerations. *Journal of Applied Psychology,* 20, 132-145.

22. Tinker, M. A. & Paterson, D. G. (1935). Studies of typographical factors influencing speed of reading: XI. Role of set in typographical studies. *Journal of Applied Psychology,* 19, 647-651.

23. Tinker, M. A. & Paterson, D. G. (1931a). Studies of typographical factors influencing speed of reading: IX. Reductions in size of newspaper print. *Journal of Applied Psychology,* 16(5), 525-531.

24. Tinker, M. A. & Paterson, D. G. (1931b). Studies of typographical factors influencing speed of reading: VII. Variations in color of print and background. *Journal of Applied Psychology,* 15(5), 471-479.

25. Tinker, M. A. & Paterson, D. G. (1931c). Studies of typographical factors influencing speed of reading: V. Simultaneous variation of type size and line length. *Journal of Applied Psychology,* 15(1), 72-78.

26. Tinker, M. A. & Paterson, D. G. (1928). Influence of type form on speed of reading. *Journal of Applied Psychology,* 12(4), 359-368.

27. Waller, R. (1991). Typography and discourse. In R. Barr, M. L. Kamil, P. B. Mosenthal, & P. D. Pearson (Eds.), *Handbook of Reading Research* (Vol II, pp. 341-380). NY: Longman.

From Documents to Discourse: Shifting Conceptions of Scholarly Publishing

Tamara Sumner
Knowledge Media Institute
The Open University
Milton Keynes, MK7 6AA, U.K.
http://kmi.open.ac.uk/~tamara
T.Sumner@open.ac.uk

Simon Buckingham Shum
Knowledge Media Institute
The Open University
Milton Keynes, MK7 6AA, U.K.
http://kmi.open.ac.uk/~simonb
sbs@acm.org

ABSTRACT

We are looking at how new forms of document interface can be used to support new forms of scholarly discourse, and ultimately, new models of scholarly publishing. The vehicle we use to conduct this research is the Digital Document Discourse Environment (D3E). D3E is an experimental system supporting the publication of web-based documents with integrated discourse facilities and embedded interactive components. We report here on two cases – an e-journal and a 'new form' of conference – where we have used D3E to promote new forms of discourse between participants. We use these cases to illustrate four principles that guide our socio-technical design actions.

Keywords: Argumentation, Digital Documents, Discourse, Electronic Publishing, Hypertext, Scholarly Publishing, Socio-technical Design, World Wide Web

INTRODUCTION

Currently, we are witnessing the beginnings of a shift from paper to digital media in the submission, review and publication of scholarly work. For many journals and conferences, it is now standard procedure for reviews and submissions to be transmitted electronically. Sometimes, automated systems are in place for matching reviewers with submissions based on keyword analysis. In a few cases, the final document version is even published electronically as a set of hypertext files available on the World Wide Web (see [12, 13] for examples). However, while various documents are becoming digital and some activities are automated, the process of scholarly publishing has remained largely unchanged. One can argue that, similar to other domains such as educational technology [24, 28], technology is most often being used to enhance traditional practices rather than to significantly rethink existing models of work.

The goal of our research is to use technology to rethink current publishing practices in order to promote new forms of discourse between participants. The vehicle we use to conduct this research is the Digital Document Discourse Environment (D3E). D3E is an experimental system supporting the publication of web-based documents with integrated discourse facilities and interactive components.

The first D3E project was to create an electronic journal on the Web (e-journal) supporting on-line peer review and embedded demonstrations. It became clear that production tools were needed to make the publishing of the journal tractable. It also became clear that there were many contexts where documents need to be discussed in different ways by different scholarly populations. This motivated the requirements for a generic publishing toolkit which could be used to generate a variety of sites. The concept of a tailorable environment was conceived, with the project's research goals being to better understand the factors that make discussions around media-rich web documents desirable and effective.

In pursuit of our research goals, we are following an iterative socio-technical design approach [21]: in addition to designing the D3E system, we also consider what processes are needed to promote and sustain changes within a specific community. To date, we have used D3E in numerous contexts, including the publication of several e-journals [5, 14], a national debate on government policy recommendations [15], and a 'new form' of academic conference [16]. Here, we report on two of these cases – JIME (an e-journal) and learning.org (a conference).

The remainder of this paper begins by discussing the motivations and design principles underlying D3E. We then use a scenario to illustrate how these principles are realised in the D3E toolkit and document interface. The heart of this paper examines how D3E has played a role in rethinking practices in two scholarly contexts.

MOTIVATION AND DESIGN PRINCIPLES

Brown and Duguid [2] contrast two models of document use – documents as darts and documents as a means of making and maintaining social groups. The 'darts' model refers to the notion of documents as a paper-based transport mechanism carrying pre-formed ideas through space and time. In the broader social model, they trace the ways documents serve as a medium for negotiation within communities, as members struggle to reach a shared interpretation. These negotiations take on different discourse forms, including discussions, debates, annotations, and even live events, such as presentations.

Current publishing practices reinforce the idea of 'documents are darts.' These practices have arisen over the last few hundreds of years from the affordances of paper and the difficulties of communicating over large geographic distances. Paper-based publishing models, such as the typical journal review process, sever all links between the document and its surrounding discourse, and between the end product and the process that shapes it. This has shortcomings in that questions go unanswered; confusions go unclarified; criticisms go undefended. Reviewers (and readers) are engaged in an imaginary debate with distant authors who are not present to respond. The dynamic cut-and-thrust of debate normally found in face-to-face contexts such as conferences and workshops is not supported.

Four Design Principles

We are using technology to explore different socially-based publishing models where documents serve as 'a medium for negotiation.' Towards this end, we are rethinking both our processes and products to support document-centred discourse. This rethinking is guided by existing research into how hypertext systems can support critical reflection. Over a period of six years, we have surveyed, prototyped and evaluated the usability and effectiveness of various argumentation and design rationale systems [3, 4, 25]. Such systems are designed to support the representation and analysis of arguments, and to capture the decisions and reasoning behind the design artifacts being discussed. From this work on pre-Web design support systems, and from our experiences using D3E, we have formulated four principles that have guided our design activities. Some of these principles are realised through system design, while others are realised through social means:

A: Avoid elaborate structuring schemes.

B: Integrate documents, demos and discourse.

C: Redesign work practices to emphasize discourse.

D: Support the new practices with tools.

Principle A: Avoid over-elaborate schemes for structuring discussions. If users classify their contributions to an on-line discussion, greater computer support can be provided. For instance, one can search for all *Theory* comments that have *Contradictory Evidence*, if those categories have been defined. A number of expressive schemes have been proposed (e.g. [7, 27]); many schemes require users to categorise contributions as *positions*, *issues*, *comments*, *pros*, and *cons*. This, however, runs the risk of burdening people with excessive representational overhead by forcing them to categorise their ideas before they are ready to. Numerous studies show that users are often unwilling and/or unable to use elaborate schemes, because the effort is too great [3, 4, 23].

Principle B: Computational tools must tightly integrate documents with their associated discourse. Many systems place the documents under development in a different application to the discussion about them (indeed we see this with many e-journals and their discussion lists). This separation hinders users from quickly accessing relevant comments when they are most needed and makes it is hard to add new comments. Likewise, tools should tightly integrate the textual parts of documents with the computational parts. Research in design support tools has shown that users need to easily bridge the separation between different representations of the design and between representations and design rationale[9, 20, 25]. In our case, we must enable users to move seamlessly between reading the document and making a comment, and between reading and interacting with an embedded demonstration.

Principle C: Work practices must be redesigned so that structured discussions are an integral product of the overall task. Studies show that people often do not contribute to discussions because it is perceived as extra work over and above what they are already required to do [11]. Successful approaches have redesigned work practices to make contributing to a discussion integral to the overall task being performed [26]. Others also advocate seeding; i.e., providing some initial contents, arguing that people find it easier to contribute to an ongoing discussion rather than starting from scratch [10]. In a journal review setting, this means redesigning the review process to require electronic threading of reviews into a shared space, and changing the traditional roles of editor and reviewer. Thus, redesigning practices is not simply about instituting new processes, it changes the roles and division of labour between community members [1].

Principle D: Tools are needed to support the new work practices. Tools are needed to make the publishing of link-rich web sites tractable. Many people may lack the technical skills, time, or inclination to engage in hand-crafting new digital document forms. Support is needed for automating the tedious and error-prone parts of the document creation process and to make it accessible to non-technical participants. Tools should be designed to make a good first approximation and then allow for humans to refine and correct the tools' output. The challenge is to create tools that are supportive, yet do not hinder the formation of new practices.

THE D3E TOOLKIT AND DOCUMENT INTERFACE

D3E consists of tools for generating and managing a site, and tools supporting the document interface (Figure 1). The Publisher's Toolkit is a Java™ application that takes HTML files (hypertext mark-up language) as input and parses these files to create new HTML files with special forms of navigation and integrated discourse facilities. The look and feel of a site is defined by creating a set of HTML template files containing D3E-specific variables that indicate where different kinds of document contents should go. In the document interface, the discourse facilities use a tailored version of HyperNews [17] (written in PERL) that we have modified to suit our design principles.

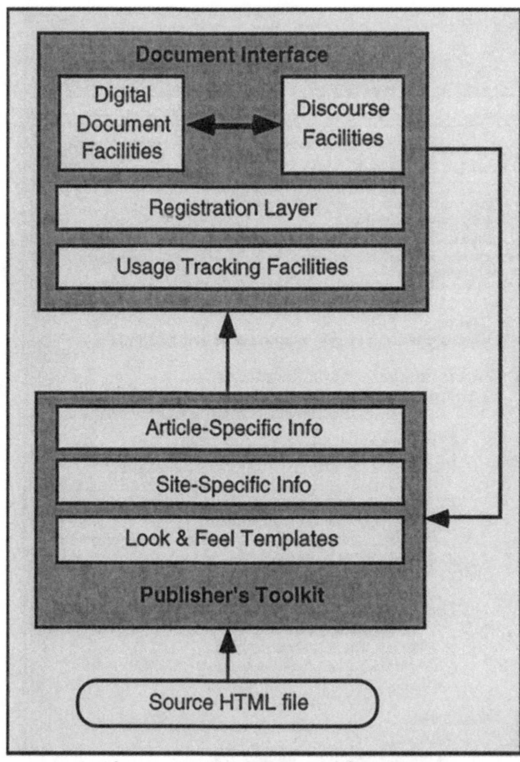

Figure 1. The D3E architecture.

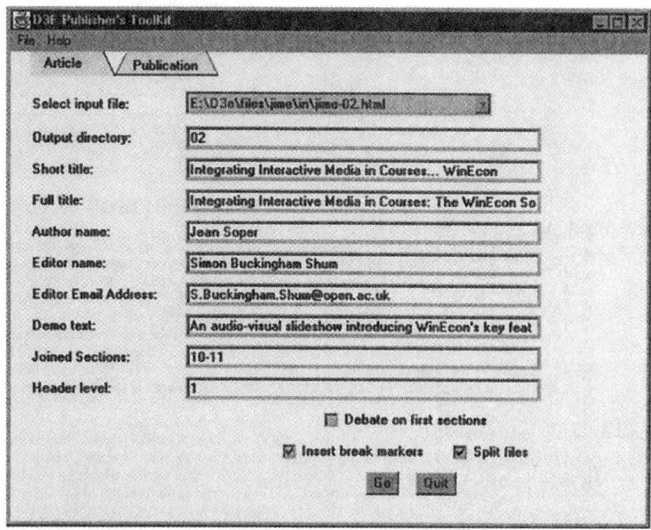

Figure 2: Article-specific information for generating the table of contents and splitting files is specified in the toolkit Article form. The Publications form is used to configure site-specific information such as the templates specifying the site's look and feel and standard topics for discussion.

We'll illustrate the basic functionality of the toolkit and the document interface using a simple scenario. Imagine a distance education setting where a tutor has asked a group of students distributed over a large geographic distance to jointly discuss a paper. The tutor imports the HTML file into the toolkit on her desktop computer by selecting an input file (Figure 2). Next, she specifies article-specific information by filling in the form with the relevant details.

On hitting the "Go" button, the toolkit takes the source HTML file and generates a new set of HTML files, creating the document interface shown in Figure 3:

- Comment icons are embedded in each article section which take the reader directly to the relevant area of the discussion space.
- An active table of contents is constructed for navigating around the article. Using the depth specified in the 'header level' field in the toolkit Article form, the toolkit parses the source file to find all <H1> and <H2> header tags and uses these tags to create the table of contents.
- The toolkit parses the source file looking for possible author-date or numeric citations. Where it detects citations, it establishes two-way links between citations and their corresponding bibliography entries. If the toolkit is configured to do so by the template files, citations and footnotes can be displayed under the Article frame when a citation link is followed.
- The source file is split up into smaller, faster loading files corresponding to sections in the article, and navigation buttons to the previous, next, and top sections are inserted at the foot of each file.
- A 'downloads' page is created, where for instance, print versions or any required plug-ins can be placed.
- Any hypertext links in the original document(s) are preserved; i.e., they still point to the same contents even though the file structure has changed.

The toolkit also generates a discussion space (right window, Figure 3) linked to the document, providing:

- An outline structure of headings matching the paper's section headings;
- Areas for general discussion (defined by the tutor in the toolkit's Publications form) are inserted at the top, for comments not specific to a particular section.
- Links back into the different sections of the article to facilitate smooth navigation.

All of this file processing is done locally, on the tutor's computer. If the tutor is not satisfied with what the toolkit has produced, she can continue to iteratively refine the document interface since the toolkit can take its own output files as input.

When she is satisfied, she moves the set of output files onto her web server and announces the location to her students. Students can now add review comments to the site by selecting a review heading, entering their comment and pressing the 'submit' button on the form provided. Students can optionally classify their comments as ones that 'agree' or 'disagree'.

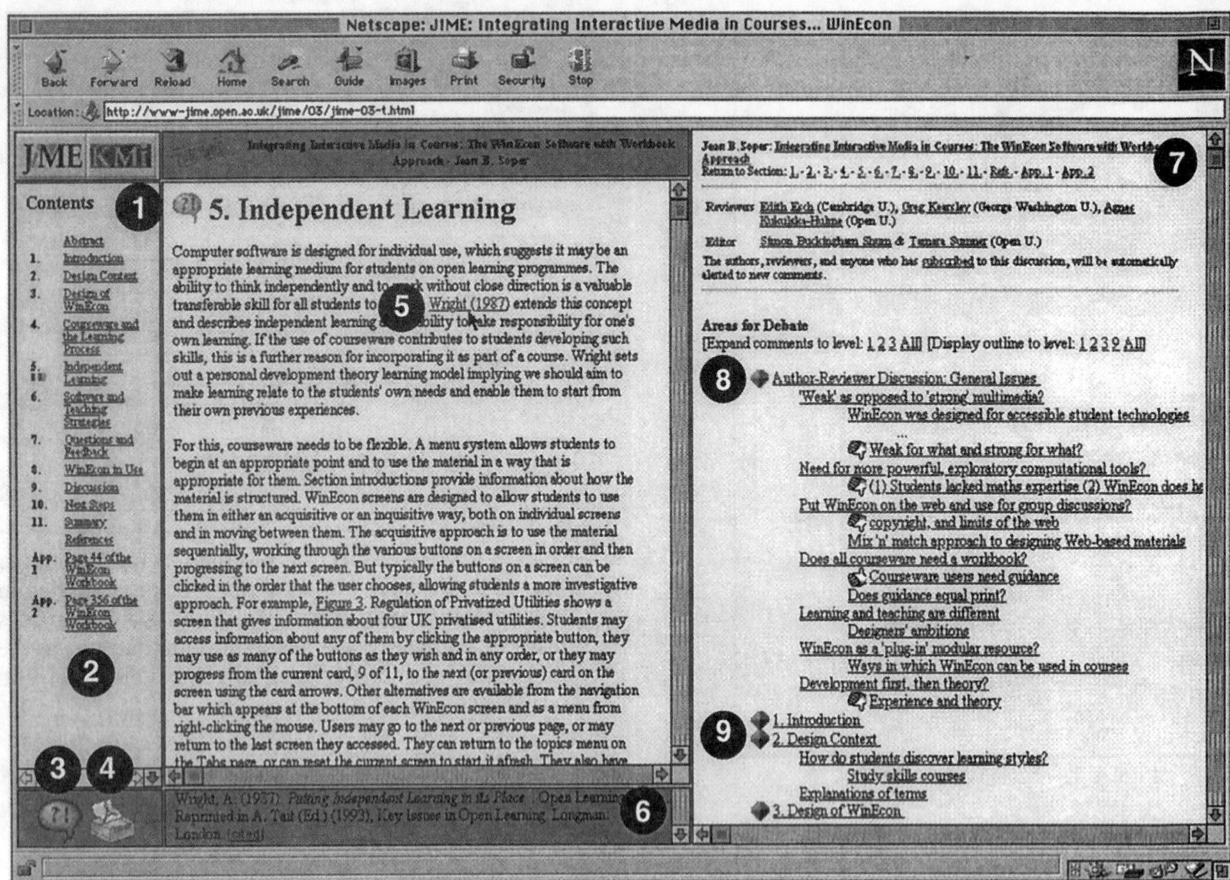

Figure 3: Output of the D3E toolkit from a source HTML article. On the left is the Article Window, on the right the Commentaries Window showing the top level outline view of discussion about the document. Key: [1] Comment icon embedded in each section heading: displays section-specific comments; [2] active contents list; [3] icon to display top level discussion outline, as shown on right; [4] icon to download Acrobat version; [5]citation automatically linked to reference in footnote window; [6] reverse link to citation; [7] links back into article; [8] general discussion heading defined in toolkit; [9] headings for section-specific comments. (Note that there are two versions of the user interface: one with tiled windows as shown, and one with overlapping windows for smaller displays).

This simple scenario illustrates how the D3E toolkit and document interface satisfy several of our design principles. First, with regard to *Principle A*, the discussion area is based on a very simple, and optional, classification scheme. All additions are classified as 'comments' by default unless 'agree' or 'disagree' are explicitly chosen. Second, with regard to *Principle B*, the toolkit embeds links in both the document and the discussion area for smoothly navigating between the two representations. The links in the document are section-specific, taking the user directly to the relevant area in the discussion space rather than to the top-level discussion page. Third, with regard to *Principle D*, the scenario demonstrates how the toolkit made constructing a site with rich linkages tractable for one person and without requiring detailed knowledge of HTML. For most documents, the publication process takes less then half an hour.

The tutor could have customized and refined the toolkit's output in a number of ways:

- The look and feel of the site can be customized by modifying the template files.
- The toolkit works in two passes which are controlled by the 'insert break markers' (pass 1) and 'split files' (pass 2) boxes shown in Figure 2. The first pass places D3E-specific tags into a copy of the source file. The second pass produces the final HTML files based on these tags. The user can stop between passes and tailor the D3E tags to modify the toolkit's output.
- The toolkit tries to automate tedious work such as automatically linking citations and references. However, there are occasionally 'potential' citations it cannot resolve. The toolkit presents the user with a list of these potential citations *and their surrounding context*. Thus, it automates what it can, and provides useful output for the user to take over when it can't.

This scenario also shows *Principle C*: the work practices of distance learning students has been redesigned to emphasise collaborative critiquing rather than individual analysis. We'll now illustrate Principle C in two scholarly contexts—an e-journal and a new form of conference.

CASE 1: JIME

We have been using D3E to publish an e-journal, "The Journal of Interactive Media In Education" (JIME). JIME is targeted at researchers and practitioners in educational technology, both in school and workplace settings. JIME has been in operation for one year and is available free of charge at [14]. Besides being a forum for work in educational technology, JIME was founded with two additional goals. First, rather than simply reading about interactive media, we wanted readers to directly experience the systems being described. Second, we wanted to foster discussions between participants from diverse backgrounds and geographic locations. We now go back in time, before the toolkit existed, and describe its co-evolution with new work practices as we tried to realise these goals.

Creating a Seed

We began by creating the D3E document interface, and decided to use the output from the review process to create an initial discussion seed. Reviewing was done in the traditional manner by independent reviewers. We then combined the reviews and entered them into the discussion space to create an initial discussion seed.

We constructed the first site, containing a single article ([8]) and its discussion space, from scratch by authoring HTML files. This article contained two embedded demonstrations that were constructed by the authors using Director™ and Shockwave™. We applied Principle B and embedded the demonstration directly in the document so that readers did not have to download a demonstration and 'run it' separately from the document (see Figure 4).

We announced this site to a limited audience (the JIME editorial board and participants of the London 1996 HCI conference) and the site received 20-30 visits a day during the open review trial period (September 1996). The purpose of the limited announcement and trial period was to gain feedback on our document interface and give us experience with the publishing process, which we could improve on before scaling up our efforts.

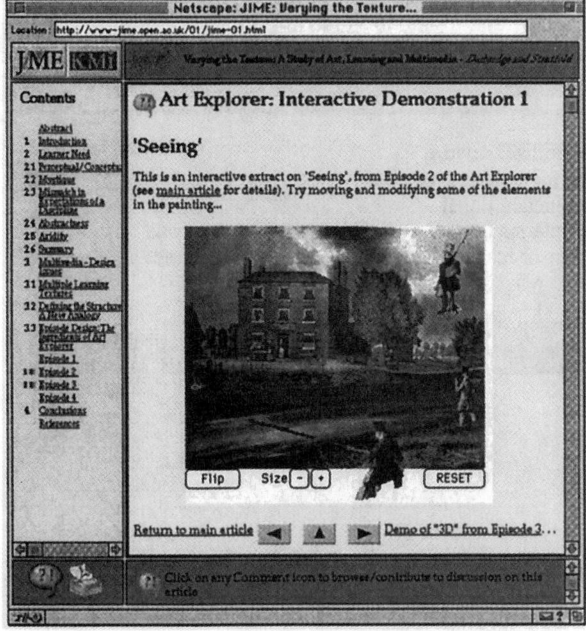

Figure 4. The interactive demonstration is embedded directly into the document.

Analyses of the log files during the trial indicated that the document interface was promising; readers were using the embedded demonstrations and viewing the associated commentary. Several participants contributed to the review debate. We viewed this as positive support for design *Principle B*, because other e-journals with demonstrations and commentary that do not provide tight integration have reported little use of either facility [18].

Eliminating Extra Work

Unfortunately, the production process had been quite demanding – requiring several days to produce the document interface (i.e., the navigation and discourse features shown in Figure 3) and to verify that the results behaved correctly. This did not include work associated with the interactive demonstrations. Clearly, this amount of per-article effort was not sustainable; tool support for the process was needed to make the publishing of the journal tractable for a small team (three people working part time). We refined the initial document interface and constructed the first version of the D3E Publisher's toolkit (containing only the Article form shown in Figure 1).

For the next two submissions, we used the toolkit to create a hidden web site and modified the review process. Reviewers entered their comments directly into the discussion area at the hidden site and authors were encouraged to participate. This change promoted a more dynamic debate, as reviewers and authors responded to each others' comments. Figure 5 shows part of a review where the key ideas of one submission were debated.

Submissions were open for public review for a one month period. While readers can add comments after this period, as a stated policy, only comments made during the period will be taken into account when producing change requirements. It is too early to be sure, but we appear to get more reader contributions during the open review period than afterwards. Knowing your comment can affect the published article may provide incentive to contribute.

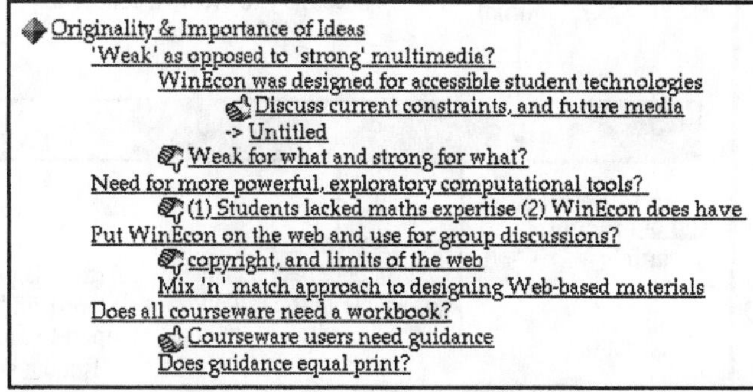

Figure 5. Outline of a thread in a review debate. 'Originality and Importance of Ideas' is a standard discussion category. Five of the contributions are from reviewers, five are from the author, one is from the editor, and two are from readers.

New Roles and Division of Labour

Figure 6 illustrates the current article lifecycle in JIME. This lifecycle changes the traditional roles and division of labour in the journal review process. The entire process is structured to promote discussion between participants, and to generate an initial discussion seed prior to the article becoming available to the public. The editor's roel is to facilitate and moderate the discussion, and manage the discussion space. As usual, editors generate change requests for authors. In JIME, these change requests take the form of hypertext accept/reject letters with embedded links back to the relevant parts of the discussion space.

At a superficial level, the publisher's role looks similar to paper-based publishing models; i.e., the publisher is marking up and making available the document. However, now the publisher creates two versions – the initial review site and the published site. This additional labour would not be feasible without a toolkit to automate most of the production process. The toolkit has dramatically reduced the time and effort to mark-up articles by several orders of magnitude: a process that took days by hand can now be done in minutes. In several cases, this aspect of the publisher's role has been assumed by the editor, and even by authors themselves wanting to fine tune the presentation of their work.

In the case of JIME, we believe a publisher role is still important even though most of the production process is automated or assumed by other participants. Many authors do not have the time or technical expertise to publish their interactive demonstrations on the web; journals wanting such components must be willing to provide technical assistance. To do so, publishers need new skills and knowledge concerning multimedia production and web publishing tools. In effect, publishers become a form of domain-specific 'translator' [19], working with authors to help them present their work effectively using interactive media. To assist in this process, we are also enriching D3E with tools to support the publishing of interactive components. One such tool, based on [22], enables authors to create narrated slide shows which can be used to give readers a guided tour through a typical use scenario.

CASE 2: LEARNING.ORG

The learning.org conference was hosted by the Office for Technology Development at the Open University. The goal of the conference was to consider the implications for United Kingdom (UK) universities of the Dearing Report recommendations [6]. Most participants were senior management staff with responsibility for the strategic direction and use of information technology within their university. Others were members of the committee that drafted the Dearing Report. Altogether, there were about thirty-five participants dispersed throughout the UK.

The Office for Technology Development wanted to use the web to enhance the value of the conference by enabling participants to make the best use of their limited face-to-face meeting time. A multi-site, three stage event with the following structure was conceived:

- Stage 1: A half day opening plenary with three speakers.
- Stage 2: Two weeks of discussion on issues raised in the plenary and in the Dearing Report.
- Stage 3: A one day meeting organised as discussion sessions around topics emerging from the previous two stages and closing plenary.

Figure 7 shows how this three stage event was carried out using a range of communication technologies. The opening plenary session consisted of a live webcast using KMi Stadium [22]. The three plenary speakers gave slide-supported talks, much as they would at any conference. Using Stadium, the talks were delivered to participants at their own universities. Using a standard web browser, participants were able to view the slides, hear the audio speech, and ask questions in an associated chat window (left side, Figure 7). As presenters switched slides, a textual marker such as "Slide 4" was inserted into the stream of comments in the chat window.

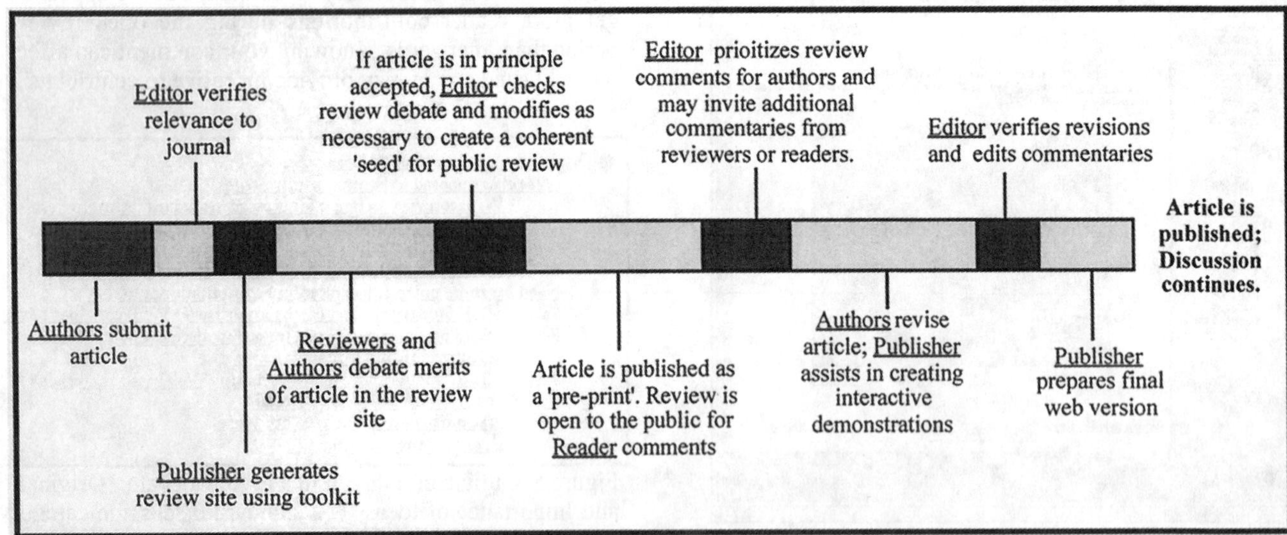

Figure 6. Lifecycle of an article under review in JIME.

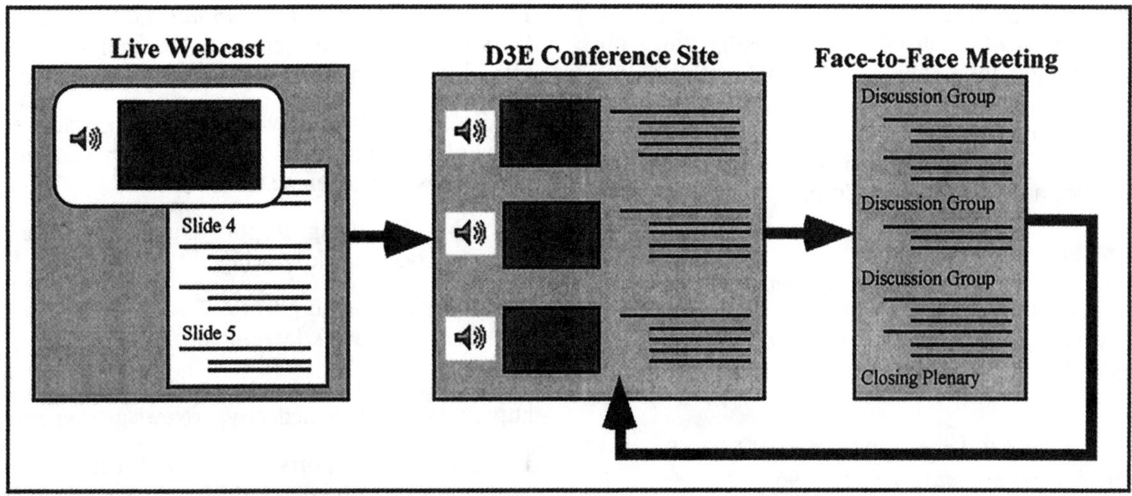

Figure 7. A new conference form: the structure of learning.org.

We used the output from the live webcast to create the initial seed for the D3E portion of the learning.org event – Stage 2. The documents published in D3E consisted of the speakers' Powerpoint™ presentations, the audio portions of their talk associated with each slide, and any comments from the chat area in the webcast (centre, Figure 7). We used the textual markers to determine the locality of comments from the webcast; i.e., comments made between the "Slide 4" and "Slide 5" markers are associated with slide 4. Slides from two of the speakers were not available until just before the webcast. Using the toolkit, we were able to publish the three slide documents and the seeded discussion space in just over a day.

Now, the face-to-face portion of the conference is able to take on a different role. Rather than focusing on delivering presentations, Stage 3 is devoted to active discussions on key topics. By supplementing these discussion groups with dedicated note-takers, the output from this stage is again, fed back into the D3E discussion space.

This process changed the roles of both the conference organisers and the participants. Participants are able to take on a more active role. In the plenaries, participants were raising and debating questions amongst themselves in the chat window *during* the talks. Rather than running out of time to discuss the issues raised (as often happens), there is plenty of opportunity to reflect on and refine the issues during the subsequent two week discussion period. The upcoming face-to-face meeting provides motivation for participants to continue to add to the ongoing debate.

Conversely, this model also requires new activities from conference organisers. Similar to JIME, with the help of the Publisher's toolkit, the production effort shifted from simply making documents available (whether papers or copies of slides), to making the discourse surrounding the documents available in an integrated interface. Our efforts were centred around quick bursts of live event, post-production activities. The goal during these bursts was to take discourse from one media form (i.e., the webcast or the face-to-face meeting) and transform it as quickly as possible to support the next stage.

CONCLUSIONS

In summary, we have described several scholarly contexts where we have used D3E to realise discourse-centred publishing practices. Using D3E, the effort behind the publishing process shifts: from making documents available, to supporting the generation and transformation of the discourse surrounding the documents. What often starts as fairly conventional document forms (e.g., a text document from a word processor converted to HTML, or a slide presentation) are progressively enriched as surrounding discourse is reified and embedded back into the documents themselves. Sometimes the discourse takes on alternate media forms such as interactive components or audio clips. The new publishing models were made possible by a combination of tool support and the redefining of participant roles. As part of this research, we have articulated four principles which we believe are useful for others considering new forms of electronic publishing and computer-mediated debate.

In [28], Veltman claims that 'recontextualising the parameters of quality" will be a key challenge facing the next generation of electronic media consumers and producers. Current publishing models emphasise document presentation in a final archival form, after lengthy and hidden deliberations. Using technology, we are considering alternate notions of quality that include making explicit other aspects of documents such as timeliness, history, and intellectual lineage. In these models, documents continually evolve to reflect the latest work, the latest event, and the reflections of others. The criteria for quality expand to include the richness and currency of the extra context. With this enriched context readily available and integrated into the document form, readers are in a better position to judge for themselves the work's relevance and quality.

This research raises many difficult questions which we can not yet answer. As future work, we will continue to build tools enabling radical process changes, to apply and refine our principles in new contexts, and to probe people's perceptions of the utility and desirability of these alternate conceptions of scholarly publishing.

ACKNOWLEDGEMENTS

Special thanks to Mike Wright and Malcolm Story for work on D3E, and John Domingue and John Rieman for their help with this paper. Java is a registered trademark of Sun Corp., Director and Shockwave are registered trademarks of Macromedia Corp., Powerpoint is a registered trademark of Microsoft Corp.

REFERENCES

1. Bellamy, R., "Designing Educational Technology: Computer-Mediated Change," in *Context and Consciousness: Activity Theory and Human–Computer Interaction*, B. Nardi, Ed., MIT Press, Cambridge, 1996, pp. 123-146.

2. Brown, J. S. and P. Duguid, "The Social Life of Documents," *First Monday,* Vol. 1, 1996, http://www.firstmonday.dk/issues/issue1/documents/

3. Buckingham Shum, S., "Analyzing the Usability of a Design Rationale Notation," in *Design Rationale: Concepts, Techniques, and Use*, T. P. Moran and J. M. Carroll, Ed., Lawrence Erlbaum, NJ, 1996, pp. 185-215.

4. Buckingham Shum, S. and N. Hammond, "Argumentation-Based Design Rationale: What Use at What Cost?," *International Journal of Human-Computer Studies,* Vol. 40, Iss. 4, pp. 603-652, 1994.

5. Buckingham Shum, S. and C. McKnight, "(Eds.) World Wide Web Usability: Special Issue, Int. J. Human-Computer Studies," Vol. 47 (1), Iss. pp. 1-222, 1997.

6. Dearing, "Higher Education in the Learning Society," http://www.leeds.ac.uk/educol/ncihe/, National Committee of Inquiry into Higher Education, UK, 1997.

7. DeRose, S. J., "Expanding the Notion of Links," *Proceedings of the ACM Hypertext'89 Conference*, Pittsburgh, PA (Nov.), 1989, pp. 249-257.

8. Durbridge, N. H. and M. P. Stratfold, "Varying the Texture: A Study of Art, Learning and Multimedia," *Journal of Interactive Media in Education,* 96 (1), http://www-jime.open.ac.uk/jime/01/jime-01.html, 1996.

9. Fischer, G., A. C. Lemke, R. McCall and A. Morch, "Making Argumentation Serve Design," *Human Computer Interaction,* Vol. 6, Iss. 3-4, pp. 393-419, 1991.

10. Fischer, G., R. McCall, J. Ostwald, B. Reeves and F. Shipman, "Seeding, Evolutionary Growth and Reseeding: Supporting the Incremental Development of Design Environments," *Human Factors in Computing Systems (CHI '94)*, Boston, MA, 1994, pp. 292-298.

11. Grudin, J., "Evaluating Opportunities for Design Capture," in *Design Rationale: Concepts, Techniques, and Use*, T. P. Moran and J. M. Carroll, Ed., Lawrence Erlbaum Associates, Hillsdale, NJ, 1996, pp. 453-470.

12. JAIR, *Journal of Artificial Intelligence Research,* Morgan Kaufmann Publishers, http://www.cs.washington.edu/research/jair/home.html.

13. JILT, *Journal of Information, Law and Technology*, University of Warwick and Strathclyde University, http://jilt.law.strath.ac.uk/jilt/issue/1997_2/default.htm.

14. JIME, "An Interactive Journal for Interactive Media," *Journal of Interactive Media in Education,* 1996, http://www-jime.open.ac.uk/

15. KMi, "Dearing Report Discussion Site," 1997, http://kmi.open.ac.uk/Dearing/

16. KMi, "learning.org," 1997, http://kmi.open.ac.uk/learning.org

17. LaLiberte, D., "HyperNews," 1995, http://union.ncsa.uiuc.edu/HyperNews/get/hypernews.html

18. Libtech, "Reports from the Electronic Libraries Programme," *Conference on UK Electronic Journals on the Internet*, University of Hertfordshire (Sept. 5), 1996.

19. Mackay, W., "Patterns of Sharing of Customizable Software," *CSCW'90: Conference on Computer-Supported Cooperative Work*, Los Angeles, CA, 1990, pp. 209-221.

20. McKerlie, D. and A. MacLean, "Reasoning with Design Rationale: Practical Experience with Design Space Analysis," *Design Studies,* Vol. 15, Iss. 2, pp. 214-226, 1994.

21. O'Day, V., D. Bobrow and M. Shirley, "The Social-Technical Design Circle," *Conference on Computer Supported Cooperative Work (CSCW '96)*, Boston (Nov. 16-20), 1996, pp. 160-169.

22. Scott, P. and M. Eisenstadt, "Stadium: Experiments in Real Telepresence," in *The Knowledge Web*, M. Eisenstadt and T. Vincent, Ed., Kogan Page, London, 1998.

23. Shipman, F. M. and R. McCall, "Supporting Knowledge-Base Evolution with Incremental Formalization," *Human Factors in Computing Systems (CHI '94)*, Boston, MA (April 24-28), 1994, pp. 285-291.

24. Sumner, T. and J. Taylor, "New Media, New Practices: Experiences in Open Learning Course Design," *In Human Factors in Computing Systems (CHI '98)*, Los Angeles (April 18-23), 1998.

25. Sumner, T. R., N. Bonnardel and B. Kallak Harstad, "The Cognitive Ergonomics of Knowledge-Based Design Support Systems," *Human Factors in Computing Systems (CHI '97)*, Atlanta, (March 22-27), 1997, pp. 83-90.

26. Terveen, L., P. Selfridge and M. D. Long, "From "Folklore" to "Living Design Memory"," *Conference on Human Factors in Computing (Interact '93 and CHI '93)*, Amsterdam (24-29 April), 1993, pp. 15-22.

27. Turoff, M., U. Rao and S. R. Hiltz, "Collaborative Hypertext in Computer-Mediated Communications," *Proceedings of the 24th Hawaii International Conference on System Sciences, Volume IV*, 1991, pp. 357-366.

28. Veltman, K., "Frontiers in Electronic Media," *interactions,* Vol. 4, Iss. 4, pp. 32-64, 1997.

The Effects of Distance in Local versus Remote Human-Computer Interaction

Youngme Moon
Massachusetts Institute of Technology
Room 14E-303
Cambridge, MA 02139-4307
+1 617 253 4921
ymoon@mit.edu

ABSTRACT

This study investigates the effects of distance on user attitudes and behavior in long-distance (networked) human-computer interaction. Two laboratory experiments are presented. In the first experiment (*N*=123), users are interviewed by a computer that they believe is either located in the same room, located a few miles away, or located a few thousand miles away. Results indicate that the greater the perceived distance, the greater the tendency to distort responses (i.e., give dishonest answers) in order to present oneself in a positive light. In the second experiment (*N*=23), the effects of distance in a persuasion situation are investigated. Results indicate that persuasion is significantly more likely to occur when the computer is perceived as being proximate, as opposed to distant. Implications for long-distance human-computer interaction are discussed.

Keywords

Distance, Networking, Proximity, Interviews, Data Collection, Remote, Local, Internet, World Wide Web, Persuasion, Advertising, Social Psychology

INTRODUCTION

Human-computer interaction is often conceptualized as a local phenomenon. Indeed, the traditional model of use in HCI studies involves a user sharing the same physical location as the computer. However, the growth in internet and world wide web activity has prompted a shift in this conceptualization: Human-computer interaction is increasingly becoming a long-distance phenomenon; that is, users often find themselves interacting with a computer that is located thousands of miles away.

This study was designed to investigate whether perceptions of geographical distance between the user and the computer influence user attitudes and behavior in human-computer interaction. Two laboratory experiments are presented below. The first experiment investigates distance effects in a computer-interviewing situation; the second experiment investigates distance effects in a persuasion situation.

THE EFFECTS OF PERCEIVED DISTANCE ON HONEST RESPONDING IN AN INTERVIEW SITUATION

It has become increasingly common for organizations to use computer networks as a convenient means of collecting data from large numbers of widely-scattered respondents. Indeed, many healthcare providers have begun to collect medical information from their patients via computer; large banking institutions routinely encourage customers to submit financial data via computer; and many companies have altered their job interview process such that applicants are required to complete a job application on the World Wide Web. Moreover, given the enhanced programming capabilities offered by internet-based software and the growing ease with which data can be submitted and collected via a network browser, this trend of collecting information – often, highly sensitive information – via computer networks seems unlikely to reverse itself anytime soon.

When an individual is interviewed via computer, the computer collecting the information may be located right in front of the respondent (in the non-networked situation), or it may be located literally thousands of miles away (in the networked situation). Does the physical distance between the respondent and the data-collecting computer affect response tendencies? The first experiment was designed to address this question.

EXPERIMENT 1

A between-subjects experiment with 3 conditions (distance: non-networked, near, far) was conducted.

Participants

Participants were 123 undergraduate students from a small, liberal arts university located in Santa Clara, California. All participants were given course credit for their participation in the study. Random assignment was used to assign subjects to conditions.

Procedure

Each participant was tested individually in a small (8' x 10') room containing a desk, a chair, and a computer.

Upon arrival to the laboratory, participants were told that the university was participating in a nationwide survey about the attitudes and personal characteristics of college students. Participants were told that the survey was being conducted by a national job recruitment (or "head-hunting") firm that was interested in determining the employability of graduating college students nationwide. Participants were also told that their answers to the survey were completely confidential, and that their anonymity would be protected at all times.

Participants were then told that the survey was to be administered via computer. The experimenter proceeded to demonstrate how the computer worked.

After delivering the instructions, the experimenter stayed in the room while the participant went through two practice items. When the experimenter was confident that the participant was comfortable using the computer, the experimenter left the room. The participant was left to complete a survey instrument, the Balanced Inventory of Desirable Responding – Version 6 [12, 13]. The BIDR is one of the most well-accepted measures of response distortion in the survey literature [14]. It consists of 40 items, stated as propositions.[1] Participants rated their agreement with each item on a seven-point scale. In addition, the computer was programmed such that only one survey item was presented to the participant at a time. Participants could not backtrack; after receiving a response, the computer was programmed to move on to the next item without offering the participant the opportunity to return to previous items. When the participant was finished, he/she exited the room and informed the experimenter that he/she was done.

The entire experiment took subjects approximately 20-30 minutes.

Manipulation of Distance

There were three distance conditions: non-networked, near and far. Participants in the non-networked condition were told by the experimenter that the survey items were originating from the computer in front of them. Participants in the near condition were told that the survey items were originating from a computer in the city of San Jose, California, several miles away. Participants in the far condition were told that the survey items were originating from a computer located in the city of Boston, Massachusetts, several thousand miles away. Participants were also told that their responses were being collected by the non-networked, San Jose, or Boston computers, respectively.

In addition, participants in the two networked conditions – the near and the far conditions – were repeatedly told that they were communicating with a "networked" computer. For subjects in the non-networked condition, the word "networked" was completely omitted from the experimenter's script.

Finally, in the non-networked condition, the survey window on the computer screen was not labeled. In the near condition, the computer screen had the words, "connection 35.167.34.467 San Jose" at the top of the survey window. In the far condition, the computer screen had the words, "connection 35.167.34.467 Boston" at the top of the survey window. This interface difference was designed to reinforce the perception, in the two networked conditions, that the participant was networked to a computer in another location.

In reality, all survey data was collected by the computer located in the same room as the participant. This computer was not actually networked; participants in the networked conditions were simply led to believe that the computer was networked. Furthermore, all participants were given identical information about the organization that was supposedly sponsoring the survey. This information did not specify the physical location of the organization's headquarters.

During post-experimental debriefs, participants were explicitly asked if they recalled the location of the computer collecting the data. All participants responded to this question correctly.

Measures

In survey research, socially desirable responding is defined as the tendency to give inaccurate responses that make oneself look good [12, 13]. The BIDR yields two scales that represent two distinct constructs associated with social desirability: Impression Management (IM) and Self-Deceptive Enhancement (SDE). IM represents the deliberate tendency to over-report desirable behaviors and under-report undesirable ones. It thus provides a direct measure of deliberate response distortion, or conscious deception (i.e., dishonesty) [12, 13]. SDE, on the other hand, is designed to measure overconfidence in one's judgments and rationality. In other words, despite the fact that SDE responses may be favorably biased, they are presumed to be honestly held self-descriptions. Because previous research [see 13] has supported the conceptual distinction between the two constructs, the two scales were analyzed as distinct criterion variables.

Both the IM and SDE scales were calculated using Paulhus's (1991) dichotomous scoring method, in which one point is given for each extreme response (in this case, 6 or 7, after reversing the negatively keyed items). High scores were thus attained only by those subjects who gave

[1] The BIDR includes statements such as, "I sometimes tell lies if I have to," "I sometimes try to get even, rather than forgive and forget," and "I never take things that don't belong to me."

exaggeratedly desirable responses. Scores on both scales had a possible range of 0-20.

Results

All analyses were based on a simple ANOVA model. In the results below, P-values reflect two-tailed significance tests.

Impression Management (IM)

With respect to the IM scale of the BIDR, an analysis of variance revealed a significant main effect for distance, $F(2, 120) = 5.27$, $p < .01$, such that mean IM scores were highest in the far condition, and lowest in the non-networked condition (see Figure 1 for comparison of means). In other words, the results showed that increased distance had a significant *negative* effect on honest responding: *the greater the distance, the greater the tendency to consciously distort responses.*

Figure 1.

Impression Management as a function of Distance

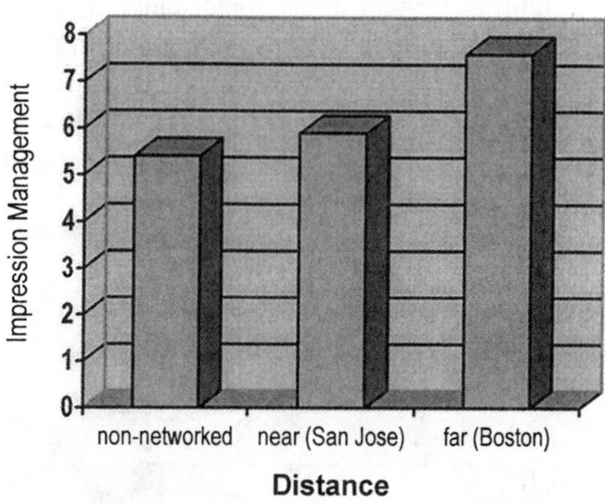

Self-Deceptive Enhancement (SDE)

With respect to the SDE scale of the BIDR, an analysis of variance revealed no effect for distance, $F(2, 120) = .01$, $p < .99$. In other words, distance had *no* effect on the tendency to be overconfident about one's abilities and judgments.

THE EFFECTS OF PERCEIVED DISTANCE ON PERSUASION

The results from Experiment 1 strongly support the idea that increased physical distance between a respondent and a computer interviewer results in an enhanced tendency to engage in response distortion, i.e., to give dishonest responses. Experiment 2 was designed to investigate the effects of physical distance in a different context.

A large proportion of long-distance computer communication is comprised of persuasive messages, either in the form of interpersonal messages or commercial advertising. Does perceived distance influence the extent to which users are persuaded by these messages?

EXPERIMENT 2

A between-subjects experiment with 2 conditions (distance: near, far) was conducted.

Participants

Participants were 23 undergraduates. All participants were given course credit for their participation in the study. Random assignment was used to assign participants to conditions. Each participant was tested individually.

Procedure

Upon arrival to the laboratory, participants were asked to complete the Desert Survival Problem [DSP; 2] using pencil and paper. The DSP is a problem-solving task that has been used in a variety of studies involving interpersonal interaction. It asks participants to rank a series of items (in this case, 12 items), according to their perceived importance in a desert survival situation.

After finishing this initial ranking, participants were taken into another room containing a terminal. The experimenter explained that the participant would have the opportunity to communicate with a networked computer about the ranking of the 12 desert survival items. This communication was to occur via computer network. In addition, participants were told that after completing the interaction with the networked computer, they would have the opportunity to change their initial ranking.

At this point, the computer set-up was explained to the participants. Participants were shown how to enter their initial rankings into the terminal, and send that information to the networked computer. The terminal then displayed another set of rankings, which the experimenter explained was the networked computer's suggested ranking of the 12 items.

The experimenter explained that there would be an opportunity to discuss each item in the order listed. For each item, the networked computer would give the participant a message regarding the ranking of that item. Participants could then respond by typing comments into a window on the terminal. When participants were ready to proceed to the next item, they were to simply click on the "next" button.

After explaining the instructions, the experimenter left the room. At this point, participant were left alone to exchange information with the networked computer about each of the 12 desert survival items.

After the interaction was complete, participants were taken into another room and given an opportunity to change their initial ranking of the 12 items. Finally, participants were given a questionnaire to fill out.

Upon completing the questionnaire, participants were debriefed, thanked, and asked not to discuss the experiment with anyone else.

Measures

In order to ensure experimental control, all of the messages from the networked computer were pre-programmed. For each item, two messages were created. The first message advised participants to rank the item lower than they had ranked it; the second message advised participants to rank the item higher. Participants received whichever message was appropriate, depending on their ranking relative to the networked computer's suggested ranking. For example, if a participants ranked an item "4" and the networked computer suggested the same item be ranked "10," the participant received the message advocating that the item be ranked lower.

Finally, the networked computer's suggested ranking was always based on the participant's initial ranking. In other words, whichever item the participant ranked as "1" was always ranked as "4" by the networked computer; whichever item the participant ranked as "2" was always ranked as "7" by the other individual, and so on. Thus, for all participants, the other individual's suggested ranking was the same distance away from the participant's initial ranking.

The Manipulation of Distance

There were two distance conditions: near and far. Participants in the near condition were told by the experimenter that the networked computer was located several miles away. Participants in the far condition were told that the networked computer was located several thousand miles away.

In addition, the window on the computer screen was labeled according to condition. In the near condition, the computer screen had the words, "35.167.34.467 connection established... 2.723 miles" at the top of the window. In the far condition, the computer screen had the words, "35.167.34.467 connection established... 2723 miles" at the top of the window.

In reality, the computer used in this experiment was not networked.

In the post-experimental questionnaire, participants were explicitly asked if they recalled approximately how far away the networked computer was located. All participants responded to this question correctly.

Measures

Persuasion

For all participants, the networked computer's suggested ranking was always the same distance away from the participant's initial ranking. However, at the end of the interaction, participants were given the opportunity to change their initial ranking. The amount of persuasion was measured as the distance between the networked computer's suggested ranking and the participant's final ranking. This was operationalized as follows: For each item, the absolute value of the difference between the participant's final ranking and the networked computer's suggested ranking was calculated. These values were summed. Lower values thus indicated more persuasion; higher values indicated less persuasion.

The other dependent variables were based on items from the paper-and-pencil questionnaire. Using these items, an *Information Quality* index was constructed, by averaging the following items: "How much did you trust the information provided by the other individual?," "How helpful was the information?," "How relevant was the information?," and "How insightful was the information?" (Cronbach's alpha = .86). Because the items in the indices were averaged, the possible range for this index was from 1 to 10.

Results

All analyses were based on a simple ANOVA model. In the results below, P-values reflect two-tailed significance tests.

Persuasion

With respect to the Persuasion measure, the analysis revealed a significant main effect for distance, $F(1, 21) = 5.40$, $p < .05$, such that mean scores were lower in the near condition compared to the far condition. Because higher scores represent less persuasion, the results indicate that *the greater the distance, the less persuasion occurred* (see Figure 2 for comparison of means).

Figure 2.
Persuasion as a function of Distance

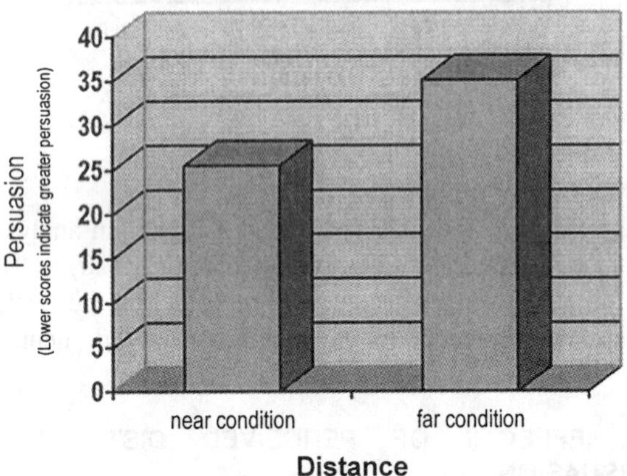

Information Quality

With respect to the Information Quality measure, the analysis revealed a significant main effect for distance, $F(1, 21) = 8.63$, $p < .01$, such that mean scores were higher in the near condition compared to the far condition. Because higher scores represent higher Information Quality ratings, the results indicate that the *users in the near condition rated the information as being of higher quality, compared to users in the far condition* (see Figure 3 for comparison of means).

Figure 3.
Information Quality as a function of Distance

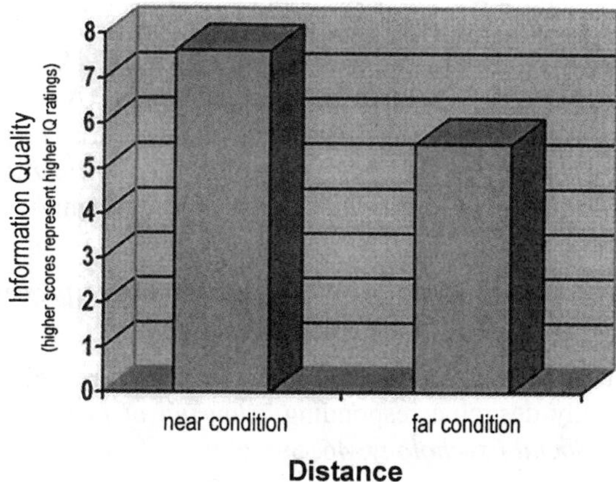

IMPLICATIONS

This study investigated the effects of physical distance on user attitudes and behavior in human-computer interaction. Based on the results from the two experiments, two conclusions can be drawn.

First, the results strongly support the idea that increased physical distance between a respondent and a computer interviewer results in enhanced response distortion. Indeed, in Experiment 1, users were significantly more likely to give deceptive answers to the distant computer compared to the proximate one.

Second, the results suggest that perceived physical distance has a significant effect on persuasion. In Experiment 2, users in the "near" condition were significantly more likely to change their ranking of the desert survival items to conform to the computer's suggestions, compared to users in the "far" condition. In addition, increased distance was negatively associated with perceptions of information quality.

These results have numerous implications, both theoretical and practical. From a theoretical standpoint, the results lend support to the theory that people respond socially to computers [15]. A series of recent studies have demonstrated that people treat computers as if they are social actors. For example, previous studies have found that people respond to computer personalities in the same way that they respond to human personalities [4, 8, 9]; that people apply gender stereotypes to computers [7]; that people engage in "polite" behavior toward computers [10, 15] and that people form team affiliations with computers [6]. All of these studies provide evidence that social phenomena – attitudes and behaviors that are traditionally thought of as being exclusively interpersonal – are also found in human-computer interaction.

Indeed, this theory provides an explanation for the results obtained in the two experiments presented above. In interpersonal interaction, people exhibit geographical biases on a regular basis – people are much more likely to confide in, be persuaded by, and be attracted to, other people they believe share their geographical background [e.g., 1, 3, 5, 11, 16]. A common example of this can be seen in the instant "bonding" that takes place between tourists in a foreign country who discover that they are from the same hometown.

In the two experiments above, users exhibited these same geographical biases in both an computer-based interview situation and a computer-based persuasion situation.

There are several important design implications of these results. One of the key design implications is that, in a computer-interviewing situation, there are significant trade-offs associated with remote, computerized data collection. No doubt, long-distance computer networks offer the ability to collect data efficiently and conveniently over great physical distances. However, these convenience benefits must be weighed against the likelihood that responses will be less honest as the physical distance between the respondent and the data-gathering computer increases. This may be of particular concern in those situations in which respondents have a distinct incentive to present a positive image, such as job applications, selection tests, etc.

However, it is important to note that it is often the case that users do not know the location of the computer to which they are connected. In this case, it is likely that there are particular variables that affect a user's *perception* of physical distance. For example, feedback latency refers to the amount of time it takes for a computer to respond to a user's input. And whereas feedback latency can often be completely unrelated to actual physical distance (it is more often related to factors such as connection speed or computer processing speed), it may be strongly related to a user's *perception* of physical distance. Other variables affecting perceptions of physical distance might include content-related variables, such as word choice, slang, references to local events and places, etc. These are all variables that are easily manipulable from a design standpoint.

The same can be said for persuasive messages that are communicated via remote networks. In this situation, variables affecting the user's perception of physical distance are likely to influence whether or not the user is persuaded by the message. Again, these variables can include content-related factors, such as verbiage, local references, etc. However, these variables can also include such factors as the domain name of the computer. For example, if an individual is connected to a computer with the domain name of "stanford.edu," it is not unlikely that he/she will assume that computer is physically located in Stanford, California, even though this may not be the case.

REFERENCES

1. Kerckhoff, A. C. (1974). The social context of interpersonal attraction. In T. L. Huston (Ed.), *Foundations of interpersonal attraction.* New York: Academic Press.
2. Lafferty, J. C., Eady, P. M, & Elmers, J. . (1974). *The desert survival problem.* Plymouth, Michigan: Experimental Learning Methods.
3. Latane, B. (1981). The psychology of social impact. *American Psychologist, 36,* 343-356.
4. Moon, Y., & Nass, C. I. (1996) How "real" are computer personalities? Psychological responses to personality types in human-computer interaction. *Communication Research, 23,* 651-674.
5. Nahemow, L., & Lawton, M. P. (1975). Similarity and propinquity in friendship formation. *Journal of Personality and Social Psychology, 32,* 205-213.
6. Nass, C. I., Fogg, B. J., & Moon, Y. (1996). Can computers be teammates? Affiliation and social identity effects in human-computer interaction. *International Journal of Human-Computer Studies, 45,* 669-678.
7. Nass, C. I., Moon, Y., & Green, N. (1997). Are computers gender-neutral? Gender stereotypic responses to computers. *Journal of Applied Social Psychology, 27,* 864-876.
8. Nass, C. I., Moon, Y., Fogg, B. J., Reeves, B., & Dryer, D. C. (1995). Can computer personalities be human personalities? *International Journal of Human-Computer Studies, 43,* 223-239.
9. Nass, C. I., Moon, Y., Fogg, B. J., Reeves, B., & Dryer, D. C. (1995). Human-computer interaction as interpersonal interaction. *Proceedings of the Computer-Human Interaction (CHI) '95 Conference,* Denver, CO.
10. Nass, C. I., Moon, Y., Morkes, J., Kim, E. Y., & Fogg, B. J. (1997). Computers are social actors: A review of current research. In Batya Friedman (Ed.), *Human Values and the Design of Computer Technology* (pp. 137-163). Stanford, CA: CSLI/Cambridge University Press.
11. Newcomb, T. M. (1961). *The acquaintance process.* New York: Holt, Rinehart, and Winston.
12. Paulhus, D. L. (1984). Two-component models of socially desirable responding. *Journal of Personality and Social Psychology, 46,* 598-609.
13. Paulhus, D. L. (1991). Measurement and control of response bias. In J. P. Robinson, P. R. Shaver, & L. S. Wrightman (Eds.), *Measures of Personality and Social Psychological Attitudes, Volume 1* (pp. 17-59). San Diego: Academic Press.
14. Paulhus, D. L., & Reid, D. (1991). Enhancement and denial in socially desirable responding. *Journal of Personality and Social Psychology, 60,* 307-317.
15. Reeves, B., & Nass, C. I. (1996). *The media equation.* Stanford, CA: Cambridge University Press/CSLI.
16. Segal, M. W. (1974). Alphabet and attraction: An unobtrusive measure of the effect of propinquity in a field setting. *Journal of Personality and Social Psychology, 30,* 654-657.

Design Evolution in a Multimedia Tutorial on User-Centered Design

Tom Carey* **Slade Mitchell**** **Dan Peerenboom*** **Mary Lytwyn**[1]

*HCI + TeleLearning Lab
University of Waterloo
Waterloo, Canada
519-885-1211 x6054
tcarey@watserv1.uwaterloo.ca

**Interactive Software Solutions
16 Lambert Crescent
Guelph, Canada
519-763-8642
smitchel@wat.hookup.net

[1] Bank of Montreal
245 Consumers Rd
Willowdale, Canada
416-224-6189
mlytwyn@ibm.net

ABSTRACT

New modes of lifelong learning in the workplace require interface designs which support new contexts for learning. We describe here a workplace learning support system for instruction in User-centered Design [UCD]. The design evolution of this system illustrates how the "why, where, when and with whom" of use affects the "what and how" of the interaction design. The tutorial system includes a multimedia Case Study, a Methods Tour of UCD techniques, and a Test Drive in which users take simulated roles in a UCD project. This paper describes how the content and features were adapted as the target audience evolved from individual learners in a career curriculum to collaborative groups within a project team.

Keywords: Training, HCI education, user-centered design, multimedia, interaction design

WHAT'S INTERESTING ABOUT THIS SYSTEM

The Learning About User-Centered Design tutorial is a multimedia system to introduce the concepts and methods of user-centered design. It went into use at the Bank of Montreal in Toronto in Fall 1997. The system contains 3 main units:

- an authentic Case Study, in which a pilot team which used UCD to develop an interactive system shares that experience
- a Methods Tour, which provides an overview and practical help for common methods in UCD
- a Test Drive, in which learners play simulated roles in a design project to experience UCD methods.

Figure 1 shows sample screens from each unit.

This paper traces the initial design evolution of the tutorial. While the UCD content and the training need remained the same throughout the project, there was a major reorientation when early prototypes were shown to user focus groups. The subsequent shift in target usage had impacts on many aspects of the interface design, and this paper will demonstrate how an awareness of these contexts of use is critical in determining individual interface features.

In addition to this general issue, the UCD tutorial system will be of interest to educators involved with workplace training, because it illustrates how new training contexts can be addressed with engaging interaction designs. The UCD tutorial system will also be of interest to individual practitioners seeking to disseminate HCI expertise within their organizations, as well as to HCI educators and trainers.

CHANGING CONTEXTS FOR LEARNING ABOUT UCD

The UCD tutorial was originally conceived as a tool for individuals who were seeking to acquire knowledge about UCD methods, as part of their personal career development or as part of a formal curriculum. The project sponsors and Bank representatives on the project team were technical professionals in the information technology development area. They had built their own knowledge of HCI from personal motivation, demonstrated the benefits through involvement in a pilot project, and wanted to use this experience to improve the resources available internally to support learning about UCD.

In the short term, the objective was to raise awareness of UCD methods and their impacts; in the long term, the objective was to link the initial product into an electronic performance support system for HCI. The Case Study success story was intended to provide the credibility needed to win acceptance of UCD. The Methods Tour was intended to make the point that deliberate choices and careful use of methods was an important component of project success. The Test Drive was seen as a mechanism for self-assessment.

A wide variety of potential users were exposed to an early prototype of the UCD tutorial concept, and their views reoriented our ideas about the target audience and how they would use the system. While the overall reactions were favorable, the focus group users were concerned that the individual motivation for self-improvement was not a sufficiently strong trigger for many of the users who could be acquiring the knowledge about UCD. The tutorial itself looked engaging, but getting people into it would be a challenge. This was particularly true for user representatives on UCD teams, their managers, and the development manager. As one of the user managers in the case study recalls in a video vignette:

"I had to continually justify why my sales reps were spending so much time in the office contributing to the design. There's no doubt in my mind that this was necessary, but from outside the process it appeared that they should have been doing more selling and less designing".

The most insightful comments for addressing this need came from a project manager who requested that the system be made available for his teams to work through at an early stage in a new project. The need to apply UCD in the imminent project would increase motivation, and conversely the opportunity to immediately apply the information would reinforce the knowledge and make it concrete.

We related this insight to research studies which have identified four distinct contexts for professionals learning in the workplace [5]:

- task-oriented, where learning is required to address immediate problems in the work at hand.
- project-oriented, where the knowledge requirements for a new project drive the learning but there is more time for reflection than in task-based contexts.
- curriculum-oriented, where learning is concerned with accreditation and has value for future assignment in new roles (e.g., promotions).
- oriented around a professional community, which can include meta issues such as the epistemology of a discipline, its relationships with related bodies of knowledge, and professional ethics.

After the focus group sessions, we redesigned the UCD tutorial system primarily for learning contexts with a project orientation and secondarily for a curriculum orientation. As the rest of the paper will now show, this seemingly small change in the context of use had substantial impacts on the resulting product. In the concluding section we outline how the other contexts of professional learning will be addressed as the UCD tutorial system evolves further.

DESIGN CHANGES FOR COLLABORATIVE USE

The original scenarios from which we designed early curriculum-oriented mockups were based around individual users who would typically access the tutorial in a Learning Center within the Bank or at home on their own time. In the revised context where the target use was in conjunction with a project team, we had the option of having learners work in collaborative groups. Use of the tutorial by small groups within the project team had the potential disadvantages of different learning styles and background knowledge, but the potential advantages of group support and group interaction.
Other research studies have illustrated the value of group use of multimedia learning support systems [3; 7]. Our own tests with small groups confirmed that collaborative use had the following benefits:

- the group's collective understanding of how to use the interface meant there was less elapsed time spent in learning about the tutorial interface itself
- by assigning learners to groups with a mix of roles from the UCD team - users, designers, developers, support staff - the different perspectives on the team became apparent during this initial tutorial
- group interactions provided a social environment and stimulated engagement with the tutorial content.

In addition, the project context allowed us to include a 'deliverable' - a memo back to the project manager, which each group produces as a report on their use of the tutorial and a position paper on how UCD could be applied in their own team project.

In the revised scenario of use, project managers introduce the UCD tutorial during an initial project team meeting and assign team members to three-person groups to work through the tutorial. Groups work on the tutorial in a Learning Center or other workplace setting, in a time slot equivalent to a project team meeting (two to three hours). In the subsequent team meeting, the project managers will lead a discussion of how UCD fits their needs, where the team will need coaching or further instruction, and who else should be included on the team - based in large part on the memos which they have received from the groups.

This change to a collaborative setting also produced some unexpected tradeoffs: we had to reduce the richness of the content and the non-linearity of the interactivity to support effective group dynamics. The next section will provide examples of these tradeoffs.

INTERACTION GENRES, TASKS AND MEDIA

Several interaction genres - story telling, guidelines and tips, role plays – were included to fit the learning model.

Story telling

It was critical to the design philosophy that the case study be clearly authentic - real people talking about their actual experiences. This required that the case study team be prepared to share both successes and setbacks, and that the case study have an engaging rhythm. We were fortunate to find a pilot case in which external pressures had caused some deviations from the UCD process which set back the schedule when the resulting designs were rejected by the users. The team treated this as a learning opportunity and were able to speak frankly about it in their video vignettes. Our test users all commented favorably on the engagement this storytelling genre produced.

Ownership was a major issue in preparing the case study: the pilot team's experiences and their reflections on it were sometimes inconsistent with the Bank's "big picture" of terminology and recommendations for UCD methods. In the end, we chose to let the team tell their own story in their own words, without commentary by UCD coaches. This preserved authenticity but at some cost in generalization.

Another issue with the case study was the use of 'talking head' video. Since the project described in the case study was already finished when tutorial development began, we were recording reflections on events rather than slices of the events in real-time. We chose a video style which preserved the dialogue flavor of our interviews with the case study team, and used large enough video windows to preserve a conversational space during tutorial use. Usability test showed that the videos were highly valued by learners - the interactions within the learning groups as they discussed the case study more than compensated for reduced interactivity from the story telling genre.

Quick fact sheets and method tips

As a prelude to a more extensive performance support system, the tutorial was to contain an overview of UCD methods. This was also intended to introduce methods which were not part of the case study. We included video vignettes from other projects to make these methods come alive with their own mini-stories. Figure 1(b) shows a sample screen from the resulting Methods Tour.

There were some problems for the groups in deciding how much information to view in the Methods Tour. We decided to provide only the 'lowest common denominator' of information, i.e., only what the user representatives needed to know for their roles in the UCD project. That left the designers and developers wanting more details, but this was left to be done in a task-oriented performance support context.

Role plays

Active learning engages learners in authentic scenarios in a 'cognitive apprenticeship' [6; 1]. The initial segments of the tutorial were relatively passive, but this was compensated for in the group interactions and the team building which was occurring. By the last unit of the tutorial, the groups were ready to tackle more substantial learning tasks.

However, it is difficult to design authentic role plays without a significant overhead for mastering the task context. Since our targeted time was limited to one project team meeting slot, we reused situations in the case study and asked learners to explain decisions rather than to generate the decisions. We also asked them to apply UCD methods to the tutorial system itself, for which we had extensive usability testing data and early design materials.

Learning model

The learning model used in the UCD tutorial is an adaptation of the Experiential Learning Cycle [4], which proceeds from observation [Case Study] through conceptualization [Methods Tour] to experimentation [Test Drive]. The upcoming project provides the final Cycle element of concrete experience.

Reflection elements are included at the end of each of the three UCD tutorial units, where the memo to the project team manager is created. In many cases, users who had skimmed through the content of the unit went back to it when they came to create their memo - with a better understanding of the extent and limitation of their own knowledge based on their ability to respond to the memo requirements.

One element we did not include in the tutorial was any meta-reflection on the learning process and in particular the process of group negotiation of navigation and responses in the memo. The results of user testing suggest that this would be a valuable addition to the tutorial, Since the group process revealed important differences in perspective amongst the various UCD project roles. The most obvious manifestation of this was the greater interest by user representatives in the test groups in listening to users from the project team, in comparison to many of the software developers in the groups tested.

INTERFACE ISSUES: INTERACTIVITY AND MEDIA

In addition to the changes in the tutorial content and style, the evolution in learning and usage contexts also produced significant changes in the interface features determining how it will be used:

User navigation choices

We reduced the level of user choice available in the initial parts of the tutorial. While this is normally the opposite of our objective as interaction designers, we found that the groups had to build internal rapport before they could tackle difficult navigational choice. In the Introduction unit there is very little user choice required. In the Case Study unit, learners could navigate by moving back and forth between events or use the navigation timeline at the bottom of the screen to move directly to an event - most groups chose to move sequentially. There was frequent discussion about the value of individual case study elements - as noted above, user representatives often wanted to listen to more of the video story segments than developers, for example. These differences in style are important elements for the project team to cope with in its own life cycle, but we were not able to incorporate specific team-building content into this tutorial.

Media elements

As the level of interactivity rose over the duration of the tutorial, we reduced the level of media richness. The Case Study has multiple video vignettes on each screen, the Methods Tour has one or two vignettes for each method, and the Test Drive has no video elements (all units have audio introductions to provide orientation for activities). We were tempted to include video segments for the coach's comments in the Test Drive, but decided to emphasize instead interactions amongst the learning group members. For individual use, we would want to have engaging media throughout.

Hypermedia

We also reduced the visibility of the hypermedia nature of the tutorial. While it is possible to move directly from a case study event using a method to a description in the Methods Tour or to a Test Drive activity using it (and back again), we removed any emphasis on this from the tutorial introduction or the visual cues. Partly this was to preserve the integrity of the case story line; partly it was to reduce the amount of choice confronting the learning groups. Another factor was that we wanted the Test Drive activities to become progressively more difficult as the groups proceeded through them, and the resulting ordering conflicted with the natural case study order. (Do the most difficult activities always take place early in the UCD process?).

RESEARCH ISSUES: MULTIMEDIA SUPPORT, RE-USE, AND INTEGRATED LEARNING

The concepts for this UCD tutorial developed out of two previous projects. The Raison d'Etre project of Carroll et al [2] demonstrated the value of authentic video reflections in "providing insight into affective, social and historical factors in design work". Our own FLUID prototype [8] had explored the use of goal-based scenarios as role plays for novice designers. The Learning About UCD tutorial applied these elements as distinct genres, and added a Methods Tour to provide an issues-based component in place of the database paradigm in Raison d'Etre.

We are continuing the research aspects of this development, to address the following questions:

i) how can multimedia engagement be most effectively employed in collaborative learning environments? We learned a number of useful lessons from the evolution of this design, but there is much more to learn as we all experiment with new media interactions.

A number of our decisions concerning media use were revised as a result of usability testing. There were three major iterations of formative evaluations, involving 31 participants in all. In the test sessions we approximated the project learning context as closely as we could, using groups of three participants from different organizational units who might be brought together for a UCD project. Participants were given a brief project scenario by way of introduction. The test system tracked and timed user actions, but the most valuable data came from observers who recorded both the content interaction and the team-building interactions within the groups. The reflection memos were also evaluated for the quality of UCD knowledge they contained.

We had originally provided some variety in the introductory media for each screen in the case study: most began with an audio segment, but on occasion a video segment was used instead. While we had expected this to be more engaging, users found it distracting. We had also planned an introduction to the navigation elements which would demonstrate simulated use of the system. However, this had the disadvantage of making the Introduction unit entirely passive. Consequently we built a navigation overview in which users select highlighted screen elements for an explanation of their function.

Early versions of the system had also contained a Timeline navigation tool which allowed users to whiz through the case at high speed and select particular event screens for more detail. While this made for attractive demos, it required too many operations to move easily between event screens. The final tutorial had a timeline which was always visible on the bottom of the screen, and provided short summaries of events on mouseover. This also allowed learners to always see what parts of the tutorial they had already examined.

ii) how suitable is the content of the tutorial for other organizations? We are working with other companies to implement UCD tutorials which follow the same learning model and re-use the design and implementation elements. Preliminary results indicate that the Methods Tour content will need adaptation for each setting. We will be experimenting with re-use of the Case Study to determine the costs and benefits of cases specific to organizations. We are also reusing the systems architecture for other project-oriented and curriculum-oriented settings, especially business process re-engineering case studies.

iii) how can the various professional learning contexts be supported by integrated tools? One immediate goal is to more effectively link an electronic performance support system into the Methods Tour, which would become an overview or front-end.

A second goal is to integrate the tutorial into a professional community context. One component is to build community ownership by maintaining the tutorial content, adding vignettes on methods and discussion groups on issues. We have already done this informally in the Test Drive: users from the testing sessions convinced us to add some of their answers to our own coach's comments.

CONCLUSIONS

The combination of Case Study, Concepts Tour and Test Drive appears to be of significant value for collaborative learning in a project context. For developers of multimedia tutorials using such authentic case studies, the evolution of our design yields the following guidelines:

• a "just-in-time" learning context requires more reflection on current work and less role play exercise

• a more collaborative usage context requires a reduction in the complexity of the navigation decisions, to allow effective deliberations by the group

• an interaction genre with more authentic story telling requires engaging media, whereas a role play exercise can rely on engaging interactions.

ACKNOWLEDGEMENTS

This research was sponsored by the TeleLearning Network of Centres of Excellence and the Bank of Montreal. We acknowledge the many contributions of the case study team, the staff who participated in focus groups and system testing, and the design and production team, especially Blair Nonnecke, Tammy te Winkel, and Mark Connolly of Convivia Interaction Design, Les Richards, Bill Milne, Pat Thompson and Aldo Caputo of the University of Guelph and Mike Roberts, Mike Hayes, Malcolm Roberts and Anne Natale of the Bank of Montreal.

REFERENCES

1. Brown, J.S., A. Collins and P. Duguid (1989), Situated cognition and the culture of learning, *Educational Researcher*, 18, 32-41.

2. Carroll, J.M., S.R. Alpert, J. Karat, M. van Deusen, M.B. Rosson (1994), Raison d'Etre: Capturing Design History and Rationale in Multimedia Narratives, *in Human Factors in Computing Systems* Proceedings, Annual Conference Series 1994, ACM SIGCHI, pp. 192-197.

3. Crooks, S.M., J.D. Klein, E.K. Jones and H. Dwyer (1996), Effects of co-operative learning and learner-control modes in computer-based instruction, *Journal of Research on Computers in Education*, vol. 29, 109-123.

4. Kolb, D. (1984), *The Experiential Learning Cycle*, Addison-Wesley Publishers.

5. Saunders, M. (1995), Researching professional learning, *Journal of Computer-Assisted Learning*, 11, 231-238.

6. Schank, R. (1994) Active Learning through Multimedia, *IEEE Multimedia*, 1(1), 69-78.

7. Semrau, L.P., K.A. Carlson, L.R. Johnson, G. Fitzgerald (1997), The Impact of Group Versus Individual Use on Multimedia-Based Instruction, poster presentation, EDMEDIA 97, World Conference on Educational Multimedia and Hypermedia, Calgary.

8. Van Aalst, J.W., T.T. Carey and D.L. McKerlie (1995), Design Space Analysis as "Training Wheels" in a Framework for Learning About User Interface Design, in *Human Factors in Computing Systems* Proceedings, Annual Conference Series 1995, ACM SIGCHI, pp. 154-161.

Figure 1(a): the first screen of the UCD Case Study. The tabs on the top left move between units, the arrows and the navigation line at the bottom of the screen move between screens of a unit such as the Case Study. Audio and video controls allow the learner to control the media.

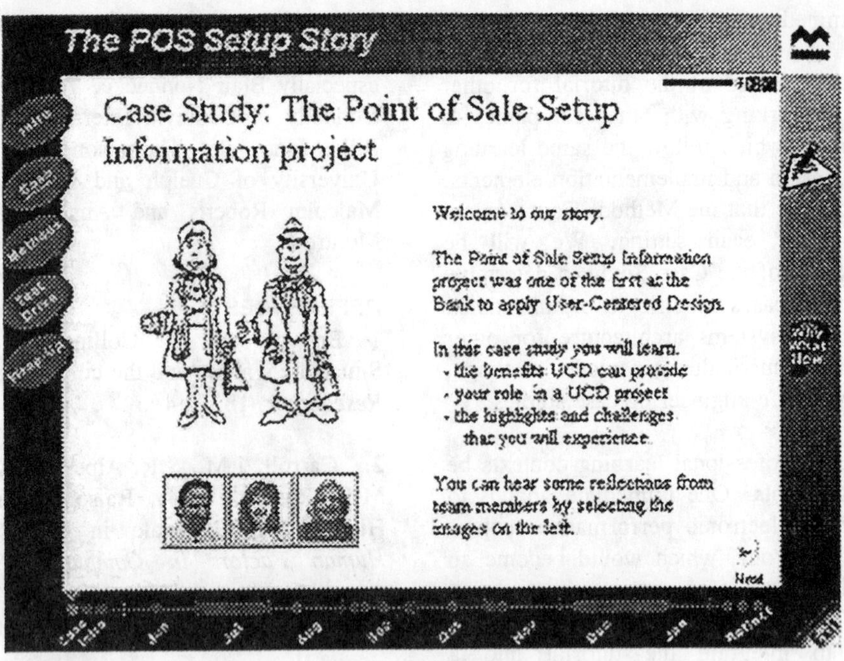

Figure 1(b): Each event in the Case Study has one or more screens of information, including an audio introduction, a text summary, and video vignettes where the case study project team reflects on their experiences with User-centered Design.

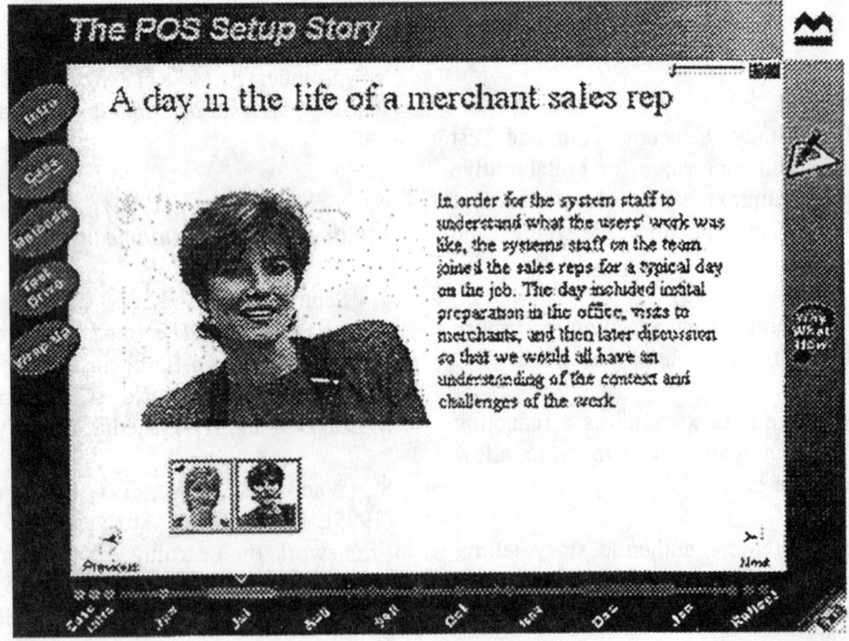

Figure 1(c): The Methods Tour provides an overview of 15 common UCD methods. For each method there is textual information about the method, a Quick Tryout exercise with relevant coach's comments on it, and video vignettes from the case or other projects using the method.

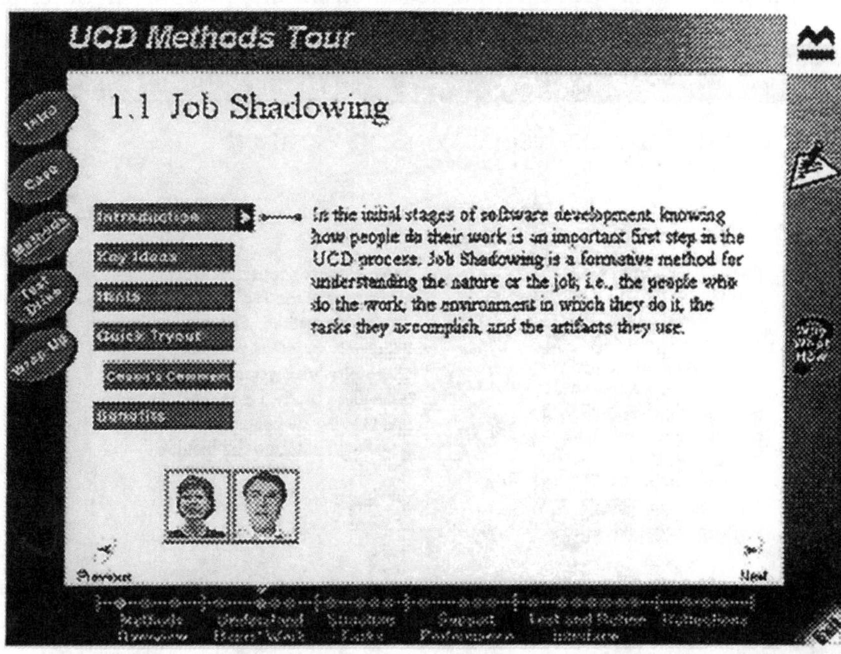

Figure 1(d): After the Case Study and the Methods Tour, learners experience a simulated role in a UCD project. The objective is to enable them to assess their team's readiness to apply the UCD methods, and to prepare for discussion on what kind of coaching or training they will require.

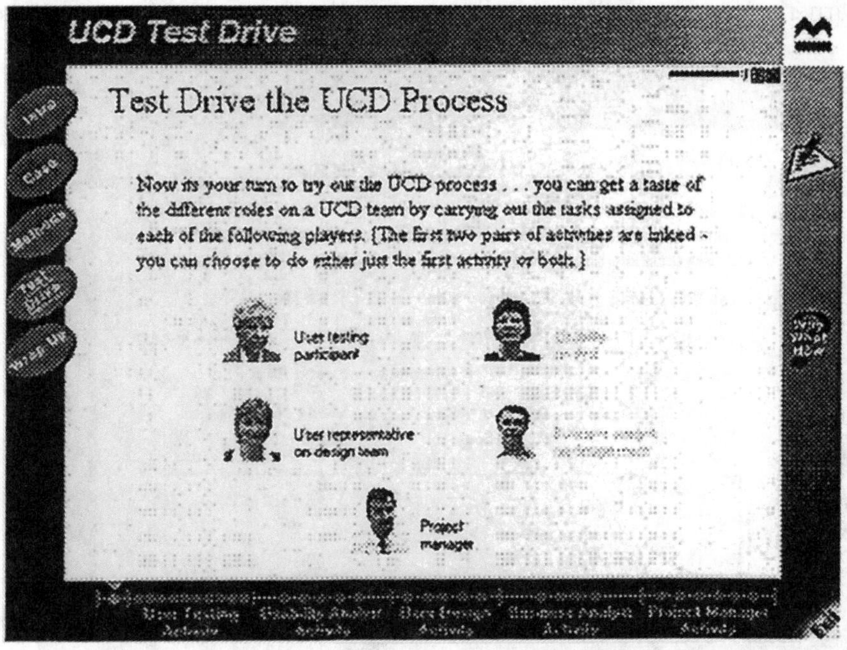

Figure 1(e): in this Test Drive activity, learners reflect on the decision to use job shadowing in the case study, as a way for designers and developers to understand users' work ("a day in the life"). After choosing strengths of this method which made it attractive in the case study project, learners are asked to match other methods with their particular strengths, to apply in other projects.

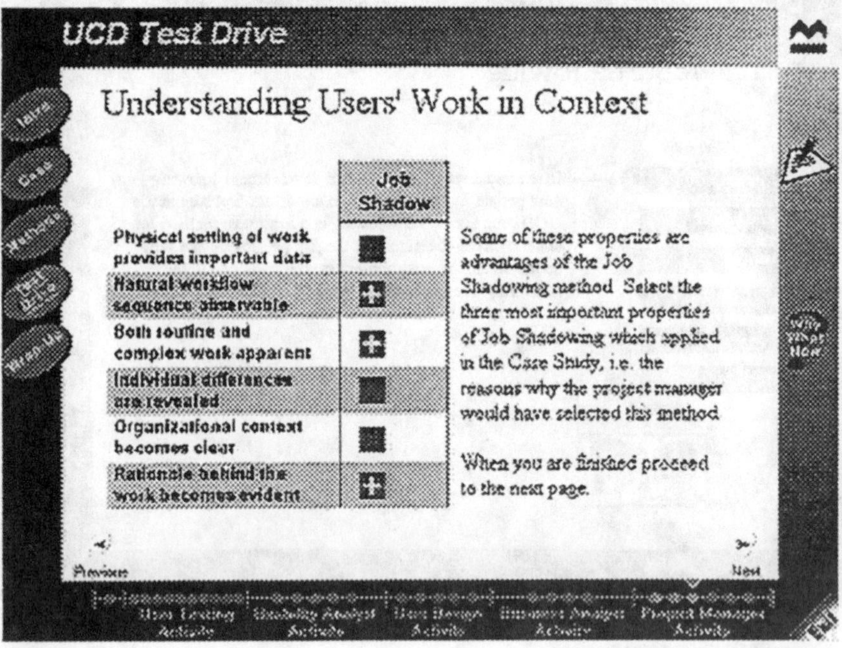

Figure 2: In the Reflection section at the end of each of the three major units, learners prepare a memo to their project manager which their thoughts on roles and methods to apply in their own project. Here learners select methods that will be useful, then are asked to explain their choices.

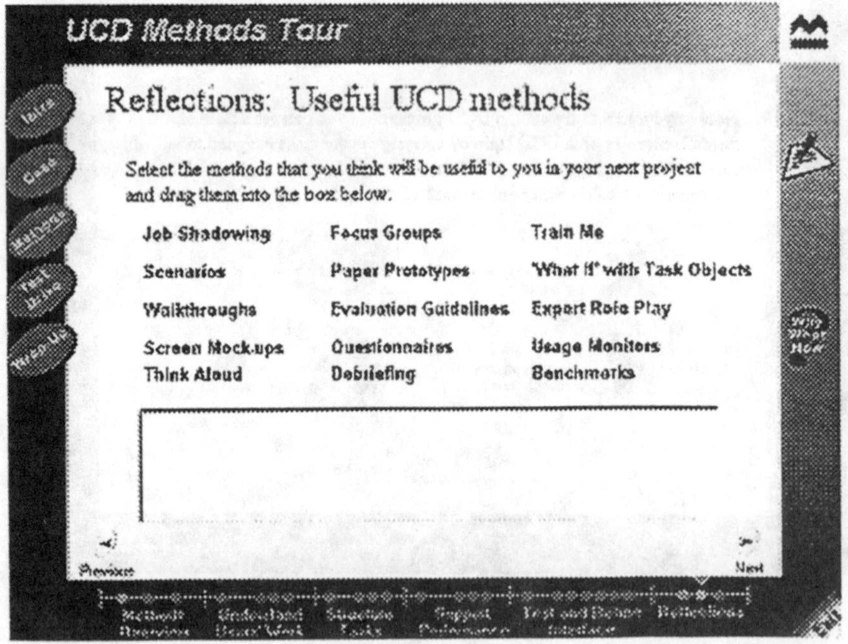

Evaluating the Location of Hot Spots in Interactive Scenes using the 3R Toolbox

Andre Plante, Shoji Tanaka and Seiki Inoue
ATR Media Integration & Communications Research Laboratories
2-2 Hikaridai Seika-cho, Souraku-gun, Kyoto, Japan 619-0288
+81 774 95 1415
{jjap, gon, sinoue}@mic.atr.co.jp

ABSTRACT

Too often in interactive pictures, movies or VR scenes where no explicit buttons exist, the user is left to find hot spots (portals, gates, links) almost at random. In any particular scene, although semantic information is present, a user may be overwhelmed by the number of possible and perfectly logical locations in which hot spots could be embedded. In this paper, we propose a new support tool based on the Highly Attractive Region Extraction Method and aimed at helping the designer identify and enhance hot spots image regions so that they become more attractive (i.e. get the user's attention). This computer tool performs an evaluation on images based on their physical features (Hue, Saturation, Lightness, Size and Contrast) and graphically shows which regions are more likely to attract a user's gaze. Based on these results, the designer can then choose to furthermore highlight a particular part of a picture or, alternatively, tone down regions that could cause confusion.

Keywords

User Interface, hot spots, Visual Communications, Interactive Movie, Image processing, navigation, Support Tool, Design

INTRODUCTION

While most interfaces rely on icons, words, menus or buttons, a growing numbers of games, interactive movies and virtual worlds rely solely on the graphical representation of a specific environment to permit user interaction. These environments can be reality or fantasy-based, depict familiar or unfamiliar objects or spaces. They can be still or in motion. They can be completely immersive as in the case of Virtual Reality experienced through a head-mounted display or simply window-based as in the case of Apple™ Quicktime VR viewed on the screen of a computer. These navigable worlds or pictures lack the familiar labels found in other types of interfaces. The lack of words or icons contributes to the depiction of a more convincing scene, but it tends to decrease the effectiveness of the manner in which the user navigates a particular content.

Now that designers can afford to create rich environments composed of many objects or use photorealistic images to create scenes, it has become more difficult for the user to find where hot spots may have been placed. The semantic information contained in a scene obviously helps the user make a decision. The representation of a door will most likely trigger the belief that there will be a hot spot at this location, although sometimes one is not available. On the other hand a user may overlook an object which the developer used as a hot spot. As an example of this, consider a navigable photo of an office: the computer screen intended to be a hot spot to another scene may be overlooked for the more obvious door on the opposite wall. The user can easily be overwhelmed by the high number of possibilities or simply fail to find all but the most obvious hot spots. To alleviate this problem, in applications where a cursor is present, routines have been implemented to modify various aspects of the cursor's behavior if it is moved over an area of the picture defined as a hot spot. The user is often compelled to stop moving and perform a "mine sweeping" motion over the whole picture to identify hot spots. Although this method is helpful in some ways, it does not address the real problem, which is one of graphic design and visual communications.

Designers, computer artists, photographers and cameramen not only must exercise good judgement in the composition of their pictures but also need a tool to analyze the physical features of their images as they are produced. These tools must show in a simple and direct manner where a user is likely to look within the frame. The designer must realize that an insignificant object, if of a certain hue and size, might detract attention from more important objects.

Some previous research on the subject of extraction of attractive regions in a picture was done by Milanese et. al [1]. They assumed that the discontinuity found inside of a picture attracts the viewer's attention. To extract those attractive regions, they first create feature maps for several physical features of the picture, then extract the discontinuous regions of each feature map. Finally the regions are integrated into a single map by using a relaxation process. Milanese et. al used a bank of difference-of-oriented-gaussians (DOORG) filters whose size are fixed to extract discontinuous regions. However, since the size of attractive regions are different within and among different pictures, it is difficult to properly extract attractive regions with filters limited to a fixed size.

Here, we propose a method that first segments the original picture into regions of various sizes. Then this method uses a discrimination function to select attractive regions from those regions. This tool automatically identifies regions with highest level of attractiveness based on physical properties (Hue,

CHI 98 Los Angeles CA USA
Copyright 1998 0-89791-975-0/98/ 4..$5.00

Saturation, Lightness, Size and Contrast) and with the help of sliders, graphically informs the designer as to why it has chosen each specific region in the image. Armed with this information the designer can interactively make the desired modifications. For example, the designer could lower the saturation of an area in order to lower its attractiveness and change the hue of another to increase it. This new feedback loop in the design process becomes absolutely necessary if one wants to produce more effective images that convey clearer navigational cues to the user.

ARTISTIC IMAGE CREATION PROCESS

Before we describe our tool in detail, it would be wise to revisit the actual process through which an image, be it a painting, illustration, 3-D scene, a photo or video, is created.

Fine Arts versus Applied Arts

Throughout the ages, artists have created images using various media. From the first cave paintings to today's computer graphics, art has been about conveying emotions and messages. Artwork is sometimes an end in itself, as in Fine Arts, or a tool to express a very specific message to an audience, as in Applied or Commercial Arts [2]. External constraints play a greater role in Applied Arts; the topic, the medium, the size of the piece and the amount of time available for production may all be decided by the client or by resource limitations. Aesthetic comparisons apart, what differentiates from Applied Arts from Fine Arts is the importance of a clear and simple communication with a specific audience.

Interface Designers and artists who produce navigable pictures or scenes should not overlook this important difference.

The Design Cycle

The design process is largely iterative in its nature, it is a series of enhancements applied after evaluation of previously accomplished steps. It is not entirely linear as a process and in that matter ressembles concurrent engineering and rapid prototyping processes.

Designers will usually create an image after some research and documentation on the subject at hand. They will research books, web sites and photo magazines, then sketch or collect whatever is relevant in a scrapbook. If this freedom is allowed, they will decide on the size and format of the image.

Photographers have a similar process in which they will scout locations and decide on the most appropriate locale.

Composition work will usually follow, while painter or illustrator have total freedom here, photographers will have only limited control over the scene at the time of the shoot. They might move a chair or ask a person to look up, but can not easily hide mountains or remove telephone wires at this stage.

Production of the artwork will then begin, illustrators might use brushes, pens or a computer mouse while photographers will use different lenses, creative filters, aperture and shutter settings.

Following this stage, post-production effects can be applied to the picture, objects can be removed and new ones merged into the frame. Creative filters can again be used at this point. This process will usually go on until the artist and the client are satisfied with the image as far as aesthetics and content are concerned.

This image might meet the artist's and the client's standards and expectations, but we argue that it might still not be optimal for navigation purposes. To insure a higher navigational optimization, we believe that a tool evaluating the physical properties of the picture should be incorporated in the later stages of production and post-production of the design process. As explained before, this tool would help the interface designer and the artist in fine-tuning the image so that the end-user will have greater success in finding hotspots in the final picture.

3R TOOLBOX

This section covers the 3R Toolbox in detail and will be followed by examples. The 3R Toolbox comprises the three following components:

- REX (Attractive Region Extraction Tool) which segments a picture into various regions.
- RAN (Attractive Region Analyzer) which evaluates these regions based on their level of attractiveness.
- RED (Region Editor) which provides the designer with a tool to increase or reduce attractiveness of specific regions in a picture.

REX

This component constitutes the core of the Highly Attractive Region Extraction Method [3] and performs the following steps:

1- Filters the noise in the picture

2- Segments the picture using the K-Means Algorithm (KMA) in a L*a*b* color space.

3- Combines segmented regions that share similar colors

4- Asks RAN to evaluate the regions

5- Outputs regions selected as attractive by RAN

The main reasons for using KMA are that it is a simple algorithm and that it can extract the general structure of a picture. When people look at a picture, they first see its rough structure. At first they ignore details, only when some points of interest are presents, will they try to focus on details. REX duplicates this behavior, and tries to extract the regions that would attract the attention of the viewers during their first exploratory glance.

Figure 4 shows an example of REX output.

RAN

As explained briefly before, this module evaluates the level of attractiveness for each region found by the REX component or specified by the user. Current image processing methods still have an extremely difficult time in recognizing meaningful objects in pictures. Since it looks only at the rough structure, RAN does not uses any semantic information to perform its evaluation, instead, it uses the physical features of a picture which contribute most to attract attention.

Pictures have many physical features, such as different colors, shapes, compositions, etc. It has been said that color plays an especially important role for attraction in general. A number of scientists and artists have studied this phenomenon, Birren [4], and Itten [5] have both written extensively on the subject. Shinsaku, et al. and Morikawa, et al. studied the attractiveness of colors [6]. They chose10 different colors from the Munsell system, arranged them on a circular surface, and asked subjects to attribute a score based on the level of attraction of each color. The above experiment was performed twice, first using a black background and later a white background to separate the colors. From the results, they concluded the following:

1) Warm colors attract more attention than cold colors and red gets high scores independent of the background

2) Highly saturated colors are more attractive

In our own previous experiments, we also found that

3) Bright colors are more attractive [7]

4) The greater the color difference between a region and its surroundings, the more attractive it also becomes

Moreover, it is obvious that

5) the larger the size of a region, the more attention it will attract.

To consider the above findings, we use the following parameters to evaluate the level of attraction of each region: Hue, Saturation, Lightness, Size ratio and Color difference between a region and its surroundings.

For the hue parameter, we assume that pure red (R,G,B=255,0,0) is the most attractive color among the warm colors according to the above finding 1). We use the HSI double-hexcone color model for calculating the hue, saturation, and lightness whose values are normalized between 0.0 to 1.0. In this color model, the hue of pure red becomes 0.0. Therefore, we use the value calculated by the following equation as the hue parameter of each region.

$$hp = 1 - \frac{h}{\pi} \quad (1)$$

(if $h > \pi$ then $h = 2\pi - h$)

where :

h : the average hue of the region.

hp : the hue parameter of the region.

For the ratio of the region to the whole picture, the following equation is used.

$$r = \frac{nrp}{npp} \quad (2)$$

where :

r : the ratio.

nrp : the number of pixels in the region.

npp : the number of pixels in the picture.

For the color difference between the region and its surrounding pixels, we calculate the value for each region with the following equations.

$$het_i = \frac{bcd_i}{\max_j(bcd_j)} \quad (3)$$

$$bcd = \sqrt{\frac{1}{n}\sum_{i=1}^{n}(pc_i - \overline{bc})^2} \quad (4)$$

where :

het : the color difference

bcd : the standard deviation of the color difference between region i and the sorrounding pixels

pc_i : the color of target pixel i

bc : the average color of the region

n : the number of target pixels

Target pixels are pixels in a rectangular region made by expanding each side of a circumscribed rectangle of a region, and they do not belong to the region.

Here, we use the rectangular region by expanding its edges by 1.5 times on each side of the circumscribed rectangle of the region.

The color difference is calculated in a L*a*b* color space.

Discrimination Function for Attraction

In order to analyze the role of each parameter mentioned above and the relationship of each parameter, we carried out experiments with 20 subjects and 50 pictures (size of 2048x1572). In the experiments, we first showed subjects the complete original picture, then showed an experimental picture, which contained an original picture and 8 attractive regions extracted by the method in [1]. Finally, we asked them to select attractive regions from segmented regions in the experimental picture.

After this experiments, we analyzed the collected data of the parameters of attractive and non-attractive regions by performing principal component analysis. As a result, the attractive regions tend to converge in the minus direction of the first principal component and in the plus direction of the second principal component.

Therefore, we use the value of the first principal component and the second principal component to discriminate between the attractive regions and the non-attractive regions. Below, we propose a discremination function for deciding whether a region is attractive or not.

$$Dis(X) = p(X \mid c_1)P(c_1) - p(X \mid c_2)P(c_2)$$

$$if \begin{cases} Dis(X) \geq 0 \rightarrow attractive \\ Dis(X) < 0 \rightarrow non-attractive \end{cases}$$

$$p(X \mid c_i) = \frac{1}{2\pi \cdot |V_i|^{1/2}} \exp\left[-\frac{1}{2}(X - \overline{X}_i)^T V_i^{-1}(X - \overline{X}_i)\right]$$

where:

X : a vector consisted of principal component values

Dis(X) : a discrimination function

$P(X|c_1)P(c_1)$: a probability of that X is attractive

$P(X|c_2)P(c_2)$: a probability of that X is non-attractive

RED

The Region Editor will allow the user to fine-tune a region to make it more or less attractive. Two modes will be built into the editor, namely: the Selection Mode and the Detail Mode.

In the Selection Mode, the user is presented with alternative solutions and selects from that series of corrected examples. The initial state of this interface is dictated by the immediate surroundings of a selected area of the image. This means that not only the selection is analyzed but also the image background around it. This information is used to pre-adjust the settings for each individual images. As an example, since the most attractive hue is different for an image with a blue background from one with a red background, the settings would differ accordingly. RED in its Selection Mode will generate several variations based on varying hue, saturation and lightness of the selected region. The user would then simply choose the preferred solution.

If the user prefers, the Region Editor will show slider bars corresponding to hue, saturation and lightness parameters. When the user modifies any of the parameters, RED will ask RAN to evaluate the region again, then it will graphically output the results so that the user can compare the attractiveness of the revised region against the whole picture.

If for artistic reasons, the user prefers to modify other parameters of the pictures, he would then go back to a commercial image processing software and when finished simply reevaluate his picture.

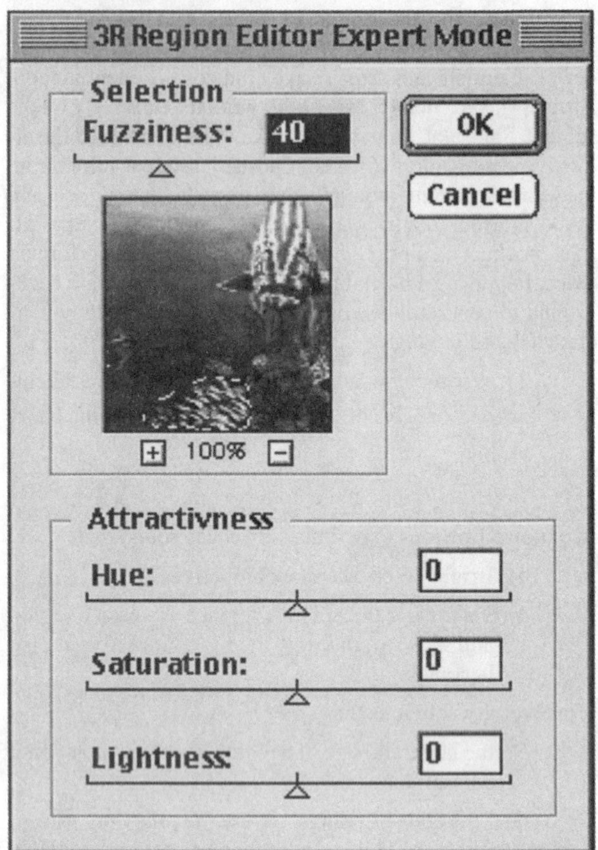

Figure 2. Detail Mode of RED

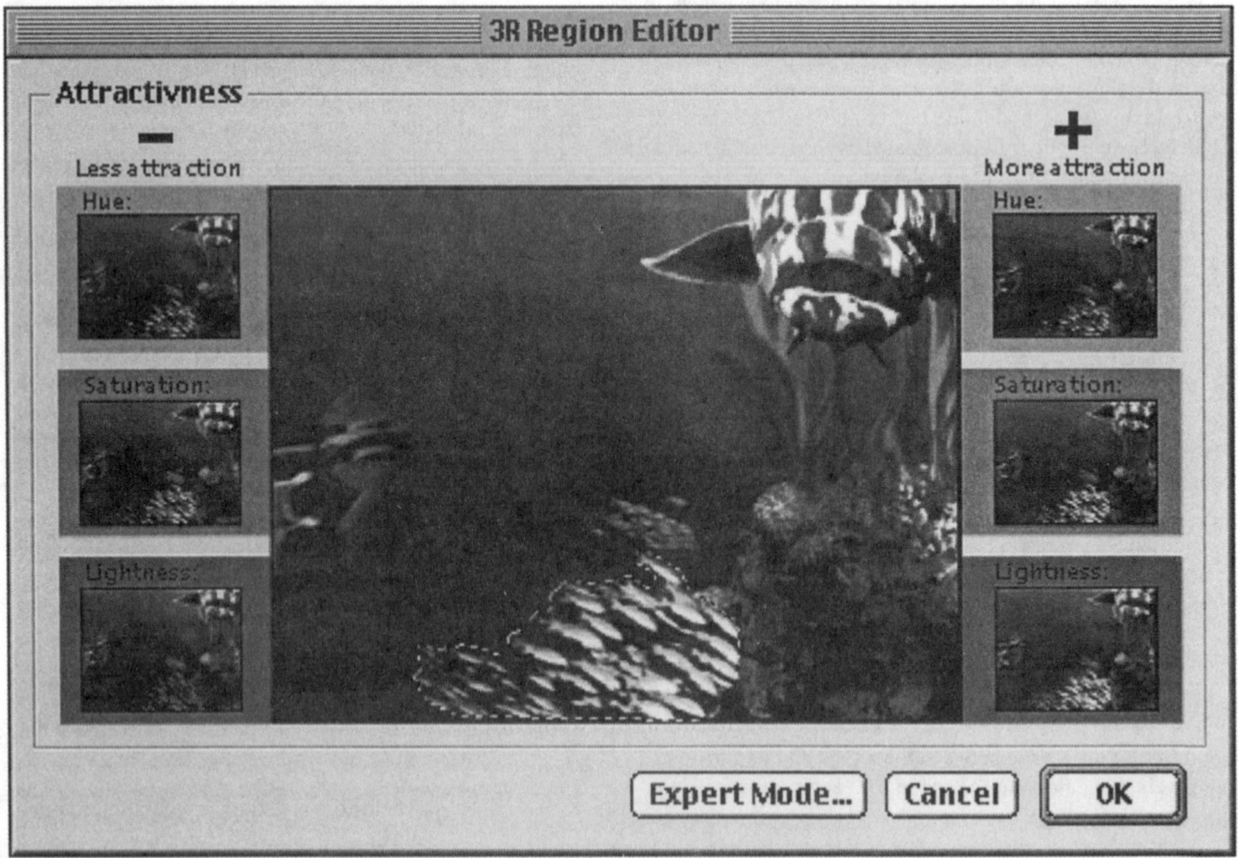

EXAMPLES

In this section, we will look at three different examples of REX evaluation.

Example 1

In the first example, the interface designer is producing an Apple™ Quicktime VR cylindrical panoramic view and has planned to locate hotspots over the volcano, the Statue of Liberty and the British telephone booths in this angle of view. (see figure 3)

Figure 3. First version of "Fujisan".

Example 1 - First evaluation

After a first evaluation of the picture with REX, the designer easily notices certain problems. As we can see in figure 4, the telephone booths generate a lot of attention but so do the dolphins, the volcano generates a little attention and the statue is totally ignored.

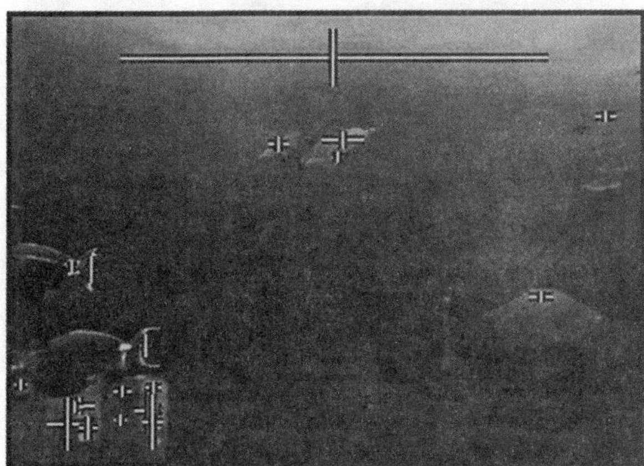

Figure 4. First version of "Fujisan" showing clusters of REX crosshairs over the telephone booths and the dolphins.

Example 1 - Revisions

With this information, the designer can revise the image by increasing the attractiveness of the volcano and the statue while reducing the effect on the dolphins. In this case, the designer has chosen to significantly brighten the volcano, move the statue in order to reduce hot spot overlap with the volcano and vary its hue and brightness. The contrast of the dolphins was reduced and as a result they better blend with the surrounding background as can be seen in figure 5.

Figure 5. Revised version of "Fujisan".

Example 1 - Second evaluation

In figure 6, the results of the evaluation performed on the revised picture show a clear improvement with still a strong cluster of crosshairs over the booths, a cluster just above the volcano and a lone but important crosshairs over the Statue of Liberty. Following these modification the dolphins are now being ignored.

Figure 6. Revised version of "Fujisan", this time showing clusters of REX crosshairs over the telephone cabins and above the volcano.

Example 2 - First evaluation

In another angle of view of the same panoramic image, the designer intends to locate hot spots over the large red fish and the pair of rays. After evaluating the picture with REX, The designer finds that a school of brightly colored yellow fishes in the lower part of the frame may distract the attention of the user

Figure 7. First version of "Fish" showing clusters of REX crosshairs over a school of yellow fishes.

Example 2 - Revisions and Second evaluation

The designer revises the picture by lowering the saturation of the yellow fishes and slightly augmenting the contrast of the two rays. Results of the second evaluation can be seen in figure 8 and on the color plate.

Figure 8. Revised version of "Fish" showing clusters of REX crosshairs over a school of yellow fishes.

Example 3 - First evaluation

The following example also illustrate a frame from a panoramic image used with Apple™ Quicktime VR. This time the designer wants to overlay hotspots on the paintings and on the door. A first evaluation shows a fairly successful image that needs little improvement (see figure 9).

Figure 9. First version of "The Gallery" showing REX crosshairs covering most of the right wall and some area of the floor.

Example 3 - Revisions and Second evaluation

None the less, the designer decides to improve the image by augmenting the contrast between the wall, the paintings and the door. The floor is also slightly retouched where it appeared too bright. Figure 10 shows the result of these modifications.

Figure 10. Revised version of "The Gallery" showing REX crosshairs on the paintings and on the door.

CONCLUSION

The designer and/or artist play an important role in facilitating navigation in the type of environments presented above. We argued that there is a design problem that can be solved via a simple evaluation and revision of the final navigable image. The modifications required for optimizing these pictures are usually simple and do not drastically change the overall look or feel of the environment depicted, but none the less will help the user in easily locating hot spot regions.

In conclusion, we strongly suggest that Designers relying solely on hot spots and the graphical representation of a specific environment as an interface add a step to their development cycle in which a physical evaluation of the images may be performed. To help in this evaluation, we proposed a toolbox based on the Highly Attractive Region Extraction Method.

REFERENCES

1. Ruggero Milanese, Harry Wechsler, Sylvia Gil, Jean-Marc Bost, Thierry Pun, "Integration of Bottom-Up and Top-Down Cues for Visual Attention Using Non-Linear Relaxation", *Proc. Computer Vision and Pattern Recognition*, pp. 781-785, 1994.
2. Edward R.Tufte, "Visual Explanations", *GRAPHICS PRESS*, 1997.
3. Shoji Tanaka, Masayuki Inoue, Michitoshi Ishiwaka and Seiki Inoue, "A METHOD FOR EXTRACTING AND ANALYZING 'KANSEI' FACTORS FROM PICTURES", *Proc. IEEE Workshop on Multimedia Signal Processing*, pp. 251-256, 1997.
4. Faber Birren, "Color & Human Response", *VAN NOSTRAND REINHOLD*, 1978.
5. Johannes Itten, "The Art of Color", *VAN NOSTRAND REINHOLD*, 1973.
6. The Color Science Association of Japan, "Color Science Handbook", 1991.
7. Shoji Tanaka, Michitoshi Ishiwaka, Masayuki Inoue and Seiki Inoue, "A Study Concerning Automatic Addition of Impression Keywords to Natural Images," *Technical Report of IEICE*, HIP96-20, pp. 19-24, Oct. 1996.

Providing Advice for Multimedia Designers

Pete Faraday & Alistair Sutcliffe
The Centre for HCI Design
City University,
London, EC1 0HB, UK
+44-171-477-8994
P.M.Faraday@city.ac.uk

ABSTRACT
The paper summarises empirical research that led to guidelines for directing the viewing/reading sequence in multimedia presentations. A method for scripting or evaluating multimedia presentations is described and illustrated with a case study. A design advisor tool based on this work is used to critique a sample MM presentation. A tool validation study with novice designers is reported.

KEYWORDS
Presentation Design, Guidelines, Tool support

INTRODUCTION

One of the problems in the design of expository Multimedia (MM) interfaces is knowing whether the presentation will successfully deliver appropriate information to the user. In a review of studies on MM instructional systems, Kozma [6] proposes a 'micro-level' approach will be required to produce effective multimedia : '...media decisions for integrated multimedia will be micro-level decisions... ... of appropriate media that can respond to specific cognitive needs and task requirements.' The problem is thus, what information can the user extract from a presentation, and how can we assist MM designers in making these micro-level decisions when producing their presentations ?

Our work has attempted to address these issues by empirically investigating attention to MM presentations and in producing design guidelines. However, experience tells us that guidelines alone are rarely effective. The paper thus also reports research on guideline delivery via methods and tools.

The paper has two main sections. The first section describes the design method we have developed to encapsulate the guidelines. Results of our previous eye tracking studies on MM presentations are summarised to introduce the guidelines and provide an example application to illustrate operation of the method and tool.

The second part of the paper describes a prototype advisor tool which embeds the guidelines as rules. The tool critiques the presentation, providing warnings and advice during authoring. The paper concludes with an evaluation of the tool's effectiveness in helping novice designers produce better MM presentations.

PREVIOUS WORK

In order to investigate the cognitive processes used in viewing an MM presentation, we performed a set of eye tracking studies upon commercial MM products. One of these studies is illustrated in figure 1. It depicts an eyetracking trace on a sequence explaining the spread of tumours via the blood system. The average fixation location for the subjects is shown as numbered locations on the screen shots (for more details of the analysis see [3]).

The eye tracking results showed that subjects initially fixated upon the large primary tumour at the centre of the screen (1), then shifted to its label (2a) when it was cued in the speech. Little order was found in shifts between the blood vessels, their labels (2b),(2c) and the primary tumour label (2a). The tumour cell was then highlighted, causing all subjects to focus on it (3). Next, the tumour cell moved through the image; and fixations tracked its path into the blood vessel (4),(5a). Finally, the tumour cell label was revealed producing a shift of fixations between the tumour cell and its label (5b).

These results demonstrated that speech cueing, highlighting objects, revealing labels and motion have strong attentional effects. To assess the effectiveness of the guidelines we had derived, subjects recall was then tested for presentations designed with and without application of the guidelines [3].

The guidelines and recall results in this case indicated a potential design problem because captions for 'primary tumour', 'blood from heart' and 'blood to heart' were all shown at once, but only the 'primary tumour' label was cued in speech possibly causing inadequate attention to the other labels. This lead to most subjects incorrectly recalling the direction of the tumour cell's movement. Reauthoring the presentation showed that application of the guidelines did improve assimilation and recall of information [3].

DESIGN METHOD

The method is underpinned by a theory of topic focus which is reasonably well understood in text [5] but less certain in images. Our own studies point to the need to actively direct the users viewing/reading sequence by drawing attention to items within a medium and to promote 'contact points' or co-references across the inter-media joins in a presentation eg between speech and text or images.

The key problem we are addressing is the design of the thread of attention that should ideally run through media of different types to deliver a coherent message :

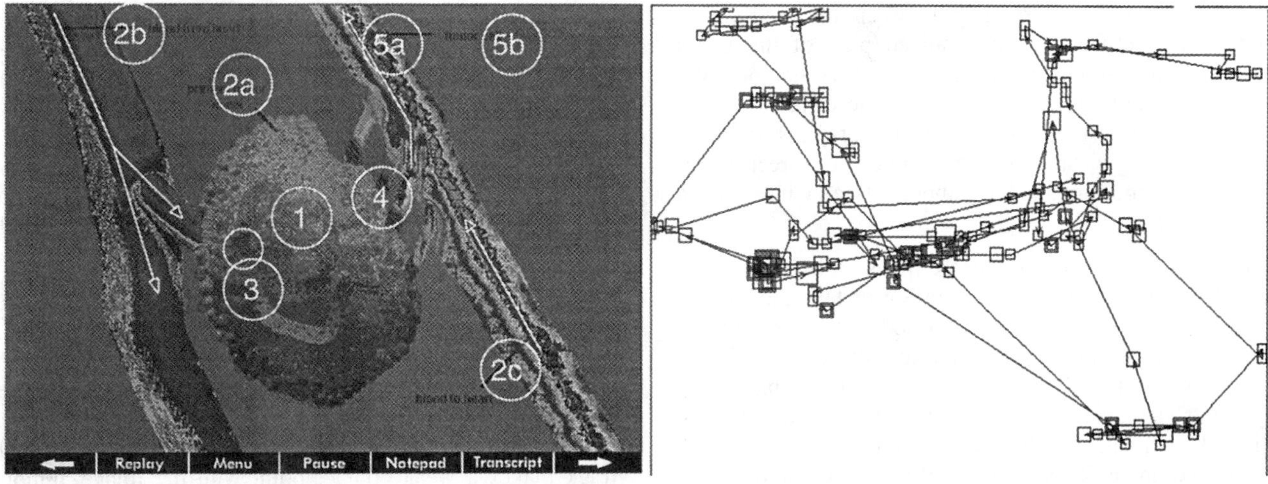

Speech : 'Metastasis resembles primary tumour development in that it is an active multistage process. Cells detach from the primary tumour mass and move into the vessels which nourish it.'

Figure 1 'Etiology of Cancer' Sequence; single subject eye track trace

- to plan the attentional thread to guide the user's viewing and reading sequence;
- to design effects and combinations of media to make important facts salient and reinforce the contact points between different media.
- to determine timing and synchronisation so that the user has sufficient time to assimilate the content.

The method guides scripting multimedia presentations and advises on the use of 'presentation effects' added to the basic script for attention control, i.e. highlighting objects, use of labels and speech references to image components. The method also guides temporal planning of media to allow sufficient time for information assimilation; and promotes reinforcement of key message components by synchronisation of audio and visual media.

Our paper based method takes a first cut media script as input. The method does advise on planning an amodal message script and media selection [8], but our focus in this paper assumes suitable media resource have already been chosen. A time line is drawn depicting which media are to be played in an approximate sequence. The message across media is planned by marking contact points between parts of the message portrayed in different media.

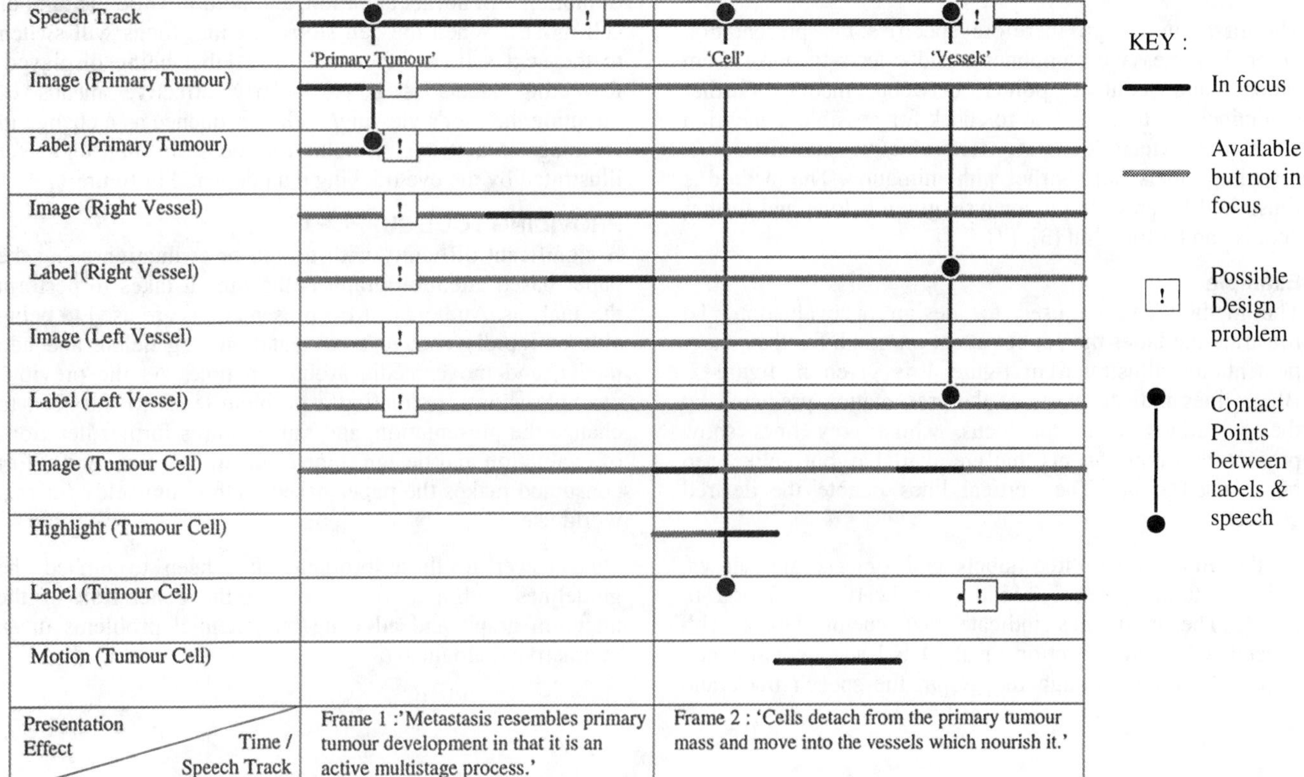

Figure 2 Example Attention Graph for 'Etiology of Cancer' sequence

This leads to a thread running between the media (see figure 2) that represents an idealised plan of the user's viewing/reading sequence through the presentation. We term this an 'attention graph'. It shows the different media on the y axis, with time on the x axis. The graph is traversed from left to right, applying guidelines to direct users' attention to important media components and inter-media contact points.

The duration of speech and video clips is set by the content selected; however, the display duration of text and images may be either user or system controlled. If the presentation sequence is to be controlled guidelines advise on minimum reading times (e.g. 120 words per minutes for simple text in large fonts) and viewing times for images. The latter are difficult to estimate as information extraction is determined by users' domain knowledge, motivation as well as by image complexity. The guidelines do account for these factors; but testing viewing times with users is strongly advised.

The next design issue is drawing attention to important information in the presentation. Guidelines suggest attention control techniques for each medium, i.e. salience and structuring effects in text, speech, image and animation. The designer walks through the presentation deciding which items are important for the overall message and applies presentation effects. At boundaries between media segments effects are specified if the contact point needs reinforcing. In some cases reference is explicit in the media content, i.e. text/speech reference to an image "look at the next photograph..", however, in many cases references have to be explicitly designed by use of labels, highlighting and adding further speech segments.

The first cut design therefore specifies the presentation order, key message components and effects to make them salient and contact points between media. Further guidelines are then applied to check for possible contention when the effects compete for selective attention, e.g. revealing labels can conflict with animation. The method is illustrated by an example analysis given below; and further details can be found in [3], [7].

Example

The method can be used for design or evaluation. To illustrate the latter the 1st cut attention graph for the cancer presentation illustrated in figure 1 is given in figure 2. Black lines indicate parts of the presentation predicted by the guidelines to be in focus, whilst grey lines show presentation components that are available, but unlikely to be focused upon. The vertical lines denote the desired contact points.

In the first frame three labels and objects are shown, 'primary tumour mass', 'blood from heart' and 'blood to heart'. The guidelines indicate that cueing labels with speech will focus attention on the label and its associated object. Walking through the graph, the speech track and primary tumour/label are marked as being candidates for initial focus. Guidelines indicate that at least 400ms should be allowed for the user to understand the image and label, if the image component and label are simple and the user has domain knowledge for rapid comprehension. Other guidelines give approximate estimates for reading times for longer texts and more complex images. The lengths of the bars in the attention graph denote viewing and reading times for the label and image.

The guidelines point to several design problems. The left and right vessel images both have labels but are presented concurrently possibly misdirecting attention. Guidelines advise that the labels should be revealed in sequence, concordant with the message script ' the tumour cell moves from the right to the left vessel'. Later in frame 2 the speech track makes a weak contact point with the image 'tumour cells detach from...and move into the vessels'. Reinforcing the message that the tumour moves from the right to the left vessel would be more effective if the label and speech references were presented concurrently following the order of the speech. The guidelines advise that labels should be revealed when cued in the speech track.

In the second frame, the guidelines indicate that focus will be drawn to the highlighted tumour cell, a desired effect because it is an important object. However there is a possible problem because display of the tumour cell label is not synchronised to form a contact point with the speech track in frame 1. The label should be shown when the tumour cell is initially referenced by speech to improve identification.

The tumour cell then begins to move in frame 2. The onset of motion will attract attention, and hold it while the tumour cell moves. When the cell stops moving, focus will switch to the next salient effect, the cell's label being displayed. Revealing labels is a particularly effective means of directing the user's viewing/reading sequence as a change in an image is a strong stimulus for focus shifting, an effect illustrated by the eye tracking data depicted in figure 1.

PROVIDING TOOL SUPPORT

A significant difficulty with design or evaluation using the paper based attention graph is the time it takes to perform the analysis. Authors of MM presentations are used to being able to rapidly change a presentation : eg delete and add media, and move media around in time. As the previous example shows, predicting a problem leads to the need to change the presentation, and thus requires further iterations of evaluation and design improvement. The time and effort consumed makes the paper based method unwieldy for real world use.

Our answer to these problems has been to embed the guidelines within a tool, enabling the generation of the attention graph and advising on potential problems in an interactive dialogue.

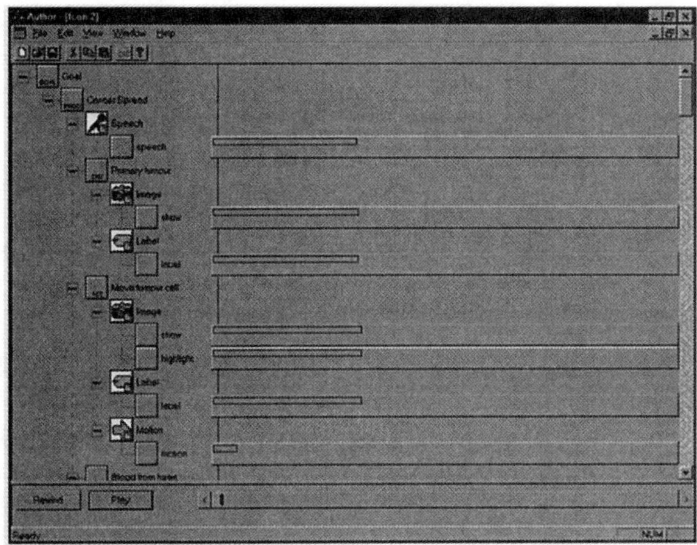

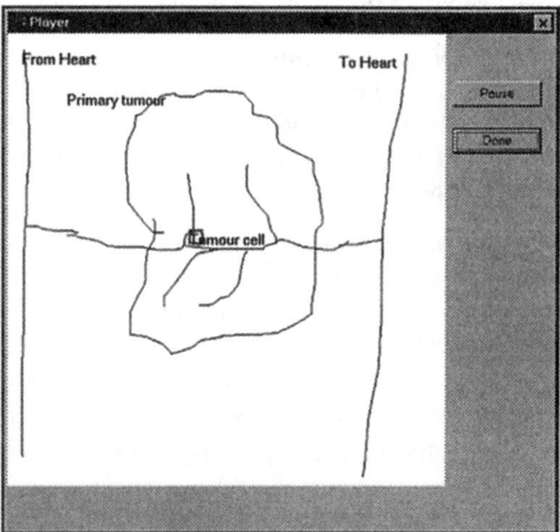

Figure 4 Screen shot of Task / Media model and timelines; sketch based play back of presentation produced

A prototype tool was built in Visual C++ and AMZI prolog under Windows 95. It has two main components, shown in figure 3. The authoring component is used by the designer to build a 1st cut script. This represents the media which are to be presented in an approximate sequence. The designer enters the script as a set of media resources that are attached to logical components of the message such as procedures, objects and actions. The designer then adds presentation effects to the script, such as speech clips, labels, images, animations and highlights, following the system's advice. Images and small scale animations may also entered as sketches to try out various designs (see figure 4 right).

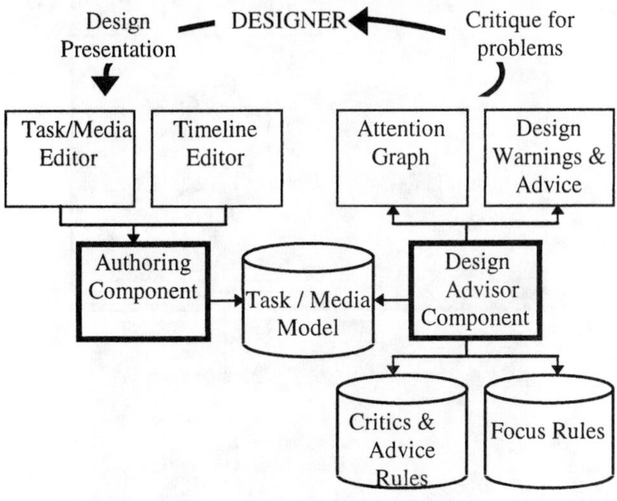

Figure 3 Tool Architecture

The start and end points of each media component and presentation effect are then set using the timeline bars. Figure 4 (left) shows the 1st cut model as a hierarchy of logical message components on the left which are attached to media components, and timeline bars specifying presentation durations. Once the 1st cut presentation has been entered, it can be played for immediate feedback

The design advisor interrogates the model formed by the authoring component and applies a set of design rules based on our guidelines to produce the attention graph and design advice.

SUPPORTING ITERATIVE DESIGN

The aim of the design advisor component is to critique the emerging presentation as the user builds up the model by adding media components, presentation effects and adjusts timing via the timeline bars. The 1st cut attention graph is produced using a set of rules which search the input script looking for presentation effects in a priority order and adding default assumptions about reading and viewing durations. These may be tailored by asking the designer questions concerning the user's profile of domain knowledge, and the complexity and importance of individual images and labels.

The critic rules search through the script finding presentations strands that are concurrent, then identify synchronisation problems and potential conflicts in attention that may arise leading to the display of warnings with design advice. The notion of a 'critic' is similar to Fischer's [4] who defined critic based advisors that do not automate design, but attempt to spot and alert users to design problems which they can then fix.

The tool allows limited adaptation of the critics and the attention graph. The designer can choose to de-activate any warnings with which they disagree. The tool also allows the designer to selectively add information concerning the media to tailor generation of the attention graph. Currently, the designer can specify that media are familiar, and thus may require short reading/viewing times; that an image (or a component) is perceptually prominent, and so will get precedence in focus; and can set the minimum viewing/reading times for a class of media.

Rule Implementation

The attention graph and critic components were built in prolog within an expert system shell. The rules used to produce the attention graph and to critique it will now be described in more detail :

a) *Initialise* : The first set of rules are used to initialise the focus search. Housekeeping rules check that focus can only be set on highlights, labels and animation when their associated image component has been displayed. The rules also create separate timelines for visual and audio media.

b) *Find a candidate start time* : The next set of rules search through the start and end times in the media model, seeking components which could potentially be in focus. The start time of one of the components is selected, based on the following salience priorities.

i) Any animation will be selected first. These rules recognise that animation have a very high attentional value and will gain focus as soon as it is released by other salient effects, and will act as an interrupt on media with lower salience, e.g. text and still image.

ii) Attention is set to highlights when they are displayed. Highlights have a lower priority than animation with an inbuilt waning factor of 200 ms, so other effects can compete for attention soon after the highlight is displayed. The tool makes provision for multiple highlight types, which can be set to different priority levels (e.g. colour icon, box surround, point by arrow).

iii) Attention is set to labels when they are displayed. Revealing labels has a lower salience than animation or highlights, and the effect wanes rapidly so other effects can complete for attention soon after (200 ms default) a label is displayed.

iv) The start time is set to media components in the absence of any salient effects or animation. Image is selected as a default over text, while other user configurable rules can discriminate between media components on criteria of window size, position, image complexity, and text formatting characteristics (size, fonts, etc.). The advisor can only work with this information if it is input by the designer, and at present we do not use this level of detail.

c) *Check visual focus priority* : Having found a candidate timeline start time, the advisor now prioritises the presentation effects throughout the script using the following rules.

i) If more than one effect can start at the same time, effects are favoured which are semantically related to the prior focus; this ensures that the current focus will move, e.g. from an image to the image's highlight or label effect.

ii) Focus is given to highlight or labels which are also referenced by speech.

iii) As salient effects finish or time-out, attention is set to any effects or components which are available, i.e. viewable by the user, but have not yet gained focus. The rules backtrack over the timelines searching for effects which did not gain focus earlier, using priority rules and then recency to adjudicate between effects with equal priority.

d) *Set focus duration* : These rules set the focus duration to allow a minimum reading time for a label/text or viewing time for an image or animation.

i) Animations are given focus for their entire duration. This is because tracking motion requires focus to be maintained.

ii) Labels are given 200 msec focus per word in the label; giving a reading rate of 2 secs for a simple sentence

iii) Longer texts are given defaults calculated at a 120 word per minute reading rate.

iv) Single, simple components in images are given 200 msec for focus.

e) *Add warnings* : A set of critic rules are applied to spot potential focus problems. These step through the presentation script testing which media components and effects may compete for the user's attention.

i) A search is made for any effects with overlapping durations which would compete for focus. These rules find any effects which have been prevented from getting focus because of competition from a dominant effect. The rules add warnings and design advice e.g. if an image is revealed during an animation, a warning will be given because the animation will block focus on the image.

ii) Inter component and effect dependencies are checked, e.g. if a label is shown, then the referenced image component is checked to ensure that it is viewable and that attention to it has not been blocked.

iii) A search is made for speech contact points to text labels. The system adds advice that labels should be shown when cued in the speech.

iv) Finally, the media model is checked to ensure that attention to each component has not been over-ridden by other components with more dominant effects.

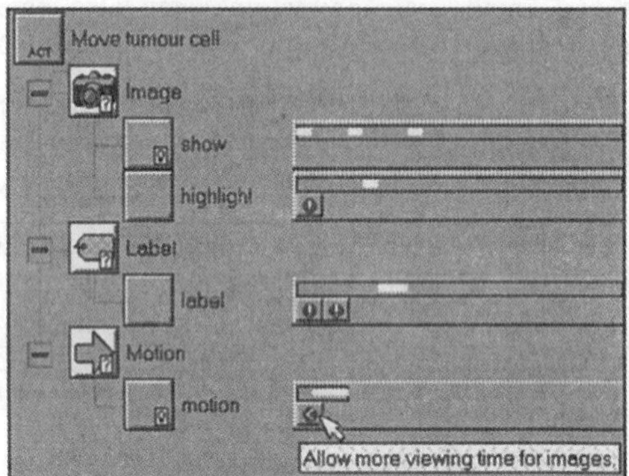

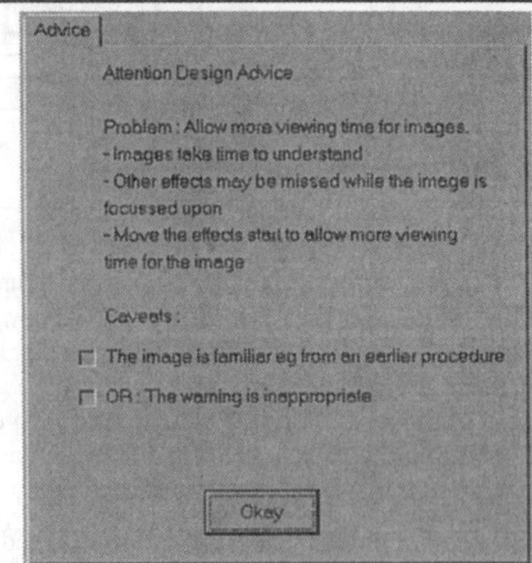

Figure 6 Tool tip and detailed advice of design problem

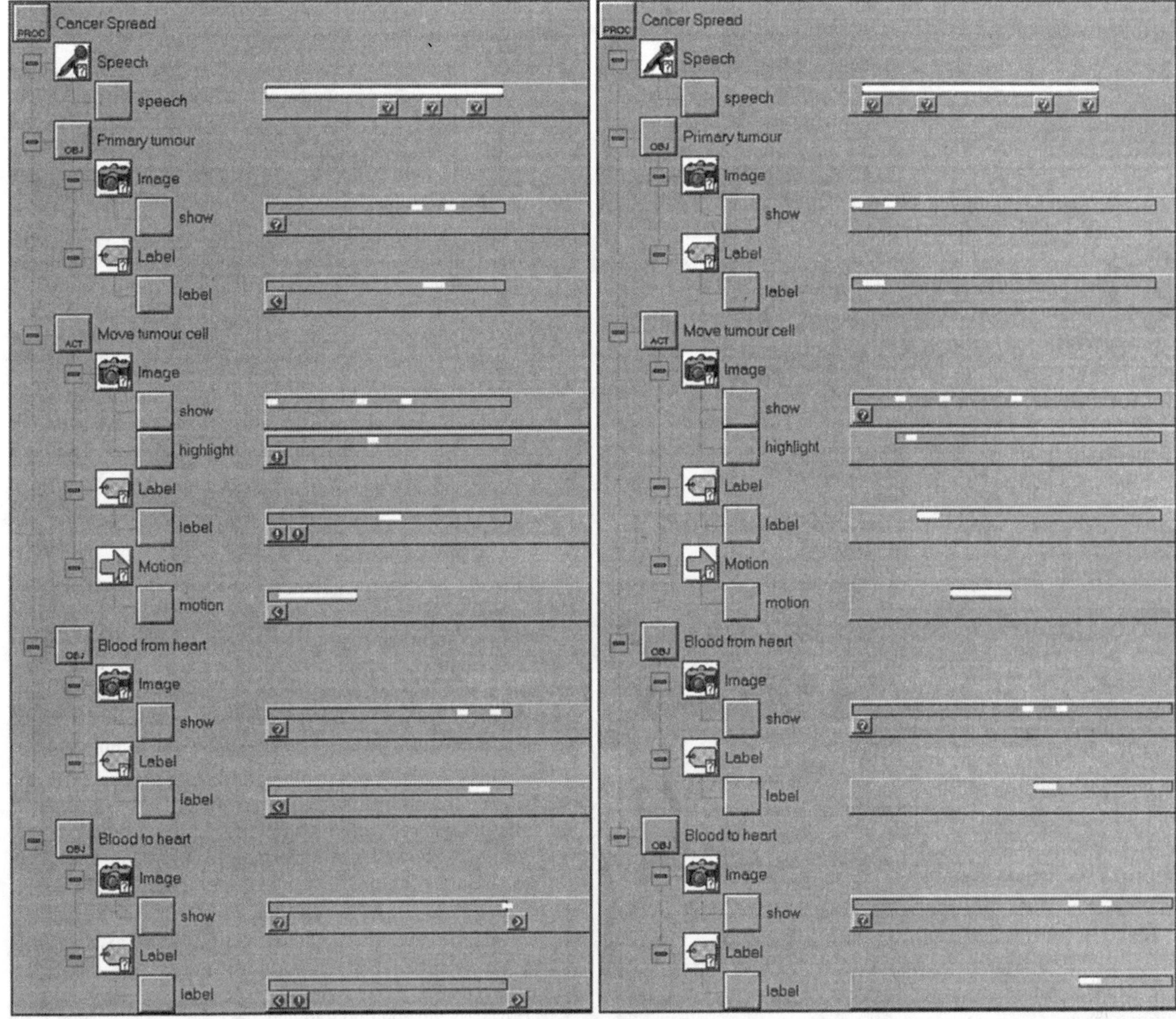

Figure 7 Default and Re-authored Presentation used in user studies

Example

Figure 7 (left) shows the attention graph for a simplified presentation for the cancer sequence, in which all the effects are shown in their initial, input state. The white lines show which part of the presentation will be in focus, and for how long. In the examples shown, simple image components require at 200msec viewing time, whilst two word labels require 400msec.

Design advice is delivered by icons, denoting potential problems. The icons provide a warning about the problem type, then give more details when clicked (see figure 6). To aid the user, different icon types are used to code warnings as related to effects either prior ('<'), post ('>') or within the timeline bar ('!'). Advice is offered using '?' icons; these do not represent problems, but suggest how to improve the presentation. If the user wishes to disable any of the warnings, this is achieved via the checkboxes on the advice dialogue (figure 6, bottom).

Walking through figure 7 (left), focus (in white) is initially given to the tumour cell image, because the animation has a higher attentional priority than the primary tumour, right or left vessel images. Focus is held on the tumour cell image for the duration of its motion. Warnings are added to the start of the other timeline bars to show that potential focus conflicts may exist because they start when the animation is running.

When the animation ends, the rules search for other effects related to the tumour cell image, hence they set focus to the cell highlight and label and allow reading time for the label. Next, focus is given arbitrarily to the primary tumour, since both it and the left and the right vessel all have the effects with the same priority level. Again, reading time is allowed for the label.

Focus then switches to the blood vessel images and labels. Note that the blood to heart image's focus bar is set beyond the end of the presentation, and that the label does not attain focus. This suggests that information in the image and label may not be assimilated by the user as insufficient time is allowed for other effects competing for attention. Warnings are added to the end of the bars to alert the designer to these problems.

By re-arranging the bars, the designer can remove the problems. Figure 7 (right), shows a re-authored version of the presentation, in which the focus contention problems have been removed. Each of the labels are revealed in sequence when cued in the speech. Reading time is allowed for each label and image before another effect is shown. The animation of the tumour cell is sequenced later in the presentation so that it does not conflict with the labels. The remaining '?' buttons remind the designer to ensure labels are shown when cued in speech, and warn that images should only be revealed together if they are related to the same topic.

EVALUATING THE ADVISOR

We conducted a within subject study using six novice designers, comparing their presentations with and without the design advisor, to test the tool's effectiveness. The subjects were given a set of sketched images, animation, labels and speech for the cancer presentation arranged in an initial script, shown in figure 7 (left). This had a simplified speech track ('The primary tumour contains a tumour cell which detaches and enters the blood stream') but was otherwise similar to the original in figure 1.

The subjects were set two problems. First, they had to produce the best presentation they could, modifying the media presentation order and durations from the default in figure 7 (left), without help from the design advisor. Once they were satisfied with their presentations, the subjects were then given the same default presentation, but with the design advisor activated.

Gold Standard Solutions	Advice Off (/6)	Advice On (/6)
i) Allow reading time for Primary Tumour label	1	6
ii) Reveal Tumour cell Label when cued in speech	2	6
iii) Reveal Tumour cell Highlight when cued in speech	5	6
iv) Allow reading time for Tumour Cell Label	1	6
v) Allow viewing time for Tumour cell Animation	2	6
vi) Reveal Blood from Heart Label when cued in speech	0	3
vii) Allow reading time for Blood from Heart label	0	4
viii) Reveal Blood to Heart Label when cued in speech	0	2
ix) Allow reading time for Blood to Heart label	0	4
Total Solutions produced	**11**	**43**

Table 1 Solutions found without and with tool advice

Results

The presentations produced by the subjects were compared against a gold standard presentation, (see figure 7 right), produced by following our design guidelines. The subject's presentations were scored against nine key problems which needed to be solved to produce the gold standard (see table 1). The subjects were not very effective in producing presentations without the design advisor (see table 1, column 1).

- Only two subjects made any attempt to reveal labels when cued in the speech; and only applied this to the tumour cell label. The blood vessel labels and tumour cell label were generally shown concurrently at the start of the presentation, rather than when cued.
- However, five subjects did correctly reveal the tumour cell highlight when cued in the speech. This suggests that subjects may have realised the importance of speech cueing, but did not apply it consistently to their presentations to reveal other labels when cued in speech.
- All subjects failed to allow sufficient reading time for labels. Only one subject attempted to sequence the labels and allow sufficient reading time before showing the next label.
- Four subjects ignored the need to allow viewing time for the animation of the tumour cell. Of these, two subjects allowed the animation to run while the blood vessel labels were cued in the speech, making the labels compete with the animation for focus. One subject allowed the animation to begin at the start of the presentation, making it difficult to focus on any labels or view the image context in which the animation took place. Another revealed the blood vessel labels when the animation started, thereby removing attention from the labels before they could be read.
- Two subjects made authoring errors. One highlighted the tumour cell without showing the tumour cell image. Another showed the tumour cell animation and label without the tumour cell image.

Qualitative questions (rated on scale 1-5)	Average Score (/5)
i) How easy did you find it move around the timeline bars ?	4.5
ii) How easy did you find it to play back the presentation ?	4.66
iii) Did you find the tools advice useful ?	3.66
iv) How much of the advice would you say was valuable to you ?	3.28
v) Could you understand what was in 'focus' ?	4.16
vi) How easy did you find it to understand the tools advice ?	3.66
vii) Could you generally relate the tools advice to the presentation ?	4
viii) How easy did you find it to fix the problems the tool found ?	3.66
ix) Did you feel that the tool helped you in producing a better presentation ?	3.66

Table 2 Qualitative scores

With the design advisor activated, (see table 1, column 2) the subjects re-arranged the presentation to solve many more of the problems which were drawn to their attention in this condition:

- All subjects organised labels to be revealed in sequence to guide the user's attention. This was in marked contrast to their original presentations, in which labels were revealed together.

- All subjects successfully set most of the labels to reveal when cued in the speech track, and allowed sufficient reading time before revealing the next label.
- All subjects allowed viewing time for the tumour cell animation, and avoiding displaying labels for its duration.
- However, only two of the subjects successfully revealed the blood vessel labels when cued in speech. Two further subjects set the labels to be revealed after the speech had completed. They justified this by suggesting that they wanted the tumour cell animation to have a longer duration, and hence moved the labels later to avoid competing with it.

Subjects were also asked to rate a number of usability issues qualitatively, shown in table 2. Analysis of the scores showed that subjects rated the tool easy to use and understood the advisor tool's representation of the focus time line. The subjects were also mildly positive that the advice of the tool was useful, that the design problems identified by the tool were fixable, and that their presentations improved.

DISCUSSION

Using the design advisor seemed to improve the presentations produced by novice designers, however the subjects' performance raised several issues.

- Subjects took far longer to author the presentation using the advisor than without. They made an average of around 30 timeline changes in the passive presentation condition 'v' 120 or more with the advisor version. This suggests that using the advisor makes the subjects take more care and try more design combinations, but does cost in time and effort. As we used a within subjects design, they may have a learning effect, however the longer times indicate the tool encourage the desigerns to be more conscientious during their second design attempt.
- Subjects suggested that at times the tool overwhelmed them with warnings and advice. The current implementation does not scope advice to a particular part of the presentation, or rate the advice in terms of its diagnostic value. Thus moving one timeline bar can generate a half dozen associated warnings, which may only be connected to one problem. These difficulties may have reduced the subject's ratings of the tool in table 2. A solution may be to rate warnings by their severity, or cluster them according to their cause. Subjects tended to ignore the more detailed design advice, in favour of the shorter summaries. The detailed advice was used as a last resort, on average only two or three times for the session.
- Two subjects tended to ignore the design advice and used a trial and error approach to removing the design problems. One reported using the tool as 'a game in which the error buttons had to be removed'. This illustrates that design advisors alone may not solve the problem, designers also require background knowledge of the problem to help them interpret advice and motivate their appreciation of why it is useful. Configurability is also important, as two subjects disagreed with one of the advisor's warning, that highlights should be revealed prior to labels, but they were able to disable the warning using the configuration facility.

CURRENT WORK & CONCLUSIONS

Multimedia design guidelines have been embedded in intelligent planners [1] and media selection advisors [2]; however we believe this is the first tool to deliver design advice which is thematically linked to the reading/viewing thread in a multimedia presentation. However, our findings are limited to novice designers whom we selected because novices generally need more assistance than experts.

In our future work we intend to assess the effectiveness of tool support for experts and, furthermore investigate the relative contributions of problem representation in the attention graph and active guidance in the advisor tool. In earlier method validation studies, we found experts accepted the representations but found the guidelines either too detailed or questioned their applicability in different contexts. It seems that tool advisors have to be approached with care; they may be useful as tutors for novices, but experts may benefit more by internalised HCI knowledge with tools that help external problem representation and manipulation. Experts may require different means of design advice delivery through example based patterns as well as increased tailorability of advice.

In spite of these limitations the tool did improve novices' designs, and it was usable. However evaluation of the tool, although demonstrating its effectiveness, also yielded a salutary lesson that tool based advice in isolation can be mistreated. Tools have to be introduced in combination with methodology and basic education about the design domain.

ACKNOWLEDGEMENTS

The Etiology of Cancer CD-ROM is copyright of American Medical Television and Silver Platter.

REFERENCES

1. Andre, E. & Rist, T. The Design of Illustrated Documents as a planning task. In *Intelligent Multimedia Interfaces*, pp 94-166, AAAI Press, 1993.
2. Bernsen, N. Foundations of Multimodal Representations. *Interacting with Computers*, 6(4), 347-371, 1994.
3. Faraday, P.M. & Sutcliffe, A.G. Designing Effective Multimedia Presentations, *ACM CHI 97*, 272-279, 1997
4. Fischer, G., Lemke, A. & Morch, A. Using critics to empower users. *ACM CHI '90*, 337-347, 1990
5. Grosz, B. & Sidner, C.L. Attention, Intention and the structure of discourse. *Computational Linguistics*, 12, 1986, 175 - 204.
6. Kozma, R.B Learning with Media. *Review of Educational Research.* 61(2), 179-211, 1991
7. Sutcliffe, A.G. & Faraday, P.M. Designing Presentation in Multimedia Interfaces. *ACM CHI'94*. 92-98, 1994
8. Sutcliffe, A.G. Task-related information analysis. *Internat. J. of Human Computer Studies*, 47(2), 23-257.

101 Spots, or How Do Users Read Menus?

Antti Aaltonen
Aulikki Hyrskykari
Kari-Jouko Räihä
Department of Computer Science
University of Tampere
P.O. Box 607 (Kehruukoulunkatu 1)
FIN-33101 Tampere, Finland
+358 3 215 6111
{aa, ah, kjr}@cs.uta.fi
http://www.cs.uta.fi/research/hci/

ABSTRACT
In modern graphical user interfaces pull-down menus are one of the most frequently used components. But still after years of research there is no clear evidence on how the users carry out the visual search process in pull-down menus. Several models have been proposed for predicting selection times. However, most observations are based only on execution times and cannot therefore explain where the time is spent. The few models that are based on eye movement research are conflicting. In this study we present an experiment where eye movement data was gathered in a menu usage task. By analyzing the scan paths of the eye, we found that menus are read in sequential sweeps. This may explain why the best models produced by previous research are hybrid models that combine systematic reading behavior with random reading behavior.

Keywords
Menu selection, visual search process, eye movement, eye tracking

INTRODUCTION

Pull-down menus (also known as drop-down menus) form one of the key components of the popular *WIMP* (Windows, Icons, Menus and Pointing devices) interfaces. Therefore it is important to understand how the users read and search menus to improve the usability of software products.

There has been a lot of research in the past about using menus in general [11], but all studies do not deal directly with pull-down menus. Pull-down menus are usually command menus and the interaction with them may differ greatly from interaction with other kinds of menus.

Menu research has traditionally focused on performance. In empirical research the easiest way to evaluate this is to measure the selection time of a specified menu item. A model can then be constructed to fit the data and to predict selection times.

A popular class of models is based on Fitts' law [2] which predicts motor response time, that is, the time required to move the pointer of a pointing device over a certain distance to a target item. The predicted time is essentially a logarithmic function of the ratio of the distance from and width of the target. Fitts' law treats the menu as a 'black box' which takes user input and after some time and a mysterious process a menu item is selected. The main drawback of such models is that they are unable to explain what actually happens during the process. Obviously, in addition to the movement of the pointing device a cognitive process is required.

The few studies that try to explain the selection process in more detail are based on analyzing eye movements during a selection task. When a subject scans a menu (or examines anything on the screen) the eyes have to remain relatively still for some period of time for the information to be processed. The points where the eye remains still are called fixations. A movement that connects two fixations is called a saccade. The pattern formed by fixations and their connecting saccades is called a scan path.

The velocity of a saccade is very high and therefore practically no information is gathered during it. The information is acquired only while the eyes are relatively still during the fixation phase. The duration of a fixation is typically 120-600 ms, while the saccades last only 30-120 ms.

Two distinct visual processes, searching and reading, can be found in every menu-related task [3, 12]. Eye movements are necessary for reading and searching because the acuity of the visual system has some limitations. The acuity of the vision is highest in the foveal region. The radius of the fovea is only one degree of a visual angle from the centre of the fixation. Beyond that the acuity decreases markedly and for example the ability to identify letters is extremely low. Therefore eye movements are needed in order to change the place of the fovea during searching and reading.

It seems natural to assume that there is a strong correlation between selection time and the number of fixations during a menu selection task. Evidence for this was found as early as 1983 [1]. However, no satisfactory explanation has been found for the number of fixations needed.

Various search strategies (systematic vs. random) have been envisioned. The number of menu items scanned during a fixation has been considered (sequential vs. parallel strategy). The resulting models are conflicting and have to rely on a combination of strategies to achieve good

CHI 98 Los Angeles CA USA
Copyright 1998 0-89791-975-0/98/ 4..$5.00

prediction level. However, none of the studies have analyzed the scan paths in detail and explained what really happens during a menu selection task. It is hard to believe that an otherwise systematic search process would be occasionally interrupted by completely random hops.

We carried out an experiment in order to understand the selection process more deeply. Twenty subjects were each given 101 tasks. Our analysis of their eye movements confirms previous findings that indeed, selection is neither systematic nor random. Our main new result is that the random component can be largely explained by the fact that given a reasonably long menu (more than just a few items), search appears to occur in alternating top-down and bottom-up sweeps. This, of course, is not very surprising, but it can form a basis for a model that is both predictive and intuitively acceptable.

The rest of the paper is organized as follows. We first review previous research that has used eye movement analysis in studying menu selection. We then describe our experiment and the methods for analyzing raw eye tracking data. The results are analyzed and presented using information visualization methods.

RELATED RESEARCH

Card's result [1] that search time depends on the number of saccadic eye movements the user makes to find a desired item is a first logical step in analysing the search process. Differences between search times are caused by difficulty in locating the target visually. This is also affected by the user's experience with the menu structure. The more familiar the user is with the menu, the fewer saccadic movements have to be made.

Several theories about the visual search patterns in menu reading have been proposed. It is interesting that two of the visual search theories are conflicting and none of them have been proven by empirical data.

The first theory concerning the search strategies is based on Card's [1] hypothesis that visual search order is completely random. Intuitively this assumption seems unnatural. MacGregor and Lee [9] suggested a systematic strategy where search is done step by step starting from the first menu item at the top of the menu until the desired menu item is found.

Hendrickson [4] studied these competing theories about search order in more detail. He observed that the visual search patterns could not be described as purely random, and not as purely deterministic, either. He concluded that menus were scanned to a large extent by systematic patterns of eye movements, and conjectured that menu scanning could be represented reasonably well as a first-order Markov process. The nature of the "systematic patterns" was not explained in the paper.

In a recent study Hornof and Kieras [5] developed and studied six computational cognitive models, which simulated the visual search strategy of a human interacting with unordered pull-down menus. The lengths of the pull-down menus in the experiment were three, six or nine items. Each menu item was a single number. The basic models studied by Hornof and Kieras were serial (one menu item processed at a time), parallel (many items processed at the same time), random and systematic search order. The last two models were combinations of the others.

The evaluation of the models was based on observed selection times in experiments run with human subjects. No eye tracking data was gathered, although the model was based on predicted eye movements. The cognitive models were evaluated with respect to how well they matched the data trends observed in the experiments.

Hornof and Kieras found that parallel search, combined with both random and systematic search, conformed very well to the observed data and based on that they suggest that:

1) people seem to process more than one item at a time, and

2) people use both random and systematic search strategies when scanning the menus.

The question that still remains is: which factors cause a diversion from a systematic search strategy into a random strategy? In fact, it may still be the case that although the hybrid model fits the data well, there is some non-random logic that explains the deviations from a pure systematic strategy. This is what we set out to study in our experiment.

THE EXPERIMENT

Task design

The experiment was carried out in our usability laboratory in two stages. In the first stage three pilot tests were performed to evaluate the usefulness of our eye tracking system for determining the visual search pattern. In the pilot test we used Corel Corporation's WordPerfect as the test program.

After the pilot tests, we proceeded to the next stage with a larger test population. We decided to change the test program used in the pilot tests into a custom made in order to vary menu structure more precisely. In our previous test program, there were too many variables that could not be studied simultaneously. For instance, we decided to exclude hierarchical menus and concentrate on linear pull-down menus. Furthermore, it was observed that indications of menu item status (*e.g.*, checkmarks to the left of the menu items) and shortcut keys caught the users' attention, even though they were not used in the selection tasks. These were excluded as well to simplify the setup. Finally, the effect of greyed out (disabled) menu items was also left as a topic for further study.

Next, we planned the menu structure. Menu items were grouped into collections of similar items. Previous research (*e.g.*, [11, 13]) clearly shows that this improves selection times, and it is a technique customarily used in current software. Group size varied from 1 to 9, with one control menu containing 20 items without any grouping. Within the groups the menu items appeared in a random order, since the groups in command menus seldom convey a structure that would be useful in searching the items within the groups.

The lengths of the menus were 3, 11 or 20 items. The upper limit of 20 items comes from the biggest single pull-down menu that we found in commonly used programs. The lower limit of 3 items is the smallest reasonable length of a menu and 11 is the rounded mean of the two extremes.

The actual items were chosen to be names or concepts that were assumed to be familiar in our subject population.

The menu structure, groups and lengths of the menus are shown in Figure 1.

Movie	Geography	Animal	Person	Music	Weather	Date	Drink	Car
Action	Capital cities	Fish	Heads of the state	Classical composers		Today	Wines	Manufacturers
Drama	Continents	Reptiles	Actors/ Actresses	Pop groups/ Artists		Winter months	Alcoholic	
Musical	Countries	Insect	Sportsmen/ Sportswomen	Songs		Spring months	Non-alcoholic	
Western		Mammals	Artists			Summer months	Beer	
Sci-fi		Bird				Autum months		
War						Days		
Historical								

Figure 1. Menu structure of the test program

The total number of tasks was 101. The tasks were divided in two categories, similar to an experiment carried out by McDonald, Stone and Liebelt [10]. The first 60 tasks were explicit commands to select a particular menu and menu item, such as "Select Person | Jack Nicholson" or "Select Date | Monday". The second category, the last 41 tasks, were so-called dictionary definitions. There was no direct cue what to select. Typical descriptions of the target item were "The leading actor in *One Flew Over the Cuckoo's Nest*" or "First workday of the week".

Test program

The test program was written in C++. The program consists of standard Windows 95 components. In the program, the tasks were placed in the top right corner of the window, just below the menu bar. This position was chosen because this way the menus did not hide the task descriptions. A screen shot of the test program is shown in Figure 2.

The test program logs the users' mouse events in pull-down menus. The logged events are menu and menu item selection as well as highlighting of an item. All these events are recorded in a log file with time stamps.

Test users

We had twenty test users. All users were right handed and they have normal vision. To get as reliable eye tracking data as possible, the subjects were chosen so that they did not need eye glasses or contact lenses. Ten test users were male and ten were female. Their average experience in using computers was 3.6 years. On the average, their experience with GUIs was 3.0 years. In the following, the eight users whose experience with GUIs was more than 3 years are called experienced users, and the twelve users with less experience are called novice users. The average experience with GUIs in these two groups was 6.9 years and 0.4 years, respectively.

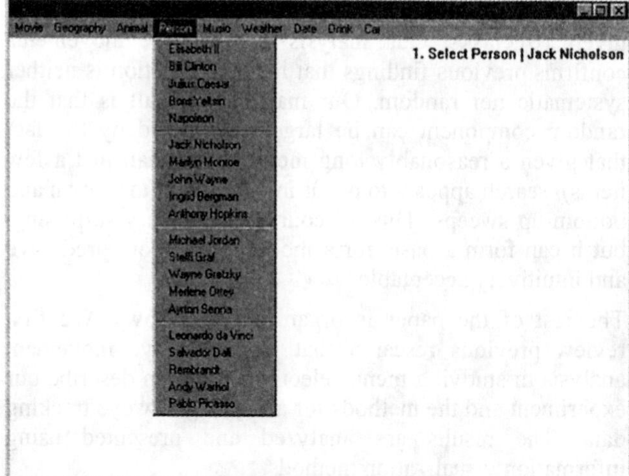

Figure 2. Screen shot of the test program.

Equipment

The computer used in this experiment was a 100% IBM-compatible PC with 90 MHz Pentium processor, 32 Mb of memory and a 17" Super VGA color monitor. The computer was used without a keyboard to prevent the user from using the shortcut keys in the pilot test, and the same setup was retained for the actual test. The operating system was Microsoft Windows 95.

The eye tracking system used in the experiment was Applied Science Laboratories model 4250R+ with floor mounted optics. The system illuminates the eye of the test user with infrared light, producing bright pupil and a corneal reflection. The system computes the distance between the centre of the pupil and the reflection. These measurements and the calibration of the system are then used to calculate the point of gaze. Similar systems have been previously used in HCI research by, *e.g.*, Jacob [7].

The system accommodates tracking mirrors and extended head movement options, which allow the subject to move his/her head more freely. This freedom makes the user feel comfortable, but it has one major disadvantage: the distance between the eye and the monitor varies. Therefore, depending on the distance of the eye and the screen, the fovea can vary from one menu item to three. However, our subjects remained reasonably still and there was very little variation in the users' distance from the monitor.

In theory, the accuracy of the eye tracking system is better than half a degree, but the human eye can change its fixation point within one degree of visual angle without physically moving the eye [7]. One degree visual angle is more than one centimetre on the screen from the typical viewing distance of a 17" monitor. A centimetre is more than the height of a menu item in Super VGA mode and therefore 640x480 resolution with 256 colors (VGA mode) was chosen for the experiment.

The computer was connected to a scan converter because the eye tracking system uses the screen as a scene. The control unit of the eye tracker superimposes the point of gaze cursor on the scene and the combined video signal is recorded using a Super VHS video tape recorder.

The test setup included a video camera. The camera recorded the users' distance from the monitor, which is relevant for the test analysis in order to calculate the size of the area visible in the fovea.

Test setup

Each test session began with an introduction of the equipment and purpose of the test. After calibration of the eye tracker the subject was first asked to read aloud two of the menus in order for us to obtain some ground data. Then the first 60 tasks were carried out. After the subject made the correct choice, a new task appeared in place of the previous one (see Figure 2). The subjects were told that this was not strictly a speed test, but nevertheless, they were asked to act promptly, in a manner that they would normally use when interacting with menus.

After the first 60 tasks there was a short break. The eye tracker was then recalibrated and the remaining 41 tasks carried out. The session ended in an interview. We first asked each subject to reproduce out of memory as much as s/he could about the contents of each menu. This was done to study the effects of learning, and is not included in this paper. Then the subjects were asked to give their own impressions of the search strategies they used, and also of the organization of the menus: did they observe the groupings, were the groupings logical, and did the subjects make use of the groupings.

On the average, the sessions lasted less than 40 minutes, varying between 30 and 55 minutes.

ANALYSIS

Initial analysis was made with the Applied Science Laboratories *Eyenal* analysis software package. The eye tracking system takes 50 samples in a second, so that tracking the eyes for, *e.g.*, 15 minutes produces 45000 points of raw data.

The *Eyenal* package can then be used to calculate the fixations from the raw data points. The algorithm uses a sliding window technique with a window size of 5 observations. We used the threshold of 120 ms for determining fixation starts as the first step in filtering the noise in the data.

Eye tracking data is never perfect. The system may loose track of the pupil or the corneal reflection, or the observation may be simply incorrect (*e.g.*, beyond the screen limits even though the subject is clearly looking at the screen). Tasks during which noisy data appeared were excluded from the analysis. Similarly, fixations that took place between tasks (from the opening of a menu to the selection) were excluded. This was done automatically by writing programs that filtered the merged log files produced by our test program and the eye tracker.

Moreover, some data could not be used because of user actions. If several menus were opened during a task, or if the user made an incorrect choice, we excluded the task from our analysis.

We realized only after the tests that leaving the tasks on the screen after the menu was opened was not a good idea. Occasionally a user started a task by opening a menu, scanned a menu for a short time, and returned to read the task description more carefully before continuing to scan the menu. Such tasks were, eventually, also excluded from the analysis. In the initial analysis phase we allowed one or two rescans of the task description. This would have produced a larger set of observations, but we chose the safe option of excluding all potentially unreliable data. There was no noticeable difference in the results.

After all this filtering, 1273 out of 2020 tasks (63%) were accepted for further analysis. We feel that the filtering was justified to obtain reliable data. A lot of data was still left for analysis; altogether there were 7928 fixations that took place during the 1273 tasks. To give an indication of the mass of data, all the fixations are plotted in Figure 3 using the Spotfire information visualization tool [6], which was used to analyze the data in more detail. It is illustrative to compare Figure 3 with Figure 1—some of the long menus clearly stand out. The size of each data point (though hardly visible) is proportional to the duration of the corresponding fixation.

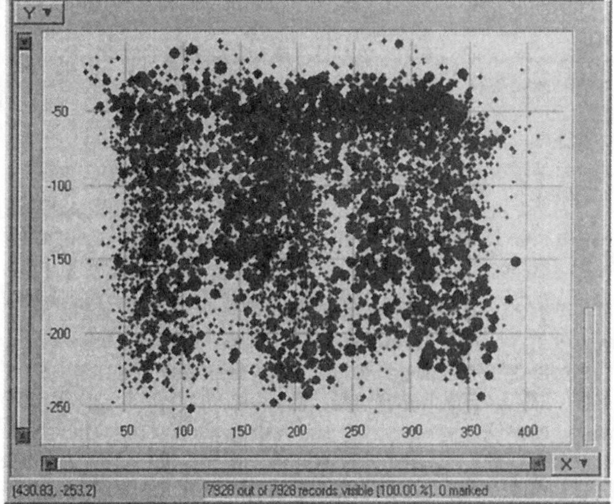

Figure 3. A plot of all the fixations that were analyzed.

RESULTS

We start by examining differences of eye movement in reading and selection tasks, and continue by showing that execution times in our tests conform to those obtained in previous research. We then analyze eye movements in more detail and show that they give additional evidence for menu search not being random. We then introduce the concept of sweeps, passes through the menu either top down or bottom up, and discuss how they explain menu reading behavior.

Vertical eye movement

To begin with, we present some data about eye movements in reading and selection tasks. Figure 4 shows side by side typical scan paths found in our experiment. The scan path on the left was created during the read-through task in the beginning of the test session, whereas the scan path on the right shows what happens during a selection task (here the user is selecting "*Staying Alive*"). The difference is remarkable. In general, the scan paths during the selection tasks followed a fairly straight vertical line, which often ran slightly to the right of the left edge of a menu. However, as Figure 3 shows, there was a lot of horizontal variation.

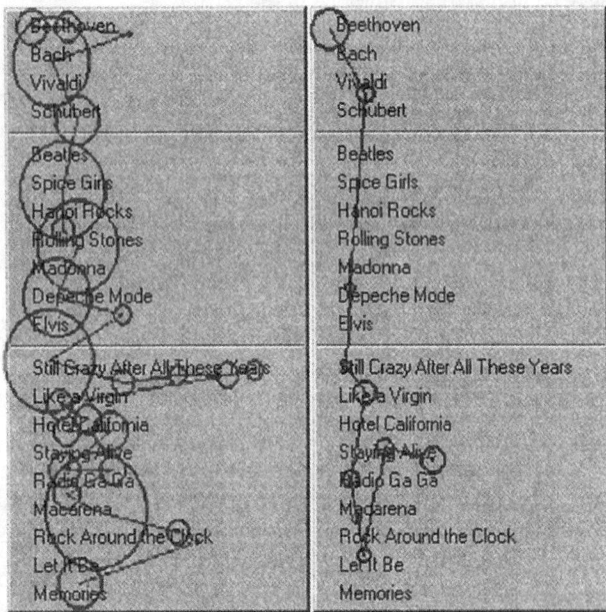

Figure 4. A test subject is reading the Music menu (on the left) and searching for "*Staying Alive*" (on the right).

The left part of Figure 4 shows that in a reading task, there was a fixation on almost every menu item, but only rarely (in case of long menu items) more than one fixation on the same level. The latter result is understandable, since from our viewing distance and with our screen setup, the fovea covered an area roughly the size of the circle in the beginning of "Depeche Mode" on the left. During selection tasks, the average saccade length in the vertical direction (over all saccades during the tasks that were analyzed) was 2.21 menu items. This supports the parallel search strategy (suggested by Hornof and Kieras [5]) where more than one menu item are processed at a time.

Selection times

Previous research has produced a fair amount of data on performance times, and it is interesting to see how our selection times fit the observations in previous studies. The selection times are plotted in Figure 5 for our three different menu lengths (3, 11 and 20 menu items).

An observation that has been made in previous studies (*e.g.*, [5]) is that there is a small drop in the time curve at the second menu item, *i.e.*, that selecting the second item is faster than selecting the first item. The phenomenon can be seen in our data, too, although not in the case of very long menus. We do not know why this is the case.

One of the main observations of our study is that producing predictive models for menu selection times is extremely difficult because of high variation between test subjects. For instance, the surprising peek at item 9 of menus with 11 items would not be nearly as high had we used median times instead of average times. The extremely long execution times of three test subjects for that particular item bias the results.

Even using the median times would not completely remove the problem, however. The ninth item in menus with 11 items was selected only once in our 101 tasks. The particular item happens to be "Bear" in the Animal menu, and the task was to select "A wild animal that likes honey"—not a particularly difficult task. But it was only the third dictionary task, so the users were not completely comfortable with the tasks at that point. A problem with eye tracking data is that variance is extremely high. Moreover, Figure 5 shows the combined results for explicit selection tasks and dictionary tasks, and for the outlying data point there were no corresponding explicit selection tasks.

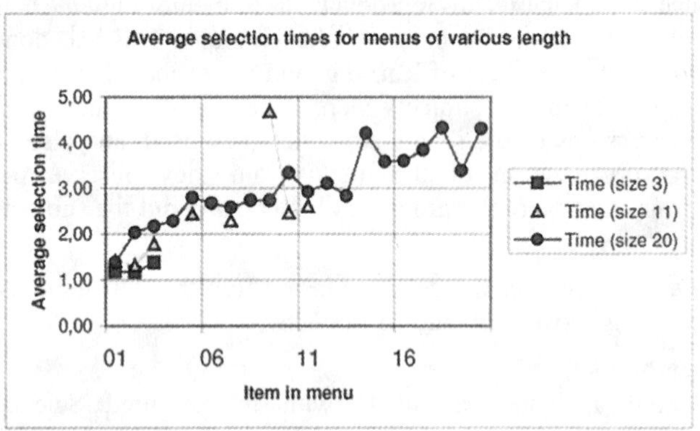

Figure 5. Average selection times for menus of various length.

Fixation patterns

We now turn to the main question of our paper: what actually happens during a selection task?

In Figure 6 we have divided the fixations in three categories. We say that a fixation is stable if its y-coordinate differs by less than half the height of a menu item from the y-coordinate of the previous unstable fixation. Thus, for instance, in the reading task in Figure 4, the fixations during the rescanning of "*Still Crazy After All These Years*" are stable, whereas the first fixation in "*Like a Virgin*" represents a down movement. Figure 6 plots the average number of down, up and stable fixations for each subject. The value on the x-axis is the total average number of fixations for that user.

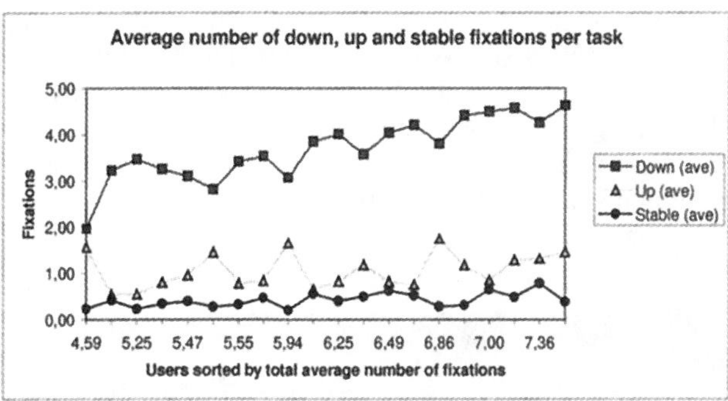

Figure 6. Down, up and stable fixations.

Figure 6 provides strong evidence that, indeed, menu search is not random. In the case of random search the number of down and up moving fixations should be roughly the same, and this is clearly not the case. It can also be seen that indeed, there are only few fixations within the same menu item, since the average number of stable fixations is below 1.

Figure 6 gives additional evidence for the fact that differences between the search strategies of different subjects can be huge. In fact, the same subject can use different strategies in different tasks. In Figure 6, the first subject (who was the fastest of all) had roughly the same number of down and up moving fixations. Next in the up/down ratio was the sixth subject, also an experienced, fast user. Clearly, these subjects used a more random and opportunistic strategy especially in the tasks that belonged to the first category.

This leads to the hypothesis that experienced users resort to different search strategies than novice users. Indeed, if we order the subjects by calculating the ratio of up and down fixations, then out of the top five subjects, four were experienced users. That is half of all experienced users.

Sweeps

If search is not random, what can explain the number of fixations and their direction? By viewing the video tapes and plotting numerous scan paths, a pattern began to emerge. It seemed that users often scanned the menus in sweeps—sequences of eye movements in the same direction. Formally, we say that a *sweep* is a sequence that consists of saccades that are stable or move in the same direction, and of the fixations that are the end points of the saccades. A down sweep starts with a saccade that moves down, and an up sweep starts with a saccade that moves up. (In the beginning of a task, a sweep may start with a stable saccade; then the first unstable saccade determines the direction of the first sweep.) For instance, the scan path on the right side of Figure 4 consists of two sweeps, the first being a down sweep and the second an up sweep.

Figure 7 shows the average number of fixations, average number of sweeps and average selection times for the test subjects.

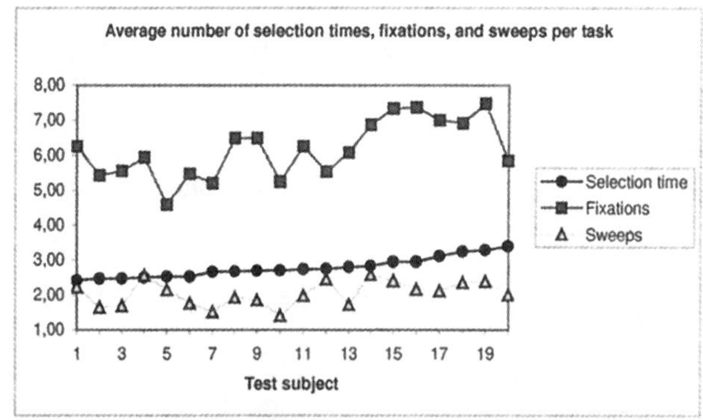

Figure 7. Average number of fixations, sweeps, and selection times (in seconds) for the test subjects.

How many sweeps should one expect to find in a scan path? By computing $E(k, n)$, the expected number of sweeps in a menu of n items and a scan path of k fixations, we could at least get information on whether the numbers seen in Figure 7 differ from what we would get with random search. Unfortunately, it is difficult to find a formula for $E(k, n)$. The expected number of sweeps without replacement (*i.e.*, when eye can never return to a previously visited menu item during a scan sequence) has been analyzed (Exercise 15 in Section 5.1.3 of [8]), but the case where replacement is allowed is harder. On the other hand, it is fairly easy to prove the asymptotic lower bound of $E(k, n) \geq k/2$. Figure 8 shows that invariably, the number of sweeps in a fixation sequence of length k is much smaller than even the lower bound of $k/2$, thereby giving evidence that sweeps do not occur at random.

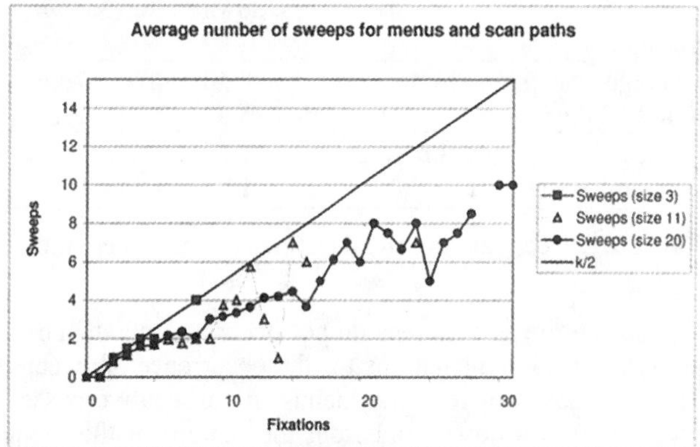

Figure 8. Observed average number of sweeps for menus and scan paths of varying length.

To summarize, sweeps do not occur at random, they fit well the behavior that can be observed in video taped tests, and they are intuitively acceptable as the basis of a model of menu search.

Altogether there were 2670 sweeps in the 1273 tasks analyzed. Average sweep length was 6.85 menu items and average sweep duration was 1.14 seconds. To get a better view of how sweeps occur, Figures 9 and 10 plot the lengths and durations of all sweeps in the analyzed tasks. The x-axis is the ordinal number of the sweep within a task. The jitter in the figures is produced to make the data points stand out.

Table 1 shows the average and standard deviation values for the same data. In some rare cases the first sweep was upwards, but even then it was short in length or duration, and the remaining sweeps followed the same pattern as the sweeps in other tasks. Therefore a total of 44 sweeps that went in the opposite direction from the general trend have been excluded from Table 1.

As shown already by Figure 7, the majority of the tasks are solved in a rather small number of sweeps. From Figures 9 and 10 we can see that after the first sweep, sweeps that take a long time disappear, and they generally take less than 3 seconds, in spite of being in some cases as long (in menu items) as the first sweeps.

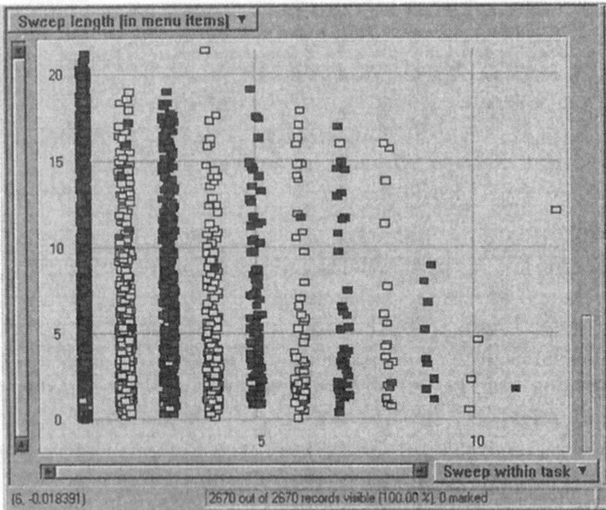

Figure 9. Lengths of sweeps (in menu items) as the function of the sweep number within task.

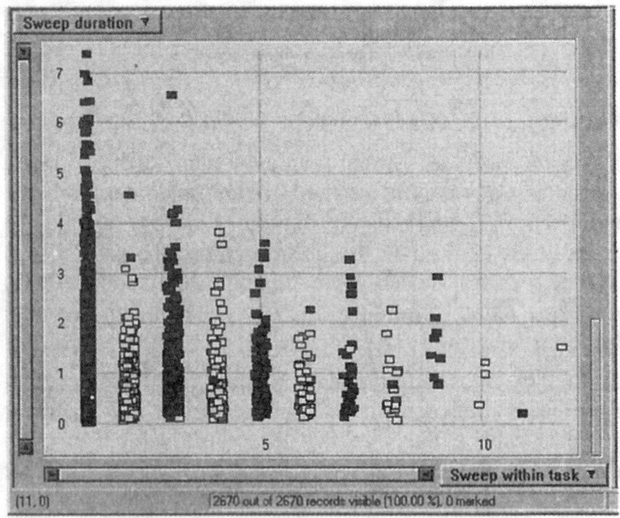

Figure 10. Durations of sweeps (in seconds) as the function of the sweep number within task.

Number of sweep within task	1	2	3	4	5	6	7	8	9	10	11	12
Direction	down	up	down	up	down	up	down	up	down	up	down	up
Sweeps	1259	609	358	174	97	56	40	19	9	3	1	1
Average sweep length	8.50	4.20	7.46	4.91	6.34	5.26	5.92	5.44	4.46	2.49	1.55	12.24
Standard deviation	5.57	3.77	5.11	4.42	4.73	5.28	5.03	5.04	2.85	2.05		
Average sweep duration	1.55	0.60	1.03	0.72	1.00	0.63	1.00	0.68	1.52	0.83	0.16	1.48
Standard deviation	1.05	0.44	0.86	0.65	0.77	0.43	0.83	0.57	0.73	0.47		

Table 1. Sweep lengths and durations by the sweep number within task.

We saw before that sweeps do not occur at random. There are two logical explanations for the occurrence of sweeps. First, the user can read the menus in consecutive passes, presumably top down, and from the bottom of the menu make a quick hop to an item higher up in the menu. Another possibility is that there are careful reading scans alternating between top down and bottom up directions.

The data (and the video tapes) give support to the existence of both reading styles. Figure 10 shows that sometimes the upward sweeps take almost as long as downward sweeps. However, Table 1 shows that in a majority of cases, upward sweeps are shorter than downward sweeps, both in length and in duration. The shorter duration is explained by the sweep being a fast hop to the top of the menu. Shorter length is partly caused by a return to a menu item that was just passed and which the user wants to recheck before proceeding.

To summarize, many reading styles emerge from the data, the most common being consecutive top down scans of the menus. The difference between up and down directions becomes less noticeable if several sweeps are needed.

CONCLUSIONS AND FUTURE WORK

Previous research has shown that menu selection times cannot be satisfactorily explained using a simple model based on any single search strategy. The models that best fit execution time data have been hybrid models combining various search strategies.

We have carried out an extensive empirical test where menu reading behavior was studied using both program log data and eye tracking data. The main observation presented in this paper has been the usefulness of sweeps, fixations moving in the same vertical direction, in explaining menu reading behavior.

The experiment produced a massive amount of data, and here we have only presented the first results. We plan to analyze carefully the effect of learning (using both observed behavior and the interviews), task type (explicit selection vs. dictionary definition), groupings, and position within both menu and group.

Initial analysis of the video tapes has also revealed interesting differences in menu reading styles when both the mouse cursor and point of gaze are studied simultaneously. Some users use the mouse cursor as a reading stick (move it from one item to the next), others leave it at the menu title and first search the target with their eyes, and yet others use the menu cursor as a landmark, leaving it to highlight the most likely candidate found so far while continuing the search with their eyes. Analyzing the reading styles used in each task could be used to create more accurate models to predict menu selection times.

Many interesting questions require further experiments. These include the effects of greyed items, marks of shortcut keys in menu items, and the effect of screen resolution.

ACKNOWLEDGEMENTS

We would like to thank all voluntary test users that made this experiment possible.

REFERENCES

1. Card, S.K. User perceptual mechanisms in the search of computer command menus, in *Proceedings of CHI'82* (Gaithersburg MD, March 1982), ACM, 190-196.
2. Fitts, P.M. The information capacity of the human motor system in controlling amplitude of movement. *Journal of Experimental Psychology 47* (1954), 381-391.
3. Graf, W., and Krueger, H. Ergonomic evaluation of user-interfaces by means of eye-movement data, in *Work with Computers: Organisational, Management, Stress and Health Aspects*, Smith, M.J., and Salvendy, G. (eds.), Elsevier Science Publishers B.V., 1989, 659-665.
4. Hendrickson, J.J. Performance, preference, and visual scan patterns on a menu-based system: Implications for interface design, in *Proceedings of CHI'89* (Austin TX, April-May 1989), ACM Press, 217-222.
5. Hornof, A.J., and Kieras, D.E. Cognitive modelling reveals menu search is both random and systematic, in *Proceedings of CHI'97* (Atlanta GA, March 1997), ACM Press, 107-114.
6. IVEE Corporation, Spotfire Pro 2.2. See http://www.ivee.com/.
7. Jacob, R.J.K. Eye tracking in advanced interface design, in *Virtual Environments and Advanced Interface Design*, Barfield, W., and Furness, T.A. (eds.), Oxford University Press, 1995, 258-288. Available as http://www.eecs.tufts.edu/~jacob/papers/barfield.html
8. Knuth, D.E. *The Art of Computer Programming, Vol. 3: Sorting and Searching.* Addison-Wesley, 1973.
9. MacGregor, J., and Lee, E. Menu search: random or systematic? *Int. J. Man-Machine Studies 26* (1987), 627-631.
10. McDonald, J.E., Stone, J.D., and Liebolt, L.S. Searching for items in menus: The effects of organization and type of target, in *Proceedings of HFS'83*, Human Factors Society, 834-837.
11. Norman, K.L. *The Psychology of Menu Selection: Designing Cognitive Control at the Human/Computer Interface.* Ablex Publishing Corporation, 1991.
12. Rayner, K. Eye movements and cognitive processes in reading, visual search, and scene perception, in *Eye Movement Research: Mechanisms, Processes and Applications*, Findlay, J.M., Walker, R., and Kentridge, R.W. (eds.), Elsevier Science B.V., 1995, 3-22.
13. Shneiderman, B. *Designing the User Interface.* Addison-Wesley, 1992, 99-137.

Visual Tracking for Multimodal Human Computer Interaction

Jie Yang, Rainer Stiefelhagen, Uwe Meier, Alex Waibel
Interactive Systems Laboratory
Carnegie Mellon University
Pittsburgh, PA 15213 USA
{yang+, stiefel, uwem, waibel}@cs.cmu.edu

ABSTRACT

In this paper, we present visual tracking techniques for multimodal human computer interaction. First, we discuss techniques for tracking human faces in which human skin-color is used as a major feature. An adaptive stochastic model has been developed to characterize the skin-color distributions. Based on the maximum likelihood method, the model parameters can be adapted for different people and different lighting conditions. The feasibility of the model has been demonstrated by the development of a real-time face tracker. The system has achieved a rate of 30+ frames/second using a low-end workstation with a framegrabber and a camera. We also present a top-down approach for tracking facial features such as eyes, nostrils, and lip corners. These real-time visual tracking techniques have been successfully applied to many applications such as gaze tracking, and lip-reading. The face tracker has been combined with a microphone array for extracting speech signal from a specific person. The gaze tracker has been combined with a speech recognizer in a multimodal interface for controlling a panoramic image viewer.

Keywords

Visual tracking, multimodal human computer interaction, skin-color modeling, face tracking, gaze tracking, lip-reading, sound localization

INTRODUCTION

While multimodal interfaces offer greater flexibility and robustness than traditional mouse/keyboard interfaces, they have been largely pen/voice-based, user activated, and operated in settings where some constraining devices are required. For truly effective and unobtrusive multimodal human-computer interaction, we envision systems that allow for freedom of movement in a possibly noisy room without the need for intrusive devices such as headsets and close-talking microphones. In order to make this goal a reality, we require not only efficient ways to integrate multiple modalities but also a better model of the human user based on a mixture of verbal and non-verbal, acoustic and visual cues. A visual tracking system can provide much useful information about users for computer systems. Using visual information and combining it with other information, it is possible to identify the message source, message target, and extract the message content. For example, a system can locate a user by merging visual face tracking algorithms and acoustic sound source localization, identify who is talking to whom by extracting head orientation and eye gaze, and extract message content by visual and acoustic speech recognition.

CHI 98 Los Angeles CA USA
Copyright 1998 0-89791-975-0/98/ 4..$5.00

In this paper, we present visual tracking techniques for multimodal human computer interaction. First, we discuss techniques of tracking human faces. A human face provides a variety of different communicative functions such as identification, the perception of emotional expressions, and lip-reading. Many applications in human computer interaction require tracking a human face. Human skin-colors can be used as a major feature for tracking human faces. An adaptive stochastic model has been developed to characterize the skin-color distributions. Based on the maximum likelihood method, the model parameters can be adapted for different people and different lighting conditions. The feasibility of the model has been demonstrated by the development of a real-time face tracker. The system has achieved a rate of 30+ frames/second using a low-end workstation (e.g., HP9000) with a framegrabber and a camera. Once a face is located, it is much easier to locate the facial features such as eyes, nostrils, and lips. This top-down approach works very well for many applications such as gaze tracking, and lip-reading. We describe some applications of the visual tracking techniques to multimodal human computer interaction. The face tracker has been combined with a microphone array for extracting speech signal from a specific person. The gaze tracker has been combined with a speech recognizer in a multimodal interface to control a panoramic image viewer.

TRACKING FACES IN REAL-TIME

Locating and tracking human faces is a prerequisite for face recognition and/or facial expressions analysis, although it is often assumed that a normalized face image is available. In order to locate a human face, the system needs to capture an image using a camera and a framegrabber, process the image, search for important features in the image, and then use these features to determine the location of the face. In order to track a human face, the system not only needs to locate a face, but also needs to find the same face in a sequence of images.

Facial features, such as the eyes, nose and mouth, are natural candidates for locating human faces. These features, however, may change from time to time. Occlusion and non-rigidity are basic problems with these features. Four basic techniques are commonly used for dealing with feature variations: correlation templates (Brunelli and Poggio, 1993; Pentland et al., 1994), deformable templates (Yuille et al. 1992), spatial image invariants (Sinha, 1994), and neural networks (Sung and Poggio, 1994; Rowley et al., 1995). These methods are computation expensive and hardly achieve real-time performance. Several systems of locating the human face have been reported. Eigenfaces, obtained by performing a principal component analysis on a set of faces, have been used to identify faces (Turk and Pentland, 1991). Sung and Poggio (1994) reported a face detection system based on clustering techniques. The system passes a small window over all portions of the image, and determines whether a face exists in each window. A similar system with better results has been claimed by Rowley et al. (1995).

A different approach for locating and tracking faces using skin-colors is described in (Hunke and Waibel, 1994; Chang et al., 1994; Yang and Waibel, 1995; Oliver et al. 1997). Color has been long used for recognition and segmentation (Ohta et al., 1980;Swain and Ballard, 1991). Using skin-color as a feature for tracking a face has several advantages. Processing color is much faster than processing other facial features. Under certain lighting conditions, color is orientation invariant. This property makes motion estimation much easier because only a translation model is needed for motion estimation. However, color is not a physical phenomenon. It is a perceptual phenomenon that is related to the spectral characteristics of electro-magnetic radiation in the visible wavelengths striking the retina (Wyszecki and Styles, 1982). Thus, tracking human faces using color as a feature has several problems. First, different cameras may generate different colors even for the same person under the same lighting condition. Second, different people have different color appearances. Finally, the color appearance of the same person may differ under different environmental conditions. In order to use color as a feature for face tracking, we have to deal with these problems.

Skin Color Modeling

Color is the perceptual result of light in the visible region of the spectrum incident upon the retina. Physical power (or radiance) is expressed in a spectral power distribution. Much research has been directed to understanding and making use of color information. The human retina has three different types of color photoreceptor cone cells, which respond to incident radiation with somewhat different spectral response curves. Based on the human color perceptual system, three numerical components are necessary and sufficient to describe a color, provided that appropriate spectral weighting functions are used.

In order to use skin color as a feature, we first have to characterize skin colors. Color can be characterized by a non-parametric model such as a color map, or a parametric model such as a distribution model. We are interested in developing a distribution model for representing human skin color distributions. The general procedure for developing a distribution model includes finding clusters, extracting features (dimensionality reduction), and determining a distribution. In order to investigate all these problems, we need a large amount of data. We have built up a database which contains about 1000 face images downloaded from the Internet and taken from our laboratory. This database covers different races (Caucasian, Asian, African American) and different lighting conditions.

Skin Color Cluster

A color histogram is a distribution of colors in the color space and has long been used by the computer vision community in image understanding. For example, analysis of color histograms has been a key tool in applying physics-based models to computer vision. In the mid-1980s, it was recognized that the color histogram for a single inhomogeneous surface with highlights will have a planar distribution in color space (Shafer, 1984). It has since been shown that the colors do not fall randomly in a plane, but form clusters at specific points (Klinker et al., 1987). The histograms of human skin color coincide with these observations. Figure 1 shows a face image and the skin-color occurrences in the RGB color space (256x256x256). The skin-colors are clustered in a small area in the RGB color space, i.e., only a few of all possible colors actually occur in a human face.

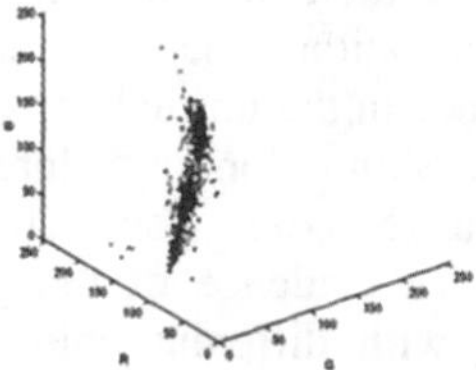

Figure 1. An example of a face image and the skin-color occurrences in the RGB space

Dimensionality Reduction

It is well known that different people have different skin-color appearances. Even for the same person, his/her skin-color appearance will be different in a different environment. In other words, many factors contribute to human skin-color appearance. In order to characterize skin-color, we hope to find a color space in which skin-colors are less variant.

For human color perception, a 3D color space such as an RGB space, is essential for describing a true color. However, a 3D space is not necessarily essential for all other problems. In the problem of tracking human faces, brightness is not important. Therefore we can remove it from the original information by normalization. Our experiments reveal that human color appearances differ more in brightness than in color itself. If we can remove the brightness from the color representation, the difference among human skin-colors can be greatly reduced. In fact, a triple $[r, g, b]$ in the RGB space represents not only color but also brightness. If the corresponding elements in two points, $[r_1, g_1, b_1]$ and $[r_2, g_2, b_2]$, are proportional, i.e.,

$$\frac{r_1}{r_2} = \frac{g_1}{g_2} = \frac{b_1}{b_2}. \quad (1)$$

They have the same color but different brightness. They can be mapped onto the same point through the color normalization (Wyszecki and Styles, 1982):

$$r = R / (R + G + B), \quad (2)$$

$$g = G / (R + G + B). \quad (3)$$

In fact, (2) and (3) define a $\mathbf{R}^3 \rightarrow \mathbf{R}^2$ mapping. the color blue is redundant after the normalization because $r+g+b = 1$.

Table 1: Comparison of mean and variance

	RGB Space	rg Space
Mean	$m_R = 234.29$ $m_G = 185.72$ $M_B = 151.11$	$m_r = 94.22$ $m_g = 81.59$
Variance	$\sigma_R = 26.77$ $\sigma_G = 30.41$ $\sigma_B = 25.68$	$\sigma_r = 4.93$ $\sigma_g = 3.89$

Another advantage of the color normalization is, we found out, that the color variance can be greatly reduced after the normalization. The same skin color cluster has a smaller variance in the normalized color space than that in an RGB space. Skin-colors of different people are less variant in the normalized color space. This result is significant because it provides evidence of the possibility of modeling human faces with different color appearances in the chromatic color space. Table 1 shows mean values and variances of the same skin color cluster in different color spaces. Obviously, the variances are much smaller in the normalized color space.

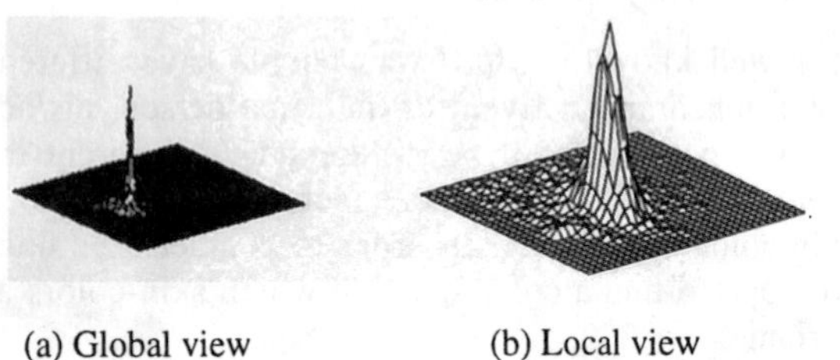

(a) Global view (b) Local view

Figure 2. Skin-color distribution of the image in Figure 1 in the normalized color space

Skin Color Distribution

We have so far revealed that human skin-colors cluster in the color space and are less variant in the chromatic color space. We are further interested in the representation of the skin-color distributions. Since we are investigating the skin-color distributions in a bivariate normalized color space, it is convenient to examine them graphically. Figure 2 shows the skin color distribution of the image in Figure 1. We have found that the shape of the skin-color distribution of a person remains similar although there is a shift in the distribution under changing lighting conditions. By closely investigating the face color cluster, we have discovered that the distribution has a regular shape. By comparing the shape of skin-color distributions with a bivariate normal distribution, we conclude that it is possible to use a bivariate normal distribution to characterize the skin-color distributions.

Goodness-of-fit Tests

Unlike most of the methods used in engineering statistics which assume a normal distribution of the measured data, we have examined whether the measured data of a sample do indeed have a normal distribution by goodness-of-fit techniques (Yang et al., 1997). Goodness-of-fit techniques examine how well a set of sample data matches with a given distribution as its population. The methods of performing a goodness-of-fit test can be an analytic or graphic approach. In the graphic approach, the most common method is Q-Q plot. We use this method to test our skin-color distributions.

The basic idea of the Q-Q plot is to use the cumulative probability of the sampling data against that of the tested distribution. A straight line indicates that we cannot reject the null hypothesis. We have tested marginal distributions and bivariate distribution. When we do marginal test, we test each variable separately against the normal distribution. When we test the bivariate distribution, we test the transformed variable against Chi-square distribution. We have built up a database which contains about 1000 face images down-loaded from the Internet and taken from our laboratory. This database covers face images of people in different races (Caucasian, African American, and Asian), genders, and the lighting conditions. Using this database, we tested the following NULL hypothesis: *human skin-color is normally distributed in a normalized bivariate space*. The results indicate that we cannot reject the null hypothesis (Yang et al., 1997).

Skin Color Adaptation

Although under a certain environment the skin-color distribution of each individual is a multivariate normal distribution, the parameters of the distribution for different people and different lighting conditions are different. A number of viewing factors, such as light sources, background colors, luminance levels, and media, impact greatly on the change in color appearance of an image. Most color-based systems are sensitive to changes in viewing environment. Even under the same lighting conditions, background colors such as colored clothes may influence skin-color appearance. Furthermore, if a person is moving, the apparent skin-colors change as the person's position relative to camera or light changes. Therefore, the ability of handling lighting changes is the key to success for a skin-color model.

There are two schools of philosophy to handle environment changes: tolerating and adapting. The most common approach for tolerating lighting changes is Color constancy. Color constancy refers to the ability to identify a surface as having the same color under considerably different viewing conditions. Although human beings have such ability, the underlying mechanism is still unclear. A few color constancy theories have demonstrated success on real images (Forsyth, 1990). On the other hand, the adaptive approach is to transform the previous developed color model into the new environment, Because the Gaussian model only has a few parameters, it is possible to update them in real-time. One way to adapt these parameters is to use a linear combination of the known parameters to predict the new parameters. The underlying theory is that a linear combination of Gaussian distributions is still a Gaussian distribution.

$$\hat{\mu} = \sum_{i=0}^{r} \alpha_i m_i, \tag{4}$$

$$\hat{\Sigma} = \sum_{i=0}^{r} \beta_i S_i, \tag{5}$$

Where $\hat{\mu}$ and $\hat{\Sigma}$ are updated mean and covariance, m and S are the previous mean and covariance, α and β are coefficients.

Based on the identification of the skin-color distribution at each sampling point, we can obtain its mean vector and covariance matrix. Then the problem becomes an optimization problem. We can use the maximum likelihood criterion to obtain the best set of coefficients for the prediction. We have investigated adapting the mean only, and adapting both the mean and covariance matrix (Yang et al., 1997).

Adapting Mean

In this case, the covariance matrix is assumed to be a constant and the mean vector μ is assumed to be a linear combination of the previous mean vectors:

$$\hat{\mu} = \sum_{i=0}^{r} \alpha_i m_i, \quad \hat{\Sigma} = \Sigma \tag{6}$$

By setting the derivatives of the likelihood function with respect to α to 0, we can obtain linear equations for solving α:

$$\sum_{k=1}^{r} m_j' \Sigma^{-1} m_k \hat{\alpha}_k = m_j' \Sigma^{-1} \bar{x}, \; j = 1 \ldots r \tag{7}$$

Adapting mean and Covariance

In this case, the both mean vector covariance matrix are assumed to be a linear combination:

$$\hat{\mu} = \sum_{i=0}^{r} \alpha_i m_i \;, \quad \hat{\Sigma} = \sum_{i=0}^{r} \beta_i S_i \tag{8}$$

In this case, there is no simple analytic solution available. An EM algorithm has been used to iteratively estimate parameters (Yang et al., 1997):

Algorithm

1. Initialization

$$\sum_{k=1}^{r} m_j' m_k \hat{\alpha}_k^{(0)} = m_j' \bar{x} \quad , \hat{\mu}_j^{(0)} = \sum_{k=0}^{r} \alpha_k^{(0)} m_k$$

$$C^{(0)} = \frac{1}{N} \sum_{k=1}^{N} (x_k - \bar{x})(x_k - \bar{x})' + \left(x_k - \hat{\mu}^{(0)}\right)\left(x_k - \hat{\mu}^{(0)}\right)'$$

$$\sum_{k=1}^{r} tr S_j S_k \hat{\beta}_k^{(0)} = tr S_j C^{(0)}, \; \hat{\Sigma}^{(0)} = \sum_{i=0}^{r} \beta_k^{(0)} S_k$$

2. Iteration

$$\sum_{k=1}^{r} m_j' \Sigma^{-1} m_k \hat{\alpha}_k^{(i)} = m_j' \Sigma^{-1} \bar{x}, \; \hat{\mu}_j^{(i)} = \sum_{k=0}^{r} \alpha_k^{(i)} m_k$$

$$C^{(i)} = \frac{1}{N} \sum_{k=1}^{N} (x_k - \bar{x})(x_k - \bar{x})' + \left(x_k - \hat{\mu}^{(i)}\right)\left(x_k - \hat{\mu}^{(i)}\right)'$$

$$\sum_{k=1}^{r} tr S_j S_k \hat{\beta}_k^{(i)} = tr S_j C^{(i)}, \; \hat{\Sigma}^{(i)} = \sum_{i=0}^{r} \beta_k^{(i)} S_k$$

3. If max ($|\beta_j(i) - \beta_j(i-1)|$) < ε for a small number $\varepsilon > 0$, stop; otherwise continue

Tracking Human Face in Real-time

A direct application of the skin-color model is to locate a face in an image. A straightforward way to locate a face is to match the model with the input image to find the face color clusters. Each pixel of the original image is converted into the chromatic color space and then compared with the distribution of the skin-color model. Since the skin colors occur in a small area of the chromatic color space, the matching process is very fast. This is useful for real-time face tracking. By combining the adaptive skin color model with the motion model and the camera model, we have developed a real-time face tracker (Yang and Waibel, 1995). The system has achieved a rate of 30+ frames/second with 305 x 229 input sequences of images on both HP and Alpha workstations. The system can track a person's face while the person walks, jumps, sits and rises. The QuickTime movies of demo sequences in different situations and on different subjects can be found on the web site http://www.is.cs.cmu.edu/ISL.multimodal.face.html.

Application to Tele-conference

An immediate application of the face tracker is to use it to automatically follow the speaker in a tele-conference. We describe a more interesting application in this subsection.

In a tele-conference, the quality of the conference greatly depends on image transmission. The bottle neck of the traffic is in the network. People have been working very hard on data compression techniques to reduce data transmission. However, there is a limitation on compression. In such a case, if we want to continue the conference, we have to discard some data. One way to do this is to skip some frames, which may result in losing important information. We want to keep the important information and discard relative unimportant data. To achieve this goal, we can add a selective function on the top of original codec to select the important information. In a tele-conference, the speaker is the center, We would like to keep updating speaker's information. Then, we could use the face tracker to track the speaker and select the region surrounding the facial area by a window. The window size is adjustable based on network bandwidth. When network traffic is good, the window is the entire image. When the network bandwidth is not enough, the window size is shrunk, and even the image is converted to grey scale. We have developed a system (Yang et al., 1996) by adding the face tracker on the top of vic, a public domain available tele-conference software. The system can provide several filtering schemes such pseudo-cropping, slicing, and blurring. Figure 3 shows how these filtering schemes work.

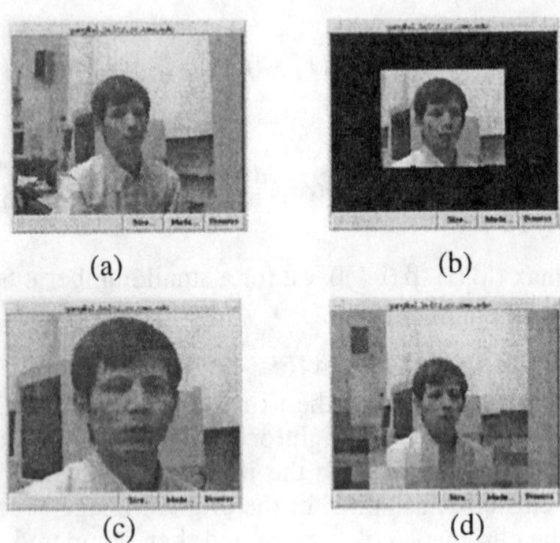

Figure 3. Different filtering schemes: (a) original; (b) pseudo-cropping; (c) slicing; (d) blurring

SEARCHING AND TRACKING FACIAL FEATURES

The face tracker can also be used as a base for other applications. Once a face is located, it is much easier to locate other features such as pupils, lips and nostrils. This top-down approach works very well for many applications. In this section, we show how to track these facial features in real-time and use them to estimate human gaze direction (Stiefelhagen et al., 1996).

Locating Facial Features

We first describe methods to locate and track the pupils, the lip corners and the nostrils within a found face.

Searching For Pupils

Assuming a frontal view of the face initially, we can search for the pupils by looking for two dark regions that satisfy certain geometric constraints and lie within a certain area of the face. For a given situation, these dark regions can be located by applying a fixed threshold to the gray-scale image. However, the threshold value may change for different people and lighting conditions. To use the thresholding method under changing lighting conditions, we developed an iterative thresholding algorithm. The algorithm iteratively thresholds the image until a pair of regions that satisfies the geometric constraints can be found.

Figure 4 shows the iterative thresholding of the search window for the eyes with thresholds k_i. After three iterations, both pupils are found.

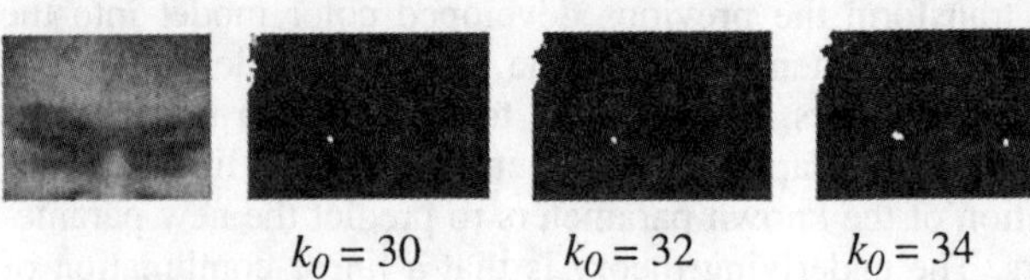

Figure 4. Iterative thresholding of the eye region

Searching For Lip Corners

First, the approximate positions of the lip corners are predicted, using the positions of the eyes, the face-model and the assumption, that we have a near-frontal view. A generously big area around those points is extracted and used for further search.

Finding the vertical position of the line between the lips is done by using a horizontal integral projection P_h of the grey-scale-image in the search-region. Because the lip line is the darkest horizontally extended structure in the search area, its vertical position can be located where P_h has its global minimum. The horizontal boundaries of the lips can be found by applying a horizontal edge detector to the refined search area and regarding the vertical integral projection of this horizontal edge image. The positions of the lip corners can be found by looking for the darkest pixel along the two columns in the search area located at the horizontal boundaries.

Searching For Nostrils

Similarly to searching for the eyes, the nostrils can be found by searching for two dark regions, that satisfy certain geometric constraints. Here the search-region is restricted to an area below the eyes and above the lips. Again, iterative thresholding is used to find a pair of legal dark regions, that are considered as the nostrils.

Tracking Facial Features

Once the facial features are located, the problems become tracking those features.

Tracking Eyes

To track the eyes, simple darkest pixel finding in the predicted search-windows around the last positions is used.

Tracking Lip Corners

Our approach to track the lip-corners consists of the following steps:

1. Search for the darkest pixel in a search-region right of the predicted position of the left corner and left of the predicted position of the right corner. The found points will lie on the line between the lips.

2. Search for the darkest path along the lip-line for a certain distance d to the left and right respectively, and choose positions with maximum contrast along the search-path as lip-corners.

Because the shadow between the upper and lower lip is the darkest region in the lip-area, the search for the darkest pixel in the search windows near the predicted lip corners ensures that even with a bad prediction of the lip corners, a point on the line between the lips is found. Then the true positions of the lip corners can be found in the next step. Figure 5 shows the two search windows for the points on the line between the lips. The two white lines mark the search paths along the darkest paths, starting from where the darkest pixel in the search windows have been found. The found corners are marked with small boxes.

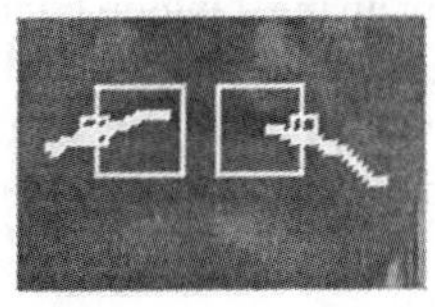
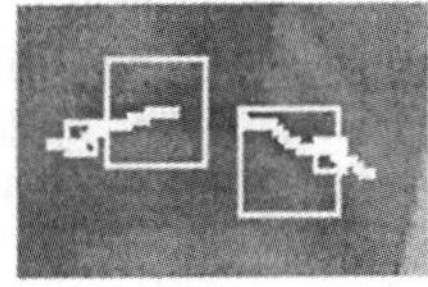

Figure 5. Search for lip corners along the line between the lips

Tracking Nostrils

Tracking the nostrils is also done by iteratively thresholding the search-region and looking for 'legal' blobs. But whereas we have to search for a relatively large area in the initial search, during tracking, the search-window can be positioned around the previous positions of the nostrils, and can be much smaller. Furthermore, the initial threshold can be initialized with a value that is a little lower than the intensity of the nostrils in the previous frame. This limits the number of necessary iterations to a small value.

However, both nostrils are not always visible in the image. For example, when the head is rotated strongly to the right, the right nostril will disappear, and only the left one will remain visible. To deal with this problem, the search for two nostrils is done only for a certain number of iterations. If no nostril-pair is found, then only one nostril is searched for by looking for the darkest pixel in the search window for the nostrils.

To decide which of the two nostrils was found, we choose the nostril, that leads to the pose which implies smoother motion of the head compared to the pose obtained choosing the other nostril.

Gaze Tracking

The locations of facial features can be used to estimate the person's gaze direction, or head pose, using a 3D model (Stiefelhagen et al., 1996).

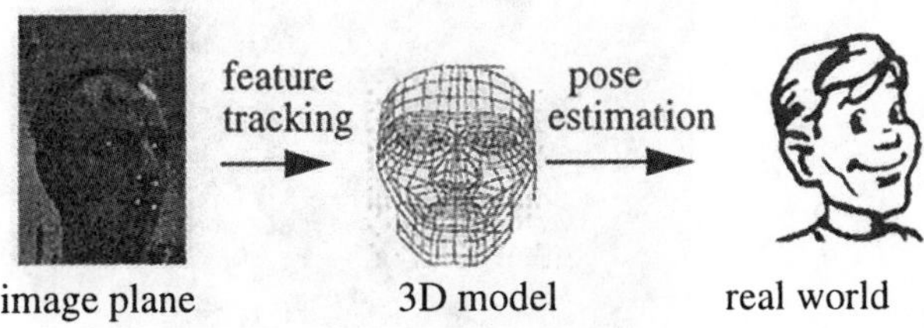

Figure 6. Gaze tracking as feature tracking + pose estimation

The basic idea is to estimate the head pose by finding correspondences between a number of head model points and their locations in the camera image as shown in Figure 6. DeMenthon & Davis (DeMenthon and Davis, 1992) developed an algorithm for estimating 3D pose of an object using as few as 4 correspondences of non-coplanar points. Since we can locate and track six non-coplanar facial features (eyes, lips and nostrils) we can compute the head pose. The current system has achieved a rate of 15 frames/second on a low-end work station (Stiefelhagen et al., 1996).

APPLICATIONS TO MULTIMODAL HCI

Human-human communication takes advantage of many communication channels. We use verbal and non-verbal channels. We speak, point, gesture, write, use facial expressions, head motion, and eye contact. However, most of current multimodal human computer interfaces have been focused on integration of speech, handwriting and pen gestures. In fact, visual information can play an important role in multimodal human computer interaction. We present three examples of multimodal interfaces that include visual information as a modality in this section.

Lip-reading

It is well known that hearing impaired listeners and listening in adverse acoustic environments rely heavily on visual input to disambiguate among acoustically confusable speech elements. It has been demonstrated that visual information can enhance the accuracy of speech recognition. However, many current lip-reading systems require users to keep still or put special marks on their faces. We have developed a lip-reading system based on the face tracker. The system first locates the face and then extracts the lip regions as shown in Figure 7.

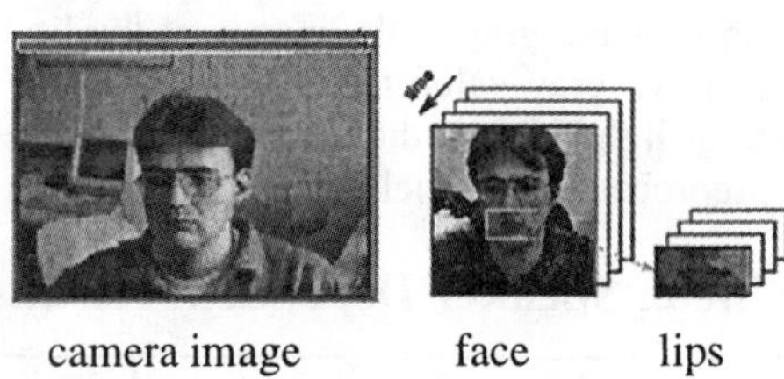

Figure 7. Basic idea of lip tracking

System Description

The system is based on a modular MS-TDNN (Multi-State Time Delay Neural Network) structure (Meier et al. 1996). The visual and acoustic TDNNs are trained separately, and visual and acoustic information are combined at the phonetic level. The system has been applied to the task of speaker-dependent continuous spelling German letters. Letter sequences of arbitrary length and content are spelled without pauses. Words in our database are 8 letters long on average. The task is thus equivalent to continuous recognition with small but highly confusable vocabulary.

Through the first three layers (input-hidden-phoneme/viseme) the acoustic and visual inputs are processed separately. The third layer produces activations for 62 phoneme or 42 viseme states for acoustic and visual data, respectively. A viseme, the rough visual correlate of a phoneme, is the smallest visually distinguishable unit of speech. Weighted sums of the phoneme and corresponding viseme activations are entered in the combined layer and a one stage DTW algorithm finds the optimal path through the combined states that decodes the recognized letter sequence. The weights in the parallel networks are trained by backpropagation. There are 15 hidden units in both subnets. The combination weights are computed dynamically during recognition to reflect the estimated reliability of each modality:

$$hyp_{AV} = \lambda_V hyp_V + \lambda_A hyp_A \tag{9}$$

$$\lambda_A = b + \frac{S_V - S_A}{\Delta S_{MaxOverData}} \tag{10}$$

$$\lambda_V = 1 - \lambda_A \tag{11}$$

The entropy quantities S_A and S_V are computed for the acoustic and visual activations by normalizing these to sum to one (over all phonemes or visemes, respectively) and treating them as probability mass functions. High entropy is found when activations are evenly spread over the units which indicates high ambiguity of the decision from that particular modality. The bias *b* pre-skews the weight in favor of one of the modalities. This bias is set depending on the signal-to-noise ratio (SNR). The quality of the speech data is generally well described by the SNR. Higher SNR means higher quality of the acoustic data and therefore the consideration of the acoustic side should increase for higher SNR-values and decrease for smaller ones. We used a piecewise-linear mapping to adjust bias b as a function of the SNR (Meier et al. 1996).

The system uses the gray-scale images of the lip region as inputs. Adaptive gray value modification is used to eliminate different lightning conditions (Meier et al. 1997). For acoustic preprocessing 16 melscale coefficients are used.

Table 2: Speaker Dependent Results

Test Set	visual only	acoustic only	combined
clean	55%	98.4%	99.5%
16dB SNR	55%	56.9%	73.4%
8 dB SNR	55%	36.2%	66.5%

Experimental Results

We have trained a speaker dependent recognizer on 170 sequences of acoustic/visual data, and tested on 30 sequences. For testing we also added white noise to the test set. The results are shown in table 2, as performance measure word accuracy is used (where a spelled letter is considered a word).

With our system we get an error reduction up to 50% compared with the acoustic recognition rate.

Panoramic Image Viewer

A panoramic image provides a wide angle view of a scene. In order to view a 360 degree panoramic image, we need to use a special viewer. In a panoramic image viewer, we need to control three parameters: pan, tilt, and zoom. The current interface uses keyboard and mouse to control them. Alternatively, we could control them by changing the positions of the viewing point., e.g., moving towards left and right, forward and backward, up and down. But it is more natural to control the panning and tilting with the gaze, and the zooming with the voice. We have developed an interface to control a panoramic image viewer by combining the gaze tracker with a speech recognizer (Stiefelhagen and Yang, 1997). With such an interface, a user can fully control the panoramic image viewer without using his/her hands. The user can scroll through the panoramic images by looking to the left and right or up and down, and he can control the zoom by speaking the commands "zoom in," "zoom in two times," "zoom out" "zoom out five times," etc. Figure 8 shows how the system works.

Figure 8. Gaze-voice controlled panoramic image viewer

Beamforming by Face Tracking

A one-dimensional microphone array allows the speech signal to be received in the half plane in front of the array. If the array is steered towards a given spot the differences of sound arrival time between the microphones are compensated for waves originating exactly from this location. By summing these aligned signals one achieves an enhancement of the desired signal while sound coming from other locations is not in the same phase and thus its audibility is deteriorated. On the other hand, if the system knows the speaker's location from visual tracking, it is possible to form a beam to select the desired sound source to enhance the quality of speech signal for speech recognition. We have demonstrated that a more accurate localization in space can be delivered visually than acoustically. Given a reliable fix, beamforming substantially improves recognition accuracy (Bub et al., 1995). Figure 9 shows the setup of the system.

Figure 9. Setup of microphone array and face tracker

CONCLUSION

In this paper we have described real-time visual tracking techniques and their applications to multimodal human computer interaction. We described how to track human faces and features in real-time. We demonstrated that systems that combine visual information other communication modalities into interfaces that are robust, flexible, and intuitive to use.

ACKNOWLEDGEMENTS

Support for this work has come from the NSF, under contract CDA-9726363, and the DARPA, under contracts N00014-93-1-0806 and N6601-97-C8553.

REFERENCES

Brunelli, R., and Poggio, T. (1993), "Face recognition: features versus templates," IEEE Trans. Pattern Analysis and Machine Intelligence, Vol. 15, No. 10, pp. 1042-1052.

Bub, U., Hunke, M., and Waibel, A. (1995), "Knowing who to listen to in speech recognition: visually guided beamforming," Proceedings of ICASSP'95.

Chang, T.C., Huang, T.S., and Novak, C. (1994), "Facial feature extraction from color images," Proc. the 12th IAPR International Conference on Pattern Recognition, Vol. 2, pp. 39-43.

DeMenthon, Daniel. F. and Davis, Larry S. (1992), "Model based object pose in 25 lines of code", Proceedings of Second European Conference on Computer Vision, Santa Margherita Ligure, pp. 335 - 343.

Forsyth, D. (1990), "A novel algorithm for color constancy," International Journal of Computer Vision. Vol. 5, No. 1, pp.5-36.

Hunke, M., and Waibel, A. (1994), "Face locating and tracking for human-computer interaction," Proc. Twenty-Eight Asilomar Conference on Signals, Systems & Computers, Monterey, CA, USA.

Klinker, G.J., Shafer, S.A., and Kanade, T. (1987), "Using a color reflection model to separate highlights from object color," Proc. ICCV, pp. 145-150.

Meier U., Hürst W., and Duchnowski P. (1996), "Adaptive Bimodal Sensor Fusion for Automatic Speechreading" Proc. Intern. Conference on Acoustics, Speech and Signal Processing, ICASSP 1996

Meier U., Stiefelhagen R., Yang J. (1997), "Preprocessing of Visual Speech under Real World Conditions" European Tutorial & Research Workshop on Audio-Visual Speech Processing: Computational & Cognitive Science Approaches (AVSP 97)

Ohta, Y., Kanade, T., and Sakai, T. (1980), "Color information for region segmentation," Computer Graphics and Image Processing, Vol. 13, No. 3, pp.222-241.

Oliver, N., Pentland, A., and Berard, F. (1997), "LAFTER: lips and face realtime tracker," Proceedings of CVPR'97, pp. 123-129.

Pentland, A., Moghaddam, B., and Starner, T. (1994), "View-based and modular eigenspace for face recognition," Proc. IEEE Conf. on Computer Vision and Pattern Recognition, pp. 84-91, Seattle, WA, USA.

Rowley, H.A., Baluja, S., and Kanade, T. (1995), "Human face detection in visual scenes," Technical Report CMU-CS-95-158, CS department, CMU, 1995.

Shafer, S.A. (1984), "Optical phenomena in computer vision," Proc. Canadian Soc. Computational Studies of Intelligence, pp. 572-577.

Sinha, P. (1994), "Object recognition via image invariants: a case study. Investigative ophthalmology and visual science," Vol. 35, pp. 1735-1740.

Stiefelhagen, R., Yang, J., and Waibel, A., (1996) "A model-based gaze tracking system," Proceedings of Joint Symposia on Intelligence and Systems (Washington DC).

Stiefelhagen, R. and Yang, J. (1997), "Gaze tracking for multimodal human-computer interaction," Proceedings of 1997 ICASSP (Munich, Germany).

Sung, K., and Poggio, T. (1994), "Example-based learning for view-based human face detection," Technical Report 1521, MIT AI Lab.

Swain, M.J., and Ballard, D.H. (1991), "Color indexing," International Journal of Computer Vision. Vol. 7, No.1, pp. 11-32.

Turk, M.A., and Pentland, A. (1991), "Face recognition using eigenfaces," Proc. IEEE Conf. on Computer Vision and Pattern Recognition, pp. 586-591, Maui, HI, USA.

Wyszecki, G., and Styles, W.S. (1982), "Color Science: Concepts and Methods, Quantitative Data and Formulae," Second Edition, John Wiley & Sons, New York.

Yang, J., and Waibel, A. (1995), "A real-time face tracker," Proceedings of the Third IEEE Workshop on Applications of Computer Vision (Sarasota, Florida, 1996), pp. 142-147 (Technical Report CMU-CS-95-210, CS department, CMU, 1995).

Yang, J., Wu, L., and Waibel, A. (1996), "Focus of attention: towards low bitrate video tele-conferencing," Proceedings of 1996 IEEE International Conference on Image Processing (Lausanne, Switzerland), Vol. 2, pp. 97-100.

Yang, J., Lu, W., and Waibel, A. (1997), "Skin-color modeling and adaptation," Proceedings of ACCV'98 (Technical Report CMU-CS-97-146, CS department, CMU, 1997).

Yuille, A., Hallinan, P., and Cohen, D. (1992), "Feature extraction from faces using deformable templates," Int. J. Computer Vision, Vol. 8, No. 2, pp. 99-111.

When My Face is the Interface: An Experimental Comparison of Interacting with One's Own Face or Someone Else's Face

Clifford Nass
Department of Communication
Stanford University
Stanford, CA 94305-2050
USA
+1 650 723 5499
nass@leland.stanford.edu

Eun-Young Kim
Department of Communication
Stanford University
Stanford, CA 94305-2050
USA
+1 650 723 2910
eykim@leland.stanford.edu

Eun-Ju Lee
Department of Communication
Stanford University
Stanford, CA 94305-2050
USA
+1 650 723 2910
ejlee@leland.stanford.edu

ABSTRACT

In this paper, we demonstrate that the effects of receiving negative evaluation from audio-visual image of oneself on a computer screen are clearly different from that of receiving someone else. When seeing the self-image, subjects claimed more responsibility for the evaluation, perceived the evaluation to be more valid and objective, and showed higher public self-awareness. Self-image subjects showed less impression management and less negative bias on recognition memory. Implications for using one's own face in virtual reality and other interfaces are discussed.

Keywords
Faces, computers are social actors, experimental research, self-image, self-attribution, impression management, memory

INTRODUCTION

Among the enormous number of visual and audio stimuli in the world, there is something very special about faces and voices. A large portion of the brain is allocated to face recognition. [7] Humans are so concerned with faces that people see faces where none may exist: A simple line drawing with two dots for eyes and a line for a mouth is readily recognized as a face [14]. Another large portion of the brain is devoted to distinguishing voices from other sounds [16]. When a person sees a face and accompanying voice, he or she makes inferences and assumptions about the person to whom the face[1] belongs. These inferences include the observed's personality, character and intention towards the person. Human faces are thus one of the most powerful human referents [25].

Of all possible faces (e.g., human, animal, imaginary), each person has one face that is in a different category from all other faces: One's own face. Since our own face is a unique marker of who we are (with the possible exception of identical twins), it is one of the most powerful suggestions of our "self."

From early childhood onward, virtually all human thoughts and behaviors are organized around the self [15, 16]. For example, at a noisy cocktail party, when someone says our name, it catches our attention [1]. In a different vein, the arguments that a person generate in a role-playing situation are more persuasive than equally good arguments provided by others [19]. Thus, a presentation of the "self" will likely be responded to differently than will other stimuli.

What is the self?

What then is "the self?" There is little consensus in the literature. Because there is nothing we can see, touch or pin down, defining the self has been difficult. We know that there is certain something called the self only through common sense and our knowledge of who we think we are and the things we believe belong to us and only us, but there are no independent measurement techniques [8].

However varied the views may be, scholars do agree that the self can be divided into several distinctive empirical selves that are distinguished from other people (e.g., physical or material self, social self, spiritual self). Although there are differences in the number and types of distinctions, one common factor is that there exists some

[1] For the purposes of concision, we use the term 'face' in this paper to refer to the combination of an animated face and an accompanying voice.

physical self [8, 12, 17]. This physical self includes the face, of course. Thus, we can assume that a key distinction that everyone makes is a distinction between one's own face and everyone else's face.

In the experiment described below, we have people interact with a video of a face on the screen. Half of the participants interact with their own face; the other half interact with someone else's face. The literature on people's distinctions between self and other, discussed below, suggest differences that we might find between these two interfaces.

Self-focused attention

Both self-awareness and self-consciousness involve directing focus of attention to various aspects about oneself, including such things as internal thoughts and feelings or how an individual thinks of oneself in relation to others [2, 5, 9]. More specifically, self-awareness is conceptualized as a state, whereas self-consciousness is a trait [2]. In this study, we are using a modified measure, self-focused attention (SFA), that combines the state aspect of self-awareness and the public and private dimensions of self-consciousness.

SFA can be seen to have two distinct dimensions: public and private [2, 9]. Public SFA is awareness of the self in relation to other people, or a concern about how others might view the person which attunes the person to the self-facets that are publicly observable. On the other hand, private SFA is the self-reflective side of awareness that tunes into inner thoughts, feelings and motives [2].

In previous studies, SFA was assumed to be heightened by exposing people to their reflections in a mirror, confronting them with their own recorded voices, or having a camera pointed at themselves [5]. So, interacting with a video of oneself can be predicted to lead to an increase in both private and public self-focused attention.

Self responsibility

Greater self-awareness has been shown to lead to greater feelings or responsibility for one's actions [6]. Thus, when an individual receives an evaluation from their own face, the individual will be more likely to take responsibility than would an individual evaluated by a different face.

Ego-enhancement

In all people, there is a basic need for self-esteem, as well as a need to protect and enhance it [23]. To ensure such ego-enhancement, people employ several strategies. For example, people may actually perceive their own performance to be better than it really is [19] or, more subtly, people may assign more importance to things they are good at, so that they may look better in the final analysis. People do these things without even being conscious of them.

If people are confronted with their own image, they will likely have a greater feeling that the behavior of the image is "their own." Thus, individuals interacting with their own face will view the behavior of the face more positively than will individuals that interact with a face that is not their own. In the particular case of evaluations, the evaluations from one's own face will seem more fair than will the evaluations from someone else's face, especially if the evaluations are negative (people are less accepting of negative information than positive information [20]).

Impression management

It is important to maintain self-esteem, because any threats to the self-concept can lead to anxiety, depression or other illness [13]. Impression management is a strategy of deliberate self-presentation to an audience. It is used to maintain a positive self-presentation to the outer world, thereby bolstering self-esteem. Because impression management is more important when confronting others as opposed to oneself, we predict that impression management will be smaller when a person interacts with one's own face as compared to when the person interacts with someone else's face [24].

Negative bias on memory

There is a general tendency for humans to remember negative information as compared to positive information [11, 20, 21]. Humans are more focused on threats than opportunities; thus, a focus on negative information has greater survival value than would a focus on positive information. Since a different person is a greater threat to an individual than they themselves are, negative information should be better remembered when it comes from someone else as compared to when it comes from oneself.

Linking the real world and the media world

In the research outlined above, people are either seeing themselves in mirrors or are led to focus on themselves. However, modern media provide the opportunity for individuals to actually *interact* with images of themselves. What leads us to believe that the prior research will carry over into the present domain of an interface with a face? The key basis for this extension of the research is *The Media Equation* [20], which demonstrates that responses to mediated presentation are remarkably similar to responses to real life. The most direct evidence for the equivalence comes from a study which demonstrates that people respond to faces on the screen in the same way as faces in real life. Specifically, it was demonstrated that faces on the screen can invade a person's body space in precisely the same way that real-life faces do: Faces on big screen, faces viewed close to the screen, and close-up faces claimed greater attention and resulted in better recognition memory [22].

Current study

The present study attempts to determine whether the literature on people's responses to reminders of themselves can be brought to bear in a circumstance in which they are interacting with a face that is their own but is behaving autonomously. This is, of course, a very different situation than either watching oneself in a mirror or on film, or in looking at a photograph of oneself.

The particular context we chose for this experiment was one in which a participant plays a computer game and receives primarily negative evaluations from either their own face or someone else's face. We chose this context for a number of reasons: 1) evaluations can be readily videotaped, 2) unlike other types of informational outputs, knowing that there are prerecorded evaluations tells one nothing about whether those evaluations are correctly applied, 3) the evaluation situation is quite common and easy to understand, and 4) negative evaluations are among the most powerful stimuli one can present [20]. Based on the previous discussion, we can adduce the following hypotheses:

1-1. Self-image participants will exhibit greater public SFA than will other-image participants.

1-2. Self-image participants will exhibit greater private SFA than will other-image participants.

2. Self-image participants will take more responsibility for the evaluations they receive than will other-image participants.

3. Self-image participants will perceive the evaluations to be more valid than will other-image participants.

4. Self-image participants will perceive the evaluations to be more objective than will other-image participants.

5. Self-image participants will exhibit less impression management than will other-image participants.

6. Self-image participants will exhibit less negative bias in memory than will other-image participants.

METHODS

Subjects

36 subjects (19 male and 17 female) from a communication course at a university participated in the experiment for partial course credit. One month before the experiment began, they were asked to fill out a questionnaire that asked about self-focus and impression management.

Participants were randomly assigned to either the self- or other-face condition. Gender was matched between the two conditions so that, for example, a female subject in the other-face condition would see the face of a female self-face condition subject. In addition, to control for the possible contamination effects of familiarity, other-face subjects were matched with a face they did not personally know (determined in pre-test).

For the experiment, an Apple Macintosh Quadra 650 with a 16-inch color monitor was used. Programming was done with Hypercard and QuickTime Movie Player.

Procedure

The experiment consisted of two phases. For the first phase, all subjects were invited to a videotaping session. They were asked to read, into a video camera, 18 evaluations (9 positive and 9 negative), 12 of which would be used in the second phase of the experiment. They were videotaped in an above-the-shoulder close-up shot so that their face would appear as the main focus of the picture. At this point, the subjects were simply told that their video clips will be used in a future phase of the experiment.

Approximately two and a half weeks later, participants were called back to participate in the second phase. Once the subjects were welcomed into the lab, they were told that they would be playing a computer game called the "Animal Game", a game that resembles "20 Questions" [10]. First, participants were asked to think of an animal, and the computer tried to guess what the animal was by probing with several yes/no questions (e.g., "Is the animal warm-blooded?"). If the computer made a correct guess (which virtually never happened), the guessing game continued for another animal. If the computer guessed wrong, the subject was asked to type in the animal he or she was thinking of and then a yes/no question that would distinguish the subject's animal from the computer's animal. At this point, the video image of self or someone else, depending on the condition, appeared on the screen and gave an audio-visual evaluation. All the subjects went through a total of 12 rounds, receiving 3 positive and 9 negative evaluations. An example of a negative evaluation is: "Your suggestion complicates the game unnecessarily" (See the Appendix for a list of the evaluations).

Before they began to play the game, participants were told that the experimenters were trying to develop a more efficient algorithm for the game. Ostensibly, the evaluations were contingent on the quality of the questions the participants suggested, but in fact, everyone received the same evaluations in the same order. After the 12 rounds (and 12 evaluations), participants filled out a paper-and-pencil questionnaire.

Measurement

For public and private SFA, we used a modified version of Fenigstein, Scheier, and Buss's self-consciousness measures [9]. Examples of public SFA items are: "I'm usually aware of my appearance" and "I'm concerned about the way I present myself." Examples of private SFA items are: "I'm usually trying to figure out myself" and "I rarely scrutinize myself" (reverse item).

Responsibility for the evaluations was assessed by the following question: "Who was more responsible for the evaluations you received – you or the computer?" Participants answered on a ten-point Likert scale ranging from "you" (1) to "the computer" (10).

The indices for perceived validity and objectivity of the evaluations are based on the question, "How well does each of these adjectives describe the evaluation session?" Responses were provided on a ten-point Likert scale ranging from "describes very poorly" (1) to "describes very well" (10). Perceived validity of the evaluation was an index comprised of six items: "accurate," "analytic," "rational," "clever," "strict" and "helpful." Perceived objectivity of the evaluation was an index comprised of two items: "objective" and "fair."

The impression management scale was derived from Paulhus's Balanced Inventory of Desirable Responding[18]. This scale is particularly responsive to demands for impression management. Examples of the items are: "I sometimes tell lies if I have to" (reverse item) and "when I hear people talking privately, I avoid listening." Answers were based on seven-point Likert-type scales (1 = "not true" to 7 = "very true").

Recognition memory was tested by presenting 18 statements that were potential evaluations and asking whether the participant heard the exact wording. Among the 18 statements, 11 statements (8 negative, 3 positive) were in fact used in the experiment while 7 new statements (4 negative, 3 positive) were added. One point was given for each statement participants recognized correctly. Negative bias on memory was computed by subtracting the sum for the positive statements from the sum for the negative statements.

RESULTS

Consistent with Hypothesis 1-1, self-image participants exhibited significantly greater public SFA than did other-image participants, even when controlling for prior levels of public SFA ($F(1, 33) = 4.30$, $p < .05$). There was no significant difference in private SFA between the two conditions ($p > .10$). Figure 1 shows the difference in means for self/other conditions for both public and private SFA.

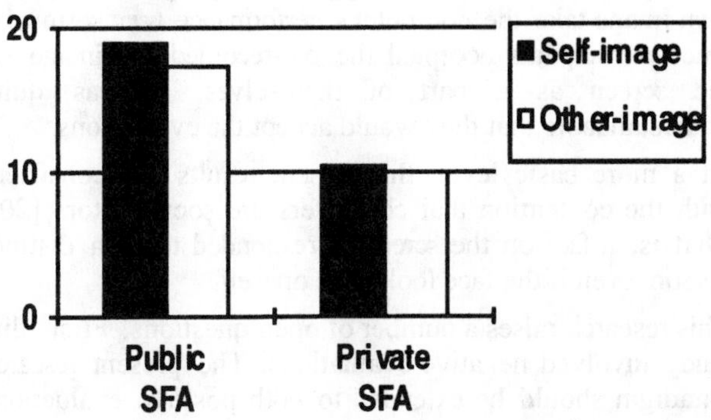

Figure 1. Comparison of means for self-image and other-image conditions in Public and Private SFA.

Self-image participants felt significantly more responsible for the evaluations than did other-image participants ($t(34) = 2.1$, $p < .05$) (See Figure 2). This finding is consistent with Hypothesis 2 and the findings that attributions to self increases when the self is the primary focus of attention [6].

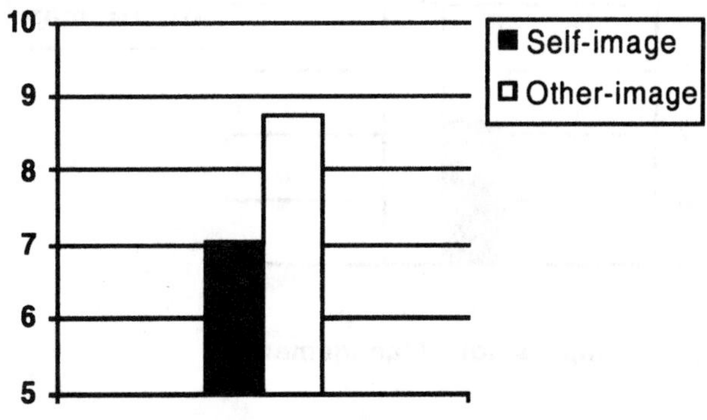

Figure 2. Comparison of means for self-image and other-image conditions in Responsibility of Evaluation.

Self-image participants perceived the evaluations as consistently more valid than did other-image participants ($t(34) = 2.0$, $p < .05$)., consistent with Hypothesis 3. As predicted by Hypothesis 4, the evaluations were perceived as significantly more objective by self-image participants ($t(34) = 2.7$, $p < .01$). The means are shown in Figure 3.

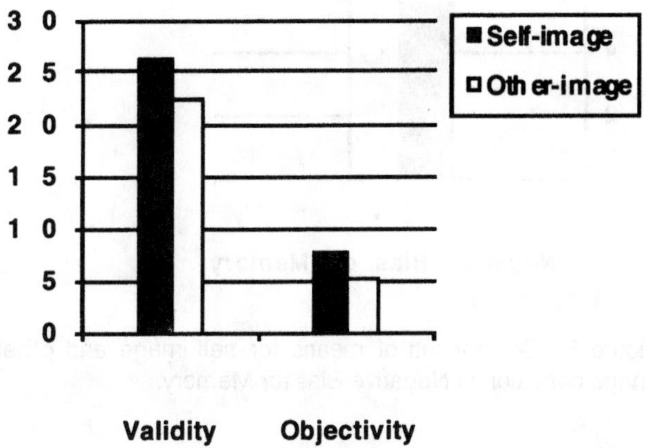

Figure 3. Comparison of means for self-image and other-image conditions in Validity and Objectivity of Evaluation.

As predicted, there was a significant difference in impression management between the two conditions (Hypothesis 5). Those who received criticisms from a stranger during the interaction exhibited greater impression management than did those who saw their own face ($t(34) = 1.8$, $p < .01$) (see Figure 4). The fact that impression management effects lingered beyond the presence of the face (or any other person) suggests that the effects of seeing one's own face are powerful.

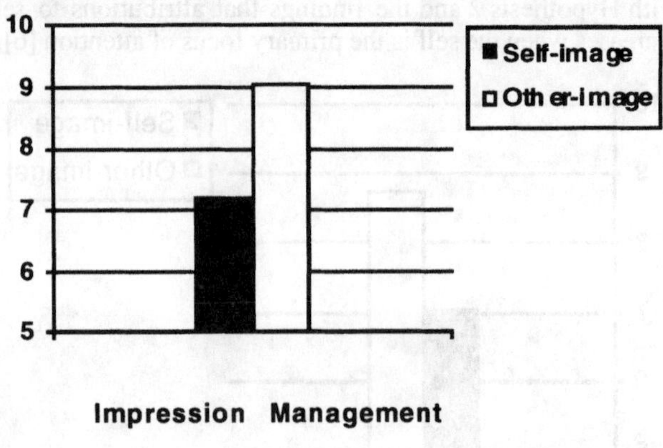

Figure 4. Comparison of means for self-image and other-image conditions in Impression Management.

Consistent with Hypothesis 6, self-image participants showed less negative bias in memory than did other-image participants. That is, self-image subjects remembered the evaluations more positively than did other-image participants ($t(34) = 2.1$, $p < .05$). Figure 5 shows the results for the negative bias on memory.

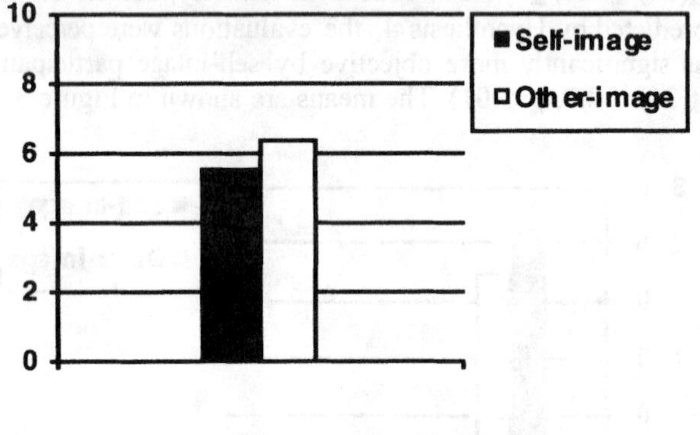

Figure 5. Comparison of means for self-image and other-image condition in Negative Bias for Memory.

DISCUSSION

It has become increasingly common for interfaces to include one or more faces. Videoconference systems inherently include faces, and often show the user's face as well as the person with whom he or she is talking. Virtual reality systems frequently include pictures of people, and sometimes display the user's own face. The programming of personal agents necessitate an interaction with "oneself;" which likely will include a pictorial representation. The rapid dissemination of MPEG ensure that more and more interfaces will display faces, including the user's own face.

While there has been intensive discussion of the advantages and disadvantages of showing faces on the screen, there has been no research on the special significance of seeing one's own face. The present study demonstrates that the placement of a user's face on the screen has a number of implications. Specifically, it changes the users' feelings about themselves and their perception of what the computer said and meant.

In general, the effects of receiving comments from one's own face are positive. Users seeing themselves are more trusting of what the computer said and believe that the computer's comments are more fair. They also remember the computer's comments more positively, another positive outcome. Thus, one may be able to reduce frustration and anger by having the user's own image present error messages. If one's own face presents information about what a piece of software cannot do, users will react to the news less negatively. The greater perceived validity and objectivity of the "self" evaluations may make this means of delivery appropriate for teaching and learning systems.

Another implication of this research concerns computer interviews. Using a computer as an interviewer for a survey, instead of a real person, has been thought to elicit more honest responses from the respondents. It is based on the reasoning -- and on a substantial body of empirical research -- that users will be less likely to exhibit impression management when answering to a computers. This research demonstrates that a video representation of an interviewer, as in Sproull *et al.* [25], will reduce the reliability of the data. However, having the interviewee respond to herself or himself might reduce these negative effects. Thus, to minimize the social desirability effects, one should use a self-image rather than a stranger's image.

These findings seem to go against the intuition that people would dismiss comments coming from a picture of themselves. "After all," the user might think, "I know that's not me on the screen; it's obviously a fake." Contrary to this view, the evidence of effects on self-consciousness and impression management, as well as the *greater* perceived validity of the evaluations, suggest that people seeing their own image take the computer's performance *very* seriously. Once participants accepted the pre-recorded self-image on the screen as a part of themselves, it was quite understandable that they would accept the evaluations.

At a more basic level, the present results are consistent with the contention that computers are social actors [20]. That is, a face on the screen is responded to as a distinct person, even if the face looks like oneself.

This research raises a number of open questions. First, this study involved negative evaluations. The present research paradigm should be extended to both positive evaluations and non-evaluative contexts. Second, each person saw only one face -- either their own or someone else's. What would happen if people saw multiple faces, as often happens in videoconferencing and virtual reality systems? Third, would these results obtain if we only used a voice, as opposed to a voice *and* a face? This is important because the addition of "self" voice prompts involves simpler and more available technology and less disk space than would presentations of one's own face.

The addition of video to computer systems opens up a world of opportunities and problems. As designers construct these worlds, they must decide how and whether the user should appear.

APPENDIX

Evaluations subjects received during the interaction

1. Not so good. You may not have the abilities to do this task well.
2. Your question steers the game in the wrong direction.
3. Your addition complicates the game unnecessarily.
4. Your question makes a useful distinction.
5. Your distinction is too arcane for a game like this.
6. Your suggestion will likely cause trouble down the road.
7. You've made a good new addition to this game.
8. Your approach will make this game more playable.
9. Your differentiation will hamper search efforts by about 28%.
10. Unfortunately, you don't seem to grasp the strategy behind this game.
11. Your question takes this game in exactly the wrong direction at this point.

REFERENCES

1. Anderson, J.R. Attention and Performance. In *Cognitive psychology and its Implications*, 4th edition. New York: W.H. Freeman and Company. 1995
2. Buss, D.M. & Scheier, M.F. Self-Consciousness, Self-Awareness, and Self-Attribution. *Journal of Research in Personality*, 10, (1976), 463-468.
3. Cialdini, R.B., & Richardson, K.D. Two Indirect Tactics of Image Management: Masking and Blasting. *Journal of Personality and Social Psychology,* 39, 3, (1980), 406-415.
4. Cooley, C. H.. *Human nature and the Social Order*. New York: Schocken Books, 1964.
5. Duval, S. & Wicklund, R.A. *A Theory of Objective Self Awareness*. New York: Academic Press, 1972.
6. Duval, S. & Wicklund, R.A. Effects of Objective Self-Awareness on Attribution of Causality. *Journal of Experimental Social Psychology*, 9, (1973), 17-31.
7. Eckman, P. (ed.). *Darwin and facial expression: A century of research in review*. New York, Academic Press, 1973.
8. Epstein, S. The Self-Concept Revisited: Or a Theory of a Theory. *American Psychologist*, 5, (1973), 404-416.
9. Fenigstein, Scheier, and Buss. Public and Private Self-Consciousness: Assessment and Theory. *Journal of Consulting and Clinical Psychology*, 43, 4 (1975), 522-527.
10. Fogg, B.J., & Nass, C. (in press). Silicon sycophants: Effects of computers that flatter. *International Journal of Human-Computer Studies*. Contact the Institute for Communication Research, Department of Communication, Stanford University, Stanford, CA 94305-2050 for copy.
11. Frijda, N. The Laws of Emotion. *American Psychologist*, 43, (1988), 349-358.
12. James, W. The Consciousness of the Self. *The Principles of Psychology*, New York: Dover Publications, (1980), 291-311.
13. Linville, P. Self-complexity as a cognitive buffer against stress and depression. *Journal of Personality and Social Psychology*, 52, (1987), 663-676.
14. McCloud, S. *Understanding Comics -- The invisible Art*, Northampton, MA: Kitchen Sink Press, Inc. 1993, 24-60.
15. Mead, G.H. *Mind, self, and society from the standpoint of a social behaviorist*. Chicago, IL: University of Chicago Press, 1934.
16. Moore, B.C.J. *An introduction to the psychology of hearing*, 2nd ed. London: Academic Press, 1982.
17. Neisser, U. Five Kinds of Self-Knowledge. *Philosophical Psychologist*, 1, 1, (1988), 35-59.
18. Paulhus. In Robinson, J.P, Shaver, P.R., & Wrightsman, L.S. (eds.). Measures of Personality and Social Psychological Attitudes. San Diego, CA: Academic Press, 1991.
19. Petty, R.E., & Cacioppo, J.T. *Attitudes and Persuasion: Classical and Contemporary Approaches*. Dubuque, IA: Wm.C. Brown, 1981.
20. Reeves, B. & Nass, C.I. *The Media Equation: how people treat computers, televisions, and new media like real people and places.* Stanford, CA.: Center for the Study of Language and Information. 1996.
21. Reeves, B.R., Newhagen, J., Maibach, E., Basil, M., & Kurz, K. Negative and Positive Television Messages: Effects of Message Type and Context on Attention and Memory. *American Behavioral Scientist*, 34,6, (July/August 1991), 679-694.
22. Reeves, B.R., Lombard, M., & Melwani, G. Faces on the Screen: Pictures or Natural Experience? Manuscript submitted to *Human Communication Research* (November, 1992).
23. Rogers, C.R. *Client-centered therapy*. New York: Houghton Mifflin. 1951.
24. Schneider, D.J. Tactical self-presentation after success and failure. *Journal of Personality and Social Psychology*, 13, 3, (1969), 262-268.
25. Sproull, L., Subramani, M., Kiesler, S., Walker, J.H., & Waters, K., When the Interface Is a Face. *Human-Computer Interaction*, 11, (1996), 97-124.

26. Wagner, U., Wicklund, R.A., & Shaigan, S. Open Devaluation and Rejection of a Fellow Student: The Impact of Threat to a Self-Definition. *Basic & Applied Social Psychology*, 11, 1, (March, 1990), 61-76.

Digital Smart Kiosk Project

Andrew D. Christian and Brian L. Avery
Cambridge Research Laboratory, Digital Equipment Corporation
One Kendall Square, Building 700, Cambridge, MA 02139
+1 (617) 692-7600 {andyc, bavery}@crl.dec.com

ABSTRACT
The Digital Smart Kiosk is an "aware" information kiosk that detects and tracks prospective clients and conveys this awareness. A single-camera vision system detects and tracks people in the kiosk's vicinity. The kiosk display contains an animated talking face, a live image from the camera, and a web browser that presents graphical and textual information. The animated talking face conveys awareness of clients and invites interaction by turning and watching prospective clients and by speaking to them. The Smart Kiosk is deployed at a local café where we are gathering usage data.

Keywords
Public kiosk, talking emotive avatar, machine vision, user interface design, information display.

INTRODUCTION
Computerized public kiosks are common sights at airports, shopping malls, and stadiums. If movies were any indication, we would interact with kiosks that see us and identify who we are, understand what we say, speak in clearly enunciated sentences, and possess friendly, "human" personalities. Our research group is periodically asked why kiosks do not have these capabilities yet. The answer is easy; although technologies exist for most of these capabilities, the technologies are not yet sufficiently robust and flexible enough for deployment in public kiosks. However, with advances in computer processing power, it is possible to create kiosks that, in real time, sense and respond to their environment.

The Smart Kiosk project was initiated at Digital to explore how advances in computer technology could be applied to improve public kiosks. Today's public kiosk has good multimedia display abilities but limited sensing capabilities. Information from a client is restricted to presses on a touchscreen or keypad and the use of magnetic cards. The presence of a client is detected by a button press or card swipe. The departure of a client can only be inferred from the lack of button presses or card swipes. This indirect method of locating the client has undesirable consequences. For example, a person may leave money at an automatic teller machine because the machine has no method of identifying a departure and hence can't warn the client.

The capability to locate a person can be used to improve the quality of an interaction. One thing we believe is important and lacking in current kiosks is the conveyance of "awareness". When two people converse, they indicate their interest in the conversation by cues such as eye contact, gestures, and vocal utterances. We hypothesize that a kiosk that is aware of clients and can convey this awareness in a socially acceptable manner will be received better than a traditional kiosk.

This document contains a description of the design, implementation, and public deployment of a prototype kiosk. The document is divided into three sections. First, a discussion of the project design criteria and how they were met. Second, a detailed description of the prototype kiosk and the software used to locate people, display awareness, and communicate. Third, a discussion of the deployment of the kiosk in a commercial setting for testing. The intent of this document is not to describe results obtained from the kiosk deployment.

PROJECT DESIGN CRITERIA
The goal of the Smart Kiosk project is to create public kiosks that sense their environment and engage clients in a personable interaction. To accurately judge the success or failure of our efforts, we determined that our kiosks should be deployed and tested outside of the laboratory in public locations. These requirements defined the three project design criteria: client awareness, information presentation to the client, and deployment.

Awareness
The kiosk should be able to detect and track people in the local area and be able to demonstrate that awareness with both visual feedback and appropriate behavior.

Detecting and tracking multiple targets in an unknown environment is a problem best solved by using machine vision. We considered other approaches, such as proximity sensors, pressure-sensitive mats, radar, or sonar. No other approach combines low cost, multiple target capability, and a self-contained solution. For example, proximity sensors have trouble resolving multiple targets. Pressure-sensitive mats require a modification to the environment (by placing a mat on the floor where clients will walk). A range-sensing radar is not cost effective and may interfere with other equipment. Machine vision is relatively inexpensive and does not require physical contact.

The kiosk contains a vision system which tracks people in the local vicinity and provides targeting information. To display "awareness" based on the targeting information, we chose an animated talking face (or avatar). People respond strongly and immediately to faces, particularly ones that turn and look at them. An animated face that watches you walk by is a strong and immediate cue that the kiosk is aware of your presence. Whether or not an animated face can be made inviting, rather than unnerving, is a subject we're exploring.

Client Interface

The kiosk should be able to present information both visually and audibly. The kiosk should engage the client in a personable interaction.

The purpose of most commercial kiosks is to provide information. Our kiosk is no different. To leverage existing technology and tools, the kiosk contains a web-browser with a touchscreen interface. The animated face used for awareness feedback is also used to provide information independently of the web-browser. The client can read the web page while listening to the animated face talk.

In theory, it should be possible to use an intelligent agent to drive the animated face. An agent could track the client's activities, offer advice, and make suggestions. However, agents require a certain amount of domain knowledge and can be difficult to set up so they enhance an interaction rather than annoy the user.

We decided to treat the animated face as a second method of presenting content. The content developer creates web pages to be displayed and speech files to be spoken by the face. The presentation is controlled by scripts written by the content developer. The scripts specify which web pages to display, what to say, and what to do if a button is pressed. The scripts also specify a temporal component; for example, if the client fails to push a button within a certain amount of time, the script can cause the face to prompt the client by speaking an appropriate and timely suggestion.

To improve the user experience, the animated face has the ability to express emotions and facial gestures, and the ability to change between different faces and voices. The animated face can take on a persona appropriate to the setting. For example, a stern news announcer when reading financial news or a perky dinosaur when singing children's songs.

Deployment

The kiosk should be rugged and reliable so that it can survive public deployment outside of our laboratory. Content should be created and maintained by non-technical people.

To properly evaluate an "aware" kiosk we had to build one and test it in a public environment. From the start of the project, we have worked closely with Cybersmith, Inc. (www.cybersmith.com), a cyber-café with branches in our local area. The Cybersmith staff volunteered to host our kiosk in their store in Cambridge, MA.

The Cybersmith store has two floors: a street-level ground floor with just a few computer stations and an upstairs floor where most of the equipment is located. The ground floor is less than half the size of the second floor. To reach the second floor, clients must climb a tall staircase (or take the elevator). This store layout frequently confuses new customers; they may not realize that there is an upstairs section of the store. This occasionally results in a potential customer walking in from the street, looking around the ground floor, and then departing without ever realizing that there was a second floor. One customer apparently visited the store regularly for more than a month before realizing that there was a second floor.

Working with Cybersmith, we decided that the best location for the kiosk would be just inside the entrance on the ground floor. The kiosk greets customers and provides information about the store and facilities. The kiosk is also used to inform regular customers of new activities and store specials, as well as providing information about the kiosk itself.

The staff of Cybersmith created their own custom content for the kiosk and gave it a uniquely "Cybersmith" look and feel. All forms of kiosk content (HTML, text/audio files for the face, and scripts) are stored on a local web server. This isolates the content of the kiosk from the implementation of the kiosk. Commercial tools are used to edit and modify the content, simplifying its creation and maintenance.

DETAILED DESCRIPTION OF SYSTEM

This section of the document contains an overview of the kiosk hardware and software, and detailed descriptions of the vision system, the animated face, and the method used to control content presentation.

Kiosk Hardware and Software Overview

A photo of the prototype kiosk is shown in Figure 1. The kiosk contains two Digital AlphaStation 500/400 computers running Digital Unix, a 21" true-color touchscreen, a color video camera, and a good set of stereo speakers. The kiosk is normally configured to run as a standalone unit, but you can connect to it over an ethernet connection to monitor its health, edit content, or upgrade software.

The Kiosk from a Client's Perspective

Figure 2 is a screen capture of what the client sees upon approaching the kiosk at Cybersmith. The display screen has four different elements, three of which are customizable by the content provider. The web browser (Netscape Navigator Gold™) occupies most of the screen on the right hand side. Large buttons are used for navigation since they are easier for a client to press than textual hyperlinks. The animated face is placed in the upper-left hand corner of the screen. The staff at Cybersmith created the character called

Figure 1: Photo of the kiosk

"Nethead Red", shown in Figure 2. The navigation bar at the bottom of the screen was also created by Cybersmith; its size and appearance can be easily altered. Finally a live image of what the camera sees is located in the middle of the left-hand side. We placed this "image display" on the kiosk because we found that clients liked seeing themselves and it helped them understand what the kiosk was doing.

From a client's perspective, a typical kiosk interaction might go as follows: The client sees the kiosk in the distance displaying random interesting photographs. The client walks towards the kiosk. When the client is approximately 15 to 20 feet from the kiosk, Nethead Red turns to watch the approaching client. As the client comes within approximately 5 feet of the kiosk, Nethead Red speaks a greeting. For example, in the morning, she might say "Good morning. Welcome to Cybersmith!" If the client pauses in front of the kiosk, the graphical display on the kiosk changes to that shown in Figure 2. The client pushes buttons and receives information about the store presented both on the web browser and by Nethead Red. If the client does not push a button within 45 seconds, Nethead Red will politely suggest that the client try pressing one of the buttons displayed on the screen. When the client walks away from the kiosk, Nethead Red says "Goodbye!" and returns to attracting new clients by displaying interesting photographs.

Kiosk Software

Figure 3 is a diagram of the kiosk software. Each box represents a separate Unix process. Processes communicate through TCP connections. The machine vision software runs on a dedicated AlphaStation 500 for performance considerations. The second AlphaStation runs the rest of the software.

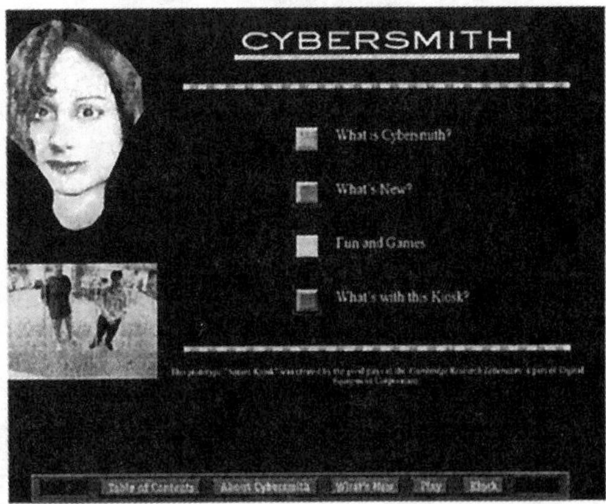

Figure 2: Image of the kiosk screen

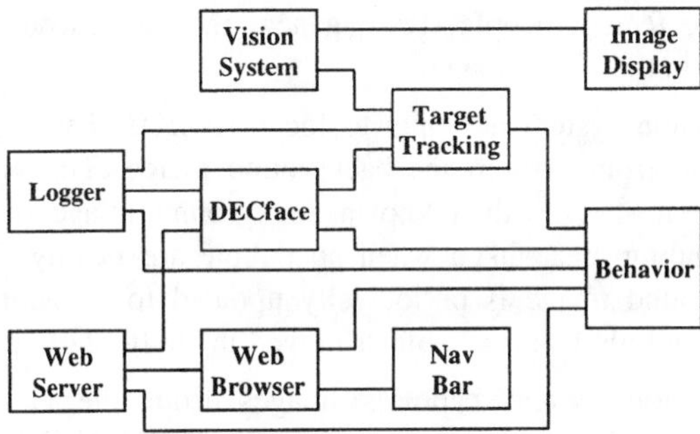

Figure 3: Software layout of the kiosk

The vision system tracks people in the vicinity of the kiosk and creates a target list. The target-tracking system turns the animated face towards the most promising target (with occasional glances at secondary targets), and notifies the behavior system when a target has stopped in front of the kiosk. The behavior system processes command scripts that specify what information is displayed in the web browser and what is spoken by the animated face. Button presses by the client are passed to the behavior system for processing in the context of the current script. All kiosk content, including behavior scripts, are stored on a local web server. All events and actions taken by the kiosk are recorded by the data logger for later analysis.

Details of the vision system, the animated face, and the scripting language used to control the kiosk are discussed in the next three sections of this document.

Vision System

The kiosk deployment location at Cybersmith, although ideal for maximizing exposure to customers, faces westward towards a busy street and large plate-glass windows. This location required a robust machine vision implementation that could adapt quickly to changing light levels and discard visual "noise" from sunlight and video displays of computers in the store.

The kiosk views the outside world through a wide-angle lens mounted on a single color camera located above the touchscreen (approximately 6 feet above the floor) and inclined downward from the horizontal approximately 30

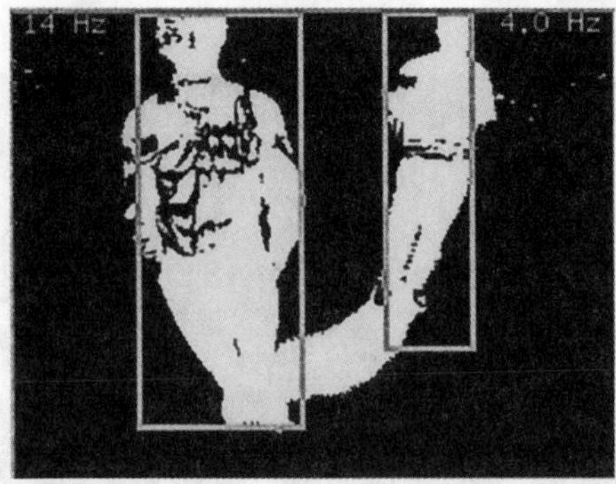

Figure 4: Mask image from the vision system

degrees. This camera can be seen on top of the photo of the kiosk shown in Figure 1. The wide-angle lens has a field of view of approximately 100 degrees horizontally and 70 degrees vertically. The camera orientation was selected so that the feet of people standing near the kiosk would be visible in the video image.

The vision system attempts to locate objects that appear different from a reference background image. The vision algorithm starts with a known background image of the surrounding area, taken when no people are nearby. This background image is periodically updated to account for changing light levels or objects moved in the field of view.

The vision system captures images from the camera, differences them from the background image in YUV color space, and locates large areas of background change. A sample mask image is shown in Figure 4, where the white regions represent places of change from the background. The preliminary set of candidate targets is screened against criteria designed to weed out non-humans: aspect ratio, approximate size, and distance from the kiosk. The distance from the kiosk can be calculated by assuming that the bottom edge of each target touches the floor and then calculating the distance to the target based on the known position and orientation of the camera.

The filtered target list is reconciled with a list of targets from prior images. Reconciliation is accomplished by comparing position, aspect ratio, approximate size, and color. Velocity estimates are calculated for targets that have been tracked for at least one frame in the past. The orange rectangles in Figure 4 mark where the vision system has decided there are valid targets.

The complete vision system runs at 15 hertz on a single AlphaStation 500/400. It does a good (but not perfect) job of tracking targets and handling occlusion (for example, when one individual passes behind another). Distance estimates based on the "standing on the floor" assumption have proven to be accurate in most lighting conditions, but the system can be fooled by dark shadows. To date, this has not been a serious problem; however we have begun work on a stereo vision system that should resolve this issue.

We found that the relatively high frame rate and wide field of view of the vision system is essential to a well-behaved kiosk. In early tests we used a lower frame rate and a camera lens with a normal field of view. In this configuration, the camera imaged a region approximately 16 feet wide and 10 feet deep. Two pathological behaviors resulted from this configuration. First, the face did not receive any tracking data until a person was within about 6 feet of the kiosk. People had the sensation of "waking up" the kiosk when they walked by. This startled some people. Second, a person crossing quickly past the kiosk did not remain in the field of view long enough for the kiosk to build up an accurate estimate of velocity before the person had actually passed the kiosk. This resulted in an awkward design choice: the kiosk could either greet the person immediately or pause briefly to determine if the person was going to stop in front of the unit. Immediate greetings annoyed people who were ignoring the kiosk. Pausing briefly convinced people that the kiosk was "slow" and "confused". Implementing a wider field of a view and a fast frame rate solved both of these problems. Now the kiosk accurately tracks people up to 20 feet away, does not talk to people who are quickly walking past, but does greet people who walk up to it and stop.

Animated Face

The animated face on the kiosk performs two separate roles. It provides a sense of client "awareness" by turning and facing the client, and it provides information to the client by speaking. The animated face used on this kiosk is an enhanced version of DECface [2-5].

DECface is a three-dimensional model of the front of a person's head with moveable eyes, mouth, and muscles. An image of a face is texture-mapped onto a wire-frame mesh. Eyeballs and teeth are mapped onto separate meshes, allowing them to move independently from the face. DECface appears to speak by synchronizing mouth, lip, and teeth movements to a synthesized voice or to a prerecorded audio track.

DECface can display emotions or moods by moving both eyelids and twelve facial muscles (shown in Figure 5). Pulling on a muscle smoothly distorts the underlying facial framework in a triangularly-shaped region. Appropriate combinations of muscle deformation, head movement, eye and eyelid movement, and mouth posture can be combined to give the impression of human emotion.

Creating a new face for DECface is a straightforward process. The designer creates an image of the face with the mouth closed, an image of an eye, and an image of the teeth. The designer uses custom tools to create and align meshes for the face, eyes, and teeth. Finally, the designer positions the muscles and adjusts their range of effect. Figure 6 shows some of the faces that have been created for DECface.

Tracking a Client

In normal operation, DECface is fed tracking information from the vision system. By default, the face is instructed to

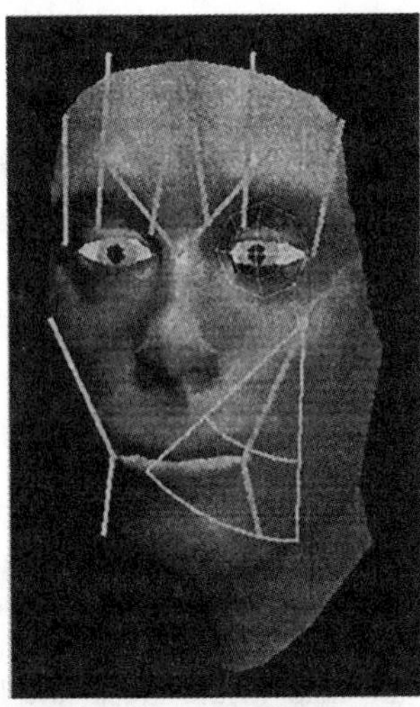

Figure 5: DECface with displayed muscles

Figure 6: Gallery of faces

turn in the direction of the person nearest the kiosk in radial distance. The face both turns from side to side and tilts up or down to accommodate tall or short people.

The actual head rotation used for tracking is linearly proportional to the angle between the perpendicular to the screen and where the target is standing. At first glance, it might seem appropriate to turn the face 20 degrees if the target person is standing 20 degrees from the perpendicular to the screen. This is inappropriate because the face is rendered on a flat screen. Strictly speaking, a face rendered with a 20 degree turn to the left visually appears to be looking to the right of any person, no matter *where* he or she happens to be standing in relation to the screen. However, in our tests we have found that turning the face about 30% of the actual angular displacement provides a compelling illusion that the face is looking at the person.

In our initial experiments the face tracked only the closest target and ignored all others. This behavior caused a few problems. First, if two people stood near the kiosk, the face would fixate on one of them and ignore the other. The second person felt "excluded" by the kiosk. Second, if those two people were roughly equidistant and moved slightly

Expression definition:

disgust:

left_mouth_up = 100%	right_mouth_up = 20%
left_mouth_down = 100%	right_mouth_down = 20%
eye_x = 5 degrees	
left_eyelid = 40%	right_eyelid = 40%;

Usage:

Hey! <disgust>Those are awful shoes you're wearing. <~disgust> How can you stand them?

Table 1: Disgust expression

forwards and backwards, the face reacted by snapping quickly back and forth between the targets.

We found that groups of people responded better to the animated face once we added a "glance" behavior and a dynamic model. The glance behavior causes the face to consistently track one target and occasionally glance for a brief period of time (usually about 300-500 milliseconds) towards other targets near the kiosk. The dynamic model gives the head mass and damping, causing it to move smoothly from target to target. Now when the face switches targets, the eyes jump to the new target and the head smoothly follows.

Face Presentation

The face can speak the contents of text files or annotated audio files. Text files are processed at run time by a speech synthesizer. Annotated audio files are recorded tracks of human speech that have been processed by speech-recognition software. The annotated audio file contains phoneme information that is used by the face to do lip synchronization.

When surveyed, kiosk users generally prefer annotated audio files to speech synthesis. However, synthesized speech has two advantages. First, it can be used to construct situation-dependent phrases (for example, "The current time is...") Second, facial expressions can be embedded within the text file. These expressions are defined in an expression data file read by the face program on startup.

Table 1 contains the definition of the expression <disgust>. This expression pulls on the mouth muscles, causes the eyes to look down by five degrees, and lowers the eyelids. The overall effect can be seen in Figure 7a. Note that the expression is applied to the face after it has said "Hey!" and is removed by the <~disgust> macro just before the final sentence is spoken.

More complicated expression macros may be defined in terms of simple expression macros and temporal duration. For example, the expression <raise-eyebrows> in Table 2 causes the face to raise the eyebrows over the course of 250 milliseconds, hold them there for 500 milliseconds, and then lower them over the course of 250 milliseconds. When used in the data file, the expression can be modified by rate and extent parameters. In this example, slowly causes the expression to take twice as long as normal and extent=75 scales the deflection of each muscle to 75% of the value

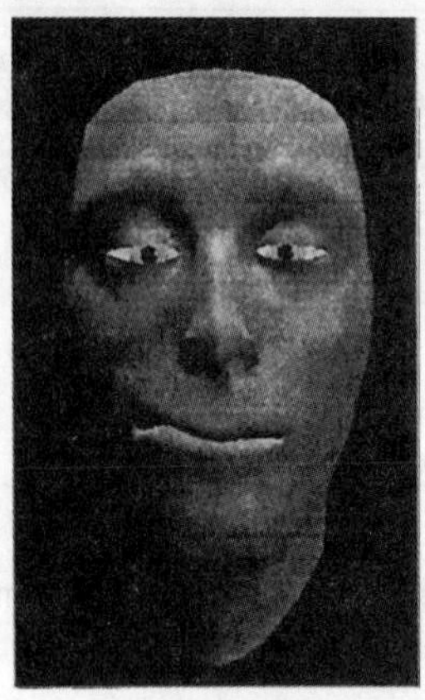
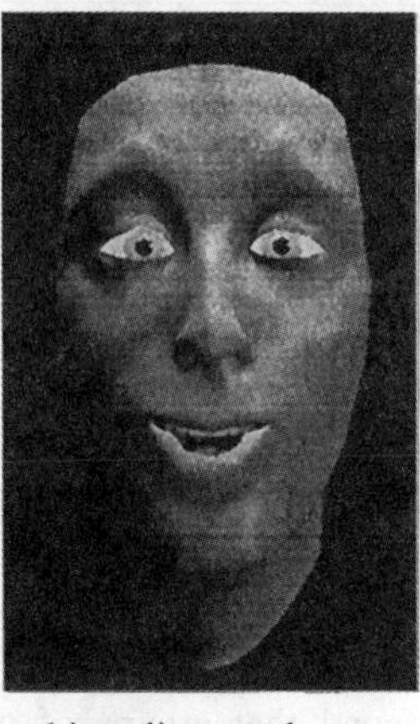

Figure 7a: DECface looking disgusted
Figure 7b: Smiling while speaking

Expression definitions:

```
smile:
  left_mouth_up = 100%   right_mouth_up = 100% ;
eyebrows-up:
  left_eyebrow = 100%    right_eyebrow = 100% ;
raise-eyebrows:
  eyebrows-up            duration = 250 ,
                         duration = 500 ,
  ~eyebrows-up           duration = 250 ;
```

Usage:

```
<smile><raise-eyebrows slowly extent=75>
Hey buddy, wanna buy a duck?
```

Table 2: Eyebrow animation

specified in the base expression. A single frame of the animation is displayed in Figure 7b.

We have trained content developers to create their own custom facial expressions and their own annotated audio files. In use, we have observed that most people find the facial expressions compelling and entertaining if they are logically tied to the content presented by the web browser.

As a sidelight, we noted that many people (particularly teenagers) feel the urge to touch the face. For our own amusement, we added a large set of phrases or expressions for the face to play back when touched (for example, "Quit poking me!") To our surprise, this addition has become extremely popular. People often stand in front of the kiosk for many minutes poking the face repeatedly.

Behavior and Scripting Language

The kiosk behavior system controls what information is displayed and spoken by the kiosk and how the kiosk responds to client inputs. The kiosk behavior is controlled at two levels: a coarse level that specifies the state that the kiosk is in, and a fine level that specifies what the kiosk should do while operating in the given state. The coarse level of the kiosk is controlled by a state machine. The fine level is controlled by scripts that specify the actions the kiosk should take.

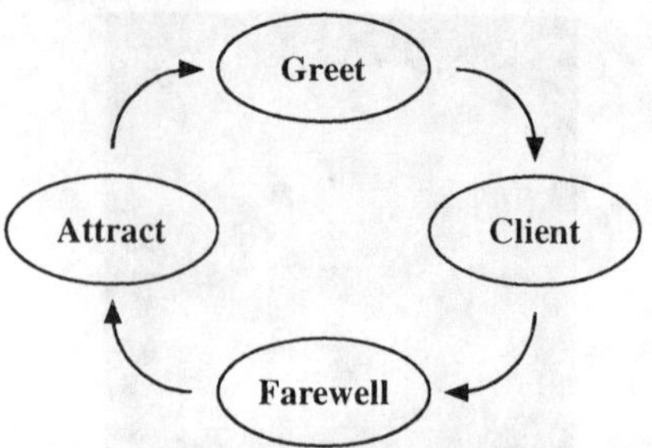

Figure 8: Core kiosk state machine

Coarse Control

At a coarse level, kiosk behavior can be represented by a state machine (Figure 8). Transitions between states are controlled primarily by events from the vision system. When no clients are near to the kiosk, the kiosk is in the ATTRACT state. In the ATTRACT state, the kiosk displays interesting images on the browser. When a potential client approaches, the kiosk switches to the GREET state and speaks an appropriately selected greeting. If the client stays near the kiosk or presses a button, the GREET state turns into the CLIENT state. When the client departs, the kiosk switches to the FAREWELL state, speaks a polite departing message, and returns to the ATTRACT state.

The kiosk behavior system is written entirely in Java. Each of the four core states is implemented as a Java module. Other Java modules representing new states can be written by a developer and dynamically loaded from the web server while the kiosk is running (using commands described in the next section). We have used the custom-state load capability to adapt the kiosk to special environments. For example, when giving a presentation about the kiosk it is advantageous to enter a custom VISIONLESS CLIENT state where exit and enter events from the vision system are ignored. This allows the presenter to demonstrate kiosk behavior without worrying about staying close enough to the kiosk to prevent an undesired transition into the FAREWELL state. The custom VISIONLESS CLIENT state took five minutes and twenty lines of Java code to write.

Fine Control

The actions of the kiosk within a given state can be controlled by a scripting language called the kiosk management language (KML). A KML file is a script of actions to take in a particular time sequence. KML contains commands for displaying HTML files in the web browser, sending audio files to the face, and sending text files to the face. A typical KML script is shown Table 3. This KML file instructs the browser to display the page `start.html` (shown in Figure 9) and has the face frown and say "Don't push the button!" If the user doesn't push the button within 10 seconds, another statement is read and the kiosk waits an additional 5 seconds before displaying `reward-page.html` and saying "Good boy!" The script then jumps to a new KML file at the `SOMEWHERE` label.

Figure 9: Displaying the page `start.html`

```
# main.kml sample file

html start.html
say <frown>Don't push the button!
pause 10000
say Don't even think about it!
pause 5000
html reward-page.html
say <smile>Good dog!

label EXIT-POINT
goto ../other-page.html @SOMEWHERE

label PUSHED-IT
html punish.html
talk punish.talk
goto @EXIT-POINT
```

Table 3: Sample KML Script

The button displayed on the `start.html` web page contains the reference `main.kml @PUSHED-IT`. Hence, if the user pushes the button, the KML script jumps to the `PUSHED-IT` label, displays the `punish.html` page, and speaks the contents of the `punish.talk` file. After the contents of the file have been spoken, the script jumps to the `EXIT-POINT` label, and from there jumps immediately to the `SOMEWHERE` label in `other-page.html`.[1]

All KML commands are described in Table 4. The last four commands described are special purpose commands used to access the Unix hardware and control software modules.

The KML scripting language has been a powerful, useful tool for controlling the kiosk behavior. For example, one popular site on our kiosk contains a database of fortunes. The KML script for that site executes a CGI program on the web server that selects a random fortune from the database, and generates an appropriate HTML file for the browser to display and an appropriate text file for the face to read. Another kiosk script uses the KML capabilities to spawn remote programs to provide basic kiosk administration tools such as calibrating the touchscreen or restarting the vision system. This script has been hidden behind a Java applet

Command	Action
html URL	Display URL in the browser.
say TEXT...	Send the TEXT string to the face. Script pauses until face finishes.
talk URL	Face speaks the content of the URL. Script pauses until face finishes.
pause DURATION	Pause for DURATION milliseconds.
label NAME	Mark an entry point.
goto URL @NAME	Jump to a new KML file, at the label called NAME.
cgi URL	Execute a CGI script for side effects
exec COMMAND...	Execute a Unix command
module ARGS...	Load a new state module. For example, VISIONLESS CLIENT.
exit	Exit the current module
send SYS ARGS...	Execute a special command on a kiosk system. For example, reset the vision background image.

Table 4: KML commands

that requires the user to enter a password before the administration page will be displayed.

Our experience has been that teaching KML to a new person rarely takes more than a few minutes, and that person will be comfortable with KML within an hour. To guarantee this ease of use, we had to restrain ourselves from making KML into a full-featured language. In future research, we may switch to using an embedded language such as Perl or Visual Basic to give the content creator greater power and flexibility.

DEPLOYMENT

Our kiosk project plan always called for public testing. Initial testing was conducted in our laboratory on a series of kiosk prototypes. As functionality was added to the kiosk, prototypes were set up in our laboratory hallways and run for weeks at a time. These prototypes helped us find bugs in the software (usually when giving demonstrations). The prototypes also helped to identify promising research directions and areas where the software or underlying algorithms needed to be improved.

Early Deployment Stages

Before deploying the kiosk at the Cybersmith Café in Harvard Square, we took two additional steps to insure that the software was sufficiently robust and mature for a public deployment. The first step was to install a kiosk staging machine in the Cybersmith headquarters. The kiosk staging machine is a single AlphaStation that runs all of the kiosk software except for the machine vision. Instead of using a camera to identify clients, the staging kiosk uses a large button labeled alternately "Client Exit" or "Client Enter". The staging kiosk is used by the Cybersmith staff to build and test their own kiosk content. Their experiences with the staging kiosk helped us debug the kiosk software and have

[1] The reward and punishment pages contain pictures of a friendly Collie and a cute Rottweiler.

suggested a number of desirable improvements. Moreover, it has been our experience that it is imperative that a staging machine be provided to anyone who is building kiosk content. Without a staging machine, people tend to build a visual web site and fail to integrate the face sufficiently into the client interaction.

The second step prior to the Cybersmith deployment was to take the kiosk on the road for a few days and see how people outside of our laboratory would react to it. We took the kiosk to the ACM SIGGraph conference in Los Angeles in the beginning of August 1997. The kiosk sat in the Digital Equipment Corporation booth at the convention for three days. Due to the crowds and erratic lighting conditions at the booth (the booth across the aisle ran a light show) it was necessary to run the kiosk continuously in the CLIENT state. The vision system did better than expected in tracking targets in the visually hostile environment of the conference, but the crowds, ever-present Digital staff members, and high ambient noise level made identifying and greeting potential clients a difficult task. Other results from SIGGraph were quite promising; we received generally positive comments and suggestions from visitors.

Cybersmith Deployment

On Thursday, 4 September 1997 the prototype kiosk was installed at the Cybersmith Café in Harvard Square. As of the time of the submission of this paper, the kiosk has been running continuously for just under 4 months. The first month of the installation was used to fix software problems, experiment with content, and make the staff at Cybersmith comfortable with the presence of the kiosk.

At the time of the writing of this paper we have not yet been able to conduct detailed analysis of the kiosk usage. However, we do have some basic usage data. During the months of October and November, 1997, a total of 1801 interactions were recorded by the kiosk at Cybersmith. An interaction consists of the vision system recording the entrance of a client, at least one button being pushed, and the vision system recording the departure of a client. The mean client duration is 137 seconds (with a median of 84 seconds). On average, a client presses 4.5 buttons per minute and visits 3.3 pages per minute.

Ongoing kiosk experimentation includes polling clients for their impressions. Originally we envisioned on-screen surveys asking for detailed feedback supplemented by personal interviews of kiosk users. Our experience quickly demonstrated that clients generally would not stand in front of the unit to answer detailed surveys, so we now restrict the on-screen survey to a single question, changed biweekly. For example, in December clients were asked if they preferred the pre-recorded human voice or a synthesized voice (and given examples of each). Of the 230 respondents, 124 selected the human voice. However, voting results should be treated with suspicion because a large percentage of the voters will vote multiple times (only the first vote is counted).

Future kiosk experiments have been planned, including: Does the "awareness" of the kiosk attract more clients? Does a talking face add value to the presentation of content? What types of faces are best? For example, animals, cartoons, photographs of real people, etc. Some preliminary work in this area has been done [1]. The current experimental plan is to vary the behavior and faces on the kiosk and analyze the usage logs. Interviews and some on-screen questions will be used to gather client's opinions.

CONCLUSIONS

We have built and deployed a public information kiosk that uses machine vision to locate prospective clients, demonstrates awareness of prospects by tracking them with an animated face, and provides information using a combination of a traditional web browser and a talking, emotionally expressive face. This kiosk has been deployed at the Cybersmith Café in Cambridge, MA for usage studies and user feedback.

Preliminary anecdotal feedback has been enthusiastic. People have reacted positively to the presence of the face. We plan on running the kiosk in the Cybersmith Café through January 1998. In the meantime, we are working on extending the kiosk to incorporate new input technologies.

ACKNOWLEDGMENTS

We would like to thank Lauren Winter-Bigelow from Cybersmith for enthusiastically supporting this project from its conception and spending so much time developing the content. We would also like to thank the research and administrative staff at CRL for their help on the project and tolerance in listening to the kiosk babble forth daily.

REFERENCES

1. Kiesler, S., Sproull, L., and Waters, K. A "prisoner's dilemma" experiment on cooperation with people and human-like computers. *Journal of Personality and Social Psychology*, 70 (1996), 47-65.
2. Lee, Y. Terzopoulos, D., and Waters, K. Realistic modeling for facial animation. *Computer Graphics* (SIGGRAPH'95), 1995, 55-62.
3. Parke, F., and Waters, K. *Computer Facial Animation.* A. K. Peters, Ltd. (1996).
4. Waters, K. and Levergood, T. An automatic lip-synchronization algorithm for synthetic faces. ACM Proceedings of the Multimedia Conference, San Francisco, California, September, 1994. 149-156.
5. Waters, K. and Levergood, T. DECface: An automatic lip-synchronization algorithm for synthetic faces. Technical Report 93/4, Digital Equipment Corporation Cambridge Research Lab, August, 1993.

Worldlets: 3D Thumbnails for 3D Browsing

T. Todd Elvins **David R. Nadeau**
San Diego Supercomputer Center
University of California, San Diego
La Jolla, CA 92093-0505
todd@sdsc.edu
nadeau@sdsc.edu

Rina Schul **David Kirsh**
Cognitive Science Department
University of California, San Diego
La Jolla, CA 92093-0515
rschul@crl.ucsd.edu
kirsh@cogsci.ucsd.edu

ABSTRACT

Dramatic advances in 3D Web technologies have recently led to widespread development of virtual world Web browsers and 3D content. A natural question is whether 3D thumbnails can be used to find one's way about such 3D content the way that text and 2D thumbnail images are used to navigate 2D Web content. We have conducted an empirical experiment that shows interactive 3D thumbnails, which we call *worldlets*, improve travelers' landmark knowledge and expedite wayfinding in virtual environments.

Keywords: 3D thumbnails, wayfinding, VRML, virtual reality, empirical study

INTRODUCTION

As the Web moves into 3D, the problem of finding one's way to sites of interest is exacerbated. Currently URLs are represented on a page or menu by sentences as in Figure 1, or by 2D thumbnail images which depict some aspect of the URL as in Figure 2. It is reasonable to suppose that interactive 3D thumbnails -- or *worldlets* -- will soon come into use. To test whether worldlets improve wayfinding we designed a psychological experiment aimed at answering the following questions:

- are menus of worldlets better than menus of text and 2D images for wayfinding ?
- what aspects of the wayfinding process are most enhanced by the use of worldlets ?

In the experiment, subjects were placed at starting locations in three virtual cities and asked to find their way to goal locations via a series of landmarks. In one city, the landmarks were described with text, in another city the landmarks were described using 2D thumbnail images, and in yet another city the landmarks were described using manipulable worldlets. We hypothesized that, compared to text and thumbnail images, worldlets would facilitate landmark knowledge and expedite wayfinding.

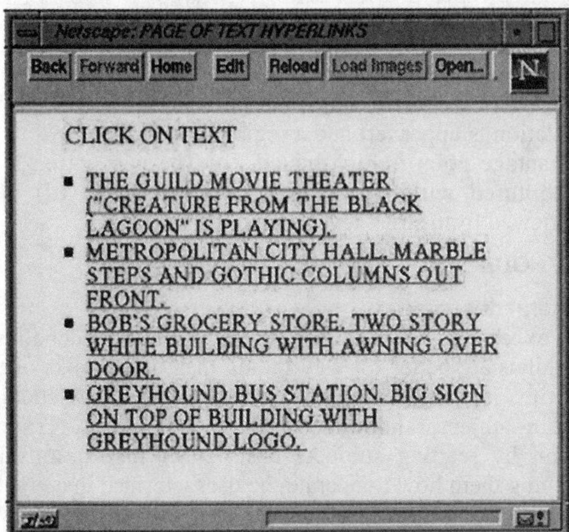

Figure 1. A Web page linking to alternative destinations within a virtual world. On this page, the destinations are represented with text.

Figure 2. On this Web page, the destinations from Figure 1 are represented as 2D thumbnail images.

WAYFINDING

Wayfinding is "the ability to find a way to a particular location in an expedient manner and to recognize the destination when reached." [11] To prevent travelers from becoming disoriented and lost, a world must contain useful wayfinding cues. Such cues enable a traveler to build a cognitive map of a region, and thereafter navigate using that map [9] [10]. A cognitive map is built from *survey, procedural*, and/or *landmark knowledge*. Survey knowledge provides a map-like, bird's eye view of a region and contains spatial information including locations, orientations, and sizes of regional features. Procedural knowledge characterizes a region by memorized sequences of actions that construct routes to desired destinations. Landmark knowledge records the visual features of landmarks, including their 3D shape, size, texture, etc. [1] [7].

Although social and engineering scientists have studied human wayfinding in the real world for many years [9] [1] [7] [4] [10] [11] [12], only recently have computer scientists investigated this subject. Satalich [13] led human subjects on a tour of a virtual building and then tested the subjects' ability to find their way to places seen during the tour. Darken [3] applied Lynch's city structure theories [9] to large sparsely featured virtual environments and then compared subjects' ability to find their way to target destinations with and without the added city structure. Witmer [17] studied route learning and found that subjects who rehearsed a route in a virtual building learned the route better than subjects who rehearsed the route verbally. Although each of these studies recognized the value of landmark knowledge for wayfinding, none studied the value of landmarks in familiarizing subjects with an environment before entering it.

Virtual cities and landmarks

3D models of large cities are becoming available for exploration via the Web [8] [2] [14]. The studies just described showed that travelers visiting such large virtual environments for the first time are easily disoriented, may have difficulty identifying a place upon arrival, and may not be able to find their way back to a place just visited.

We hypothesized that by enabling a traveler to become familiar with landmarks before visiting an environment, the traveler will be better prepared to: (1) find their way to destinations of interest, (2) recognize destinations upon arrival, and (3) find their way back to previously visited places. More generally, we believe that directions are more effective if presented using landmarks, and specifically using 3D landmarks. This is in keeping with Wickens' claim that virtual environment search tasks are difficult because "often the object of the search is specified in a format different from and more abstract than its rendering in the virtual environment." [16] Worldlets address this problem by representing the object of the search in the same 3D format as the virtual environment, thereby giving searchers first-person experience with virtual world landmarks.

WHAT ARE WORLDLETS

In two previous papers we described our preliminary worldlet design, implementation, and pilot study [5] [6]. Like a 3D photograph, a worldlet is associated with a viewing position and orientation, and captures a snapshot of the 3D shapes (usually landmarks) falling within the viewpoint's viewing volume. Worldlets can be explored and manipulated in the same way that virtual worlds can be explored and manipulated. Incorporated into a VRML browser, a guidebook or list of worldlets enables a world traveler to view landmarks and landmark context from multiple vantage points. Seeing the landmarks presented in worldlets may help a traveler select destinations of interest and navigate unfamiliar worlds.

Figure 3 depicts the process of constructing a *spherical* worldlet from a fragment of a virtual city surrounding a central viewpoint position. Once captured, worldlets can be browsed, manipulated, and explored in a number of ways.

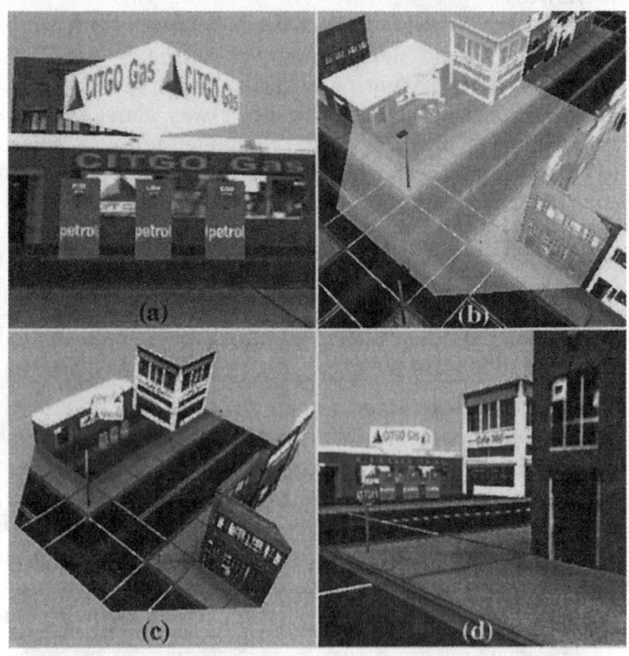

Figure 3. Construction of a worldlet. A gas station landmark in a virtual city (a) viewed from a vantage point in the street. (b) Viewed from above, the gas station is upper left and a region around the previous vantage point is highlighted. (c) The gas station is captured within a spherical worldlet, and (d) is viewed from street level within the worldlet.

METHODS

General description

The experiment was designed to test whether guidebooks of worldlets are better for wayfinding than guidebooks of text and images, and if so, why are they better. A standard within-subject randomized design was used. Training began by reading subjects a series of instructions and teaching them how to operate the user interface in a practice three block by three block virtual city. Next, subjects were allowed to spend unlimited time in this city becoming familiar with the controls and the on-line guidebooks. Each subject was then asked to find their way to a brightly colored goal kiosk, via one landmark, in three practice cities, each five blocks by five blocks. In one city, the guidebook represented each landmark with a paragraph of text, in another city the landmarks were represented as 2D thumbnail images, and in a third city the landmarks were represented in a spherical worldlet. The guidebooks only contained landmark information; subjects were given no procedural or survey information. Although the thumbnail and worldlet guidebook had the same appearance, as shown in Figure 4, the worldlets in the worldlet guidebook could be explored and manipulated.

Figure 4. The image and worldlet guidebook looked like this, however, subjects were able to interactively explore the worldlets in the worldlet guidebook.

Parameter	Constant value	Comments
City dimensions	10x10 blocks	100 total blocks
Building lots per block	20 on perimeter of block	building footprint varies
Distance from start to goal	1200 meters	past 100 12 meter-wide lots
Landmarks per city	9, including goal kiosk	ordered in guidebooks
Distance between landmarks	1.5 blocks	+/- 0.25 block
Travel speed	5 meters/second	slow driving speed
Types of landmarks	8	1 of each kind in each city
Turns required to reach goal	5	left and right turns
Radius of information	~20 meters	see city design section
Landmark positions	3 on corner, 5 midblock	goal is midblock
Goal building	yellow/red striped kiosk	6 sided, viewpoint invariant

Table 1. Although the arrangement of buildings, landmarks, and routes were different in each city, their basic structure in terms of city design and landmark layout was kept constant to allow for controlled comparision. Subjects moved at a fixed speed in all cities.

After completing the practice tasks, the experiment began and subjects were asked to find their way to the goal kiosk via eight ordered landmarks in three ten block by ten block virtual cities. Performance in these three cities was timed and the subject's location, orientation, and actions were recorded at one second intervals. Subjects visited the test cities in a random order to counterbalance possible learning effects. Each of the cities and landmarks were different and unique.

Before the computer portion of the experiment, subjects filled out a brief questionnaire on their prior experience with computers. After the experiment subjects answered written questions about the strategies they used while finding their way, and how difficult they found the task using each of the guidebooks. Subjects also completed spatial and verbal neuropsychological tests during a separate session.

Constants

The major independent variable in this experiment was the type of guidebook used (text, image, worldlet). Parameters concerned with city design and landmark layout, as described in Table 1, were held constant.

City design

Our primary goal in designing the virtual cities was to preserve as many elements of a real city as possible. Toward this goal we developed a pseudo-random city generator that produced cities based on a regular street grid with pavement roads and sidewalks between the blocks. Each block contained up to twenty buildings, side-by-side around the block perimeter. Using a cache of 250 building designs, buildings were randomly selected and placed on city blocks. Many non-landmark buildings were repeated between and within the cities. Rendering requirements were reduced by programming buildings to make themselves invisible when farther than three blocks from the current viewpoint. To prevent subjects from seeing buildings turning on and off in the distance, we added fog to the environment.

Cities contained parks, parking lots, and other civic features but did not contain cars or street signs. The landmarks were placed so that a subject could not shortcut the route and would never have to make an exhaustive search; i.e. as long as they carefully looked down each possible path for familiar landmarks and landmark context, they could always determine in which direction to proceed. No landmarks were located within one block of the perimeter wall that surrounded each city.

Radius-of-information

Radius-of-information was the most difficult parameter to make constant across the three guidebooks. Given that text, 2D images, and worldlets are different representations, they do not convey an equivalent quantity and quality of landmark information. We determined, while building the guidebooks for the pilot study, that using a radius of twenty meters produced the most nearly equivalent set of guidebooks. For the text guidebook this meant describing in words the landmark, the building or structure directly across the street, the building on each side, and whether the landmark was on a corner or not. Thus our textual description of a landmark with a twenty meter radius read as follows:

> Citgo Gas Station. Citgo's red gas pumps are at a corner location. Next door is the Cafe 360 in a beige colored building, and across the street is the Lumbini Restaurant in a red brick building.

For the image guidebook, a twenty meter radius meant positioning the camera across the street from the landmark so that the captured thumbnail image would contain the buildings or structures on the left and right of the landmark. For the worldlet guidebook, setting the information radius simply meant setting the yon clip plane to cut away 3D shapes further away than twenty meters while capturing a spherical worldlet. Image and worldlet camera locations were selected so as not to suggest a direction of approach to the landmark.

Figure 5. The main city window.

Hardware and software design

The experiment was conducted using a standard 19 inch Silicon Graphics monitor. Stereo glasses were not used. A main city window displayed the city in a VRML browser user interface modified for the experiment. Subjects used keyboard arrow keys to move forward and backward a fixed distance on each key press, and to turn left and right by a fixed angle on each key press. In the worldlet guidebook, subjects used the arrow keys in the same manner to move around in the worldlet. Collision detection prevented subjects from passing through buildings and other objects in the city.

Subjects pushed a Start button before starting, a Landmark button each time a landmark was reached, and a Stop button upon reaching the goal kiosk. Subjects pushed a Guidebook button, located near the Start button, to display the guidebook. Subjects practiced operating all of these buttons in practice cities prior to beginning the experiment. The windows were designed so that when the guidebook (Figure 4) was open, the main city window (Figure 5) was completely occluded and no movement could be made.

Lessons learned from the pilot study

Our pilot study design and results are described in [5]. From the pilot study we learned that landmarks cannot be more than two blocks apart or subjects frequently resort to an exhaustive search of the neighborhood. We also learned that some subjects will take much longer than other subjects to complete the task and that the task difficulty and length must be designed while keeping the slower wayfinders in mind.

Subject instructions

The following is a subset of the instructions read to the subjects. Instructions 3 and 4 were repeated before beginning each city.

1. The guidebook contains a series of landmarks that you probably want to follow, since traveling past these landmarks will lead you to the goal kiosk.
2. When you are at a landmark, you may have to walk as far as one or two blocks before you will be able to see the **next** landmark.
3. Your task is to locate the goal kiosk as quickly as possible. Go as fast as you can, but be careful to not get lost
4. Remember, you can look at the guidebook as often as you like

Subjects

Subjects were primarily University of California, San Diego students from a number of major departments. Ages ranged from 18 to 36, with a mean age of 24. Fourteen males and twelve females completed the experiment. Results from four other subjects had to be excluded from our data because the subjects became lost in one or more of the cities. All subjects were computer literate, but had varying degrees of experience with virtual environments.

Neuropsychological tests

To provide an independent measure of a subset of the subjects' cognitive abilities, subjects were tested in a separate session, using two standardized subtests from the Wechsler Adult Intelligent Scale - Revised (WAIS-R) [15].

The Vocabulary subtest, comprising part of the WAIS-R Verbal subtests, was used to assess the subject's verbal ability. Performance was scored according to standardized procedures based on the subject's degree of familiarity with a list of up to 35 words and their elegance of expression [15].

The second test was the Block Design subtest comprising part of the WAIS-R Performance subtests. The test was used to assess the subjects' constructional-spatial ability, and was administered in the standardized manner [15].

Analysis

A one-way repeated measures analysis of variance (ANOVA) was performed for each of the dependent variables and the overall times and distances. The within-subjects variable was the landmark description type with three levels: text, image, and worldlet. Post-hoc analyses were done using the Scheffé test for differences in sample means. Correlation analysis was performed across the scores of the neuropsychological tests and the scores of the wayfinding tests. We adopted a significance level of 0.05 on all analyses unless otherwise noted.

RESULTS

Our primary result was that people spend more time consulting the worldlet guidebook than the other guidebooks, but require less time to reach the goal when using the worldlet guidebook. The following specific findings tell us more about the component activities that benefitted from worldlet use.

Time and distance measures

Figures 6 through 9 show time and distance measures where the independent variable (type of guidebook) is displayed as white, grey, and black bars along with the standard error of the mean (SEM). Figure 6 shows the mean overall time and distance required to reach the goal kiosk. Figure 7 breaks the overall time into its components. Figure 8 gives the forward and backtracking distance components. Figure 9 shows the mean number of times that each type of guidebook was opened. Figure 10 diagrams the subjects' scores on the Wechsler neuropsychological tests.

Analysis of variance followed by Scheffé post hoc tests were performed for the different measures. Table 2 summarizes these results.

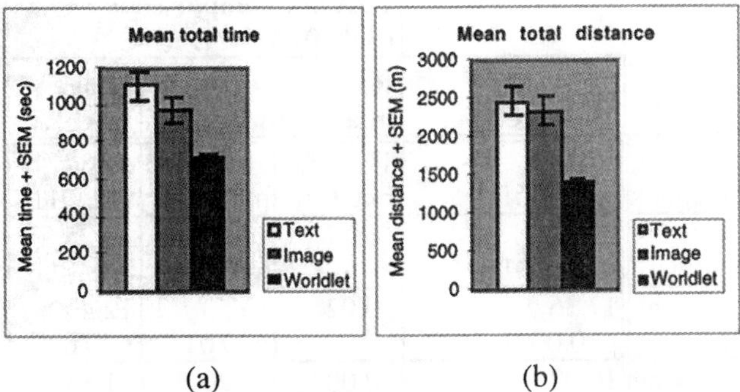

(a) (b)

Figure 6. (a) Mean total time. The overall time spent traveling to the goal was significantly less using the worldlet guidebook than when using the text ($F(1,24)=9.89$, $p<0.01$) or image ($F(1,24)=4.63$, $p<0.01$) guidebooks. (b) Mean total distance. The overall distance traveled using the worldlet guidebook was significantly less than the distance traveled using the text ($F(1,24)=11.41$, $p<0.01$) or image ($F(1,24)=8.93$, $p<0.01$) guidebooks.

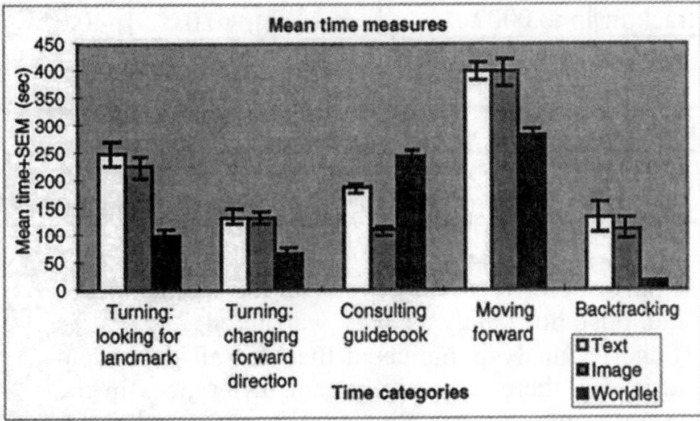

Figure 7. *Turning: looking for landmark* is time spent standing in one location. *Turning: changing heading* is time spent changing forward direction. *Consulting guidebook* is time spent with the guidebook on screen. *Moving forward* is time spent traveling over new ground. *Backtracking* is time spent retreating. Note that time spent consulting the worldlet guidebook is significantly greater than time spent consulting the text or image guidebook. Also note that time backtracking is near zero when using the worldlet guidebook.

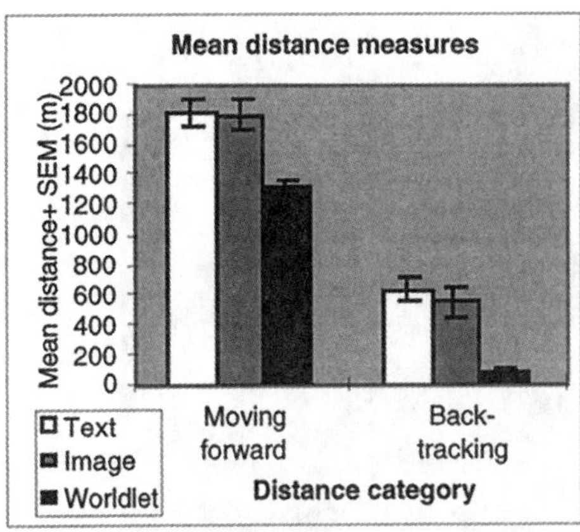

Figure 8. The mean distance moving forward while using the worldlet guidebook is significantly less than the forward distance covered while using the text or image guidebook. Backtracking distance is almost non-existent for the worldlet guidebook task.

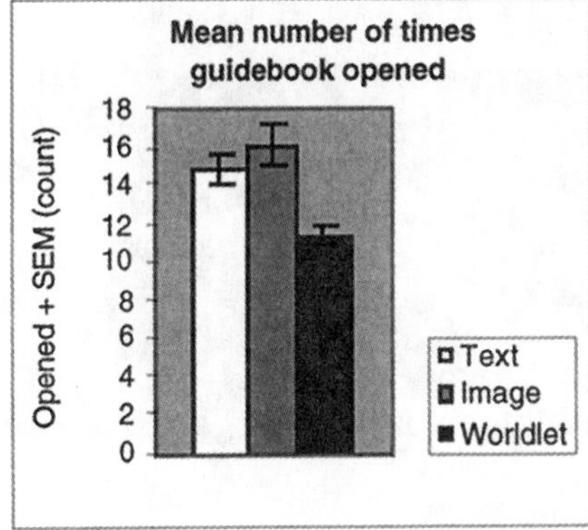

Figure 9. Subjects opened the text and image guidebooks on average 15-16 times while seeking the eight landmarks enroute to the goal kiosk. The worldlet guidebook was opened 11 times on average.

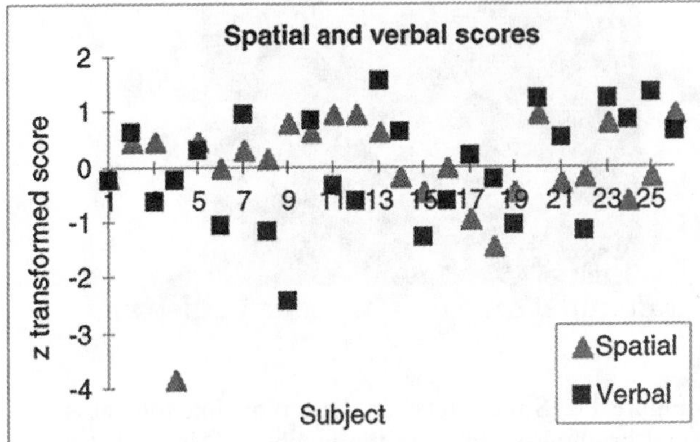

Figure 10. Z transformed spatial and verbal scores from the neuropsychological tests. Before applying the z transform, the mean spatial test score was 45, and mean verbal test score was 55.

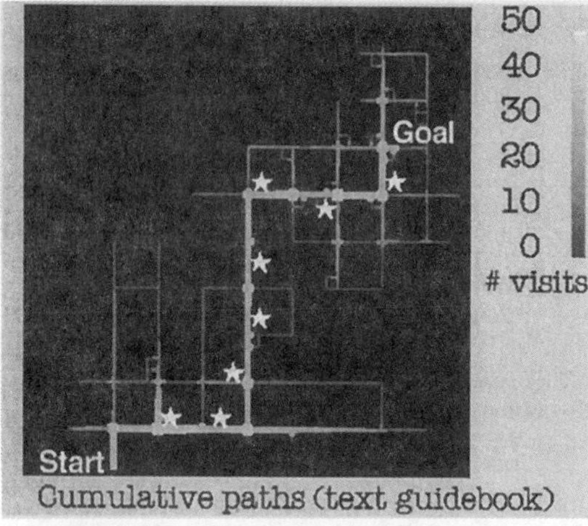

(a)

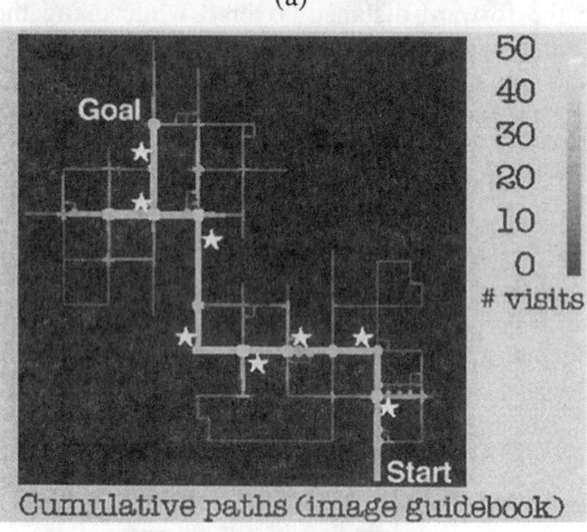

(b)

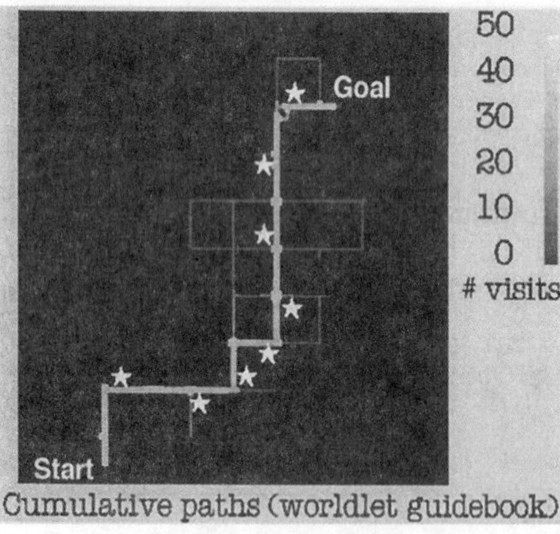

(c)

Figure 11. Street plots. In these plots line thickness and brightness indicates the number of times that a street was traversed. In (a) and (b) the 26 subjects traversed some streets 47 times indicating backtracking. (a) and (b) also exhibit circuitous trails. In (c) very little backtracking occurred, and circuitous trails are minimal.

Street plots

Figure 11 shows plots of the streets traversed by the 26 subjects in the three test cities. The thickness and brightness of each street line indicate the total number of times that the street was traversed. For example, wider brighter streets indicate heavily used avenues. Backtracking can increase the number of street traversals beyond the expected minimum of 26. The starting point and goal kiosk are indicated on each plot, and landmarks enroute to the goal are marked with a star (☆).

		Post hoc comparisons (Scheffe F-test)		
Time	**ANOVA**	**text vs. image**	**text vs. worldlet**	**image vs. worldlet**
consulting guidebook	55.59 * p<0.0001	19.66 * p<0.001	8.84 * p<0.01	54.88 * p<0.011
looking for landmark	21.61* p<0.0001	0.47	18.69 * p<0.001	13.25 * p<0.01
changing heading	17.36 * p<0.0001	0.02	13.53 * p<0.01	12.49 * p<0.01
moving forward	16.02 * p<0.0001	0.003	12.20 * p<0.01	11.83 * p<0.01
back-tracking	9.55 * p<0.0003	0.22	8.26 * p<0.01	5.86 * p<0.01
overall	10.34 * p<0.0002	0.98	9.89 * p<0.01	4.63 * p<0.01
Distance				
moving forward	15.33 * p<0.0001	0.05	12.23 * p<0.01	10.72 * p<0.01
back-tracking	10.19 * p<0.0002	0.23	8.84 * p<0.01	6.21 * p<0.01
overall	13.65 * p<0.0001	0.15	11.41 * p<0.01	8.93 * p<0.01
Guidebook				
opened	15.27 * p<0.0001	1.04	7.59 * p<0.01	14.26 * p<0.001

Table 2. Our ANOVA indicated that there were significant differences between all the sample means and post hoc analysis was warranted. Post hoc (Scheffe) analysis indicated that, for all dependent variables, there were significant differences in the sample means of the text versus worldlet performance, and thumbnail versus worldlet performance. Performance using the text versus image guidebooks was not significantly different except that time spent consulting the text guidebook was significantly greater than time spent consulting the image guidebook. In each table cell, the upper number is the F value, and the lower number is the p value. Asterisk indicates significance p<0.05. Time and distance measures are explained in the captions for Figures 6-9.

Subjective measures

As part of the written questionnaire administered after the experiment, subjects were asked how difficult the search task was using each of the different types of guidebooks.

Responses were scattered, however, a clear trend in favor of the worldlet guidebook was evident.

	Text	image	worldlet
Very easy	0	2	11
Easy	10	8	9
Doable	10	8	6
Difficult	5	7	0
Very difficult	1	1	0
Median	Doable	Doable	Easy

Table 3. Subjects were asked to rate the difficulty of the search task using the three different types of guidebooks.

Correlation analysis

One surprising finding was a high inverse correlation (-0.77, p=0.01) between spatial skills and the time spent consulting the text guidebook. Subjects with good spatial abilities seemed able to form a mental picture of a landmark on the basis of textual description more quickly than subjects with lower spatial abilities. This is not the case for image and worldlet guidebooks.

We expected to find a negative correlation between spatial skills and overall travel time in the thumbnail and worldlet guidebook cities. The data did not support this, nor did they support another of our hypotheses that there would be a positive correlation between verbal skills and the performance in the text guidebook city. Verbal skills made no difference in overall wayfinding time.

Additional observations

Many subjects said that the tasks were harder than they had imagined, and afterwards several said that they felt tired. No subjects complained of motion sickness. Most subjects required seventy minutes or more to finish all aspects of the computer-based part of the experiment.

We observed subjects to use three general types of strategies while deciding what direction to go from a street intersection:

1. Look down each street from many viewpoints within the intersection, until a landmark or landmark context is seen.
2. Look down each street and if nothing looks familiar, search exhaustively in each direction until the next landmark is found.
3. Look down each street and if nothing looks familiar, try going one half block in each direction and look again.

Subjects using strategy #1 seemed to find their way more quickly and with less backtracking than subjects who used strategies #2 and #3. Another strategy, described by some subjects on their written questionnaire, involved viewing a landmark in the worldlet guidebook from many distant vantage points in the hopes that one of the vantage points would be similar to the direction from which they would actually approach the landmark in the city. We observed that some subjects often forgot what it was they were looking for, and so had to open the guidebook momentarily to remind themselves.

Not surprisingly, landmarks with signs such as "Grocery Store" and landmarks painted with more highly saturated colors seemed easier to find than other types of landmarks. Also, after passing all the landmarks, several subjects exclaimed that they had lost all sense of direction within the world.

A final unexpected result is that there were many similarities between the text and image guidebooks. The text and image guidebooks were only significantly different in the time subjects spent consulting them. Considering that text and images represent landmarks in very different ways, we expected differences in time and distance measures.

Major findings

1. As we predicted, the total time spent traveling to the goal was significantly less using the worldlet guidebook than when using the text or image guidebooks.
2. Subjects spent significantly more time studying the worldlet guidebook than the text or image guidebook.
3. Increased worldlet study time was more than compensated for by a reduction in the time required to reach the goal. Using the worldlet guidebook, subjects traveled on average 55% faster than when using the text guidebook, and 38% faster than when using the image guidebook.
4. Increased worldlet study time also allowed subjects to move more directly to the goal and reduced backtracking time to almost zero. This is shown diagramatically in Figure 11 where Figures 11a and 11b show brighter wider streets than Figure 11c. Figure 11c also exhibits fewer detours and less wandering than Figures 11a and 11b.

We postulate that compared to the landmark knowledge gained from text and image guidebooks, the improved landmark knowledge built while consulting the worldlet guidebook enabled subjects to refer less frequently to the guidebook. This postulation is further supported by examining worldlet guidebook results:

- Subjects spent significantly more time studying the worldlet guidebook than the other types of guidebooks
- When using the worldlet guidebook, subjects traveled faster, more directly, and with more skill, to the goal kiosk
- Subjects' median rating for the difficulty of the search task was 'Easy' when using the worldlet guidebook.

CONCLUSION

We know of no studies that have considered the comparative advantages of different types of guidebooks for wayfinding. Intuitively, one would predict that 3D thumbnails make better guidebooks for 3D worlds than do text and 2D thumbnail images, and indeed, this is what we found. We wanted, however, to identify the component activities in using guidebooks that most benefited from 3D elements. Perhaps of greatest interest was our finding that worldlets enabled subjects to find their way in complex environments with almost no backtracking. By spending more time studying the worldlets in their guidebooks, they spent less time looking around, re-orienting themselves, conducting exhaustive searches, and performing similar time-wasting activities. We must be cautious, however, in what we conclude since worldlets contain more information than text or 2D thumbnail images. To control for this difference in information content, more experiments are necessary.

Future work

We would like to investigate the comparative advantages of worldlet guidebooks for wayfinding tasks in corresponding virtual and real world environments (both urban and rural). We are also considering an experiment to evaluate tandem use of traditional 2D maps and landmark guidebooks.

ACKNOWLEDGMENTS

Our appreciation goes to Planet 9 Studios (http://www.planet9.com) for the use of their city building textures. Thanks to John Moreland and Mike Bailey for technical assistance on this project, and thanks to Suzi Feeney for collaborating in the pilot study design. UCSD librarian Debbie Cox and her staff were invaluable in locating references. Thanks also to John Helly and Reagan Moore for their support. San Diego Supercomputer Center is funded by NSF, grant ASC 8902825, the University of California, the State of California, and industrial partners.

REFERENCES

1. Appleyard, D.A., "Why buildings are known," *Environment and Behavior*, 1969, 1, 131-156.
2. Art+Com, "The cybercity Berlin project", http://www.artcom.de/projects
3. Darken, R. P., and Sibert, J. L., "Wayfinding strategies and behaviors in large virtual worlds," in *Proceedings of the ACM CHI 96 Conference*, Vancouver, BC., April, 1996, 142-149.
4. Downs, R. J., and Stea, D., "Cognitive maps and spatial behavior," in *Image and Environment*, Chicago: Aldine Publishing Company, 1973, 8-26.
5. Elvins, T.T., Nadeau, D.R., Kirsh, D., "Worldlets - 3D thumbnails for wayfinding in virtual environments,"in *Proceedings of the ACM User Interface Software and Technology Symposium*, Banff, Canada, October, 1997, 21-30.
6. Elvins, T.T., "Wayfinding in layered information worlds," Short paper in *Proceedings of the CODATA Euro-American Workshop on Data and Information Visualization*, Paris, France, June, 1997, 6-7.
7. Goldin, S.E., Thorndyke, P.W., "Simulating navigation for spatial knowledge acquisition," *Human Factors*, 1982, 24 (4), 457-471.
8. Liggett, R., Friedman, S. and Jepson, W., "Interactive design/decision making in a virtual urban world: visual simulation and GIS," in *Proceedings of the 1995 ESRI User Conference*, Environmental Systems Research, July, 1995 http://www.esri.com/base/common/userconf/proc95
9. Lynch, K., *The Image of the City*, M.I.T. Press, 1960.
10. Passini, R., *Wayfinding in Architecture*, Van Nostrand Reinhold, NY, second edition, 1992.
11. Peponis, J., Zimring, C., and Choi, Y.K., "Finding the Building in Wayfinding," *Environment and Behavior*, 1990, 22 (5), 555-590.
12. Presson, C.C., Hazelrigg, M.D., "Building Spatial Representations Through Primary and Secondary Learning," *Journal of Experimental Psychology: Learning, Memory and Cognition*, 1984, 10, 716-222.
13. Satalich, G. A., *Navigation and Wayfinding in Virtual Reality: Finding the Proper Tools and Cues to Enhance Navigational Awareness.*, Masters Thesis, Department of Computer Science, University of Washington, 1995. http://www.hitl.washington.edu/publications/
14. University College London Center for Advanced Spatial Analysis, "Virtual London: a proposal," http://www.geog.ucl.ac.uk/casa/vl.html
15. Wechsler, D., *WAIS-R Manual,* The Psychological Corporation, Harcourt Brace Jovanovich, Inc., 1981.
16. Wickens, C., and Baker, P., "Cognitive Issues in Virtual Reality," Chapter 13 in *Mental Models and Human-computer Interaction,* Editors Woodrow Barfield and Thomas Furness III, Oxford University Press, 1995, 514-541.
17. Witmer, G.G., Bailey, J.H., Knerr, B.W., Parsons, K.C., "Virtual spaces and real world places: transfer of route knowledge," *Int. J. Human-computer Studies*, 45, 1996, 413-428.

Evolving Video Skims into Useful Multimedia Abstractions

Michael G. Christel, Michael A. Smith, C. Roy Taylor, David B. Winkler
Carnegie Mellon University
Pittsburgh, PA 15213 USA
+1 412 268 7799
{christel, msmith, crt, dwinkler} @cs.cmu.edu

ABSTRACT
This paper reports two studies that measured the effects of different "video skim" techniques on comprehension, navigation, and user satisfaction. Video skims are compact, content-rich abstractions of longer videos, condensations that preserve frame rate while greatly reducing viewing time. Their characteristics depend on the image- and audio-processing techniques used to create them. Results from the initial study helped refine video skims, which were then reassessed in the second experiment. Significant benefits were found for skims built from audio sequences meeting certain criteria.

Keywords
Video abstraction, evaluation, digital video library, video browsing, video skim, empirical studies, multimedia

INTRODUCTION

With increasing computational power and storage capacity, the potential for large digital video libraries is growing rapidly. The World Wide Web has seen an increased use of digital video, and digital video remains a key component of many educational and entertainment applications. As the size of accessible video collections grows to thousands of hours, potential viewers will need abstractions and technology to help them browse effectively and efficiently through this new wealth of information.

A *multimedia abstraction* ideally preserves and communicates in a compact representation the essential content of a source video. Examples include brief titles and individual "thumbnail" images that, when selected appropriately, facilitate operations on the corresponding source [3]. Another common approach presents an ordered set of representative thumbnail images simultaneously on a computer screen [3, 5, 6, 9, 11, 15, 17, 18]. While these abstractions have proven useful in various contexts, their static nature ignores video's temporal dimension. In addition, they often concentrate exclusively on the image content and neglect the audio information carried in a video segment. Our preliminary investigations suggest that the opposite emphasis offers greater value.

We define "video skim" as a temporal, multimedia abstraction that incorporates both video and audio information from a longer source. A video skim is played rather than viewed statically, and a two-minute skim may represent a 20-minute original. Our goal for video skims goes beyond merely motivating a viewer to watch a full video segment; we seek to communicate the essential content of a video in an order of magnitude less time.

During the past few years, the Informedia Project has developed and integrated speech recognition, image processing, and natural language techniques for processing video automatically [7, 16]. We are applying these techniques to extract the most important content from a video, that is, its significant images and words, and using that content as components for its video skim [13]. This paper reports on two experiments that examined ways to improve upon simple, mechanistic skimming techniques.

GENERATING SKIMS

One straightforward method for creating skims would simply increase the frame rate across the whole video. This "fast forward" approach might achieve a tenfold decrease in viewing time, but would seriously degrade coherence [14], both perturbing the audio [4] and distorting image information.

The skims described here, however, all preserve the source video's frame rate and differ only in the rules used for selecting "important" audio and video components. Our skim-generating procedures automatically select and concatenate original video and audio data into new, shorter presentations, as Figure 1 shows.

The most basic of these methods "subsamples" a source video, skipping frames at fixed intervals and keeping, for example, the first 10 seconds of each 100. The selected pieces are then concatenated and played back at the original frame rate. Figure 2 illustrates how source components map to a skim. While dropping video at regular intervals will likely delete essential information [16], this technique is trivial to implement and so serves as the default skim (DEF) in the studies reported here.

More ambitious methods analyze image, audio, and language information to differing degrees. An image-centric skim (IMG), for example, emphasizes visual content, decomposing the source into component *shots* [6, 11, 15, 17, 18], detecting "important" objects, such as faces and text [12, 13], and identifying structural motion within a shot [13]. Image heuristics, including weighting heavily those frame sequences with significant camera motion and those showing people or a text caption, prioritize shots for inclusion in the skim [13]. Metarules avoid overlapping regions and provide uniform coverage of the source video. Shots are repeatedly added to a skim until it reaches a threshold size, such as one-tenth of the full video.

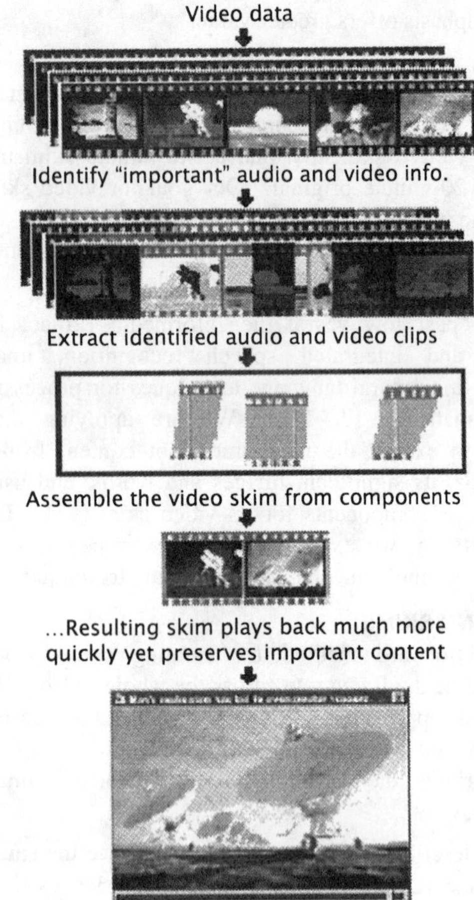

Figure 1. Generalized video skim creation process

Component shots for an image-centric skim may be quite abbreviated, however, and audio synchronized with brief shots will be short as well. Replaying audio components thus selected tends to yield a choppy presentation of partial words and noises. Pilot testing revealed such audio to be disconcerting and frustrating. The IMG skim design tested here maintains its singular emphasis on image analysis by incorporating an improved audio track, namely the same, subsampled audio as in the default (DEF) skim.

The structure of an audio-centric skim (AUD) derives solely from audio information. Automatic speech recognition and alignment techniques [7] register the audio track to the video's text transcript. A link-grammar parser developed at Carnegie Mellon identifies noun phrases within the transcript, and term-frequency, inverse-document-frequency (TF-IDF) scoring ranks them [13]. Words that appear often in a particular document but relatively infrequently in a standard corpus receive the highest weight. Noun phrases with many such words are judged "key phrases" and are assumed to contain the source video's most important audio information. Key phrases and their associated image frames are repeatedly added until the skim reaches a threshold size.

An "integrated best" skim (BOTH) merges the image-centric and audio-centric approaches while maintaining moderate audio/video synchrony. Top-rated audio regions are selected as in the AUD skim; hence, for a given source video, audio portions of AUD and BOTH skims are identical. The audio is then augmented with imagery selected — using IMG heuristics — from a temporal window extending five seconds before and after the audio region. This bounded window forces selection of visual components different from those in an IMG skim and aligns them more closely with the audio than in the IMG design. While the audio and video components of a BOTH skim may not be precisely synchronized, each attempts to capture the most significant information of its type.

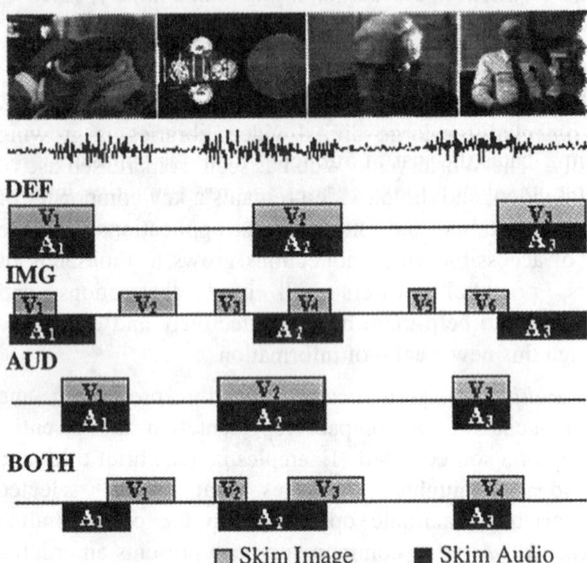

Figure 2. Audio/video alignment in skims (Exp. 1)

EXPERIMENT ONE

Our first experiment examined the use of these four different video skims on two tasks:

- Factfinding, where subjects used skims to locate video segments that answered specific, content-related questions.
- Gisting, grasping the essence of a video through its skim, where subjects matched skims of a longer video with representative text phrases and single-frame images for that longer video.

These tasks represent two complementary facets of video information retrieval. Factfinding tends to emphasize analytic processing, focusing attention to find a specific image or phrase within a larger context. Gisting, on the other hand, emphasizes synthetic processing to distill content, as in scanning a set of search results to narrow the scope of further, more detailed examination.

Subjects

Forty-eight Carnegie Mellon students (31 male, 17 female) from several majors and programs volunteered for the study, responding to an electronic call for participation in the spring of 1997. Each received $5 and spent about an hour with the system. A background questionnaire found that the subjects were, in general, "very comfortable" with computers but had little prior experience with digital video.

Materials

The video material was drawn from three public television series: "The Infinite Voyage", "Planet Earth", and "Space Age." This material was carefully documented to a fine level of granularity for delivery with the Informedia system to a high school in the Pittsburgh area [2]. The documentation was done manually and then checked and corrected for accuracy, without any knowledge that it would be later used in skim experiments. For these documentaries, every 1.6 minutes of video, on average, are represented by a short text phrase and a thumbnail image. These manually chosen representative images and manually generated text phrases serve as the gist of a video for our experiment. Ideally, after watching a video skim that fully communicates the gist of a longer video, the subject would be able to select all text phrases and representative images that belong to that longer video.

Design

Each of the skims was one-tenth the length of its source video and built from segments averaging three seconds duration (Figure 2). This 3-second "grain size" equals the average duration of key phrases used in the AUD and BOTH skims. The study compared the following four types of skims:

- DEF, the default, subsampled skim, comprising seconds 0-3 of the source video, then seconds 30-33, seconds 60-63, 90-93, etc.
- IMG, "best video" skim
- AUD, "best audio" skim
- BOTH, "integrated best" skim

Procedure

Subjects participated in the study individually. Each used a computer with a 17-inch color monitor, keyboard, mouse, and headphones. Each subject completed the factfinding task four times, once for each skim type, and the gisting task eight times, viewing each skim type twice. Subjects thus viewed skims of 12 different videos. We used a repeated measures design in a 4×4 Latin Square configuration to balance any learning effect between treatments [8].

In the factfinding task subjects were given a question and asked to navigate to that region of a video presenting the answer. While seeking the answer region, they could toggle between the skim and the full video. A potential $25 bonus encouraged them to work quickly.

After each factfinding exercise with a skim type, we asked subjects to evaluate the interface using a subset of the QUIS instrument [10], including such nine-point Likert scales as "terrible-wonderful" and "dull-stimulating." We also invited the subjects to type open-ended comments.

In the gisting task subjects watched a video skim without the option of switching to the normal video presentation. After watching each skim, they chose from text-phrase and thumbnail-image menus those items that best represented the material covered by the skim. The menus were populated with the independently validated text phrases and representative images.

Results

At the 0.05 level of significance, the four skim types yielded no differences in mean accuracy or speed on either factfinding or gisting. This result was surprising to us, since we expected the default skim to produce slower and less accurate performances than the other three skims. Pilot studies had shown us that users found the default skim "jerky," "too hard to follow," and "too jumpy."

There were also no significant (0.05 level) differences between the QUIS answers concerning user satisfaction for the four skim types.

EXPERIMENT ONE ANALYSIS

Several factors may have contributed to the lack of observed differences among skim types:

- All the tested skims used a small grain size. Even if the IMG, AUD, and BOTH skims had successfully identified and incorporated "important" segments, those components may have been too brief to communicate content effectively. Thus fine granularity may have masked differences among skim designs, leading subjects to consider all the skims essentially equivalent.
- The source videos were fairly short, 8 to 12 minutes, so skims ran 48 to 72 seconds. While these skims reduced viewing time by 7 to 11 minutes over watching the full video, perhaps the benefits of compaction become significant only for longer source video segments. Maybe 30-minute videos and 3-minute skims, for example, would work better for showcasing skim benefits.
- Two of the skim designs failed to preserve audio/video synchrony, a lack that may have distracted users enough to offset any benefits these skims provided over the other types.

- Users expressed difficulty in seeing the low-resolution thumbnail images, which occupied only 1/16 the area of the skim and source-video images.

REDESIGNING SKIMS

We addressed these shortcomings by:

- Modifying the key-phrase selection process and extending the average grain size from three to five seconds.
- Generating skims from longer, half-hour source videos.
- Improving audio/video synchronization in the "integrated best" skim.
- Using larger images in our gisting instrument (352×240 pixels, the same resolution as the MPEG-I video).

Our main concern in redesigning skims was granularity. User feedback in the first study indicated that all skims appeared disjointed and that the audio, in particular, was too choppy for easy comprehension.

Where our initial approach to audio segmentation relied solely on transcript analysis, for our second study we grouped words into phrases using signal power. Other researchers have similarly used speech signal characteristics to produce compact audio representations [1]. This analysis calculates the power of an audio sample as:

$$Power = \log\left(\left(\frac{1}{n}\right) \bullet \sum \left(Si^2\right)\right)$$

where Si is the signal intensity — low frequencies pre-emphasized — within a 20 ms frame, and n is the count of frames averaged. A low power level indicates little active speech, and we inserted segment breaks where power dropped to the average minimum in a trailing 0.5-second window. Thus the audio signal itself delineates utterance beginnings and endings.

The resulting phrases are typically longer than those selected in our first study. For example, Figure 3 shows a case where the noun-phrase approach would isolate the first eight words of a seventeen-word sentence. The power method, however, selects the full sentence.

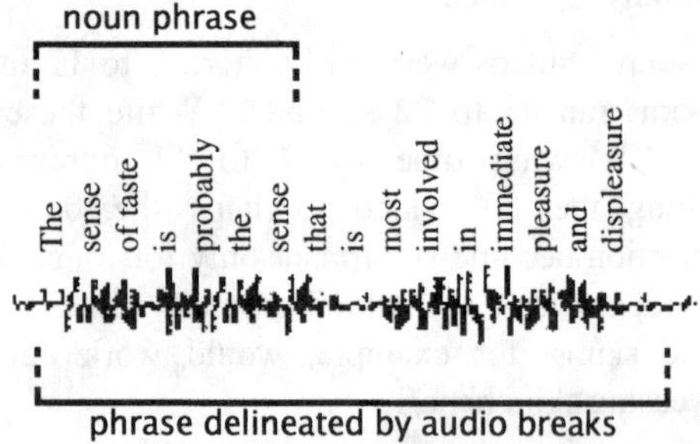

Figure 3. Audio regions based on parsed noun-phrases (Experiment 1) and signal-power segmentation (Exp. 2)

Detected utterances shorter than eight seconds are included unchanged. Words within a selected utterance constitute a candidate phrase, and phrases are scored using TF-IDF weighting, as before. Skims are built from the highest scoring phrases and, for the documentary videos used in these studies, average five seconds in length.

Another major concern with skims from our first study was synchrony between audio and video in the image-centric (IMG) and integrated best (BOTH) skims. For a given audio phrase these skims included images from a window considerably broader than that corresponding to the audio. For our second study we limited image adjustments to substitute only neighboring video for audio regions near shot breaks or blank video frames.

Pilot testing of our revised skims revealed that:

- People questioned the benefits of skims relative to using the full video.
- People found choppy audio more annoying than choppy video.
- Some people took the extreme position that the audio carries the entire gist for a movie and that two skims with the same audio track will produce similar results, regardless of the video content.

This feedback directly affected the design of the subsequent skim study conducted in September 1997.

RECONSIDERING TASKS

The factfinding task in our first experiment may have failed to distinguish among skims because it underutilized their temporal aspects. Our goal with skims is to communicate essential imagery and narrative. However, for locating a particular fact within a video, a skim's coverage may be more critical than how well it captures important parts. Sophisticated skim designs may offer little inherent advantage over more mechanistic ones that provide uniform coverage, abstractions such as our default skim (DEF) or simultaneous, static displays of representative thumbnail images [6, 9, 11, 15, 17, 18]. Showing where query-matching words occur within a video's transcript also may aid navigation to a point within a video more directly than a skim [3]. Rather than attempt to justify the use of skims for navigation, we decided to address only the issue of gisting in our subsequent skim study.

Our first experiment measured gisting through both text and image questionnaires. The text was not taken verbatim from the video, but rather was composed by Informedia staff members to serve as video descriptors for library delivery and use [2]. The same text representations are used again to measure gisting in Experiment Two.

For gisting images to complement the text phrases, we might have, ideally, developed a pictorial questionnaire that summarized a video without explicitly including any of its contents. Since this goal presented significant practical difficulties, we chose instead to use representative images carefully selected *from* the video and independently validated.

In our first experiment some skims incorporated such representative images while others, in fact, did not. For example, the DEF skim of a 12-minute video may have contained eight such images, while the AUD skim of the same source may have omitted them all. Viewers of this DEF skim have essentially an image recognition task, since they have seen the images being presented to them in the just-watched skim video. Viewers of this AUD skim would face the more difficult, although more authentic gisting task of determining whether the eight images could be part of the source video condensed in the skim. We wished to eliminate that variance in tasks.

For the image-gist instrument in our second experiment, we used only representative images that appeared in all skim treatments, so that, across all treatments, our pictorial questionnaire tested image recognition only. Subjects were asked to determine whether the image was part of the video they had just seen.

EXPERIMENT TWO

Our second study employed five experimental treatments: four skim types — each 7.5 times shorter than the associated video — and a fifth treatment that showed the full source video itself. The level of compaction in these skims extracted approximately eight seconds per minute of video, a capture ratio essentially determined by our power-based audio segmentation technique.

Subjects

Twenty-five Carnegie Mellon students (16 male, 9 female) from several majors and programs volunteered for the study, responding to an electronic call for participation. Each received $7 for spending about eighty minutes with the system. As in Experiment One, a background questionnaire revealed that the subjects were, in general, "very comfortable" with computers but had little prior experience with digital video.

Materials

The video material was drawn from the same three public television series as used in the first study, with manually generated text phrases and chosen representative images again serving as the gist of a video for our experiment.

Design

The five treatments in this experiment were:

- DFS: a default skim using short components and comprising seconds 0-2.5 from the full source video, then seconds 18.75-21.25, seconds 37.5-40, etc.
- DFL: a default skim using long components and consisting of seconds 0-5, then seconds 37.5-42.5, seconds 75-80, etc.
- NEW: our redesigned, "integrated best" skim
- RND: "best audio" with reordered video
- FULL: complete source video, with no information deleted or modified

Figure 4 shows how source components map to these four skims. Two variants of our default skim (DFS and DFL) tested grain-size effects. DFS components were 2.5 seconds, and DFL used segments twice as long. The "new integrated best" design (NEW) had the same average granularity as DFL, constrained image regions to contiguous frames, and limited synchronization offsets to minor shifts between associated video and audio regions. A fourth skim type (RND) addressed the effects of extreme synchronization differences. It used the same audio and video as NEW but reversed video-component ordering, so that audio and video corresponded only at mid-skim.

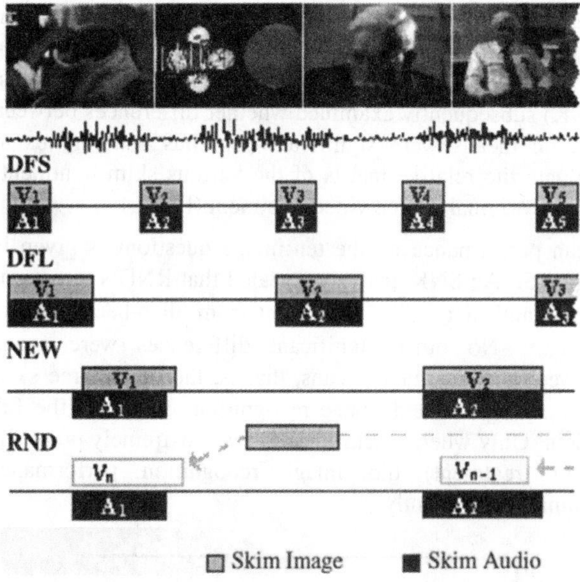

Figure 4. Audio/video alignment in four skims (Exp. 2)

Procedure

Subjects participated in the study individually, as in the first experiment. Each used a computer with a 17-inch color monitor, hardware support for smooth full-motion video playback, and headphones. All materials were presented online. After entering background information and reading the instructions, the subject viewed a short video skim of a popular movie to get acclimated to skim presentations. We used a 5×5 Latin Square configuration to balance any learning effect between treatments [8]. Thus we repeated the following procedure five times, using a different source video and treatment on each iteration:

1. The subject watched a video without interruption. For DFS, DFL, NEW, and RND, a presentation lasted about four minutes; the FULL video ran approximately 30 minutes. One-fifth of the subjects saw DFS first, one-fifth saw DFL first, etc.
2. The subject answered three Likert-scale questions taken from QUIS [10] plus three subjective questions concerning opinions about the just-completed video.

3. The interface then presented ten images, one at a time, each at the same resolution as the video. Subjects selected "yes" or "no" based on whether they recognized the image as one from the video.
4. The interface presented 15 text phrases, one at a time, and for each the subject selected "yes" or "no" to indicate whether that text phrase summarized information that would be part of the full source video. This is the same metric used in the first experiment.

Finally, we asked each subject how well the video had prepared him or her for the just-completed questions and invited them each to type comments concerning this particular video treatment.

Results

Analysis revealed significant ($p < 0.01$) differences in mean performance on text gisting and image recognition among the five video treatments. A Student-Newman-Keuls test (SNK) subsequently examined whether differences between specific means were significant [8], thus enabling us to evaluate the relative merits of the various skim treatments and the original source video treatment (FULL).

Mean performance on the ten image questions is given in Figure 5. An SNK analysis revealed that RND's mean was significantly ($\alpha = 0.05$) different from all other treatment means. No other significant differences were found between the treatment means, that is, the other three skim treatments promoted image recognition as well as the full video. Only when synchronization was extremely poor (the RND treatment) did image recognition performance diminish significantly.

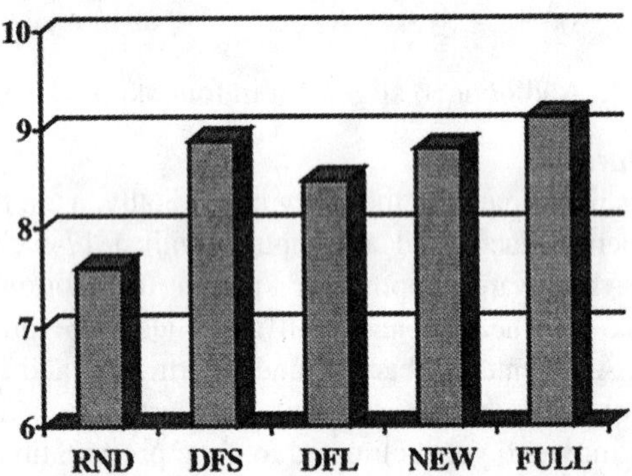

Figure 5. Mean scores for image recognition

The mean performance for the 15 text-gist questions, given in Figure 6, was generally worse than that for the image recognition questions. This difference is likely due to the fact that while the images in question were actually shown during the presentation, subjects neither saw nor heard the text.

Testing the text-gisting means with SNK revealed that FULL's mean was significantly ($\alpha = 0.05$) different from the other four treatment means. The subjects understood the essence of a video better when they saw the full version rather than a video skim. The NEW mean was also significantly different from the RND mean, with no other significant differences found between the treatment means.

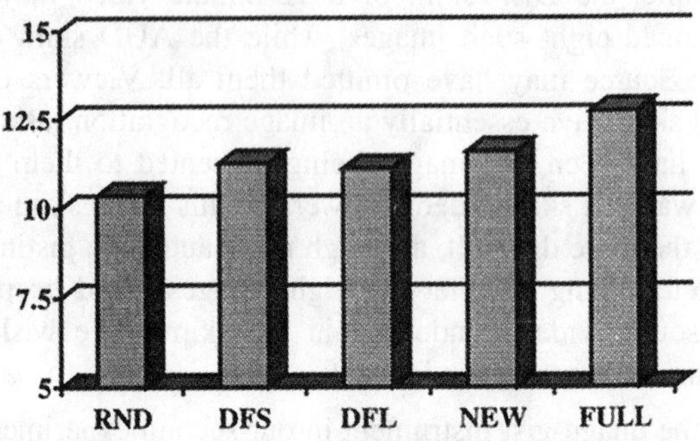

Figure 6. Mean scores for text phrase identification

Figure 7 shows mean subjective responses to the three QUIS questions used in this experiment, each with different shading. On these nine-point scales "1" mapped to "terrible," "frustrating," or "dull" and "9" to "wonderful," "satisfying," or "stimulating," respectively. The trend revealed here shows the FULL treatment to be the most preferred, followed in order by NEW, DFL, and then DFS or RND.

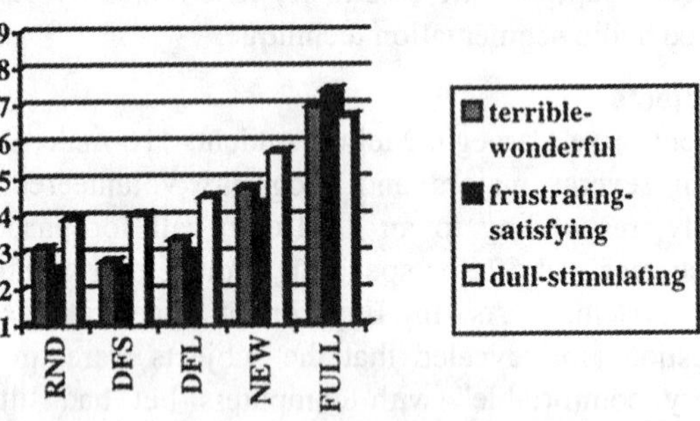

Figure 7. Mean scores for three QUIS subjective ratings

We added two nine-point scales to measure the subject's perception of audio and video quality ("1" = "poor audio" and "poor video"), with mean scores presented in Figure 8.

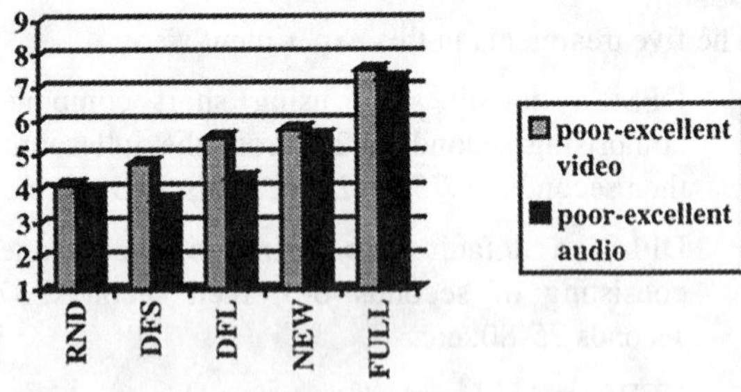

Figure 8. Mean scores for audio/video subjective ratings

The subjects were directly asked how well they felt the video skim did in communicating the essence of a longer video segment. This question was only asked following the viewing of one of the skim treatments, and the mean results from the nine-point scale ("1" = "inadequately") are shown in Figure 9. The subjects were also asked how well they felt the video treatment informed them for answering the text and image questions. These mean results ("1" = "poorly informed") are shown in the figure as well.

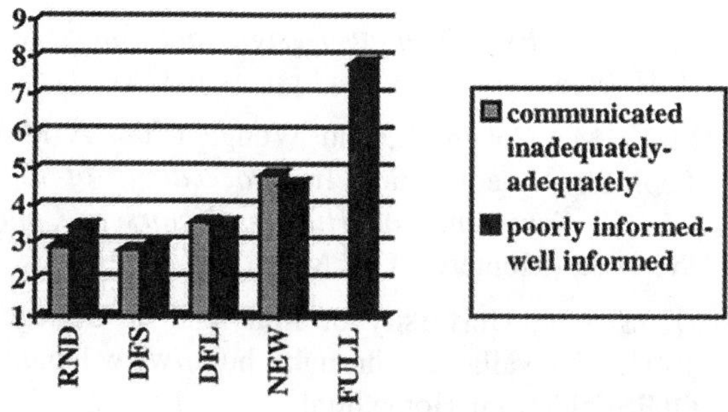

Figure 9. Mean scores for additional subjective ratings

Analysis of variance for the Latin Square design for all seven subjective questions showed significant ($p < 0.01$) differences in mean ratings among the five video treatments. Testing the means with SNK revealed that FULL's mean was significantly ($\alpha = 0.05$) different from all other treatment means and that, for six of seven cases, NEW's mean was significantly different from all other skim treatment means. For the seventh case ("poor-excellent video") NEW's mean was still the greatest of the skim treatment means and significantly different from all but the DFL treatment mean.

The subjects' open-ended comments supported these results as well. An informal classification of the 59 open-ended comments offering a favorable or critical opinion produced the distribution shown in Figure 10.

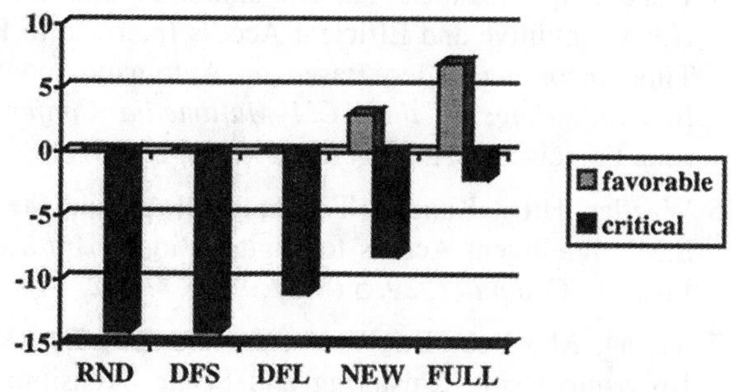

Figure 10. Count of open-ended comments by treatment

DISCUSSION

Clearly, the subjects preferred the full video to any of the skim types in the second experiment. However, subjects favored the NEW skim over the other skim treatments, as indicated by the subjective ratings. These results are encouraging, showing that incorporating speech, language, and image processing into skim video creation produces skims that are more satisfactory to users.

The RND skim distinguished itself as significantly poorer than NEW on the text-phrase gisting instrument, despite the fact that both RND and NEW use identical audio information. This result shows that the visual content of a video skim does have an impact on its use for gisting and so addresses a point raised during earlier pilot studies.

The DFS and DFL skim treatments did not particularly distinguish themselves from one another, leaving open the question of the proper grain size for video skims. The larger grain size, when used with signal-power audio segmentation, produced the NEW skim that *did* distinguish itself from the other skims. If the larger grain size is used only for subsampling, however, it yields no clear objective or subjective advantage over short grain size skims, such as DFS. In fact, both DFS and DFL often rated similarly to RND, indicating perhaps that *any* mechanistically subsampled skim, regardless of granularity, may not do notably well.

While our first study found no significant differences between a subsampled skim and a "best" audio and video skim, the second study uncovered numerous statistically significant differences. The primary reasons for the change can be traced to the following characteristics of the audio data in the latter experiment:

- Skim audio is less choppy due to setting phrase boundaries with audio signal-processing rather than noun-phrase detection.
- Synchronization with video is better preserved.
- Grain size has increased from three seconds to five.

Although the NEW skim established itself as the best design under study, considerable room for improvement remains. It received mediocre scores (4-6) on most of the subjective questions, and its improvement over the other skims may reflect more on their relatively poor evaluations than on its own strengths. NEW did distinguish itself from RND for the image recognition and text-phrase gisting tasks, but not from the DFS and DFL skims.

FUTURE WORK

Image components for skims merit further investigation. Our NEW skim achieved smoother audio transitions but still suffered abrupt visual changes between image components. Perhaps transitions between video segments should also be smoothed — through dissolves, fades, or other effects — when they are concatenated to form a skim.

Other researchers have focused exclusively on image-based video abstractions [5]. Such strategies typically decompose video into shots and represent each shot with a selected image [6, 11, 15, 17, 18]. Concatenating these representative images yields a form of video skim that provides full coverage of all component shots with duration proportional to the time for displaying each image [5]. Such skims resemble "automatic slide shows" where still images appear sequentially. The skims investigated here, however, more resemble "video digests" that are "played." Combining the two approaches would produce a visually dense representation with complementary audio. Further study is required to determine whether more uniform coverage offsets the loss of temporal flow and audio/video synchrony.

Finally, we have focused on general-purpose skims. Work on other multimedia abstractions has shown the benefits of exploiting context to tailor representations [3]. For example, given a query, a skim emphasizing target regions that contain matches may prove more effective than a general-purpose skim. We intend to explore such context-based skims in future work.

ACKNOWLEDGMENTS

This material is based on work supported by the National Science Foundation, DARPA, and NASA under NSF Cooperative Agreement No. IRI-9411299. Michael Smith is supported by Bell Laboratories. Numerous Informedia Project members contributed to this work, including Howard Wactlar, Takeo Kanade, Alex Hauptmann, Michael Witbrock, Craig Marcus, Naomi Dambacher, Jayshree Ranka, and Bruce Cardwell. Special thanks go to Ellen Hughes, Yuichi Nakamuri, Bryan Maher, Ricky Houghton, and Laurel Margulis for their invaluable assistance. Finally, we thank Informedia Project partner QED Communications for the video source material.

REFERENCES

1. Arons, B. SpeechSkimmer: Interactively Skimming Recorded Speech. In *Proceedings of the ACM Symposium on User Interface Software and Technology.* (Atlanta, GA, Nov 1993), 187-196.

2. Christel, M.G., and Pendyala, K. Informedia Goes To School: Early Findings from the Digital Video Library Project. *D-Lib Magazine* (September 1996). URL http://www.dlib.org/dlib/september96/09contents.html.

3. Christel, M.G., Winkler, D.B., and Taylor, C.R. Improving Access to a Digital Video Library. In *Human-Computer Interaction: INTERACT97, the 6th IFIP Conf. On Human-Computer Interaction.* (Sydney, Australia, July 14-18, 1997).

4. Degen, L., Mander, R., and Salomon, G. Working with Audio: Integrating Personal Tape Recorders and Desktop Computers. In *Proceedings of the ACM CHI'92 Conference on Human Factors in Computing Systems.* (Monterey, CA, May 1992), 413-418.

5. Ding, W., Marchionini, G., & Tse, T. Previewing Video Data: Browsing Key Frames at High Rates Using a Video Slide Show Interface. In *Proceedings of the International Symposium on Research, Development & Practice in Digital Libraries.* (Tsukuba Science City, Japan, November 1997), 151-158.

6. Hampapur, A., Jain, R., and Weymouth, T. Production Model Based Digital Video Segmentation. *Multimedia Tools and Applications, 1* (March 1995), 9-46.

7. Hauptmann, A.G., and Witbrock, M.J. Informedia: News-on-Demand Multimedia Information Acquisition and Retrieval. In *Intelligent Multimedia Information Retrieval,* M. Maybury, Ed. 1997, AAAI Press/MIT Press: Menlo Park, CA.

8. Lee, W. *Experimental Design and Analysis.* 1975, W.H. Freeman & Co.: San Francisco, CA.

9. Mills, M., Cohen, J., and Wong, Y.Y. A Magnifier Tool for Video Data. In *Proceedings of the ACM CHI'92 Conference on Human Factors in Computing Systems.* (Monterey, CA, May 1992), 93-98.

10. *QUIS 5.5b.* University of Maryland at College Park, 1994. Available through http://www.lap.umd.edu/QUISFolder/quisHome.html.

11. Pfeiffer, S., Lienhart, R., Fischer, S., and Effelsberg, W. Abstracting Digital Movies Automatically. *Journal of Visual Communication and Image Representation, 7,* 4 (Dec 1996), 345-353.

12. Rowley, H., Baluja, S. and Kanade, T. Human Face Detection in Visual Scenes. Carnegie Mellon University, School of Computer Science Technical Report CMU-CS-95-158 (Pittsburgh, PA, 1995).

13. Smith, M., Kanade, T. Video Skimming and Characterization through the Combination of Image and Language Understanding Techniques. In *Computer Vision and Pattern Recognition.* (San Juan, PR, 1997).

14. Stevens, S. Next Generation Network and Operating System Requirements for Continuous Time Media. In *Network and Operating System Support for Digital Audio and Video,* R. Herrtwich, Ed. 1992, Springer-Verlag; New York.

15. Taniguchi, Y., Akutsu, A., Tonomura, Y., and Hamada, H. An Intuitive and Efficient Access Interface to Real-Time Incoming Video Based on Automatic Indexing. In *Proceedings of the ACM Multimedia Conference.* (San Francisco, CA, November 1995), 25-33.

16. Wactlar, H.D., Kanade, T., Smith, M.A., and Stevens, S.M. Intelligent Access to Digital Video: Informedia Project. *Computer, 29,* 5 (May 1996), 46-52.

17. Yeung, M., Yeo, B., Wolf, W., and Liu, B. Video Browsing Using Clustering and Scene Transitions on Compressed Sequences. In *Proceedings of IS&T/SPIE Multimedia Computing and Networking* (1995).

18. Zhang, H.J., Tan, S., Smoliar, S., and Yihong, G. Automatic Parsing and Indexing of News Video. *Multimedia Systems, 2,* 6 (1995), 256-266.

Navigation Guided by Artificial Force Fields

Dongbo Xiao and Roger Hubbold

Department of Computer Science
University of Manchester
Manchester M13 9PL, United Kingdom
roger@cs.man.ac.uk

ABSTRACT

This paper presents a new technique for controlling a user's navigation in a virtual environment. The approach introduces artificial force fields which act upon the user's virtual body such that he is guided around obstacles, rather than penetrating or colliding with them. The technique is extended to incorporate gravity into the environment. The problem of negotiating stairs during a walk-through has also been investigated with the new approach. Human subjects were tested in experiments in which they experienced three different kinds of navigation: unconstrained, simple constrained and assisted by force fields. The results demonstrate that the force-field technique is an effective approach for effective, comfortable navigation.

KEYWORDS: 3D interfaces, virtual environments, collision avoidance, navigation, force fields.

INTRODUCTION

An important feature of virtual reality is the facility for users to move through a virtual environment in a natural and easily controlled manner. Natural navigation methods contribute to a sense of presence, cited by some researchers as a defining attribute of VR [1]. The illusion of presence can be lost through unnatural experiences during a walk-through. This can be caused by poor interactive metaphors or by experiences which are not consistent with the user's everyday understanding of the real world. Several attempts have been made to develop new metaphors for walking through virtual environments [2, 3, 4, 5]. However, intuitive metaphors are only able to solve part of the walk-through problem. The other part concerns how to provide a virtual environment with more realistic properties so that the user's walk-through can be more natural and comfortable. Unconstrained motion is sometimes desirable, indeed liberating, since less concentration is needed in the control of motion. However, the physical world is full of solid objects and we do not expect to penetrate these when we collide with them. Thus, in situations where realistic, real-world behaviour is required, more constrained navigation methods are called for.

In this paper, we present a technique for assisting a user's navigation in a virtual environment. The method we have devised incorporates several new features. We use *force fields* to guide a user past objects in the environment. This idea is combined with a simple, but efficient, form of *collision avoidance* which guarantees that users cannot pass through solid objects. The method also offers a straightforward way of incorporating *gravitational effects*, and effective assistance to negotiate stairs.

The technique we present is a general solution: it does not rely on any explicit (semantic) knowledge of the virtual environment, such as 'this is a staircase'. The technique for climbing stairs can also be employed to climb on top of other objects – a chair, for example – provided that it is low enough for the user to 'step' on. The algorithm can be implemented for a variety of primitive shapes as long as they are convex (non-convex shapes can be constructed by assembling convex primitives), and works well with complex and dense environments. It does not require any complicated interactive metaphors or devices, and can be used for immersive environments as well normal 3D workstations.

We present results from experiments we have performed which compare the new algorithm with two other methods: unconstrained navigation, and navigation using only collision detection. These demonstrate that the force-field technique is an effective approach for comfortable navigation.

RELATED WORK

One of the problems of unconstrained navigation, particularly in complex or cluttered environments, is that it is very difficult for a user to control a virtual body which has no mass or other natural attributes. When attempting to find one's way past objects without any haptic feedback, one is relying totally on visual cues, and this is doubly difficult if the field of view is restricted – a common situation with many head-mounted displays. As a result, the user often encounters unnatural experiences, such as walking through objects like walls. Particularly confusing is the act of mistakenly walking backwards through a wall, when the world suddenly disappears from view. A direct approach to solving this problem is to make objects solid, that is to introduce some form of collision detection [6] to prevent users from passing through objects. While this avoids the more obvious problems, such as walking through a wall backwards, it does not make the actual task of steering a course through an environment any easier. It is still relatively easy to get stuck against small objects which are not in one's immediate field of view.

Consideration of this problem led us to the idea of using a force field around objects to guide the user. The idea was motivated by the work of Bouvier and Guilloteau [7], who used a flocking algorithm [8] for simulation of crowd control in a virtual environment. Force-field methods have been applied previously to path planning in robotics [9, 10, 11, 12]. In robotics, in addition to repulsive forces surrounding objects, an attractive force from a designated target plays an important role in 'pulling' the robot in the desired direction. However, generally, the robot's target is known in advance, so that a force field for the whole environment can be precalculated. With *interactive* navigation, the control of movement should respond to the user's input and this cannot be pre-planned. Instead of passively responding to the environment or following a given path, the user's intention during the walk-through may be arbitrary and varying, so a different approach is needed. Egbert and Winkler [13] proposed a force-field technique for computer animation, which used a vector field around objects to prevent collisions between them. However, interaction with a user was not considered. Furthermore, as we shall see later, a force field alone is not sufficient to prevent collisions with objects.

Since the work reported here was conducted, our attention has been drawn to the work of Jacobson and Lewis [14]. Our experiments and ideas are very similar to theirs, although they do not use force fields.

THE FORCE-FIELD GUIDED APPROACH

The fundamental idea in the new approach is that each object in a virtual environment is surrounded by a repulsive force field. Each field extends to a pre-determined distance – a *region of influence* – beyond which no force is applied. If the user is close enough to an object to be inside its region of influence, the object creates a repulsive force to resist any attempt of the user to get closer to the object in question. In this way, the force field around an object forms a barrier to prevent the user from getting too close to the surface of the object, and also assists the user to make effective movement in order to avoid the object.

The differences between the new approach, the unconstrained approach, and another which simply detects collisions, are illustrated in Figure 1 with a simple scene. Suppose the user is moving forwards and approaching an obstacle. The user will walk through and penetrate the obstacle with the unconstrained method (Figure 1a), or be stopped at the edge of the obstacle with the simple collision avoidance method (Figure 1b). With the guidance of a force field, the user will move slightly sideways, avoid the obstacle, and carry on going forward (Figure 1c).

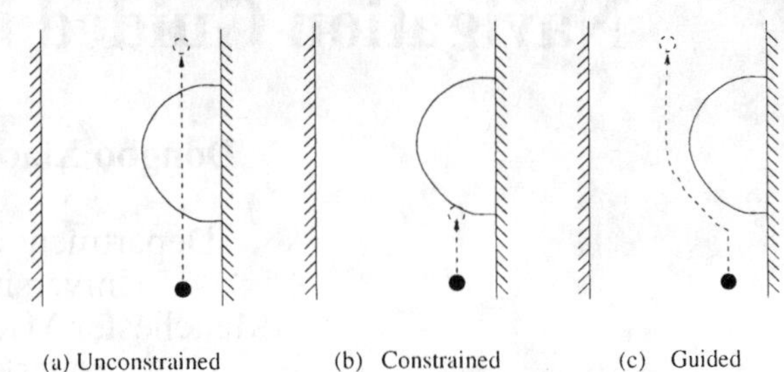

Figure 1: Three types of walk-through

User's Control of the Motion

The user's intended motion is specified interactively as a force, which is determined by the user's virtual body orientation, velocity and acceleration. The user's input is supplied with a 3D mouse containing a Polhemus Fastrak sensor. Inputs from the mouse can be mapped to suitable ranges to give easy control of direction and velocity. To move forwards, the user pushes the mouse forwards, while keeping a button depressed. This results in a forward force applied to the virtual body. Pushing the mouse further forward generates a larger force, causing acceleration. Pulling it backwards generates a backward force. Similarly, a sideways translation of the mouse results in a corresponding sideways force on the virtual body. Twisting the mouse about a vertical axis induces a rotational (steering) movement, permitting a change of direction.

These forward or backward, sideways and rotational movements can all be applied simultaneously, giving quite precise control. Releasing the button allows the mouse to be moved without generating any input forces. Thus, at any time, a user can stop moving by releasing the mouse button, and can restart with a new frame of reference by pressing the button again.

The Force Field around an Object

The force field exerted by an object is represented by a single force along the shortest path between the object and the user's virtual body. The magnitude of the force is a function of this path length.

Initially, we planned to use an inverse square law to control the force, but we discovered that the sudden increase in repulsion as the user approached objects made this method difficult to control interactively. After experimentation, we finally opted for a linear force field, in which the repulsive force is inversely proportional to the shortest distance between the user's virtual body and the object in question. At the edge of the region of influence the force drops to zero. The force and distance parameters can be scaled to suit the user's virtual body size within the environment.

Computing the Resultant Force on the Virtual Body

If the user is not close to any objects – that is, if he or she is outside their regions of influence – then movement is completely controlled by the user. Otherwise, the next 'step' is decided by combining the force applied by the user with the forces exerted by nearby objects. We discovered that naively combining all of the forces, to obtain a resultant force upon the virtual body, led to cases where the result was uncomfortable for the user. For example, the mere presence of a nearby object could cause movement when the user actually wanted to stand still. Three rules were therefore derived to govern the force computation:

1. If the user does not apply any force to the virtual body, with the mouse, then it remains stationary. This is important as it means users are always completely in control of movement. You won't get pushed around if you happen to stand next to objects which apply a force, unless you also apply a force.
2. Objects only push *against* the direction in which the user tries to move. Thus, if you attempt to move forwards through an object, the movement will be resisted. The same will happen if you try to go backwards through something. But, if you stand with your back to a wall and then walk forwards, the wall will not exert a force.
3. In simple mechanics, component forces would normally be summed to produce a resultant force. Here, the effect of this would be that two adjacent objects would create a double force, repelling the user strongly. In regions of the environment with many small objects clustered together, unacceptably large forces would result. To prevent this, we resolve each separate object force into components in the direction of the user's input force – the direction he would move in the absence of any other forces, which we term the *major direction* – and the directions normal to this. Only the *maximum* positive and negative components in each direction are then considered. Any force from behind the user is ignored and the other components are resolved to produce a final direction and distance of movement.

There remains one final detail of motion control which must be addressed: the problem of oscillation. Consider the case where a user is approaching a wall. As the wall gets closer it exerts an increasing, repulsive force. If the wall is approached cautiously, the forward force applied by the user and the repulsive force from the wall reach a point of balance and movement stops. But if the wall is approached more rapidly, it is easy to pass beyond this equilibrium state, so that the force exerted by the wall greatly exceeds that applied by the user. When this happens, the user is repelled strongly and bounces back from the wall. This backward movement reduces the opposing force, and the user moves forwards again. Unless some kind of damping is introduced the user may end up in a state of oscillation. In practice, this can be considerably exacerbated by the user's natural reaction, which is often to move the mouse either forwards or backwards to try to bring the situation under control. Such oscillations are visually distressing and make precise control very difficult.

To counteract oscillations, we take the following steps. First, we identify the *major direction* of the user's motion. Note that this is not necessarily the direction in which the user's virtual body is pointing, because sideways as well as forward and backward movements are permitted. We discovered empirically that oscillation control is only necessary in the major direction. In fact, we do not wish to damp forces which are normal to this, as it is these which provide the predominant 'steering' effect from the environment.

Next, in the major direction, if the opposing force from an obstacle is greater than that applied by the user, we limit the magnitude of the net force in this direction. This is done by scaling (damping) the force difference according to the shortest distance to the obstacle, thereby reducing the net repulsion. This override mechanism guarantees that the user will come to a stop progressively without being too strongly repelled by the object. The parameters which control the relative strengths of the force fields, the oscillation damping, and the user input can all be tuned to achieve an appropriate 'feel' for a given type of environment.

Collision Avoidance

If we were to use only force fields it would still be possible for a user to collide with objects, or even to pass completely through them, by 'pushing' hard enough with the 3D mouse. This is because our algorithm works incrementally, re-evaluating the force fields each time a step is made. To prevent such violations we establish a *safe region* around the user at each step. As long as the user's next step is inside this safe region, we can guarantee that no collision will occur. Any movement which is to move the user further beyond the safe region will be limited.

Figure 2 shows how the safe region is computed. First consider the left-hand half of the figure, which shows a single object, **O1**, and the current position of the user. Note that for simplicity, the user has been represented as a single point, although in the implementation more complicated body representations are also supported. The circle surrounding the user represents the range of movement which could be made under the control of the user's input, assuming that there are

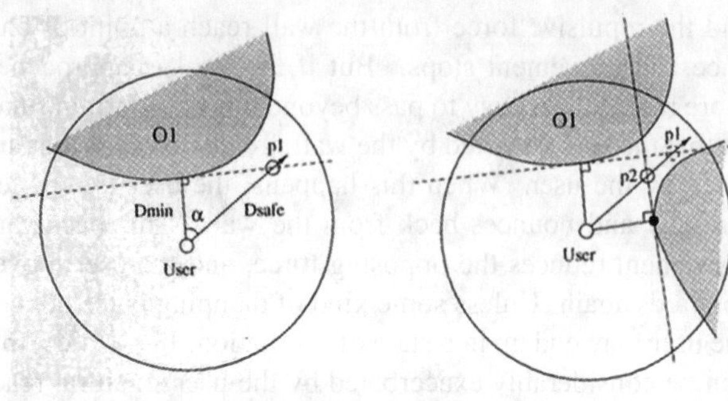

Figure 2: Safe region

no objects nearby. In this case, after taking account of the net forces acting upon the user, the intended direction of movement is towards the point **p1**. But we must check whether this would result in a collision with **O1**. Because objects are convex (or can be decomposed into assemblies of convex shapes), it is safe to move anywhere in the half-space defined by the tangent plane at the point on the object closest to the user, shown dotted in the figure. Thus, the user can safely move as far as **p1** in this example.

The right-hand half of Figure 2 shows how the addition of a second object, **O2**, further limits safe movement to the point **p2**, computed in the same manner. In fact, it is easy to see that the safe region is the intersection of the half-spaces defined by the shortest distances to each object, and that the safe step is the minimum of the distances computed in this way.

This is a conservative solution because there are cases where a user is able to move beyond the computed safe region without any collisions with objects. But this has proved to be quite acceptable in practice. The user is slowed down when close to objects and this feels very natural. It can be seen that the safe distance, **Dsafe** depends on the angle between the intended motion and the tangent plane, shown as α in the figure. Therefore, if the user moves parallel to a surface, such as a wall, no slowing down results. Once all nearby objects have been checked in this way, the user's position is updated, and the whole process is repeated.

Gravity and Staircases

A benefit of the force-field approach is that it is very simple to incorporate gravity. During normal operation, a downward gravitational force is applied to the virtual body. Horizontal (or inclined) surfaces, such as floors or stair treads, apply an upward force which counteracts this gravitational force. Unless the user provides an additional upward force, the virtual body's 'weight' and the upward force from the surface balance and the user can move smoothly across horizontal surfaces. Walking over a cliff or a hole in the floor removes the supporting force and the user falls vertically downwards. Thus, gravity can be included very inexpensively by treating it as an extra, constant force applied to the user's virtual body.

Vertical movement of the 3D mouse controls an additional upward force which can be used to overcome gravity. To facilitate smooth motion over flat surfaces, the vertical input from the mouse has a built-in 'dead space' so that small movements have no effect. Supplying a larger upward movement with the mouse overcomes gravity and permits users to 'jump in the air'. However, this takes them away from the supporting surface, and the repulsive force is therefore reduced as the distance increases. So, unless this jump causes them to land on another surface, the gravitational force will bring them down again.

Walking down a staircase is simple – the user moves forwards and the gravitational force causes them to drop from one step to the next. Thus, no special processing is necessary to deal with walking downstairs. However, to climb a staircase, the user must push forwards and upwards with the mouse. It is difficult to move the virtual body to the next step without colliding with the front of the next step. Therefore, in order to be able to clear a step, the upward movement is computed and applied *before* the forward motion. Then, provided that the user has arrived above a step, the application of gravity will cause them to drop back onto its horizontal surface. Before display, these vertical and horizontal movements are combined to form a single motion of the virtual body.

Searching for Nearby Objects

To avoid exhaustive testing of all objects in a model, we use hierarchical bounding volumes [15] for locating objects in the vicinity of the user. The search space is adjusted according to the user's speed of movement. The same data structures are used for control of culling and level-of-detail display. Therefore the algorithm is efficient, both for display and force computation.

Our implementation uses a system called MAVERIK [16], in which the behaviour of environments is customised using callback functions. MAVERIK already supports a number of different geometric primitives, including polygons, polygon meshes, cylinders, spheres, cones, tori, and boxes. Adding new primitives is straightforward, requiring only that appropriate methods be registered for certain operations (such as a display method). In order to compute the shortest distances and half-spaces for force evaluation and safe region testing, we register a callback function to perform these evaluations for each type of primitive.

EXPERIMENTS AND RESULTS

To test the new technique. we have conducted experiments with fifteen volunteer subjects, including both experienced users of VR and complete novices. We set them the task of following a prescribed route around a model of a house containing two floors, a dog-leg staircase, and some furniture. The route involved walking around and between tables and chairs, passing between the furniture and the walls, going upstairs, passing around more furniture, going back downstairs, and returning to the starting position. The gaps between some pieces of furniture were deliberately made quite small, so that good navigation control was necessary to squeeze between them.

In the experiments we compared the force-field method with free navigation, which is totally unconstrained, and also with simple collision detection. In the former case users could walk through objects and the goal was to see how well they could follow a specified route, to measure the time taken and the number of collisions. In the case of simple collision detection, the user could move freely in uncluttered regions, but movement towards an object was prevented once the user came into contact with that object. The routes taken by a typical subject (number 7) in the three types of navigation are illustrated in Figures 4, 5, and 6, together with snapshots of the user's track on the stairs. The radius of the point plotted at each position is proportional to the time the subject stayed at the position, either for looking around, turning, or because of getting stuck there.

Each subject was tested with the three different methods – unconstrained (UC), collision detection (CD), and force-field (FF) – but with the order varied. Each experiment was repeated three times, totalling nine tests for each person, and 135 tests in the complete set. Each time, subjects were asked to complete the same route in the shortest possible time. The route and the time taken were recorded, and codes were instrumented to measure display frame rates and collisions in a post-processing phase. From these we were able to analyse other factors, such as the time spent without moving (looking around, or stuck in corners), and the processing requirements of the algorithms. We also interviewed each subject and asked them to rate their subjective views of each trial. During the experiments they were given no information about which method they were testing, but they were allowed a brief, preliminary practice session, using unconstrained motion, to familiarise themselves with the basic motion control using the forward, backward and twisting movements of the mouse.

The experiments were conducted using stereoscopic projection onto a screen of 2.5 metres diagonal dimension, viewed with passive, polarising glasses. Subjects sat in front of the screen and controlled motion with a 3D mouse containing a Polhemus sensor, as described previously. The software executed on a Silicon Graphics Crimson VGXT workstation with output through a videosplitter interface.

Here, we have space only to summarise some of the main results. A more detailed analysis is available from the authors [17], including correlation analysis, and a separate analysis of the performance of experienced and inexperienced users.

Timing Results

Table 1 shows the mean times taken by subjects to complete the route using each of the three methods. There is quite a large standard deviation, which is to be expected with a mixture of experts and novices. It can be seen that the force-field method is marginally quicker than totally unconstrained navigation and significantly better than the collision detection method. Further analysis allows us to draw other conclusions about the time taken for the different methods:

Method	Mean Time	Standard Deviation
UC	3'22"	1'19"
CD	4'56"	2'09"
FF	3'17"	1'35"

Table 1: Timings for different methods

- With the unconstrained method, users were able to move through the scene quite rapidly. Although they were told that they should attempt to avoid furniture and other obstacles, they did in fact make many collisions. One reason why the force-field method comes out best is that with unconstrained navigation users strayed outside the house or underneath the stairs (see Figure 4), which was very disorientating and therefore cost them time. As well as the simple timings, we have analysed the routes taken by users, and measured the times taken along the routes. Cases where users were disorientated show up very clearly in this analysis. The absolute path length with the UC method was 320 units, compared with 286 for CD and 292 for FF. The longer path length for the UC method is a result of users straying off-course. Although the path length for the CD method was shorter, users spent a significant amount of time without moving, either because they were stuck, or because they needed to look around to get their bearings.

- With the CD method, users frequently became stuck in corners (Figure 5). Corners exist where chairs protrude from underneath tables and where furniture is placed against the wall. With CD, the only way to escape such corners is to move backwards or sideways. With the FF approach, the force fields tended to guide them past such situations, resulting in a superior performance (Figure 6).

As an aside, it is interesting to note that because users have a more restricted field of view with the projection system than they would have in the real world, they tended to wrongly estimate the positions of objects which had passed out of their field of view. Thus, in turning to walk around a table, users would often turn *before* they had actually cleared the obstacle. With UC navigation, this resulted in a collision, and with CD it sometimes caused them to get stuck.

Collisions

The CD and FF methods guaranteed that users could not pass *through* objects. In analysing collisions in the unconstrained method, we distinguished penetration of external boundaries – passing through walls, for example – from colliding with furniture. The reason for this is that users were relatively unconcerned about the effects of passing through furniture. We attribute this to the fact that their eye-level was above the top of the furniture, so that such collisions did not affect their view of the scene. However, penetration of external boundaries usually results in a discontinuity in the view. In the results which follow, penetration of the floor is only included in the statistics if the viewpoint goes below the floor. Minor violations, where the lower part of the body penetrates the floor have not been included, as they do not affect the view and do not appear to seriously disorientate the user, although they can result in a 'child's-eye' view of the scene.

For the UC method, in only 3 tests out of the total of 45 were subjects able to complete the route without penetrating boundary objects. On average in each test the subject collided with furniture 7.3 times and passed through external boundaries (floors, walls and ceilings) 2.7 times. More than half of the penetrations of boundaries occurred on the staircase (1.6 times on average), indicating the difficulty of negotiating the stairs, while at the same time staying inside the walls on either side. Users ended up outside the house 1.7 times on average.

Subjective Analysis

As well as collecting data about timings and collisions, we asked our users for their subjective views of the methods. They were asked to rate four aspects of each method: general ease or difficulty of navigating on the level, ease of going upstairs and downstairs, and visual comfort. Under each heading, users were asked to score their experience on a scale of 1 to 5:

1	Very bad (very difficult to navigate, ...)
2	Bad (quite difficult to navigate, ...)
3	Average
4	Good (easy to navigate, ...)
5	Very good (very easy to navigate, ...)

Figure 3 shows a histogram of the aggregate scores for the four aspects, for each of the three different methods (maximum score of 20), while Table 2 summarises the separate scores (maximum score 5 for each). There was no significant difference in visual comfort, although the FF approach scored slightly above the other methods. We attribute this to the smoothing effect of the guided motion. But for the other three scores, which are all related to ease of control, the FF algorithm was rated significantly above the UC and CD methods. Force-field navigation obtained the highest mean overall response with the smallest standard deviation. Subjectively, it was clear that the greatest difficulty occurred

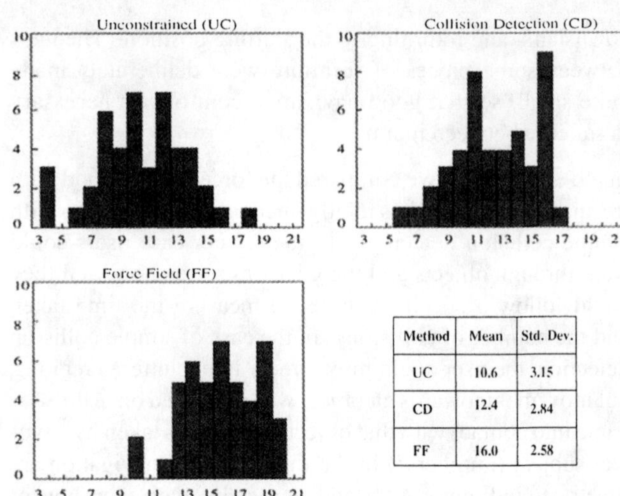

Method	Mean	Std. Dev.
UC	10.6	3.15
CD	12.4	2.84
FF	16.0	2.58

Figure 3: Histograms of overall responses to three methods

while negotiating the stairs. Going downstairs is particularly easy with the FF method – the user simply moves forwards and drops down under the force of gravity.

Method	*Mean Response*			
	Visual	*Navigating*	*Upstairs*	*Downstairs*
UC	3.15	2.47	2.10	2.05
CD	3.14	2.85	2.86	2.90
FF	3.70	4.29	4.19	4.28

Table 2: Mean scores for four aspects

Improvement with Practice

To see whether users managed to improve with practice, we compared their performances in each round of tests. As might be expected, the time required to complete the route improved in each case. Table 3 summarises the mean times. By the third series of tests there seems little to choose between the unconstrained and force-field methods.

	Time		
Method	*Round1*	*Round2*	*Round3*
UC	4'	3'11"	2'59"
CD	6'07"	4'34"	4'13"
FF	3'43"	3'08"	2'57"

Table 3: Average time taken in three rounds

However, as noted previously, with the unconstrained method, users made many collisions with furniture and penetrations of boundary objects. Table 4 shows how performance varied over the three rounds with the unconstrained method. Although there was some improvement in collisions with furniture, penetrations of boundaries actually became worse as users attempted to complete the task more quickly. With unconstrained movement, considerable concentration is required to avoid collisions, and users found this quite tiring.

Round	Collisions with Furniture	Boundary Penetrations	
		Total Number	On Stairs
Round1	8.13	5.53	3.33
Round2	7.27	5.07	3.13
Round3	6.47	5.80	3.40

Table 4: Collisions and penetrations in different rounds

CONCLUSION

We have proposed a new method for navigation in virtual environments which combines force fields and collision avoidance. Experiments in which we compared the new method with unconstrained navigation and simple collision detection show that the force-field algorithm out-performs these other methods, both objectively and subjectively. It guarantees a collision-free walk-through, while providing assistance in navigating around obstacles and negotiating stairs, and gravity comes free. The algorithm is simple to implement and efficient in execution.

ACKNOWLEDGEMENTS

The authors wish to thank their colleagues in the Advanced Interfaces Group for their support, enthusiasm and encouragement. Continued work on these methods is funded by the UK Engineering and Physical Sciences Research Council, grant number GR/K99701. We are also grateful to one of our industrial collaborators, Sharp Laboratories of Europe Ltd, who provided us with the stereoscopic projection system.

REFERENCES

[1] Mel Slater and Martin Usoh. Representations systems, perceptual position, and presence in immersive virtual environments. *Presence*, 2(3):221–233, 1993.

[2] K. M. Fairchild, B. H. Lee, J. Loo, and L. Serra. The heaven and earth virtual reality: Designing applications for novice users. In *Proc. IEEE Virtual Reality Annual International Symposium(VRAIS)*, pages 47–53, sept 1993.

[3] Frederick P. Brooks Jr. Walkthrough Project: Final Technical Report to National Science Foundation Computer and Information Science and Engineering. Technical Report TR92-026, Computer Science Department, University of North Carolina at Chapel Hill, 1992.

[4] H. Iwata and K. Matsuda. Haptic walkthrough simulator: Its design and application to studies on cognitive map. In *The 2nd International Conference on Artificial Reality and Tele-existance, ICAT 92*, pages 185–192, 1992.

[5] Mel Slater, Martin Usoh, and Anthony Steed. Taking steps: The influence of walking technique on presence in virtual reality. *ACM Trans. on Computer-human Interaction*, 2(3):201–219, September 1995.

[6] Steven M. Drucker and David Zelter. Intelligent camera control in a virtual environment. In Wayne A. Davis and Barry Joe, editors, *Proc. Graphics Interface '94*, pages 190–199. Canadian Human-Computer Communications Society, May 1994.

[7] E. Bouvier and P. Guilloteau. Crowd simulation in immersive space management. In M. Göbel and J. David and P. Slavik and J.J. van Wijk, editor, *Virtual Environments and Scientific Visualization '96*, pages 104–110. Springer-Verlag/Wien, 1996.

[8] Craig W. Reynolds. Flocks, herds, and schools: A distributed behavioral model. In Maureen C. Stone, editor, *Computer Graphics (SIGGRAPH '87 Proceedings)*, volume 21, pages 25–34, July 1987.

[9] O. Khatib. Real-time obstacle avoidance for manipulators and mobile robots. In *Proceedings IEEE Robotics and Automation Conference*, pages 500–505, 1985.

[10] Ronald C. Arkin. Motor Scheme-based Mobile Robot Navigation. *The International Journal of Robotics Research*, pages 92–112, August 1989.

[11] J. Borenstein and Y. Koren. Real-time obstacle avoidance for fast mobile robots. *IEEE trans. on Systems, Man, and Cybernetics*, 19(5):1179–1187, 1989.

[12] B.H. Krogh. Integrated path planning and dynamic steering control from autonomous vehicles. *Proc. IEEE Int'l Conf. on Robotics and Automation*, pages 1664–1669, April 1986.

[13] Parris K. Egbert and H. Winkler. Collision-free object movement using vector fields. *IEEE Computer Graphics and Applications*, 16(4):18–24, July 1996.

[14] Jeffrey Jacobson and Michael Lewis. An experimental comparison of three methods for collision handling in virtual environments. In *Proc. Human Factors and Ergonomics Society Conference*, 1997.

[15] Timothy Kay and James Kajiya. Ray tracing complex scenes. *ACM Computer Graphics*, 20(4):269–278, 1986.

[16] Roger Hubbold, Dongbo Xiao, and Simon Gibson. MAVERIK – The Manchester Virtual Environment Interface Kernel. In M. Göbel and J. David and P. Slavik and J.J. van Wijk, editor, *Virtual Environments and Scientific Visualization '96*, pages 11–20. Springer-Verlag/Wien, 1996. ISBN 3-211-82886-9.

[17] Dongbo Xiao. *Interactive display and intelligent walkthrough in a virtual environment.* PhD thesis, Department of Computer Science, University of Manchester, October 1997.

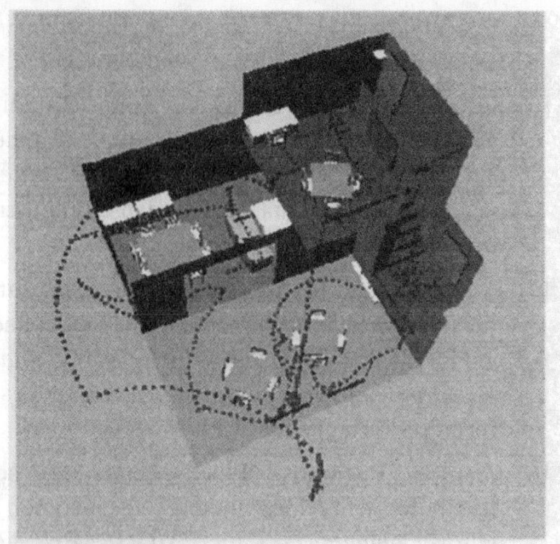
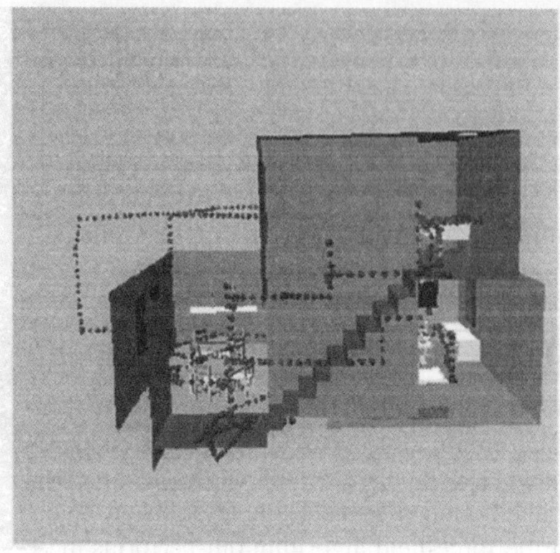

Figure 4: A typical route with the unconstrained approach

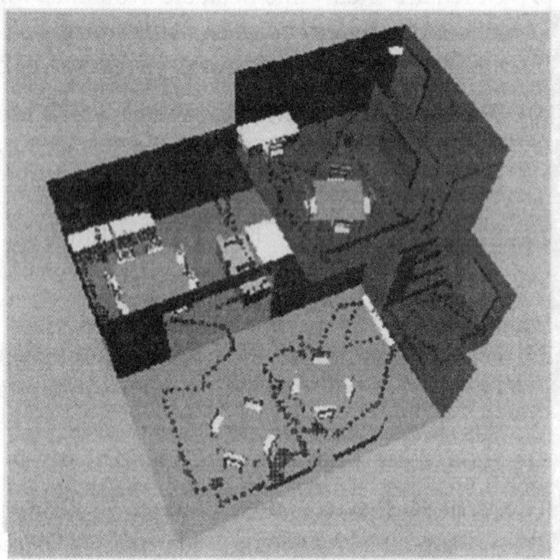
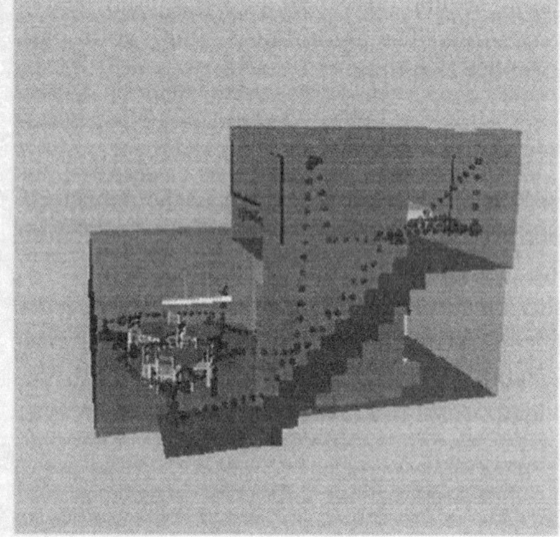

Figure 5: A typical route with the simple constrained approach

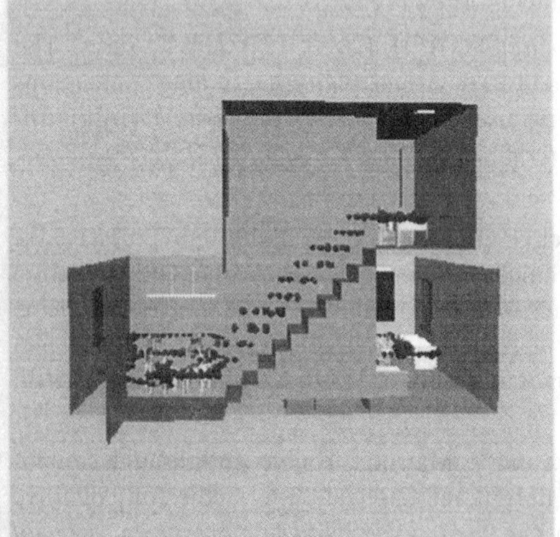

Figure 6: A typical route with the force-field approach

The Design of Guided Learner-Adaptable Scaffolding in Interactive Learning Environments

Shari L. Jackson, Joseph Krajcik, Elliot Soloway
College of Engineering, School of Education, School of Information
University of Michigan
1101 Beal Ave.
Ann Arbor, MI 48109, USA
http://hi-ce.eecs.umich.edu/
E-mail: shari_jackson@alum.mit.edu, krajcik@umich.edu, soloway@umich.edu

ABSTRACT
The learner-centered design of software suggests the need to design scaffolding—fadeable supports—in educational tools. We describe an approach, Guided Learner-Adaptable Scaffolding (GLAS), in which the learner controls the fading of scaffolding, with guidance and support provided by the system. Using GLAS, we have developed a tool, TheoryBuilder, that supports learners in building and testing dynamic models of complex systems. We have conducted extensive classroom testing with students who used the tool several times throughout a year. An analysis of the data demonstrates the success of the GLAS approach in developing an adaptable tool to support the diverse and changing needs of learners.

Keywords
Learner-Centered Design, Scaffolding, Fading, Adaptable Interfaces, Education Applications.

INTRODUCTION
To address the needs of a population of users who are also learners, in our recent work we have proposed a new methodology for the *learner-centered design* (LCD) of software [9, 10]. Learners often require extra support and motivation to engage in unfamiliar tasks. Learners are a diverse population, varying in knowledge, skills, interests, and learning style. And finally, learners will *learn*—as they grow and develop understanding and expertise over time and through interaction with the software, their needs for software support and functionality will change as well.

The needs of learners suggest the use of *scaffolding* in educational software. Scaffolding refers to support provided so that the learner can engage in activities that would otherwise be beyond their abilities. Scaffolding, as provided by human tutors, has been well-established as an effective means of supporting learning [2, 8]. Building scaffolding into software offers the opportunity to provide for diversity through individualized support that accommodates learners of different skills, backgrounds, and learning styles, and to support growth by making more powerful functionality available as the learner develops expertise.

A critical component of scaffolding is that it be capable of fading; as the learner's understanding and abilities improve, the computer, much like a human tutor, needs to back off and give the learner more autonomy, fewer hints, etc. In the field of educational software research, scaffolding is a new concept that is still being defined [2, 4, 9, 10]. Many techniques have been explored that provide various supportive structures for learners, but typically that support does not fade within the software itself.

The question of how to design scaffolding—fadeable supports—is informed by research in the field of adaptive and adaptable interfaces. *Adaptive* interfaces can be implemented as scaffolding that changes automatically using a model of the learner's understanding. The main problem is that an extensive model of the learner's knowledge may be hard to specify or evaluate in more open-ended domains. The alternative, *adaptable* interfaces, suggests scaffolding faded by the user. One problem is that it may be hard for the learner to make fading decisions. To address this, the software can be designed to provide information and advice, and to encourage self-evaluation, helping the student to measure his or her progress and understanding [6]. Another issue is that the learner needs to understand what the options are [3]. The question of how to design scaffolding is still an open one, although some combination of adaptive and adaptable fading appears to be the appropriate direction for future research.

We have therefore developed a design approach that we call *Guided Learner-Adaptable Scaffolding (GLAS)*. GLAS is designed as discrete, fine-grained scaffolding of various types, faded under control of the learner, with guidance from the software to aid the learner in making informed decisions. We have developed scaffolding design and fading mechanisms, based on the GLAS approach, for a wide range of scaffolding types.

GLAS has been applied to the design of TheoryBuilder, which is the successor to Model-It, a tool that we developed to support the complex and educationally valuable task of scientific modeling [5, 10]. Research with Model-It provided us with a great deal of information about the kinds of supports and functionality that learners need to engage in modeling activities. TheoryBuilder incorporates a broad range of scaffolding to specifically target those needs. And whereas Model-It's supports generally did not fade,

TheoryBuilder implements the GLAS approach, providing fading of each of its scaffolds under the learner's control.

TheoryBuilder has been thoroughly tested in actual classroom use with 100 students over several projects throughout a school year. Data collected include the models that the students constructed and videotapes of student conversations and software use. In-depth analysis of this data is used to evaluate the success of the GLAS approach.

Model-It

TheoryBuilder, also called Model-It 3.0, represents the next phase of our research with Model-It—a tool to make modeling accessible to high school science students [5]. The basic components of each tool are the same. Students construct, verify, and analyze qualitative models by linking together the factors that comprise high-level objects.

To build a model, a student begins by creating objects, and choosing photos or pictures to represent them. Next the student defines factors, measurable quantities or characteristics associated with each object. Then the student defines the relationships between factors, either qualitatively, (Figure 1) or quantitatively, by clicking on the points of the graph or inputting a table of values.

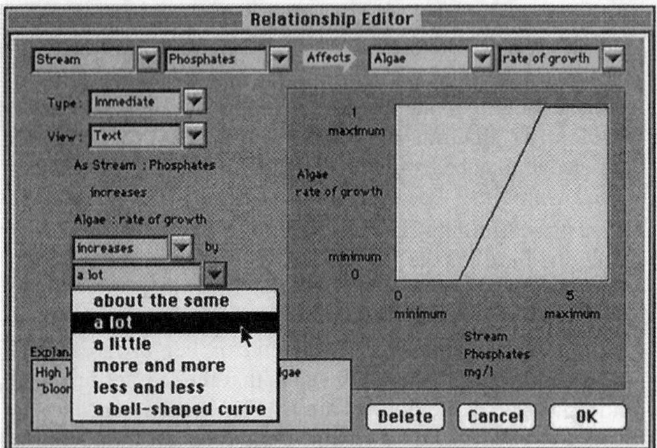

Figure 1: Qualitative relationship definition

Once objects, factors, and relationships have been defined, students can run their models, using meters and graphs to view factor values. While a model is running, students can change the value of factors in real-time and see the results (Figure 2). Student can view their model either with a high-level "world" view of the objects in the model, or an interactive "map" view in which icons representing each object's factors are linked together with arrows that represent the relationships.

Previous Research

Versions of Model-It have been used by hundreds of 14 to 15-year-old students at a local school over the past four years. Four classroom studies have been conducted, in each of which students were asked to design and create their own models. These models typically exhibited reasonable scientific validity and significant complexity. Students appropriately focused on high level concepts—defining the factors in the system and the relationships between them, running simulations with different factor values, and

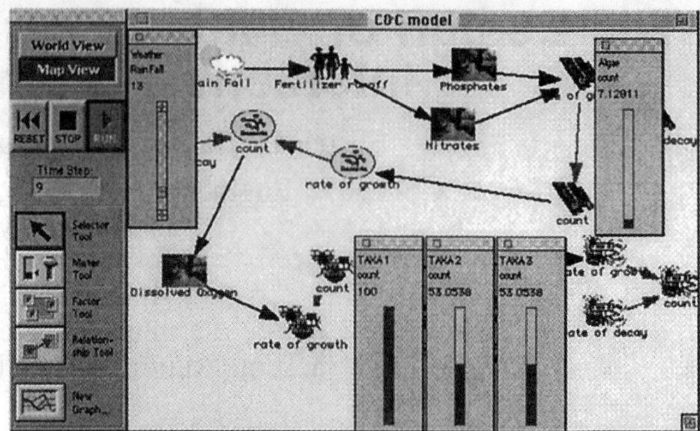

Figure 2: Map view, running a simulation with the model

determining the validity of the results. Students were comfortable expressing themselves qualitatively, and were able to conceive of a relationship, then quickly add it to their model. We found significant evidence that Model-It can make modeling accessible to pre-college science students. [5, 10, 11].

Our research also suggested areas where students would have benefited from additional support to learn the task and to engage in modeling activities. For example, we found that some students required more support in order to understand and engage in the cognitive activities associated with modeling—e.g., planning, making predictions, testing and evaluation [11]. Interviews and video of students identified areas of confusion for novice learners, as well as ideas for other advanced functionality that might be useful.

TheoryBuilder, the next phase of our project, had two goals. First, to broaden the range of supports provided by the program, in order to address the issues highlighted by our research. And second, to specifically address the idea of what it means to implement scaffolding in interactive learning environments, by designing supports that can be faded as the learner's understanding and abilities improve.

APPROACH

We propose a particular approach to the design of scaffolding in software: *Guided Learner-Adaptable Scaffolding (GLAS)*. The design is *learner-adaptable* because, in keeping with the goal of designing learning environments as tools with which the learner designs and creates artifacts (as opposed to, e.g., tutoring programs in which the software directs the interaction), the learner will also be in control of deciding to change and fade scaffolding. The design is *guided*, because of the potential need for guidance from the system (to supplement, not replace, the classroom teacher) in making those decisions. The goal is for the student, with the software's help, to be able to take on some of the responsibility for his or her learning.

For purposes of our research, and based on the literature [2, 4, 8], we have defined scaffolding as covering the following three categories: supportive scaffolding, reflective scaffolding, and intrinsic scaffolding. For each, we describe its purpose, its implementation in TheoryBuilder and its fading, summarized in Table 1.

Scaff. Type	TheoryBuilder Implementation	Fading
Supportive Scaffolding	Guiding through subtasks (e.g., plan before building, test periodically). Coaching and modeling throughout the software, providing context-sensitive help and examples.	Guiding faded with "Stop Reminding Me" button. Coaching, modeling invoked by learner; "faded" as not invoked.
Reflective Scaffolding	Eliciting articulation with forms and prompts for: • Planning: stating goals of model, ideas for building it. • Explanations for objects, factors, and relationships. • Testing: predicting before test, evaluating result of test. • Evaluating: deciding how well the model works, what could be changed.	Optional and available. "Faded" as ignored. Also linked to guiding scaffolding - reminders to fill in each form - faded with "Stop Reminding Me" buttons.
Intrinsic Scaffolding	Multiple, linked representations (from simple to advanced): • Factor definition (qualitative text labels, numerical values) • Relationship definition (textual, graphical, table, rate) • Viewing model (world view, map view) • Viewing factor values (meters, graphs) Hiding complexity, but making advanced options available: • Weighting - set relative weights of relationships. • Delay - specify time duration for relationship to take effect. • Combining - combine effects of relationships in different ways (e.g., sum, product, difference, maximum, minimum)	"View" menus let user switch between representations. Often different views are displayed simultaneously as linked representations. "Options" buttons open structured dialog boxes that allow options to be turned on and off, with associated help to guide the learner in making decisions.

Table 1: Fadeable scaffolding strategies and their implementation in TheoryBuilder

Supportive scaffolding

Supportive scaffolding is support for doing the task. The task itself is unchanged; scaffolding is provided alongside the task, to offer advice and support. As supportive scaffolding is faded, the task is the same as before, but the expectation is that the learner has internalized the concepts which had been scaffolded. This kind of scaffolding, which includes guiding, coaching, and modeling, is the most often referred to as scaffolding in the literature [e.g., 2, 8].

In TheoryBuilder, guiding scaffolding is provided through messages which appear when appropriate, and which can be faded through a "Stop reminding me" button (Figure 3). If the learner continues to neglect a task after fading a reminder, a message will eventually appear: "I know you asked me not to remind you about this, but I noticed that you haven't been..." In keeping with our learner-centered approach in which the learner is in control of the tool and not vice versa, these reminders are suggestions; they do not force the learner into an action, and can be ignored.

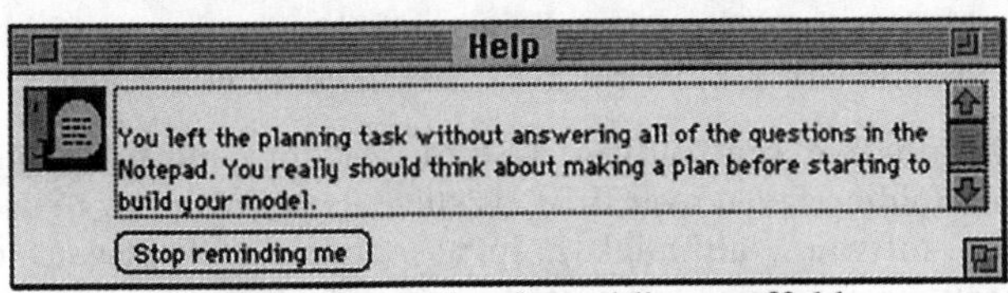

Figure 3: Example of a guiding scaffold

Coaching and modeling scaffolds provide help and examples explaining the various modeling concepts. They are invoked through contextualized help buttons that appear throughout the software, usually as "?" (e.g., Figure 4) or "Show me an example". They display help using both text and pictures. Being passive scaffolds, these buttons do not fade per se, but rather are faded simply through not being invoked.

Reflective scaffolding

Reflective scaffolding is support for thinking about the task (e.g., planning, making predictions, evaluating). It also doesn't change the task itself, but instead makes the activity of reflection explicit by eliciting articulation from the learner. As Norman asserts, reflective cognition, the mode of "comparison and contrast, of thought, of decision-making," is essential for learning, although more rarely supported by technology [7].

Reflective scaffolding in TheoryBuilder is provided by a Notepad that appears alongside the main window, and by description fields that are part of each component's editing window. The learner reflects by typing plans, descriptions, predictions and evaluations into appropriate fields of the Notepad, as relevant for each subtask. Many of the guiding scaffolds refer to these text fields, prompting the learner to fill them in when appropriate, (e.g., Figure 3). Another passive scaffold, the text fields themselves do not fade, but once the reminders are faded they are more easily ignored.

Intrinsic scaffolding

Intrinsic scaffolding is our name for supports that change the task itself, by reducing the complexity of the task and focusing the learner's attention (e.g., training wheels on a bicycle, outlines in coloring books), or by providing mechanisms for visualizing or thinking about a concept (e.g., maps and models for visualization). Intrinsic scaffolding can be designed simply by providing the option of a beginner mode, as in the Training Wheels word processing program [1] or KidPix's (Broderbund) option of "Small Kids Mode." Ideally, however, scaffolding should support more gradual fading [8]. As the scaffold fades, the task is changed, but associations should remain so that the learner can progress from simpler, more structured, or more concrete tasks to variations in which more of the underlying complexity or abstractness is introduced.

Intrinsic scaffolding is implemented in TheoryBuilder as defaults which hide all but the simplest tools from the novice learner, but make advanced features available as the learner grows and develops expertise. Intrinsic scaffolding is manifested as different views and representations of model components, or different sets of enabled controls and tools. Figure 4 shows the mechanism by which the learner fades intrinsic scaffolding for the relationship editor by turning on advanced options that were previously hidden. The dialog also provides guidance for selecting appropriate options by showing what each option will let the user do. Other advanced features are listed in Table 1.

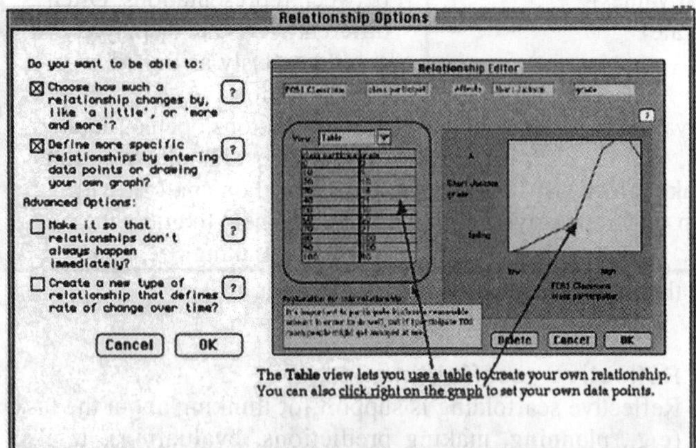

Figure 4: Example of the fading mechanism for intrinsic scaffolding for the Relationship Editor.

Other Supports

TheoryBuilder also includes other supports that make the task more accessible, but which cannot be called "scaffolds" by our definition because they do not fade within the program. Some of these features are: Task-switching controls (Plan, Build, Test, Evaluate) that identify and the task and provide different sets of tools for each subtask; labels on relationship arrows that display the graph or type of relationship; and the ability to test parts of a model by highlighting specific relationships, as a debugging aid.

METHODS

We worked with four classes of 9th graders (about 100 14 and 15-year-olds), who used TheoryBuilder for three modeling projects in their science class. Each project lasted about four hours over one week; projects were scheduled about two months apart over the school year. For each project, the students worked in pairs to build models that represented their understanding of some aspect of the topic currently being studied. The specific goal, content and structure of their models was determined by the students themselves. Formal instruction on the software was minimal: for the first project, students were introduced to the program via a one-hour, self-paced tutorial, and in successive projects, a 20-30 minute demo and discussion, supplemented by handouts, was used to make students aware of advanced features of the program.

For the first half of the year, the class studied stream ecology. For the first modeling project, in November, students built models of the physical and biological factors of a stream, and for the second, in January, students chose their own topic relating to some aspect of the whole stream ecosystem, including physical, biological, and chemical factors. In the spring, the class studied weather and global climate issues such as acid rain, global warming, and the greenhouse effect. For the third modeling project, students chose a research question based on these issues, used the internet to search for information, and built models to demonstrate their theory or understanding about the topic they had researched, using data from their research where appropriate. They presented these models to the class.

Data collected from all students included the models created for each project, and software-generated log files that record student interactions with the program. This data has been used to compile statistical information about the use of scaffolding and fading mechanisms over time.

In order to achieve an in-depth understanding of students' usage of and reactions to the software, a focus group of 11 students was chosen as a representative subset. For this focus group, process video was collected continuously during each project, consisting of audio recordings of their conversations coupled with video recordings of their computer screen interactions. Post-interviews were conducted to further clarify their motivations and solicit reactions to specific scaffolding and fading mechanisms.

To compile user profiles, video of each focus student was analyzed and episodes involving use of or reactions to scaffolding and fading mechanisms were recorded and categorized. By observing changes and fading of scaffolding over time, we can identify reactions to specific scaffolding components, and overall, the success of the GLAS approach in supporting students adapting and fading the software to meet their changing needs.

RESULTS

The data from these studies is currently being evaluated. Preliminary analysis of the full set of models indicates that the software was quite successful. For the first project students were able to use the basic program to build useful models with only brief instruction, aided by the supportive scaffolding, and shielded by the intrinsic scaffolding from the potentially confusing array of options. In successive projects, a short introduction to advanced features was sufficient for students to choose to fade selective scaffolds and build larger, more complex, and more accurate models.

Supportive scaffolding: Use of coaching and modeling scaffolding faded over time, as students learned how to use the software, although help associated with advanced features continued to be used as these features were turned on. For the first project we tried having some help appear automatically the first time the student encountered a concept, but it appeared that students mostly ignored the help unless they had invoked it themselves.

More students faded guiding scaffolds over time as they learned the task; by the third project 63% of the students had turned off at least one reminder. Others simply learned to ignore the reminders. (Regrettably, there was no mechanism for remembering student preferences between projects, so all reminders were initially turned on at the start of each project). In general, in later projects students tended to ignore all supportive scaffolding unless they had invoked it themselves (e.g., by clicking on a help button).

Table 2 shows how often each reminder was faded, for each project. The reminder to test the model periodically was the most commonly faded, by 45% of the students in the second and third projects. This reminder first appeared after three relationships had been created or modified, and every five relationships thereafter, so it was the most frequently encountered, and perhaps thereby most frequently became annoying. Despite turning off the reminder, however, students tested their models more frequently in later projects, suggesting that they had retained the strategy. Other reminders, such as to open meters or to fill in descriptions and explanations, were faded less frequently, probably because students usually did these tasks without prompting and so encountered the reminders less often.

Guiding Reminder	Proj 1	Proj 2	Proj 3
Fill in plan before building	1	9	8
Describe objects	0	6	5
Describe factors	2	9	11
Explain relationships	2	9	14
Test periodically	3	20	19
Predict before testing	1	14	18
Open meters before testing	2	5	7
Assess results after testing	3	14	18

Table 2: Number of models (out of 45) in which each reminder was faded, over the three projects.

Reflective scaffolding: Students were required by the teacher to fill in the text fields that comprise reflective scaffolding (plans, descriptions, explanations, evaluations) as part of their grade. As a result, rather than fading, there tended to be increased and more thoughtful usage of these fields in successive projects. The exceptions were the prediction and assessment questions that accompanied the testing task, which were not printed out and therefore not graded. The result was that students tended to skip these questions in later projects, and in fact, as Table 2 shows, the guiding reminders to fill in these fields were the second and third most commonly faded supportive scaffolds.

As further evidence that students had developed the habit of filling out reflective scaffolding, we saw that even though there was no reminder to fill in the explanation field for the advanced weighting and combining editor, students who used it still tended to write an explanation.

Intrinsic scaffolding: More students faded the intrinsic scaffolding, i.e., used more of the advanced features, in later projects as they developed expertise, as shown in Table 3. For the first project the only options used by any students were the most basic: 20% of the student pairs used the option of specifying the slope of a relationship, and 9% used the table option to draw their own relationship graph. By the third project 85% of the models used one or both of those options, and of the most advanced options, 41% used delay and 26% used rate relationships, 28% used the weighting tool, and 11% used the combining function to calculate the product or difference of two factors' effects.

	Number	Slope	Table	Delay	Rate	Weighting	Combinations
1	0	20	9	0	0	0	0
2	37	78	54	30	4	20	0
3	50	72	37	41	26	28	11

Table 3: Percentage of models using each advanced option, over the three projects.

The table option was used most often in the second project, because the textbook used for that topic included a number of applicable graphs, while for the third project, on climate, the resources used by students usually did not include that level of detail. The third project did see the most use of the other advanced options, even the rate relationships which our previous research showed was rarely ever used. Here, though, owing perhaps to the growth of expertise due to the increased time students had spent with the program, many students were able to use rate relationships to model such temporal phenomena as the release of ozone-depleting gasses or the melting of the polar ice caps.

User Profiles

In this section, we present a qualitative analysis of two students from our focus group. These two students represent the diversity of our learner population, having very different backgrounds, approaches, and learning styles.

User Profile 1: Greg

Greg is mathematically and logically inclined, even enrolled in a higher level math course than most of his classmates. He was quick to learn the program, and from the first day, branched out to explore and try new ideas. He was thoughtful about model-building, reasoning about chains of relationships.

Figure 5 shows the model Greg built for project 3. Greg had read that an increase in global temperature would increase storm severity, and he built a model to express his theory about why this would occur: that flooding would cause greater humidity in coastal areas as compared to inland areas, and this difference would create a pressure differential that would increase storm severity.

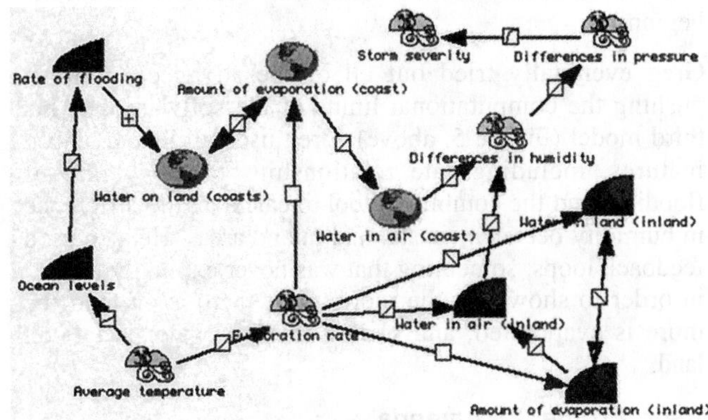

Figure 5: Greg's model for Project 3

Supportive scaffolding: Greg used the coaching help buttons frequently in the first project as he explored the program, and thereafter only rarely, to learn about new advanced features. In a post-interview he said that the buttons were most helpful early on, but they were "nice to have around." The reminders were also used most at the beginning. During the first project, Greg read and followed reminders five times, but in the second and third projects, Greg was more impatient with the reminders and used the "Stop reminding me" button to fade most of them.

Greg's reaction to the reminder to test was particularly interesting. The first day learning the program, he never tested the model, ignoring all reminders, saying that he wanted to finish building relationships first. The second day, building a new model, he decided to try following the testing reminder, and it led him to discover a mistake in his model. Having learned that testing can help catch errors early, Greg continued to test periodically in later models, internalizing the habit even after fading the reminder.

Reflective scaffolding: Greg was impatient with the reflective scaffolds, describing himself as a "verbal thinker" and feeling that he already had the whole model planned out in his mind, and just wanted to build it. He thought the testing questions were "pointless, because I can think of what I expect to happen and compare it to what happens without writing it down." Indeed, he did state very good predictions out loud and test his model against them. On the other hand, he wrote very good explanations, and said that he particularly enjoyed filling in the evaluation because he was proud of his model.

Intrinsic scaffolding: Greg explored advanced options from the first project, and used the guiding information in the dialogs to learn what the options would do. Still, he didn't choose to turn on all the advanced options (fading the intrinsic scaffolds) at first. For example, he read the Factor option for numerical values and decided "we don't need that." Later in the project, he did find a need to use numbers, and went back to the dialog to turn it on, using the associated help to figure out how to use it. In post-interviews, Greg said that while he understood that options were hidden so as not to confuse students who didn't want to use them, he didn't think it would've confused him, and if he were the only user he would like them all on from the beginning.

Greg eventually tried out all of the advanced options, pushing the computational limits of the software. For his third model (Figure 5, above), Greg used all the advanced features, including rate relationships to show rate of flooding, and the combining tool to calculate the difference in humidity between coastal and inland areas. He also used feedback loops, something that was never explicitly taught, in order to show that the more water there is on land the more is evaporated, and in turn the less water is left on land.

User Profile 2: Amanda

Amanda describes herself as "not comfortable with computers." Nevertheless, she applied herself to the modeling task and tried to learn the software, focusing on what was necessary to get a good grade. She had a very good understanding of the scientific content, wrote detailed scientific explanations, but didn't always understand how to translate her knowledge into a model.

Figure 6 shows Amanda's third project, which shows the human impact on ozone depletion, and suggests that alternatives to CFC-producing products could help alleviate the problem. When asked how her use of the program had changed over time, Amanda said that even though she tried to keep things simple, she felt "we understood it better now and I think we did a more thorough, better job on this one."

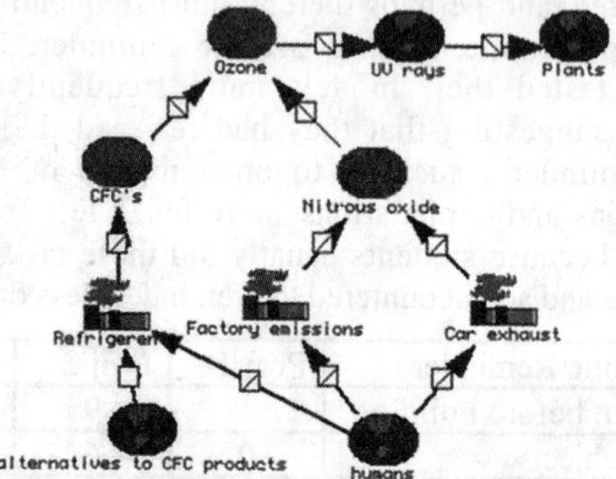

Figure 6: Amanda's model for Project 3

Supportive scaffolding: Amanda used the coaching help buttons most in the first project, and later only to learn about advanced options such as weighting. She seemed to prefer to get help from the teacher or paper handouts. She thought that the guiding reminders were definitely helpful at the beginning, and even by the third project when she mostly ignored them, she never faded them, saying that they "didn't bug me 'cause I knew I could turn them off whenever I wanted."

Reflective scaffolding: Amanda spent a lot of time writing detailed descriptions and explanations of the components of her model and how they related. She thought that writing explanations for each relationship "helped so that you felt like you could explain the model more... and it made the relationships clear in your mind, 'cause you knew exactly how everything affected everything." Amanda even felt that planning ought to be required, because if not she might skip it, and then not be making the best use of her time. She also liked the evaluation questions because it helped her plan what to say in her presentation.

Intrinsic scaffolding: Amanda used some advanced features, but tended to stick with the simpler layers of functionality that were easier for her to understand. During the building of her second model, a fellow classmate "helped" her by turning on all the advanced relationship options, and the teacher, looking at their model, suggested and showed them how to use the Table view. She and her partner tried to follow others' suggestions, but on their own they stayed with the most basic options. When asked what she thought the program would be like if it started with all the advanced options visible, she said "I think it would have been confusing.... But if it would've been explained really well, probably we could've done it, I don't know."

She said about her third model that they had chosen a simple project and just used what they needed to make it work. Her goal was to get the basic model working, and add advanced options later. In fact, although they did not use the slope, table, or delay features that had been suggested to them in the previous project, they did choose to add weighting and combining at the end to make their model more accurate.

Weighting had a relatively simple interface (Figure 7) and was conceptually intuitive. As Amanda said, "We want to weight it so nitrous oxide has less of an effect on ozone depletion than CFC's do." The combining option was more awkward and required mathematical insight in order to recognize the need for it. The problem was that she wanted her model to show that CFC's are high only if there are both a large human population and low usage of non-CFC producing alternatives. She had discovered during testing that the default which averaged the effects was not working, although it was hard to understand why. With help, Amanda was able to change the combining function to "product" and achieve her goal, but when asked later if she understood it she said "I understand the concept of what we did, but I might not have been able to do that on the model."

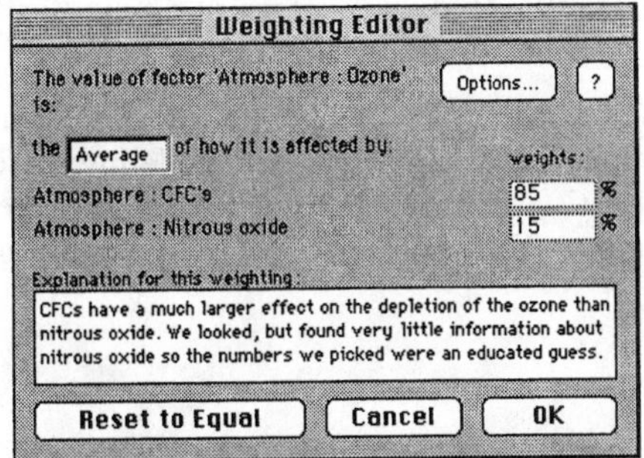

Figure 7: Weighting in Amanda's 3rd model

Discussion

In analyzing the effectiveness of GLAS, we recall first our fundamental motivation in designing learner-centered software—to make the task accessible. This goal was certainly achieved; almost all students were able to build reasonably accurate models to represent their understanding of the topic being studied. Second, the motivation for providing *scaffolding* was to allow students to gradually adapt the software to meet their changing needs. Here, too, we feel that the design was generally successful. Students turned off or ignored help features that they no longer needed, and accessed more advanced features as they felt ready. Both Greg and Amanda learned and changed their usage of the program over time, and each was able to adapt the program in different ways to meet their individual needs.

Greg and Amanda were most different in their fading of intrinsic scaffolding and use of advanced features. We had learned from our research with Model-It that the tool was successful where students could think in terms of the domain concepts, not "programming" a model, but representing their ideas in a way that was natural to them. Similarly, we find that the advanced features designed into TheoryBuilder were successful in proportion to how qualitatively and conceptually they were presented. For example, the advanced option of *delay* allowed students to specify whether a relationship ought to happen "immediately, quickly, or slowly." Underneath, this was a complex mathematical function, but it is presented in terms the students understand, so it became one of the most frequently used features.

Another option, *weighting*, was a little more advanced but it still fit well with students' thinking, and was used correctly by many students. Students found the interface understandable, although a qualitative option might also have been useful since students might not have quantitative data (e.g., in Figure 7, Amanda writes that "CFC's have a much larger effect on the depletion of the ozone than nitrous oxide" but the specific weighting values they chose were "an educated guess").

The combining option, however, was purely mathematical, and few students could follow there on their own. In presenting the combining option to the class, we had given the example that if the combined effect depends on two factors both being active, than a product might be most appropriate. Scaffolding could be designed along these lines, to bridge from conceptual to mathematical representations. Students might specify the desired effect (e.g., by filling in sentences about when x is high and y is low, then z is {low, medium, or high}). Once students had mastered this level, fading from conceptual to mathematical could help them see how their ideas are translated into equations.

CONCLUDING REMARKS

One goal of this research is to take what we have learned about scaffolding and fading design and propose some general design guidelines. For example, we suggest that an interface that presents lots of options will initially confuse many users who are new to the task, even if there are useful defaults. Instead, allowing users to choose the options they want to use will help them tailor the interface in ways that make more sense to them. Through our analysis, we hope to identify a set of guidelines and context for their use.

A future direction for research is to focus more on the computer's role in helping the user make fading decisions. For example, the system may be able to provide feedback about the appropriateness of the current level of scaffolding, by identifying and informing the learner of problems that might have been caused by fading too much too rapidly, and suggesting alternative scaffolding options. Even open-ended tools that have no content knowledge can, like TheoryBuilder, still provide procedural scaffolding using knowledge of general and modeling-specific problem-solving strategies. The learner's self-evaluation can also be taken into account—if the learner can articulate, through predictions, how he expected his model to behave, the system may then be able to help the learner in modifying the model to meet his expectations [6].

In summary, the advantage of tools with scaffolding—fadeable layers of support—is to provide learners with an adaptable interface to fit their learning approach and changing needs. Learners take on more of the responsibility for doing the task as they are ready to do so, fading supports that are no longer necessary, and selecting advanced levels of functionality as they want access to more complex tasks.

ACKNOWLEDGMENTS

This research has been supported by the National Science Foundation (RED 9353481 and IRI 9117084), the National Physical Science Consortium, and the U. of Michigan.

REFERENCES

1. Carroll, J. M., & Carrithers, C. (1984) Training Wheels in a User Interface, *Communications of the ACM,* Vol. 27, No.8, August, 800-806
2. Collins, A. (1996) Design Issues for Learning Environments, in S. Vosniadou, E. DeCorte, R. Glaser, & H. Mandl (Ed.) *International perspectives on the psychological foundations of technology-based learning environments*, Lawrence Erlbaum Assoc., Hillsdale, NJ
3. Fischer, G. (1993) Shared Knowledge in Cooperative Problem-Solving Systems - Integrating Adaptive and Adaptable Components, in M. Schneider-Hufschmidt, T. Kuhme, & U. Malinowski (Eds.), *Adaptive User Interfaces: Principles and Practice,* North-Holland, Elsevier Science Publishers B.V., Amsterdam
4. Guzdial, M. (1995). Software-realized scaffolding to facilitate programming for science learning. *Interactive Learning Environments*, 4(1), 1-44.
5. Jackson, S. L., Stratford, S. J., Krajcik, J. S., Soloway, E. (1996) Making Dynamic Modeling Accessible to Pre-College Science Students. *Interactive Learning Environments,* 4(3), 1994, pp.233-257
6. Nathan, J. N., Kintsch, W., & Young, E. (1990) A Theory of Algebra Word Problem Comprehension and its Implications for Unintelligent Tutoring Systems, (Technical Report 90-02) Institute of Cognitive Science, University of Colorado, Boulder
7. Norman, D. (1993) *Things That Make Us Smart: Defending Human Attributes in the Age of the Machine*, Addison-Wesley Publishing Co., Reading, MA
8. Rogoff, B. (1990) *Apprenticeship in thinking: Cognitive development in social context.* New York: Oxford University Press
9. Soloway, E., Guzdial, M., & Hay, K. E. (1994) Learner-Centered Design: The Challenge for HCI in the 21st Century, *Interactions*, Vol. 1, No. 2, April, 36-48
10. Soloway, E., Jackson, S. L., Klein, J., Quintana, C., Reed, J., Spitulnik, J., Stratford, S. J., Studer, S., Eng, J., & Scala, N. (1996) Learning Theory in Practice: Case Studies of Learner-Centered Design. In *ACM CHI '96 Human Factors in Computer Systems,* Vancouver.
11. Stratford, S. J. (1996) Cognitive and other conceptual activities in dynamic modeling: case studies of cognitive modeling activities in precollege classrooms. Unpublished Ph.D. dissertation, U. of Michigan.

ARTEMIS: Learner-Centered Design of an Information Seeking Environment for K-12 Education

Raven Wallace, Elliot Soloway, Joseph Krajcik, Nathan Bos, Joseph Hoffman, Heather Eccleston Hunter, Dan Kiskis, Elisabeth Klann, Greg Peters, David Richardson, and Ofer Ronen

University of Michigan

School of Education
610 East University
Ann Arbor, MI 48104
313-647-7877
ravenmw@umich.edu

School of Information
550 East University
Ann Arbor, MI 48104
313-936-1562
soloway@umich.edu

ABSTRACT

Learners use software for different reasons and with differentskills and motivations than other users. Using concepts of learner-centered design (LCD), we developed a user interface for supporting learners as they use digital information resources in inquiry-based science classrooms. Learner needs are categorized in five areas: content knowledge, technology knowledge, strategic and metacognitive knowledge, and motivation. Results of research on problems encountered by students as they engage in information seeking are used as the basis for applying LCD, by identifying some specific problem areas learners encounter: engaging in a process, generating search terms, staying on task, and evaluating information. Solutions offered through the Artemis interface are described.

Keywords

Learner-centered design, information seeking, digital libraries, K-12 Education

INTRODUCTION

In the fall of 1995, researchers from the University of Michigan Digital Library (UMDL) began observing use of digital resources in 6th and 9th grade classrooms to gain understanding of classroom uses and learner needs for information seeking. Initially, students used Web browsers and search engines in their science classrooms to complete inquiry-based assignments. Our observations convinced us that standard Web tools are not adequate for learners as they engage in information seeking in classrooms. For example, search engines return too many hits, and too many of them are useless or irrelevant; students lack a stable context in which to work and are easily lost or distracted; and Web browsers are disconnected from software which lets students use what they find. Artemis is an interface designed in response to our classroom observations, to support K-12 students access and use information in the University of Michigan Digital Library.

This problem is of particular interest for two reasons. First, we are addressing a user population – K-12 learners – which is often overlooked in the user-centereddesign of general software tools. Second, the growing enthusiasm for connecting schools to the Internet, and the increasing ubiquity of connected classrooms, create a pressing need for closer scrutiny of the design and use of tools which contribute to educationally sound uses of the vast and heterogeneous resources available on the Internet. This paper describes the rationale for the design of Artemis, including an overview of the UMDL; explanation of our conception of learner-centereddesign; description of the contexts for initial implementation of Artemis and the learning problems associated with those contexts; and explanation of the solutions Artemis provides to the problems of learning with digital information resources. The design which has been through three major revision cycles, has followed an iterative process, with revision of the software based on observation of use in classrooms and test environments.

THE UMDL/MYDL PROJECTS

Artemis is part of the University of Michigan Digital Library Project (UMDL), a project of the Digital Libraries Initiative. The project's mission is to create an architecture and software infrastructure for development of a digital library open to multiple, heterogeneous collections. The structure and contents of collections are constrained only by their ability to communicate with agents in the UMDL infrastructureabout contents, search protocols, and other metadata. The UMDL project includes testbed collections in the domains of earth and spacescience.

Within the agent architecture of UMDL, multiple interfaces are allowed, each with its own agent which communicates with other agents in the UMDL infrastructureto find information, to negotiate prices for copyrighted information, to browse collections and thesauri, and to register materials. [1] Just as different collections can be specialized by content domain or user characteristics, so interfaces to UMDL can address particular user groups. Artemis is an example of such an interface, designed particularly for K-12 students learning through a process of inquiry.

Middle Years Digital Library (MYDL) focuses on deployment of UMDL in middle school classrooms, following the initial deployment of UMDL in high school classrooms. Between 1995 and 1997, researchers observed over 1000 students in over 30 sixth and 15 ninth grade classrooms as they learned to find and use digital information resources. Classes began by using Web browsers and resources while UMDL was being developed, with initial tests of Artemis beginning in February, 1997. [2]

TWO KEY ASPECTS: LEARNER NEEDS AND INFORMATION SEEKING

Learner Needs

The principles of learner-centered design (LCD) [3] recognize the fact that students differin a number of ways from professionals who use computational software. Table 1 provides a summary of the dimensions of learner needs which require particular scrutiny as part of a process of learner-centered design (LCD). Each dimension is more fully explained below.

Unlike professionals using software to do their job, learners do not initially know the content with which they are engaging. They lack *domain knowledge* and must be supported as they engage in inquiry, in ways that allow them to build coherently on any background knowledge they have. A related area of difference between learners and other users is in their *technology knowledge.* Students may need particular help in using new technologies to insure that the tool is the background, not the purpose of the learning. In order to learn content they may need strategies particular to the type of work they are doing. For example, they may need to learn to read a graph, or to interpret a map. Thus, students differ in terms of their *strategic knowledge* both generally (i.e., strategies for reading and comprehending text) and specifically within the domain of investigation (e.g., reading a map.)

Another area of difference between learners and other users is in *metacognitive knowledge*. This refers to students knowledge of strategies for monitoring their progress and thinking about their thinking. Metacognitive strategies include asking themselves such questions as "Have I seen this before?" "Where am I in this process - what do I need to finish?" "Do I understand this?" [4] Metacognitive knowledge implies the abilitiy to assess one's content knowledge and learning strategies. This is clearly a type of knowledge which students lack in varying degrees, and which teachers provide in the normal course of teaching.

Finally, learners differfrom other users in terms of their *motivation.* While professionals in a field are committed to their work and use software tools to accomplish a task, students are often not similarly motivated. Technology must help sustain engagement by supporting complex activities so that students can focus on substantive cognitive issues and problem solving.

Domain (content) knowledge: How can the software help the learner recall prior knowledge and build on what she knows?

Technology (tool) knowledge: How can the software meet learners at varying levels of technological expertise in ways that keep the learner focused on substance, not on the tool?

Strategic knowledge: How can the software help the learner use strategies he possesses, and learn new strategies appropriate to the task at hand?

Metacognitive knowledge: How can the software assist the learner in keeping track of her goals, monitoring her progress, etc.?

Motivation: How can the software help the learner stay engaged and motivated?

Table 1: Five Dimensions of Learner Needs

These five dimensions are considered as they apply to the particular requirments of learners as they engage in information seeking in an electronic environment.

Information Seeking

Information Seeking in Inquiry

Our research has focused on providing tools, pedagogy, and contexts for students to engage in inquiry, with information seeking as one part of the process. Inquiry can include many types of investigations from experiments to observations, from using primary resources to reading what others have written. Key to the concept of inquiry is that students engage in sustained investigations of questions of interest to them. [5, 6] The major challenge of including digital information resources in inquiry-based learning is to provide tools which allow students to embed information seeking in a sustained process. This means allowing for not only one-shot queries when the user is looking for a simple answer, but also complex exploration of information spaces when the user is trying to understand a complex problem. [7]

Typically, the information seeking process includes posing a question, exploring for information, refining the question, finding information, organizing and evaluating what is found, synthesizing information, and, finally, using the information. [2, 7] These steps are not followed linearly, but rather, feedback from each phase may used to reiterate a previous step, or to jump to a new step. For example, the cycle of exploring, refining the question, and looking for information may be repeated many times until a satisfactory, focused question is formulated. For a user, each piece of the information seeking process might be thought of as a separate task, and differentsoftware tools might be used for different pieces of the process. Historically, computer systems have provided tools for information seeking in pieces, focusing on limited aspects of the process. For example, search engines address the phase of looking for information; word processors address using information; Web indexes help with browsing; bookmarking programs are for organizing. However, for a

Information Seeking	Dimensions of Learner Needs				
	Domain knowledge	Technology knowledge	Strategic knowledge	Metacognitive knowledge	Motivation
Engaging a in process	*Persistent Workspace* *Driving Question Folders*		*Driving Question Folders* *Past Results*	*Past Results*	*Persistent Workspace* *Recommendations*
Generating search terms	*Broad Topics* *Collections*	Overall design supports growth in technology knowledge by building on common design metaphors	*Broad Topic* *Past Resultss*	*Broad Topics*	*Broad Topics*
Staying on task	*Persistent Workspace* *Collections*		*Persistent Workspace* *Past Results*		*Collections*
Evaluating information	*Driving Question Folders* *Collections*		*Driving Question Folders* *Collections*	*Driving Question Folders* *Collections* *Past Results*	*Recommendations*

Table 2: Artemis Features: Dimensions of Learner Needs and Information Seeking

learner, whose purpose is to learn from the information encountered, not just to find a specific piece of information, the task is the entire process, and it must be supported as a whole. The support should allow the student to focus on the content, not on the technology. For students, especially at younger ages, simultaneous use of multiple pieces of software is not an option. In addition to cognitive issues, the hardware available in schools often cannot effectively support the information seeking process through use of multiple programs.

Empirical Basis for Understanding Information Seeking

As a first step toward understanding how to support information seeking for students, we implemented Web-based units in 6th and 9th grade science classrooms. We used three major sources of data:

- Process video uses a video recorder to capture everything that students see on their computer monitors through a video-out connection, and combines this with audio recording of conversations between students stationed at the computer. Process video allows fine-grained studies of students collaboratively searching for information.
- Classroom observations follow focus groups of students over time in the course of their classroom activity (which includes Artemis searching). Student groups are monitored across inquiry-based science projects, as well as longitudinally over the year. Following students over time allows study of students' developing competencies, and preferences-over-time, and also allows us to assess the larger impact of Artemis-provided information in inquiry-based science.
- Structured interviews of students and teachers were used in conjunction with other observations. Observers watch students in the course of a search recorded on process video, or over the course of a longer project, and question students or teachers on aspects of their search, inquiry processes, and attitudes toward the tools.

During the one to three week projects, students posed questions and looked for information on the Web and in their school libraries to complete their assignments, which varied from writing a report to creating a multimedia document. Detailed observations of focus students were obtained by recording their on-line activities with process video. We followed ten pairs of middle school students doing four projects, and six pairs of high school students doing three projects during the 1996-7 school year. Analysis of the video records is ongoing, but initial results of analysis of these records, along with observations of similar projects during the 1995-6 school year, highlighted four major aspects of information seeking in which students need support. [8-11] These are described below, and are related back to the five dimensions of learner needs. Table 2 gives an overview of these aspects the information seeking as they related to the dimensions of learner needs, indicating the Artemis feature which addresses each dimension.

Engaging in a process. Students often interpret the task of information seeking as one of getting one "right" answer or a perfect source. Rather than trying to solve a problem and increase their understanding of the content area, they work to finish, reducing their goal to "schoolwork." This is a problem related to all areas of student motivation and knowledge. They need some base level content knowledge to be able to ask an interesting question and to deal with content they encounter. They need strategic knowledge of a variety of types. For example, they need strategies for reading on-line material, for planning their progress toward completion of their project, and for keeping track of what they find.

Generating search terms. Lacking background knowledge, students often have trouble generating any keywords other than those used in their question. More generally, keyword selection is problematic because of the nature of language and of search systems: e.g., exact string matching ignores meaning and choice of keywords exactly determines what is returned to the user. [12, 13, 14] An inability to generate synonyms, either because of a lack of background knowledge or because of a misunderstanding of the significance of the particular keyword chosen, can completely thwart a student's progress. This problem relates to student's content, technological, and strategic knowledge.

Staying on task. Students can be easily distracted in an environment such as a computer-rich classroom or lab in which accountability is low because of the variety of tasks students are engaged in and the high ratio of students to teacher. Lack of success can decrease student interest in staying on task, and lack of understanding of content can make it difficult for students to focus. This is a problem of domain knowledge and motivation.

Evaluating information. Accustomed to the textbook model, in which students merely look up the answer and take it as given, students may have neither skills, knowledge, nor inclination to critically evaluate information they find. This is a problem of content, strategic, and metacognitive knowledge.

LEARNER-CENTERED DESIGN: ADDRESSING KEY ASPECTS

The incorporation of features which address the needs of learners within the problem space of the learning at hand is central to LCD. These features can be of two types: learner supports and scaffolds. We use the term "learner supports" to refer to features that are inherent in the software, but which are specifically included to support learning. Examples of learner supports might be a spell checker which helps students identify and correct misspellings, or a graphical overview of an information space which helps the learner understand the knowledge domain in question. Learner supports may be useful to professionals, but are in some sense essential for learners. They are passive supports, in that they do not interactively intervene in the student's behavior, but rather are available as an integral part of the software.

"Scaffolding," on the other hand, refers to features which support learning, but which fade as the learner grows in knowledge and skills. [15] An example of scaffolding might be an interactive help screen which prompts the student through the steps of a process with decreasing frequency as the student becomes successful. Scaffolding can also be passive, for example, functionality providing simplified views of a problem. The distinguishing characteristic of scaffolding is that it fades over time, becoming unavailable or invisible to the user as the user becomes more expert. The purpose of scaffolding is to enable the learner to do complex things on her own once the scaffolding has faded. A vivid example of scaffolding is training wheels on a bicycle: they provide support for the beginner, can be altered as the child learns, and finally are removed altogether when no longer needed.

In the design of Artemis, we include learner supports, but, in the initial releases, no scaffolds. Our intention is to continue observation and analysis of Artemis in use, and consider addition of scaffolds as we understand more about the information seeking needs and contexts of learning of students in inquiry-based environments.

Learner-centered design methodology employed in the design of Artemis includes analyzing the learning context and learner needs in light of research on learning and teaching. In this instance, the context is information seeking with digital resources in science classrooms. The special problems of this context are described above. The five dimensions of learner needs, along with the identified aspects of information seeking, provide the basis for understanding the task from the perspective of the learner. Our methodology requires that we work closely with teachers in classrooms to iteratively modify our designs based on actual uses by students.

ARTEMIS DESIGN

Our observations of students using Web browsers for inquiry confirm that information seeking is a complex process which is often not attended to in K-12 education. [7,10,13] We designed classroom contexts and Web environments to support students' reflective use of Web resources, and yet students short-circuited our efforts as they sought to make sense of their assignments and of the inherent difficulties of finding useful information in a complex environment. The design of Artemis is in large part a response to the difficulties we observed in the four general categories above, and in many small, specific instances. Overall, we found that it is imperative for students to be able to accomplish multiple tasks within a single computer environment so that their work does not become fragmented, and so they can pick up where they left off when they return to the computer day after day. We sought to design learner supports which made it possible for students to use Artemis as part of a reflective approach to using digital information, concluding that providing scaffolds early in the design cycle might be too limiting. Our stance as educators led us to believe that the role of the teacher along with the classroom and school contexts determines how even the best software is used, and we opted not to try to predict what scaffolds would become most important until we had extensive observation of the software in use in the classrooms of expert teachers. The most important learning supports of the Artemis interface in its initial design, and their relation to the needs of learners and the particular problems of information seeking, are described below, shown in Figure 1, and summarized in Table 2.

Persistent Workspace

The *Persistent Workspace* provided through Artemis retains student work from session to session. In particular, a record of searches with their results (in the form of live links to actual documents) and the *Driving Question Folders* (described below) with live links to documents are stored on a UMDL server and are available through a user name from any computer with access to the Web. The *Persistent Workspace* is important because it can help students engage in information seeking as a sustained process over time, an important aspect of inquiry and one which is quickly forgotten if students focus only on query, submitting keywords and "getting good hits." Even for reflective students, fifty minute class periods make it difficult to make progress in finding useful information, especially if they need to start over each day.

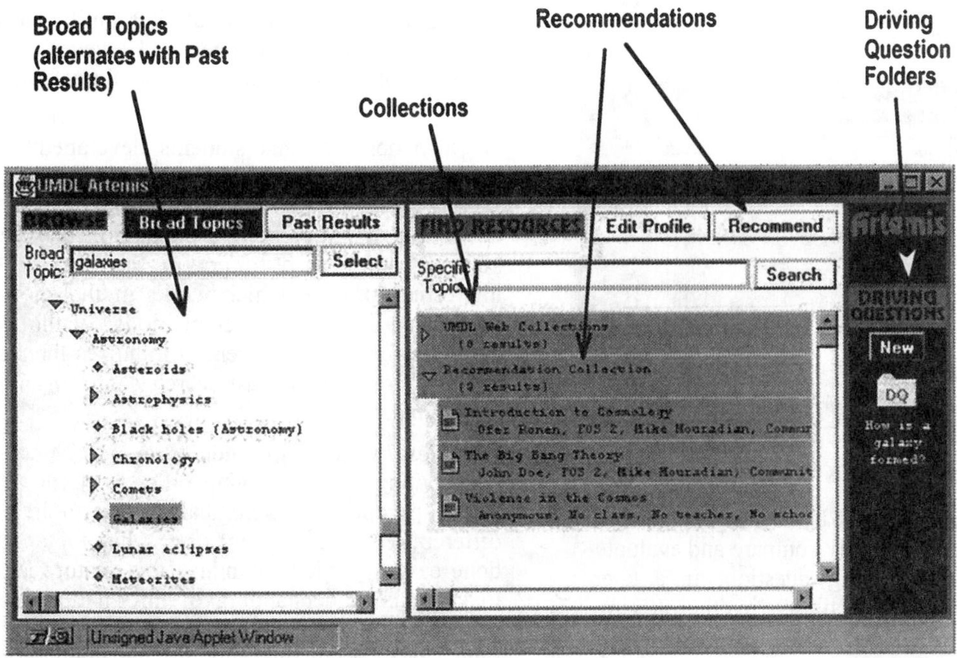

Figure 1: The Artemis Interface

Seeing what they have done before can not only help students avoid redundant searches, but can also reinforce the notion that they are engaged in a process of exploring, finding, and evaluating information, not racing to finish.

The *Persistent Workspace* supports growth of students strategic and metacognitive knowledge, as well as helping them build content knowledge.

In classrooms, we observed a disconnect between querying and actually looking at and evaluating information, which students have trouble bridging. In fact, we have observed that students act as if anything they find about the subject they are searching for is acceptable: they do very little evaluation of content. The idea of a persistent workspace is to give them a way to retain information about what they have already done, and to work with information as they need it. The persistence not only provides information over time, but also reinforces the idea that information seeking is more than just getting the right keywords

Driving Question Folders

Driving Question Folders (Figure 2) are created by students to store links to items they find interesting. They function like a bookmark file, but are a visible part of the interface. Items are placed in a folder by dragging and dropping from the Search window. Students can make multiple folders which can reflect different areas of interest, or refinements of an initial question. Because they are part of the *Persistent Workspace*, the folders are accessible day after day, from any computer the student is working on.

An important concept of inquiry-based learning is that students work on questions of interest to them, sometimes described as "authentic" or "driving" questions. We use the term driving question, defined by one middle schooler as "A question that drives you crazy until you get the answer." In posing such a question, the student may start with a general area of interest, and narrow it down as she finds interesting information. Or, alternatively, she may find that her interests change as she encounters new information, and change her question altogether. These folders allow flexibility in storing links, and may help students focus on the substance of what they find. They can create multiple folders, reflecting a refinement of their original question, or a new area of interest. The folders are part of the persistent workspace, and thus can be used across multiple work sessions, adding items or looking in more detail at items already found. This provides support for engaging in a process

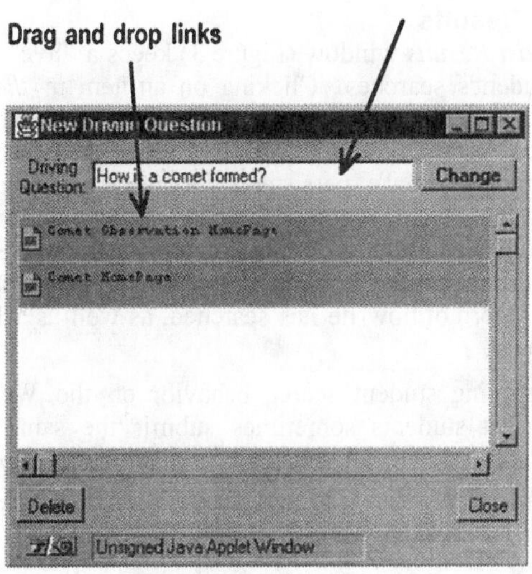

Figure 2: Driving Question Folders

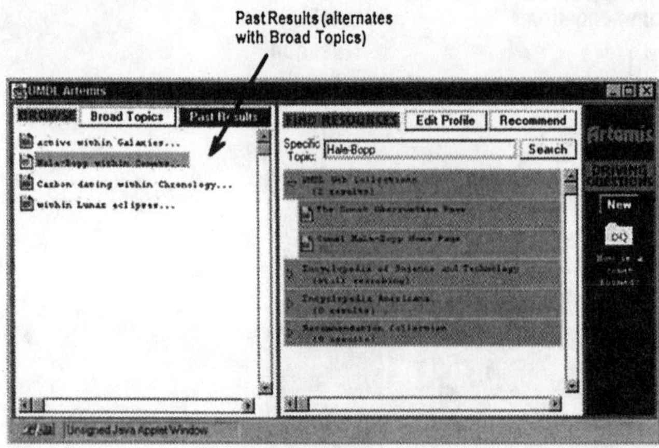

Figure 3: Past Results in Artemis

and may help students stay on task by making organizing easier. It also allows them to readily compare and evaluate resources about a specific driving question. In a later release, a note pad will be available in the driving question folder.

Driving Question Folders support learning content knowledge by helping students focus on the question. Needing to put things in folders helps them think about what information fits with their question and what other related questions they might usefully pursue. We have observed that without a strong focus, students often ramble around in content without paying much attention to what they know, or what they are trying to learn. Strategic knowledge is supported by providing them with ready ways to organize what they found, as well as to refine their question. These are strategic skills which have proven difficult for students to use on the Web. Metacognitive knowledge is supported through the persistence of the *Driving Question Folders*, allowing later reflection on what they found, where they are in accomplishing their goals, and what they need to do next.

Past Results

The *Past Results* window (Figure 3) keeps a "live" list of the student's searches. Clicking on an item in *the Past Results* window shows the results in the *Search* window. The results are actually stored on the UMDL server as part of the student's persistent workspace, so what they see in the Search window is identical to their original search. In addition, the broad topic and keywords used when the search was submitted are shown, so the student has a record of how he has searched, as well as what he has found.

In observing student search behavior on the Web, we found that students sometimes submit the same query repeatedly, and are often unaware that they have done so. One reason for their repetition may be that they come to see information seeking as a task of creating a perfect query, one which gets them exactly what they want. This is reinforced by the unmanageable number of sites returned through Web search engines, leading to the feeling that there is no point in looking at sites until you are dealing with a manageable number. However, Web search engines typically offer little support for actually refining a query.

We also observed that students developed a strategy of recording keywords as if they provided an index to Web sites. That is, if they found a good site, instead of writing down the URL or creating a bookmark, they recorded the keywords they used to get to the site. This is an interesting strategy which works in the short term and says much about their mental model of the Web. The *Past Results* feature in a sense formalizes their strategy by actually making their past searches into an index of what they found.

Past Results can help students avoid useless repetition, contributing to their staying on task. It can also be used in an appropriate pedagogical context to help them use different keywords, by making what they have already done easy to review. Finally, this feature can contribute to students' understanding of information seeking as a process, by allowing them to see their own process over time. Past Results thus supports development of strategic and metacognitive knowledge, addressing all four aspects of information seeking on which we have focused.

Broad Topics

The *Broad Topics* window (Figure 1), which alternates *with Past Results* in one corner of the Artemis window, consists of a list of topics organized by domain. The topics serve two types of functions, one internal to the UMDL system, and the other directed toward the learner. Within UMDL, broad topics are actually a controlled vocabulary used to register materials in some collections within the library. As explained below, the broad topics shown were selected to register the particular collection designed by UMDL researchers for K-12 classrooms, and they are taken from the SEARS headings, a well known subject heading system for school libraries. Agents within the UMDL architecture translate these broad topics to topics in other vocabularies (that is, other sets of terms used to register collections), and can automatically broaden or narrow searches if no results are found.

From the perspective of the user, broad topics present a hierarchy of terms which can be browsed or searched as the first step in creating a query. UMDL uses the broad topics selected by the user as keywords when a search is submitted. If specific topics are also entered, UMDL searches on those keywords as well. The topics are searchable - entering a word results in highlighting all instances of that word in the Broad Topics window.

From the perspective of learning, the *Broad Topics* window is intended to help students generate keywords and recall prior knowledge, and it gives them a view of the structure of the content area they are exploring. Students who ask questions that interest them often end up exploring content areas about which they know very little. The result is that they can have a lot of trouble thinking of any terms outside of the language of the question they have posed. That is, if the question is, "how hot is lava?" they may try to use the keywords "hot" and "lava" for their search. For them, *Broad Topics* works something like an on-line thesaurus, letting them explore related terms, jogging their memory and perhaps their interest in related topics.

We see Broad Topics as a support for learning content knowledge as described above, and also for development of strategic and metacognitive knowledge, and helping with student motivation. It presents a strategy for generating search terms and gives students a concrete way to think about what they know and what they need to know. As support for motivation, it can provide them with alternatives - differentterms with which to search - possibly avoiding some of the frustration of getting stuck using search terms that aren't working without being able to think of alternatives.

Collections

UMDL consists of multiple collections, related by a focus on earth and space science. In the testbed are a journal collection from UMI (ProQuest Direct); the "Web Collection," a collection of Web sites created for K-12 students; a collection of referencematerials including the Encyclopedia of Science and Technology, and Grolier's Encyclopedia Americana; and the "Recommendation Collection" (which is described in the next section.) The Web itself is also a collection of UMDL by virtue of having a UMDL agent which searches the Web when queries are submitted. Once a query is submitted, returns are grouped by collection, showing the number of returns within each collection. This provides an initial grouping of returns, helping make the return set manageable.

The Web Collection consists of Web pages identified by librarians as particularly suited for students in the pilot deployment of Artemis, 6th and 9th grade earth and space science students. Librarians located, evaluated, and abstracted readable material with appropriate content. They also looked specifically for information that was designed to take advantage of the web environment, not simply marked up textbook pages. They sought pages with interactivity, animated illustrations, forms to communicate and respond with web authors. These sites are registered in a special UMDL collection using controlled vocabulary from the Broad Topics list. The Web Collection is designed to insure that students have successful searches as a way to help motivate them to stay on task.

Observations of students using general Web search engines indicate that students get frustrated by the numerous, often irrelevant, sites returned from even fairly specific searches. Irrelevant results also lead to distraction from their task, as students follow useless links. The Web Collection approach is similar to the tried and true approach of libraries, in which collections appropriate to the user population are made available.

Each site in the Web Collection includes an abstract written by the librarians. The abstract appears when the student picks the link from the search results list, allowing them to get a quick overview of the site without the time cost of actually linking to the page. This feature is another way to help keep students on-task. In addition, it provides an aid to their evaluation of the site.

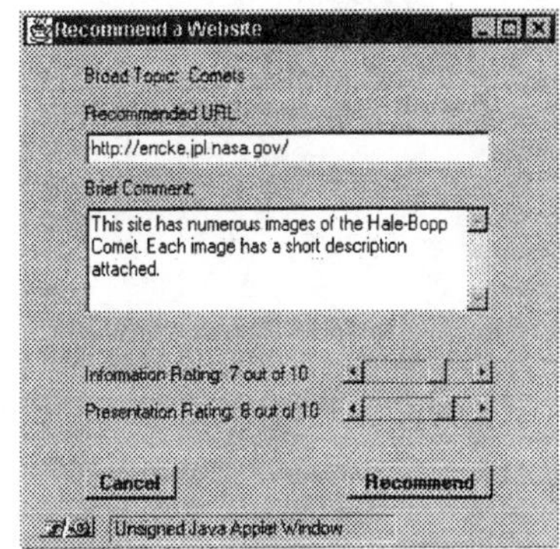

Figure 4: Making a Recommendation

The various feature of UMDL collections support students in engaging in a process, staying on task, and evaluating information.

Recommendations

The *Recommendations* feature lets students and teachers recommend good resources. Figures 4 and 5 show how recommendations are set up, while the results of recommendations are shown in the search window of Figure 1.

In our classroom experiences with students using the Web, one approach which was beneficial was to create our own Web pages with good starting points selected by UMDL librarians in collaboration with teachers. This experience resulted in the Web collections described above, and the *Recommender*. The *Recommender* automates the process of making targeted collections, and incorporates them into the UMDL as a registered collection.

A teacher or student can recommend resources by using the window shown in Figure 4. The recommended sites are compiled into a recommendation collection which is a searchable collection within UMDL. Using the Profile window (Figure 5) to set criteria, a user making a query can ask for recommendations based on characteristics of the person making the recommendation or the topic. For example, a class list of recommended resources can be created by the teacher. She can have her class set their preferences to get her recommendations. When they enter queries, the system searches her recommendations for matches to their query, and these appear as search results in the Recommendation collection.

Recommendations is another feature which can be used to help students evaluate information they find. On the one hand, they can read evaluations from others about a site they are interested in. On the other hand, they may be asked to make recommendations to others, a process which involves explicit evaluation. This supports both strategic and metacognitive knowledge. We also expect that being able to contribute recommendations, and see what peers and teachers think about sites will motivate students as they work.

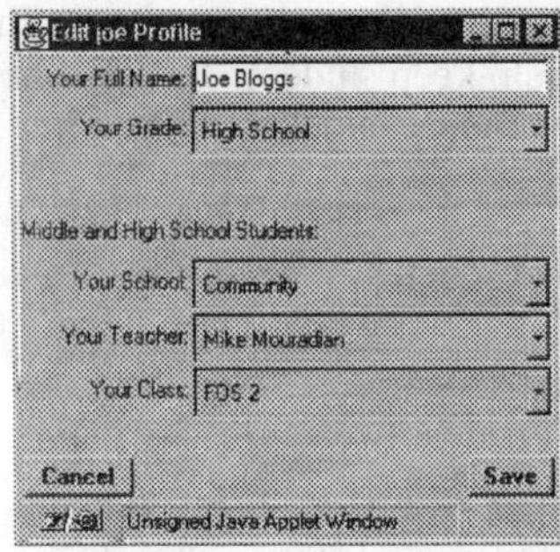

Figure 5: User Profile for Recommendations

EVALUATION

Evaluation of the first release of Artemis as described in this paper is being conducted during the 1997-98 school year in middle and high schools. Log file data and process video records of student use are being collected and analyzed for system functionality and interface usability. For example, we are looking at patterns of use by high school students to determine proportion of time spent submitting and sorting through searches compared to time spent reading and evaluating material found; and we are looking for use of specific supports such as the Driving Question folders and Past Results. Feedback from field data is being used to rework the interface for a new release in the spring of 98.

DISCUSSION

There are very high expectations for the value of the digital resources, and particularly the Internet, in education. Unfortunately, currently the Internet is used, for the most part, as a mechanism to deliver electronic versions of textbooks: "go to the following Web site and answer the following 5 questions." In order to truly realize the potential of the digital information resources for learning and teaching, learners will need software that supports them in their use of those resources, and enables students to go beyond simply answering teacher-given questions, supporting them as they engage in substantive inquiry.

Artemis is one attempt at using learner-centered design ideas to produce a learning environment that does support students in such inquiry activities. As the foregoing has documented, the design is well rationalized; we have attempted to take into consideration cognitive, social, and motivational issues in the design of Artemis' functionality and supports. Our next round of data on the use of Artemis will enable us to revise, yet again, the interface and better hone the learner-centered design guidelines and processes.

ACKNOWLEDGMENTS

The authors wish to thank the students and teachers who participated in the UMDL/MYDL research projects from 1995-1998. This work was supported by the NSF/DARPA/NASA Digital library Initiative (Cooperative Agreement IRI-9411287); by a grant from NSF NIE for the Middle Years Digital Library (RED-9554205) and by the University of Michigan.

REFERENCES

1. Atkins, D.E., Birmingham, W. P., Durfee, E. H., *et al., Toward Inquiry-Based Education Through Interacting Software Agents.* Computer, 1996. **29**(5): p. 69-76.

2. Wallace, R., J. Krajcik, and E. Soloway, *Digital Libraries in the Science Classroom: An Opportunity for Inquiry.* D-Lib Magazine, 1996 (http://www.dlib.org/dlib/september96/umdl/09wallace.html).

3. Soloway, E., M. Guzdial, and K.E. Hay, *Learner-centered design: The challenge for HCI in the 21st century.* Interactions, 1994. **1**(2): p. 36-48.

4. Paris, S.G. and P. Winograd, *How metacognition can promote academic learning and instruction,* in *Dimensions of thinking and cognitive instruction,* B.F. Jones and L. Idol, Editors. 1990, Lawrence Erlbaum Associates: Hillsdale, N. J. p. 15-51.

5. National Research Council, *National Science Education Standards.* 1996, Washington, DC: National Academy Press. 262.

6. Blumenfeld, P.C., *et al., Motivating Project-based learning: Sustaining the doing, Supporting the Learning.* Educational Psychologist, 1991. **26**(3 & 4): p. 369-398.

7. Kuhlthau, C.C., *The process of learning from information,* in *The virtual school library: Gateway to the information superhighway,* C.C. Kuhlthau, Editor. 1996, Libraries Unlimited, Inc.: Englewood, CO. p. 95-104.

8. Wallace, R., *On-line information seeking in a sixth grade classroom.* In revision, 1997.

9. Hoffman, J.L., Kupperman, J., Wallace, R. *On-Line learning materials for the science classroom: Design methodology and implementation.* Paper presented at *AERA* 97, Chicago.

10. Wallace, R. and J. Kupperman. *On-line search in the science classroom: Benefits and possibilities.* Paper presented at *AERA* 97, Chicago. (ERIC # ED407252)

11. Soloway, E. and R. Wallace, *Does the internet support student inquiry? Don't ask.* Communications of the ACM, 1997. **40**(5): p. 11-16.

12. Greene, S.L., Devlin, S.F., Cannata, P. E., Gomez, L. M., *No IFs, ANDs, or ORs: A study of database querying.* International Journal of Man-Machine Stuidies, 1990. **32**: p. 303-326.

13. Furnas, G. W., Landauer, T. K., Gomez, L. M., Dumais, S. T. *The vocabulary problem in human -system communications,* Communications of the ACM, 1987. **30**: p. 964--971

14. Marchionini, G., *Information seeking in electronic environments.* Cambridge Series on Human-computer Interaction, ed. J. Long. 1995, Cambridge: Cambridge University Press. 224.

15. Wood, D., J.S. Bruner, and G. Ross, *The role of tutoring in problem-solving.* Journal of Child Psychology and Psychiatry, 1975. **17**: p. 89-100.

Building an Electronic Learning Community: From Design to Implementation

Anne Rose*, Wei Ding, Gary Marchionini*, Josephus Beale, Jr., Victor Nolet

Digital Library Research Group
Human-Computer Interaction Laboratory*
University of Maryland, College Park, MD 20742
http://www.learn.umd.edu

{arose, weid, march, melc, vnolet}@learn.umd.edu

ABSTRACT

The University of Maryland at College Park in cooperation with the Baltimore City Public Schools and several partners is working to build an electronic learning community that provides teachers with multimedia resources that are linked to outcome-oriented curriculum guidelines. The resource library contains approximately 1500 videos, texts, images, web sites, and instructional modules. Using the current system, teachers can explore and search the resource library, create and present instructional modules in their classrooms, and communicate with other teachers in the community. This paper discusses the iterative design process and the results of informal usability testing. Lessons learned are also presented for developers.

Keywords

digital libraries, learning communities, dynamic query, java, video

INTRODUCTION

Educators have become increasingly interested in understanding the role technology can play in the classroom. One goal of the U.S. Department of Education's Technology Challenge Grant program is to demonstrate how public school-university-business consortia can cooperate to improve educational outcomes through enhanced technology. One of the projects funded, the Baltimore Learning Community (BLC), is a collaborative effort among the University of Maryland at College Park (UMCP), Johns Hopkins University (JHU), and the Baltimore City Public Schools (BCPS). The goal of this five year demonstration project is to create a learning community through the use of high quality educational resources and high-speed networking. The JHU component (The Baltimore Initiative) focuses on interactive video conferencing. The goal of the UMCP component (Maryland Electronic Learning Community) is to provide teachers with multimedia resources and link their use to outcome-oriented curriculum guidelines [4][5][6]. Constructivist learning theory is one of the educational philosophy that underlies this project [2]. This paper focuses on the technology component of the Maryland Electronic Learning Community.

For the past two years, the University of Maryland has been working with a team of middle school science and social studies teachers from three Baltimore City Public Schools and several partners including Discovery Communications, Inc., the U.S. Archives, the Space Telescope Institute and Apple Computer to build an electronic learning community. From a technology standpoint, this has thus far involved installing four or more computers in each of 12 classrooms; linking those machines and teachers at home to the Internet; creating a digital library of 1500 multimedia educational resources; and developing a prototype system that allows teachers to explore and search the resource library, build and present instructional modules, and exchange ideas with other teachers in the community (via email and video conferencing).

Classroom Setup

Apple Computer provided 40 Macintosh PowerPCs for use in the classrooms. Each classroom is equipped with 3-4 Macintosh 5200 computers capable of displaying MPEG video and a teacher machine, a Macintosh 5400 computer with a 4gb hard drive. Each classroom also has two 27 inch "s-video" monitors that can be used for classroom presentation. Currently, the machines in each school are networked via an ethernet LAN with a dial-up connection to an Internet service provider. High-speed networking solutions, such as fiber or hybrid wired/wireless solutions, are being investigated for the full implementation years of the project. Since teachers do much of their planning at home, they have also been provided with Internet access at home and when necessary, with modems and computers.

Digital Library

The resource library is a collection of videos, texts, images, web sites, and instructional modules that cover a wide range of social studies and science topics. Each resource is digitized, indexed, and added to the project database. These resources have been collected from several sources including Discovery Communications, Inc. which is providing up to 100 hours of digitized video, the U.S. Archives, and the Space Telescope Institute. The selection of which resources to include in the community has been driven primarily by the teachers and their curricula. Teachers specifically requested several hundred images from the U.S. Archives and provided input to Discovery on what video programming to include. Discovery clears digitization rights and provides MPEG files based on segmentation (2-3 minute clips) done by UMCP staff. At the end of Fall 1997, six hours of video were included in the database and twelve additional hours had been segmented and indexed and were in the MPEG process. Selected websites are indexed after they are checked for student suitability and publisher stability.

The indexing process involves mapping a resource to one or more topic-outcome pairs. Currently, over 10,600 pairs are mapped to the 1500 resources. We chose to index by topic-outcome pairs because teachers currently select and organize materials by topic (e.g., space, ecology) but they organize their lesson plans according to the Maryland Statewide Performance Assessment Program (MSPAP) outcomes. A specific goal of this project is to help teachers develop more outcome-oriented lessons. Consider the science outcome "unifying concepts and processes". Anything that demonstrate the links/connections between a concept and the process that illustrates it is indexed by this outcome like a video clip that describes how humans need food to have energy (concept) and then explains how the food is converted to energy (process of digestion). We chose to use the outcomes proposed by the national science and social studies teacher organizations because this would allow our resource library to be shared with other states in the future.

Prototype System

For the past two years we have been working toward our goal of building an integrated system that supports resource exploration, module construction and presentation, and community exchange. Using the current prototype, teachers have created almost 100 modules on topics ranging from "Being a Space Explorer" to "Interpreting the Boston Massacre" to "The Bountiful Chesapeake". The rest of the paper discusses the iterative design process and the results of informal usability testing. Lessons learned are also presented for developers.

DESIGN PROCESS

Because the project is a longitudinal, demonstration project that aims to influence human behavior, a user-centered, iterative design process was adopted to "grow" a system according to the needs of an evolving community of users. We knew that we wanted to provide rich system support for a variety of resources and communication venues, but could not overload busy teachers who have a wide range of previous computer experience with a full-featured system. Moreover, we knew that over the five years of the project, the technological capabilities and costs (especially with respect to high-speed networking) would change dramatically. Thus, multiple phases were defined and this briefing focuses on interface developments in the first phase of the overall project. The first two years of work have involved three major iterations, which are detailed below.

Iteration 1: Concept Prototype

By the end of the project, the resource library is expected to grow to over 50,000 objects so the first prototype focused on the problem of how teachers could explore and search the available resources. In addition to the traditional keyword search strategy, we chose to use the dynamic query approach [1] because we thought it would encourage teachers to explore the library, not just search for specific resources. Dynamic query (DQ) applications support fast and easy exploration of data by allowing users to make queries by adjusting sliders and selecting buttons while the search results are continuously updated in a visual display (e.g., x/y scatterplot, map, etc.).

The aim of this prototype was to provide a tangible platform for discussing the pedagogical functionality for exploring the resource library and to introduce the dynamic query interface. We chose to develop the prototype using the PC-based Visual Basic because it allowed us to demonstrate our ideas to teachers very quickly. The data displayed was entirely mocked up for demonstration purposes.

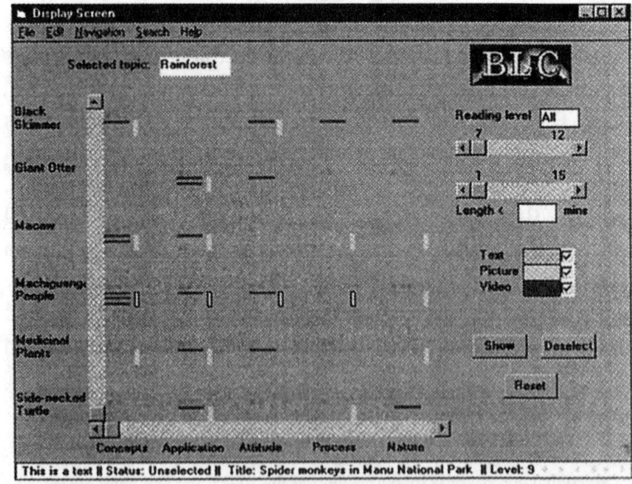

Figure 1. Visual Basic prototype of explorer component

To start, a subject (e.g., science, social studies) and a topic (e.g., chemistry, geography) were selected. Then the resulting resources were shown on an x/y display where the x axis showed outcomes and the y axis showed subtopics (Figure 1). Selecting a topic-outcome region displayed detailed bibliographic information for the selected resources. The axes were chosen to help teachers map their current practice of searching for materials by topic to outcomes of student learning which are the basis of assessment. A drawback of the x/y display was the number of resources mapped to the same point so we needed a strategy for handling this overlap (iteration 2). Controls also illustrated how users could filter the display by reading level (for text), resource type, and length.

Teachers' initial reactions to the explorer component were positive so we proceeded to build a WWW based system that teachers could actually use to create and present instructional modules.

Iteration 2: Web Prototype

Whereas the concept prototype focused solely on the search function, the web prototype considered three main functions: planning instructional modules (module construction component), searching for resources to use in modules (explorer component), and using the completed modules in class (presentation component). Thus, we created the first prototypes of the module construction and presentation components, and continued the development of the explorer component. Other components such as teleconferencing will be added in coming years.

The first module construction prototype used a simple HTML-based, form fill-in style interface with five main sections: a general heading section, a before instruction section, a during instruction section, an after instruction section, and a reflections section (Figure 2). The information contained in each of the sections was based on teacher input. A direct link to the MSPAP outcomes was provided so outcomes could easily be copied and pasted into teacher's modules. This approach also allows other states to plug in their outcomes very easily and with minimal change.

The first presentation prototype displayed a simple HTML module summary that allowed teachers to display resources by clicking on their URL links and to print out hard copies of their modules. After using the presentation component, teachers requested the addition of a simple slide show function that would make it easier to display the resources during class.

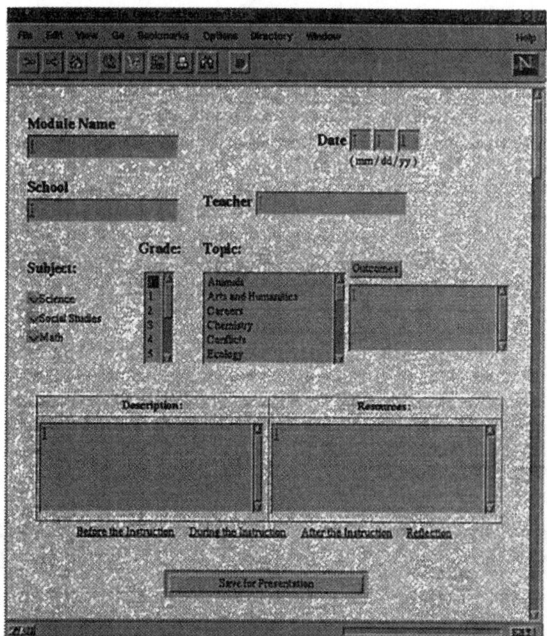

Figure 2. First module construction prototype

In continuing the explorer development, we moved from the conceptual Visual Basic prototype to a functional Code Warrior prototype that could run on Apple Macintoshs (Figure 3). Our intent was to integrate the explorer component with the other components by making it a Netscape plug-in. Major design changes included displaying overlapping resources as bar charts color coded by type, using real resource data, and providing image and video previews (four static key frames). We are using software that automatically detects scene changes to help automate the key frame selection process [3].

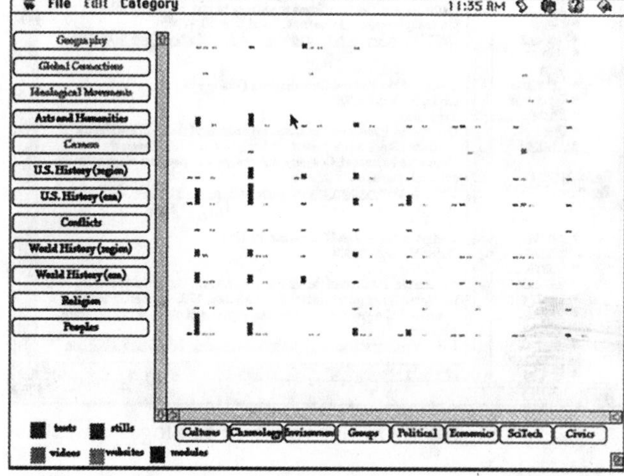

Figure 3. Code Warrior prototype of explorer component

Even though the display was very sparse initially, it allowed us to visualize which topics and outcomes had more resources and the quantity of various resource types (e.g., images, videos, etc.). Selecting a bar caused a popup window to appear with a list of titles and a preview specific to the given object (see Figure 4 for an example of a video object).

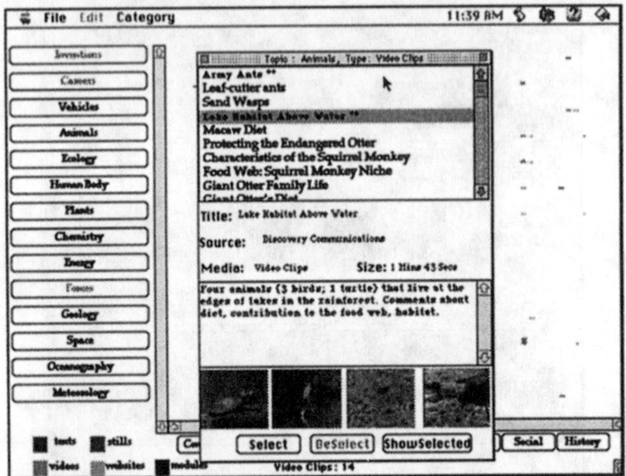

Figure 4. Popup details window showing static key frame video preview

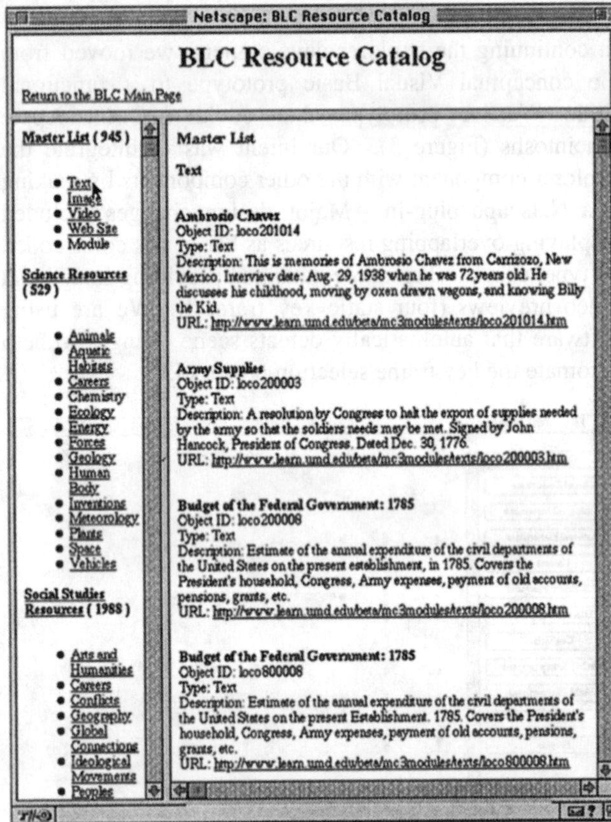

Figure 5. On-line resource catalog

Even though the Code Warrior version of the explorer was functional, it was still not integrated with the module construction component and had to be run as a standalone application. However, teachers were still able to begin creating their own modules by typing in the URLs for the resources they wanted to use. As an alternative to the paper catalogs some teachers were using to find resources in the library, we created a simple HTML resource catalog that allowed them to search, print, and view resources online (Figure 5). This simple, interim solution enhanced the usability of the current system for many of the teachers during the 1996-97 academic year.

Iteration 3: Beta System

In the beta system, all the components were integrated to work from the main BLC web page and re-implemented in Java. Our original intention was to create a Netscape plug-in from the Code Warrior explorer but given the rapid development of Java tools and the difficulties of creating plug-ins for Netscape in a project where components would change each year, we decided to re-implement all the components in Java. This allowed us to build an integrated suite of tools available on the WWW with the added advantage that the tools would be platform independent (for the most part). This opportunity also allowed us to incorporate many significant design changes recommended by the teachers into the revised components. Overall, we tried to minimize the amount of scrolling and reduce popup windows whenever possible. Screen real estate was also an issue since teacher machines could only display 640x480 pixels.

In the module construction component, we added tabs for quick access to sections, multiple mechanisms for adding resources (e.g., explorer, resource catalog, personal resources (not in resource library)), and a section for controlling access level (read/write permissions) (Figure 6). This version not only added new functionality for the teachers but also greatly compacted the design.

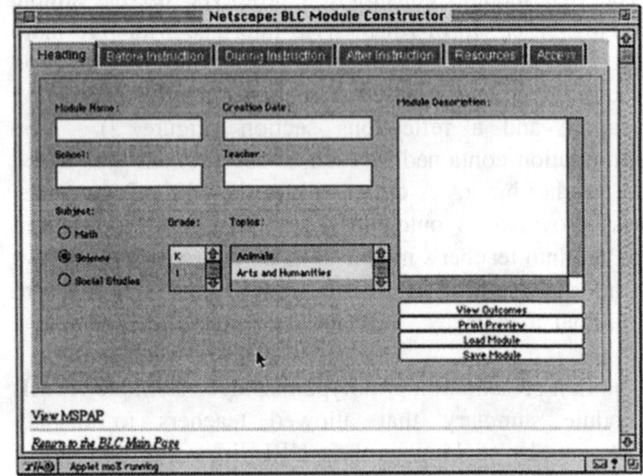

Figure 6. Java version of module construction

New functionality was also added to the explorer component (Figure 7) such as color coding by different attributes (e.g., type, source, etc.), changing axis attributes (e.g., topic, outcome, type, source, etc.), and "slide show" video previews that do not limit the number of key frames (Figure 8). In addition to bar charts, the explorer now supports jittered starfield displays (another alternative to

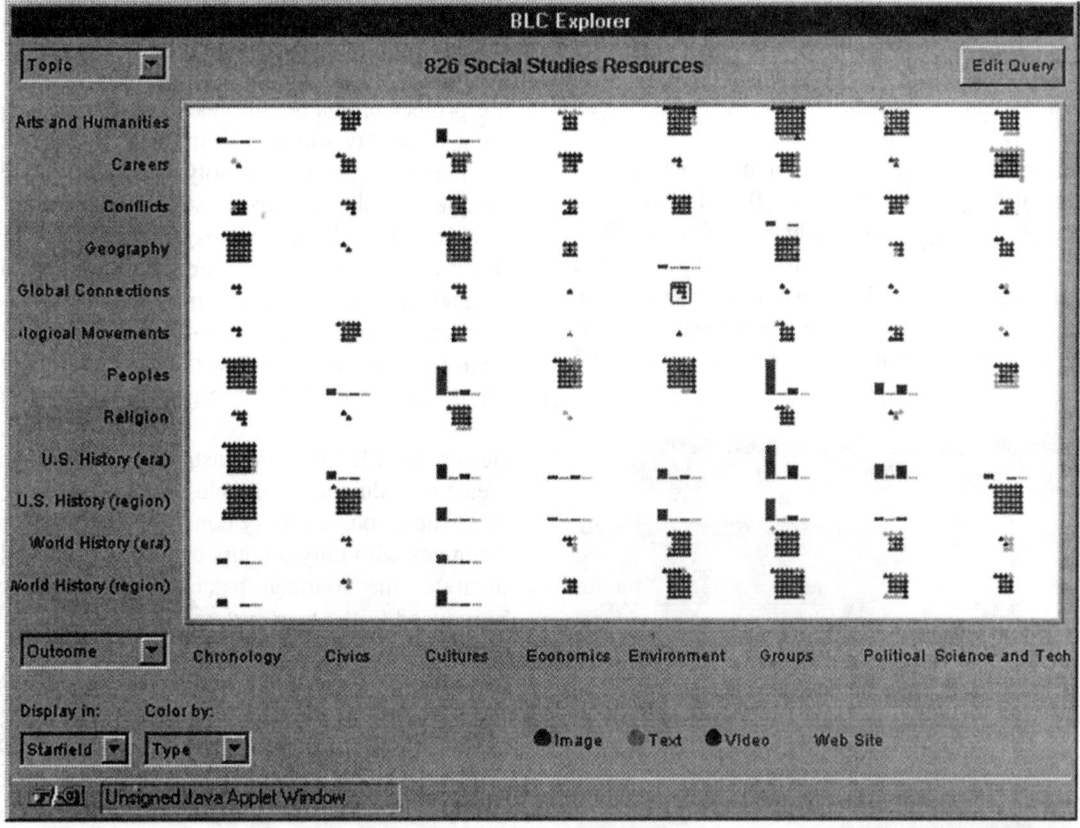

Figure 7. Java version of explorer showing available social studies resources in "jittered" display

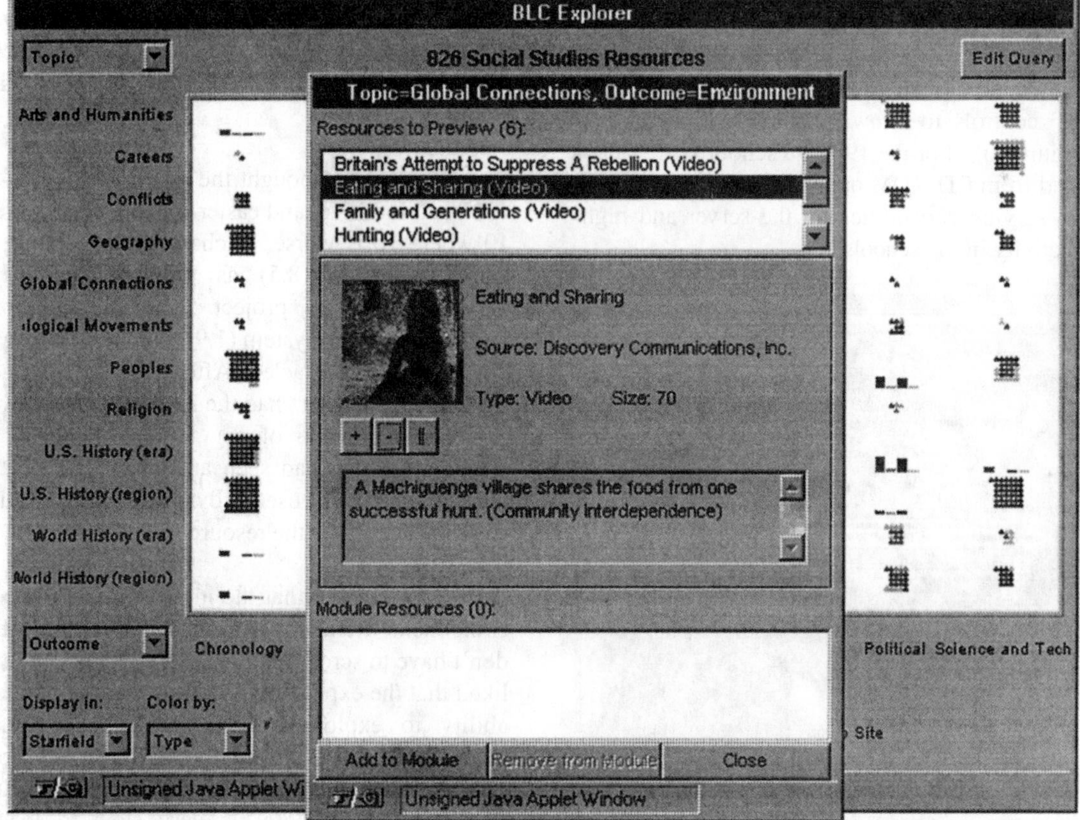

Figure 8. "Slide Show" video preview

the overlap problem) where all the resources mapped to the same point are shown by color coded dots circling the point. When too many resources are mapped to the same point (>50), a bar chart is shown.

Controls for querying by subject, type, source, and keyword are also provided (Figure 9). Initially the explorer supported dynamic querying (as a user manipulated a query control the display results on the starfield were updated simultaneously) but because of slow network speed users are now required to submit their queries (by pressing a button) before the results are displayed.

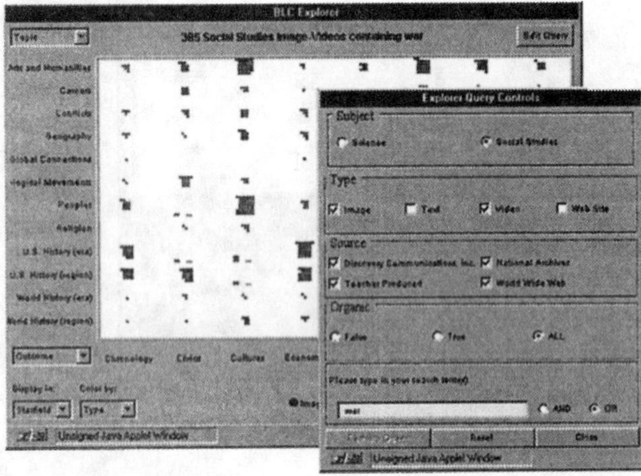

Figure 9. Query controls for filtering explorer display

Major changes to the presentation component included providing quick access to module sections and adding "slide show" controls to allow teachers to present their modules (Figure 10). For the 1997-98 school year, videos will be loaded from CD-ROM or local hard disk while we install video serving capabilities on the server and high-speed connectivity in the schools.

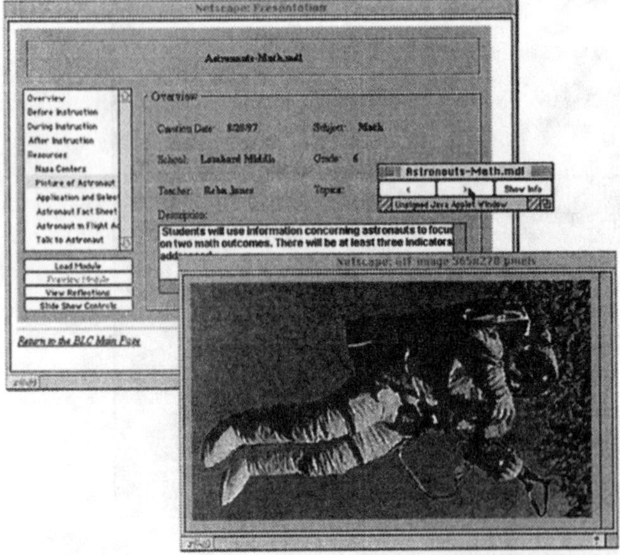

Figure 10. Java version of Presentation component

INFORMAL USABILITY TESTING

In addition to after school in-service meetings and periodic visits to the classrooms during the school year, the project brings all the teachers together each summer for a three day summer institute. At the 1996 institute, teachers used the web prototype components to construct sample modules and made suggestions for what became iteration 3. Since the explorer component was not functional, they used paper catalogs and web search engines to locate objects. During the 1996-97 school year, teachers mainly used web resources and some images in their modules while we worked on adding video to the library and developed the beta system.

Before the 1997 summer institute, teachers were asked to create a module using the old system (iteration 2). At that time, the resource library consisted of approximately 1000 resources with only 6 hours of indexed video. During the institute, the fourteen teachers who participated were introduced to the beta system and used it to enhance their existing modules by adding video and to construct new modules. The concept of what constituted a module varied from teacher to teacher. Some modules contained slide shows of several images or video clips, while others integrated non-computer tasks and were meant to span several days. The project leader for the teachers demonstrated how the system could be used to create a module very quickly. In 8 minutes, he created a module for discussing the patterns evident in a series of cities (images) by using the explorer to select resources. After he presented his module, we noticed more teachers trying the explorer rather than depending only on the resource catalog.

Overall, teachers thought the new components were more compact, intuitive, and easier to use. On a scale from 1 to 10 where 10 is worse, teachers rated planning time (9.4) and class time (8.5) as their biggest problems in implementing this project in their classrooms. The complexity of the system (1.9) and the software (3.3) were not considered obstacles. After using the new components for one day, teachers had the lowest comfort level with the explorer (3.9 out of 5) which was not surprising considering they had seen and reacted to prototypes but had never actually used a dynamic query application and were used to using the resource catalog.

One teacher noted that the improved module construction component (iteration 3) was "easier to use because you don't have to scroll up and down so much." Teachers also liked that the explorer was "compact, color coded" and the ability to explore/search by topic. Another teacher commented: "The dittered dots allowed me to know the general idea of how the resources are distributed." However, the explorer is very slow to load so some teachers preferred to copy and paste resource information from the resource catalog. Teachers also "surf the web" to find resources since the resource library is not very large yet. The slide show feature was definitely the most popular improvement to the presentation component.

During a discussion of when and how the modules will be used in September and October, one teacher noted: "I think the BLC project has taught me a great deal about how to use the technology in the classroom as a tool and not as a play toy for my students. They really get involved with learning." Another interesting observation echoed by several project staff was how teachers went to other teachers for help rather than always depending on a staff member -- a sign of an emerging community.

It was not surprising that teacher's reactions were very positive since they had been involved in the design of the system from the beginning. However, several usability issues did emerge during the institute that will be incorporated into future versions. Some of these are simple oversights or features not completed in time for the summer institute, but others require new functionality.

1. Allow users to edit personal resources - Initially, users could only add and delete personal resources so if they needed to make a change, like changing a URL that is out of date, they had to delete the resource then add it again with the new information. Teachers were constantly frustrated when they wanted to make minor adjustments to the personal resources that they included in their modules. Functionality to edit personal resources has been added in the latest version.

2. Move the save/load buttons in the module construction component to the bottom - At first the save/load buttons were only visible in the heading section so several teachers lost their work because they forgot to save their modules. The buttons have now been moved to the bottom of the tabbed panel and are visible from all sections. Messages to warn users of any unsaved changes will also be added in the future.

3. Add functionality to print hard copy of module - Teachers are required to turn in lesson plans that take a significant amount of time to prepare. This functionality was missing from the system initially but adding it has made using the system much more practical for the teachers.

4. Add a field to indicate the intended length of a module - Now that more modules are being created and teachers are sharing their creations with others, it would be useful to know the length of instruction, an hour or a few weeks.

5. Implement word wrap – Word wrap is not implemented in the module construction component and only primitively in the presentation component. This seemingly minor functionality causes the teachers a fair amount of frustration since they format their text in the module construction component then see it displayed very differently in the presentation component (due to inconsistent implementation and different sized text boxes). We realized this would be an issue before summer institute but did not have the time to add and coordinate word wrap.

6. Load the resource library more quickly in the explorer – One of the chief complaints when using the explorer is that it is too slow to load. Currently, the resource library is loaded from a flat file stored on the server. As the resource library grows, the problem will only worsen so we need a solution that will scale up. Some of the alternatives we are investigating include using more efficient data structures or a real database engine.

In addition to the summer institute, teachers have started having weekly professional education workshops that allow them to discuss how they are using the components in their classrooms with other teachers and get help with any problems they are having. The University is also using this forum as an opportunity to educate teachers about the indexing process so we can start migrating this task over to the teachers. We have also started looking at web server logs to understand when teachers are using the system and which components are used most often.

LESSONS LEARNED

After three iterations, we learned several important (and sometimes surprising) lessons that can benefit future developers.

Provide alternative search strategies - Providing different alternatives (e.g., explorer, resource catalog, keyword search) for teachers to search for resources enhanced the overall usability of the system by allowing users to choose the tool that best suits their work style, their computing environment, and the task at hand. The explorer's dynamic query interface provides an overview of all the available resources and allows users to search and explore using a variety of controls but its current implementation requires a fairly fast CPU with sufficient memory. Teachers working at home on slower machines through modem connections would more likely prefer to use the resource catalog or a simple keyword search. Using the resource catalog or keyword search is sufficient when searching for a specific resource. Some teachers may even prefer to work from a hard copy of the resource catalog that they can read at their leisure.

Provide "quick fixes" until functionality is available – There is always a tradeoff between waiting for a fully functional system and implementing interim solutions. Some developers may view interim solutions as a waste of time since they will be discarded when the final system is developed but in our case we were not only building a system but we were also building a community. Communities are defined by personal involvement so it is important for users start using the system early and contribute to its design on an ongoing basis. In the coming year, we plan on installing video streaming software on the server. In the mean time, the system has been configured to play videos from CD-ROMs given to the schools. The resource catalog was another interim solution that was built while the integrated explorer component was being developed. User reaction to the resource catalog was so positive that we decided to keep it in the current version even though the explorer was functional. These interim solutions have allowed teachers to use the system while development continues and in some cases have altered the system design.

1500 resources is very small – Collecting, cataloging, and indexing is a very time consuming process. Currently, it is being done by a few UMD graduate students. Even with 1500 resources it is still hit or miss whether teachers find what they need. For some topics, like space, there is a lot of material but for others there is very little. One benefit of using the explorer is that teachers can see how the resources are distributed. For example, there are currently more social studies resources than science resources and most of the videos are on science topics. Discussions regarding the process for contributing resources to the community library are ongoing.

Seemingly minor functionality can become a major usability roadblock – Most of the suggested changes were things we planned on fixing in the future but it was still surprising how much frustration they caused. Some of the problems were present in previous versions but had only come to the foreground in the beta prototype. This is most likely because teachers were now presented with an integrated system that they could really start using in their classrooms so they were more focused on usability.

Building a community takes time – It is no surprise that in many systems like ours the biggest challenges are social and political, not technical. While there are several technical challenges we still need to tackle, our ultimate goal is to build an electronic learning community. Early on we provided teachers with instructional tools and email in an effort to help "grow" our community. As the community grows and teachers become more comfortable with the technology, the system will continue to evolve and teachers will become even more active participants in the design process. By working with the early adopters, we hope to hasten the adoption of the system by others teachers.

CONCLUSION

In three iterations we went from a concept prototype that illustrated our ideas to a beta system that teachers actually use to create instructional modules. Involving teachers in the design process early on has enhanced the usability of the system and has helped "grow" the community. As designers we have learned the value of providing alternative strategies for performing tasks, the benefit of interim solutions, how time consuming it is to build a library, and that it is difficult to build a community. As teachers start using their modules more extensively in their classrooms, the system design will continue to evolve. Our current efforts are focused on collecting additional resources, implementing video streaming on the server, responding to teacher feedback, and assessing the impact of the project on teaching and learning. The system will continue to grow along with the community.

ACKNOWLEDGMENTS

We acknowledge the support of the U.S. Department of Education Technology Grant (#R303A50051) to the Baltimore City Public Schools. Thanks are due to the BCPS teachers and UMCP faculty and students who form the BLC community.

REFERENCES

1. Ahlberg, C., Williamson, C., & Shneiderman, B. Dynamic queries for information exploration: An implementation and evaluation. *Proceedings of CHI '92*, (Monterey, CA, May 3-7, 1992), ACM Press, 619-626.

2. Kafai, Y. & Resnick, M., *Constructivism in practice: designing, thinking, and learning in a digital world.* Lawrence Erlbaum, Mahwah, NJ, 1996.

3. Kobla, V., Doermann, D., & Rosenfield, A., Compressed domain video segmentation. *Technical Report CAR-TR-839*, University of Maryland, 1996.

4. Marchionini, G., Nolet, V., Williams, H., Ding, W., Beale, J., Rose, A., Gordon, A., Enomoto, E., & Harbinson, L. Content + Connectivity => Community: Digital Resources for a Learning Community. *Proceedings of Digital Libraries '97*, (Philadelphia, PA, July 23-26, 1997), ACM Press, 212-220.

5. Nolet, V., Marchionini, G., Enomoto, E. Full Motion Video and Dynamic Query in a Networked Learning Community. *Proceedings of EDMEDIA '97*, (Calgary, June 14-19, 1997), AACE, 777-78.

6. Pea, R., Computer support for knowledge building communities. In T. Koschmann (Ed.) *Computer support for collaborative learning: Theory and practice of an emerging paradigm.* Lawrence Erlbaum, Mahwah, NJ, 1996.

Quantifying the Effect of User Interface Design Features on Cyberstore Traffic and Sales

Gerald L. Lohse
The Wharton School of the University of Pennsylvania
1319 Steinberg Hall - Dietrich Hall
Philadelphia, Pennsylvania 19104-6366
(215) 898-8541
lohse@ wharton.upenn.edu

Peter Spiller
McKinsey & Company, Inc.
Koenigsallee 60C
40027 Duesseldorf, Germany
0049 211 1364 395
Peter_Spiller@mckinsey.com

ABSTRACT

Given the resources needed to launch a retail store on the Internet or change an existing online storefront design, it is important to allocate product development resources to interface features that actually improve store traffic and sales. Using a regression model, we predict store traffic and dollar sales as a function of interface design features such as number of links into the store, image sizes, number of products, and store navigation features. By quantifying the benefits of user interface features, we hope to facilitate the process of designing and evaluating alternative storefronts by identifying those features with the greatest impact on traffic and sales.

Keywords

Electronic commerce, Internet retail store design, WWW, economic value, regression analysis, shopping, marketing

CYBERSHOPPING

The promises of online shopping, touted by the popular press, include convenient access to greater amounts of information that enhances consumer decision making and easy penetration of greater markets for the merchants. Numerous articles equally bemoan these promises. With titles such as "Online shopping – Virtually Impossible!" critics are quick to point out that expectations are not being met [5]. As one cybershopper stated, "I imagined that buying clothes online would be as easy as clicking on a outfit and having it appear on my doorstep. But after the third time I waited more than five minutes for a fuzzy picture to download and then sifted through the information, I realized that the technology has not caught up with my imagination." Regrettably, the number of shoppers and total sales are still marginal, in part, because of poor interfaces and store navigation [4,12].

Account managers, production staff and merchant partners should not assume customers do not want an item in an Internet retail store if it is not selling. Nor should they conclude that a poor response to a given store design is because of the merchandising mix. It is important to take a harder look at the possible relationship between poorly selling items and screen design and layout. Could customers be having a tough time wading through the screens? Can customers find what they want in the stores? Are customers aware of what products are in the stores? After all, diligence in browsing a store is not a virtue Internet retail marketers should expect from their customers.

While store traffic and sales are adversely influenced by poor interface features, it is important to document and quantify how much sales are impacted as well as to understand the underlying consumer behavior. The number of levels between the store entrance and end product, the number of browsing modes, such as searching by brand or by price, as well as the consistent design of lists and menu bars should influence consumer buying behavior in an online marketplace. Using a regression model, we examine the relationship between interface design features and traffic and sales data in order to quantify tradeoffs among different interface redesign alternatives. The model explains variance in store traffic and sales as a function of differences in interface design features. This can be used to assess the existing store and to improve features that are below average. It can also answer questions such as: "What is the value of implementing a search function into a site?" or "What is the value of having a product featured on the home page of a store?". This type of data provides some arguments for redesigning Internet retail stores. Even small improvements in traffic and conversion rates can have a huge influence on sales. This research identifies store and interface features that impact online store traffic and sales.

RESEARCH METHODOLOGY

Survey Sampling

A previous classification of Internet retail stores by Spiller and Lohse [14] identified five distinct types of online retail stores: super stores, promotional stores, plain sales stores, one page stores and product listings. In the current research, we focus on **Super Stores**. Super Stores have a large selection of products. Available information is extensive, including information about the company, ordering, gift services and "What's new?" sections. The numbers of extra appetizer and customer-care features such as feedback or access to sales representatives are also more extensive. Most Super Stores have a product index or a search function. Super Stores also provide the most text information for each product of any store group from our previous study. Number of products on product pages is small with most stores displaying only one product per page. The corresponding page length is one screen page in most cases. Product selection and ordering is supported by a shopping cart metaphor. Some examples of Super Stores noted in the Spiller and Lohse [14] study include: L.L. Bean, Land's End, Spiegel, Online Sports, J.C. Penney, Shoppers Advantage and Service Merchandise. Super Stores are analogous to magalogs [9].

Given the confidential nature of the dependent measures, monthly traffic (number of visits) and monthly sales in dollars, sampling was dependent upon the availability of data from a cybermall. As such, this survey is not a random sample of Super Stores. It does, however, represent a reasonable cross-section of online retail stores. Service stores offering financial services or information for sale were not considered. Stores that had changed significantly since May 1996 were also excluded from the survey. Thirty-two interface features were measured for the resultant set of 28 online retail stores in August 1996.

Retail Store Attributes

Electronic shopping incorporates many of the same characteristics as "real" shopping. Thus, we examined the marketing literature to identify attributes that shoppers consider when patronizing a retail store. Berry [3] empirically identified a number of attributes using a mail survey. May [8] emphasized the importance of the retail stores' image. Lindquist [6] categorized store components into functional areas such as merchandise selection, price, store policies and store layout. His attribute list is a compilation from 26 researchers in this field.

We adopted the store attributes identified by Lindquist. These attributes are categorized into four groups: merchandise, service, promotion, and convenience. Table 1 summarizes the 32 interface variables.

Merchandise variables measure product selection, assortment, quality, guarantees, pricing and the number of product categories. The number of hierarchical store levels was a proxy variable for the number of product categories. Information about the quality of the goods includes guarantees, order information, and shipping and return information.

Merchandise:
1 total number of different products in the store
2 number levels between home page and the shopping home page
3 levels between shopping home page and the end product page
4 number of screen pages of information about ordering, quality, shipping, and guarantees.

Service:
5 gift services (e.g., wrapping, reminders, certificates)*
6 Is there an FAQ section on product related questions?*
7 number of screen pages of company reputation information
8 average length of text description about products (sampled over several pages from each category)
9 Access to salesclerk service (sum of 4 binary variables: email, phone, customer feedback, mailing list)
10 extra product information (number of screen pages on product usage as well as extra information, lotteries, contests)
11 help on product size selection (e.g., charts, tables)*

Promotion:
12 hours promotion per month on cybermall entrance
13 hours promotion per month on all other locations
14 average percent price discount (based on the regular or reference price given)
15 serial position in the cybermall list of stores (alphabetic position in an A-Z listing)
16 number of featured products on the home page (sampled on 8/17/96)
17 total number of featured products at "end of aisles" (sampled on 8/17/96)
18 Is a "what's new" section available?*

Convenience:
19 number of links to store from other screens in the mall
20 number and type of different shopping modes (e.g. by brand or by price)
21 average number of items per product menu listing (average over all listing levels)
22 number of lists that have to be scrolled (number of lists longer than the list box)
23 are products' prices already given in the listings?*
24 type of product lists: basic, with pictures, with buttons, with pictures and buttons

Interface Variables
25 menu bars consistent on all pages (every page has search, top of department, top of store, etc.)*
26 homogeneity of product listings in each department (List contains product or product + other information)*
27 difficulty of shopping mode accessibility -- how many actions? (one click=1; otherwise=0)*
28 background color or pattern on the home page (0=white or gray, 1=color, 2=pattern or texture, 3=picture)
29 help screens available on interface usage*
30 image size on the home page (cm^2)
31 number of buttons on the home page
32 product list type (1=icon, 2=icon+text, 3=text, 4=picture+text).

* a binary variable coded presence or absence of feature

Table 1: 32 Online retail store features surveyed.

Service is very important for online stores [13]. Service information includes whether the store featured any gift services, a frequently asked questions (FAQ) section, company information, the information provided for the average product (e.g., information that is accessible to the customer when talking to a sales representative), a feedback section, help on the product-size selection, featured questions in the order form to "get to know" the customer, merchandise return, and credit policies.

Promotion variables record sales, advertising, and features that attract customers. Promotions include frequent buyer schemes, appetizer information such as magazines or lotteries and links to other sites. The existence of a "What's New?" section was another promotion measure.

Convenience variables include store layout and organization features. Arnold et al. [1] extended the convenience attributes to include ease of navigating through the store and a fast checkout. Stores featuring a deep hierarchy of levels had to provide tools to easily navigate the store. In online stores, navigability can be supported by features such as search or browse functions. Providing product indices or a site index also greatly enhances the feeling of "knowing where you are" in an interface. Browsing and navigation capabilities of an Internet retail store also include the number of modes to shop the store (by brand, price, department), and convenience during checkout in an online store.

Interface variables survey whether consistent menu bars were in place on all pages. We analyzed whether stores offered any initial help for customers shopping their store. This included help information about the store's navigation or the use of ordering features such as a shopping cart function.

The second author coded all store variables using a standardized checklist (see Appendix A in [14]). The reliability of the coding was tested *post hoc* using a random sample of 42 retail Web sites. Using Cronbach alpha, inter-rater reliability between the second author and a research assistant was 0.818.

We counted the total number of screen pages and full text lines that contained related information. Full text lines were adjusted to reflect different font sizes and frames. A *post hoc* analysis of a random sample of 14 retail Web sites found a high correlation (r = 0.98) between line count and word count. Thus, line count is a reasonable approximation for word count.

Regression Diagnostics

Because regression models with too many variables and too few observations leads to potential collinearity problems, we reduced the number of variables in both models. Using stepwise regressions, we first identified variables that had no impact in either of the models. Non-significant variables were then deleted and no longer considered in our final models. Table 3 lists 13 predictor variables eventually used in a traffic model that used number of visits per month as the dependent variable, and a sales model that used monthly dollar sales as the dependent variable.

Collinearity among the independent variables causes the model to be unstable when deleting or adding variables to the model. If two or more variables are completely collinear (i.e., one variable can be written as a linear combination of the others), the model is not full rank and regression coefficients can not be calculated. A measure for collinearity in multiple regression models is the variance inflation factor, VIF_i, which should be smaller than 10 for all variables [7]. This criterion was easily met for all variables. In our model, another measure of collinearity, the condition index, was below the critical value of 30 [2, p. 105]. Plotting residuals versus predicted sales and visits did not reveal any patterns in the residuals. The White Test for heteroskedasticity [15] let us maintain the null hypothesis that errors are homoskedastic and independent from the regressors (prob>chi-square was 0.85 for the traffic model and 0.42 for the sales model).

The quality of our estimates varied across the variables. The standard error, which is a measure of confidence, was relatively high due to the small number of stores in our survey. In order to overcome these limitations, we would need to survey more stores with a greater variance in the interface features.

It is also important to note that the statistical model does not detect causalities. The model reveals correlations that might stem from a causal relationship, but correlations might also be completely accidental. We do not know whether advertising promotions *caused* more traffic and higher sales. We can only observe from our specific data that more promotion was associated with more traffic and higher sales. A causal model would require a detailed theory about all of the factors influencing these measures.

DISCUSSION OF RESULTS

The summary statistics for both models are highly significant (Table 2). The overall F-test is significant for both models at $\alpha<0.0001$. R^2 values measure the percentage of total variance in the data that can be explained by each independent variable. The variables in the traffic model explain 89.3% of all variance in the store traffic data; the sales model explains 86.8% of the variance in dollar sales data. The usual R^2 value can only improve by adding more variables to the model, even when their contribution is very small or accidental. The adjusted R^2 value takes into account the number of variables in the model. Adding more variables with small contributions will therefore worsen the adjusted R^2 values. Hence adjusted R^2 is a less biased measure for the variance explained by the model; therefore, we use it in our interpretations.

Model	DF	F Value	Prob > F	Adjusted R^2
Traffic	13	18.260	0.0001	0.883
Sales	13	14.648	0.0001	0.832

Table 2 Summary regression statistics for both models

Table 3 summarizes the variables used in the regression analysis. The column titled *Standardized Estimate* shows the beta weights calculated for each model. A one standard deviation change in one of the independent variables produces a X_i standard deviation change in the dependent variable. By measuring all of the independent variables in standardized units, the relative impact on the dependent variable can be compared directly. Also, the regression estimates in dollars per month or visits per month are not shown to protect the confidentiality of these data. The columns headed Prob>|t| show the significance of individual variables in the regression.

1. Additional products in the store attract more traffic

Each additional product in the store yields additional store traffic. Apparently, shoppers have an idea or some experience of what products they might find in each store. If they are looking for a particular product, they are more likely to find it in a larger store, suggesting that they tend to prefer larger stores to smaller ones. The variable explains 17% of all variance in the number of visits data and is significant (α<0.0001). Interestingly, store size did not have a significant effect on dollar sales. It seems that more products result in more traffic to the store, but the additional traffic did not result in higher sales. Perhaps, consumers can not find what they want once they are in the store. This also implies that big stores are no better than small stores at converting traffic into sales.

2. Featuring a FAQ section in the store is associated with more traffic

The second variable records whether the store features a frequently asked question (FAQ) section about the company or its products. The variable is significant in the traffic model. This suggests that, on average, stores having a FAQ section generate more visits per month, compared to those stores without this section. However, again, it is important to emphasize that we can not

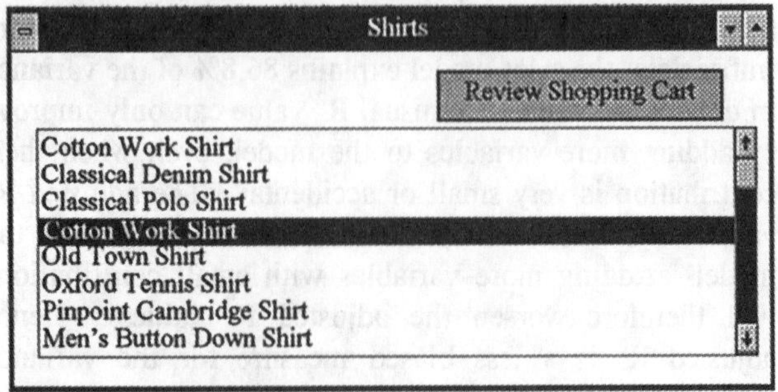

Figure 1: Scrolling menu showing a basic product list.

determine if it is a causal relationship. A possible explanation for this outcome is that the bigger stores received so many email messages per day that they felt that implementing a FAQ section would be helpful in reducing the cost of this interaction. With this interpretation, the FAQ variable is more of a descriptive indicator for store traffic. In this sense, the FAQ feature is a result of the store's size, not an independent variable that led to more traffic. The variable had no significant effect on sales.

3. Providing a feedback section for the customers is associated with lower traffic and higher sales

The feedback parameter suggests that having this feature decreased traffic but increased dollar sales. Providing a way for customers to comment on catalog services and interface features is considered to be a method for improving the interface [13]. But it is not quite clear how having a feedback section can influence sales. The results might again be due to the small number of stores that featured this section. Also, assuming that established feedback sections already result in improved services and interfaces, this feature might explain higher sales to some extent.

4, 5, 6. Improved product lists have a tremendous effect on sales

We expect that any improvement over the basic product list window would yield better sales since shoppers could navigate the store much more easily and are exposed to more featured products on their way through the store. All product list improvements had a significant impact on either dollar sales or store traffic. Product lists account for 61% of the variance in monthly sales. Product lists also explain over 7% of the variation in store traffic. Thus, improving product lists and store navigation features had the most impact on sales.

- The basic product list consisted of a scrolling menu listing products (Figure 1).
- An improved version of this list displays either a featured product or a related image adjacent to any product list.
- Another list contains additional buttons to navigate the store, such as a home page or a search button.
- The most sophisticated list windows uses both images and extra navigation buttons.

7. A greater number of "store entrances" yields additional visits and sales

Links from a greater number of subcategory listings should have a positive impact on visits. These additional links from other locations in the cybermall can be seen as additional "store entrances" or even branches of the store as they offer multiple ways to access a store's home page. We expect that any additional appearance would facilitate navigation and increase sales. The regression

		Descriptive Statistics				Traffic Model			Sales Model		
	Variable	Min	Max	Mean	Std	Standardized Estimate	Prob>|t|	Adj R^2	Standardized Estimate	Prob>|t|	Adj R^2
	Intercept					0.0000	0.0066		0.0000	0.4278	
1	Number of products	56	22,000	1264	4202	1.1810	0.0001	0.170	-0.2682	0.1972	n.s.
2	FAQ section available	0	1	.143	.36	1.5548	0.0001	0.451	0.1876	0.3785	n.s.
3	Feedback section	0	1	.107	.32	-0.7292	0.0001	0.091	0.3674	0.0348	0.081
4	Lists with button + picture	0	1	.071	.26	0.4966	0.0044	0.037	0.8369	0.0001	0.579
5	Lists with pictures	0	1	.214	.42	0.2872	0.0028	0.039	0.1728	0.0702	n.s.
6	Lists with buttons	0	1	.071	.26	-0.0957	0.591	n.s.	0.5059	0.0201	0.027
7	Store "entrances"	1	7	2.61	1.42	0.3535	0.0025	0.068	0.4122	0.0017	0.101
8	Shopping modes	1	5	2.71	1.15	-0.3435	0.0206	0.013	-0.1390	0.3573	n.s.
9	Appetizers	0	43	10.03	12.43	-0.2548	0.0531	n.s.	-0.0653	0.6327	n.s.
10	Promotion hours	1	30	9.89	9.07	0.1702	0.0339	0.014	0.2235	0.0146	0.044
11	No. featured products	0	5	1.21	1.17	-0.1613	0.1091	n.s.	0.1146	0.2915	n.s.
12	Number of levels	2	7	4.36	1.37	-0.1461	0.1969	n.s.	-0.0321	0.7925	n.s.
13	Consistent menu bars	0	1	.18	.39	-0.1978	0.2611	n.s.	-0.3234	0.1062	n.s.

Table 3 Variables used in the regression (n.s. means the variable was not significant)

found that each additional listing was associated with additional visits and sales.

Of course, there was an upper limit to the number of links into the store. The maximum number of "entrances" in our data was seven. The variable can not be extrapolated beyond this point. The significance of this variable suggests that shoppers frequently used other entrances to locate a particular store. The variable explains 7% of the variance in traffic data and 10% of the variance in dollar sales data.

8. The number of shopping modes has no impact on sales

Additional shopping modes should enhance the navigation capabilities of the interface and also segment customers who, for example, prefer to shop by brand or by price. The variable had no significant effect on dollar sales and a negative effect on the number of visits.

We can only hypothesize the reason for this outcome. It might be due to our data coding. The variable only codes the *number* of different shopping modes, not their quality. A sophisticated search function is considered the same as a very simple list. Many of the smaller cybermall stores feature several simple modes, such as lists by price or alphabetically, but none of them offered more advanced shopping modes such as a search function. Still, they score higher on this variable due to their many simple shopping modes than a better store with fewer but more sophisticated modes. It might have been more accurate to weigh a search function higher than an alphabetical list. On the other hand, we also defined binary variables coding a search function or a A-Z list and did not find a significant effect of these variables. As mentioned before, the likelihood for type II errors, rejecting true hypotheses, is relatively high due to the small number of stores in the survey.

9. Appetizer information has no significant effect on traffic or sales

Nearly all the stores provided some information about the company, featured additional information or appetizers, or offered additional services. We hypothesize that the amount of these services would positively impact sales and visits. We coded whether the store provides any additional information over the basic product catalog, such as information on the usage of its products, on health, or other issues customers might be interested in. The variable was not significant in either model. Either consumers do not need and search for this kind of information, or they do but this does not alter the probability of purchasing anything. Whether consumers use appetizer information screens can be determined by analyzing browsers' navigation paths in server log file data.

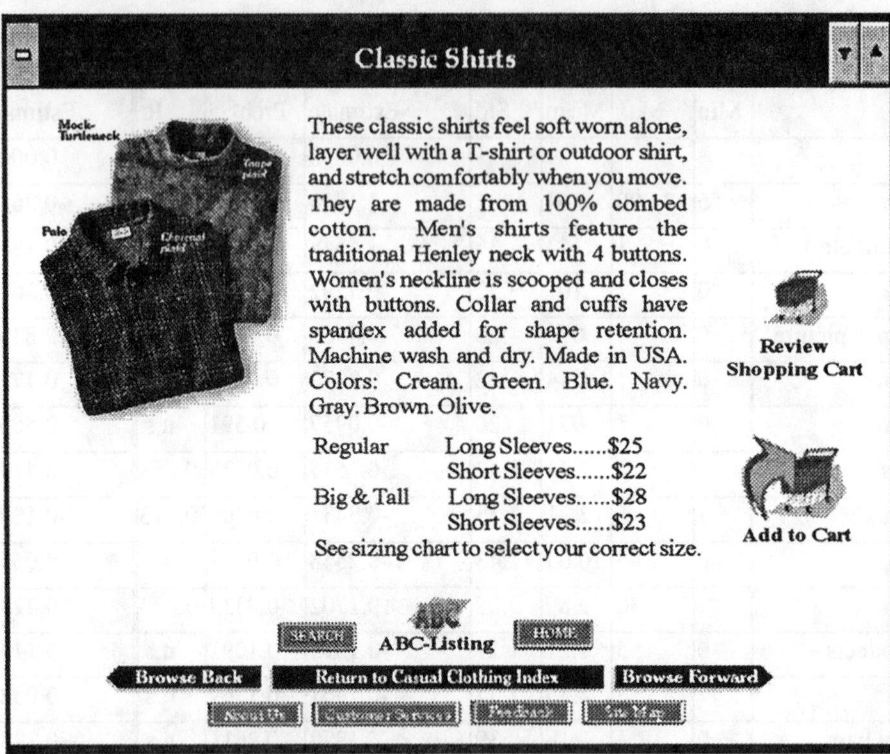

Figure 2: End product page with consistent navigation buttons and icons.

10. Promotion on the Cybermall entrance screen generates traffic and sales

Each hour of promotion on the cybermall entrance screen resulted in additional visits and generated additional sales for the store. The variable is significant in both models at the level $\alpha<0.05$. Four percent of the total variance in dollar sales and 1.4% of the total variance in store traffic can be explained by this variable.

However, the conversion from these ads to *store traffic* is very low. The low conversion to store traffic is probably a function of the end product page design. Promotional ads directed customers directly to an individual product. Often, the remainder of the store was not accessible from these individual screens. There is no navigation path available to navigate from any specific product screen into the store to see some other products or the store's home page. Figure 2 shows an end product page with navigation buttons to browse other areas of the store. The browse forward and browse back buttons allow customers to navigate from one end product page to another. Without such buttons, the consumer can not look at merchandise adjacent to this promotion item nor can they access information about the company's reputation, returns policies, etc.

Customers either purchase the promotion product and enter the store afterwards to search for some additional products, or they do not purchase the product and never enter the store. In this sense, these ads provide a reminder or motivate the customer to patronize the store. Promotional activities for particular products in real stores always aim to give shoppers an incentive to patronize the store and to buy some other products as well. The cybermall home screen promotion does not capitalize on these effects very well because there is no direct navigation path available from end product pages to browse other products in the store.

11. The number of featured products along the departmental navigation path has no significant effect

A higher number of featured products along the usual path from the home page to end product pages should have a positive effect on sales. These featured products can be seen as the aisle products in a retail store.

We did not find a significant effect of the number of featured products in the online store on sales. The variable also was not significant in the traffic model. We did not study the copy quality of these featured ads. Assuming that online shoppers are merely attracted by featured products, it might be concluded that most online shoppers are actively searching for particular products in the product lists, no matter how many "advertised products" they see on their way through the store. This, however, is in conflict with findings from a cybermall user focus group survey. Most users in this survey stated that they only dropped into the stores to browse whether or not they found anything interesting. Very few declared they were looking for something particular.

It would be interesting to look at actual purchases in this context. Featured products might have a great impact on customers but at the same time cannibalize on other products in the store, leaving total sales almost unchanged. Unfortunately, we could only look at aggregate sales data in this survey. But this is certainly a promising area for future research.

12. The number of levels between home page and end product pages has no significant effect on visits and sales The number of levels between the home page and end product pages should have a negative effect on sales because shoppers will have difficulty finding products. We assumed that too many levels between home page and end products would be confusing for shoppers and would reduce buying. This hypothesis must be rejected from our data. The variable was not significant in either model. We tested different level-definitions and eventually used the average number of levels between store entrance and end products in the models. The parameter estimates for the variable are not significant. In order to test this hypothesis more accurately, more similar stores in terms of size (but differing in their level number) should be evaluated.

13. Consistent menu bars have no significant effect in the models

The variable, recording whether the stores featured consistent menu bars on the pages, was not significant in either model. A consistent menu bar meant that every product page in the store had a consistent set of store navigation icons. For example, these might include search the store, move to any other department, top of store, etc. Interface consistency is generally considered to be important from a human-computer interaction perspective [10, 11]. However, it is very hard to code consistency into variables. Studying additional variables describing the concept of consistency, such as the menu organization, wording and consistent use of colors and icons might yield a different result. It may also be the case that in the context of all the other factors influencing traffic and sales, consistent menu bars had a small, non-significant impact.

LIMITATIONS OF THE REGRESSION ANALYSIS

The implications of the small sample size were mentioned a number of times throughout the text. Having only 28 different stores in the sample limits the overall confidence in the parameter estimates as well as increases the probability for type II errors in testing hypotheses. A larger number of stores in the sample is necessary to overcome this problem.

Another serious limitation in this study stems from the heterogeneity of shops we surveyed. The regression models do not distinguish between stores on the basis of product types or brands. Implicitly, we assume that the effects we found do not differ for stores selling flowers and stores selling computers, for example.

IMPLICATIONS FOR STORE DESIGN

These preliminary results suggest that improving the browsing and navigation capabilities of stores and especially product lists can generate significantly higher traffic and sales per store. Additional product list information such as price, a thumbnail image, and a longer descriptive product name had the largest impact on sales. We speculate that this facilitated purchase decision making at the point consumers initially view the product.

This is particularly important as we did not find an effect for other storefront variables such as image size, background patterns, or the number of buttons on the storefront screen. It appears that a user interface that facilitates browsing product lists is more important for generating sales than a "fancier" storefront.

The results outlined above can be applied to improve the cybermall in two different ways. First, identify features that cause poor performance. Second, concentrate any interface redesign effort on interface features that we identified to have an impact on traffic and sales. The implications of the interface features can be grouped as follows:

Navigation

The cybermall store interface does not enable shoppers to browse products easily. Shoppers have to use product lists, open a particular product, go back to the product list, and open another product screen when they want to compare different products in sequence. Also, if consumers arrive at end product screens via promotion advertisements, there is no navigation path available to navigate from this specific product screen into the store to see some other products. The regression suggests that improving these browsing and navigation capabilities of the stores and especially the product lists will facilitate sales. Featuring products on list screens and providing additional buttons to navigate from these list screens to other store departments or the store entrance facilitates traffic and sales. We would suggest an interface redesign priority on improving these lists with featured products and navigation capabilities.

Promotion

Promotion on the cybermall entrance screen increased sales for stores. Promoting stores in the cybermall entrance increased traffic only by a small amount. Some types of these promotions had no significant effect in the regression. The impact of promotions should be studied in more detail. Is there an effect of the copy text? Are bigger and fewer ads more effective? How can the cybermall customize these promotions to individual users by linking them to demographics or purchase histories? Is there an efficient model for the future allocation of these promotions to stores?

We did not study the impact of advertisements placed in the remaining cybermall content with hyperlinks to stores. No data about these ads were available. Yet, offering additional store entrances in the form of additional links positively impacts store traffic. Additional ads throughout the cybermall content that represent extra "store entrances" will improve traffic into stores.

Providing additional appetizers or customer services to attract browsers had no effect on traffic or sales in the regression. This research suggests that the provision of this additional information should not be a design priority.

Store Size

Larger stores attract more traffic. But as we have also seen, this traffic does not necessarily translate into higher sales. One reason for this outcome is that consumers may not find products they are looking for in larger stores. Improved search functions or other shopping modes should overcome this low conversion to sales. These shopping modes also segment consumers who search by price or by brand. However, the regression did not reveal an effect of the shopping modes we surveyed. Since only a few stores offered customers multiple modes of shopping, we assume that the sample size was not sufficient to show any effect of these shopping modes. By linking sales data to users' ZIP codes and demographics, future research could examine whether particular customer segments prefer shops that allow them to shop, for example, by price or by brand.

Store size is also reflected in the number of hierarchical levels between the store entrance and the product pages. In some stores, the consumer had to pass seven screens before arriving at the final product screen. The statistical analysis of the data did not reveal a negative effect of too many of these levels. Either the sample size was again too small to show an effect, or consumers do not bother to navigate several screens to arrive at the products sought.

Store Presentation

We did not find an effect of "store presentation" variables, such as image sizes, background patterns or the number of buttons on the storefront. Consumers want to find products quickly and effortlessly. It appears that no amount of "sparkle" in the presentation of products can overcome a site design with poor navigation features.

While this research analyzes and quantifies the impact of different cybermall interface design features on traffic and sales, it does not provide any detail about converting traffic into sales. Analyzing clickstream and browsing navigation data could provide understanding of how to increase profitability of online markets.

REFERENCES

1. Arnold, S. J.; Ma, S.; Tigert, D. J. A comparative analysis of determinant attributes in retail store selection. *Advances in Consumer Research*, Association for Consumer Research, 5 (1977), 663-667.
2. Belsley, David A., Kuh, Edwin, and Welsch, Roy E., *Regression Diagnostics: Identifying Influential Data and Sources of Collinearity*, John Wiley, New York, 1980
3. Berry, L. J. The components of department store image: A theoretical and empirical analysis. *Journal of Retailing*, 45, 1 (Spring 1969), 3-20.
4. Jarvenpaa, S. L. and Todd, P. A. Consumer reactions to electronic shopping on the World Wide Web. *International Journal of Electronic Commerce*, (1997), 1, 2, 59-88.
5. Glamour, September 1996, p 232.
6. Lindquist, J. D. Meaning of image. *Journal of Retailing*, 50, 4 (Winter 1974-1975), 29-38.
7. Mason, Charlotte H. and Perreault, William D. Jr., Collinearity, Power and Interpretation of Multiple Regression Analysis, *Journal of Marketing Research*, Vol. 28 No. 3 (August 1991), p. 268-280.
8. May, E. G. Practical applications of recent retail image research. *Journal of Retailing*, 50, 4 (Winter 1974-1975), 15-20.
9. Morris-Lee, J. Push-pull marketing with magalogs. *Direct Marketing*, 56, 2 (June 1993), 23-26, 47.
10. Nielsen, J. *Usability Engineering*. Cambridge, MA: Academic Press, 1993.
11. Polson, P. G. The consequences of consistent and inconsistent user interfaces, in: Guindon, R. (ed.). *Cognitive Science and its Application for Human-Computer Interaction*. Hillsdale, NJ: Lawrence Erlbaum, 1988.
12. Ridgon, J. Caught in the Web. *Wall Street Journal*, (June 17, 1996) R14.
13. Sandberg, J. Making the sale. *Wall Street Journal*, (June 17, 1996) R6.
14. Spiller, P. & Lohse, G. L. (*forthcoming*). A classification of Internet retail stores. *International Journal of Electronic Commerce*, 2, 2.
15. White, Halbert, "A Heteroskedasticity-Consistent Covariance Matrix Estimator and a Direct Test for Heteroskedasticity," *Econometrica*, Vol. 48 No. 4 (1980), p. 817-838

Interactive Advertising: Patterns of Use and Effectiveness

Kirsten Risden, Mary Czerwinski, Stephanie Worley, Lynda Hamilton, Joe Kubiniec

Microsoft
One Microsoft Way
Redmond, WA 98052 USA
+1 425 703 4882
marycz@microsoft.com

Hunter Hoffman[1], Nancy Mickel[2]
Elizabeth Loftus[3]

Human Interface Technology Laboratory[1]
Department of Psychology[2, 3]
University of Washington
Seattle, WA, 98195-2142
+1 206 616-1496
hunter@hitl.washington.edu

ABSTRACT

The number of people exploring the World Wide Web is growing dramatically. Many companies are interested in the potential of advertising on the web, but there is little research to guide their decision. The present study demonstrates the concept of a corporate sponsored website as a promising direction for web advertisers. Advertisements for products targeting 10-14 year-olds were presented as web games and inserted into a prototype website. For example, in one ad, players scored points by actively steering toward the advertised product with their web video-game car, while dodging undesirable obstacles on the road (sound effects included). For comparison, subjects also watched a TV ad for the same product embedded in a TV program. One day later, tests showed that web ads positively influenced how easily the advertised brand came to mind compared to TV ads and compared to no-ad controls. The effectiveness of interactive web ads for influencing consumers' memory in this preliminary study suggests that it merits more attention as a potentially viable medium for advertising. Factors that could contribute to the advantage for web ads are discussed.

Keywords

Interactive Ads, TV, World-Wide Web, Engagement, User Interface Design

INTRODUCTION

The number of Americans using the World Wide Web continues to grow at an astounding rate. While only 9.4% of US households were online in 1995, 45% of all U.S. households are projected to have web access by the year 2002 [4]. A few companies are already profiting from this trend but many US companies are just beginning to explore the best way to capitalize on this new medium. Web advertising is one attractive option that many companies are considering. While the amount of money being invested in web advertising is presently modest and exploratory, spending is projected to grow dramatically as the number of users increases. Jupiter [4] projects that 10 billion dollars will be invested annually in web advertising by the year 2002, up dramatically from the 37 million spent in 1997.

Despite these projections, many companies are wondering whether advertising on the web can actually be effective and, if so, how to make it as effective as possible. This includes not only the companies whose products are advertised but also the companies whose web sites display the ads. Most web advertising currently involves banner ads; usually a rectangular graphic set at the top or bottom of a web page. These are commonly found at the gateways to the web (e.g., default start pages for browsers such as Microsoft's Internet Explorer or Netscape's Navigator, as well as so-called portal sites such as Yahoo and Excite) and presently account for 80% of all advertising revenue [3]. Although passive exposure to a banner has its own influence [2, 5], banners are often limited in how creative they can be and in the amount of information they can convey on their own. As a result, the actual purpose of many banners is to entice users to click through to the advertised company's website where they interact directly with the product information. However, getting a large number of viewers to a single website is difficult and in some ways counter to the goals of the companies that house the ads. Only 3%-13% of the visitors to a website [9] click into a banner, and those that do may not ever come back to the website that hosted the ad. This of course runs counter to the desires of the ad-hosting company.

Recently, researchers and advertisers have proposed corporate sponsorship of web sites, modeled after corporate sponsorship of popular TV programs. In this alternative approach, a company's ad is displayed in several places on

CHI 98 Los Angeles CA USA
Copyright 1998 0-89791-975-0/98/ 4..$5.00

the hosting site. Some of these ads are actually undisguised entertainment attractions designed to be fun. Users click the ad to interact directly with product information (i.e., they are taken to another web page within the hosting site for the interaction). When users are finished interacting with product information, an exit button takes them back to the originating page of the sponsored website. This benefits both the company sponsoring the website and the company that owns the website being sponsored. The hope is that there is a greater chance that users will click through to the product information, but less of a chance that users will click away from the hosting website when they do so. The present study demonstrates the viability of this concept for product sponsorship of a website targeted at 10 to 14 year-olds. Advertisements for products that are popular with this age group were inserted into a prototype website. Users could click through a small banner icon to interact with the product information. In keeping with the nature of the website itself, the product information was presented as a game.

Despite the benefits of sponsorship such as those described above, advertisers may still wonder whether web advertising can be effective when deciding where to spend their advertising dollars. This study also addresses that question by comparing the effects of web and television advertising on subjects' brand awareness and product choice behavior. There is a great deal of psychological evidence to suggest that the interactivity afforded by web-based advertising is likely to result in superior memory for products advertised in this way. According to educational technologists, interaction facilitates learning and memory for visual information [1, 7]. Furthermore, a recent study demonstrated better understanding and memory for an activity when children performed the activity themselves, as opposed to observing or hearing a narration of the activity [6]. To the extent that superior understanding and memory for ad content underlies product awareness and product choice, interactive, web advertising should be more effective than traditional methods of advertising, such as television. However, to our knowledge, ours is the first controlled laboratory study to directly investigate the effects of interactive, web-based advertising in comparison to other advertising mediums.

In this study, subjects watched a traditional TV ad as a commercial in a popular half-hour TV show. In another condition of the study, they also visited an interactive website that aggregated several age-appropriate activities. On the home page, subjects could choose from 4 activities, or they could click on a small icon, which encouraged them to play the ad game when they hovered or "rolled over" it with their mouse. These ad games were based loosely on the message expressed in the television ad counterpart. For example, a TV ad that involved driving was turned into an interactive web game where players scored points by actively steering toward the advertised product with their car, while dodging undesirable obstacles on the road (sound were included). One day later, we measured the influence of these same television and web ads on brand awareness, as well as product choice. We predicted that interactive ads would influence brand awareness and product choice more than TV ads or a no ad control condition.

EXPERIMENTAL DESIGN AND METHODOLOGY

Subjects

The subjects were 70 individuals aged 12-13 years old. Approximately half of the subjects were girls (n = 36) and half of the subjects were boys (n = 34). They were recruited from the Microsoft subject pool, and only subjects with intermediate computer skills were selected to participate. All participants received a gratuity of one computer game software package per day of participation.

Design & Materials

The pool of critical items included two fruit drinks, Fruitopia and Snapple, and two candy bars, Twix and Kit-Kat. On Day 1 every subject was exposed to one fruit drink ad and one candy bar ad, with one of the critical items shown via TV and the other critical item presented via the website (based on random assignment). Put another way, each subject saw only one ad from each product category. One ad was presented on the web and one on the TV (e.g., Fruitopia TV-Twix Web was possible, but Fruitopia TV-Snapple web was not). The web ads conveyed the same message as their television counterparts, but enabled active interaction with the product information. We manipulated which ad was conveyed in which medium, which medium occurred first, and also the order of tasks on Day 2.

Procedure

On Day 1 of the study, subjects came in groups of three to a room located at the Microsoft headquarters. They were given a preliminary overview of the research. Informed consent was gathered, and subjects were told their computer screens would be videotaped. Subjects were told that in anticipation of the convergence of TV and the World Wide Web in the future (e.g., MSNBC); we were trying to figure out the best way to combine them. Then subjects engaged in a two-part session involving both TV and web use.

If subjects were assigned to view television first, they read some instructions telling them that they were about to watch a TV program and they would be asked some questions about it. They were explicitly told that while watching the TV material they could laugh but they could not talk with one another. Then they watched a 30-minute video, which included a *Seinfeld* episode, with TV ads interspersed within the episode. The ads were placed midway and at the end of the Seinfeld episode. Except for a critical TV ad about either a fruit drink or a candy bar, the other ads were for network promotion rather than product promotion. The critical ad appeared only once and was always 30 seconds in length.

If subjects were assigned to the web ad condition first, they instead began by reading instructions telling them that they were about to explore a website for kids their age. They were explicitly told that they should not look at each other's screens or talk to one another and that they would be told to stop after 30 min. Then they spent 30 min. exploring an area for 10 to 14 year-olds on The Microsoft Network. They were not allowed to go to other places on the Web. Web ads were available at all times during this 30-minute session, and could be accessed by clicking on an animated anchor icon. An animated anchor consisted of an icon representing the product. When subjects rolled over the icon, it animated, and displayed instructions (e.g., "Click here for the Fruitopia game.") An audio segment representing the product also played when subjects rolled over the anchor. In addition to the advertisement, four online games and activities were accessible within the area for subjects to interact with. In the web condition, subjects were free to explore the web ad, and/or any of the 4 web activities (non-ads) on the site, for any length of time they chose, going back and forth between them at will.

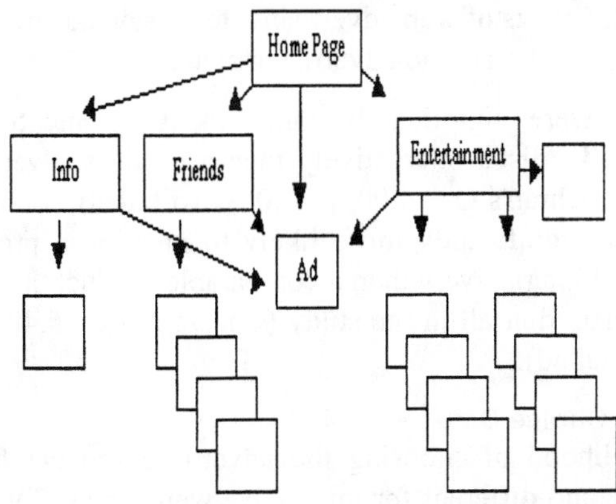

Figure 1. Site map of the website used in this study.

Figure 1 provides a site map of the website. As indicated subjects could access an ad from the home page and from any of three "section pages". The cascading boxes depict the number of pages within each activity area. For simplicity, links within activity areas are not shown.

Approximately half the subjects viewed the TV episode first, followed by use of the web site, and half used the website first and then got the TV episode. After the TV and website experiences, subjects were given a partial debriefing, and asked to return the next day. Subjects thought the next session was a completely different study, as it was carried out in a different building and had a different title in their correspondence. To enhance this perception, a different experimenter administered the second session to help disguise the true purpose of the experiment (the true purpose of Day 2 was to test the influence of the ads experienced on Day 1).

On Day 2, the new experimenter greeted the subject and gave the cover story that Microsoft was interested in the subject's help in designing products that would appeal to kids their age. Then they engaged in a two-part session. If they were assigned to do the *brand awareness task* first, they were given a booklet of 8 pages, each with its own category heading at the top, and five spaces for responding. The categories were Name of Clothing Stores, Insects, Brands of Candy Bars, Colors, Brands of Toothpaste, Parts of a Building, Brands of Fruit Drinks, and Vegetables. Subjects were asked to write down the first 5 items for each category that they could think of, in the order that the items came to mind. Examples were given to clarify the instructions. Brands of fruit drinks and brands of candy bars were the two target categories. The other brand categories were fillers used to reduce the saliency of the target categories and disguise the intended purpose of the study. The positions of the critical categories, fruit drinks and candy bars, were counterbalanced to occur in either the 3rd or 7th positions.

If subjects were assigned to do the *product choice task* first, they were taken to a small equipment room one at a time, under the impression that they were getting a snack to take to a snack room for a short break. They were shown a table with five candy bars in front, and four fruit drinks in back. The right-left serial position of the products was randomized for each subject. Subjects were told they could take one drink and one candy bar. They did so individually, as the only one in the choice room, with their back to the experimenter. After the subject had been taken to a third room, the experimenter returned and recorded which products the subject had taken. Subjects who began with the *brand awareness task*, next did the *product choice task*. Subjects who began with the *product choice task* next did the *brand awareness task*.

At the end of this session, subjects answered an open-ended question inquiring what they thought the experimenters were trying to figure out (encouraging them to guess if necessary). They filled out some other forms not relevant to the present study, were fully debriefed, and given a gratuity.

RESULTS

Use of Interactive Web Ads

One initial analysis concerns whether and to what extent the subjects in the web phase of Day 1 were exposed to the critical ads. To determine this, we first eliminated from all analyses five subjects who revealed that they had detected the purpose of the study and realized that Day 2 was testing the influence of Day 1 activities. This left 65 subjects in the experimental groups who participated in both days of the study. The mean number of times that the ad anchor was rolled over, the mean number of times the ad anchor was clicked and the mean length of time spent interacting with the ad content was calculated for these 65 subjects and is shown in Table 1. The finding that 89% of the subjects visited the ad at least once compares very favorably to banner ads which have reported rates of users clicking into them of only between 3 and 13%[1] [9]. Moreover, subjects had comparatively frequent and lengthy exposure to the product information, both in terms of the number of times they received the effects of rolling over the anchor, the number of times they interacted with the ad content, and the length of time they spent in such interactions. Thus, it appears that the model of web advertising used in this study is an effective way to expose users to advertising content.

Rates of interactive ad use (standard deviations in parentheses)	
Percentage of subjects who visited the ad at least once.	89%
Average number of anchor rollovers per session.	4.79 (2.56)
Average number of visits to an ad per session.	2.10 (1.47)
Average length of visit in minutes (excludes subjects who did not go in at all.)	3.33 (2.99)

Table 1. Measures of interactive ad use.

Brand Awareness Data

The first comparison of interest is whether experiencing an ad, either via TV or on the web, influenced the extent to which the product being advertised came to mind in response to the product category label (e.g., fruit drinks). We calculated the proportion of subjects who mentioned the critical product on Day 2, for each of the exposure conditions from Day 1.

These calculations were made only for the 35 subjects who had the *brand awareness task* first because a significant effect of test order was found, (t (52) = 2.71, $p < .01$, SE = .18). Subjects who participated in the *product choice task* first were more likely to name an advertised product as a category member in the *brand awareness task*. To ensure that *product choice* did not contaminate *brand awareness*, only data from children who did the *brand awareness task* before the *product choice task* were included in subsequent analysis of the brand awareness data. Since each advertised item (e.g., Fruitopia) had an unadvertised counterpart (e.g., Snapple), the proportion of subjects who mentioned the unadvertised products could also be calculated as a within-subject control condition for the *brand awareness* measure. This gave baseline rates, (e.g., the proportion of subjects who would have thought of Snapple even without any Day 1 advertising). The mean proportion of subjects mentioning the critical item in each condition is shown in Figure 2.

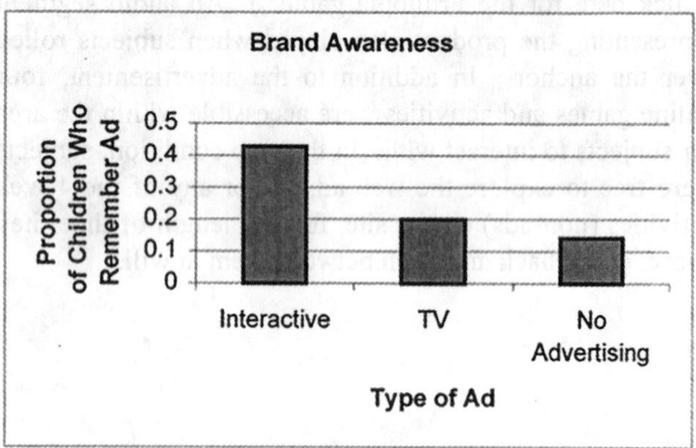

Figure 2. Effects of web advertising, television advertising, and no advertising at all.

Subjects were significantly more likely to mention a product advertised interactively than a product advertised on TV (Cochran's Q = 4.00, $p < .05$, two tailed). Subjects were also significantly more likely to mention a product advertised interactively than a comparable product that was not advertised at all in the study (Cochran's Q = 5.40, $p < .05$, two-tailed).

Product Choice Data

The likelihood of choosing the advertised product for a snack was no different for interactive web ads vs. TV ads. Kids chose the product advertised interactively 22% of the time and the product advertised on television 23% of the time. These rates did not differ significantly and were very close to the chance probability of choosing the advertised products (chance calculated as an average over drinks (1/4) and candy bars (1/5) was 22.5%)

CONCLUSION AND FUTURE WORK

This study demonstrates the viability of a "sponsorship" model of web advertising and indicates that interactive web ads can influence children's memory for advertised products more effectively than TV ads, and more effectively than no ads. The subjects in this study interacted

[1] This difference is likely due, in part, to the fact that our subjects were required to stay within a circumscribed set of websites designed to simulate the "sponsorship model" as opposed to being able to "surf the net" at large.

with product information extensively. As a result, the brand names of products advertised interactively were more prominent in subjects' memories than if they had not used the web advertisements. The effectiveness of interactive web advertising for influencing consumers' awareness of products in this preliminary study suggests that it merits more attention as a potentially viable medium for advertising.

No significant advantage was observed with regard to the product choice measure used in this study; however, this has traditionally been a less sensitive measure of ad effectiveness (Rust, Personal communication). This is because it is more difficult to control all the variables affecting behaviors like product choice. Packaging, subjects' prior experience with the brand, what they are feeling like at the time the data are collected and a range of other variables act on the behavior, create noise, and make it more difficult to detect underlying patterns. A study that controls for these variables may be necessary to show an effect of advertising on product choice. It may also be the case that our current set of interactive advertisements was not potent enough to produce an effect. By applying what we have learned about designing for this genre during this, our first attempt, we may be able to build ads which influence memory and product choice.

Initial Hypotheses

The logical next question to ask is why the interactive web ads had the effect they did? The answer to this question may help us understand the critical factors for success in an interactive ad. We would then be able to replicate success repeatedly in our ad designs on the web. In this section of the report, we discuss our initial hypotheses about what made these interactive ads effective, describe further analyses that could provide more definitive answers, and point to possibilities for studies that could provide further information about effective ad design.

There are several factors that likely influenced the effectiveness of the interactive web ads used in this study. The opportunity for high rates of exposure to the ad content afforded by the sponsorship model, both through roll over and clicking through to the actual ad content, was undoubtedly critical to the effectiveness of the ads. When we initially piloted the ads, none of the subjects clicked into them! We subsequently changed the anchors to be obviously "clickable", to set up expectations for fun, and to use highly directive language (e.g., "Click here for the Snapple game!"). These changes resulted in the currently reported rate of 89% of the children clicking into the ads and should be adopted by designers interested in effectively getting users into ad content.

The frequency and length of time the subjects spent interacting with the content is also likely to have contributed to the effectiveness of the ads. However, although one clear advantage of web ads over TV ads is that subjects can spend more time in them, sheer amount of exposure is unlikely to be what distinguishes effective web ads from ineffective web ads. To explore this, initial analyses examined the number of times subjects rolled over the ad anchor and the total number of minutes of exposure to ad content. These results indicated that there was no difference in ad exposure between subjects who remembered the web ad and subjects who did not. This is consistent with the finding [6] that the number of times an event is directly experienced has little effect on children's recall of the event. In contrast, the structure of the information (e.g., whether the relationships between parts of the event make for a coherent whole) tends to be of critical importance to children's ability to recall an event [8]. This suggests that more fine-grained analyses that take a qualitative look at how our subjects used the interactive ad content, what they remembered about the ads themselves, and how those factors related to brand awareness may provide better information about the kinds of design features that make these ads effective. Analysis of the video tapes of subjects using the ads and analysis of free and cued recall data that were also collected at the end of the Day 2 activities can be used to determine what was most salient about the ads. The results of these analyses may help guide the design of effective interactive ads for the Web.

Further Studies

We had many initial questions about interactive advertising that were tabled in favor of the issues we chose to focus on for this research. One question we had at the outset was whether the effectiveness of interactive advertising would depend on the age of the user. Another interesting question regarded the effectiveness of interactive advertising across repeated exposures. Several well-known psychological findings suggest that the factors that influence effectiveness may change over repeated experience with ads. Finally, it seems likely that advertisements presented in different kinds of media will interact. For example, although pitted against one another in the present study, TV ads and interactive web ads will likely work synergistically in the real world. The influence of a web ad would likely be enhanced by subsequent exposure to TV ads, and TV ads may be more engaging after interacting with a complementary web ad. The best way to use interactive and TV ads conjointly for maximal effectiveness is an additional question that should be explored in further research. Corporate investment in empirical research on the fundamentals of web advertising will accelerate the maturation of this potentially influential medium.

ACKNOWLEDGMENTS

We would like to thank Kevin Larson for his assistance with preparing this paper in the format for a CHI submission and Amy Tsai for her help running subjects.

Thanks to George Robertson for his helpful comments on an earlier draft of this paper. We would also like to thank Ellen Gasca, and the usability test coordinators, as well as the participants in this study, for their time and efforts in scheduling repeat visits to the lab for this research.

REFERENCES

1. Anderson, J.R., Corbett, A.T., Koedinger, K.R., & Pelletier, R. (1996). Cognitive tutors: Lessons learned. Pittsburgh, PA: Carnegie Mellon University Unpublished manuscript.
2. Briggs, R., and Hollis, N. (1997). Advertising on the Web: Is there response before click through? *Journal of Advertising Research, March/April* 33-45.
3. Jupiter report cited by *Cyberatlas*, (1997). http://www.cyberatlas.com/advertising.html.
4. Jupiter (1997). The 1997 Online Kids Report. *Jupiter Communications*, NY., http://www.jup.com.
5. Maddox, L.W., and Mehta, D. (1997). The role and effect of web addresses in advertising. *Journal of Advertising Research, March/April*, 47-59.
6. Murachver, T., Pipe, M., Gordon, R., Owens, J.L., and Fivush, R. (1996). Do, show and tell: Children's event memories acquired through direct experience, observation and stories, *Child Development*, *67*, 3029-3044.
7. Psotka, J. (1995). Immersive tutoring systems: Virtual reality and education and training. Available as an HTML document from http://www.hitl.washington.edu
8. Van den Broek, P. (In press). Discovering the cement of the universe: The development of event comprehension from childhood to adulthood. In P. van den Broek, P. Bauer, & T. Bourg (Eds.) *Developmental spans in event comprehension and representation: Bridging fictional and actual events.* Hillsdale, N.J.: Erlbaum.
9. Voight, J. Beyond the banner. *Wired, December*, 1996.

Persuasive Computers: Perspectives and Research Directions

BJ Fogg

Stanford University
Box 8338, Stanford, CA 94309 USA
bjfogg@stanford.edu, bjfogg@acm.org
www.captology.org

Sun Microsystems
901 San Antonio Road, MPK17-105
Palo Alto, CA 94303 USA
b.j.fogg@sun.com

ABSTRACT

The study of computers as persuasive technologies (called "captology") was introduced at CHI 97 as a new area of inquiry. This paper proposes definitions, perspectives, and research directions for further investigation of this field. A persuasive computer is an interactive technology that attempts to change attitudes or behaviors in some way. Perspective 1 describes how computers can inherit three types of intentionality: endogenous, exogenous, and autogenous. Perspective 2 presents the "Functional Triad," which illustrates that computers can function as persuasive tools, media, and social actors. Perspective 3 presents a "levels of analysis" approach for captology, which include varying levels from individual to societal. Perspective 4 suggests a simple method for exploring the design space for persuasive computers. Perspective 5 highlights some ethical issues inherent in persuasive computing. The paper concludes by proposing seven directions for further research and design.

Keywords

persuasion, captology, media, computers as social actors, ethics, design methods, computers as persuasive technologies

INTRODUCTION

At CHI 97, a special interest group meeting gathered a number of participants who were interested in exploring the domain of computers and persuasion [6]. We agreed to call this area "captology" (built from an acronym for Computers As Persuasive Technologies), with the graphic in Figure 1 serving as a reference point for this domain.

The discussion on captology at the CHI 97 SIG proved fruitful and enlightening, with participants concurring that captology was an intriguing area for further research and design. The group also agreed that this domain had not yet been adequately defined or addressed by researchers and practitioners of human-computer interaction. We found that our discussion suffered at times because we lacked key definitions and frameworks for understanding captology. The purpose of this paper, therefore, is to contribute to the CHI community's understanding of persuasive computing by proposing definitions, perspectives, and research directions for the field of captology.

CHI 98 Los Angeles CA USA
Copyright 1998 0-89791-975-0/98/ 4..$5.00

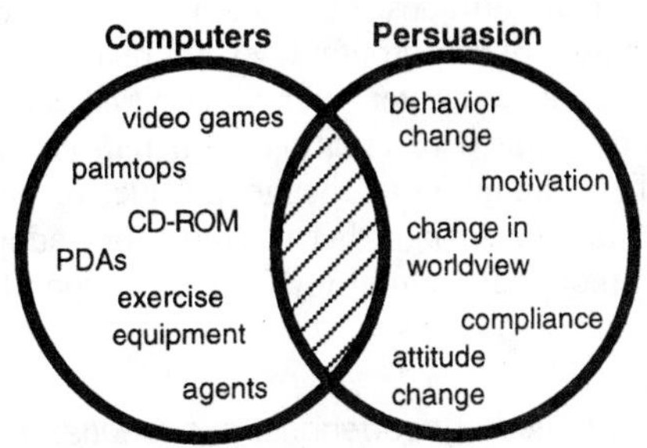

Figure 1: Captology describes the shaded area where computing technology and persuasion overlap.

This paper first presents five perspectives on computers and persuasion. They include the following:

- Perspective 1: Definition of persuasive computers
- Perspective 2: A functional view of persuasive computers
- Perspective 3: Levels of analysis for captology
- Perspective 4: The design space for persuasive technologies
- Perspective 5: Ethics of computers that persuade

Each of these five perspectives provides a different way to view persuasive computers, while also describing examples of relevant technologies. After setting forth the five perspectives on persuasive technologies, this paper concludes by outlining seven profitable directions for further research in the area of persuasive computers.

To be clear, this paper makes a contribution by articulating a range of approaches to captology. It is the role of later work to expand and revise the ideas proposed in this paper.

PERSPECTIVE 1: DEFINITION OF PERSUASIVE COMPUTERS

What is a persuasive computer?

Simply put, a persuasive computer is an interactive technology that changes a person's attitudes or behaviors. This definition works well in many cases, but a more thorough definition gives a better understanding of persuasive computing.

The psychology literature suggests many definitions for the word "persuasion" [e.g., 24, 36]. After reviewing the work of persuasion scholars, I've synthesized the various definitions to define "persuasion" as "an attempt to shape, reinforce, or change behaviors, feelings, or thoughts about an issue, object, or action."

Persuasion and intentionality

One key point in this definition is that true persuasion implies an **intent** to change attitudes or behaviors; in other words, persuasion requires intentionality. Therefore, not all behavior or attitude change is the result of persuasion. For example, a rain storm may cause people to buy umbrellas, but the storm is not a persuasive event because it has no intentionality associated with it. (However, if an umbrella manufacturer could somehow cause rain, then the rain storm might qualify as a persuasive tactic.)

Because machines do not have intentions [8], a computer qualifies as a persuasive technology only when those who create, distribute, or adopt the technology do so with an intent to affect human attitudes or behaviors. To be clear, the persuasive nature of a computer does not reside with the object itself; instead, a computer being classified as "persuasive" depends on the context of creation, distribution, and adoption. I propose that if an intent to change attitudes or behaviors is a factor in the creation, distribution, or adoption of a technology, then that technology inherits a type of intent from human actors.

Three types of intent: endogenous, exogenous, and autogenous

For the purposes of captology, I propose three kinds of inherited persuasive intent: endogenous, exogenous, and autogenous. According to my definitions, a computer technology inherits **endogenous** intent when a designer or producer creates a technology with intent to persuade users in some way. A computer technology inherits **exogenous** intent when one person provides another person with a computer technology in an attempt to change that person's attitudes or behaviors. A computer technology inherits **autogenous** intent when a person chooses to use or adopt a technology in order to change his or her own attitudes or behaviors. Table 1 makes this idea clearer.

Type of intent	Where intent comes from	Example
endogenous "from within"	Those who **create** or **produce** the interactive technology	Health-Hero video games are designed to persuade children to develop good health habits [17].
exogenous "caused by external factors"	Those who **give access** to or **distribute** the interactive technology to others	A mother may give her son a Palm Pilot PDA in hopes that he will become more organized.
autogenous "self-produced"	The person **adopting** or **using** the interactive technology	A person may buy and use a calorie-counting computer device to help change his or her own eating behavior.

Table 1: Three types of intent with examples

Although the above categories aim to distinguish among types of persuasive technologies, I recognize that these categories are not always precise, and they are not always mutually exclusive. Indeed, making inferences about intentions is tricky business—we may infer intent where there is none, or we may fail to perceive intent when intent does indeed exist. Furthermore, it is quite possible that a given interactive technology may fall into more than one category. Despite the potential ambiguities, I find these three categories helpful in better understanding the range and roles of persuasive computing technologies.

PERSPECTIVE 2: A FUNCTIONAL VIEW OF PERSUASIVE COMPUTERS

While Perspective 1 provides an "intentional" framework for persuasive computers, Perspective 2 presents what I call a "functional" view. To explain Perspective 2 clearly, I first describe the basics of the "Functional Triad." I then show how this framework can provide key insights into the study of persuasive computers.

The Functional Triad

I propose that today's computers function in three basic ways: as **tools**, as **media**, and as **social actors**. Researchers and designers have often discussed variants of these functions [e.g., 18, 22, 33], usually as metaphors for computer use. However, I suggest that these three categories are more than metaphors; they are basic ways that people view or respond to computing technologies. I refer to these three areas as "functions."

As a **tool**, the computer (or the computer application or system) provides humans with new ability or power, allowing people to do things they could not do before, or to do things more easily [28, 29].

Computers also function as **media** [13, 30, 32], a role that has become more apparent and important in recent years [30, 34]. As a medium, a computer can convey either symbolic content (e.g., text, data graphs, icons) or sensory content (e.g., real-time video, simulations, virtual worlds).

Computers can also function as **social actors** [12, 16, 25, 32]. Users seem to respond to computers as social actors [25] when computer technologies adopt animate characteristics (physical features, emotions, voice communication), play animate roles (coach, pet, assistant, opponent), or follow social rules or dynamics (greetings, apologies, turn taking).

Mapping the functions

One way to view these three functions simultaneously is to map the three categories into two dimensions. Of course, in all but the most extreme cases, these functions mix and blur in any one given interactive technology. However, consciously mapping interactive technologies into a triangular space I call the "Functional Triad" generates insight into the roles and relationships of different computer technologies. Figure 2 represents the Functional Triad with some prototypical examples.

Persuasion and the functional view of computers

Although the functional triad is a useful framework for understanding computer technologies in general, adopting this functional view of computers yields specific insights for analyzing persuasive interactive technologies.

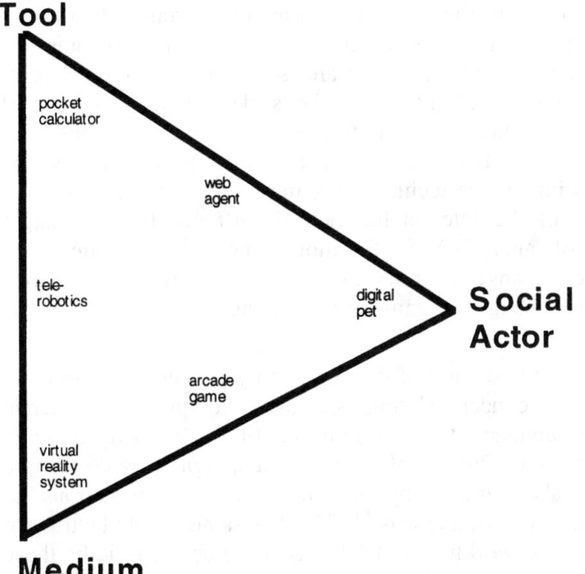

Figure 2: The Functional Triad with examples

By viewing a computer technology as a tool, one can then ask how tools can be persuasive devices. In other words, "How do tools change attitudes or behaviors?" While this question deserves more detailed exploration, one preliminary answer is that tools can be persuasive by (1) reducing barriers and thereby increase the likelihood of a certain behavior [2, 11], (2) increasing self-efficacy by making a certain behavior seem achievable [2, 17], (3) providing information that allows informed decisions [19], and (4) shaping a person's mental model by channeling behavior in a certain pattern.

One could also pose similar questions about the other two functional areas for computers: "What makes computers as media persuasive?" and "What makes computers as social actors persuasive?" [4, 5, 20]. While this paper will not fully answer these questions, Table 2 highlights some persuasive affordances in each of the three functional areas:

Function	Essence	Persuasive affordances
computer as **tool** or **instrument**	increases capabilities	• reduces barriers (time, effort, cost) • increases self-efficacy • provides information for better decision making • changes mental models
computer as **medium**	provides experiences	• provides first-hand learning, insight, visualization, resolve • promotes understanding of cause/effect relationships • motivates through experience, sensation
computer as **social actor**	creates relationship	• establishes social norms • invokes social rules and dynamics • provides social support or sanction

Table 2: Three computer functions and their persuasive affordances

Examples in each functional area

As the Table 2 shows, computers functioning as tools, media, or social actors can change attitudes and behaviors through different means. Examples of persuasive computers in each category follow:

Example of computer as persuasive tool

Polar Heart Rate Monitor [www.polar.fi]: This exercise device sounds an alarm when a person's heart rate falls outside a pre-set zone. The device not only can motivate a person to change behavior during exercise, but it may also increase self-efficacy about one's ability to exercise effectively (thus increasing likelihood of adherence to an exercise program).

Example of computer as persuasive medium

HIV Roulette [www.exploratorium.edu]: A computerized exhibit at the San Francisco Exploratorium allows visitors to make hypothetical choices about sexual behavior and then vicariously experience how those choices would affect their chances of contracting HIV. This exhibit attempts to motivate people to avoid unsafe sexual behaviors.

Example of computer as persuasive social actor

"5-A-Day Adventures" [www.dole5aday.com]: This CD-ROM, designed for children, features a character named HB who guides users through the application. HB encourages users to eat more fruits and vegetables, and he praises them for compliance.

Functional view illuminates affordances

The functional view of persuasive computers offers key insights into the different affordances of persuasive computers. Not only does this framework help differentiate among persuasive computers (as well as among different aspects of a single persuasive technology), but this perspective can also provide researchers with guidance for primary and secondary research efforts.

PERSPECTIVE 3: LEVELS OF ANALYSIS FOR CAPTOLOGY

The third perspective I propose for understanding computers as persuasive technologies is one that directs specific attention to various levels of analysis for both computer use and behavior/attitude change.

Levels of analysis: Not just individuals

Most people think of computer use as it applies to an individual—an individual interacts with or through a computer. The same holds true for notions of persuasion: An individual changes his or her attitudes or behaviors. In both cases, this level of analysis focuses on the individual. Even though both computer use and persuasion are often thought to be most germane to individuals, other levels of analysis besides the individual level can generate important insights in researching and designing computing technologies.

In recent years, HCI researchers have done admirable work in conceptualizing computer use on a level of analysis other than individual [see reference 10 for resources; see also www.acm.org/sigchi/cscw98]. Usually referred to as "computer-supported cooperative work," this area examines computing as it pertains to groups or organizations (group and organizational levels of analysis). It is important for the HCI community to continue defining and exploring the various levels of analysis related to computer use.

The fields of public information campaigns and health promotion interventions have also done notable work in conceptualizing different levels of analysis [e.g., see 1]. The levels of analysis from these fields include—

- intraindividual level
- interindividual level (dyads, couples, friends)
- family level
- group level
- organizational level
- community level
- societal level

To be sure, previous HCI work has examined computing at all of the above levels, but our field can benefit from more clearly differentiating these different levels and from deliberately using these levels more often as a driving force in researching or designing computing technologies. HCI and captology have much to gain from viewing computing from these various levels of analysis.

Different levels of analysis cause different variables to be salient, which generates new insights in research or design. The different levels also draw on different theoretical frameworks, methodologies, and measures. For example, persuasion on the individual level is conceptualized and measured differently than persuasion on the community level. Although examining each level as it applies to persuasive computers is beyond the scope of this paper, Table 3 gives some examples to help illustrate this point.

Level of analysis	Computer artifact, application, or system	Behavior change of interest
individual	Baby Think It Over (A computerized doll that requires care. Designed to teach teens about the difficulties of parenting [www.btio.com])	To motivate an individual to be more sexually responsible so he or she doesn't become a teenage parent.
family	Home video game system (A parent may want her family to interact more with each other rather than passively watching TV.)	To increase family interactions (possibly measured by number of conversations, frequency of eye contact, etc.)
organizational	Remote work system (A computer system that allows people to work effectively from home.)	To reduce absenteeism. To increase employee retention.
community	Ride-sharing system (A community paging network that allows people to coordinate ride sharing with minimal prior planning.)	To reduce the community's use of private cars. To reduce traffic congestion and pollution.

Table 3: Levels of analysis, technologies, and behavioral outcomes

The table shows that, at least in principle, certain technologies are best suited for different levels of analysis—some are individual-level technologies and some are community-level technologies. (Admittedly, today's default view is biased toward computers as individual-level devices; however, advances in online technology are making community and societal interactive technologies more common. To be sure, the rise of the Internet has helped shift our focus to larger levels of analysis.) Furthermore, the table implies that behavior change is not just an individual-level variable: families change, organizations change, and communities change.

Although this section of the paper only begins to explore the benefits of conceptualizing persuasive computers at different levels of analysis, the potential benefit to HCI and captology is substantial. Public information campaign researchers have accomplished much by conceptualizing interventions at different levels of analysis [1, 26]. The same should be true for those of us working in HCI-related fields, especially those interested in researching or designing interactive technologies that promote beneficial social changes [27].

PERSPECTIVE 4: THE DESIGN SPACE FOR PERSUASIVE TECHNOLOGIES

The previous three perspectives propose frameworks for better understanding persuasive computing technologies. Although the ideas from the previous sections serve as analytical tools to study existing persuasive computing technologies, these frameworks can also serve a useful **generative** purpose. In other words, the previous frameworks can help create ideas for new types of persuasive computing technologies. When used for their generative powers, the three previous perspectives contribute to my fourth perspective: the design space for persuasive technologies.

The captology design space is large and relatively unexplored. Because captology presents a new perspective on the role of computers, it is relatively easy to conceptualize new technologies, or to add persuasive enhancements to existing technologies.

To approach this design space methodologically, I propose a two-step process: (1) identify domains and issues of interest, and (2) use the above frameworks to gain new perspectives.

Identifying domains and issues

My searches in the academic literature indicate that most existing computer systems which attempt to change attitudes or behaviors fall into just a few categories: health, mental health, and education [e.g., see 31]. My efforts to identify persuasive interactive technologies in today's marketplace also showed health as a central domain. Of course, health and education are still excellent areas for research and design of persuasive technologies, but many other domains remain relatively unexplored.

When my students and I set out to identify appropriate domains for captology, we first made an extensive list of pervasive social or personal problems. We then clustered the problems and nested them under broader headings. In this exercise we developed a long (though not exhaustive) list of domains in which persuasive computer technologies may serve a useful role. Table 4 contains a brief excerpt from our list (see www.captology.org for more domains).

Domain	Issues
safety	• safe driving • wearing bike helmets • substance abuse
environment	• recycling • conservation • bicycle commuting
personal management	• time management • study habits • personal finance

Figure 4: A sample of domains for persuasive computers

Using captology frameworks

Once a person selects a domain or issue, the next step in exploring the design space for persuasive computers is to use the captology frameworks described in this paper to generate a variety of perspectives and ideas about the selected domain or issue. For example, one might ask the following questions:

Levels of analysis: What do different levels of analysis offer to this issue or problem? Which level of intervention is likely to be most productive?

Functional Triad: What functional areas will the persuasive technology leverage? Should it focus on computer as tool, medium, social actor, or combinations of the three?

Intentionality: For this issue or domain, what are the possibilities for endogenously, exogenously, or autogenously persuasive interactive technologies?

An example of using these frameworks in design exploration follows.

Example: Recycling paper products

For this example, I have chosen **recycling** as the issue to address using persuasive technology. Specifically, this example focuses on recycling paper products.

Levels of analysis perspective: One can profitably conceptualize recycling paper at various levels: individual, family, organization, or community. Of these levels, I have chosen the organizational level for this example. The goal, then, is to explore the possibilities for creating a persuasive technology for increasing paper recycling behavior at the organizational level. (At this point one might then study various issues for more insight: organizational culture, barriers to recycling, etc.)

Functional Triad perspective: One would also explore how the three different functions of computers (tools, media, social actors) might profitably motivate paper recycling behavior. Even on the organizational level, many ideas are possible. For this example, one might propose the following:

A computer acting as a **tool** could weigh the recycled paper in the organization and calculate the number of trees saved from recycling efforts. Other types of calculations are also possible (trees saved per week, oxygen produced by the saved trees, etc.). Knowing this information might motivate people in the organization to recycle their paper products more.

The computer acting as a **medium** could then render an image of a tree growing as paper is added to the recycling container. (The image might be on the recycling container itself.) Seeing the tree grow in size might provide motivation to recycle because the image helps people visualize a cause/effect relationship in recycling.

The computer as **social actor** could audibly thank people each time they added paper to the recycling container. A more extreme idea is to have an anthropomorphic tree that smiles or tells humorous stories in response to recycling efforts.

Intentionality perspective: The recycling technology described above would inherit both **endogenous** persuasive intent (from the designers of the device) and **exogenous** persuasive intent (from the management team that provides the technology for rest of the organization).

To further explore the design space, one might profitably ask, "How might an **autogenously** persuasive technology function in this organizational setting?" Because this design example focuses on the organizational level, autogenous intent would imply that the organization as a whole (not just the management) would choose to adopt a technology to change their collective recycling behavior.

Design explorations generate insight

Exploring the design space for persuasive computers is often an enlightening process. Especially if one has no intentions of turning ideas into marketable products, one can push the envelope of the design space to illuminate new theoretical areas of persuasive computing. As the above example shows, the two-step method of (1) identifying domains/issues and then (2) applying the captology frameworks is a simple process that yields rich—and often surprising—results.

PERSPECTIVE 5: ETHICS OF COMPUTERS THAT PERSUADE

Ethics is yet another perspective from which to view computers as persuasive technologies. Adopting an ethical perspective on this domain is vital because the topic of computers and the topic of persuasion both raise important issues about ethics and values [7, 15, 36]. Therefore, when the domains of computers and persuasion merge (as they do in captology), the ethical issues are sure to play a crucial role. This section presents examples of some ethically questionable technologies, proposes ethical responsibilities for designers of persuasive computers and captology researchers, and discusses the importance of educating about persuasion.

Persuasive technologies that raise ethical questions

Most examples of persuasive computers in this paper are technologies that promote widely held conceptions of the "good" [23]: a computerized doll motivates responsible sexual behavior, a CD-ROM encourages eating fruits and vegetables, a ride-sharing technology cuts down on pollution in a city.

However, persuasive technologies can also serve ignoble purposes. Table 5 contains examples of persuasive computing that may be ethically questionable, along with a brief gain/loss analysis for stakeholders (which is, admittedly, highly subjective).

Summary of persuasive technology in question	Stakeholder analysis
A computerized slot machine uses animation and narration to make the gambling experience more compelling.	**gain**: manufacturer and casinos **loss**: individuals (money, time)
A computer system records employees' activities on the Web.	**gain**: company **loss**: employees (privacy, trust)
A computer system monitors restaurant employees' hand washing behavior after using the restroom.	**gain**: restaurant patrons **loss**: employees (privacy, trust)
A software installation seems to require registration with the company in order to complete the installation. The software automatically dials company to download personal information.	**gain**: company **loss**: individual users (personal information)

Table 5: A simple stakeholder analysis of some persuasive technologies

I believe that the simple gain/loss analysis in Table 5 helps show why the above technologies could be ethically questionable. In most cases above, companies stand to gain profit or information, while individuals stand to lose money, privacy, or freedom. In contrast, a simple gain/loss analysis for the other persuasive computers in this paper would likely show gains for all stakeholders, including individuals.

Ethics of distributing or creating computers to change attitudes or behaviors

The ethical implications for those who design persuasive technologies are similar to the ethical implications for other persuaders in society (e.g., sales people, coaches, counselors, religious leaders, etc.) [15]. Because values vary widely, no single ethical system or set of guidelines will serve in all cases, so the key for those designing persuasive interactive technologies is gaining a sensitivity to the ethical implications of their efforts. High-tech persuaders would do well to base their designs on a defensible ethical standard. At the very least, a few core values should apply to all persuasive computing designs, such as avoiding deception, respecting individual privacy, and enhancing personal freedom.

Ethics of studying persuasive computers

The ethical implications for those who study persuasive computers are somewhat different from those for designers. I propose that those who study persuasive technologies have a responsibility to play a watchdog role for the HCI community, in particular, and for technology users, in general. Ethical actions for those who study persuasive computers fall into four categories:

1. **Identify artifacts and techniques**. By using the various frameworks suggested in this paper, a researcher can better identify persuasive technologies, as well as the persuasive strategies a technology uses.

2. **Examine effectiveness and effects**. Researchers should also assess the effectiveness (the intended impact) and the effects (the unintended side-effects) of persuasive technologies or strategies.

3. **Disclose findings**. Those who study persuasive computers then have an obligation to disclose their findings.

4. **If needed, take or advocate social action**. Finally, if a computing artifact is deemed harmful or questionable in some regard, a researcher should then either take social action or advocate that others do so.

Education is the key

I propose that the best approach regarding the ethics of computers and persuasion is to educate widely about this new area of research and design. Education about captology helps people in two important ways: First, increased knowledge about persuasive computers allows people more opportunity to adopt such technologies to enhance their own lives, if they choose. Second, knowledge about persuasive computers helps people recognize when technologies are using tactics to persuade them. In the end, the best path for captology is the same as the path taken by various persuasion researchers [15, 24, 36]: Educate widely about persuasion. This paper represents one effort to bring such issues to light.

RESEARCH DIRECTIONS FOR CAPTOLOGY

Because captology is a relatively new field of inquiry, many questions about computers and persuasion remain unanswered. To help move the field forward, I propose seven directions for research and design that will yield the greatest understanding of persuasive computers in the shortest amount of time.

Seven profitable directions for captology

Direction A: *Captology should focus on interactive technologies that change behaviors.*

As stated earlier, my definition of persuasion is "an attempt to shape, reinforce, or change behaviors, feelings, or thoughts about an issue, object, or action." Although this is a good definition, it is too broad to be useful in focusing research and design in the early stages of captology. Therefore, at this point people involved in captology would do well to pursue **behavior change** as the test and metric for persuasive computers.

Behavior change is a more compelling metric than attitude change for at least three reasons: (1) behavior change is thought to be more difficult to achieve than attitude change [15, 36], (2) behavior change is more useful to people concerned with real-world outcomes [9, 31, 36], and (3) one can measure behavior change without relying on self-reports [9] (attitude change measures hinge on self-reports).

Direction B: *Captology should follow the well-established CHI tradition of adopting and adapting theories and frameworks from other fields.*

While captology has the potential to generate new theories and frameworks—as demonstrated to some degree in this paper—those of us who study computers as persuasive technologies would do well to find extant persuasion theories and frameworks and investigate how they apply to captology. For example, Aristotle certainly did not have computers in mind when he wrote about the art of persuasion, but the ancient field of rhetoric can apply to captology in interesting ways.

The field of psychology—both cognitive and social—has a tradition of examining different types of persuasion and influence. The theories and methods from psychology transfer well to captology, enriching the field. In addition, the field of communication has a history of examining the persuasive effects of media and other types of message sources. Specifically, the applied domain of public information campaigns has a set of theories and practices that give insight into the study of persuasive computers.

Direction C: *Captology should examine and inform the design of interactive technologies that are specialized, distributed, or embedded.*

While the typical computer of today lives on top of a desk and requires a keyboard and a monitor, people involved in captology would do well to focus mainly on technologies that are **specialized**, **distributed**, or **embedded** [for more on the concept of ubiquitous computing, see references 3 and 34].

From my vantage point, the most interesting interactive technologies today seem to fall in at least one of these three categories. And it seems that most persuasive technologies of the future will not be associated with desktop computers; they will be specialized, distributed, or embedded. If this is true, then it would be a relatively poor use of time to examine existing desktop applications or to design persuasive programs solely for desktop computers. Persuasive situations occur most frequently in the context of normal life activities—not when people are seated at a desktop computer.

Direction D: *Captology should focus on endogenously persuasive technologies.*

I've proposed three types of persuasive technologies: endogenously persuasive (those designed with persuasive goals in mind), exogenously persuasive (those used to persuade another person), and autogenously persuasive (those used to persuade oneself). Understanding **endogenously persuasive technologies** seems more essential to understanding captology than the other two types. According to my definition, endogenously persuasive technologies were created with an intent to change attitudes or behaviors. As a result, the strategies and techniques to persuade are embedded in the technology itself. In contrast, the other two types of persuasive technologies—exogenous and autogenous—rely heavily on external factors for their persuasive power.

Direction E: *Captology can learn from other media but should steer clear of comparing computer persuasion with persuasion from other media.*

Although captology has much to gain from other media research (such as effects of video, print, radio, etc.), comparing computer persuasion with persuasion from other sources seems to be a dead end. Many studies have attempted to do this, and virtually all of them contain serious weaknesses [for a longer discussion of this claim, see 14].

Although a researcher can clearly determine that computer program X is more persuasive than video Y or pamphlet Z, these results hold only for artifacts X, Y, and Z—not for comparing computers, videos, and pamphlets in general. One problem is that too many variables are at play in cross-media studies; as a result, no useful theory comes from this type of research [21].

In order to avoid this well-traveled dead-end road, those involved in captology research should compare the persuasive effects of one aspect of computing technology with other aspects of computing technology.

Direction F: *Captology should focus on both "what is" and "what could be."*

Captology should focus both on existing persuasive technologies and on potential persuasive technologies. A fairly good number of persuasive technologies already exist. Research into the impact, uses, and implications of these technologies can yield valuable insight for the field.

But captology also has a strong generative component. Because this field provides a new lens for viewing computing technology, captology generates insights about novel possibilities for computers, as well as new ways to bring about attitude and behavior changes.

Direction G: *Captology should be pursued with ethical issues and implications in mind.*

The study of computers as persuasive technologies raises important ethical questions. This is understandable and inescapable, given the fact that persuasion has long been an area for ethical debate, and that computer technology has raised recent ethical questions. As with any other means of persuasion, one could compromise values and ethics intentionally or unintentionally. Therefore, those who study persuasive technologies should have a sound understanding of the ethical implications of this field. A subfield on the ethics of persuasive computing is a worthy and important endeavor.

SUMMARY

This paper has defined captology and has articulated five different perspectives for studying computers as persuasive technologies. This paper also proposed seven directions for future research. While these perspectives and research directions may be superseded by better ideas and new perspectives, this paper lays the groundwork for taking significant steps forward in understanding this new field.

ACKNOWLEDGMENTS

Cliff Nass, Byron Reeves, Terry Winograd, and Phil Zimbardo have been instrumental in my work on persuasive computing.

REFERENCES

[1] Atkins, C., & Wallace, L. *Mass Communication and Public Health*. Newbury Park, CA: Sage, 1990.

[2] Bandura, A. *Social Foundations of Thought and Action: A social cognitive theory*. Englewoods Cliffs, NJ: Prentice Hall, 1986.

[3] Buxton, W. "Living in Augmented Reality: Ubiquitous media and reactive environments." Web URL: www.dgp.utoronto.ca/OTP/papers/bill.buxton/augmentedReality.html

[4] Fogg, B.J. & Nass, C.I. "How Users Reciprocate to Computers: An experiment that demonstrates behavior change." In *Extended Abstracts of CHI'97*, ACM Press, p. 331-332.

[5] Fogg, B.J. & Nass, C.I. "Silicon Sycophants: The effects of computers that flatter." *International Journal of Human-Computer Studies* (1997), 46, 551-561.

[6] Fogg, B.J. "Captology: The Study of Computers as Persuasive Technologies." In *Extended Abstracts of CHI'97*, ACM Press, p. 129.

[7] Friedman, B. *Human Values and the Design of Computer Technology*. New York: Cambridge University, 1997.

[8] Friedman, B., and Kahn, P. "Human Agency and Responsible Computing: Implications for Computer Systems Design." *Journal of Systems Software*, 17:7-14, 1992.

[9] Graeff, J., Elder, J., and Booth, E. *Communication for Health and Behavior Change*. San Francisco, CA: Jossey-Bass, 1993.

[10] Honeycutt, L. *Resources on Computer-Supported Cooperative Work*. http://www.dcr.rpi.edu/cscw.html

[11] Huddy, C., Herbert, J., Hyner, G., & Johnson, R. "Facilitating changes in exercise behavior." *Psychological Reports*, 1995, 76(3), 867-875.

[12] Kay, A. "Computer software." *Scientific American, 251*, (1984), 53-59.

[13] Kozma, R. "Learning with media." *Review of Educational Research, 61*, (1991), 179-211.

[14] Kuomi, J. "Media comparison and deployment: A practitioner's view." *British Journal of Educational Technology*, 1994, 25(1), 41-57.

[15] Larson, C. *Persuasion: Reception and responsibility*, 7th ed. Belmont, CA: Wadsworth Publishing, 1995.

[16] Laurel, B. *The Art of Human-Computer Interface Design*. Reading, MA: Addison-Wesley, 1990.

[17] Lieberman, D. "Interactive Video Games for Health Promotion." In *Health Promotion and Interactive Technology*, eds, R. Street, W. Gold, & T. Manning. Mahwah, NJ: Lawrence Earlbaum, 1997.

[18] Marcus, A. "Human communication issues in advances UIs." *Communications of the ACM*, 36(4), 1993, 101-109.

[19] Mutschler, E. "Computer assisted decision making." *Computers in Human Services*. 1990 6(4), 231-250.

[20] Nass, C. I., Fogg, B. J., Moon, Y. "Can computers be teammates?" *International Journal of Human-Computer Studies, 45*, 1996, 669-678.

[21] Nass, C. I. and Mason, L. "On the Study of Technology and Task: A variable-based approach." In J. Fulk & C. Steineld (eds.), *Organizations and Communication Technology*, 46-67. Newbury Park, CA: Sage, 1990.

[22] Patton, P. "User interface design: Making metaphors." *I.D. Magazine*, April, 1993, 62-65.

[23] Rawls, J. *A Theory of Justice*. Cambridge: Harvard University Press, 1971.

[24] Reardon, K. *Persuasion in Practice*. Newbury Park, CA: Sage, 1991.

[25] Reeves, B. & Nass, C. *The Media Equation: How people treat computers, television, and new media like real people and places*. New York: Cambridge University Press, 1996.

[26] Rice, R. and Atkin, C. *Public Communication Campaigns*. Newbury Park, CA: Sage, 1989.

[27] Salmon, C. *Information Campaigns : Balancing social values and social change*. Newbury Park, CA: Sage Publications, 1989.

[28] Schneiderman, B. *Designing the User Interface*. New York: Addison Wesley, 1987.

[29] Sheridan, T. *Telerobotics, Automation, and Human Supervisory Control*. Cambridge, MA: MIT Press, 1992.

[30] Steuer, J. "Defining virtual reality: Dimensions determining telepresence." *Journal of Communication*, 1992, 42(4).

[31] Street, R., Gold, W., and Manning, T. *Health Promotion and Interactive Technology*. Mahwah, NJ: Lawrence Erlbaum, 1997.

[32] Turkle, S. "Who am we?" *Wired Magazine*, 1996, January, 148-202.

[33] Verplank, B., Fulton, J., Black, A., & Moggridge, B. *Observation and Invention: Use of Scenarios in Interaction Design*. Tutorial at INTERCHI'93, Amsterdam, 1993.

[34] Weiser, M. "The computer for the 21st century." *Scientific American*, 1991, 265(3), 94-104.

[35] Winograd, T. "The design of interaction." In P. Denning & R. Metcalfe (Eds.). *Beyond Calculation: The next fifty years of computing* (pp. 149-161) New York: Springer-Verlag, 1997.

[36] Zimbardo, P. and Leippe, M. *The Psychology of Attitude Change and Social Influence*. New York: McGraw Hill, 1991.

Student Readers' Use of Library Documents: Implications for Library Technologies

Kenton O'Hara, Fiona Smith, William Newman & Abigail Sellen
Xerox Research Centre Europe
Cambridge Laboratory
61 Regent St., Cambridge, CB2 1AB, U.K.
<surname>@cambridge.rxrc.xerox.com

ABSTRACT
We report on a study of graduate students conducting research in libraries, focusing on how they extract and record information as they read. By examining their information recording activities within the context of their work as a whole, it is possible to highlight why students choose particular strategies and styles of recording for what these activities provide both at the time of reading and at subsequent points in time. The implications of these findings for digital library technologies are discussed.

KEYWORDS
Reading, annotation, note-making, paper, documents, digital documents, digital libraries, design, information recording

INTRODUCTION
As is shown by the emergence of specialist conferences, research projects, and journals, in recent years there has been a growing interest in the topic of "digital libraries". This growth is set to bring about significant changes in information services and library policies which, in turn, will impact on the work practices of library users. In order to better understand the impact of these changes, it is first necessary to have an understanding of the kind of work that library users carry out. Such an understanding can also guide the design of new digital technologies in support of library work. Hopefully, by doing so, these new technologies can be made more sensitive to the needs and current practices of library users.

The need to understand the requirements and work practices of library users is one that is very much recognised in the literature. Indeed there are many examples of user-centred approaches to the design of technology for the "digital library" [e.g. 4, 8, 17, 20]. However, much of this end-user research generally has a very narrow focus [1]. With the odd exception [e.g. 11, 13], user-centred approaches have concentrated primarily on how users search for and retrieve information. As such, much of the design effort in the field has been aimed at providing support for these activities.

CHI 98 Los Angeles CA USA
Copyright 1998 0-89791-975-0/98/ 4..$5.00

As we will show in this paper, however, there is a great deal more document-related work that occurs once library users have retrieved their documents, and these activities have received far less attention in the literature. By underplaying these activities, the field ignores the need to gain a more comprehensive understanding of the work that library users engage in; more importantly, it ignores how all these document activities have a mutual influence on each other. We would argue that library users' activities need to be examined within the context of their work as a whole if we are to really understand how we can design technology to support them.

The purpose of this paper is to extend our notions of the work of library users by focusing on their reading activities, and more specifically by focusing on their "information recording" activities. By "information recording" we mean the way readers extract and record information from a source text, mainly through notes, annotations and photocopies. Because of this interest, we focus on library users (in this case graduate students) reading for research purposes as a representative sample of intensive library users. We examine their information recording activities within the broader context of their library work so as to highlight the contingencies and motivations that underlie them.

The Literature
The information recording activities of undergraduate students, such as note-making and annotation, have received considerable attention over the last 25 years. Much of this effort has been driven by the "encoding-review" framework of the learning benefits of note-making established by DiVesta and Gray [2] with the aim of identifying the circumstances under which information recording activities have positive, neutral and negative effects on learning behaviour. Particular attention has been devoted to understanding the effects of note-making on learning from lectures. Reviews of the literature [6, 9, 10] have revealed mixed findings, but on the whole, the evidence suggests that when positive effects are demonstrated, reviewing information in one's notes has a stronger influence on learning than the information gleaned during the course of actually making the notes. A smaller effort has extended some of the findings to information recording from text-based information sources. These again have demonstrated some of the

positive effects on learning of information recording activities such as underlining and note-making, with the stronger influence attributed to review aspects [e.g. 5, 7, 12].

This paradigm, while useful in some respects, may be directly responsible for the often conflicting nature of the findings in the field, by not respecting the range of functions that particular information recording strategies may have in different situations [12]. As Van Meter, Yokoi and Pressley [18] have noted, very little effort has been aimed at understanding note-making from the perspective of those who actually undertake the activity in terms of the various contingencies of their work as a whole that motivate their choices on different occasions (some exceptions include [3, 14, 19]). The study reported here is motivated along similar lines to Van Meter et al.'s [18] analysis of students' perspectives of note-making during lectures but focuses on information recording from text-based sources within libraries. Such a perspective can offer ways of generating new hypotheses about the document activities of library users, particularly in relation to annotation and note-making. In doing this, the aim is to help identify new opportunities for improving the design of digital library systems and technologies to support the document activities of library users.

METHOD

Participants

Participants in this study were 25 PhD students in the arts and humanities at Cambridge University at varying stages of their studies. All were volunteers who responded to an advertisement placed in some of the college libraries, and each was paid £25.00 for their participation.

The Libraries

The Cambridge University library system is made up of many libraries dispersed across the city. In addition to the main University Library, which houses the principal collection of materials, there are over 100 libraries linked in some way with the University, with the other major ones being the Scientific Periodicals Library, the University Medical Library, and the Squire Law Library.

Procedure

Participants were asked to complete a diary of their document-related activities during a working day at the library as well as any document-related research activities undertaken elsewhere. They were given pre-printed diary sheets on which to record details about their research activities including: the nature of a research activity, the time taken, the documents and sources used, any accompanying support activities such as note-making or photocopying, and the place where the activity was conducted. At the end of their working day (or the next morning if they worked late in the evening) they were interviewed for approximately 1 hour. The initial part of the interview was used to get a basic sense of the nature of the research being undertaken by participants, in order to help ground the later discussions about their document-related activities. The activities in the diary were then used as a basis from which to guide the remainder of the interview, during which participants were asked to elaborate upon their research activities and the motivations behind them were explored. The interview focused in particular on what, how and why information from the materials in the library was recorded and subsequently used.

A FRAMEWORK

From an initial analysis of the interviews and diary data we found it helpful to first sketch out a high-level model of the document related activities of library users at different stages of their research work (Figure 1). While such a view is clearly over-simplified, it nevertheless demonstrates how scholarly research may be characterised as a complex process of searching, information retrieval, reading, information extraction and recording by annotation and note-taking, information review, and writing new compositions (such as papers or thesis chapters). Many of these processes are iterative and there are potentially large time gaps between different stages, e.g. months or even years. Some of the activities take place in libraries, some at home, and some in other places.

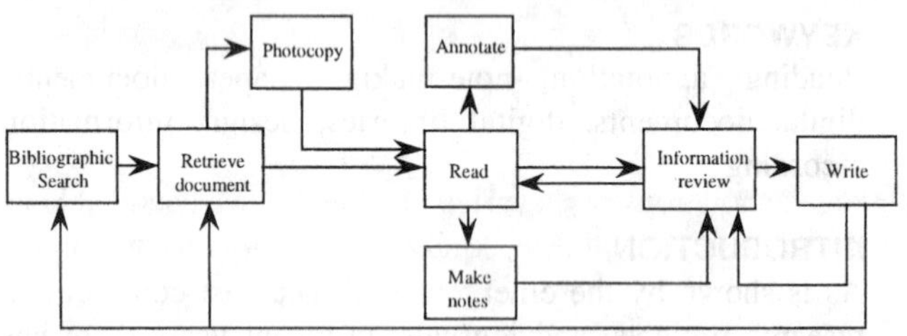

Figure 1. A model of document related activities of library users at different stages of their research work.

Outlining the context of the researchers' work in this way then provided a useful framework within which we could further analyse and understand in more detail the data from the interviews and diaries. It also helped us to understand the interdependencies that may arise within library users' activities, and consequently the choices and decisions that they make. For example, consider a researcher wanting to read a new article in a current periodical that is not available for loan. The researcher must either read it in the library or make a photocopy so as to be able to take it home. Because it is forbidden to mark up the original volume, if no photocopy is made, the researcher cannot annotate the document, but rather must take notes on a separate document so as to get the information home where it is used to help write a thesis chapter. These notes may be on paper or on a laptop. If the notes are on a laptop, this may allow notes and quotations recorded to be directly re-used in the thesis chapter. However, because of the limitations of screen space there will be problems laying out the notes for the purpose of cross referencing while writing. Conversely, if the notes are on paper this may facilitate review, but require information from notes to be re-entered into a computer if used when writing. From this it can be seen how decisions taken during document activities early on in the process can affect document activities at later stages of the researcher's work.

FINDINGS

With this framework in mind, we proceeded to carry out a more in-depth analysis of readers' information recording activities. Here we focus on summarising participants' descriptions of their activities from their diary data, from the interviews we conducted, and from looking at and discussing their notes and annotations. We first present the findings in terms of the *nature* of the information they recorded and then in terms of the various *methods* by which they recorded it. Throughout, we comment on how these activities were shaped by readers' awareness and consideration of the larger context of their research-related document activities.

The nature of the information recorded

Before exploring the issues of just how this information was extracted and recorded, it is first of interest to describe the kinds of information readers were recording in more detail. These we were able to uncover both through the interviews themselves and by "walking through" our researchers' notes and annotations with them.

As is illustrated by the example in Figure 2, the nature of the information recorded by the researchers in their notes and annotations was varied. However, we were able to distinguish four basic kinds of information recorded: paraphrased content, verbatim information, readers' thoughts and ideas in response to a text, and bibliographic information.

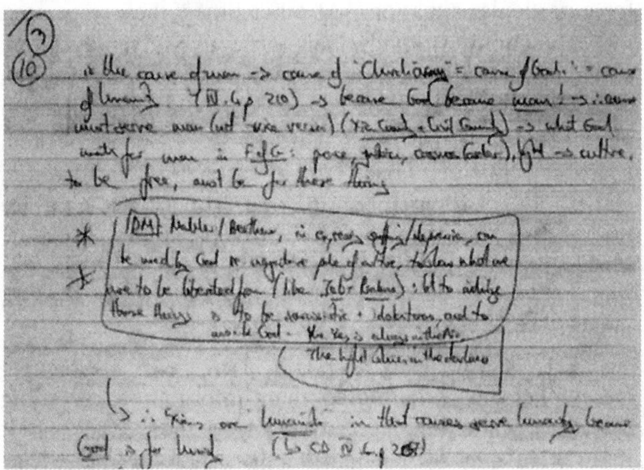

Figure 2. An extract from the notes of a researcher in the study.

Paraphrased Information. The recording of paraphrased material was essentially exclusively done by note-making. Traditional views in the literature have tended to associate the use of paraphrased material with greater cognitive demand than the recording of verbatim information (see [18] for a review). Comments from subjects did indicate that paraphrased information was indeed seen by them as demanding greater cognitive effort, but this in turn was something they claimed facilitated concentration and engagement with a text.

However, this was only one reason for choosing to make paraphrased notes. Other reasons had to do with supporting subsequent review of the notes. For example, a large proportion of readers' notes were made up of paraphrased material from the source text capturing key aspects of the content they thought that they were unlikely to remember later unaided.

The researchers also said that paraphrasing allowed them to convert the content of what they were reading into language that was clearer to them. This not only facilitated the encoding of the information, but also made subsequent review of the information much easier. Paraphrasing was especially flexible here in allowing information to be condensed by varying degrees (ranging from simple rewording to capturing the gist of an article in a single sentence according to the level of detail required). Furthermore, because meaning rather than form was the most important consideration, the paraphrased material was frequently recorded in personalised shorthand (see line 4 in Figure 2: "F of G".) and using graphics in order to reduce the time costs of the information recording.

The researchers also made use of structural organisation here. Most of the hand-written notes we examined were found to be very structured, helping to organise information both for encoding and for review purposes. Various formatting techniques were used, such as colour or underlining to emphasise subtitles and keywords, or to distinguish quotations from paraphrased notes. Indentations and bulleted lists were used to represent and organise ideas of different levels of structural status within the text.

Verbatim Information. Verbatim material was extracted and recorded in notes, as annotations, and through the use of photocopies. In contrast to paraphrased material, the literature has tended to associate verbatim information recording with less cognitive effort and familiarity with content area (see [18] for a review).

However, this view is undermined by the fact that, in the readers' notes we observed, verbatim material was very much interspersed with paraphrased material. It was clear that, for various reasons, participants consciously chose to record certain pieces of information in verbatim format. Further, with verbatim material, while participants did indicate that they thought the actual recording of the information was relatively "brainless", it was clear that the researchers' engagement with the text when choosing the information was a thoughtful and deliberate process.

One reason our researchers gave in choosing to record information verbatim was in anticipation of quoting it in their own written work. For this reason, participants were often very specific about bibliographic details, and putting page numbers against quotations was common. Quotations within notes also acted as objects which they could then refer to, allowing the nature of the researchers' own comments and ideas to be more indexical in style. That is, the verbatim extract often formed the context that was then "pointed to" by a reader's comments.

Our sample of researchers was also aware that their views, ideas and interpretations would sometimes change over time. This was another factor that they stated in deciding to make verbatim recordings. Verbatim text allowed them to "revisit" a text or sections of a text within the context of new knowledge and to check or modify their initial interpretation of the text.

Finally, another reason participants gave for verbatim recording was to record texts where the texts themselves were the objects of analysis. Important information might be contained within the style of a text and an author's use of particular words and phrases, rather than just in the ideas represented by the text. In such cases, a high level of accuracy was required in the recording process, so as not to lose the subtleties or distort the meaning.

Readers' Remarks. Interspersed with the paraphrased and verbatim information made directly from the source text were the readers' own thoughts, ideas and critical views in response to the text. The recording of these thoughts, comments and ideas was often not necessarily specified in any complete or grammatical manner. Rather, they seemed inextricably bound to ideas in the text and knowledge in the readers' heads, their purpose being to cue this information rather than to record it in some final form that could be directly re-used. As such, both style and meaning of such remarks was extremely personalised.

With hand-written notes, many of the researchers were careful to make sure that their own thoughts and ideas were visually distinct from those of the author by using various mechanisms such as colour, asterisks, initials and square brackets to make (see Figure 2.). Reasons given for this included the need to avoid plagiarism when using notes for writing as well a way of making these remarks immediately discernable when reviewing them before writing.

Readers' thoughts and ideas were also recorded as annotations, which were generally placed in the margins of the (mainly photocopied) document. As with the hand-written notes, the nature of these annotations was not such that they recorded large amounts of information in any complete manner. Rather, single words or brief incomplete phrases were used, the meaning of which was dependent upon the textual context within which they were placed. The parts of the text to which they were tied was indicated by spatial coproximity, as well as underlined or circled portions of text, both in combination and isolation. Remarks or thoughts written in the margins were therefore not separately interpretable, but rather derived their meaning from their combination.

Bibliographic Information. The recording of bibliographic information was of two kinds. The first related to the document being read at the time. Many participants were careful to invest time and effort at the reading stage to record the full bibliographic details associated with their source materials such as title and page numbers of the source text (see the circled "10" in Figure 2.). This was partly to construct the bibliography of subsequent writings such as research papers and partly to enable reference back to the original sources for contextual clarification if necessary. The second form of bibliographic information recorded related to potentially useful articles cited in the source text. This was to facilitate subsequent search and retrieval of new material at some later time, the researchers not generally wanting to interrupt their current tasks more than was necessary.

Methods of recording information

As we have already seen, recording information can be broadly categorised as involving note-making, annotating texts, and photocopying texts (often for subsequent annotation or note-making purposes). Although participants had their preferred methods, these tended not to be used in any mutually exclusive fashion. Rather, each researcher would use a mixture of these different methods in an attempt to optimise the level of functionality they would attain from their information recording activities, both at that time of reading and when subsequently reviewing or using the information.

Sometimes different methods were treated as alternatives with the relative trade-offs being consciously calculated for a particular situation. At other times, they were used in conjunction to provide their respective advantages and compensate for respective disadvantages. For example, some participants made notes but still kept backup photocopies of the source texts in case it became necessary to refer back to it later for clarification, elaboration, or re-interpretation of information. A further reason was that some notes were not written to allow interpretation in isolation from the photocopied text but rather would make indexical reference to information in the photocopy.

Researchers also monitored their information recording activities while reading and changed them mid-task if they were felt to be inefficient. For example, one researcher reported that because her notes became too detailed while reading a particular text she decided to stop taking notes and photocopy it. The following discussion aims to set out the major characteristics of the different methods which impact on readers' decision making about the optimal strategy for recording information.

Annotation. Annotating a text was seen as a time efficient way of focusing the reader's concentration on a text by engaging the reader in a dialogue with the text. The recording of information could be done very quickly when compared with hand-written notes, making annotation a favourable choice in time critical situations and when large amounts of information needed to be read. Annotations were quick because comments could be made with reference to a pre-existing text using pointers and indexes to that text. For this reason, annotation was viewed by some of the researchers as more "continuous" with the reading itself, requiring fewer shifts in concentration than with note-taking. However, some researchers viewed it as less beneficial than note-making in terms of encoding the important information from the text.

> "I prefer to annotate and underline, basically, because it's less hassle, but I don't mind writing things as long as it's not too much. I just feel that taking hand-written notes is really slow and I think it's OK if you have to learn it - then it's good to write it out by hand. But if you don't have to actually learn it, and it's just for research and no one is examine you on it, then I prefer to zap across it with a highlighter."

Annotation was also sometimes chosen because of the way that it supported information review. Firstly, it reduced the amount of material that required review by allowing readers to select out important material at the time of reading. In addition, annotations could be easily distinguished from the source text when re-reading, thereby facilitating the retrieval of important points and comments. Furthermore, the co-proximity of the context and markings was seen by some researchers as useful, in that it made the source text and recorded information easy to integrate. The source text also provided additional context for clarification and elaboration of material when reviewing information. However, because annotations were necessarily tied to the text, they could not be collated and offered little in the way of re-organising material in the text. Additionally, limited space would sometimes restrict the detail with which thoughts and comments could be made. While this facilitated the quick recording of ideas, it sometimes made comments difficult to understand during later review, which also impacted on its choice as a recording technique.

Owing to the restrictions on writing on library texts (though these were not strictly adhered to), the use of annotations to record information from library texts often required the researcher to first obtain a photocopy of the source text on which they could then write. As such, this method of recording information would often incur financial and temporal costs that restricted its use in some circumstances.

Note-making. Like annotations, notes were used because of the way that they encouraged dialogue with the text and thereby the processing of the information in the text.

> "If I have a pencil in my hand or something and can jot in the book...I find it helps me concentrate... I think a lot of writing it down is just to fix it in my head really."

Notes offered the researchers greater flexibility over the nature of information recorded (e.g. a choice of paraphrased over verbatim material), the detail in which it was recorded, and over the organisation of the information. The organisation was considered important for the researchers in terms of encoding and review functions of information recording. Notes could be used to bring information from disparate sources together in a unified format and to condense information, making re-reading and cross-referencing during writing more efficient. Notes were also chosen because they did not cause any permanent damage the source text.

While generally more time consuming than making annotations, the financial costs of note-making were dramatically less than photocopying and annotation. In some circumstances, however, making hand-written notes was also seen as less time consuming. For example, recording small amounts of information from a text such as a short quote or a few key points would often not justify the costs of a trip to the photocopier to allow annotation.

> "So I think "Do I get up, go down 3 flights of stairs, go off and get a photocopy card, stand in a queue for the photocopier, just to photocopy this one page. And so often I will just write it out because its actually quicker just to write it out rather than go though all that."

Nevertheless, there was evidence that researchers would choose to incur the time costs of note-making because they believed that taking notes forced them to think about exactly what was relevant and to encouraged deeper processing of the information. This, in turn, would make the information easier to review at the point when it came to be used. As the comment below illustrates, there was a belief that quicker, easier ways of recording information counteracted these benefits:

> "In a way having the technology to be able to photocopy, write, scan - in a way it makes you do too much. If you can do things fast you tend to do things more. You tend not to think about it and have hard criteria about what you actually choose to write."

For the majority of participants, notes tended to be hand-written on paper of various formats (only 2 subjects used a laptop for note-making). One reason for this was related to how they would subsequently use their notes. For example, notes were often used during the writing process for planning and cross-referencing. Previous studies have shown how paper is generally the preferred medium for supporting these kinds of activities [15] and this was consistent with the preferences of the researchers studied here.

> "I have the file open, I take a lot of these sheets out and spread them all around... using some paper [for reference], writing on others and occasionally looking for references."

A further reason for using paper notes was that, as an information recording medium, paper notes were easily transferable across work locations (although, of course, this was not always true of the sources). For example, one participant continued working on a particular research activity that was started earlier in one library, while staffing the issue desk later in a different library. Another researcher used reference cards to record the details of articles or references that she came across while reading, whether at home or in the library.

Photocopying. Photocopying a text provided researchers with a personal resource that removed various constraints, such as borrowing restrictions, availability, and the ability to mark up texts. It also provided researchers with greater flexibility over when, where and how they interacted with a text. Photocopying was seen as a time efficient way of recording large amounts of information but not very suitable for recording small text extracts. This was due to the relatively large costs of going to the photocopier and queuing. Additionally, photocopying small amounts of information was sometimes seen as a problem from the point of view of organisation within a larger set of notes. In some circumstances, the photocopied text would stand alone as a resource but, in general, photocopies formed the basis for further information recording such as annotation and note-making

A number of participants stated that they would only photocopy those texts that they felt were particularly important and that they would be likely to refer back to or which were particularly dense with information. Other decision criteria were based on the text type. For example, one participant stated that she would only photocopy information from primary sources and not from secondary sources, while another participant would only photocopy those articles which reviewed a particular subject area. The physical characteristics of a text also affected participants' photocopying decisions; articles from large, heavy bound journal volumes were sometimes photocopied to avoid have to carry the complete volume home.

Summary: Functions of Information Recording

In summary, careful examination of *what* information readers record in libraries, and *how* they record that information reveals a range of different purposes they are serving in the course of their research work as a whole. Some of these are tied to the immediate context of the reading task itself, while others are more temporally removed from the reading and recording context to some subsequent point in time for use of that information. The important point here is not just that there were multiple purposes that motivated information recording, but rather that researchers were aware of the complex inter-relationship between these goals and the nature, format and medium used for their information recording.

Information recording to focus attention and facilitate encoding. One way in which information recording supported participants' learning was that it encouraged them to focus attention on the text and to maintain a level of concentration necessary for understanding. The task of information recording demanded more active involvement with the information in the text, creating a deeper level of cognitive processing that facilitated encoding. This was not just due to the task of selecting the important ideas but also the critical assessment of these ideas. In addition, by recording their own thoughts and ideas in response to the text, participants linked this information to their existing framework of knowledge.

Information recording for clarification and interpretation. Certain information recording activities were used for the purposes of clarification and interpretation. Translations of foreign words or paraphrasing of obtuse language was one level at which clarification might be provided. A second level was the use of information organisation (e.g. bulleted lists) to clarify information in the text, such as making it clearer for the reader to understand and encode.

Information recording for mapping out directions for literature review. New references and directions to pursue were often found when reading, which needed to be followed up at a later date. By recording these bibliographic details through highlighting, note-making, or making reference cards, the researchers mapped out a means by which they could span the related literature in the future. Such information could also act as a reminding device, prompting a researcher to go and look up certain articles. The bibliographic information recorded itself became the subject of annotation at these later points in time, for example, the shelf location information was written against it.

Information review and re-use. Reviewing information at some later point in time was one of the reasons for making notes. These notes were used to re-acquaint researchers with a corpus of material, which, in some cases, might have been brought together from disparate sources to form a single source. The review of information was considered by researchers as important for learning and in preparation for writing a new document. Recorded information might also be used during the writing process for the purpose of cross-referencing, as well as the direct use of recorded information such as quotations and bibliographic references.

A portable resource. Another reason for information recording was to researchers to transcend the constraints of the various locations in which they either wanted or needed to work. Recording information provided participants with a personal resource, the use of which was not restricted by opening hours, borrowing rights or availability. It allowed information to be transported to different locations, thereby allowing participants the freedom and flexibility to work with the information whenever, wherever and in whichever ways that they wanted. For example, a number of researchers had word processors at home on which they wrote new documents. By recording information of texts stored in the library, the researchers could the move the information from its source location (library) to where it was to be used to support writing (e.g. home).

DISCUSSION AND IMPLICATIONS FOR DIGITAL LIBRARY TECHNOLOGIES

This study has shown how we can offer a more comprehensive understanding of library users by examining their various document activities within the broader framework of their work as a whole. In particular, it has helped demonstrate the sometimes complex inter-relationships between information recording behaviour and other aspects of research work such as reading, information review, writing, and information search. It has shown how researchers' awareness of these interrelationships can have an impact on their information recording behaviour. Further, it has begun to help us map out the space of decision making criteria (e.g. time costs, financial costs, accuracy, level of retention resulting from recording information etc.) that govern such things as what information is recorded, in how much detail, the type of recording method, and the medium used.

From a design perspective, this type of understanding provides a useful resource with which to think about and critically assess the role of technologies in libraries at several different levels. At a relatively simple level, by allowing us to specify a range of document related activities that take place within a library during the course of academic research, the analysis has highlighted new areas where we might consider introducing technological support for the researcher in the library.

At another level, where the analysis has addressed the relationships and mutual dependencies between different activities, it becomes possible for us to consider how technologies designed to support one particular activity (e.g. note-making) may have knock-on consequences for the performance of other activities at different stages of the research process (e.g. information review). This allows us to consider the impact of technologies on the outcome of the research process as a whole which, after all, is the ultimate concern of the user.

Finally, by highlighting the parameters within which researchers make their decisions about their research behaviour at different stages of the research process we can delimit the design space with a richer set of criteria to be considered when developing new technologies. Additionally, while some of these decision making parameters remain difficult to measure in any meaningful and controlled manner, they can nevertheless provide the means by which to think about the evaluating of the introduction of new technologies into libraries.

To illustrate, let us consider the following example where a researcher is making notes from a paper text. For any verbatim piece of text to be recorded, the transcription process is tedious and time consuming. At the first level this suggests that a potentially useful technology might be a hand held scanner, for example, because it could save time spent transcribing.

If we go on to consider the second level where the relationships and mutual dependencies are considered, the use of a handheld scanner affects other aspects of the note-making and research process:

- By shifting the researcher to on-line note-making, it becomes more difficult to create the more free-form and idiosyncratic style of paraphrased information and reader comments that might normally be interleaved with verbatim information.
- Difficulties may be caused during the search and retrieval stages when the reader needs to takes notes to a catalogue and annotate them with shelf location information which can subsequently be taken to the shelf as a memory aid.
- At the information review stage, certain benefits may result from having notes on-line such as the ability to search notes electronically but difficulties may arise when trying to read the notes in any intensive way which is likely at this stage [15].
- At the writing stage, having verbatim information on-line will be of benefit when incorporating a quotation within the researcher's written work by obviating the need to retype. However costs may come about from the need to check for OCR accuracy. Also at this stage having information on-line may lead to problems for information organsiation and cross-referencing where notes need to be laid out in space [15]. This may require the information to be printed out on paper.

Moving on to the level of the decision parameters such as time costs, financial costs, accuracy of recording and extent to which information is retained due to information recording, we can think about the situation in the following terms:

- The hand held scanner can reduce time that would be spent transcribing but is likely to increase time spent creating free-form paraphrased notes and comments by making it more cumbersome.
- It could be argued that by reducing the time cost to record verbatim information (and potentially the financial cost of photocopying) the researcher may become less selective in terms of the amount of information recorded. This can have a negative impact on the processing of information in the text and therfore the extent to which it is retained beyond the recording stage.
- Consequently, time spent reviewing may increase by making review more necessary and by reducing familiarity with the information space such that the researcher spends more time trying to locate information in the notes.
- By having the notes on-line, time costs may be reduced through electronic search but this needs to be traded off against the ease of manipulating and arranging paper notes. This could be overcome by printing out the notes but this merely transfers financial cost to another stage of the research process.
- At the writing stage, time costs may be saved having information in electronic form for easy re-use in new

compositions. However, this needs to be weighed up against time spent checking for and correcting errors from imperfect OCR accuracy.

This illustrative example clearly involves a certain amount of speculation, but nonetheless we would argue that this framework provides a more systematic way of analysing the potential impact of new library technologies.

CONCLUSIONS

The study has shown how it is useful to take a broader view of library use which goes beyond information access; in this case considering the whole range of activities that involve information recording and extraction which happen once library users have found the books and documents they want. Further, we have shown that by examining information recording within the context of researchers' work as a whole, we can gain new insights into the motivations and decision parameters that influence the nature of research activities as well as the mutual dependencies and interrelationships between different stages of the research process. While the study focussed on a small subset of library users, namely postgraduate students in the arts and humanities, the activities uncovered would appear to be common to more general forms of document intensive work. As such the implications should have more wider applicability. We hope that the study has provided a useful way to help designers to think about design and evaluation of new technologies for supporting library work in a digital future.

REFERENCES

1. Barry, C. (1996) The Digital Library: The needs of our users. *Proceedings of International Summer School on the Digital Library*, 5th Aug., 1996, Tilburg University, The Netherlands.

2. DiVesta, F.J. and Gray, S.G. (1972) Listening and notetaking. *Journal of Educational Psychology, 64,* 278-287.

3. Erickson, T. (1996) The design and Long Term Use of a Personal Electronic Notebook: A Reflective Analysis. *Proceedings of CHI '96, Conference on Human Factors in Computing Systems, Vancouver*

4. Fox, E.A., Hix, D. Nowell, L.T., Brueni, D.J., Wake, W.C. and Heath, L.S. (1993) Users, User Interfaces, and Objects: Envision a Digital Library. *Journal of the American Society for Information Science, 44,* 480-491.

5. Haenggi, D. & Perfetti, C.A. (1992) Individual Differences in Reprocessing of Text. *Journal of Educational Psychology, 84,* 182-192.

6. Hartley, J. (1983) Notetaking Research: Resetting the Scoreboard. *Bulletin of the British Psychological Society, 36,* 13-14

7. Kardash, C.A. & Kroeker, T.L. (1989) Effects of time of review and test expectancy on learning from text. *Contemporary Educational Psychology, 14,* 323-335.

8. Kiestra, M.D. Stokmans, M.J.W. and Kamphuis, J. (1994) End-users searching the on-line catalogue: the influence of domain and system knowledge on search patterns. *Electronic Library, 12,* 335-343.

9. Kiewra, K.A. (1985) Investigating note-taking and review: A depth of processing alternative. *Educational Psychology, 8,* 336-374.

10. Kiewra, K.A. (1989) A review of note-taking: the encoding storage paradigm and beyond. *Educational Psychology Review, 1,* 147-172.

11. Levy, D. and Marshall, C. (1995) Going Digital: A look at Assumptions Underlying Digital Libraries. Communications of the ACM, 38(4), 77-84.

12. Lonka, K. Lindblom-Yvonne, S. and Maury, S. (1994) The effect of study strategy on learning from text. *Learning and Instruction, 4,* 253-277.

13. Marshall, C. (1997) Annotation: from paper books to the digital library. *Proceeding of Digital Libraries '97*, Philadelphia, Pennsylvania.

14. Monty, M. L. (1990) *Issues for supporting notetaking and note using in the computer environment.* Doctoral Dissertation, University of California, San Diego.

15. O'Hara, K. and Sellen, A.J. (1997). A Comparison of Reading Paper and On-line Documents. *Proceedings of CHI '97, Conference on Human Factors in Computing Systems,* Atlanta, GA.

16. Adler, A., Gujar, A., Harrison, B., O'Hara, K. and Sellen, A.J. (1997) A Diary Study of Daily Reading Activities: Design Implications for Digital Reading Devices. CHI '98, proceedings, Los Angeles, CA

17. Smithson, 1994; Information Retrieval Evaluation in Practice: A Case Study Approach. *Information Processing and Management, 30,* 205-221.

18. Van Meter, P., Yokoi, L. and Pressley, M. (1994) College students' theory of note-taking derived from their perception of note-taking. *Journal of Educational Psychology, 86,* 323-338.

19. Wilcox, L.D., Schilit, B.N. and Sawney, N.(1997) Dynomite: A Dynamically Organised Ink and Audio Notebook. *Proceedings of CHI '97, Conference on Human Factors in Computing Systems,* Atlanta, GA.

20. Wood, F., Ford, N., Miller, D., Sobczyk, G. and Duffin, R. (1996) Information Skills, searching Behaviour and cognitive styles for student learning: a computer assisted approach. *Journal of Information Science, 22,* 79-92.

A Diary Study of Work-Related Reading: Design Implications for Digital Reading Devices

Annette Adler [1], Anuj Gujar [1], Beverly L. Harrison [1], Kenton O'Hara[2], Abigail Sellen[2]

[1] Xerox Palo Alto Research Center
3333 Coyote Hill Rd.
Palo Alto, CA. 94304, USA
<adler, agujar, beverly>@parc.xerox.com

[2] Xerox Research Centre Europe
(formerly Rank Xerox Research Centre)
61 Regent St., Cambridge, CB2 1AB, UK
<ohara, sellen>@xrce.xerox.com

(Authors are listed alphabetically)

ABSTRACT
In this paper we describe a diary study of how people read in the course of their daily working lives. Fifteen people from a wide variety of professions were asked to log their daily document activity for a period of 5 consecutive working days. Using structured interviews, we analysed their reading activities in detail. We examine the range of reading activities that our subjects carried out, and then present findings relating to both common characteristics and variation across the sample. From these findings, we discuss some implications for the design of digital reading devices.

KEYWORDS
reading, writing, paper documents, digital document readers, design, diary study, field study, electronic books, virtual paper, user behaviour

INTRODUCTION
Technological advances in recent years have meant that digital display media are becoming more "paper-like". Wireless, lightweight digital displays are now more mobile and portable than ever. The quality and readability of the screens themselves are quickly approaching the brightness, resolution and contrast of plain paper. New techniques for stylus-based entry are making possible more paper-like interactions, such as allowing richer and more flexible mark-up and manipulation of digital documents.

Such advances have sparked a flurry of interest in developing digital devices for reading, as evidenced by a growing number of new projects using terms such as "portable document reader", "electronic book", "electronic encyclopaedia", "virtual paper", and "electronic paper". However, developers of these devices are faced with some difficult decisions. If they are to design devices for reading, what are the kinds of reading they should aim to support, who are the people that they should support, and how should they best support these reading activities? The fundamental problem is that the task of "reading" is far too general and ubiquitous: reading takes on a range of forms, is done for a variety of purposes, and is embedded within and related to many other document-based activities. These activities, of course, will also vary depending on whether one is considering reading at work or at home, and will depend on the kind of work environment one considers.

The purpose of the study reported in this paper is to begin to answer these questions in a systematic, empirical way, within real work settings. While not discounting reading for leisure, this study focuses on work-related activities, whether they happen "at work" or in the home. We deliberately chose a sample of people who have very different types of jobs, across a range of different vertical markets. We did this because we were interested in exploring the range and diversity of work-related reading activities, as well as any commonalities that might nonetheless emerge despite this diversity. Our approach was to ask subjects to keep daily logs of their document activities, and then to unpack and expand these descriptions through structured interviews (a method successfully used previously, e.g., [2, 9]).

From this diary study comes a rich database of both descriptive materials as well as quantitative measures. In this paper, we present some selected findings addressing the following issues, which we feel have important implications for the design of digital devices for reading:

- A description and taxonomy of the range of reading activities and writing activities that occurred in the working lives of our sample.
- A discussion of common findings across our sample, most notably the predominance of reading in conjunction with writing, the predominance of paper-based document activity, and the degree to which reading activities occurred across multiple, independent reading surfaces.
- A discussion of the ways in which these people in different professions varied with respect to their reading activities.

Throughout these discussions we draw attention to what these findings mean in terms of design requirements for devices which aim to support on-line reading.

The Literature
To our knowledge there are no existing studies that attempt to characterise and quantify the range of reading activities that occur within real work settings, especially with an eye to the design of new technologies. There have been many attempts in the management science and business literature

CHI 98 Los Angeles CA USA

to analyse the various activities of office workers (see [4], for a review), but such analyses do not focus on reading activities, *per se*.

There is also a great deal of literature within psychology and human factors exploring the issue of how people read. Within psychology, the emphasis is mainly on modelling the reading process for specific kinds of reading tasks, and in strictly controlled laboratory situations. Having said that, there have been attempts to develop taxonomies of reading activity ([5, 6]). However, these are not derived from work settings and are more concerned with theoretical rather than practical implications of this categorisation. Within human factors, studies of reading do concern themselves with the practical application of reading, but much of the emphasis concerns on-line versus paper-based reading (e.g, see [1, 3]), again most frequently using short laboratory tasks testing psycho-perceptual parameters.

METHOD

Pilot Study

In order to develop a taxonomy of reading activities and to refine our methodology, we first ran a pilot study using 10 members of our respective laboratories, including ourselves, as "subjects". The initial taxonomy of reading activities was developed using a search of the literature [7]. Pilot subjects logged their document activities for 5 consecutive days (50 days worth of data). We then applied our taxonomy to each of these logs. All five co-authors discussed the data and the categories assigned, to produce consistency in the application of our taxonomy and some degree of inter-judge reliability. Based on these data, we refined the categorisation scheme, and developed a set of questions to ask our subjects in follow-up interviews. As a result of this pilot study, we also found it important to develop a taxonomy of writing activities in order to capture the range and extent to which writing occurred in conjunction with reading.

Choice of Subjects

This study was intended to be exploratory and, as such, we wished to gather broad and rich information about diverse reading activities that people carried out related to their work, across a wide variety of professions, representing a range of vertical markets.[1] In choosing subjects, we also took account of three factors for which we wanted a representative range:

- Mobility: We selected people whose jobs were predictably mobile across several locations (e.g., surgeon, anaesthetist, lawyer), unpredictable in terms of location (e.g., contract airline pilot, real estate agent), and generally centrally based in one location (e.g., accountancy assistant, warden).
- Location: We selected people from a variety of "activity locations" such as traditional offices, retail offices, home offices (i.e., self employed or working from home), and other work sites (e.g., cars, client sites, operating rooms).
- Collaboration: We selected people who were different in the extent to which their work habits involved synchronous collaboration. Subjects worked as part of a tightly organised team (e.g., surgeon, organ transplant ward co-ordinator/nurse), loosely organised shifts (e.g., warden), or groups (e.g., lawyers). In other cases, subjects were primarily independent workers (e.g., optician, architect, real estate agent).

These criteria were partly derived from previous marketing analysis for portable document reading devices. They also represented issues the co-authors felt to be of critical importance to reading behaviour in this exploratory investigation. Based on these criteria, our final subject pool comprised: a contract airline pilot, a general surgeon, an organ transplant ward coordinator/nurse, two anaesthetists, a residential architect, a real estate agent, two lawyers (a director and an associate), a warden of a half-way house, an accountancy assistant, an optician, a marketing manager, an executive from a small start-up company, and a social worker.

Diary Method

Fifteen subjects were asked to log their daily document activities during the course of their working day, for five consecutive days. It was explained that by "document" we meant any sort of document, whether it be paper-based documents ranging from books to post-it notes, or electronic documents ranging from computer-based documents to the use of pagers or palmtops. We focused on documents that required the reading or writing of text. We asked subjects to log any document activity, not just reading activities. Further, we asked them to estimate the duration of each activity and to note this down on their log forms.

At the end of each day, an interviewer used a structured form in order to expand on the description of each activity and to note down more details such as what types of documents were used, whether the activity was collaborative, where the activity occurred, and what additional tools were used. Interviews typically took from 1/2 hour to 3 hours, depending upon the number of activities listed for the day.

By the end of the study we had 72 days worth of data across subjects. (The nurse worked only a 3-day shift, and the start-up executive 4 days that particular week.)

DATA ANALYSIS

The first step in the analysis was to apply our reading and writing taxonomies to the data. Classification of subjects' document activities into reading and writing categories relied, as much as possible, on subjects' own descriptions of their activities. However, in some cases, it was necessary to break down a single activity (as described by a subject) into multiple sub-tasks if the activity noted was discovered to involve multiple, distinct reading and writing components. As much as possible this was done within the context of the interviews and through discussion with the subjects.

Initial classification for both reading and writing activities was carried out by the interviewer of each subject. However, this was done with all experimenters/interviewers present so that ambiguous or difficult classifications could be discussed and agreed upon. Several sample logs were done jointly by all experimenters to ensure consistency in the

[1] Clearly at some future point, deeper investigation of any one of these professions using many representative subjects would be of value. As it stands, with the possible exception of our cluster of medical professionals, this small and varied sample makes it impossible to generalise about any one professional group in particular. However, patterns across the whole sample are particularly suggestive given this diversity.

application of categories. Because this was an exploratory study with no specific *a priori* hypotheses in mind, we did not attempt to establish more formal inter-rater reliability using independent judges. We found that the reading and writing taxonomies could be unambiguously applied to most activities, though in some cases multiple categories needed to be applied to a single activity. Generally, the five experimenters felt that the categorisations were consistently applied, and any inconsistencies that did arise were "caught" and corrected in the course of the many subsequent analyses we carried out.

In order to obtain quantitative data on what proportion of their time subjects spent carrying out different reading or writing activities, the times associated with each activity involving reading and/or writing were analysed. Early in the course of the study we found it was difficult to obtain separate timing data for reading and writing within any given document-related activity. For example, a subject could tell us they spent 80 minutes reading and annotating a document, but not just how much of that time was spent reading as opposed to writing within that activity. Thus, we had little choice but to use the overall total duration of the document activity reported for each of the reading and writing sub-components. This means that the quantitative data we report will tend to overestimate the *actual* reading and writing times that occurred. However, the data reported do give an indication of the amount of time that people spent engaged in activities in which reading or writing activities either featured strongly, or acted in a supportive role.

RESULTS AND DISCUSSION

In general, if we assume a 40 hour work week for our subjects, we found that the document-related activity time they reported accounted for an average of approximately 82% of their working week, ranging from 23% (for the nurse) to 94% (the accountancy assistant). Such figures are comparable (though somewhat lower) to findings for knowledge workers in a "document-intensive" work setting [9]. Clearly, even in our diverse sample, document-related activities played an integral and central role in people's work, regardless of profession.

Reading in order to identify (ID) Glancing at a document only in order *to identify* which document it is.

Skimming (SK) Reading rapidly in order to establish *a rough idea of what is written*, and to decide whether anything is useful, or whether anything needs to be read in more detail later.

Reading own text to remind (REM) Reading *specifically* in order to remind oneself of what to do next, e.g., a To Do list, shopping list, Post-It note.

Reading to search/answer questions (SAQ) Reading to search for particular information: to answer a question, for reference, or to obtain information necessary to make a decision. *Goal-directed: the reader is sampling information in the text which satisfies the goal of the search.* Ranges from very simple goals to complex decision-making or problem-solving tasks.

Reading to self inform (SI) Reading for the purpose of furthering general knowledge *without any specific goal to which the information will be applied.*

Reading to learn (LE) Reading with the goal of being able to relate or apply information at a later date. This can refer to reading to review the basic concepts for discussion, or it can be much more reflective in nature.

Reading for cross-referencing (CR) Cross-referencing documents in order to integrate information. Includes reading from multiple sources or reading from one source. It can be for the purpose of writing, and may well include some editing activities.

Reading to edit or critically review text (ED) Reading in order to monitor what has been written in terms of content, style, grammar, syntax, and/or overall presentation. Includes editing one's own text, seeing how one's own text fits into a collaborative document, or the review of the text of others.

Reading to support listening (LI) Reading in order to support listening to someone else talk (e.g., following a presentation by looking at a series of slides).

Reading to support discussion (DI) Referring to text during a discussion in order to establish a mutual frame of reference and focus for discussion. Usually takes place in a synchronous collaborative situation (e.g., sitting around a table).

Figure 1. Categories of reading used in the analysis.

Reading Categorisation

Within subjects' document-related activities, reading occurred on average in 70% of them, pointing to the importance and also ubiquity of this kind of document activity. It is perhaps not surprising, then, that reading takes on many different forms within our data. The taxonomy of reading activities that we applied is described in Figure 1.[2]

The percent of time spent on document activities in which these reading activities occurred is shown in Figure 2, averaged across all 15 subjects. This includes activities where reading occurred by itself and where reading occurred in conjunction with writing.

As can be seen, the reading that occurred in our sample covers a broad spectrum of activity. For example, they range from "lightweight" sorts of reading activities such as quick glances to identify documents (ID), skimming (SK), and reading to remind (REM), to more intensive sorts of reading such as reading to learn (LE) or reading to edit text (ED). The reading activities reported also covered a range of different kinds of goals such as reading to search or answer questions (SAQ) or reading to self-inform (SI). They occurred in situations where people were working alone, as in reading to learn (LE), or in group situations, as in reading to supporting listening (LI) or discussion (DI).

Sketching out this range of reading activities has a general message for designers of digital reading devices which is that it is vital to understand precisely what is meant by supporting "reading". As varied as these categories are, the requirements for supporting one type of reading as opposed to another can be quite different. From Figure 2, we can see that for much of the work day, our subjects were involved in rapid and goal directed types of reading such as skimming (SK) and searching to answer questions (SAQ). This points to the need to consider digital reading devices that support fast and flexible search, manipulation and navigation. The predominance of cross-referencing activity points to the

[2] While our original taxonomy derived from the literature contained additional categories (e.g., reading in order to tell a story, reading for enjoyment, reading to follow instructions), the above list resulted from practical application to the work-related activities produced by our subjects. No doubt other categories might be necessary with a different sample of people, or in looking at reading for leisure, for example.

need for multi-document manipulation and viewing capabilities (CR). Finally, the high frequency of reading in support of discussion (DI) highlights the extent to which reading activity takes place in the context of other people using documents to support and provide a shared focus for that discussion. These kinds of reading can be contrasted with the simplified notion of a digital reading device as something which supports linear and continuous reading of single documents, such as books, by people who are alone. Certainly this does occur (as the categories SI and LE indicate), but the proportion of time spent in such activities is low by comparison.

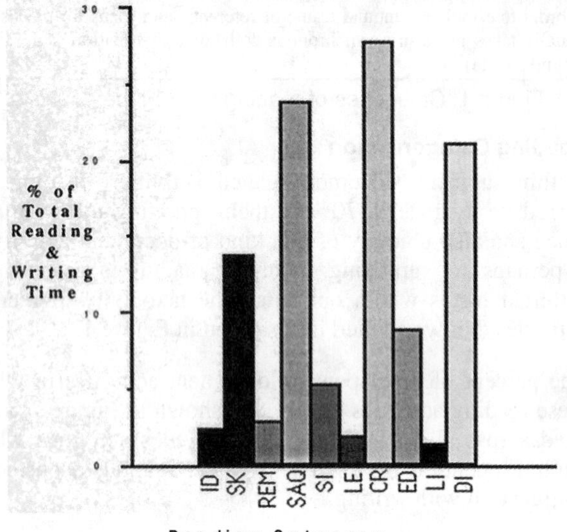

Figure 2. Reading Category Analysis

However, one may quite reasonably question the granularity of the above breakdown, especially if we are interested in specific design requirements for digital reading devices. It may be that this level of description is too broad for these purposes. To explore this issue further, we looked in more detail at the three categories of reading which occurred most frequently across our sample: the "skimming" (SK), "searching to answer questions" (SAQ), and the cross-referencing (CR) categories. Here, we will discuss only the first "sub-analysis" by way of illustration.

Analysis of Skimming (SK)

Within the skimming category (SK), we identified three sub-categories:

(1) *Sorting* refers to skimming which typically occurred when subjects sorted through mail to determine what further action was needed, if any (e.g., reply, forward, throw away, file). This quick glancing to categorise documents also occurred when tidying up or filing away documents.

(2) *Proofing* refers to a fast check of the contents of a document to ensure no items are missing or to quickly get the basic information out of a document. This more goal-directed kind of skimming includes examples such as glancing at medical records to familiarise oneself with content, reviewing patient histories, or looking over blue prints or flight plans, without actually searching for any particular item.

(3) *Browsing* describes a sub-category of skimming which occurred mainly with newspapers, magazines, or journals where subjects said they did not read in detail but rather only to obtain a general sense of an article's content and extent. Typically this type of skimming appeared to have no immediate goal in mind to further apply what was being read (as do proofing or sorting).

Overall, no one kind of skimming dominated the data, with sorting occurring 38% of total time spent skimming, proofing occurring 31% of the time, browsing 28%, and "other" 3% of the time. What this analysis does indicate, though, is that categories within the reading taxonomy we have derived need to be examined more closely to understand the implications for design.

For example, in order for digital reading devices to support a sorting activity, one would require rapid and simple ways of moving through a "pile" of items or documents, such as showing the size of the electronic pile, with the topmost item always visible, and the possible destinations where items can be dropped into categorised piles. On the other hand, proofing typically occurs *within* a document. Devices supporting proofing require fast and simple page-by-page turning mechanisms. They should also provide a means of highlighting critical information *in situ* to preserve document context while giving the reader faster access to summary impressions of the document content. This is different from merely providing abstracts or summarised information separate from the context. Finally, the browsing sub-category occurs both within and across documents. Devices supporting this activity need to support both the rapid and simple page turning required within a document and a simple mechanism for switching documents. Browsing could take advantage of technology that highlights features of the articles, highlights critical segments, and/or provides brief summarisation. Functions similar to news clipping services might be used to provide overviews.

In summary, while the taxonomy that we applied to the data is useful in distinguishing amongst broadly different kinds of reading tasks, in order to use this categorisation scheme to help specify design requirements, some further sub-categorisation may well be necessary within each reading "type".

Commonalities across Subjects

Given the diversity of people, professions, and work settings represented in this study, and given the range of reading activities that emerged, it is instructive to ask whether these reading activities exhibited any common characteristics, despite the underlying variation, from which we might draw some general design implications. Here we highlight three issues in particular: the extent to which reading (and writing) was paper-based, the degree to which reading took place in conjunction with writing, and the use of multiple "display" surfaces in the course of reading and writing.

Paper Versus On-Line Reading and Writing

In order to examine the extent to which reading and writing activities were paper-based as opposed to being carried out using on-line tools, we classified each reading or writing activity as falling into one of three categories: paper-based, on-line, or presentation-based. *Paper-based* reading and writing included such items as drawings, blue prints, flight plans. *On-line* reading and writing tended to be computer-based but included specialised equipment with screens such as medical monitors and weather machines for flight reports. In this category we also included situations where subjects moved between on-line and paper media. Third, we separated out *presentation* type media which included videos, 35mm slides, and overheads.

Analysis across all subjects showed that paper-based reading and writing accounted for 85% of people's total activity time. On-line reading and writing make up about 13% of the total time, and presentations only 2%.

These figures are especially interesting in light of the fact that all of our subjects had computers with essential data which required them to use the computers for at least some portion of their work. One can surmise that at least in some situations, the choice of paper over an available on-line alternative is because paper supports their particular reading and writing tasks better, and that the on-line alternatives simply fail to provide the same critical affordances as paper [8], [9]. The next two findings, the degree to which people write as they read, and the use of multiple documents during reading, provide some insight into this issue.

Reading in Conjunction with Writing

Early on in our analysis, it soon became clear that, within a given document activity, reading frequently co-occurred with some kind of writing. To assess the extent to which this occurred, we tabulated the total time for activities in which reading alone occurred (without writing), as against the total time in which reading occurred with writing. We found that, while there is significant variation, reading was accompanied by writing most of the time. In fact, for 8 of the 15 subjects, reading occurred with writing over 75% of the time and up to 91% of the time. For all but one subject, reading was more often accompanied by writing than not. In order to better understand what kinds of writing were occurring in our sample, we applied the taxonomy shown in Figure 3.

Creation Writing to create a new document or writing to modify an existing document.

Note-taking Writing in an abbreviated and unstructured way, usually in order to serve an intermediate or temporary purpose rather than to create a final document.

Annotation Marking on top of an existing document to relate the marks to their surrounding context.

Form-filling Filling in structured forms or writing in a prescribed, structured way, such as filling in a register.

Updating Updating calendars or schedules.

Figure 3. Categories of writing used in the analysis.

One design implication which comes from this analysis is that if one is to design a digital reading device, it makes little sense to think of reading in isolation from writing.

The breakdown of writing activities occurring in the context of reading, averaged over all subjects, is shown in Table 1.

Writing Category	% Total Reading & Writing Time
Creation	16.4%
Note-taking	21.7%
Annotation	26.4%
Form-filling	33.9%
Updating	1.6%

Table 1. Percentage of different writing activities (done in conjunction with reading), averaged over all subjects.

As shown in Table 1, writing includes far more than the creation or modification of stand-alone documents. It appears that a significant amount of time, at least in our sample, was spent form-filling while reading, or annotating documents while reading them, or taking notes in the course of reading. Thus it appears that a digital reading device which does not support what is mostly pen-based marking either in conjunction with, or on top of documents, will have limited value if one is seeking to support a wide range of work-related reading activities.

Cross-Document Use

The final common finding that emerged that we will discuss is the use of multiple documents during reading. As is indicated by the dominance of the reading category "cross-referencing", it appeared that subjects were carrying out a great deal of their reading and writing activities using multiple documents in parallel with each other.

In order to examine this issue more closely, all of the subjects' reading and/or writing activities were categorised as using a single surface for reading and/or writing or whether multiple display surfaces were in use concurrently for reading and/or writing activities. In this analysis, a display surface was defined as an independent, tangible surface such as a computer screen or piece of paper. In order for them to be classified as used concurrently, it had to be clear that the surfaces were being used side-by-side for the same activity. Here, flipping back and forth within a document was not counted as a case of parallel, concurrent usage. Multiple windows on a computer were considered a special case of page flipping and not concurrent usage. (Windows usually needed to be switched around to bring any one into the foreground to be read, much like page flipping.)

When analysed on the basis of total document-related activity time, we found that 52% of the time subjects used a single surface for reading, writing, or a combination of reading and writing, such as annotating a document while reading it. This means that 48% of the time they used *at least two display surfaces* concurrently. To explore this cross-document activity in more detail, we further categorised these activities as follows:

- *Independent Reading and Writing Displays:* Activities in which one display was used primarily for writing while cross-referring to or reading from another independent display.
- *Multiple Reading Displays:* Activities in which no writing occurred but in which two or more displays were read with reference to each other in parallel in the same activity.
- *Multiple Reading Displays plus Writing:* Activities in which two or more displays were used for reading with

reference to each other, as described above, but in which a writing activity also took place, either on a display also used for reading or on a separate display.

The breakdown of this cross-document use for all 15 subjects is shown in Table 2. As can be seen, the majority of cross-document activity involved reading in combination with writing, and the biggest portion of that involved the reading of more than one document. In these cases, writing either occurred on a separate document or occurred on one of the documents also being read.

Multiple Document Category	% Total Reading & Writing Time
Independent reading & writing surfaces	19.1%
Multiple surfaces for reading only	3.9%
Multiple surfaces for reading plus writing	25.1%

Table 2. Breakdown of use of multiple display surfaces as a percentage of total activity time involving reading or writing.

Just why these sorts of activities were so frequent is best explained by looking in more detail at what subjects were doing when reading and writing using multiple documents. This can be summarised as follows:

- *Extracting information.* One reason separate notes or form-filling occurred while cross-referring was to extract information from the document being read - as a list of reminders for themselves, to draw attention to some subset of the information in the document being read, or to instruct others to do things. Sometimes information was extracted in order to keep a separate record of it. Extracting information could also involve some degree of transformation of that information, such as using a separate piece of paper as a computational workspace, or for writing summaries, or plans of action.
- *Integrating information.* Another major reason for cross document activity was to integrate information from other sources. This could be in the service of constructing another document. Subjects referred across documents both for specific facts and figures, and also for general ideas and themes. Cross referencing was also done when updating one document using another, such as updating figures in a database, incorporating paper-based changes into an electronic version, or using old "To Do" lists to create new ones. Finally, information integration across documents was done to make decisions, by considering information from multiple different sources.
- *Consistency checking.* A third reason for cross document activity was to ensure that one document was consistent with another. This could involve checking for consistency amongst facts and figures, or could involve checking for consistency in language or format.
- *Critiquing or making comment.* Finally, cross document activity also took place when subjects had to critique, comment or refer to a document in order to write another.

One clear implication from this is that the sorts of activities described above somehow need to be supported in digital reading devices if they are to satisfactorily replace current practice. Either this needs to be accomplished by providing at least two readable/markable display surfaces, or the ability to carry out these various activities has to be supported in other ways. For example, one could imagine, and indeed there already exist, on-line facilities for ensuring consistency (i.e., templates ensure format consistency). Interfaces are being developed which accomplish some of the kinds of information extraction tasks subjects reported doing with multiple documents. For example, the Dynomite notebook [10, 11, 12] allows certain kinds of information such as action items and reminders to be indexed and automatically compiled separately from the document in which they are embedded. However, it may be that the multiple display, "paper-like" approach is, in the final analysis, a much more parsimonious approach to supporting the whole range of tasks that subjects accomplish by using more than one document.

Variation Across Subjects

Up to this point we have been focusing on commonalities that emerged across our subject sample, and some general design implication. Of course in such a varied collection of people, across such a wide range of professions, one would expect interesting differences in the ways in which they read, in the ways in which they combine reading with writing, and in other aspects of where and how reading occurs. These are especially important to understand if, as a designer, one wishes to target a specific set of "users" in a particular vertical market. Of course, one cannot make such generalisations about the needs of an entire profession or vertical market on the basis of our small sample, but it is nonetheless interesting to look more closely at the inter-subject variation that did occur to get some sense of how different people's needs might be. While we are forced to be brief in our discussion of these issues, we will concentrate on four aspects of that variation: the "top" reading and writing categories for each subject, degree of sharing, and mobility.

Table 3 shows, for each subject, which reading and writing categories featured most strongly. Specifically, it considers which of the reading and writing categories constituted the highest percentages of total reading and writing activity time for each subject.

Table 3 also shows the extent to which each subject tended to engage in shared document viewing. We considered the shared viewing of a document either to be a single document which two or more people gather around to see simultaneously or multiple copies of a single document which people read simultaneously as a reference. Here, sharing involved either the joint reading of a document (such as when people are reviewing case histories or medical charts together), the joint writing of a document (such as where several people may be viewing a document and dictating modifications or additions to one person), or combined reading and writing such as is typical of joint authorship situations where a document is reviewed and annotated in a collaborative setting.

From this analysis we found that subjects fell into 3 different clusters: "high" sharers were those where shared viewing occurred for over 50% of their activities; "medium" cases were those people in which shared viewing occurred for about 50% of their activities; and "low" sharers were those for whom shared viewing occurred for less than 50% (and in this case less than 30%) of their activities.

The final dimension represented in Table 3 is that of "mobility". Here, all reading activities were classified according to where they took place: in the subject's office (including offices located in subjects' homes), within the site where the subject's office was located, or outside of the building or site. We found that subjects could then be grouped on the basis of the amount of time spent on reading activities falling into these three categories. Nine subjects fell into the "non-mobile" group, meaning that the largest percentage of time spent in reading activities was done at the desk in the office; two subjects were primarily "locally mobile" in that the largest percentage of their activities were within the office site but outside of their office; and two subjects were mostly "remotely mobile" in carrying out most of their activities involving reading outside of the site containing their office. Two further subjects we classified as "combination" cases, where approximately half of their time was spent at their desk and half was spent being remotely mobile.

Subject	Top Reading Category	Top Writing Category	Shared Viewing Category	Mobility Category
Architect	Edit/Review	Creation	low	combinat'n
Pilot	Cross-Ref	Note-take	medium	remote
Warden	Cross-Ref	Form-Fill	medium	non-mobile
Account. Ass't	Cross-Ref	Form-Fill	low	non-mobile
Lawyer (Assoc)	Cross-Ref	Creation	low	non-mobile
Lawyer (Dir.)	Discussion	Annotate	medium	non-mobile
Optician	Discussion	Form-Fill	high	non-mobile
Social Worker	Discussion	Note-take	high	non-mobile
Market'g Mgr	Discussion	Annotate	high	combinat'n
Start-Up Exec.	Discussion	Creation	medium	remote
Real Est. Agent	Search/Ans	Note-take	low	non-mobile
Nurse	Search/Ans	Form-Fill	low	non-mobile
Doctor	Search/Ans	Form-Fill	low	non-mobile
Anaesthetist 1	Search/Ans	Form-Fill	low	local
Anaesthetist 2	Search/Ans	Form-Fill	low	local

Table 3. Four dimensions of inter-subject variability.

The first interesting feature of this analysis is to note the similarities amongst the four medical personnel in our sample (doctor, 2 anaesthetists, and nurse). All can be characterised as form-fillers, whose main reading task is one of searching through documents for facts, results, instructions, and other specific kinds of information, often in order to complete those forms. This kind of document activity is something they do on their own (although the documents they interact with are generally jointly authored in themselves). Note, however, that these medical professionals differ in the degree to which they are based in an office, with the anaesthetists generally using public or shared spaces in which to carry out their document work.

A second interesting group of subjects is those who spend a great deal of time reading in support of discussion (lawyer-director, optician, social worker, marketing manager and start-up executive). As one might well expect, these people are also in the "high" or "medium" shared viewing categories. Having said that, they vary in their mobility, and engage in very different kinds of writing activities. For example, the optician is mainly form-filling as a result of discussion with clients, while the social worker mainly took free-hand notes. The marketing manager relied very heavily on the annotation of the documents around which the discussions were centred in order to record pertinent facts, or to write reminders for herself.

The third "group" which emerges is what one might call the "cross-referencers". However, on closer inspection of their data, the nature of the cross-referencing these subjects carried out was actually quite different from subject to subject. For example, the accountancy assistant spent most of her time cross-referencing to check for consistency amongst figures, the pilot was integrating and extracting from multiple documents to plan routes and check flight information, the warden was mainly extracting information for form-filling, and the lawyer-associate was mostly cross-referencing to check language and format of documents in the creation of new ones. While one might surmise that such heavy use of multiple documents is best suited to an office environment where papers can be spread out in space, obviously remotely mobile workers engage in this sort of activity too, as the case of the pilot demonstrates.

The first implication of this overview of inter-subject differences is that one might conceptualise a range of different kinds of portable, digital reading devices. For example, some might be specifically geared toward providing users with an armoury of different kinds of flexible search and navigation features for people whose main reading task is that of quickly browsing through information, or finding and getting access to specific kinds of information. Digital devices obviously have the potential to confer many benefits here, especially in terms of increased access to more information, and to more up-to-date information. At the risk of over-generalising, it appears that medical practitioners are one group of users who might benefit from this sort of device. For example, in medical settings, paper documents are often problematic in that patient's notes are often out of date, information needs to come from many different departments, and forms get lost. Digital reading devices specifically designed to allow quick, flexible access to information could have an important impact here, especially if careful consideration is given to the ways in which medical practitioners currently search through documents.

Another "kind" of digital reading device is one that is designed with collaborative use in mind. This will affect both hardware and software requirements. For example, the viewing angle of the screen will be an issue here. One can imagine exploring a range of possibilities for allowing multiple pen input, and for providing software which supports joint marking and editing. Our data suggest that such a device might be used across a range of different job types.

The group of cross-referencers suggests that some people may be more heavily in need of multiple display surfaces than others in their work. Thus a "two-screen" version of a device might well find its niche naturally within some professions. However, judging by the degree to which multiple displays were used across our whole sample, we can surmise that at least two functionally interlinked screens might be more generally useful, for the whole range of reasons we have outlined.

As a final comment on inter-subject variation, the data on the amount of reading carried out away from the desk strengthens the case for the need for truly mobile reading devices (see also [3] for empirical results confirming the dimensions of this). Even for the 9 "non-mobile" subjects, 6 of these people spent from 13-40% of their time doing reading activities away from their home office. (The optician, warden, and social worker were entirely desk-based.) Obviously there are a range of reasons why people are office-based, and we can only guess at the extent to which these figures would change if they had technologies available which enabled them remote access to the document tools and resources currently only found in their offices.

CONCLUSION

We have shown how a diary study can allow the collection of both descriptive and quantitative data on reading activities within the context of people's working lives. Further, we have used our analysis to draw out several different design implications for the design of new technologies in support of reading. These can be summarised as follows:

- The linear, continuous reading of single documents by people on their own is an unrealistic characterisation of how people read in the course of their daily work. Reading takes on a variety of different forms, serves a range of different goals, and is carried out in many different ways, as the 10 reading categories we have identified illustrate.
- Looking in detail at the way reading is carried out within any one reading category can offer guidance in specifying a range of design requirements.
- Reading occurs more frequently in conjunction with writing than it does in isolation. Thus, it appears that writing (in a variety of forms) is an integral part of work-related reading. Designers need to seriously consider the importance of developing reading devices which also support the marking or writing of documents during the reading process.
- Almost half of all the document activities which involved reading involved the concurrent use of multiple "display surfaces" for reading, or reading in conjunction with writing. This points to the need to consider how single display devices can support the range of cross-document activities people carry out. It also emphasises the importance of considering the benefits of designing devices which are based around the use of multiple, digital displays.
- Inter-subject variation suggests the potential for a range of kinds of digital reading devices. Examples include a reading device specifically developed to support goal directed searching and browsing (such as was characteristic of our medical personnel), and a reading device designed for collaborative use.

In drawing attention to these issues, we hope that we have illustrated the value of studying reading behaviour in detail, and in the context of day to day working life. While guesswork and intuition can result in very successful design solutions, we suggest that grounding design in empirical data can be a productive, more systematic way forward. At the very least, it can help us to clarify our assumptions, and ask important questions about who we are designing for, and what is the nature of the current working practices we are aiming to augment or change for the better.

ACKNOWLEDGEMENTS

We are grateful to all of our subjects for taking part in this study and allowing the intrusion into their daily working lives. We also wish to thank Marge Eldridge for comments on this paper and assistance in setting up the study, Joe Sullivan and his group at FX-PAL for providing additional financial and moral support, and Tom Moran for comments on the paper, input on the study design, advice and support.

REFERENCES

1. Dillon, A. (1992). Reading from paper versus screens: A critical review of the empirical literature. *Ergonomics, Vol. 35(10)*, 1297-1326.
2. Eldridge, M. & Newman, W. (1996). Agenda benders: Modelling the disruptions caused by technology failures in the workplace. *Proceedings of CHI '96, Companion Vol.* New York: ACM Press, 219-220.
3. Gujar, A., Harrison, B. L., and Fishkin. (1997). A Comparative Empirical Evaluation of Display Technologies for Reading. Submitted to *CHI'98* papers.
4. Hirscheim, R.A. (1985). *Office Automation: A Social and Organisational Perspective.* John Wiley and Sons, Chichester, New York.
5. Kintsch, W. and van Dijk, T.A. (1978). Toward a model of text comprehension and production. *Psychological Review, 85,* 363-394.
6. Lorch Jr., R.F., Lorch, E.P. & Klusewitz, M.A. (1993). College students' conditional knowledge about reading. *Journal of Educational Psychology, 85,* 239-252.
7. O'Hara (1996). *Toward a typology of reading goals.* XRCE Technical Report No. EPC-1996-107. Xerox Research Centre Europe, Cambridge, UK.
8. O'Hara, K., & Sellen, A.J. (1997). A comparison of reading on-line and paper documents. *Proceedings of CHI '97.* New York: ACM Press.
9. Sellen, A.J., & Harper, R.H.R. (1997). Paper as an analytic resource for the design of new technologies. *Proceedings of CHI '97.* New York: ACM Press.
10. Shilit, B., Golovinchinsky, G. and Price, M. (1997). Beyond Paper: Supporting Active Reading with Free-form Digital Ink Annotations. Submitted to *CHI'98* papers.
11. Wilcox, L., Schilit, B., and Sawhney, N. (1997). Dynomite: A dynamically organised ink and audio notebook. *Proceedings of CHI '97.* New York: ACM Press, 186-193.
12. Bly, S., Wilcox, L., Chui, P., and Gwizdka, J. (1997). Finding Information in Ink and Audio Notes: A Study of Indexing. Submitted to *CHI'98* papers.

Beyond Paper: Supporting Active Reading with Free Form Digital Ink Annotations

Bill N. Schilit, Gene Golovchinsky, Morgan N. Price
FX Palo Alto Laboratory, Inc.
3400 Hillview Ave., Bldg. 4
Palo Alto, CA 94304
+1 650 813-7322
{schilit, gene, price}@pal.xerox.com

ABSTRACT

Reading frequently involves not just looking at words on a page, but also underlining, highlighting and commenting, either on the text or in a separate notebook. This combination of reading with critical thinking and learning is called *active reading* [2]. To explore the premise that computation can enhance active reading we have built the XLibris "active reading machine." XLibris uses a commercial high-resolution pen tablet display along with a paper-like user interface to support the key affordances of paper for active reading: the reader can hold a scanned image of a page in his lap and mark on it with digital ink. To go beyond paper, XLibris monitors the free-form ink annotations made while reading, and uses these to organize and to search for information. Readers can review, sort and filter clippings of their annotated text in a "Reader's Notebook." XLibris also searches for material related to the annotated text, and displays links to similar documents unobtrusively in the margin. XLibris demonstrates that computers can help active readers organize and find information while retaining many of the advantages of reading on paper.

Keywords

Paper-like user interface, reading online, affordances of paper, pen computing, dynamic hypertext, document metaphor, information retrieval

INTRODUCTION

Computers, once expected to create a paper-less office, have instead produced ever-increasing quantities of paper documents. Dataquest predicts that 1,344 billion pages will be generated by printers and copiers in the US in 1997 [15]. This statistic suggests that people are not using computers to read. Whereas paper is lightweight, inexpensive, and easy to annotate, interfaces for reading online typically involve clumsy interactions with bulky desktop monitors.

Although reading online presents a number of problems, we will show that integrating computation with reading also presents novel opportunities for improving the reading process. Thus there is a tension between the advantages provided by computation and the advantages provided by paper: the choice depends on the reader's goals. For reading a romance novel at the beach, low weight and portability are essential, and it is unlikely that computation could provide any real benefit. For more dynamic types of reading, however, computation may be desirable.

Active reading is the combination of reading with critical thinking and learning, and is a fundamental part of education and knowledge work. Active reading involves not just reading *per se*, but also underlining, highlighting and scribbling comments, either on the text itself or in a separate notebook [2]. Readers use these marks to organize their reading for later review and retrieval. In addition, active reading often requires readers to move from one text to another to satisfy their information needs.

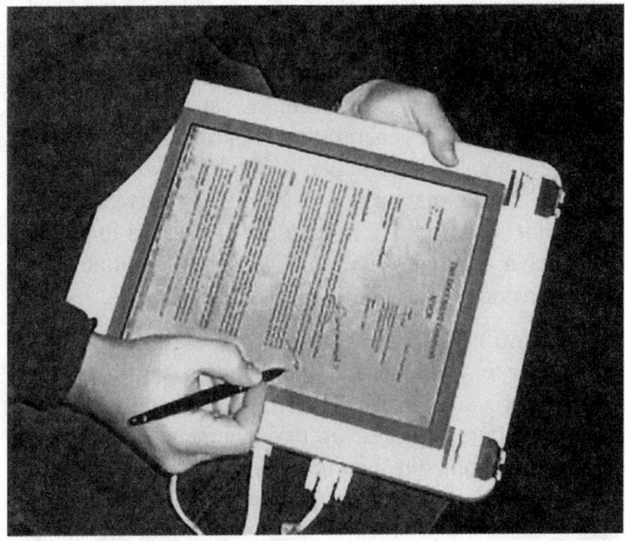

Figure 1: XLibris prototype in a reader's lap

We have built an "active reading machine," XLibris, to explore the premise that computation can enhance active reading. To make reading online acceptable, XLibris implements a paper document metaphor (see Figure 1) that provides key affordances of paper. To go beyond paper and make reading online desirable, XLibris helps readers organize and retrieve information. By exploiting the existing practice of free-form ink annotation, XLibris provides these benefits with minimal additional effort from the reader. To apply these advantages to existing documents, XLibris allows input of both paper and digital documents. Indeed, an active reading machine would likely be used together with desktop computers (e.g., for writing) and with paper (e.g., for some forms of collaboration).

The rest of this paper is organized as follows. We describe active reading practices, and the problems with reading online. We then describe the XLibris system in detail, and conclude with a discussion of related and future work.

ACTIVE READING

The combination of reading with critical thinking is a fundamental part of education and knowledge work. This activity is practiced by students learning a textbook discipline, by lawyers processing discovery documents, researchers keeping "up to date," by analysts finding answers to specific questions, by executives cleaning out their inboxes, and by citizens deciding how to vote. Active reading is a skill that most literate people share.

Today, active reading is a "craft skill" rather than a formal academic discipline. Even though critical reading is a key part of learning from a text, reading is rarely included in school curricula beyond the elementary level. Nevertheless, improving the skills of learning from and finding information in a text has occupied educators for centuries. More recently, Mortimer Adler's *How to Read a Book* [2]—part of the Great Books campaign—presented a methodology for active reading in great detail.

Adler and other educators recommend pigeon-holing a text, skimming the contents, reading at different speeds, marking (underlining, highlighting, starring) important information, and in general, "carrying on a conversation" with the author. For example, scribbling "Norman would disagree!" in the margin is part of a dialog between reader and author. These practices have been observed in real use in a number of studies [21, 16, 1, 22] that are summarized in the remainder of this section.

Note Taking Practices

Readers write. Marks made while reading aid understanding, memorization and later retrieval. Readers generate marks in different places: on the document, in a separate notebook, or sometimes on loose-leaf paper or note cards. We use *annotation* to refer to marks on (or attached to) reading matter, and *notes* to mean marks that are not co-located with the text to which they refer. The tradeoffs between annotations and notes are discussed below.

Annotations

Many people annotate directly on paper documents while they are reading. When people do not want to mark in their books (or in borrowed reading matter), they may write on removable Post-It™ notes or on slips of paper. Readers tend to scribble short comments in margins; they draw asterisks to make an important statement stand out; they highlight, underline or circle key words or phrases [16].

The advantages of annotating directly on the page are convenience, immersion in the document context, and visual search. Annotating documents does not disrupt the flow of reading. Also, annotations contain more information because they occur within the "context" of the document. Marks such as "!" or "?" or "not true!" may represent various levels of agreement with adjacent text. Finally, annotations stand out visually, allowing readers to scan for them.

The major disadvantage of annotations is that they become lost in the piles of papers and books. Annotations only work well when you *see* them on the document page.

Notebooks

Some readers use a bound notebook to store their notes in one place. People use notebooks to record facts, figures, and key points, to copy interesting quotes, and to jot down ideas. Readers can review their notebooks to study and to understand what they have read. Over time, a notebook becomes a reader's *catalogue raisonné*, containing annotations and thoughts about documents that have been read. Additionally, flipping through the pages in a notebook is a rapid way to review information across documents.

Although notebooks provide the reader a broad overview of their reading, they often lack details and depth. Readers must recreate the note's context—the document name, page number, idea, quotation, etc.—in the notebook. Writing "yes!" in the margin is a useful annotation, but in a notebook it must be accompanied by substantially more information. Copying this context into a notebook can be tedious, time-consuming and error-prone. Incomplete notes may not be comprehensible later, and may also create problems of attribution.

Note Cards and Loose-leaf Paper

People also use index cards and loose-leaf paper to write notes while reading. The advantage of unbound notes is that they can be arranged and reorganized flexibly. For example, authors often organize their notes by topic or to fit an outline.

The problem with unbound notes is the effort required to create and to manage them. As with a notebook, there is no context available from the document, but there is also no context available from surrounding notes. Furthermore managing dozens of note cards can be a chore in itself.

In summary, all three places for marking—on the page, in notebooks, on unbound paper—are used not just to record information but also to organize it. Annotations highlight key information but tend to be lost in piles of paper. Notebooks are reviewed easily, but taking notes is tedious and error-prone. Unbound notes can be reorganized flexibly, but require even more effort by the note taker.

Finding related material

Finding related material and moving from one text to another is also part of active reading. For example, an ecology student studying the effects of acid rain in the Appalachian Mountains decides to search the Internet for information on the economy of West Virginia. A doctor reading up on a drug she's never prescribed decides to follow a reference to a study of its side effects.

This activity of finding related materials while reading is often disconnected from the main activity. Typical information retrieval interfaces force users to suspend their reading activity to identify and then to retrieve related documents. References found in paper documents are even more time-consuming to track down. Although hypertext was designed to address some of these problems, authors cannot anticipate the information needs of all readers. Ironically, although readers' interests change fluidly, interfaces for moving from reading to finding and back to reading again tend to be time consuming and disruptive.

THE CHALLENGES OF ACTIVE READING ONLINE

People typically print long documents to read them, rather than reading them on the computer. Why does this happen? What affordances does paper provide that are lacking online? A number of researchers [5, 12, 18, 21] have studied these issues; we summarize applicable results below.

Tangibility

Tangibility refers to the physical properties of sheets or stacks of paper that allow them to be held, moved, folded, rotated, etc. Readers move their documents around in space to improve legibility [5], to adjust perspective or gain objective distance [12], and to ease and speed up handwriting [11]. In contrast, reading online typically means reading from a monitor on a desk.

The physical nature of paper also affords effortless navigation [18]. For example, readers can look at the previous page while marking on the current one, sense the length of a document by its thickness and weight, and sense location in a book by the thickness of the sides.

Free-form ink annotation

Free-form ink annotation refers to the ease of marking on paper. Annotating with a pen requires little cognitive overhead compared to typing or to selecting text with a mouse and issuing a command. Annotation is an important part of active reading, yet it tends to be very difficult online [1, 18].

Furthermore, annotations on paper are conceptually and visually separate from the underlying document. In contrast, text annotations online often blend in with surrounding text or change document layout.

Page orientation

Page orientation refers to the fixed division of paper documents into pages and the fixed spatial layout of those pages. Page layout conveys the organization of the document and supports navigation, skimming, and spatial memory [6].

This "sense of the document" is often lost online [12, 18]. One problem is that the landscape orientation of typical monitors does not allow a full page of text to be displayed. This leads to awkward view scrolling and zooming. In addition, scrolling views (e.g., Web browsers, text processors) that do not respect fixed page layout can make it difficult to read a document non-linearly.

Multiple displays

Reading at work often involves using several documents—paper and/or digital—together, each with their own display [1]. Paper provides an unlimited number of physical displays because it is cheap. Most computers provide multiple virtual displays, but existing windowing systems are too cumbersome to support reading from several documents [18].

Sharing

Paper is directly sharable. More than one person can view and interact with a single piece of paper at a time; people can hand over a paper document in person; and people can see what others are doing with paper documents [21].

Legibility

Although legibility is a common explanation for why people prefer reading on paper, legibility does not appear to be a significant factor. Many studies in the 1980's found significant differences in reading speed or proofreading accuracy between CRT displays and paper, but these differences shrink or disappear with modern high-quality CRTs [5, 10].

MEETING THE CHALLENGE OF READING ONLINE

Supporting all of the advantages of paper described above in an active reading machine seems to be impossible. It is also unnecessary: our goal is to improve active reading, not to replace paper. Readers will use active reading machines together with paper and traditional computers, and documents will move back and forth as best supports people's work. This suggests that active reading machines need not necessarily provide multiple displays or support sharing directly.

Instead we have focused our attention on tangibility, free-form ink annotation, and page orientation. To provide these affordances, XLibris combines a pen tablet display with a paper document metaphor. Together, these allow XLibris to emulate the physical experience of reading and marking on paper: the reader can hold a scanned image of a page in their lap and mark on it with digital ink.

Pen Tablet Display

XLibris runs on a paper-like tablet computer. A tablet is a lightweight (1–2 kg) device that combines a high-resolution flat-panel display and a pen. The devices come in two varieties: tablet displays connected to conventional computers, and standalone, portable pen computers.

Tangibility

Unlike CRT monitors, tablets are graspable physical objects. Although 1–2 kg is heavier than most books, tablets are light enough to put in one's lap, comfortable to write on, and movable. By movable we mean that they can be tilted easily, shifted around, etc., within a small space such as an office. This distinguishes tablets from portable computers (e.g., laptops) that can be packed up and transported from place to place, but may not be conveniently movable once unpacked for use. Conversely, a tethered device—a tablet connected to a stationary computer or source of power, or a book on a chain in a library—may be movable but not portable.

Physical widgets incorporated into the tablet can further enhance tangibility. For example, Harrison *et al* [14] have mounted pressure sensors on the top corners of the XLibris prototype's case (Figure 1). Readers turn pages by thumbing across these sensors (from left to right or from right to left), mimicking page turning in a paper document.

Paper document metaphor

XLibris uses the *paper document metaphor* to capture several important characteristics of paper documents. The metaphor includes a display that emulates the appearance of a sheet of paper, an interface for viewing pages in the linear order of the document, the ability to mark in any place on any page, and cues about the size of a document and about the reader's location within it.

XLibris reinforces this user interface metaphor through the form factor of the device. The tablet and the pen complement the software interface to create a richer, more tangible document reading experience.

XLibris differs radically from standard WIMP interfaces. This is reflected not only in the document metaphor, but also in fundamental differences in interaction between a desktop computer and a tablet. Although the mouse and the pen serve similar purposes, they have quite different affordances. Furthermore, screen space in XLibris is at a premium because tangibility requires a small form factor, and also because document pages require all the pixels that current display technology provides.

User interface design principles

As we designed the XLibris system, we identified several design principles that should pervade and structure the user interface. These principles included a transparent ("No UI" UI) user interface and modeless interaction.

XLibris provides a minimal interface with a few commands for turning pages, changing views and selecting ink and highlighter colors. The richness of the interaction is derived from the form factor of the device and from the ease and familiarity of making marks with a pen. The intent was to create a transparent user interface that users would accept implicitly without the typical and frustrating process of "learning the UI."

For review only; please do not cite or distribute.

Beyond Paper: Supporting Active Reading with Free-form Digital Ink Annotations

Bill N. Schilit, Gene Golovchinsky, Morgan N. Price
FX Palo Alto Laboratory, Inc.
3400 Hillview Ave., Bldg. 4
Palo Alto, CA 94304
+1 650 813-7322
{schilit, gene, price}@pal.xerox.com

ABSTRACT
Reading frequently involves not just looking at words on a page, but also underlining, highlighting and commenting, either on the text or in a separate notebook. This combination of reading with critical thinking and learning is called *active reading* [1]. To explore the premise that computation can enhance active reading we have built the XLibris "active reading machine." XLibris uses a high-resolution pen-tablet display along with a paper-like user interface to support the key affordances of paper for active reading: the reader can hold a scanned image of a page in his lap and mark on it with digital ink. To go beyond paper, XLibris monitors the free-form ink annotations made while reading, and uses these to organize and to search for information. Readers can review, sort and filter clippings of their annotated text in a "Reader's Notebook." XLibris searches for material related to the annotated text, and displays links unobtrusively in the margin. XLibris demonstrates that computers can help active readers organize and find information while retaining many of the advantages of reading on paper.

Keywords
Paper-like user interface, reading online, affordances of paper, pen computing, dynamic hypertext, document metaphor, information retrieval

INTRODUCTION
Computers, once expected to create a paper-less office, have instead produced ever-increasing quantities of paper documents. Dataquest predicts that 1,344 billion pages will be generated by printers and copiers in the US in 1997 [12]. These statistics suggest that people are not using computers to read. Whereas paper is lightweight, inexpensive, and easy to annotate, interfaces for reading online typically involve clumsy interactions with stationary desktop monitors.

Although reading online presents a number of problems, we will show that integrating computation with reading also presents novel opportunities for improving the reading process. Thus there is a tension between the advantages provided by computation and the advantages provided by paper: the choice depends on the reader's goals. For reading a romance novel at the beach, low weight and portability are essential, and it is unlikely that computation could provide any real benefit. For other types of reading, however, computation may be desirable.

Active reading is the combination of reading with critical thinking and learning, and is a fundamental part of education and knowledge work. Active reading involves not just reading *per se*, but also underlining, highlighting and commenting, either on the text or in a separate notebook [1]. Readers use these marks to organize information for later review and retrieval. In addition, active reading often requires readers to move from one text to another to satisfy their information needs.

We have built an "active reading machine," XLibris, to explore the premise that computation can enhance active reading. XLibris has three major features: the paper document metaphor, a "Reader's Notebook" for organizing annotated documents, and margin links for serendipitous discovery of related material.

XLibris emulates the physical experience of reading a document on paper. The metaphor of a paper document pervades the design: the hardware approximates the form factor of a pad of paper, and the software supports a paper-like interface. Readers hold a lightweight pen tablet that displays one page of a scanned or printed document at a time. As on paper, readers can mark anywhere on the page.

To go beyond paper, XLibris monitors free-form ink annotations that readers make as part of their existing reading practice. These annotations, meaningful to the reader, can also be meaningful to the system. The system can use the extent of the annotations to determine the text they refer to. That text may then serve as a representation of the reader's interests. Thus, free-form digital ink can provide a transparent, low cognitive overhead user interface for enhancing active reading with computation.

Figure 2. An annotated document page in XLibris

An essential aspect of ink on paper is its lack of modality: you can write anything you want, anywhere on a page, in any order. In XLibris, therefore, users can scribble notes, draw figures, and annotate text, all without switching modes or applications. In contrast, conventional graphical user interfaces use widgets to produce a highly structured interaction, and typically force users to adapt to the structure of applications.

Similarly desirable is the ability to perform the same task in different ways. Users prefer interfaces that provide multiple navigation options (i.e., queries, hypertext links, buttons, etc.) to interfaces with fewer navigation mechanisms [8]. Although the destination in each case may be the same, different interface actions may be appropriate for different goals, or the choice may depend on a user's prior experience. Thus we designed XLibris to support a variety of navigation mechanisms interfaces; they will be discussed in detail in the "Support for navigation" section, below.

Page orientation

XLibris maintains page layout by using tablets in portrait mode and devotes the entire display to a single page (Figure 2). XLibris uses page turning rather than scrolling to move between pages of a document. Page turning is preferred to scrolling because it preserves the visual characteristics of pages (enhancing visual memory) and because it is more consistent with the paper document metaphor.

XLibris provides visual feedback about the length of the document and about the reader's location within the document using "location guides" (Figure 2). These are small widgets at the top corners of the page that indicate visually the approximate size of the document, the reader's position in the document, and whether there is a following or a preceding page. Location guides are similar to Book Emulator's black page edges [3] but take up far less space; their design will be refined based on experimental evaluation.

Free-form ink annotation

XLibris supports free-form ink annotation directly on the page, anywhere on the page. We believe that the ability to make unstructured, idiosyncratic marks is a key aspect of a paper-like user interface. Although such marks may not have explicit meaning to the computer, they have rich meaning to the user and thus support episodic memory. XLibris provides different colors of highlighters and pens to increase users' flexibility of expression.

Operating XLibris

In the real world, we envision our active reading machine coexisting with personal computers and with paper, and we see documents moving freely between these three media. In our current system, readers can "print" from their desktop computer into XLibris and can scan paper documents into XLibris. Similarly, we envision XLibris printing to paper or exporting text and images for use in desktop applications.

Navigation

One of the design guidelines we identified was that XLibris should support multiple navigation mechanisms. We have implemented the following: readers can turn pages using the pressure sensors until the desired page is reached; a "document view" showing thumbnails of all pages simultaneously can be used to select the desired page (Figure 3); or the "Reader's Notebook" view (see next section) can be used to find a page with a familiar annotation. A view history allows user to backtrack through the reading session in time. We also envision using the location guides to riffle through pages.

Figure 3: The document view shows page thumbnails, including annotations, for the entire document.

XLibris uses small page images, or thumbnails, instead of generic icons to represent links to pages and documents. Although almost entirely illegible, the thumbnails retain the layout information and reveal the idiosyncratic annotations when they are present. Thus readers can identify marked-up pages or pages with distinctive figures or unusual layouts from the thumbnail, without following the link.

XLibris also provides a "workspace view" to help readers navigate between documents. The workspace view (Figure 4) displays a thumbnail (with a shadow that indicates document size) for each of the reader's documents. Each thumbnail is linked to the first page of the corresponding document.

Figure 4: The workspace view shows all of the reader's documents. Each document has a drop-shadow that indicates its approximate length.

Command Invocation

Readers using XLibris can ink on the page with a pen, turn pages by thumbing on the case, follow links by tapping with the pen, and invoke commands from a menu. Currently the commands include selecting a pen, highlighter or eraser, toggling margin links, or moving to one of the views described above.

Figure 5: "Silk screen" menu at bottom of page

We have explored three styles of command menus. Initially we implemented a circular pie menu that popped up when users tapped while holding down the pen barrel button. Since users found this awkward, we replaced the button with a "dwell" gesture: pressing the pen down and holding it stationary brings up the pie menu. Dwell menus should not interfere with writing because dwell is not part of paper practice: holding a pen in one spot on paper causes bleeding. We also designed the menu as a set of silk screen buttons, emulated by a button bar at the bottom of the display, as shown in Figure 5.

ENHANCING READING WITH COMPUTATION

XLibris provides a paper-like user interface based on the document metaphor, but some functions of an active reading machine should not be entirely paper-like. For example, active links do not exist in paper documents, and paper notebooks cannot be reorganized dynamically. Although these features are not present "verbatim" in the document metaphor, they are not inconsistent with it. For example, people have physically cut out sections of documents to generate clipping files, and there is a scholarly tradition of putting references to related works in the margins of a document. These existing practices are reinterpreted in XLibris in a computational manner, as described below.

The Reader's Notebook

The Reader's Notebook is a notebook of clippings derived from readers' annotations. The Reader's Notebook combines the advantages of annotating directly on the page, of taking notes in a separate notebook, and of organizing index cards. Furthermore, the Reader's Notebook overcomes the limitations of its paper cousins: as with paper documents, readers mark on the page, in the context of the document, and without tedious and error-prone copying of information. As with a bound notebook, readers can review concise annotations by time. Finally, as with note cards, flexible filtering and sorting of the view allow readers to reorganize their information as their needs change.

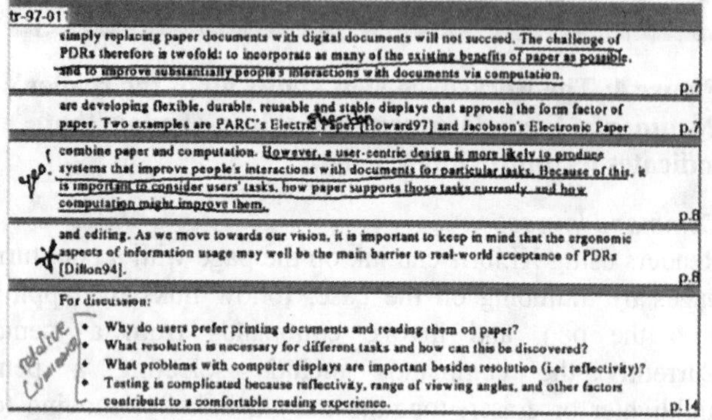

tr-97-011

simply replacing paper documents with digital documents will not succeed. The challenge of PDRs therefore is twofold: to incorporate as many of the existing benefits of paper as possible, and to improve substantially people's interactions with documents via computation. p.7

are developing flexible, durable, reusable and stable displays that approach the form factor of paper. Two examples are PARC's Electric Paper [Howard97] and Jacobson's Electronic Paper p.7

combine paper and computation. However, a user-centric design is more likely to produce systems that improve people's interactions with documents for particular tasks. Because of this, it is important to consider users' tasks, how paper supports those tasks currently, and how computation might improve them. p.8

and editing. As we move towards our vision, it is important to keep in mind that the ergonomic aspects of information usage may well be the main barrier to real-world acceptance of PDRs [Dillon94]. p.8

For discussion:

- Why do users prefer printing documents and reading them on paper?
- What resolution is necessary for different tasks and how can this be discovered?
- What problems with computer displays are important besides resolution (i.e. reflectivity)?
- Testing is complicated because reflectivity, range of viewing angles, and other factors contribute to a comfortable reading experience. p.14

Figure 6: The Reader's Notebook shows annotated clippings of documents laid end-to-end. Clippings are labeled with document title and page number, and are linked to the corresponding pages.

The Reader's Notebook (Figure 6) extracts annotated clippings and lays them end-to-end in a separate, multi-page view. Each clipping is linked to the annotated page, so the reader can move fluidly between notes and documents. Each clipping includes some surrounding text and is labeled with document title and page number to help the reader understand the meaning of the marks.

How much text should be shown with each annotation? Clippings are derived from the bounding boxes of annotations by expanding them horizontally to the width of the page, and by expanding them vertically to include complete words. Clippings that overlap are merged together.

The Reader's Notebook can display clippings from one document or from all documents, and can be sorted and filtered. By default, clippings are sorted by time, so that new information appears at the end, as in a paper notebook. Clippings can also be sorted by page number. Searching through clippings sorted by page number is analogous to rummaging through a pile of paper documents, but should be faster because readers need not deal with less important (un-annotated) information.

Finally, readers can filter the clippings by ink color to search for different kinds of marks or to group related items together. Many readers already use different pens to mark different types of information. For example, some lawyers highlight "pro" information in green and "con" information in red.

Margin Links

XLibris supports a novel type of *serendipitous* retrieval. Consider a library containing large collections of documents arranged by topic. As people walk to the shelf for a particular book, walls of related books surround them, making it possible to find interesting material accidentally. This serendipity in finding books in a library is a common and often rewarding experience. Magazines and journals sometimes provide the same function. Unfortunately, in both paper and online environments, finding related materials while reading is often disconnected from the main activity.

Margin links provide serendipitous access to related documents *during* the reading process. As readers mark up documents, the system finds documents related to annotated passages and presents links unobtrusively, in the margin. Each anchor is a thumbnail image of the target page (see Figure 7).

Link creation does not disrupt the reading process. The reader is free to disregard the suggestion and to continue reading. The intent is to provide a modeless link suggestion mechanism, and to allow readers to follow the links at their leisure, rather than at the time that the links are identified.

Query-mediated links

Query-mediated links derive a query from a user's interaction with a document and use that query to identify related documents. Golovchinsky [9] has shown that query-mediated links based on explicitly selected words and passages are effective in supporting information exploration tasks.

Similarly, XLibris computes margin links from the words, phrases and passages that are implicitly selected by the reader's marks. Each mark is converted in turn into a text selection, a full-text query, and a best-matching passage. The system adds a margin link to the best match if its similarity value (or belief score) is above a threshold.

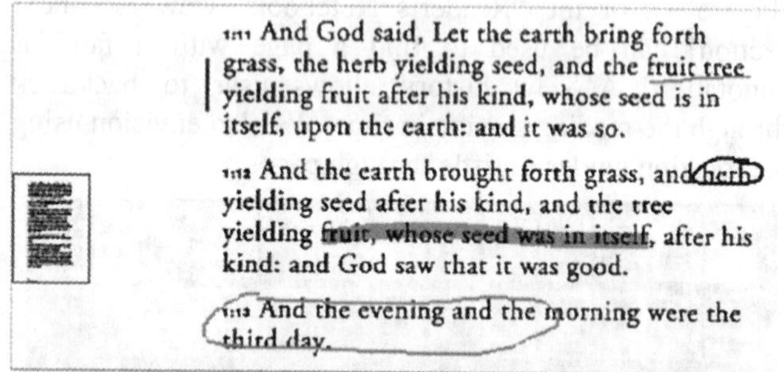

1:11 And God said, Let the earth bring forth grass, the herb yielding seed, and the fruit tree yielding fruit after his kind, whose seed is in itself, upon the earth: and it was so.

1:12 And the earth brought forth grass, and herb yielding seed after his kind, and the tree yielding fruit, whose seed was in itself, after his kind: and God saw that it was good.

1:13 And the evening and the morning were the third day.

Figure 7. Examples of highlighting, underlining, circling, and margin annotations. Each annotation generates a query. If a good match is found, XLibris adds a margin link (rectangle on the left) that shows the thumbnail of the destination page.

Query-mediated links require sources of appropriate documents for retrieval. Although our prototype implementation relies on the reader's private collection, commercial digital document repositories are becoming available. The ACM and the IEEE already publish their journals and conference proceedings electronically, and the

Columbia University Press has announced online access to their academic publications. Institutional memory repositories and other private collections can also serve as sources of documents.

Ink annotations as queries

XLibris recognizes several distinct ink patterns from which queries are computed. These include underlined words, circled words, circled passages, and margin annotations (Figure 7). Each type of annotation results in a different query for the search engine. Marks that select specific words translate into queries that emphasize those words over others in the same sentence. Marks that select longer passages generate queries that search for similar phrases. Currently, a separate query is computed for each stroke; we envision grouping ink by time and type of annotation.

In summary, margin links allow the reader to stumble into information serendipitously—without any explicit interaction—in the context of their reading. This contrasts with interfaces for browsing or information exploration, which separate information gathering from in-depth reading and require readers to describe their interests more explicitly.

IMPLEMENTATION

XLibris is implemented in C++ and the Win32 API, and runs on Windows 95/NT. The program takes over the entire display, and does not use any Windows widgets. Instead, XLibris defines a small set of widgets, renders them to an in-memory bitmap, rotates the bitmap, and copies it to the display device. In this way, XLibris uses a landscape device in portrait mode.

Our current hardware platform is a Mutoh 12.1" (30.7 cm) diagonal 1024x768-pixel tablet display tethered to a PC [17]. XLibris displays documents as 100-dpi 64-color bitmap images shrunk slightly to fit into the aspect ratio and size of this display. Although the margins are clipped slightly on each side, enough space remains for annotations. Documents containing 10 point text or larger are quite readable.

In order to treat scanned-in paper documents and printed digital documents identically, XLibris uses an "image + text" file format [19, 4]. The image supports rendering independent of the source of the document. The text, inferred from print commands or from OCR, is tied to the image by a bounding box for each word. This "text" supports information retrieval, and is never shown to the reader directly.

RELATED WORK

Most previous attempts to improve reading with computation have focused on creating new media—hypertext or hypermedia—that redefine the documents being read as well as the act of reading, placing them in a separate world from existing books and paper documents. This contrasts with our approach of supporting paper practices and paper-based documents.

A number of systems have explored digital ink annotation. Wang Freestyle [7] provides free-form ink annotation on a fixed page of information, but does not use computation to enhance the ink. Wolf et al. [23] built a "Paper-like Interface" consisting of a pen tablet display that supported traditional computer applications rather than active reading, and used gestures rather than annotations. The collaborative text editor MATE [13] interprets free-form ink revision marks as editing commands at the user's request, or allows users to specify their own interpretation. XLibris' Reader's Notebook is similar to the ink property index in Dynomite [22], but XLibris organizes the underlying document, not just the ink.

The Lectrice project at DEC SRC [4] designed and built a document reader intended to be an alternative to reading on paper. However, Lectrice did not provide free-form digital ink annotation or support active reading.

The Remembrance Agent [20] finds documents related to the last few lines typed into a text editor. Whereas the Remembrance Agent supports writing, XLibris supports reading by generating margin links from ink annotations and the underlying document.

CONCLUSIONS AND FUTURE WORK

We began with the premise that computation can enhance active reading. Toward this end we explored the task of active reading and the affordances of paper for reading. We formulated a set of challenges for reading online that must be overcome, and also a set of opportunities that computation provides.

We have designed and implemented the XLibris "active reading machine." XLibris implements a paper document metaphor that includes a page-oriented display, document-like navigation, ink annotation, and cues indicating document size and location within the document. These software features are complemented by the affordances of the pen tablet device on which XLibris runs. The tangibility of the device reinforces the document reading experience.

XLibris allows users to mark up documents in a manner analogous to writing on paper, but then goes beyond paper by letting readers review, sort and filter clippings of their annotated text in a "Reader's Notebook." In addition, XLibris monitors the free-form ink annotations made while reading, and uses them to discover the reader's interests. XLibris searches for material related to the annotated text, and displays links unobtrusively as "margin links."

We have begun a paper-based study comparing reviewing annotations in the Reader's Notebook with reviewing annotations on the document. In the future, we plan to deploy XLibris and evaluate its use in a real work setting. The main obstacle that must be overcome first is seamless scanning and printing into XLibris.

Although we have not completed our user evaluation, we are encouraged by our observations thus far. XLibris provides a natural, paper-like user interface and people find the computational enhancements powerful and compelling.

ACKNOWLEDGEMENTS

We thank Beverly Harrison, Anuj Gujar, Roy Want and Kim McCall for integrating the pressure sensors into XLibris. We thank DEC SRC for making their Lectern document format publicly available. We thank members of the Xerox PARC PDR team for comments and suggestions. We thank Joe Sullivan and Jim Baker for supporting this research.

REFERENCES

1. Adler, A., Gujar, A., Harrison, B.L., O'Hara, K., and Sellen, A. (1998) A Diary Study of Work-Related Reading: Design Implications for Digital Reading Devices. In *Proceedings of CHI98* (Los Angeles, CA, April 1998), ACM Press.
2. Adler, M.J. and van Doren, C. (1972) *How to Read a Book.* Simon and Schuster, New York, NY.
3. Benest, I.D. (1990) A hypertext system with controlled hype. In *Hypertext: State of the Art,* R. MacAleese and C. Green (Eds.), Intellect, Oxford, UK, pp. 52-63.
4. Birrell, A. and McJones, P. Virtual Paper. Available at www.research.digital.com/SRC/virtualpaper/home.html
5. Dillon, A. (1992) Reading from paper versus screens: a critical review of the empirical literature. *Ergonomics,* 35(10), pp.1297-1326.
6. Dillon, A. (1994) *Designing Usable Electronic Text.* Taylor and Francis, London, UK.
7. Francik, E. (1996) Rapid, Integrated Design of a Multimedia Communication System. In *Human-Computer Interface Design*, M. Rudisill, *et al.*, (Eds.), Morgan Kaufman, San Francisco, CA.
8. Golovchinsky, G. (1997a) Queries? Links? Is there a Difference? In *Proceedings of CHI97*, (Atlanta, Georgia, March 1997), ACM Press, pp. 407-414.
9. Golovchinsky, G. (1997b) What the Query Told the Link: The integration of hypertext and information retrieval. In *Proceedings of Hypertext '97* (Southampton, UK, April 8-11), ACM Press, pp. 67-74.
10. Gould, A., Alfaro, L., Barnes, V., Finn, R., Grischkowsky, N., and Minuto, A. (1987) Reading is slower from CRT displays than from paper: attempts to isolate a single-variable explanation. *Human Factors,* 29(3), pp. 269-299.
11. Guiard, Y. (1987) Asymmetric Division of Labor in Human Skilled Bimanual Action: The Kinematic Chain as a Model. *Journal of Motor Behavior,* 19(4), pp. 486-517.
12. Haas, C. (1996) *Writing Technology: Studies on the materiality of literacy.* Lawrence Erlbaum Associates, Mahwah, NJ.
13. Hardock, G., Kurtenbach, G., and Buxton, W. A. (1993) A Marking Based Interface For Collaborative Writing. In *Proceedings of UIST '93.* ACM Press, pp. 259-266.
14. Harrison, B.L., Fishkin, K., Gujar, A., Mochon, C., and Want, R. (1998) Squeeze me, Hold me, Tilt me! An Exploration of Manipulative User Interfaces. In *Proceedings of CHI98* (Los Angeles, CA, April 1998), ACM Press.
15. Johnson, A. (1997) Fax Trends. *Office Equipment and Products,* July 1997, p. 25.
16. Levy, D.M. and Marshall, C.C. (1994) Washington's White Horse? A Look at Assumptions Underlying Digital Libraries. In *Proceedings of Digital Libraries '94.* Texas A&M University Press, College Station, TX.
17. Mutoh (1997) Mutoh America Inc. Available at www.mutoh.com
18. O'Hara, K. and Sellen, A. (1997) A Comparison of Reading Paper and On-Line Documents. In *Proceedings of CHI97* (Atlanta, GA, March 1997), ACM Press, pp. 335-342.
19. Phelps, T.A. and Wilensky, R. (1996) Towards Active, Extensible, Networked Documents: Multivalent Architecture and Applications. In *Proceedings of Digital Libraries '96,* ACM Press. Pp. 100-108.
20. Rhodes, B.J. and Starner, T. (1996) A continuously running automated information retrieval system. In *Proceedings of The First International Conference on The Practical Application of Intelligent Agents and Multi Agent Technology (PAAM '96)*, London, UK, April 1996, pp. 487-495.
21. Sellen, A. and Harper, R. (1997) Paper as an Analytic Resource in the Design of New Technologies. In *Proceedings of CHI97* (Atlanta, GA, March 1997), ACM Press, pp. 319- 326.
22. Wilcox, L.D., Schilit, B.N., and Sawhney, N. (1997) Dynomite: A Dynamically Organized Ink and Audio Notebook. In *Proceedings of CHI97* (Atlanta, Georgia, March 1997), ACM Press, pp. 186-193.
23. Wolf, G.C., Rhyne, J.R., and Ellozy, H.A. (1989) The Paper-like Interface. In *Designing and Using Human-Computer Interfaces and Knowledge-Based Systems*, G. Salvendy and M.J. Smith (eds.), Elsevier Science Publishers, Amsterdam, The Netherlands, pp. 494-501.

Bullseye! When Fitts' Law Doesn't Fit

Naomi Friedlander, Kevin Schlueter and Marilyn Mantei

Department of Computer Science
University of Toronto
10 Kings College Road
Toronto, ON
Canada M5S 4G4

{naomi, kevins, mantei}@dgp.toronto.edu

ABSTRACT

Today's GUI interfaces require considerable visual attention for their operation. Consequently, interface events use up precious screen real estate and disenfranchise blind users from current software usage. If interfaces move to the realm of auditory and tactile designs, these problems are mitigated. However, it is not clear how much useful HCI research, particularly performance time models, will transfer from the visual to the non-visual. This paper attempts to answer a small part of this question by considering performance time models for menu selection in a non-visual bullseye menu. We chose to study non-visual bullseye menus because we have found them to be highly useful in non-visual interfaces: they can serve as effective non-visual replacements for several visual linear menus.

MOTIVATION

Standard GUIs rely heavily on the visual modality, because it is an efficient and effective means of interaction between humans and machines. The PC of today includes a large CRT that can display high resolution graphics, but may not include high-quality speakers (or even a sound card) for emitting sounds. Tactile input/output device are not generally included either. One may think that the reason for the overwhelming popularity of visual interfaces and the rarity of non-visual ones is that non-visual interfaces are simply not needed in today's mainstream applications. We argue that non-visual interfaces are indeed needed, for several important reasons.

Blind Users Compute Too

Users who have a visual impairment are at an extreme disadvantage. The WIMP interface provides feedback that is almost all visual. Sounds are sometimes used in this interface, but only for special purposes such as to attract the attention of the user. Some work has been performed on creating non-visual interfaces, but the emphasis of current research remains with the visual modality.

CHI 98 Los Angeles CA USA

Screen Space is a Precious Resource

If a particular display mechanism has low resolution or is designed be small, such as that of a PDA or another hand-held device, then for the sake of efficiency, the display space should be used only for output which cannot be conveyed any other way. Even in systems with large resolution screens, displayed information sometimes covers other information which the user may want to see. For example, when a users pulls down a linear menu is activated, the menu may cover important information on the screen. Thus screen space should be considered a precious resource.

Visual Overload

Although the resolution of today's monitors is a vast improvement over the CRT's of the past, users still suffer from fatigue effects caused by looking at computer displays for a long period of time, such as dry eyes or difficulty focusing on the screen. These fatigue effects are a symptom of visual overload. If some of the visual components of interaction were replaced by non-visual components, visual overload would decrease, and users may suffer less from these fatigue effects.

Non-visual Interfaces May Be More Intuitive

One of the main goals of interaction design is to render the interface as intuitive as possible. In our everyday environments humans receive a variety of stimuli playing upon all senses, including aural and tactile, and we instinctively respond to these stimuli. If computing systems take advantage of these instinctive responses, they will be more intuitive to use.

Non-visual Interfaces May Support the Visual Task

Users tend to perform better on user interface tasks they are familiar with. Hence learnability plays a central role in the usability of an interface tool. Some users may find that learning via the visual channel is effective, while others may not. We can make thus user interfaces more learnable for more users by supplying learning cues in multiple modalities.

MODELLING USER PERFORMANCE IN NON-VISUAL INTERFACES

Much research has been done on modelling user performance in visual interface tasks, helping both HCI researchers predict behaviour during task execution and interface designers build better interaction tools. Non-visual interface elements have also been developed, but there has been little work on modelling them. This paper provides a modest remedy. It proposes an effective non-visual user interface element called a *bullseye menu.* It then proposes and evaluates two performance time models for selecting an item from it. One of these models is Fitts' Law, which is commonly used to model performance time for visual menu selection tasks. The other is a simple linear model, which states that the time to select from this menu is a linear function of the index of the target ring. Perhaps surprisingly, Fitts' Law is shown to be inferior in this particular instance of a non-visual user interface task.

THE BULLSEYE MENU

A bullseye menu is a series of concentric *circles* divided into *sectors.* We call the region between two neighbouring concentric circles a *ring*. Each ring has a corresponding *index*: The index of the ring containing the first set of menu items is 1, the index of the ring containing the second set of menu items is 2, etc. The direction and distance a user moves a pointing device (in our case, a stylus) from a floating origin determines the menu category. For example, selection in ring 1 in the upward sector might correspond to selecting the "File: New" command, and selection in ring 3 in the right-hand sector might correspond to selecting the "Edit: Copy" command. The bullseye menu can be implemented both visually and non-visually. Figure 1 depicts selection from it.

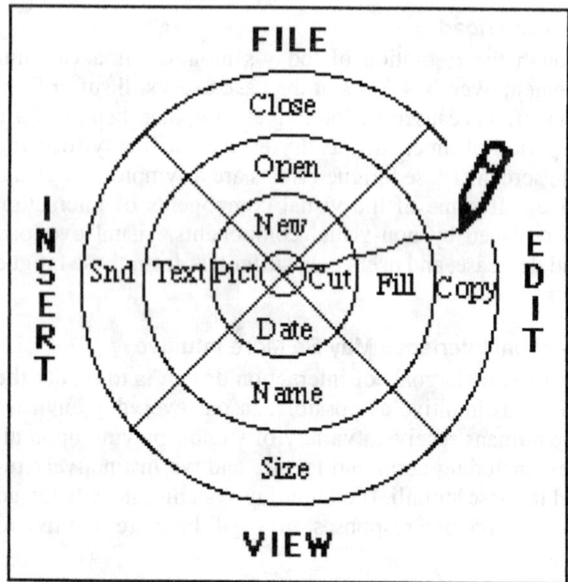

Figure 1: Selection from a bullseye menu.

A Visual Version

In the visual implementation, the system displays a menu in response to some user interface event, such as putting pressure on a stylus. The user visually locates the target selection, moves the cursor to it, and upon seeing that the cursor is in the target area, performs some action to select that item. Clearly, we can model this task using Fitts' Law [3].

A Non-visual Version

Our non-visual version is similar to the visual one, except the menu is not displayed and a non-visual cue signals when the user rolls the cursor over a circle. Thus, after activating the menu, the user moves the cursor in the direction of the item s/he wishes to select and counts the number of non-visual cues. For example, if the user knows that "Edit:Copy" is in ring 3 in the right-hand sector, s/he might press a mouse button and move the mouse to the right for three signals to select that particular menu item.

A bullseye menu therefore serves as a good basis for non-visual menu selections for two reasons. There is no need to move the mouse to a certain position before making a menu selection. Also, it is possible to handle a large number of menu selections or handle the menu selections represented by a number of linear menus in a straightforward and easily understandable fashion.

STUDYING PERFORMANCE TIME

We decided to consider two different types of non-visual cues in our study: a simple "beep" sound and a tactile pulse, which was provided by a relay connected to the parallel port of the PC and controlled through the interface code (see [4], [5]). Since we were only interested in selection time and not search time, our study was designed so that the user need not think about the location of the target item: its position was explicitly given by specifying the index of the target ring and the direction to move.

Two Possible Performance Time Models

An important criterion for determining the value of an interface is establishing how well users perform when interacting with it. Developing an appropriate model for user performance helps us predict the efficiency and effectiveness of interface usage. We can directly compare one interface to another by comparing their performance time models.

In the next subsections we give a short description of Fitts' Law, a short description of an alternative, "linear" model, and discuss which may be more appropriate for modelling performance times in a non-visual bullseye menu.

Fitts' Law

Fitts' Law [3] predicts that the time for a user to move a pointing device to a *target* from a *starting point* is logarithmically proportional to the distance to the target and inversely logarithmically proportional to the size of the target. The original Fitts' Law formula has been updated by Mackenzie [6]. We used Mackenzie's version for our experiment.

We can use Fitts' Law to measure the effectiveness of visual menus [8] by computing that menu's mean time to target. We can then compare this to the mean times of other menu systems to determine relative effectiveness.

Boritz, Booth and Cowan [4] performed what is probably the most relevant Fitts' Law study to non-visual bullseye menus. They showed that Fitts' Law is a good predictor of the time to target for circular menus and that time to target is affected mainly by target size and distance, and only slightly by direction. This effect is small enough that it is possible to use one set of Fitts' law constants for all directions.

We thus considered Fitts' Law to be a possible performance model for selection from a non-visual bullseye menu. There is an analogous physical movement – a user moves toward a target and homes in on it. The direction to the target is already known, and through aural or haptic feedback, the user is aware of when the cursor is in the target area. It also appeared that menu selection could be modelled by Fitts' Law from casual observation of the task. We observed that when users select from a non-visual menu they tend to move the stylus more quickly through the inner rings of the menu, and slow down when the target ring is close. These changes in the speed of movement are comparable to deceleration in a Fitts' Law task. We also noted that Fitts' Law has often been used to model visual menus. We therefore considered it worthwhile to investigate whether it can adequately model non-visual bullseye menus.

Why Consider an Alternative to Fitts' Law?

There are characteristics of visual Fitts' Law tasks that are quite different from non-visual bullseye menu selection. First, Fitts' Law tasks generally involve visual, instead of auditory or tactile feedback. It was unclear whether these communication channels are sufficiently similar to the visual channel for Fitts' Law to apply. With visual feedback, the user is constantly aware of the exact position of the target. With tactile and auditory feedback, the user can only approximate the position of the target, given the distance s/he has already moved the stylus and the speed at which the stylus is moving.

Second, typical Fitts' Law tasks have no intermediate targets between the original position of the pointing device and the target. The feedback signals at each of the inner circles on the path to the target in a non-visual bullseye menu can be considered intermediate targets. If the user wishes to select from ring 4, then s/he knows s/he must detect 4 feedback signals in order to reach it. The first three signals are intermediate targets: they must each be reached before the fourth (and ultimate) target is reached. The user aims for the first signal, then the second, then the third, and finally the fourth, and then stops. It seems likely that the presence of these intermediate targets has on effect on user performance.

The Linear Model

The linear model discussed in this paper predicts that the mean time to hit a target is a linear function of inputs (possibly including the size of the target and the index of the target ring), rather than a logarithmic function, as in Fitts' Law. Our literature review uncovered only one other instance of a linear model being used for predicting time to target, Accot and Zhai [1]. They point out that while Fitts' Law adequately describes performance time for most pointing tasks, it inadequately describes performance time for trajectory-based pointing tasks. They describe a "steering law" which states that the time to select a target along a trajectory is a linear function of the width of the path and length of the distance travelled to the target. They perform a series of experiments involving various angles of movement and differing "tunnel" widths in which the cursor must be moved. The results show that this "steering law" does indeed explain user behaviour in trajectory-based tasks.

Although this work involves visual tasks, it is related to the task of selecting from the non-visual bullseye menu. The "tunnels" through which Accot and Zhai's users travelled constrained an otherwise unrestrained motion: users moved the pointing device with more prudence.

The same restrained motion may exist in the task of selection from a non-visual bullseye menu. Each signal produced by traversing a circle on the way to the target ring must be counted, and therefore may be considered an intermediate target. These intermediate targets may act as speed regulators: the user must accurately count the number of signals traversed, which might cause the speed of movement to be more constant or more restrained. Also, there is a ceiling on how fast humans can count: users need to move the stylus slowly enough so that they can count the signals. Since the target position in a non-visual bullseye menu is ambiguous, users must carefully keep track of their orientation in the menu in order to avoid over- or undershoot. A constrained movement similar to that found in trajectory-based visual pointing tasks may therefore result, which prompted us to investigate the possibility of a linear model of performance.

An intuitive explanation of the difference between these two models is as follows. Imagine a driver looking for a parking spot in a busy parking lot. S/he finds one and wishes to reach it before any other drivers have a chance to park there. S/he drives quickly to the spot but applies brakes in time so that s/he won't drive past the spot. This scenario is analogous to a Fitts' Law task – the user moves toward the target quickly but applies a stopping function to avoid overshoot. Imagine another scenario: a driver with failing headlights wishes to find a spot in the fourth row of an unilluminated parking lot at night time, and knows s/he must cross four speed bumps to get to it. The driver proceeds slowly enough to count the speed bumps (and to avoid damage to the automobile) in order to know when s/he reaches the fourth row. This scenario is analogous to a linear model: the driver's speed is more constant and regulated – the time to reach the fourth row of parking spots is a linear function of the number of speed bumps to cross.

THE EXPERIMENT

The aim of the experiment was to determine, for both tactile and auditory feedback, whether times to target aggregated over all users could be better modelled by Fitts' Law or a linear function of the index of the target ring.

Experimental Design Overview

The experiment used a four-factor, 7 x 3 x 4 x 2 design. The first factor was number of signals to target. Number of signals to target varied from 1 to 7. We considered it important to vary the target ring so that we could be assured that the hypothesis was proved for a variety of target distances. The second factor was ring width. Ring widths were 2.5 mm, 4.2 mm and 5.8 mm. We chose to vary the width of the ring between trials so that the data would include a variety of target sizes. It should be noted that we did not vary the widths of the rings within each trial: in other words, for each trial, the circles in the menu were equidistant. The third factor was direction. Directions were up, down, left and right. This variable was used for another study, but was not considered in determining the best performance time model. The fourth factor was type of nonvisual feedback, auditory or tactile. The dependent variable in the study was the time to reach the menu target. Both correct trials and error trials involving overshoot and undershoot were used in the analysis.

Subjects

Twelve subjects between the ages of 19 and 46 participated in this study. They were all undergraduate or graduate students in the Department of Computer Science at the University of Toronto. Eight subjects were male and four were female. All except one of the participants had 4 or more years of experience with computers on a daily basis, and one had two years of experience. Nine of the participants had 4 or more years of experience with a mouse on a daily basis, one had 1 year of experience, one had 2 years of experience, and one had 3 years of experience. All except one participant had little or no experience with a stylus in the past, and one had some experience.

Apparatus

We used an NEC PowerMate V100 pentium computer, a WACOM Digitizer II tablet, and the tactile feedback mechanism described in Friedlander, Schlueter and Mantei [4]. The operating system was Windows 95. We used the standard Windows system beep for the auditory feedback. We also used a fan to cool the tactile feedback mechanism. The tablet driver was developed by LCS/Telegraphics for the Wintab^{TM} 16- and 32-bit API. The experiment was implemented using Visual C++^{TM}.

Method

The experiment consisted of four one-hour sessions. The sessions were on four consecutive days – we wanted subjects to have one night's sleep in between sessions to alleviate fatigue effects and at the same time to ensure that any learning that had taken place during that day's session would not be forgotten. Each participant attended all four sessions at approximately the same time over the four days. These times varied between participants but were always between 9 am and 6 pm. Each session took one hour. The experiment type (auditory vs. tactile feedback) was alternated between sessions, and the feedback type used on the first day was counterbalanced over the 12 subjects.

Each *trial set* consisted of 32 trials. It began with 4 practice trials, where the user was instructed to move in one of four directions for 4 signals. These practice trials were not included in the data analysis: they were included so that users could familiarize themselves with the particular ring width used in that trial set before the actual trials took place. The remaining 28 actual trials were unique combinations of the 4 directions and 7 target ring indexes in random order. One block of trials contained three trial sets: at the beginning of the experiment each of the three ring widths was randomly and uniquely assigned one of the three trial sets; thus, in each block, each trial set used a particular ring width once in random order. The order in which each ring width was tested was maintained for each block of trial sets within that particular session. The first two sessions consisted of 10 blocks, and the last two consisted of 13 blocks. (As users became better at the selection task, they could perform the task more quickly, and we could fit more trials in a one-hour session.) We were only interested in measuring performance and not learning. Thus, only the last two sessions were analyzed.

For each trial, a black compass was displayed at the center of the screen (Figure 4), with the north, south, east and west arms marked "N", "S", "E" and "W" respectively. The centre of the compass contained a letter (either N, S, E, W) and a number (1 to 7) indicating the direction and ring index of the target selection. The compass arm corresponding to the direction (denoted by the letter at the center) was highlighted in red. The user was to place the stylus anywhere on the tablet, press down the stylus button, move the stylus in the given direction for the given number of signals (either tactile pulses or beeps) while keeping the stylus button pressed, and release when the target was reached. An error tone was played if the user missed the target. A message indicating whether the user's error rate was acceptable was displayed at the bottom right-hand side of the screen ("Error rate is OK." or "Error rate is a little high."). A count of the number of errors of the last 10 trials was used as the error rate: if 20% or more of these trials were unsuccessful, the error rate was considered high, otherwise the error rate was considered satisfactory. The purpose of displaying whether the error rate was acceptable was to ensure that users did not become too careless in performing the selection task. The screen display used in the experiment is shown in Figure 2.

The Hypothesis

Our hypothesis, H, is: the mean time to select a menu item from a non-visual bullseye menu aggregated over multiple users and multiple trials is linear to the index of the target ring, as opposed to following Fitts' Law. The null hypothesis, H_{null}, is the negation of H.

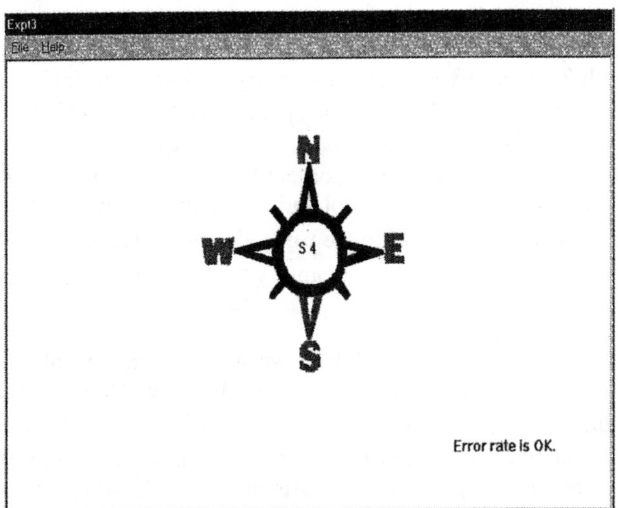

Figure 2: The Experiment Interface. According to the directions at the centre of the compass, the user is to move downwards for four signals.

To elaborate, Fitts' law in this case predicts that

$$MT = a + b \cdot \log_2\left(\frac{A}{W} + 1\right)$$

where A is the distance to target, MT is the time to target, and W is the size of the target. (The values of a and b are determined through linear regression.) We define r to be the width of a ring, and all rings have equal widths. Mackenzie discusses applying Fitts' Law to two-dimensional tasks [7] via two different methods: one by designating the width of the target as the trace of the approach vector through the centre of the target and the other by choosing the smaller of the width and height of the target. This work helped us to determine the target size of non-visual bullseye menu items: we set W, the size of the target, to the length of the one-dimensional trace of the stylus moving in a line perpendicular to the tangent of the ring. The length of this trace is the ring width, r. Thus, the width of the target is:

$$W = r$$

The distance to the target is measured from the starting point to the midpoint of the target ring. Thus, if the index of the target ring is x, then the distance from the centre of the menu to the midpoint of the target is the width of that ring; is the sum of the x-1 intermediate ring widths plus half the target ring width. Therefore, the distance from the starting point to the centre of the target is a multiple of the distance between the rings:

$$A = r(x - 0.5)$$

Thus, for our experiments, Fitts' Law becomes:

$$MT = a + b \cdot \log_2(x + 0.5)$$

The Linear model is much simpler:

$$MT = a + b \cdot x$$

As in Fitts' Law, MT is the mean performance time, and a and b are constants determined from linear regression.

The linear model can be best compared to Fitts' Law by noting that one obtains the former from the latter by removing the logarithm. The implication is that MT increases more quickly with increasing x in the linear model than in Fitts' Law.

In both cases, we average the data over ring size and the index of the target ring; thus, twenty-one data points are generated for our regression analysis. The analysis compares the actual mean time to target to the calculated mean times to target in both the linear and Fitts' Law models.

RESULTS

We tested our hypothesis separately for each feedback mechanism. For both auditory and tactile feedback, a simple regression analysis was performed on the nonerror cases and the overshoot/undershoot error trials. The results of this are shown in Figure 3 and Figure 4. It appears from these that the linear model is more accurate for both modalities. Looking at the linear model regression fits, we see that the data points are everywhere distributed evenly on both sides of the fitted line. In the Fitts' Law regression fit, the central data points sag below the fitted line, while the outermost data points fall above it. These observations are confirmed by the r-squared

Regression Analyses – Auditory Feedback

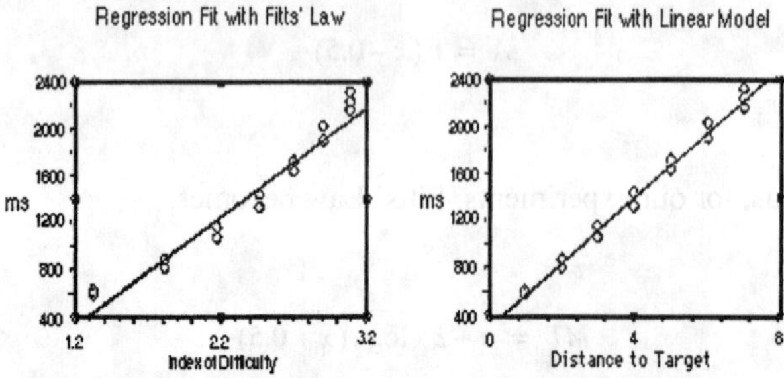

Figure 3: A comparison of the regression analyses of the observed data vs. Fitts' Law and the linear model in the auditory feedback case.

Regression Analyses – Tactile Feedback

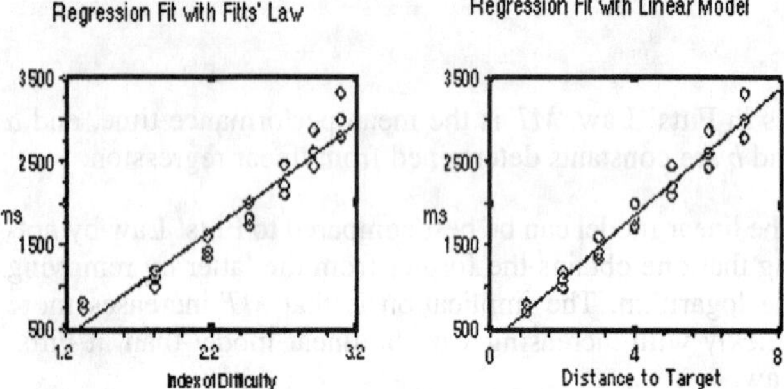

Figure 4: A comparison of the regression analyses of the observed data vs. Fitts' Law and the linear model in the tactile feedback case.

error terms for the regression. These values can be found in Figure 5.

	Auditory Feedback	Tactile Feedback
r^2, Linear vs. Observed Data	0.992	0.968
r^2, Fitts' vs. Observed Data	0.949	0.931

Figure 5: Resulting r^2 values from regression analysis, Fitts' Law vs. Observed Data and Linear Model vs. Observed Data, in both the auditory and tactile cases.

However, these observations are not enough to confirm our hypothesis. We need to verify that the difference in regression fits is significant. This was done as follows:

Both the linear model and Fitts' law are of the form $T = a + Db$, where *a, b* are constants, and *D* is the Index of Difficulty for the Fitts' Law comparison and the index of the target ring for the linear model comparison. It is therefore true that the *D* term in both Fitts' Law and the linear model are positively correlated with *T*. Asking which of the regression lines fits the data most closely is therefore equivalent to asking which of the *D* terms is most positively correlated with *T*. In our experiment, the values for r_F (the correlation coefficient for Fitts' Law) and r_L (the correlation coefficient for the linear model) are 0.996 and 0.974 respectively for auditory and 0.984 and 0.965 for tactile. Hotellings' T-test can be used to determine the probability that the true value of r_F is greater than or equal to the true value of r_L. This is equivalent to determining the probability that our null hypothesis is true.

To perform Hotellings' T-test, we need two more values. One is the coefficient of correlation between D_F and D_L, which we will call $r_{F,L}$. We calculated this to be 0.985, for both tactile and auditory experiments. The other is *N*, the number of data points in the regression analysis, which is 21 (7 target ring indexes * 3 ring widths). The quantity given by [5]:

$$t = (r_L - r_F)\sqrt{\frac{(N-3)(1+r_{F,L})}{2\left(1 - r_{F,L}^2 - r_L^2 - r_F^2 + 2r_{F,L}r_Lr_F\right)}}$$

is therefore a T distribution with 18 degrees of freedom. For the auditory experiment, $t = 6.78$. Thus,

$$p[t \geq 6.78] = p[H_{null}] < 0.0005$$

In the tactile feedback case, $t = 2.64$. Thus,

$$p[t \geq 2.64] = p[H_{null}] < 0.01$$

In both cases, the null hypothesis is rejected: the linear model is a better predictor of performance time than Fitts' Law.

IMPLICATIONS

A linear model for performance time fits selection in a non-visual bullseye menu more closely than Fitts' Law. We can think of two reasons for this. Users tend to restrain movement when performing this task in order to count accurately. They also seem to prefer counting at a particular speed, and adjust their movements in order to do so.

The better fit of the linear model means that performance times for non-visual bullseye menu selections are likely not as fast as for equivalent visual bullseye menus, for which selection times are modelled by Fitts' Law. In Fitts' Law tasks, performance time increases logarithmically with increased distance. They will thus be increasingly superior to performance times that are linear functions of distance as the distance to the menu selection increases. However, this also implies that there may be little difference when selection distances are short. Thus, UI designers should put frequently accessed menu items near the centre of a non-visual bullseye menu. It may also be wise for them to increase the number of sectors, so that more selections are closer to the centre.

Our results are evidence that selection tasks are performed differently when simple non-visual feedback is given instead of visual. Probably because the former gives less information to the user than the latter, selection tasks cannot be performed as efficiently. It is interesting to ask whether and how the non-visual feedback we describe can be augmented to improve user performance so that it is equivalent to visual feedback. Perhaps information about distance travelled can be communicated progressively using various qualities of sound, such as frequency and timbre. Users may then be able to "home in" on their selection as they can when they can see it. One could measure the degree of improvement achieved by enhancing the non-visual feedback by comparing performance time data to that predicted by the linear model and by Fitts' Law. The linear model would serve as the baseline, and Fitts' Law would be the presumed upper bound. Our performance time model for our simple non-visual feedback task is not that far from that for the equivalent visual feedback task (i.e. a linear model is closer to a logarithmic model than a quadratic or cubic one). We are thus optimistic that enhancing non-visual feedback will bring user performance close to that of visual feedback.

It should be noted that the results from the regression analysis of the Fitts' Law case are quite good: in both the auditory and tactile cases the r^2 value of these analyses are higher than 0.9. Without consideration of the linear model it would be quite understandable to assume that Fitts' Law is the best predictor model for the task at hand. An important implication of our work is that Fitts' Law should not be the only performance model tested for new user interface tasks. Even if it fits the task quite well, there may be a better choice.

CONCLUSIONS

Using non-visual bullseye menus, dependence on visual feedback in menu selection can be eliminated at the cost of increased performance time, if users are able to memorize the configuration of the menu.

The mean time for non-visual bullseye menu selection follows a linear function of the ring number rather than Fitts' Law when feedback is given at equidistant intervals. This is likely due to the constraining effect of counting the signals. In spite of the limited information conveyed by non-visual feedback in comparison to visual feedback, the performance time model is not as different as one might expect. This suggests that user performance with enhanced non-visual feedback can closely approximate that with visual feedback, especially when the distance to the target is not large.

FUTURE WORK

Consider other non-visual menu designs

A bullseye menu is essentially a pie menu modified to permit more efficient selection from a large number of options. Both of these characteristics make bullseye menus attractive for non-visual interfaces. Marking menus [6] [7] have very similar properties and are thus a logical alternative for non-visual menus. It would be interesting to implement marking menus non-visually to study their advantages and disadvantages vs. bullseye menus as well as to see if a non-visual performance model for them differs from a visual one.

Consider an alternative predictor model

Walker [9] found that times to select from a pull-down menu were always better than those for a walking (or cascading) menu. Walking menus involve a series of Fitts' Law targets (one in each linear portion of the configuration) rather than just one target in the corresponding pull-down menu. The amount by which the series of start-up times increased total performance time was longer than the amount by which the series of targets with shorter distances reduced it. Perhaps the intermediate targets of a non-visual bullseye menu are analogous to the intermediate targets in a visual walking menu. Thus, future work may include developing a predictor model for selection from a non-visual bullseye menu as a summation series of Fitts' Law tasks, one for each of the intermediate targets (i.e. the intermediate signals perceived) on the way to selecting the non-visual bullseye menu target item.

Consider directional influences.

This work does not take into account directional influence on performance time. It would be useful to verify whether the linear model predicts performance time better than Fitts' Law for each direction, rather than just for data aggregated over all directions.

Implement a real non-visual bullseye menu

The experiment discussed in the thesis used an abstraction of the selection task in a non-visual bullseye menu. It would be useful to construct and conduct usability studies on an actual instance of such a menu, and do some longitudinal data collection on performance to study learning effects. A preliminary implementation could also have 4 sectors and 7 rings, and each of the sectors could correspond to a familiar menu, such as File or Edit. The menu could be activated by a right-button mouse click, and if no mouse movement is detected within a certain dwell time (perhaps 500 milliseconds) a corresponding visual bullseye menu would appear to remind the user of the menu configuration.

Several aspects of the implementation of non-visual bullseye menus can be studied. Learning can be explored. Expert performance can be compared to expert performance in other menu systems. Studies of user satisfaction can be performed to see what elements of non-visual bullseye menus they find appealing, and what elements do not work well. The auditory feedback implementation on adjacent machines could be problematic for users: studies can be performed on this type of interference and which types of sounds to select to minimize interference.

Rerun experiment on blind participants

The original goal of the research into non-visual bullseye menus was to develop an interface for the visually impaired. Although the results of our experiment indicate that the non-visual bullseye menu is a viable menu system which allows users to make "eyes-free" selections, we have not verified that it can be used by visually-impaired users. We would like to rerun the experiment on only visually-impaired participants, and perform some usability studies for this target group.

Rerun the experiment with slight changes to investigate particular performance issues

Our experiment did a somewhat basic analysis of selection in a vanilla bullseye menu. The menu always had four sectors, and the circles were equidistant. We only implemented two non-visual feedback mechanisms, and didn't look into their visual equivalents.

Part of this paper discusses Fitts' Law as a possible model for human performance. The linear model fit better, but perhaps this was due to the fact that the circles of the bullseye menu were equidistant. Would Fitts' Law be more suitable for a bullseye menu that had distances between circles increase logarithmically? Would performance improve if the non-visual feedback were enhanced to give users more precise information about the position of the pointing device? Having more sectors potentially decreases the distance to the selection and reduces the advantage that visual bullseye menus have over non-visual ones. However, does increasing the number of sectors make selection in non-visual bullseye menus more difficult? Investigations such as this would give researches more insight into the workings of Fitts' Law and the effect of non-visual feedback.

REFERENCES

1. Accot, J. & Zhai, S. Beyond Fitts' Law: models for trajectory-based HCI tasks. *Proceedings of the CHI '97 Conference on Human Factors in Computing Systems*, New York: ACM.

2. Boritz, J., Booth, K. S., & Cowan, W. B. (1991) Fitts's law studies of directional mouse movement. *Proceedings of Graphics Interface '91*, 216-223.

3. Fitts, P. M. (1954) The information capacity of the human motor system in controlling the amplitude of movement. *Journal of Experimental Psychology*, 47, 381-391.

4. Friedlander, N., Schlueter, K. & Mantei, M. (1997) A bullseye menu with sound feedback. *Proceedings of Human Computer International '97*, New York: Elsevier.

5. Friedlander, N., Schlueter, K. & Mantei, M. (1997) Easy tactile feedback at bargain basement prices. *Companion Proceedings of the CHI'97 Conference on Human Factors in Computing Systems Extended Abstracts*, 308-309, New York: ACM.

6. Guilford, J. P (1973). *Fundamental Statistics in Psychology and Education*. USA: McGraw-Hill.

7. Kurtenbach, G. & Buxton, W. (1993) The limits of expert performance using hierarchical marking menus. *Proceedings of the CHI'93 Conference on Human Factors in Computing Systems,* New York: ACM.

8. Kurtenbach, G., Sellen, A. & Buxton, W. (1993) An empirical evaluation of some articulatory and cognitive aspects of "marking menus." *Human Computer Interaction*, 8(2), 1-23.

9. Mackenzie, I. S. (1991) Fitts' law as a performance model in human-computer interaction. Doctoral dissertation, University of Toronto.

10. Mackenzie, I. S. & Buxton, W. (1992) Extending Fitts' law to two-dimensional tasks. *Proceedings of the CHI '92 Conference on Human Factors in Computing Systems*, 219-226, New York: ACM.

11. Norman, K. L. (1991) *The Psychology of Menu Selection: Designing Cognitive Control of the Human/ Computer Interface*. New Jersey: Ablex Publishing Co.

12. Walker, N. (1991) Optimizing speed and accuracy of menu selection: a comparison of walking and pull-down menus. *International Journal of Man-Machine Studies*, 35, 871-890.

Cognitive Function Analysis for Human-Centered Automation of Safety-Critical Systems

Guy A. Boy
European Institute of Cognitive Sciences and Engineering (EURISCO)
4, Avenue Edouard Belin, 31400 Toulouse, France
+33.5.62.17.38.38
boy@onecert.fr

ABSTRACT

The Cognitive Function Analysis is a methodology supported by a mediating tool for the human-centered automation of safety-critical systems [4]. It is based on a socio-cognitive model linking the artifact being designed, the user's activity, the task to be performed, and the organizational environment. Cognitive functions can be allocated to humans or machines. They are characterized by their role, context definition and associated resources. The methodology is supported by active design documents as mediating representations of the artifact, the interaction description and cognitive function descriptors being designed, redesigned and used as usability criteria to evaluate the distribution of cognitive functions among humans and machines. This methodology enhances user-centered and participatory design, and traceability of design decisions. It was successfully tested on three main applications in the aeronautics domain. One of them is presented.

Keywords

Active documents, aeronautics, evaluation, function allocation, automation, organizational memory systems, participatory design, safety critical systems.

INTRODUCTION

Automation has been mostly constructed and applied by engineers in the past. Human factors people have brought new principles and methods to test the usability of complex systems during the design process. However, end users are only one concern. Automation needs to be considered in a broader sense than just user-centered automation [1] because it should be done for the benefit of the largest range of people including users, designers, support people and trainers. Participatory design and traceability of design decisions (design history) is consequently a crucial issue [7], in particular, for the design and management of safety-critical systems. Safety-critical systems include, for example, critical-care, nuclear, emergency, military and aerospace systems. They are characterized by the following list of non-exhaustive issues: time-pressure, complexity, risk assessment and human reliability. A wrong function allocation in such systems may result in catastrophic accidents. The paper will first introduce an agent-oriented cognitive engineering model. Subsequently, the concept of cognitive function will be developed. Human-centered automation will be described in terms of cognitive function allocation among humans and machines along four fundamental dimensions: task, artifact, user and environment. Active design documents supporting the Cognitive Function Analysis (CFA) will be presented and illustrated as mediating tools that support the allocation process. An aeronautical example will illustrate the use of CFA. Conclusions and perspectives will be given in the balance of the paper.

AGENT ORIENTATION: A COGNITIVE ENGINEERING MODEL

Both human and machine agents have cognitive functions

Safety-critical systems such as aircraft currently include a tremendous amount of computer software. Previous human-machine interaction that was energy-intensive has now evolved towards human-computer interaction that is information-intensive. The nature of interaction is quite different to the point that new jobs (represented by specific cognitive functions) have emerged. An aircraft pilot has become a manager of what can best be thought of as artificial agents. He or she needs to coordinate, trust, supervise and cooperate with these agents. Several traditional human factors principles and approaches have also become obsolete because the paradigm of a single agent, as an information processor, is no longer appropriate. Multi-agent models [13] are better suited to capture the essence of today's information-intensive safety-critical systems. A human agent interacting with a software agent [5] must be aware of:

- what the other agent has done (history awareness);
- what the other agent is doing now and for how long (action awareness);
- why the other agent is doing what it does (action rationale awareness);
- what the other agent is going to do next and when (intention awareness).

These four situation awareness issues correspond to the most frequently asked questions in advanced cockpits [25]. Agent-to-agent communication has been described by many authors working in the domain of highly automated systems [1, 16]. Several attributes were used to describe automation. Among them, in addition to basic usability principles [17], and from our experience in aeronautics, the following were found important in multi-agent human-machine communication:

- prediction, i.e., ability to anticipate consequences of actions on highly automated systems;
- feedback on activities and intentions;
- autonomy, i.e., amount of autonomous performance;
- elegance, i.e., ability not to add additional burden to human operators in critical contexts;
- trust, i.e., ability to maintain trust in its activities;
- expertise-intensive versus common-sense interaction;
- programmability, i.e., ability to program and re-program highly automated systems.

The AUTO pyramid

An artifact is a physical or conceptual human-designed entity useful for a given class of users to perform specific tasks. Carroll and Rosson discussed transactions between tasks and artifacts in the human-computer interaction world [8]. It is sometimes very difficult to know if the task defines the artifact or if the artifact defines the task. In reality, users' profiles, tasks and artifacts are incrementally defined to satisfy a specific objective. The task and the user are usually taken into account implicitly. Task can be modeled from a task analysis or a model of the process that the artifact will help to perform. A specified task leads to a set of information requirements for the artifact. Conversely, the artifact sends back its own technological limitations according to the current availability of technology. Users can be incrementally taken into account in the design loop either through the development of descriptive or analogous user models. User modeling can be implicit or explicit, and leads to the definition of appropriate user profiles. When a version of the artifact and the task are available, a user can use the artifact to perform the task. An analysis of the user activity is then possible, which contributes to adapt both the task, procedures and training, and artifact ergonomics. The artifact-user-task triangle [4] implicitly defines an incremental approach to design/evaluation that is similar to the spiral model for software development [2].

Artifact design and use are defined not only from a local ergonomics viewpoint, but also from management and organizational viewpoints both in the short term and the long term. Global ergonomics expends the triangle to a pyramid by introducing a fourth concept: organizational environment. The *artifact-user-task-organizational environment* (AUTO) pyramid introduces three additional issues (Figure 1): the designed artifact emerges in the environment, and the environment evolves from the integration of the artifact; the task requires the organization of new jobs, and the environment sends back new roles; users using the artifact to perform the task in the organizational environment determine social issues.

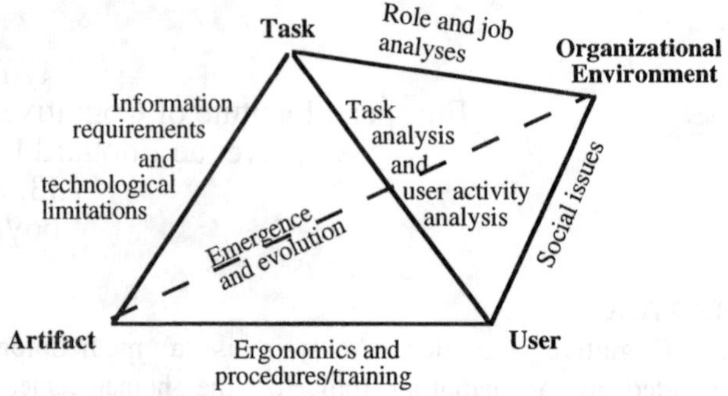

Figure 1. The AUTO pyramid.

Cognitive function definition

In highly dynamic complex automated systems, users develop cognitive skilled processes that are very context-sensitive. These numerous skills can be approximated by cognitive functions. By definition, a cognitive function enables its user to transform a (prescribed) task into an activity (effective task). It represents a human cognitive process that has a role in a limited context using a set of resources. The role of a cognitive function covers the concept of responsibility (who is in charge?) Eliciting a cognitive function requires one to specify its context of use (where and when this function is relevant and usable?) Unlike goal-driven models, such as GOMS [6], that tend to valorize smaller numbers of methods, context-driven models such as cognitive functions try to elicit organization of context patterns that facilitate the access to the right cognitive function at the right time. Cognitive functions are incrementally categorized according to context. A cognitive function is implementable when it is linked to right resources that are cognitive functions themselves. With respect to the AUTO pyramid (Figure 2), these resources can be user-based (e.g., knowledge and skills), task-based (e.g., checklists or procedures), artifact-based (e.g., artifact level of affordance [18]) or organizational environment-based (e.g., delegation to other agents).

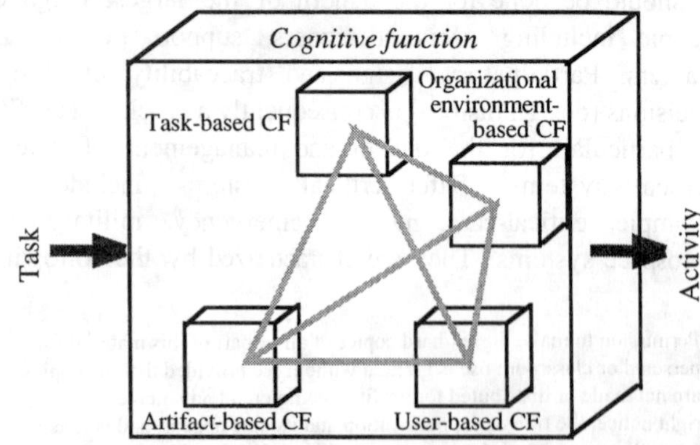

Figure 2. Four types of cognitive function components.

An important issue is to make the constraints explicit enough to guide the decisions during the design process. Cognitive functions are experimentally elicited by interpreting the deviations between the task and user activity in terms of role, context and resources. Examples of high-level cognitive functions are: situation identification, decision making, planning, and actions coordination.

HUMAN-CENTERED AUTOMATION OF SAFETY-CRITICAL SYSTEMS

The procedure-interface duality

In safety-critical systems, operational procedures are used in either normal or abnormal situations. Operational procedures are supposed to help operators during the execution of prescribed tasks by enhancing an appropriate level of situation awareness and control. It is usually assumed that people tend to forget to do things or how to do things in many situations. Procedures are designed as memory aids. In abnormal situations, pilots need to be guided under time-pressure, high workload and critical situations that involve safety issues. Procedures are often available in the form of checklists that are intended to be used during the execution of the task (it is shallow knowledge that serves as a guideline to insure an acceptable performance), and operations rationale that needs to be learned off-line from the execution of the task (this is deep knowledge that would induce too high a workload if it was interpreted on-line.) The main problem with this approach is that people may even forget to use procedures! Or they anticipate things before the execution of a procedure. People tend to prefer to use their minds to recognize a situation instead of immediately jumping on their checklist books as they are usually required to do in aviation, for instance [9]. In other words, people are not necessarily good procedure followers. They want to be in control [1]. Ultimately, if the user interface includes the right situation patterns that afford the recognition of and response to the right problems at the right time, then formal procedures are no longer necessary. In this case, people interact with the system in a symbiotic way. The better the interface is, the less procedures are needed. Conversely, the more obscure the interface is, the more procedures are needed to insure a reasonable level of performance. This is the procedure-interface duality issue.

Example of advanced cockpit automation

Prior to the integration of flight management computers (FMCs) onboard aircraft, pilots planned their flights using paper and pencil technology. An FMC is a real-time database management system where flight routes are stored. It enables the pilot to program or recall a flight route and adapt it to the current flight conditions. This machine-centered flight management is programmed to define a vertical profile and a speed profile, taking into account air traffic control requirements and performance criteria. Once a flight route is programmed into the system, the FMC drives the airplane by providing setpoints to the autopilot. The FMC computes the aircraft position continually, using stored aircraft performance data and navigation data [11]. The same kind of example was studied by Irving et al. using the GOMS approach [14], and experimentally by Sarter and Woods to study pilots' mental load model and awareness of the FMC [19]. An analysis of the cognitive functions involved in the use of the Multifunction Command and Display Unit (MCDU), the user interface of the FMC, enabled us to elicit a set of cognitive functions categorized according to the AUTO pyramid.

Programming a flight plan using a MCDU is a complex cognitive function that may be decomposed into several layers of simpler cognitive functions. Only task-based and artifact-based cognitive functions are elicited first. User-based and organizational environment-based cognitive functions are subsequently added to describe user's assets and problems as well as environmental issues. For instance, the *Preflight* task-based cognitive function is decomposed into three task-based cognitive functions *Setting up*, *Flight plan preparation*, and *Performance*. *Setting up* is then decomposed into two task-based cognitive functions *System status check*, and *Navaids deselection*. *System status check* is conditionally (*If A/C Status page is not displayed*) decomposed into four artifact-based cognitive functions *Depress 'DATA' key*, *Select 'A/C STATUS'*, *Check Database period of validity*, and *Check Clock/Date*. Anytime a cognitive function is elicited, its role and context of use are also described or refined.

An easy-to-use user interface usually results in affordable artifact-based cognitive functions. Most pilots find the MCDU difficult to learn and use. This complexity of use can be illustrated using two kinds of observations. First, the pilot needs to push keys, browse menus that can be more or less complicated due to the depth or recursion of these menus, i.e., artifact-based cognitive functions are often complicated. Second, pilots delegate complex cognitive functions, such as minimizing the distance between two geographical waypoints or satisfying a constraint imposed by air traffic control, to onboard computers that help manage the flight, i.e., task-based cognitive functions delegated to the machine are complex and require the involvement of information-intensive cognitive functions such as situation awareness and supervisory control [20].

Cognitive function allocation

The first step of CFA involves eliciting, constructing and chaining cognitive functions that are involved in a specific task. A second step involves a set of principles and guidelines that guide cognitive function allocation among agents, and help understand the repercussions of this allocation. These repercussions can be expressed in terms of new cognitive functions created and new relations between agents. The development of new tools can facilitate the execution of such cognitive functions by taking over part of the job currently done by humans.

Formalizing cognitive function allocation is a means of better understanding and controlling automation according to a list of automation goals such as those proposed by Billings for the air transportation system [1]: *safety*: to conduct all operations, from start to end, without harm to persons or property; *reliability*: to provide reliable operations without interference from environmental variables; *economy*: to conduct all operations as economically as possible; and *comfort*: to conduct all operations in a manner that maximizes users' and related persons' health and comfort. Human-centered automation principles should be clearly defined, e.g., technology-mediated human-human communication can be greatly enhanced by directing tedious and time-consuming cognitive functions towards the machine, and cognitive functions that keep user awareness and control of the situation towards the human.

CFA provides a theoretical basis supporting a current debate on direct manipulation versus interface agents [21]. Artifact-based cognitive function transfer from the user to the machine usually defines an automation that enhances direct manipulation. Task-based cognitive function transfer from the user to the machine defines an automation that enhances task delegation to a software agent. It distributes the responsibility of the task between the human and the machine. The way task-based cognitive function transfer is understood by designers is crucial because it defines the user's role and context of use of the machine. This is why a careful CFA is required to define roles, context of use and resources of each cognitive function involved in the human-machine interaction of safety-critical systems. For instance, it is often crucial that users perceive the level of autonomy of the designed artifact. The result is that the context of use of a cognitive function must be incrementally co-constructed by both designers and users in a participatory design framework that is proposed in the next section.

ACTIVE DESIGN DOCUMENT SUPPORT

Active design document definition

CFA is supported by a cooperative use of active design documents. Exploiting the procedure-interface duality issue and the AUTO pyramid, an active design document is defined by three aspects [3]:

- *interaction descriptions*–the symbolic aspect, which conveys ideas and information, e.g., the description of a procedure to follow; this aspect of an active design document is related to the task involved in the use of the artifact; it defines the *task space;*
- *interface objects* connected to interaction descriptions–the emotive aspect, which expresses, evokes, and elicits feelings and *attitudes*, e.g., a mockup of the interface being designed; this aspect is related to the interface of the artifact that provides interactive capabilities; it defines the *activity space*;
- *contextual links* between the interaction descriptions and the interface objects, e.g., annotations or comments contextually generated during tests; this aspect is related to the user and the environment in which the artifact is used; it defines the *cognitive function space.*

Development of active design documents

After a first active design document is designed and developed (interface objects and interaction descriptions), a first round of analysis determines the first contextual links. Such an analysis is based on the evaluation of observed or reported human-machine interactions produced by typical users. An active design document can be refined either by: revising interaction descriptions under the requirements of previously generated contextual links and possibly the modification of interface objects; modifying interface objects under the requirements of previously generated contextual links and possibly the modification of interaction descriptions; or generating contextual links to provide information on flaws and relevant comments of the congruence between interaction descriptions and interface objects. Active design document creation and refinement is guided using usability principles and criteria that are based on domain requirements. In particular, contextual links are generated and structured according to these usability principles and criteria. They can be generated as: free text, quantitative and qualitative evaluations based on specific criteria and constraints.

Evaluation using cognitive function descriptors

Measuring is evaluating. A measurement is always based on a model or a theory. It can be subjective or objective according to the confidence that we have in both the model and the measurer. For a long time, human and social sciences implicitly acknowledged that quantitative measures were good (objective) evaluation tools. Unfortunately, quantification works on a closed-world and do not take into account unanticipated events very well. Thus, there was a need for a new type of approach. The expert system approach has revealed a new type of model based on the use of qualitative expertise. Instead of having a specified metrics, e.g. metrics in statistics, a few domain experts are required to provide their knowledge. Experts or key informants are usually good evaluators when they are provided with the right things to evaluate. They are also able to extend the initial set of criteria. This approach is thus more open-world and enables evaluation to take into account unanticipated events. Its weakness is that experts are subjective, based on their background, experience, skills and situation awareness. The choice of a (small) number of evaluators is thus crucial. It is guided by a good mix of common sense and domain knowledge.

The description of a cognitive function by a domain expert is often a good measure of the quality, relevance and usability of an artifact. Cognitive functions are elicited with respect to their role, context and associated resources. They are described by cognitive function descriptors (CFDs) that are measurable attributes constructed from domain knowledge and usability attributes of multi-agent human-machine environments (already provided in this paper). CFDs should be clearly defined in order to be further compared and widely accepted. In other words, a CFD has the following properties: two CFDs provided by two experts A and B should be comparable, i.e., expressed properties should be clearly defined and consistent in both CFDs; this is a comparison issue; any CFD template should be defined according to current cognitive engineering results and the terminology of the application domain; this is a standardization issue. CFDs are usually defined from observation in work situations and in meetings of experts. The following CFDs constitute a potential list of usability criteria for HCA in the MCDU/FMC domain: *long-term memory* (LTM): necessary effort to recall the way to execute an instruction; *data affordance* (DA): information relevance and capacity to guide the user on the next action to perform; explicit data enable the user to minimize his or her memory effort and workload before starting the next action; *data readability* (DR): data representation, format and font; *feedback* (FB): system reaction after each action of the user; *data format* (DF): consistency between data format and insertion-identification procedure; *error tolerance* (ET): human error possibility, importance of its consequence and its recovery ease; *keystroke number* (KN): number of keystrokes to perform an action; *recursion levels* (RL): number of recursion levels to perform an action. In addition, each qualitative CFD is typically evaluated according to a five-value scale: 1: excellent; 2: good; 3: medium; 4: poor; 5: unacceptable. An example of evaluation results included in a contextual link of an active design document is provided in Table 1.

Cognitive Function Level 1	Cognitive Function Level 2	LTM	DA	DR	FB	DF	ET	KN	RL
WIND ENTRY: format error	- if F-PLN page not displayed DEPRESS F-PLN key	3	2		1			1	+1
	- DEPRESS 'NEXT PAGE' key	5	3		1			1	+1
	- SELECT 'VERT REV WPT'	3	2	4	1			1	+1
	- ENTER & INSERT 'WIND'	1	2	4	1	3		8	
	Total						4	**11**	**3**
RECOVERY									
- erase message 'FORMAT ERROR'	- DEPRESS 'CLR' key	5	3		1			1	
- erase invalid data	- DEPRESS 'CLR' key 5 times	3	2		1			5	
- enter corrected data	- ENTER & INSERT 'CORRECT WIND'	2	1	4	1	3	5	5	
	Total							**11**	

Table 1. An example of CFA results for a classical MCDU.

Incremental generation of active design documents

In the FMC experiment, the general trend was to move from a generic MCDU interface, e.g., including generic functions keys, to an integrated interface that includes affordable interface objects. These affordable interface objects are hypermedia objects that can be easily modified during the design process, and include relevant properties and behaviors that are specified from the first CFA results. Figure 3 presents an example of an alternative interface for programming the FMC. In this kind of interface, waypoints and trajectories are interface objects that have properties and behaviors. For instance, the preprogrammed waypoint TRS1 can be changed into the waypoint TRS2 by simply selecting it. When TRS2 is selected, the trajectory is automatically redrawn. Main advantages of interface objects direct manipulation are:

- quick access to the appropriate information;
- easy understanding of what to do (i.e., natural interaction with interface objects);
- immediate feedback, visualization of usual objects, and affordance to assess them against expected results.

In other words, the pilot does not have to search for waypoints by browsing FMC pages using a classical MCDU. He or she directly manipulates meaningful objects that appropriately react to provide immediate possible configurations. The example provided in Figure 3 shows that a new interaction device is necessary to manipulate interface objects such as waypoints. The trackpad was chosen for environmental reasons. A second cognitive function analysis was then performed. Results are presented in the form of tables (Figure 3). The first observation of this table shows that scores are closer to 1 than to 5,... as expected!

Participatory design and traceability issues

Active design document generation and maintenance concretizes Muller's arguments in favor of *participatory design* [16]: to combine diverse sources of expertise; to formalize the ownership and commitment by all of the people who will eventually work on or with the designed artifact; to participate in decision-making by the people who will be affected by the design decisions. Active design documents are shareable prototypes of the real artifacts being designed that can be used by real users to assess their usability. Prototypes should be familiar to users. Their limitations should be clearly identified. A shareable prototype should be understandable by all the members of the design team and keep them on a common track. Active design documents enable the design team to share concepts by writing and reading their expression in the form of multimedia objects. They are incrementally modified to harmonize mutual understanding of design team members. The basic difference between the classical human-factors-oriented design and participatory design is that instead of analyzing the existing user organization and the application area, design team members learn from each other. Active design documents define an active *external memory*. They are incrementally modified according to possible design options, human factors evaluation criteria and organizational requirements. In the CFA approach, modifications are induced from interaction among design team members. Active design documents may come to dead ends as well as evolve into currently valid documents describing the artifact. Corresponding document evolution is kept to preserve design history.

Basically, in the beginning of the design process, active design documents may have large interaction descriptions that document a preliminary task analysis, roughly sketched interface objects, and contextual links mainly defined by early design rationale. Later in the life cycle of the artifact, active design documents interface objects become more sophisticated and user-friendly, interaction descriptions should become minimal, and contextual links richer in comments and feedback from tests. The shorter and crisper interaction descriptions are, the easier the interaction with interface objects is. An important issue is to handle the growth of contextual links. This is precisely where traceability problems arise. We call *traceability* the process that enables one to recall design decisions and the various alternatives as well as why these alternatives were not chosen. Contextual links are used to implement an indexing mechanism. They should be classified, generalized, and incrementally simplified in order to be efficiently used. A first solution is to group them by viewpoint.

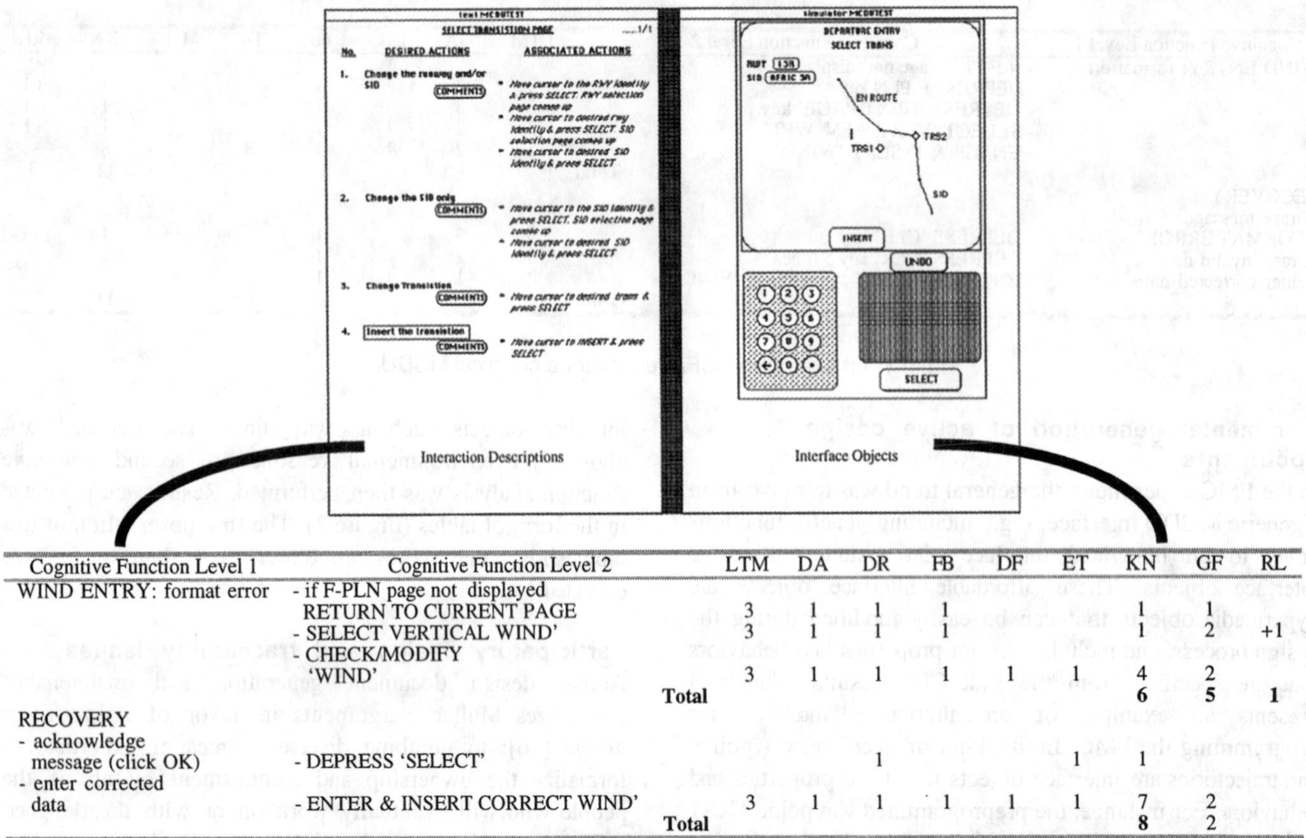

Cognitive Function Level 1	Cognitive Function Level 2		LTM	DA	DR	FB	DF	ET	KN	GF	RL
WIND ENTRY: format error	- if F-PLN page not displayed RETURN TO CURRENT PAGE		3	1	1	1			1	1	
	- SELECT VERTICAL WIND'		3	1	1	1			1	2	+1
	- CHECK/MODIFY 'WIND'		3	1	1	1	1	1	4	2	
		Total							**6**	**5**	**1**
RECOVERY - acknowledge message (click OK)	- DEPRESS 'SELECT'				1			1	1		
- enter corrected data	- ENTER & INSERT CORRECT WIND'		3	1	1	1	1	1	7	2	
		Total							**8**	**2**	

Figure 3. Example of a MCDU alternative interface, the associated procedure (interaction description) and the content of a contextual link expressed in the form of a CFD table (the whole imbedded in an active document).

RELATED WORK

Depending on the type of behavior, two types of analysis are possible:

- A goal-oriented task analysis involves a hierarchic decomposition of goals into subgoals, and so on until basic actions are found and executed. The corresponding scientific approach is top-down, based on analytical descriptions. It usually attempts to model internal cognitive mechanisms of a single agent, and to describe exhaustively the goal space.
- An event-oriented task analysis involves an incremental composition of events into sub-contexts and contexts. The corresponding scientific approach is bottom-up, based on observation protocols of situated actions [22]. It usually attempts to model multi-agent interaction within an organizational environment, and to describe exhaustively the context space.

When a human performs a task, his or her behavior is opportunistic, i.e., both intentional and reactive. In the control of complex dynamic systems, human operators need to be and are opportunistic. They need to be ahead of the machine (goal-driven anticipation) and respond quickly to events that are not anticipated (event-driven reaction). With respect to some typical events they may change their strategies, i.e., their goal-driven behavior. CFA differs from GOMS techniques [6, 14] because it attempts to incrementally model contexts of use of both human and machine cognitive functions. Since safety-critical systems such as aircraft induce both intentional and reactive behaviors, CFA is very appropriate to study and describe situation awareness, human errors, cooperation, coordination, for instance.

	Goal-oriented task analysis	Event-oriented task analysis
Human behavior models	Intentional and deliberative	Reactive and explicative
Approach	Top-down based on analytical descriptions	Bottom-up based on cooperative observation protocols and interactions with users
Modeled process	Internal model of an agent	Interaction between several agents
Goal space	Strongly defined, limited by the granularity of the description	Loosely defined
Context space	Loosely defined	Strongly defined, limited by the granularity of the description

Table 2. Goal- versus event-oriented task analysis.

Table 2 presents the advantages and drawbacks of these two different task analysis approaches. Goal-driven approaches are well adapted to analyze problem solving. Event-driven approaches are better suited to analyze problem formulation or problem setting (situation patterns) in complex system environments. Indeed, a problem is characterized by a problem statement and a problem solving process leading to a solution. Everybody knows that a well stated problem is already half solved and this is well adapted to (successful) reactive behavior. Moreover, when a beginner starts to learn a particular domain, he or she starts learning problem solving methods (analytical knowledge) which he or she will improve incrementally simply by augmenting and improving these methods, and also by improving the way he or she formulates problems. In a cognitive function analysis, the emphasis is put more on problem formulation, and then context, than on problem solving. Problem formulation, like problem solving, is an incremental process that again calls for Pasteur's 'prepared mind.' But it is not a magical or mysterious process [15]. CFA combines both goal- and event-oriented analyses within a single framework uspported by active design documents.

CFA is a global approach that considers the task as part of an overall framework that also includes the artifact, the user and the organizational environment. In other words, the task cannot be isolated from the actual work that includes a description of three types of contraints, i.e., roles, contexts and involved resources. Similarly, Vicente and Pejtersen [24] propose a constraint-based approach to work analysis (that focuses on flexibility and broad scope of applicability), instead of an instruction-based approach to task analysis (that focuses on efficiency of task performance). A constraint-based approach does not tell you the right way to do your task. It just lists constraints. As in CFA, this approach leads also to a functional description for human-machine systems.

Active design documents support sketching [12] as mediating tools for design team members. They also enable one to trace design decisions based on the evaluation of cognitive function descriptors. From this perspective, CFA has similarities to *Raison d'Etre* [9]. CFA contributes to the creation and maintenance of a living design memory [23].

CONCLUSIONS AND PERSPECTIVES

This paper has presented a methodology for human-centered design of highly automated safety-critical systems. It focusses on cognitive function allocation using a combined analytical and situated (empirical) methodology to human-centered automation.

CFA enables the investigator to describe cognitive functions with respect to the constraints and limitations imposed by the artifact, the user, the task, and the organizational environment.

CFA attacks the difficult issue of function allocation. It enables the description of how new technology influences distributed cognition by using a participatory design tool both mediating creativity and evaluation, and accounting for design history. Since it is very difficult and sometimes impossible to predict design-induced errors that lead to incidents or accidents, incremental evaluations and refinements are mandatory during the overall life cycle of an artifact. Active design documents offer the opportunity to users and other parties involved in the life-cycle of an artifact to formally influence its design. CFA supported by the effective use of active design documents provides descriptions of possible interaction, design rationale and evaluations linked to the actual artifact.

By enabling the visualization of interaction descriptions, interface objects and cognitive functions involved in the use of the artifact being designed, the design team is likely to anticipate and discover more contexts of use, more appropriate resources to perform the task and cooperative features required within the organizational environment. Since automation always leads to the definition of new roles, and possibly jobs for users, CFA offers a framework to elicit and analyze these new roles and changes. In particular, CFA is useful to analyze and possibly anticipate new risks in safety-critical systems.

The traceability of design rationale and associated human-factors-oriented evaluations represents a real asset for the organization that develops an artifact. Active design documents are designed and refined from the beginning to the end of the artifact life-cycle. A remaining important issue is to justify time and money spent in the implementation of CFA in a large-size industrial organization. Estimated development costs should be compared to the costs of late modifications of the artifact, incidents and accidents due to design flaws, and unnecessary training or maintenance. An evaluation framework, such as proposed by Zimmermann and Selvin [26], should be set up to assess the methodology against organizational requirements and current needs.

ACKNOWLEDGMENTS

Hubert L'Ebraly, Thierry Broignez, Meriem Chater, Mark Hicks, Christophe Solans and Krishnakumar greatly contributed to the current state of the CFA methodology at EURISCO, Aerospatiale and British Aerospace. Thank you all. Jonathan Grudin, David Novick, Helen Wilson and anonymous reviewers provided astute advice towards improving the quality of this paper.

REFERENCES

1. Billings, C.E. (1991). *Human-centered aircraft automation philosphy*. NASA TM 103885, NASA Ames Research Center, Moffett Field, CA, USA
2. Boehm, B.W. (1988). A spiral model of software development and enhancement. *IEEE Computer*, Vol. 21, no. 5, May, pp. 61-72.
3. Boy, G.A. (1997). Active design documents. *Proceedings of ACM DIS'97 Conference*. ACM Press, New York.
4. Boy, G.A. (1998). *Cognitive Function Analysis*. Ablex Publishing Corporation, Greenwich, CT.
5. Bradshaw, J. (1997). *Software Agents*. MIT/AAAI Press, Cambridge, MA, USA.
6. Card, S.K., Moran, T.P. & Newell, A. (1983). *The Psychology of Human-Computer Interaction*. Lawrence Erlbaum.
7. Carroll, J.M. and Moran, T. (1991). Introduction to this special issue on design rationale. *Human-Computer Interaction*, Lawrence Erlbaum Associate, Inc., Vol. 6.
8. Carroll, J.M. & Rosson, M.B. (1991). Deliberated Evolution: Stalking the View Matcher in Design Space. *Human-Computer Interaction*, Lawrence Erlbaum Associate, Inc., Volume 6, pp. 281-318.
9. Carroll, J.M., Alpert, S.R., Karat, J., Van Deusen, M.S. & Rosson, M.B. (1994). Raison d'Etre: Capturing design history and rationale in multimedia narratives. *Proceedings of the ACM CHI'94 Conference*. (Boston, April 24-28). New York: ACM Press, pp. 192-197, 478.
10. De Brito, G., Pinet, J. & Boy, G. (1997). *Checklist use in new generation aircraft.* EURISCO Technical Report no. T-97-042.
11. FCOM-A320 (1997). *Flight Crew Operation Manual A320.* Airbus Industrie, Toulouse-Blagnac, France.
12. Fischer, G., Nakakoji, K. & Oswald, J. (1995). Supporting the evolution of design artifacts with representations of context and intent. *Proceedings of Designing Interactive Systems (DIS'95).* ACM Press, pp. 7-15.
13. Hutchins, E. (1995). How a Cockpit Remembers its Speeds. *Cognitive Science*, 19, pp. 265-288.
14. Irving, S., Polson, P. & Irving, J.E. (1994). A GOMS analysis of the advanced automated cockpit. *Human Factors in Computing Systems. CHI'94 Conference Proceedings*. ACM Press, pp. 344-350.
15. Langley, P.W., Simon, H.A., Bradshaw, G. & Zytkow, J.M. (1987). *Scientific dicovery; An account of the creative process*. MIT Press. Boston, MA.
16. Muller, M. (1991). Participatory design in Britain and North America: Responding to the «Scandinavian Challenge». In *Reading Through Technology, CHI'91 Conference Proceedings*. S.P. Robertson, G.M. Ohlson and J.S. Ohlson Eds. ACM, pp. 389-392.
17. Nielsen, J. (1993). *Usability engineering*. Academic Press. London.
18. Norman, D.A. (1992). Turn Signals are the Facial Expressions of Automobiles. Reading, MA: Addison-Wesley.
19. Sarter, N.B. & Woods, D.D. (1994). Pilot interaction with cockpit automation II: An experimental study of pilots' mental model and awareness of the Flight Management System. *International Journal of Aviation Psychology*, 4, pp. 1-28.
20. Sheridan, T.B. (1984). Supervisory control of remote manipulators, vehicules and dynamic processes: experiment in command and display aiding. *Advances in Man-Machine Systems Research*, J.A.I. Press, 1, pp. 49-137.
21. Shneiderman, B. & Maes, P. (1997). Direct manipulation vs. Interface agents. *interactions*, November-December, volume IV.6.
22. Suchman, L.A. (1987). *Plans and situated actions. The problem of human-machine communication*. Cambridge, England: Cambridge University Press
23. Terveeen, L.G, Selfridge, P.G. & Long, M.D. (1995). Living design memory: Framework, implementation and lesson learned. *Human-Computer Interaction*, Volume 10, pp. 1-37.
24. Vicente, K. J., & Pejtersen, A. M. (in preparation). *Cognitive work analysis: Towards, safe, productive, and healthy computer-based work*. Mahwah, NJ: Erlbaum.
25. Wiener, E.L. (1995). The focus of automation: Which tasks should be automated. *EURISCO Industrial Summer School on Human-Centered Automation*. Saint-Lary, France.
26. Zimmermann, B. & Selvin, A.M. (1997). A framework for assessing group memory approaches for software design projects. *Proceedings of DIS'97*. August 18-20, Amsterdam, The Netherlands.

Delegation and Circumvention: Two Faces of Efficiency

Suresh K. Bhavnani
School of Architecture
Carnegie Mellon University
Pittsburgh PA 15213 USA
+1 412 363 8308
suresh@andrew.cmu.edu

Bonnie E. John
HCI Institute
Carnegie Mellon University
Pittsburgh PA 15213 USA
+1 412 268 7182
Bonnie.John@cs.cmu.edu

ABSTRACT
Throughout history, inefficient methods to use devices have been replaced by more efficient ones. This shift typically occurs when users discover how to *delegate* work to the powers of a tool, and to *circumvent* its limitations. Strategies of delegation and circumvention, therefore, appear to be the core of efficient use. To show how this approach can explain the relationship between tools and strategies in complex computer systems, we describe five ways to perform a real-world drawing task with current as well as future tools. We then present five corresponding GOMS models that demonstrate the value of efficient strategies when compared to the observed behavior of a professional CAD user. We conclude by presenting a generalized framework to characterize efficient strategies and discuss its relevance to design and training.

Keywords
Strategies, CAD, GOMS, efficiency, productivity.

INTRODUCTION
Records from early civilizations show that humans throughout history have developed devices and processes to assist in the efficient performance of tasks. The Sumerians, for example, first began to write on clay tablets by scratching marks on their surface. Over 700 years, this method of writing gradually changed into the cuneiform script comprising of wedge-shaped marks pressed into clay with a reed stylus. Historians suggest that this change was largely motivated by scribes who discovered that pressing marks into the clay instead of scratching upon its surface was not only faster, but also more durable over time [11].

While the Sumerians may have had the luxury to gradually develop a more efficient method of writing on wet clay, today's users of computer tools have far less attention and time resources to become efficient. As complex applications such as CAD and word-processors continue to explode with a profusion of new tools, users level off into sufficient usage patterns that tend not to exploit potential efficiencies. Furthermore, several longitudinal and real-world studies suggest that neither good design nor experience can ensure that users move from a sufficient to an efficient use of computer tools [4, 6, 8, 14].

CHI 98 Los Angeles CA USA
Copyright 1998 0-89791-975-0/98/ 4..$5.00

Based on observations of real-world use of complex systems, we have argued that *strategies* hold the key to efficient usage, and identified several that were shown to be not only powerful, but also generally useful across applications [3, 4]. However, we need a more systematic approach to understand the relationship between computer tools and efficient strategies. Similar to frameworks that help us understand and prevent errors through better design [15, 16], this paper defines a framework to help us understand and identify efficient strategies.

We begin by analyzing examples from history to understand the relationship between tools and the strategies to use them efficiently. These examples suggest that as new and more powerful tools evolved in the past to improve product and performance, they often presented new limitations either due to inherent constraints, or due to the new tasks that were attempted. The efficient use of such tools therefore required a combination of *delegation strategies* that exploited the powers of these tools, as well as *circumvention strategies* that dealt with their limitations. The circumvention strategies transformed either the process, or the task, or triggered the development of a more powerful tool, in which case the process repeated.

To show how the relationship between tools and strategy is relevant to computer usage, we analyze a real-world CAD task performed by a user during an ethnographic study [2]. Starting from how such a drawing task would be done using manual tools, we explore the effect of the increasing sophistication in CAD tools on strategies to complete the task. In order to test the hypothesis that these strategies are actually efficient and of value to users, we present the results from five GOMS models. These models range from how the user performed the task on a current version of the system, to how the same task could be done in future versions. The analysis demonstrates that regardless of how powerful computer systems become, their efficient usage requires delegation and circumvention strategies. However, while these strategies can have strong effects on product and performance, they may not be obvious to even experienced computer users.

We then present a framework of strategies focused on iterative tasks, and show how it can be generalized. In conclusion we discuss how such a framework could be used to explain the relationship between tools and strategies to users, as well as to help designers more systematically explore the effects of their designs.

CIRCUMVENTION AND DELEGATION IN HISTORY

There are numerous examples throughout history that show the relationship between tools and efficient methods to use them. The following three illustrate some important concepts about efficient methods.

According to surviving records, most scribes of ancient civilizations either wrote from right to left or from top to bottom. But around the fifth century BC the Greeks began a dramatic reversal; for a period their writing zigzagged horizontally in a style known as boustrophedon (as the ox plows), before they settled down to the modern style of writing in English from left to right [7, 11]. What might have caused this gradual but radical shift?

Historians and calligraphy scholars note that this change coincided with the replacement of the reed brush by the reed pen as the dominant writing tool [11]. The reed pen, whose tip, if cut and used properly, offered a more precise way of making marks on papyrus. However, unlike the reed brush, the reed pen could easily catch in the fibers of rough papyrus. Historians hypothesize that the Greeks, over a period of 200 years, realized that it was more efficient to pull the reed pen across the rough papyrus rather than to push it. For a right-handed scribe, this meant writing from left to right. Therefore the Greeks used new methods to exploit the hard material of the reed pen to be more precise, and overcame its limitation by changing the direction of writing.

At a later stage in the history of writing, the reed pen and papyrus were replaced by the much more precise quill and smooth parchment, both of which offered a new range of possibilities to the medieval scribe. Illuminated manuscripts of that era show extremely detailed floral and abstract patterns in brilliant colors. But these elaborate decorations greatly increased the time to produce such books as demonstrated by the Book of Kells from Ireland, which was never completed [11]. One of the incomplete pages reveals how its illuminators had sped up the process. This page, like others, contained several independent patterns that had to be painted in many colors. Although the illuminator could have completed each pattern in turn with all its colors, the page shows that all patterns across the page had been painted with yellow. By finishing *all* areas of one color, the painter had reduced tool switching between paint brushes or color. In addition, this procedure may have allowed the yellow paint to dry on the first pattern while subsequent patterns were painted yellow; consequently another color paint could be applied immediately after the last pattern's yellow was complete. Despite this task organization, such processes still remained time-consuming, and the replication of books was laboriously slow.

The production of books was radically changed with the invention of the printing press. With the advent of this new technology, the construction and replication of individual pages could be done far more rapidly compared to the manual process. However, early printers in Germany took time to realize that the way to exploit the iterative power provided by the press was by *not* adding anything to the copies. For instance, many early books tried to copy the style of scribed manuscripts by hand-painting first letters of paragraphs on pages *after* they were printed. Later printers abandoned this approach, making the book production process far more efficient.

The above examples provide several insights into the evolution of efficient methods. First, none of the efficient methods employed were absolutely necessary to complete the tasks but were employed as they improved either the quality of the product, or performance of the tasks. Because such methods are *goal-oriented* and *non-obligatory,* they have been defined as *strategies* [4, 17].

Second, each new tool offered new or increased powers and, by using the tools efficiently, users could exploit these new powers. These methods can therefore be referred to as *delegation strategies*. In the case of the reed pen and quill, by using proper strategies to prepare and use the tools, users could delegate precision to the tools; with the printing press, users could delegate the iterative task of replication to the printing process.

However, new limitations often accompany new powers, either due to inherent constraints in the tool, or when new tasks are attempted with the new tools. When users perceive such limitations, they may make a change to the process (such as the change in writing direction by the Greeks), or move to another tool (such as the printing press). These transformations can therefore be regarded as *circumvention strategies*.

While the above explanation of circumvention and delegation strategies through history is plausible, what relevance does it have to the evolution of computer tools and the strategies to use them? Moreover, are the efficient strategies to use these tools obvious to experienced users?

THE EFFECT OF DRAWING TOOLS ON EFFICIENT STRATEGIES

To demonstrate how drawing tools affect strategies, we present a real-world task performed by a CAD user during an ethnographic study [2]. This task and user behavior is typical of 9 other users currently being analyzed [1] (for example, see [2] and [3] for the analysis of another user's interaction from the same data). One of the users from that study, "L1", had more than 2 years experience in using a CAD system called MicroStation™ (version 4). His task was to edit a drawing containing ceiling panels in an architectural plan that overlapped air-condition vents. Such repetitive tasks are common during the detail drawing stage of a building design. As vents go vertically through ceiling panels, they both cannot occupy the same space. Therefore, as shown in Figure 1, the task is to remove all the line segments representing ceiling panels that overlap the rectangles representing the air-condition vents.

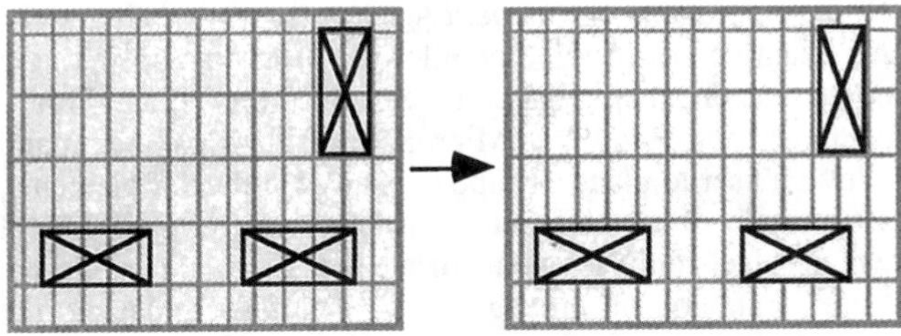

Figure 1. The panel clean-up task requires all ceiling panel lines that overlap the air-condition vents to be modified.

The vents and panels are defined in two different drawing files that are simultaneously displayed on the screen to reveal their overlap. The vents (shown here in black), were placed in a file by an engineer, and are displayed on the screen by L1 as a REFERENCE FILE, where elements can be viewed and selected, but not edited. The panels (shown in gray), were placed by an architect and viewed by L1 as an editable file. L1 can therefore modify the panels with respect to the vents. (This separation of information is necessary to enable architects and engineers to perform tasks independently and at different stages of the design process).

The file has 21 such vents, all of them similar to those shown in Figure 1. L1 zoomed in and panned a single window in order to frame sets of these vents to work on. The rectangle around the vents in Figure 1 represents a typical example of such a window setup, with 3 of the 21 vents showing. The remainder of this paper will refer to editing the panels overlapping these three vents as the *panel clean-up task.*

Depending on the tools available to an architect, the panel clean-up task can be performed in several ways[1]. To understand the relationship between tools and efficient ways to perform the task, we begin by describing strategies to use simple drawing tools available in manual drafting as well as in CAD, and progress towards more sophisticated CAD tools that either exist or are being prototyped. At each stage we shall explore the powers and limits of the tools and discuss efficient strategies to deal with them. It is important to remember that more sophisticated tools usually appear *in addition to* less sophisticated tools in complex computer applications. Thus, users always have a choice of strategies, some of which may have been efficient in older versions of the application, but which are inefficient relative to the new tools.

[1] There are at least two ways that obviate the panel clean-up task. The first is to draw the panel lines only *after* the vents have been placed. But this is not a general solution as the locations of vents typically change during the evolution of the design, in which case the architect has no option but to modify all the panel lines again. The second approach is to make the vents opaque and place them *over* the panel lines, therefore masking the overlap. While this approach could produce a correct printed out drawing in some CAD systems, it does not produce an accurate CAD model on which other operations such as automatic dimensioning can be performed. The strategies presented in this paper assume that the panels and vents can be placed in any order, and the task requires an

Powers and Limits of Precision Tools

It is well-known that manual drafting tools provide users with the ability to create precise graphic elements. For example, the T-square provides constraints to the movement of a pencil and enables a user to draw precise horizontal and parallel lines. Therefore, given a T-square and a set-square, a user can *delegate* the act of achieving precision in horizontal and vertical lines to the tools. With such manual drafting tools, one way to perform the panel clean-up task is to erase a segment of each line to an approximate distance, followed by precisely redrawing the lines to meet accurately at the vents.

As shown in Figure 2a, this approach to the panel clean-up task can also be performed on CAD using equivalent precision tools. The DELETE-PART-OF-ELEMENT tool could cut each panel line, and EXTEND-TO-INTERSECTION could extend it precisely to the boundary of the vent. We call cutting and extending each line in turn an instance of the *Sequence-by-Element* strategy.

The Sequence-by-Element strategy is sufficient for a small number of elements. However, when this strategy is used for iterative tasks with many elements, which are typical in the production of architectural designs (e.g., our user had to clean up 21 vents, each with about four overlapping elements), they can offer little assistance beyond precision. The delete and extend tools offer only the ability to apply single operations to single elements, and therefore have to be repeatedly applied to each line overlapping each vent. One way to circumvent this limitation, at least partially, is to reorganize the task by reducing the number of times a tool is switched. Therefore, instead of selecting the DELETE-PART-OF-ELEMENT tool and applying it to a line, then selecting EXTEND-TO-INTERSECTION and applying it to the line, a more efficient method as shown in Figure 2b, is to delete segments of *all* relevant lines, followed by an extension of *all* the erased lines to meet the vent boundary. We call this method an instance of the *Sequence-by-Operation* strategy.

Sequence-by-Operation addresses the problem of repeated tool-switching in the Sequence-by-Element strategy, but no matter how these tasks are reorganized, precision tools just cannot assist much in iterative tasks. A more general approach to circumvent the limitation of precision tools is to use an entirely different set of tools, which allow the delegation of iteration.

Powers and Limits of Iteration Tools

A wide range of applications such as CAD, spreadsheets, and word-processors provide assistance for iterative tasks through *aggregation.* Aggregation refers to the ability to group disjoint elements in various ways and to manipulate these groups with powerful operators [4]. There appear to be three types of aggregation tools: those that allow for the application of single operations on element aggregates, the application of operation aggregates on single elements, and the application of operation aggregates on element aggregates. We call the general class of strategies to use these tools the *Aggregate-Modify* (AM) strategies.

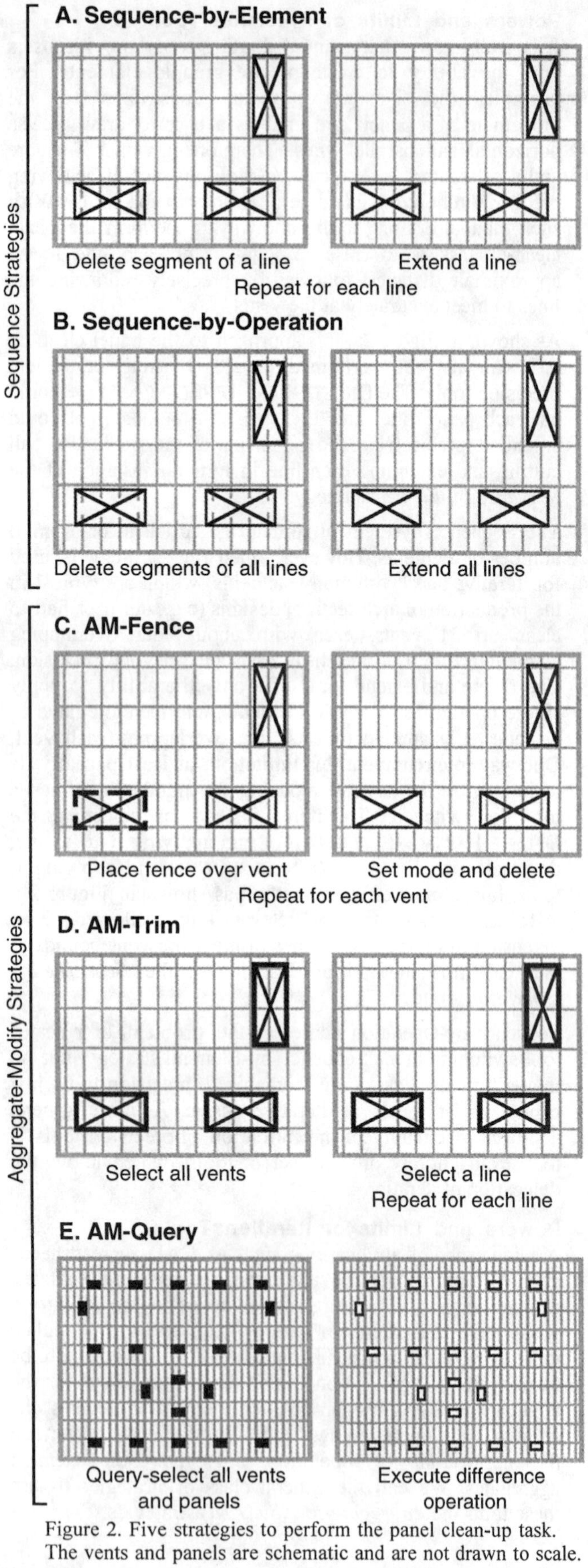

Sequence Strategies

A. Sequence-by-Element

Delete segment of a line
Extend a line
Repeat for each line

B. Sequence-by-Operation

Delete segments of all lines
Extend all lines

Aggregate-Modify Strategies

C. AM-Fence

Place fence over vent
Set mode and delete
Repeat for each vent

D. AM-Trim

Select all vents
Select a line
Repeat for each line

E. AM-Query

Query-select all vents and panels
Execute difference operation

Figure 2. Five strategies to perform the panel clean-up task. The vents and panels are schematic and are not drawn to scale.

Single Operations on Element Aggregates

An example of a tool that allows a user to apply single operations on an aggregate of elements is the PLACE-FENCE command provided by MicroStation™. This command allows a user to place a shape over any number of elements, set a mode of element selection (such as the CLIP-MODE which selects only segments of elements that are inside the fence boundary in the aggregate, therefore replacing the extend operation) and manipulate or modify the resulting set.

As shown in Figure 2c, the FENCE tool could be used to perform the panel clean-up task. To use the FENCE tool, the user must place a rectangular fence on top of the vent by accurately selecting its vertices, setting the CLIP-MODE, and then applying the delete operation to the aggregate. The computer responds by deleting all the element segments within the boundary of the fence. (Since the vents are in a REFERENCE FILE, they will be unaffected by this operation). The crucial aspect of this strategy is to aggregate before modification, which relieves the user from operating on each element. However, the fence tool requires single operations (for example FENCE DELETE) to be independently applied to element aggregates, and there can be only one fence active at a time.

Operation Aggregates on Single Elements

One way to circumvent the single-operation limitation of the FENCE tool is to use the TRIM tool instead. With this tool, a user can select any number of "cutting elements" which define the limits to which intersecting elements will be deleted. Therefore the delete and the extend operation are aggregated for the user over all the vents. However, to disambiguate which segment of an intersecting line is to be deleted, the command requires the user to click on the appropriate segment of each element.

These new powers and limitations allow for a different instantiation of the AM strategy. As shown in Figure 2d, this new tool could be used by first selecting all the vents. When the TRIM command is invoked, the selected vents are interpreted as the limits to which the lines must be modified. As the user selects each line, the aggregated operation is applied to each line by deleting *and* extending each line. Therefore, while this new command addresses the limitation of the fence command which does not aggregate operations, it forces the user to once again iterate over single elements.

Operation Aggregates on Element Aggregates

The fundamental limitation of the FENCE and TRIM tools is that they deal with primitive elements such as lines and shapes, forcing the user in this case to deal with each vent.

Circumventing the limitations of FENCE and TRIM for complex iterative tasks requires a different paradigm of CAD, where users do not place lines and shapes, but *domain objects* such as ceiling panels and vents. As these objects would reside in a database, users could perform sophisticated searches using queries enabling the aggregation and manipulation of information in a much more powerful way [18]. For example, as shown in Figure 2e, one can imagine a command that allows a user to retrieve *all* occurrences of ceiling panels and vents that overlap. This aggregate of vents and panels can be processed by using another command to perform a difference operation between the geometry of each panel and the vents that it overlaps.

The above strategies can be organized in a matrix as shown in Figure 3.

THE VALUE OF EFFICIENT STRATEGIES

Although Figure 3 allows easy identification and classification of sequence and AM strategies, it remains to be shown that the AM strategies are actually more efficient for real-world tasks, and whether they have value for real users. To rigorously understand the effects of strategies on performance, we conducted an NGOMSL analysis (a variant of GOMS [5] described in [12]) on all five strategies to perform the panel clean-up task. Each model implemented one of the strategies in Figure 2 down to the keystroke level. For example, the goal hierarchy (excluding keystrokes for the lowest subgoal) for the AM-Fence strategy (Figure 2c) is shown below:

Goal: Edit Design
. Goal: Modify Multiple Objects *(Repeat for all vents)*
. . Goal: Determine Strategy *(In this case, AM)*
. . . Goal: Execute Aggregate-Modify Strategy
. . . . Goal: Aggregate Objects
. . . . . Goal: Place Fence
. . . . Goal: Modify Objects
. . . . . Goal: Delete Elements
. . . . . . Goal: Set Clip Mode
. . . . . . Goal: Execute Delete Command

The execution times predicted by the NGOMSL models were then compared to L1's real-world behavior to determine the potential for improved productivity.

A GOMS Comparison of Five Strategies

The five NGOMSL models developed using GLEAN [19] (a GOMS interpreter), produced estimates for the execution times for each of the strategies on the panel clean-up task for three vents. As shown in Figure 4, the execution time drops as more and more iterations are delegated to the computer. While Sequence-by-Operation saves some time by grouping operations, the AM strategies produce greater time savings by delegating iteration.

The analysis however revealed one unexpected outcome. The AM-Trim model predicts a time of almost 17 seconds less than the AM-Fence model. This was initially puzzling

Operations		Elements		Strategies
Single	Agg.	Single	Agg.	
X		X		Sequence-by-Element Sequence-by-Operation
X			X	AM-Fence
	X	X		AM-Trim
	X		X	AM-Query

Figure 3. Five iteration strategies based on combinations of functionalities.

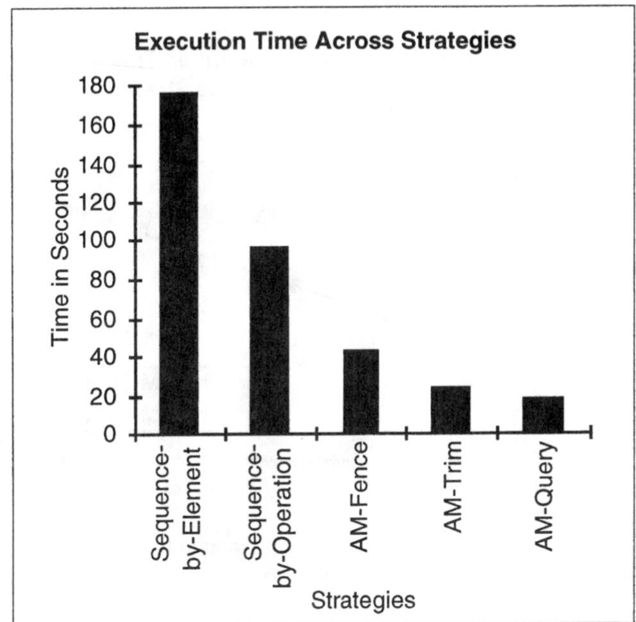

Figure 4. Comparison of the predicted execution times for different strategies to perform the 3-vent panel clean-up task. The AM-Query strategy modifies the panel lines that overlap all 21 vents instead of just 3.

as we expected the selection of individual lines to be more time consuming than using a fence. Investigating the details of this prediction revealed a general principle of these strategies. The models were most sensitive to an increase in the largest undelegated iteration. As shown in Figure 3, the Sequence and AM-Trim models did not support element aggregation and therefore were most sensitive to the number of panel lines. Because the AM-Fence model could not aggregate over operations, it was most sensitive to the number of vents. The AM-Query strategy aggregates over both elements and operations, so its model is neither sensitive to the number of vents nor number of lines, and the time shown in Figure 4 for 3 vents would be the same for the entire 21-vent task. The AM-Trim model and the AM-Fence model are therefore in competition because the number of lines more or less offsets the number of vents in the 3-vent task.

To test this hypothesis, a series of AM-Trim models were executed while keeping the number of vents constant and increasing the number of lines. Figure 5 shows that the predicted execution time for the AM-Trim model is equal to that of the AM-Fence model at around 32 lines, but this time steadily increases as the number of lines increase. Therefore, when the number of lines is small, and the operations are restricted to cut and extend, the TRIM tool is advantageous. But when the number of elements increases, the FENCE tool produces better performance. Our 3-vent example task involves 11 lines, so the TRIM tool wins in Figure 4.

How L1 Performed the Panel Clean-up Task

Figure 4 shows a factor of nine reduction in time from the least efficient strategy to the most efficient strategy. But this theory-based information is only valuable to users if they are not already using efficient strategies. To understand the

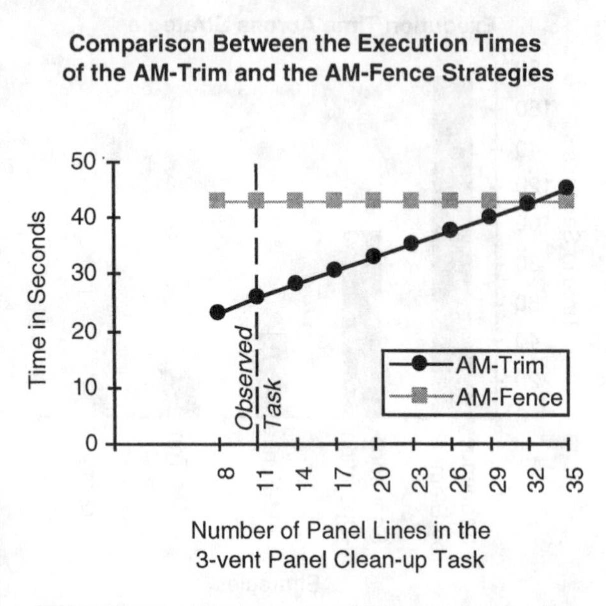

Figure 5. While the execution time for the AM-Fence strategy remains constant, the execution time for the AM-Trim strategy is directly proportionate to the number of panel lines.

potential for productivity improvement, we examined L1's behavior in the context of the specific application he used. MicroStation™ version 4, provided aggregation of elements with the FENCE tool, but no tools for the AM-Trim or AM-Query strategies. However, although L1 had previously used the FENCE tool (based on our ethnographic data), he consistently used the Sequence-by-Operation strategy to delete and extend each line that overlapped all of the 21 vents. The Sequence-by-Operation model is within 11% of the error-free[2] real-world data. If L1 had used the AM-Fence strategy to cut and extend groups of lines, it would have taken him 40% of the time to complete the task.

In addition, L1 committed many errors which added 20.33 seconds to the error-free time. He committed both errors of omission and commission. First, he did not notice that a panel line located very close to the boundary of the upper right-hand vent overlapped the vent; he had to return to it after the rest of the lines had been cut and extended. Second, he accidentally selected a panel line just above the lower right-hand vent instead of the actual vent boundary, thereby extending a panel-line to the wrong location. This error of commission went undetected and the drawing was inaccurate after he completed the task. Finally, he committed many slips in the selection of panel and vent lines, which required him to repeatedly re-select to get exactly the line he wanted.

L1 could have used the AM-Fence strategy with a SNAP mouse option (where the cursor jumps to the closest intersection thereby delegating precision to the computer) to accurately place the fence over the vent. With this procedure *all* element segments within the fence, regardless of how visually close they were to the vent boundary, would have been selected. The errors related to precise line selection, and those of not noticing lines that had to be cut and extended, would not have occurred. This would have reduced performance time *and* increased accuracy.

The above analyses demonstrate two important points. First, when work is delegated to the computer, there are fewer opportunities for errors. Second, even experienced users such as L1, doing extremely repetitive tasks, tend to miss opportunities to delegate work to the computer.

We are not alone in observing that users do not use efficient strategies to delegate iteration to computers. Other studies in CAD [13], as well as in other domains such as spreadsheet use [6, 14] show similar results where users performing iterative tasks also missed opportunities to delegate iteration to computers. The above analyses of strategies to deal with iterative tasks, their effects on performance, as well as the empirical data, provided the basis to develop a generalized framework for iteration that might be useful across domains.

THE ITERATION FRAMEWORK

As discussed earlier with reference to Figure 3, the different tools to assist in iteration could be characterized in terms of single or aggregate operators applied to single or aggregate elements. It is combinations of these functionalities that produce various designs of tools which, in turn, require particular strategies to exploit them. Figure 6 is an extension of Figure 3 to include these relationships in a more detailed framework. Each row defines a particular combination of operator and element types, which is directly related to what can and cannot be delegated to the computer. The strategies emanate from these powers and limitations. The Aggregate-Modify strategies (shaded gray), exploit the power of iteration tools by delegating iteration. Circumvention strategies can range from transforming a task decomposition as demonstrated by the move to the Sequence-by-Operation strategy, to using an entirely different set of tools (moving to a different row in the framework, if the tools exist). CAD tools are shown as examples.

Because the framework shows the explicit relationship between abstract functionalities, tools, and strategies, it can be applied in four different ways: to identify strategy-instantiations in other domains, to explore the design of tools, to describe behavior, and to train users in the repercussions of strategies.

Identification of Strategy Instantiations

Since the iteration framework is structured around abstract functionalities instead of specific tools, it can be used for any application where these particular sets of functionalities appear. For instance, using a STYLES tool on multiple paragraphs in a word-processor can be seen as instantiation of the fourth row in the matrix. The efficient strategy to perform such a task is to define a style with multiple attributes such as bold and italic (aggregate operations), and

[2] The error-free time (105.7 sec.) was calculated by subtracting the time L1 spent to commit, search for, and recover from errors (20.33 sec.), plus unexplained behavior (0.53 sec.), from the total time (126.56 sec.) he spent editing the 3 vents.

Operations		Elements		Example	Powers	Limitations	Efficient Strategies
Single	Agg.	Single	Agg.	CAD Tools	Delegated		
X		X		Line-manip. tools	Precision	Iteration cannot be delegated	Sequence-by-Operation
X			X	Fence, Fence Delete	Iteration over elements	No iteration over operations	AM-Fence
	X	X		Shift-Select, Trim	Iteration over operations	No iteration over elements	AM-Trim
	X		X	Query, Boolean Op.	Iteration over operations and elements	No Propagation	AM-Query

Figure 6. The iteration framework showing the relationship between abstract functionality, tools, and strategies for tasks requiring multiple operations on multiple elements. Precision tools (shown in white) cannot delegate iteration. This limitation can be partially circumvented by reorganizing the task as described by the Sequence-by-Operation strategy, but more fully addressed by using iteration tools with AM strategies (shown in gray). Iteration tools themselves have various limitations which can be circumvented by using increasingly sophisticated iteration tools, or through the use of future propagation tools (not shown).

apply them to multiple paragraphs (aggregate elements), particularly if there are many iterations of this task.

Design of New Tools

To demonstrate the use of this framework to inform design, consider the TRIM tool. The specific operation of this tool was taken from MicroStation™ version 5, and as shown in Figure 6, its limitation is that it does not allow aggregation over elements.

The previous analysis overcame this limitation by going to an entirely new paradigm for CAD where domain-objects are manipulated in a database (a paradigm used by several architectural research projects). However, the framework pinpoints the limitation, which inspires a re-design without changing underlying paradigms. In this re-design, a more specific version of the TRIM tool could allow the selection of closed shapes which could act as cookie cutters on all elements that overlap them. Since the lines to delete would be encompassed by the closed shapes, this would be unambiguous and not require the user to identify each segment. Given this modification, the user could now select all vents and delete all overlapping elements in one step, effectively delegating all iteration to the computer.

Description of Behavior

The framework can also be used to describe how users interact with a system. Since the framework provides a continuum of powers starting from no delegation to the delegation of iteration over operations and elements, one can identify explicitly the level at which a particular user performs a particular task. Instructors could use this information to diagnose lack of knowledge on the part of the user and decide which concepts (e.g., aggregation of operations) and skills to teach (e.g., use of the TRIM tool).

Design of Training

We believe that there is nothing inherently wrong with the way new tools evolve. Often metaphors of older technologies are the only way to start exploring a new technology as its development, usage, and exploration go hand-in-hand. But we do think that the way tools are *introduced* requires a more systematic approach, and when efficient strategies shift, users must be made explicitly aware, not of just *what* the new tools are (as is currently done), but also *how* they directly affect the nature of tasks.

The framework could therefore be used to design training. For instance, users can be taught to recognize opportunities to delegate work to computer powers, as well as to circumvent their limitations Exercises could focus on planning and what we have called *Learning-to-See* (elements and operations to profitably aggregate). In addition, users can do tasks using several different strategies in order to demonstrate the differences in performance these strategies afford. Here, exercises could focus on execution and what we call *Learning-to-Do.* We are currently exploring this approach of Learning-to-See and Learning-to-Do in a course on CAD for architecture graduate students.

TOWARDS A GENERAL FRAMEWORK OF EFFICIENT STRATEGIES

Clearly there are other powers of computer applications beyond precision and iteration. Thus, we are developing a larger framework of which the iteration framework is just a small segment. In addition to precision and iteration, we are currently investigating other powers such as propagation, visualization, and generation as discussed below.

Powers and Limits of Propagation Tools

Although future iteration tools that operate on domain objects with queries are powerful, they also have limitations. For instance, each time a change in the vent layout occurs, the user must remember to make the appropriate changes to panels. Furthermore, these tools can provide little help if the engineer decides to move the vents *after* the panel lines have been modified. Depending on the way the vents are moved, the panel lines could be in complete disarray; some would be partially overlapping the vent, and some not touching them at all. This would force the user into a labor-intensive process to search for, and extend each cut line that did not terminate at a vent.

One way to overcome these limitations is to provide the power of constraint propagation. With tools of propagation, one can imagine future systems where ceiling panels "know" about their relationship to vents and vice versa, and any change in vents can automatically propagate to the ceiling panels. However one can already expect problems to emerge in such systems. For instance, once ceiling panels are modified, they could violate some other constraint leading to endless cycles of propagation where the user is completely out of control. Tools and strategies to circumvent such limitations will therefore have to be defined.

Powers and Limits of Visualization Tools

One of the most important powers that make computer applications useful to architects is the power of visualization. With this power, users can visualize complex objects such as buildings in many different ways without having to alter the underlying representation. However the screen size of most current systems puts a severe constraint on how much information can be viewed at the same time. Users often face the trade-off between visual detail and the scope of information displayed on the screen. One way to circumvent this limitation in CAD is to have two windows: one to always provide an overview of the entire building, and the other zoomed far into the details of a section. Procedures for easily navigating between these views already occur in many CAD systems like MicroStation™. However, as with the iteration strategies, our data showed that L1 did not use this useful circumvention strategy and spent unnecessary time panning and zooming looking for the panel lines that had to be modified.

Powers and Limits of Generation Tools

While iteration and propagation can modify and replicate existing elements, computer applications with powerful algorithms can also generate new kinds of information not explicitly provided by the user. For example, future systems will enable users to explore designs generated by computers based on constraints and rules [10]. However such systems incur huge overheads in their setup and modification, and appear to be useful mainly for recurring problem types (e.g., floor plans of hospitals, dorms, barracks). Therefore they may require a whole new set of strategies that have yet to be encountered.

CONCLUSION

Strategies of delegation and circumvention appear to be the core of efficient use of complex systems. Understanding the relationship between abstract functionality, tools, and strategies can assist us in the development, training, and efficient use of complex applications such as CAD. Our analysis showed that regardless of how sophisticated CAD tools may become in the future, it appears they will always have powers as well as limitations, which users must learn to delegate and circumvent.

ACKNOWLEDGMENTS

This research was supported by the National Science Foundation, Award# IRI-9457628. The views and conclusions contained in this document are those of the authors and should not be interpreted as representing the official policies, either expressed or implied, of NSF, or the U. S. Government. The authors acknowledge the contributions of O. Akin, U. Flemming, J. Garrett, H. Simon, G. Vallabha; and Bentley Systems, Inc. for the academic edition of MicroStation™.

REFERENCES

1. Bhavnani, S. K. How Architects Draw with Computers: An Analysis of Real-World CAD Usage, *Ph.D. dissertation* (in preparation) Carnegie Mellon University, Pittsburgh.
2. Bhavnani, S.K., Flemming, U., Forsythe, D.E., Garrett, J.H., Shaw, D.S., and Tsai, A. CAD Usage in an Architectural Office: From Observations to Active Assistance. *Automation in Construction* 5 (1996), 243-255.
3. Bhavnani, S.K., and John, B.E. Exploring the Unrealized Potential of Computer-Aided Drafting. *Proceedings of CHI '96* (1996), 332-339.
4. Bhavnani, S.K., and John, B.E. From Sufficient to Efficient Usage: An Analysis of Strategic Knowledge. *Proceedings of CHI '97* (1997), 91-98.
5. Card, S.K., Moran, T.P., and Newell, A. *The Psychology of Human-Computer Interaction.* Hillsdale, NJ: Lawrence Erlbaum Associates, 1983.
6. Cragg, P.B. and King, M. Spreadsheet Modeling Abuse: An Opportunity for OR? *Journal of the Operational Research Society* 44 (1993), 743-752.
7. Denman, F. *The Shaping of our Alphabet.* Alfred A. Knopf, New York, 1955.
8. Doane, S.M., Pellegrino, J.W., Klatzky, R.L. Expertise in a Computer Operating System: Conceptualization and Performance. *Human-Computer Interaction* 5 (1990), 267-304.
9. Flemming, U., Bhavnani, S.K., John, B.E. Mismatched Metaphor: User vs. System Model in Computer-Aided Drafting. *Design Studies* 18 (1997), 349-368.
10. Flemming, U., Woodbury, R. Software environment to support early phases in building design (SEED): Overview. *Journal of Architectural Engineering, ASCE,* 1(4) (1995), 147-152.
11. Jackson, D. *The Story of Writing.* Taplinger Publishing Co., Inc., 1981.
12. Kieras, D. A Guide to GOMS Model Usability Evaluation using NGOMSL. in M. Helander & T. Landauer (eds.) *The handbook of human-computer interaction* (Second Edition). Amsterdam: North-Holland (in press).
13. Lang, G.T., Eberts, R. E., Gabel, M. G., and Barash, M.M. Extracting and Using Procedural Knowledge in a CAD Task. *IEEE Transactions on Engineering Management,* 38 (1991), 257-68.
14. Nilsen, E., Jong H., Olson J., Biolsi, I., Mutter, S. The Growth of Software Skill: A Longitudinal Look at Learning and Performance. *Proceedings of INTERCHI '93.* (1993), 149-156.
15. Norman, D. *The Design of Everyday Things.* Doubleday, New York, 1988.
16. Reason J. *Human Error.* Cambridge University Press, 1994.
17. Siegler, R.S., Jenkins, E. *How Children Discover New Strategies.* Lawrence Erlbaum Associates, New Jersey, 1989.
18. Snyder, J., Aygen, Z., Flemming, U. and Tsai, J. SPROUT - A modeling language for SEED, in *Journal of Architectural Engineering, ASCE,* 1(4) (1995), 195-203.
19. Wood, S. *GLEAN - GOMS Language Evaluation and Analysis.* University of Michigan, 1995.

Digital Manipulatives: New Toys to Think With

Mitchel Resnick, Fred Martin, Robert Berg, Rick Borovoy, Vanessa Colella, Kwin Kramer, Brian Silverman
MIT Media Laboratory
20 Ames Street
Boston, MA 02139 USA
+1 617 253 0330
{mres, fredm, rberg, borovoy, vanessa, khkramer, bss}@media.mit.edu
http://el.www.media.mit.edu/groups/el/

ABSTRACT
In many educational settings, manipulative materials (such as Cuisenaire Rods and Pattern Blocks) play an important role in children's learning, enabling children to explore mathematical and scientific concepts (such as number and shape) through direct manipulation of physical objects. Our group at the MIT Media Lab has developed a new generation of "digital manipulatives"—computationally-enhanced versions of traditional children's toys. These new manipulatives enable children to explore a new set of concepts (in particular, "systems concepts" such as feedback and emergence) that have previously been considered "too advanced" for children to learn. In this paper, we discuss four of our digital manipulatives—computationally-augmented versions of blocks, beads, balls, and badges.

Keywords
Education, learning, children, ubiquitous computing

INTRODUCTION

Walk into any kindergarten, and you are likely to see a diverse collection of "manipulative materials." You might see a set of Cuisenaire Rods: brightly colored wooden rods of varying lengths. The colors and lengths of the rods are carefully chosen to engage children in explorations of arithmetic concepts and relationships. Children discover that each brown rod is the same length as two purples—or four reds. On the next table, you might see a set of Pattern Blocks. Children can use these polygon-shaped tiles to create mosaic-like patterns—and, in the process, learn important geometric concepts.

As children build and experiment with these manipulative materials, they develop richer ways of thinking about mathematical concepts such as number, size, and shape. But there are many important concepts that are very difficult (if not impossible) to explore with these traditional manipulative materials. In particular, traditional manipulatives generally do not help children learn concepts related to dynamics and systems. Usually, these concepts are taught through more formal methods—involving manipulation of abstract symbols, not physical objects. As a result, these concepts are accessible only to older students, with more mathematical expertise.

This paper discusses a new breed of manipulative materials that we call "digital manipulatives." These new manipulatives—with computational power embedded inside—are designed to expand the range of concepts that children can explore through direct manipulation, enabling children to learn concepts that were previously considered "too advanced" for children. The paper begins with a brief history of the educational uses of manipulative materials, then discusses several digital manipulatives that our research group has developed.

LEARNING WITH MANIPULATIVE MATERIALS

The idea that physical objects might play an important role in the learning process is a relatively new idea. Until the 19th century, formal education focused almost exclusively on lectures and recitations. One of the first advocates for "hands-on learning" was the Swiss educator Johann Heinrich Pestalozzi (1746-1827). Pestalozzi asserted that students need to learn through their senses and through physical activity, arguing for "things before words, concrete before abstract" [12].

Friedrich Froebel, who created the world's first kindergarten in Germany in 1837, was very influenced by Pestalozzi's ideas. Froebel's kindergarten was filled with objects for children to play with. Froebel developed a specific set of 20 "gifts"—physical objects such as balls, blocks, and sticks—for children to use in the kindergarten. Froebel carefully designed these gifts to help children recognize and appreciate the common patterns and forms found in nature. Froebel's gifts were eventually distributed throughout the world, deeply influencing the development of generations of young children. Indeed, Frank Lloyd Wright credited his boyhood experiences with Froebel's gifts as the foundation of his architecture [2].

Maria Montessori extended Froebel's ideas, developing materials for older children and inspiring a network of schools in which manipulative materials play a central role. In an effort to create an "education of the senses" [10], Montessori developed new materials and activities to help children develop their sensory capabilities. Montessori hoped that her materials would put children in control of the learning process, enabling them to learn through personal investigation and exploration.

CHI 98 Los Angeles CA USA
Copyright 1998 0-89791-975-0/98/ 4..$5.00

Jean Piaget provided an epistemological foundation for these educational ideas. Piaget theorized that children must first construct knowledge through "concrete operations" before moving on to "formal operations" (e.g., [13]). During the past decade, a new wave of research has suggested that Piaget, if anything, understated the importance of concrete operations. Sherry Turkle and Seymour Papert, for example, have argued for a "revaluation of the concrete," suggesting that "abstract reasoning" should not be viewed as more advanced than (or superior to) concrete manipulations [22].

Today, manipulative materials are well-established in the classroom, especially in the early grades. Education journals are filled with papers on ways of using manipulative materials in the classroom—papers with colorful titles such as "Lima Beans, Paper Cups, and Algebra" [8] and "Activities to Grow On: Buttons, Beads, and Beans" [5].

DIGITAL MANIPULATIVES

Different manipulative materials engage children in different types of thinking. According to an old saying: "Give a person a hammer, and the whole world looks like a nail." Similarly, give a child Cuisenaire Rods, and arithmetic relationships become more salient for the child. Give a child Pattern Blocks, and geometric relationships become more salient.

Our goal in designing new "digital manipulatives" is to make a new set of concepts salient for children. Our basic strategy is to embed computational and communications capabilities in traditional children's toys. By using traditional toys as a starting point, we hope to take advantage of children's deep familiarity with (and deep passion for) these objects. At the same time, by endowing these toys with computational and communications capabilities, we hope to highlight a new set of ideas for children to think about.

In particular, we believe that children, by playing and building with these new manipulatives, can gain a deeper understanding of how dynamic systems behave. Until recently, dynamic systems have been studied primarily at the university level, using advanced mathematical techniques like differential equations. Computer-based modeling environments—such as Stella [20], StarLogo [15], and Model-It [7]—have made it easier for pre-college students to model and explore systems phenomena (such as feedback and emergence). We expect that digital manipulatives will make these ideas accessible to even younger students, enabling students to explore these ideas through direct manipulation of familiar physical objects. Such explorations would not be possible with traditional (non-computational) manipulative materials. Computation and communication capabilities play a critical role: they enable physical objects to move, sense, and interact with one another—and, as a result, make systems-related concepts more salient to (and manipulable by) children.

Our development of digital manipulatives can be seen as part of a broader trend within the CHI community. CHI researchers have long recognized the value of providing users with "objects" to manipulate, but they have traditionally focused on "virtual objects"—as in object-oriented languages and direct-manipulation graphical interfaces. It is only in recent years that CHI researchers have shifted attention to physical objects. In research efforts variously described as "ubiquitous computing," "computer-augmented environments," and "things that think," researchers are now exploring ways of adding computational capabilities to everyday objects ranging from notepads and desktops to eyeglasses and shoes [4, 6, 24, 25].

Our research on digital manipulatives is part of this trend, but it focuses explicitly on the use of objects to support learning and education. Our primary goal is not to help users accomplish some task faster or more effectively, but rather to engage them in new ways of thinking. In short, we are interested in Things That Think only if they also serve as Things To Think With.

This research can be viewed as an extension of our previous work on LEGO/Logo [14], a robotics construction kit commercialized by the LEGO toy company and now used in more than 20,000 schools in the United States. With LEGO/Logo, children can write computer programs to control their LEGO constructions. Elementary-school students have used LEGO/Logo to build and program a wide assortment of creative machines, including a programmable pop-up toaster, an automated amusement park, and a machine that sorts LEGO bricks according to their lengths. In these projects, students build with an enhanced set of LEGO parts (including motors and sensors), connect their constructions to a personal computer (using wires and an interface box), then write Logo computer programs to control the actions of their constructions.

In LEGO/Logo, wires are both a practical and conceptual nuisance, limiting not only what children can build but also how they think about their constructions. In our new work with digital manipulatives, we get rid of the wires and embed computational capabilities directly in the toys themselves. We continue to use Logo as the primary programming environment. But Logo programs can be downloaded directly into these new toys (typically via infrared communication), so that the toys function autonomously.

The next four sections describe digital manipulatives that we have created by adding computation to four traditional children's toys—blocks, beads, balls, and badges. These projects are in varying stages of development. Some of these new manipulatives have already been used extensively by children; others are still in the early prototype stage.

BLOCKS

We began our work on digital manipulatives by embedding computation in LEGO bricks—creating Programmable Bricks [9, 16]. Each Programmable Brick has output ports for controlling motors and lights, and input ports for receiving information from sensors (e.g., light, touch, and temperature sensors). To use a P-Brick, a child writes a Logo program on a personal computer, then downloads the program to the P-Brick. After that, the child can take (or put) the P-Brick anywhere; the program remains stored in the P-Brick.

Figure 1. Two elementary-school students test the behaviors of their Programmable Brick "creature."

In our initial work in schools, students have used Programmable Bricks to create autonomous "creatures" that mimic the behaviors of real animals (Figure 1). For example, one group of fifth-grade students created a LEGO dinosaur that was attracted to flashes of light, like one of the dinosaurs in Jurassic Park. To make the dinosaur move toward the light, the students needed to understand basic ideas about feedback and control. The program compared readings from the dinosaur's two light-sensor "eyes." If the dinosaur drifted too far to the left (i.e., more light in the right eye), the program made it veer back to the right; if the dinosaur went too far right (more light in the left eye), the program corrected it toward the left.

This type of feedback strategy is typically not taught until university-level courses. But with the right tools, fifth graders were able to explore these ideas. The students also considered the similarities (and differences) between animals and machines. Were their LEGO creatures more like animals? Or more like machines? They compared their robots' sensors to animal senses, and they discussed whether real animals have "programs" like the ones they wrote for their robotic creatures [17].

Our newest Programmable Bricks, called Crickets, are roughly the size of children's Matchbox cars and action figures (Figures 2 and 3). Each Cricket contains a Microchip PIC processor and is capable of two-way infrared communications. Children can use Crickets to create communities of robotic creatures that interact with one another. We have found that children, by teaching their creatures to communicate with one another, can learn general principles about communication. When a child programs a Cricket-based creature to communicate with a second creature, the child must have a good model of what the second creature already "knows." The general lesson: to communicate well, you must develop a model of your audience. This idea might seem obvious, but it is often ignored in interactions among people, and thus is an important lesson for children to learn.

Recently, we have begun a new science-education initiative using Crickets [18]. Many science-education researchers emphasize the importance of children developing their own scientific investigations (rather than carrying out pre-scripted experiments, as is common in many classrooms). We go a step further, encouraging students to use Crickets to create their own scientific instruments to carry out their investigations. For example, two elementary-school girls used Crickets to build a bird feeder that keeps track of the birds that visit. When a bird lands, it pushes a touch sensor, which triggers a LEGO mechanism, which depresses the shutter of a camera, taking a picture of the bird. Our initial studies indicate that students, by building their own scientific instruments, not only become more motivated in science activities, but also develop critical capacities in evaluating scientific measurements and knowledge, make stronger connections to the scientific concepts underlying their investigations, and develop deeper understandings of the relationship between science and technology.

Figure 2. A Cricket (with LEGO figure to show scale)

Figure 3. Creature with two built-in Crickets, which communicate with one another to synchronize their motion

BEADS

In recent years, beads have become increasingly popular among children, especially young girls. There are entire stores with nothing but bins of beads of varying colors and sizes. Children string beads together to create colorful necklaces and bracelets.

With traditional beads, children create colorful but *static* patterns. Our Programmable Beads (Figure 4) are designed to engage children in creating *dynamic* patterns. Each Programmable Bead has a built-in microprocessor and light-emitting diode (LED), and it communicates with its neighboring beads by simple inductive coupling. String beads together in different ways and you get different dynamic patterns of light. Some beads pass the light to the next bead along the string, other beads reflect the light back, still others "swallow" the light. Some beads pass the light with a particular probability. A slight change in the behavior or placement of one of the beads can lead to an entirely different pattern of activity in the overall collection.

Children can work with the beads at two different levels. For starters, they can string together pre-programmed beads (each with a fixed behavior), and observe the dynamic lighting patterns that arise from the interactions. More advanced users can write new programs and download them into the beads.

A string of Programmable Beads can be viewed as a physical instantiation of a one-dimensional cellular automata [21]. In cellular automata, each cell changes its state based on the states of its neighboring cells. Cellular automata have proved to be a rich framework for exploring "emergent phenomena"; simple rules for each cell can lead to complex and unexpected large-scale structures. But cellular automata seem best suited as a tool for mathematicians and computer aficionados, not for children. The idea of writing "transition rules" for "cells" is not an idea that most children can relate to. Programmable Beads allow children to explore ideas of decentralized systems and emergent phenomena in a more natural way, through the manipulation of physical objects.

Figure 4. A necklace of Programmable Beads

We believe that Programmable Beads can provide a meaningful and motivating context for children to begin thinking about probabilistic behaviors. Imagine a bead that passes the light to the next bead half of the time but reflects the light back to the previous bead the other half of the time. By stringing a set of these beads together, children can explore random-walk behaviors. What if you then add a bead that passes the light three-quarters of the time and reflects it just one-quarter of the time? How will that change the overall dynamic pattern? Most children (indeed, most people) have poor intuitions about such systems. Our hypothesis is that children who grow up playing with Programmable Beads will develop much richer intuitions about probabilistic behaviors.

Programmable Beads also provide a context for children to learn about "programming paradigms." There are two very different ways to think about programming the beads. Paradigm 1: Children can program the behaviors of the beads themselves, telling each bead to turn its light off or on based on its neighbors' lights. Paradigm 2: Children can program a "process" that jumps from bead to bead (e.g., turn on this bead's light for two seconds, then jump two beads down the string and turn on that light for three seconds). The important point is not for children to learn which of these paradigms is better (in fact, neither is inherently better). Rather, the important lesson is that there are often multiple approaches for describing behaviors, each with its own advantages.

BALLS

Probably the most popular of all children's toys is the ball. How could computation possibly improve the ball? We are exploring that question with our BitBall—a transparent, rubbery ball (about the size of a baseball) with a Cricket, accelerometer, and colored LEDs embedded inside.

To customize a BitBall (Figure 5), a child writes a program on a desktop computer (using a modified version of Logo), then downloads the program to the BitBall via infrared communication. A child can program a BitBall to turn on its LEDs based on its motion, as detected by the accelerometer. One child, for example, might program a BitBall to flash its red light whenever it undergoes a sharp acceleration or deceleration (i.e., whenever it is thrown or caught). Another child might create a ball that "wants" to be played with: If the ball doesn't experience any sharp accelerations for a certain period of time, it begins flashing its lights in an effort to attract someone to play with it. We have found that children are quick to attribute intentionality to the BitBall, even when it is running the simplest of programs. When children program the BitBall themselves, they develop a better understanding of how seemingly-intentional behaviors can arise from just a few simple rules.

Since the BitBall (via its Cricket) can send and receive infrared signals, children can also program BitBalls to communicate with other electronic devices. For example, students have programmed the BitBall to send its acceleration data to a MIDI synthesizer in real time, in an effort to "hear the motion" of the ball (with, for example, acceleration mapped onto pitch).

BitBalls can also be used in scientific investigations. A BitBall can store its acceleration data and later upload the data to a desktop computer for analysis. For example, students have dropped a BitBall from the top of a building, then used the acceleration data to figure out the height of the building. Such investigations can lead to a deeper understanding of kinematics. One group of students (in this case, university students) threw a BitBall in the air and graphed the acceleration data in an effort to find the top of the trajectory. They discovered that there was no change in acceleration while the ball is in flight, so it was impossible to determine the top of the trajectory from acceleration data alone. The students had previously studied gravity and acceleration in physics class, but they were not able to apply their classroom knowledge to this real-world context. We believe that experience with the BitBall will help students develop an understanding of acceleration that they can more easily transfer to new contexts.

It is important to note that the BitBall is significantly different from most commercial toys with embedded electronics. Some companies, for example, sell yo-yos that turn on a light while they are moving. We believe that such toys are different from the BitBall along an important dimension. The light-up yo-yo is pre-programmed to always do the exact same thing. It is a one-trick toy. The BitBall gives much greater flexibility and creative power to children. With the BitBall, children themselves decide how the toy should behave.

Figure 5. The BitBall

BADGES

Many children like to wear badges (such as a sheriff's badge) and buttons with slogans. Our Thinking Tags are based on these traditional badges, but they have built-in electronics so that they can communicate with one another (via infrared communication)—and also change their displays based on those communications.

We first developed the Thinking Tags (Figure 6) for a conference (for adults) at the Media Laboratory. The Thinking Tags served as name tags, but each tag also contained information about the interests and opinions of its wearer. When two people met, their badges exchanged information and turned on lights to show how much the two people had in common. In this way, the badges acted as a conversational prop to get people talking with one another. Other research labs have also developed "smart badges" (e.g., [23]), but our Thinking Tags are different in an important way: While other badges are designed to support interaction between people and machines (e.g., to track the location of a person within a building), our Thinking Tags are designed to facilitate communication among people. And, indeed, the Thinking Tags have proved successful as a catalyst for conversation [1].

More recently, we have begun to use Thinking Tags in educational applications with pre-college students. In particular, we have organized "participatory simulations" in which students themselves play roles within simulations [3, 19]. For example, some students have used Thinking Tags to simulate the spread of an epidemic, with an electronic "virus" jumping from one student's Thinking Tag to another. Some students start as the (unknowing) carriers of the disease, while others are immune to the disease. Over time, more and more students become "infected" with the disease. The challenge is for the students to develop theories to explain the spread of the virus. Does the disease have a latency period? Is transmission probabilistic? Are some people more susceptible than others? As part of their analysis, students can get additional data from their Thinking Tags, which keep track of who each person has interacted with and when. Often, the students "rerun" the simulation, resetting their badges to their initial states and testing a different set of interactions.

Students, of course, could do similar explorations with on-screen computer simulations. But we have found that the first-person nature of the Thinking-Tag activities provides a more meaningful framework for students to investigate systems concepts (at least initially). In particular, the Thinking-Tag activities encourage "collaborative theory building," in which groups of students work together to develop and test new theories.

We have run similar activities using somewhat different metaphors. In one case, we explained that ideas (or "memes") could jump from one badge to another. Some people were "resistant" to new ideas; others were active carriers. The goal was to help people develop a better understanding of how ideas spread through a population—and also to engage them in thinking about the similarities (and differences) between the spread of disease and the spread of new ideas.

Our latest version of the Thinking Tag has a built-in two-line display, so that people can display text messages on their badges. In one of our participatory simulations, each person was able to store up to seven memes on their badge. When you met another person, your badge interacted with the other person's badge and "decided" which of your memes to display to the other person—based on which memes the other person had previously seen and selected. Meanwhile, if you saw a meme you liked on another person's badge, you could simply push a button on your own badge and add the meme to your personal collection. The badges collected data so that students could later analyze the patterns of social interaction and meme propagation. Social scientists have long been interested in these types of patterns, but they have lacked the tools needed for rigorous data collection and analysis. Thinking Tags fill that gap.

This type of activity is very different from traditional science-education activities. Science is usually taught as a process of detached observation of phenomena, not active participation within phenomena. We believe, however, that role-playing can play a powerful role in science education—especially in the study of systems-related concepts. Our preliminary analysis indicates that participatory simulations (supported with Thinking Tags) leads to a richer learning experience than is possible with traditional computer-simulation activities—or with traditional group activities without computer support.

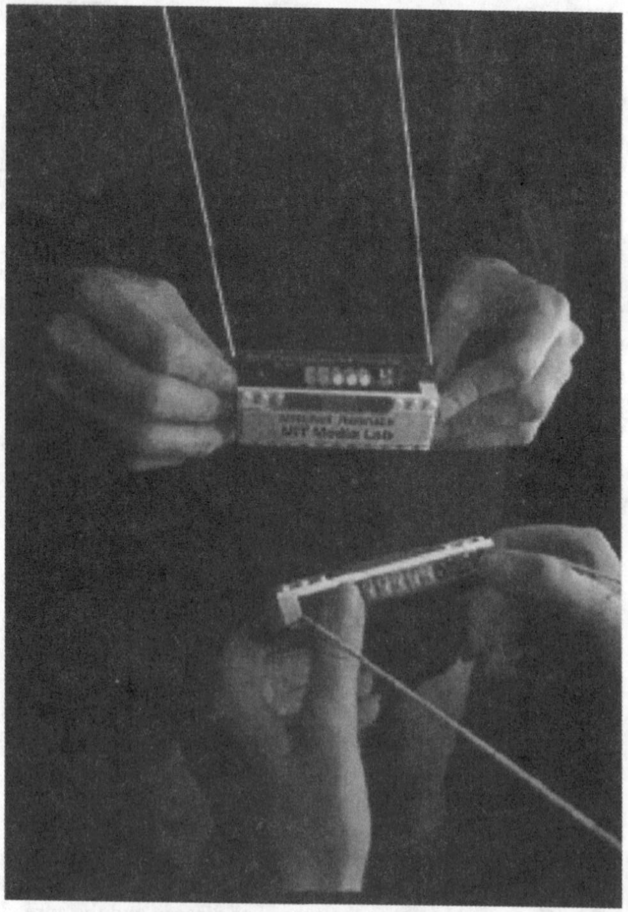

Figure 6: Thinking Tags

LOOKING AHEAD

We view these new blocks, beads, balls, and badges not as a set of separate projects, but as an integrated family. The same underlying software environment is used for programming all of these new toys, and the toys are designed to communicate and interact with one another. A BitBall, for example, can send information (via infrared) to the Thinking Tags—in effect, using the Thinking Tags as a remote display peripheral. Our goal is to create a unified "community of things" that children can use in a wide variety of explorations and design activities.

Our work with digital manipulatives is still in the preliminary stages. Our plan is to conduct more in-depth empirical studies of how and what children learn through their interactions with digital manipulatives. In particular, we plan to investigate: What types of programming paradigms and interfaces are needed to help children program digital manipulatives? Are children able to understand how and why patterns arise from interactions among the digital manipulatives (e.g., the emergent lighting patterns that arise along a necklace of Programmable Beads)—and, if not, what new tools and support materials should we provide to help children make sense of those patterns? In what ways do the "surface features" of our digital manipulatives (e.g., the packaging for the beads) influence how children use them? In what ways do we need to rethink classroom organization and practices if we want to use digital manipulatives in classroom settings?

We expect that these studies will yield ideas for the redesign of our current digital manipulatives—and the design of new ones. More broadly, we hope that these studies will help us to develop a richer theoretical framework for understanding the role of physical objects (and, in particular, computationally-enhanced physical objects) in the learning process.

ACKNOWLEDGMENTS

The Programmable Bricks and Crickets have been developed primarily by Fred Martin, Brian Silverman, and Robbie Berg. The Programmable Beads have been developed primarily by Kwin Kramer and Rick Borovoy. The BitBalls have been developed primarily by Kwin Kramer, Robbie Berg, Fred Martin, and Brian Silverman. The Thinking Tags have been developed primarily by Rick Borovoy, Fred Martin, Vanessa Colella, Brian Silverman, and Kwin Kramer. Mitchel Resnick has supervised the projects and developed the conceptual framework of "digital manipulatives." This research has been supported by generous grants from the LEGO Group, the National Science Foundation (grants 9358519-RED and CDA-9616444), and the MIT Media Laboratory's Things That Think and Digital Life consortia.

REFERENCES

1. Borovoy, R., McDonald, M., Martin, F., and Resnick, M. (1996). Things that blink: Computationally augmented name tags. *IBM Systems Journal 35*, 3, 488-495.
2. Brosterman, N. (1997). *Inventing Kindergarten*. New York: Harry N. Adams Inc.

3. Colella, V., Borovoy, R., and Resnick, M. (1998). Participatory Simulations: Using Computational Objects to Learn about Dynamic Systems. Demonstration session, *Proceedings of CHI '98*, ACM Press.

4. Eisenberg, M., Mackay, W., Druin, A., Lehman, S., and Resnick, M. (1996). Real Meets Virtual: Blending Real World Artifacts with Computational Media. Panel session, *Proceedings of CHI '96*, ACM Press.

5. Gonzolis, A. (1992). Activities to Grow On: Buttons, Beads, and Beans. *Instructor 101*, 7, 51.

6. Ishii, H., and Ulllmer, B. (1997). Tangible Bits: Towards Seamless Interfaces between People, Bits, and Atoms. Paper session, *Proceedings of CHI '97*, ACM Press.

7. Jackson, S., Stratford, S., Krajcik, J., and Soloway, E. (1996). A Learner-Centered Tool for Students Building Models. *Communications of the ACM 39*, 4, 48-49.

8. Loewen, A.C. (1991). Lima Beans, Paper Cups, and Algebra. *Arithmetic Teacher 38*, 8, 34-37.

9. Martin, F. (1994). *Circuits to Control: Learning Engineering by Designing LEGO Robots*. Doctoral Dissertation. Cambridge, MA: MIT Media Laboratory.

10. Montessori, M. (1912). *The Montessori Method*. New York: Frederick Stokes Co.

11. Papert, S. (1980). *Mindstorms: Children, Computers, and Powerful Ideas*. New York: Basic Books.

12. Pestalozzi, H. (1803). *ABC der Anschauung, oder Anschauungs-Lehre der Massverhaltnisse*. Tubingen, Germany: J.G. Cotta.

13. Piaget, J. (1972). *The Principles of Genetic Epistemology*. New York: Basic Books.

14. Resnick, M. (1993). Behavior Construction Kits. *Communications of the ACM 36*, 7, 65-71.

15. Resnick, M. (1994). *Turtles, Termites, and Traffic Jams*. Cambridge, MA: MIT Press.

16. Resnick, M., Martin, F., Sargent, R., and Silverman, B. (1996). Programmable Bricks: Toys to Think With. *IBM Systems Journal 35*, 3, 443-452.

17. Resnick, M., Bruckman, A., and Martin, F. (1996). Pianos Not Stereos: Creating Computational Construction Kits. *Interactions 3*, 6, 41-50.

18. Resnick, M., Berg, R., Eisenberg, M., Turkle, S., and Martin, F. (1996). Beyond Black Boxes: Bringing Transparency and Aesthetics Back to Scientific Instruments. Proposal to the National Science Foundation. Available from MIT Media Laboratory.

19. Resnick, M., and Wilensky, U. (1997). Diving into Complexity: Developing Probabilistic Decentralized Thinking through Role-Playing Activities. *Journal of the Learning Sciences 7*, 2.

20. Roberts, N., Anderson, D., Deal, R., Garet, M., and Shaffer, W. (1983). *Introduction to Computer Simulation: A System Dynamics Modeling Approach*. Reading, MA: Addison-Wesley.

21. Toffoli, T., and Margolus, N. (1987). *Cellular Automata Machines*. Cambridge: MIT Press.

22. Turkle, S., and Papert, S. (1990). Epistemological Pluralism. *Signs 16*, 1, 128-157.

23. Want, R., Hopper, A., Falcao, V., and Gibbons, J. (1992). The Active Badge Location System. *ACM Transactions on Information Systems 10*, 1, 91-102.

24. Weiser, M. (1991). The Computer for the 21st Century. *Scientific American 265*, 3, 94-104.

25. Wellner, P., Mackay, W., and Gold, R. (1993). Computer Augmented Environments: Back to the Real World. *Communications of the ACM 36*, 7, 24-26.

When the Interface is a Talking Dinosaur: Learning Across Media with ActiMates Barney

Erik Strommen
Microsoft Corporation
One Microsoft Way
Redmond, WA 98052, USA
+1 425 936 6380
erikstr@microsoft.com

ABSTRACT
ActiMates™ Barney™ represents a new form of interactive learning product for two- to five-year old children: a small computer that looks like an animated plush doll. He can be used as a freestanding toy and, by means of a wireless radio link, he can interact with PC-based software and linear videotapes. In each mode, Barney takes advantage of children's social expectations about playmate performance to engage the user in learning interactions. The theory and practice behind Barney's performance in each mode (freestanding, with the computer, and with the television) are described, as well as how key research results shaped the interface across the different modes.

KEYWORDS: learning, interface, children, interactive media

INTRODUCTION

A theory of interactive learning

Recent theory and research in children's learning has emphasized the importance of social interaction as a mechanism for mental growth [18,23,24]. A key learning process identified by this school of thought is a type of social intervention called *scaffolding*. Scaffolding is the process whereby an adult or more mature peer supports a child's acquisition of a new skill by providing assistance at key points during the execution of the skill itself, in a form of collaborative effort. An example of scaffolding might be helping a child learn to count by filling in numbers in the count sequence when the child is unable to remember them, or manually guiding the child's finger to each object being counted while counting along, to structure the task as it is executed. The metaphor of the scaffold is meant to capture the temporary and transitional nature of the learning intervention. Just as a scaffold is gradually removed from a new building as it is completed and can stand on its own, support of the child is gradually reduced as repeated effort leads to mastery of the new skill.

A critical part of scaffolding as a learning intervention is the use of language. Language in this framework gives form to thought by guiding and directing mental processes. Young children are thought to acquire concepts and abilities by gradually internalizing the verbal support and direction of others, until they become capable of guiding their own behavior using the same skills and strategies that were initially provided externally [4].

Applying scaffolding theory to educational technologies for children

Scaffolding theory holds great promise for educational technologies, because of the strong parallels between the nature of the user interface and the nature of scaffolded learning. Learners control the pace and course of action in scaffolded learning efforts, just as they do in their use of interactive technologies. And scaffolding requires context-specific responses to repeated efforts over time, something that computers can provide very well. The key limitation in translating this model of learning into technology use has always been its fundamentally social nature, and its heavy reliance on language. Most computer interfaces are strictly visual, relying on a small screen with two-dimensional images controlled by some form of pointing device – a form of interaction that is hardly social. Even when a small, talking character is included in the graphical interface itself, the abstract nature of the interface often fails to evoke the basic social expectations of cooperation and verbal engagement that make scaffolding possible.

ActiMates Barney (hereafter simply A/Barney) represents a unique interface that uses the social dynamics of pretend play to integrate technology and learning. By virtue of being an animated plush doll who resembles and behaves like a familiar media character, A/Barney taps into powerful pretend play and toy experiences common to early childhood. Young children 'animate' dolls and other objects on their own, treating them as if they are sentient and responding to them in ways that mimic familiar social interactions (comforting a 'crying' doll is a classic example) [1]. Using speech and movement, A/Barney invokes similar pretend responses as an interface strategy. While there have been other attempts to use a concrete character as an interface for young children's interactive learning [5,6], A/Barney is the first to rely so heavily on language and social interaction in its design.

The goal of A/Barney's design was to use the social mimicry of pretend play, combined with the differential responsiveness of interactive technologies, to provide scaffolded learning experiences for young children, both during toy play and in combination with other learning media. The remainder of this article describes the application of scaffolding theory to the content and design of each of A/Barney's modes of interaction, and the iterative design and research process that shaped the feature set included in the final product.

THEORY INTO PRACTICE: ONE DINOSAUR, THREE WAYS

The core interface across all three of A/Barney's modes is A/Barney himself. A/Barney is a 13" animated plush doll. Motors provide simple arm and head movement, and a small loudspeaker provides audible speech. A/Barney's interface is a set of five sensors: Four touch sensors (one in each hand and foot), and a light sensor located in his left eye. A ROM chip hidden in his body allows him to respond to children's inputs by moving and speaking using pre-recorded, digitized speech and programmed motion. A/Barney interacts with other media using an internal radio transceiver similar to that of a walkie-talkie. When a special transmitter is attached to a TV and VCR, he can receive new speech and motion from encoded videotapes that play as the child is watching the video. When a transmitter is attached to a PC running encoded CD-ROMs, A/Barney both receives and transmits data. He both receives new speech and motion content from the computer and transmits inputs from his own sensors back to the computer, as well. In this way, A/Barney not only reacts to children's actions as they use software with a conventional pointing device such as a mouse, but children's actions on his sensors also affect what happens in the software.

The task of creating an integrated model for A/Barney's performance as a pretend playmate who could be integrated into a variety of electronic media interactions presented a novel design challenge. It required defining a set of conventions for interacting with A/Barney that were both consistent across all modes of use *and* flexible enough to accommodate the context-specific variations each type of interaction required. Consistency was created by building the interface conventions around the one element that remained constant across all modes of use: A/Barney himself. In practice, this meant that even though A/Barney's freestanding toy mode performance differed from that in the other modes in important ways, it was this mode that set the standard for his performance when watching television or playing at the computer.

A/Barney as a freestanding toy

The research conducted on A/Barney during the development of his freestanding toy mode generated the design principles that guided the development of his other modes. These principles can be summarized as three simple maxims.

Playmates should be directive, but friendly

In freestanding toy mode, A/Barney is assumed to be the child's sole playmate, and his interactions are designed to promote the child's direct engagement by being conversational and familiar. He refers to the child using the pronoun "you," and to their joint activities using the shared pronoun "we." Research on adults using phone interfaces and on speech in the software interface has found that direct queries (for example, "What would you like to play?") prompt user responses less often than do explicit directives [16,21]. Building on these findings, A/Barney does not ask questions as part of his verbal interface. Instead, he makes simple directive statements such as: "Cover my eyes to play Peek-a-boo!" "Squeeze my middle toe to sing a song!"

Testing of A/Barney's games and activities demonstrated that the use of concrete directives was an effective interface strategy, but also revealed that it had a significant drawback in the social context of a two-person play dyad: over time, the directives had the unintentional effect of making A/Barney seem bossy and task-driven. It often seemed that every statement he made was an instruction, particularly when no game or song was active, and he was prompting the child to select an activity. This constant browbeating quickly reduced children's interest during free play use. To remedy this situation, A/Barney's interface instructions were intermingled with a set of compliments and positive other-directed statements having no functional value, such as "This is fun!" "I like playing with you!" "You're my special friend!", and so on. Adding these phrases to the interface made A/Barney seem much less task-oriented, and as forms of unconditional praise, they bolstered children's pleasure during interactions as well.

To each sensor, it's own function

Early testing of the doll's sensor interface with young children clearly demonstrated two critical facts. First, children easily understood that acting on A/Barney's body parts (eyes, hands, and feet) initiated interactions. They responded immediately to requests such as "Squeeze my hand to play a game!" for example, by reaching for A/Barney's hand and squeezing it, then waiting expectantly for him to speak. However, children of this age were consistently unable to use A/Barney's sensors in any combinations, simultaneous or sequential, as part of an interface. That is, children could not be asked to squeeze both a hand and foot sensor together to start a game, nor could they be asked to first cover A/Barney's eye and then squeeze his hand in a two-step sequence. These results led to a highly simplified design, whereby each class of body part (feet, hands, and eyes) is dedicated to one and only one class of response. Given children's inability to reliably identify left and right at this age [12], left and right were not differentiated in the interface – both hands, both feet, and both eyes are treated redundantly.) There are three types of interaction:

A/Barney's feet are dedicated to songs. Squeezing the touch sensors in either of A/Barney's feet causes him to sing one of 16 familiar preschool songs (*The wheels on the bus*, *If you're happy and you know it*, and so on.).

A/Barney's hands are dedicated to activities and games. Squeezing the sensors in either of A/Barney's hands causes him to randomly do one of the following: recite nursery rhymes, pose simple queries that require no response ("Is it raining outside? I like rainy days and sunny days!" and so on), or engage the child in an imitation game using animal sounds or simple motor movements. There are a total of 12 different interactions in all.

A/Barney's eyes are dedicated to the game of peek-a-boo. Peek-a-boo was designed as an open-ended series of alternating "It's dark" / "It's light" responses. When A/Barney detects a loss of light, he responded with an 'It's dark' comment such as "Where did everybody go?" "Now I can't see you!" or "It sure is dark!" After playing an "It's dark" comment, when A/Barney detects an increase in light, he responds with an "It's light" comment: "Peek-a-boo, I see you!" "Oh, there you are!" and so on.

The effectiveness of dedicating sensors to functions by their location on his body was assessed by having children return repeatedly to play with A/Barney over several months, for different studies. When children returned, they were asked to make A/Barney sing a song, play a game, or play peek-a-boo. The results were striking: even after just a single session, most children recalled exactly which sensor started a given function, and executed it confidently and reliably.

Everything interrupts everything else

A key element of play is the intrinsic motivation derived from its self-directed form [17]. Similarly, in social pretend play children experience a feeling of control as the participants jointly create play events [7]. How could A/Barney mimic this responsivity? The answer came from studying two key elements of children's patterns of interaction with A/Barney: their deliberate disruption of ongoing interactions, and their conscious searching for favorite songs or games as part of their play.

Children's typical performance during play sessions was to squeeze A/Barney's hand or foot, and then play or sing along with whatever activity or song A/Barney produced. Since he randomly varied the items in his hand and foot menus and moved through all items before repeating any, the selections were always different with each round of use. This variety of presentation kept children's interest high. However, during many play sessions, particularly after children had become familiar with A/Barney's offerings, they frequently did something striking: they started a given song or game, only to then deliberately try to terminate it by acting on a different sensor. In A/Barney's early designs, such user-initiated interruptions were not part of the interface. Interruptions were viewed as accidents to be avoided, so once a song or game was started, it had to be completed before a new activity could be selected. But the research clearly documented children purposefully trying to stop a song by starting a game, for example, or trying to stop a game they themselves had started in order to play peek-a-boo, and so on. Even within the game of peek-a-boo, a similar play pattern was observed. Children would cover A/Barney's eyes, and then uncover them while he was still speaking, to stop his speech mid-utterance.

In addition to the deliberate interruptions, another pattern of interaction was for children to try to force A/Barney to play one specific game or song they desired, by trying to squeeze the same sensor repeatedly. Children spontaneously squeezed his toe several times in a row to find a specific song, for example, in efforts that mimicked cycling through the tracks on an audio CD. They showed a similar preference for finding particular games. As with cross-sensor interruptions, A/Barney's early interfaces did not support this form of searching, and children's reactions to their limited choices were very consistent: diminished interest. Their attention wandered as they waited for unwanted songs or games to end; several children actually became aggressive with A/Barney as well.

The lesson was obvious. Interruptive functions had not been included in the design because it had been assumed children would 'play along' with A/Barney. Instead, children expected the opposite: A/Barney was supposed to play along with *them*. Subsequently, all of A/Barney's interfaces were changed such that (1) any action on any sensor caused A/Barney to change what he was doing to the function associated with the triggered sensor; and (2) repeated inputs on a single sensor cycled the content of that sensor's menu. These changes increased A/Barney's responsiveness to child action, and subsequent testing showed that it increased the length and tempo of children's play with him. It also introduced a new risk: unintentional interruptions. This was especially true of the light sensor, since it responds to changes in light level – something not always due to user action. The new risk was judged acceptable, however, because of the overall enhancement A/Barney's responsiveness brought to the quality and tone of children's interactions with him.

A/Barney at the computer

A/Barney's interactions with the computer provided a striking opportunity to expand his repertoire of functions. Once the PC transmitter establishes the two-way radio link with A/Barney, all of his intelligence becomes a subset of the computer's processing power, and his internal functionality is suppressed. At the PC, therefore, his intelligence is limited only by the power of the PC itself. New speech can be transmitted to him as needed from specially designed software, and his sensors can be assigned entirely new functions as well – even combined with keyboard or mouse inputs, to allow for a variety of different interactions.

The content of A/Barney's interactions at the computer was shaped by reviewing the literature on cooperative learning methods used with computers in formal instruction in schools [10,13,14,20]. Cooperative learning, like scaffolding theory, stresses the social context and verbal interaction among learners. These studies provided insight into the dynamics of situations where social interactions take place around the computer as the common focus of attention. This research also documented the types of verbal interactions used by learning partners, especially thinking aloud during task execution, praise, and hints, which are most effective in promoting learning and mastery. The cooperative learning literature did not, however, provide insight into how A/Barney, as a simulacrum with his own interface, should be integrated with the computer. Was it possible to create interfaces that combined A/Barney's sensors with mouse use and integrated him closely with software content?

An initial test of a mixed interface, using A/Barney and the mouse together in a simple counting task, provided important guidance. All of the subjects were familiar with A/Barney from previous tests, and all were computer users in their homes. When they played with A/Barney in his freestanding mode at the start of the testing session, they interacted with him directly, attending to him visually, listening to him, and acting on his sensors. When it was time to use him with the computer, however, their performance was markedly different. They sat A/Barney next to them by the computer, and then immediately stopped interacting with his sensors and grasped the mouse, while gazing expectantly at the computer screen. When he spoke to them, they demonstrated an unexpected ability to listen to him while using the mouse at the same time. When A/Barney commented on their actions with the mouse, or gave instructions for pointing and clicking, children kept their eyes onscreen, yet responded to him with smiles and comments, and most importantly, by using the mouse as he asked.

When he asked children to use both his sensors and the mouse together for software tasks, however, a host of problems emerged. Children would inadvertently move the cursor when they released the mouse to grasp his sensors, forcing them to have to recover its location before going on with the activity. They were easily confused by the sequence of events, as well. When, exactly, were they to use the mouse versus A/Barney's sensors? In an attempt to coordinate the two interfaces, some children adopted a strategy of keeping one hand on the mouse and one on A/Barney, an awkward posture that degraded their cursor control, especially when they chose to keep their dominant hand on A/Barney and their other hand on the mouse. But perhaps the most striking result of the study was a strong transfer of expectations about *content*. Children expected that if they squeezed A/Barney's foot during software use, for example, he would respond as he did in freestanding toy mode: He would sing a song. This expectation persisted even if A/Barney had explicitly indicated otherwise in his comments. In other words, children did not expect A/Barney to change his behavior just because a computer was present.

Based on these results, the software and A/Barney's role in it were deliberately designed to build on children's existing expectations, not only about A/Barney, but about software use as well. Subsequent testing refined the elements of this design, producing a media-specific extension of the original principles created for freestanding toy mode.

From playmate to coach

The social dynamics of shared computer use differ from those of shared play. In shared play, the play partner is the focus of attention. In shared computer use, both partners focus their attention on the computer instead. Since A/Barney's goal is to stimulate the child's learning while using the computer, *his reactions and comments are all about the child's performance using the computer.* Unlike freestanding toy mode, in computer mode he never attempts to draw the child into playing with him, except during long periods of mouse inactivity. When the child is using the mouse interface, A/Barney responds to the child's actions in several specific ways, all primarily verbal, that mimic those that research indicates are used by effective learning partners:

<u>Giving content hints</u> – If the child is asked to select a triangle from a set of shapes and makes an error, for example, A/Barney provides additional information, such as the fact that triangles have three sides.

<u>Praising performance</u> – A/Barney congratulates the child whenever a right answer is selected, regardless of number of errors or time on task. He also makes task-specific compliments, such as "You have a good memory!" on memory tasks, "You sure know your letters!" on letter tasks, and so on.

<u>Modeling performance</u> – When A/Barney takes his turn during open-ended tasks, he models the cognitive and interface performance children can use. On a coloring task, for example, he might say, "I think I'll color this part yellow!" and change a section of the drawing.

<u>Articulating patterns</u> – During open-ended activities, A/Barney recognizes simple logical and sequential patterns in the child's performance and identifies them verbally. If a child has used all the same color during a coloring activity, for example, A/Barney comments on that fact. If the child squeezes A/Barney's hand after the comment, he will take a turn and continue the child's pattern, while verbally reinforcing it: "You used a lot of red. I'll color this part red, too!"

To each interface its own function

To keep the integrity of A/Barney's interactions, his role at the computer was transformed from that of direct play partner to the less-dominant role of coach, or sidekick. His own functions are carefully segregated from computer control. To this end, although A/Barney reacts to the child's performance, the onscreen activities are supervised and directed not by A/Barney, but by onscreen characters in the software itself. Everything related to computer control is done with the mouse, and the onscreen characters relay all relevant interface information to the child: where to click, the goal of the task, and so on. A/Barney remains true to his freestanding performance, but with a new twist. His feet remain an interface for songs, for example, but now the songs are new tunes, written as joint performances shared by both A/Barney and the onscreen characters together. A/Barney's eyes remain a dedicated peek-a-boo interface, but now the onscreen characters play along, covering and uncovering their eyes along with A/Barney and reacting appropriately (saying "Peek-a-boo!" when A/Barney's eyes are uncovered, for example). A/Barney's hands remain an interface for games, but now the games are onscreen in the software in the form of simple, linear vignettes. During structured tasks like drill activities, hand squeezes result in brief onscreen lessons related to the game content that are executed in squeeze-by-squeeze fashion, just like freestanding mode games. During open-ended activities like drawing or building collages with shapes, hand squeezes result in A/Barney "taking a turn" – coloring a section of the drawing himself, or adding his own shape, and reflecting on his action.

Everything interrupts everything else redux

Subsequent testing with young children demonstrated that their interactions with A/Barney and the software were highly similar to their interactions with A/Barney alone in one key respect: they showed a strong tendency to 'graze' across the different functions available to them. They might, for example, use the mouse to solve a problem, then squeeze a toe to sing along with a song, then play peek-a-boo, and then use the mouse again. As in their freestanding play performance, deliberate interruptions were common. To accommodate this pattern of performance, all of A/Barney's interactions were designed to be modular and mutually exclusive. The mouse was integrated into the universal-interruptibility design established in freestanding mode, and followed the same rules. Just as with the other sensors, a mouse click terminated any ongoing interactions and started the next event associated with the object the child clicked on.

A/Barney with the television

Research on learning from television has established that young children comprehend more program content when their viewing is supplemented by the comments and questions of older peers or adults [3,8,9]. This form of interaction, described as 'co-viewing,' is almost completely verbal. In TV mode, A/Barney performs this function through the use of specially encoded videotapes and a transmitter attached to a VCR. Unlike PC mode, however, A/Barney's comments on video content are fixed. Being part of the tape, the comments are the same each time the tape plays, and the child's actions on A/Barney cannot affect what happens on the tape or what A/Barney says about it.

From playmate to co-viewer: Less is more

Similar to PC mode, A/Barney's performance in TV mode is not the dominant role of playmate, but the less-engaged role of viewing partner. A/Barney and the child again share a common focus of attention, but this time it is the television. Children typically sat or lay with A/Barney while watching the television. Since A/Barney's goal in this mode is to promote comprehension of video content, his comments are like those in PC mode: his speech is directed to the child, but he is reacting to what is happening on the screen. He never draws attention to himself or his functions. He promotes comprehension by scaffolding TV viewing in a variety of ways:

Directing attention – A/Barney says things such as "Watch this!" or "Oh, look!" when important events are shown onscreen.

Modeling involvement – A/Barney reacts to onscreen content with appropriate responses such as surprise ("Oh, my!"), and emotional responses to events (cheering at good news, expressing concern when hearing bad news, and so on). He also sings along with songs, counts along with onscreen characters, and recites the alphabet with them.

Querying the child – A/Barney asks questions about events onscreen that are designed to promote children's thought, such as predictions ("What do you think will happen next?"), requests for identification ("What's that?" "Who's that?"), and preference queries (such as "Would you like to do that?").

Using vocabulary words – A/Barney labels objects onscreen such as letters and numbers, and identifies the colors or names of specific objects, as appropriate.

Encouraging physical participation – A key element of preschool learning is musical engagement and physical activity. During musical events onscreen, A/Barney sings along with songs and explicitly encourages the child to imitate the dancing of onscreen characters, saying "Spin all around!" or "Wave your arms!" as songs are underway.

Research with children watching a program while A/Barney delivered these comments demonstrated that they were highly effective. Similar to their performance during computer use, children showed an ability to divide their attention, listening to A/Barney's spoken comments *and* watching onscreen events at the same time. Several children responded verbally to A/Barney's questions, or repeated his comments to others watching along with them during the testing session. Even when children did not show an overt response, their eye movements revealed that they were listening to A/Barney and processing his comments as they kept their eyes onscreen.

The research also revealed that the frequency and timing of co-viewer comments was a critical design element. Educational programming for young children is designed to maintain attention by being fast-paced and full of sights, sounds, and action. Fitting A/Barney's observations into such content without his talking over onscreen events was difficult to accomplish. Testing clearly indicated that too many comments distracted children by competing with action on the screen. A low frequency of comments was best; A/Barney's individual prompts were novel enough to catch children's attention but not so frequent as to be disruptive. In terms of timing, the most significant discovery was the need to allow children plenty of time to react to what A/Barney said. Attention directives, for example, needed to happen before, not during, the events they were targeting. A comment that was synchronous with the event it was targeting was ineffective because children's latency to focus their attention was too long, and the event would end too quickly to be processed.

Sensor functions should fit the social context

TV mode raised a troubling design issue for A/Barney: what was the appropriate role for his freestanding functions, such as songs? In PC mode, these functions were preserved and augmented by keeping them intact and integrating them into the software content itself. This design had the virtue of both keeping A/Barney's interface consistent and at the same time keeping the child's attention focused on the computer screen, even if his songs and games were not a part of the actual computer task. The linear nature of video content precluded this design from the start. A song on demand during TV viewing could not be integrated into what was on the screen; it would be a distraction, creating exactly the opposite of what was intended in the co-viewing educational model.

One possible solution was to simply deactivate A/Barney's sensors during TV viewing. This meant he would comment on what he was watching, but would not respond to child action. Testing of this scenario, however, showed it was inadequate. Children acted on A/Barney's sensors far less often than during freestanding play or PC play, but when he failed to respond they were perplexed. Why was A/Barney talking, yet not responding to their actions? His lack of responsiveness actually became a distraction in itself, as children turned their attention to A/Barney and tried to elicit a response from him and began ignoring the content of the program they were viewing.

The key to the correct design came from a careful review of how, exactly, children engaged not only A/Barney, but also their parents, during tests of TV mode. Unlike their interactions with A/Barney in freestanding mode or PC mode, children did not give their full attention to A/Barney when they interacted with him in TV mode. Rather, they tended to reach over and act on A/Barney absently, as a secondary behavior during viewing. What was striking what that they tended to act on their parents in the same way, *often with an identical action.* If they patted their parent's arm while viewing, for example, they also patted A/Barney. The parent's response, typically a brief recognitory action (a return pat, a stroke, etc.), typically satisfied children. Would they be satisfied with a similar, abbreviated response from A/Barney?

Subsequent testing revealed that this was in fact the case. If the children squeezed A/Barney's hand or foot, all he had to do was make a friendly comment ("I like watching TV with you,") or give a generic, TV-specific attention directive ("What's happening on the TV?"), and children were content. No children protested or asked why A/Barney did not play games or sing while watching TV if his hands or feet were squeezed. Peek-a-boo, however, was a different story. Although it was played more laconically, children still expected that A/Barney would respond to having his eyes covered – especially during an activity that depended on being able to see. In the TV viewing context, in fact, covering A/Barney's eyes seemed to be a sort of teasing behavior that children enacted with a mischievous grin, as if they were deliberately obstructing his view. To accommodate this specific interaction, peek-a-boo was kept fully functional in TV mode, and TV-specific comments such as "I can't see the TV!" were added to A/Barney's repertoire – changes that satisfied children in subsequent tests.

Interruption and the limits of pretend

TV mode differs from A/Barney's other modes in one important way. Unlike freestanding toy mode and PC mode, where children's own actions are the focus of A/Barney's attention, in TV mode A/Barney is reacting to the content of the program being viewed. Yet for him to be responsive to children, and be consistent with his behavior in other modes, all child-initiated actions still take precedence over his reactions to the TV program, and interrupt them. Squeezing a foot or hand causes him to interrupt his TV comments and give one of special recognitory phrases, and covering his eyes makes him play Peek-a-boo.

Peek-a-boo presents an unusual case, however. In his other modes, keeping A/Barney's eyes covered for a long period of time leads to a termination of peek-a-boo. In freestanding play, A/Barney stops making comments about not being able to see and prompts the child to play a game or sing a song. In PC mode, the end of peek-a-boo results in either the same reaction from A/Barney or a request for mouse action from the onscreen character. Auto-termination of the game makes sense in these modes, because there is no expectation that A/Barney needs to be able to "see" to play his games or sing songs. In TV viewing, however, A/Barney's being able to "see" was a key element of the pretend engagement and ending peek-a-boo automatically raised difficult issues. If A/Barney were put under a blanket and left there, for example, should he terminate peek-a-boo and start talking about what was on the television, even though his vision would still be obstructed? Should peek-a-boo be different during TV viewing, and never terminate until A/Barney's eyes are uncovered, to maintain the pretend illusion of his having vision?

The decision was made that the dangers of maintaining the pretend illusion outweighed the benefits in this scenario. A/Barney's performance in TV mode needed to be consistent with his pretend-based design, but to keep it consistent on this point created unacceptable risks. To take just one possible situation, if A/Barney's light sensor became disabled and peek-a-boo did not auto-terminate, he would never be able to interact with the TV at all. Poor lighting conditions could also prevent him from interacting with the TV, even with the sensor intact. Being consistent across modes and auto-terminating peek-a-boo, even thought it violated the logic of pretend in TV mode, was judged an acceptable trade-off in light of the possibility that all of his TV interactions would be put at risk otherwise.

CONCLUSIONS

Consistency and context in interface design

Shaping A/Barney's interactions to provide educational content appropriate to each mode while maintaining consistency in his interface proved to be the biggest design challenge facing this product. Consistency is critical to a good interface, because it makes interaction predictable and reliable, resulting in less demand on user working memory and less effort spent on learning the rules of task execution [2,19]. Yet the demand characteristics of each of A/Barney's learning modes required that some context-specific changes in the interface be made, if the learning objectives appropriate to each interaction were to be met. The issues associated with altering A/Barney's interface to fit changes in his functions can be considered as a modern variant of the classic "mode" problem faced in early text-editor design [11,15]. In the era before graphical interfaces, the design challenge was that a change in software mode (from editing lines of code to running the program, for example) often meant a change in the functions of a single interface. The F1 key, for example, might mean "cut" in editing mode but then mean "abort" in run mode. The arbitrary nature of the function changes, and the lack of visual feedback that the mode had changed, created confusion among users and led to high rates of error.

For A/Barney, the challenge was similar: functional changes in A/Barney's role meant changes in his interface that would be invisible to the child user. A/Barney's interface design avoids making these changes confusing because he can do what software interfaces cannot: make the changes fit the demands of the social context in which he and the child are participating, so that they seem obvious and natural instead of arbitrary and artificial. Accomplishing this goal required not only a careful analysis of existing research on learning in social contexts, but also extensive study of young children's interactions with A/Barney himself.

The pretend playmate as an interface convention

ActiMates Barney is able to scaffold children's learning across three distinct social contexts because his performance in each context matches their expectations of the social dynamics of each interaction. As a freestanding toy, he interacts directly with the child; as a TV co-viewer, he watches along and attends to the television; and as a learning partner at the computer, he offers assistance, encouragement, and observation. These forms of engagement would not succeed unless children were willing to "play along" with the idea that Barney is a social being, and that his behavior should be consistent with the friendly, supportive, and wiser play partner he portrays on his television program.

It would also not have succeeded if children's expectations about social interactions, both one-on-one and with electronic media, were not so clearly differentiated. Indeed, perhaps the most striking aspect of the research and design on this product is the finding of just how elaborate and detailed children's patterns of engagement with different media are, even at three years of age. Barney's interface in each mode had to be carefully refined to match children's existing social repertoires for each – repertoires that were divergent in surprisingly subtle ways. By mimicking the performance children expect from a play partner across different social contexts and in the company of different media, A/Barney is able to maintain an integrity of purpose and interface even as his specific functions and interactions vary.

ActiMates Barney succeeds as a learning product by conforming to the demands of the situation and to the expectations of his users, just as an intelligent, respectful play partner should. And in this way he suggests an important lesson for future interface designs, especially those based on social conventions. Whether it is an intelligent agent who shops for you, or one that tutors you as you learn, technology interaction is a form of consensual play-acting where both the user and the technology have specific roles to play. Such shared pretend is a form of true partnership and collaboration, and achieving that level of user engagement is the ultimate goal of interface design. It seems particularly fitting that a product designed for our youngest users, for whom pretend play itself is a way of learning about the world, should remind us of this simple fact.

REFERENCES

1. Bretherton, I. and Beeghly, M. Pretence: Acting 'as if.' In J.J. Lockman and N. L. Hazen (Eds.) *Action in Social Context: Perspectives on Early Development*. Plenum Press, NY, 1989, pp. 239-271
2. Brown, C.M. *Human-computer interface design guidelines*. Ablex Publishing Co., Norwood, NJ, 1988.
3. Collins, W.A, Sobol, B.L. & Westby, S. Effects of adult commentary on children's comprehension and inferences about a televised aggressive portrayal. *Child Development*, 52, 1 (1981), 158-163.
4. Diaz, R.M., and Berk, L.E. (eds.). *Private Speech: From Social Interaction to Self-Regulation.* Lawrence Erlbaum Associates, Hillsdale, NJ, 1992.
5. Druin, A. Noobie: The Animal Design Playstation. *SIGCHI Bulletin*, 20, 1 (1988), 45-53.
6. Druin, A. Physical Multimedia Environments. In A. Druin and C. Solomon (eds.). *Designing Multimedia Environments for Children.* John Wiley and Sons, NY, 1992, 176-191.
7. Forys, S.K.S., and McCune-Nicolich, L. Shared pretend: Sociodramatic play at 3 years of age. In I. Bretherton (ed.). *Symbolic Play: The Development of Social Understanding.* Academic Press, NY, 1984, 159-191.
8. Haefner, M.J. and Wartella, E.A. Effects of Sibling Coviewing on Children's Interpretations of Television Programs. *Journal of Broadcasting and Electronic Media*, 31, 2 (1987), 153-68.
9. Huston, A.C., Donnerstein, E., Fairchild, H., Katz, P.A., Murray, J.P., Rubinstein, E.A., Wilcox, B.L., and Zuckerman, D.M. *Big World, Small Screen: The Role of Television in American Society.* University of Nebraska Press, Lincoln, NE, 1992.
10. Johnson, D.W. and Johnson, R. *Learning Together and Alone: Cooperation, competition, and individualization.* Prentice-Hall, Englewood Cliffs, NJ, 1975.
11. Jones, M K. *Human-Computer Interaction: A Design Guide.* Educational Technology Publications, Englewood Cliffs, NJ, 1988.
12. McCarthy, D. *Manual for the McCarthy Scales of Children's Abilities*. The Psychological Corporation, Cleveland, OH, 1972.
13. Mevarech, Z.R., Silber, O., & Fein, D. Leaning with computers in small groups: Cognitive and affective outcomes. *Journal of Educational Computing Research*, 7 (1991), 233-243.
14. Nastasi, B.K. and Clements, D.H. Social-cognitive behaviors and higher-order thinking in educational computing environments. *Learning and Instruction (special issue on cooperative learning and computers)*, 2 (1992), 215-238
15. Norman, D. Design Principles for Human-Computer Interfaces. In A. Janda (ed.), *Human Factors in Computer Systems. Proceedings of the ACM SIGCHI Conference* (Boston MA, December 1983), North-Holland, Amsterdam, 1-10.
16. Resnick, P., and Virzi, R.A. Relief from the Audio Interface Blues: Expanding the Spectrum of Menu, List, and Form Styles. *ACM Transactions on Computer-Human Interaction*, 2, 2 (June 1995), 145-176.
17. Robson, S. "Best of all I like Choosing Time": Talking With Children About Play and Work. *Early Child Development and Care*, 92, (1993), 37-51.
18. Rogoff, B., & Gardner, W. Adult Guidance of Cognitive Development. In B. Rogoff and J. Lave (eds.). *Everyday Cognition: Its Development in Social Context.* Harvard University Press, Cambridge, MA, 1984, 95-116.
19. Shneiderman, B. *Designing the Human Interface: Strategies for Effective Human-Computer Interaction.* Addison-Wesley Publishing Co., Reading, MA, 1987
20. Slavin, R. E. Cooperative Learning. *Review of Educational Research*, 60 (1980), 315-342.
21. Strommen, E.F. "What did he say?": Speech output in preschool software. In *Proceedings of NECC'91* (Phoenix AR, June 1991), International Society for Technology in Education, Eugene, Oregon, 149-151.
22. Tudge, J.R.H., Winterhoff, P.A., & Hogan, D.M. The Cognitive Consequences of Collaborative Problem Solving With and Without Feedback. *Child Development*, 67(6, 1996), 2892-2909.
23. Vygotsky, L. S. *Mind in Society: The Development of Higher Psychological Processes.* Harvard University Press, Cambridge, MA, 1978.
24. Vygotsky, L. S. *Thought and Language.* M.I.T. Press, Cambridge, MA, 1967.

PRoP: Personal Roving Presence

Eric Paulos **John Canny**

Department of Electrical Engineering and Computer Sciences
University of California, Berkeley
Berkeley, CA 94720-1776, USA
paulos@cs.berkeley.edu jfc@cs.berkeley.edu

ABSTRACT

Current internet applications leave our physical presence and our real-world environment behind. This paper describes the development of several simple, inexpensive, internet-controlled, untethered tele-robots or PRoPs (Personal Roving Presences) to provide the sensation of tele-embodiment in a remote real space. These devices support at least video and two-way audio as well as mobility through the remote space they inhabit. The physical tele-robot serves both as an extension of its operator and as a visible, mobile entity with which other people can interact. PRoPs enable their users to perform a wide gamut of human activities in the remote space, such as wandering around, conversing with people, hanging out, pointing, examining objects, reading, and making simple gestures.

Keywords

Tele-action, tele-presence, tele-conferencing, tele-embodiment, telecommunications, tele-robotics, gesturing, tele-work, robotics, computer-mediated human–human interaction.

INTRODUCTION

We already live in a society accustomed to ubiquitous telecommunications [4]. Telephones are in every office, cellular phones are in many automobiles, and many individuals are reachable at any time via a pager or personal phone. More recently, the internet has increased our tele-connectivity by allowing us to exchange text, images, sound, and video with anyone whose interests we share, professionally or socially.

But obviously something is missing from these tools compared to direct human contact. This difference is so important that we expend a great deal of time and money traveling to experience these direct contacts. There is something about the extended experience of "being there" and the gamut of activities that we can perform when physically present that makes us prefer to be there in person.

CHI 98 Los Angeles CA USA

We do not believe that we can ever replace true human-human interactions, nor is it our goal to do so. However, we do feel that it is possible to identify and distill a number of human behavioral traits or skills that are inherent to human communication, understanding, and interaction. Employing computer networking and robotic technologies to implement these traits, our goal is to ultimately provide a compelling overall experience for both the remote and local users and more importantly to create a usable system for tele-embodiment.

Why Tele-embodiment?

PRoPs allow human beings to project their presence into a real remote space rather than a virtual space, using a robot instead of an avatar. This approach is sometimes called "strong telepresence" or "tele-embodiment" since there is a mobile physical proxy for the human at the end of the connection. We coined the term *tele-embodiment* to emphasize the importance of the physical mobile manifestation.

Our approach differs fundamentally from more traditional versions of strong telepresence which involve an anthropomorphic proxy or android. Instead, PRoPs attempt to achieve certain fundamental human skills without a human-like form. More importantly, our research is driven by the study and understanding of the social and psychological aspects of extended human–human interactions rather than the rush to implement current technological advances and attempt to re-create *exact* face-to-face remote human experiences.

Why Not Video Teleconferencing?

While standard internet-based video teleconferencing provides an arguably more realistic interface than many other forms of telecommunications, it is more of an enhancement to existing technology rather than a new form of communication. With video teleconferencing we find ourselves fixed, staring almost voyeuristically through the gaze of an immovable camera atop someone's computer monitor. As actions and people pass across the camera's field of view, we are helpless to pan and track them or follow them into another room. The result is a "one-sided" experience where the remote user feels immersed but there is no physical presence at the remote end with which people can interact. In essence we still lack mobility and autonomy. We cannot control what we see or hear. Even if we had cameras in every room and the ability to switch between them, the experience would still lack the spatial continuity of a walk around a building.

We claim users want a more realistic perception of physical remote embodiment. We realized the importance of immersing the PRoPs user in the remote space by providing continuity of motion and control of that motion. These elements provide the user the visual cues necessary to stitch together the entire visual experiences into a coherent picture of a building and its occupants. Our system also supports various levels of communications and interaction between the PRoP user and the remote world's inhabitants. Furthermore, our system is accessible to any user on the internet with standard software running on currently existing computer architectures.

Outline

This paper first reviews previous and related work in telepresence and personal, remote interaction devices. However, discussion of some related research is postponed until more appropriate sections of the paper. We then describe the implementation and design of airborne and later terrestrial PRoPs. We discuss the results of our use of these devices and identify several important elements in providing a compelling tele-embodied experience. Next we confront several relevant social issues involving PRoP development. Various future PRoP design plans are investigated. Finally, we complete the paper with a summary of PRoPs, their contributions, and importance.

PREVIOUS AND RELATED WORK

Methods of achieving telepresence[1] are not new with one of the first electrically controlled mechanical teleoperational systems being developed by Goertz [6] in 1954. Since then a variety of applications for tele-operated robotics have been explored [16]. However, most of these system are designed for a single specific task and are quite complex. They also typically require special purpose dedicated hardware and a highly trained operator to control and interact with the mechanism in the remote environment. In our system we strived to constrain its development so that it would be accessible to a wide audience without additional, expensive, or extraordinary hardware. In essence, telepresence[2] for the masses.

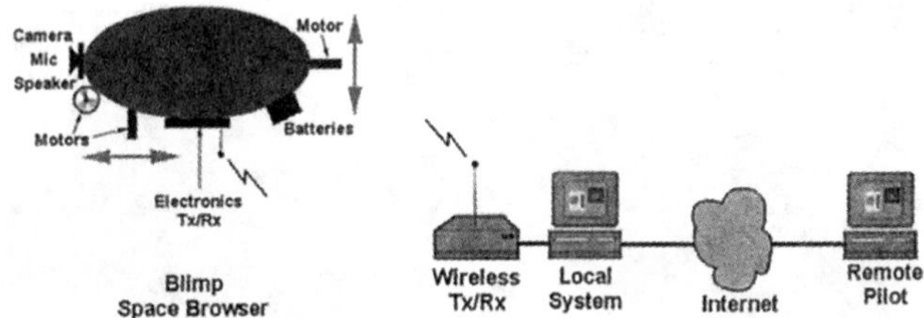

Figure 1: System overview of the basic space browser (or blimp PRoP) hardware configuration.

The exponential growth of the WWW over the past several years has resulted in a plethora of remote controlled mechanical devices which can be accessed via the WWW. Goldberg [7] developed a 3 DOF (Degree Of Freedom) telerobotic system where users were able to explore a remote world with buried objects and, more interestingly, alter it by blowing bursts of compressed air into its sand filled world. Soon afterwards, we developed Mechanical Gaze [13], a tele-robotic system where uses could control a camera's viewpoint and image resolution to observe various museum artifacts placed within the robot's workspace. By 1995, Goldberg had developed another telerobotic system called the TeleGarden [8] in which WWW users are able to observe, plant, and nurture life within a living remote garden. As of this writing, well over several hundred interesting mechanical devices are connected to the WWW with more spawning daily.

Social and psychological aspects of extended human-human interactions motivate the design of our PRoPs and we have identified a wide range of research in this area. Shared spaces and human interaction with video walls such as the VideoWhiteboard [17] designed at Xerox PARC and later Ishii's ClearBoard [9] are fundamental to designing usable PRoPs. We are also interested in the use of video in tele-connecting individuals which has been nicely explored by Kraut and Fish [10; 5] and others [3].

AIRBORNE PROPS: SPACE BROWSERS

The first PRoPs were simple airborne tele-robots we named *space browsers*. A space browser is a helium-filled blimp of human proportions or smaller with several lightweight motors directly connected to small propellers and no other moving parts. On board the blimp is a color video camera, microphone, speaker, simple electronics, and various radio links (see Figure 1). The entire payload is less than 600 grams (typically 400–500 grams). Our design choice was to use the smallest sized blimps that could carry the necessary cargo, thus making them easily maneuverable down narrow hallways, up stairwells, into elevators, and through doorways. At present we have iterated

[1] "To convey the idea of these remote-control tools, scientists often use the words *teleoperators* or *telefactors*. I prefer to call them *telepresences*, a name suggested by my futurist friend Pat Gunkel." [12]

[2] More specifically we are referring to tele-embodiment, tele-robotics, or tele-action. This is to avoid the ambiguity caused by the term *telepresence* which has grown in recent years to describe not only systems involving distant real spaces (*i.e.* tele-robotics) but also distant virtual spaces or VR.

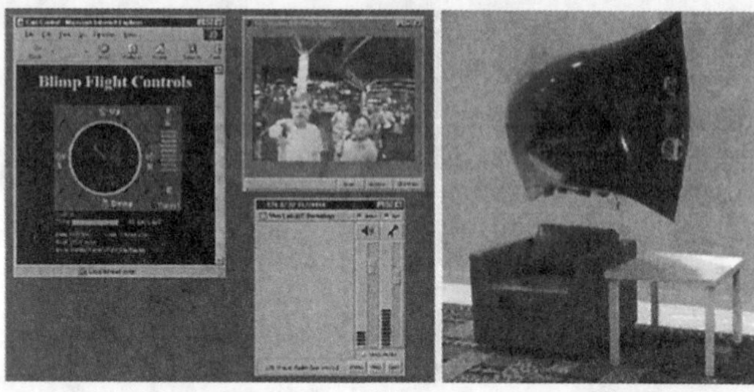

Figure 2: The remote pilot's Java interface with live audio and video (left) and a blimp PRoP in flight (right).

through several different configurations. Blimps ranging in size from 180x90 cm to 120x60 cm and shapes such as cylinders, spheres, and "pillow shaped" have all been flown. The smaller blimps consume about the same space as a standing person and are thus well-suited for moving into groups of people and engaging in conversation with minimal disruption. Even under full power a blimp moves at human walking pace. Figure 2 depicts one of the "pillow shaped" blimps in flight.

A user, anywhere on the internet, can use a simple Java applet running within a Java-enabled browser to pilot the blimp (see Figure 2). As they guide the blimp up and down or right and left the blimp delivers, via wireless communications, live video and audio to the pilot's machine through standard free tele-conferencing software that runs on a standard PC. The pilot observes the real world from the vantage of the blimp while listening to the sounds and conversations within close proximity to the blimp. The pilot converses with groups and individuals by simply speaking into the microphone connected to their desktop or laptop computer, the sound delivered via the internet and then a wireless link to the blimp's on-board speaker.

Problems with Blimps

Space browsers are far from perfect in that they are currently quite high maintenance. Stringent weight limitations allow for only a small amount of batteries to be carried on-board, yielding flights of about an hour before batteries need replacement. Although replacement is quick and rather straightforward, this process still prevents the blimp from operating continuously, as we would desire. As a result, remote conversations and explorations are often cut short.

Furthermore, piloting the blimp is often awkward. Typically the blimp exhibits erratic behavior and the sensation is more like swimming or floating than walking. Another problem is that unlike other robots, blimps are nearly impossible to bring to a complete halt.

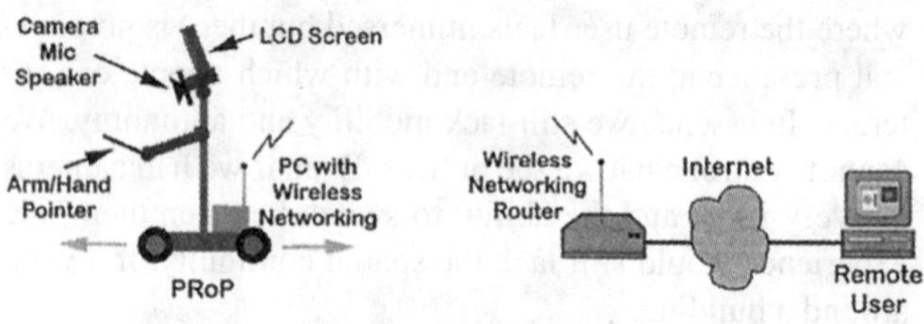

Figure 3: System overview of a Surface Cruiser (or cart) PRoP hardware configuration.

Some Solutions

Typically, a user wants to maintain a constant height while flying around, but instead must manually burst the lift motor at regular intervals to maintain that height. To solve this we have incorporated a simple lightweight sonar device onto the blimp to help maintain a constant height. Likewise, various simple aerial acrobatics such as nice ninety-degree turns and flying forward without rotating slightly left or right are difficult. In an attempt to solve this we have incorporated a simple, inexpensive electronic compass weighing less than 25 grams. Both the compass and sonar are carried on board and thus are not susceptible to the network delays experienced by the pilot attempting to correct these problems remotely. There is addition information [14] available for readers wishing to acquire more information about these airborne PRoPs.

TERRESTRIAL PROPS: SURFACE CRUISERS

Leveraging off of our previous research with airborne PRoPs, we developed terrestrial four-wheeled *surface cruisers* or *carts*. These carts are designed from simple remote-control vehicles with modifications to slow them to human walking pace and a 1.5 meter vertical pole to provide a realistic human vantage for the camera. On board the cart is a color video camera, microphone, speaker, color LCD screen, a few simple custom electronics, and various drive and servo motors. The basic system layout for the cart system is shown in Figure 3. Unlike the blimps, carts can travel outdoors, require less maintenance, and provide much longer battery life. Carts also carry a complete PC on-board with wireless networking hardware attached. Thus the multiple radios previously required to operate the blimp coalesce into a single wireless signal on carts. Furthermore, we leverage off of wireless communication infrastructures already in existence, greatly extending the inhabitable world of carts. A recently designed cart is shown in Figure 4.

RESULTS

The various PRoP design choices have been guided largely through trial and error experiments with the actual devices. Obvious methods of communication such as audio and video were part of our original design. However, after

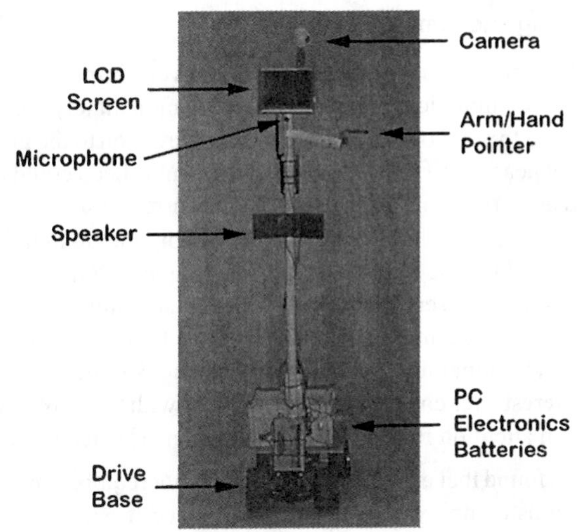

Figure 4: A cart PRoP with camera head, video LCD screen, controllable "arm/hand" pointer, microphone, speakers, and drive-able base.

extended use of these PRoPs it was clear that many important, and often subtle, elements were missing from the experience.

Through this evolutionary development we have been able to identify several behavioral traits which we consider essential to providing the most compelling overall experience for both the remote and local PRoP user. In the following subsections we iterate these elements and discuss their role in creating convincing tele-embodiment. While some of them may seem obvious, there are others that we have found to be surprisingly important and far less evident.

Audio

Perhaps the most apparent element of communication, two-way audio allows users to engage in remote conversations. Audio is also the channel whose usefulness is most susceptible to quality degradation from reduced network bandwidth and/or network packet loss. An unexpected result was the importance of background "noise" near the PRoP. The experience of using the PRoP was noticeably more compelling when users were able to gauge the general mood of the remote location by receiving a variety of subtle aural cues such as doors opening, elevators arriving, people approaching, nearby conversations, music playing, automobile traffic, wind blowing, etc.

Video

A visual portal into the remote space is another obvious element of the immersive experience. Video is also the most demanding tele-embodiment trait in terms of network bandwidth consumption and processor usage. Despite the increased resource consumption, color video is far superior to grey-scale for distinguishing details and identifying objects and locations remotely as well as for providing a more realistic perception of the remote space. The effects and tradeoffs of video and image quality and its resulting perception by humans has been extensively studied by Reeves and Nass [15].

We learned that sophisticated video compression algorithms are essential to make video signals usable. Surprisingly, in many cases the overall quality of the resulting video is far less important than the ability of that video to provide subtle information about the motions, actions, and changes at the remote location. When the user is navigating or when significant amounts of activity are occurring within the camera field of view, the importance of high video frame rates dominates over the resulting video quality. We learned that during times of "high video activity" the resulting compressed video signal should convey to the remote user at least an approximate representation of the remote motion and/or activity. However, during periods of small temporal video activity such as when the user is conversing with an individual, examining an object, or reading a sign, it is clearly the overall quality of the video signal that dominates over frame rate.

On several occasions PRoP drivers lost their way in a familiar hallway. Users performed a two-step process to orient themselves. First, using the high-frame-rate low-quality video, users steered the PRoP towards a door name-tag or room number sign. Accurately positioning the PRoP in front of such a room marking is prohibitively difficult without the use of high-frame-rate video to provide visual feedback to the user. Second, when motion stopped, the user requests high-quality low-frame-rate video which is used to easily resolve the name on the door (or room number), thus identifying their location in the building.

This led us to identified the need for at least two levels of video resolution or "Telepresence with Extra Eyes" [18]. The system should provide a wide angle view similar to the human eye for navigating and recognizing people (and objects) and also a smaller field of view for reading text on paper, white-boards, doors, and computer screens.

We noticed that with only one-way video, PRoPs can be mistaken as tele-operated surveillance tools or autonomous reconnaissance drones. Both of these tasks are far from the intended application of PRoPs. We removed this video-asymmetry by adding a small (15 cm diameter) LCD screen with a video feed from the remote user. This two-way video is also an appropriate mechanism for transmitting a richer representation of the remote user through their facial gestures and expressions. When bandwidth is a problem and the screen is used only to display a still image of the remote user, we find that it still succeeds in conveying the identity and existence of the remote user.

Mobility

Mobility, and in fact all of the remaining behavioral traits, are notable PRoP enhancements to standard video teleconferencing. While the space browsing blimps possess more mobility (*i.e.* flying in the third dimension), the carts are actually much more effective PRoPs. The main reason is that blimps actually provide too much freedom and no mechanism to stop. That is, the blimps, despite several on-board sensors, are unable to hold a fixed position while the cart PRoPs can easily halt and interact with a group of people.

So how sophisticated should the mobility be? We found that simple car-like navigation of a PRoP on the ground was fairly straightforward for a user to understand and control though a relatively simple interface. It also provided enough freedom for users to maneuver within (and outside of) buildings. This was the simple design of our first PRoP.

However, since human interactions occur where humans can travel, PRoPs must be able to reach much of the world accessible to humans. Again, we are not attempting to create an android or anthropomorphic robot so we will not handle what we call dextrous human motions. In particular PRoPs do not need to climb fences, swing from ropes, leap over ditches, repel down cliffs, slide down poles, *etc.*

Our basic philosophy is that PRoPs should be able to access the *majority* of locations most humans inhabit daily. Aiming for simplicity, we feel that PRoPs should be able to perform simple locomotion through fairly benign terrains such as mild inclines, curbs, stairs, and small variations in ground surface (*i.e.* sidewalks, grass, dirt, *etc.*). This includes traveling outdoors and also means that PRoPs must be be untethered (*i.e.* wireless). It is also important to impede the overall speed of the PRoP, typically through various gear reductions, to roughly mimic human walking pace.

Directed Gaze

Although remote users can see, hear, and move around, navigating remains a tedious task and does not facilitate the ability to quickly glance around a room to get a feel for its size, occupants, *etc.* This problem is remedied by incorporating a small movable "head" (*i.e.* a camera on a controllable pan-tilt platform) onto the PRoP. Our device is similar to the GestureCam [11] which allows a remote participant in a conversation to have direct control of his or her visual field of view. This relatively simple PRoP "head" provides a vitally important element of human communication, direction of attention or gaze as discussed by several researchers [2; 9]. This allows PRoPs to perform human-like conversational gestures such as turning to face someone in order to see them, address them, or just give attention to them. These actions are also visible to people interacting locally with the PRoP and provide simple gestural cues to let individuals know when they are being addressed or looked at by the remote user.

Pointing and Simple Gesturing

We learned quickly that gestures are very important for human communication. Remote users immediately found the need to point out a person, object, or direction to the individual near the PRoP. Although the movable head could be used as a crude substitute, it lacked the correct visual gestural aesthetic of pointing and was often ambiguous to individuals watching the PRoP. We added a simple 2 DOF pointer so that remote users can point as well as make simple motion patterns. These motion patterns allow the PRoP user to express additional non-verbal communications gestures such as interest in a conversation, agreement with a speaker, or to gain attention for asking a question in a crowded room.

We found that adequate pointing does not require a mechanism as complex as a human hand, since it is gross motion and not dexterity that is needed for the social function of gesturing. We have also been exploring several optional "arm/hand" designs to accomplish basic gesturing functions. More complex gesture interfaces and mechanisms are an important piece of our long term research agenda.

There has been a significant amount of research into gesture *recognition*. These systems typically aim to identify a human motion, typically made with a mouse, and interpret it as a known gesture. For example, a quick up-down motion of the mouse may be recognized as the "scroll page" gesture. However, we are making a conscious choice to use such symbolic descriptions of gestures only as a last resort. Instead we prefer to use continuous input devices like mice and joysticks to provide direct gestural input from the user to the PRoP. For example, compare typing text to a speech synthesizer, with spoken text transmitted through a speech compression algorithm. The synthesis approach may provide clean-sounding speech at low bandwidth, but all nuance and emotional content is lost. Similarly, music which is generated by computer from an annotated musical score is lifeless compared to music played by a human from that score, even if the recording mechanism is identical (*i.e.* MIDI).

We believe that any human communication beyond the very simplest cannot be ascribed a unique or personal meaning. We are further motivated by Wittgenstein who succinctly expressed that communication is about *connotation* (what the communication could mean) and not about *denotation* (some particular meaning). Post-structural literary theory underlines the importance of social, political, and historical context in the understanding of any text. It illustrates just how complex the meaning of short "symbolic" text can be. It also explains why symbolic representations such as text are capable of such great richness.

In fact it is not really surprising that through these crude devices and narrow communication channels, that rich and complex communication is possible. Recall that actors transmit their gestures to audience members tens of meters away, dancers and mimes work without speech, and puppeteers work without a human body at all. All of us use the telephone without a visual image of our interlocutor. Our task in gesture transmission is to isolate the key aspects of gesture so as to preserve meaning as closely as possible. Some factors are clearly important, such as time-stamping to preserve synchronization and velocity. Others, such as mapping human degrees of freedom to robot "arm/hand" degrees of freedom are much less so.

Reflexivity

The ability of a user to experience their own existence and actions through the PRoP turns out to be an extremely important element in providing a compelling tele-visit. When users could point the camera downward and actually see the wheels and base of the PRoP there was a noticeable improvement in the quality of the immersive tele-experience. Likewise, the experience was enhanced when users could steer the wheels, move forward and backwards, or position the pointer while visually watching the actions that resulted from their commands. Imagine if you were able to give commands to your arms and legs but never sense the result? Clearly, the experience would be lacking a significant element which we call *reflexivity*.

There is also reflexivity in the audio channel. In fact the importance of full-duplex audio, that is the ability to hear and speak at the same time, allows the remote user to hear their own voice when speaking. Users also use this mechanism to regulate the tone or volume of their voice to suit the acoustical or aural mood of the remote space the PRoP is inhabiting.

Limited resources such as bandwidth can inhibit reflexivity and distract from the immersive experience. This occurs when network delays cause the user to feel detached from the PRoP. The lag between moving the control joystick or mouse and seeing the results can sometimes be several seconds. By then the PRoP may have wandered far from where the user intended. The impression that the user gets its that the PRoP has "a mind of its own" which is exactly the opposite of an immersive experience. Expected technological advances will eventually solve this problem. However, substantial transmission delays are going to be a fact of life on the internet for at least a few more years. That means that real-time control of PRoPs over the internet will continue to be cumbersome.

Physical Appearance and Viewpoint

Although not anthropomorphic, we observed that PRoP design is loosely coupled to a few human-like traits which are important visual cues for successful communication and interaction. Clearly, a small ground-based robot conveys a rodent-like perspective of the world. However, a large robot is typically unable to navigate down narrow hallways, pass through doors, and impedes normal human traffic flow in a building. Furthermore, larger more industrial-type mobile robots are also more likely to frighten people, detracting from their use in human communication and interaction.

Since they stand in as a physical proxy for a remote user, it makes sense that PRoPs should be roughly the same size as a human. We attached a 1.5 meter vertical pole at the center of the PRoP to provide a realistic human vantage for the camera. In general we have found that the positioning of various attachments on the PRoP (*i.e* head, pointer, arm, *etc.*) should have some correspondence to the location of an actual human body part that provides the equivalent functionality. Also, all of the communication channels should be from the point of view of the PRoP (*i.e.* from on-board the tele-robot). It does not suffice to simply have a camera someplace in the room where the PRoP is currently located.

We have also experimented with the overall height of the PRoP after discovering that it was intimidating to people shorter than the camera head on the PRoP. It is still to early in our research to determine the useful range of heights or overall torso designs that facilitate human interaction with PRoPs.

Browsing and Exploring

When designing PRoPs we found that even with all of the previously discussed traits, it is essential to allow a remote user to wander, explore, and travel throughout buildings and spaces in much the same manner as humans normally do. It is this higher level browsing and exploring behavior that is perhaps the most important element of tele-embodiment.

PRoPs should allow users to search for an individual or a particular location such as a laboratory, office, or conference room. They should support exploration and wandering, where the user has no specific target. This behavior is intended to mimic the action of walking around a location noting the names and functions of rooms, wandering around looking for people they want to visit, or checking out the progress of experiments in a laboratory.

When exploring and browsing, the user can automatically generate a spatial time-line or "visual scrapbook" of the visit. By simply recording high-quality still images as the user travels with the PRoP, a rich context of the visit can be generated. For example, a user may record that they met their friend X in the south hallway of a building, then went to Professor Y's office, then went for coffee at the cafe down the street, *etc.* The visual time-line that is created assists the user in remembering the visit and in acquiring an overall feel for the remote space.

More importantly, browsing and exploring are autonomous operations performed by a remote user and do not require any support from individuals in the remote space, beyond the availability of the PRoP itself. The benefit of this is that PRoPs can be installed and used in a location with little overhead and disruption to the inhabitants of the remote space. A remote PRoP user can also be given a tour of the remote space by one of its local occupants. In fact either or both the visitor and guide may be PRoPs. Overall, a wide gamut of human activities can be performed without any local assistance such as attending meetings, seminars, conferences, discussions, *etc.*

Hanging Out

A surprising but important social function is the ability to simply hang out. We know that physical presence often improves the length, quality, and priority of one-on-one group interactions. This is a purely social phenomenon. In many work situations, individuals are willing to talk to you for a much longer period in person than they would be willing to do over the phone. When phone and in-person communications collide, most people try to terminate the phone call so they can return to their live interlocutor. We would like to better understand the factors that influence this preference and see where a PRoP presence fits into the priority ordering.

A visit to a remote place is an extended activity in which a person shares space with others. During this time, the task being performed by each person changes, and there may or may not be tasks in common at any given moment. These tasks serve as additional stimuli for communication between the individuals, leading to multiple communication episodes with different subjects.

SOCIAL ISSUES

Although PRoPs provide interesting new methods of remote interaction, there are also numerous social issues that must be carefully addressed before PRoPs become ubiquitous tele-embodiment tools. In this section we discuss a few immediate and obvious concerns in this research area.

Safety

When control of a physical mechanical system is accessible by anonymous individuals, great precautions must be taken to insure the safety of people and objects sharing the space with the PRoP. We are all aware of the interest in hacking into computers and manipulating, stealing, or destroying digital data. One can easily image the fascination of taking control of a potentially dangerous device to use to one's own ends.

Unlike many other robots, it is vital that safety be a primary concern when designing PRoPs. We propose a teleoperational variation on Asimov's first law of robotics[3] which stipulates that at no time should a PRoP ever be capable of injuring a human being, regardless of the action or inaction of the remote tele-operator.

The tele-robot's abilities, physical attachments, and even the basic construction must all be considered. Even an out of control PRoP must safely interact with humans and property. Since we desire these tele-robots to co-habitate with humans, this constraint is of the utmost importance. For example, even a seemingly un-threatening and safe, but slightly heavy, tele-robot may accidentally be knocked over near a stairwell, causing it to tumble recklessly down the stairs, and impact an innocent human in the stairwell. The importance of the safe co-habitation requirement cannot be overstated as it relates fundamentally to the acceptance, approachability, friendliness, and interactivity of PRoPs and humans.

Privacy and Security

As fascinating as a floating blimp or cruising cart is, it is somewhat disconcerting when you wonder who may actually be at the other end of the connection. Should that person be allowed to access to the space occupied by the PRoP? We envision a system to easily provide secure access to PRoPs using techniques not to different from those currently used to limit access to your individual files and computer hardware. People would invite individuals into their local space by issuing them a digital token that would authenticate and validate individual access to the local PRoP and hence the space. Also, although they are designed to be small and agile so that they can navigate within a building, PRoPs have no super human abilities that enable them to pass through walls, push elevator buttons, unlock doors, or for that matter even open a closed door.

CURRENT AND FUTURE RESEARCH

Current and future research plans center around enhancing the overall quality of the experience delivered by the PRoP and its functionality as a communication tool. We have had only limited experience with pointers on the PRoPs and would like to experiment with richer gesturing devices. We expect these to be more mechanically complex than the simple 2 DOF pointer, but we are still unsure of the actual design, methods of use, or quality of gestures we can produce.

We are also studying human physiology to better understand the dynamics of the human hand and arm. Similar research is being conducted using simulated dynamical systems to prototype simple gestural mechanisms. We plan to design dynamic regularizers (perhaps using simple PID controllers on the motors) that translate simple mouse gestures into resulting "arm/hand" dynamics on the the PRoP that mimic human arm/hand motions. The goal is to provide realistic and thus recognizable human gestures on the PRoP.

[3]"A robot may not injure a human being or, through inaction, allow a human being to come to harm." Handbook of Robotics, 56th Edition, 2058 A.D., as quoted in *I, Robot* by Asimov [1]

Certain common tasks are far too cumbersome using the current system. For example, navigating down to the end of a long hallway requires constant user attention and subtle command tweaking to avoid colliding with the walls. Our plan is to design a simple system that allows for a more intuitive point and move-to mode. A user would simply click on the video image causing the tele-robot to move to the corresponding location on the ground plane.

We expect that our simple click-and-move system will lack the accuracy of a high performance (and expensive) tele-robotic system. In fact it will likely require a few refinements in the positioning as the robot moves down the hallway. However, the benefit of moving through large areas using only a few mouse clicks would relieve the user of a tremendous burden and increase the overall functionality of PRoPs.

We would also like to be able to record higher quality images at certain locations, save them, and use them to mosaic the larger room or space. Mosaicing may also occur automatically when the PRoP is idle or when it detects an interesting event such as an extended conversation. These higher quality images server as a "scrapbook" of the interesting episodes during the user's PRoP tele-visit.

As described in the results section, there are distinct situations in which a PRoP should trade off video frame rate for resolution. We would like to be able to automatically detect these events and control the level of trade-off in the video compression algorithm. Currently, controlling this trade-off requires user intervention.

So far our cart PRoPs have not been able to negotiate stairs. We currently have several simple tread-based robot designs that we hope can be constructed to allow PRoPs to use stairs and travel over curbs.

CONCLUSION

Our claim is that PRoPs provide an extremely useful, functional, powerful new tool for supporting human communication and interaction at a distance. They enable a variety of important work and social tele-activities far beyond what we perform currently with our computers and networks.

PRoPs are also an ideal platform for studying computer-mediated human interaction because they operate in existing social spaces and can interact with groups of humans. Despite our limited experience using PRoPs, we have been able to identify several factors that we consider vital to providing the most compelling overall experience for both the remote and local users. This is why our research draws as much on the sociology of group interactions as on sensing and actuation techniques. In fact we need the former to drive our choices for the latter.

Interestingly, we found that the absolute performance of the PRoP hardware is less important that the human activities that it enables or impedes. In fact the technologies needed to construct compelling and highly immersive tele-embodiment PRoPs already exist, and they are surprisingly inexpensive. The space browser prototype cost under two-thousand US dollars and the carts only slightly more. With their low cost and enormous commercial potential, we feel that it is quite possible that such devices will someday become ubiquitous home computer accessories.

ACKNOWLEDGMENTS

This research was supported by BMDO, grant number N00014-96-1-1200 administered by ONR. We would also like to thank the following individuals for numerous enlightening personal discussions surrounding this work: Ken Goldberg, Mark Pauline, Scott Fisher, James Landay, Benjamin Zorn, and Allison Woodruff.

References

[1] Asimov, I. *I, Robot.* Garden City, N.Y. : Doubleday, 1950.

[2] Donath, J. The illustrated conversation. In *Multimedia Tools and Applications* (March 1995), vol. 1.

[3] Finn, K., Sellen, A., and Wilbur, S., Eds. *Video-Mediated Communication.* L. Erlbaum Associates, 1997.

[4] Fischer, C. S. *America Calling: A Social History of the Telephone to 1940.* University of California Press, 1992.

[5] Fish, R., Kraut, R., Root, R., and Rice, R. Evaluating video as a technology for informal communication. *Communications of the ACM 36*, 1 (1993), 48–61.

[6] Goertz, R., and Thompson, R. Electronically controlled manipulator. *Nucleonics* (1954).

[7] Goldberg, K., Mascha, M., Gentner, S., Rothenberg, N., Sutter, C., and Wiegley, J. Robot teleoperation via www. In *International Conference on Robotics and Automation* (May 1995), IEEE.

[8] Goldberg, K., Santarromana, J., Bekey, G., Gentner, S., Morris, R., Sutter, C., Wiegley, J., and Berger, E. The telegarden. In *SIGGRAPH* (1995).

[9] Ishii, H., and Kobayashi, M. Clearboard: A seamless medium for shared drawing and conversation with eye contact. In *ACM SIGCHI* (1992).

[10] Kraut, R., Fish, R., Root, R., and Chalfonte, B. Informal communication in organizations: Form, function, and technology. In *ACM Conference on Computer-Supported Cooperative Work* (1988).

[11] Kuzuoka, H., Kosuge, T., and Tanaka, M. Gesturecam: a video communication system for sympathetic remote collaboration. In *ACM Conference on Computer-Supported Cooperative Work* (October 1994).

[12] Minsky, M. Telepresence. *Omni 2*, 9 (June 1980).

[13] Paulos, E., and Canny, J. Delivering real reality to the world wide web via telerobotics. In *IEEE International Conference on Robotics and Automation* (1996).

[14] Paulos, E., and Canny, J. Ubiquitous tele-embodiment: Applications and implications. *International Journal of Human-Computer Studies/Knowledge Acquisition* (1997). Special Issue on Innovative Applications of the World Wide Web.

[15] Reeves, B., and Nass, C. *The Media Equation: How People Treat Computers, Television, and New Media Like Real People and Places.* Cambridge Univ Press, 1996.

[16] Sheridan, T. B. *Telerobotics, Automation and Human Supervisory Control.* MIT Press, 1992.

[17] Tang, J., and Mineman, S. Videowhiteboard: Video shadows to support remote colaboration. In *ACM SIGCHI* (1991).

[18] Yamaashi, K., Cooperstock, J. R., Narine, T., and Buxton, W. Beating the limitations of camera-monitor mediated telepresence with extra eyes. In *ACM SIGCHI* (1996).

Coincident Display Using Haptics and Holographic Video

Wendy Plesniak and Ravikanth Pappu
Spatial Imaging Group, MIT Media Laboratory
Cambridge, MA
{wjp,pappu}@media.mit.edu

ABSTRACT

In this paper, we describe the implementation of a novel system which enables a user to "carve" a simple free-standing electronic ***holographic*** image using a force-feedback device. The force-feedback (or ***haptic***) device has a stylus which is held by the hand like an ordinary cutting tool. The 3D position of the stylus tip is reported by the device, and appropriate forces can be displayed to the hand as it interacts with 3D objects in the haptic workspace. The haptic workspace is spatially overlapped and registered with the holographic video display volume. Within the resulting ***coincident visuo-haptic workspace***, a 3D synthetic cylinder is presented, spinning about its long axis, which a person can see, feel, and ***lathe*** with the stylus. This paper introduces the concept of coincident visuo-haptic display and describes the implementation of the lathe simulation. After situating the work in a research context, we present the details of system design and implementation, including the haptic and holographic modeling. Finally, we discuss the performance of this prototype system and future work.

KEYWORDS

Haptics, holography, electro-holography, autostereoscopic display, offset display, coincident display.

INTRODUCTION

To recognize the intimate dialog between materials and the skilled eyes, hands, and intuition of the craftsperson is to acknowledge the enormity of the technology and interaction design tasks which still lie ahead of us. Ideally, we would rally the full exploratory and manipulative dexterity of the hand, and the rich sensory capabilities of both hand *and* eye to the tasks we engineer for.

Consider the domain of *traditional craft*, in which gaze and touch convene in the same location: vision directs the hand and tool; the hand senses, manipulates tools and coaxes material to take an envisioned form. Such tight alliance of eye and hand has traditionally been fundamental to tasks in which material is artfully worked into form, and a similar condition may hold for other domains as well, like surgery, component assembly, or repair and maintenance training.

Yet, in most computer-assisted applications, the hands manipulate a pointing device while the gaze is turned to a screen. Such *offset* display configurations, which direct eyes displayward and hands to controllers elsewhere, comfortably and naturally facilitate some activities (like driving a car, playing a musical score, or moving a cursor with a mouse). In such familiar manual tasks, vision is useful for transporting the arm/hand to an object, but manipulation can often proceed quite well either in the absence of vision (after physical contact is made) or with the monitoring of visual feedback provided elsewhere. However, this may not be the best paradigm for all tasks—especially, those which are harder to control, require constant and precise visual and haptic monitoring and near-constant manual response.

In this paper, we describe an early prototype system which *spatially reunites* the focus of eye and hand and also takes a step toward bringing materials-working pleasure to computer-assisted design. While there are several conventional kinds of visual display hardware suitable for coincident visuo-haptic display of 3D information—head tracked LCD shutter glasses or head mounted displays (HMDs) combined with stereo computer graphics for instance—and while many of these visual display options currently offer adequate image quality and frame rate, they are cumbersome to wear and have attendant viewing problems. Instead, we are using a prototype glasses-free *autostereoscopic display* which allows untethered movement throughout the viewzone.

This prototype display device, MIT's second-generation holographic video (*holovideo*) system, is capable of rendering moving, monochromatic, free-standing, three-dimensional holographic images. Currently, this device has its own shortcomings, but many will be addressed by future research and routine advances in technology. For position tracking and force display, we use the Phantom™ haptic interface, a three degree-of-freedom (d.o.f) mechanical linkage with a three d.o.f passive gimbal that supports a simple thimble or stylus used by the hand. The haptic and visual workspaces are physically co-located so that a single, free-standing multimodal image of a cylinder to be "carved" is presented.

In the coincident workspace, a user can see the stylus interacting with the holographic image while feeling forces that result from contact with its force model (Figure 1). As the user pushes the tool into the simulated cylinder, it deforms in a non-volume-conserving way and an arbitrary surface of revolution can be fashioned. Ultimately, the finished computer model can be dispatched to a 3D printer providing an actual hardcopy of the design (Figure 5b). In effect, a user "sculpts light" and produces a physical result.

With these combined apparati and supporting computation, we are beginning to investigate high-quality multimodal dis-

CHI 98 Los Angeles CA USA
Copyright 1998 0-89791-975-0/98/ 4..$5.00

play and interaction that is more *Newtonian* than *symbolic*, which may be preferable for tasks which have traditionally been practiced in this fashion.

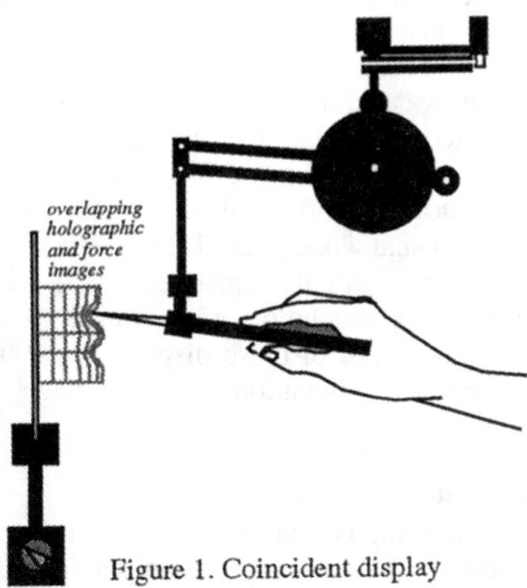

Figure 1. Coincident display

BACKGROUND

One well-established approach to joining the eyes and hands in a coincident workspace is to employ manipulable "wired" physical objects as controllers for digital objects or processes. Several research efforts are investigating the use of physical handles to virtual objects by attaching interfacing sensors or other electronics to real objects. These *tangible* objects then act as *physical controllers* for virtual processes, providing whole-hand interaction and rich visuo-haptic feedback that seems both natural and obvious. In these applications, a participant perceives his or her own body interacting with physical interface objects, but usually *also* monitors the action-outcome on another separate display or in the ambient environment.

One such project, called Graspable User Interface: Bricks [12], employed basic physical objects called "bricks" which were physical instantiations of virtual objects or functions. Once a brick was attached to a virtual object, the computational model became itself *functionally graspable*. A brick might be used, for instance, to geometrically transform a virtual object to which it was attached, availing direct control through physical handles. Tactile and kinesthetic feedback are also present and exploitable with such an interface; thus the ability to operate quickly and efficiently, using two-handed input is possible. Extending this work to incorporate a small set of differentiable geometries and material textures among the bricks could increase a person's ability to identify and manipulate the bricks without having to look at them. This could afford visual attention the luxury of continuously monitoring the application state displayed elsewhere.

Two additional systems which give primacy to both eyes and hands in manipulatory space should be mentioned; one is Wellner's Digital Desk project at EuroPARC [14] and the other is Ishii's metaDESK project at the MIT Media Laboratory [13]. Both provide desktops on which physical and digital information commingle, and accept either gestures made with hands / pencils (Digital Desk) or the manipulation of active objects (metaDESK) as input.

The Digital Desk project represents an attempt to render the computer desktop onto a real desk surface, and to merge common physical desk-objects with computational desktop functionality. The system employs a video projector situated above the desk for display of information, and a nearly co-located camera to monitor a person's movements in the workspace. Hand gestures are interpreted by a computational vision algorithm to be requests for various utilities that the system offers.

The metaDESK project attempts to physically instantiate many of the familiar GUI mechanisms (menus, windows, icons, widgets, *etc.*) in the form of tangible user interfaces (TUI's). The mapping between physical icons and virtual ones can be literally or poetically assigned; for instance placing a small physical model of MIT's Great Dome on the desk surface might cause an elaborate map of MIT to be displayed. In addition to summoning the map to the display and indicating its position, the physical Great Dome icon can be moved or rotated to correspondingly transform the map.

The metaDESK system design includes a flat rear-projected desk surface, physical icons and functional instruments for use on the surface. The state of these physical objects is sensed and used as application input. Not only can the state of virtual objects be changed by manual interaction with physical objects, but part of the display itself can be "hand-held" and likewise manipulated. The metaDESK project underscores the seemingly inexhaustible palette of ideas for instrumenting interactive space, harkening to the rich set of sensibilities and skills people develop from years of experience with real world objects, tools, and their physics.

A wide variety of virtual reality (VR) and augmented reality (AR) application areas such as telesurgery, maintenance repair and training, computer modeling and entertainment employ haptic interaction and high-quality computer graphics to study, interact with or modify data. Here, many applications employ *instrumented* force-feedback, rather than physical objects and whole-hand interaction, and trade off sensory richness for flexibility in physical modeling and visual / force rendering.

Most existing applications offset the visual and manual workspaces, but several diverse efforts to conjoin eye and hand in interactive applications exist. An example thematically related to our work is the compelling "Virtual Lathe" described and presented at the SIGGRAPH'92 conference by Michael Deering [10]. In this demonstration, a head-tracked stereo display showed a virtual stock, spinning about its long axis, which a person could interactively lathe using a 3D mouse in the shape of a rod. The demonstration required a participant to wear LCD shutter goggles for stereo viewing, but had no provision for force feedback.

A very interesting system which incorporates force feedback but no stereo viewing has been demonstrated by researchers at Carnegie Mellon University [9] called the

WYSIWYF (What You See Is What You Feel) display. The visual display behaves like a moveable "magic window", interposed between the viewer's eyes and hand, and through which the hand can be seen interacting with a virtual, tangible scene. The work employs a six degree-of-freedom haptic manipulator and monographic visual rendering to combine three pieces of information in this final coincident display: a video image of the operator's hand/arm, the computer graphically rendered scene, and the accompanying force model. The visual display is a color LCD panel with a CCD camera attached to its backplane. This display/camera unit can be moved with respect to the physical scene, while vision-based pose estimation is employed to determine its new orientation. The display shows a computer graphic view of the synthetic scene generated from the newly-computed viewpoint, composited with a live Chroma Keyed image of the operator's hand/arm moving behind the display and interacting with the haptic device. This display cannot currently reproduce correct occlusion relationships between the hand/arm and virtual objects and provides only monocular cues to scene depth (no stereo viewing or head-tracked motion parallax is available).

In other systems which employ a coincident workspace, the use of a half-silvered mirror to combine an image of the CRT's pixel plane and the haptic workspace is a historically popular and frequently used technique. One such example is the "Virtual Workbench" [8], developed at the The Virtual Environment Technologies for Training (VETT) Group at MIT's Research Lab for Electronics. This system, used to study human sensorimotor capabilities and to develop training applications, employs a Phantom haptic interface and the half-silvered mirror technique with stereo computer graphics for coincident 3D display. Representing correct occlusion relationships between the hand and simulated objects is a problem in this display configuration too. Additionally, the workspace that can actually be shared by the visual display and the hand is depth-limited in stereoscopic systems; inherent in these displays is an accommodation-convergence mismatch—a functional disengagement of several systems of the eye which normally function in cooperation. If scene depth is not designed well for the display's particular viewing geometry, eye strain, headaches and unfuseable stereo images can result. Of course, the very purpose of combining the manual and visual workspace is to visually monitor the hand (or hand-held tool) and its interaction with the object or material. Consequently, the ability to keep both the displayed object and the hand in visual focus is essential, and careful design must be employed to render it so.

Holographic displays eliminate this particular design problem by permitting a viewer to freely converge and accommodate to any point in the display volume. The combination of haptics and holography was first investigated by researchers at De Montfort University for an object inspection task [1]. Visual display was provided by a reflection transfer hologram which presented an aerial image of a control valve. A Computer Controlled Tactile Glove (CCTG) provided coincident haptic display of the same data. Similar informal experiments in combining reflection transfer holograms with force-feedback were also performed by researchers at the MIT Media Laboratory's Spatial Imaging Group. In all of these efforts the interacting hand could literally block the reflection hologram's illumination and prevent image reconstruction.

This problem was addressed by employing full-parallax edge-illuminated holograms in combination with the Phantom for the inspection of static 3D models [4]. The edge-illuminated hologram format allowed hand movements in any part of the visual workspace. Thus a viewer could haptically explore the spatially-registered force model while visually inspecting the holographic image details over a wide field of view. All of these displays were static, however; no dynamic modification could be made to the data presented.

SYSTEM DESIGN

Marrying haptics and holovideo permits us to render simple *dynamic* scenes in the user's manipulatory space, the domain of real objects. Two separate modules comprise the computation which feeds the displays; a *haptics module* that performs force modeling, and the *holovideo module* which pre-computes holograms and drives rapid local holographic display updates based on changes to the model. The haptics and hologram modules are organized by the *Workspace Resource Manager* (WRM) which is notified of geometry changes imparted to the spinning cylinder by the user's hand, and requests hologram updates to local regions of the visual display where changes have occurred. The haptics and hologram modules rely upon separate and characteristically different representations of the cylinder, which are carefully spatially and metrically registered. From the point of view of the user, who is holding the stylus and pressing it into the holographic image, a single multimodal representation of the simulation can be seen and felt changing in response to the applied force. The system overview is shown below in Figure 2.

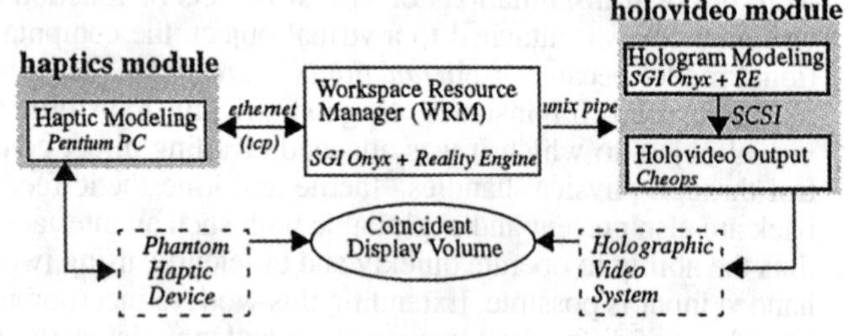

Figure 2. System overview

Haptic Modeling

Research in haptics modeling is yielding methods to model the surface and bulk properties of materials, and the computational forces generated as we mechanically interact with them. The fidelity with which computational haptics is currently able to render both the pleasing *feel* of a material interacting with our tools, and the mechanical *cues* that relay information about object and material integrity is rapidly progressing.

Our haptic device can display force to the user's hand according to its position-based interaction with the computational models describing the object's geometry, bulk and tactual properties. Six encoders on the device provide positional information resolved to approximately 0.1 mm, and three servo motors provide force display up to roughly eight Newtons, within a workspace of about 290 x 400 x 560 mm^3.

The haptic cylinder, initially and in subsequent stages of "carving", is represented as a surface of revolution with two caps. It has a mass of 1 gram, an algorithmically defined vertical grating as surface texture, static and dynamic frictional properties, stiff spring bulk resistance, and rotates about its axis at one revolution per second. The cylinder model straddles a static haptic plane (which spatially corresponds with the physical output plane of the holovideo optical system); the haptic plane is modeled with the same bulk and frictional properties as the cylinder. Currently, the haptics simulation is run on a Pentium PC with an average servo rate of 1500Hz.

The radius profile of the surface of revolution is represented as a cubic B-spline curve with 28 control points, all of which are initially set to the same radius value (25mm) to let us begin with a cylinder. The curve evaluated between the middle 21 points defines the profile of the cylinder body; the remaining top three and bottom four points lie beyond the actual extent of the cylinder, and serve to "lock" the shape at its top and bottom, respectively. Control points are modified as force is exerted on the shape at height *h*, between control points P_i and P_{i+1}. A new radius for the surface of revolution at this height can be computed by evaluating the nonuniform rational B-spline formulation.

The cylinder can be felt spinning beneath the user's touch, and when pressed with enough force (*i.e.,* when the surface has been penetrated by some threshold distance Δ) the surface deforms. A very simple method for surface deformation is used: the two control points straddling the penetration location are displace toward the central cylinder axis by a fraction of the penetration distance. The upper point is displaced by $tk\Delta$, and the lower by $(1-t)k\Delta$, with t being the normalized distance between the contact point and the lower control point, used in the B-spline formulation. The closer control point is displaced by a greater distance. If contact occurs directly on a control point, then that point alone is displaced by $k\Delta$. Thus, control point displacement modifies the circumference of the cylinder at height *h*, as force is interactively applied.

The parameters k and Δ can be adjusted to make carving the rotating cylinder require more or less force. A minimum radius of 15mm is enforced, so that once the surface has deformed this much, the control points update no further. The control point density, 4.17 points/cm, was experimentally determined to be high enough to accommodate local model changes, yet sparse enough to avoid unstable deep notching of the haptic surface.

Holographic Video Modeling

We employ the second generation of holovideo in this work [5, 6]. This system is capable of displaying monochromatic, horizontal-parallax-only (HPO) images in a volume of 150 x 57.5 x 150 mm^3, and the viewing angle is 30°. The 3D image produced by holovideo supports the most important depth cues: stereopsis, motion parallax, occlusion, and many pictorial and physiological cues to depth.

For the present purpose, we may consider holovideo to be a black box which accepts two inputs: a *computer-generated hologram* (CGH) and light. The output of the black box is a 3D *holographic image* whose visual and geometrical characteristics depend on how the CGH was computed. Each CGH contains an enormous amount of data—36 megasamples (at 1 byte per sample) apportioned into 144 hololines of 256 kilosamples each. The CGH is made available to the display via a framebuffer. Because holovideo has a non-standard display format, an image-processing system developed at the MIT Media Lab, *Cheops*, was extended to support it. Cheops has three different module types: processor, input/memory, and output, and an optional memory module provides up to 0.5 Gbytes local to the system. These modules are interconnected by two linear buses. One of these buses, the Nile bus, is capable of sustained high bandwidth (>100 Mbyte/sec.) transfer of samples and the second, the Global bus, is capable of 32 Mbyte/sec. transfer [7].

IMPLEMENTATION

Haptics Module

The Workspace Resource Manager (WRM) running on the SGI/Onyx initializes its own model of the surface of revolution, which starts as a cylinder of desired height and radius. It then initiates the haptic simulation by making client calls to the haptics server on the Pentium PC. These calls request creation of a haptic cylinder of the same height and radius at a desired location. The haptics module commences physical simulation of this spinning cylinder, and computes collisions of the Phantom tip with the computational model. Based on these collisions, forces are computed and displayed to the operator's hand, and any resulting shape modifications are reflected in the model update.

Any changes in the cylinder's underlying B-spline representation are automatically communicated from the haptics module to the WRM approximately 30 times per second. The information sent contains the location where change begins on the curve (the number of the bottom-most control point), and values of the six affected control points, ordered from bottom to top. It is assumed that model changes occur reasonably slowly, so that no more than six control points are updated within 0.033 second. Since computing a deformation means updating at most two control points surrounding the point of contact, our communication rate means that we can only guarantee reporting accurate model changes from contact in a region 6.9 mm high within an update interval. Though this assumption usually puts us within the realm of normal interaction speed, eventually, communicating a variable

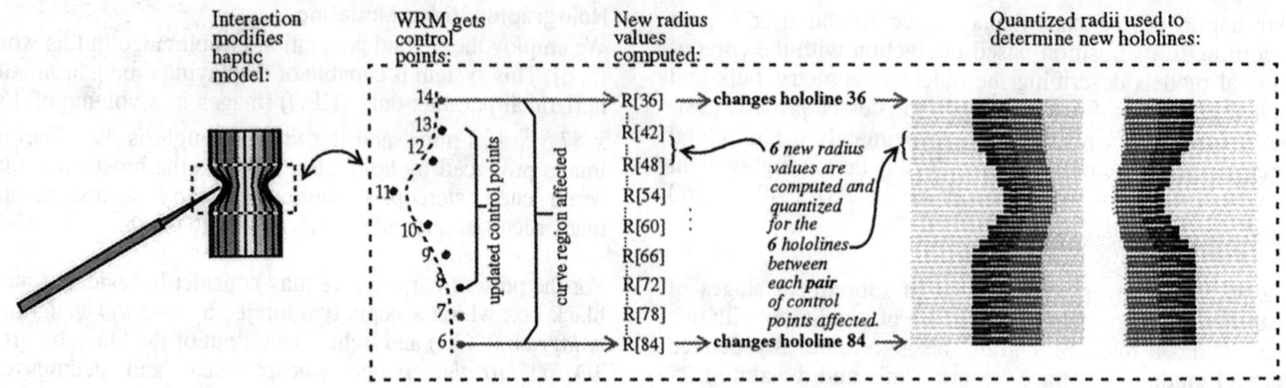

Figure 3. Determining which display lines are affected by changes in haptic model

number of control points to reflect the precise region of change would be more robust, and future work will implement this change.

Workspace Resource Manager

Once the WRM receives the message, the changed control points are used to update its own representation of the radius profile. The WRM determines which lines of the holovideo display will be affected by the updated region of the curve. Since the final holographic image will span 120 lines of the display, we maintain a state vector, **R**, with 120 elements whose values represent the exact radii of the surface of revolution at corresponding display lines. A set of six holovideo display lines correspond to the space between any two adjacent control points in the WRM's model. If as many as six control points have changed, it is necessary to recompute radii for the 48 display lines spanning *eight* control points, between which the curve will have been affected (Figure 3). These new radius values are reflected in the state vector **R**. In the current implementation, the WRM's model can also be rendered to a graphics display using SGI's Graphics Library for debugging purposes, and to provide a means for remotely monitoring a user's performance.

Because it is not yet possible to compute 36 Mbyte holograms in real time [3], we decided to pre-compute five cylinder holograms for use in updating the display, as explained shortly. Each hologram displays a cylinder with a different radius, the initial cylinder, and four progressively smaller ones, r_{cyl} (mm) = {25.0, 22.5, 20.0, 17.5, 15.0}, ending with the minimum-radius cylinder. All holographic cylinders are 47.9 mm high. These holograms, from largest to smallest radius, are loaded sequentially into the Cheops memory module. It would be possible to compute a fewer *total* number of lines if we omitted visual texture from the object or restricted texture to be periodic. At system start-up, the cylinder with the largest radius is displayed. As the initial haptic cylinder is carved, a visual approximation to the resulting surface of revolution is assembled on the display by loading the appropriate lines from each of these five separate holograms.

First we must determine *how many* and *which* lines we should change on the holovideo display. The number of display lines that require updating will vary, depending on exactly which model control points are displaced. In regions near the top or bottom of the carved shape, a smaller region of the curve contributes to the visible extent of the shape, so fewer display lines will require change. The new radius values in **R** corresponding to changed display lines are quantized to match one of the set of five holographic cylinder radii, and each is assigned a radius code based on its quantized value as shown below:

radius (mm)	25.0	22.5	20.0	17.5	15.0
code	5	4	4	2	1

A message, which contains the number of the hololine marking the start of the update region, the number of lines that need to be updated, and the radius codes of each new line, is sent to the holovideo output module on Cheops. In order to minimize the display update time, we are currently updating a maximum of 32 hololines per cycle, representing only the display lines between the original six control points sent by the haptics module.

Holovideo Indexing

Upon receiving the update message, the holovideo output module must instruct Cheops to collect the appropriate hololines and dispatch them to the display. This is accomplished by indexing into the memory module with the radius code to determine the correct cylinder to display, and then writing the corresponding hololine to the output card (Figure 4). The final holographic image is assembled using hololines from the five individual holograms. It must be noted that this method of hologram assembly is valid only for HPO holograms; for full-parallax holograms, the entire hologram would have to be recomputed. In the absence of the computation and communication bandwidth necessary to update fully-computed holograms in real-time, pre-computed hologram indexing enables rapid, local updating.

RESULTS AND DISCUSSION

Simulation Results

When an operator carves the holographic surface of revolution with the Phantom, the hologram image changes

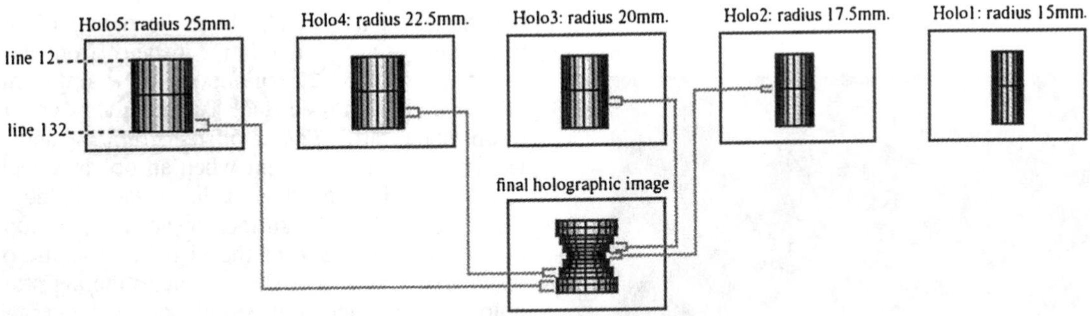

Figure 4. Method of assembling final holographic image

due to force apparently applied by the tip of the stylus. The resulting shape can be explored by moving the stylus tip around the surface without exerting too much force. Physical objects in the workspace may also be explored, so that both physical and simulated forces can be displayed to the operator alternatively in the same workspace. When the operator maintains the correct viewing distance for holovideo, the perception of a single multimodal stimulus is quite convincing. Images of an operator interacting with the image are shown in Figure 5.

System Lag

A compelling multimodal representation depends heavily on minimizing, to imperceptible levels, the time lag between the operator effecting changes in the haptic model and the result of that change appearing on the visual display [11]. A reasonable visual update rate (20+ frames per second) is not currently possible on holovideo, principally due to the speed at which we can communicate with and update the display. The effect of the resulting system lag, on the order of 0.5 sec., is that an operator can *see* the stylus tip penetrating into the holographic surface before the surface is apparently subtracted away. Higher bandwidth spatial light modulators, efficient data compression techniques, improvements in computation speed, and higher bandwidth data pipelines will all help to alleviate this problem in future generations of the holovideo system.

Since the visual display is holographic, the full range of horizontal parallax is always available in the viewzone; no lag is encountered with motion of the operator's head. Additionally, no special eyewear is necessary to perceive the stereo information.

Differences in the Visual and Haptic Renderings

Our haptic simulation models a spinning surface of revolution, but the visual representation does not spin. In order to represent a spinning holographic image, we need to be able to update all the hololines spanned by the image at a reasonable rate. As mentioned above, our system currently suffers a low frame rate with the update of only 32 lines; thus we choose to forgo animating the spinning of the holographic surface. When visual update can be more rapid, this visual animation will eventually be included.

When the stylus tip is touched to an image detail on the holographic surface, touch, stereopsis and motion parallax reinforce the perception that the stylus and the holographic surface detail are spatially co-located. However, as is the case for all HPO holograms, the lack of vertical parallax causes a slight vertical shift that increases with image depth to accompany vertical head motion.

Haptic Differences Between Simulation and Real Task

Differences between the haptic feedback in our simulation and the feeling of carving on an actual lathe are important to note. Among them are that the simple material properties we currently simulate are quite different from those of wood or metal moving against a cutting tool. Additionally, since a "cut" applied at an instantaneous position on the cylinder surface results in a surface modification that extends around the *entire* shape circumference, the user does not experience the feeling of continuously removing material as the shape spins under the stylus. Of course, one obvious departure from reality is the 90° change in orientation of the lathe axis.

Sensory Conflicts

Unless idiosyncratic physics are intentionally being modeled, all sensory modalities employed in a spatial display should act in concert to depict some basic rules that, based on our experience, physical objects usually obey. We have observed some important rules, and undoubtedly more still need to be considered:

- the volumes of real or virtual objects should not interpenetrate,
- occlusion, stereopsis, and motion parallax cues should report the same depth relationships,
- visual and force images of *objects* should have "stable" spatial and temporal properties (no perceptible temporal intermittence, spatial drift, or wavering)
- optical and haptic material properties, as represented, should be compatible (a surface that *looks* rough shouldn't *feel* soft and spongy),
- all multisensory stimuli should appear to arise from a single source, and all should be in precise spatial register.

If *inter*modality or *intra*modality sensory cues yield conflicting information about the physical location and

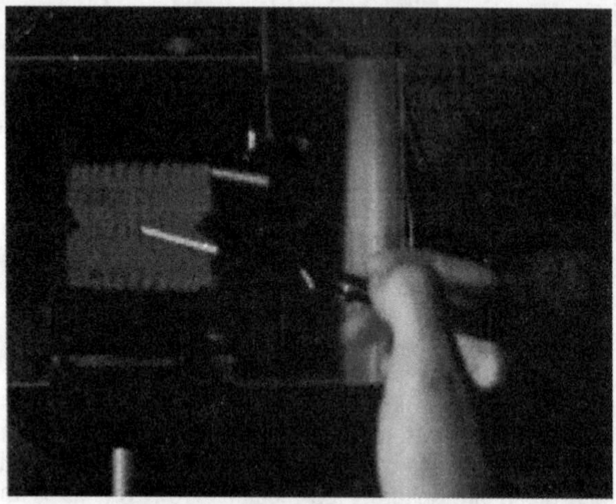

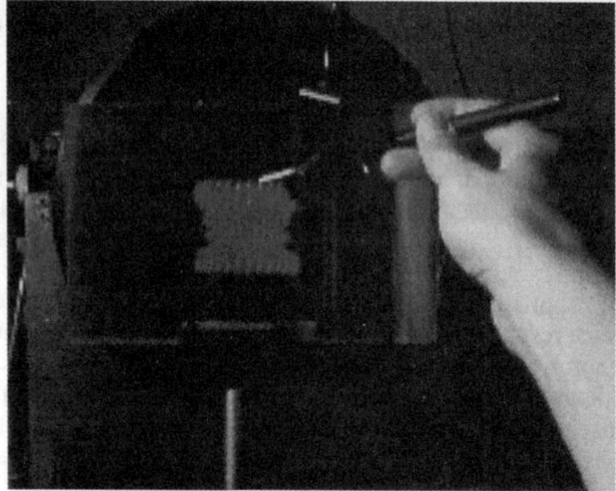

Figure 5a. Interactive carving in the coincident workspace

Figure 5b. Physical hardcopy from a Stratasys 3D printer

boundaries of an object, about the nature of its material properties, or about its relative distance from the observer, the impression of the simulation as a single multimodal event can be compromised. Two conflicts which are most troublesome are *spatial misregistrations* and *occlusion violations*. At the moment when an operator feels that the stylus tip is in contact with the surface, if the tip is seen either penetrating the surface or not making contact at all due to misregistration of the visual and haptic output, the visual discrepancy is striking. Due to the lag present in the holovideo pipeline, our simulation is vulnerable to this problem when the operator is actively carving the surface.

Allowing interaction between the output of optical projection systems, like holograms, and an operator's hands (plus physical objects or instruments), permits object depth relationships to occur which violate occlusion rules obeyed by the physical world. Normally, when we see the image of one object blocking the image of another from view, we understand that the occluded object is farther from our eyes. In our system, it is possible to interpose part of the stylus between the holographic image and physical output plane of the holovideo optical system, thus blocking the image from the line of sight between the viewer and stylus. In this event, it appears that the farther object (stylus) occludes the nearer (holographic image). This anomalous cue is strong enough to confuse perception, even when correct depth reporting from stereopsis and motion parallax is available.

ONGOING / FUTURE WORK

Currently, we are working on improving the fidelity of materials simulation, and modeling a more realistic haptic representation of carving. We are developing algorithms for computing smooth-shaded and visually textured holographic images. Also, we are modifying our pipeline to write hologram lines directly to the memory module to increase our visual display update rate. When we can update the holovideo display more rapidly, our general results will improve markedly and simulating more complicated dynamics becomes a tractable pursuit.

It is important to note that evaluating affordances in a system that spatially unites manual interaction and visual display, and determining whether performance (for some tasks) is *truly enhanced* in such a workspace requires a rigorous comparison between offset and coincident display formats. While it is premature to consider performance testing or user preference evaluation using the system described here, a controlled study could be made presently by using, for instance, a more conventional stereoscopic display and a Phantom.

Certainly, electronic holography and force feedback technologies still present us with many fundamental engineering challenges, and evaluation of their mutual efficacy should be carried out after these challenges have been addressed.

CONCLUSION

We have described an interactive multimodal spatial imaging system in this paper. We have situated the system in a research context and outlined the requirements of such a coincident workspace system. The component haptic and holographic subsystems were described and the implementation of the whole system was detailed. Both the benefits and problems raised by using a coincident display format were discussed.

Our belief in the importance of high-quality visual and haptic cues as well as the attentive dialog between vision, hands, tools, and the material they manipulate is at the root of the work presented here. The coincident-workspace system takes a step toward giving primacy to the skilled eyes and hands of the craftsperson and offers, for further inquiry, a possible interaction technology for future digital design studios.

ACKNOWLEDGEMENTS

We would like to thank the Honda R&D Company, NEC, IBM, the Digital Life Consortium at the MIT Media Lab, the Office of Naval Research (Grant N0014-96-11200), Mitsubishi Electric Research Laboratories, and the Interval Research Corporation for their support of this research. We would also like to acknowledge valuable conversations with members of the Spatial Imaging Group and the community at the MIT Media Laboratory, especially Professor Stephen Benton, Professor Hiroshi Ishii, Carlton Sparrell, Michael Halle, and John Underkoffler. We also thank Bill Verplank for inspiration and valuable discussion, and Yael Maguire for his 3D printing effort.

REFERENCES

1. Jones, M.R.E., The Haptic Hologram, *Proceedings of SPIE, Fifth International Symposium on Display Holography,* Vol. 2333, pp. 444-447, 1994.

2. McCullough, M., Abstracting Craft: the practiced digital hand, the MIT Press, Cambridge, MA, 1996.

3. Pappu, R., *et al.*, A generalized pipeline for preview and rendering of synthetic holograms, in S.A. Benton, ed., *Proceedings of the IS&T/SPIE's Symposium on Electronic Imaging, Practical Holography XI*, 1997.

4. Plesniak, W., Klug, M., Tangible holography: adding synthetic touch to 3D display, in S.A. Benton, ed., *Proceedings of the IS&T/SPIE's Symposium on Electronic Imaging, Practical Holography XI*, 1997.

5. St. Hilaire, P., "Scalable Optical Architectures for Electronic Holography", Ph.D. Thesis, MIT Program in Media Arts and Sciences, Massachusetts Institute of Technology, 1994.

6. Underkoffler, J., "Toward Accurate Computation of Optically Reconstructed Holograms", S.M. Thesis, Media Arts and Sciences Section, Massachusetts Institute of Technology, 1991.

7. Watlington, J., *et al.*, A hardware architecture for rapid generation of electro-holographic fringe patterns, in S.A. Benton, ed., *Proceedings of the IS&T/SPIE's Symposium on Electronic Imaging, Practical Holography IX*, 1995.

8. Wiegand, T.E.v., The Virtual Workbench & the Electronics Training Task. Internal memo, 1994. VETT project at MIT/RLE, 77 Massachusetts Ave. MIT, Cambridge MA 02139-4307, http://mimsy.mit.edu/.

9. Yokokohji, Y., Hollis, R.L., Kanade, T., Vision-based Visual/Haptic Registration for WYSIWYF Display. International *Conference on Intelligent Robots and Systems,* pp. 1386-1393, 1996.

10. Deering, M., High Resolution Virtual Reality. Proceedings SIGGRAPH'92, *Computer Graphics*, Vol. 26, No.2, pp. 195-202. July 1992.

11. Mark, W.R., *et al.*, Adding Force Feedback to Graphics Systems: Issues and Solutions. *Computer Graphics Proceedings, Annual Conference Series, ACM SIGGRAPH*, pp. 447-452, 1996.

12. Fitzmaurice, G., Ishii, H., Buxton, W., "Bricks: Laying the Foundations for Graspable User Interfaces," *Proceedings of Conference on Human Factors in Computing Systems (CHI '95), ACM*, Denver, May 1995, pp. 442-449.

13. Ishii, H. and Ullmer, B., "Tangible Bits: Towards Seamless Interfaces between People, Bits and Atoms," *(CHI '97), ACM*, Atlanta, March 1997, pp. 234-241.

14. Wellner, P., Mackay, W., and Gold, R., "Computer Augmented Environments: Back to the Real World," *CACM*, Vol. 36, No. 7, July 1993.

The Structure of Object Transportation and Orientation in Human-Computer Interaction

Yanqing Wang and Christine L. MacKenzie
School of Kinesiology
Simon Fraser University
Burnaby, BC V5A 1S6
Canada
+1 604 291 5794
{wangy, cmackenz} @move.kines.sfu.ca

Valerie A. Summers and Kellogg S. Booth
Department of Computer Science
University of British Columbia
Vancouver, BC V6T 1Z4
Canada
+1 604 822 2218
{summers, ksbooth} @cs.ubc.ca

ABSTRACT
An experiment was conducted to investigate the relationship between object transportation and object orientation by the human hand in the context of human-computer interaction (HCI). This work merges two streams of research: the structure of interactive manipulation in HCI and the natural hand prehension in human motor control. It was found that object transportation and object orientation have a parallel, interdependent structure which is generally persistent over different visual feedback conditions. The notion of concurrency and interdependence of multi-dimensional visuomotor control structure can provide a new framework for human-computer interface evaluation and design.

Keywords
Direct manipulation, input device, multi-dimensional control, visuomotor control, visual conditions, information processing, interface design, virtual reality.

INTRODUCTION

Object manipulation is a basic operation in human-computer interaction (HCI). Modern computer technology advances towards affording multi-dimensional object manipulation. A virtual environment can typically provide at least six degrees of freedom of control for a graphic display with a controller. The spatial state of a rigid object in a multi-dimensional space can be completely described by its location and orientation. By definition, the spatial state of an object's location is independent from that of its orientation at the descriptive level. Accordingly, the spatial state of an object can be changed with object translation and object rotation processes in a parallel or serial pattern. For example, a robotic manipulator can be programmed to move an object to the same predetermined position with an arbitrary order of translation and rotation. If, however, a human hand is the manipulator, as is the case of direct manipulation with a pointing device, the relationship between object transportation and object orientation is no longer so simple [5]. Two streams of research are related to the relationship between object transportation and object orientation. One is on the structure of interactive graphic manipulation in HCI derived from the perceptual structure of visual information, and the other is research on the hand prehension in human motor control. One important question is, what is the natural structure of control for object translation and rotation. There is not a ready answer to this question from previous research. This study address this question by exploring the structure of object transportation and object orientation by the human hand in the context of human-computer interaction, and therefore provides implications for human-computer interface design.

Perceptual structure of visual information and the control structure of input devices

According to the theory of perceptual structure of visual information by Garner, a multi-dimensional object can be characterized by its attributes into two categories: integral structure and separable structure [3]. Visual information has an integral structure if its attributes can be perceptually combined to form a unitary whole, e.g., lightness and saturation of a color. If visual object attributes demonstrate perceptually distinct and identifiable dimensions, they are separable. For example, the lightness and size of an object have a separable structure. The type of the perceptual structure of an object can be determined by direct similarity scaling methods. An integral structure shows Euclidean distance, while a separable structure demonstrates city-block distance in the perceptual attribute space.

Jacob and his colleagues extended Garner's notion of integral and separable structure to interactive tasks by observing that manipulating a graphic object is simply the changing of values of its attributes [6]. They reasoned that since the attributes of an object define a perceptual space, changing these values is the same as moving in real time within the perceptual space of the object. They predicted that the interaction movement in an integral space should be Euclidean, straight-line distance between two points, and movement in a separable space should be city-block and run parallel to the axes. In turn, the pattern of Euclidean distance and the city-block distance indicates the type of the perceptual structure.

Jacob et al. also extended the notion of integral and separable structure to describe the attributes of an input device, based on whether it is natural to move diagonally across all dimensions [6]. With an integral device, the movement is in Euclidean space and cuts across all the dimensions of control. A separable device constrains movement along one dimension at a time, showing a city-block pattern. They hypothesized that human performance improves when the perceptual structure of the task matches the control structure of the device. They conducted an experiment in which subjects performed two tasks that had different perceptual structures, using two input devices with correspondingly different control structures, an integral three-dimensional tracker and a separable mouse. The integral task was the control for a graphic object's location and size, and the separable task was the control for object's location and brightness (greyscale). Their results converged to support their hypothesis. They concluded that the interplay between task and device was more important in determining performance than either task or device alone. The framework proposed by Jacob et al. has a significant influence in today's human-computer interaction research, particularly, in the area of computer input devices evaluation and design [1][9][16].

However, the notion of the integral and separable structure is not automatically applicable to multi-dimensional object manipulation including object transportation and orientation by the human hand. The original notion of integral and separable structure by Garner only deals with intrinsic properties of a visual object, such as the size and color [3]. The location and orientation of an object are extrinsic properties. Furthermore, recent research shows that humans may have two separate visual systems, one for perception, the other for action [4]. This evidence suggests that the perceptual structure of an object may not be the same structure of the interaction movement of an object. It is arguable whether or not a structure in a perceptual space can be extended to an interactive space. Jacob et al.'s framework has not explicitly addressed the relationship between object transportation and orientation [3]. Ware found that subjects could easily achieve simultaneous object transportation and orientation using a 6DOF controller, but some other researchers reported that it was rather difficult for humans to transport and orient an object at the same time [14]. The relationship between object transportation and orientation remains an open question.

Natural prehension by the human hand

On the other hand, there is substantial motor control research on natural prehension with focus on the relationship between hand transportation (reaching) and orientation (grasping) [8]. Jeannerod's "independent visuomotor channels" hypothesis states that there may be independent neural pathways controlling hand reaching and grasping separately [7]. Furthermore, the reaching component may be more related to the extrinsic properties (e.g., location) of a target object, while the grasping component may be more related to the intrinsic properties (e.g., size) [7]. The independent visuomotor channels hypothesis was developed originally for the phase of prehension before the hand makes contact with a target object (see [8] for a description of phases of grasping). A recent review by Paulignan and Jeannerod demonstrated neural, biophysical and behavior evidence supporting this hypothesis [10]. The empirical data showed that object location (extrinsic property) affected the hand reaching component and object size (intrinsic property) affected the grasping component separately. However, since object transportation and object orientation are both extrinsic properties, it is inappropriate to draw conclusions on the relationship between object transportation and orientation based on visuomotor channels theory. Further, human prehension with an object in hand such as operating a mouse in HCI, where tactile information is available, can be very different from grasping prior to contact with an object [2][4][11][12]. These considerations warrant further investigation into the relationship between object transportation and orientation by the human hand in HCI.

Research hypotheses

We argue that an interface design should not only accommodate the perceptual structure of the task and control structure of the input device, but also the structure of motor control systems. However, research in HCI generally does not address the motor control aspect of human-computer interaction per se. At the same time, motor control researchers do not examine object transportation and orientation in the context of HCI. The assumptions underlying the theoretical framework by Jacob et al. and two independent visuomotor channels theory by Jeannerod appear to point in opposite directions. Based on the notion of integral and separable perceptual structure, object transportation and orientation could be integrable because the spatial attributes are generally considered integral [3][6]. On the other hand, the hypothesis of independent visuomotor channels suggests that it is likely to make the control of object transportation and orientation separable [7]. Results regarding the relationship between object transportation and orientation are not conclusive from both streams of research.

Object transportation and orientation can be described as two processes in the tempo-spatial domain. Jacob et al.'s framework is related to the aspect of the time courses between two processes, while studies in motor control emphasize on the aspect of the interaction between two processes. We propose a new framework to encompass both aspects of the relationship between object transportation and orientation processes.

We define a structure of object transportation and orientation in terms of concurrency and interdependence between two processes. The concurrency indicates the relationship between the time courses of two processes, either in parallel or in serial. The notion of parallel and serial is similar to that of integral and separable by Jacob et al., but in a multi-dimensional visual motor control space. If two processes occur simultaneously, they are parallel. As a special case of parallel, if one process contains the other one, the longer process dominates the shorter one. Interdependence reflects the interaction between object transportation and orientation processes. If the inputs of one processes affects the outputs of the other process, two processes are interdependent.

Our main research hypothesis is that object transportation and orientation have a parallel and interdependent structure. We also expect that object transportation and orientation processes show different weights in object manipulation and one process may dominate the other. We further hypothesize that, as visual feedback conditions change, the structure of object transportation and orientation may change. An experiment was conducted to test above hypotheses.

METHOD

Experimental setup

A virtual environment (The Virtual Hand Lab) was set up for this experiment, as shown in Figure 1. A stereoscopic, head-coupled graphical display was presented with a Silicon Graphics Indigo RGB monitor. A half-silvered mirror was placed parallel to the computer screen and the table surface. The image on the screen was reflected by the mirror, and then was perceived by the subject as if it was on the table surface. There was a light under the mirror (not shown in the figure) to control the visual conditions. When the light was on, the subject could see through the mirror, and thus the visual feedback of the hand and the wooden cube was present. When the light was off, the subject could see neither his/her hand nor the wooden cube. For both conditions, the graphic target was always visible, with a black background on the computer screen.

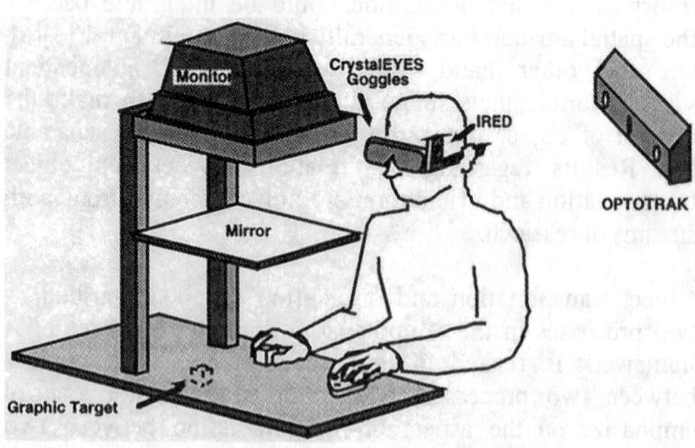

Figure 1. The Virtual Hand Lab.

The subject was comfortably seated at a table, with the forearm at approximately the same height with the table surface. The body was about 30 mm away from the front edge of the table. The subject was wearing CrystalEYES Goggles to obtain a stereoscopic view of an image. Three infrared markers (IREDs) were fixed to the side frame of the goggles, and individual subject eye positions were calibrated relative to these markers. The movements of the head were recorded with an OPTOTRAK motion analysis system (Northern Digital, Inc.), which measured the three-dimensional position of the IREDs on the goggles. The stereoscopic, head-coupled, graphic display was updated at 60 Hz with 1 frame lag of OPTOTRAK co-ordinates. The target image was a graphic, wireframe cube projected on the table surface. The 30 mm graphic cube was positioned at one of three locations and two orientations. The object to be manipulated was a wooden cube with the size of 30 mm * 30 mm * 30 mm, the same as the target cube. The wooden cube weighted 11 grams. Two IREDs were placed on the top of the wooden cube, IRED 1 at the center and IRED 2 diagonally 15 mm away from IRED 1. Data from the OPTOTRAK were sampled and recorded at 60 Hz by a Silicon Graphics Indigo Extreme computer workstation. A thin physical L-frame (not shown in the figure) was used to locate the starting position of the wooden cube, at the beginning of each trial. A mouse was operated with the subject's left hand to control the start and end of a trial.

Subjects

Eight university student volunteers were paid $20 for participating in a two-hour experimental session. All subjects were right-handed, and had normal or corrected-to-normal vision. Subjects all had experience using a computer.

Procedure

The task was to align or dock a small wooden cube with the graphic target cube. Manipulation tasks were designed that required both object transportation and orientation, under different visual feedback conditions. The subject held the wooden cube with the right hand, with the thumb and index finger in pad opposition on the center of opposing cube faces which were parallel to the frontal plane of the body. To start a trial, the subject pressed the mouse left button, with the left hand; this generated the graphic target cube on the table top, 30 mm, 100 mm or 200 mm from the starting position, and rotated by 22.5 or 45 degrees from the frontal plane of the subject. The subject was asked to match the wooden cube to the graphic target cube as fast and accurately as possible. When the subject was satisfied with the match, he/she pressed the mouse middle button to end that trial. Trials were blocked by two visual conditions: without visual feedback (only the graphical objects were visible), or with visual feedback (the subject's hand and the physical cube were also visible). Four subjects started with the visual feedback condition, and the other four started with the no visual feedback condition. Target location and orientation were randomized within a block. For each experimental condition, 15 trials were collected. At the beginning of the session, subjects were given two trials of practice for each experimental condition.

Data analysis

OPTOTRAK 3-D position data collected from two IREDs on the top of the wooden cube are analyzed here. Data were filtered with a 7 Hz low-pass second-order bi-directional Butterworth digital filter to remove digital sampling artifacts, vibrations of the markers, and tremor from the hand movement. Original IRED position data were interpolated and filtered only once, and then were used for the following data manipulation including angular data generation. A computer program determining the start and end of a pointing movement was used for the transportation and orientation processes separately, based on criterion velocities [5]. The start and end of each process were then confirmed by visually inspecting a graph of the velocity profile. A trial was rejected if the program failed to find a start and end or there was disagreement between experimenter's visual inspection and the computer's results. This case usually occurred when subject made a false start.

Primary dependent measures of object manipulation were Movement time (MT), transportation time (TT), Orientation Time (OT), and spatial errors of object translation and rotation to the target. MT was defined as the task completion time, which should be equal to or greater than the longer one between the transportation and orientation processes. TT was the transportation time determined with translation data from IRED 1 at the center of the cube top. OT was determined with data calculated from the horizontal rotation of the cube around IRED 1. Results of spatial errors were reported elsewhere by Wang et al. [13], and are shown in this paper.

ANOVA was performed on the balanced design of 2 visions (V) * 3 distances (D) * 2 angles (A) with repeated measures on all three factors. We also examined the effects of target location and orientation under each vision condition. Two-way ANOVAs were performed, separately, with full vision of the hand and the object and without the hand and the object in view. In the vision condition, the experiment setup provided a realistic visual world and an unconstrained control for six degrees of freedom of object manipulation. Therefore, the performance under the vision condition was considered to be "natural", while the no vision condition was considered to be visually "impoverished". Separate data analyses for each visual condition as well as a comparison between two visual conditions were performed for this study.

RESULTS

We examine the structure of object transportation and orientation in terms of concurrency and interdependence between two processes. Within each, the natural performance, where visual feedback of action was available, is discussed first. Then the results of the object manipulation are reported where visual feedback of the hand and the object was unavailable. Finally, a comparison between two visual conditions will be made.

Concurrency

Concurrency with vision of the hand and object

Total movement time (MT) in the vision condition had an average value of 776 ms. The average transportation time (TT) was 766 ms in the visual feedback condition, only 10 ms shorter than the total task completion time (MT). The average orientation time (OT) was 479 ms in the vision condition, 297 ms shorter than MT ($F(1, 7) = 155.27$, $p < .001$). Apparently, the average MT was much less than the sum of average TT and OT.

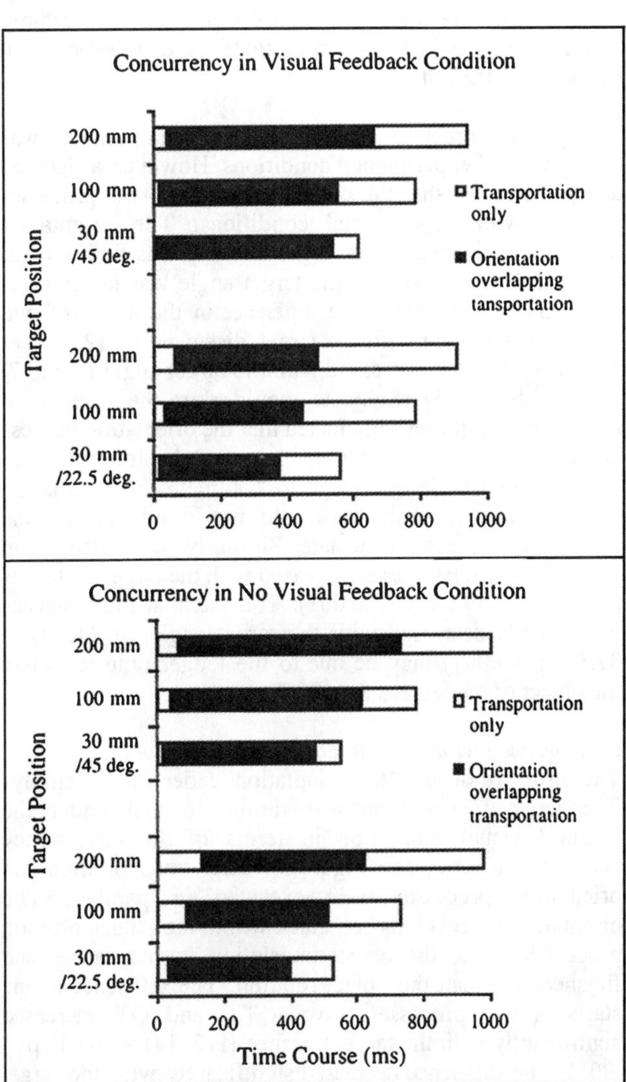

Figure 2. Time courses of object transportation and orientation processes. White areas indicate transportation only. Dark areas are orientation overlapping transportation.

The concurrency of the time courses between two processes in the vision condition is shown in the top part of Figure 2. Experimental results clearly demonstrated that object translation and object rotation were processed in parallel in the time domain. In general, object manipulation first started with the object transportation process. After a very short period, an average of 30 ms, the orientation process started, joining the transportation process. The simultaneous execution of two processes remained for an average period of 479 ms until the orientation process finished. The transportation process continued another 257 ms on average and object manipulation ended. Statistics showed a significant earlier start ($F(1, 7) = 10.27$, $p < .001$) and later end ($F(1, 7) = 186.26$, $p < .001$) of the transportation process than the orientation process. The transportation process took totally 287 ms longer than the orientation process ($F(1, 7) = 155.27$, $p < .001$). Nevertheless, the total task completion time was mainly determined by object translation, that is, the transportation process was the critical path.

The parallel structure of natural object manipulation was stable over all experimental conditions. However, a detailed analysis showed that the overlap portion of two processes changed with experimental conditions. The orientation process took longer as the target distance was further ($F(2, 14) = 15.56$, $p < .001$) or the target angle was larger ($F(1, 7) = 76.26$, $p < .001$). The difference in the starts of two processes increased with the target distances ($F(2, 14) = 7.96$, $p < .01$), but decreased with the target angle ($F(1,7) = 8.96$, $p < .05$). Subjects would start the orientation process earlier if they anticipated that the orientation process could be longer. On the other hand, if the transportation process could be long enough to complete the orientation process within it, subjects would not mind starting the orientation process a little late. Similarly, the difference in the ends of two processes increased with the target distances ($F(2, 14) = 39.34$, $p < .0.001$). The fact that the difference in the ends decreased with the target angle ($F(1, 7) = 37.85$, $p < .001$) may be due to the longer time to orient the object of 45 degrees than 22.5 degrees.

Concurrency with no vision of the hand and object
The structure of object manipulation under the "visually-impoverished" condition was similar to that under the "natural visual" condition in terms of the concurrency between two processes (Figure 2). The transportation and orientation processes were executed in parallel. The orientation process was contained within the transportation process, that is, the object translation started earlier and finished later than the object rotation. The difference in the starts of two processes between TT and OT increased significantly with the target distance ($F(2, 14) = 16.01$, $p < .001$). The difference decreased significantly with the target angle ($F(1, 7) = 40.86$, $p < .001$). The difference in the ends of two processes between TT and OT increased significantly with the target distance ($F(2, 14) = 10.17$, $p < .01$). The difference decreased significantly with the target angle ($F(1, 7) = 13.22$, $p < .01$). Overall, there were no differences in MT between two visual feedback conditions.

Effects of visual feedback on concurrency
Effects of visual feedback on object manipulation were examined with pooled data over two vision conditions. ANOVA was performed with repeated measures on vision condition, target distances and target angles. The difference in the concurrency between the two vision conditions can be generally examined by comparing the top part with the bottom part of Figure 2.

Deprivation of vision of the hand and the object significantly delayed the start of the orientation process relative to the start of the transportation process, $F(1, 7) = 8.05$, $p < .05$. The average difference between the starts of two processes increased from 30 ms in the vision condition to 64 ms in the no vision condition. The starting difference was also affected by an interaction between the vision and the target distance ($F(2, 14) = 5.71$, $p < .05$), the interaction between the vision and the target angle ($F(1, 7) = 13.77$, $p < .01$). Vision had no significant effects on the difference in the ends of two processes between TT and OT.

Interdependence
Interdependence with vision of the hand and object
During object manipulation, the target distance was assumed to be the input for the transportation process with the output of TT, while the target angle was the input for the orientation process with the output of OT. As shown in Figure 3, it was not surprising that TT increased significantly with the target distance ($F(2, 14) = 65.25$, $p < .001$), and OT increased significantly with the target angle ($F(1, 7) = 76.26$, $p < .001$). However, it was found that the input for each process affected the output of the other process. Changes in the target distance had a significant effect on the OT ($F(2, 14) = 15.56$, $p < .001$), while changes in the target angle affected the TT significantly ($F(1, 7) = 7.51$, $p < .05$). As a general trend, both TT and OT increased as the requirement of either object transportation distance or object orientation angle increased. Accordingly, the total movement time (MT) increased significantly with both target distance ($F(2, 14) = 66.46$, $p < .001$) and target angle ($F(1, 7) = 10.89$, $p < .05$). It seemed that the effects of the target distance were more pervasive on the OT than vice versa. Object transportation and orientation processes were thus interdependent on each other.

Interdependence with no vision of the hand and object
Similar effects were found in the "visually impoverished" condition. Object manipulation completion time, MT, increased with the target distance ($F(2, 14) = 101.11$, $p < .001$) and the target angle ($F(1, 7) = 9.10$, $p < .05$). Both processes contributed to the MT, but the transportation process was the critical path to determine the MT. TT increased with the target distance ($F(2, 14) = 103.00$, $p < .001$) and the target angle ($F(1, 7) = 8.43$, $p < .05$). The object rotation affected the object translation, showing the interdependence of TT on the target angle. Both the target distance ($F(2, 14) = 30.10$, $p < .001$) and the target angle ($F(1, 7) = 42.29$, $p < .001$) had main effects on OT. OT as an output of the object rotation increased with the object translation. An interaction between the target distance and the target angle was also found ($F(2, 14) = 8.36$, $p < .001$). The difference in OT between two target angles seemed to increase with the target distance. OT thus not only depended on the orientation process, but also depended on

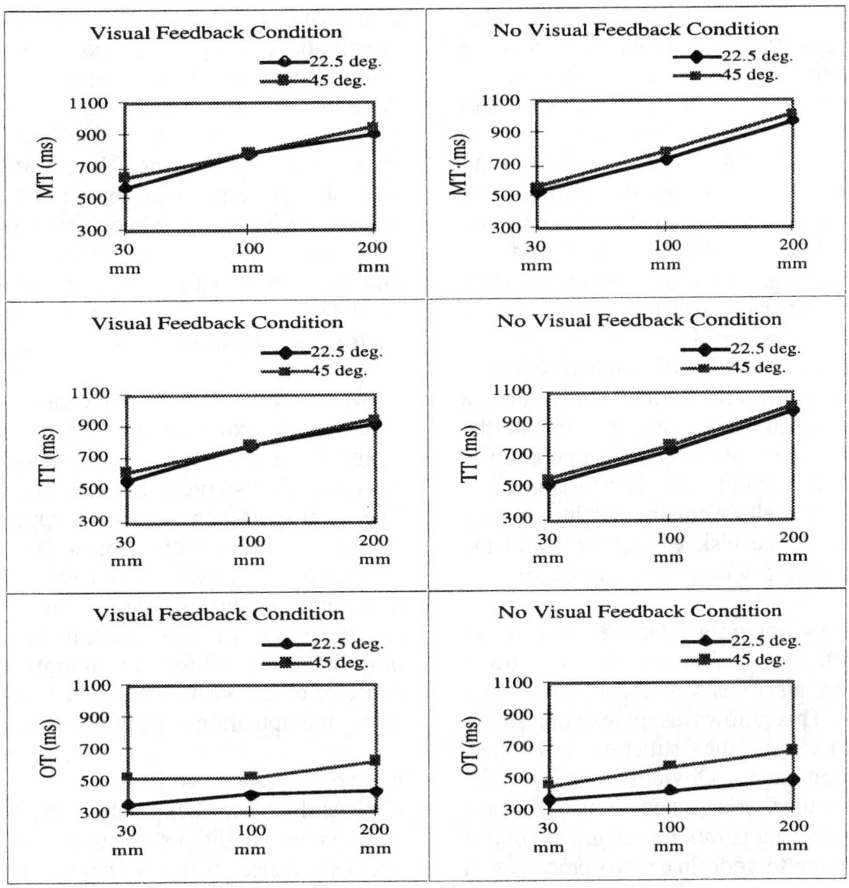

Figure 3. Total movement time (MT), transportation time (TT) and orientation time (OT) under various experimental conditions.

the transportation process. The interdependent structure of two processes was persistent over visual conditions.

Visual effects on interdependence

As shown in Figure 3, TT and OT presented a similar pattern for vision conditions in relation to target location and orientation variables. Visual conditions of the hand and object did not have main effects on both object transportation and orientation times. However, Vision conditions showed interactions with the target distance and rotation angle of the target. There was also a three-way interaction among the vision, target distance and the target angle, $F(2, 14) = 7.11$, $p < .001$.

DISCUSSIONS AND CONCLUSIONS

Parallel structure

These results demonstrated a parallel structure of object transportation and orientation, supporting our research hypothesis. The total object manipulation time was less than the sum of object translation time and rotation time. There was a large portion of overlap between object transportation and orientation processes where object manipulation cut across the object translation dimension and rotation dimension simultaneously, showing a Euclidean distance in the space. In this sense, object transportation and orientation seemed to have characteristics of a integral structure, according to the notion by Jacob et al. [6].

However, our results also indicated that even though object transportation and orientation processes were in parallel, they were not completely overlapped from the beginning to the end. Usually the object orientation started a little late and completed quite early compared with object transportation, and the final stage of movements reflected only object transportation portion. On average, the time course of object transportation contained that of object orientation, that is, object transportation dominated object orientation. This evidence made object transportation and orientation distinct and identifiable, and therefore suggested a separable structure based on the definition of a perceptual structure [3] [6]. Even though, as recognized by Jacob et al., "Integral and separable define two classes of perceptual structure that mark the endpoints of a continuum rather than forming a sharp dichotomy", a structure should not be described as both integral and separable.

The interpretation to the mechanism underlying the parallel structure of object transportation and orientation has to be extended beyond the notion of integral and separable. We attribute our results to the structure of visuomotor control rather than only the perceptual structure of visual information. Object manipulation is not involved with visual information alone, and therefore the structure of tasks cannot be dictated by only visual information. Indeed, our results show that the vision condition of the hand and object interacts with the target attributes jointly to affect object manipulation performance, rather than acts alone. Haptic and kinesthetic information have a strong role to play in object manipulation tasks as well. Human separable visual systems for perception and action imply that a structure of an object in a perceptual space may not be the same one in an interactive space [4]. Object manipulation as a goal-directed movement should take into account the attributes of the target as well. Actually, all information including visual display of the task environment and the manipulator may be relevant to determine the structure.

The notion of concurrency not only addresses whether or not object transportation and orientation occur simultaneously, but also identifies where and when each process starts and ends. This allows us to explore subtle but important differences in the structure of object transportation and orientation. Obviously, a parallel structure is more efficient than serial one in terms of the task completion time. To achieve a parallel structure in object manipulation, subjects have to coordinate two processes in the temporal domain. It was interesting to note that the difference between the starts of transportation and orientation was very short, 30 ms in the vision condition, but consistently increased with the target distance. This observation was unlikely to be a result from the on-line adjustment after object manipulation started because the time was too short for a feedback adjustment. A possible interpretation is that subjects formed a plan to start the orientation process earlier if the transportation process would be shorter so as to achieve an efficient parallel structure. This interpretation is consistent with the fact that the orientation process started earlier when subjects anticipated a longer object rotation. It seemed that there was a need to allocate enough time for on-line correction on object transportation in the last phase of the movement. Evidence shows that the time course of one process of object manipulation has to be planned in coordination with that of the other process. In conclusion, object manipulation is a unitary visuomotor output with a coordinated control for object translation and rotation.

Interdependent structure

Evidence from this study does not support the extension of Jeannerod's "independent visuomotor channels" hypothesis to the structure of object transportation and orientation by human hand [7]. In contrast, our results showed a strong interdependence between object transportation and orientation processes. The object translation time depended on not only the target distance, but also the target orientation angle, and vice versa. These results are consistent with recent research on hand transportation and orientation [2][11]. This indicates that even though the spatial states of object translation and rotation can be described separately within a coordinate system, the two processes of object translation and rotation are executed interactively by humans. Note that Jeannerod's empirical data for grasping was based on grasp aperture, not orientation of grasp. Object size (an intrinsic property) affects grasp aperture but object orientation (an extrinsic property) affects both transportation and orientation of the hand. This is an important distinction, both for motor control and HCI researchers.

It was evident that the increase in object translation requirements extended the object rotation time, while a larger object rotation resulted in a longer object translation. However, the two processes did not affect each other evenly. The transportation process appeared to have more significant effects on object manipulation than the orientation process. Evidence showed that the transportation time course contained the orientation time course so that TT was determinant of MT. Quite a long time was allocated for transportation only during the last phase of object manipulation. TT was the critical path for object manipulation with two processes.

Effects of visual conditions

In general, object manipulation structure was similar under two vision conditions in terms of the concurrency and interdependence between transportation and orientation processes. When the visual feedback on the hand and the object was deprived, same as in the visual feedback condition, the transportation time course contained the orientation time course, and two processes were interdependent on each other. These results were unexpected. This means that the visual feedback information of the manipulator and the object being manipulated is not important for forming the structure of object transportation and orientation. In another word, the parallel and interdependent structure of object manipulation is persistent to changes in visual feedback conditions. One possible explanation is that, given the target location and orientation, the structure is already programmed before the start of the movement. Another explanation is that the structure is insensitive to the difference between proprioceptive feedback and visual feedback. This topic deserves further investigation. Deprivation of visual feedback of the object and the hand increased spatial errors of object translation and rotation, but the effects were more significant on the translation errors than the rotation errors (see Wang et al [13] for detail].

Implications for HCI design

Human-computer interfaces should be designed to accommodate the natural structure of object manipulation. Constraints or interruption on the integration of object manipulation may result in a structural inefficiency. For example, in case a parallel structure of transportation and orientation processes is transformed into a serial structure, the total task completion time may increase significantly even though the completion time for each process is still the same. At the same time, if the main goal of interface design is to achieve the "naturalness" or realism such as virtual reality, remaining the natural structure of human object manipulation will be particularly important.

A hand-centered approach can be beneficial for evaluating and designing input devices, especially multi-dimensional pointing devices. This study shows that the orientation control can be totally integrated to the transportation control, and the transportation control is the critical path for task completion. These features of hand prehension should be carefully considered for the input device design.

In a virtual environment design, the quality of visual presentation of a controller may not be as important as that of other graphic objects. For example, if we want to design a 6DOF virtual hand, a stick-like hand may do the same job as a fully rendered hand with graphic skin, and be more cost effective.

In conclusion:

1. Object transportation and orientation have a parallel, interdependent structure that can be fully understood only in the human visuomotor control system.

2. The structure of object transportation and orientation is generally independent of visual feedback conditions.

3. The object transportation process dominates the object orientation process.

4. The research on control structure for object manipulation provides an appropriate framework for HCI design.

References

1. Balakrishnan, R., Boudel, T., Kurtenbach, G. and Fitzmaurie, G. (1997). The rockin' mouse: integral 3D manipulation on a plane. Proceedings of the Conference on Human Factors in Computing Systems CHI '97 /ACM, 311-318.

2. Desmurget, M., Prablanc, C., Arzi, M., Rossetti, Y. and Paulignan, Y. (1996). Integrated control of hand transport and orientation during prehension movements. Exp. Brain Res., 110, 265-278.

3. Garner, W. R. (1974). The Processing of information and structure. Lawrence Erlbaum, Potomac, Md.

4. Goodale, M.A., Jakobson, L.S and Servos, P. (1996). The visual pathways mediating perception and prehension. In Hand and Brain, ed. by Wing, A. M., Haggard, P. and Flanagan, J. R., 15-31, New York: Academic Press.

5. Graham, E.D. and MacKenzie, C.L. (1996). Physical versus virtual pointing. In Proceedings of the Conference on Human Factors in Computing Systems CHI '96 /ACM, 292-299.

6. Jacob, R. J. K., Sibert, L. E., McFarlane, D. C. and Mullen, M. P. Jr. (1994). Integrality and separability of input devices. ACM Transactions on Computer-Human Interaction, 1 (1), 1-26.

7. Jeannerod, M. (1984). The timing of natural prehension movements. Journal of Motor Behavior, 16, 235-254.

8. MacKenzie, C.L. and Iberall, T. (1994). The grasping hand. Amsterdam: North-Holland.

9. MacKenzie, I.S., Soukoreff,. R.W. and Chris, P. (1997). A two-ball mouse affords three degrees of freedom. Extended Abstracts of the Conference on Human Factors in Computing Systems CHI '97 /ACM, 303-304.

10. Paulignan, Y. and Jeannerod, M. (1996). Prehension movements - the visuomotor channels hypothesis revisited. In Hand and Brain, ed. by Wing, A. M., Haggard, P. and Flanagan, J. R., 265-282, New York: Academic Press.

11. Soechting, J. F. and Flanders, M. (1993). Parallel, interdependent channels for location and orientation in sensorimotor transformations for reaching and grasping. Journal of Neurophysiology, 70 (3), 1137-1150.

12. Soechting, J. F. and Tong, D. C. and Flanders, M. (1996). Frames of reference in sensorimotor integration - Position sense of the arm and hand, In Hand and Brain, ed. by Wing, A. M., Haggard, P. and Flanagan, J. R., 151-168, New York: Academic Press.

13. Wang, Y., MacKenzie, C. L. and Summers, V. (1997). Object manipulation in virtual environments: human bias, consistency and individual differences. Extended In Abstracts of the Conference on Human Factors in Computing Systems CHI '97 /ACM, 349-350.

14. Ware, C. (1990). Using hand position for virtual object placement. The Visual Computer, 6, 245-253.

15. Zhai, S. and Milgram, P. (1993). Human performance evaluation of manipulation schemes in virtual environments. In Proc. of the first IEEE Virtual Reality Annual International Symposium, Seattle, 155-161.

16. Zhai, S. and Milgram, P. and William Buxton (1996). The influence of muscle groups on performance of multiple degree-of-freedom input. In Proceedings of the Conference on Human Factors in Computing Systems CHI '96 /ACM, 308-315.

Quantifying Coordination in Multiple DOF Movement and Its Application to Evaluating 6 DOF Input Devices

Shumin Zhai
IBM Almaden Research Center
650 Harry Road, San Jose, CA 95123, USA
+1 408 927 1112 zhai@almaden.ibm.com

Paul Milgram
Dept Mech. & Ind. Eng., University of Toronto
Toronto, Ontario, Canada, M5S 3G8
+1 416 978 3662 milgram@mie.utoronto.ca

ABSTRACT

Study of computer input devices has primarily focused on trial completion time and target acquisition errors. To deepen our understanding of input devices, particularly those with high degrees of freedom (DOF), this paper explores device influence on the user's ability to coordinate controlled movements in a 3D interface. After reviewing various existing methods, a new measure of quantifying coordination in multiple degrees of freedom, based on movement efficiency, is proposed and applied to the evaluation of two 6 DOF devices: a free-moving position-control device and a desk-top rate-controlled hand controller. Results showed that while the users of the free moving device had shorter completion time than the users of an elastic rate controller, their movement trajectories were less coordinated. These new findings should better inform system designers on development and selection of input devices. Issues such as mental rotation and isomorphism vs. tools operation as means of computer input are also discussed.

Keywords

Input devices, interaction techniques, evaluation methods, 6 DOF control, rotation, mental rotation, 3D interfaces, virtual environments, motor control, coordination.

INTRODUCTION

Computer input control has traditionally been evaluated using speed (e.g., task completion time) or accuracy (e.g., error rate) as performance measures. As we move to broader topics such as drawing [2], two handed input [8] and high degree-of-freedom (DOF) control, these measures become insufficient to capture the complete quality of input performance.

Driven by the need in 3D user interfaces, much research has been done to evaluate various multiple DOF input devices [see 6, 7, 15, 14 for reviews]. Many fundamental questions on multi-DOF input, however, remain to be scientifically addressed. Can users simultaneously control all 6 degrees of freedom? Or do users actually control fewer degrees of freedom at a time? Can one 6 DOF device be substituted with multiple lower DOF devices? Rice et al [12] observed that controlling 6 DOF with one hand is difficult. Some teleoperation systems, such as the Shuttle Remote Manipulator, also known as the "Canadarm", require two-handed operation: one hand for rotation control and the other for translation control. O'Hara [9] contradicted such an observation and found little performance difference between two 3 DOF controllers and one 6 DOF controller. To answer these questions on a firm scientific ground, we first need to define informative measures beyond speed and accuracy. One of them is the degree of coordination among the multiple degrees of freedom.

COORDINATION MEASURES

For a given trial of motor performance, such as an athlete's movement or a trial of docking in 3D space, people can often agree if it is coordinated. The research challenge here is how to reflect consensual and intuitive understanding by quantitative measures. In the case of multiple degrees of freedom input control, the following measures have been considered as indices of coordination.

Simultaneity. For a task that involves multiple degrees of freedom, coordinated control may require all the degrees of freedom simultaneously activated. Percentage duration that multiple degrees of freedom are co-activated can therefore be a measure of coordination. The drawback of the simultaneity measure is that it does not account for the magnitude of the control actions in each degree of freedom. As long as all of the degrees of freedom are activated, regardless the amount of input generated, the trial is considered coordinated by this measure.

Time-on-target and correlation. In a 3 DOF pursuit tracking task, Ellson [3] recorded *simultaneous* time-on-target (STOT) in all pairs of degrees of freedom as well as all three at once, in addition to TOT (time-on-target) in each of the component dimensions. He then compared STOT scores with the *products* of the component TOT scores. His argument was that if the percent STOT was *equal* to the product of the component TOTs, then the components may be considered independent (uncoordinated). If greater, they were positively correlated (coordinated); if less, negatively correlated (discoordinated). Senders [13] extended Ellson's approach. He computed an approximation of the product-moment correlation coefficient of two separate degrees of freedom as a measure of coordination. Recently, Zhai and Senders [17, 18] extended the time-on-target and correlation measures to 6 DOF tracking tasks and found that subjects tended to have coordinated trials when using a 6 DOF isometric or elastic rate control device. However, both TOT and correlation as coordination measures have drawbacks. One of them is that these two measures do not account for perfect trials. If a trial is 100% simultaneously on target with zero tracking error in all degrees of freedom at all time, the TOT coordination measure will give an uncoordinated result (STOT equals to the product of component TOTs) and correlation become meaningless since errors in all degrees of freedom are zero.

EFFICIENCY AS COORDINATION MEASURE

We propose *efficiency* as a measure of quantifying coordination in multiple degrees of freedom. For a task that involves N degrees of freedom, the trajectory that has the shortest length in that N dimensional space is considered the most coordinated movement. For simplicity, let us examine trajectories on a 2D space, as illustrated in Fig. 1. In order to move from Point A to B in this space, two variables x and y have to be changed from x_A to x_B and y_A to y_B respectively. Supposing we had an input device that has two separate 1 DOF controls, as in an Etch-a-Sketch toy, one possible trajectory would be AC-CB, as a result of moving in the x dimension first and in the y dimension second. In such a case, the two degrees of freedom are completely uncoordinated, because x and y are not moved at the same time, resulting in a longer trajectory than necessary. With an integrated 2 DOF device such as a mouse, one may produce a trajectory *l* that is close to the straight line AB. Trajectory AB is the shortest and most efficient among all possible trajectories. It can also be considered most coordinated in the sense that x and y move simultaneously at the *same relative pace*. Any deviation from the path AB can be considered a result of imperfect coordination, which will result in a longer trajectory. In light of this analysis, we define the translation inefficiency, i.e. the amount of "work wasted", as an inverse measure of translation coordination.

$$\frac{\text{Length of actual path} - \text{Length of shortest path}}{\text{Length of shortest path}} \quad (1)$$

By this definition, trajectory *l* in Fig. 1 is better coordinated than trajectory AD-DB, which is in turn better coordinated than AC-CB.

The same definition of coordination coefficient can be easily generalized to translations in 3D space simply by measuring 3D instead of 2D Euclidean distances. Fig. 2 shows (top curves) an example of the 3D application.

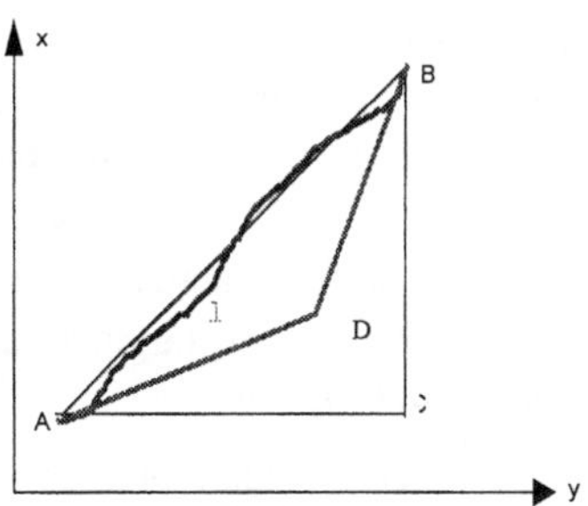

Fig. 1: Coordination with 2 degrees of freedom

To generalize the coordination measure to rotation in 3D space is less straightforward, however. The parameters commonly used in engineering (Euler angles), pitch, yaw, roll, are often misleading [1]. A more valid metric is *rotation vector*. Define the initial mismatch between a cursor and a target (both are 3D objects in 3D space) to be

$$\mathbf{Ø_A} = \phi_A \mathbf{n}_A = (\phi_{Ax}, \phi_{Ay}, \phi_{Az}) \quad (2)$$

where $\mathbf{Ø_A}$ is the rotation vector signifying an angle ϕ_A of

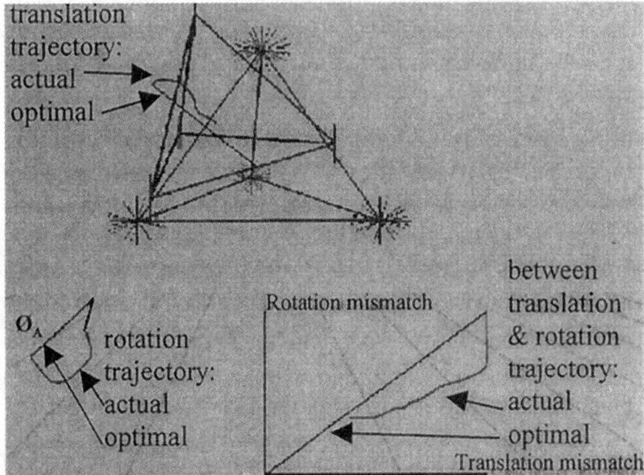

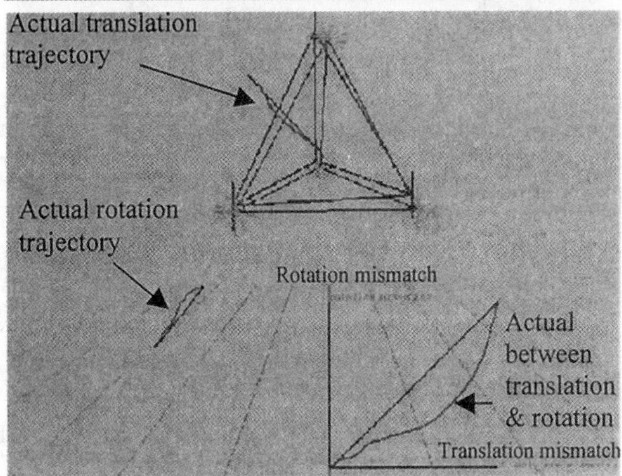

Fig. 2. Coordination measurements superimposed on to a 6DOF docking task. Top: a trial in progress. Bottom: a completed trial. The ratio between actual and optimal trajectory in translation(3D), rotation(3D), and between translation-rotation spaces(2D) quantify the degree of coordination.

rotation about $\mathbf{n}_A$, where $\mathbf{n}_A = (n_x, n_y, n_z)$ is a unit vector defining the axis of the rotation in x, y, z frame of reference, then the *minimum* amount of rotation that the cursor has to go through to reach the target is ϕ_A (Fig. 2). The ratio between ϕ_A and the actual amount of rotation of the cursor upon reaching the target is defined as the rotation coordination coefficient:

$$\frac{\text{Amount of actual rotation - Initial rotation mismatch}}{\text{Amount of actual rotation}} \quad (3)$$

When one can control all 3 rotational degrees of freedom with *perfect* coordination, the rotation mismatch between the cursor and the target will be reduced from $\phi_A \mathbf{n}_A$ to $0\ \mathbf{n}_A$, *without changing the direction of the mismatching rotation vector*. Otherwise, if the 3 rotational degrees of freedom cannot be controlled *simultaneously at the same relative pace*, at an instant of time t the mismatch will be $\phi_t \mathbf{n}_t$ ($\mathbf{n}_t \neq \mathbf{n}_A$), causing a larger amount of actual cursor rotation (Fig. 2, actual trajectory).

The two coordination coefficients defined above deal with translation and rotation separately but do not reveal the coordination aspect between translation and rotation taken together. In other words, a trial can be perfectly coordinated with respect to both its translation trajectory and rotation trajectory, but the rotation and the translation may not necessarily be performed at the same time. Hence, a third coordination factor is defined in the translation-rotation (2D) space which has two dimensions. One is the translation distance, d_t, between the cursor and the target centers of mass, and the other is the rotation mismatch ϕ_t (the magnitude of rotation vector) between the cursor and the target (See Fig. 2). Note that both d_t and ϕ_t are function of time, which define a 2D trajectory over the course of an experiment trial.

Defining coordination by optimality in fact has been proposed in the human motor control literature. For example, Flash and Hogan have measured coordination by the minimum jerk (rate of change of acceleration) for arm movement [4].

COORDINATION IN TWO CLASSES OF 6 DOF INPUT DEVICES: AN EXPERIMENT

Having defined the efficiency measure of coordination, we applied it in two experiments to investigate two 6DOF input devices, the Fingerball and the EGG[1] (Fig. 3).

The Fingerball, similar in shape and size to the 3Ball of Polhemus, represents a class of isotonic (free moving) 6 DOF input devices. Previous study showed that the Fingerball is superior to glove-based devices, due to the fact that one can use both the fingers and the arm/wrist to manipulate the degrees of freedom [16]. The EGG (Elastic General–purpose Grip) represents a different class of 6 DOF devices that are constrained on desktop and work in rate control. In comparison to the commonly used isometric rate controlled desktop device such as the Spaceball™, the EGG offers a slight advantage at the early learning stage due to richer proprioception [15].

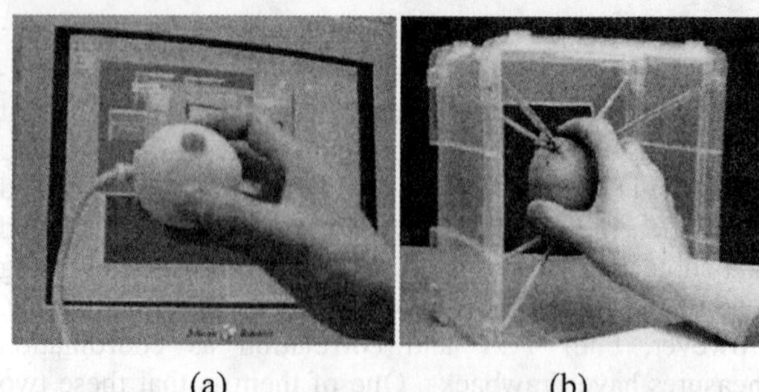

(a) (b)

Fig. 3. Two 6 DOF devices used in the experiments. (a) The Fingerball is a free moving, position controlled input device and (b) The EGG is a desktop, elastic rate controlled device. The two experimental devices were based on the same 6 DOF magnetic sensor, Ascension Bird™.

Fig. 4. Experimental Set-up

Experimental Set-up

Experimental Platform and Display

The experiment was conducted with a desktop 3D virtual environment. In order to ensure that the task performance was driven predominantly by differences in input controller conditions rather than by difficulties in perceiving depth information, binocular depth cue was implemented by means of a 120 Hz sequential switching stereoscopic display, together with perspective projection and occlusion (Fig. 2, 4).

Experimental Task

A 6 DOF docking task, illustrated in Fig. 2 and 5, was used for this experiment. (The coordination displays in Fig. 2, superimposed onto the docking task, were not visible to the subjects). In the experiments, subjects were asked to move a 3D cursor as quickly as possible to align it with a 3D target. The cursor and the target were two

[1] The experiments also included an isometric 6 DOF device (the Spaceball™). Due to space limit, this paper only analyzes and reports results with regard to the Fingerball versus the EGG.

tetrahedra of equal size (4.2 cm from the center to each vertex). The edges and vertex markers (bars and spherical stars) of both tetrahedra were colored so that there was only one correct match in orientation. The stars on the target indicated the acceptable error tolerance for each vertex (0.84 cm). During the trial, whenever a corner of the cursor entered into the tolerance volume surrounding the *corresponding* corner of the target, the star on that corner changed its color as an indication of capture. Whenever all four corresponding corners stayed concurrently matched for 0.7 seconds, the trial was deemed completed. At the end of each trial, the trial completion time was printed on the screen. The beginning of each trial was signaled with a long auditory beep and the end of each trial was signaled with a short beep.

At the beginning of each trial, the cursor appeared in the center of the 3D space while the target randomly appeared in one of 8 pre-set locations and orientations. The 8 trials were divided into two sets of 4 trials. In one set of the trials the cursor and the target were mismatched in orientation about axes that were parallel with the viewer's primary coordinates (X, Y, Z). In another set the orientation mismatches were about arbitrary vectors that did not coincide with the X, Y, Z coordinates. Recent research in mental rotation [10] has shown that humans cannot effectively perform mental rotation about arbitrary 3D axes. We hypothesized that once interaction (manipulation) is allowed, subjects should be able to find the correct rotation path. Note that the magnitude of mismatch of both translation and rotation in each trial in one set correspond to a trial in the other set, so the total amount of translation and rotation are equalized in the two groups.

Experimental Design

Both experiments used between-subject design in order to avoid asymmetrical skill transfer between devices [11]. In Experiment 1, each device group had 16 subjects, none of them had prior experience with using 6 DOF input devices.

Each experiment had 5 repeated tests, which consisted of randomly shuffled 8 trials (with initial locations and orientations as described earlier). Test 1 started after a short demonstration and two warm-up trials. Test 2, Test 3, Test 4, and Test 5 started 10, 20, 30, and 40 minutes after the beginning of Test 1 respectively. Practice trials (with completely random initial locations and orientation) were given between the tests. The entire experiment lasted about 1 hour for each subject.

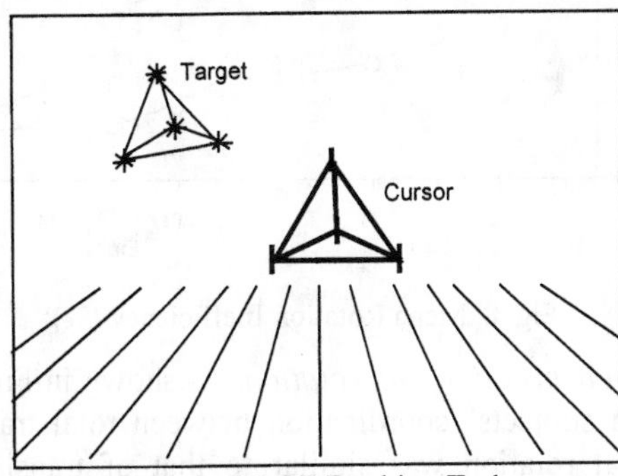

Fig. 5. 6 DOF Docking Task

A follow-up experiment, Experiment 2, was conducted for two reasons. First, we wanted to see effect of retention and extended practice. Second and more importantly, we wanted to know if a coordination difference between the two devices still exists if we give explicit instructions emphasizing coordination.

16 subjects (8 in each device group) who participated in Experiment 1 were called back two months later in Experiment 2, which started with the same instruction as in Experiment 1. After regaining their skills in Test 1 and Test 2, subjects were instructed (through demonstration and explanation) to perform the trials as coordinated (producing smooth and short trajectory) as possible, while trying to complete each trial as quickly as possible.

As a motivating tactic, before Test 3 of Experiment 2, completion times were displayed to the subjects after each trial and each test. After Test 2 of Experiment 2, these were displayed together with coordination measures.

Experimental Results and Discussion

The results of statistical analyses of data collected in the two experiments are summarized in Table 1.

Completion time. As shown in Fig. 6, for both experiments, the mean trial completion time of the free position control (Fingerball) group was significantly shorter than that of the elastic rate control (EGG) group. (Due to space constraint, all F-test degrees of freedom and significance level are summarized in Table 1).

Particularly worth noting is that after Test 2 in Experiment 2 when the emphasis on coordination was given, the subjects sacrificed their completion time in order to make more coordinated movements (Test 3). As they gained more practice, however, the completion time continued to improve.

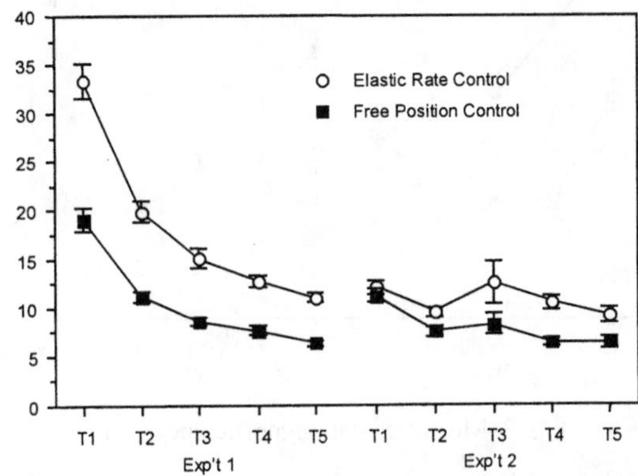

Fig. 6. Mean trial completion time with standard error bars

Table 1: Summary of Experiment 1 Variance Analyses

	Independent variable	Device		Exp't Phase		Device X Phase		Rotation Type		RType X Device	
		$F_{1,30}$	P <	$F_{4,120}$	P <	$F_{4,120}$	P <	$F_{1,30}$	P <	$F_{1,30}$	P <
Exp't 1	Completion Time	30.8	.0001	232.8	.0001	.116	.97 *NS*	27.6	.0001	.96	.33 *NS*
	Translation Inefficiency	44.4	.0001	56.4	.0001	1.7	.15 *NS*	35.1	.0001	.26	.61 *NS*
	Rotation Inefficiency	24.7	.0001	68.2	.0001	.197	.93 *NS*	58.0	.0001	16.2	.001
	Between Tran & Rot	18.0	.0005	94.5	.0001	1.20	.32 *NS*	13.1	.005	.308	.58 *NS*
	Total Transport	18.7	.0005	83.2	.0001	1.78	.14 *NS*	39.4	.0001	.772	.39 *NS*
		$F_{1,14}$	P <	$F_{4,56}$	P <	$F_{4,56}$	P <	$F_{1,14}$	P <	$F_{1,14}$	P <
Expt 2	Completion Time	5.31	.05	13.8	.0001	2.54	.06 *NS*	26.8	.0001	14.3	.005
	Translation Inefficiency	36.3	.0001	42.7	.0001	1.30	.27 *NS*	3.99	.07 *NS*	3.17	.10 *NS*
	Rotation Inefficiency	27.1	.0001	33.5	.0001	2.84	.05	40.8	.0001	38.2	.0001
	Between Tran & Rot	14.7	.005	5.58	.0001	4.42	.05	2.18	.16 *NS*	6.72	.05
	Total Transport	22.7	.0005	54.2	.0001	2.82	.05	24.8	.0005	13.9	.005

Translation. Fig. 7 illustrates the mean translation inefficiency measured in the experiments. In contrast to the trial completion time data, for both experiments, the free moving position control device was significantly (Table 1) less efficient than the elastic rate control device. Subjects significantly improved their translation coordination over the five tests in each experiment, particularly after Test 2 of Experiment 2 when emphasis on coordination and efficiency was given. In terms of magnitude, on average the initial translation trajectories were 300% (free position control group) or 200% (elastic rate control group) longer than the optimal path. At the end of Experiment 2, the mean inefficiency of the elastic rate control group was reduced to 43.3% but that of the free position control group was still at 88.7%.

The lesser degree of coordination of the free moving position control device is plausible. First, position control is directly proportional to hand/finger movement and thus constrained to anatomical limitations: joints can only rotate to certain angle. In contrast, with an elastic rate control device, a small amount of hand movement is mapped onto the velocity of the cursor movement. The integral transformation (from velocity to cursor position) in rate control makes the actual cursor movement a step removed from the hand anatomy.

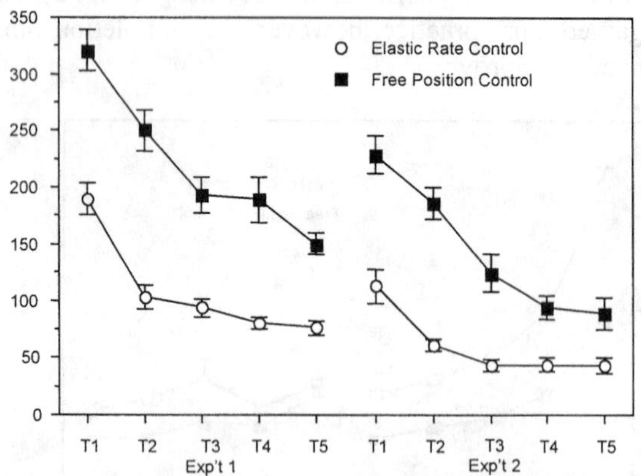

Fig. 7. Mean translation inefficiency (%)

Secondly, the integral transformation in rate control is a low pass filter that removes the higher frequency noise, producing smoother trajectories than position control. This also contributes to the higher efficiency of rate control.

Rotation. Fig. 8 illustrates the mean rotation inefficiency of the two devices. Similar to translation inefficiency, for both experiments, the rotational inefficiency with the free position control device was significantly higher than with the elastic rate control device (Table 1). Subjects also significantly improved their rotation performance over the five tests in each experiment. At the end of Experiment 2, the mean rotation inefficiency of the free position group was reduced to 97.3% and elastic rate control group reduced to 70.4%.

Note that subjects' rotation inefficiency was much higher than that of translation, up to 580% in Test 1 of Experiment 1 by the free position control group. One possible reason is that humans can not effectively do mental rotation of 3D objects. In other words, subject might not be able to figure out the ideal rotation axis before they manually trying out the movement. We will return to this issue shortly.

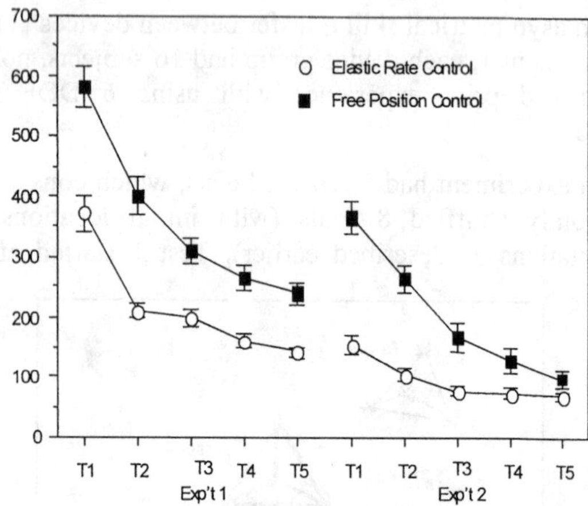

Fig. 8. Mean Rotation Inefficiency (%)

Between translation and rotation. As shown in Fig. 9, the trend in subjects' coordination between total translation and total rotation was similar to that of translation or rotation. The rate control group was significantly more efficient than the position control group in *both* experiments, although the magnitude of the difference was reduced after the instruction change during Experiment 2. At the last test, the inefficiency of the rate and position control group was 26.7% and 36.8% respectively. Interestingly, the mean percentages of "wasted" movement in the translation-rotation space were in fact lesser than in the translational space and rotational space, suggesting that there is little reason to separate translation and rotation control into two hands, as in some telerobotic systems.

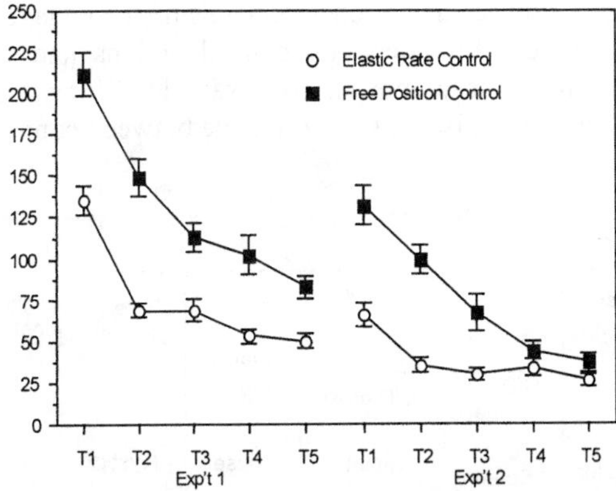

Fig. 9. Inefficiency in translation-rotation space

Total Transport. The above three measures separately indicated users' efficiency with the two 6 DOF input devices in translation, rotation, and between translation and rotation. The total transport, defined as the line integral of the four vertices of the cursor tetrahedron, was used as an integrated measure of coordination in 6 degrees of freedom. Same as the conclusions drawn from the previous three measures, the rate control device was significantly more efficient (or more coordinated) than the position control device. Practice and instructional emphasis improved efficiency with both devices and the difference between the two was reduced by the instruction, but the final difference was still significant. At the last test of the Experiment 2, the inefficiency of the rate control group was 65.4% and that of the position control group was 96%.

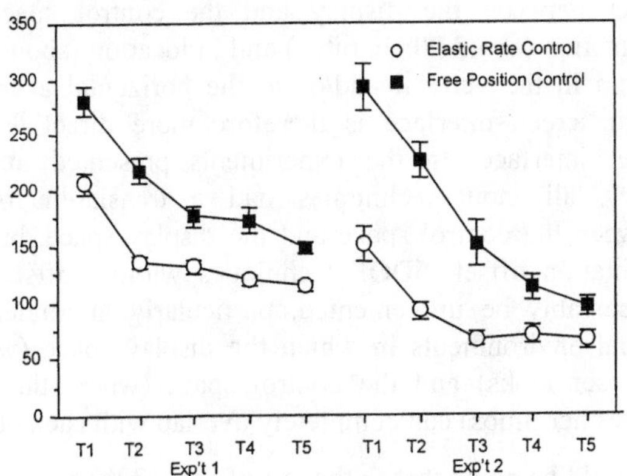

Fig. 10. Inefficiency in total transport

The impact of 3D mental rotation. As recent studies in mental rotation have shown [10], human subjects are incapable of mentally rotating objects in *3D* space. This is particularly true when the rotation axis does not coincide with viewer's primary axes. In Parson's experiments, subjects did not perform better than chance in mentally finding the correct rotations about arbitrary 3D axes. In our experiments, it is indeed true that the subjects were significantly less efficient in trials with arbitrary initial rotation mismatch than in trials with rotation mismatch about primary axes. Fig. 11 shows such an impact.

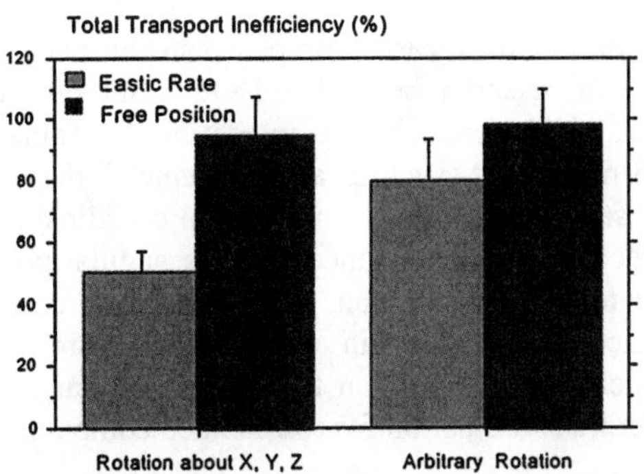

Fig. 11. The impact of rotation type on total movement (total transport data from the last test of Experiment 2)

In not a single trial in our experiments, however, were the subjects unable to successfully complete a trial both in translation and in rotation, including trials in practice sessions when the rotation mismatches are randomly generated and not repeated. The reason, in our view, lies in interaction, the interaction between action and cognition. Note that to be able to manipulate still needs the involvement of mental rotation, the probability to match the target by random manual exploration could not be high. We should point out that the focus of this study is not on mental rotation, although interesting research can be carried in such a direction with the current paradigm.

A greater efficiency difference between the two devices was found when the trials involved rotations only about viewer's primary axes. This is again plausible: for arbitrary rotation trials, the rotation inefficiency was partially caused by physically searching the correct rotations. For trials that were mismatched about the primary rotation axes, subjects can mentally find the correct rotation more easily so the advantage of the rate control device that may enable higher degree of coordination was better revealed in such trials.

CONCLUSIONS AND GENERAL DISCUSSIONS

The efficiency based coordination measure

Although the experiment showed that the efficiency based measure of coordination was sensitive enough to reveal performance differences, this is not necessary the only "correct" measure to quantify coordination in multiple degrees of freedom. One possible argument against such a measure is that it is a *definition*, not a validated conclusion about coordination. The critical issues are whether it is an arbitrary definition or a definition in agreement with our common sense judgement of coordination, and furthermore, if the definition is informative. We think both are true. Another drawback of the efficiency measure is that other factors besides manual coordination, such as the mental rotation factor presented above also contribute to the trajectory efficiency, although one can argue that coordination simply includes a cognitive component.

The coordination measure proposed in the paper can be applied to research beyond 6 DOF input devices. For instance, it is conceivable to define coordination of human movement (such as arm movement) that involves N joints. If we defined N dimensional coordination space with each axis as the distance from the angular position of a joint to its goal position, then a perfectly coordinated movement should result in a straight line from the initial mismatch to (0, 0, ...0) in that space. Similarly, we can also define coordination for two-handed computer input.

Isomorphic manipulation vs. tool operation

By applying the efficiency based coordination measure to input device evaluation, we begin to gain insights into the characteristics of 6 DOF input devices that have not been rigorously demonstrated before. Our experiments showed that while the 6 DOF free moving position control device was faster in docking task completion, the elastic rate control device produced more efficient or coordinated trajectories. The difference was true even after emphasis on coordination was explicitly given to the subjects. The contrast between the pros and cons of the two types of devices tested illustrate a more general philosophical issue on computer input device design: isomorphism (direct manipulation) versus tool-using that has been informally debated by researchers [5]. As shown in Fig. 12, there is in fact a continuum on the dimension of directness[2]. The most dominating factor to directness of an input method is the transformation from the *control space* to *display space*. The more mathematically complex this transformation is, the more indirect the input technique is. Input techniques with first order (rate control) or higher order control dynamics are indirect "tools". With these techniques, one or more integrals are involved in the mathematical mapping from the control space (user's control actions) to the display space (cursor movements). The elastic rate controller (EGG) used in the experiments is such an example.

Moving to the left of Fig. 12, input devices become more direct. For position control techniques, the mathematical transformation from the control space to the display space is a multiplication, which is simpler than integration. Among position control techniques, *absolute* devices, such as a 2 DOF digitizing tablet or the 6 DOF Fingerball in Experiment 4 are more direct than *relative* devices, such as a 2 DOF mouse or the 6 DOF glove [16]. Relative devices require a clutch mechanism to engage and disengage the link between control actions and cursor movements. For a mouse, for example, lifting it from mouse pad will disengage the linkage between control and display.

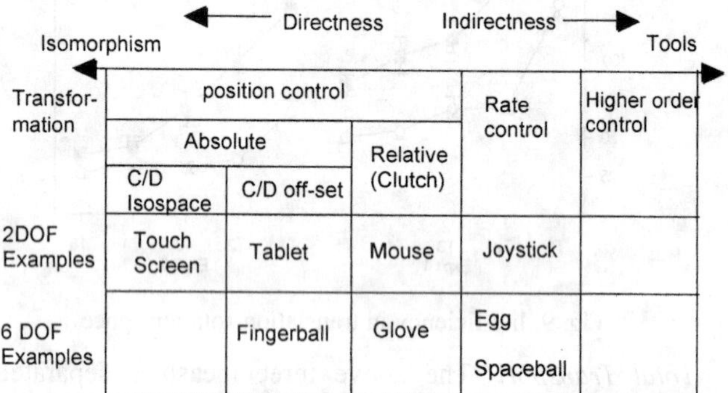

Fig. 12. Isomorphism - tool continuum: A taxonomy of classifying input devices according to directness of transformation from control space to display space

Another factor that affects the directness of position control techniques is the control-display (C-D) ratio. When the C-D ratio is 1, the multiplication operation is reduced to an assignment (copying) operation, which makes the input control more direct than when the C-D ratio is not 1.

There is still another factor that makes some absolute position input techniques more direct than the others: the orientation or location *offset* between the control space and the display space. Both a touch-screen and a tablet are absolute position control devices but the latter has an offset between the display and the control space in orientation (about 90° in pitch) and in location (about 20 - 40 cm in the vertical and/or in the horizontal axes). A touch screen interface is therefore more direct than a tablet interface. In the experiments presented in this paper, all input techniques had a translation offset between the control space and the display space, but no orientation offset. 6DOF techniques without offset can conceivably be implemented, particularly in immersive virtual environments in which the display space (where the user looks) and the control space (where the user moves her limbs) can completely overlap with each other.

It should be noted that to the left of Fig. 12 there are input devices that are even more direct. These are the position control devices with force-reflecting capabilities. The

[2] Fig. 12 can be viewed as an input device design space or taxonomy. For proposals and discussions of input taxonomy, see W. Buxton "Lexical and Pragmatic Considerations of Input Structure" *Computer Graphics* 17 (1); J. Mackinlay, S.K. Card, G.G. Robertson "A Semantic Analysis of the Design Space of Input Devices" *Human-Computer Interaction vol 5* pp145-190.

ultimate isomorphic input controller is one that allows force feedback in all directions, to recreate what we would feel when manipulating real 3D objects directly with our bare hands. In other words, the ultimate isomorphic interfaces are completely "transparent" to the user.

It is important to note that there are both advantages and disadvantages to techniques on each end of the isomorphism - tool continuum, as illustrated by our coordination experiments. In daily life, we prefer to perform many tasks with our bare hands. Even with a glove, the small "transformation" between the hand and the actual manipulation may be undesirable on some occasions. On the other hand, we do frequently use various tools, sometimes as simple as rulers, wrenches, screwdrivers, etc., for precision, for power and for overcoming some of our other physical limitations. In general, more isomorphic (more direct) designs are more intuitive and require less learning. Such devices are needed for applications where an explicit learning period is perhaps not available, such as commercial video games where users should be able to walk-up and play immediately. The disadvantages with such isomorphic designs lie in possible fatigue, coarseness of the control action, and anatomical limitations of the human limb. In contrast, less direct, tool-like devices may take more time to learn but may be more efficient in terms of reduced fatigue, coordinated motions, and fewer physical limitations of the human limb. Such designs can be more suitable for tasks of long duration, such as in teleoperation and image visualization.

ACKNOWLEDGEMENTS

The experiments presented here were conducted at the ETC lab of the University of Toronto. The study was made possible by a research grant from ITRC, a center of excellence of Ontario. We thank our co-grantee Bill Buxton for his support and close collaboration. We also like to thank the IBM Almaden Research Center for supporting the first author to continue and complete this study.

REFERENCES

1. Altmann, S. L. (1986). *Rotations, Quaternions, and Double Groups*. Oxford: Clarendon Press.
2. Accot, J. and Zhai, S., Beyond Fitts' Law: Models for trajectory-based HCI tasks, *Proc. CHI'97*, 295-302.
3. Ellson, D. C. (1947). *The independence of tracking in two and three dimensions with the B-29 pedestal sight*. Report TSEAA-694-2G, Aero Medical Laboratory.
4. Flash, T., Hogan, N. The coordination of arm movements: An experimental confirmed mathematical model, *The Journal of Neuroscience*, Vol 5, No. 7. 1688-1703, 1985.
5. Green, M., Bryson, S., Poston, T. & Wexeblat, A, Hands off my VR: the role of gestures in VR (panel session). *Proc. of Virtual Reality Software and Technology (VRST 1994)*, 267-268.
6. Hinckley, K., Tulio, J., Pausch, R., Proffitt, D, Kassell, N., Usability Analysis of 3D Rotation Techniques, to appear *Proc. of ACM Symp. UIST'97*, 1997.
7. Jacobus, H. N., Riggs, A. J., Jacobus, C. J., & Weinstein, Y. (1992). Implementation issues for telerobotic handcontrollers: human-robot ergonomics. In M. Rahimi & W. Karwowski (Eds.), *Human-Robot Interaction* . London: Taylor & Francis.
8. Kabbash, P., Buxton, W., Sellen, A., Two-handed input in a compound task, *Proc. CHI'94*, 417-423.
9. O'Hara, J. (1987). Telerobotic control of a dexterous manipulator using master and six-DOF hand controllers for space assembly and servicing tasks. *Proc. Human Factors Society 31st Annual Meeting*.
10. Parsons, L., Inability to reason about an object's orientation using an axis and angle of rotation. *Journal of Experimental Psychology: Human Perception and Performance*, 1995, Vol.21, No.6, 1259-1277.
11. Poulton, E.C., Unwanted asymmetrical skill transfer effects with balanced experimental designs. *Psychological Bulletin, 66* 1 (1966), 1-8.
12. Rice, J. R., Yorchak, J. P., & Hartley, C. S. (1986). *Capture of satellites having rotational motion. Proc. Human Factors Society 30th Annual Meeting*
13. Senders, J. W., Christensen, J. M., & Sabeh, R. (1955). *Comparison of single operator's performance with team performance in a tracking task* (TN-55-362): Aero Medical Laboratory, Wright Air Development Center.
14. Ware, C. Using hand position for virtual object placement, *the Visual Computer*, 1990, Vol 6, 245-253
15. Zhai, S. (1995). *Human Performance in Six Degree of Freedom Input Control.* Ph.D. Thesis, Univ. of Toronto. Http://vered.rose.toronto.edu/people/shumin.html
16. Zhai, S., Milgram, P. Buxton, W., The influence of muscle groups on performance of multiple degree of freedom input control, *Proc. of CHI'96*.
17. Zhai, S., Senders, J.W., Investigating Coordination in Multidegree of Freedom Control I: Time-on-Target Analysis of 6 DOF Tracking, to appear in *Proc. Human Factor Ergonomics Society* 1997.
18. Zhai, S., Senders, J.W., Investigating Coordination in Multidegree of Freedom Control II: Correlation Analysis of 6 DOF Tracking. *ibid*

An Efficient Text Input Method for Pen-based Computers

Toshiyuki Masui

Sony Computer Science Laboratory Inc.
3-14-13 Higashi-Gotanda
Shinagawa, Tokyo 141-0022, Japan
+81-3-5448-4380
masui@csl.sony.co.jp

ABSTRACT

Pen-based computing has not yet taken off, partly because of the lack of fast and easy text input methods. The situation is even worse for people using East Asian languages, where thousands of characters are used and handwriting recognition is extremely difficult. In this paper, we propose a new fast text input method for pen-based computers, where text is not composed by entering characters one by one, but by selecting words from a menu of candidates created by filtering the dictionary and predicting from context. Using our approach, users can enter Japanese text more than twice as fast as recognition-based and other existing text input methods. User studies and detailed analysis of the method are also given.

KEYWORDS: Input devices, Pen-based input, Predictive interface, Hand-held devices, International interfaces, POBox

INTRODUCTION

Although a variety of pen-based computers are available these days, they are not as widely used as keyboard-based computers, partly because entering text is much harder on pen-based machines. Traditionally, handwriting recognition techniques and the soft keyboard (virtual keyboard displayed on the tablet of a pen computer) used to be the main techniques for entering characters on pen-based computers, although other techniques have also been proposed[4][6]. However, using any of these techniques takes much longer to enter text than with a standard keyboard.

The situation is worse for East Asian languages such as Chinese, Japanese, etc. These, unlike European languages, have thousands of character faces. Even with a keyboard, it is not easy to enter a character. A variety of techniques for entering text into computer have been investigated. The most widely-used Japanese input technique is "Roman-Kanji conversion" (RKC), in which a user specifies the pronunciation of a word with an ASCII keyboard, and the system shows the user a word with the specified pronunciation[1]. If the word was not the one that the user intended to use, the user types a "next candidate key" until the correct word appears as the candidate.

On almost all the pen-based computers available in Japan, either RKC or handwriting recognition is supported. Text input is slow and tiring using either of the techniques, for the following reasons. Specifying the pronunciation of every input word using a soft keyboard takes a lot of time, and the user must convert the pronunciation to the desired Kanji strings with extra keystrokes. Handwriting recognition has more problems. First, the recognizer has to distinguish between thousands of characters, often making errors. Many of the characters in the character sets have similar shapes, so it is inherently difficult to make recognition reliable. Second, in many cases, users do not remember the shape or the stroke order of Kanji characters, even when they have no problem reading them. Finally, writing many characters with many strokes on a tablet is very tiring. With these difficulties, it is believed to be difficult to enter Japanese text faster than 30 characters a minute on pen-based computers, which is several times slower than using keyboards.

We have developed a new pen-based text input method called *POBox* (Pen-Operation Based On eXample), where users can efficiently enter text in any language, using menus, word prediction and approximate pattern matching. The remainder of this paper demonstrates the details of POBox.

STRATEGIES FOR RAPID TEXT ENTRY

There is a big difference between the speed of typing on keyboards and pointing to characters on soft keyboards of pen-based computers. Computer users can easily type more than five characters per second, while it is very difficult to touch three character keys per second, accurately on the soft keyboard of a pen-based computer. In contrast, the speed of selecting an item from a list is faster with a pointing device, and many keyboard-oriented text editors (e.g. Emacs) now have mouse interfaces. For this reason, forcing the user to enter many characters should be avoided on pen-based computers, while a better approach should allow the user to select a word from a list of candidates, in a minimum number of penstrokes. We took the following approach.

[1]Japanese characters consist of two character sets. Kanji characters, imported from China, contain both meaning and pronunciation, while Kana characters only represent pronunciation.

CHI 98 Los Angeles CA USA
Copyright 1998 0-89791-975-0/98/ 4..$5.00

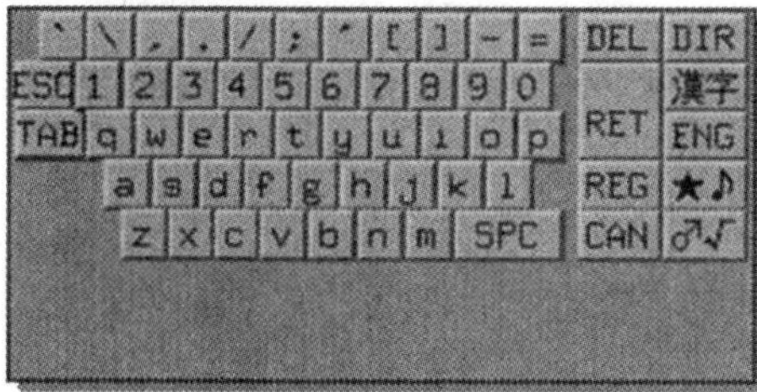

Figure 1: Initial display.

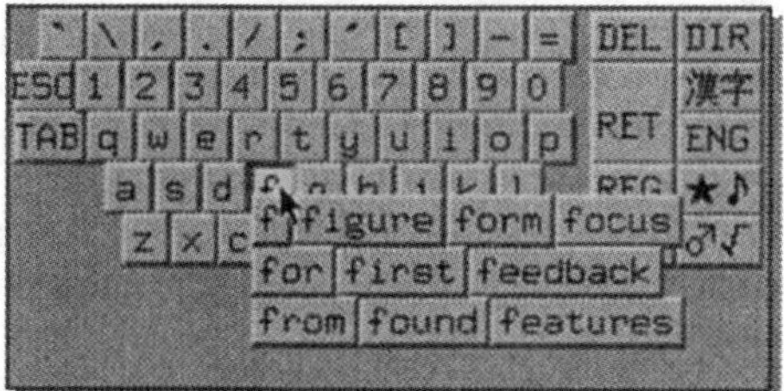

Figure 2: Selecting the "F" key.

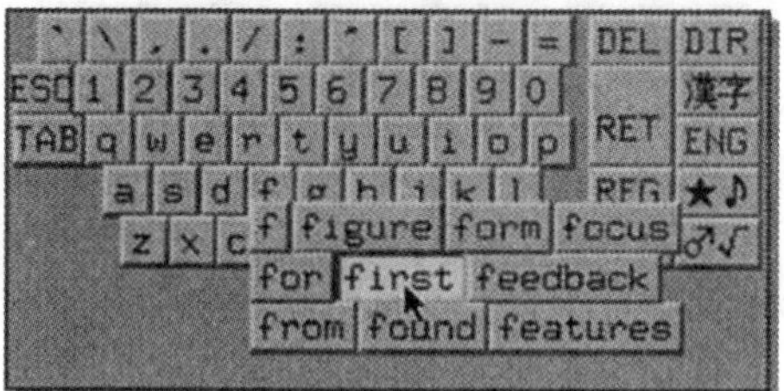

Figure 3: Selecting "first" by dragging.

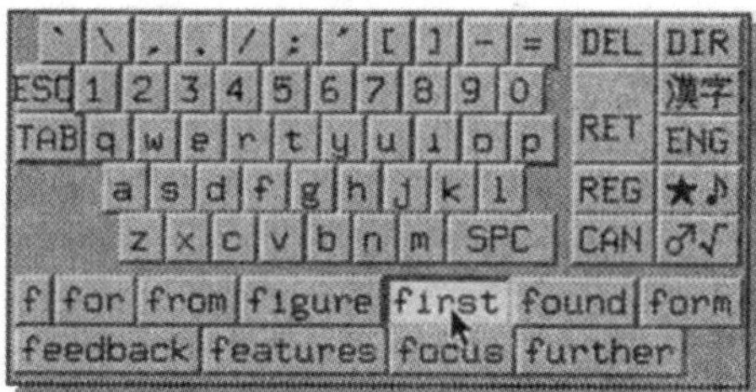

Figure 4: Selecting "first" after releasing the pen from the tablet.

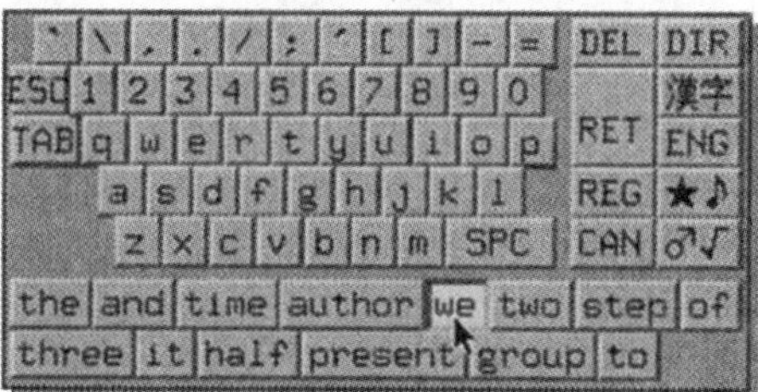

Figure 5: Selecting "we" after selecting "first".

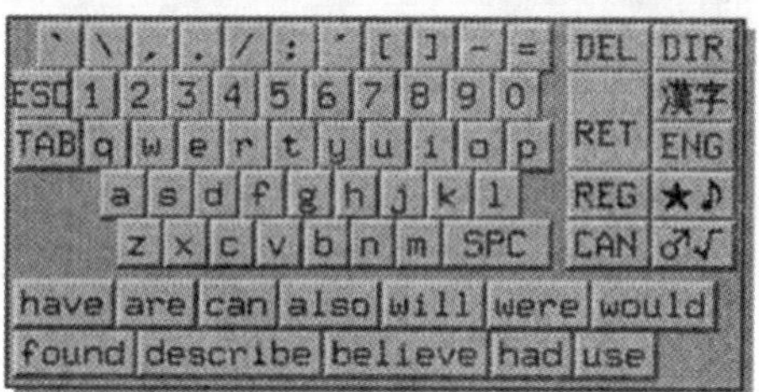

Figure 6: After selecting "we".

Using dynamic menus to show candidates and select words: The desired word can be picked up directly from a pulldown or popup menu.

Dynamic query for dictionary search: As soon as the user specifies a portion of the pronunciation or the spelling of a word using the soft keyboard on the tablet, POBox shows a menu of candidate words that match the input.

Using term frequency and example phrases: The words which are most likely to appear at the insertion point in the text are shown at the top of the menu. The likelihood is calculated from the term frequency and context. For example, since the word "interface" tends to come after "user," it appears at the top of the menu after the user has selected "i" as the first character following "user."

Dynamic approximate string matching for selecting candidate words: If the pattern specified by the user does not exactly match any of the words in the dictionary, POBox automatically performs approximate string search based on the following two strategies. One is *spatial approximation*, where adjacent characters on the soft keyboard are treated equally in the search. This strategy is effective especially when the soft keyboard is small and precise selection is difficult. For example, if the user failed to tap the right position of a soft keyboard and selected "**`dtns`**" to enter "**`dynamic`**," no word in the dictionary matches "**`dtns`**" and POBox automatically searches the dictionary using the less strict pattern "**`[ersdfxc][rtyfg][hjbnm][weasdzx]`**," based on the arrangement of ASCII keyboard. ("**`d`**" key is surrounded by "**`e`**," "**`r`**," "**`s`**," "**`f`**," "**`x`**" and "**`c`**" keys.) This pattern matches words like "**`synergy`**" and "**`dynasty`**," but since "**`dynamic`**" has higher term frequency than these words, it is shown in the candidate word list for the selection. The other is *pattern matching allowing errors*. This strategy is effective when the user does not remember the correct spelling or the pronunciation of a word. In this case, POBox automatically looks for words whose spelling or pronunciation is closest to the pattern and shows them as candidates. Users can even specify only a portion of a word to get the desired word in the candidate list.

Simple dictionary adaptation: Newly selected words are put at the top of the dictionary, and are likely to be shown at the top of the menu so that the dictionary reflects the characteristics of the current text.

EXAMPLES

Entering English Text

First, for explanatory purpose, we show how to use POBox for entering English text, although POBox is more effective for entering Japanese and other East Asian languages. We used the ACM CHI'95 Electronic Proceedings CD-ROM to create an English dictionary with term and phrase frequencies. We extracted plain text files from all the HTML files in the CD-ROM, counted the occurrences of words and word combinations, and created the dictionaries by sorting the entries by frequency order. The remainder of this section uses the sentence (*"First, we show our technique for entering English text."*) as the sample input text for our example.

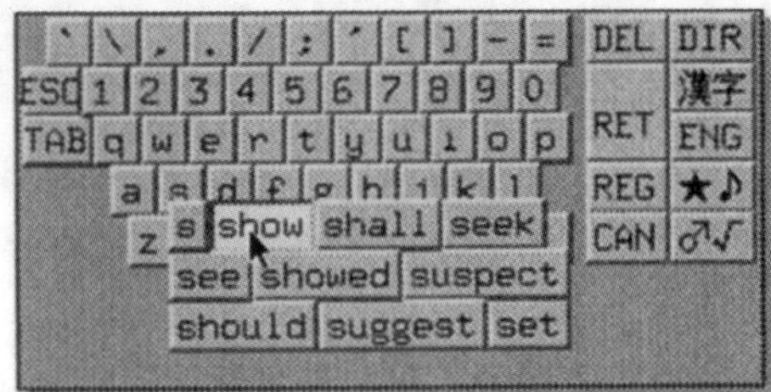

Figure 7: Selecting "show" from the menu.

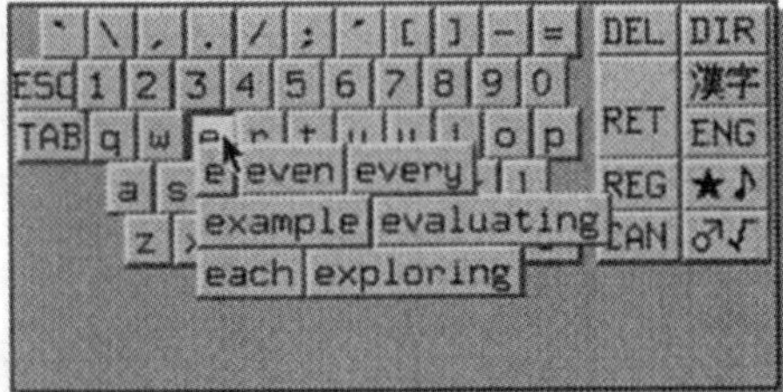

Figure 8: Selecting the "E" key.

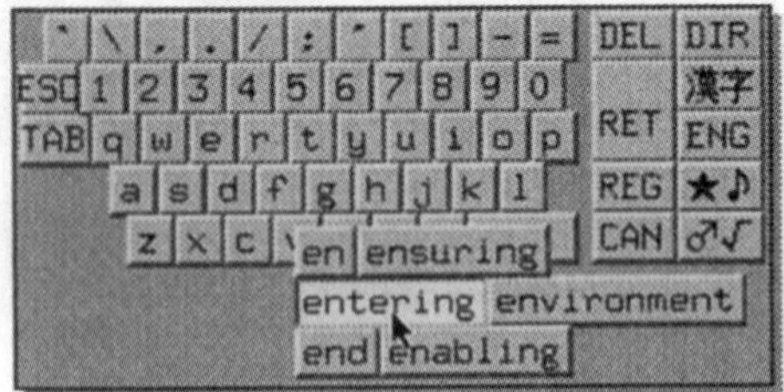

Figure 9: Moving to the "N" key and selecting "entering".

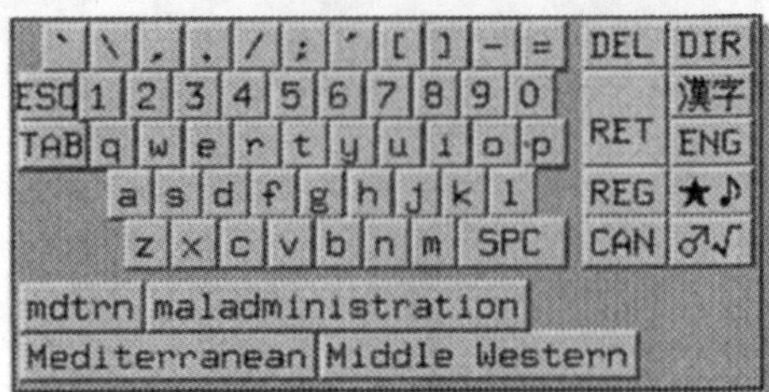

Figure 10: Specifying "mdtrn" to get "Mediterranean".

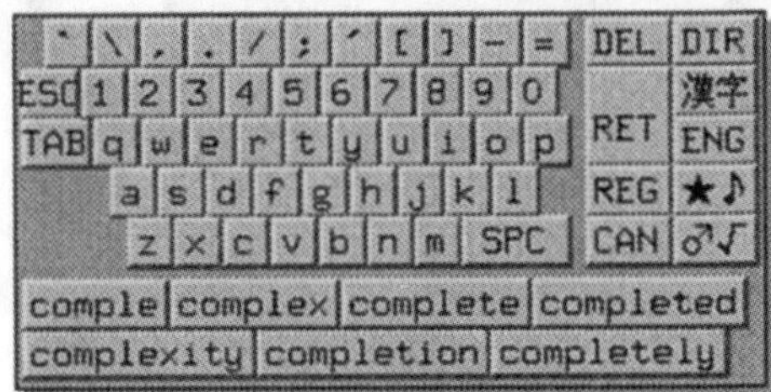

Figure 11: After specifying "comple".

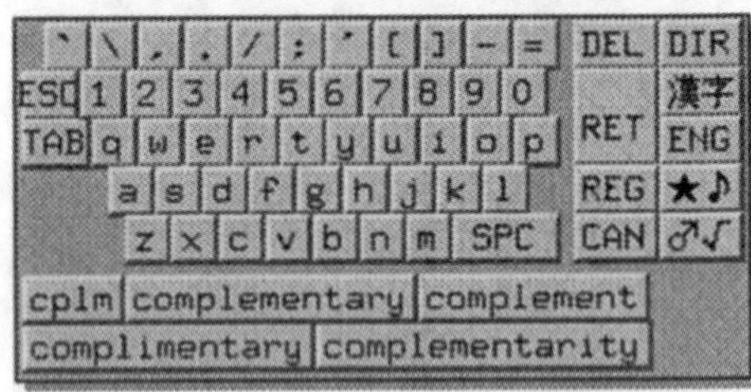

Figure 12: After specifying "cplm".

Figure 1 shows the startup display of POBox. When the user touches the "F" key, the display changes to Figure 2, showing the frequently used words that start with "F" in a pulldown menu. Since the word "first" is a frequently used word and is found in the menu, the user can drag the pen and highlight the word "first" as shown in Figure 3, and then take the pen off the tablet to complete the selection. Alternatively, if the user does not make a selection from the pulldown menu of Figure 3, he can choose the desired word from the popup menu as shown in Figure 4.

After selecting "first", the display changes to Figure 5. In the menu at the bottom, the words that often come after "first" are listed in order of frequency. The word combination "first the" appears 27 times in the CHI'95 CD-ROM, "first and" and "first time" appear 20 times, etc. Since the next word, "we," happens to be in the list because "first we" appears 13 times in the CD-ROM, the user can directly select "we" by touching it in the menu. After selecting "we", the display changes to Figure 6. In this case, "show" is not found in the menu, but it can be selected from the pulldown menu by touching the "S" key as shown in Figure 7.

After this, "our", "technique" and "for" can be selected in a similar manner. Touching the "E" key does not make the system display the next intended word ("entering") as shown in Figure 8, but touching the "N" key next narrows the search space of the dictionary and "entering" then appears in the menu for the selection (Figure 9).

From start to finish, the user only had to tap the tablet 15 times to enter the phrase "First, we show our technique for entering." Notice that the user made no spelling errors with this method, since all the input words were taken from the dictionary.

Using Approximate String Matching

With the approximate string matching feature, even when the user does not specify the correct spelling of a word, there is a good chance of finding the desired word among the candidates. Also, the user can specify only part of the spelling to find the desired word. For example, if the user does not remember the spelling of "Mediterranean," he can specify "mdtrn" to see the list of words which are close to the pattern and then can find the right word in the list (Figure 10.)

The same technique can be used to enter a word that has a common prefix. If the user tries to enter "complementary" and specifies "comple," he still cannot find the word in the candidates in Figure 11, since there are many commonly used words that begin with "comple." Instead, the user can specify the characters that better represent the word. As shown in Figure 12, the user can obtain "complementary" by specifying "cplm," although other patterns such as "cpmt" will also work.

Entering Japanese Text

With POBox, users can enter Japanese text much more easily than RKC and handwriting recognition systems. We show the example by using "以下に本手法を用いた文章入力例を

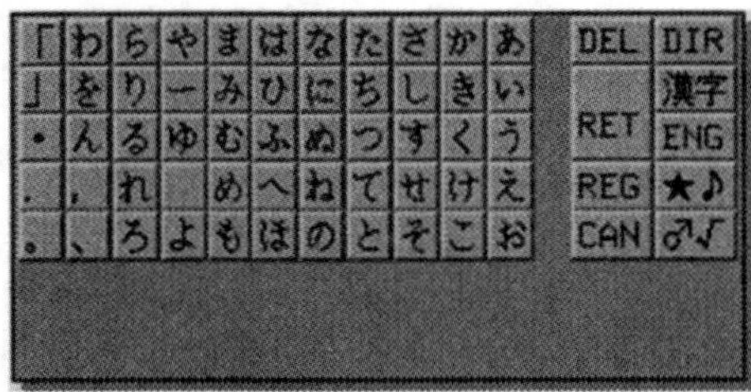

Figure 13: Initial display in Japanese input mode.

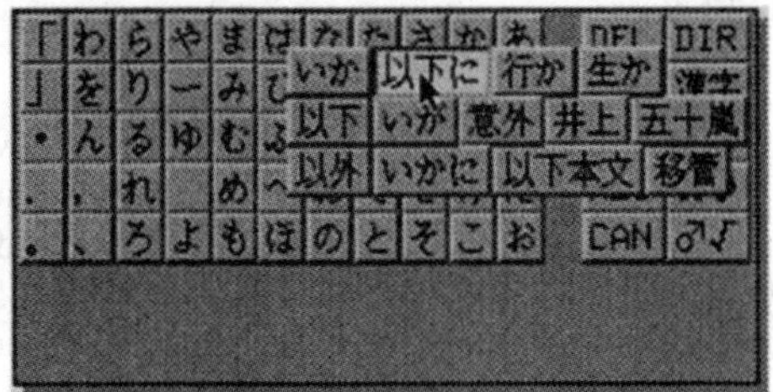

Figure 14: Selecting "以下に".

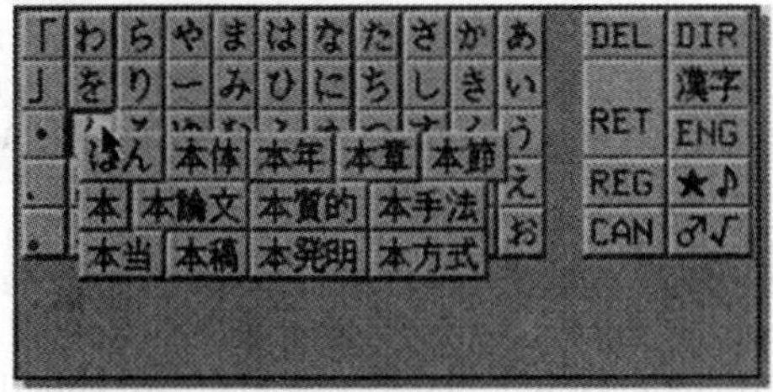

Figure 15: Before selecting "本手法".

示す"[2] as a sample Japanese input text. Figure 13 shows the initial display of POBox in Japanese input mode. A Hiragana character table is displayed for entering pronunciations, instead of the Roman alphabet in English mode.

The pronunciation of the first word "以下に" is "いかに"(i-ka-ni), and the user can select the word by choosing "い"(i) and "か"(ka) from the Hiragana keyboard, just like in the English example. Figure 14 shows how the user can select the word "以下に" with the pulldown menu. The user can select the next word "本手法" (pronounced "hon-shuhou") after selecting its pronunciation "ほ"(ho) and "ん"(n).

In this way, the user can enter Japanese text by specifying the pronunciation of the first portion of the word and then selecting the desired word from the menu, just like specifying the spelling for English words. The user can input the phrase "以下に本手法を" in 7 penstrokes, whereas the ordinary RKC method requires at least 20 penstrokes.

DETAILS OF THE ALGORITHM

Dictionaries and Word Prediction

The word dictionary is a set of 2-tuples {word, spelling/pronunciation} sorted by the term frequency of the word. The top portion of the English word dictionary is shown in Figure 16. Since "the" appears more often than any other word in the corpus, it resides at the top of the dictionary, with its spelling "THE." The phrase dictionary is a set of 3-tuples {context, word, spelling/pronunciation} sorted by the phrase

[2] "Here, we show an example of entering text using this method"

Word	Spelling/Pronunciation
the	THE
of	OF
to	TO
and	AND
...	...

Figure 16: Word dictionary.

Context	Word	Spelling/Pronunciation
of	the	THE
in	the	THE
to	the	THE
...	...	...
as well	as	AS
into	the	THE
...	...	...

Figure 17: Phrase dictionary.

frequency. Here, "context" means the word(s) that precede the input word. The top portion of the initial phrase dictionary is shown in Figure 17. Of all the phrases (lists of more than one words), "of the" occurs most often and hence appears at the top of the phrase dictionary.

Whenever possible, POBox checks the context and the characters specified by the user, and generates the list of candidate words for the next user input. First, it checks the phrase dictionary and looks for the dictionary entries whose context match the current context and whose spelling match the user input. If such entries are found, POBox puts them into the candidate list. Then it checks the word dictionary and looks for entries whose spelling match the user input. If no entry is found in both of the dictionaries, POBox tries to find more candidate words by performing approximate string matching described in the next section. After the user selects a word from the menu, the newly selected word and phrase are put at the top of the dictionaries.

A middle-sized natural language dictionary usually has 20,000 to 50,000 word entries, which occupies less than 500KB of memory without compression. With appropriate compression and indexing techniques, a word dictionary plus a phrase dictionary can easily be packed into 1MB of memory.

Approximate String Matching

Our approximate string matching algorithm is based on Baeza-Yates' "shifter algorithm"[1], with our extensions for allowing errors and handling simple wildcard characters. The shifter algorithm is also used in an approximate string matching program **agrep**[7] (an extension to **grep** on UNIX), where wildcard characters are treated differently from ours. In our algorithm, we limit the wildcard to the basic "**.***" pattern in order to achieve simple and fast processing.

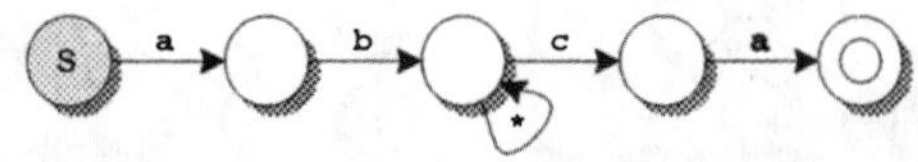

Figure 18: A state transition machine which accepts "**ab.*ca**".

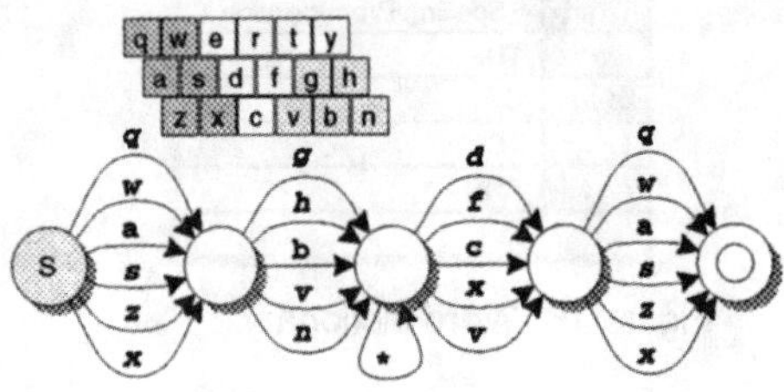

Figure 19: A state transition machine with spatial approximation

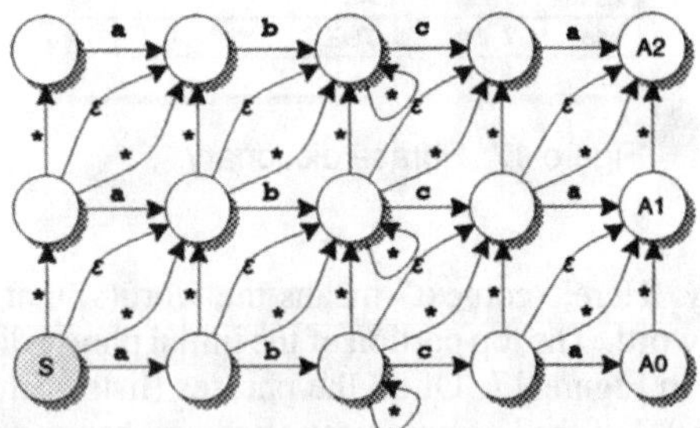

Figure 20: State transition machine which allows errors.

Figure 18 shows a nondeterministic state transition machine which accepts a regular expression "**ab.*ca**". In the shifter algorithm, a bit string is used to represent the status of this state machine. For example, the initial state is represented as "**10000**", and it becomes "**11000**" after accepting an "**a**".

The state machine can be extended to perform spatial approximate search by adding transitions by adjacent characters (Figure 19.) The state machine can also be extended to allow errors by adding extra rows of states as shown in Figure 20. A0 is the accept state with no errors, and A1 and A2 are the accept states with one and two errors, respectively. Like most spelling correctors, POBox treats character insertion, deletion and substitution as errors. Figure 21 shows the state transition by "**abracadabra**". After reading "**ab**", state A2 becomes active, showing that "**ab**" matches "**ab.*ca**" with two errors. After reading "**abra**", state A1 also becomes active, showing that "**abra**" matches "**ab.*ca**" with one error.

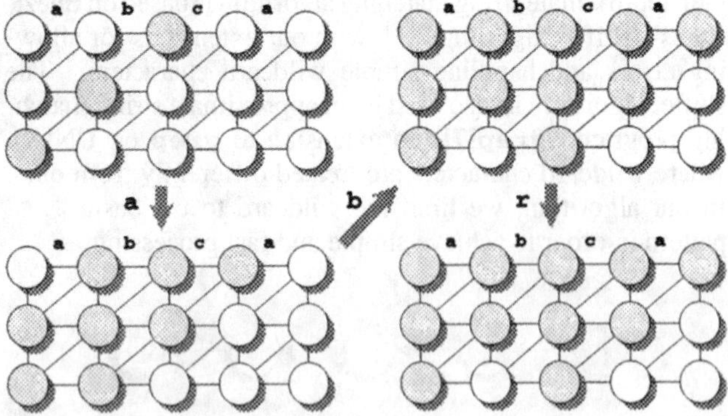

Figure 21: State transition by "**abracadabra**".

This state transition can be calculated with simple logic and shift operations. For a short pattern with small ambiguity, POBox first creates a deterministic state transition table from the nondeterministic state transition diagram like the one shown in Figure 20, and uses the transition table instead, for faster processing. For example, the state machine in Figure 20 can be converted to a deterministic state transition table with 32 states.

EVALUATION

POBox currently runs on UNIX(X11), Windows95, Newton, Java VM, and Pilot. POBox for Pilot is the latest version, distributed to the public on the Web[3] since July 1997, and downloaded by more than 10,000 people in two months. Since it is the most widely-used version of POBox, we used it for the evaluation, although it lacks the pulldown menu feature because of its limited processing power.

A set of inquiries asking the user's background and impressions of POBox was also presented on the Web page for downloading POBox, and 1,057 people answered the questions. Among the 967 people with experience in both POBox and Japanese handwriting recognition systems, 126 people (13.0%) said they feel that POBox is as efficient as handwriting recognition systems, and 796 people (82.4%) said POBox is more efficient. Among the 899 people with experience in both POBox and RKC systems, 118 people (13.2%) said they feel that POBox is as efficient as conversion-based systems, and 718 people (80.1%) said POBox is more efficient. Several people sent back comments saying that they feel POBox is the most effective pen-based Japanese input method they have ever used.

To obtain more reliable data, we asked POBox users who answered the inquiry to compare the text input time using POBox and other handwriting recognition systems[4]. Of these users, we selected approximately 300 people who seemed to have reasonable experience with both POBox and handwriting recognition systems, independent of their performance on the two systems, and 31 people agreed to perform the experiment and sent back the test results. All of them are adult male, and most of them are engineers in various Japanese companies. About half are in their thirties, three are in their forties, all of them having enough experience on both POBox and handwriting recognition systems.

We asked the participants to measure the entry time of a sample Japanese text consisting of 53 Kanji/Kana characters and 2 punctuation characters, under the following conditions:

1. writing the text on paper.
2. entering the same text using POBox.
3. entering the text using conventional RKC.
4. entering the text using the participants' favorite Kanji handwriting recognition systems on any architecture.

[3] http://www.csl.sony.co.jp/person/masui/POBox/pilot.html

[4] We offered calling cards (a value of approximately $5) to the participants as a token incentive to perform the test seriously.

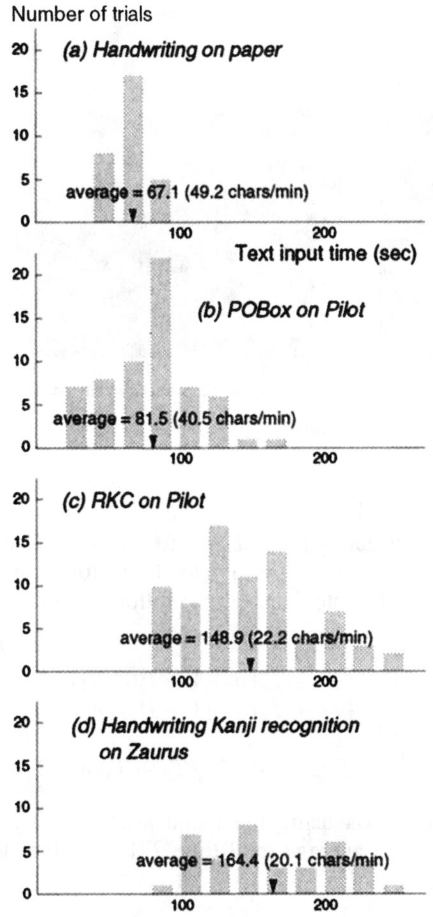

Figure 22: Distribution histograms of text input time using different methods.

The second and third tests were performed on the Pilot, which does not have a Kanji handwriting recognition system. Therefore, we asked the participants to use their favorite recognition systems, instead.

Among the 31 participants, 10 people used the same handwriting recognition system available on a Zaurus PDA[5] (made by Sharp). Other people used various handwriting recognition systems on PCs and other PDAs, but the recognition time was longer than on the Zaurus. The summary of the test result is shown in Figure 22. Since not all participants completed all experiments for the same number of times, the area of the histogram differ among the tests.

Input Speed Comparison

Most of the participants could write the sample text on paper faster than with any of the electronic text input methods. (The average was about 50 chars/min.) Writing speed does not vary significantly between people. On the other hand, the text input speed using Zaurus' Kanji handwriting recognition system does vary considerably from person to person, the average being about 20 chars/min. This is much slower than writing on paper, because of the recognition error and difficulty of writing on a tablet. No correlation was observed between the speed of writing on paper and the speed of entering text using handwriting recognition systems.

The average text input speed using POBox was about 40 chars/min, which is approximately twice as fast as conventional RKC or Zaurus' handwriting recognition system. While the fastest handwriting recognition times observed were shorter than the slowest POBox users, every individual tested performed better with POBox than with the handwriting recognition system.

Approximate String Matching

We have not advertised the approximate string matching feature very much on the Web page, but 448 people (43.4%) of the users noticed this feature. Of these 448 users, only 30 of them (6.7%) answered that approximate string matching was not useful for them.

DISCUSSIONS

Stochastic Analysis of the Dictionary

The total number of words in the CHI'95 CD-ROM is about 650,000, and the distribution of the frequency conforms well to Zipf's rank-frequency law. From the data, the probability of finding the desired word in the candidate menu after entering the top portion of the spelling can be calculated by summing up all the frequencies of words that appear in the menu after each penstroke. This is the case when using POBox without the prediction from context feature. The result is shown in Figure 23.

When the system shows 10 candidates after each penstroke, about 53% of the input words can be found in the menu after specifying one character, and about 92% of words can be found after three penstrokes. This means that 92% of the words can be entered with four penstrokes, while about 50% of the words in the CHI'95 CD-ROM consist of more than four letters. This result shows that the menu-based text input method of POBox is effective even without the prediction mechanism.

The same analysis for the Japanese dictionary is shown in Figure 24. Since about 50 Hiragana characters are used for

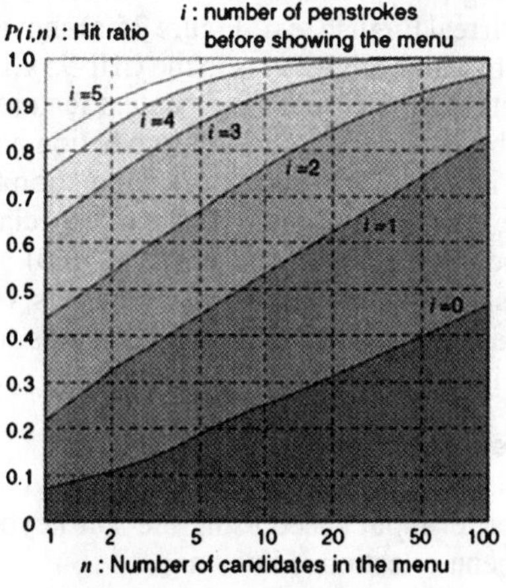

Figure 23: Probability of finding the desired word in the menu (English text).

[5]Zaurus was the most popular PDA in Japan at the time this experiment was performed.

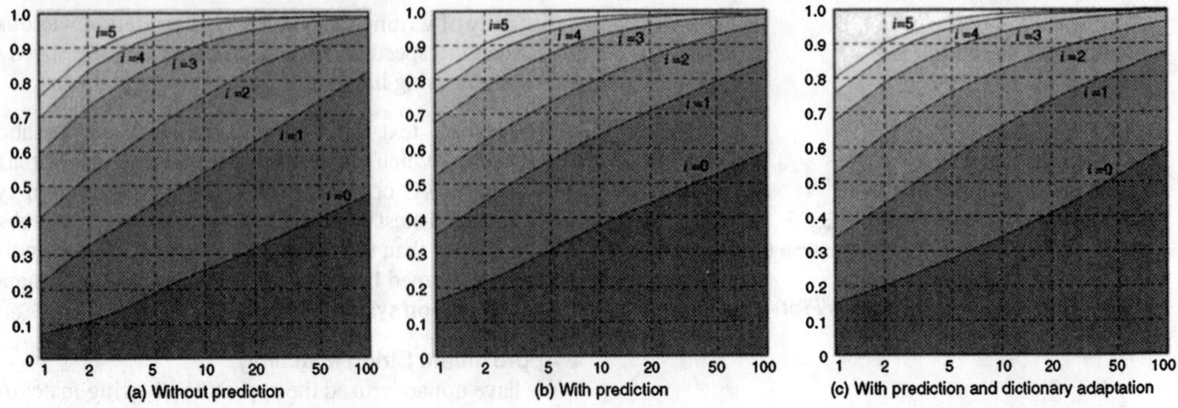

Figure 25: Probability of finding the desired word in the menu.

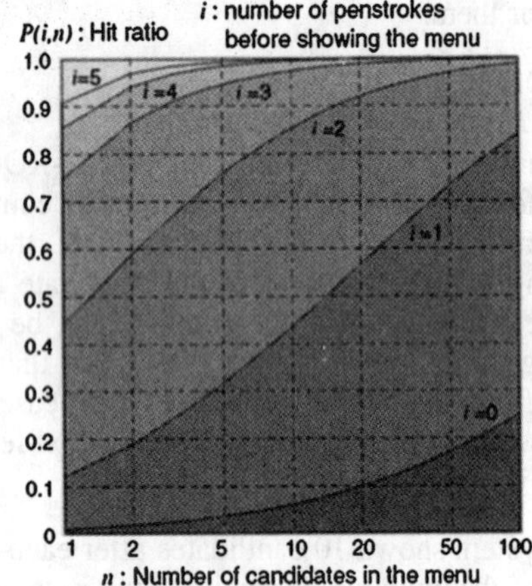

Figure 24: Probability of finding the desired word in the menu (Japanese text).

Japanese text input, most of the desired words can be found in the menu after two or three penstrokes, while more than four penstrokes are required using ordinary Kanji-conversion methods.

Dynamic Analysis

More accurate hit ratio of POBox menus can be calculated by simulating the prediction and adaptation mechanisms of POBox with real English text. Figure 25(a) shows the hit ratio calculated by using all the texts in the CHI'95 CD-ROM. The hit ratio with the prediction from context feature is shown in Figure 25(b), and the hit ratio with prediction and dictionary adaptation is shown in Figure 25(c). Prediction from context is effective for increasing the hit ratio, especially when no input is specified for selecting words ($i = 0$). In this case, POBox displays the correct word among its 10 candidates 38% of the time, whereas this number drops to 26% when prediction is not used.

Input Speed Estimation

Text input speed can also be estimated by dynamic analysis if the character input speed using the soft keyboard and the speed of menu selection is known.

From the dynamic analysis shown above, the hit ratio $P(i, n)$ of finding a word in the menus with n items after selecting i characters is known. If it takes T_k for a user to input one character and it takes $T_s(n)$ to select an item from the menu with n items, the average total time for entering a word ($T(i, n)$) can be calculated by the following formula:

$$\begin{aligned} T(i,n) &= T_s(n) \\ &+ (T_k + T_s(n))(1 - P(0,n)) \\ &+ (T_k + T_s(n))(1 - P(1,n)) \\ &+ \dots \\ &= T_s(n) + \textstyle\sum_{j=0}^{\infty}(T_k + T_s(n))(1 - P(j,n)) \end{aligned}$$

If the user starts using the menu after entering at least i characters, the average total time $T(i)$ is calculated by the following formula:

$$T(i,n) = i \cdot T_k + T_s(n) + \sum_{j=i}^{\infty}(T_k + T_s(n))(1 - P(j,n))$$

We assume that $T_s(n)$ is proportional to n and T_k is a constant value, since POBox shows a menu of candidates according to the probability of the words, and the user cannot tell the ordering of the words in the menu beforehand. We calculated $T(i, n)$ using $P(i, n)$ for the two cases of slow and fast character input.

Slow Character Input: Figure 26 shows the calculated average time for entering a word where character input speed is slow and $T_s(n)$ can be estimated to be $n/10$ and T_k is the constant 1. In this case, without prediction, the minimum text input time is obtained when $i = 1$ and $n = 3$, which means using a three-entry menu after one penstroke without a menu. With prediction, the input time is minimized when $i = 0$ and $n = 3$, which means using a three-entry menu from the start. This is because frequently-used words are displayed at the top of the menu even before the user specifies characters for filtering the dictionary. The estimated average time for entering words is smaller with prediction than without prediction.

Faster Character Input: Figure 27 shows the average time for entering a word, where character input speed is faster than the previous example and $T_s(n)$ is estimated to be $n/3$. In this case, minimum input time is obtained when $i = 0$ and $n = 1$, which means predicting one word every time after entering a character.

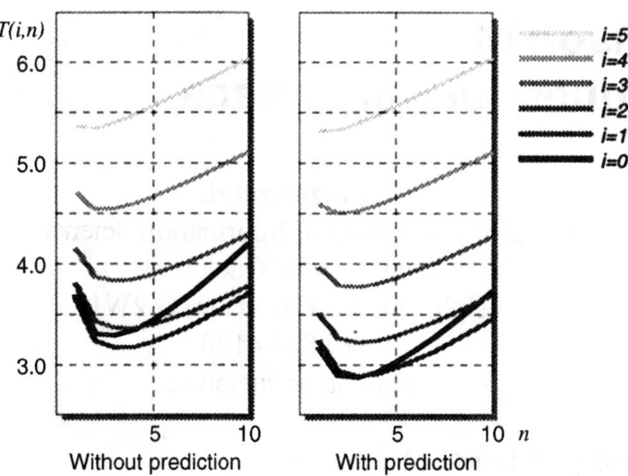

Figure 26: Text input speed estimation with slow character input. ($T_k = 1, T_s(n) = n/10$)

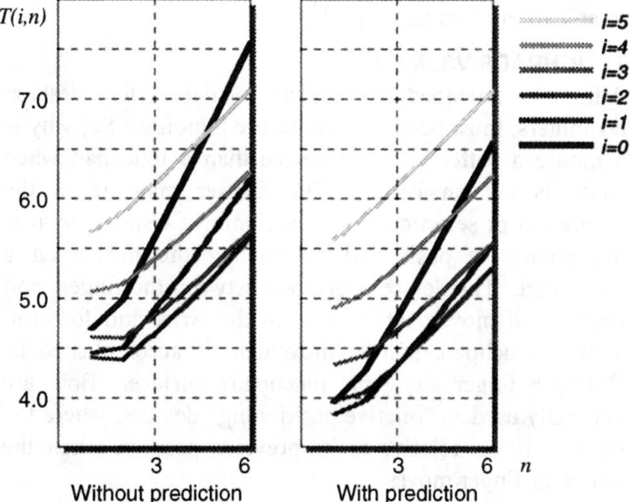

Figure 27: Text input speed estimation with faster character input. ($T_k = 1, T_s(n) = n/3$)

In this manner, the fastest method for entering text depends on the relation between $T_k/T_s(n)$ and $P(i,n)$. Roughly speaking, when $T_k/T_s(n)$ is very small (character input is very fast) as with a keyboard, the fastest way of entering text is entering characters without the use of menus. On the other hand, if $T_k/T_s(n)$ is very large (character input is very slow), using menus with many entries is faster. The two cases shown in Figure 26 and Figure 27 are between these extremes, and POBox supports the entire spectrum.

Related Work

Darragh's Reactive Keyboard[2] predicts the user's next keystrokes from the statistical information gathered by the user's previous actions and shows the predicted data for the selection. Unfortunately, the Reactive Keyboard is not usually useful for experienced computer users, since they can type much faster than selecting candidates from the menu. On pen-based computers, however, people cannot enter characters as fast as with keyboards, thus predictive methods like POBox and the Reactive Keyboard are useful. By integrating existing common GUI tools with the prediction mechanism, POBox can greatly reduce the time for text input on pen-based computers, especially for Japanese and other languages where direct text input is not possible.

Greenberg[5] argued that it is convenient to put frequently used tools close at hand, and showed that this technique is useful for issuing text commands in his WORKBENCH system. POBox resembles the WORKBENCH system in that both frequently used words and recently used words always appear close at hand at the top of the candidate list for quick selection.

Fukushima et al.[3] showed that input word prediction can reduce the search space and the number of penstrokes for handwriting recognition of Japanese texts. Although they reported that their prediction system could reduce input penstrokes from 10 to 40 percent, problems with handwriting recognition still remain and the text input speed does not increase dramatically.

CONCLUSIONS

We developed a new fast text input method for pen-based computers based on dynamic query of the dictionary and word prediction from context. With our method, the speed of text input on pen-based computers greatly increases and for the first time, pen computing becomes a viable alternative to keyboard-based input methods.

ACKNOWLEDGEMENTS

We would like to thank Jun Rekimoto and Jeremy Cooperstock for giving us many valuable suggestions. We also thank many POBox users who actually used it, sent comments to us, and performed the evaluation tests.

REFERENCES

1. Baeza-Yates, R. A., and Gonnet, G. H. A new approach to text searching. *Communications of the ACM 35*, 10 (October 1992), 74–82.

2. Darragh, J. J., Witten, I. H., and James, M. L. The Reactive Keyboard: A predictive typing aid. *IEEE Computer 23*, 11 (November 1990), 41–49.

3. Fukushima, T., and Yamada, H. A predictive pen-based Japanese text input method and its evaluation. *Transactions of Information Processing Society of Japan 37*, 1 (January 1996), 23–30. in Japanese.

4. Goldberg, D., and Richardson, C. Touch-typing with a stylus. In *Proceedings of ACM INTERCHI'93 Conference on Human Factors in Computing Systems (CHI'93)* (April 1993), Addison-Wesley, pp. 80–87.

5. Greenberg, S. *The Computer User as Toolsmith.* Cambridge Series on Human-Computer Interaction. Cambridge University Press, March 1993.

6. Venolia, D., and Neiberg, F. T-Cube: A fast, self-disclosing pen-based alphabet. In *Proceedings of the ACM Conference on Human Factors in Computing Systems (CHI'94)* (April 1994), Addison-Wesley, pp. 265–270.

7. Wu, S., and Manber, U. Agrep - a fast approximate pattern-matching tool. In *Proceedings of USENIX Technical Conference* (San Francisco, CA, January 1992), pp. 153–162.

A Comparison of Three Selection Techniques for Touchpads

I. Scott MacKenzie
Dept. of Computing & Information Science
University of Guelph
Guelph, Ontario Canada N1G 2W1
+1 519 824 4120 x8268
smackenzie@acm.org

Aleks Oniszczak
Dept. of Computing & Information Science
University of Guelph
Guelph, Ontario Canada N1G 2W1
+1 519 824 4120
aoniszcz@uoguelph.ca

ABSTRACT

Three methods of implementing the select operation on touchpads were compared. Two conventional methods — using a physical button and using "lift-and-tap" — were compared with a new method using finger pressure with tactile feedback. The latter employs a pressure-sensing touchpad with a built-in relay. The relay is energized by a signal from the device driver when the finger pressure on the pad surface exceeds a programmable threshold, and this creates both aural and tactile feedback. The pressure data are also used to signal the action of a button press to the application. In an empirical test with 12 participants, the tactile condition was 20% faster than lift-and-tap and 46% faster than using a button for selection. The result was similar on the ISO-recommended measure known as throughput. Error rates were higher with the tactile condition, however. These we attribute to limitations in the prototype, such as the use of a capacitive-sensing touchpad and poor mechanical design. In a questionnaire, participants indicated a preference for the tactile condition over the button and lift-and-tap conditions.

Keywords

Touchpads, pointing devices, input devices, tactile feedback, Fitts' law

INTRODUCTION

Since notebook computers are usually operated in constrained spaces, mice are generally not used as the systems' pointing device. Until recently, most notebooks included either a trackball or an isometric joystick as a pointing device. Apple was the first company to incorporate a touchpad in a notebook computer, and many other companies have since chosen touchpads over joysticks or trackballs. A touchpad implements the select operation either using physical buttons (as with mice) or using a "lift-and-tap" technique.

This paper presents an empirical evaluation of a new selection technique for touchpads that is based on tactile feedback. The work is a continuation of a design described in an earlier short paper [11].

TOUCHPADS VS. MICE

Although touchpads are also available for desktop computers, most people prefer to use a mouse. So, why is a mouse a better pointing device than a touchpad when space is not an issue? The answer may lie in the separation of selection from positioning. Using a mouse, the pointer is positioned by moving the mouse on a mousepad. The device is gripped between the fingers and thumb and movement occurs via the wrist and forearm. With a touchpad, pointer movement is accomplished by sliding a finger along the touchpad's surface. Both are generally used as "relative positioning" devices, where the pointer moves relative to its previous position when the device or finger moves.

For a mouse, selecting is the act of pressing and releasing a button while the pointer is over an icon or other screen object. Double clicking and dragging are related operations that also require pressing a button. There are two common implementations for selecting with touchpads: (a) using physical buttons, or (b) using lift-and-tap. Both inherit problems we are attempting to correct in our tactile touchpad.

Physical Buttons

Most touchpads include physical buttons that are typically operated with the index finger or thumb. If an index finger is used, the finger must move frequently between the touchpad and the buttons and this impedes performance compared with the same procedure using a mouse. If the thumb is used, then positioning and selecting proceed in concert, as with a mouse; however, the result may be sub-optimal because of interference between the muscle and limb groups engaged. A similar problem has been noted for trackballs [12], wherein high error rates (particularly for dragging tasks) are attributed to the "closeness" of the muscle and limb groups required for the separate acts of positioning and selecting. With a mouse, on the other hand, positioning occurs primarily via the wrist and forearm, while selecting occurs primarily through the fingers. Thus, the limbs and muscle groups are separate for each task and tend not to interfere.

Lift-and-Tap

Because of the problem noted above, most touchpads also support "lift-and-tap" as an alternative to pressing buttons. However, this is perhaps replacing one problem with another. We'll illustrate this by considering the basic transactions with computer pointing devices. According to Buxton's three-state model of graphical input [4], these can be modeled by three states:

State 0 out-of-range (the device/finger is elevated)
State 1 tracking (pointer movement)
State 2 dragging (movement with button depressed)

These are identified in Figure 1, annotated for mouse interaction.

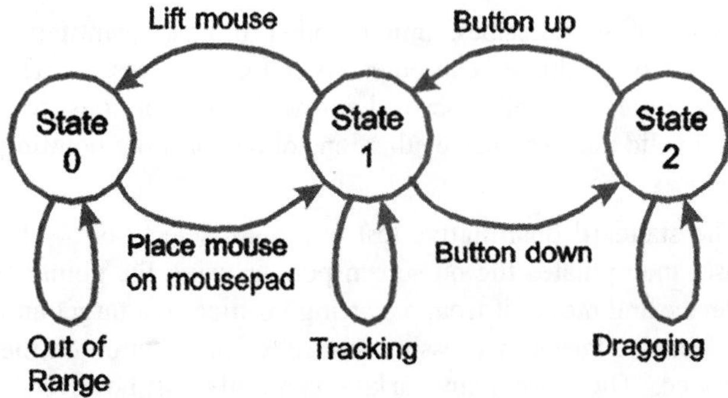

Figure 1. Buxton's three state model of graphical input with labels appropriate for mouse interaction

For touchpads and mice, pointer motion occurs in state 1, the tracking state. The comparison becomes interesting when we consider the state transitions required for clicking, double clicking, dragging, and clutching. (Clutching is the act of lifting the mouse or finger from the mousepad or touch surface and repositioning it.) Figure 2 identifies the state transitions for the most common operations for a mouse and a lift-and-tap touchpad. A few observations follow. In general, operations require more state transitions with a lift-and-tap touchpad than with a mouse. A simple click on a mouse begins and ends in state 1, whereas on a touchpad it begins in state 1 and ends in state 0. To return to pointer positioning (state 1), the finger must resume contact with the pad, and if this occurs too quickly a dragging operation occurs. Note as well that clutching on a lift-and-tap touchpad is confounded with clicking and dragging. This is not the case with a mouse.

Operation	Mouse	Lift-and-tap Touchpad
Pointer Positioning	1	1
Single Click	1-2-1	1-0-1-0
Double Click	1-2-1-2-1	1-0-1-0-1-0
Dragging	1-2	1-0-1-0-1
Clutching	1-0-1	1-0-1

Figure 2. State transitions for common operations using a mouse and a lift-and-tap touchpad.

THE TACTILE TOUCHPAD

In view of the preceding discussion, it is worth exploring alternate, perhaps better, implementations for state transitions. One possibility is to implement them by pressing harder with the pointing/positioning finger. A mouse button provides aural and tactile feedback when it is pressed, and this is an important component of the interaction. Similar feedback may be elicited from a touchpad by means of a mechanical solenoid or relay positioned under the pad and activated with an electrical signal to create a "click" sensation in the fingertip. Since a mouse button clicks both when pressed and when released, the same response is desirable for a tactile touchpad to achieve a more natural feel.

To prevent spurious clicks, the transitions should include hysteresis. That is, the state 1-2 pressure level that maps to the button-down action should be higher than the state 2-1 pressure level that maps to the button-up action. This is illustrated in Figure 3. The correct thresholds must be determined in user tests.

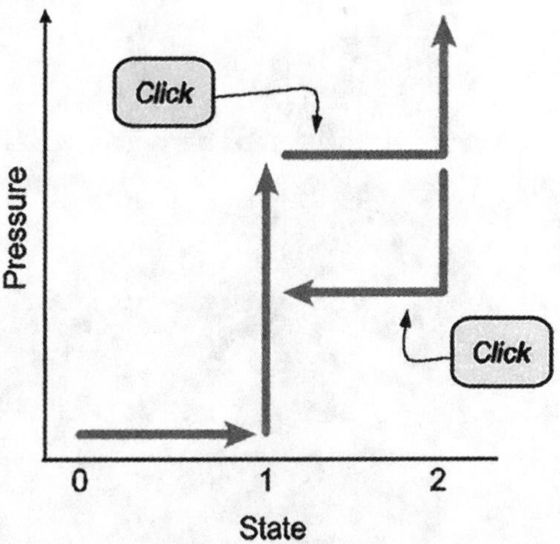

Figure 3. Pressure-state function. A click is generated for state 1-2 transitions and for state 2-1 transitions.

There is prior work on embedding a solenoid under a mouse button to create tactile feedback. A study by

Akamatsu and MacKenzie [1] found significant reductions in movement times for target selection tasks using a modified mouse incorporating tactile feedback as compared to an unmodified mouse. Using a Fitts' law analysis of the data, it was found that the tactile condition produced the highest throughput of all tested conditions. It was surmised that similar results would be achievable with the tactile touchpad. One can provide aural feedback through the computer's existing sound system. However, we feel the combination of spatially-placed aural and tactile feedback at the finger tip is preferable to spatially-displaced audio-only feedback using the system's loudspeaker, although the latter is worthy of investigation.

Our tactile touchpad is illustrated in Figure 4. For our prototype, we cut a hole in the bottom of a Synaptics T1002D capacitive touchpad and installed a Potter & Brumfield T90N1D12-5 relay. A wooden platform attached to base provides space for the relay. The relay is controlled by signals sent from the host's parallel port.

(a)

(b)

Figure 4. The tactile touchpad. (a) top view. (b) bottom view.

The Synaptics touchpad includes an *x-y-z* mode in which the *z*-axis information is the applied pressure. Our software uses *z*-axis information to determine when to energize and de-energize the relay. In informal tests with pilot subjects we determined that, of the 256 pressure levels detected by the touchpad, a value of 140 with a hysteresis value of 5 produced an acceptable response — one similar to the feel of a mouse button.

ISO TESTING OF POINTING DEVICES

Although there is an abundance of published evaluations of pointing devices in the disciplines of human-computer interaction and human factors, the methodologies tend to be ad hoc, and this greatly diminishes our ability to interpret the results or to undertake between-study comparisons. Fortunately, there is an emerging ISO standard that addresses this particular problem [8]. The full standard is ISO 9241, "Ergonomic design for office work with visual display terminals (VDTs)". The standard is in seventeen parts, and some have received approval as a DIS (draft international standard). Part 9 of the standard is called "Requirements for non-keyboard input devices". As of this writing it is in the CD (committee draft) stage.

ISO 9241-9 describes, among other things, quantitative tests to evaluate computer pointing devices. The procedures are well described and will allow for consistent and valid performance evaluations of one or more pointing devices.

The standard quantitative test is a point-select task. The user manipulates the on-screen pointer using the pointing device and moves it from a starting position to a target and selects the target by pressing and releasing a button on the device. There are many variations on this test; however, a simple reciprocal selection task is easiest to implement and allows for a large quantity of empirical data to be gathered quickly. The task is "reciprocal" because the user moves the pointer back and forth between targets, alternately selecting the targets. The selections are "blocked" with multiple selections per task condition.

As the point-select task is carried out, the test software gathers low-level data on the speed and accuracy of the user's actions. The following three dependent measures form the basis of the subsequent quantitative evaluation:

Movement Time. Movement time (*MT*), or task completion time, is the mean time in seconds or milliseconds for each trial in a block of trials. Since the end of one trial is the beginning of the next, the movement time is simply the total time for a block of trials divided by the number of trials in the block.

Error Rate. Error rate (*ER*) is the percentage of targets selected while the pointer is outside the target.

Throughput. Throughput (*TP*) is a composite measure, in "bits per second", based on both the speed and accuracy of performance. The measure was introduced in 1954 by Paul Fitts [5], and it has been widely used in human factors and experimental psychology ever since.[1] See [16] [9] for extensive reviews.

Throughput, as specified in the ISO draft standard, is calculated as follows:

$$Troughput = \frac{ID_e}{MT} \tag{1}$$

where

$$ID_e = \log_2\left(\frac{D}{W_e}+1\right) \tag{2}$$

The term ID_e is the effective index of difficulty, and carries the unit "bits". It is calculated from D, the distance to the target, and W_e, the effective width of the target.

The term MT is the movement time to complete the task, and carries the unit "seconds". Thus, throughput carries the unit "bits per second", or just "bps".

The use of the "effective" width (W_e) is important. W_e is the width of the distribution of selection coordinates computed over a block of trials. Specifically,

$$W_e = 4.133 \times SD_x \tag{3}$$

where SD_x is the standard deviation in the selection coordinates measured along the axis of approach to the target. This implies that W_e reflects the spatial variability or accuracy that occurred in the block of trials. As a result, throughput is a measure of both the speed and the accuracy of the user's performance. In some sense, throughput reflects the overall efficiency with which the user was able to accomplish the task given the constraints of the device or other aspects of the interface.

It is important to test the device on difficult tasks as well as easy tasks; so, multiple blocks of trials are used, each with a different target distance and/or target size.

METHOD

Participants

Twelve participants (5 male, 7 female) were used in the study. All participants were right handed, and all used computers with graphical user interfaces on a daily basis. Two participants had prior experience with touchpads.

Apparatus

A 166 MHz Pentium-class system with a 17" color monitor was used. The *Ctmouse* mouse driver for DOS, version 1.2, was used for all but the tactile touchpad condition. For the latter, a custom driver was written to implement the special features of the tactile condition.

[1] Fitts used the term "index of performance" instead of throughput. The term "bandwidth" is also used.

The experiment used custom software known as the *Generalized Fitts' Law Model Builder* [15]. The software executes under DOS and interacts with the system's pointing device through the installed mouse driver.

All three selection techniques used the same device, a modified Synaptics T1002D touchpad, as described earlier. Standard features of the touchpad include two physical buttons and a lift-and-tap button emulation in firmware.

For each block of trials the experimental software presented a new target condition. Two rectangles of width W separated by distance D appeared. A crosshair pointer appeared in the left rectangle and a red X appeared in the opposite rectangle denoting it as the current target (see Figure 5.)

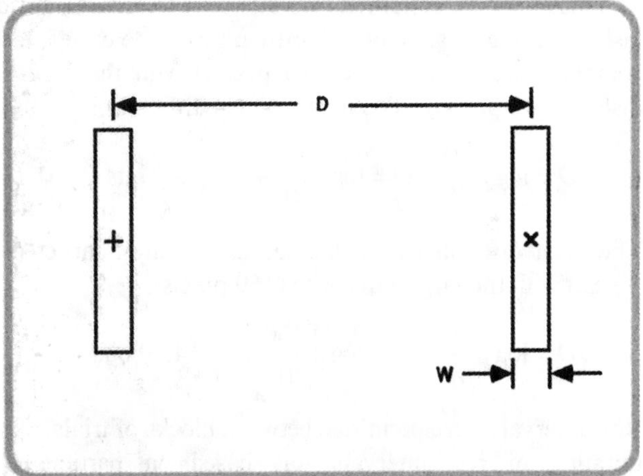

Figure 5. Experimental condition.

Procedure

Participants were instructed to move the pointer by moving their index finger on the touchpad surface. Specifically, they were instructed to move the pointer as quickly and accurately as possible from side to side alternately selecting the target using the current selection technique.

As each target was selected the red X disappeared and reappeared in the opposite rectangle. This helped synchronize participants though a block of trials. If a select operation occurred while the pointer was outside the target, a beep was heard to signal an error. Participants were instructed to continue without trying to correct errors. For each task condition, participants performed 20 selections.

Before gathering data, the task and the selection technique were explained and demonstrated to the participants. Participants were given a block of warm-up trials prior to data collection.

Design

The experiment was a 3 × 3 × 3 × 3 × 20 within subjects design. The independent variables were as follows:

Selection Technique	button, lift-and-tap, tactile
Block	1, 2, 3
Target Distance	40, 80, 160 pixels
Target Width	10, 20, 40 pixels
Trial	1, 2, 3 ... 20

The conditions above combined with 12 participants represent a total of 19,440 trials. To minimize skill transfer, the presentation of the selection techniques was counter balanced. The target distance/size conditions were blocked. Each block consisted of nine distance/size combinations presented in random order. For each condition, participants performed 20 trials in succession.

The distance/size conditions were chosen to create a set of tasks covering a range of task difficulties. The easiest task combines the largest target (40 pixels) with the shortest distance (40 pixels). The index of task difficulty is

$$ID = \log_2\left(\frac{D}{W}+1\right) = \log_2\left(\frac{40}{40}+1\right) = 1.00 \text{ bits} \qquad (4)$$

The most difficult task combines the smallest target (10 pixels) with the largest distance (160 pixels):

$$ID = \log_2\left(\frac{D}{W}+1\right) = \log_2\left(\frac{160}{10}+1\right) = 4.09 \text{ bits} \qquad (5)$$

Rest intervals were permitted between blocks of trials. The duration of rest intervals was based on participants' discretion. All three selection techniques were tested in a single session lasting about an hour. At the end, participants were given a brief questionnaire on their impressions of the three selection techniques.

RESULTS AND DISCUSSION

Since the experiment employed a within-subjects design, a Latin Square was used to balance potential learning effects. However, there remained the possibility of asymmetrical skill transfer [14] from one selection technique to the next based on the order of presentation. This was tested for and was found not to have occurred, as the effect for order of presentation was not statistically significant on all three dependent measures (movement time, error rate, throughput, $F_{2,9} < 1$).

The grand means on the three primary dependent measures were 1641 ms for movement time, 6.6% for error rate, and 1.17 bps for throughput. The interaction technique and block effects on these measures are reported in the following sections.

Speed and Accuracy

The tactile selection technique had the lowest movement time per trial at 1345 ms. The other conditions were slower by 20% for lift-and-tap (1611 ms) and by 46% using the physical button (1967 ms). These differences were statistically significant ($F_{2,18} = 47.6, p < .0001$).

Exactly the opposite ranking was observed on error rates, however. Using a button for the select operation, the error rate was 4.1%. It was 1.4× higher using lift-and-tap (5.8%) and 2.4× higher using the tactile condition (9.9%). However, these differences were not statistically significant ($F_{2,18} = 2.27, p > .05$).

The results for speed and accuracy are shown in Figure 6. Overall performance is better toward to bottom-left of the figure.

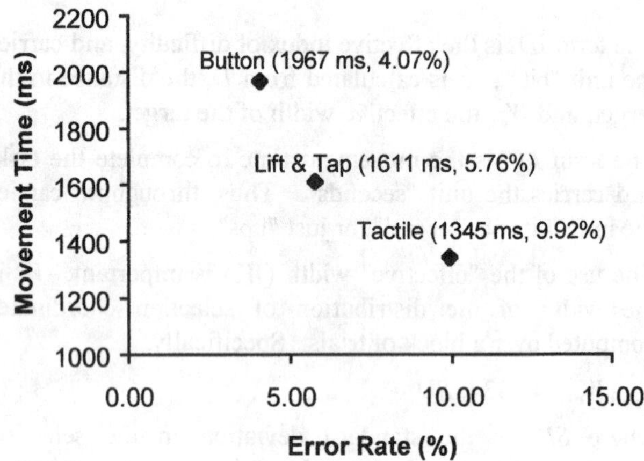

Figure 6. Results for speed and accuracy

Throughput

A strong analysis of the effect of selection technique is obtained by the dependent measure throughput, because it reflects both the speed and accuracy of performance and because it is the measure recommended in the ISO draft standard, 9241-9. The highest throughput was observed in the tactile condition at 1.43 bps. The other conditions exhibited lower throughputs by 25% for lift-and-tap (1.07 bps) and by 31% using a button (0.99 bps). See Figure 7. The differences were statistically significant ($F_{2,18} = 18.0$, $p < .0001$).

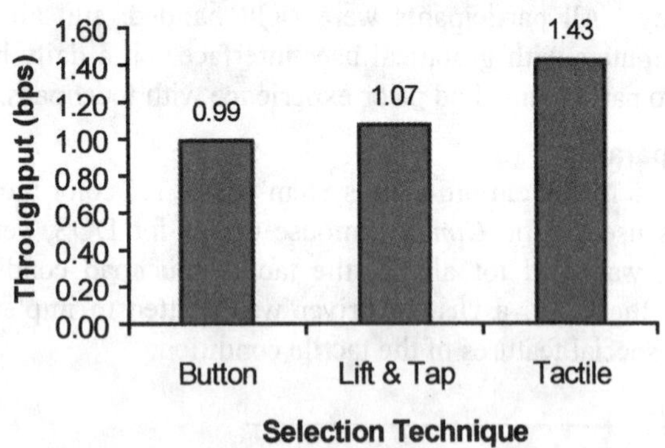

Figure 7. Throughput by selection technique

These measures for throughput are on the low side when compared to other pointing devices. We have conducted other unpublished studies using the same experimental conditions, and have obtained measures in the range of 3.0-4.5 bps for mice and 2.0-3.5 bps for trackballs. Published figures for throughput are also higher, in general. A 1991 study reported 3.3 bps for a Kensington trackball, 4.5 bps for an Apple mouse, and 4.9 bps for a Wacom stylus [12], while a 1993 study found throughput equal to 4.3 bps for the mouse [13]. Rates less than 4 bps are not uncommon, however (e.g., [2, 7, 10, 3, 6]).

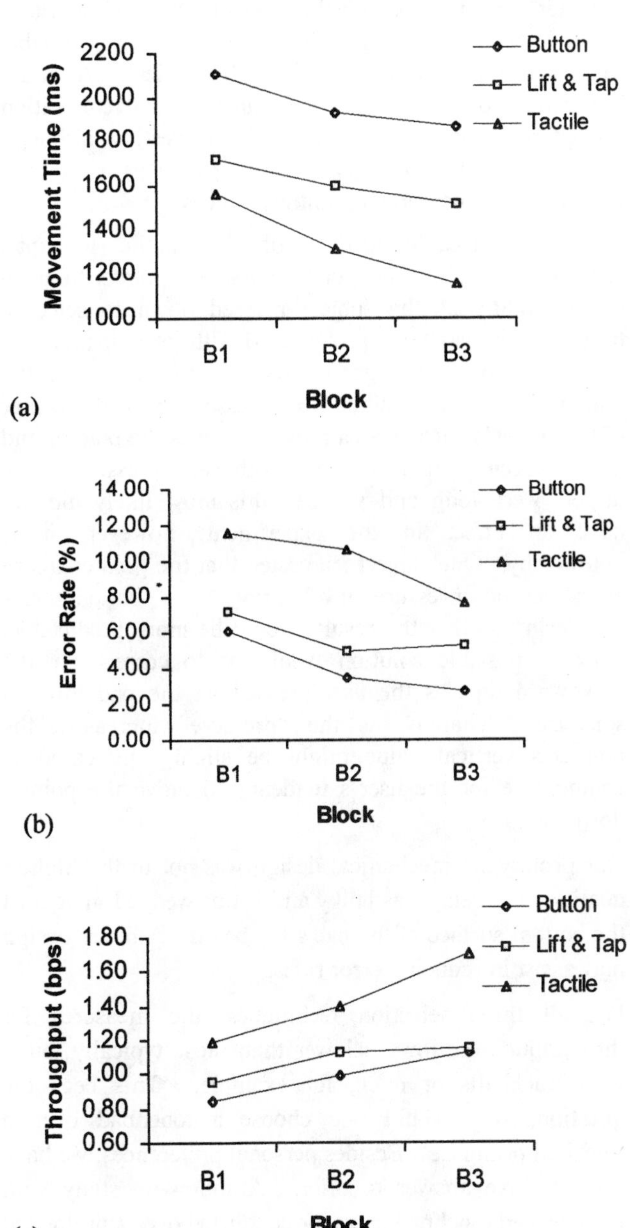

Figure 8. Block by interaction technique for (a) movement time, (b) error rate, and (c) throughput.

Learning Effects

For each selection technique, participants performed three blocks of trials in succession. Each block consisted of 20 trials on each of the nine randomly presented target conditions (180 total trials). It is worthwhile, therefore, to examine the effect of "block" on the three dependent measures, since this reflects the extent to which participants improved with practice. As well, a block × selection technique interaction effect may be present, indicating different learning patterns across devices.

The main effect of block was statistically significant for movement time and throughput, but not for error rate. The reverse pattern emerged for the block × selection technique interaction, which was significant for error rate, but not for movement time or throughput. These patterns are best illustrated through figures (see Figure 8).

The pattern in all three parts of Figure 8 looks favorable for the tactile selection condition. The improvement in performance is clearly seen in each figure, and it is most dramatic from block 2 to block 3 (although the block × interaction technique effect was not statistically significant). With continued practice, the tactile condition is likely to improve. On error rate — the only measure on which the tactile condition faired poorly — it might even "catch up", although this could only be determined in a prolonged study.

Outliers

Since the error rates were somewhat high, we decided to investigate further. We identified a category of response called "wrong-side outliers". These are selections that occurred on the wrong side of the display. For example, if the goal was to select the target on one side of the display and the selection occurred before the pointer was halfway to the target, the selection was on the wrong side of the display. This is a gross error. We call these "outliers" because they are outside the normal range of variations expected in participants' behavior. A wrong-side outlier can occur for several reasons, such as double-clicking on a target or inadvertent lifting or pressing with the finger during pointer motion.

Overall, button selection had the fewest wrong-side outliers (178, 2.75%), followed by tactile (245, 3.78%) and lift-and-tap (253, 3.90%). Comparing the percentages with the overall error rates given earlier, we see that wrong-side outliers, formed a significant portion of the overall errors.

The number of wrong-side outliers, by selection technique and block is shown in Figure 9.

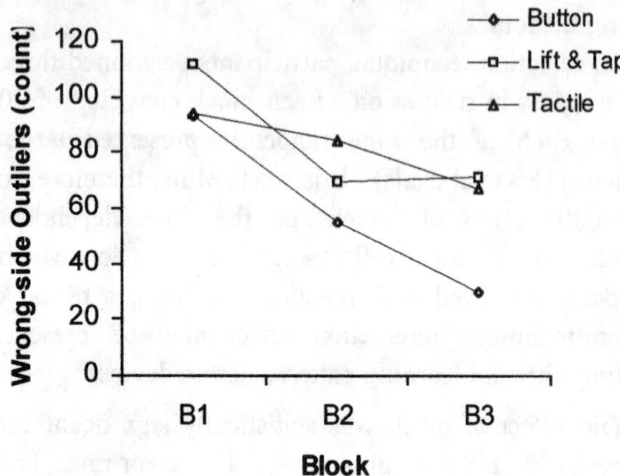

Figure 9. Wrong-side outliers by block and selection technique

The good showing of the button technique is likely due to the clear separation of pointer movement from target selection. Since movement and selection are more integrated with the lift-and-tap and tactile conditions, higher rates for wrong-side outliers are expected.

Questionnaire

At the end of the experiment, participants were given a questionnaire. For each selection technique, they were asked to provide a rating on their speed perception, their accuracy perception, and their overall preference. They entered a score from 1 (slowest, least accurate, liked the least) to 4 (quickest, most accurate, liked the most). The results are shown in Figure 10. Each cell is the total score for twelve participants, with higher scores preferred.

Selection Technique	Speed Perception	Accuracy Perception	Overall Preference
Button	3	15	5
Lift-and-tap	15	13	15
Tactile	19	15	17

Figure 10. Questionnaire results. (Note: Scores are totals of participants' ratings; higher scores are better.)

Participants liked the tactile selection technique. (This was evident in their comments, as well.) Tactile selection ranked 1st for speed perception, 1st (tied) for accuracy perception, and 1st for overall preference. It is noteworthy that on accuracy participants rated the tactile condition equal to, or better than, the other conditions even though it had the highest error rate. This could be due to the higher measures for throughput, which reflect the overall ability of participants to complete their tasks.

The Potential for a Tactile Touchpad

The Synaptics touchpad's method of deriving pressure data is indirect since it senses the capacitance between the finger and the pad. Pressure is derived from the area of the user's finger contacting the surface of the pad. Since one's finger flattens on the pad with increased pressure, the device takes advantage of this correlation. As a consequence, users with small fingers must press harder than users with large fingers. Participants with particularly large fingers required a more delicate touch than they preferred. This may account for the increased error rate of the tactile touchpad condition.

A better version of our touchpad would use true pressure-sensing technology, and such products are now available (e.g., the *VersaPad* by Interlink Electronics). A future replication of this experiment utilizing a calibration procedure at the onset would also be interesting, although this is generally not considered acceptable as a required procedure in commercial pointing devices.

Another noticeable artifact of the tactile touchpad condition was a tendency for the on-screen pointer to move down slightly as the subject pressed down to select a target. This was most pronounced with participants who held their pointing finger relatively perpendicular to the touchpad's surface. When they pressed down, the center of the finger's surface area moved towards the bottom and the onscreen pointer "dipped" with each press. As the targets were long and vertical, this most likely did not have an effect in the experiment; however, it is noteworthy. One subject suggested that the pointer freeze at a certain pressure level prior to a button press registering so that the results would be more predictable. Another possible solution would be to correct for the downward dips as the user pressed on the pad through software. That is, as the "pressure" increased, the pointer's vertical value might be slightly increased to compensate for the user's tendency to move the pointer downwards.

Our prototype's mechanical design was not of the highest quality. The relay was bulky and it was wedged-in against the bottom surface of the pad's PC board. A better design may assist in reducing error rates.

For all three selection techniques, the measures for throughput were low — lower than those typically found with trackballs or mice, for example. This begs the question, why would one choose a touchpad over a trackball or mouse? Besides personal preferences, we have no definitive answer to offer. A follow-up study with experienced touchpad users, or conducted over a prolonged period of time, might shed light on this; it would help answer the question, *can* a touchpad be as good as a other pointing devices (using throughput as the criterion)?

CONCLUSION

Although touchpads are not likely to supplant mice on the desktop, our results have implications for portable computer usage, and further refinements may make the tactile touchpad closer to a mouse in performance.

The tactile touchpad was found superior to both the lift-and-tap mode touchpad and button mode touchpad in terms of movement time and throughput. Although the error rate was higher than with the other touchpad conditions, it was not generally noticed by the participants and the overall flow of information (viz., throughput) was higher even with the increased error rate. With design improvements, the use of embedded tactile feedback in a touchpad can facilitate simple interactions such as pointing and selecting.

ACKNOWLEDGEMENTS

We thank Joe Decker of Synaptics for providing the touchpads and technical documentation for our prototype. Helpful comments and suggestions were provided by members of the Input Research Group at the University of Toronto and the University of Guelph. These are greatly appreciated. This research is funded by NSERC of Canada.

REFERENCES

1. Akamatsu, A., and MacKenzie, I. S. Movement characteristics using a mouse with tactile and force feedback, *International Journal of Human-Computer Studies 45* (1996), 483-493.
2. Balakrishnan, R., and MacKenzie, I. S. Performance differences in the fingers, wrist, and forearm in computer input control, In *Proceedings of the CHI '97 Conference on Human Factors in Computing Systems.* New York: ACM, 1997, pp. 303-310.
3. Boritz, J., Booth, K. S., and Cowan, W. B. Fitts's law studies of directional mouse movement, In *Proceedings of Graphics Interface '91.* Toronto: Canadian Information Processing Society, 1991, pp. 216-223.
4. Buxton, W. A. S. A three-state model of graphical input, In *Proceedings of INTERACT '90.* Amsterdam: Elsevier Science, 1990, pp. 449-456.
5. Fitts, P. M. The information capacity of the human motor system in controlling the amplitude of movement, *Journal of Experimental Psychology 47* (1954), 381-391.
6. Gillan, D. J., Holden, K., Adam, S., Rudisill, M., and Magee, L. How does Fitts' law fit pointing and dragging? In *Proceedings of the CHI '90 Conference on Human Factors in Computing Systems.* New York: ACM, 1990, pp. 227-234.
7. Gillan, D. J., Holden, K., Adams, S., Rudisill, M., and Magee, L. How should Fitts' law be applied to human-computer interaction? *Interacting with Computers 4.3* (1992), 291-313.
8. ISO. *Ergonomic requirements for office work with visual display terminals (VDTs) - Part 9 - Requirements for non-keyboards input devices*, International Organisation for Standardisation, 1997.
9. MacKenzie, I. S. Fitts' law as a research and design tool in human-computer interaction, *Human-Computer Interaction 7* (1992), 91-139.
10. MacKenzie, I. S. Movement time prediction in human-computer interfaces, In *Proceedings of Graphics Interface '92.* Toronto: Canadian Information Processing Society, 1992, pp. 140-150.
11. MacKenzie, I. S., and Oniszczak, A. The tactile touchpad, In *Extended Abstracts of the CHI '97 Conference on Human Factors in Computing Systems.* New York: ACM, 1997, pp. 309-310.
12. MacKenzie, I. S., Sellen, A., and Buxton, W. A comparison of input devices in elemental pointing and dragging tasks, In *Proceedings of the CHI '91 Conference on Human Factors in Computing Systems.* New York: ACM, 1991, pp. 161-166.
13. MacKenzie, I. S., and Ware, C. Lag as a determinant of human performance in interactive systems, In *Proceedings of the INTERCHI '93 Conference on Human Factors in Computing Systems.* New York: ACM, 1993, pp. 488-493.
14. Martin, D. W. *Doing psychology experiments*, 4th ed. (Pacific Grove, CA: Brooks/Cole, 1996).
15. Soukoreff, W., and MacKenzie, I. S. Generalized Fitts' law model builder, In *Companion Proceedings of the CHI '95 Conference on Human Factors in Computing Systems.* New York: ACM, 1995, pp. 113-114.
16. Welford, A. T. *Fundamentals of skill*, (London: Methuen, 1968).

A Multiple Device Approach for Supporting Whiteboard-based Interactions

Jun Rekimoto
Sony Computer Science Laboratory Inc.
3-14-13, Higashi-gotanda, Shinagawa-ku, Tokyo 141 Japan
Phone: +81 3 5448 4380
Fax: +81 3 5448 4273
E-Mail: rekimoto@csl.sony.co.jp
http://www.csl.sony.co.jp/person/rekimoto.html

ABSTRACT
In this paper, we propose a multiple-device approach for supporting informal meetings using a digital whiteboard. Traditional digital whiteboard systems often suffer from a limited capability to enter text and the handling of existing data. The large display surface of the whiteboard also makes traditional GUI design ineffective. Our proposed approach provides a hand-held computer for each participant which serves as a tool palette and data entry palette for the whiteboard. Just as an oil painter effectively uses a palette in his/her hand, this hand-held device offers an easy way to create a new text/stroke object, to select existing data from a network, to select pen attributes, and to control the whiteboard application. This paper also reports our experience with the digital whiteboard systems using a proposed multi-device architecture.

KEYWORDS: Multi-computer user interfaces, Pick-and-Drop, digital whiteboard, Ubiquitous Computing, CSCW

INTRODUCTION

During an informal group meeting or at a small lecture, a whiteboard often serves as the central communication medium. Participants gather in front of the whiteboard, and anyone can quickly scribble some text or a diagram to visualize and share his or her thoughts. Similarly, a computerized whiteboard (also called a digital whiteboard), such as the Xerox LiveBoard system [5], is considered to be an important device for computer supported collaboration.

A digital whiteboard is not just a large computer display. In addition to the actual information drawn on it, the physical actions of participants, such as their pointing gestures, are also important.

Recently, many manufactures have been selling affordable LCD projectors and whiteboard-sized tablets. By combining these devices, one might be able to configure an affordable pen-sensitive whiteboard-sized display. However, without a proper understanding of whiteboard activities, such a system would fail become a usable collaborative medium.

Tivoli [13] was one of the first software systems that focused on supporting collaborative activities on a digital whiteboard. During the design and testing of the Tivoli software, several UI research issues relating to digital whiteboards became apparent. We believe that some of these topics can be addressed by enhancing the software design of the system, however others will probably require changing the physical system configuration.

In this paper, we propose a different way to utilize digital whiteboards more effectively by distributing some of the whiteboard functions to a palm-top computer for each participant (Figure 1). We also provide an easy and direct data transfer method between a palm-top and a whiteboard. This palm-top computer works as a tool palette, a remote commander, a text entry box, as well as a temporary data buffer during whiteboard-based collaboration.

DESIGN PROBLEMS OF EXISTING DIGITAL WHITEBOARDS

In our laboratory, we have installed and used a combination of a WACOM Meeting Staff whiteboard (capable of sensing an electronic pen) and a computer projector, as a digital whiteboard. We also have tried several whiteboard emulation systems, as well as off-the-shelf GUI applications on this configuration. During this trial, we immediately noticed a number of limitations that hamper effective collaborative activities when using a digital whiteboard (some of these are also discussed in [5, 13]). These problems can be summarized as:

Text entry is difficult.

During normal whiteboard-based discussions, we frequently write on the board with a marking pen. However, this fundamental activity is not well supported by a digital whiteboard. With the limited precision and tracking rate of current digital whiteboards, writing text using an electronic pointing device is not as successful as on a conventional whiteboard. The resulting pen strokes and characters are often shaky and hard

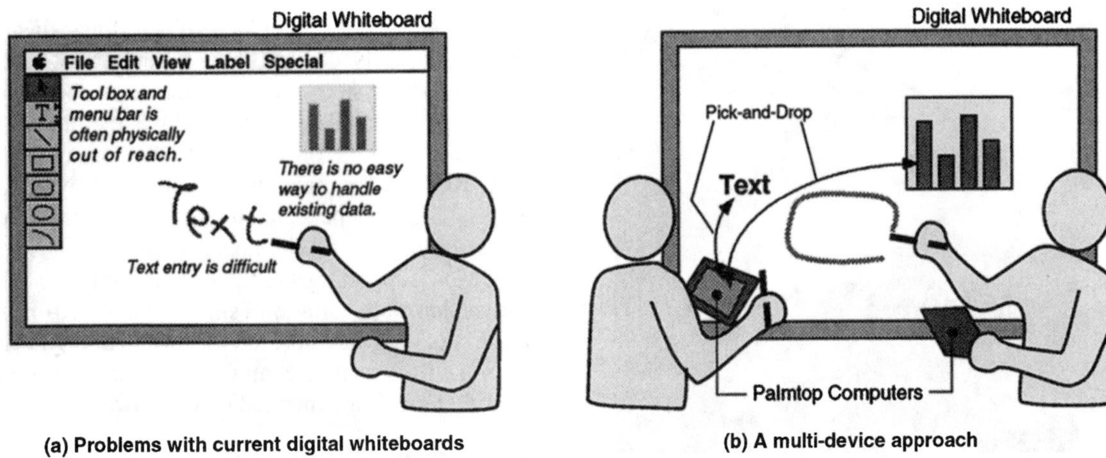

(a) Problems with current digital whiteboards

(b) A multi-device approach

Figure 1: The basic difference between traditional and multi-device approaches to whiteboard user interfaces

to read, not only for a computer (i.e., handwritten recognition software), but also for humans (Figure 2). For this reason, some users hesitate to write characters on a digital whiteboard, preferring to draw very rough diagrams or strokes instead.

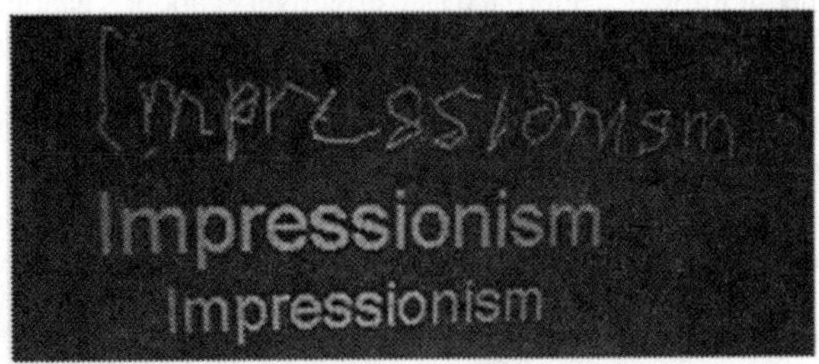

Figure 2: Handwritten text vs. printed fonts on a digital whiteboard

Some digital whiteboard systems provide a keyboard located just below the whiteboard (e.g., Xerox LiveBoard), but this layout causes other problems. Only one user can enter text at a time, and doing so requires an unnatural posture. Furthermore, users must also specify the text insertion point on the display using some other method.

One may argue that it is not necessary to provide computer-recognizable characters during an informal meeting; handwritten characters are enough. However, this limitation kills the great potential of computerized whiteboards. If participants can easily enter digits on a spreadsheet, for example, they can take advantage of capabilities offered by computerized whiteboards that are unavailable on physical (non-computer) ones. Recognized characters are far easier to move, copy, erase or search than unrecognized strokes. Recognized texts are also valuable for retrieving information from meeting logs.

Handling of existing data is also problematic.
During whiteboard sessions, participants often need to search for and display existing information from their private online storage, or from public information services such as the World Wide Web (WWW). However, it is quite irritating and disturbing to the flow of the discussion to wait for one participant to retrieve some desired information while monopolizing the surface of the whiteboard.

Large display size makes current GUI design ineffective.
Using a large screen size can be of itself a problem. Many applications designed for desktop-size displays normally have a menu bar at the top and toolbar(s) at the top or left of the window. As Buxton humorously observed in his talk at CHI'97, this layout causes an out-of-reach problem when used on a wall-sized display. One may have to jump up or walk toward the toolbox or menu bar position, often by displacing other standing participants.

Interactions with the whiteboard become a bottleneck.
Most existing whiteboard applications are designed to be used by one user at a time. As a result, these applications seldom allow simultaneous multiple selections by two or more users. Pop-up and pull-down menus are similarly limited. These single-threaded features prohibit parallel activities among collaborators (e.g., two users entering text segments on different portions of the whiteboard). Given this bottleneck, participants must wait for one user to finish a specific activity. However, this constraint is often violated by mistake. For example, if one participant issues a copy command without waiting for the completion of the other participant's copy-and-paste operation, confusion may result.

A MULTI-DEVICE APPROACH

After considering the present situation, we concluded that a multi-display configuration can potentially solve many of these problems. Existing digital-whiteboard systems have tried to address every problem by enhancing the design of user interfaces only on a whiteboard. However, we feel that if some of the whiteboard functions were given to the participants via hand-held devices that it would offer a simple, yet powerful solution to the problems discussed above. Like an oil painter effectively using a palette in his/her hand to draw a picture on canvas, our proposed approach provides a

Figure 3: The Pick-and-Drop operation: To transfer data between devices, a user first taps the pen on an object in the first display, then taps again on another display. During this operation, the pen virtually "holds" the data providing an illusion of manipulating digital data as if it were a physical object.

palmtop-sized pen computer (also called a Personal Digital Assistant or PDA) to each participant and allows the user to enter data and manipulate applications on a whiteboard through this PDA. This PDA is used to prepare new text segments, to select existing data, and can be used as a tool palette for controlling the state of the application on the whiteboard.

A participant can use the same pen for manipulating his/her PDA and a whiteboard. For easy data transfer between a PDA and a whiteboard computer, we also developed a direct-manipulation method called *Pick-and-Drop* [14]. Pick-and-Drop is an extended concept of the commonly used drag and drop. With this technique, a user picks up an object on one computer display with a stylus, then drops it on a (possibly different) computer display (Figure 3). For example, a user can select or create text on the user's own PDA and pick-and-drop it at any desired location on the whiteboard. From an implementation point of view, data is transferred through the network, but from the user-interface point of view, this technique allows a user to pick up digital data as if it were a physical object (refer [14] for more detailed description).

This multi-device approach naturally solves many whiteboard-based system problems.

Text Entry

To add a text object to the whiteboard, the user first creates the message on his/her own PDA, then picks it up with the stylus and attaches it at the desired position on the whiteboard. Users can also choose their preferred text input method (e.g., handwritten recognition, soft-keyboard, or simplified stroke input methods such as Unistroke [8] or Graffiti [2]).

This feature might also be more beneficial to Japanese (and perhaps to most of multi-byte language) users, because they normally rely on a dictionary-based input conversion system for text entry (i.e., enter text as an alphabetical-notation, and interactively convert it into Chinese characters using a conversion system). Dictionaries used for input conversion are often highly personalized; people normally register many words to the dictionary to improve conversion accuracy. Keyboard-commands for controlling the input method are also highly dependent on the user's personal preference. Consequently, no single input method can satisfy all users. However, supporting multiple input methods and multiple conversion dictionaries on a single whiteboard display would make situation far more confusing. The multi-device approach solves such a contradiction. Users can simply use their preferred input method on their own PDAs.

This work style also has affinity with brainstorming methodologies such as the KJ-method. With such methods, participants each write their own ideas on small paper cards, and then spread them on a large table for organizing them. Similarly, using a multiple-device approach, people can dynamically create a text segment during discussion and attach it on the whiteboard.

Handling of Existing Data

The multi-device approach also effectively supports handling of existing data. A user can search for data on his/her own PDA, without disturbing other participants' activities. Once the user has found the data, it can be transferred it to the whiteboard using a Pick-and-Drop. Similarly, teachers can prepare lecture notes (a list of texts and graphic elements) on their PDAs, and attach them one-by-one during their lectures.

Separation of Personal and Public Workspaces

It is natural to assume that participants might not want to display every piece of information on the whiteboard. For example, during a lecture or a presentation, a presenter might prefer not to display a slide sorter window on a public screen. The multi-device approach is a natural way of separating such personal workspaces from a public display. A presenter could have a slide list on his/her palmtop, select the next slide on-the-fly, then drop it on the whiteboard screen. Similarly, some interactions that are not directly related to the current discussion, such as browsing a help menu, can be better placed on a personal palmtop device. The user might also be able to have a personal work buffer on a PDA to temporarily store text / graphics elements.

Application Control

Instead of placing tool palettes or menu bars on the whiteboard, Participants would have their own tool palettes on a PDA. For example, a user could select pen color or brush width by clicking on tool icons on the PDA, then draw on the surface of the whiteboard with selected pen attributes. Users would not be bothered by the out-of-reach toolboxes on the whiteboard. Having a personal toolbox would also support multiple pen attribute selection naturally; each participant could select pen attributes independently and the state of all pen attributes would be indicated as highlighted tool icons. If only one set of tool palettes is supplied on a whiteboard, it

Figure 4: A multi-device whiteboard system in action (above: digital drawing in an oil-painter's style, below: collaborative diagram making using pen attributes and text entry palettes)

becomes difficult to display each participant's pen state.

AN EXPERIMENTAL MULTI-DEVICE WHITEBOARD SYSTEM

System Configuration

To realize the proposed multi-device approach described in the previous section, we developed a digital whiteboard system by combining a WACOM Meeting Staff whiteboard, an EPSON ELP-5000 LCD projector, and a PC for controlling both. The Meeting Staff whiteboard can sense the existence and the position of an untethered electromagnetic pen. It also distinguishes up to three different pens. Pen stroke information is sent to the PC through a serial cable, and the PC draws stroke images on the surfaces of the whiteboard through the projector.[1] Note that users can also use normal marking pens on the surface of the whiteboard. Thus, the user can mix digital data with physical (non-electronic) writing/drawing on the same whiteboard.

Each user is also provided with a palm-sized computer called

[1] To relate the two coordinate systems (the whiteboard's and the projector's), a calibration tool has been developed. At the beginning of the session, a user points to four known points on the surface of the whiteboard with his/her pen. This information is then used to correctly convert position information on the whiteboard into the correct position on the projector.

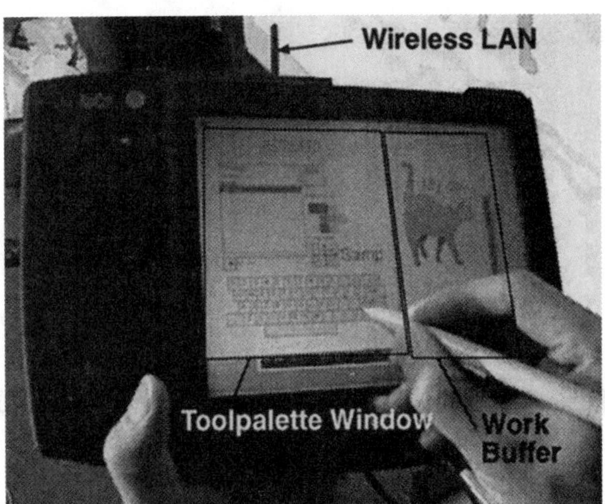

Figure 5: Close-up of M-Pad, a palmtop computer for controlling the digital whiteboard: The window at the left serves as a tool palette, and the window at the right acts as a temporary work buffer. The user can easily transfer information between these windows and the whiteboard by using Pick-and-Drop operations.

the *M-Pad*, which is based on the Mitsubishi AMiTY-SP pen computer, as his/her own tool palette. Since the M-Pad also supports the same pen technology as the whiteboard, the user can manipulate the palm-top computer and the whiteboard with the same pen. The palmtop and whiteboard computers are connected by a spread spectrum wireless network. Users can directly interchange digital objects by using the Pick-and-Drop operation with any participating computer.

M-Draw: A Multi-Device Drawing Tool

Based on the above hardware configuration, we also have developed an experimental multi-device whiteboard tool written in Java called the *M-Draw* (a Multi-device Drawing tool) (Figure 4). The whiteboard part of the M-Draw is simple; there is just a canvas window. With a pen, a user can draw free-form diagrams or handwritten texts on the canvas window, like other ordinary digital/physical whiteboards.

Adding to this basic functionality, users can also use the M-Pad palmtop computer to control the M-Draw application (Figure 5). During operation, the user normally holds this device with his/her non-dominant hand, and use a dominant hand for manipulating a pen.

The window on an M-Pad is split in two. The main window (the left window of Figure 5) is a multi-page tool panel. A user can flip to several tool-palette pages by selecting page tabs on top of the window. Figure 6 shows samples of these tool panels. Using these panels, the user can

- Select pen color, width, and other attributes (dashed-line, etc.) from the pen palette,
- select a prepared diagram element on the picture palette,
- draw a free hand stroke and pick it up on the stroke palette, and
- prepare text segments on the text entry palette.

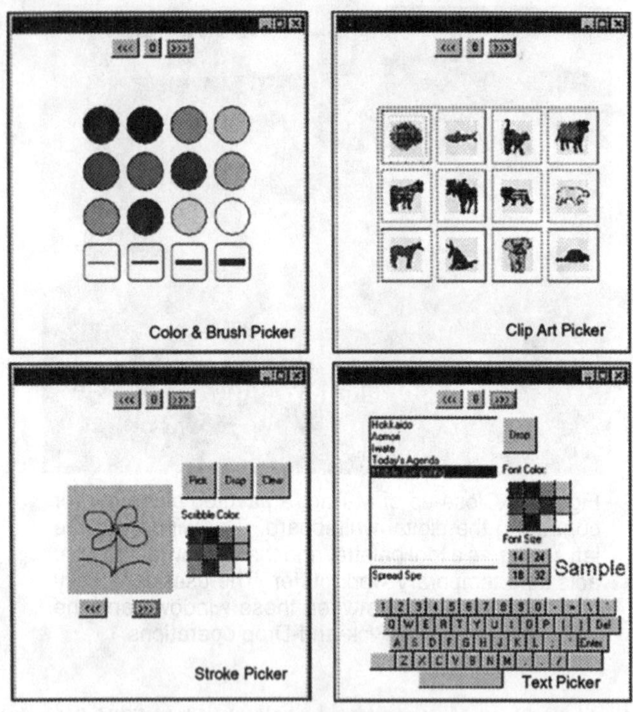

Figure 6: Tool palette examples

Once a user has selected or created a data item on the palmtop computer, he/she can pick it up with the pen and drop it at a desired location on the whiteboard. The user can also change pen attributes by tapping on the pen attribute palette on the M-Pad. This work style is a natural adoption of oil-painting using a (physical) palette.

The other window on the M-Pad (the right window of Figure 5) is a temporary work buffer. A user can store several data elements in this window, and paste it to the whiteboard using a Pick-and-Drop operation.

Early User Study

Using this M-Draw system, the author and other colleagues in the laboratory have experimentally tried several collaborative activities including a group meeting (2 or 3 people attended) and a small-size lecture (one presenter used a whiteboard and others audited). Though the functionality of the system was immature, they appreciated the natural separation of the whiteboard and the palmtop. Figure 7 is a typical user operation sequence during a collaborative session. As shown in this diagram, users effectively utilized the personal (palmtop) and the shared (whiteboard) workspaces.

Most of the users felt the benefit of having printed texts on the whiteboard. These are far easier to read than handwritten characters, and also aesthetically pleasing. M-Pad offers an easy and quick way to make "printed" characters of preferred font size and color. We realized, with surprise, that we have had to use handwritten characters on traditional digital whiteboards, only because there were no other (easier and quicker) ways to write a text.

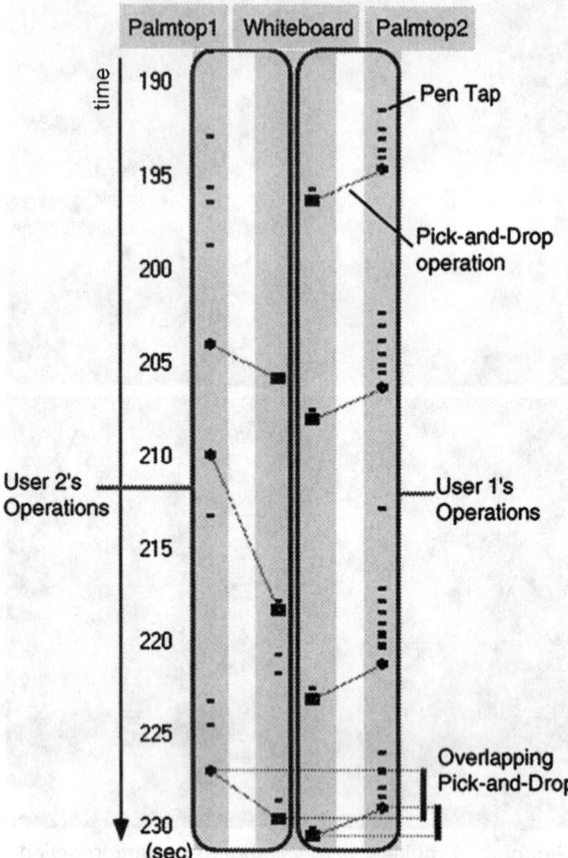

Figure 7: The pattern of pen operations by two participants during a collaborative drawing session

One participant found it effective to use the work buffer on the M-Pad to duplicate data on the whiteboard. He first Picked-and-Dropped it to the work buffer on the M-Pad, then repeatedly used this method to return the information to the whiteboard. To encourage this work style, a copy of the data remains on the M-Pad after the Pick-and-Drop operation. Similarly, after transferring a newly created text from the text entry palette to the whiteboard, the text remains on the item list of the palette; therefore the user can quickly duplicate previously created text items.

It turned out to be quite impressive during the lecture style session to pick up and drop text or diagrams, one-by-one, from a prepared data list on the M-Pad. The lecturer could freely decide which data should be displayed next, according to the flow of his/her talk. The result was a mixture of whiteboard-based lecture style with digital presentation information. Such an effect is not possible using only traditional presentation software.

We did noticed that some of functions should not be placed on a palmtop units. Some design decisions were obvious. For example, if a tool button for flipping a drawing surface is located on a palmtop computer, a participant might surprise other participants by unexpectedly clicking on the flip button. These buttons should be placed on a shared working space.

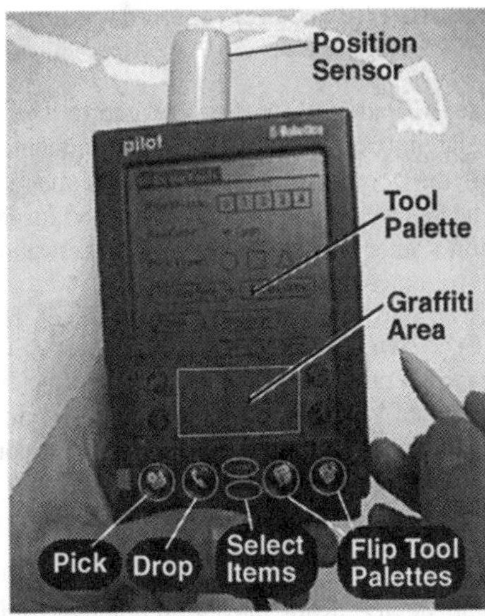

Figure 8: The second generation M-Pad based on PalmPilot

Figure 9: A lecture style session

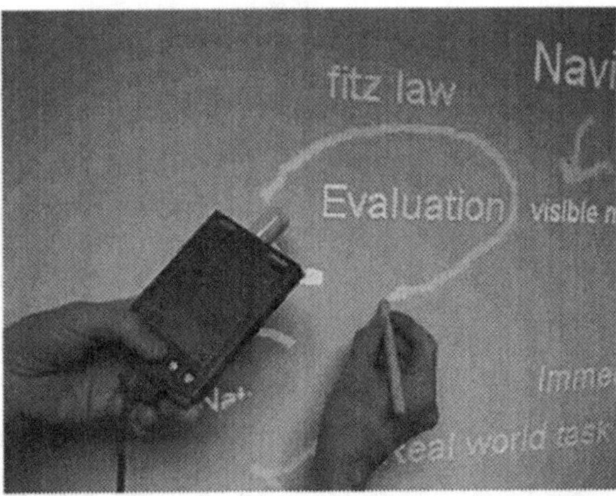

Figure 10: Select-and-Paste: Pasting a selected item on the M-Pad with one hand. Note that the other hand is using a stylus.

Figure 11: M-Pad is used as a physical Toolglass: A user changes text size and color by clicking-through the M-Pad.

Others were not clear. If we put too many functions on the palmtops, users tend to keep concentrating on their own palmtop devices, thus degrading mutual awareness among the participants. We feel that there are many UI design issues when distributing functions among multiple devices, however these are still under investigation and require more detailed user studies.

Some of the users complained about the weight of the palmtop device. The device we are using is an off-the-shelf pen computer and it weights 850g. This weight might not be practical for a long meeting session.

Finally, we also observed that the Pick-and-Drop function within a same whiteboard surface, often worked better than drag-and-drop, particularly when the user had to move data for a long distance (e.g., from corner to corner). Drag-and-drop forces a user to keep the pen-tip in contact with the board during the entire operation, and this feature is not suitable for a large display surface.

The Second Generation System Design

Based on comments from early users, we are currently developing a second-generation M-Pad device. Since the users' main concern was weight, we decided to use a much lighter hand-held unit. Our choice is the 3Com / U.S.Robotics PalmPilot [4] that weights only 160g, less then one fifth of the previous device.

Figure 8 shows the second version of our M-Pad device. Unlike the first version, this palmtop device itself has a position-sensing device, so the location of the device can be measured if the device is close enough to the whiteboard surface. It also has several physical buttons to control the operation. These buttons are used for selecting data, flipping tool palette pages, and making pick or drop operations.

The combination of the light weight device and the physical buttons enables a new usage of the M-Pad, one we call the ''select-and-paste'' technique. Using this new palmtop device, a user can select data and attach it to the whiteboard by using one (normally a non-dominant) hand, leaving other hand free for normal writing or drawing (Figure 10). The user can also create a new text element by using a soft keyboard, or the simplified stroke recognition system (Graffiti [2]) on the palmtop.

One of the tool palette pages can be used to modify the attributes of data items on a whiteboard. That is, the user places a hand-held device near the data item on the whiteboard, then taps one of the attribute buttons (color, font size, etc.) with the pen (Figure 11). It is a physical variation of the click-through GUI technique (e.g., Toolglass [1]).

Although the new version is more practical than the previous PC-based version, especially in terms of the weight, there are some design-tradeoffs between the two. Since the first version is a full-fledged PC, the user was able to retrieve any online data from the network using FTP, a web browser, or any other PC applications. These data can be picked up and attached to the whiteboard. On the other hand, with the new version it is not impossible, but not very practical to operate such complicated GUI applications on such a small-size display. [2]

RELATED WORK

Our work has been influenced by the vision of Ubiquitous Computing (UbiComp) [17], where many computers, jointly working together, can help people and their real world activities. While UbiComp mainly focuses on ''computation in the background'', the topic of this paper concentrates more on designing ''foreground'' interfaces and interaction techniques using multiple computers and devices.

Xerox LiveBoard [5] and its meeting software Tivoli [13] are pioneering research efforts for designing a digital whiteboard and its user interfaces. [13] mentions several differences between traditional desk-top GUIs and desirable UIs for whiteboard systems, which also partly motivated our work. Nakagawa et al. also discusses the user interfaces for the large screen display, and proposed several GUI widgets for such environments [12].

The Spatial Data Management System (SDMS) [3] is a well known multi-modal system that uses hand pointing and voice commands. SDMS is also has a multi-device configuration. Information is displayed on a wall-sized projection display and the operator uses a small touch-sensitive display mounted on the armrest of a chair. Although the user manipulates two different screens to perform a single task, information exchange interfaces between these devices has not be sufficiently studied.

The PARC TAB is a palm sized computer that was developed at Xerox PARC as part of the Ubiquitous Computing project [16]. It is also used in an multi-display environment. For example, the PARC TAB can be used as an tele-pointer for the LiveBoard. However, direct manipulation technique between the PARC TAB and the LiveBoard was not seriously considered.

The use of the M-Pad work buffer is related to the application on The DigitalDesk [18], a computer augmented desk consisting of the combination of a desk, a camera, and a projector. The PaperPaint application developed for the DigitalDesk allows select-and-copy operations between paper and a projected image.

The PDA-ITV system [15] proposes the usage of a PDA as a commander for interactive TV. Although it uses two different displays for one task, the roles of PDA and TV are static; PDA always acts as a commander for the TV. Inter-computer manipulation was not considered. For example, it is not possible to grab information from the TV screen and drop it to the PDA.

Our hand-held device using the PalmPilot has some similarity to the spatially aware palmtop computer called the Chameleon [6]. Chameleon senses its location in a physical space with an attached 3D sensor, and gives appropriate information related to that position. Our PalmPilot version also shows property information on a display object when the palmtop device is close enough to that object.

The idea of blurring virtual and physical spaces is becoming popular recently. The graspable UI [7] introduced a brick, a small physical object that can be attached to a virtual object on the screen. Tangible UI [11] also extends this concept, and coins a term ''phicon'' (PHysical ICON). Our innovation to this area is the introduction of multiple computer user interfaces, and the notion of digital information transfer in a physical world. Using pick-and-drop, the user can pick up digital information as if it were a real object, and transfer it across device boundaries.

Finally, this work is also an extension to our previous research called the Pick-and-Drop [14]. Pick-and-Drop allows information transfer across computer boundaries with a direct manipulation interaction technique. Although our system also uses Pick-and-Drop for data transfer, the focus of this paper is on a user interface for supporting whiteboard-based interactions and not just on general data transfer among computers.

CONCLUSION AND FUTURE DIRECTIONS

In this paper, we have described existing problems with the current digital whiteboard systems and have proposed a solution to them. Our proposed multi-display approach has shown to be a natural separation of personal and public work spaces, and encourages parallel activities during whiteboard-based activities. This approach is also a solution for the design of user interfaces using a large-display surface.

There are several ways to extend our proposed method. Immediate possibilities are to extend our system into a distributed environment such as a shared whiteboard, video conferencing, and connection to the WWW. Since the multi-

[2] The screen resolution of PamlPilot is 160×160 (pixel).

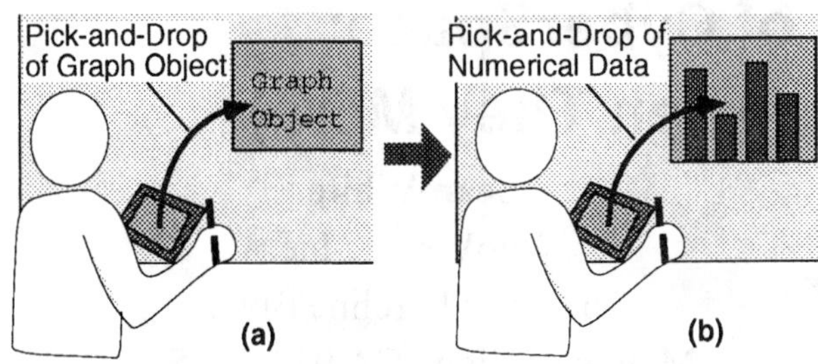

Figure 12: Pick-and-Drop of an active object: The user first attaches a business graph object to the whiteboard (a), then picks-and-drops numerical data on that object (b).

device approach is a fundamental improvement to whiteboard interfaces, it should be possible to combine this technique with other applications such as a meeting support tool or a group decision making tool. In particular, we are interested in combining a multi-device approach with a drawing tool that has interactive beautification capabilities (such as [9]).

Another possible extension is to add a mechanism for handling active objects (such as JavaBeans [10]) to the system. That is, the user can pick up an object from the palmtop device and attach it on the whiteboard. For example, he/she first picks up a business-graph object, drops it on the whiteboard, then he/she can also pick up other numerical data and drop it on the business-graph object (Figure 12). The appearance of the graph object would change according to the dropped data.

ACKNOWLEDGMENTS
We would like to thank Toshiyuki Masui and Jeremy Cooperstock for their helpful discussions and valuable comments on the draft. Nobuyuki Matsushita and Yuji Ayatsuka contributed the photographs in this paper and the video production. We are also in debt to Mario Tokoro and Toshi Doi for their continuing support on our research.

REFERENCES

1. Eric A. Bier, Maureen C. Stone, Ken Pier, William Buxton, and Tony DeRose. Toolglass and Magic Lenses: The see-through interface. In James T. Kajiya, editor, *Computer Graphics (SIGGRAPH '93 Proceedings)*, volume 27, pp. 73-80, August 1993.

2. C. H. Blickenstorfer. Graffiti: Wow! *Pen Computing Magazine*, pp. 30-31, 1995.

3. R. A. Bolt. Put-That-There: voice and gesture at the graphics interface. *ACM SIGGRAPH Comput. Graph.*, Vol. 14, No. 3, pp. 262-270, 1980.

4. 3Com Corporation. PalmPilot home page. http://www.usr.com/palm/, 1997.

5. Scott Elrod, Richard Bruce, Rich Gold, David Goldberg, Frank Halasz, William Janssen, David Lee, Kim McCall, Elin Pedersen, Ken Pier, Jhon Tang, and Brent Welch. LiveBoard: A large interactive display supporting group meetings, presentations and remote collaboration. In *CHI'92 Proceedings*, pp. 599-607, 1992.

6. George W. Fitzmaurice. Situated information spaces and spatially aware palmtop computers. *Communication of the ACM*, Vol. 36, No. 7, pp. 38-49, July 1993.

7. George W. Fitzmaurice, Hiroshi Ishii, and William Buxton. Bricks: laying the foundations for graspable user interfaces. In *CHI'95 Conference*, pp. 442-449, 1995.

8. D. Goldberg and C. Richardson. Touch-typing with a stylus. In *Proc. InterCHI '93*, pp. 80-87. ACM, 1993.

9. Takeo Igarashi, Satoshi Matsuoka, Sachiko Kawachiya, and Hidehiko Tanaka. Interactive beautification: A technique for rapid geometric design. In *Proceedings of UIST'97*, October 1997. to appear.

10. Sun Microsystems Inc. JavaBeans home page. http://java.sun.com/beans/, 1997.

11. Hiroshi Ishii and Brygg Ullmer. Tangible Bits: Towards seamless interfaces between people, bits and atoms. In *CHI'96 Proceedings*, pp. 234-241, 1997.

12. M. Nakagawa, T. Oguni, T. Yoshino, K. Horiba, and S. Sawada. Interactive dynamic whiteboard for educational applications. In *International Conference on Virtual Systems and Multimedia (VSMM) '96*, pp. 479-484, September 1996.

13. Elin R. Pedersen, Kim McCall, Thomas P. Moran, and Frank G. Halasz. Tivoli: An electronic whiteboard for informal workgroup meetings. In *Proc. InterCHI '93*, pp. 80-87. ACM, 1993.

14. Jun Rekimoto. Pick-and-Drop: A Direct Manipulation Technique for Multiple Computer Environments. In *Proceedings of UIST'97*, October 1997. to appear.

15. Stott Robertson, Cathleen Wharton, Catherine Ashworth, and Marita Franzke. Dual device user interface design: PDAs and interactive television. In *CHI'96 Proceedings*, pp. 79-86, 1996.

16. Roy Want, Bill Schilit, Norman Adams, Rich Gold, Karin Petersen, John Ellis, David Goldberg, and Mark Weiser. The PARCTAB ubiquitous computing experiment. Technical Report CSL-95-1, Xerox Palo Alto Research Center, March 1995.

17. Mark Weiser. The computer for the twenty-first century. *Scientific American*, Vol. 265, No. 3, pp. 94-104, 1991.

18. Pierre Wellner. Interacting with paper on the DigitalDesk. *Communication of the ACM*, Vol. 36, No. 7, pp. 87-96, August 1993.

The First Noble Truth of CyberSpace: People are People (Even When They MOO)

Diane J. Schiano
Interval Research Corporation
1801 Page Mill Road
Palo Alto, CA 94304 USA
+1 650 842 6099
schiano@interval.com

Sean White
WhoWhere? Inc.
1675 N. Shoreline Blvd.
Mountain View, CA 94043 USA
+1 650 938 4400
swhite@cs.stanford.edu

ABSTRACT

This paper presents major findings from a large research project designed to carefully characterize what "life in LambdaMOO" (a classic social MUD) is like for many of its members. A "convergent methodologies" approach embracing qualitative and quantitative, subjective and objective procedures was used. A rich, extensive database was produced, from which robust patterns could emerge, be considered in context and assessed with some confidence. Results are discussed in terms of four broad categories of interest: 1) users and use, 2) identity 3) sociality and 4) spatiality. These data should help inform the discourse on, and design of, online communities in the future.

KEYWORDS

Virtual communities, MUDs, social computing, network community, identity, shared space, virtual worlds

INTRODUCTION

Imagine logging in to your network server and reading the following:

```
>You enter the Living Room. It is very bright, open and airy here, with large plate-glass windows looking southward over the pool to the lush gardens beyond. On the north wall, there is a roughly-hewn stonework fireplace. The east and west walls are almost completely covered with large, well-stocked bookcases...
...An entrance in the northwest corner leads to the kitchen...
>You see the Cuckoo Clock, the Cockatoo, the Scrabble Game and a Map of LambdaMOO here...
>DreamWeaver, HardCore & CeLeRY are here...
>DreamWeaver looks your way and smiles warmly.
>DreamWeaver says,"Hi, you new around here? :-)"
```

This is a simulated screenshot illustrating a kind of online interaction that thousands of people experience every day when they log into a social MUD ("Multi-User Domain"). MUDs are a large and growing Internet phenomenon, reflecting one approach to the quest for greater personal connection and community on the Internet. MUDs evolved from early text-based adventure games in the hopes of providing a richer sense of place and "presence" than conversational mechanisms (chat, email) alone can provide [10][11]. MUDs and MOOs ("MUDs, Object-Oriented"), typically still text-based, are shared, persistent, navigable virtual environments in which user-created characters and scriptable objects can interact with one another in surprisingly rich and compelling ways. MUDs now number in the hundreds, with tens of thousands of members world-wide [15]. The screenshot above was derived from LambdaMOO--one of the oldest, largest, and most well-known online communities in use today [4][5]. LambdaMOO is a purely "social"--as opposed to fantasy/adventure (e.g., TrekMUSE) or research/education (e.g., MediaMOO)--MUD [3]. Note how different the kinds of interaction suggested in the screenshot are from anything email or chat lines could easily afford.

CHI 98 Los Angeles CA USA
Copyright 1998 0-89791-975-0/98/ 4..$5.00

A great deal of media attention--and social science research--has been focused on social MUDs recently, and some popular and even provocative claims have emerged. For example, MUD "addiction" (logging in for extremely extended periods of time) is assumed to be a widespread phenomenon [11][15]. Identity--and gender--play with multiple characters (or "morphs") has been portrayed as the primary preoccupation of MUDding, perhaps to the point of promoting a 'post-modern fragmentation of the psychological sense of self' [1][6][14][15]. Others view MUDs as a form of "great good place"[11]--a public, social alternative to home and work of the sort that the sociologist Oldenburg [12] considers essential to community development. Finally, it is commonly held that spatiality, the ability to navigate and explore, gives MUDs an especially compelling sense of place or "presence"[11].

Research reports in which such claims are made can be richly evocative, insightful--and often deeply critical of traditional "objective" psychological research methods [1][3][15]. However, the generality of these claims are difficult to assess, both because they tend to be based primarily on qualitative, anecdotal methods and because of a tendency to use only a small sample of participants, selected either without regard to representativeness or with the explicit intent to highlight diversity rather than giving a sense of what is common to the community as a whole.

In the research project to be described here, our aim was to characterize aspects of "life in LambdaMOO" as experienced by a large proportion of members. We chose to study LambdaMOO in part because much of what's been claimed about social MUDs in general has been based on LambdaMOO (or its direct descendants) in particular. We applied an inclusive, hybrid "convergent methodologies" approach, embracing qualitative and quantitative, subjective and objective methodologies, since each has its strengths as well as weaknesses. A rich, extensive database was created from which robust patterns emerged and could be contextualized and assessed with some confidence. This paper reports major findings (from 3 primary studies) in four broad categories of interest: 1) users and use, 2) identity 3) sociality and 4) spatiality. In each category, we focus on empirical findings which, in providing a close characterization of "life in LambdaMOO" also serve to test some popular "hype-otheses" regarding social MUDding.

METHOD

Participants

All participants were active members of LambdaMOO, a social MUD created and maintained by Pavel Curtis of Xerox PARC since 1990. With over 7,000 members worldwide, it is perhaps the oldest and largest MUDs extant. Access is freely available through a widely publicized telnet address. LambdaMOO has grown rapidly, developing its own social and "cultural" norms [4][5].

Procedures

This was a large, multi-year, multi-study project. The results presented here come from 3 major studies performed primarily in 1994-5, when LambdaMOO provided perhaps the most sophisticated and freely accessible form of online community available. A wide variety of additional methods (with largely converging results) were also used, but space constraints preclude discussing them all in this paper.

Online Survey

For one week, all logins to LambdaMOO were given an invitation to participate in a research survey. MOOers could freely accept, decline or delay participation. Upon acceptance, they entered a "survey room" for uninterrupted survey administration. Approx. 30 questions addressed four categories of interest; various response formats were used. 558 players responded to at least some questions; 515 completed the survey (78% male; 22% female).

Personal Interviews

The survey contained a call for local residents to participate in a follow-up interview conducted by the author. Twelve volunteers (8 male, 4 female) participated in discussions conducted in an unstructured, conversational manner, with questions aimed at evoking a rich sense of each person's experience in LambdaMOO and their views on issues in the categories of interest. Sessions typically lasted 1.5-2 hours, and included a brief map-drawing task. Interviewees' experience estimates ranged between about 1 and 4+ years; mean experience was 19.5 months. Ages ranged from 15-45 yrs; mean age was 26; modal age, 28. Character and user names were changed to protect privacy.

Logging Study

Public status information on character and room objects for the entire system was logged at approximately one minute intervals, 24 hrs/day for approximately two weeks. This procedure allowed precise characterization of "who was where when", including time logged on, user first-connect date, character (morph) count and presenting gender. To protect privacy, no data identifying individual users or the content of interactions were recorded. Two logging studies were conducted over an interval of several months; this report focuses on the data from the second study, which included recording of idle times. Data on over 4,000 users—approximately 6,000 characters (excluding guests), of which 55% were primarily "male-presenting", 34% "female-presenting", 10% other, were taken during a total logging period of 348 hours (25541 time-stamped samples). Data from users seen for less than 10 samples were excluded, leaving a total of 3122 users included in the analysis.

RESULTS & DISCUSSION

The major findings of this project are presented below in terms of the 4 categories of interest: users and use, identity, sociality and spatiality. Statistical analyses of the survey data include chi-square analyses (primarily on forced-choice responses) as well as analyses of variance (ANOVAs). Note that due to rounding errors, not all percentages total to exactly 100%; also, degrees of freedom for error terms vary since not all respondents answered all questions. All results in this project were analyzed for gender and experience effects (and their interactions). For the survey analyses, gender was given by direct report and estimated number of hours in character served as the experience measure. In the logging study, user identities were not known, so we relied on character information to inform the gender and experience analyses. The gender variable used is the modal presenting gender ("MP gender") of all characters of a given user. Since MOOers can specify a wide variety of "genders", MP genders were categorized into 3 groups: primarily "male-presenting" (55%), "female-presenting" (34%) and "other" (neither; many of these were neuter, the default). Experience was estimated by first-connect date for a given user in any character. For ease of analysis and clarity of presentation, experience level was divided into quartiles for the logging study.

In general, for conciseness, only significant effects are reported here; failure to report a gender, experience or interaction effect for any specified analysis implies that it was not statistically significant. Experience effects are reported in terms of an omnibus test over all values of the variable. Results of pairwise comparisons of means are available upon request.

I. User and Use Characteristics

The online survey included several questions on user characteristics. The reported proportion of males (78%) to females (22%) is consistent with previous estimates [4].

	AGE					
GENDER	< 16	16-18	19-21	22-24	25-27	27+
Female	01%	09%	36%	23%	14%	14%
Male	04%	09%	36%	19%	13%	19%
ALL	03%	09%	36%	20%	13%	18%

Table 1: Age and Gender Distribution of Survey Respondents.

Table 1 shows the distribution of survey respondents by reported age and gender. As expected, most members are college age, but the range is fairly wide. Similar distributions are found for males and females.

Respondents were asked to estimate "about how many hours (in total) have you been on LambdaMOO" in terms of five response categories: <=10,10-100,100-500,500-1000 and 1000+ hours. The distribution of experience by gender for each of these categories is given in Table 2. Modal experience level for both genders fell into the 10-100 hr. range, but the median experience level was in the 100-500 hr. category. The fairly high proportion of relatively inexperienced players may reflect increased public awareness due to recent publicity on LambdaMOO. Note that estimated number of hours in character served as the measure of experience for analyses of survey data. While the analyses included all five levels of experience, for clarity of presentation in this paper, data from only the extremes--"novices" (<=10hrs) and "experts" (1000+hrs)--are presented in further tables of results given below.

	EXPERIENCE (HRS IN CHARACTER)				
GENDER	<=10	10-100	100-500	500-1000	1000+
Female	09%	27%	23%	23%	14%
Male	06%	33%	28%	14%	18%
ALL	07%	32%	27%	16%	17%

Table 2: Experience and Gender of Survey Respondents.

Related Experience

To get some idea of the kinds of related experience or skills LambdaMOOers may have, survey respondents were asked to "rate your experience level for each activity" on a 7-pt scale (1="never tried it", 4="intermediate", 7="expert"). Results are shown in Table 3. Overall, the ratings tend to fall in the lower intermediate range; ratings of programming experience are somewhat higher. Significant gender differences in these ratings were found for computer programming ($F(1,513)=62.46$, $p<.001$), video games ($F(1,513)=27.65$, $p<.001$) and "real-life" role-playing games (e.g., "Dungeons & Dragons") ($F(1,513)=23.07$, $p<.001$). Males gave higher ratings than females in each case, but only video games showed a significant (LambdaMOO) experience effect ($F(4,510)= 2.81$, $p<.05$).

RATED (1-7) EXPERTISE:	ALL	FEM	MAL	NOV	EXP
Programming	4.3	3.1	4.6	4.3	4.5
Video Games	3.9	3.1	4.1	3.7	4.2
RPGs	3.6	2.7	3.8	3.4	4.2
Other MUDs	2.9	2.7	2.9	2.8	3.3
Other OLCs	3.5	3.6	3.4	3.6	3.6

Table 3: Rated Experience with Specified Activities.

Two further ratings of special interest include that of experience with "other MUDs" and with "other on-line communities (e.g., chat lines)". The overall ratings are in the low-to-moderate range, with those for other OLCs slightly higher than for MUDs. These results do not support the view that MUDding typically involves simultaneous activity in multiple MUDs [15]. Our interviewees reported some experimentation with other MUDs, but primary involvement in only one at a time. (One exception to this rule experimented with several MUDs and considered himself an established member of two). A significant (LambdaMOO) experience effect was found on ratings of experience with other MUDs ($F(4,510)=2.63$, $p<.05$).

Learning Strategies

LambdaMOO can be fairly intimidating to the uninitiated, at least at first. One survey question asked "which did you rely on *most* for guidance when first learning to use LambdaMOO?". Five forced-choice response alternatives were provided, as shown in Table 4. The pattern of results differed reliably by gender (χ^2 (4, N = 558) = 40.69, $p <$ .001). Males were more likely to have sought online guidance, from written material or an online person. Females focused more on personal guidance, online or "in real life". A significant effect of experience was also found (χ^2 (16, N = 559) = 29.89, $p < .05$); experts tended to have relied on help from an online person followed by online written materials, while this order was reversed for the less experienced. Interview reports suggest that this may in part reflect that the MUD was smaller and more friendly towards (relatively much rarer) newcomers earlier on.

LEARNING STRATEGIES:	ALL	FEM	MAL	NOV	EXP
Online Written	31%	14%	36%	43%	18%
OfflineWritten	03%	00%	04%	00%	06%
Online Person	38%	51%	33%	29%	41%
Real-Life Person	14%	23%	12%	14%	18%
Trial and Error	14%	09%	17%	29%	23%

Table 4: Primary Source of Guidance for Learning

Activities on the MUD

A set of questions asked participants to "estimate the percentage of time" spent in various activities (see Table 5). The largest estimate by far was that for social interaction, where a significant gender effect was found ($F(1,564) = 7.32$, $p <.01$), as might have been expected [13]. Experience was associated with more time socializing ($F(4,560)=6.02$, $p < .001$) and building ($F(4, 561) = 11.77$, $p < .001$) and less time exploring the space ($F(4, 563) = 9.54$, $p < .001$). These results converge well with interview reports.

%TIME ESTIMATES:	ALL	FEM	MAL	NOV	EXP
Social Interaction	59%	66%	57%	41%	66%
Exploring	14%	11%	15%	37%	05%
Building	14%	11%	15%	05%	17%
Gaming	07%	07%	07%	10%	05%
Other	06%	04%	06%	07%	07%

Table 5: Estimates of % of Time in Various Activities.

MUD Addiction?

The logging data provide direct measurements of time spent logged in to LambdaMOO. Figure 1 shows time online in terms of the mean number of hrs/day spent on LambdaMOO by both user experience quartile and MP gender. Overall, users spent a mean of 1.13 hrs/day (or about 8 hrs/week) logged in. Note that this is a very liberal estimate of MUD activity, since it does not take idle time into account. Idle times can be extensive; MUDders commonly report "multitasking"–MUDding while working or performing other tasks. Yet even with this very liberal measure, less than 5% of users were online for over 20 hrs/wk, despite highly publicized suggestions that MUDding for "up to 80 hrs/week may not be uncommon" [15]. A reliable increase with experience ($F(3, 3110)=7.66$, $p<.05$) and experience x MP gender interaction ($F(6, 3110) =1.90$, $p<.05$) were also found. Thus, while many people may spend substantial time in LambdaMOO, and while a small proportion of them may well do so excessively at least some of the time (e.g., during exam periods), the evidence clearly does not support widespread addiction.

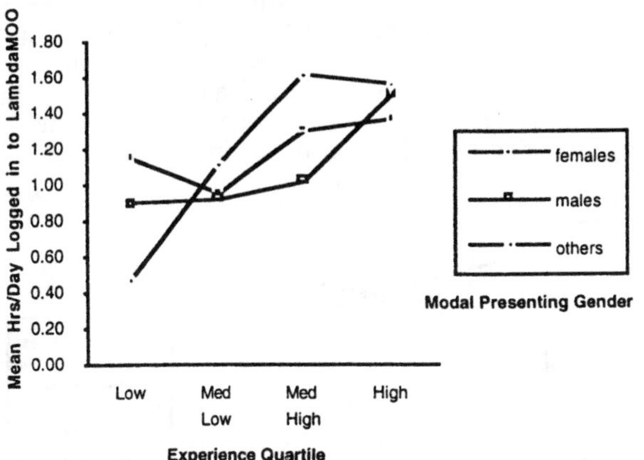

Fig 1: Mean Hrs/Day Logged in to LambdaMOO (Unadjusted for Idle Time)

The picture that emerges here is of a population of users who are mostly male, fairly young, and with some experience programming, playing video games, etc. In general, reported experience with other online communities is moderate, that with other MUDs is slightly lower. Social interaction appears to be the major activity, increasing with experience. Many members may spend several hrs/wk logged on LambdaMOO--which is substantial but not especially surprising for this population. There is little evidence of widespread addiction.

II. Identity

Preferred Mode of Self-Representation

While LambdaMOO is a purely text-based MUD, related systems are being developed incorporating audio, video and/or graphical animation. To explore preferred mode of self-representation, we asked "if you had the choice, which of these alternatives would you choose to use as your self-representation in a system like LambdaMOO?" Results are shown in Table 6. Interestingly, text was most popular overall, followed by animated character; video came in a distant third. Of course, text is the familiar mode for MUDders; a great appreciation for the rich potential of written language was also apparent in the interviews. Males and females showed differing patterns of results here ($\chi^2(3, \underline{N} = 515) = 8.12, p < .05$); females preferred text most by far while males chose text and animation equally. Experienced users preferred text ($\chi^2(16, \underline{N}=559) = 29.89.12, p < .05$).

PREFERRED MODE:	ALL	FEM	MAL	NOV	EXP
Text	42%	50%	38%	29%	47%
Audio	07%	04%	08%	00%	06%
Video	14%	09%	15%	14%	18%
Animation	38%	36%	38%	57%	35%

Table 6: Preferred Mode of Self-Presentation.

A further question asked "in a system where you saw images of the characters, how important would it be for your character to look like you?". Responses were given in terms of ratings on a 7-pt scale (1=not important at all, 4=intermediate, 7=extremley important). Overall, mean ratings were moderately low (3.3); still, females (3.6) gave significantly higher ratings than males (3.1) did ($F(1,513)=5.49$, $p<.05$). The gender differences in the pattern of responses to these two questions are supported by interview reports; taken together, they suggest that while women may be less likely to prefer image-based representations overall, if images are to be used, women may prefer more realistic self-representations.

Identity and Role-Play

Sherry Turkle claimed that "you are who you pretend to be" in the MUD, and that "there is no unitary voice...the self is...multiplied without limit." [14]. We explored the issue of identity and role-play in various ways in this project. In the survey, as shown in Table 7, slightly less than half the respondents answered "yes" to a question asking if "you have more than one character (including morphs)". Thus, overall, a slight majority of respondents report having only 1 character (a significant decrease with experience was found ($\underline{F}(4, 510) = 25.53$, $p < .001$)). In a follow-up question, only those who reported more than one character were asked to give "the total number of characters (including morphs)"; the overall mean for this response was 5. This number appears to be misleadingly high, both from interview reports and from considering the distribution of the data. A small proportion of users gave extremely large numbers in response to this question, driving the mean up.

CHARACTER QUESTIONS:	ALL	FEM	MAL	NOV	EXP
>1 Character?	49%	54%	47%	00%	70%
If >1, Total #	05	04	05	02	06
Role- Playing	2.7	2.5	2.8	2.7	2.6

Table 7: Responses to Queries re. Characters

To some extent, this might reflect honest answers to the "letter" if not the "intent" of the question—one interviewee used an algorithm to randomly vary the capitalization of letter sequences in his main character's name, thus creating a large number of different (or at least differently spelled) morphs. When extreme values (over 20) were excluded from the analysis, the mean decreased to 2. This was also the mode of the distribution. A reliable increase with experience was found ($F(4,249)=3.59$, $p<.001$); the fact that morphs accumulate unless deliberately deleted might have contributed to this effect. Further evidence on character use will be presented with the logging study results.

A final survey question on the topic of identity and role-playing was: "Do you ever feel that you are role-playing your character (rather than 'being yourself')?". A 7-pt response scale was again used (with 1=never, 4=about half the time, 7=always). Responses to this question were fairly low, with an overall mean of 2.7. This finding accords well with interview reports in which most people said they generally "speak with their own voice" or "are themselves" on LambdaMOO; this will be discussed further below.

Every person we interviewed reported having one primary character on LambdaMOO. These tended be slightly distorted, perhaps idealized or fanciful versions of one's view of oneself [4]; most interviewees expressed concern that the description of the primary character should match how they think of themselves. One exception to this rule had a character humorously described as a vegetable but still reported "being himself" in LambdaMOO. Another man made a point of representing himself "as himself" in character, with the one exception of changing his stated gender to female. He said this was initially done almost on a lark, to explore how it would affect his reception by others (the received wisdom is that female characters get "hit on" but also helped more). This was the only interviewee (and one of a very few of anyone we spoke with) who reported a primary character of the opposite sex in the MUD (not including "others"). He reported this to be a fascinating experiment, but began to experience great difficulty as time went on, since he had become known in LambdaMOO and built up friendships in his "female" form and began to fear that these friends would feel betrayed if he ever revealed himself to be male. Yet he also felt increasingly inauthentic in these intimate relationships by not doing so. Almost all our interviewees claimed to not role-play their primary character; our most highly experienced interviewee said "I don't (sic) know hardly anyone... who role-plays."

Secondary morphs appear to serve more as short-term, special-purpose tools or costumes than true alternative identities, often used for comedic effect. For example, a commonly reported, if cruel, "game" played among male newbies is for a more skilled male user to assume a seductive female character and later make embarrassing revelations about his unwitting victim. Of course, role-play is a complex concept that occurs along a continuum; one older woman living in a remote area with little social contact reported having a young, sexy secondary character that she occasionally used to "live a little"; but when asked if she thought of the character as an "alter-ego", she replied "Well, it was supposed to be an attempt at humor...." Interestingly, she also reported that many MUDders refused to take her character seriously since it was so stereotypical; she was often assumed to be male "in real life".

Many interviewees reported that over time, they felt a growing awareness of social pressures to maintain the accountability afforded by a single primary identity. As one person put it, "pseudonymity is not anonymity". The sociologist Goffman [9] argued that long-term social cohesion requires stability of self-presentation (including one's appearance, behavior, home and possessions). In a "real" community, concern for one's reputation exerts strong control over the behavior of the individual. Only in ephemeral, anonymous, low-risk situations are social constraints loosened enough to experiment in role-playing with strangers. To the extent that LambdaMOO provides a "real", persistent sense of community, the social constraints described by Goffman should hold. Interview reports suggest that reputation is indeed the currency of the MUD; in general, programming skill and creativity are highly valued, but observing "MUD manners" and showing a willingness to help others is also important. Character appearance, behavior, home and possessions are used to get an impression of what the player is "really like"; deception can be despised. Moreover, a strong interest in getting to know other MUDders "in real life" was expressed (many interviewees had joined BAM, the "Bay Area MOOers" club). Thus, as in the case of the male interviewee who had posed as a female, over the long term, the price of real intimacy may be authenticity.

While the interaction between identity and sociality cannot be discussed at length here, it should be noted that the issue has been surprisingly neglected by previous researchers. Many have focused instead on the personal, psychological significance of "acting out" behaviors that are risky or difficult "in real life", such as gender-swapping or sexual experimentation [6][14][15]. Ironically, the "social laboratory for experimentation with the constructions and reconstructions of the self" that Sherry Turkle and others see in the MUD may be more characteristic of short-term sociality among strangers ("guests" and "newbies") than among those seeking to become community members--or even just to make real friends in the virtual world.

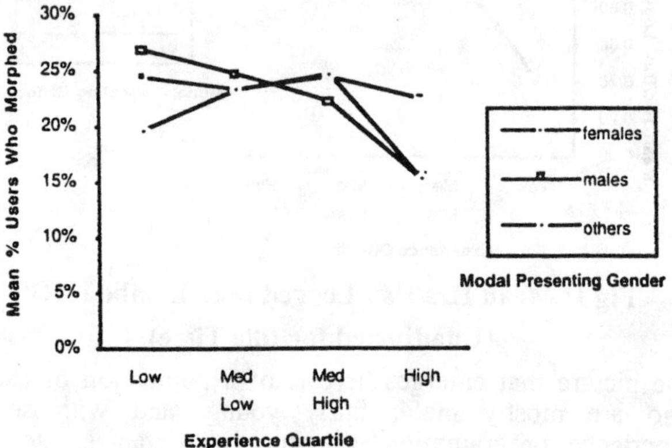

Figure 2: Mean % of Users Changing Character

Identity change

The logging data provide information regarding frequency of identity change, and therefore some sense of relative use of characters. The time-stamped logs show that less than 25% of players *ever* morphed identity–changed character– over the entire 2-week observation period. Of those who did, less than half *ever* changed gender. These data are shown in Figure 2, by experience level and MP gender. A significant effect of experience was found. Users who did morph used a total of 3 characters on average, but the vast majority of their time (mean=81.44%, sd=17.7) was spent in a single "main character". These data are shown in Figure 3; significant (though small) effects of experience ($F(3,689)=2.82$, $p<.05$) and an experience x MP gender interaction ($F(6,689)=2.77$, $p<.05$) were also found.

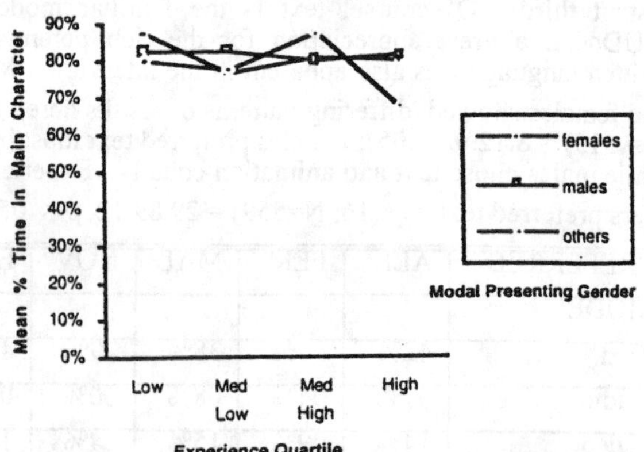

Figure 3: Mean % Time in Main Character (For Morphers)

Taken together, the patterns of results discussed above suggest that while deep explorations of multiple identities may be a major activity for some LambdaMOOers some of the time, this is *not* the primary preoccupation of most members. Indeed, failure to find some identity play (at least over the short term) would be more surprising in a group containing such a large percentage of adolescents under such little social constraint. The strong prevalence of the single primary character converges well with reports of social pressures constraining identity over the long term; further research on the relation between online identity and sociality—especially over time—is clearly needed.

III. Sociality

Sociality was cited as the primary reason for MUDding by all our interviewees. LambdaMOO's peculiar ability to afford a wide range of creative yet constrained forms of social expression and interaction was also widely appreciated. As described above, most survey respondents reported spending most of their time in social interaction; perhaps not surprisingly, estimates were higher overall for females and showed a reliable increase with experience.

A Great Good Place?

Interview and logging data suggest that most 'personal' socializing in LambdaMOO is done in pairs or small groups, typically privately. Figure 4 shows the mean number of active companions (awake users in the same room simultaneously) per user, by experience level and MP gender. Mean number of companions overall was only 1.48; and a reliable decrease with experience ($F(3,31098)=10.16$, $p<.05$) was found. Thus, while sociality seems to play a primary role in "life in LambdaMOO", these results suggest that it may be typically expressed in a more intimate, private form than characterizations of the MUD as a commons or "great good place" [11] would imply. Further evidence is given below.

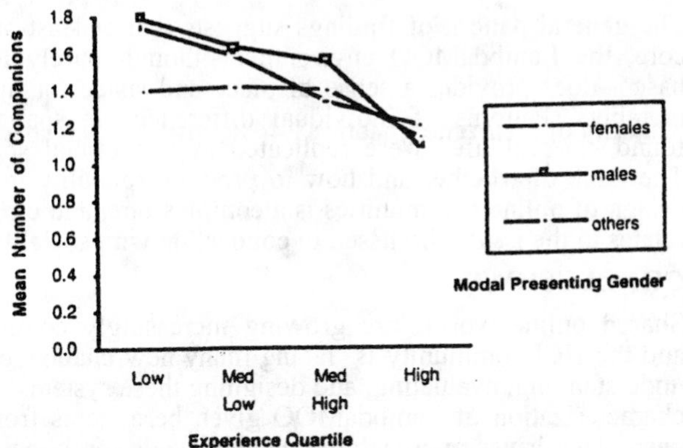

Figure 4: Mean Number of Active Companions per User

In LambdaMOO, location has strong implications regarding who one might be with and the kind of social interaction one might be engaged in. Time-stamped logs show that one place where users spent considerable time was their own private spaces, or "homes." Home-ownership was nearly universal among LambdaMOO members (mean=99%) in the second logging study (up from 78% in the first study, which might reflect an increasing general tendency to build a home immediately upon creating a character to join the MUD). Shared home-ownership, though easy to do, was so extremely rare as to be negligible. Overall, homeowners spent about half (49%) their active time at home. A highly reliable increase in time spent at home was found with increasing experience ($F(3,3062)=40.32$, $p<.0001$), and significant effects of MP gender ($F(2,3062)=3.18$, $p<.05$), and experience x MP gender interaction ($F(6,3062)=2.42$, $p<.05$) were observed. A trend for "females" to spend more time at home than "males" ($F(1,2747)=2.76$, $p=.09$) did not reach significance (although it did in the first logging study, where "females" were also significantly more likely to own a home).

Note that since the home is a separate room, conversations within it are private in that they cannot be simply "overheard" by others. Moreover, security conditions at home are controlled by the homeowner. Most interviewees reported using a security system of some sort to limit access to their homes; otherwise anyone else could, say, teleport in at any time. Security was typically accomplished by simply specifying those who are–or are not--allowed entrance. Interview reports also suggest a resolution to the apparent contradiction of findings which suggest that increased experience is associated both with more time spent socializing and with an increased likelihood to be observed be at home, often alone. Highly experienced interviewees reported commonly communicating from home via "remote channels", paging and MOO-mail. The affordances of staying home include the ability to monitor multiple remote conversations at once--or focus on building a program--while still remaining accessible to friends who might check in. We were told that this is fairly widespread among expert users, and this is at least consistent with the data we have.

When not at home, LambdaMOOers spent a mean of 23% of their time in public rooms (with a strong decrease with experience ($F(3,3098)=14.05$, $p<.0001$) and a trend for "males" to be in public more than other MP genders; in the first logging study, both effects were highly significant). Thus about 77% of their time was spent in private rooms, the vast majority of which are homes (one's own or another's). Interviewees described public spaces primarily as places to meet people, especially initially; many said that most of their "in person" interactions take place with 1 or 2 others, typically in the privacy of someone's home. However, most interviewees also said that they had felt more comfortable in public spaces in earlier times, when the community was much smaller and more closely-knit.

Overall, the pattern of findings strongly suggests that sociality is expressed by LambdaMOO members largely–although not solely--through personal interactions in private circumstances. This tendency may be somewhat greater for females, at least initially, and seems to increase with experience. Our interviewees suggest that most public spaces in LambdaMOO may function more as a way to meet new people or as an occasional diversion than as somewhere to repair to regularly, especially for more experienced members. This pattern converges well with results found in survey data on social patterns among university students [13] who do not report spending a large percentage of free time socializing in "great good places" (also known as "third places", alternatives to the home and work/school place; the British local pub is often cited as a prime example). Of course, as Oldenburg [10] might argue, the creation of such places might well promote greater social cohesion in the community.

LambdaMOO as a whole does not seem to qualify as a "great good place"; the prevalence of small, private, exclusive interactions is especially uncharacteristic. But some features of "great goodness" are found in it: conversation as a primary activity, high accessibility even at "off hours", and a capacity for providing both a playful mood and psychological support [10]. Interview reports suggest that LambdaMOO's "great goodness" may have peaked early on, when it was a quite small community in which it was possible (and comfortable) to regularly repair with your friends to The Living Room or The Hot Tub and feel that on at least some level you knew and were known by many of the people there. The issue of how "great goodness" might be supported on the large scale, perhaps through the creation of neighborhoods with local hangouts of the third kind, is of primary significance for designers of shared virtual worlds [7]. But the data presented here indicate that we should be sure not to neglect the primary importance: private, personal spaces in online communities.

IV. Spatiality

Sense of Place and Space

Does LambdaMOO provide a stronger sense of "place" than other text-based forms of communication can provide? Interviewees uniformly agreed that it does, although speculations as to why differed. Some cited the ability to navigate and interact with objects, others the great visual detail given in descriptions. Several survey questions explored the sense of place and space afforded by LambdaMOO. Respondents were asked to rate how often "you feel like you are 'in another place' when you are on LambdaMOO" on a 7-pt scale (1=never, 4=about half the time, 7=always); results are shown in Table 11. The overall mean fell in the intermediate range; a reliable increase with experience was found ($F(4, 548) = 2.67, p < .05$). Similar results were found for how often "you have a fairly detailed image of that place while you're 'there'." No gender differences were observed in these questions focusing on images and felt experience of place [12].

PLACE & SPACE	ALL	FEM	MAL	NOV	EXP
Another Place	4.5	4.5	4.5	3.9	4.9
Image	4.4	4.4	4.4	3.9	4.5
Mental Map	50%	41%	54%	29%	65%
Custm Nav	45%	36%	47%	14%	65%
Lost	2.8	2.9	2.8	4.2	2.2

Table 11: Survey Results on Place and Space.

But how strong can a spatial metaphor be in a purely text-based realm? Spatiality is a complex and controversial issue in LambdaMOO; to complicate matters, only the public core of LambdaHouse and its environs are now reliably navigable. In recent years, many users have built homes which can only be reached by "teleporting", commands which automatically move characters between locations. Locations can be specified by a room name/number or by a character to "join". Emphasizing the role of the MUD as a social space, interviewees report "joining" as a common mode of transport. The effect of relaxing requirements for spatial navigation is a topic of great controversy among experienced users; many feel that navigation promotes "presence" and even community.

When survey respondents were asked "do you have a 'mental map' of LambdaMOO?", slightly more than half answered "yes". Individual differences in spatial cognition observed in the "real world" were replicated [12]; reliable effects of both gender ($F(1,544) = 5.75, p<.05$) and experience ($F(4,541)=9.79$,$p<.001$) were found. Another question asked "have you customized your navigation in LambdaMOO in any way?". Overall, somewhat less than half of respondents answered "yes" to this question. A gender effect ($F(1,542) = 5.48, p<.05$), and a strong increase with experience ($F(4,539) = 10.32, p<.001$) were found. The experience effects might reflect in part that more experienced members may have joined LambdaMOO when navigability was the rule. A final question asked how often "you ever find yourself 'lost' in LambdaMOO". Overall ratings are fairly low; no reliable gender effect was observed but the decrease with experience was still found ($F(4,540) = 23.85, p < .001$). Perhaps those who navigated less had less opportunity to get lost. Interviewees report navigating little after an initial exploratory stage, yet do still feel they have retained a good sense of the space.

Logged location data recorded "who was where" during the observation period. A related logging analysis assessed the relative extent of "travel" by members of LambdaMOO. The average user was observed in 8.9 different rooms. This differed with MP gender ($F(2,3379) = 17.85, p < .001$) such that "males" traveled most and "others" least, and sharply decreased with experience ($F(3,3379) = 66.73, p < .001$). A significant interaction was also found ($F(6,3379) = 4.76, p < .001$). Since navigation involves passage through intermediate rooms, it is not surprising to find that males traveled more and that experience was associated with decreased travel. These data converge well with many of the findings discussed above. Additional survey questions and the map-drawing task were used to probe the nature of the "mental models" users have of the space. Patterns of errors in spatial memory were complex, and performance was not high overall, but the expected gender and experience effects were generally replicated, as were common spatial framework patterns (e.g., greater accuracy for front/back than left/right) [12].

The general pattern of findings suggests that at least at its core, the LambdaMOO environment--though purely text-based--does provides a sense of place and space for many members. Patterns of individual differences in spatiality found "in real life" were replicated in this virtual space. The issue of whether and how to promote spatiality in the design of online communities is a complex one, and closely relates to the issues discussed in connection with sociality.

CONCLUSIONS

Shared online worlds are growing increasingly common, and the HCI community is facing many new challenges in understanding, evaluating, and designing these systems. The characterization of LambdaMOO given here stems from a deep, data-driven approach that we believe is sorely needed in this field. Many of our results directly address specific issues cited in calls for further research to inform design [8] and because they provide empirical results, can be used as a basis for direct comparisons with alternative systems.

One of our major "lessons from LambdaMOO" with direct implications for design is the strong focus on social interaction, which seems to only increase with experience, even to the point of superseding any interest in navigating the space. As Whyte, an urban planner (cited by Donath [8]), pointed out for designing real spaces, "What attracts people most, in sum, is other people. If I labor the point, it is because many spaces are designed as though the opposite were true and as though what people liked best are the places they stay away from." Our findings suggest that design in virtual spaces should similarly focus on supporting social interaction in order to function effectively. Otherwise, people may well find ways to circumvent design elements in order to foster the social practices in which they are most interested.

In some sense, this project serves as a "case study" of a research program incorporating a synergy of qualitative and quantitative, subjective and objective methodologies in the attempt to understand what "life was like" for most people in a given online community at that time. While causal conclusions must be made with great care, robust patterns of convergent observations derived from this approach can be accepted with some confidence. The general observation that major patterns of behavior in this text-based virtual world do not depart radically from those in "real life", while perhaps not especially surprising, should nonetheless underscore for researchers and designers alike the value of putting one's hypotheses to empirical test. The results also highlight the basic import of a theme pointed out by Randy Farmer in 1992 [8]. Even in cyberspace, people are people.

ACKNOWLEDGMENTS

Many thanks to E. Bewersdorff, H. Colston, P. Curtis, B. Fuson, J.Loftus, S. Mainwaring, M. Millis, and all MOOers.

REFERENCES

1. Allen, C. *Virtual Identities: The Social Construction of Cybered Selves.* Ph.D. Dissertation, Northwestern University, June 1996.
2. American Psychological Association. Ethical principles of psychologists and code of conduct. *American Psychologist, 47,*(1992),1597-1611.
3. Cherny, L. *The MUD register: Conversational modes of action in a text-based virtual reality.* Ph.D. Dissertation, Stanford University, December 1995.
4. Curtis, P. MUDding: Social phenomenon in text-based virtual realities. *Intertrek,* 3(3), (1992), 26-34.
5. Curtis. P. and Nichols, D. *MUDs Grow Up: Social Virtual Reality in the Real World.* Paper presented at the meeting of the Third International Conference on Cyberspace, Austin TX, 1993.
6. Dalaimo, D. M. *The Simulation of Selfhood in Cyberspace.* Unpublished doctoral dissertation, University of Nevada, Las Vegas, 1995.
7. Donath, J. *Inhabiting the virtual city: The design of social environments for electronic communities.* Ph.D. Dissertation, MIT, 1996.
8. Farmer, F. R., *Social Dimensions of Habitat's Citizenry.* 1992.http://www.communities.com/company/papers/citizenry.html
9. Goffman, E. The Presentation of Self in Everyday Life. New York: Doubleday, 1959.
10. Oldenburg, R. *The Great Good Place.* New York: Paragon House, 1991.
11. Rheingold, H. *The Virtual Community: Homesteading on the Electronic Frontier.* New York: Addison-Wesley Publishing, 1993.
12. Schiano, D. J. *Mental models of "MUDs": Just like being...where?".* Psychonomics Society, Chicago, 1996.
13. Schiano & Colston. CMC and *Community on Campus.* Society for Computers in Psychology; Philadelphia, PA, 1997.
14. Turkle, S. Constructions and reconstructions of self in virtual reality: Playing in MUDs. *Mind, Culture and Activity, 1*(3), (1994), 158-167.
15. Turkle, S. *Life on the screen: Identity in the age of the Internet.* New York: Simon & Schuster, 1995.

Are Newsgroups Virtual Communities?

Teresa L. Roberts
Sun Microsystems, Inc.
901 San Antonio Road, M.S. MPK 16-107
Palo Alto, CA 94303 USA
+1 650 786 4455
troberts@eng.sun.com

ABSTRACT

Online groups have been described as "virtual communities," although commentators differ on the amount of group feeling that they observe online. This paper reports on a survey that investigated to what extent people who post to 30 widely-varying online groups experience community online. Results show that two-thirds of respondents did indeed perceive a sense of belonging to their group. Beyond that, dimensions analogous to those of geographic communities were studied, and differences were found among the groups in those dimensions. The best predictors of these dimensions tended to be the time and effort individuals put into the groups. These dimensions added up to a unified statistical "Community" factor. Although the newsgroups did not turn out to vary significantly with this factor, individuals' experiences in their groups did. For women, their experience could be predicted by the thoroughness with which they read the group; for men, their experience could be predicted by the prevalence of women on the group.

Keywords

Virtual community, newsgroups, Internet, social computing.

INTRODUCTION

In his book *The Virtual Community*, Howard Rheingold waxes poetical about the potential of people who are dispersed geographically to find a sense of community online:

> "... whenever [computer-mediated communication (CMC)] technology becomes available to people anywhere, they inevitably build virtual communities with it." Rheingold, [5]

Other writers, however, see potential dysfunction:

> "What's missing from this ersatz neighborhood? A feeling of permanence and belonging, a sense of location, a warmth from the local history. Gone is the very essence of a neighborhood: friendly relations and a sense of being in it together." Stoll, [9]

Many of the commentators on the Internet are themselves heavy users of the net, and write based on that experience. Others (e.g., Turkle [10]) choose to focus on individuals representing subcultures that are most foreign to the mainstream offline culture, and hence may not accurately represent the majority online experience. This study endeavors to ask a broad cross-section of Internet users about their own experiences and perceptions.

We ask to what extent "community" exists among casual users of the Internet. And what are the variables that foster this sense of community?

For practical reasons, this particular study looked only at newsgroups, which are bulletin-board-like forums that individuals can post to and that anyone can later read. The research questions apply equally to other technologies, including e-mail groups and real-time forums.

RELATED WORK

There is a growing literature that studies the use of the Internet. Much of it is descriptive, recording what kinds of behaviors occur online. This paper focuses on quantitative studies that also elicit the *prevalence* of such behaviors.

M. Smith [8], in one of the earliest studies of online behavior, found that the WELL did have the capability to produce "collective goods," although it struggled with socializing its members.

Parks and Floyd [4] surveyed a variety of newsgroups to identify the prevalence and characteristics of friendships that were initiated online. Out of a 33% response rate, they found that 61% of the respondents reported having formed friendships online. They found that women were more likely than men to have participated in an online friendship. The individual's duration and frequency of participation *in that newsgroup* were the factors that best predicted the prevalence of friendships. They found that friendships that were begun online often moved to other media. Wysocki [13] did a similar study of the relationships that people developed over Prodigy newsgroups and a private sexually-oriented bulletin board. In contrast to Parks, she found no overall differences between women and men. She found that relationships developed at a faster rate and had smaller differences in women's and men's roles, compared to face-to-face.

C. Smith *et al.* [7] looked at 83 episodes of behavior control on 5 newsgroups. They found that the tenor and frequency of reproaches varied according to the type of offense and the individual newsgroup, and that the response from the offender varied by the style of the reproach. They found few differences between women and men, although their groups contained few enough women that they wondered if the women there were representative of women as a whole.

In the converse approach, the HomeNet field trial [3] starts with a sampling of people at home and examines their behavior online. This makes possible more longitudinal

CHI 98 Los Angeles CA USA
Copyright 1998 0-89791-975-0/98/ 4..$5.00

studies of the same set of individuals. They have found that communication, rather than information or entertainment, drives Internet use, although they have not yet studied behavior in online groups.

DEFINITION OF "COMMUNITY"

The word "community" has been used in a metaphorical sense for long enough that it doesn't have a precise meaning:

> "Usages such as 'the scientific community' and 'the jazz community' tend to be metaphorical efforts to convey a kind of psychological unity. Moreover, it seems generally agreed that this 'sense of community' is a highly variable condition when it does occur, differing from one individual to another and from group to group. As such, it might be preferable to regard it wholly problematic and subject to empirical determination." Schnore, [6]

To build a working definition for the present study, we could define community in a variety of ways. First and most straightforward would be to define "community" as a simple sense of group cohesion and individual belonging. We will look at that aspect of community, but we would also like a richer definition, one that has more potential for analyzing its components and for predicting attributes that might tend to foster the community feeling.

One approach is to define "community" in terms of isolated villages. Such communities are primarily defined simply by their geography. But these communities have a purpose: making the lives of their residents easier. As such, they support such processes as the generation and transportation of goods and services, communication, mutual support, self-regulation, and protection against outsiders. Smith [8], in studying "collective goods" and self-regulation online, used a definition based on this aspect of community.

An alternative approach to defining "community" might be to base it on other kinds of groups of people. *Primary groups* are defined to be small, emotionally-involving groups that people identify with, such as family or friendship groups; primary groups are an end in themselves. *Secondary groups* are impersonal groups with a specific purpose, like committees and sports clubs. Wellman [12], in studying "The Community Question," used a definition much like a primary group to identify individuals' "communities" within modern metropolitan areas.

Finally, entire networks of social relations might be analyzed. Garton *et al.* [1] gives an overview of such methods.

For the purpose of this study, the author has chosen to use the former approach: a more literal analogy to geographic communities. The working definition of "community" for use in this study contains the following dimensions:

- Cohesion: the sense of there being a group identity and that the respondent belongs to the group.
- Effectiveness: the impact that the group has on the members' lives and on the outside world.
- Help: the perceived ability of members to ask for and receive various kinds of help.
- Relationships: the likelihood of group members interacting individually, including forming friendships.
- Language: the prevalence of specialized language.
- Self-regulation: the ability of the group to police itself.

METHODOLOGY

This study consisted of choosing a widely-varying set of newsgroups, and a widely-varying set of individuals who participated in the newsgroups. Surveys were e-mailed to the chosen participants, and the results analyzed. These steps are described in detail below.

Choice of Newsgroups

Because the point of this study was to learn about a broad cross-section of newsgroup users, newsgroups with widely varying characteristics were chosen. There were three dimensions along which the chosen newsgroups varied:

Topic: The newsgroups were categorized into the following general topic areas:

- Living: *e.g.*, family, health, support groups.
- Issues: *e.g.*, social issues, politics, religion.
- Recreation: *e.g.*, hobbies, sports, television, erotica.
- Professional: *e.g.*, computers, education, medicine.

The topic was determined by skimming the content of the newsgroup, and by looking at the purpose described at the Usenet Info Center [11].

Traffic:

- Range of 5-10 messages per day.
- Range of 20-40 messages per day.
- More than 80 messages per day.

Traffic was first estimated by looking at the number of messages available at the time on the University of Colorado's [CU] server. It was confirmed from the statistics at the Usenet Info Center.

Proportion of women and men posting:

- At least 75% of the messages from women.
- Range of 40-60% of the messages from women.
- Less than 25% of the messages from women.

The sex ratio of postings was estimated by looking at all of the postings currently on CU's server. The author assigned a sex to the sender using the following heuristics:

- Strongly sex-linked names (Linda, Howard) were assigned to the appropriate sex. Clearly ambiguous names (Chris, Marty) were assigned "unknown." Names that were usually associated with one sex but that could be applied to the other (Leslie, Sam) were assigned to the more common sex.
- Non-English names unfamiliar to the author were assigned "unknown."
- Initials, surnames, company names, and codes were assigned "unknown."
- Multiple owners of the account (Bill and Mary Smith) were assigned "unknown."
- Pseudonyms were assigned to the appropriate sex if they were strongly sex-linked (MachoMan, SusiesMom), but were assigned "unknown" otherwise (MarchHare).

Messages were spot-checked for the signature inside the message matching the From field of the message. Very few inconsistencies were found.

Newsgroups were disqualified from consideration for the following reasons:

- The proportion of messages that were crossposted to other newsgroups, as reported by the Usenet Info Center, was greater than 30%. Groups with a lot of crossposting are less likely to have their own character.
- The sex of the sender could not be determined for more than 30% of the postings. In such cases, the sex proportion of the group could not be classified accurately enough.
- The newsgroup was local to a city or campus. The purpose of this study was to learn about groups in which the participants could not interact easily in person.
- The group consisted only of informational postings (job listings, sexy pictures), and not discussion.
- The discussion was not primarily in English.

Out of 5221 newsgroups that were on CU's server in the spring of 1996, 2607 (49.9%) had enough traffic to be considered and were not local groups. The five traffic bands (the three listed above and the two between the bands being considered) divided the newsgroups into segments of roughly equal sizes.

The author randomized the order of the 2607 newgroups, and then looked at them in order, to identify one newsgroup for each of the 36 slots determined by the three dimensions given above (4 topics X 3 traffic levels X 3 sex proportions).

Difficulty arose in finding heavily-female newsgroups. Out of the first 50 randomly-selected newsgroups, the mean proportion of postings from women was only 14%. (This occurred at a time when the Georgia Tech study [2] of the World Wide Web showed 31.5% female usage. The different media seem to have very different appeal to women.) Despite a decision to loosen the definition of each of the bands of female participation, only 30 of the 36 slots for newsgroups could be populated. (All subsequent analyses were performed using numerical percentages of female participation, not the nominal groupings.)

The chosen newsgroups are shown in Table 1.

	Living	Issues	Recreation	Professional
Low Traffic	---	bionet.women-in-bio	---	sci.med.transcription
	misc.kids.vacation	soc.net-people	rec.crafts.dollhouses	k12.ed.soc-studies
	misc.health.arthritis	bit.listserv.seasia-l	misc.transport.rail.misc	comp.sys.apollo
Medium Traffic	soc.support.fat-acceptance	---	alt.tv.x-files.creative	---
	rec.arts.books.childrens	soc.feminism	alt.arts.ballet	bit.listserv.buslib-l
	alt.suicide.holiday	misc.rural	alt.sports.baseball.tor-bluejays	comp.publish.prepress
High Traffic	soc.couples.wedding	soc.women.lesbian-and-bi	rec.arts.tv.soaps.cbs	---
	alt.support.mult-sclerosis	alt.pagan	bit.listserv.words-l	---
	misc.consumers.house	alt.society.generation-x	alt.guitar.tab	comp.os.os2.apps

Table 1 Chosen newsgroups. Within each cell, the top newsgroup is the female group, the middle one mixed, and the bottom one male. "---" indicates that there was no newsgroup with these characteristics.

Choice of Participants

Participants for each newsgroup were chosen among people who had posted to that newsgroup within the previous week. Because of the publicly-readable characteristic of newsgroups, it was not possible to identify people who read the group without posting. People were only chosen if their message had not been crossposted to another group, because it's impossible to tell what newsgroup was intended to be the primary recipient of crossposted messages.

An attempt was made to find 6 people of each sex per newsgroup. This was not always possible in newsgroups that were primarily populated by one sex.

People were selected in order to maximize the variation in posting frequency. Within each sex, the two people who posted the most were chosen, 2 people who had posted only once, and 2 people who posted near the geometric mean between the most and least frequent posters.

In total, 330 participants were chosen, out of a possible 360 (30 newsgroups X 2 sexes X 6 participants per sex). Out of these, 161 were female and 169 were male.

Procedure

The survey was e-mailed individually to each of the participants in May 1996. Surveys were to be returned by e-mail to the author. Respondents were invited to use an anonymous mailing service to return the surveys if they preferred, but none did.

RESULTS

Demographics of Respondents

Of the 330 surveys sent out, 107 were returned, for a response rate of 32%. Of women, 59/161 (37%) returned their surveys; of men, 47/169 (28%) returned theirs.*

Sex: Of the respondents, 55% were female and 45% male. Only one person claimed to be of a sex different from what the author had expected.

Age: Respondents ranged in age from 14 to 69, with the distribution shown in Table 2.

Marital status: 38% were single, 52% were married, and 8% were divorced or widowed.

* In addition, 8 respondents declined politely, 4 objected more strenuously to the survey, and 1 complained to the researcher's postmaster. Five of the addresses were undeliverable, despite having been posted from within the previous week.

Age Range	Count	%
10-19	7	7
20-29	34	32
30-39	28	26
40-49	26	24
50-59	7	7
60-69	4	4

Table 2 Age distribution of respondents.

Family responsibility: 74% were not responsible for children, 9% had a preschool child, 7% had a child aged 7-12, and 9% had a teenager. (Where there were multiple children, only the youngest is counted here.)

Internet experience: Table 3 shows the distribution of experience on the Internet and with the newsgroup that the respondents were being asked about. (In statistics that use these data as independent variables, individuals who were more than 3 standard deviations out were omitted as outliers because they dominated the regression statistics. The values for the outliers are given in the last column of the table; these 6 values came from 3 individuals. The values of the Maximum, Mean, and Standard Deviation shown here do not include the outliers.)

	Min	Max	Mean	S.D.	Outliers
Months reading any newsgroups	0	90	20.0	17.2	
Number of professional lists	0	16	3.1	3.3	30, 100
Hrs/week on prof'l lists	0	20	2.9	4.0	
Number of personal lists	0	45	6.1	7.0	100
Hrs/week on personal lists	0	30	5.9	6.2	
Number of lists posted to	0	28	4.4	4.0	100
Months reading this group	0	60	12	12	
Hours/week on this newsgroup	0	18	3.3	3.3	30, 45

Table 3 Respondents' experience with the Internet. "Lists" refers to both newsgroups and e-mail lists.

Attention to this group: Table 4 shows the frequency with which the respondents say they attend to this newsgroup. In addition, 18% reported that they read every message, 33% read most messages, 42% read all headers but read only a fraction of the messages, and 7% skimmed the headers.

	Daily	Weekly	Monthly	Less
Read	81	14	4	1
Post	19	34	29	18

Table 4 Percentage of respondents who read and post to this newsgroup with these frequencies.

Sense of Belonging

The simplest definition of "community" is just whether the participants feel a personal sense of belonging, and whether they perceive a sense of closeness in the group. Table 5 shows responses to these two questions. Two-thirds of the respondents did feel that they belonged, and more than half perceived closeness in the group. Several of the respondents who said that they did not feel they belonged to the group that was being asked about volunteered that there were other groups where they did feel they belonged.

	1	2	3	4	5
Belong to the group	7	17	9	33	34
Group has closeness	4	9	25	45	14

Table 5 Sense of belonging to the group and closeness within the group. On a 5-point scale, 1=not at all, 3=neutral, 5=very much. Numbers are percentages of respondents.

For people who said that they felt like they belonged to their newsgroup, we asked how long it took for them to feel that way. The mean reported time was 2.4 months, with a standard deviation of 2.6 months. The median and mode times were both 1 month.

Individual Dimensions: Results and Predictors

Next we look in more detail at the individual dimensions that we posited might add up to a "community" analogous to geographic communities. For each of these dimensions, we first look at how strong that factor is across all of our newsgroups. Table 6 shows the distributions of the dimensions; each dimension is discussed individually below. The last row of the table is discussed in the section entitled Global "Community" Factor.

Dimension	1	2	3	4	5
Cohesion	1	25	38	24	0
Effectiveness	0	3	43	37	6
Help	9	26	24	15	8
Relationships	65	13	8	5	4
Language	6	29	25	10	21
Self-regulation	11	18	36	30	--
Community	21	34	28	12	5

Table 6 Prevalence of each dimension across all newsgroups. Values in the table are percentages of respondents in each quintile. The column labeled 1 gives the lowest quintile and 5 the highest. (Self-regulation could only be divided into quartiles; see text.)

Next, for each dimension we ask whether that dimension varies significantly across the newsgroups. Table 7 shows overall results from analyses of variance, which will be discussed below.

Finally, 20 variables were examined to see which ones might be significant in predicting differences among the respondents. (Note that this is a statistical prediction only. It does not tell us cause and effect.) First, a further analysis of variance was run on the 2 categorical dimensions "newsgroup topic" and "sex of the respondent." Then a stepwise regression on 18 numerical variables was done. (Stepwise regression is a tool that finds the best predictors in a step-by-step manner. It is useful in situations when predictors are mutually correlated, to avoid finding redundant effects.) All tests were done separately for female and male respondents; while there was no main effect for sex, and dividing the data reduces the power of the statistics, there were enough differences between the sexes to justify the division. Results of this analysis are given in Table 8, and are discussed in the subsections below. (Results are shown for all tests in which $p<.05$. Even though large numbers of tests were performed, the author made the judgment to leave the level of significance at .05, having seen the decrease in sensitivity due to the splitting by sex. A conservative reader may wish to discount all effects with p values larger than .01.)

Dimension	*p*-value for differences across Newsgroup
Cohesion	.08
Effectiveness	.25
Help	<.0001
Relationships	.0002
Language	<.0001
Self-Regulation	<.0001
Community	.17

Table 7 Analysis of variance results: probability that differences in each dimension across newsgroups can be explained by random chance.

Predictor Variables	Cohesion	Effective-ness	Help	Relation-ships	Language	Self-Regulation	Commu-nity
Time/effort in this newsgroup							
Months reading the group	---/---	---/---	.008/.03	<.0001/<.0001	---/---	---/---	---/---
Frequency of posting	---/---	---/---	---/---	.0003/.005	.0004/---	---/.0004(-)	---/---
Thoroughness of reading	.0002/---	.006/---	.009/---	---/---	---/---	---/---	.006/---
Frequency of reading	.002/.03	---/---	---/---	---/---	---/---	---/---	---/---
Hours per week	---/---	---/---	.001/.001	---/---	---/---	---/---	---/---
Time&effort on the Internet							
Hr/week on personal lists	---/---	---/---	<.0001/---	.004/.006	---/---	---/---	---/---
Number of personal lists	---/---	---/---	---/---	---/---	.02/---	---/---	---/---
Hr/wk on prof'l lists	---/---	---/---	---/---	---/---	---/---	---/---	---/---
Number of prof'l lists	---/---	---/---	---/---	---/---	---/---	---/---	---/---
Number of lists posted to	---/---	---/---	---/---	---/---	---/---	---/---	---/---
Mo. reading newsgroups	---/---	---/---	---/---	---/---	---/---	---/---	---/---
Attributes of the newsgroup							
Topic	---/---	---/---	.02/.005	---/---	---/---	---/---	---/---
% postings from women	---/.02	---/.03	---/---	---/---	.03/.05	---/---	---/.02
Traffic level (msgs/day)	---/---	---/---	---/---	---/---	<.0001/.01	<.0001(-)/---	---/---
Narrowness of topic	---/---	---/---	---/---	.04(-)/.002(-)	---/---	---/---	---/---
% postings w/ sex known	---/---	---/.002	---/---	---/---	---/---	---/---	---/---
% crosspostings	---/---	---/---	---/---	---/---	---/---	---/---	---/---
Demographics of respondent							
Family responsibility	---/---	---/---	---/.05	---/---	---/---	---/---	---/---
Age	---/---	---/---	---/---	---/---	---/---	---/---	---/---
Sex	---	---	---	---	---	---	---

Table 8 Statistically significant predictors (p<.05) from stepwise regression (and from analysis of variance for the categorical variables Topic and Sex). Values are probabilities that the distribution could be caused by random chance. For each pair of values, the first value is for female respondents and the second for male respondents. "(-)" means that the relationship was in the negative direction.. "---" means that that predictor was not statistically significant.

Cohesion

Three questions were used to elicit the group cohesion. Two are the ones shown in Table 5: belonging to the group and a sense of closeness in the group. These both had fairly positive results. The third question was about stability of the group. The most common response, from 62% of the respondents, was that the group contained a mix of oldtimers and newcomers. Combining the answers to these questions resulted in a moderate value for group cohesion, as shown in the first row of Table 6.

The analysis of variance that compared the Cohesion dimension across newsgroups showed only a marginally statistically significant difference.

For predicting the variation among the respondents, we see in Table 8 that for women the frequency and thoroughness of reading this newsgroup were the significant predictors.

For men, the predictors were the presence of women in the group and the respondents' frequency of reading the group.

Effectiveness

Three questions were used to elicit the group's effectiveness. Two were ratings of how well the group met its own purpose and how well it met the respondent's needs. These questions got positive answers from 86% and 85% of the respondents respectively. The third measurement was a count of how many functions the group tried to accomplish. Most groups were rated as only having one or two of the four potential purposes (exchanging information was a function of the group for 82% of respondents, chatting for 59%, mutual support for 39%, and causing change in the world was a funtion for only 15%). Combining these three questions results in the distribution shown in the second row of Table 6: moderately positive ratings, fairly tightly distributed. The analysis of variance showed no significant differences among the newsgroups.

Differences among the respondents' ratings were predicted, for women, by thoroughness of reading the group, and, for men, by the presence of women in the group and by the proportion of writers whose sex was identifiable.

Help

Respondents were asked to mark which of various kinds of help they thought they could ask for and get within the newsgroup. These were divided into the categories of informational help, emotional help, and real-world help. The combined rating is the count of different kinds of help they marked. The third line of Table 6 shows a wide spread among the responses, with somewhat more responses on the low end than the high. Differences among newsgroups were statistically significant.

Further analysis shows that newsgroup topic is a significant predictor of these differences: the Issues and Living topics get the high ratings and Recreation and Professional the low ratings. Also significant are the amount of time the respondents spend on the list and how long they've been reading it. For men, those with younger children perceive that they can get more help online.

Relationships

Respondents were asked how many people from this newsgroup that they'd

- exchanged one-on-one e-mail with,
- met face-to-face, and
- considered to be friends.

(Responses for each question that were larger than 20 were changed to 20, the high end of the smooth distribution, to keep outliers from dominating the statistics.) Responses to these three questions were added together, and the distribution of the result is shown in the fourth row of Table 6. While the distribution is skewed toward the low end, there are still substantial numbers of people who have had interactions of varying intensity with large numbers of people they've met online. Differences among newsgroups were statistically significant.

Of the respondents to this survey, 39% said that they'd made at least one friend in this newsgroup. All but one of these people said they considered the closest friend that they'd met through this list still to be a friend. The mean lifetime of that friendship so far was 6 months.

Predictors for the number of individual relationships were duration of time with the group, frequency of posting to the group, and time spent on personal e-mail lists and newsgroups. Groups that interpreted their topic broadly, rather than keeping to a narrow focus, also fostered individual relationships.

Language

Two questions asked how frequently internet jargon and language specialized to this newsgroup were used in the group. The results are shown in the fifth row of Table 6. Few groups used no jargon at all, but otherwise the spread was wide. Differences among newsgroups were statistically significant.

The primary predictors for the use of specialized language were the traffic level on the list and the visibility of women. For women, two additional predictors were how frequently they themselves posted to the group and how many personal lists they were on.

Self-regulation

One question asked how much difficulty the group had with inappropriate behavior. The distribution of the answers to that question are given in the sixth row of Table 6 (since only four answers were offered, there is no fifth quintile in the results). There was a wide range of responses, with the majority being fairly positive. Differences among newsgroups were statistically significant.

Predictors for the effectiveness of the group's self-regulation differed between women and men. For the women, higher traffic predicted poorer regulation. (This predictor actually just missed being statistically significant for the men, also.) For the men, the more they posted, the less they perceived effective self-regulation in the group.

Global "Community" Factor

If we believe that the dimensions discussed above add up to a common whole that we might call "community," statistical techniques can help us find it.

First, correlations were done among the dimensions, with the results shown in Table 9. We see that most of the dimensions are positively correlated and that the correlation among those dimensions is in the range of 0.3 to 0.5. Self-regulation, however, is negatively correlated with the rest of the dimensions, with a magnitude of 0 to 0.3.

With that kind of correlation among the dimensions, a factor analysis was able to identify a factor that combines these dimensions. This "Community" factor is described in Table 10. It explains 46% of the variance among the respondents' data, and is statistically significant at a level of $p<.0001$.

The same analyses were done for this Community factor as for all other dimensions. Quintiles in Table 6 show that the

	Coh.	Eff.	Help	Rel.	Lang	Reg.
Cohesion	1.00	0.43	0.46	0.32	0.36	-0.03
Effectiveness	0.43	1.00	0.49	0.27	0.42	-0.11
Help	0.46	0.49	1.00	0.43	0.45	-0.23
Relationships	0.32	0.27	0.43	1.00	0.43	-0.29
Language	0.36	0.42	0.45	0.43	1.00	-0.29
Self-regulation	-0.03	-0.11	-0.23	-0.29	-0.29	1.00

Table 9 Correlation coefficients among the dimensions.

Dimension	Factor Weight
Cohesion	.67
Effectiveness	.70
Help	.79
Relationships	.68
Language	.75
Self-regulation	-.40

Table 10 Factor that combines the dimensions into "Community." R^2=.46, p<.0001.

distribution of "Community" tended to be grouped at the low end of the scale, and to tail off at the high end. In fact, the newsgroup soc.support.fat-acceptance stood out as a clear outlier at the high end. Differences among the newsgroups were not found to be statistically significant on the whole, however.

Among the individual respondents, two variables did predict Community. For women, the predictor was the thoroughness with which they read the newsgroup. For men, the predictor was the prevalence of women posting to the group.

DISCUSSION

This study succeeded in getting information from a wide range of Internet users. Respondents represented a broad age range, although young and elderly people were underrepresented compared to the population as a whole. Respondents were both single and married, but parents were underrepresented. There was a wide range of experience with the Internet, with distribution skewed toward new users, as is true of net users as a whole.

The amount of time respondents reported spending on the newsgroup that this survey asked about is substantially larger than the time they spend on an average newsgroup (3.3 hours *vs.* 1 hour per week, respectively). This makes sense because the participants were picked based on showing enough commitment to their newsgroup to post to it. Thus the results of this study should be recognized to apply to active participants in groups; they may not be so applicable to passive readers.

In the simplest sense, "community" might be defined as a feeling of belonging to a group, and/or a belief that the group has a sense of closeness. With this definition, the newsgroups studied here clearly demonstrated community: 66% of the respondents said they they felt as if they belonged to the group, and 59% said that their group had a feeling of closeness. Although this feeling of belonging is far from universal, it does seem to be held by a large enough proportion of the population to be an important attribute of these groups.

The analysis of dimensions analogous to geographic communities generated a wealth of data.

- Cohesion: Respondents did feel a sense of group cohesion, even though the membership in the group was changing. Thoroughness of reading the newsgroup was the primary predictor of the perception of cohesion.
- Effectiveness: The groups were perceived as being fairly effective at meeting their purpose and their members' needs. There were no significant differences among this set of groups in this area. The predictors for individual respondents were an odd mix, with women thinking better of the group if they read it more thoroughly, and with men thinking it more effective if more women and fewer sex-ambiguous people post.
- Help: Ability to ask for and get help varied greatly. The main difference was that some groups were meant for informational help only, while others also offered emotional and real-world assistance. Time spent in the newsgroup was the primary predictor of how much help people felt they could get. Interestingly, men who had greater family responsibilities perceived that they could get more help from their groups than childless men.
- Relationships: Most respondents had had individual interactions with members of the list, and one-third had developed friendships. Not surprisingly, the length of time a person had been corresponding on the list and their level of activity (*i.e.*, visibility) determined the likelihood of their having had individual interactions. This is consistent with Parks and Floyd's [4] results, although the frequency of friendships found here is smaller.
- Language: Internet jargon and specialized language within the newsgroups were common. They were more likely on high-traffic lists, and, interestingly, on lists with a higher prevalence of women.
- Self-regulation: This dimension tended to operate in the opposite direction of the other dimensions, suggesting that for groups to allow for a group feeling and effectiveness, they must not be too tightly regulated.

The above dimensions add up to a statistical factor that one might call Community. Surprisingly, Community did not vary significantly among the newsgroups. This seems to be largely because while the newsgroups did vary in most of the dimensions, different groups were strong on different dimensions. Instead, it turned out that Community seemed to be more a function of the individual respondents, and in fact, it explained almost half of the variance in their data. This suggests that one's experience with a newsgroup has as much to do with one's own behavior as with the characteristics of the group. This seemed particularly true among women, where the thoroughness with which they read the newsgroup was the best statistical predictor of their experience of Community. The story is a little less clear for men, for whom the prevalence of women on the group is the best predictor of Community. (One must note that what the men are cuing in on here is not necessarily the possibility of relationships with women in their newsgroups. Prevalence of women did not predict the Relationships dimension. Instead, it predicted men's perception of Cohesion, Help, and specialized Language.)

The other interesting side of Table 8 is the set of variables that did *not* turn out to be predictors. Demographic variables and experience on the Internet as a whole were not good predictors of people's perceptions of these dimensions of community.

CONCLUSIONS

This work demonstrates empirically that there is indeed a sense of "community" in newsgroups among active participants, both a sense of belonging and a set of dimensions analogous to geographic communities.

In predicting the values of the different "community" dimensions, the most frequent predictors had to do with the amount of time and effort that the individuals devote to the group. The cause/effect relationship here undoubtedly goes in both directions: the more effort one puts in, the more one gets out of participating, and conversely, the less satisfied one is, the less effort one is likely to devote to the group. This phenomenon is particularly prevalent for women.

A less predictable factor is that the presence of women posting to the group was a positive predictor, mostly for the men. This suggests that the increasing presence of women on the 'Net will make it a more pleasant place for everyone.

FURTHER WORK

The newsgroups chosen for this research were deliberately chosen to be broadly representative of the types of newsgroups available on the Internet. But the decision to include only groups that had smaller amounts of crossposting and had large percentages of senders whose sex could be identified (and who hence were mostly using ordinary names) effectively excluded a large segment of available newsgroups. Since crossposting and pseudonyms are often regarded as symptoms of a more freewheeling nature, or even dysfunction, in newsgroups, it is quite likely that the newsgroups omitted from this study might have different characteristics from those described here. More research is needed in this direction.

Another major limitation is the restriction to primarily-English groups. Extension of the work to non-English-speaking cultures is needed, to make our understanding of the Internet more complete.

This research reports on data collected in May 1996. With the rapid expansion of the Internet, it is quite possible that the results obtained here will change as the population on the 'Net changes. The fact that length of time online did not correlate with the dimensions studied here suggests that there might not be any such changes, but future changes should nevertheless be monitored.

Finally, this study gathered data only on one type of Internet group: newsgroups. Similarities and differences with other types of groups should be explored: real-time groups who populate chat forums, e-mail groups, and interactive forums on the World Wide Web.

ACKNOWLEDGMENTS

A substantial portion of this work was done while the author was on sabbatical at the Institute of Cognitive Science, University of Colorado, Boulder, Colorado, USA. The author thanks ICS and Peter Polson for their support. The author would also like to thank Sun Microsystems for support since then.

Many people have contributed to discussions of the research methodology and data analysis presented here. They include Marita Franzke, Robin Jeffries, Clayton Lewis, Anne McClard, A. Kartik Mithal, Jakob Nielsen, Malcolm Parks, Scott Robertson, Carrie Rudman, and John Thomas. Special thanks go to Mac Parks for enabling the author to base her survey on his.

REFERENCES

1. Garton, L., C. Haythornthwaite, and B. Wellman. Studying Online Social Networks. *J. of Computer-Mediated Communication 3*, 1, (June 1997).
2. Graphics, Visualization, & Usability Center, Georgia Institute of Technology. *GVU's 5th WWW User Survey*. http://www.cc.gatech.edu/gvu/user_surveys/survey-04-1996.
3. Kraut, R., W. Scherlis, T. Mukhopadhyay, J. Manning, S. Kiesler. The HomeNet Field Trial of Residential Internet Services. *Comm. of the ACM 39*, 12 (Dec. 1996), 55-63.
4. Parks, M., and K. Floyd. Making Friends in Cyberspace. *J. of Computer-Mediated Communication 1*, 4 (Mar. 1996).
5. Rheingold, H. *The Virtual Community: Homesteading on the Electronic Frontier*. HarperPerennial, New York, 1993.
6. Schnore, L.F. Community. In Smelser, N.J. *Sociology: An Introduction*. Wiley, New York, 1967.
7. Smith, C.B., M.L. McLaughlin, and K.K. Osborne. Conduct Control on Usenet. *J. of Computer-Mediated Communication 2*, 4 (March 1997).
8. Smith, M.A. *Voices from the WELL: The Logic of the Virtual Commons*. Masters Thesis, UCLA, Department of Sociology, 1992. Available online at http://www.ssc-net.ucla.edu/soc/csoc/virtcomm.htm.
9. Stoll, C. *Silicon Snake Oil: Second Thoughts on the Information Highway*. Doubleday, New York, 1995.
10. Turkle, S. *Life on the Screen: Identity in the Age of the Internet*. Simon & Shuster, New York, 1995.
11. Usenet Info Center. http://sunsite.unc.edu/usenet-i/home.html.
12. Wellman, B. The Community Question: The Intimate Networks of East Yorkers. *American Journal of Sociology 84*, 5, (1979), 1201-1231.
13. Wysocki, D.K. *Somewhere Over the Modem: Interpersonal Relationships Over Computer Bulletin Boards*. Doctoral Disseration: University of California at Santa Barbara, Sociology Department, 1996.

Communication and Information: Alternative Uses of the Internet in Households

Robert Kraut	*Tridas Mukhopadhyay*	*Janusz Szczypula*	*Sara Kiesler*	*William Scherlis*
1-412-268-7694	1-412-268-2307	1-412-268-6096	1-412-268-2848	1-412-268-8741
robert.kraut @cmu.edu	tridas @andrew.cmu.edu	jslm @andrew.cmu.edu	kiesler+ @andrew.cmu.edu	scherlis @cs.cmu.edu

Human Computer Interaction Institute
5000 Forbes Avenue
Carnegie Mellon University
Pittsburgh, PA 15213, USA

ABSTRACT

The Internet has been characterized as a superhighway to information and as a high-tech extension of the home telephone. How are people really using the Internet? The history of previous technologies that support interpersonal communication suggests that communication may be a more important use and determinant of participants' commitment to the Internet than is information acquisition and entertainment. Operationalizing interpersonal communication as the use of electronic mail and information acquisition and entertainment as the use of the World Wide Web, we analyzed longitudinal data from a field trial of 229 individuals in 110 households during their first year on the Internet. The results show that interpersonal communication is a stronger driver of Internet use than are information and entertainment applications.

Keywords: interpersonal communication, family communication, social impact, computer-mediated communication, Internet, World Wide Web, online services, user studies, technology adoption, Email

INTRODUCTION

Before the 1990s, few households had computers, and home omputers were used primarily by white collar men to do office work (Venkatesh & Vitalari, 1992). Today, computers have diffused much more widely, as measured by the number of households that own a computer, the number of people within households who use a computer, and the number of different tasks to which home computers are applied (Venkatesh, 1996). In 1993, a third of all US households owned a computer and over 60% of the richest quartile did so (Anderson, Bikson, Law, & Mitchell, 1995). By 1996, a significant proportion of these home computers were being used for online connections to the Internet. One estimate puts Internet penetration in 1996 at about 12% of U.S. households (NPD Group, 1996). The Internet is a new household technology, and, if the public press is to be believed, it portends large changes in the ways people live their lives.

CHI 98 Los Angeles CA USA
Copyright 1998 0-89791-975-0/98/ 4..$5.00

More so than with other technologies, the impact of the Internet will not simply flow from features of the technology. Computers and the Internet are highly adaptable and can support many different kinds of use. Since the Internet could provide very different kinds of services to citizens, its effects will depend on which ones they use. This paper is an attempt to understand how people use the Internet at home.

Contrasting information and entertainment with interpersonal communication

In this paper, we make a primary distinction between Internet services primarily used for *interpersonal communication* as compared with those used for *information and entertainment*. If the history of the telephone, radio, and television is any guide, either communication or information and entertainment could dominate residential use of the Internet and, accordingly, will influence how the Internet develops and what social impact it has. Both communication and information uses of the Internet have the potential to open up relatively encapsulated households to influences from the larger society and to bind households to it, although in quite different ways. Even if both categories of use are embraced, each may appeal to different types of people, may engage people differently, may offer different satisfactions and rewards, and, as a result, may have different effects on society and different implications for technology and policy development.

This paper operationalizes the distinction between information and entertainment as compared with interpersonal communication by comparing how people differentially use the World Wide Web and personal electronic mail, the two most popular of all Internet resources. We recognize that this operationalization is not perfect. Motives for using any Internet service may be mixed, and different software can be used for several services. Nonetheless, it is the case that electronic mail and the World Wide Web have a history of supporting "interpersonal communication" and "information and entertainment" applications, respectively.

Although data networking technology was not initially built for the purpose of connecting people, electronic mail (Email) was an early innovation in these networks; the first messages were sent over the precursor to the Internet in 1969 (Leiner et al., 1997), and Email as a communication medium has undergone only minor changes since its inception. Communication through Email is personalized, spontaneous, and interactive; senders can specify who they want their recipients to be and tailor their messages to them, taking into account their prior interactions and the nature of the relationship. These conversational and relationship-oriented attributes of Email make it engaging. Historical accounts of the telephone suggest that demand for interpersonal communication is highly elastic. Whenever inter-personal communication becomes easier or cheaper, people communicate more (Mayer, 1977).

Contrasted with Email, the World Wide Web (the Web) is a relatively new technology and is still rapidly evolving. The basic software behind the Web was created in 1992 in a high energy physics research laboratory so scientists could offer data and results to others (Leiner et al., 1997). In comparison to Email, the Web is more like broadcast media—billboards, magazines, radio, and television—although on the Web, almost anyone can publish. Information and entertainment on the Web are generally posted in a public place and available to anyone who happens by. The postings are minimally interactive. If their content is tailored to recipients at all, it is typically to broad audience characteristics, not to particular people. These features of the Web may make information and entertainment services less engaging and less important to people than interpersonal communication services. Historical evidence suggests that consumer demand for information and entertainment is comparatively flat, at least as compared to interpersonal communication. When a new broadcast medium, like the video cassette player, becomes available, people tend to decrease the amount of time they devote to older media, such as theaters, for acquiring the same information (Carey, 1989).

If either interpersonal communication or information and entertainment dominate people's use of the Internet, one would expect this preference to be reflected in several measures of usage—popularity of one type over the other, priority of access within sessions, consistent use over time, generalization to other uses, and continuation of usage rather than dropping service. Based on the history of the residential telephone (e.g., Fischer, 1992) and the use of the Internet in organizational settings (e.g., Sproull and Kiesler, 1991), we expect that people will have a preference to use the Internet for interpersonal communication.

We tested these ideas with computer-generated usage records from the HomeNet field trial. We also tested predictions about variation among people suggested by demographic differences in the use of the residential telephone. Adult women and teenagers of both genders are the heaviest users of the residential telephone (Brandon, 1980). Both preference and opportunity may account for these demographic correlates of telephone use. Women, as part of their sex-role obligations, often take responsibility for maintaining the family's social networks; women also say they enjoy talking on the phone and think the phone is especially helpful for socializing (Dimmick, Sikand, & Patterson, 1994). Also, because women are less likely than men to work outside of the household, they may find more opportunities to talk on the phone. Teenagers are at a life stage when they are developing their personal social networks and have substantial free time. These same factors—the value placed on sociability and the availability of free time–may cause women and teenagers to be heavier users of the Internet for interpersonal communication than adult men.

The effects of experience

Peoples' overall preferences for Email or the Web could be examined by simply averaging their usage of each service over a year's time. However, doing so would obscure the dynamics of usage over time—i.e., of the early experiences that may lead to later uses and the influence of one type of use on the other. Are the people who experiment with Email in their first months of Internet use the same people who are using Email at the end of the year? Does their use become routinized and less variable? This pattern (that early use predicts later use) is true of many innovations, but it may be especially true of the Internet because the technology is both more adaptable and more complex than many household devices. The most useful applications of the Internet often must be discovered by those who use them. Many consumer products, such as the electric toothbrush or VCR, have a narrow range of uses that are relatively easy to envision before purchase. By contrast, the protean character of the computer, with its large number of computing applications, variety of Internet information, and global reach to people, contributes to a relative ambiguity about what home computers are good for. It is perhaps for these reasons that many people cannot accurately predict how they will use their computer at the time they first get one for their home (Kraut et al., 1996).

Under these circumstances, people's early successes using home computers and the Internet are likely to have substantial impact on their later use. They will begin using them, we think, by exploring a few applications (perhaps those easiest to use or those recommended by others). In organizational settings, the introduction of new technology often leads some employees to commit substantial time and attention to investigating the possibilities of the technology, and it is often an event that disrupts ongoing routines. But exploration is relatively short-lived, as new routines come to assert themselves (e.g., Eveland & Bikson, 1987; Tyre & Orlikowski, 1994). In households, one or more family members might devote time to getting their computer set up and learning how to connect to the Internet. Success in doing so and interesting outcomes would reinforce some continued usage. Eventually, however, the demands of family, work, school, and household chores should reclaim some of the time that had been allocated to learning the computer and exploring

Internet possibilities, and old diversions—favorite TV shows, hobbies, and socializing—would reassert themselves.

To examine whether peoples' use of the Internet would crystallize with experience, we included a time dimension in all of our analyses. We expected variability in Internet use to decrease with experience, predictability of use to increase with experience, and that the influence of external influences on use (such as the degree to which other family members are using the Internet) would decrease with experience. Our hypotheses suggest all of these patterns may be stronger when people discover Email early.

METHOD

The data analyzed here come from HomeNet, a field trial of residential Internet use, in which a sample of 110 demographically diverse households (229 individuals)[0] were given Internet access during 1995 and 1996 in exchange for providing a variety of data about their use of the Internet and their beliefs about it. When the present analyses were conducted, all participants had received access to the Internet for at least a year. Details of the field trial and the sample are available in Kraut et al., 1996.

Data collection

The data we report on for this paper come from four sources: (a) computer-generated usage records of Internet use, (b) questionnaires completed approximately every three months, (c) an archive of public news group messages, and (d) videotaped home interviews with 25 households. Kraut et al (1996) provides more detail about data collection.

(1) Computer-generated usage records

Households were given access to the Internet on a staggered schedule. (The first family received an Internet account in March, 1995, and the last family received an account in March, 1996.) To allow for comparisons across the entire sample, the data reported here encompass the first 52 weeks after the Internet accounts in any household first became operational. The usage data have been summed on a weekly basis to increase reliability.

We derived the following metrics from the usage records:

Sessions: The number of discrete sessions per week a participant logged into the Internet. A session is the interval between an authentication to our Internet server and a log out.

[0] The 110 households contained 386 individuals but only 258 were over 10 years old, requested an Internet account, and agreed to participate in the data collection. Of these, only 229 actually filled out the pretest questionnaire and used the Internet at any time during the trial. The number of respondents fluctuates with analyses because people moved into and out of households (e.g., students who went away to college) and some participants sometimes failed to complete questionnaires.

Internet hours: The total hours in a week in which a participant logged into the Internet. It is the sum of the length of the sessions in a week.

Electronic mail use: We recorded the sessions in which participants sent or read electronic mail and the number of Email messages they sent and received.

Because our concern in this analysis was to contrast interpersonal communication with information and entertainment, we included only messages in which a participant was an explicit recipient. The excluded messages were typically ones broadcast to a distribution list to which the participant had subscribed and which did not address the recipient by name. We believe these messages reflect a mix of interpersonal communication and information distribution. For the same reason, we excluded reads and posts to computer bulletin boards and news groups.

World Wide Web use: We recorded the number of unique World Wide Web domains or sites visited per week (a domain or site is an Internet protocol address, such as www.disney.com). Our metric for total volume of World Wide Web use is the number of different domains accessed during the week. The average number of weekly domains visited and the average number of weekly html pages visited were very highly correlated (r=.96).

(2) Social influences on use

We included two factors that might expose participants to other people's use of the Internet and, by this route, influence participants' amount and style of use. One is a measure of Internet use by other household members; the second indicates the percentage of time that schools were in session.

Other household members' usage: We expected family members would influence one another but did not predict the direction of this influence. Modeling could lead to a positive influence, whereas competition for the computer or family specialization could lead to a negative influence. We included measures of the extent to which other participant members of the household used the Internet during a particular week in terms of the number of hours they were connected, the number of Web sites they accessed, and the number of personal electronic messages they sent and received.

School days: The school year schedule has a large impact on how students and their parents spend their time, so we included a measure of the percentage of days during the week that were school days. Since business holidays are often geared to school vacations, this measure is also a proxy for vacations for non-school households. This measure was 0 for weeks during summer vacation and ranged from 0 to 100 during the academic year.

(3) Additional measures

Early vs. late time period: We included an index that represented the number of weeks that a participant had access to the Internet and dichotomized it so that 0 indicates the first 26 weeks of the trial and 1 represents weeks 27 through 52. Conclusions about the importance of time, however, were the same whether we treated week or half year as the unit.

Individual differences and other control variables: Previous literature and exploratory analyses of our own data suggested additional variables that might predict the extent to which people would use the Internet. To evaluate alternative explanations, we included the following variables when creating models estimating Internet usage in a particular week: *gender* (female versus male), *generation* (< 19 versus >=19 years old), *race* (minority versus white), and self-reported *computer skill.*

Sample type: This dummy variable specifies how the household was recruited. HomeNet's first sample of families was selected after contacting students in high school journalism programs; the second sample of families included members of local community activist groups.

RESULTS

To examine how use changes with time, we will first present descriptive statistics showing the amount and variability of total Internet usage during participants' first year in the trial. The primary dependent measure is the number of hours each week that participants used the Internet (which is an index of aggregate Internet use). Next, we will differentiate electronic mail and World Wide Web use to test hypotheses that compare participants' use of the Internet for inter-personal communication versus for information and entertainment.

Interrelationships among measures of Internet use

To determine if our differentiation of electronic mail from web use was sensible, we correlated our three major usage variables with the unit of analysis being an individual's behavior during a week. Internet hours during a week correlated highly with both personal electronic mail messages sent and received (r=.81) and with Web sites visited (r=.73). However, Email use was only moderately correlated with Web use (r=.53). These two services have enough independence so that they could have different causes and different effects.

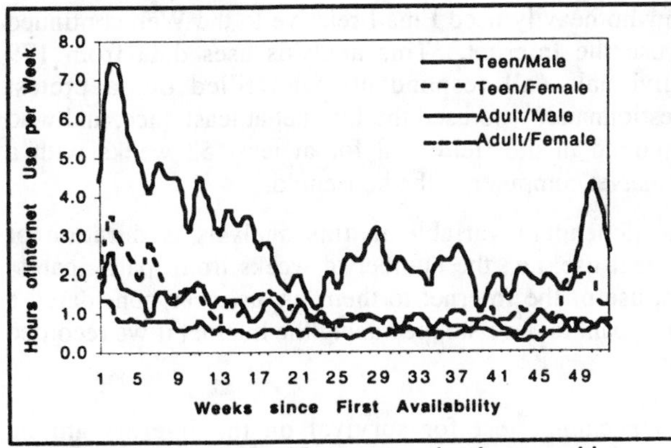

Figure 1: Weekly hours of Internet use by demographic group.

Note: To compensate for skewed data, entries are Winsorized means of data from the middle 80% of the sample.

Preference for Email versus the Web

The most direct way of demonstrating the relative preferences for interpersonal communication versus information and entertainment is to see whether people used their Email application more than they used their Web browser[1]. Overall, participants preferred using Email to the Web. Participants used Email in 44% of their Internet sessions,[2] but used the Web in only 25% of the sessions. Within sessions involving both Email and the Web, participants accessed their Email before they accessed the Web 75% of the time. These analyses support our predictions that Email is more popular than the Web and that Email takes priority in Internet sessions. In only one respect did indicators favor the Web; sessions involving the Web (including downloading) were longer than sessions involving Email. (Means are 40 minutes for Web sessions versus 34 minutes for Email sessions.)

Predicting hours of Internet use

Figure 1 shows demographic differences in Internet usage and an overall decline in weekly use after the first weeks. We analyze these time trends in more detail below.

We used time series regression analyses to examine the influences on a participant's hours of Internet use each week. We used a Mixed Model regression, available from the SAS Institute (Littell et al., 1996), to carry out a panel design. The dependent variable was the hours that a participant was connected to the Internet during a week. Both participant and week were repeated factors modeled as random effects; week was a repeated variable with an autoregressive component of order one. Independent variables included: race, gender, generation, the gender x generation interaction, sociability, computer skill, school days, other household members' hours of use, time period, lagged connect hours, and the interaction of time period with computer skill, household, and lagged connect hours. Individual differences and period were modeled as fixed effects. This design is equivalent to a random effects model for an unbalanced panel. To allow comparisons between size of effects, all variables were standardized to a mean of zero and a standard deviation of one.

Our major goal in this analysis was to understand what influence participants' use of the Internet at one week had on their use in a subsequent week, holding constant a

[1] Note that participants in this field trial could neither send nor retrieve electronic mail via their Netscape browser.

[2] This estimate of Email use is systematically low. Because of the peculiarities of the mail package participants used, our probes recorded electronic mail use only if participants opened their mailboxes to read or send messages. If participants connected to the Internet but discovered that they had no mail waiting and then disconnected, the probes would not record their use of electronic mail in that session.

number of control variables. The coefficient for lagged hours of Internet use represents a stability coefficient, which summarizes the week-to-week predictability over a year of use. To examine whether stability increased with time, we included the interaction of the lagged hours of use with the early-late period variable. We expected that the stability coefficient would be larger in the second half of the year than the first.

The results for the control variables were similar to those we found in earlier research with a smaller sample (Kraut et al., 1996). Males used the Internet for more hours per week than females(β=.06, p<.05), and teenagers used it more than adults (β=.08, p<.01). The effects of gender did not differ for teens and adults (β=.02, p>.10). Race and sociability did not significantly predict computer use.

Participants who possessed more computer skill before the field trial started were heavier users of the Internet throughout the trial (β=.09, p<.01). Surprisingly the effect of self-reported pre-existing skill did not decline with time period (β=.01, p>.10). The positive coefficient, although not significant, shows that the difference between skillful and less skillful people in weekly usage of the Internet was at least as large in the second half of the trial as it was initially.

Participants used the Internet more during weeks when other members of their households were also using the it, suggesting moderate social influence (β=.04, p<.01). The coefficient for time period shows that on average participants' level of use dropped during the course of the year (See Figure 1; β=-.02, p<.05).

As one would expect, heavy Internet use was habitual. By far the strongest predictor of week-to-week variation in the numbers of hours a participant devoted to Internet use one week was the number of hours that the participant spent on the Internet the preceding week (β=.48, p<.001). However, the absence of a significant interaction between time period and lagged connect hours suggests that participants were not gradually developing stable patterns of Internet usage (β=-.00, p<.50). The week-to-week predictability of Internet use was equally strong in the first and last 6 months of the trial period.[3]

Stability of Email and Web use

To determine the relative stability of Email and Web use, we conducted time series analyses similar to the one we just described, but using the number of personal Email messages each week and number of Web sites visited each week as dependent variables. We included Email and Web usage measures lagged at a one week interval. To test comparative stability, we examined whether the stability coefficient (i.e., the standardized beta weights showing whether use in one week predicted use in a subsequent week) was larger for Email or for the Web.

[3] The interaction of time period with lagged connect hours also remained nonsignificant when we used a finer granularity for time— a week rather than 26 weeks.

Both Email use and Web use were stable over time, but stability was substantially greater for Email (β=.62, p<.001) than for the Web (β=.26, p<.001). That is, one can predict a participant's current Email use from his or her use in the prior week much better than one can predict a participant's current Web use from his or her prior Web use (for the difference t=11.0, p<.001).

Generalizability of Email and Web use

To examine generalization (i.e., whether use of Email or the Web leads to greater overall use of the Internet), we added Email and Web usage measures lagged at a one week interval to the model predicting weekly hours of Internet use. While controlling for hours using the Internet in a prior week and other variables, this analysis estimates whether exceptionally heavy or light Email or Web use in a prior week changes the total number of hours participants use the Internet in the current week.

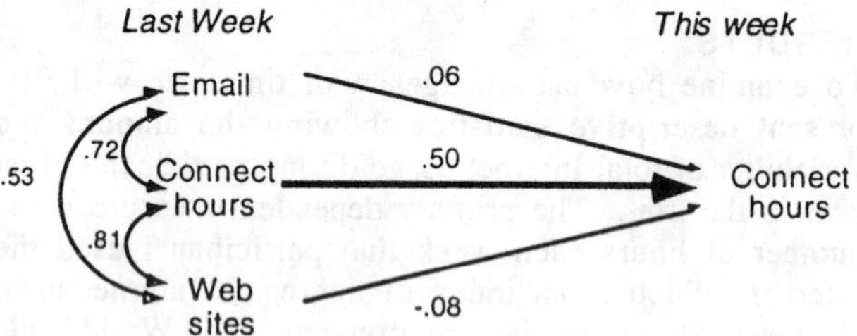

Figure 2: Influence of electronic mail use and World Wide Web use on subsequent Internet use.

Note: Numbers are standardized beta weights.

Figure 2 summarizes the relevant coefficients. When participants sent or received more Email than their average during one week, the next week they logged into the Internet for more time than than was usual for them. In contrast, following weeks in which they used the Web more than average, they decreased their subsequent hours of Internet use. (β_{Email}=.06 versus β_{Web}=-.08; for the difference t=2.8, p<.05).

Survival analysis

We conducted a survival analysis to examine how long people who heavily used Email relative to the Web continued to use the Internet. This analysis uses data from 179 individuals—all respondents who filled out a pretest questionnaire, who used the Internet at least once, and who remained in the field trial for at least 52 weeks with a HomeNet computer in the household.[4]

The dependent variable in this analysis is duration of Internet use, i.e., the number of weeks from participants' first use of the Internet to their last use. We considered a participant to have stopped using the Internet if we recorded

[4] We cannot test for survival on the Internet among participants who never used it. Other participants were dropped from this analysis because they left their household (e.g., through marital separation or going to college) or because the household computer left the household (e.g., a student taking the computer to college).

no Internet activity during weeks 49 through 52. Because the data are right censored at 52 weeks, we used a survival analysis with the Kaplan-Meier method to examine whether greater relative Email use (vs. Web use) led to longer survival on the Internet. To measure Email use relative to Web use, we created a ratio: We standardized Email use (number of messages sent and received) and Web use (the number of web sites visited), divided the former by the sum of both (Email and Web), and then separated participants into low and high relative Email users on the basis of a median split.

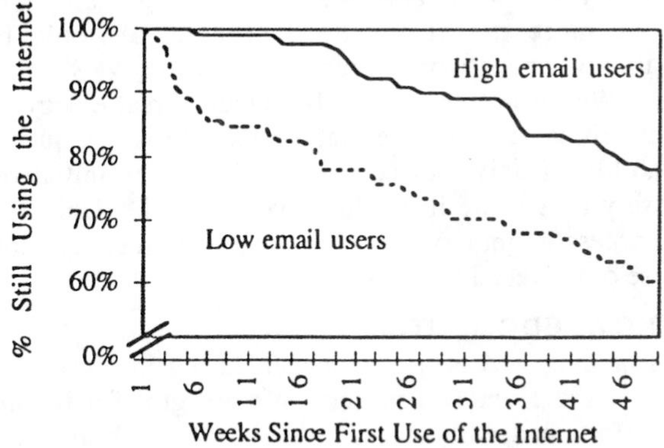

Figure 3. Internet survival by relative Email use

Note: The sample has been divided by median split into those for whom Email is a relatively high or low percentage of all Internet use.

N = 179

Figure 3 shows a plot over time of the proportion of high and low relative Email users who continued to use the Internet during the first year of their Internet subscription. People who use Email more than they use the Web were more likely to continue using the Internet over the course of a year than were people who use the Web more than Email. Seventy-eight percent of the participants with the high Email ratio were continuing to log on to the Internet after a year, compared with only 60% of participants with a low Email ratio (Log-rank chi-square = 8.6, df = 1, p = .003). The high Email users had an average duration on the Internet of 44.5 weeks, compared with 37.8 weeks for the low Email users. Note that the differences in survival come about because a disproportionate number of low Email users dropped out early, within two or three months of first logging on. After four months, the gap between low and high Email users stays constant. The implicit decision to stay or quit seems to have been made early during participants' experience with the Internet. Presumably, the relatively low Email users may not have had enough contact with the Internet early on to discover a sustaining use.

DISCUSSION

Analyses of the HomeNet data provide strong support for the importance of interpersonal communication as compared to information and entertainment in driving people's use of the Internet at home. First, participants preferred Email over the Web. They used Email in more Internet sessions and used Email first in sessions where they used both Email and the Web. Second, participants' use of Email was more stable from week to week than was their Web use. Third, use of Email at one time seemed to increase overall Internet use at a subsequent time, but use of the Web seemed to depress it. Finally, those who used Email more heavily than they used the Web were more committed to the Internet in general. That is, a smaller proportion of them discontinued Internet use during the first year.

Our expectation that early use of the Internet would shape later use was not supported. While we found strong evidence that Internet use became habitual, we found no evidence that predictability in use increased with time.

Why is Email important to people?

One explanation for this pattern of results is that the messages people send and receive by Email sustain dialogues and ongoing relationships with family, friends, and coworkers. These dialogues and relationships tend to be unbounded; that is, they often extend beyond the electronic medium and have no *a priori* stopping time. Participants described a variety of people with whom they had relationships—grandparents, members of the soccer team, teachers, people they met in chat groups. Even in the absence of standing relationships, dialogues conducted by Email have an obligatory character that helps to make them self-perpetuating. It is considered rude to fail to respond to a message.

By contrast, using the Web often satisfies a bounded goal, and may even exert negative pressure for revisits, as when a game is already downloaded, a weather report is obtained, or a homework assignment is completed. In analyses not reported in this paper, we tested this idea by examining participants' loyalty to Email addresses and Web domains over time and found that people were two or three times more likely to reuse an Email address than they were to revisit a Web domain, even a year after its first use.

Interviews with participants in the trial suggest that most (but not all) of the time Email relationships preceded participants' use of the Internet, and Email was just one mechanism that they used to maintain them. For example, we frequently heard of teenagers sending Email to friends whom they have just seen at school.

In other cases, Email energized a pre-existing relationship that had languished. These were ongoing personal relationships that became more intense because of the convenience of electronic communication.

The analyses we report here did not explicitly examine group communication through listservs, news groups, chat services, MUDs or IRCs (Internet Relay Chat). Our interviews, however, suggest that electronic groups may be the primary mechanism by which people start new relationships online. Unlike telephones and more like face-to-face interactions in public settings, electronic groups on the Internet comprise semi-public places where strangers can observe each other privately for awhile ("lurk") and strike up conversations either in the same forum or more privately through Email to particular discussants with whom they identify. Hence, electronic groups provide safe places in which to strike up relationships.

Our analyses do not imply that interpersonal communication is the only resource of value on the Internet. Certainly, a number of participants in our study continued to use the Internet for over a year while sending or receiving virtually no electronic mail. We think of the Internet as a portal through which people have access to a rich array of other people, information, and experience. The depth and diversity of the resources available there mean that virtually anyone could potentially find something or someone to interest him or her. However, finding the most personally relevant resources often requires skills, guidance, and perseverance. Email activity may be one factor that increases the perseverance that allows individuals to find personally relevant resources on the Internet. This speculation is consistent with our finding that the gap in Internet survival between relatively high and low Email users does not increase after four months. It is as if electronic mail keeps people coming back to the Internet until they discover some interest that will sustain their use.

Implications for social impact, technology design, and policy

Our analyses suggest that interpersonal communication does and will continue to dominate residential use of the Internet. If this proves to be the case, then implications for understanding the social impact of the Internet, of providing useful Internet applications, and for public policy choices are large. The commercial development of Internet services and public policy initiatives to date have probably over-emphasized information and entertainment and under-emphasized interpersonal communication.

Computer scientists see the most challenges and most opportunities for the Internet in the burgeoning amount of multimedia data that the Internet makes available to its users; entrepreneurs see them in the Internet's potential as a vehicle for retail sales. Currently on the Internet, applications for finding people are far less common, sophisticated, or accurate than applications for finding information and products. Online directories of Email addresses are far less comprehensive than online directories of telephone numbers. Search services on the Internet, like Yahoo, Alta Vista, InfoSeek, and Lycos, grew from sophisticated industrial and government-funded research programs in information retrieval; they are well known and heavily used. The initiative on digital libraries, funded by the National Science Foundation and DARPA, has a goal of making pictures, graphs, and video images as easy to search and retrieve as text. Comparable search capabilities for finding people based on their attributes are far less well supported. (See the research on collaborative filtering, e.g., Resnick & Varian, 1997, for an interesting exception.) Our data suggest that current design initiatives are imbalanced with respect to what people really want.

Information and entertainment perspectives have also dominated most policy debates about the Internet. For instance, the Federal Communications Decency Act of 1996–struck down by the US Supreme Court (1997)--reflected a widespread concern over children's possible exposure to pornography over the Internet. In contrast, public policy discussion about issues relevant to interpersonal communication has been scant. Consider, for example, the issue of universal access. In the first half of the twentieth century, both industry and the federal government instituted policies to foster universal access to telephone service, subsidizing residential and rural phone subscribers through subscription revenues from businesses or urban areas. One goal was to make the telephone network more useful for the nation as a whole by capitalizing on network externalities (Katz & Shapiro, 1994). We do not prejudge whether universal electronic mail is critical, but believe that a public debate about the desirability of universal access and the policy initiatives necessary to achieve it would be very useful.[5] Universal email access might have benefits to the nation comparable to those of universal phone service.

ACKNOWLEDGMENTS

Jane Manning was project manager during the formative stages of the HomeNet project. We are grateful for her skill, effort, and enthusiasm. Vicki Lundmark and Rob Theilke also provided valuable support in later stages of the project. HomeNet has been supported by grants from Apple Computer, AT&T, Bell Atlantic, Bellcore, Hewlett Packard, Intel, Carnegie Mellon University's Information Networking Institute, Interval Research, The Markle Foundation, the National Science Foundation (Grant #IRI-9408271), the NPD Group, the U.S. Postal Service, and US West. Farallon Computing and Netscape Communications contributed software. The HomeNet project would have been impossible without support from Carnegie Mellon University's Computer Services Group.

REFERENCES

Anderson, Robert H., Tora K. Bikson, Sally A. Law, & Bridger M. Mitchell, *Universal Access to E-Mail: Feasibility and Societal Implications.* MR-650-MF. Rand Corporation, Santa Monica, CA, (November, 1996).

Brandon, Belinda. The *effects of the demographics of individual households on their telephone usage.* Ballinger, Cambridge, MA, (1980).

Carey, John. "Consumer adoption of new communication technologies." *IEEE Communications Magazine*, 27, (1989), 28-32.

Dimmick, John, Jaspreet Sikand, & Scott Patterson, "The gratifications of the household telephone." *Communications Research*,, 21, 5(1994), 641-661.

Eveland, J. & T. Bikson, "Evolving electronic communication networks: An empirical assessment." *Office: Technology and People*, 3, (1987), 103-128.

[5] Anderson et al. (1996) represents one of the few policy analyses of this issue insofar as we are aware.

Fischer, Claude S. *America Calling*. University of California Press, Berkeley, CA, (1992)

Katz, Michael L. & C. Shapiro, "Systems competition and network effects." *Journal of Economic Perspectives*, 8, 2(1994), 93-115.

Kraut, R., W. Scherlis, T. Mukhopadhyay, J. Manning, J., & S. Kiesler, "The HomeNet field trial of residential Internet services." *Communications of the ACM*, 39, (1996), 55-65.

Leiner, Barry M., Vincton G. Cerf, David D. Clark, Robert Kahn, Leonard Kleinrock, Daniel C. Lynch, Jon Postel, Larry G. Roberts, & Stephen Wolff, *A Brief History of the Internet* (Version 3.1). (1997, Feb. 20). http://info.isoc.org/internet-history/

Littell, R. C., G. A. Milliken, W. W. Stroup, R. D. Wolfinger. SAS *System for Mixed Models*, SAS Institute Inc., Cary, NC., (1996).

Mayer, M. "The telephone and the uses of time." . In I. de Sola Pool (Ed.) *The Social Impact of the Telephone*. MIT Press, Cambridge, Massachusetts, (1977), pp. 225-245.

NPD Group, *National Survey of Hardware Ownership*. Author, Port Washington, NY, (1996).

Resnick, Paul, Varian, Hal R., "Recommender Systems: Introduction to the Special Section." *Communications of the ACM*, 40, 3(1997), 56-58.

Sproull, Lee & Kiesler, S. *Connections :New Ways of Working in the Networked Organization*. Cambridge, MA: MIT Press (1991).

Tyre, Marcie & Wanda Orlikowski, "Windows of opportunity: Temporal patterns of technological adoption in organizations." *Organizational Science*, 5, 1(1994), 98-119.

Venkatesh, Alladi. Computers and interactive technologies for the home: Their use and impact—past, present, the future. *Communications of the ACM*, 39 (1996), 47-54.

The *Vista* Environment for the Coevolutionary Design of User Interfaces

Judy Brown
Victoria University of Wellington
P.O. Box 600
Wellington, New Zealand
+64 4 471 5328
Judy.Brown@mcs.vuw.ac.nz

T.C. Nicholas Graham, Timothy Wright
Dep't of Computing and Information Science
Queen's University
Kingston, Ontario, Canada
+1 613 545 6526
{graham,wrightt}@qucis.queensu.ca

ABSTRACT

User centered design requires the creation of numerous design artifacts such as task hierarchy, task-oriented specification, user interface design, architecture design and code. It is increasingly accepted that such artifacts cannot be created in isolation, but instead incrementally coevolve, where information obtained from the development of one artifact contributes to the development of the others. In user interface development, these artifacts are typically developed by different people with different backgrounds, hindering the communication necessary for coevolution. This paper demonstrates how different design artifacts can be linked, exposing their common elements. Such links can be developed despite the differing points of view and differing levels of detail of the design artifacts. This paper describes *Vista,* a prototype tool for examining the links between design artifacts, and demonstrates how making these links explicit supports coevolutionary design.

Keywords

Task-analysis, task-oriented specification, user-interface, architecture, methodology

INTRODUCTION

User-centered design consists of a set of steps such as task analysis, user interface design, task-oriented specification, and implementation. Each step results in a design document that expresses information contributing to the usability of the resulting system. In the software engineering community, it is widely acknowledged that these steps cannot realistically be performed in strict sequence, but are instead carried out concurrently [2,7,13,16]. In the development of user interface software, the requirements of iterative refinement make the need for concurrent development even more pronounced.

If there is continuous feedback between the evolving design representations, each design activity can benefit from information derived in the other steps. For example, user interface design benefits from task analysis; problems in the task analysis can in turn be revealed during user interface design, allowing benefit to be derived in both directions. Fischer et al. [7] refer to concurrent design with multidirectional information flow as the *coevolution* of a set of design artifacts.

Figure 1 shows part of a process for the coevolutionary design of interactive systems. HCI designers and software engineers concurrently produce a set of design artifacts contributing to the system's implementation. These artifacts include task hierarchy, user interface design, task-oriented specification (in the User Action Notation [11]), software architecture and code. A complete process would involve the user community, for example through usability testing.

In our experience, the communication central to coevolutionary design is hindered by the difficulties of relating the design artifacts. Designers cannot see how knowledge from one design artifact can be applied to other artifacts if they cannot easily correlate the information provided in the two artifacts. Designers have difficulty correlating design artifacts since they express information from different points of view (e.g., the users' view vs. the implementer's view) and at different levels of abstraction (e.g., code is much more detailed than architecture) [8].

This paper shows how different user interface design artifacts can be linked to expose their common elements, facilitating the communication on which coevolutionary design is based. To support these links, we have developed *Vista,* a tool that allows designers to simultaneously navigate hyperlinked task hierarchy, task-oriented specification, software architecture and code documents. In Vista, links are developed partly by hand and partly through automated analysis of the design artifacts. The paper is organized as follows. We first introduce an application to be used as an example throughout the paper. We then introduce the design representations supported by the method. The following section explains how these artifacts are linked in *Vista.* The final section analyses the effectiveness of linking design artifacts in supporting coevolutionary design of user interfaces.

CHI 98 Los Angeles CA USA
Copyright 1998 0-89791-975-0/98/ 4..$5.00

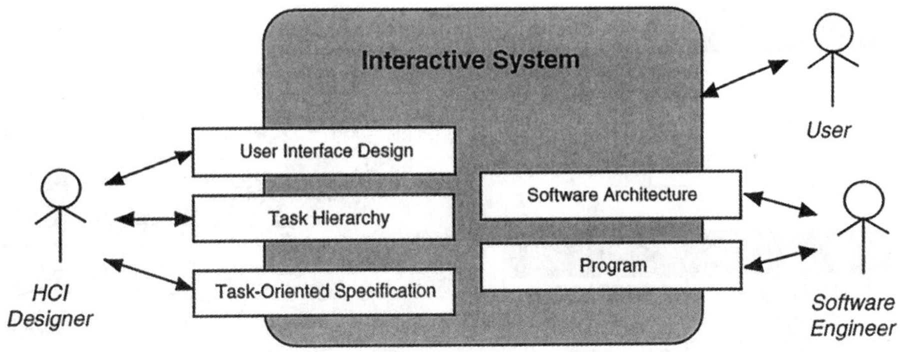

Figure 1: Coevolutionary design of interactive systems. The design process leads to a set of artifacts, which are developed iteratively and incrementally. Improvements in one artifact contribute to improvements in the others. Different artifacts represent the point of view of different participants in the design process.

Figure 2: A collaborative tool for annotating videos.

VIDEO ANNOTATOR

Throughout the paper, we use the example of a groupware video annotation tool [9] to illustrate the use of coevolutionary design. The video annotator allows a group of people to review a video that has been previously recorded and add textual and graphical annotations to frames of interest. All participants in the session see the video playing, and see the annotations of other participants as they are added in real time. Standard VCR controls allow the video to be stopped, fast-forwarded and reversed. A *gestalt* view shows a timeline of the video, in which vertical lines indicate where frames have been annotated. When a participant clicks on one of the vertical lines, the view of all participants moves to the corresponding annotated frame. The annotator was developed to support the collaborative analysis of taped usability testing sessions.

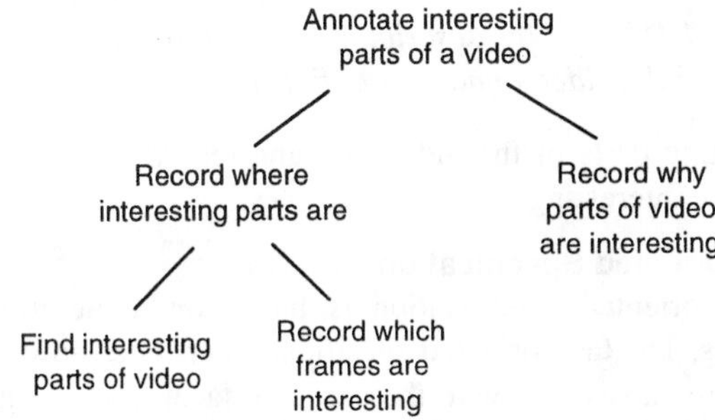

Figure 3: An excerpt from the hierarchical task analysis developed for the video annotator of figure 2.

DESIGN ARTIFACTS

In order to demonstrate how different design notations can be linked, we first review the notations supported by our *Vista* tool and used in the process of figure 1. We concentrate on the three notations of task hierarchy, task-oriented specification and user interface architecture. We chose these notations for the initial version of Vista because they are well defined and because we believe that tool support for these notations could help them become more widely used. We hope to extend Vista in the future to handle other forms of design artifact, such as screen designs, scenarios and videos of usability testing sessions.

Task Analysis

Task analysis is widely used as a means of codifying the goals and tasks of the intended user community [1, 5, 14]. A design artifact resulting from task analysis is a hierarchical task decomposition.

Figure 3 shows an abbreviated task hierarchy for developing an annotated video transcript. The main task is to add annotations to interesting parts of the video. A task hierarchy such as this one shows how the main goal of the users can be decomposed into subtasks that help to achieve this goal. For example, in figure 3, the main goal is decomposed into the subtasks of noting where the

TASK Annotate interesting parts of a video
USER ACTIONS
Record where interesting parts are ‖ Record why parts of video are interesting

TASK Jump to annotation		
USER ACTIONS	INTERFACE FEEDBACK	INTERFACE STATE
~[annotation_mark] Mv	Display current frame and current annotations	Current frame := frame for annotation mark
M^		

Figure 4: UAN tables describing how two tasks are carried out using the video annotator of figure 2.

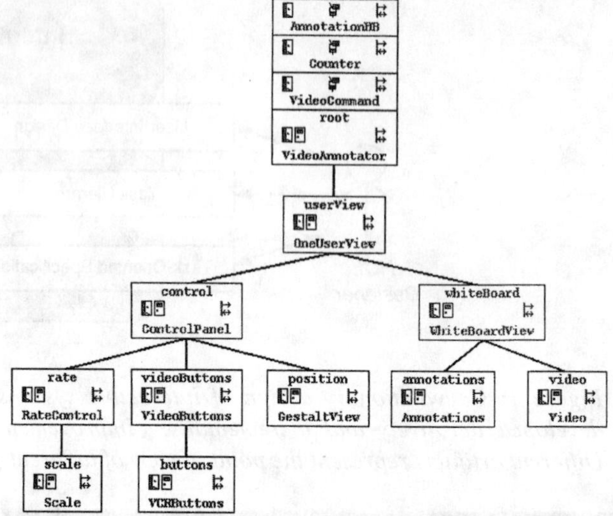

Figure 5: An excerpt from the software architecture of the video annotator of figure 2.

interesting parts of the video are, and recording *why* these parts are interesting.

Task-Oriented Specification

A task-oriented specification is based on a hierarchical analysis. The task-oriented specification encodes how these tasks are carried out with the user interface, from the point of view of a user of the system. In the User Action Notation (UAN) [11], tasks are encoded in a tabular format. Figure 4 shows how the main goal of the system is encoded as a UAN task: in order to annotate interesting parts of the video, the user records where the interesting parts are, and records why those parts are interesting. These are specified under the heading of *User Actions*, as they represent the actions that the user performs in order to carry out the task. The two subtasks are connected by the "‖" symbol, indicating that they may be carried out in any order, or even concurrently.

Task-oriented specifications explain how a user carries out these tasks with the user interface. For example, part of navigating the video involves jumping to a frame that has already been annotated, perhaps to add new annotations. This task is shown in figure 4. The user moves over one of the annotation marks in the gestalt view of the video (~[annotation_mark]) and depresses the mouse button (Mv). The video annotator jumps to the selected frame and shows the correct annotations. The *Interface Feedback* column specifies how the system responds to the user's actions; the *Interface State* column records (in natural language or pseudo-code) the effects of the user's actions on the internal state of the user interface. Finally, the user releases the mouse button (M^), completing the task.

UAN specifications provide precise descriptions of the dynamic aspects of user interfaces. They show how a system is used by walking through the tasks that users wish to perform, showing precisely what users may do, and showing how the user interface responds to the user's actions. The UAN is a useful tool to HCI designers, as it allows the behavior of a user interface to be documented prior to implementation. UAN specifications provide a basis for evaluating user interface designs using cognitive walkthrough.

User Interface Architecture

Software architectures provide a means of decomposing complex systems into smaller parts, simplifying implementation, evolution and maintenance. A number of software architecture styles have been proposed to help in the development of interactive software, particularly the development of multiuser and multimedia applications [3,9, 12,17]. By using an existing architecture style, software engineers benefit from high-level structuring techniques developed by others.

In *Vista*, we use the Clock architecture style for developing user interfaces [9]. This architecture style provides high-level support for distribution, networking, concurrency control and multimedia, freeing developers from low-level programming details. As with a number of other modern architecture styles for user interfaces, Clock architectures are organized as layered model-view-controller (MVC) [15] clusters.

Figure 5 shows an excerpt from the Clock architecture implementing the video annotator. The architecture structure is compositional: the video annotator is composed of one *userView* per user; the user view is composed of a control panel (*control*) and a white board (*whiteBoard*). The architecture is composed of components, which are responsible for processing user inputs and maintaining the display. For example, *video* displays the current video frame, while *annotations* displays any annotations that have been made on that frame. Components may be augmented with *ADTs* which contain application data. For example, the

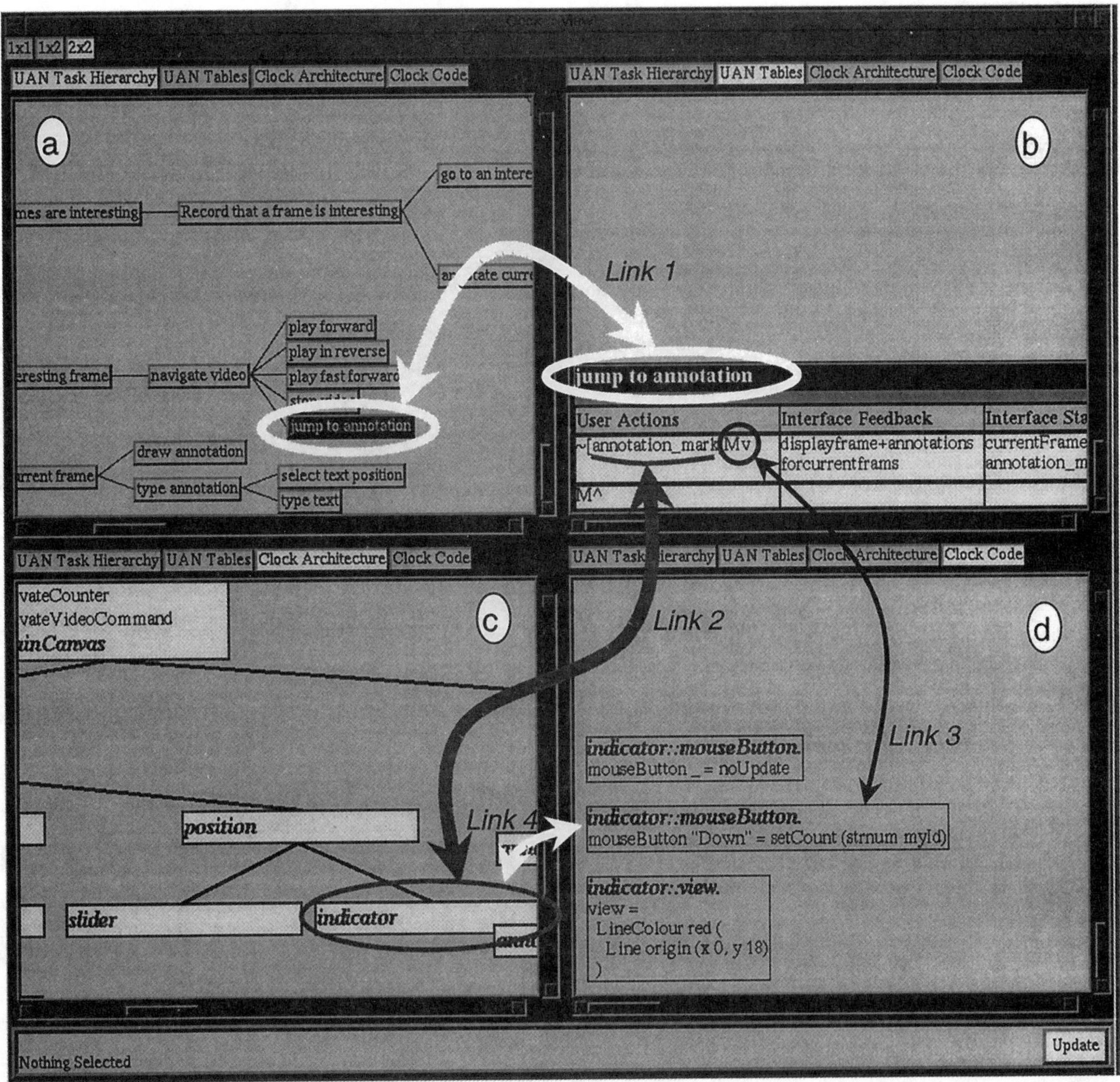

Figure 6: Linked views in Vista. A designer has selected four views of the video annotator application: (a) the task hierarchy; (b) the task-oriented specification in the UAN; (c) the Clock architecture of the application, and (d) the Clock code. The Vista display has been annotated to show some of the links between the design representations. This display has been hand-annotated to show some of the links available to designers and developers.

root component is augmented with the *VideoCommand*, *Counter* and *AnnotationsDB* ADTs. The *AnnotationDB* ADT records which frames are annotated and how, while the *Counter* ADT represents the frame counter.

Components communicate via messages. For example, the *position* component responds to mouse button input (when a user clicks an annotation mark to move to a previously annotated frame.) *Position* uses methods defined in AnnotationDB and Counter to update the display.

Task-oriented and architectural specifications capture similar information. They both specify the functionality of the user interface, but from different points of view. The next section discusses the links between UAN task-oriented specifications and Clock architectures.

LINKS BETWEEN DESIGN REPRESENTATIONS

Figure 6 shows four views of the video annotator as displayed within the *Vista* environment. These views show the design and implementation of the *gestalt* timeline of the video annotator (figure 7). The *Vista* display is split into

Figure 7: The gestalt view of the video annotator (excerpted from figure 2).

four panels showing (a) the hierarchical task-analysis, (b) the UAN task-oriented specification, (c) the Clock architecture and (d) the Clock code of the gestalt view.

The gestalt view supports the task of navigating the video, shown in the task hierarchy panel (*a*). The UAN table of panel *b* shows that users perform this task by selecting an annotation mark along the timeline. The timeline is implemented by the *position* architecture component (shown in panel *c*). The detailed Clock code for this component is shown in panel *d*.

The views of these four panels are connected by hyperlinks, so that when designers click on information in one panel, the corresponding information is shown in the other panels. Figure 6 has been annotated to show four of the hyperlinks available to designers. For example, clicking on the "jump to annotation" task in panel *a* pops up the corresponding UAN table in panel *b* (link 1 in figure 6).

Designers may tile the *Vista* display into one, two or four panels, allowing them to select between more views and bigger panels.

The next section describes the links between the user-centered UAN task-oriented specification and the system-centered Clock architecture specification. Links between other specifications are not as complex. The section explores how the UAN concepts of *context*, *user action*, *interface feedback* and *interface state* are linked to the architectural concepts of *components*, *input events*, *view methods* and *ADTs*.

Linking UAN Contexts to Architecture Components

Clock architecture components implement UAN contexts. For example, in the task "Jump to annotation" of figure 6, the UAN context *annotation_mark* is implemented by the *indicator* architecture component. In *Vista*, clicking on *annotation_mark* in the UAN table highlights the *indicator* component in the architecture view.

Identifying which architecture component implements each UAN context is non-trivial. The HCI designer and the software engineer may have given the same entity a different name (as in the example above). Another problem is that UAN contexts and architecture components do not match on a one-to-one basis. Architecture designers do not necessarily create a new component whenever the UAN specification identifies a new context. Figure 8 shows how one architecture component can implement more than one UAN context. The *button* component of the video annotator supports the *play forward* and *play in reverse* tasks by implementing the *fwd_button* and *rev_button* contexts identified in the UAN task oriented specification. *Vista*

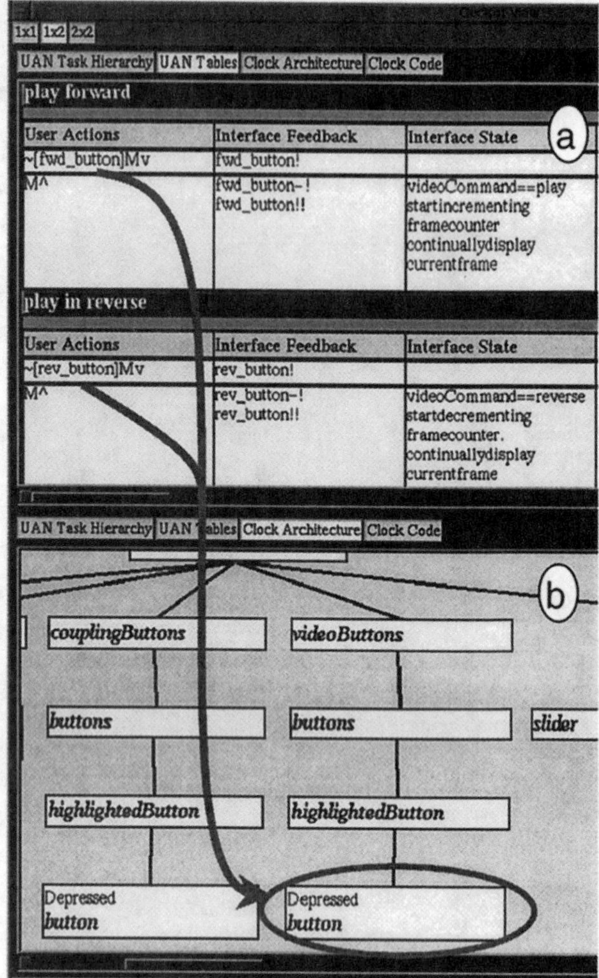

Figure 8: UAN contexts fwd_button and rev_button are both implemented by the button architecture component.

solves the two problems described above by statically binding contexts to components.

Linking UAN Actions to Architecture Components

In a UAN dialogue specification, user actions specify what inputs users perform in order to carry out their task. User actions occur within contexts. For example, in order to jump to a previously annotated frame in the video, the user positions their pointer over an annotation mark (~[annotation_mark]) in the gestalt view and then depresses the mouse button (Mv). The "Mv" action therefore occurs in the context of the annotation mark. User actions are processed by the architecture component implementing the action context. The *indicator* component implements the annotation mark context, and therefore processes the "Mv" user action. Figure 6(d) gives the code of the *mouseButton* method contained in the *indicator* component. The method responds to a mouse button "down" action by issuing a *setCount* message, which updates the current frame number.

User actions are therefore linked to the components that implement those actions. Clicking on the "Mv" symbol in figure 6(b) displays the method that handles mouse button events (link 3), and highlights the component that contains the method (link 4).

Linking UAN Interface Feedback Specifications to Component Views

The column in a UAN table labeled "Interface Feedback" specifies how the display should change in response to user input. The software engineer uses this information to implement the view methods of architecture components. In the video annotator, clicking down on any of the control buttons (*play*, *fast-forward*, etc.) highlights the button. In the UAN, we indicate that the forward button should be highlighted when depressed by writing "fwd_button!" in the *Interface Feedback* column (figure 8(a)). In the architecture, highlighting is implemented by the *button* component (figure 8(b)). When the *button* component receives the mouse button input (not shown), it changes the appearance of the button, providing feedback to the action of depressing the mouse.

In *Vista*, clicking the "fwd_button!" text in figure 8(a) highlights the button component of figure 8(b) which implements the appearance of the play button.

Linking UAN Interface State to ADTs

User actions can cause displays to change but they can also trigger state changes. In the UAN, these state changes are specified using pseudo-code in the "Interface State" column of the UAN table. States are implemented in Clock architectures as abstract data types (ADTs), which are attached to architecture components. The state that is referenced in the pseudo-code of the UAN tables can then be linked to the ADTs implementing the state.

For example, in figure 8(a), the UAN specifies that clicking on the *rev_button* should change the video command state to reverse ("videoCommand == reverse"). The video command state is implemented by the *VideoCommand* ADT located in the root of the architecture tree (figure 5). *Vista* implements links between interface state and ADTs. For example, clicking on the *videoCommand* text in figure 8(a) highlights the *VideoCommand* ADT.

This section has shown that four diverse artifacts from the user-centered design of user interfaces can be effectively linked. The links between design representations are complex, due to their differing points of view and differing levels of detail. The next section discusses how the ability to display these complex relationships aids in the coevolutionary design of user interfaces.

ANALYSIS

The last section showed how the *Vista* tool exposes the common elements of different design artifacts by linking these artifacts. In this section, we discuss how linking design artifacts supports the coevolutionary design of user interfaces. Our experience with *Vista* has been gained from four case studies: the development of a critical path planning application, the video annotator, a simple video player, and of *Vista* itself. Each of these case studies involved a group of people working on different aspects of the design and implementation, and each involved coevolution. Two of the applications are complex, two involve multimedia, and two are real-time groupware applications. We illustrate the benefits of links through examples from the video annotator application, and by discussing our experience in applying *Vista* to its own development.

Linking design artifacts helps designers collaborate in two ways: by helping to bridge gulfs of communication, and by adding value to the artifacts each designer uses.

Links aid communication among designers by showing how parts of one design artifact are reflected in others. This helps designers quickly locate parts of other design artifacts that are of interest to them, allowing them to access information in the artifact without having to read and understand it in its entirety.

We shall separately consider how links are helpful to HCI designers and to software engineers.

How Links Help HCI Designers

Linking design artifacts helps HCI designers by revealing the state of development, providing feedback on the implementation of the task specification, and by helping with the analysis of the complexity of the user interface design.

Reveal the State of Development

Linking the design artifacts developed by software engineers to those developed by HCI designers helps communicate the state of development to the HCI designers. HCI designers can see what features have been provided to implement their designs, and how far the implementation has progressed. Even if the HCI designer does not understand the details of an architecture, seeing its complexity gives the designer feedback on the feature's implementation cost. This feedback can aid discussions on whether user interface features should be redesigned to reduce the difficulty of their implementation.

For example, HCI designers can see that the task of navigating the video is implemented in components implementing a set of arrow buttons, and by the gestalt view.

Support Continual Refinement of Task Hierarchy

Task descriptions are not static entities, but instead evolve as understanding of users' tasks improves, and as the tasks themselves evolve as new technologies and processes are introduced in the workplace. Implementation helps in refining the understanding of how users perform their jobs, and how users will change their work patterns following the introduction of the system under development. Ideally, this information should be fed back to the HCI designers who perform the task analysis. Links between architecture and task-oriented specification can help facilitate this feedback.

We experienced this feedback in the development of the *Vista* tool itself. *Vista* was originally developed in order to demonstrate how links could be found between different design artifacts. The original task analysis underlying *Vista* paid little attention to how designers would actually use the tool to build systems. Once the first prototype had been built, it became evident that a tool of this form would be useful to developers. The task analysis was revised to better show how the tool would be used to support coevolution.

One concrete improvement to *Vista*'s design that resulted from this process was the identification that links need to be preserved as the structure of the architecture evolves. Architecture structure evolves significantly throughout coevolutionary design. The need to automatically maintain links throughout this evolution was not demonstrated in the original task analysis, but became clear when the second task analysis was developed. This in turn identified a significant flaw in the design of the *Vista* tool itself.

Indicate Complexity and Design Parsimony

Links between tasks and architecture components show what components are required to implement a task. The number of components gives some measure of the complexity of the task-action mapping. The links from task-oriented specification to architecture therefore augment the information present in the task-oriented specification, providing useful additional information to the HCI designer.

Similarly, linking architecture back to task hierarchy gives a measure of the parsimony of the user interface design, showing how many tasks are supported by a single component.

For example, the task hierarchy for the video annotator (figure 3) shows separate tasks for annotating a frame and for identifying that a frame is interesting. *Vista* shows that these tasks are in fact carried out by the same mechanism of annotating a frame, as implemented by the *Whiteboard* architecture component.

How Links Help Software Engineers

Linking design artifacts helps software engineers by helping to keep the perspective of the user visible throughout implementation. We found that links help keep design rationale visible and aid in implementation.

Keeps the Design Rationale Visible

Links between task hierarchy and architecture help to record design rationale. Links clearly show the implementer what tasks a user interface feature is meant to support. This helps the implementer assess the importance of keeping the feature as designed. In particular, user interface features may have been designed to support more than one task. In the heat of implementation, a software engineer may lose track of these multiple contexts of use, and optimize a feature for one kind of use. Links from architecture to task hierarchy avoid this problem by revealing to implementers all contexts of a feature's use.

For example, the gestalt view of the video annotator (figure 7) can be seen as an aid to navigation. The gestalt view requires a difficult custom implementation, since it cannot be based on standard widgets provided with user interface toolkits. An implementer might be tempted to substitute a different navigation mechanism that is easier to implement. The task hierarchy (figure 3) shows, however, that a major task of users is to find out what parts of a video are interesting. The gestalt view supports this task – wherever annotations form a cluster in the gestalt view, a segment of the clip is interesting. A different interaction technique might support the navigation function of the gestalt view, but not the analysis function of identifying interesting segments of the video. By linking the task-oriented specification to the architecture view, the two functions of the gestalt view are clearly shown.

Aiding Implementation

User interface implementation is complex, and can be greatly helped by the precise descriptions provided by UAN specifications. Our experience with programmers using UAN specifications has shown, however, that programmers complain about the length of UAN specifications, the distance of UAN specifications from their code, and the difficulty of locating relevant parts of UAN specifications [8]. Linking architecture and code to UAN specifications helps programmers find what parts of the task-oriented specification are relevant to the part of the system under development. The precise specifications are then readily available and the chances of forgetting important requirements are reduced.

Task-oriented specifications provide a reminder of the user's perspective. It is helpful to implementers to be able to quickly retrieve this perspective through *Vista*'s hyperlinks.

RELATED WORK

The work described in this paper draws on a wide body of related research in task analysis, task-oriented specification and software architecture. It is widely accepted that coevolutionary design is a natural and preferred design process [2,4,6,7,10,13,16].

The importance of task analysis in implementation is widely recognized [5]. Diaper [6] links task analysis with entity modeling by automatically generating entity life history matrices. Adept [14] is a tool for automatically generating user interfaces from task modeling artifacts which has been used in the domain of medical applications. In our earlier work, we showed how software architectures can be methodically derived from task-oriented specifications [8].

Vista depends on the inclusion of software architecture design in the development process. Software architecture provides a high-level abstraction for code that makes links more clear. In recent years, there has been substantial work in demonstrating the importance of software architecture in the development of interactive systems [3,9,12,17]. The architecture styles that have been proposed all have common elements: a hierarchical structure representing the compositional structure of the user interface, and a reliance on implicit invocation (through constraints or view triggers) for display updates. This convergence of basic features in user interface architecture styles suggests that *Vista*'s linking techniques could be applied to implementation languages other than Clock.

CONCLUSIONS

This paper has shown that design artifacts developed to produce user-interfaces can represent radically different views of a system under development. We have described two design artifacts that represent a user-centered perspective and an implementer's perspective of a system under development. We described the links between these two design artifacts in some detail. We then presented a tool called *Vista* that was developed to help designers explore design artifacts through these related links.

We presented a view of the development process of a system that suggests that design artifacts coevolve. We have shown how this is the case with the two design artifacts we focused on in this paper. We believe that coevolution of design artifacts can be supported by tools like *Vista* that visually display user-interface design artifacts and their links.

The work with Vista is ongoing. We are currently researching how links can be created and maintained in a more automatic manner than our current approach. A new Java-based version of Clock is being developed, which should allow Vista to be migrated to a more conventional programming language.

ACKNOWLEDGMENTS

The video annotator example [9] was programmed by Tore Urnes. This work was partially supported by the Natural Science and Engineering Research Council, the Information Technology Research Centre and Communications and Information Technology Ontario.

REFERENCES

1. Berry, R., Isensee, S. and Roberts, D. *OVID: Object View and Interaction Design,* Tutorial notes for CHI97.
2. Booch, G. *Object-Oriented Analysis and Design with Applications, 2nd ed.* The Benjamin/Cummings Publishing Company, Inc. 1994.
3. Coutaz, J., PAC: an object-oriented model for dialog design, *Proceedings of INTERACT'87,* 431-436, 1987.
4. Curtis, B. *...But You Have to Understand, This Isn't the Way We Develop Software at Our Company.* MCC Technical Report STEP-203-89. May 1989.
5. Diaper, D. Task observation for Human-Computer Interaction. In Diaper, D., editor, *Task Analysis for Human-Computer Interaction.* Ellis Horwood, 1989.
6. Diaper, D. Integrating HCI and Software Engineering Requirements Analysis. *SIGCHI Bulletin* 29, 1, 41-50.
7. Fisher, G., Redmiles, D., Williams, L., Puhr, G.I., Aoki, A. and Nakakoji, K. Beyond Object-Oriented Technology: Where Current Approaches Fall Short. *Human-Computer Interaction,* 10,1, 79-119, 1995.
8. Graham, T.C.N., Damker, H., Morton, C., Telford, E. and Urnes, T., *The Clock Methodology: Bridging the Gap Between User Interface Design and Implementation.* York University Technical Report CS-96-04, 1996.
9. Graham, T.C.N. and Urnes, T, Integrating Support for Temporal Media into an Architecture for Graphical User Interfaces, in *Proceedings of ICSE'97,* ACM Press, 172-183 ,1997.
10. Graham, T.C.N., Viewpoints Supporting the Development of Interactive Software, in *Proceedings of Viewpoints 96,* ACM Press, 263-267, October 1996.
11. Hartson, H.R., Siochi, A.C. and Hix, D. The UAN: A user-oriented representation for direct manipulation interface designs. *ACM Transactions on Information Systems* 8, 3, ACM Press, 181-203, July 1990.
12. Hill, R.D., Brinck,T., Rohall,S.L. and Patterson,J.F. The *Rendezvous* language and architecture for constructing multiuser applications. *ACM Transactions on Computer-Human Interaction* 1,2, 81-125, June 1995.
13. Jacobson, I. *Object-Oriented Software Engineering: A Use Case Driven Approach.* Addison-Wesley, 1992.
14. Johnson, P., Johnson, H. and Wilson, S. *Rapid Prototyping of User Interfaces Driven by Task Models in Scenario-Based Design: Envisioning Work and Technology in System Development.* John Wiley & Sons Inc., 1995.
15. Krasner, G. and Pope, T., A Cookbook for using the Model-View-Controller Interface Paradigm. *Journal of Object-Oriented Programming,* 1,3, 26-49, 1988.
16. Parnas, D.L. and Clements, P.C., A Rational Design Process: How and Why to Fake it. *IEEE Transactions on Software Engineering* SE-12,2, 251-257, Feb. 1986.
17. Taylor, R.N., Nies,K.A., Bolcer,G.A., MacFarlane,C.A., Anderson, K.M. and Johnson, G.F. Chiron-1: A Software Architecture for User Interface Development, Maintenance, and Run-Time Support. *ACM Transactions on Computer-Human Interaction,* 2,2, 105-144, 1995.

Tools For Incremental Development of Educational Software Interfaces

Wolff Daniel Dobson
The Institute for the Learning Sciences &
Department of Computer Science
Northwestern University
Evanston, IL 60201
+1 847 491 3500
wolff@cs.nwu.edu

Christopher K. Riesbeck
The Institute for the Learning Sciences &
Department of Computer Science
Northwestern University
Evanston, IL 60201
+1 847 491 3500
riesbeck@ils.nwu.edu

ABSTRACT

In this paper we describe the evolution of an educational software tool designed to let non-programmers build content-rich learning environments. Version 1 was a wholly model-driven authoring environment, but was unpopular with authors as they were forced them to build up-front domain representations before prototyping their interfaces. Version 2 uses a GUI method of interface development while the model is developed incrementally and as needed. In this version, authors built less of a model overall, but were more satisfied with the results. This paper discusses the natures of the two approaches to model-building and how they are authored.

Keywords

Educational software, interface design, interface tools, intelligent systems, INDIE, goal-based scenario.

INTRODUCTION

For computer-based instruction to have a noticeable effect on the world's educational landscape, educators will need to build thousands of software "lessons" in thousands of different, unrelated fields. Anyone who can write a textbook (or small group of such authors), if armed with a video camera and a good software development tool, should be able to build multimedia educational software.

INDIE, developed and used at ILS, is an attempt at such an educational-software-building tool. The systems INDIE builds have enough intelligence to be able to offer the student a variety of choices and to critique those choices. The topic of this paper is the problem of building tools for authors that scale easily from simple interface interactions to a well-represented domain model without significant re-implementation at each stage of design and without significant programmer involvement. Both of these issues, as demonstrated with the INDIE tool, tend to be difficult problems when building educational software.

INDIE: WHAT THE STUDENT SEES

INDIE builds a particular kind of educational software, a case-based, learning-by-doing style of program called a Goal-Based Scenario (GBS). A GBS is a simulated world in which students, under the watchful eyes of coaches, experts, and critics, try to achieve a set of goals. Students are given these goals, an initial situation, specific tools for information collection and management, and a way to communicate their claims and knowledge. The pedagogical rationale behind GBSes can be found in [3,4].

Figure 1: Lake temperature results in *Volcano Investigator*

As the student works on the problems presented, the system tracks what's happening. As needed or requested by the student, the system uses experts captured on video to guide, coach, critique and give real world examples of similar situations. A GBS is not a typical classroom setting; it is supposed to be like learning on the job, only better because experts are available all the time for help and review.

The INDIE tool builds a certain subclass of GBS learning environments that centers around diagnosis tasks. Students are given an urgent problem that needs diagnosing (such as a patient with an unknown illness), and then given tools to gather information about the case (tests to run on the patient, documents to inspect, and so forth). After investigating the case, students make a claim about the case and build a report from the evidence they have collected to prove it.

Along the way, students can ask for help and browse a richly-indexed multimedia hypertext network called an ASK system[1]. The central idea in ASK systems is that all information is linked to other information via follow-up questions. For example, if an expert in a video clip mentions how volcanoes are caused by magma being forced to the surface during earthquakes, follow-up questions might be, "What is magma?" and "What causes earthquakes?"

INDIE Example: Volcano Investigator

An example of a current INDIE project is "Volcano Investigator," where the student plays the role of an expert volcanologist brought in to decide whether or not a town at the foot of a volcano should be evacuated.

After hearing an introduction, students can run six different tests on the volcano. Each one provides evidence, in the form of itemized points, that appears in the notebook to the side of the screen. Figure 1 shows an example of a student seeing the result of a lake temperature test.

After gathering this test-based information, students can submit their suggestion (evacuate now, don't evacuate, or evacuate soon) to the mayor of the town. They choose a claim, then drag points from their notebook to a report to support this claim. The mayor comments on the proposal, and then the students' work is critiqued by an on-screen co-worker. The critiquing mechanism (the "critiquer") comments on whether or not the claim is well-supported, looking for missing, irrelevant, or conflicting evidence points in the report (Figure 2).

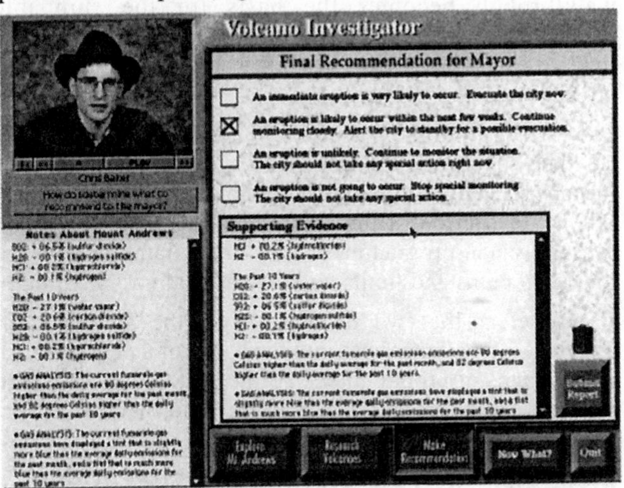

Figure 2: Submitting a report in *Volcano Investigator*

Domain Modeling

To have the student learn about the domain, authors need to be able to model it in software. A solid model gives students the opportunity to interact with "the real thing," so to speak, and gives the GBS a good basis for remediating the student. Authors then need tools to let them model the world, provide feedback to students, and let students have access to experts.

More importantly, the model should allow for smooth scale-up. If a program is just a collection of screens with buttons connecting them, each addition of a scenario or a test would require linearly more information. Instead, we'd like development times where building the first scenario or test takes the longest, and building each additional scenario or test costs asymptotically less.

With this definition of INDIE and its intent, we can now answer the question, how do INDIE projects get built and who builds them?

THE GBS DESIGN PROCESS

Staff and students at the Institute for the Learning Sciences have built eight GBSes with INDIE, and from those experiences we have revised our tool quite heavily to support that process. Based on these projects, we have divided development into the following stages of tool use:

1 Pre-tool. Authors collect information about their domain from experts and books in preparation for doing a full design. At this point, they usually work on white boards or notebooks.

2 Storyboard: Authors concretely envision what the program will look like. They use paper or programs like Powerpoint or Director to make a linear sequence of screens, each screen showing one or two mouse clicks in the demonstration. Although the introduction to the scenario is usually complete, tests and remediation are usually extremely sketchy.

3 First Walkthrough: Authors animate their storyboard, this time doing a higher-fidelity mockup of the interface. For non-tool projects, this can be built in Director or Supercard, with working buttons, some movies, and functional art. The path through the program is still mouse click to mouse click and extremely linear. Some expert video is shot but most of it has not been indexed into the ASK system.

4 Prototype of first scenario: A nearly-complete scenario is built. The conceptually hard parts are designed (such as all the tests and the structure of the critiquing), but the application often supports only two or three different paths through the content (often corresponding to different demo lengths for different audiences). The application is implemented on the final delivery platform.

5 Shrinkwrapped system: This is a delivery-level system. Full content is available, all tests are running, the critiquer is complete, and enough supporting material has been entered such that all claims can be successfully supported or disconfirmed.

Applications will go through several iterations within stages and across them.

An important thing to note is that frequently projects never get past the first few stages. Projects developed by students, depending on the project size, last one to five months, which generally isn't enough time to build shrinkwrapped systems. Often prototypes are built as research projects or proposals, and after the proposal is demonstrated, the project never gets any further.

Investing time at the beginning of a project in model infrastructure can pay off later when finishing the program. However, if the project isn't going to be finished, why spend the time on infrastructure? This problem was key to the failure of our first tool, INDIE 1.0.

INDIE 1.0: A MODEL-DRIVEN-APPROACH

The first iteration had a strong task model of the tasks in a diagnosis scenario. The model was divided into several different modules:

- *The Problem Selector:* Students choose a scenario to work on–in Volcano, it was which mountain to work on.
- *The Lab:* Students run tests and talk to experts in the field, collecting information.
- *The Argument Constructor:* Students make claims to the clients in the simulation, suggesting different courses of action or diagnosises (i.e. "The volcano is going to erupt tomorrow.")
- *The Critiquer:* Students hear feedback from the client, telling them what is wrong with their submitted claims and letting them ask questions about them.

Each one of these modules had a default interface layout–one or two "screens" for each, and then specific buttons for each kind of interaction: one button per scenario, one button per possible thing to say back to the client, and so forth. If authors wanted to add a scenario button, they would edit the problem-selection module to add another scenario, and a button would be automatically added to the scenario-selection screen. Our goal was to automatically supply the interface so that authors could concentrate on the content.

Authors found INDIE 1.0 very restrictive for several reasons. First, the tool built applications that didn't look the way they wanted them to look, and changing that "look" required the INDIE programming team to reprogram the interface.

Also, and probably more importantly, building the modules' model representations didn't work well. Authors, who had been drawing screens on paper and Powerpoint in the late stages of the idea phase, were suddenly forced to understand the INDIE model representation, and construct objects in it. For example, to make a specific test show a specific result, authors had to create:

- a test (such as finding the content of the gases emitting from a volcano)
- a set of scenario facts (such as that the volcano is about to erupt)
- a prop that could be tested (such as some volcanic gases)
- a table that specifies the results that occurs when the student runs this test on this prop in this scenario

Unfortunately, all that the authors wanted to say was, "When this button is pressed, play this movie." Defining interactions in the model (such as the results of tests, the relationship between available help and the tests, and getting critiquing running) required a fair amount of time, yet authors frequently rebuilt them due to design changes. In other words, rapid prototyping was difficult. Design iterations took full-time consulting from the INDIE programming team and much planning by authors.

On one project slated to use this version of INDIE, project-assigned programmers built an interactive walkthrough in Supercard rather than INDIE. The walkthrough had no model. They did this because, like all teams, they had a limited amount of time, and it was easier and faster to mock something up in Supercard than to use INDIE.[1]

The Trouble With Mock-Ups

The problem with building a mock-up in Supercard or Director is that turning such a prototype into a shippable program requires a complete re-implementation of the program in a new tool (probably INDIE). Supercard and Director use languages and representations that are largely scripting tools. To support INDIE questions, answers, rules, widgets, and screens, complete with hyperlinked data, nested structures, and modern model/interface separation is well beyond the scope of a scripting language. So, after spending time and effort building such a mock-up, helpful as it was in the early stages, there would be little or no reuse of this artifact in the final product outside of a few bits of art and video.

The major issue for product delivery is to consider the total length of time on the project. If the project is completely re-implemented in a new tool, a very large portion of the time spent building the mock-up will be wasted, thus increasing the total project length. If authors started building on the final delivery platform from the beginning, the time spent on walkthroughs isn't wasted; the walkthrough becomes the basis for the shippable application. However, authors couldn't afford to spend the time up front due to short deadlines at the beginning of the project.

Even worse from the perspective of final delivery, authors are likely to (and did) design interface and model interactions that are difficult or impossible to implement for real as they felt no restrictions from their mock-up tool. Authors, especially non-programmers, who aren't familiar with the tool's strengths and limits will construct almost anything.

It was clear that we needed to get the authoring of storyboard-level interfaces into the hands of authors and out of the hands of programmers. At the same time, we had to preserve the authoring of the model information that the full-scale application would require.

INDIE 2.0: IF YOU CAN'T BEAT SUPERCARD...

Thus, there were three problems with INDIE 1.0's model-driven approach to authoring that we needed to address:

- Authors had trouble getting the "look" they wanted while manipulating the model.

---

[1] The other three projects in the first version of the tool were built within the tool from the start, although with extremely heavy support from the INDIE programming team.

- Rapid prototyping of ideas was difficult and time-consuming.
- Authors would duplicate effort between building prototypes and their final products.

Essentially, we wanted authors to have free rein to prototype, but have their application scale-up to a completed application without having to lose the work they did on their prototype.

Simple Interface Editing

To give authors the look they wanted, we made building the interface entirely separate from constructing the model representation. Interfaces are now built with Supercard-like buttons, pictures, and movie-players. Authors can drag different widgets off a palette, re-size them, change their attributes, then test them immediately by switching from an interface-designing mode to a system-test mode.

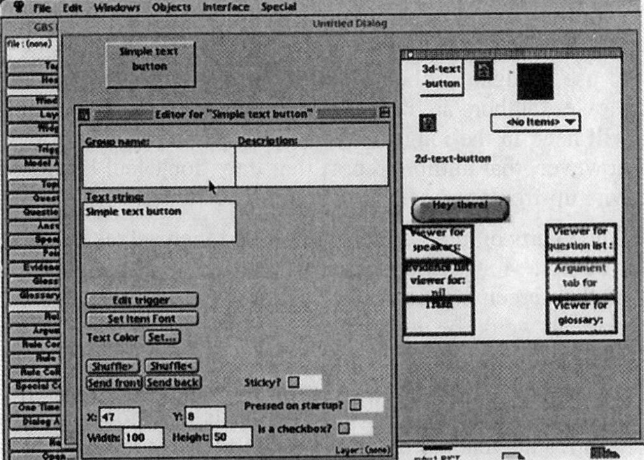

Figure 3: The INDIE tool visual editor

In this example, the author has created a "Go to map" button and is editing its attributes. The attribute editor is accessed simply by double-clicking the widget. Widgets can be grouped into "layers," which can be shown or hidden as a unit, giving authors the ability to make reusable screens and sub-screens.

Simple Interface Action Editing

Though interfaces can be very complicated, what happens in the interface in an INDIE application can be broken down into three classes:

- Show or hide a screen or some subportion of a screen, or else switch windows entirely.
- Play a movie.
- Make one or more ASK questions visible on screen as clickable buttons.

Examples of these from the Volcano project include:

- Show the result of a lake temperature test (show a picture and play a movie explaining it, then add a list of follow-up questions),
- Respond to the press of a button that says "Go to the lake" (show a group of widgets, then play a guide movie).

We supported this by allowing authors to create event response lists. Entries in a system-wide table associate an event (which can be a model- or interface-level event) to a list of screens, movies, and help questions that can appear. Each line in the table, which is a combination of event and a response to it, is called a "trigger." Any time an event occurs, the system looks up in the table for a matching event pattern and then executes what it finds in the response list. These triggers are constructed with a fill-out form that can be seen later in the paper.

The trigger-editing form is a simple visual programming system that most authors are able to grasp quickly. Authors don't have to learn any syntax or construct a list of commands from scratch; they can just fill in the blanks. The blanks are the same as those listed above: play a movie, show this list of questions, and show or hide some group of widgets on screen. If an author wants to show a sequence of responses (such as several introductory movies in a row), he or she can chain together several triggers at any length for very long interactions.

Modgets: When Triggers Aren't Enough

Though triggers are invaluable for letting authors construct and prototype interface ideas, they are only useful when building navigation, introductions, and conclusions. They aren't sufficient for the more complex responses necessary in sophisticated educational software. For example INDIE applications contain frequent on-screen help. It appears as clickable buttons on screen, as in Figure 4.

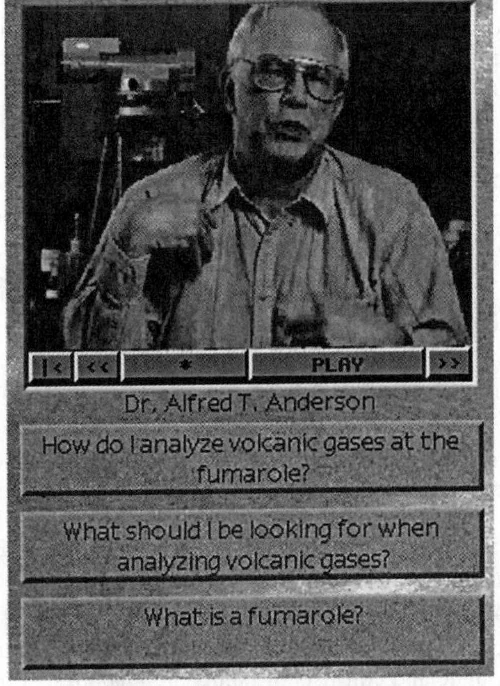

Figure 4: An ASK Modget

All INDIE applications have this sort of just-in-time ASK system. It consists of a list of clickable question buttons and an area where answers appear. When a question is "asked" (i.e. the button is clicked on), a *media item* (movie, text, or picture) response appears in the box above the list of questions. After the media item plays, a list of follow-up questions to it appear below it. These follow-ups have their own answers with follow-ups, which can lead students into a vast web of interlinked questions and answers.

Authors *could* build each question as a separate button widget whose trigger shows the appropriate movie and then shows other widgets, but this would become extremely cumbersome since there are usually hundreds of ASK questions in an INDIE project.

Instead, authors drag out a pair of widgets from the palette. The first is called an "answer-viewer." Answer-viewers show answers (i.e. any kind of picture, text, or movie). Any answer that is "shown" is played in the answer-viewer widget. There can be many different viewers and authors can, for each answer, choose in which viewer the answer will play.

The second widget is a "question-viewer." It is resizeable and supports different looks and styles of question button. Authors can specify multiple question viewers, and then associate each question with a viewer.

Answer-viewers and question-viewers are called in INDIE parlance "modgets," which is a term that combines "model" and "widget." Modgets are widgets that have a predefined interface interaction with the underlying model. They show what is happening in the model for certain kinds of objects: questions and answers, in this case.

When a student clicks on a question button, the answer for the question the button represents is declared shown. The answer's follow-up questions are declared visible. An answer-viewer then shows the correct media item while the buttons for follow-up questions appear in the appropriate question-viewers. This is shown in Figure 5.

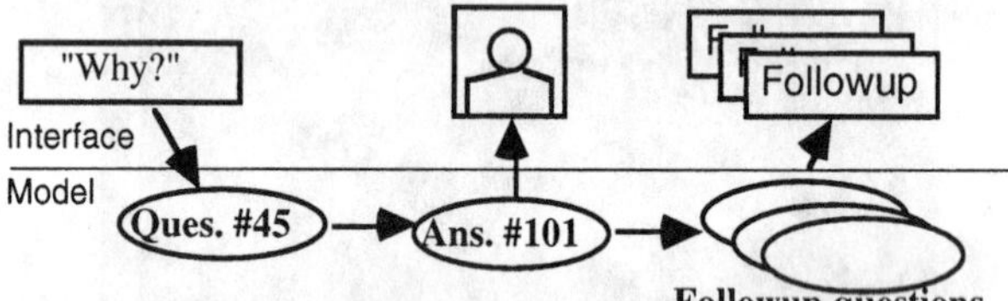

Figure 5: Model/interface interactions when asking questions

Questions and answers are model objects that are authored separately with a database-like tool.

This is a big win for authors–they only have to author two widgets, yet they can scaleably add hundreds of questions to their ASK systems. This sort of scaleability is why we have a model in the first place, and what differs INDIE from Supercard and its ilk.

Other modgets

There are other modgets, such as those that let students manipulate and edit lists of points in *notebooks*. A point is a sentence or two of text which summarizes the contents of a media item or describes the results of a test. It can act as evidence for or against an argument. A point first becomes visible when the student has seen the answer or result that it describes. Eventually, students will drag these points from a working notebook (where they appear as the students explore) to reports that argue for or against claims.

Notebook modgets (which represent working notebooks as well as reports) work in a similar manner to question-viewer modgets–each point is associated with a notebook, and when a point is made visible, a draggable text item is added to the viewer. Notebooks, aside from having editable properties like font and size and repositionable, automatically support dragging and dropping between them.

There are also glossary modgets, trash modgets (where students drag points when they want to remove them from a notebook), and argument-status modgets that show whether or not students can go on to the next scenario. All of these modgets indicate the state of the model, and are quite similar to model-view-controllers [2].

Scaleable Representations

The intent of modgets is almost to "sneak" representation into authors' early design stages. Authors of INDIE projects know they need questions, answers (both in response to questions and as general media items), and notebooks. The easiest way to put them in storyboards and walkthroughs is to use modgets. When making the modgets show text or movies, authors are in fact building parts of the model they will need in the long run. The modgets are visual enough, however, that authors report that they don't feel burdened with up-front representation building.

Some parts of an interface do not lend themselves easily to modgets. Modgets work best when there is a small section of the screen where some homogenous action will take place. It would be difficult, for instance, to come up with a modget that would represent tests. A test can be anything from looking through a microscope to feeling every part of a dog for injuries. Conceptually, tests are model objects with results that are based on which scenario the student is currently working on, which is a structure found in most domains. However, the *look* of the test is quite varied. For these, authors tend to depend on combination of widgets and conditional triggers.

SCALING UP CONDITIONAL BEHAVIORS

In early design stages (up to and including first walkthrough), authors tend to build interfaces for non-modget interactions that work much like the simplest Supercard interfaces: press this button, see this movie, and then put up these questions. Press another button, see another movie and show another screen. In this manner, authors can quickly construct a demopath while not building and rebuilding a model.

As the program grows in complexity, authors need to make the interface respond conditionally to clicks, but one of the goals from the INDIE 1.0 experience is to make sure authors have to duplicate effort as little as possible.

There are several different kinds of conditionality in INDIE:

- Show different introductions and conclusions when scenarios start or end.
- Show different advice/critique movies depending on what is missing, conflicting, or irrelevant in the students' reports.
- Show different test results and help questions depending on what scenario the student is in.

At the first walkthrough stage, the buttons that would normally handle this sort of conditionality are "hardwired": "On CLICKED: `Run lake temperature test' button, play movie #45 and show these 3 follow-up questions." A scaleable authoring tool should make turning this interaction conditional a smooth process and require little or no re-authoring.

Example

INDIE's event-based architecture makes it possible to make this change without losing the work the author already did. For the test example, an author might need to make the temperature test work for several different mountains instead of just for Mt. Andrews.

Currently, the "test" is in a push-button arrangement, as so:

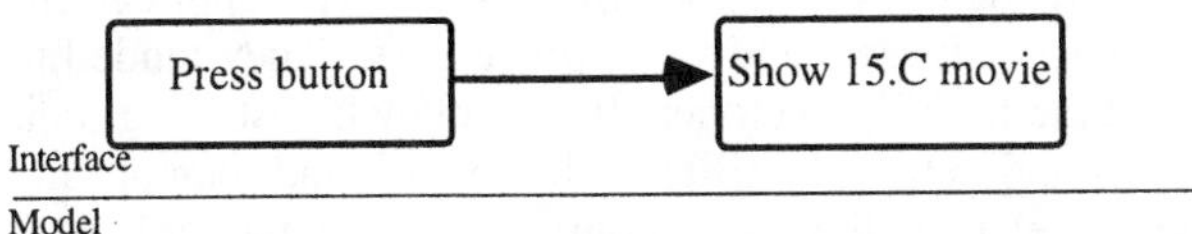

Figure 6: A "hardwired" test

The author would like to instead have the internal structure look like this:

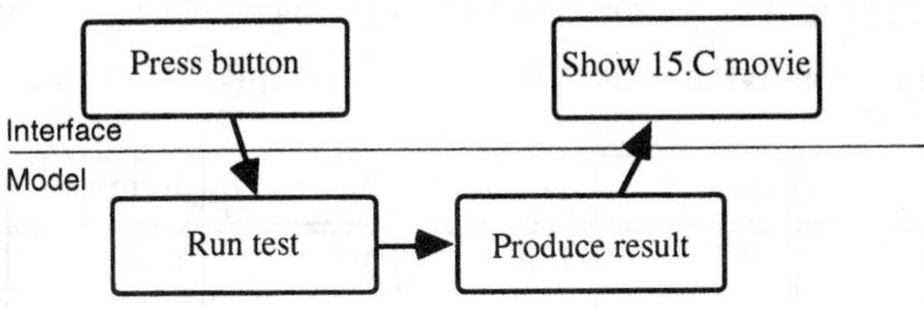

Figure 7: A test that uses the model

To do this, the author needs to do the following steps:

1. Create a temperature test object.
1. Create a scenario object, "Mt. Andrews Scenario."
2. Create a "Lake Temperature" test object.
3. Define a result object for the "Lake Temperature" test for the Mt. Andrews scenario called "15.2 °C".
4. Make the trigger that plays the 15.2 °C movie execute when the result created in step 3 is generated.
5. Make the button's trigger run the test.

Re-authoring triggers in INDIE

At first, the author might have a hardwired trigger like this:

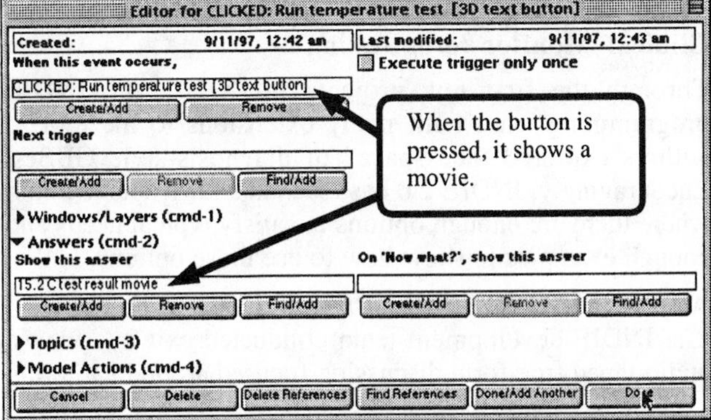

Figure 8: A hardwired trigger

To make this test conditional on the scenario, the author would first make a scenario object. Scenario objects only consist of a name.

Then he or she would add a test object:

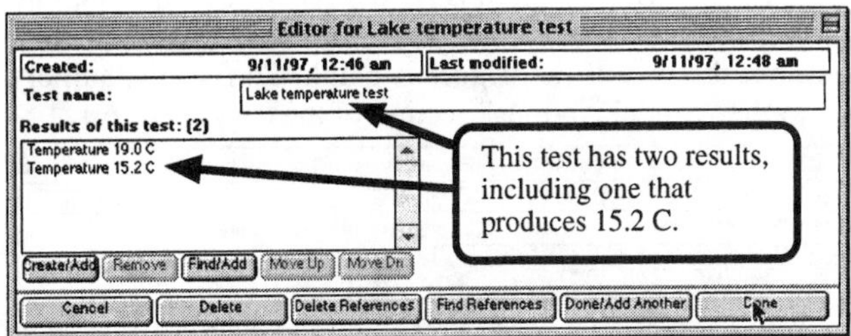

Figure 9: Test editor

The author then specifies a result. Results are named, such as "Temperature 15.2 °C" and "Temperature 19.0 °C". Each result object has an editor like this:

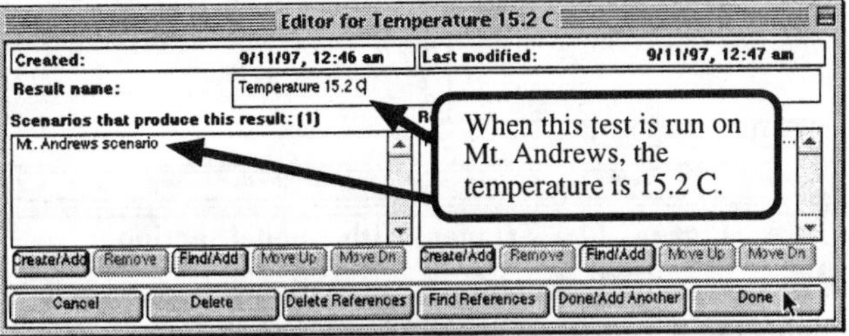

Figure 10: Result editor

For a result, authors specify what scenario will produce this result. Here, the "Mt. Andrews" scenario will cause the 15.2 C° result to appear.

Scenarios, tests, and results are model objects that don't appear on screen nor do they have associated modgets. Authors make students aware of changes in these model objects through triggers with special kinds of events. These *model events* include:

- Test-result generated event
- Scenario chosen event
- Critiquing-rule fired event

In this example, the author can re-author his or her old trigger to execute when the 15.2 °C test result is generated. The author opens the trigger editor, and with a visual editor selects the event "TEST RESULT: 15.2 C". The resulting trigger now reads:

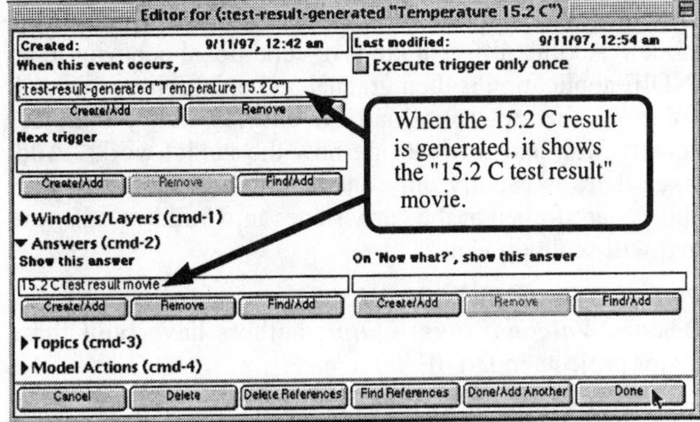

Figure 11: Test result trigger

Finally, the author needs to connect the clicked button to the running of the test. Authors edit the trigger for the "Run temperature test" button event by pressing the "Edit Trigger" button again on that button's attribute editor. Given that currently there is no trigger for this button, one is automatically generated. The event slot is already filled out, but the rest of the trigger is blank. To fix this, authors go to the "Model Actions" section of the trigger editor:

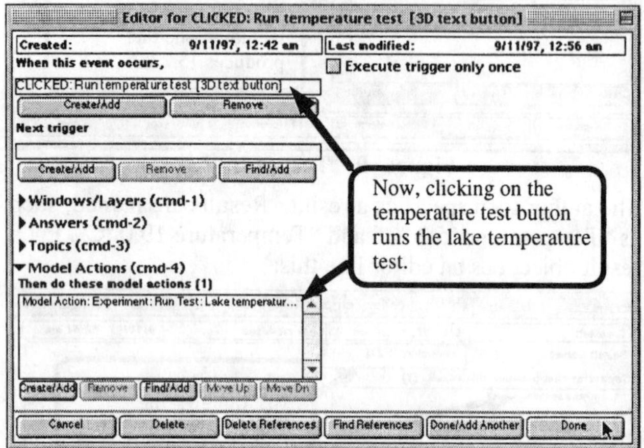

Figure 12: Trigger with model action

A model action is a command that allows the interface to connect to non-modget model objects. In this case, authors would click on the "Create/Add" button and visually select the model action "RUN TEST" and, through a few dialog windows, choose the test object they have created. Now, pressing the "Run temperature" test will act conditionally depending on which scenario had been chosen.

Although in this example, the author has built a fair bit more model structure than the author had before, *no work was duplicated.* This author used his or her old trigger, and now adding a new scenario would only require authoring a new result and result trigger. Authors of multi-scenario applications reported they frequently made use of this flexibility.

Other Conditional Behaviors

Other conditional behaviors are constructed in a similar manner to model actions and events. Authors can use model actions to select which set of critiquer rules should be used or to indicate to the model that the student has chosen to switch scenarios.

We restrict all conditional behavior to occur through the model. Adding different kinds of conditional behavior to an INDIE application is then gradual and only done as needed, reducing the up-front load on authors' time, both for construction and for learning how the model works. And, since there is usually only one way to add such behavior, authors are forced at the early stages into building software that will scale up well.

PROJECTS BUILT IN INDIE

Besides *Volcano Investigator*, authors have built three major projects in INDIE 2.0 to date:

- **Immunology Consultant:** Medical students are in the role of an immunologist with a difficult case to solve, and they use tests and interviews to figure out what is wrong with her.
- **Is It A Rembrandt?:** Art history students have to determine whether each of three paintings is painted by Rembrandt or is a forgery by inspecting the style of the painting, its provenance, the signature, and so on.
- **Nutrition Clinician:** Medical students have to determine what nutritional deficiencies each of 3 patients has, what the medical implications are, and what needs to be done to remove the deficiencies.

Authors of these projects were experienced ILS staffers who had worked on one or more GBS projects before starting with INDIE, but had no experience with the INDIE tool. They had no previous programming experience (most had liberal arts degrees) but had strong skills with applications such as spreadsheets and word processors. They tended to contact the INDIE developers frequently when starting their projects and getting familiar with the tool, and then around once a week once they were comfortable with the tool.

All of these systems have at least 15 different screens, ranging from introductions, tests, interviews, ASK zoomers, ASK browsers, report-building, and feedback. Each project took from 5 to 10 months to complete.

This table summarzies the relative complexity of each project:

	Immun.	Volcano	Nutrition	Remb.
ASK nodes	217	150	600	620
Triggers	162	187	612	334
Points	120	36	1000	514

Table 1: Relative sizes of four INDIE projects.

INDIE application sizes are dominated by graphics and video. **Rembrandt**, for example, has around 60MB of pictures (largely uncompressed) and nearly 4 gigabytes of video consisting of nearly 500 clips of experts. **Nutrition** has 3 gigabytes of video.

INDIE 2.0 has additionally been used by four groups of graduate students, both Ph.D. and masters, in course projects. These projects tend to go through the third stage, First Walkthrough. **Volcano Investigator** was the most successful of these student projects, built by first-year masters students in an intensive project in 4 months. Others include **KERMIT** (ecology), **Car Repair,** and **Clinical Monitor** (drug testing).

Through the first few projects in INDIE, the INDIE programming team built many extensions to the tool as authors explored the "space" of diagnosis-style GBSes. Encouragingly, INDIE 2.0 has reached a fairly stable point, where there are enough options to satisfy typical needs and enough examples to show how to use those options.

AUTHORING EXPERIENCES IN INDIE

The INDIE development team conducted exit interviews, audio-taped free-form discussion focused around authoring experiences, with authors from each group. They reported the following major points:

- Most teams (usually groups of 3) had one person use the tool to build the interface, with the other students working on contacts with experts. Frequently other authors on the team would use the tool briefly for some targeted task, such as ASK system constructing and linking.
- Outside of using Powerpoint or paper for proposal-level storyboarding, all four teams used the INDIE tool as their primary development environment. This was one of our stated main goals of this project. Authors said that they liked INDIE precisely because it is so flexible in comparison to other more model-driven GBS tools available to them.
- It took teams from four days to two weeks to get comfortable with the tool to the point where they were able to construct their demopaths for presentations late in the Storyboard stage. This indicated that authors rapidly gained familiarity with the tool. Authors emphasized how easy they felt it was for them to get started with the tool.
- Two INDIE projects, Rembrandt and Nutrition, have been scaled up from initial demopaths to full-fledged multi-scenario shippable applications. These projects will be used by Northwestern University students beginning fall of 1997. Neither team reported significant re-authoring while moving from a single scenario to several scenarios (outside of a technical point about background images).

CONCLUSION

INDIE 2.0 has proven to be easy for authors to work in. With gradual scale-up, authors can move smoothly through the stages of educational software design, starting from late storyboarding and continuing to the final, shippable application, all without spending large amounts of time re-implementing between stages. Triggers provide a way for non-programmers to specify behavior in the "when this button is pressed, play this movie" mode, but scale gracefully up to the stage where authors want "when this button is pressed, do the right thing." We are looking forward to working on even more richer models for more complex interactions with INDIE. Also, researchers in other domains that are interface-heavy at the beginning and content-heavy at the end could be informed by our experience with INDIE, such as multimedia non-educational hypertext, data-rich websites, and MIS database front-ends.

A general lesson can be extracted from our experiences with INDIE that applies to tools for authoring intelligent (or at least model-based) applications. The problem in such tools has always been balancing the long-term representational needs of the applications with the short-term needs of the authors. The authors want to prototype their interfaces quickly and easily, but typical interface builders let authors envision interactions way beyond what current intelligent systems can support. On the other hand, if you force authors to do up-front knowledge representation before interface prototyping, they will use other tools first and use your tool late and inefficiently, if at all.

Two techniques were used in INDIE 2.0 to resolve this conflict. First, by representing surface-level interface actions with event-based response triggers, authors can author interface actions as easily as in other systems. Later, as needed, they can incrementally refine these hardwired responses into model-based responses. Second, with modgets, authors can quickly and directly incorporate certain commonly used model-based widgets, such as evidence notebooks and lists of questions, ready for instant scale-up.

ACKNOWLEDGMENTS

We'd like to acknowledge significant effort and contributions on the part of Seth Tisue (ASK network tools and software development); Steven Silverstein, Abigail Sher, Bridget Weise (Immunology); Brendon Towle and Joe Herman (editor tool kit); John Sangimino, Jeff DeSmet, Faith Fuqua-Purvis (Volcano); and Brian Davies and Steven Feist (graphics tools).

This work has been supported in part by the Defense Advanced Research Projects Agency, monitored by the Office of Naval Research, under contracts N00014-90-J-4117 and N00014-91-J-4092. The Institute for the Learning Sciences was established in 1989 with the support of Andersen Consulting.

REFERENCES

1. Ferguson, W., Bariess R., Birnbaum, L., and Osgood, R. ASK Systems: An approach to story-based teaching. In *Proceedings of the 1991 International Conference on the Learning Sciences*, L. Birnbaum, Ed. Evanston, IL, Aug. 1991), 158-164.
2. Goldberg, A. Information Models, Views, and Controllers. *Dr. Dobb's Journal* (July 1990), 54-60.
3. Schank, R. Goal-based scenarios: A radical look at education. *Journal of the Learning Sciences 3*, 4(1994), 429-453.
4. Schank, R., Fano, A., Jona, M., and Bell, B. The design of goal-based scenarios, *Journal of the Learning Sciences 3*, 4(1994), 305-345.

Visual Task Characterization for Automated Visual Discourse Synthesis

Michelle X. Zhou **Steven K. Feiner**
Department of Computer Science
Columbia University
500 West 120th St., 450 CS Building
New York, NY 10027
+1 212 939 7000
{zhou, feiner}@cs.columbia.edu

ABSTRACT

To develop a comprehensive and systematic approach to the automated design of visual discourse, we introduce a visual task taxonomy that interfaces high-level presentation intents with low-level visual techniques. In our approach, visual tasks describe presentation intents through their visual accomplishments, and suggest desired visual techniques through their visual implications. Therefore, we can characterize visual tasks by their visual accomplishments and implications. Through this characterization, visual tasks can guide the visual discourse synthesis process by specifying what presentation intents can be achieved and how to achieve them.

Keywords

Automated design of graphics, visual discourse, visual task characterization.

INTRODUCTION

Handcrafting effective visual presentations can be extremely expensive and time-consuming, especially if the presentations are to be customized for individual users and situations. Therefore, researchers are developing computational approaches to automating the design process. The work described here addresses the general task of designing *visual discourse*, a series of connected visual displays [32], of which a single display or a series of static displays may be considered special cases.

If an approach is to create effective presentations, it must accomplish a set of presentation *intents* associated with the discourse [3, 21, 23, 8]; for example, it may inform a user about some fact *x* or enable a user to search for information *y*, which we will notate as Inform<?x> or Search<?y>. One design approach, which we are investigating, involves the formulation of a set of rules to select appropriate visual techniques based on the presentation intents. However, it is difficult to formulate general rules that can directly relate high-level presentation intents, such as Inform<?x>, to low-level visual techniques, such as Highlight<?x>.

Based on a variety of visual presentations from different sources (e.g., [22, 26, 27, 10, 28]), and our own work on visual discourse synthesis [32], we believe that there is a level of abstraction midway between presentation intents and low-level visual techniques. We refer to this level of abstraction as a *visual task taxonomy.* Unlike presentation intents, visual tasks *directly* indicate the desired visual effects. For example, the visual task Locate<?x, ?locator> signifies that an object ?x be visually located relative to another object, ?locator. However, visual tasks are *not* visual techniques, as they may imply related visual techniques without specifying exactly *how.* For example, the visual task Focus<?x> may imply that visual techniques such as Enlarge<?x> or Highlight<?x> could be used to focus attention on ?x, but without specifying which technique to use.

On one hand, visual tasks can be grouped together to uniformly describe how to accomplish various presentation intents. On the other, as visual tasks imply desired visual techniques, they enable abstraction beyond the concrete details of lower-level visual techniques, while still maintaining close enough contact with these techniques. Therefore, visual tasks could be considered as *abstracted* visual techniques, which can be achieved by a set of lower-level techniques. Consequently, high-level presentation intents and low-level visual techniques are tied together through visual tasks: a presentation intent could be accomplished by certain visual tasks, which then imply the visual techniques to achieve them.

As visual tasks serve as an interface between presentation intents and low-level visual techniques, they can be characterized along two dimensions: visual accomplishments and visual implications. *Visual accomplishments* specify the presentation intents a visual task could achieve, while *visual implications* indicate the visual techniques a visual task may imply. Using the visual task taxonomy, visual discourse synthesis first tries to interpret the presentation intents using a set of visual tasks; then, based on the implications of these visual tasks, it suggests a set of visual techniques to achieve the presentation intents.

In the rest of this paper, we first discuss related research and compare these approaches with ours. Next, we introduce and analyze our visual task taxonomy. To demonstrate its utility, we provide concrete examples that illustrate how visual tasks are used in automated visual discourse synthesis. These examples are automatically generated by a knowl-

This research is supported in part by DARPA Contract DAAL01-94-K-0119, the Columbia University Center for Advanced Technology in High Performance Computing and Communications in Healthcare (funded by the New York State Science and Technology Foundation), the Columbia Center for Telecommunications Research under NSF Grant ECD-88-11111, and ONR Contract N00014-97-1-0838.

edge-based visual presentation system called IMPROVISE (Illustrative Metaphor Production in Reactive Object-oriented VISual Environments). IMPROVISE uses a hierarchical planning approach [32] to automatically generate coherent visual discourse in two application domains: computer network management and hospital patient record summarization. Finally, we present our conclusions and suggest future research directions.

RELATED WORK

To characterize different visual presentations and capture the relationships between presentation intents and visual cues, researchers have developed various taxonomies (e.g., [7, 13, 24, 29, 10]). Unlike our visual task taxonomy, previous taxonomies either broadly categorize the functions of pictures without examining their specific visual organizations (e.g., [7, 13]), or only describe conceptual relationships between *information-seeking goals* and various visual techniques (e.g., [29, 10]). Of these researchers, only Sutcliffe et al. [24] briefly mention four specific visual tasks (e.g., Highlight and Classify).

For the purpose of automated visual discourse synthesis, researchers have classified various user information-seeking goals (e.g., [3, 21, 8]) or communicative acts (e.g., [1, 17, 23]). Although information-seeking goals or communicative acts serve different design purposes [20], they are similar in the sense that they both specify high-level presentation intents. To bridge the gap between high-level presentation intents and low-level visual techniques, a set of intermediate specifications is usually constructed.

One type of specification, known as *perceptual operators* (e.g., [3, 8]), indicates the perceptual tasks to be performed by the user in a visual environment. There are significant differences between a perceptual operator and a visual task. To achieve presentation intents, perceptual operators emphasize what a *user* needs to do (e.g., *search* for an object), while visual tasks describe what needs to be carried out by a visual *presentation* (e.g., make the object of search be in *focus*). In this sense, the visual task operates one level *below* the perceptual operator to signify the desired visual effects. Whereas perceptual operators are usually employed sequentially, visual tasks can be specified in parallel to achieve multiple visual effects simultaneously.

Closest to our visual task specifications are *visual acts,* such as style strategies in [23], visual operators in [1], and graphic acts in [17]. Like visual tasks, visual acts *directly* specify the visual effects. By our definition, however, visual acts such as Highlight, Zoom, and Include are more like low-level visual techniques than *abstracted* visual tasks. Instead of presenting an abstraction of various visual techniques, these visual acts are usually employed directly to achieve communicative intents, even though some of their parameters (e.g., a Highlight color) may be determined in the application stage. Moreover, since systems that use visual acts deal mainly with real-world objects (e.g., [1, 23]) or existing presentations (e.g., a database of maps in [17]), they focus on visual manipulation instead of visual creation. Therefore, they rarely include or describe visual acts that can be used to create visual presentations from scratch (e.g., visual symbol encoding acts in graph creation). In comparison, our visual task taxonomy presents an abstraction above low-level visual techniques and addresses both visual creation and manipulation.

It is also worth noting that the *pragmatic directives* proposed by Marks [16] are different from any of the taxonomies mentioned above. They more or less directly imply the underlying visual organization or layout (e.g., a particular network path or a hub), but do not imply or suggest any of the low-level attribute encodings. In contrast, our visual task taxonomy covers both high-level visual organization and low-level visual symbol encoding tasks.

VISUAL TASK CHARACTERIZATION

Building on previous work [29, 10, 17, 24], we have derived a taxonomy of visual tasks, shown in Figure 1. Like a visual act, each visual task is described by two parts: an act and a set of arguments to act on. We have refined each type of visual task so that it can be accurately described and effectively employed to achieve presentation intents. These refinements could be interpreted as *particular ways* of achieving the task. For example, the visual task Identify<?x, ?identifier> could be refined using one of the four more specific visual tasks to indicate a particular way of *identifying* an object:

Name: identify ?x using its name
Portray: identify ?x by its portrait (image)

\# Relational visual tasks
- **Associate**<?x, ?y>
  - Collocate<?x, ?y>
  - Connect<?x, ?y>
  - Unite<?x, ?x-part>
  - Attach<?x, ?x-part>
- **Background**<?x, ?background>
- **Categorize**<?x1, ...,?xn>
  - MarkDistribute<?x1, ..., ?xn>
- **Cluster**<?cluster, ?x1, ..., ?xn>
  - Outline<?cluster>
  - Individualize<?cluster>
- **Compare**<?x, ?y>
  - Differentiate<?x, ?y>
  - Intersect<?x, ?y>
- **Correlate**<?x1, ..., ?xn>
  - Plot<?x1, ..., ?xn>
  - MarkCompose<?x1, ..., ?xn>
- **Distinguish**<?x, ?y>
  - MarkDistribute<?x, ?y>
  - Isolate<?x ?y>
- **Emphasize**<?x-part ?x>
  - Focus<?x-part ?x>
  - Isolate<?x-part ?x>
  - Reinforce<?x-part ?x>
- **Generalize**<?x1, ..., ?xn>
  - Merge<?x1, ..., ?xn>
- **Identify**<?x, ?identifier>
  - Name<?x, ?name>
  - Portray<?x, ?image>
  - Individualize<?x, ?attr>
  - Profile<?x, ?profile>
- **Locate**<?x, ?locator>
  - Position<?x, ?locator>
  - Situate<?x, ?locator>
  - Pinpoint<?x, ?locator>
  - Outline<?x, ?locator>
- **Rank**<?x1, ..., ?xn, ?attr>
  - Time<?x1, ..., ?xn, ?t>
- **Reveal**<?x-part ?x>
  - Expose<?x-part ?x>
  - Itemize<?x-part ?x>
  - Specify<?x-part ?x>
  - Separate<?x-part ?x>
- **Switch**<?x, ?y>

\# Direct visual organizing and
\# encoding tasks
- **Encode**<?x>
  - Label<?x>
  - Symbolize<?x>
    - Quantify<?x>
    - Iconify<?x>
  - Portray<?x>
  - Tabulate<?x>
  - Plot<?x>
  - Structure<?x>
  - Trace<?x>
  - Map<?x>

Figure 1. Visual task taxonomy

Individualize: identify ?x using its unique attributes
Profile: identify ?x using its profile

We characterize visual tasks along two dimensions: visual accomplishments and visual implications. *Visual accomplishments* describe the type of presentation intents that a visual task might help to achieve, while *visual implications* specify a particular type of visual action that a visual task may carry out.

Visual Accomplishments

Informational visual presentations are usually charged with one of two intents [2, 20]: the presentation is intended either to simply convey a presenter's message to a user or to help the user accomplish certain perceptual tasks such as *search* or *verify*. Based on this distinction, visual tasks could be classified into two categories at the highest level: visual tasks that help the presenter to *inform* the user and tasks that *enable* the user to perform visual *exploration* or *computation*. Visual tasks that *inform* could be further distinguished as to whether they help to *summarize* or to *elaborate* information. Similarly, visual tasks that enable a user to *explore* or *compute* could be further classified by whether they aid the user to *search* for a particular object, to *verify* a fact, or to *differentiate* or *sum* different values.

As listed in Figure 2, many visual tasks could help to achieve different presentation intents at once in different ways [13]. For example, the visual task Compare<?x, ?y> could aid in accomplishing the intent Inform<?x> by indicating the similarity between ?x and ?y (Intersect<?x, ?y>), and could also help to achieve the intent Verify<?x> by showing a difference (Differentiate<?x, ?y>). To decide which visual tasks may be used to achieve what presentation intent, we pair presentation intents and corresponding information categories together [9] (e.g., Verify<object-composition>). Then we infer how the specific presentation intent could be accomplished *visually*, based on both rhetorical and visual design principles [22, 18, 15, 26, 27, 19, 28]. For example, Verify<object-composition> requires displaying an object and its components. Thus, the visual task Reveal<?x> could facilitate perceptual verification.

In addition to information categories, many other factors, such as the audience or presentation environment, will also affect the mapping between presentation intents and visual tasks. For example, informing a nurse about a patient's postoperative status may require accomplishing visual tasks such as Locate<devices, patient-body> (locate medical devices in context of the patient's body) and Itemize<drugs> (list all administered drugs). In contrast, informing a doctor about the same patient may involve visual tasks such as Trace<operation-events> (order events during the operation temporally) and Categorize<drug1, ... purpose> (categorize all administered drugs by purpose).

Therefore, visual task classification by visual accomplishments based on information categories alone is incomplete. Other factors, such as the user model, must be taken into account to establish a comprehensive mapping between presentation intents and visual tasks. Here, we focus on discussing the general *domain-independent* connections between presentation intents and visual tasks, and hope that such a broad characterization will serve as a starting point in visual discourse synthesis. By accounting for the factors mentioned above, more accurate mappings and refined characterizations for specific domains can then be formulated based on these general guidelines (see Section **EXAMPLES**).

Thus far, we have roughly characterized various visual tasks by their accomplishments. Next we introduce a finer-grained categorization of visual tasks by their visual implications.

Visual Implications

Cognitive psychologists have conducted extensive studies to understand human visual perceptual behavior and reveal how visual cues can affect or direct perception (e.g., [25, 6, 12]). Based on these studies, a set of principles for visual perception and cognition has been formulated. From the standpoint of visual discourse synthesis, we have summarized three types of visual perception and cognition principles: visual organization, visual signaling, and visual transformation. The *visual organization* principle suggests how people visually organize the world and perceive it as a coherent whole (e.g., [25, 6, 12]). The *visual signaling* principle explains how people tend to interpret visual cues and infer their meanings (e.g., [6]). The *visual transformation* principle explains how people switch attention and adapt to visual changes (e.g., [31]).

Directed by these principles, we could categorize various visual tasks by their visual implications: whether they imply certain types of *visual organization*, certain ways of *visual signaling*, or certain paths of *visual transformation*. Based on these implications, a visual discourse synthesis system may use visual tasks to sketch the visual organization of the presentation, and to search for appropriate visual signaling or transformation techniques with which to encode information in a new presentation or modify an existing one. Moreover, we could formulate partial plans in advance for

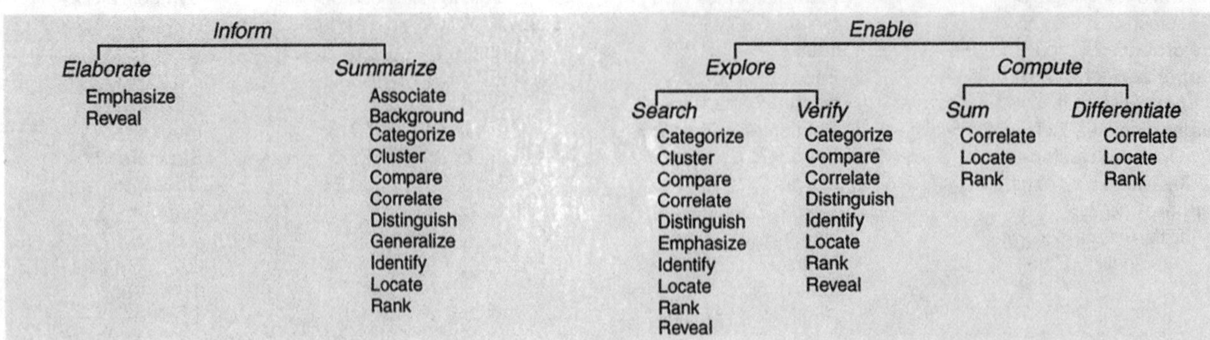

Figure 2. High-level presentation intents (*italic*) and visual tasks (roman) that achieve them

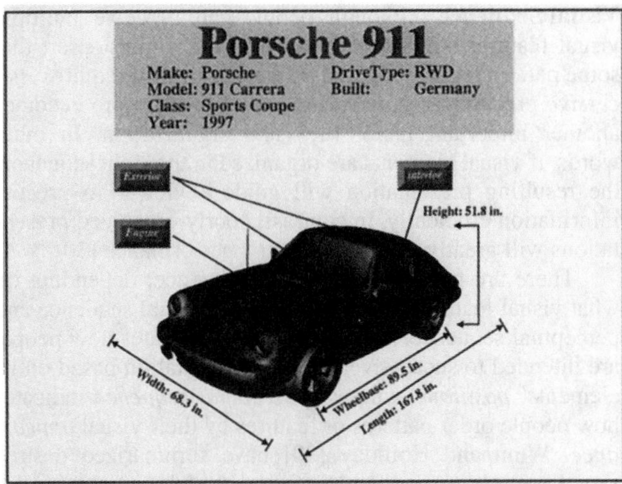

Figure 3. Present information about a car to a customer

each type of visual task, using lower-level visual techniques [32]. For example, if we know that the visual task Focus implies attracting attention, and that visual techniques such as Highlight or Enlarge attract visual attention, then these techniques could become different subplans to achieve Focus.

Visual Organization

Visual organization could be described from several aspects such as overall pattern or sequence of the organization (e.g., [30]), preattentive features of the organization (e.g, [25]), and various visual relationships among visual elements (e.g., [11, 12]). Generalizing from this previous work, we have compiled a comprehensive set of features to describe various aspects of visual organization: visual grouping, visual attention, visual sequence, and visual composition.

Visual grouping is concerned with how visual patterns could be grouped together so people can perceive them as groups. *Visual attention* asserts what distinct features enable people to perceive them preattentively and effortlessly. *Visual sequence* indicates how visual patterns influence people to scan presentations in a particular order, while *visual composition* focuses on explaining different ways of composing lower-level visual elements into more complex visual structures. Next, we describe how various visual tasks are characterized by these four aspects.

Visual Grouping. According to gestalt psychology, people group different visual elements together by certain patterns: proximity, similarity, continuity, and closure [19].

Proximity states that objects that are spatially close will be perceived as being together. For example, Figure 3 presents information about a car to a customer. Below the presentation's title, it is easy to perceive two groups corresponding to two columns: make, model, class and year are in one group, and the rest in another. The visual task Cluster can be used to indicate this grouping. Based on their semantics, these visual tasks imply visual grouping by proximity:

Associate: associated objects perceived as a group by proximity
Cluster: spatial clusters perceived as groups by proximity
Locate: locator and objects being located are grouped by proximity

Similarity asserts that objects that are presented with similar visual appearance will be perceived as a group. In Figure 4, sales centers are encoded as dark spheres and branches as light cones. At first glance, two groups emerge: the spheres and the cones. This particular grouping is accomplished through the visual task MarkDistribute<?centers, ?branches>, which *categorizes* various objects by visual appearance. Several visual tasks enforce grouping by similarity to achieve certain visual effects:

Categorize: objects in the same category grouped by similarity
Cluster: objects in the same cluster grouped by similarity
Distinguish
- **MarkDistribute:** similarity helps to distinguish groups

Continuity suggests that people tend to group objects and their continuations together as a whole. Figure 5 displays engine data in the form of a pull-down menu below the *Engine* button. A pull-down menu can be interpreted as a *continuation* of a button that reveals more information when the button is pressed. In this case, the engine button and its pull-down menu continuation are easily perceived as a group. The visual task Itemize<engine-data>, a special case of Reveal<engine-data>, precisely describes the intended grouping. These visual tasks imply visual grouping by continuity:

Associate
- **Connect:** two objects are each other's continuation
- **Attach:** attachment is a continuation of another object

Locate
- **Outline:** a spatial or temporal extent marked as a continuation

Reveal
- **Expose:** internals depicted as spatial continuation
- **Itemize:** set members depicted as conceptual continuation
- **Specialize:** specifications depicted as conceptual continuation

Closure implies that people tend to group things together as a coherent whole when they are in a closed form. As depicted in Figure 4, the map used as the locator (Locate<nodes, map>) presents a closed form to group everything together as a network so they are not perceived as unre-

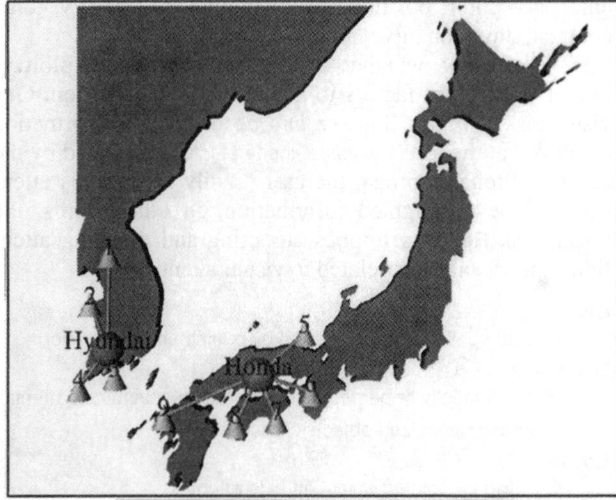

Figure 4. Car sales network

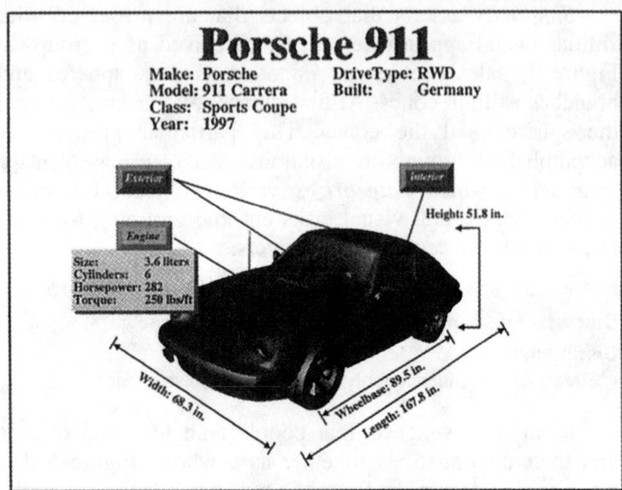

Figure 5. Reveal information about a car's engine

lated entities. Other visual tasks suggesting closure are:

Cluster
 Outline: visual clusters indicated by closed form
Locate: locator presents objects in a closed form

Besides proximity, similarity, continuity, and closure, *symmetry* groups objects by a sense of "good form" [11]. However, since the definition of "good form" may depend on factors such as the viewer's visual literacy, we do not discuss it here.

Visual Attention. Cognitive psychology studies have shown that people are usually drawn to special visual features when they gaze at visual presentations (e.g., [25, 6]). As the process of recognizing these features does not require conscious attention [25], it is important to know what types of visual tasks imply such *preattentive* features. Using this knowledge, presentation systems could employ these visual tasks to achieve related presentation intents, and use appropriate visual techniques to accomplish these tasks.

Since we focus only on visual features independent of their semantics, our visual tasks are concerned only with *syntactic emphasis* as defined by Goldsmith [6]. Goldsmith summarizes eight important visual factors that help syntactic emphasis: color, position, size, isolation, complexity, tonal contrast, directionality, and implied motion.

We examine whether a visual task implies exploiting any of these eight factors to attract or direct attention. One visual task of Figure 3 is to *reinforce* the general information displayed at the top (Reinforce <general-info>). Directed by the color and tonal contrast, the user readily focuses his attention on the highlighted information. In other words, the visual task Reinforce implies attracting and directing attention. The visual tasks related to visual attention are:

Cluster
 Outline: spatial clusters marked by outline attract attention
Distinguish
 Isolate: spatially or perceptually isolated objects attract attention
Emphasize: emphasized objects attract attention
Locate
 Pinpoint: pinpointed object attracts attention
 Outline: marked spatial or temporal extent attracts attention

Visual Sequence. Although people can perceive multiple visual features simultaneously, cognitive studies assert that some pattern recognition and interpretation still requires *successive* processing [25]. *Visual sequence* therefore becomes another important factor in visual organization. In other words, if visual elements are organized in the right sequence, the resulting presentation will guide a viewer to process information efficiently. In contrast, poorly organized presentations will greatly impair a viewer's performance [30].

There are two types of visual sequence, depending on what visual features produce the order: spatial sequence and perceptual sequence. *Spatial sequence* indicates how people are intended to successively scan a presentation based on its elements' *positions*, whereas *perceptual sequence* indicates how people order patterns or features by their visual *appearance*. Winn and Holliday [30] have summarized desired visual sequences used in charts, graphs and diagrams. Goldsmith's experiments [6] have also indicated how certain visual patterns guide ordered perception.

Based on their results, we recognize a set of visual tasks that imply certain visual sequences in presentations. For example, one of the visual tasks to be carried out in Figure 3 is to use the general car description (e.g., make and model) to *identify* the car. In this case, the description is encoded as the presentation's title and placed at the top. This arrangement already implies a visual sequence: read the description first, then the rest. In fact, all types of Identify will imply a similar sequence: read the *identifier* first, then the *object* being identified. Likewise, all types of Emphasize tasks also suggest a particular visual sequence: read the emphasized objects first, then the rest. These visual tasks imply a visual sequence:

Emphasize: emphasized objects and the rest are ordered
Identify: identifier and objects being identified are ordered
Rank: objects are ordered by rank

Visual Composition. The last factor that affects visual organization is visual composition. *Visual composition* indicates how different visual elements are pieced together to form a coherent whole based on their relationships. Visual tasks express these relationships and eventually determine their corresponding spatial and perceptual relationships. For example, the visual task Expose is carried out in Figure 6 to reveal a car's engine. The *constituent* relationship between the car and its engine is conveyed by showing the engine spatially inside the car. Similarly, other types of Reveal also imply different types of spatial composition (e.g., Itemize<engine-data> in Figure 5). Not only does Reveal imply certain ways of composing visual elements, but visual tasks such as Identify, Associate, and Correlate also suggest various types of visual composition:

Associate: associated objects imply being placed together visually
Correlate: correlated objects imply composite visual structure
Identify: object and its identifier imply a particular arrangement
Reveal: objects being revealed imply visual composition

Visual Signaling

As abstracted visual techniques, visual tasks usually *imply* desired visual structures or encodings without explicitly naming them. Nonetheless, some visual tasks may *directly* specify the desired visual structures or encodings at the user or application's request (e.g., *chart* these data). Whereas visual organization describes the *framework* of the presentation, *visual signaling* indicates the more concrete visual *contents* of the presentation. For example, visual tasks may specify that information be presented *symbolically* (e.g., the car model in Figure 3) rather than *textually* (e.g., the engine table in Figure 3), or in a *cartogram* (e.g., Figure 4) instead of a *structure diagram* (e.g., Figure 3).

Based on the level of detail, we divide visual signaling into two types: visual structuring and visual encoding. *Visual structuring* specifies the type of display [7, 14], while *visual encoding* emphasizes visual symbol encoding, such as using visual variables (e.g., color, size, and shape) to encode an object or its attributes.

Visual Structuring. We have combined several visual display taxonomies [7, 30, 11, 14] to categorize the displays in which we are interested. Based on this display categorization, we recognize five types of visual tasks: Tabulate, Plot, Structure, Trace, and Map. They imply five types of visual display:

Tabulate: implies organizing information in a tabular chart

Plot: implies organizing quantitative information in conventional graphs, such as a bar graph or line graph.

Structure: implies organizing information in a structure diagram by showing the structures of the objects

Trace: implies organizing information in a process diagram or time chart by temporal order.

Map: implies organizing information by geographic location

Visual Encoding. In a visual representation, an object can either be named in a textual format, encoded by a visual variable, or depicted by a realistic image. We refer to these three types of encoding as *labeling* an object, *symbolizing* an object, and *portraying* an object, respectively. Thus, three visual tasks Label, Symbolize, and Portray correspond to three different visual encodings. In addition, Symbolize could be further refined to Quantify or Iconify an object, depending on what visual variable is involved. For example, Quantify implies that the object may be encoded effectively using the visual variable *size*, but not by *shape* or *color* [2, 4], while Iconify implies that the object may be encoded by shape or color [14].

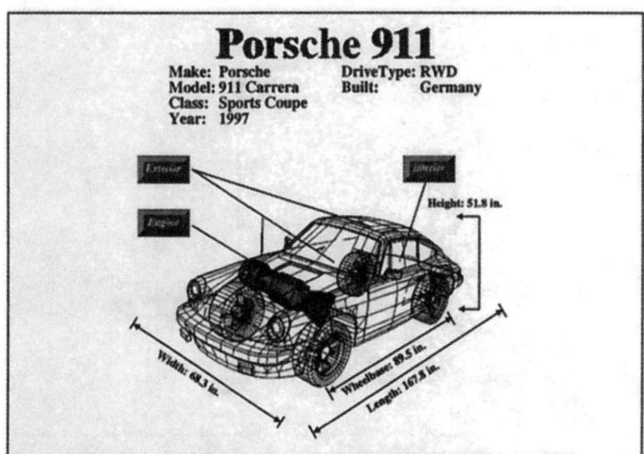

Figure 6. Reveal a car's engine

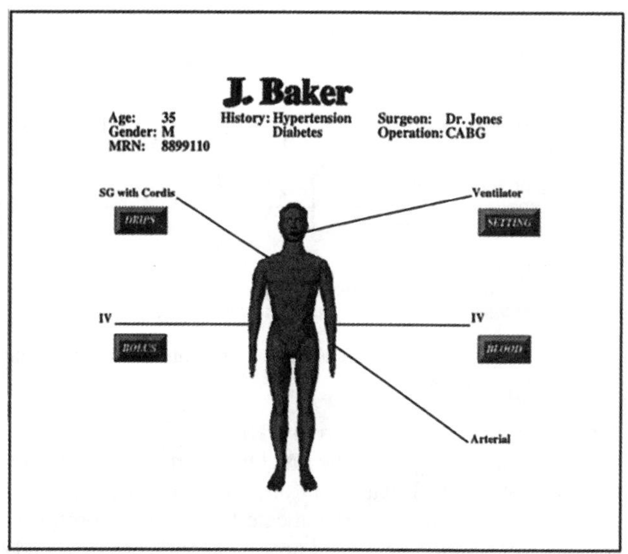

Figure 7. Present a patient's information to a nurse

Visual Transformation

To ensure visual discourse coherence, visual transformation cannot be ignored [32]. Visual transformation can help integrate new information into the current display to achieve *unity*; or gradually transform the current display into a new one to achieve *continuity*. We need to identify which visual tasks imply visual transformation, and subsequently, determine how to achieve these transformations.

We recognize two types of visual transformation: visual modification and visual transition. *Visual modification* asserts that the current display has been modified either to achieve a new task or accommodate a new piece of information. *Visual transition*, on the other hand, indicates visual effects [31] that bridge a gap between two completely different presentations (e.g., a cross-fade).

Examining our visual tasks, we are able to determine that some imply visual modification, and others visual transition. For example, various types of Reveal tasks indicate visual modifications by adding more detailed information to the current display (e.g., Itemize), while tasks such as Generalize may suggest visual modifications by merging different components together. As shown in the following table, only the visual task Switch implies a visual transition.

Emphasize: may imply transformation by modifying emphasized objects

Generalize: implies transformation by merging components

Reveal: implies transformation by adding new information

Switch: implies transition by switching from one scene to another

EXAMPLES

Figure 7 *summarizes* for nurses a patient's status after a coronary artery bypass graft (CABG) operation, while Figure 9 *summarizes* and *elaborates* for doctors a patient's post-operative status. Using these two examples, we demonstrate how IMPROVISE formulates visual tasks based on their visual accomplishments, and how it determines visual techniques based on their visual implications. We focus here on explaining the use of visual tasks in visual discourse synthesis, having described IMPROVISE's inference mechanism in our

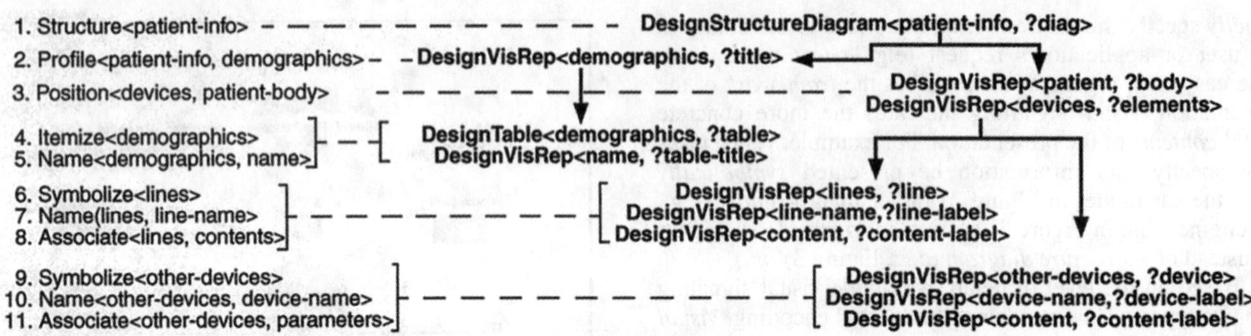

Figure 8. Visual tasks and their corresponding visual techniques used in designing Figure 7

previous work [32].

Present Patient Information to a Nurse

As shown in Figure 8, the first task formulated by IMPROVISE is to Structure all patient information together, since our informal design studies [5] indicated that nurses prefer all relevant information be placed near a patient's physical body and displayed at once (rather than successively revealed). This task could be directly specified as a user directive, or inferred from a set of rules, as it is in IMPROVISE:

If: Summarize<?info> & Audience<Nurse>
then: Arrange<?info, ?structure> & IsPhysical<?structure>
If: Arrange<?info, ?structure> & IsPhysical<?structure>
then: Structure<?info>

Based on domain information, two more tasks are formulated: using demographics information to *identify* other information, and using the patient's body to *locate* all medical devices. In particular, while the demographics provides a *profile* of the patient information (task 2 in Figure 8), the medical devices are *positioned* relative to the body (task 3). As IMPROVISE continues, additional visual tasks are formulated to more concretely describe the intended visual relationships among different components (tasks 4–11). Based on user preference, tasks 4–5 involve *itemizing* all demographics information and using the patient name to *name* it. As both infusion lines and other devices must be physically located, tasks 6–11 specify the desired *symbolic* representations for all medical devices that should also be *named* and *associated* with their respective contents or parameters.

Once the visual tasks are formulated, IMPROVISE tries to determine visual techniques for accomplishing them. As mentioned in the last section, Structure implies constructing a structure diagram (DesignStructureDiagram in Figure 8), which is capable of conveying a physical structure (e.g., the patient body) and expressing the spatial coordinates for related objects (e.g., medical devices) [30, 14]. DesignStructureDiagram produces an "empty" structure diagram, and other visual tasks help refine it. Task 2 (Profile) indicates that the demographics become the *title* of the diagram as an identification, while task 3 (Position) makes the patient body become the *core* of the diagram, about which other information can be located. Based on visual tasks 6–11, the design of the structure diagram becomes more complete: Every medical device (e.g., SG with cordis) is symbolized using a line, identified by its textual name, and associated with its contents (e.g., DRIPS button) or parameters.

Present Patient Information to a Doctor

Unlike nurses, doctors in this situation prefer to see events arranged along a time line (Trace<events>). But similar to the nurse's example, the demographics information is used to Identify other information. In this particular example, the presentation should also depict the correlation among the event's time, location, and tasks performed (Correlate<?time, ?location, ?tasks>) at the doctor's request. Moreover, to *elaborate* the patient's bypass status, IMPROVISE formulates three tasks: Outline<status-time>, Itemize<status>, and Focus<bypass-time>. Not only must the presentation communicate the abnormal bypass time qualitatively (e.g., *prolonged*), but it must also Specify the time value quantitatively (e.g., *3 hrs.*). Based on these tasks and object relationships, IMPROVISE is also able to infer that the bypass event itself should also be in focus (Focus<bypass>) as the status is *part of* the bypass event.

While the task Trace<events> implies using a time chart (DesignTimeChart) to organize all events, task Correlate refines the chart by providing its axes (Figure 9). Furthermore, all events are encoded as boxes and placed on the chart. To Itemize the bypass status and Focus on the bypass time, all status information is listed in a panel with bypass time information highlighted. The bypass event block is highlighted and the status information is outlined along the time axis to accomplish Focus<bypass> and Outline<status-time>. Furthermore, the bypass time is also stressed quantitatively by using the time axis to achieve Specify<bypass-time>.

CONCLUSIONS AND FUTURE WORK

We have identified and presented a set of visual tasks that can serve as an interface between high-level presentation intents and low-level visual techniques. This set of tasks is summarized based on our careful analysis of a wide range

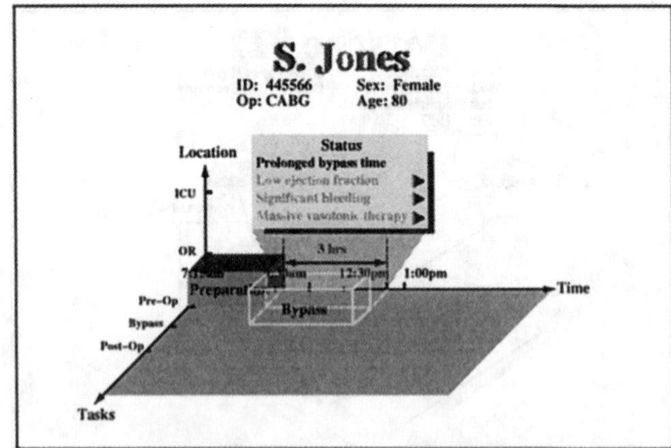

Figure 9. Present a patient's information to a doctor

of visual presentations (e.g, [26, 27, 10, 28]) and integration of both rhetorical and visual design theories (e.g., [22, 18, 30, 15, 11, 19]). Moreover, these task specifications are being used in our experimental visual discourse synthesis system IMPROVISE to test their practical value.

To use visual task specifications in automated visual discourse synthesis, we have characterized them by their visual accomplishments and implications. In the course of synthesis, a presentation system can formulate a set of visual tasks based on their accomplishments to achieve presentation intents, then select the appropriate visual techniques based on their implications to achieve these tasks. Two different examples generated by IMPROVISE illustrate the visual-task-oriented synthesis process.

To construct a complete visual discourse synthesis system, visual task characterization must be combined with other areas of research, such as data characterization and visual principle modeling [20]. Formal user studies will also be essential to provide a more comprehensive and accurate evaluation of the current set of visual tasks. For example, we would like to determine how well users can employ the visual task descriptions to describe visual presentations, and the range of presentations they can describe.

REFERENCES

[1] E. Andre and T. Rist. The design of illustrated documents as a planning task. In M. Maybury, editor, *Intelligent Multimedia Interfaces*, chapter 4, pages 94–116. AAAI Press/The MIT Press, Menlo Park, CA, 1993.

[2] J. Bertin. *Semiology of Graphics*. Univ. of Wisconsin Press, Madison, WI, 1983. (trans. by W.J. Berg).

[3] S. Casner. A task-analytic approach to the automated design of graphic presentations. *ACM Trans. on Graphics*, 10(2):111–151, 1991.

[4] W. Cleveland and R. McGill. Graphical perception: Theory, experimentation, and application to the development of graphical methods. *Journal of the American Statistical Association*, 79:531–554, 1984.

[5] M. Dalal, S. Feiner, K. McKeown, D. Jordan, B. Allen, and Y. alSafadi. MAGIC: An experimental system for generating multimedia briefings about post-bypass patient status. In *Proc. 1996 AMIA Annual Fall Symp*, pages 684–688, Washington, DC, October 26-30 1996.

[6] E. Goldsmith. *Research Into Illustration: An Approach and A Review*. Cambridge University Press, Cambridge, 1984.

[7] B. Hunter, A. Crismore, and P. Pearson. Visual displays in basal readers and social studies textbooks. In D. Willows and H. Houghton, editors, *The Psychology of Illustration: Instructional Issues*, volume 2, chapter 5, pages 116–158. Springer-Verlag, New York, 1987.

[8] E. Ignatius, H. Senay, and J. Favre. An intelligent system for task-specific visualization assistance. *J. of Visual Lang. and Computing*, 5:321–338, 1994.

[9] P. Johnson, H. Johnson, R. Waddington, and A. Shouls. Task-related knowledge structures: Analysis, modelling, and application. In D. Jones and R. Winder, editors, *People and Computers IV, Proc. of British SIGHCI*, pages 35–61. Cambridge University Press, 1988.

[10] P. R. Keller and M. M. Keller. *Visual Cues: Practical Data Visualization*. IEEE Computer Society Press and IEEE Press, 1993.

[11] S. Kosslyn. Understanding charts and graphs. *Applied Cognitive Psychology*, 3:185–226, 1989.

[12] W. Levie. Research on pictures: a guide to the literature. In D. Willows and H. Houghton, editors, *The Psychology of Illustration: Basic Research*, volume 1, chapter 2, pages 1–50. Springer-Verlag, New York, 1987.

[13] J. Levin, G. Anglin, and R. Carney. On empirically validating functions of pictures in prose. In D. Willows and H. Houghton, editors, *The Psychology of Illustration: Basic Research*, volume 1, chapter 2, pages 51–86. Springer-Verlag, New York, 1987.

[14] G. Lohse, K. Biolsi, and H. Rueter. A classification of visual representations. *Communications of the ACM*, 37(12):36–49, 1994.

[15] W. Mann and S. Thompson. Rhetorical structure theory: Towards a functional theory of text organization. In *TEXT*, volume 2, pages 243–281. Springer, 1988.

[16] J. Marks. A formal specification scheme for network diagrams that facilitates automated design. *J. of Visual Languages and Computing*, 2(4):395–414, 1991.

[17] M. Maybury. Planning multimedia explanations using communicative acts. In M. Maybury, editor, *Intelligent Multimedia Interfaces*, chapter 2, pages 60–74. AAAI Press/The MIT Press, Menlo Park, CA, 1993.

[18] K. McKeown. *Text Generation*. Cambridge University Press, London, 1985.

[19] K. Mullet and D. Sano. *Designing Visual Interfaces*. SunSoft Press, Mountain View, CA, 1995.

[20] S. Roth and W. Hefley. Intelligent multimedia presentation systems: Research and principles. In M. Maybury, editor, *Intelligent Multimedia Interfaces*, chapter 1, pages 13–58. AAAI Press/The MIT Press, Menlo Park, CA, 1993.

[21] S. F. Roth and J. Mattis. Automating the presentation of information. In *Proc. IEEE Conf. on AI Applications*, pages 90–97, 1991.

[22] C. Schmid. *Handbook of graphic presentation*. The Ronald Press, New York, 1954.

[23] D. Seligmann. *A Visual Language for Automated 3D Graphics Generation*. PhD thesis, Columbia University, New York, NY, 1993.

[24] A. Sutcliffe and J. Darzentas. Use of visual media in explanation. In M. Tauber, D. Mahling, and F. Arefi, editors, *Cognitive Aspects of Visual Languages and Visual Interfaces*, chapter 2, pages 105–132. Elsevier Science B.V., Amsterdam, 1994.

[25] A. Treisman. Perceptual grouping and attention in visual search for features and for objects. *J. of Experimental Psychology: Human Perception and Performance*, 8(2):194–214, 1982.

[26] E. R. Tufte. *The Visual Display of Quantitative Information*. Graphics Press, Cheshire, CT, 1983.

[27] E. R. Tufte. *Envisioning Information*. Graphics Press, Cheshire, CT, 1990.

[28] E. R. Tufte. *Visual Explanations: Images and Quantities, Evidence and Narrative*. Graphics Press, Cheshire, CT, 1997.

[29] R. Wehrend and C. Lewis. A problem-oriented classification of visualization techniques. In *Proceedings of the First IEEE Conference on Visualization: Visualization 90*, pages 139–143. IEEE, Los Alamitos, CA, October 1990.

[30] W. Winn and W. Holliday. Design principles for diagrams and charts. In D. Jonassen, editor, *The Technology of Text*, volume 1, pages 277–299. Educational Technology Publications, Englewood Cliffs, NJ, 1982.

[31] H. Zettl. *Sight Sound Motion: Applied Media Aesthetics*. Wadsworth Publishing Company, Belmont, CA, second edition, 1990.

[32] M. Zhou and S. Feiner. Top-down hierarchical planning of coherent visual discourse. In *Proc. IUI'97*, pages 129–136, Orlando, FL, January 1997.

Visualizing the Evolution of Web Ecologies

Ed H. Chi[†], James Pitkow, Jock Mackinlay, Peter Pirolli, Rich Gossweiler, Stuart K. Card
Xerox Palo Alto Research Center
3333 Coyote Hill Road
Palo Alto, CA 94304 USA
{echi,pitkow,mackinla,pirolli,rcg,card}@parc.xerox.com
([†] current address: echi@cs.umn.edu, University of Minnesota, Computer Science Department,
200 Union St. SE Room 4-192, Minneapolis, MN 55455)

ABSTRACT

Several visualizations have emerged which attempt to visualize all or part of the World Wide Web. Those visualizations, however, fail to present the dynamically changing ecology of users and documents on the Web. We present new techniques for Web Ecology and Evolution Visualization (WEEV). Disk Trees represent a discrete time slice of the Web ecology. A collection of Disk Trees forms a Time Tube, representing the evolution of the Web over longer periods of time. These visualizations are intended to aid authors and webmasters with the production and organization of content, assist Web surfers making sense of information, and help researchers understand the Web.

Keywords

World Wide Web, visualization, log file analysis, temporal analysis, information ecologies, hypertext, documents.

INTRODUCTION

Currently, producers, organizers, and users of content on the World Wide Web must use technologies that are spartan in providing cues that would make their lives easier. For comparison, the librarian or experienced user of a physical library can usually tell, with some ease, the general layout of content, figure out which books are of greatest interest to the community (e.g., by the wear on the book spines), and figure out what's timely or deadwood (e.g., by looking at the circulation check-out stamps inside the book covers). The organizers and authors of such content may use such cues as data for different purposes, to structure content in more appealing and useful ways.

It is important to note that these cues are not just about the content: they are about the relationships among content (e.g., the books themselves), their topology (e.g., layout in physical and topical space), and use (e.g., circulation). To use a biological metaphor, such a complex set of relations form an *ecology* among users and their information environment, and its change through time is a form of *evolution*. Here we present visualization techniques that provide cues that enhance the understanding of relationships among Web content, topology, and usage through time. These techniques are examples of Web Ecology and Evolution Visualization (WEEV). Such techniques should aid users in finding content, keeping track of it, making sense of it, and understanding its timeliness. The techniques should also help authors, sponsors, and site administrators understand how content is being used and the effectiveness of their designs.

Visualizations of entire information spaces as large as the World Wide Web have been pursued by various researchers [7,8,17]. However, most systems have yet to deal with the larger problem of how these information spaces evolve over time. The problem is more difficult because: 1) the ecology of these information spaces changes rapidly, and 2) the size of these information spaces grows explosively within the time span that we are interested in examining.

In this paper, we introduce a new visualization called the *Time Tube*. The Time Tube organizes and visualizes the evolution of Web sites. For the purpose of this paper we will explore the application of Time Tubes to the Xerox WWW site (www.xerox.com), a medium sized *time-extended document ecology* (7,500 items across a 30 day period). Time Tubes are composed of one or more *Disk Trees*, which represent the hyperlink structure of a Web site. Figures 1 and 2 show the Time Tube and Disk Trees, respectively.

These new visualizations are designed to assist users in the difficult task of understanding the complex relationships and interactions among the production and consumption of information within Web sites. If we divide tasks into three levels:

Level 1: (Local) Finding some specific content

Level 2: (Comparison) Comparing information at two places

Level 3: (Global) Discovering a trend or pattern

then most Web interaction methods focus on Level 1 tasks. One of the goals of WEEV techniques is to address tasks at Levels 2 and 3.

CHI 98 Los Angeles CA USA
Copyright 1998 0-89791-975-0/98/ 4..$5.00

Different communities of Web users are likely to share at least some common questions and tasks. For instance, consider these questions about the usage and structure of the Web (this list is by no means exhaustive):

Usage

- How has information been accessed? How frequently? How recently? What is the most/least popular information?
- Where do people enter the Web site? Where do people spend time on the site? How long do they spend in the site?
- How do they travel within the site? What are the most popular paths? What is the road least traveled?
- Who are the people accessing the site? From which geographic location? From what high level domain (.com, .edu, etc.)?

Structural

- What information has been added? Modified? Deleted? Remained the same, but moved?

Another set of common questions might arise concerning the relations among usage and structure. For example, Web site administrators and content providers are often curious about the following:

- How is new information accessed? When does it become popular? When does it die?
- How does the addition of information change the navigation patterns within the site? Can people still navigate to desired information?
- Would a site benefit from a redesign? Was the redesign of a site effective? What about minor redesigns and restructuring?
- Do people look for deleted information? Could unused information be deleted or relegated to cheaper storage?

While the WEEV system we developed was designed to answer questions such as those above, here we restrict ourselves to only a subset, and use the Xerox Web site in our examples. Before describing the Time Tube system and demonstrating how the Time Tube and Disk Trees help answer these questions we describe the underlying mapping of data to visualizations.

Figure 1: Time Tube shows the evolution of a time-extended document ecology (**www.xerox.com** during April 1997). This Time Tube is composed of four Disk Trees, each representing one week of April.

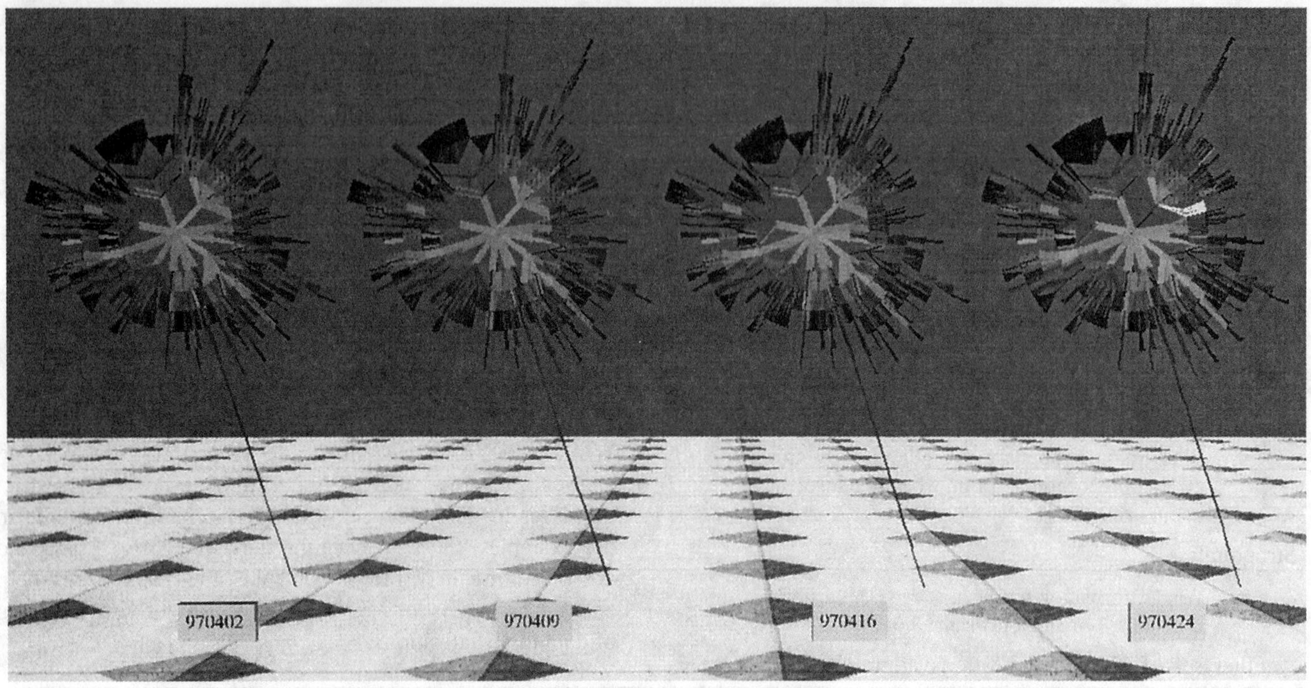

Figure 2: Each of the four **Disk Tree** shows a discrete time slice of a Web ecology (**www.xerox.com**, April, 1997).

FROM RAW DATA TO USEFUL ABSTRACTIONS

We can think of information visualization as involving a set of mappings from some Base Data set, in some idiosyncratic representation through possibly intermediary representations to some Analytic Abstraction appropriate for insight or communication and then into a Visualization representation suitable for visual analysis and communication with the user.

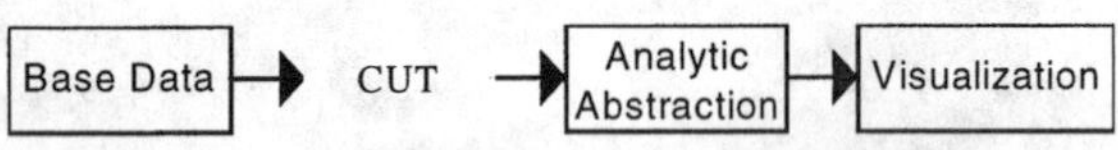

Current attention within the Web measurement community centers around the number of times items are requested (hits) and hyperlink topology. In the case of the Web, our previous work [13] has shown that it is much more useful to organize an intermediate representation CUT based on Content (C), Usage (U) and Topology (T). In addition to the explicit linkages among documents, the intermediate CUT representation can be used to create implicit relationships with a much more richly connected space.

Previous work has tended to focus on CUT elements in isolation. Early work on information retrieval of document collections, for example, focused on Content, usually represented as document vectors [16]. Later work, e.g., [4] considered Topology, especially in the form of explicit hypertext links. But we have argued [13] that a richer set of analysis can be preformed by combining Content, Topology, and Usage.

We further extend these analyses by examining changes through time. Such data more directly address deeper and more difficult questions like "Was newly added information well consumed?" and "What faddish trends occur within our site?" Here we concentrate on Topology and Usage computed over time, deriving these from available data and mapping these into an Analytic Abstraction that can be mapped into an information visualization.

RELATED SOLUTIONS

Although the Web has grown rapidly, one can easily argue that the state-of-the-art tools for the analysis of WWW logs have not. Many of the commercially available analysis programs perform the same functionality as the earliest descriptive statistics reporting programs like Kevin Hughes' *getsites*, released during the summer of 1993 [9] and the earliest access log visualization programs like WebViz and WebSpace [14,7].

Analyses

Essentially, modern day log file analysis programs provide spreadsheet-like descriptive summaries of Web site activity. A typical package [12,10] reports the number of times an object was requested, simple characterizations of the machines requesting objects from the site, entry and exit points, and temporal summaries of the requests on a per hour basis. Most packages also create charts that summarize the descriptive data. It is important to note though that while these systems are able to read several months worth of WWW access data, reports are usually only produced on a per-day basis.

Visualizations

Recently, several analysis packages have emerged that provide visualizations of an entire site [3,1]. While Accure Insight™ primarily focuses on the real-time monitoring of Web sites, the Astra SiteManager™ (ASM) concentrates on the structure and usage of a site. Since ASM provides the closest functionality to Time Tubes, we briefly review the functionality of ASM.

ASM provides the analyst with a split screen display, with one part dedicated to visualizing the site and the other towards textual descriptions of the site. The topology of a site is gathered by walking the structure of a site via a spider. Pages and links are displayed using a 2-D cone-tree layout scheme similar to [6]. In this scheme, WWW objects are laid out along a circle with the space occupied by each object being proportional to the number of children it contains. The layout is recursive in the sense that the same circular layout is used for the children of an object. Users are able to interactively zoom-in and zoom-out of the visualization and collapse and expand the children of a page.

With ASM, the analyst is able to create daily maps of a Web site based upon the crawls of the site and the site's usage. The system enables user-specified filtering based upon several parameters (e.g., media type, origin of link, etc.) and colors usage according to user-specified thresholds (e.g., blue for low usage, pink for more active usage, and red for high usage items). Additionally, support is available to help understand the structural changes to a site. This is accomplished by color-coding additions, deletions, and changes that occur between two maps and displaying the result as a single graph.

Although ASM provides many useful functions, it does not easily answer questions about evolving Web ecologies. First and foremost, the system has difficulty visualizing a large number of documents, such as those within the Xerox site[1]. A considerable amount of screen real estate is consumed at the expense of displaying the link structure among documents. This effect is further amplified as pages with a large number of children are allocated a circle with a large radius (The large radius is necessary to separate all the children).

Another limitation is that the system only permits the visualization of a site at a single point in time, making it very difficult to make comparisons across times. Additionally, no mechanism is provided that allows *differences* in usage to be identified as well. Without the basic ability to identify usage and structure differences, one can not expect to readily understand how these dimensions change across time.

BASE DATA AND ANALYTIC ABSTRACTIONS

For our exploration of the evolution of a Web ecology, we examined data for the Xerox Web site for a one-month period starting April, 1997. Content providers for the Xerox site contributed 889 new items (11%), bringing the site to a total of 7,588 items by the end of April. For each day, additions, modifications, and deletions of content to the site were monitored and the corresponding structural changes recorded. Additionally, the daily usage logs from the site were collected. The combined data set was chosen to be large enough to be a significant challenge to visualize without being so large as to incur extreme computational penalties during the exploration phase.

We derive the Base Data from the link information extracted from WWW pages and from the usage log information collected by Web servers. WWW servers are instrumented to record relevant transactional information in the Common Log Format (CLF) [11]. For each item requested, the Web server logs the following information:

Server Log (CLF format)

{<Requesting host IP address or DNS name>,
<The remote logname of the user.>,
<User authenticated name>,
<Time to nearest sec>,
<name of object requested>,
<HTTP version>,
<HTTP method invoked>,
<Bytes transferred>,
<HTTP status code returned>}

While additional transaction information is now available since the advent of CLF, e.g., user agent, referrer, cookie, etc., our efforts concentrate only on the information contained in CLF.

The topology information is stored in a custom hyperlink database, where a complete snapshot of the topology is captured daily. The format used to store the topology is as follows:

Topology (custom)

Day1: {URL1: {<link> <link> ...}
{URL2: {<link> <link> ...} ...
Day2: {URL1: {<link> <link> ...}

From the Base Data representation, we construct a CUT representation.

Topology

URL1: {day1: <link> <link> ...}
{day2: <link> <link> ...} ...
URL2: {day1: <link> <link> ...}
{day2: <link> <link> ...} ...

[1] Unfortunately we are not able to include a screen shot of the ASM's presentation of the Xerox Site for comparison due to a bug in the ASM's Web crawling spider that caused it to infinitely recurse the Xerox Site.

...

Usage

URL1: {day1: <freq>, day2: <freq>, ...}

URL2: {day1: <freq>, day2: <freq>, ...}

...

Finally, to support the visualization, we build an Analytic Abstraction by mapping the CUT structures into trees aggregated over time forming combined trees over all weeks, where each node has the following attributes:

{ <freq over 1 week>, <age of node>, <status- (added, modified, deleted> <relation to other nodes>}

WEB ECOLOGY AND EVOLUTION VISUALIZATION

In analyzing the linkage structure of the Web, we are often interested in the shortest number of hops from one document to another. Breadth-first traversal transforms the Web graph into a tree by placing a node as closely to the root node as possible. After obtaining this tree, we then visualize the structure using the Disk Tree technique.

Instead of having a different layout for each Disk Tree, we use a combined layout for all trees. We do this by taking into account of all of the documents that ever existed in the entire time range of the time tube, then computing a single Disk Tree layout that is then used across all of the Disk Tree slices. This produces a layout that remains consistent across Disk Trees.

Disk Tree Visualization

The Disk Tree uses a circular layout to visualizing the hierarchy. Each successive circle denotes levels in the tree. The layout algorithm runs in two passes. In the first pass, the algorithm traverses the entire hierarchy using post-order traversal. At each node, the algorithm calculates the number of leaf nodes in that subtree. So we know the total number of leaves in this tree. We then calculate the amount of angular space each leaf node should be allocated (360/Total # of Leaves). In the second pass, the algorithm traverses the hierarchy using breadth-first traversal. At each node, it allocates the amount of angular space for that node by looking to see how many leaf nodes are rooted at that subtree. In this manner, each leaf node is guaranteed a fixed amount of angular space. The result is shown in the figure below. Each concentric circle is a new level in the tree.

We can gain increased understanding of visualizations by paying attention to the choices made in mapping data into visual presentations [5]. In our use of Disk Trees to visualize the Web site, the computed hierarchy is mapped (see Figure 2):

Analytic Abstraction		*Visualization*
Treelinks	→	a line mark in X and Y
Page access frequency	→	line size and brightness
Page lifecycle stage	→	color (new page = red; continued page = green; deleted page = yellow)

Because of the large number of nodes and because of its importance, page access frequency is double-coded. This has the effect of making the diagram visually simpler and allows the diagram to separate out three hierarchical levels of attention: (1) Documents added or deleted in a week standout highlighted in yellow or red. (2) Frequently visited parts of the Web site (thick bright green) form a noticeable foreground. Finally, (3) low frequency areas of the Web site seem to recede into the background.

The Disk Tree has several advantages: First, the structure of the tree is visualized compactly, with the pattern easily recognizable. Second, when viewed straight on or at slight angles, there are no occlusion problems since the entire layout lays on a 2D plane. Third, unlike Cone Trees, since it is a 2D technique, we can utilize the third dimension for other information, such as time, or a 3D glyph at each node. Lastly, the circularity is aesthetically pleasing to the eye.

The visualization itself actually validates the choice of our transformation algorithm—breadth first traversal. Notice that the high traffic areas are concentrated near the root node. This means that the algorithm places easy to reach nodes starting from the root node. As the document gets farther and farther away from the root node, the document has a lesser possibility of being accessed.

Time Tube Visualizations

Using Disk Trees, we can utilize the third dimension to represent time. In the Time Tube visualization, we layout multiple Disk Trees along a spatial axis. By using a spatial axis to represent time, we see the information space-time in a single visualization, thus facilitating easy sense making on the entire information space-time. Essentially in Figure 2 we are reusing the X dimension, once as part of the layout of the Disk Tree and again to represent the passage of time.

Treelinks	→	a line mark in X and Y
Time	→	an area on X

The mapping of multiple variables is mitigated if the Disk Trees are turned as in Figure 1. By making the Disk Trees be 2D in a 3D world, we get additional flexibility in the mapping at the cost of perspective distortions and lower readability.

Slices in the information space-time of Figure 1 are actually not laid out parallel to each other. Each slice is rotated so that it occupies the same amount of screen area as other slices. Because of perspective effects, if each slice were parallel to each other, then slices in the center would occupy smaller amounts of space than slices on the side.

Also, we would see the front side of the slices that are on the left side of the viewing frustum, and the backside of the slices that are on the right side of the viewing frustum. By carefully monitoring the viewing degree of interest, we can also emphasize certain slices, and de-emphasize others to get a focus+context effect.

Another interesting variant of the Time Tube is to stack the Disk Trees in the Time Tube and then fly through the tube, or similarly, to play the Disk Trees one after another in time order so as to create an animation of change. That is, instead of mapping time into space, we just map it into time.

Time → time.

This method is more compact, hence the Disk Trees can be larger, and it engages the motion detection capabilities of the human perceptual system. The detection of change and the interpretations of series of changes are enhanced at the cost of the ability to do comparisons between different points in time.

Interaction Model

The system allows users to interact with the visualization in various ways:

- By clicking a button, the system rotates all of the slices so that we are viewing it head-on, as shown in Figure 2.
- Clicking on a slice brings that slice to the center focus, thus allowing us to view that week's worth of data in more detail. That slice is also drawn on a transparent circular background, so the slices in the Time Tube are still visible.
- Using a "Flick-Up" gesture, the slice goes back into the Time Tube.
- Using a "Flick-Down" gesture, the slice becomes the floor (at a slight angle).
- Right-clicking a node zooms to the local area of that node to show more detail. Hitting the home key sends the user back the global view. This enables a "Drill-Down" operation that is of favorite among analysts. The rapid exploration of local patterns is of great interest to them.
- We can also use the mouse to poke around in the slices. When a mouse is over a node, that node is highlighted in all of the slices. In addition, a small information area shows the details on that node. This interaction is like brushing your finger through the Time Tube, seeing the detail of the point of interest.
- While poking around with the mouse, you can also instruct the program to notify the Netscape browser to bring up that particular page. Making this into a novel web-surfing tool!
- When the mouse is activated on a particular node, the 1-hop links are also shown using blue lines.
- Another button changes the point of view so that we are viewing straight down the Time Tube.
- We can also see an animation of each successive slice shown head-on. This maps the time dimension of the data into a time dimension in the visualization.

REAL-WORLD ANALYSIS SCENARIOS

Given the ability to visualize usage patterns on web sites, analysts can now answer some interesting questions. We started this paper by motivating a number of questions that site administrators, content producers, and users may have about the behavior of a specific Web site. Given the space limitations, we will focus on the following questions with respect to the Xerox Web site, and answer them in order:

1. What devolved into deadwood? When did it? Was there a correlation with a restructuring of the Web site?
2. What evolved into a popular page? When did it? Was there a correlation with a restructuring of the Web site?
3. How was usage affected by items added over time?
4. How was usage affected by items deleted over time?

Deadwood

In our previous work [15], we motivated the notion of the time-course desirability of information. That is, information is subject to various patterns of faddishness across time. For example, while some pages remain perennially popular, the desirability of other information decreases over time, i.e., becomes deadwood. Content providers need to be made aware of the utility of their material. Popular information needs to remain accessible whereas information that has lost its appeal can be removed, relegated to cheaper storage devices, given a face-lift, or integrated into other content.

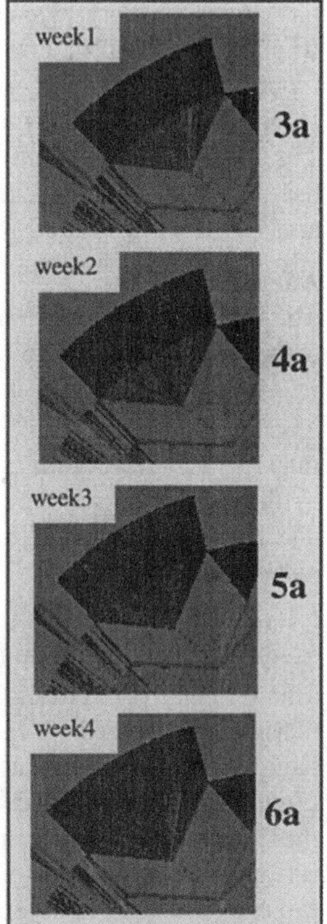

The wide fan in Figure 3a corresponds to a set of product safety information. During the first week, the partial green color of the area reveals moderate usage of the information. As time progresses (Figures 4a, 5a, 6a), the area becomes darker and darker revealing that the material is becoming less and less popular. While Time Tube does not inform us in this case *why* the material lost its popularity, it does clearly identify the change in usage and enables further exploration.

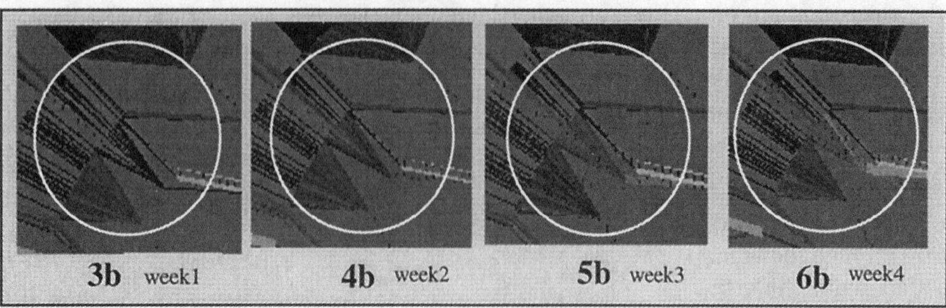

The Rise of Information

Fortunately, not all material becomes deadwood. Each year, Xerox publishes a Fact Book that contains all relevant product, service, and financial information for the current year. For 1997, the Fact Book was published online prior to the month of April but received very little attention from users of the site. This is shown in Figure 3b, where the black coloring of the pages in the Disk Tree reveals that the pages existed but were not receiving much traffic. Due to a modification during the second week within the site that helped promote attention to the 1997 Fact Book (Figure 4b), the area becomes noticeably greener indicating increased traffic to the area. In each successive week (Figure 5b and 6b), the Fact Book continues to become more and more popular and the corresponding area in the Disk Trees becomes greener and greener. In this case, Time Tubes enabled the quick verification that a minor redesign was able to successfully influence the traffic to an area of the site.

Addition of Items

The addition of new material into a document ecology competes with other items for attention. Therefore, one would like to know how the addition of new information affects global usage across time. It is possible that the new material is never used, or it may become wildly popular. Without an understanding of the evolution of the topology and the usage patterns, this determination cannot be easily performed.

Using the Xerox Web site Time Tube visualization in Figure 4c, we see the addition of a press release announcing a new family of Xerox products. In Figure 4, we see that the node is colored black in the first week, indicating the page does not yet exist. In Figure 4c, the red line depicts the introduction of the press release into the Web site. By brushing this area in Figure 4c, we are able to drill down and discover that usage in the third week skyrocketed from 1 access to 871 accesses. In week four (Figure 6c), additional red lines indicate that more related press releases were added. From this example, we are able to understand the impact of a series of important press releases on the Xerox Web site. The addition of this material positively affected the usage, probably indicating a well-received product line.

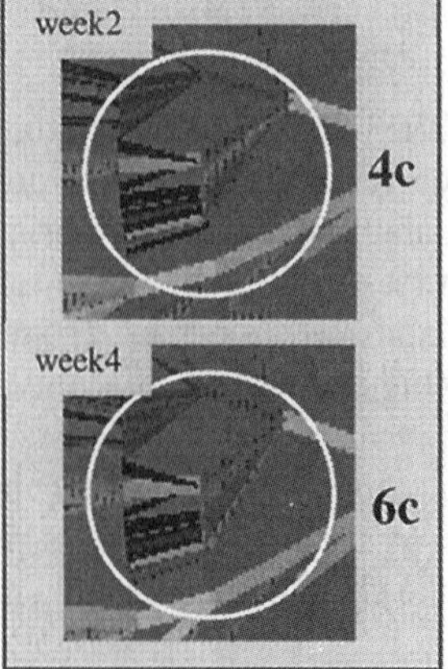

Deletion of Items

Equally interesting as the incorporation of new material into a Web ecology is the deletion of material from that ecology. The deletion of material not only affects the content within the site, but potentially the navigational structures that enable users to get from one portion of the Web site to another as well. Clearly, the haphazard deletion of material can negatively impact the usability of a site. Both end-users as well as administrators can profit from being made aware of deletions.

The area displayed in Figure 5d corresponds to Xerox print drivers information. The green color and the width of the lines indicate that the material is well-used. The root of the branch serves as the navigational hub to pages in this area, and has a direction from the Xerox home page. During the fourth week, a different navigation path replaced the direct link from the Xerox home page to the main driver page. The Disk Tree in Figure 6d shows the link from the home page to the driver page as black, indicating no usage of that link. Despite this dramatic change in topology, usage of the driver area remained strong (notice the subtree remains green). The yellow lines in Figure 6d indicate that a subset of the driver information was deleted in the fourth week. From this example, we can see the deletion of material and navigation redesign did not negatively affect the overall usage of driver information.

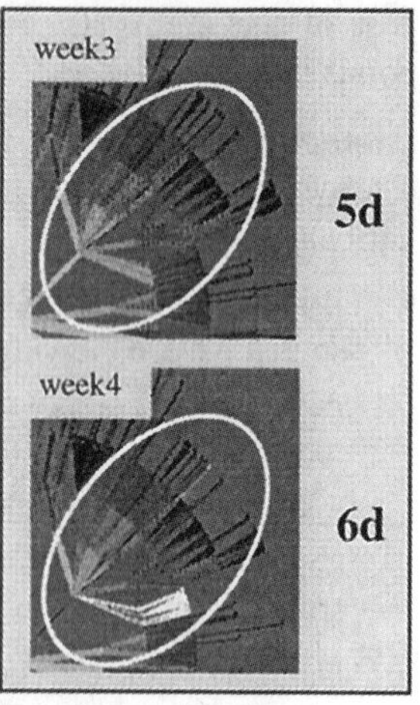

GENERAL DISCUSSION

We have presented the Disk Tree and Time Tube as examples of Web Ecology and Evolution Visualization (WEEV) techniques. These techniques are designed to provide users with visual cues about patterns and trends in the relationships among content, topology, and use over time. There remain many limitations to the current system that need to be addressed. For instance, there is no simple method for presenting abstracts or summaries of node content—the current system just presents URLs. Despite these limitations, our scenarios illustrate that the techniques reveal information that is not readily available otherwise.

The scenarios showed how it is possible to see the birth and death of information structures on the Web environment.

Moreover, the scenarios showed how activity in the information environment often begets activity in the user community, and vice versa. Each adapts to the other, since the survival of information depends on the interest it receives, and lives of users are simplified by getting the best information at the lowest effort. The WEEV techniques presented here are aimed at enhancing our understanding of the patterns of dependency and adaptation among documents and use.

While it would be nice to have developed a system that is able to answer all of the possible questions dealing with the interactions between usage and structure of Web sites, we readily recognize several limitations of Time Tubes.

Since we used a global layout (laying out every node that ever existed during the time period), the documents and links did not shift from disk to disk. This made temporal comparisons much easier, but masked the movement of documents (for example, moving from /xps/driver.html to /driver.html). This movement is not directly apparent in this visualization because

1. The document always exists, and therefore has one representation in the global layout.
2. May continue to have similar usage patterns even after being moved, so its color brightness does not change.

As potential future work, we can imagine creating visualizations that show before-and-after views and how documents shifted around.

CONCLUSION

Given the infancy of the Web, it is not surprising that the interactions and relationships within Web ecologies are not very well understood. The visualization system presented in this paper pushes the capabilites of current Web analysis programs in the amount of data it is able to handle as well as making the evolutionary patterns of Web ecologies more apparent. As the World Wide Web continues to grow in the number of users and the number of documents made accessible, the problem of understanding the correlations between the producers of the information, the charateristics of the information, and the users of the information will most likely remain. While the Time Tube was able to address several real world analysis scenarios that are not possible with other systems, we look forward to expanding the capabilites of the Time Tube, and as a result, our understanding of Web ecologies and other time-dependent document ecologies.

ACKNOWLEDGMENTS

This work was supported in part by Office of Naval Research contract N00014-96-C-0097 to Peter Pirolli and Stuart Card.

REFERENCES

1. Accrue Insight™. http://www.acrue.com (1997).
2. Andrews, K. Visualizing Cyberspace: Information Visualization in the Harmony Internet Browser. In: *Proceedings of Information Visualization '95.* (1995).
3. Astra SiteManager™. http://www.merc-int.com (1997).
4. Botafogo , R.A, Rivlin, E. and Schneiderman, B. Structural analysis of hypertexts: Identifying hierarchies and useful metrics. *ACM Transactions on Information Systems,* 10(2):142-180 (1992).
5. Card, S. K. and Mackinlay, J. The structure of the information visualization design space. InfoVis '97. IEEE Symposium on Information Visualization. (1997).
6. Carrière, J. and Kazman, R. Interacting with huge hierarchies: Beyond cone trees. In: *Proceedings of Information Visualization '95.* (1995).
7. Chi, E. H. WebSpace Visualization. http://www.geom.umn.edu/docs/weboogl/. The Geometry Center, University of Minnesota. (Also appeared in First WWW Conference, Chicago, 1994)
8. Hendley, R.J., Drew, N.S., Wood, A.M., and Beale, R. Narcissus: Visualizing information. In: *Proceedings of Information Visualization '95.* (1995).
9. Hughes, K. *getsites* (software no longer supported), private communication (1997).
10. Interse Market Focus™. http://www.backoffice.microsoft.com (1997)
11. Luotonen, A. The common logfile format. *CERN httpd user manual.* (1995)
12. net.Genesis. net.Analysis™. http://www.netgen.com (1997)
13. Pirolli, P., Pitkow, J. and Rao, R. Silk from a sow's ear: Extracting usable structures from the web. In: *Conference on Human Factors in Computing Systems (CHI '96),* Vancouver, Canada (April 1996).
14. Pitkow, J. and Bharat, K. WebViz: A tool for World Wide Web access log visualization. In: *Proceedings of the First International World Wide Web Conference.* Geneva, Switzerland (May 1994).
15. Pitkow, J. and Pirolli, P. Life, Death, and Lawfulness on the Electronic Frontier. In: *Conference on Human Factors in Computing Systems (CHI '97).* p. 383-390. Atlanta, Georgia. (April 1997).
16. Salton, G. *The SMART Retrieval System—Experiment in Automatic Document Processing.* Prentice Hall, Englewood Cliffs, (1971).
17. Wise, J., J. Thomas, K. Pennock, D. Lantrip, M. Pottier, Anne Schur, and Vern Crow. Visualizing the Non-Visual: Spatial analysis and interaction with information from text documents. . In: *Proceedings of Information Visualization '95.* (1995)

Hi-Cites: Dynamically Created Citations with Active Highlighting

Michelle Q Wang Baldonado*
Xerox Palo Alto Research Center
3333 Coyote Hill Road
Palo Alto, CA 94304 USA
baldonad@parc.xerox.com

Terry Winograd
Gates 3B
Stanford University
Stanford, CA 94305-9035 USA
winograd@cs.stanford.edu

ABSTRACT

The original SenseMaker interface for information exploration [2] used tables to present heterogeneous document descriptions. In contrast, printed bibliographies and World Wide Web (WWW) search engines use formatted citations to convey this information. In this paper, we discuss *hi-cites*, a new interface construct developed for SenseMaker that combines the benefits of tables (which encourage the comparison of descriptions) and citations (which facilitate browsing).

Hi-cites are dynamically created citations with active highlighting. They are useful in environments where heterogeneous structured descriptions must be browsed and compared with ease. Examples beyond digital libraries include product catalogs, classified advertisements, and WWW search engines.

We have performed an evaluation of hi-cites, tables, and citations for tasks involving single attribute comparisons in the digital-library domain. This evaluation supports our claim that hi-cites are valuable for both comparison and skimming tasks in this environment.

Keywords

Hi-cites, dynamic citations, highlighting, digital libraries, information visualization, browsing

INTRODUCTION

Look for a book entitled "Physics" in most library card catalogs and you will be amazed at the number of books bearing that name. Fortunately, library catalogers describe documents by recording values for a wide variety of characteristic attributes. Library patrons can learn the author, publication year, number of pages, and the Library of Congress subject heading for each of the "Physics" books that have entries in a library's card catalog.

Users who perform information exploration in digital libraries spend much time perusing document descriptions of the kind found in library card catalogs. However, the descriptions come from an ever-growing variety of sources. Information may come not only from on-line library catalogs but also from video archives, World Wide Web (WWW) search engines, music indices, e-mail archives, map databases, and much more. The structured descriptions obtained from these sources can be heterogeneous in two ways. First, these sources may employ different conventions for describing documents. For example, USMARC defines one set of descriptive attributes, while Z39.50 Bib-1 defines a different set. In the Stanford Digital Library Project, we have addressed this problem through the development of a metadata architecture [1] that accommodates different descriptive attribute sets as well as services for translating descriptions from one attribute set to another.

A second type of document-description heterogeneity revolves around document genre. The choice of attributes for a document's description often depends on its genre. Document descriptions for music recordings are likely to include information about performers, tempo, and style; descriptions for WWW pages are likely to include information about URL and file size. The SenseMaker interface has been designed with this second style of heterogeneity in mind. The overall goal of SenseMaker is to support the contextual evolution of a user's interests during information exploration in the digital library (see [2] for more details). This paper focuses solely on how to present the heterogeneous document descriptions obtained while interacting with SenseMaker.

TABLES AND CITATION SETS

The original SenseMaker interface presented search results (document descriptions) in a table whose columns were dynamically defined by users. Tables encourage users to compare descriptions in terms of a particular attribute, due to our visual disposition to use whitespace and proximity as perceptual grouping cues [5]. Focusing on a single attribute while browsing a collection allows users to gain an overview of the collection with respect to that attribute. For example, focusing on *publication location* while browsing a collection of results produced by a search for "ODA" might lead the user to observe that much work on ODA has taken place in Europe. This style of overview is particularly useful in heterogeneous environments where document descriptions come from widely varying contexts. In a pilot user study performed on the original SenseMaker interface (in which users gathered references for a hypothetical term

* When this paper was first submitted, the author was a Ph.D. student at Stanford University.

paper on a given topic), users explicitly mentioned this ability to see all values for a particular attribute at once as one of the features that they particularly liked.

Figure 1 shows an excerpt from the original table-based version of SenseMaker. Each row in the table corresponds to one document. Each column in the table stands for an individual attribute of the document.

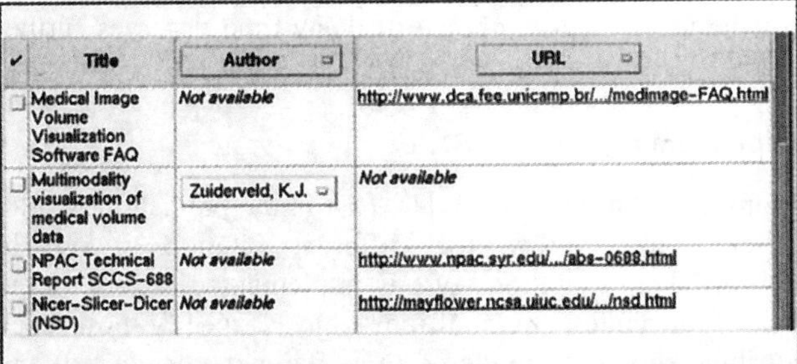

✓	Title	Author	URL
	Medical Image Volume Visualization Software FAQ	*Not available*	http://www.dca.fee.unicamp.br/.../medimage-FAQ.html
	Multimodality visualization of medical volume data	Zuiderveld, K.J.	*Not available*
	NPAC Technical Report SCCS-688	*Not available*	http://www.npac.syr.edu/.../abs-0688.html
	Nicer-Slicer-Dicer (NSD)	*Not available*	http://mayflower.ncsa.uiuc.edu/.../nsd.html

Figure 1: Excerpt from Table-Based Version of SenseMaker

As this figure illustrates, a tabular view of heterogeneous document descriptions is often sparse. We have *URL* values but no *author* values for results from WWW search engines, and vice versa from citation databases. The multiplicity of "*Not available*" values is distracting to users. Furthermore, users must almost always use horizontal scrolling since screen space disappears quickly when each attribute requires its own column. Skimming is also difficult due to the spatial discontinuities that are characteristic of tables.

In contrast to tables, formatted bibliographies require less screen space and provide a spatially continuous flow of information. A bibliographic citation concatenates just the attribute values that are available for the document it describes. Furthermore, these citations make use of conventions that indicate for each value what its associated attribute is. These conventions may rely on fixed order (most bibliographic styles prescribe a particular order for citation elements) and may also use visual cues such as font style. A typical citation appears in Figure 2.

Strunk, W. Jr. and White, E. B. *The Elements of Style.* Third edition. Macmillan Publishing Co., Inc., New York, 1979.

Figure 2: Typical Citation

In this figure, italics are used for book titles, while the order of author, book title, edition, publisher, publication city, and publication year is conventional. The demarcating punctuation marks between items serve to delineate and identify each item in the citation as well.

In the publishing world, standard bibliographic styles are used for traditional written works, such as books, magazine articles, newspapers, memos and more. Formatted bibliographies can be generalized to accommodate nontraditional document descriptions as well (e.g., descriptions of videos, software, e-mail, maps, people, etc.). We call such a generalized bibliography a *citation set.* Note that most World Wide Web search engines present their results as citation sets (see Figure 3) .

1. Philadelphia Online | Return to MARS
Shuttle astronauts back on Earth, mission finally accomplished. By MARCIA DUNN ASSOCIATED PRESS. CAPE CANAVERAL, Fla. (AP) - Space...
http://www3.phillynews.com/packages/mars/shut17.asp - size 5K - 15-Aug-97 - English - *Translate*

2. JPL Mars Pathfinder - Video from KSC
Mars Pathfinder - KSC Video Feeds. Automatically reloads every 90 seconds, or click on reload for newest images. PATHFINDER at Complex 17B. Mars...
http://www.ksc.nasa.gov/payloads/missions/pathfinder/old-video.html - size 1K - 3-Dec-96 - English - *Translate*

Figure 3: AltaVista Citations

The gain in browsing ease offered by citation sets (due to the compactness and visually identifiable structure of citations) is offset by a loss in ease of comparison of available items. In this paper, we define and propose *hi-cites*, a novel interface idea that promises to improve browsing by combining the benefits of citation sets with the benefits of tables. The SenseMaker interface has been revised to make use of hi-cites instead of tables.

HI-CITES

Hi-cites, dynamically created citations with active highlighting, are a hybrid of citation sets and tables. They are like citation sets in that they concatenate visually marked attribute values (subject to wraparound), treating attribute values as though they were words and phrases in a single sentence. Definable citation styles encapsulate the ordering, marking, and rendering rules required for this display. For example, one citation style might stipulate that *title* appear before *author*, while another might change that ordering. In addition, one citation style might mark an *editor* value with the suffix "ed.," while another might use the suffix "(editor)." Finally, a citation style might specify that article *titles* are quoted while journal *titles* are italicized.

Hi-cites are like tables in that they facilitate the perceptual grouping of all values of a particular attribute. Specifically, users can highlight* in red all values for an attribute by pausing for a short period of time over that attribute with the mouse (see the next section for a detailed discussion of this affordance). Figure 4 shows both *title* highlighting and *publisher* highlighting. Note that it substitutes reverse video for color so that the highlighting can be represented in a black-and-white figure.

In addition to enabling highlighting, the point-plus-delay affordance also allows users to find out the name of each attribute. If a SenseMaker user were to move her cursor over a *title* attribute value and pause, then all *title* values would be highlighted. In addition, the name *Title* would

* The name hi-cite derives from the words "highlight" and "citation."

Strunk, W. Jr. and White, E. B. *The Elements of Style*. Third edition. Macmillan Publishing Co., Inc., New York, 1979.

Morris, W. and Morris, M. *Morris Dictionary of Word and Phrase Origins*. Harper and Row, Publishers, New York, 1977.

Strunk, W. Jr. and White, E. B. *The Elements of Style*. Third edition. Macmillan Publishing Co., Inc., New York, 1979.

Morris, W. and Morris, M. *Morris Dictionary of Word and Phrase Origins*. Harper and Row, Publishers, New York, 1977.

Figure 4: Two Sets of Hi-Cites (actual hi-cites make use of color rather than reverse video for highlighting)

show up in a temporary rectangular pop-up box. This result is shown in Figure 5.

This "help" feature is important for cases where users are not familiar with the chosen attribute marking conventions. For example, a newcomer to geographic information sources may not be familiar with the conventional marking of latitude and longitude, and thus may need to discover what the pieces of a geographic citation are.

Affordances

The hi-cite affordance for highlighting an attribute and for discovering an attribute's name (point-plus-delay over an individual attribute value) is similar to that needed to initiate "tool tips" in Windows applications. The choice of this affordance was made after comparing it to a number of other possibilities. In an early design that we considered, the affordance was simply moving the mouse over an attribute value, similar to the affordance for Macintosh "balloon help" [8]. However, we discovered that this was distracting to the user. Furthermore, the interaction between scrolling and skimming was problematic. Consider the situation where a user wants to skim all titles in the collection of document descriptions (not just those that fit into the current window). If moving the mouse over an attribute value causes highlighting to occur, then the act of moving the mouse to the scrollbar is likely to cause the desired highlighting to be lost.

We rejected the possibilities of highlighting on single-click or double-click on the grounds that they would conflict with the design languages [7] of Web browsers and GUIs, both of which are already well-known and familiar to our intended user community. In particular, single-click maps onto "follow link" in Web browsers, while double-click maps onto "open" in GUIs.

Finally, we debated making the affordance something less familiar, such as typing a letter over the attribute value (e.g., "h" for highlight); right-clicking and then either automatically highlighting or bringing up a pop-up menu (as in Windows); or doing a combination of special key (e.g., the Apple key or the Control key) and clicking. In all of these cases, the affordance would be learnable, but it was unlikely that users would "stumble" across the affordance. We felt that highlighting was so crucial to hi-cites that ease of discovery was as important of ease of learning. Thus, we decided to use the point-plus-delay affordance, even though the delay means that highlighting is not as fast as it could be for the user. Clearly, choice of delay time deserves further study.

Implementing Citation Styles

Many different citation styles exist in the publishing world. Hi-cites also allow for different citation styles. In SenseMaker, a citation style is implemented as an ordered list of attributes. In addition, objects specify how each attribute should be rendered (e.g., italicized or quoted) and marked (e.g., with a suffix "ed."). In our implementation, attribute values can be rendered as links (pointers) to the actual attribute values. This use of links in citations has already become common practice in the reference sections of documents on the World Wide Web. For example, articles in the on-line D-Lib magazine (http://www.dlib.org/) often include bibliographic citations that have hypertext links to the referenced works. Similarly, the result format for the various WWW search engines is an implicit citation style that contains links.

Including link information in the rendering-style object also allows local values that are particularly long to be accessible via a link rather than directly integrated into the citation. Consider for example the difference in expected lengths of a title, abstract, and full text of a document. Titles are usually fairly short in length and are almost always listed in on-line citations. Abstracts are usually on the order of one to two paragraphs. In many electronic card catalogs, the user has a choice of a terse or verbose presentation of citations, where the abstract is listed in only the verbose style. Finally, full text is almost never included directly in the citations of an on-line catalog, but may be available via a special command. The ability to have links in citations changes the design space in that it makes it possible to have longer values readily accessible without giving up screen space.

In non-textual domains, such as video, the "citation" for a video clip may be a multimedia sequence of images and text rather than an attribute-value style citation. In general, the question of how to display succinct representations of multimedia documents is an open area for research. We believe that at least some of the hi-cite principles are applicable to this domain. For example, the last hi-cite that appears in Figure 5 is a description of a video. It contains a *title* attribute, which is common to all of the displayed hi-cites, but it also contains a number of genre-specific attributes (e.g., *filmstrip*) that are accessible via links. An alternative to this citation style might inline the *filmstrip* value for each video directly into the hi-cite.

RELATED WORK

Highlighting

The use of highlighting as a mechanism for bringing a user's attention to a particular piece of information on the screen has been carefully studied by the human factors community. From this perspective, highlighting is defined as any visual characteristic that causes the highlighted piece of In addition to color, highlighting can include boxing, inverse video, blinking, and other techniques. Several studies have shown that color highlighting is useful for the visual-search task [3, 6]. Although no definitive answer has emerged on how to choose a color for highlighting, some studies show the perceptual salience of red [6]. In addition to choosing a color for highlighting, designers must also consider the amount of color in the interface.

One issue that has received great attention in highlighting studies is the effect of mis-highlighting information, or what happens when information is highlighted but the user does not wish to focus on it. In general, a high rate of mis-highlighting can override the benefits obtained from highlighting [6]. These findings are good evidence for the importance of user control in hi-cites. The fact that a hi-cite user can quickly and easily control what piece of information is highlighted means that the user can ensure that highlighting always matches the current focus of attention. These study results also indicate the need for SenseMaker users to be able to turn off highlighting completely in the interface, a feature that is not currently implemented.

One possible alternative to hi-cites is to differentiate the attributes within a citation by displaying each of them in a different color (e.g., red for *title*, blue for *publication date*). In this case, dynamic highlighting would not be necessary. Users could compare values for an attribute by focusing on the color corresponding to that attribute. However, this strategy requires addressing the issue of color blindness. Furthermore, we found informally in experimenting with prototypes that a multiplicity of colors in the interface was often distracting and detracted from our ability to perform perceptual grouping for a given attribute. This anecdotal evidence, combined with the literature on the effects of mis-highlighting, convinced us to design for dynamic, single-color highlighting rather than for static, multi-color highlighting.

Keyword-in-Context Indices

Another alternative to our hi-cite design originates in the pioneering work of H.P. Luhn on keyword-in-context indices (KWIC indices) [4]. A typical keyword-in-context index has one entry for each keyword of each indexed work's title. These titles are presented "in context," meaning that they are presented sandwiched in between the surrounding words from the title. The keyword entries themselves are aligned in a single column. In a classic keyword-in-context index, there was a limit on how many characters could be displayed. Therefore, a fixed number of characters from the prefix to the keyword could be included to its left and a fixed number of characters from the keyword to the suffix could be included to its right. An example of a keyword-in-context index appears in Figure 4.

In KWIC indices, position is used to highlight a piece of structured information. "The initial letters of the alphabetized keywords form a column which guides the eye when scanning for desired words" [4, p. 289]. In other words, the "highlighting" mechanism of keyword-in-context is alignment rather than color. This reliance on alignment means that tables are more similar to keyword-in-context indices than to hi-cites.

In a static display, highlighting by alignment is easier for scanning than highlighting by color since the eye does not need to rove across the page. However, dynamically changing what is highlighted is much more disruptive for highlighting by alignment than for highlighting by color since it causes the rearrangement of all the visible document descriptions.

In the heterogeneous digital-library domain, users are likely to change what is highlighted quite often. It is for this reason that we hypothesize that hi-cites are better suited for skimming document descriptions in this environment than are KWIC indices. Hi-cites keep document descriptions globally constant in space throughout the browsing process while still allowing perceptual grouping by color.

```
ve Survey of the Radio, Phonograph, and Television Habits in
te Manual of the Edison Phonograph
                    The Phonograph and its Inventor, Thomas
ete Library of American Phonograph Recordings
    The Edison Improved Phonograph
            The Fabulous Phonograph; from Edison to Stereo
e Patent History of the Phonograph, 1877-1912: A Source Book
                        Recollections of Thomas A. Edison: A
```

Figure 4: A Keyword-in-Context Bibliographic Index

EVALUATION

Hi-cites are modeled after both citation sets and tables. Citation sets are easier to skim than tables since they take up less screen space and provide a more spatially continuous flow of information. Hi-cites are so close in appearance to citation sets that it is reasonable to believe that they are also easier to skim than tables. Tables are better than citation sets for the comparison of attribute values since they facilitate perceptual grouping. Hi-cites are different enough from tables that an evaluation is necessary to determine if they are also better than citation sets for this task. Before conducting such an evaluation, we enumerated the following hypotheses about the differences we expected to find among tables, citation sets, and hi-cites for tasks that involve looking for particular attributes within a set of document descriptions or for performing single attribute comparisons of document descriptions.

- Task-completion times will be fastest for tables, then hi-cites, then citation sets
- Perceived task-completion times will be fastest for tables, then hi-cites, then citation sets
- Error rates will be smallest for tables, then hi-cites, then citation sets
- Hi-cites will be the preferred condition since they allow for rapid answering of the questions as well as for quick skimming.

With these hypotheses in place, we constructed an experimental design that allowed us to determine their validity.

Experimental Design

Fourteen subjects participated in our evaluation of hi-cites. All subjects were from Stanford University and were paid for their time. Thirteen of the subjects were either undergraduates or graduate students. One subject was a Stanford staff member in the Computer Science Department. No subjects were students in the Computer Science Department, although the majority were students in the sciences.

The study compared three different presentation styles: tables, citation sets, and hi-cites. Each subject completed a practice task (where textual and oral help were provided), and then proceeded to complete two actual tasks (no help provided). Each task had three steps, where each step involved viewing a new collection of document descriptions in a particular presentation style and then answering questions about those descriptions. Step order and the pairings between collections and presentation styles were varied randomly. The questions asked in each step were of the following types (and were always presented in this fixed order):

- How many descriptions have the word X in the title?
- How many descriptions have publication locations listed?
- How many descriptions have the publication date Y?

All of these questions require that a user consider the document collection from the perspective of a particular attribute. We opted for providing users with this standard set of questions rather than providing a real-world task because we felt that these questions ensured that users would indeed perform attribute-based comparisons and obtain attribute-based overviews of the document collection (the focus of our evaluation, as well as a useful strategy in real digital-library tasks). Also, these question-based tasks were amenable to statistical comparison.

The time to complete each step and the error rate for each step were measured automatically. At the end of each task, subjects were also asked to rank each presentation style in terms of perceived speed. Finally, at the completion of the study, subjects were asked to compare/contrast orally the different styles and to choose one as preferred.

Experimental Results

Completion times

The comparison of completion times for each condition used the average of each subject's Task 1 time and Task 2 time. This average compensates for potential differences in the ease of learning each step, since step order was varied randomly for each subject. A one-way repeated-measures ANOVA on these average completion times ($F = 7.52$, $p = .003$) showed that the three conditions differed significantly at the .005 significance level. At significance level .05, the *post hoc* Student-Newman-Keuls test showed that the average completion times for tables and hi-cites were not significantly different. However, the average completion times for tables and citation sets and for hi-cites and citation sets were significantly different. Thus, tables and hi-cites are significantly faster for these tasks than are citation sets. The completion times for each condition, averaged across all subjects, are presented in Table 1.

Table 1: Average Completion Times (in seconds)

Tables	Citation Sets	Hi-Cites
43.081	51.969	45.477

Error rates

A one-way repeated-measures ANOVA on the error rates (again, averaged over the two tasks) showed no significant difference among the error rates ($F = .24$, $p = .786$). The error rates for each condition, averaged across all subjects, are presented in Table 2.

Table 2: Average Error Rates (number of wrong answers ÷ 3)

Tables	Citation Sets	Hi-Cites
0.10	0.13	0.11

Rankings of perceived completion times

In addition to looking at the actual differences in average completion times for each of the conditions, we also looked at perceived differences in completion times. Users' perceptions of time do not always match up to real time. Furthermore, a user's perception that an interface is fast and facile can make a crucial difference in whether or not an interface will be used, no matter what the actual performance metrics might be for the interface.

A one-way repeated-measures ANOVA* ($F = 10.72$, $p < .005$) showed that the means for the average rankings (1 is fastest; 3 is slowest) were not equal. At a significance level of .01, the Student-Newman-Keuls test showed that all differences were significant. Hi-cites were perceived to be faster than tables, and tables were perceived to be faster than citation sets. The average rankings for each condition are shown in Table 3.

Table 3: Average Rankings of Perceived Completion Times (1 is fastest; 3 is slowest)

Tables	Citation Sets	Hi-Cites
1.82	2.68	1.50

Preferences

Subjects specified their overall preferred presentation style at the end of the session, not at the end of each task. This data was analyzed using a t-test, where the null hypothesis was that the probability of a subject choosing a condition as preferred was 1/3. The observed proportions of preference assignments for each condition appear in Table 4. Computing t for each condition showed that the observed proportions of preference assignments for hi-cites and citation sets were significantly different from 1/3 at the .05 level, but that the observed proportion for tables was not significantly different from 1/3 at the .05 level.

Table 4: Observed Proportions of Preference Assignments

Tables	Citation Sets	Hi-Cites
4/14	0/14	10/14

User feedback

At the end of a session, each subject was asked not only to select a presentation style as preferred, but also to compare and contrast all of the presentation styles. This feedback served to contextualize the preference choices with a concrete sense of why subjects found their preferred style to be useful and also gave a good indication of what was easy or hard to do in the other presentation styles. Overwhelmingly, subjects were enthusiastic about the value of hi-cites. They particularly liked the way color guided their eye to the "right place" in the collection. However, they found much to like about tables also. They pointed out that tables arranged the information in a format that would be very convenient to browse if it all fit on the screen. The need to scroll horizontally in tables was the most frequent complaint about their use. Subjects explained their difficulties with citation sets in terms of problems with honing in on the right piece of information in a description. They felt that color and space served to mark attributes well, but that slight changes in format and relative position were not good perceptual markers. A sampling of subject comments appears in Table 5.

Table 5: Sampling of Subject Comments

Hi-cites	caught my eye; much easier to go by color than location
	really great; focus on particular area; red drew visual attention
	with a lot of text, it just hops out at you
	stuck out compared to other ones
	don't know where to find first one (or there might not be a location)
Tables	hard to use because you need to scroll
	liked having it all mapped out
	nice; knew where to look
	maybe easier except you can't see it all on the screen
	everything structured in such a way you could do the same thing easily
Citation Sets	confusing; hard to pick out information being asked for
	more time to sort out information
	didn't really like them; just slower to get through
	tedious to read through words to look for information
	had to look through everything

* Technically, the use of the ANOVA is problematic here since the observations are not independent. However, the ANOVA is still the most useful statistic for this situation to the best of our knowledge.

Discussion

Before conducting the experiment, we set forth the following hypotheses about tables, citation sets, and hi-cites.

- Task-completion times will be fastest for tables, then hi-cites, then citation sets
- Perceived task-completion times will be fastest for tables, then hi-cites, then citation sets
- Error rates will be smallest for tables, then hi-cites, then citation sets
- Hi-cites will be the preferred condition since they allow for rapid answering of the questions as well as for quick skimming.

Statistical analysis of our experimental results leads to the following conclusions:.

- Task-completion times are faster for tables and hi-cites than for citation sets, but there is no significant difference between tables and hi-cites
- Perceived task-completion times are faster for hi-cites, then tables, then citation sets
- Error rates do not differ significantly among tables, citation sets, and hi-cites
- Hi-cites are the preferred condition

Our experimental results were somewhat surprising in that hi-cites either outranked tables or were not sufficiently different from tables in all cases. Thus, we can conclude that hi-cites are indeed a hybrid between tables and citation sets in that they:

- allow for ease of comparison
- allow for ease of skimming

Ease of comparison is demonstrated by our experimental results. Ease of skimming stems from the fact that hi-cites and citation sets are both compact representations of information that take up less screen space and are more spatially continuous than tables.

CONCLUSION

We have proposed the concept of hi-cites: dynamically created citations with active highlighting. The generation of hi-cites relies on access to attribute-value encodings of documents. The appearance of hi-cites is governed by citation styles that dictate what attributes should be presented, in what order they should be listed, and how they should be rendered and marked. Users control the active highlighting of hi-cites through a "tool tip" affordance. Point-plus-delay on any attribute value causes all values for that attribute to be highlighted in the citation set. We have chosen red color highlighting for hi-cites based upon our understanding of previous highlighting studies.

We have argued that hi-cites combine the benefits of both bibliographic citations and tables. The evaluation that we have performed supports our claim for a particular set of tasks and conditions. More insight into hi-cites could be gained by devising experiments to compare hi-cites to KWIC indices, to measure the ease of discovery for the point-plus-delay affordance currently used for hi-cites, and to determine the effects of different styles of highlighting (e.g., reverse video vs. red) in this context.

This paper has focused on the role of hi-cites in SenseMaker, an interface to a heterogeneous digital library. We believe that hi-cites can be useful in other environments that require heterogeneous structured descriptions to be browsed and compared with ease. Examples beyond digital libraries include product catalogs, classified advertisements, and World Wide Web search engines.

ACKNOWLEDGMENTS

This work is supported by the National Science Foundation under Cooperative Agreement IRI-9411306. Funding for this agreement is also provided by DARPA, NASA, and the industrial partners of the Stanford Digital Libraries Project.

We would like to thank Cliff Nass and Vicky Reich for their valuable advice on experimental design and statistical analysis.

REFERENCES

1. Baldonado, M., Chang, C. K., Gravano, L., and Paepcke, A. Metadata for digital libraries: architecture and design rationale, in *Proceedings of DL '97* (Philadelphia PA, July 1997) ACM Press, 47-56.
2. Baldonado, M.Q.W., and Winograd, T. SenseMaker: An information-exploration interface supporting the contextual evolution of a user's interests, in *Proceedings of CHI '97* (Atlanta GA, March 1997) ACM Press, 11-18.
3. Brown, T.J. Visual display highlighting and information extraction, in *Proceedings of the Human Factors Society 35th Annual Meeting* (1991), 1427-1431.
4. Luhn, H.P. Keyword-in-context index for technical literature (KWIC Index). *American Documentation* XI, 4 (1960), 288-295.
5. Nielsen, J. *Usability Engineering*. Academic Press, Boston, MA, 1993.
6. Philipsen, G. Effects of six different highlighting modes on visual search performance in menu options. *International Journal of Human-Computer Interaction* 6, 3 (1994), 319-334.
7. Rheinfrank, J., and Evenson, S. Design languages, in T. Winograd (ed.), *Bringing Design to Software*. Addison-Wesley, Reading, MA, 1996.
8. Sellen, A., and Nicol, A. Building user-centered online help, in B. Laurel (ed.), *The Art of Human-Computer Interface Design*. Addison-Wesley, Reading, MA, 1990.

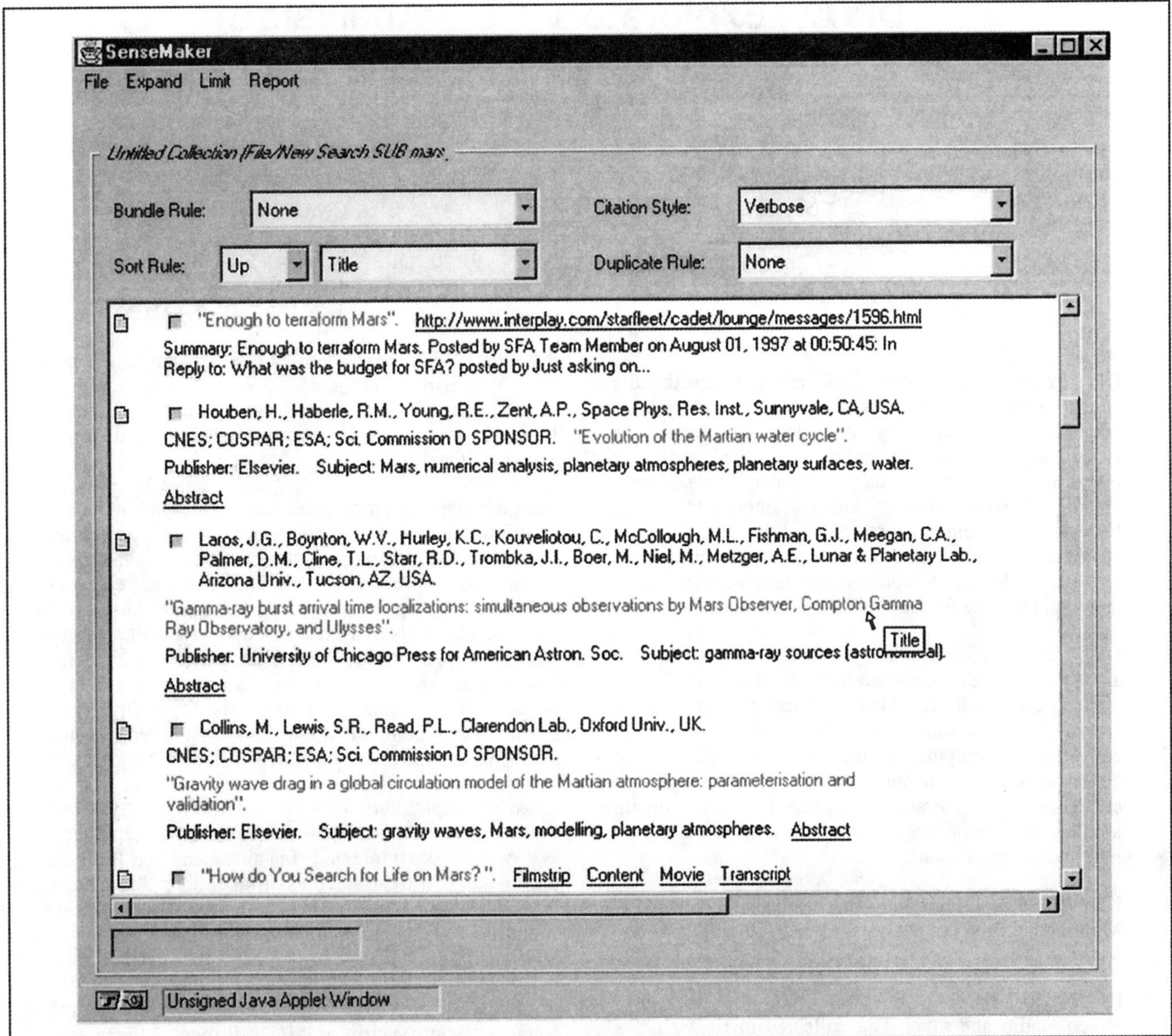

Figure 5: Hi-Cite Version of SenseMaker (*titles* are highlighted in red)
The heterogeneous set of documents described includes articles, WWW pages, and videos.

DIVA: Exploratory Data Analysis with Multimedia Streams

Wendy E. Mackay [1,2]

Michel Beaudouin-Lafon[2]

Centre d'Études de la Navigation Aérienne[1]
Orly Sud 205
94542 ORLY AÉROGARES
FRANCE
mackay@lri.fr

Laboratoire de Recherche en Informatique[2]
URA CNRS 410
LRI - Bâtiment 490 - Université de Paris-Sud
91 405 ORSAY Cedex - FRANCE
mbl@lri.fr

ABSTRACT

DIVA supports exploratory data analysis of multimedia streams, enabling users to visualize, explore and evaluate patterns in data that change over time. The underlying stream algebra provides the mathematical basis for operating on diverse kinds of streams. The streamer visualization technique provides a smooth transition between spatial and temporal views of the data. Mapping source and presentation streams into a two-dimensional space provides users with a direct manipulation, non-temporal interface for viewing and editing streams.

DIVA was developed to help us analyze both qualitative and quantitative data collected in our research with French air traffic controllers, including video of controllers at work, audio records of telephone, radio and other conversations, output from tools such as RADAR, and coded logs based on our observations. Although our emphasis is on exploratory data analysis, DIVA's stream architecture should prove useful for a wide variety of multimedia applications.

KEYWORDS: Exploratory data analysis, Hypermedia, Multimedia, Protocol analysis, Streams, Stream algebra, Video

INTRODUCTION

Video, audio and other data collected in field studies continue to be cumbersome to manage and analyze. We are interested in the problem of how to compute with a variety of these multimedia data types: to visualize, explore, analyze and evaluate relationships among streams of data.

Early systems to support analysis of video records were influenced by hypermedia, which is a logical extension of hypertext. Originally proposed by Vannevar Bush (1945), the basic approach organizes text into separate chunks that are linked together. Hypermedia adds images, audio and video, using hypermedia links (Conklin, 1987) to organize them. Hypermedia has become the dominant metaphor for managing multimedia data and is used in a wide variety of applications, including multimedia documents (Buchanan & Zellweger, 1992), education (e.g., Denning, 1997), games (e.g., Myst) and of course, the World Wide Web. An early tool for analyzing video data, VideoNoter (Trigg, 1989, Roschelle & Goldman, 1991) begins with data streams, and then uses hypermedia links to organize the relationships among different aspects of the data.

Another approach emphasizes streams instead of chunks of information. Rather than treating all data as chunks and converting naturally-continuous information such as video into discrete units; all data can be treated as streams, mapping naturally-discrete objects onto event streams. The analysis system can operate on all data in a uniform way, exploring directly the patterns that emerge from the streams. Hypermedia lets users start and stop streams; the stream approach lets them highlight, examine and compute upon the patterns within and among streams.

EVA, the Exploratory Video Annotator, (Mackay, 1989, Mackay & Davenport, 1989) was based on this approach. We were not interested in authoring multimedia documents that treat video as "illustrations that move". Instead, we were interested in helping researchers annotate and visualize patterns and relationships among time-based multimedia data. EVA's stream metaphor derived from our work on Muse, a multi-media authoring language originally designed at Digital Equipment Corp. and enhanced significantly at MIT's Project Athena (see Hodges & Sasnett (1993) for a description).

One of the authors (Mackay, 1989) suggested that the exploratory data analysis techniques pioneered by Tukey (1977) (see Hartwig & Dearing (1979) for a concise summary) are more appropriate for examining video data than the standard statistical techniques used in controlled laboratory studies. Sanderson and her colleagues (Sanderson et al., 1994, Sanderson & Fisher, 1994) have pursued this idea extensively, coining the term Exploratory sequential data analysis (ESDA) for systems that support the exploration of multimedia data. Several systems have been developed to support the analysis of video data, including Harrison (1991), Olson et al. (1994), Chua & Ruan (1995), and Plaisant et al. (1996). Other researchers working in related areas such as video conferencing have developed similar tools, e.g. the tools developed at Xerox PARC, including Where Were We? and its successors (Minneman & Harrison, 1993, Minneman et al., 1995, Moran et al., 1997), Marquee (Weber & Poon, 1994), and TimeWarp (Edwards & Mynatt, 1997).

CHI 98 Los Angeles CA USA

Research context

Our current research (Mackay & Fayard, 1997a) seeks to provide air traffic controllers with the benefits of networked computing without forcing them to give up their successful existing work artifacts, in particular, paper flight strips. We began with a four-month field study, following a team of controllers at the Paris en route control center (Athis Mons). We are now analyzing over 100 hours of coded event streams, based on researchers' observations, approximately 50 hours of video of controllers at work, with corresponding radio, telephone and local conversations, output from RADAR and other devices, and copies of relevant artifacts, particularly paper flight strips.

We use exploratory data analysis techniques to identify and analyze both qualitative and quantitative aspects of this data and are particularly interested in finding patterns that occur across media types. For example, Figure 1 shows two controllers writing simultaneously on two different flight strips, a relatively rare event. We are interested in understanding the circumstances that surround such situations. Are there other patterns of activity correlated with this one? Are the controllers more or less likely to talk to each other? Are they likely to perform other activities at the same time? Can we predict this pattern from other recurring patterns, e.g., stressful situations? Are there any events that help predict when this occurs?

Figure 1 : Two air traffic controllers writing at the same time on different flight strips.

Discovering the answers to these and related questions not only increases our understanding of the complexity of their work, but also helps us better understand how to create tools that support rather than interfere with their existing work practices, addressing problems without adding unnecessary costs (Mackay & Fayard, 1997b).

This article describes DIVA, a system designed to support computing with streams of multimedia data, enabling users to visualize, explore, analyze and evaluate patterns of data that change over time. We present the underlying system architecture, which involves a common representation for multimedia streams and an algebra for manipulating them. We next present the user interface, which provides interactive temporal and spatial views of the data. Throughout, we use examples from the air traffic control project to illustrate the interface to DIVA and explain how various stream operations work and why they are useful. We conclude with a summary of the contributions of DIVA and directions for future research.

STREAM ALGEBRA

DIVA uses the same stream metaphor as the earlier EVA system, with a more powerful set of operations derived from a stream algebra. Others have used algebras to deal with time-based data. For example, Algebraic video (Duda et al., 1996) defines an algebra to describe the spatial and temporal composition of video segments. However, the operators they use are different from DIVA, since the purpose of their system is the production of video presentations, not the analysis of time-based data. Rivl (Swartz & Smith, 1995) is a language that also focuses on video data and production tasks by providing graphical operators to create complex presentations.

This section describes the DIVA algebra, with examples derived from air traffic control data. The algebra is based on the notion of multimedia ***streams*** and a set of operators to create, modify, play and present streams.

A stream s of type T is defined as a sequence (t_i) of $n+1$ clock times and a sequence (v_i) of n values:

$$s = (t_1\text{: } v_1,\ t_2\text{: } v_2,\ \ldots,\ t_n\text{: } v_2,\ t_{n+1})$$

The sequence (t_i) is increasing, so the stream can also be viewed as a sequence of *stream segments* $[t_i, v_i, d_i]$. The duration of the segment is $d_i = t_{i+1} - t_i$. The values v_i are either undefined (denoted as $\bot$) or a value of type T, e.g. boolean, integer, text or image. The value of a stream s at time t is noted $s@t$ and is defined as follows :

- **if** $t < t_1$ or $t \geq t_{n+1}$ **then** $s@t = \bot$
- **if** j is such that $t_j \leq t < t_{j+1}$ **then** $s@t = v_j$

The empty stream, noted () is a stream whose value is undefined for any time *t*.

Example

If we begin with a video clip of two air traffic controllers writing on two paper flight strips, as in Figure 1, we have one stream of video data:

s.video = (1:00:00: frame0, 1:00:01: frame1,
1:00:02: frame2, ... , 1:03:00).

A data log is another type of stream, consisting of a series of boolean values that indicate the precise times at which specific events occur. For example, a boolean stream can identify every situation in which a controller writes something on a flight strip:

s.write = (1:00:05: on, 1:00:09: off, 1:02:49: on,
1:02:57: off, 1:03:00).

Session transcripts can be represented as a series of subtitles. For example, a text stream might identify every radio conversation between the radar controller and the pilot, with the specific text appearing as the value associated with each time segment:

s.radio = (1:00:21: "Maintain flight level",
1:00:34: ⊥,
1:01:58: "Climb to level 310",
1:02:04: ⊥, 1:03:00).

Streams can contain any type of values. For example, the RADAR screen presents a 2-dimensional view of the location of a set of airplanes moving in a 3-dimensional space. We can define a stream for each airplane that contains its position over time.

Normalizing streams

Before computing with streams, it is useful to normalize them: segments with a duration of 0 are removed, successive segments with the same value are merged, and leading and trailing segments with value ⊥ are removed. In other words, if two segments with the same value are adjacent to each other, the normalized stream contains a single, longer segment. All streams in this discussion are assumed to be normalized. We define the *extent* of the stream as the interval $[t_1, t_{n+1}]$ of its normal form.

Normalizing streams provides a canonical representation of a stream so that, for example, we know that two streams are equal if and only if their normal forms are the same. Normalizing streams also minimizes storage and reduces processing costs.

Stream expressions

New streams can be created from existing streams by *stream expressions*, comparable to the expressions used to compute a cell from other cells in a spreadsheet. Given n streams $s_1, s_2, \ldots s_n$ of types $T_1, T_2, \ldots T_n$ and a function $f : T_1 \times T_2 \times \ldots T_n \to T$, the stream expression $f(s_1, s_2, \ldots s_n)$ is a stream s of type T such that :

$$s@t = f(s1@t, s2@t, \ldots sn@t) \text{ for all } t$$

It is assumed that $f(\bot, \bot, \ldots \bot) = \bot$.

A common stream expression is *editing* : a source stream *s* and an edit stream *e*, both of type *T*, are combined with the following *edit* function:

edit (vs, ve) = **if** (ve = ⊥) **then** vs **else** ve

The resulting stream is the same as the source stream except that it is replaced with the edit stream where the edit stream is defined (Figure 2).

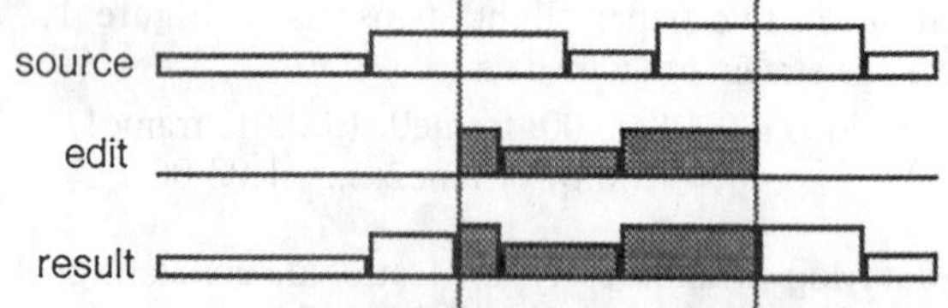

Figure 2: Editing a stream. Time goes from left to right. Each rectangle is a stream segment.

Example

Usually, we use at least two researchers to code the activities. Some situations are ambiguous and we might have to discuss the final analysis. This technique allows us to work with one of the annotation streams made by one researcher and modify it based on the annotation stream created by another researcher.

Insertion and deletion

Like editing, insertion and deletion are common operations on streams (Figure 3). Inserting a segment into a stream creates a new, undefined segment and offsets the subsequent segments accordingly. Usually, the inserted part is then replaced with the *edit* operation described above. Deletion removes and/or shortens segments so that a given interval is removed from the stream. The *offset* operation is a short-hand for inserting or deleting a segment before the start of the stream. The offset *d* can be positive or negative so that an entire stream can be offset forward or backward in time.

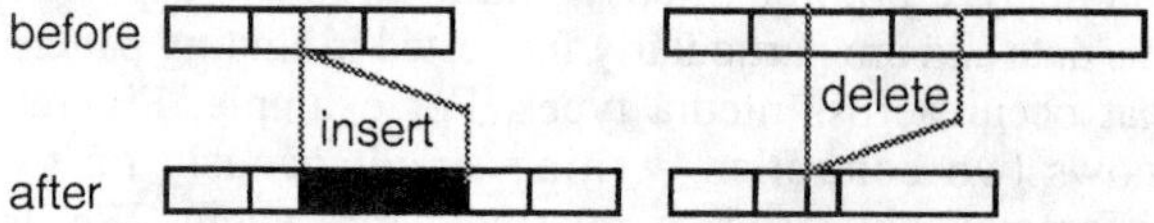

Figure 3: Inserting and deleting stream segments.

Example

We need to present collections of examples of activities observed in our data. For example, we have a video that presents a series of clips of controllers writing on strips, pointing to the strips, and rearranging the strips. When we videotape a new session, we can easily insert new examples of these activities into the existing set of streams.

Time filtering

It is often useful to analyze when a given condition occurs before or after another condition. We call this operation *time-filtering* and define it as follows:

s1 = v1 **within** [d, d'] **of** s2 = v2

It creates a boolean stream *s* defined as follows:

- $s@t = \bot$ if $s1@t \neq v1$
- $s@t = true$ if $\exists\, t', t+d < t' < t+d'$ and $s2@t' = v2$
- $s@t = false$ otherwise

The resulting stream describes when an occurrence of *v1* in stream *s1* occurs close to an occurrence of *v2* in stream *s2*. The interval [d, d'] defines how close (or how far apart) we want the values to occur (Figure 4).

A variant of time filtering uses a condition that tests whether the whole segment containing *v2* in stream *s2* is within the time interval defined by [d, d']. These conditions generalize Allen's (1984) algebra on time intervals by introducing the notion of temporal vicinity (specified by *d* and *d'*). This is necessary for the type of data analysis we are interested since we need to be able to look for events that occur at times close to each other.

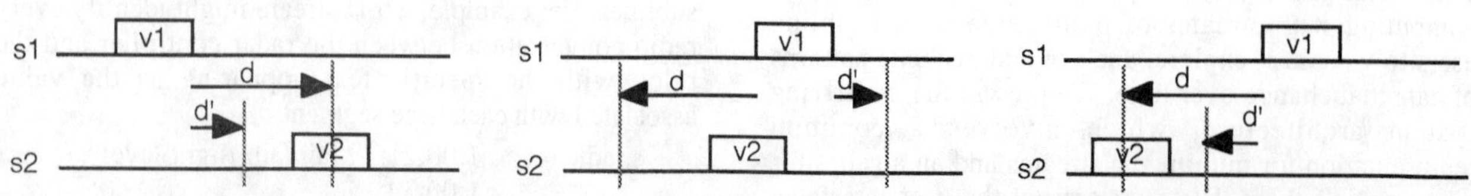

Figure 4: Time filtering. Left: v1 before v2 (d>0, d'>0); Center: v1 close to v2 (d<0, d'>0); Right: v1 after v2 (d<0, d' <0)

Example
When two controllers interact with the same set of strips at the same time, it is an indication of a "charged" situation. We can find out if there is always a corresponding rise in the number of new flights or an increase in conversations between the radar controller and the pilot, just prior to this event. We can then perform a time series analysis on the result with an external tool to determine which activities cluster together and whether or not we can predict the occurrence of some activities based on the occurrence of others.

Stretching segments
The last operation defined by the algebra stretches the segments of a stream by a duration *d*. Each segment is extended at the beginning and at the end by *d* if the adjacent segment is undefined. Stretching is very useful to create a control stream (see below) that includes some context around a specified set of clips (Figure 5).

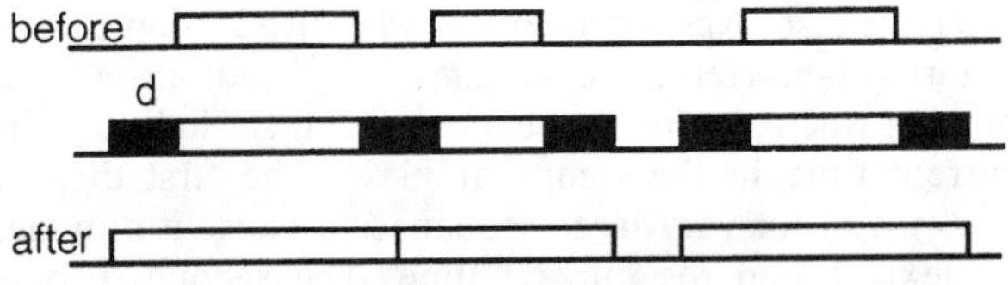

Figure 5: Stretching a stream by d.

Playing streams
In order to play a stream, it must be bound to a *time base*. Several streams are synchronized by binding them to the same time base. A time base is defined by a start time, a stop time and a rate. It generates a time value that changes over time at a pace defined by its rate. The rate is a real number that specifies whether the time base runs forward or backward at slow, normal or fast speed or whether it is stopped (like the jog-shuttle of a VCR).

A time base can have a *control stream*: the time base skips undefined segments of the control stream as it runs, making it easy to play sequences of clips not originally adjacent to each other in the original streams.

Example
If we are interested in looking at situations where more than one controller writes at the same time on a strip, we create a stream identifying this condition, stretch it by 1 or 2 seconds, and use the resulting stream as the control stream. We can then view in succession all clips in which more than one controller writes at the same time.

Time warping
A more sophisticated method of controlling playing is to define the mapping between the time delivered by the time base and the time used to index the streams. This mapping is defined by a stream called the *warping stream*. Values of a warping stream *ws* are pairs (t, r) of time values and rates. Let *tb* be the time delivered by the time base (called the *playing time*) and let $[t_i, v_i, d_i]$ be the segment of the warping stream such that $t_i \leq tb < t_i + d$. Then $ws@tb = v_i = (t, r)$ where *t* is a time and *r* is a rate. The warping *tw* of time *tb* is defined as $tw = t + r^*(tb\text{-}t_i)$.

Time warping of a segment is illustrated in Figure 6. The slope of the diagonal line indicates the rate. If the slope is 45°, the rate is 1 and the clip plays at normal speed. If the slope is under 45°, the clip plays in slow motion, while if the slope is over 45° the clip plays in fast motion. Finally if the diagonal appears in the other direction, the clip plays backward (at a rate determined by the slope).

Time warping makes it possible to take any combination of clips from the streams and play them in any order and at any rate (Figures 7a and 7b).

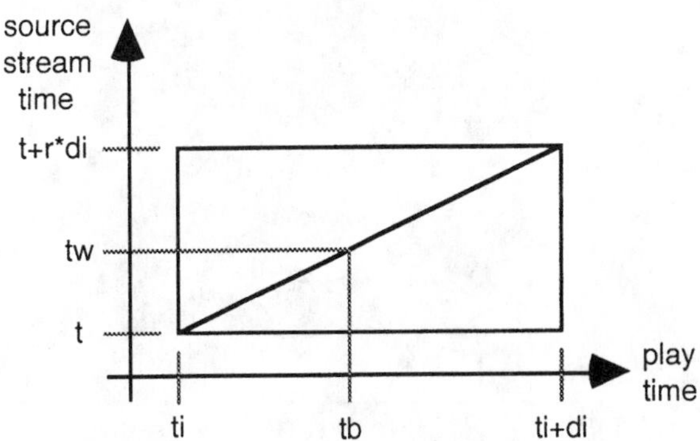

Figure 6: A segment of the warping stream.

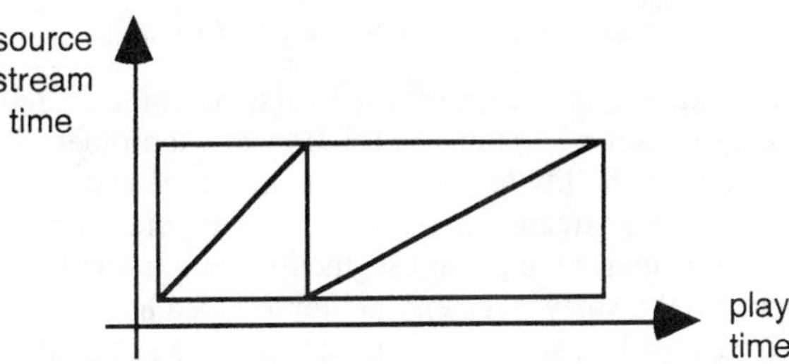

Figure 7a: A warping stream that plays a clip twice: first at normal speed and then in slow motion.

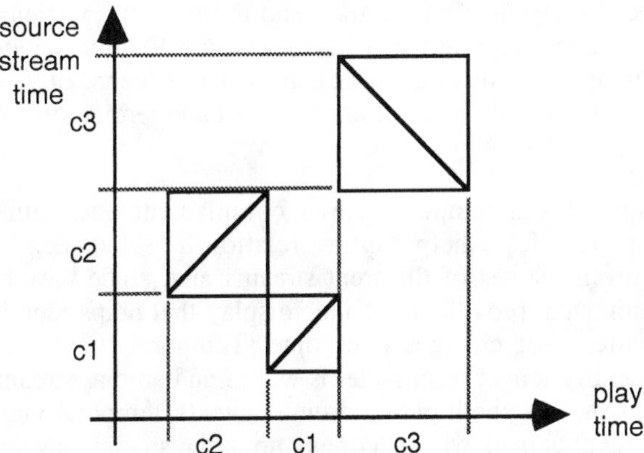

Figure 7b: A warping stream that plays the stream segments c1, c2, c3 in the order c2, c1, c3. c1 and c2 play at normal speed; c3 plays backwards.

DIVA USER INTERFACE
Like EVA and later Video Mosaic (Mackay & Pagani, 1994), DIVA provides two views of the stream data: temporal and spatial. Spatial views show the current value of a set of streams at the current time of their time base. Figure 8 shows an example with a video stream in the middle, boolean streams on the left side and text streams at the bottom. Two air traffic controllers are writing on the strips at the same time (stream 2W). The radar controller is telling the pilot to "Maintain flight level" (stream Rad) and the corresponding boolean stream for talking to the pilot (stream R>P) is on. No one is

speaking on the telephone (stream Tel), and the activity code for conversations between the two controllers is off (stream R>O). Other activity codes, including pointing to the RADAR (PR), adjusting the Digitatron (PD) and adjusting the RADAR image (MC) are also off. Note that these activity codes are defined by the user.

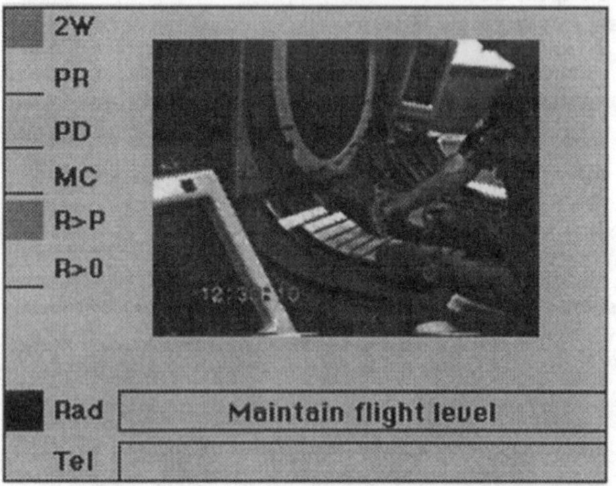

Figure 8: Spatial view of a set of streams.

Temporal views show abstracted versions of the changing state of a set of streams in relation to each other. This gives us the ability to "lay out time in space" and interact with various streams in parallel. The temporal view of a stream displays the stream segments along a timeline. In horizontal display, segments are represented by rectangles whose position, size and color represent the segment time interval and value. A boolean stream can be displayed by assigning a different color to its true and false segments or by appearing and disappearing. An integer stream can be displayed as a histogram and more complex streams can combine color and height (Figure 9). For a video stream, the temporal view can present a sequence of video "best frames", as is often done in commercial systems such as Adobe Premiere.

Spatial and temporal views complement each other. Spatial views help capture relationships between the current values of different streams and, since they are animated, provide a dynamic display that helps identify patterns of changes over time. Temporal views help identify longer term patterns within and among streams. By showing both past and future events, temporal views help anticipate what is coming up in the spatial views.

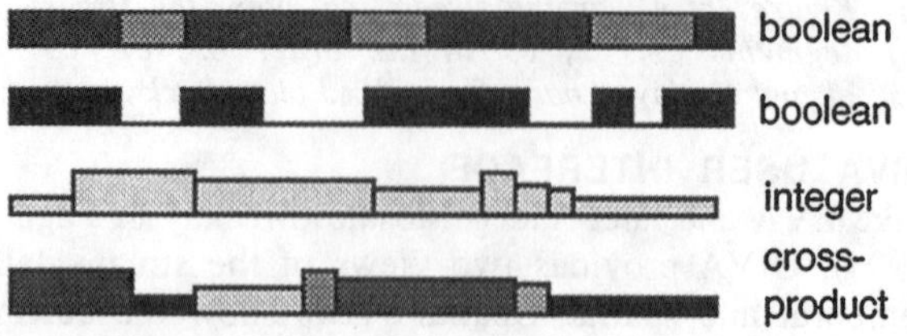

Figure 9: Temporal views for different streams.

Streamer display

In order to better visualize and interact with streams, DIVA integrates both types of views into a single display. We were influenced by the video streamer (Elliot, 1993), which generates a stream from a video sequence by offsetting the edges of each video image. Cruz & Hill (1994) have also used this technique to visualize changes in audio level and button states in a video conferencing application. We have generalized this technique to display the changes in multiple streams of any type.

Figure 10 (next page) illustrates the smooth transition between the spatial and temporal views. The streamer display includes a spatial view in the center of the main window and a temporal view around it. When the set of streams is played, the temporal view streams up or down (depending on whether it is played forward or backward) so that the spatial view in the central display is always positioned correctly relative to the streams: streams along the edge of the spatial view seem to leave a trace that corresponds to the temporal view. When the temporal view is "streaming", the parts to the left and top of the central screen show a trace of what has already occurred whereas the parts to the right and bottom of the central screen show what is about to occur (Figure 11-a).

We have also experimented with the display depicted in Figure 11-b. Here, the streams are fixed: instead of moving when playing the sequence, a cursor indicates the current time in the temporal view. The first display works well for very large sequences because it provides context around the current time. The second display collapses long streams into a small screen space, reducing accuracy for both the display and the interaction. Either display makes it easy to detect changes in state as the image "streams" forward or backwards in time.

On a 21" screen, the streamer display can accommodate a large number of streams: up to 2 video streams, 5 to 10 text streams and 30 activity streams. The user can decide which streams to display and can define groups of streams that can be displayed or hidden together. The bottom of the display (not shown) contains a VCR-like interface to control the time base. Any stream can be designated as the control stream and warping streams can be edited in a separate window.

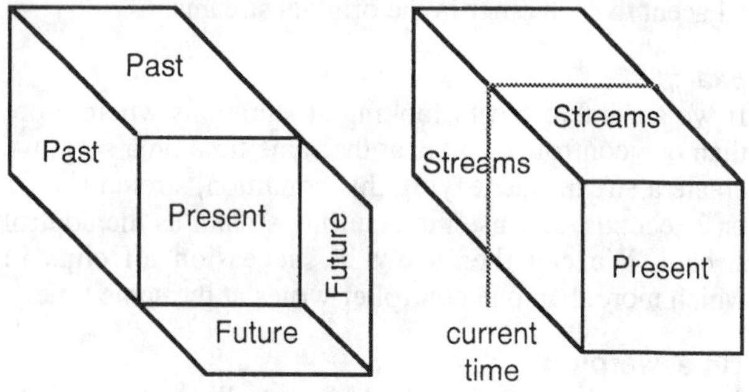

Figures 11a & 11b: A comparison of two display strategies for linking spatial and temporal views.

Creating streams

Creating streams from external sources

Streams can be created from files in various formats: recorded video or audio signals, a column or row from a spreadsheet, a text file, the output of devices such as the Digitatron or the RADAR, etc. Figure 10 shows actual data imported from an Excel spreadsheet. Streams can also be exported to these file formats, which makes it easy to use spreadsheets or statistical analysis packages to conduct other kinds of data analysis.

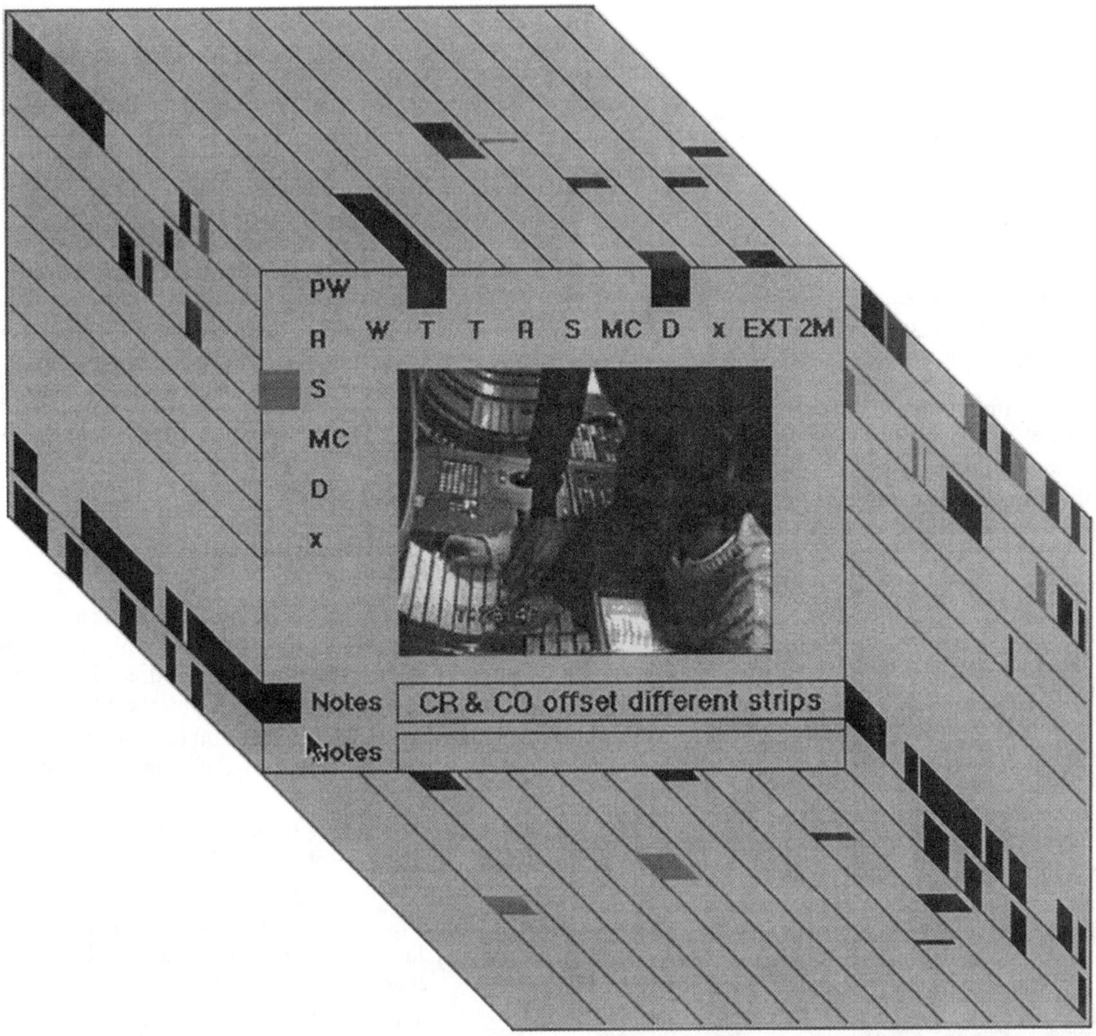

Figure 10: DIVA main display. The spatial view is in the center and the temporal view is on the sides. When the time base is running, the spatial view is constantly updated and the temporal view streams from bottom-right to top-left.

Creating streams by direct input

Streams can also be created explicitly by the user: the user defines the type and names of the stream in the stream's creation box (Figure 11). The user can then work in *live mode* by starting the time base and clicking the value buttons in the creation box to create segments. Each click creates a segment that starts at the time of the click. The user can also work in *off-line mode* by selecting a start and stop time in the time base control panel and a value in the stream creation box. This creates a new segment in the stream with the specified times and value. Several streams can be created simultaneously by opening as many creation boxes as necessary, and keyboard equivalents can be defined for each stream to speed up input.

For example, to code the data in a video stream, a user may create a set of binary streams that identify specific activities of the controllers. The user creates a stream and specifies its short and long names (e.g. "2W" and "Two controllers writing simultaneously"), its type (boolean) and its colors (e.g. green and red). The user then starts the time base and records stream values by clicking the on/off/undefined buttons in the creation box at the appropriate times. Since the rest of the interface is active, the user can see the other streams play in the main display, especially the video streams.

Figure 11: Stream property box

Creating streams with the stream algebra

Streams can also be created with the stream algebra. After selecting the "expression" type in the stream's creation box, the user can enter a stream expression using any of the operators of the stream algebra. By default, the resulting stream is re-computed every time a stream that appears in the expression is changed, as in a spreadsheet.

For example, if the user is interested in seeing the video segments in which two controllers are writing on the flight strips at the same time (stream 2W) and the radar controller is talking to the pilot (stream R>P), the user can perform a logical *and* between the two relevant streams:

2W = on *and* **R>P = on**

The resulting stream shows situations in which both events occur simultaneously. In order to find situations where the two controllers write at the same time shortly after the radar controller talks to a pilot, the expression uses time filtering:

2W = on *within* [0, 2s] *of* **R>P = on**

The user can further investigate these events by stretching the stream to provide context, making it the control stream and playing the result.

Editing Streams

DIVA allows the user to edit existing streams in several ways, depending on the type of the stream and the scope of the edit. Streams that result from stream expressions cannot be edited directly since they are re-computed each time one of their dependent streams is modified. However the stream expression itself can be edited to re-create the stream.

Editing segments

The value of a segment can be changed by clicking on it when it is visible in a temporal or spatial view. The start and stop times of a segment can be changed in a temporal view by selecting a segment and dragging or resizing it. They can be changed in a spatial view by selecting the view when the segment is visible and setting the start and stop times in the time base control panel. Such editing is used mostly to fine-tune a stream after it has been created in live mode.

Editing streams individually

More radical editing is achieved by creating an "edit" stream with one of the stream creation methods (usually live mode) and using the "edit" operation of the stream algebra on the original stream. This modifies the original stream and creates an "undo" stream that can re-generate the previous version of the stream from the modified version with the same "edit" operation of the stream algebra. This is often used to re-record a part of a stream that is incorrect.

Editing multiple streams

The stream algebra can be used to apply the same operation to a set of streams. This is mostly used with the insert, delete and time-warping operations to reorganize the contents of a set of related streams. For example, once a specific set of events has been identified, all the irrelevant segments in all the streams can be deleted to keep only the interesting material.

Editing warping streams

Editing the warping stream is performed in a separate window similar to the display in Figure 7. Clips can be reordered, stretched or shrunk by direct manipulation. Several warping streams can be created and edited, but at most one can be designated as the current warping stream.

IMPLEMENTATION

The first prototype of DIVA was implemented in Tcl/Tk (Ousterhout, 1994), which allowed us to validate the key concepts of DIVA: stream algebra, streamer display and time-warping. The second version (currently under development) is implemented on the Apple Macintosh as a set of extensions to Tcl/Tk, which allows us to reuse parts of the prototype. We use QuickTime (Apple Computer, 1993) to implement the time base and to play audio and video streams. The stream algebra is implemented in C++ for better efficiency. The current version is functional and we are re-implementing a larger part of the system in C++.

SUMMARY AND CONCLUSIONS

DIVA provides a significant advance over the earlier EVA system at both the architectural level and the user interface level. The major contributions at the architectural level include:

1. A stream algebra that provides a simple but mathematically powerful model of streams and operations upon them,
2. Precise and powerful control and editing functions such as time warping and time filtering.

DIVA's user interface is designed to support the generation and analysis of not only the multimedia streams themselves, but the relationships among them. The major contributions at the interface level include:

1. The smooth transition between the temporal and spatial views of the data, using the streamer visualization technique,
2. The ability to browse, edit and modify the data using either view (temporal or spatial) or the stream algebra,
3. The two-dimensional direct manipulation interface for editing streams, using spatial rather than temporal views, and
4. The ability to use an external package to perform statistical computations, such as identifying correlations, on the results of stream operations.

Informal evaluations using data from our study of air traffic controllers have shown the power of linking the spatial and temporal views. Compared with a spreadsheet display, the dynamic aspect of streaming gives an entirely different perspective on the data. We were also able to isolate key events using the stream expressions. We plan to conduct more in-depth evaluations of DIVA as we analyze additional data sets.

DIVA is clearly designed to support a particular kind of interaction with multimedia data, i.e. exploratory data analysis. Yet the stream algebra and the streamer interface should be useful for a variety of other multimedia applications, including analysis of video conferencing, editing for multimedia presentations, educational applications and games.

ACKNOWLEDGEMENTS

Thanks to Eddie Elliot and Glorianna Davenport for conversations about the streamer technique, which we found to be a wonderful solution to our interface problem. Also, thanks to Anne-Laure Fayard for all her work on data coding and analysis and to the members of Equipe 9West at Athis Mons en route air traffic control center, for generating all that data!

REFERENCES

Apple Computer (1993) *Inside Macintosh - Quicktime.* Reading, MA: Addison Wesley.

Allen, J.F. (1984) Towards a general theory of action and time. *Artificial Intelligence.* **23**, pp. 123-154.

Buchanan, M.C. and Zellweger, P.T., (1992) Specifying Temporal Behaviour in Hypermedia Documents, in *Proc ECHT'92*, European Conference on Hypermedia Technology, Milan, Italy.

Bush, V. (1945) As We May Think. *Atlantic Monthly* , July issue, pp.101-108.

Chua, T.S. & Ruan, L.Q. (1995) A Video Retrieval and Sequencing System. *ACM Transactions on Information Systems.* 13(4), pp. 373-407.

Conklin, J., (1987) Hypertext: A Survey and Introduction, *IEEE Computer*, 20(9), pp. 17-41.

Cruz, G. & Hill, R. (1994) Capturing and playing multimedia events with streams. In *Proc. Multimedia '94*, pp. 193-200, ACM.

Denning, P.J. (1997) How we will learn. In *Beyond Calculation: The Next Fifty Years.* pp. 267-286. New York, NY: Copernicus.

Duda, A., Weiss, R., & Gifford, D.K. (1996) Content-based access to Algebraic Video. *IEEE Multimedia.*

Elliott, E.L. (1993) *Watch-Grab-Arange-See: Thinking with Motion Images via Streams and Collages.* MIT MS Visual Studies Thesis.

Edwards, W.K. & Mynatt, E.D. (1997) Timewarp: Techniques for autonomous collaboration. In *Proc. CHI '97 Human Factors in Computing Systems.* pp.218-225. Atlanta, GA: ACM.

Harrison, B. (1991) Video annotation and multimedia interfaces: from theory to practice. In *Proc. Human Factors Society 35th Annual Meeting*, pp. 319-323.

Hartwig, F. & Dearing, B.E. (1979) *Exploratory Data Analysis.* Beverly Hills, CA: Sage Publications.

Hodges, M.E. & Sasnett, R. (1993) *Multimedia Computing: Case Studies from MIT Project Athena.* Cambridge, MA: Addison-Wesley.

Mackay, W. E., & Davenport, G. (July, 1989) Virtual Video Editing in Interactive Multimedia Applications, *Comm. ACM*, 32(7), pp. 802-810.

Mackay, W. E. (October, 1989) EVA: An Experimental Video Annotator for Symbolic Analysis of Video Data, *ACM SIGCHI Bulletin*, 21(2), pp. 68-71.

Mackay, W.E. and Pagani, D. (October 1994). Video Mosaic: Laying out time in a physical space. In *Proc. Multimedia '94.* San Francisco, CA: ACM.

Mackay, W.E. & Fayard, A.L. (1997a) HCI, Natural Science and Design: A Framework for Triangulation Across Systems. In *Proc. DIS '97, Designing Interactive Systems*, Amsterdam: ACM.

Mackay, W.E. & Fayard, A.L. (1997b) Radicalement nouveau et néanmoins familier: Les strips papiers revus par la réalité augmentée. In *IHM'97 Actes 9èmes Journées sur l'Interaction Homme-Machine.*, Poitiers, France: Cépaduès Editions.

Minneman, S. and Harrison, S.R.(1993) Where Were We: Making and using near-synchronous, pre-narrative video, In *Proc. Multimedia '93*, pp. 1-6, Anaheim, CA: ACM.

Minneman, S., Harrison, S., Janssen, B., Kurtenbach, G., Moran, T., Smith, I. & van Melle, W. (1995) A confederation of tools for capturing and accessing collaborative activity. In *Proc. Multimedia '95.* San Francisco, CA: ACM.

Moran, T., Palen, L., Harrison, S., Chiu, P., Kimber, S., Minneman, S, van Melle, W., & Zellweger, P. (1997) I'll get that off the audio: A case study of salvaging multimedia meeting records. In *Proc. CHI '97 Human Factors in Computing Systems.* Atlanta, GA: ACM.

Olson, G.M., Herbsleb, J. & Rueter, H. (1994) Characterizing the sequential structure of interactive behaviors through statistical and grammatical techniques. *Human-Computer Interaction*, 9(3), pp. 427-472.

Ousterhout, J.K (1994) *Tcl and the Tk Toolkit.* Reading, MA: Addison-Wesley.

Plaisant, C., Milash, B., Rose, A., Widoff, S., Shneiderman, B. (1996) LifeLines: Visualizing Personal Histories. In *Proc. CHI'96, Human Factors in Computing Systems.* pp. 221-227. Vancouver, BC: ACM.

Roschelle, J. & Goldman, S. (1991) VideoNoter: A productivity tool for video data analysis. *Behavior Research Methods, Instruments and Computers.* 23, pp. 219-224.

Sanderson, P., Scott, J., Johnston, T., Mainzer, J., Watanabe, L., James, J. (1994) MacSHAPA and the enterprise of exploratory sequential data analysis. (ESDA), *International Journal of Human-Computer Studies*, 41(5), pp. 633-681.

Sanderson, P. & Fisher, C. (1994) Exploratory sequential data analysis: foundations. *Human-Computer Interaction*, 9(3), pp. 251-317.

Swartz, J. & Smith, B. (1995) A resolution-independent video language. In *Proc. Multimedia '95*, San Francisco, CA: ACM.

Tukey, J.W. (1977) *Exploratory Data Analysis..* Reading, MA: Addison-Wesley.

Trigg, R.H. (1989) Computer Support for Transcribing Recorded Activity. *ACM SIGCHI Bulletin*: Special Issue on Video as a Research and Design Tool, 21(2), pp. 72-74.

Weber, K. & Poon, A. (1994) Marquee: A Tool for Real-Time Video Logging. *Proceedings of CHI'94, Human Factors in Computing Systems.* pp. 58-64. Boston, MA: ACM.

National Geographic Unplugged: Classroom-Centered Design of Interactive Nature Films

Brian K. Smith
MIT Media Laboratory
20 Ames Street, E15-313
Cambridge, MA 02139 USA
+1 617 253 6537
bsmith@media.mit.edu

Brian J. Reiser
School of Education and Social Policy
Northwestern University
Evanston, IL 60208 USA
+1 847 467 2205
reiser@nwu.edu

ABSTRACT

Designing computer-based learning environments must account for the context in which activity occurs, the tasks that students perform, and the tools that facilitate these tasks. When designing for school use, it is also crucial to consider how the software will be integrated into the organization of the classroom workplace and how teacher practices influence the adoption and success of interactive learning environments. This paper discusses our experiences in designing and deploying an interactive video tool to high school classrooms. We stress a classroom-centered design that tries to integrate usable software with interactions that occur "outside of the box" to alter traditional school learning.

Keywords

Children, collaborative learning, educational applications, interaction design, multimedia, social issues, video.

INTRODUCTION

This paper focuses on the design of an interactive video system called *Animal Landlord*. Developed for high school biology classrooms, students interact with digital video clips showing the Serengeti lion hunting its prey to learn concepts in behavioral ecology such as resource competition, social organization, and optimal foraging theory. The system provides computational tools to help students extract "field data" from the video, create narrative explanations of the observed behaviors, and, ultimately, generalize explanatory models accounting for the causal influences on lion predation and prey evasion. Students become documentary narrators, using the software tools to interpret and explain visual events.

Our goal is to change the typically passive viewing of documentary films into a problem solving task, where students interact with computer tools to observe and explain complex, visual behaviors. In some sense, this means changing the nature of classroom activity. The traditional view of learning is one where students passively absorb information transmitted by a teacher, a textbook, or a film [6, 12, 20]. In contrast, we would like to see students develop their own understandings through inquiry, interpretation, and argumentation with peers. Computational media can provide rich, interactive environments to explore and construct ideas, but they must also provide explicit help for students, as they are not accustomed to these types of reasoning in classroom settings.

The issue is to introduce computer technologies into classrooms in ways that benefit teaching and learning. We have been influenced by a learner-centered design framework [20], acknowledging that the tasks students perform, the tools needed to perform these tasks, and the context in which activity occurs all contribute to the success of computer-based learning environments. In addition, developing usable software is not enough to ensure learning. We must also account for the roles of teachers and non-technological media, introducing our computer systems into the existing work cultures of schools — classroom-centered design, if you will. By integrating the engineering of computer software with the reengineering of the classroom workplace, we hope to improve learning practices.

We review the design iterations of Animal Landlord, focusing on changes resulting from an increasing awareness of the relationship between context, tasks, and tools. We highlight features of the classroom setting and their influence on the overall interaction. In particular, we suggest that teachers, as well as students, are users of computer-based learning environments as a result of their important role in instruction. We also stress the social collaborations taking place around the computer and the use of non-technological media in facilitating learning.

PRODUCING INTERACTIVE NATURE FILMS

Our research concerns the development of learning environments to help students engage in inquiry around actual, scientific research issues [8, 21]. We provide environments where students can generate and test hypotheses and create causal explanations of complex phenomena. Standard laboratory activities in high school classrooms provide some opportunities for this kind of problem solving, but they tend to prescribe the exact data to be collected, hypotheses to be tested, and conclusions to be drawn [4]. Our environments are meant to extend these structured laboratories by providing more open-ended avenues for students to reason about complex problems.

Why Film?

Animal Landlord's curriculum deals with the hunting behaviors of the Serengeti lion. When we ask students how often they think lions successfully capture their prey, their predictions are quite high (50-90%). In reality, only 15-30% of all attempted hunts actually result in a successful capture [14]. This mismatch between the lion's mythology and scientific observations raises curiosity and sets the stage for learning topics in behavioral ecology such as social organization, resource competition, variation between individuals and species, and environmental pressures. To understand why lion hunting success is lower than expected, one needs to understand the causal interactions between the lion, its prey, and the environment.

Nature documentary films provide a good medium for observing such behaviors, but they tend to provide topical overviews and surface accounts of behavior, neglecting many interesting domain processes in favor of straightforward outcomes. For instance, a film might mention that a creature performs a particular behavior without going into the complexities of why it does so. Narration is the primary source of knowledge in these films [3, 22], yet there is a great deal of implicit information in the video that students could observe and explain for themselves.

We use these films as the basis for our curriculum because students and teachers are accustomed to viewing them in classrooms. We were hoping this familiarity would ease the transition to new activities and ways of learning. We can use their knowledge of the information found in documentary narrations to develop new understandings of what these narratives could be. Essentially, we are trying to hold one aspect of the learning culture constant — the video — while changing another — the activity around video.

Nature films also hold a wealth of "raw data" that can be observed, analyzed, and explained scientifically. Students can become multimedia researchers [5], decomposing these films into salient events, analyzing and drawing connections between these events, and collaborating with others to construct meaningful representations of the visual data. In a sense, students can study nature films to learn about behavior in the same ways that behavioral ecologists study animals in their natural habitats.

A number of existing software environments assist students in learning by interacting with video. Some of these allow students to take quantitative measurements of objects and actions directly from digital video [3, 14, 15], encouraging the development of mathematical ideas around real-world phenomena. Many authoring environments allow students to express ideas by creating various multimedia presentations [1, 5, 11]. There is also a focus on establishing learning collaborations by using video as data to coordinate group activities [2, 9]. These projects shift students away from the passive viewing of video by creating tasks requiring construction and/or interpretation of multimedia artifacts.

Our work is motivated by these systems but differs in our emphasis on qualitative modeling of causal phenomena. With Animal Landlord, students create explanatory narratives for a corpus of video clips. To do this, they view documentary footage seeking answers to an assigned question (*e.g.*, "Why is the lion a 'bad' hunter?"). Instead of simply watching films, students capture and manipulate video frames as a primary data source. Gradually, they move from raw video footage to working with evidence in the form of significant frames. As students and teachers collaborate to argue over and refine ideas posed through the video, an interactive experience emerges around nature films.

Classroom-Centered Design

A learner-centered design framework suggests that the design of effective learning environments must take into account the context in which software is used, the tasks that students will perform, the tools provided to engage in these tasks, and the user interface to these tools [20]. The central claim is that explicit supports, or *scaffolds*, can be embedded in software to help learners accomplish tasks that might otherwise be beyond their abilities. These scaffolds make problem solving strategies explicit for students. For instance, we will discuss several ways that we have tried to scaffold students through the steps of decomposing behaviors into smaller, constituent actions.

In designing Animal Landlord, we had to consider more than the software itself. It is often tempting to computerize all of the learning scaffolds, but this can lead us to overlook many of the resources that classrooms offer. Teachers play a role in student learning, and we need to involve them in the design process and the overall interaction. As well, schools have social and work cultures that cannot be ignored [6, 16, 17]. Often, these existing practices offer better task solutions than software implementations. In a sense, we have engaged in classroom-centered design, distributing tasks and tools between the computer, the teacher, and existing work materials (*e.g.*, chalkboards, videocassettes, and so on).

This classroom-centered design emerged through collaboration with ecologists, students, and teachers. Ecologists helped us understand the tasks that they perform and the sorts of reasoning required when observing and explaining animal behavior. Teachers helped us interpret the classroom context, co-developing activities and offering insights into their expectations of student performance. Finally, student interviews and analyses of their work helped us scaffold tasks with tools. Below, we discuss tasks, tools, and context and how our design partners influenced curriculum development.

Tasks

We collaborated with behavioral ecologists early in the design of Animal Landlord to understand how they conduct field observations. After several working sessions with them, we developed a sense for the strategies that help them focus their investigations of behavior. This expertise was distilled into an investigation model that attempts to capture important features of their observation and argumentation [21]. In particular, the model makes explicit the components of the investigation task and the salient features of an ecological argument.

In practice, a behavioral ecologist might begin by cataloguing the behaviors in a hunt (*e.g.*, stalking, chasing, scanning) to understand the space of activity. Behavior patterns begin to emerge as actions found in different hunts are compared. For instance, lions may not stalk in some percentage of their hunting attempts. When variations are found, it is useful to look for selection pressures that may account for the behavior. A lion may break into a chase without stalking if it is close to its prey or if there is dense vegetation in the area. Generally, this leads to additional questions requiring additional observational data (*e.g.*, "How close is 'close enough'?). Finally, considering the costs and benefits of actions by relating them to strategic factors can lead to evolutionary explanations of behavior.

This can be thought of as four subtasks that are useful for analyzing and interpreting complex behaviors:

- Decompose complex behaviors into smaller, related actions.
- Compare similar events to look for variations.
- Identify factors responsible for these variations.
- Relate factors to behaviors to form an evolutionary explanation.

These subtasks can be performed whether the phenomenon is being observed in the Serengeti or on a computer screen. Behavioral ecologists understand this process and seem to follow it when interpreting the causal structure of complex behavior. High school students do not have this expertise, and we have tried to help them through the process by providing effective scaffolds for each individual subtask.

Tools

Our design tries to lead students through the elements of this investigation model, helping them to make sense of complex, visual data. A software annotation tool focuses students on the first subtask, detecting intermediate actions that lead to an outcome. Comparing and identifying strategic factors that vary across events are also facilitated through a tool that allows annotated films to be compared against one another. A modeling activity at the end serves to link everything together, forming a qualitative explanation of hunting behavior. These tools were iteratively refined through discussions with students and teachers and observations of classroom activity.

However, some of the tools are not computational. For instance, we have students draw relationships between strategic factors and hunting behaviors with pencil and paper and then write their diagrams on large posterboards. We also make extensive use of videotape (in addition to the digital video on the computer) during classroom discussions. Two issues were considered when deciding whether to embed scaffolds directly into the software. First, although software should assist task performance, it is possible to eliminate learning benefits by having the computer do too much [13]. It is beneficial for students to construct ideas, and this often means doing so without computational scaffolds. Second, observations of classroom work practices often suggested that software was not the best medium for the tools, and we discuss this below.

Context

Schools and classrooms are organizations with elaborate work practices, and successful software environments must respect these practices [6, 16, 17]. For instance, although students are the target audience, it is equally important to consider teachers as users of the system. At the simplest level, teachers are the ones judging the software's utility in their classrooms — if they do not approve of it, students will never see it. More importantly, designing for active classroom participation requires teachers to facilitate activities, as students need guidance when learning and collaborating. Teachers orchestrate classroom activities "outside of the box", and their role in the learning environment effects learning outcomes. In short, teachers are users too.

Large numbers of students sit in classrooms, and things often get noisy and chaotic. Rather than trying to build individualized systems for such settings, we have tried to leverage off of the social interactions in the classroom, developing activities that allow students to collaborate and argue around the computer tools. Such collaboration can be useful when observing and interpreting video, as students are more likely to make their thoughts explicit, pose alternative ideas, and critically interpret and learn from their colleagues. Because computer monitors offer limited viewing space, some tasks are best achieved through traditional media such as blackboards, posters, and so forth. As we mentioned earlier, some of the tools in the Animal Landlord intervention are paper constructions because it is easier for large groups of students to gather and discuss ideas around them.

ANIMAL LANDLORD

In this section, we discuss the result of integrating context, tasks, and tools by describing the evolution of Animal Landlord over several iterations. We have conducted four, week-long user trials with 300+ students in twelve, introductory biology classrooms. During each iteration, we looked to see what kinds of activities were occurring in the classroom, focusing on the conversations taking place, the teacher's role in sustaining these conversations, and the products created by students. We describe the iterations and the design changes resulting from observations of students and teachers interacting with the curricular materials.

Trial 1: Annotation

Animal Landlord provides nine video clips, each depicting different ways that lions obtain their prey. These 1-2 minute segments vary across factors such as size and composition of the lion/prey groups, prey species, time of day, hunting methods (stalking, ambushing), and hunt success or failure. This allows students to make comparisons between films to identify strategic factors influencing hunt outcomes and their range of possible values. For example, students might notice that the size of the hunting party changes across films, and that this seems to be related to the size of the prey animal being captured.

Groups of 3-4 students work with these clips, presented as QuickTime video without narration on the computer, and use a tool which allows them to capture and annotate frames of the film to explain their significance. Their task is to develop a model of how lions (and their prey) behave during hunting episodes that will later be used to think about how evolution led to these behaviors. The first step towards this is to interpret and articulate plot structures for the film clips. Students must observe visual events, decide which events contribute to hunting success or failure, and annotate each event with an explanation of its significance.

In early meetings with teachers, it was suggested that students were not accustomed to decomposing complex behaviors into constituent parts, that they would think of hunting as a simple outcome — the predator eats or goes hungry. Our initial implementation probed this hypothesis by simply giving students a QuickTime movie viewer coupled to a text document as a tool. Students could click on a button to transfer the current video frame to the text document for annotation. We noticed that students would generally grab the final frame of the video and make comments such as, "The lion failed its hunt because it was slower than the warthog." In talking to the students that produced these minimal annotations, it appeared that they were aware of other influences on the hunts, but they were accustomed to articulating final outcomes rather than causal relationships.

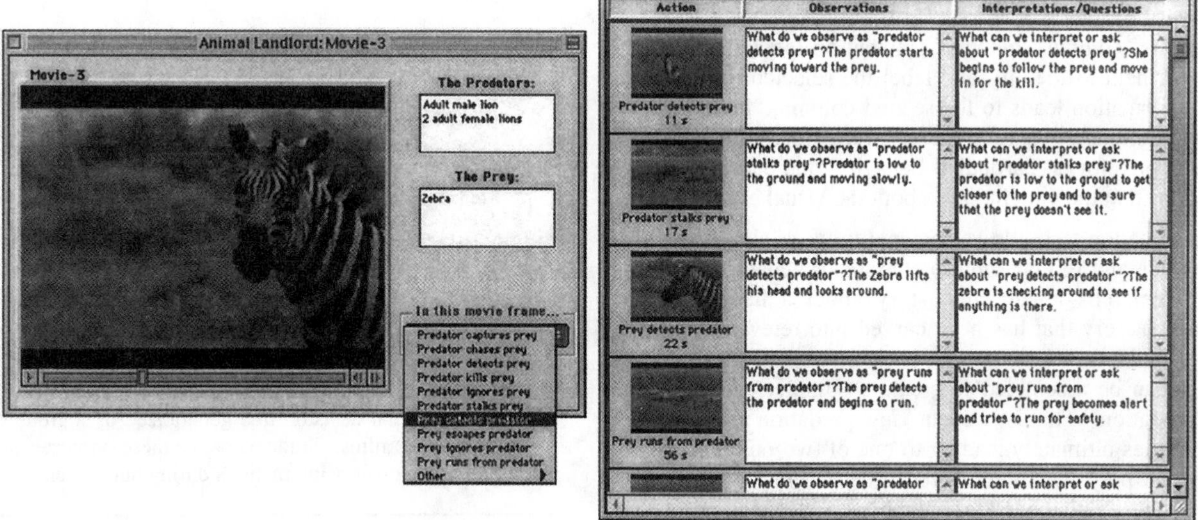

Figure 1: Animal Landlord's movie viewer and annotation tool by the fourth user trial. The exposed menu is used to label movie frames from a palette of actions. The frame is sent to the annotation window on the left where students make observations and interpretations around the event. Alternatively, students can drag and drop frames from the movie viewer to the annotation window.

Trial 2: Annotation Revisited & Decision Variables

It appeared that our teachers were correct, that students would not spontaneously generate detailed annotations. To provide more structure for students, our second trial provided an explicit scaffold in the form of a menu of possible interactions between predator and prey (Figure 1). Since students were only marking the film outcomes, we felt that suggesting intermediate actions might motivate them to attend to these in the films. The quality of their annotations changed dramatically as a result. Not only were they able to identify the features present in the menu, but they also identified additional, more subtle features (which can be added to the menu and shared with other groups), possibly because they stood out against those events listed on the action menu.

The menu focuses students on possible action choices, but we also felt that the task needed to be modeled for students. We created a videotape of hunting segments that the class would view before the computer activities. The first of these clips showed chimpanzees hunting red colobus monkeys; it is the only film in our curriculum containing a narration. Teachers lead students through an in-depth analysis of the hunt events, and they also point out pros and cons of the narration. For instance, this particular film clip does an excellent job of explaining the social interactions of the chimpanzees. On the other hand, it mentions that chimps hunt in the wet season without explaining why that might be. Teachers pull out these subtle distinctions in the quality of explanations and use them to model what they expect of students during computer work. In addition, they refer to the chimpanzee film throughout the week to help students understand the various subtasks of the investigation model.

The remaining clips on the videotape show the lion in action, and teachers use these to reinforce the lessons learned from the chimpanzee hunt. They also try to get students to generate the items on the action selection menu as they watch the videotape, giving the modeling activity a constructive flavor. This initial classroom discussion and the action selection menu work together to scaffold students through the annotation process.

Figure 1 also shows the annotation window where students explain each event that they captured. Initially, there was a single text pane, and students would write annotations such as, "The predators changed their mind and let the prey get away because they are in a playful mood." These comments conflate observations of the film with possible inferences or conclusions. In traditional science classrooms, students are rarely taught to distinguish between observations and inferences [10], so we created the two types of annotations seen in the figure. In the "Observations" column, students comment on the actions that allowed them to identify and label the selected behavior. This information leads to the second column, "Interpretations/Questions", where students make inferences about the reasons for a particular behavior and/or can note questions that they might have about the visual events.

The annotation task allows students to work closely with video data and to make interpretations of behaviors. But every film tells a particular story about a hunting encounter, a story that has been carved into relevant events by the students. The next task is to understand how these stories can be assembled to create a complete picture of lion predation. That is, we can view predation as a space of activities ultimately leading to one of two outcomes — either the prey is captured or it escapes [7]. Along the path to these outcomes are a number of "decision points" influencing the predator's success or failure. Mapping this space is useful for understanding the interactions between the predator, its prey, and the environment.

We felt that we could leverage off of students' existing annotations by asking them to revisit the nine films, this time looking for variables that might influence hunting success (*e.g.*, time of day, number of predators) and adding these to their original annotations. Students quickly rebelled, saying that they had already done this task, yet there was no evidence of this in their work. It became clear through discussions with the students and teachers that there was a problem with the task implementation, namely that students are not accustomed to refining existing work. School cultures do not always encourage iterative refinement of work products; students are used to completing assignments and never dealing with them again. This aspect of schooling forced us to rethink the nature of the task and to design a *new* product that would encompass this deeper level of analysis.

Trial 3: Decision Trees

Students continued to annotate plot structures in the third trial. To encourage comparison across films, we asked students to create "decision trees", simple graphs of all possible activities that could occur in a hunt. The graphical representation encourages students to connect hunting actions, generating the space of possible alternatives. It is also a more explicit representation of the task that students had rebelled against in the previous trial. And because students perceived this as a very different task than annotating video, they were more than willing to cooperate.

Initially, we had students create these trees offline, on large sheets of poster paper — Figure 2 shows an example decision tree created by students from three of the films. Essentially, students create qualitative models of predator-prey interactions, specifically looking at decisions made during predation. These models are similar to those found in the ecological literature [7] and are used in class discussions to explore evolutionary reasons for behavior.

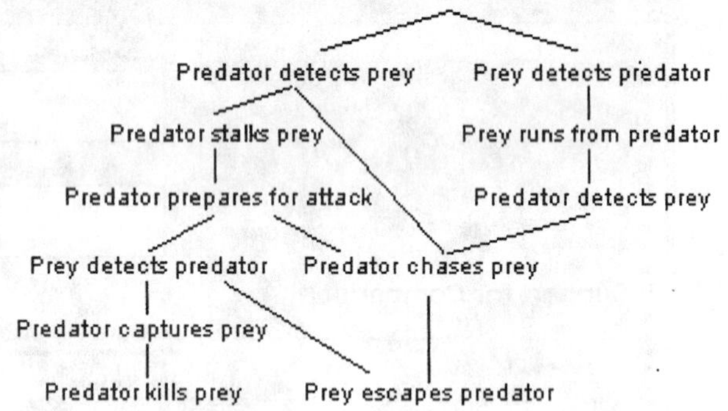

Figure 2: A partial decision tree generalized by a group of students from three films. Students create these on poster paper to highlight predator-prey interactions during hunting encounters.

It is also useful to consider the strategic factors associated with each node in the tree. For instance, a successful stalk relies on a number of factors, such as the amount of cover available, the sensory devices of the target prey, and so on. As students construct their decision trees, they also identify selection pressures influencing the shape of the hunt space. These pressures were generally written on separate pieces of paper but were also attached to the trees themselves.

We saw a great deal of collaboration around the creation of the decision trees. Different groups of students were assigned to become "experts" on certain films. Groups would shift throughout the classroom, exchanging ideas and revising their explanations based on feedback from other groups. By annotating videos, students had an opportunity to be media producers. During the construction of the decision trees, they became media critics, arguing about the validity of each other's annotations. The software became a conversational prop in these encounters, a way for students to back their critiques with evidence. It was quite common to see students using the annotation window's picture icons to click back to a frame, play the video at that spot, and argue about some aspect of behavior — "The lion trips, and then the wildebeest trips, and *that's* how it makes the kill."

In this user trial, the tasks performed by students changed, but the software support remained the same. We had planned to develop graphical tools for creating the decision trees, but after observing the classroom activity around their creation, we decided against it. Creating posters is part of the school work structure, and students seemed to enjoy walking away from the computers to present their work in a familiar format. As well, the posters were displayed around the room, providing artifacts for whole-class conversations.

Teacher involvement is crucial during decision tree construction. At times, they call class discussions to think about the meaning of the trees, generally using the chimpanzee film as an example. They lead students through discussions of possible evolutionary reasons for the tree structures (*e.g.*, Why do the female lions do most of the hunting?). They also select nodes in the trees to talk about optimal foraging and energy (*e.g.*, Why do the predators decide to give up the chase?). Eventually, they help students use the trees and strategic factors as "predictive" models. Students watch additional video clips, try to fit them into their models, and revise their structures where necessary.

Trial 4: Support for Comparison

Sometimes while creating decision trees, students would get tangled in syntactic details, focusing more on layout design than the meaning of the layout. Students commented that it was difficult to keep track of the branching tree structure by comparing printouts of their annotations. It seemed that they needed a way to look globally at their individual work products, so in our fourth user trial, we introduced a comparison "light table" (Figure 3).

Instead of going from annotations to decision trees, students now converse about their initial annotations after loading them into this light table. Each column shows a film's annotations, and students can select particular actions in the grid to see where similar events occur across films (Figure 3 shows the light table aligned at "Prey runs from predator"). Lining up similar actions in the light table often reveals differences in the surrounding states that may be important to understanding the hunt space. For instance, in some cases, a predator might not stalk before chasing; this may suggest something about the conditions required to initiate the action. Students also argued over the classification of events, sometimes clarifying terms ("What do you mean it's being *sneaky*? How can you *measure* sneaky?"), sometimes decomposing events even further ("Crouching and stalking are different because stalking means the lion is moving.").

We could have used the light table to generate decision trees for students, since the action labels are privy to the system. We did not for reasons discussed earlier — the software should not automate tasks where learning can take place [13]. The social cooperation that occurs as students make sense of hunting behaviors with the light table is crucial to the learning interactions. It appears that students were developing sophisticated notions of behavior through negotiations around the light table and decision trees.

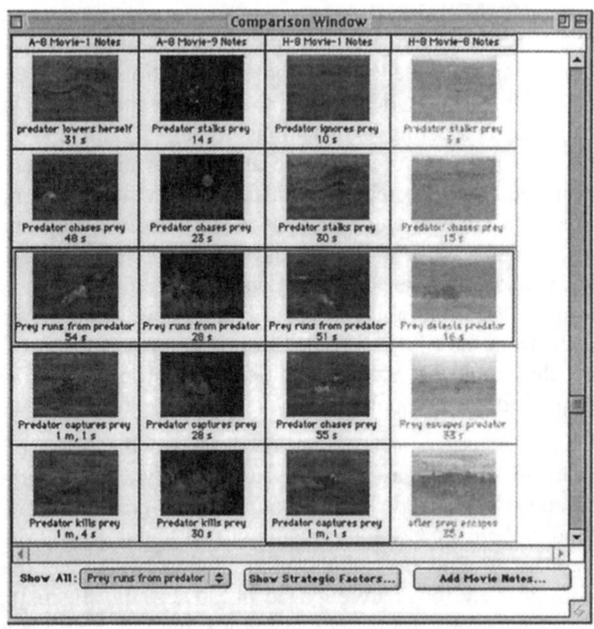

Figure 3: Animal Landlord's comparison light table. Students can align actions that occur across films. This table is aligned on "Prey runs from predator", and all films containing the action are highlighted in yellow. The film on the right does not contain the action, hence its column is grayed out.

For example, herbivore vigilance is an active area of research in behavioral ecology [7, 15], yet we have never seen it mentioned in high school biology textbooks. Nevertheless, several groups noticed patterns of prey animals alternating between feeding and scanning for predators. As students noticed these patterns by aligning events in the light table, the teacher would prompt them to form theories about how often animals need to scan, differences in scan times for different animals, and why these lead to evolutionary advantages. If the computer simply created a decision tree, it is doubtful that such learning opportunities would spontaneously arise. More so, this sense of discovery seemed to encourage students to share their findings with others; again, this is something that typically does not occur around nature film viewing.

Throughout the four trials, we have reshaped the curricular activities to encourage small-group and whole-class discussion and theory construction. The computer-based annotation and comparison tools allow students to create props for argumentation. In addition, videotapes and poster diagrams act as learning props. Teachers facilitate learning as they talk with students in small-group or whole-class discussions, directing their activities and encouraging argumentation around their findings. Yet, they are responding to student inquires, and, indeed, the issues raised in each classroom depend very much on the observations that students make. Ultimately, learning seems to emerge from student-initiated discussions moderated by teachers and fueled by observations made on the computer. This is very different than traditional lab activities in classrooms where teachers drive discussions.

PRELIMINARY RESULTS

The benefits of the Animal Landlord curriculum seem to stem from its reflection of the investigation model described earlier. Students come to realize that there can be multiple, competing explanations for an organism's behaviors, and structures like the annotations and the decision trees help to emphasize differences in student work. The light table proved to be a valuable asset during student collaboration, for they could easily inspect intermediate actions and detect salient variations. By scanning films in the light table, strategic factors could also be derived from the films. The decision trees provided a product that could be used in additional classroom activities apart from the computer.

It is obvious from classroom observations that fourteen-year-old students are motivated to watch videos of large creatures chasing down and eating larger creatures. Although there were some initial concerns about gender differences around the subject of predation, we found that both girls and boys are engaged in the activity. Focusing on a single topic for a week is atypical in high school, and teachers were surprised that 15-20 minutes of video could hold student attention. They also felt that the time was well spent and that their students gained valuable experiences in conducting their own investigations and collaborating to produce explanatory models.

We have collected data in the form of student and teacher interviews, work products, classroom video, and pre/post tests. We are still analyzing these data, and we have reported results from our final user trial concerning the pre/post tests elsewhere [19]. The open-ended essay questions used in the pre/post tests were drawn from university-level biology examinations and administered to students before and after the Animal Landlord intervention.

Consider one of these essay questions: What limits the amount of prey consumed by a predator? Initially, students wrote responses such as, "If they're not hungry, they won't eat," and "They know they have to save food." At the completion of the curriculum, their responses focused more on the behaviors of the creatures and tended to be more causal. Students articulated more points (*e.g.*, size of prey) for each question on the posttests (mean improvement from 2.4 to 3.9, $p < .001$). There were also more justifications (*e.g.*, size of prey is important because large animals may be difficult to subdue) for these points after working through the curriculum (mean improvement from 1.2 to 2.4, $p < .001$). These posttest justifications also contained more references to behavioral ecology issues such as interactions between organisms, environmental pressures, and energy consumption. And, in contrast to research showing that students often use less causal reasoning *after* viewing nature films [18], we see a significant increase in causal justification in our posttest results.

FUTURE WORK

It appears that students are learning to articulate scientifically plausible explanations during the Animal Landlord intervention. Further data are required to better understand these outcomes. For instance, we did not have a control classroom, so we cannot say whether there are learning gains beyond more traditional methods of instruction, including the standard viewing of nature films. It is clear that our students are discussing ideas that are deeper than those found in traditional nature films, but if such films *were* to mention these topics, would students learn just as much? We suspect that the actual interpretation of video contributes to the development of strategic reasoning around biological concepts, and we are now recruiting additional classrooms to help us investigate these issues.

Although we have only dealt with clips of lion predation in classrooms, Animal Landlord was designed to handle arbitrary visual content, and it is relatively straightforward to change the video clips and action selection menus using standard resource editors. However, simply changing the media does not ensure that additional domains will fit into the current investigation structure. To test the generality of our approach, we are working with additional examples of animal behavior for students and teachers. We are also developing interpretive activities in the arts and humanities to see what additions are necessary to make sense of visual data in domains unrelated to animal behavior. We expect that the general annotation and comparison tasks will be applicable in these areas, but much of the external, classroom supports will need to be revised.

Finally, after a week of activity, students produce film annotations and decision trees, but they never create text narrations similar to those in nature films. We will soon implement tools for students to sequence the original video clips, add audio tracks, and ultimately produce a documentary film that can be transferred to videotape. Moving the student-authored presentations "out of the box" so that they can be shared outside the classroom should be a powerful motivator.

CONCLUSION

In designing and testing Animal Landlord, we have developed a better understanding of the interaction between classroom work contexts, tasks, and tools and how this relates to the success of computer-based learning environments in schools. Instead of solely creating computational tools for students, we have tried to distribute activity throughout the classroom culture, taking advantage of teacher expertise and existing non-technological media. In doing this sort of classroom-centered design, it appears that we were able to alter work practices to promote social collaboration amongst students and teachers, collaborations that led to an interactive learning experience around nature films.

ACKNOWLEDGMENTS

This work is funded by a Cognitive Studies in Educational Practice Grant from the James S. McDonnell Foundation, a Patricia Roberts Harris Fellowship, and a National Science Foundation training grant. Ben Loh, Josh Radinsky, Bill Sandoval, Franci Steinmuller and Iris Tabak have also contributed to the thinking on classroom-centered design. We would like to thank Pamela Lentine for assisting with the curriculum design and deployment, our teacher collaborators, Sharon Cannavino, Phil Hiller, Karen Olson, and Maria Vermiglio, and ecologists Hans Landel and David Scheel for their expertise on behavior and lions. Thanks also to Marina Umaschi Bers and our anonymous reviewers for suggestions on earlier drafts of the paper.

REFERENCES

[1] Baecker, R., Rosenthal, A.J., Friedlander, N., Smith, E., & Cohen, A. (1996). A multimedia system for authoring motion pictures. In *ACM Multimedia '96 Proceedings*, (pp. 31-42). New York: ACM Press.

[2] Bellamy, R.K.E. (1996). Designing educational technology: Computer-mediated change. In B.A. Nardi (ed.), *Context and Consciousness: Activity Theory and Human-Computer Interaction*, (pp. 123-146). The MIT Press: Cambridge, MA.

[3] Erdman, B. (1990). The closely guided viewer: Form, style, and teaching in the educational film. In E. Ellsworth & M.H. Whatley (eds.), *The Ideology of Images in Educational Media: Hidden Curriculums in the Classroom*, (pp. 27-42). Teachers College Press: New York.

[4] Germann, P.J., Haskins, S., & Auls, S. (1996). Analysis of high school biology laboratory manuals: Promoting scientific inquiry. *Journal of Research in Science Teaching*, 33(5): 475-500.

[5] Goldman-Segall, R. (1995). Deconstructing the Humpty-Dumpty myth: Putting it together to create cultural meaning. In E. Barrett & M. Redmond (eds.), *Contextual Media: Multimedia and Interpretation*, (pp. 27-52). The MIT Press: Cambridge, MA.

[6] Hawkins, J. (1993). Technology and the organization of schooling. *Communications of the ACM*, 36(5): 30-37.

[7] Lima, S.L. & Dill, L.M. (1990). Behavioral decisions made under the risk of predation: A review and prospectus. *Canadian Journal of Zoology*, 68: 619-640.

[8] Loh, B., Radinsky, J., Reiser, B.J., Gomez, L.G., & Edelson, D.C. (to appear). The Progress Portfolio: Promoting reflective Inquiry in complex investigation environments. To appear in *Proceedings of Computer Supported Collaborative Learning 97*. Toronto, Canada.

[9] Nardi, B.A., Kuchinsky, A., Whittaker, S., Leichner, R., & Schwarz, H. (1996). Video-as-data: Technical and social aspects of a collaborative multimedia application. *Computer Supported Collaborative Work*, 4: 73-100.

[10] Norris, S.P. (1985). The philosophical basis of observation in science and science education. *Journal of Research in Science Teaching*, 22(9): 817-833.

[11] Pea, R.D. (1991). Learning through multimedia. *IEEE Computer Graphics & Applications*, 11(4): 58-66.

[12] Pea, R.D. & Gomez, L.M. (1992). Distributed multimedia learning environments: Why and how? *Interactive Learning Environments*, 2(2): 73-109.

[13] Rappin, N., Guzdial, M., Realff, M., & Ludovice, P. (1997). Balancing usability and learning in an interface. In *Proceedings of CHI 97*, (pp. 479-486). New York: ACM Press.

[14] Schaller, G.B. (1972). *The Serengeti Lion: A Study of Predator-Prey Relations*. Chicago, IL: University of Chicago Press.

[15] Scheel, D. (1993). Waiting for lions in the grass: The usefulness of scanning and its effects during hunts. *Animal Behaviour*, 46: 695-704.

[16] Schofield, J.W. (1995). *Computers and Classroom Culture*. New York: Cambridge University Press.

[17] Schwab, R.G., Hart-Landsberg, S., Reder, S., & Abel, M. (1992). Collaboration and constraint: Middle school teaching teams. In *Proceedings of Computer Supported Collaborative Work 92*, (pp. 241-248). New York: ACM Press.

[18] Silverstein, O. & Tamir, P. (1993). The role of imagery in learning biology science through television. In *Selected Readings from the Symposium of the International Visual Literacy Association*. Delphi, Greece.

[19] Smith, B.K. & Reiser, B.J. (1997). What should a wildebeest say? Interactive nature films for high school classrooms. In *ACM Multimedia 97 Proceedings*, (pp. 193-201). New York: ACM Press.

[20] Soloway, E., Jackson, S.L., Klein, J., Quintana, C., Reed, J., Spitulnik, J., Stratford, S.J., Studer, S., Jul, S., Eng, J., & Scala, N. (1996). Learning theory in practice: Case studies of learner-centered design. In *Proceedings of CHI 96*, (pp. 189-196). New York: ACM Press.

[21] Tabak, I., Smith, B.K., Sandoval, W.A., & Reiser, B.J. (1996). Combining general and domain-specific strategic support for biological inquiry. In *Proceedings of the Third International Conference on Intelligent Tutoring Systems*, (pp. 288-296). London: Springer Verlag.

[22] Wetzel, C.D., Radtke, P.H., & Stern, H.W. (1994). *Instructional Effectiveness of Video Media*. Hillsdale, NJ: Lawrence Erlbaum Associates.

New Media, New Practices: Experiences in Open Learning Course Design

Tamara Sumner
Knowledge Media Institute
The Open University
Milton Keynes, MK7 6AA, UK
http://kmi.open.ac.uk/~tamara
T.Sumner@open.ac.uk

Josie Taylor
Institute of Educational Technology
The Open University
Milton Keynes, MK7 6AA, UK
J.Taylor@open.ac.uk

ABSTRACT
We explore some of the complex issues surrounding the design and use of multimedia and Internet-based learning resources in distance education courses. We do so by analysing our experiences designing a diverse array of learning media for a large scale, distance learning course in introductory computing. During the project, we had to significantly rethink the design and production of our learning resources as we *shifted from a paper-based teaching model to an interactive teaching model.* This shift entailed changes to our design products (to promote more effective media use by learners) and changes to our design practices (to foster consistent media use and design across a large and distributed team). Course designers and course students alike needed help in breaking out of paper-based models of learning to obtain maximum benefit from the interactive teaching model.

Keywords: Design, Distance Education, Educational Technology, Lifelong Learning, Multimedia

INTRODUCTION

Recently, there has been a realisation of the importance of lifelong learning to the envisioned knowledge-based economies of the next century [7]. With this realisation, there has been an explosion of interest in new forms of teaching and learning made possible by new technology – particularly on-line distance education and multimedia learning environments. These two areas are perceived as offering the potential to promote lifelong learning by supporting flexible learning, fostering learner control, and stimulating learner engagement. Given these perceptions, it is not surprising that many educational institutions, including our own, have started or announced plans to 'put their courses on-line' and make 'significant use of new media.'

In this paper, we unpack these phrases and explore some of the complex issues surrounding the design and use of 'new media' in large-scale distance education courses which consist of learning resources distributed across numerous media and technologies. Students work with a wide array of on-line tools: standard office productivity tools, various kinds of communication software, World Wide Web-based hypermedia, and specialised learning environments tailored to particular curricular needs. In this situation, it is a challenge for both course designers and learners to effectively manage the media-mix to achieve their educational objectives [4]. We focus on related *design and use* issues such as:

- Should we design for media redundancy or media complementarity?
- What forms of media integration are necessary or desirable?
- Can we transfer existing materials to new media or must we engage in substantial re-design?
- What new design and production practices may we need to adopt?

We examine these issues by critically analysing our experiences in designing and evaluating a large scale open learning course in introductory computing at The Open University in the UK. This course uses a wide range of technologies and media to deliver to students, in their homes, a full year's worth of learning activities in object-oriented programming, software design, and networked computing.

After describing our particular course and open learning setting, we examine our preliminary experiences with the initial course materials during formative testing. Next, we show how developing an explicit interactive teaching model helped us understand and resolve the problems we encountered, one of which was students' lack of orientation and confusion with respect to the roles of various media. This we addressed through the development of an interactive Course Map. We then reflect on the design and use issues outlined above and distil several lessons based on our experiences. Finally, we examine the consequences of these lessons for educators moving to technology-based teaching, and more broadly, designers of diverse media 'systems'.

SETTING: THE NEW COURSE

Since the late 1960's, The Open University (OU) has been providing mixed media, distance education courses combining printed texts, television, video, audio, and home-laboratory kits. Materials are centrally produced to an academically high standard, and presented in an open learning style that is accessible to people with no previous academic qualifications. After signing up for a course, students receive by post a course pack containing all necessary study materials. While materials are designed to support independent learning, students are not entirely on their own and are assigned to small tutor-groups of 20 students. They communicate with tutors and other students via telephone, e-mail, and computer conferencing, only occasionally meeting face-to-face.

The specific setting is the development of a new first-year undergraduate course called "Computing: An Object-oriented Approach." Such introductory courses often have between 3000 and 5000 students enrolled. This course is being developed in the Computing Faculty by a large, multi-disciplinary course team composed of about thirty academics, software developers, editors, graphic designers, and television producers. Our roles, as academics specialising in HCI and educational technology, were two-fold. First, we were responsible for evaluating the usefulness and usability of the new course resources under development. Second, we served as consultants to the team on media use. In the remainder of this section, we give an overview of the initial design goals and resources created for this course. A discussion of the pedagogical motivations can be found in [9].

Initial Design Goals

Obviously, one set of design goals related to enabling students to meet the educational aims of the course – to develop a solid understanding of object-oriented design and programming, networked computing, and software design. However, the course team also wanted students to have 'philosophical thoughts' and perceive both the software they used and the software they created as designed artifacts, necessarily embodying trade-off decisions between competing goals and objectives. Thus the course needed to be designed to encourage students to look at software artifacts from multiple perspectives, and to critically examine real world applications related to what they do in the course.

A second set of design goals was based on the OU charter of supporting 'open learning'; that is, allowing for and designing for students with diverse backgrounds who need to study in their own time and place. Students will have extremely diverse backgrounds in key areas such as previous experiences with academic study, programming, and computing in general. Thus, materials and tools must be designed to accommodate different levels of expertise and experiences with software and new media.

To support studying in their own place, learning resources must be designed to take into account the capacity, performance, and cost constraints of a student's typically moderate specification home computing kit (e.g., 8 megabytes of RAM) [4]. Also, students are unwilling to spend large amounts of time on-line with their modems given the price of telephone services in the UK (pay per minute for local calls). To support studying in their own time, materials need to be designed so that students can accurately estimate and plan the time needed for computer-based activities.

Initial Course Resources

By fall of 1995, the course team formulated the course goals and pedagogical approach and identified most of the resources (Table 1). The course would be structured around a printed text with accompanying practical work contained within Smalltalk LearningBooks (Figure 1) based on the notebook metaphor provided in the LearningWorks Environment™.

Table 1. Initial course resources.

Course Resources
Printed Texts
Smalltalk LearningBooks Programming Environment
Set Book: Parsons & Oja [6]
Eleven Television Programmes
Two Multimedia Titles – 'The Object Shop' and 'Grumble's Grommets'
Electronic Glossary
World Wide Web Site
Computer Conferencing
Email
Personal Productivity Tools

There would also be multimedia CD-ROMs, web activities, and television programmes. As with other OU courses, the printed text produced by the team would serve as the 'backbone', integrating the concepts covered by other resources and directing students to other resources. Additionally, the team constructed an initial web site which provided general course information and replicated some of the text materials in hypertext form.

PRELIMINARY EXPERIENCES

The team had produced draft texts and prototype LearningBooks for about the first third of the course and wanted feedback on their initial course design before proceeding further. So for the next six months, until April of 1996, we analysed our preliminary experiences with the new course. One strand of our activity consisted of detailed analyses of existing resources, whilst the other focused on empirical evaluations with users.

We brought together specialists from the course team in key design and production areas: educational technology,

HCI, television, software development, graphic design, and text production to form a Media Group.

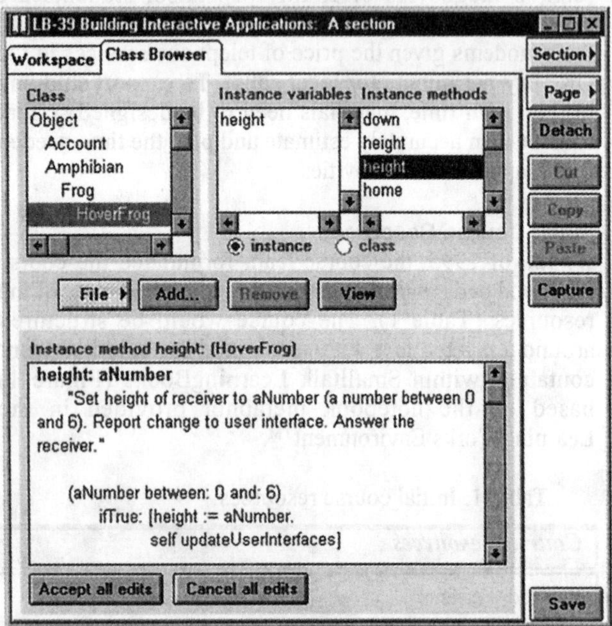

Figure 1. Notebook sections contain microworlds and programming tools, such as this Class Browser, that the team created for the course.

The group's task was to advise the larger course team: (1) how multimedia could be used to promote more active learning, (2) how to make use of the World Wide Web and (3) on the practicalities of producing resources given time and budget constraints. The Media Group conducted a series of resource analyses focusing on the contents of and relationships between the printed texts and LearningBooks, and between the printed texts and web resources. Our analyses highlighted potential use and production problems stemming from existing media redundancy and resource integration practices.

"Inscribed' into the structure of the printed texts was an implicit model of use which assumed that students were using the texts and their computer-based LearningBooks side-by-side in a highly interleaved fashion, reading a little, then programming a little. All the supporting context for the programming activities – problem statements, hints, solution approaches – were embedded in the print. Authors had been inconsistent in the granularity of their interleavings (with some authors going for larger 'chunks' before switching activities and others smaller). From a use perspective, we were concerned about forcing students to work in this interleaved fashion: it promoted dependence on textual materials, made it difficult for learners to estimate the time needed for computer-based activities, and was place-bound requiring students to read next to their computer. From a production standpoint, we were concerned at the tight, dependent coupling between the two media that arose from interleaving. This style of resource integration resulted in lots of media redundancy: the texts were filled with LearningBook-specific instructions and screen dumps. As the software evolved, the texts needed to be updated. This was problematic given the widely differing production time periods of the two media. (Texts often have to be ready a year in advance for printing and, due to costs, are rarely modified and reprinted.)

The team wanted advice on whether to render the printed text in hypertext form and make it available at the course web site. Again, there were concerns over production issues arising from this level of media redundancy, such as initial mark-up costs and maintaining consistency between the different media versions (print and web). More importantly, it wasn't clear if this approach provided any added value for learners or whether they would even make use of this type of resource.

In the same period, we conducted two forms of empirical evaluations on existing course materials: longitudinal surveys and open-ended interviews. The surveys looked at whether people were able to learn with the resources. Fourteen people, similar to the expected student population, were paid to act as students and 'take' the course using the preliminary materials. Each person was given the necessary computer hardware and software for the duration of the testing. As 'students' worked through each chapter in their homes, they filled in a questionnaire about the resources and the subject matter.

We also conducted open-ended, semi-structured interviews with eight of these testers. These interviews focused on trying to understand students' experiences working and learning with the computer-based resources. We asked them in detail about how they studied, how they organised their on-line work and study time, and their experiences using particular tools such as Smalltalk, email, and the web. Where possible, we asked students to show us their notes, filing system, diaries, etc. and explain them to us. Here, we will not consider these studies in detail but instead will focus on the findings that influenced our design (see [8] for more details).

Analyses of the survey data showed that overall things were going fairly well. About half of the students were able to do the practical programming activities and seemed to grasp the various object-oriented concepts with no significant problems. Unfortunately, other students were having difficulties, particularly those students with little prior experience with technology. Despite their initial enthusiasm, they were not making effective use of their computer-based course resources and instead were relying heavily on the paper-based materials. The interview data provided converging evidence and identified several areas of concern:

- Some students had little confidence in their ability to work and learn with the computer-based resources. Several had long-standing prior anxiety about computers and this was slow to change. Others had experienced setbacks, e.g., a difficult installation or 'web' session, that had shattered their confidence.

- Many students felt disoriented and had difficulty judging progress through electronic materials.
- Nearly all students were unclear about the role of the various resources in the course and how they should be using them to support their learning.
- While they could use resources to carry out specific activities, many had difficulties making connections between practical activities and larger conceptual issues. As a result, they tended to develop isolated, piecemeal views of their computer resources.
- Some students were relying heavily on reading texts. The interleaving approach led some to believe they could read about programming rather than actually doing it. Some reported difficulties using the texts side-by-side with the LearningBooks.
- Some students rarely visited the web site since the materials there were redundant to their printed text.

We believed that many of the problems uncovered during these preliminary experiences were rooted in tacit paper-based models of teaching and learning which underlay the current design, and was promoted by interleaving. Lack of confidence with technology was also a contributing factor, reducing people's willingness to experiment with new ways of learning.

DEVELOPING AN INTERACTIVE TEACHING MODEL

Our evaluations indicated that *students* needed help breaking out of paper-based learning habits in order to capitalise upon the new resources. Specifically, learners needed: orientation support to feel more confident and in control of their learning process, bridging support to help relate specific activities to conceptual knowledge, and assistance fostering active learning habits. Basically, a framework was needed that defined a consistent task and support structure, encompassing both traditional and electronic media.

Conversely, the *course team* also needed help to break out of paper-based teaching and production practices. In paper-based courses, work practices are organised around a waterfall model of authoring: successive drafts of material are refined by academics over long periods of time and then handed over to editors and graphic designers to be produced. With computer resources, production is distributed and interdisciplinary, with parallel developments going on in different organisational areas by different media specialists. The course team needed a framework to guide both present and future course resource development. Such a framework should foster consistent production of materials across a large, distributed team and promote new models of working and divisions of labour across media specialists.

The tool the Media Group used to think about these inter-related use and production concerns was the development and refinement of an 'interactive teaching model.' This evolving model consisted of collections of representations, mock-ups, use scenarios, and prototypes that served as 'objects-to-think-with' as we considered possible new resource designs. We began by focusing on learners and their activities and developed models that helped make explicit:

- types and distributions of activities across resources,
- transitions between different resources in envisaged use situations, and
- where students may need support in adopting a new model of learning.

Changes to chapter structure

At the chapter level, we explored ways of moving the problem-solving contexts out of the text and into the LearningBooks to create a clearer distribution of activities across the resources. Figure 2 shows a set of mock-ups we created in April 1996 to demonstrate a new use scenario along these lines. We took an existing chapter and 'moved' problem framing and solution materials into separate LearningBook pages surrounding each programming problem. We added a special page at the front of each LearningBook called an 'agenda'. Similar to other systems [5, 10], we used the agenda to provide learners with 'support for practical action.' To support bridging between practical action and general concepts, we embedded hypertext links in the agenda, and other LearningBook pages, to concepts presented in an electronic glossary.

This particular redesign is based on the principle of media complementarity; i.e., that each resource should fulfil a unique function and support different activities. It addressed the production concerns due to integration by interleaving, and seemed to promote a more active learning style by reducing learner dependence on detailed instructions embedded in the text. For this scenario, the team was concerned with whether there were sufficient learner benefits to justify the re-working of existing texts and the extra programming effort required. They asked the Media Group to develop a working prototype of the model and test it with learners using the next chapter going out in May of 1996 for testing – Chapter 19. We did so, and conducted follow-up phone interviews with the testers. The response to the new chapter-level task structure was very positive. One student felt that the new approach "finally gave them a chance at success."

Developing the prototype involved changes to the LearningBook software and changes to the printed text. To function in a new role as a complementary resource, the printed text needed to be significantly rewritten. The editors and graphic designer undertook most of the restructuring and re-writing of both media. The HCI and educational technology specialists looked at how the problem context needed to be modified as it moved from printed text to software. The software developer modified the LearningBook software to support the addition of the new hypertext pages by editors.

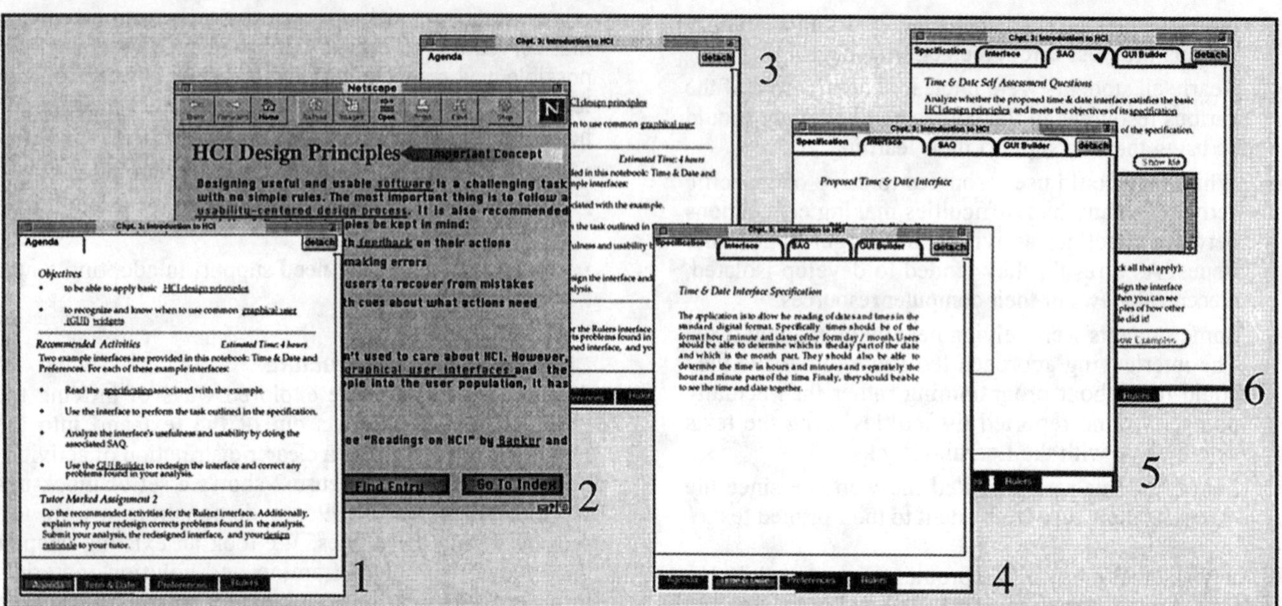

Figure 2. Mock-ups in a use scenario showing how the learner moves between the different resources during a programming session.

Since all the various Media Group specialists had contributed to developing the prototype, we were able to collectively analyse our experiences and produce authoring guidelines and ideas on new divisions of labour to promote the consistent production of the new resource structure. For example, the authoring guidelines offered advice on how to write the problem context pages in the LearningBooks to promote more active learning. Changes to the division of labour included recommendations for editors to become involved much earlier during production and assist academics in producing the hypertext pages. As time progressed, this part of the model was progressively refined by the larger course team as they produced more chapters.

Changes to course structure

At the course-level, we used architecture diagrams to help us analyse different resource configurations (Figure 3). These diagrams helped us see the amount and types of integration being built into the course as we analysed various production and use concerns. Figure 3 shows the current course configuration. The Course Map and the web-based Study Calendar integrate, either by reference (dotted lines) or by computational links (solid lines), all the course resources. When other resources change, these need to be updated. There are computational links between the LearningBooks and hypertext Glossary, and between the CD-ROMs and Glossary supporting smoother work flows between these resources. Now, the integration between the printed text and the LearningBooks is primarily through conceptual linking using common examples or problem domains. For instance, to help students bridge between a conceptual treatment of inheritance (an object-oriented concept) in the texts and activities where they create their own inheritance network, resources rely on a similar ecosystem inheritance example.

The web serves as a digital library for materials not available elsewhere, such as time-sensitive information and updates for all resource types. This use of the web as a periodic delivery mechanism is consistent with the design goal of limiting the time students must spend on-line due to high telephone costs. The only form of media redundancy left in the course is the Glossary which is replicated in both the printed text and in hypertext. Many students would not bother to use an electronic glossary while reading the printed texts.

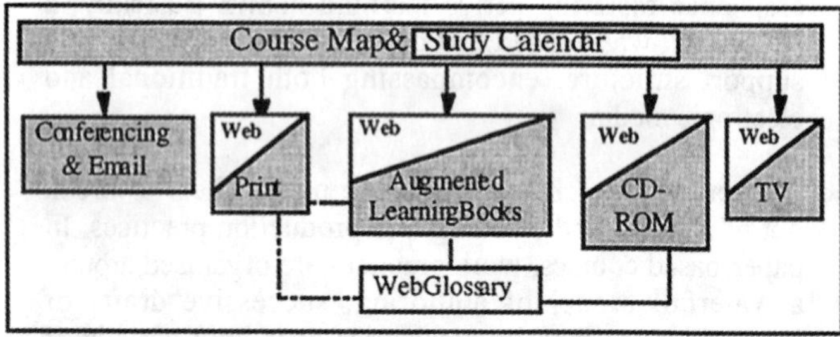

Figure 3. Course architecture diagram showing resource integration and web complementarity.

Table 2 shows the final functions associated with the media as a result of this process of re-design and refinement. The materials are both complementary and overlapping, with each resource playing an important role in the overall course. While some media may support overlapping objectives, each does so in a different way. These different ways include supporting different learning styles (i.e., experiential versus reflective cognition) or providing a different perspective on the same material (e.g., the printed texts take a theoretical look at networks whereas when using 'Grumble's Grommets', students design a network using today's existing technologies).

Table 2. Course resources and their different functions.

Course Resources	Function in Course
Printed Texts	Provides the conceptual and theoretical learning materials in the course; designed to give the students a 'good read' without requiring being on-line.
Smalltalk LearningBooks	Provides the practical materials supporting learning-by-doing activities related to programming, object-oriented concepts, and software design.
Parsons & Oja	Provides much practical information on computer hardware, software, and networked computing and relates many general ideas in these areas and to existing real-world applications.
Eleven Television Programmes	Contextualises students' activities to real-world problems and applications. Programmes feature interviews with designers, users, and clients.
Multimedia Titles	Provides two experiential, learning-by-doing environments in object-oriented concepts (Object Shop) and networked computing (Grumbles Grommets).
Electronic Glossary	Supports linking of terms and ideas into larger concepts and, by integration with the Smalltalk environment, linking of practical actions with concepts.
World Wide Web Site	Serves as the course library containing complementary course materials and materials of a timely nature, new updates to course resources, and pointers to further background materials.
Computer Conferencing	Supports general communication among participants and the necessary discourse between group members during collaborative group working.
Email	Supports student - tutor communication and electronic assignment submission.
Course Map and Study Calendar	Helps clarify the role of resources in the course, integrates resources, promotes more effective media use by linking academic objectives with practical action, fosters learner confidence with new media.
Productivity Tools	Word processors and drawing tools are used for written and design work.

Our interactive teaching model helped us reflect on what models of learning we may be building into the resources and where students may need support in adopting a new model. The redesign of the LearningBooks created a new model of learning at the chapter-level and the agenda pages made the new model explicit. However, our evaluations uncovered broader course-level learner problems concerning lack of orientation and clarity about the overall role of different learning resources in the course, which appeared to have a negative impact on learner confidence and motivation. We explored ways to address these issues through the creation of an Interactive Course Map. Our design goal was to create a multimedia map with 'welcome tour' that students could use in the early part of the course to get a feel for how to work and study using the course resources. We developed several prototypes exploring different styles of representation and eventually refined and tested the prototype shown in Figures 4 and 5.

The colours and fonts were chosen to match those used in the course's printed text and web site. Thus, resources have a familiar and consistent look, regardless of the media. The Map (Figure 4) is composed of three main areas: a course content area (right-hand pane), a course resources area (left-hand pane), and a tour area (video window, top left). The course resources area provides students with an overview of how a particular resource will be used in the course and global advice about how to study with the resource for this particular course.

The course content area supports orientation by laying the structure of the course bare and reflects the block structure of the course. Pressing the Block 1 button at the top level (shown in Figure 4) brings up the two panes shown in Figure 5. Each block area is structured into two panes – the Block Overview pane (right-hand side) and the Weekly Resource pane (lower left). The Block Overview pane shows how each study week is composed of one or more chapters. Clicking on any chapter title will bring up a third level pane containing a chapter description which focuses on learning goals and high-level tasks. The left side of the Resources pane shows what tools and resources are used to achieve the learning goals or complete that week's tasks. Making connections between learning objectives and resource activities is supported by the interplay between these two panes.

The Map operates on a principle of 'self-disclosure' [2] – two guided tours are available, in which a member of the course team (whose head appears in the video pane, top left) talks students through different aspects of the course structure or resources, whilst simultaneously the map illustrates what is being said. The General Course Tour outlines *all* the course resources and students are advised to watch this at the start of the course, before they do anything else. There is also a Block 1 Tour which introduces learners to the multiple media structure of chapters; i.e., printed text, LearningBooks, and web pages.

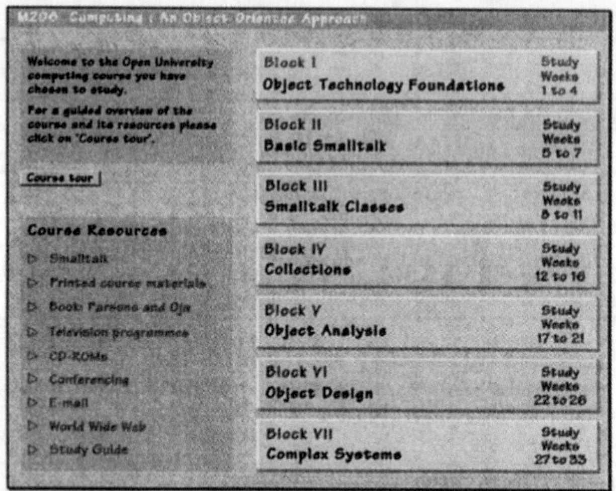

Figure 4. Top level view of the Course Map

We have completed formative testing of the map using six volunteers. To summarise our results, all participants were very enthusiastic and positive about the overall look and feel of the map, and had very few problems navigating, easily finding the things we set them to look for. All six participants described the tours as 'helpful' in the following specific ways: for taking them through the structure of the course phase by phase, for introducing the media and for showing them how to use the map itself. All participants said they would probably listen to all, or parts, of the tours several times. As a result of using the Map (with tours), 5 out of 6 participants were able to clearly articulate the structure of the course and the rather complex structure that 'chapters' might have (e.g. printed text, electronic learning books, web pages and television programmes). Additionally, everyone was able to articulate the general role of major resources in the course; i.e., that conferencing was for communicating with other students and tutors, while the web was a resource area for getting updates to course materials. We regard this as a measure of success. A full-fledged Course Map based on this prototype is currently being developed.

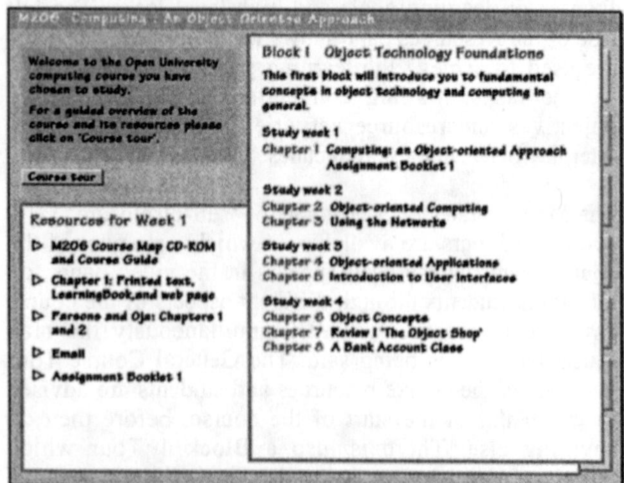

Figure 5. Course content area in the map visible after selecting 'Block 1' in Figure 4.

REFLECTIONS

In the Introduction, we articulated several issues surrounding the design and use of 'new media' in large-scale distance education courses. Here, we reflect on how we resolved these issues in our project and generalise some lessons based on our experiences.

Lesson 1: Design for media complementarity. Media redundancy (replicating the same materials in different media) did not help our learners or our production process. Many learners will not bother to access digital resources that are in more readily available paper form. Replicating materials can be a production nightmare; changes to content in one media will necessitate changes across all media to preserve consistency (a problem Green describes as viscosity [3]). We designed for complementarity based on learner activities and the media's time-base for modifications. Thus, we concentrated all materials supporting programming activities in the LearningBooks and used the course's web site as a digital library containing materials that change from year-to-year.

Lesson 2: Resource integration is important for learners, but how you do it affects your ability to evolve resources independently. Integration refers to the coupling between different resources. Referential integration (e.g., showing a picture or description of one resource inside another) greatly complicates the production process. In the original 'interleaving' approach, the referential integration between the LearningBooks and the printed text meant we could not evolve the software without re-writing the texts. Now, the integration is primarily through conceptual linking using common examples or problem domains. We also confined integration into specific components such as the Course Map and Study Calendar. This serves mainly to isolate the locus of possible viscosity effects; thus, rather than having to adjust several resources, efforts can be focused on keeping the Map and Calendar up-to-date.

Lesson 3: Be aware of models of working and learning you may be inscribing into the resources. As more educators move their teaching materials on-line, there is a likelihood that tacitly held models of teaching and learning refined for traditional media (e.g., paper- or lecture-based) will be inscribed into resources. We found it useful to explicitly articulate and reflect on what new model of learning we were trying to create and to analyse the resources we were producing from this perspective.

Lesson 4: Be prepared to rethink, restructure, and redesign your learning resources. If you design for complementarity and avoid referential integration (a common practice in paper-based teaching), you will need to restructure your learning resources. If you are trying to promote a new model of working and learning, you will inevitably need to rethink and redesign as well.

Lesson 5: New models of working and learning require new practices, from both course designers and learners. Our learner evaluations and production analysis activities helped us to understand current practices. The interactive teaching model helped us reflect on future use and production scenarios. The challenge is how to transform current practices in order to these future scenarios? In our case, the academics, editors, software developers, and graphic designers used the mock-ups and authoring guidelines to help rethink the division of labour within the production community.

Fostering new learning practices is always a difficult task. In our case, it is even trickier given our distance education setting: we will never meet learners face-to-face and their learning situation is distant and uninspectable. We attempted to foster new practices through resource redesign (e.g., the LearningBooks) and study support tools (e.g., the Course Map). While initial tests were promising, success remains to be validated during actual course presentation. However, we can – and do – confidently assert that many students will always need help!

Lesson 6: A Media Group can be helpful, but form the group early in the course design process. The most important function of the Media Group was to help the course team engage in self-reflection about their design products and practices. To do so, we undertook a variety of evaluation and analysis activities, looking at both use and production issues. We used these activities to provide a starting point for further rethinking and redesign by the team themselves. In the vein of participatory design [3], our key contributions were to construct representations, mock-ups, and prototypes that served to ground their redesign process and to help them reflect on how their practices might need to change.

While these lessons arose out of our very specific experiences, we feel they are applicable to other situations. Educators considering moving existing materials to new media forms, whether in traditional classroom or distance education settings, could benefit by thinking about resource complementarity, integration, and how to promote new learning practices. At the organisational level, educational institutions considering how to promote new practices could consider the Media Group option. Yokam et. al. ([11] in [1]) discuss how teachers learn new practices in special 'classrooms of tomorrow' but have difficulties transferring their new skills back to their own classrooms. The Media Group option side-steps the transfer problem by making the teacher's own context the locus of the re-thinking activity. Finally, our lessons are relevant to the publishing community, who are also creating products (educational and otherwise) using multiple media; i.e., combinations of books, CD-ROMS, and web-based resources. Our experiences indicate that the current trend towards media redundancy is problematic from both production and use perspectives.

In summary, we have described and analysed our experiences creating a new large-scale, media-rich distance learning course. These experiences opened our eyes to the shortcomings of previously implicit practices; a lifetime of practices honed for paper-based courses didn't transfer well to new media for either learners or designers. The new media required new practices, and we used our 'full battery' of HCI techniques to understand the changes that needed to be made. We do not claim that either our design process or the resulting course resources are without flaws, or even that we carried out all our own lessons faithfully and consistently. But we will certainly use these lessons as a starting point in our future course designs.

ACKNOWLEDGEMENTS

We thank the M206 course team, Diane Mole, other members of the Media Group, and the Open University Production Centre /BBC for their generous support during this project. Thanks to John Rieman, Simon Buckingham Shum, and John Domingue for comments on earlier drafts.

REFERENCES

1. Bellamy, R. K. E., "Designing Educational Technology: Computer-Mediated Change," in *Context and Consciousness: Activity Theory and Human–Computer Interaction*, B. Nardi, Ed., MIT Press, Cambridge, 1996, pp. 123-146.

2. DiGiano, C. and M. Eisenberg, "Self-Disclosing Design Tools: A gentle introduction to end-user programming," *Symposium on Designing Interactive Systems (DIS '95)*, Ann Arbor, MI (August 23-26), 1995, pp. 189-197.

3. Green, T. R. G., "The Cognitive Dimension of Viscosity: a sticky problem for HCI," *Human-Computer Interaction – INTERACT '90*, 1990, pp. 79-86.

4. Laurillard, D., "Multimedia and the changing experience of the learner," *British Journal of Educational Technology,* Vol. 26, Iss. 3, pp. 179-189, 1995.

5. Lemke, A. C. and G. Fischer, "A Cooperative Problem Solving System for User Interface Design," *Proceedings of AAAI-90, Eighth National Conference on Artificial Intelligence,* , pp. 479-484, 1990.

6. Parsons, J. and D. Oja, *New Perspectives in Computer Concepts – Comprehensive Edition,* International Thompson Publishing, Albany, Second Edition, 1996.

7. Dearing Report, "Higher Education in the Learning Society," http://www.leeds.ac.uk/educol/ncihe/, National Committee of Inquiry into Higher Education, United Kingdom, 1997.

8. Sumner, T. and J. Taylor, "Coping with Virtuality: Steps toward a Personal Learning Manager," *1997 UNESCO Workshop on Virtual Learning Environments*, Open University (UK), In press .

9. Woodman, M. and S. Holland, "From Software User To Software Author: An Initial Pedagogy For Introductory Object-Oriented Computing," *First ACM SIGCSE/ SIGCUE Conference on Integrating Technology into Computer Science Education*, Barcelona (June), 1996.

10. Wroblewski, D., T. McCandless and W. Hill, "DETENTE: Practical Support for Practical Action," *Human Factors in Computing Systems (CHI '91)*, New Orleans (April 27 - May 2), 1991, pp. 195-202.

11. Yokam, K., F. Wilmore and D. Dwyer, "Apple Classrooms of Tomorrow Report," in *Situated Teacher Development: ACOT's Two-Year Pilot Project*, 1994.

Investigating the Capture, Integration and Access Problem of Ubiquitous Computing in an Educational Setting

Gregory D. Abowd, Christopher G. Atkeson, Jason Brotherton, Tommy Enqvist, Paul Gulley & Johan LeMon
GVU Center & College of Computing
Georgia Institute of Technology
Atlanta, GA 30332-080 USA
+1 404 894 7512
{abowd, cga, brothert, tommyy, paulg, johan}@cc.gatech.edu

ABSTRACT

In this paper, we describe efforts to develop and evaluate a large-scale experiment in ubiquitous computing applied to education. Specifically, we are concerned with the general problem of capturing a rich, multimedia experience, and providing useful access into the record of the experience by automatically integrating the various streams of captured information. We describe the Classroom 2000 project and two years of experience developing and using automated tools for the capture, integration and access to support university lecture courses. We will report on observed use of the system by both teachers and learners and how those observations have influenced and will influence the development of a capture, integration and access system for everyday use.

Keywords

Ubiquitous computing, educational application, capture, integration and access of multimedia

INTRODUCTION

The interest in ubiquitous computing has surged over the past few years, thanks to some influential writings [17, 18] and plenty of experimental work. One of the potential features of a ubiquitous computing environment is that it could be used to record our everyday experiences and make that record available for later use. Indeed, much of our everyday lives is spent listening to and recording, more or less accurately, the events that surround us, only to have that one important piece of information elude us when we most need it.

There is a value to using computational resources to augment the inefficiency of human record-taking, especially when there are multiple streams of related information generated by a group of people. It is virtually impossible for a human to record all aspects of such a rich interactive experience. Computational support can also automate the relationships between various streams of information, so that one stream of information, such as notes taken during a meeting, can be used to index into another stream, such as the audio track from the same meeting. In this way, an integrated, multimedia record of an experience can aid in the recall of the meaning or significance of past events.

We have just outlined the general capture, integration and access problem for ubiquitous computing [2]. Tools to automate the support for capture, integration and access can replace an activity humans are not good at (e.g., recording) with other, more suitable tasks (e.g., summarizing, and interpreting).

As Weiser points out, "Applications are of course the whole point of ubiquitous computing." [18] It is not enough to identify the general problem of capture, integration and access for ubiquitous computing. We are compelled to explore and understand it better through specific applications. Over the past two years, we have examined this problem within the context of university education, in a project called Classroom 2000 [1]. The objective of the Classroom 2000 project is to create an environment to capture as much of the university classroom experience as possible. We have developed tools to automate the production of on-line lecture notes that integrate the various streams of information common to the classroom experience.

We have built a special-purpose classroom and iteratively developed a suite of tools. Over the past 18 months, our systems have been used regularly in a dozen undergraduate and graduate courses. This paper reports on our observations of how a capture, integration and access system is used and how it impacts teaching and learning practices, and further issues on how the system has evolved over time and how we see it evolving in the future.

Ultimately, we want to use our experience with Classroom 2000 to:

- Demonstrate to researchers in ubiquitous computing the importance of engineering robust systems that can be the basis of large-scale and long-term studies; and
- Inform educators on how ubiquitous computing technology can be used to improve both the teaching and learning experience.

BACKGROUND

History of capture, integration and access

Our work has been greatly influenced by previous research at Xerox PARC in ubiquitous computing [17,18] and tools to support electronic capture and access of collaborative activities [4,11,12,13]. We want to provide the students with a way to capture more personal notes through some form of an electronic notebook. The Marquee note-taking prototype developed at PARC [16], the Filochat prototype developed at Hewlett-Packard Labs [19], and the Dynomite personal note-taking environment from FX-PAL [20] come close to what we wanted to have in the hands of the students. Another possibility is to augment the capabilities of a traditional paper notebook, as done by Stifelman [15]. We have experimented with personal notebooks, but our most significant experience has been support for public display surfaces in the classroom using a large-scale electronic whiteboard like the Liveboard [4].

The integration of text with audio or video is critical to our work, and this is a popular research theme for those interested in information retrieval and content-based access to multimedia. A recent posting to the corpora mailing list (corpora@hd.uib.no) lists a number of research and commercial systems to align textual transcripts to audio and video archives. This linking between text and audio greatly enhances search capabilities, but it is only useful when a textual transcript is available, a process that currently requires much post-production effort.

When it is not practical to produce such a transcript, we rely on the implicit relationship between an audio stream and time-stamped pen strokes or keystrokes. This time-based relationship directly supports the task of a user browsing a set of notes that was taken during a class and asking "What was the lecturer talking about when this was being written?" This form of integration is exploited by the note-taking prototypes mentioned above, as well as other work at MIT's Media Lab [7] and at Apple [3].

The assumption in all of the preceding work in this area was that only one person will ever access the recorded notes and associated audio or video streams. Our work, in contrast, assumes that captured information in the classroom supports a number of people, bringing up issues of sharing public records and preserving the security of private notes.

Educational technology

It is important to place the problem of capture, integration and access within the larger context of educational technology. Much effort to introduce technology in the classroom equates to placing a workstation in front of each student. This is appropriate for some classes, but we want to investigate the usefulness of alternative pen-based interfaces that are amenable to the presentation and handwritten note-taking activities that occur in most classrooms.

We consciously decided to support the lecturing and note-taking activities that already occur in the majority of university classes. An important part of our research methodology is to put a system into use quickly and with a variety of users. Only through long-term use will we be able to observe the impact of our system on teaching and learning. It is much more practical to provide an initial system, therefore, that requires relatively little change in the practice of the users. Over time, we fully expect that our systems, if useful, will evolve to be used in ways that we did not and cannot predict.

A problem with educational software is content generation. Years of effort can go into producing a single course module that represents only a fraction of a student's educational experience. Every year, however, universities provide thousands of hours of instruction in a myriad of subjects. By viewing the classroom experience as a multimedia authoring session, we simplify content generation. It is feasible that over time a number of captured classes can themselves be packaged in a way to augment future educational objectives. We leverage heavily off of the World Wide Web as a delivery mechanism for this content. This more active use of the Web infrastructure is in tune with some recent educational technology work [10,14,5].

Proper research in educational technology has a foundation in some theory of learning that is backed by empirical results. In our case, we are focussed on the learner in a typical lecturing situation. A very common task for the learner is to take notes and to use those notes as a study guide [8]. Kiewra et al. [9] explain that note-taking is a complex task which allows little time for generative processing (active learning) to occur, and that review of the notes allows for more deeper understanding and reflection. A recent study [6] of the relationship between note-taking, review and student ability showed that students with high working memory capacity performed better in classes when they primarily listened during lectures and reviewed notes provided by the lecturer. These theories on note-taking and the somewhat surprising result lend credence to our intuitions. Providing better ways to capture the classroom experience can improve learning if students are encouraged to listen and engage in the lecture with confidence that notes will be provided afterwards.

Evaluation

Several of the research prototypes cited above have been subjected to some form of evaluation to determine both usability (do users find the system simple to use for the purpose it was designed) and usefulness (does the system enhance the user's ability to perform some task). The two most substantial evaluation studies have been conducted at PARC and Hewlett-Packard. For a two-year period at PARC, a suite of tools was used to support a process of intellectual property management [12,13]. At Hewlett-Packard, the Filochat system was evaluated in field and laboratory studies, generating both qualitative information on the reaction of users to the technology and also quantitative information comparing the accuracy, efficiency and confidence of Filochat with paper-based and dictaphone systems [19].

The evaluation in this paper is largely qualitative and based on 18 months use of various prototypes in actual courses. This paper reports experience from use in a dozen courses within the undergraduate and graduate Mathematics and Computer Science curriculum at Georgia Tech. During that time, we have administered questionnaires to students and teachers, tracked student usage of the system (both anonymously and with student identification) conducted ethnographic style interviews with some students, and observed videotapes of lectures. All of this data collection has been used to help us modify the capabilities of the system based on user requests and to help us better understand over time how the system is being used and why. It is unwise to conduct quantitative experiments to gauge the impact on specific learning outcomes prior to having such an understanding.

THE CLASSROOM 2000 SYSTEM

Fielding a ubiquitous computing system that is robust enough for everyday use in a classroom environment is a very challenging prospect. The engineering issues can easily outweigh the research challenges. Initially, the effort involved to support a single class was so great that we were only able to experiment with one class per quarter. Over time, we were able to streamline all features of the system to support many changes at a time. We have identified four separate phases of the system execution and built or bought tools to support those phases. The phases are briefly described below.

Pre-production

Before a lecture begins, some lecturers prepare a presentation as a series of slides or even Web pages. In this pre-production phase, we are very concerned with providing a simple way to reuse existing classroom material. Our electronic whiteboard supports the annotation of GIF images. We modified some public domain UNIX scripts to convert Postscript output to a series of GIF images that can then be loaded into our electronic whiteboard system. Recently released commercial applications, such as PowerPoint 97, have built-in conversion utilities that also allow for the creation of high-quality GIF images from presentation slides.

Live recording or capture phase

Once a lecture starts, we want to record as much information as possible. Since most teachers use some sort of blackboard or whiteboard during a lecture, we provide an electronic whiteboard to capture what is presented and written. We have written several whiteboard programs for pen-based computers, the latest of which is called ZenPad, a client-server Java system. The front-end client of ZenPad, shown in Figure 1, runs as a Java applet inside a Web browser. An earlier Visual Basic prototype whiteboard, ClassPad is discussed in [1]. ZenPad provides a very minimal interface that maximizes the actual screen surface for writing. Earlier prototypes provided more functionality to the end user, but those features were not

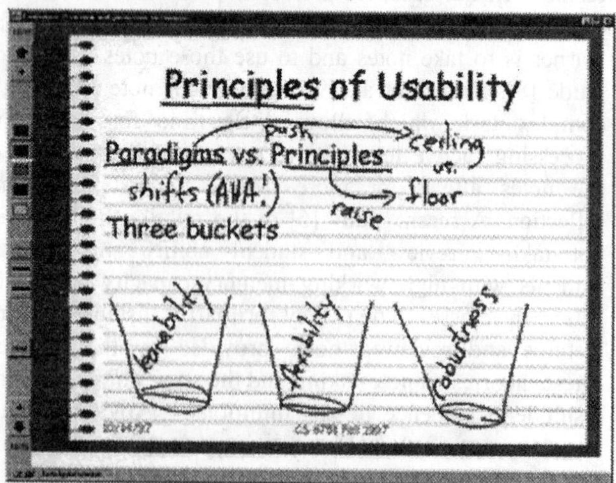

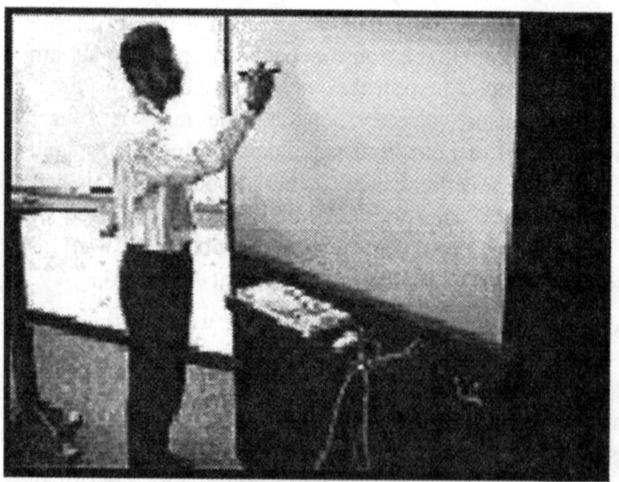

Figure 1 The ZenPad electronic whiteboard. On the left, we show prepared slides over which the teacher can write. On the right, we show ZenPad being used on a Liveboard in an actual class lecture.

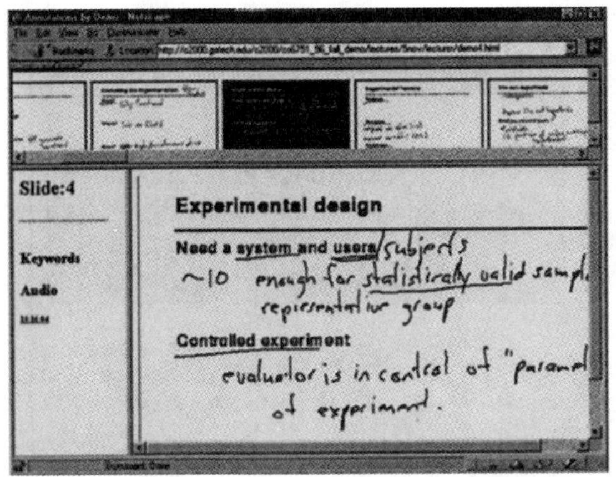

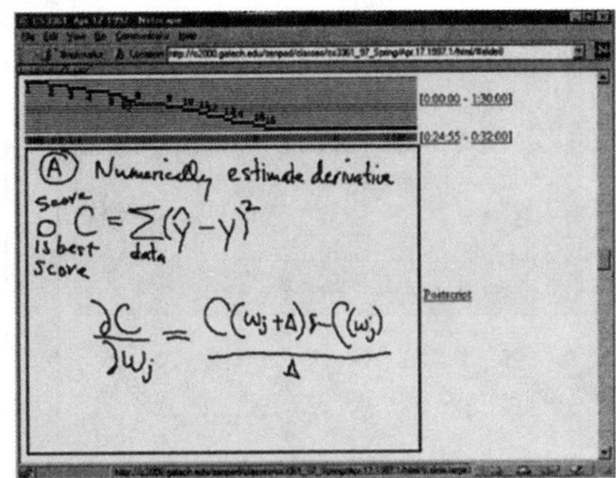

Figure 2 Sample access interfaces. The left-hand example shows thumbnail images to allow for quick browsing of all slides. Selecting a particular thumbnail brings up that. To the left of the magnified slide are links that will pull up an audio player (RealAudio) at the time the selected slide was visited during the lecture. The sample interface on the right presents a continuous scrollable display of all slides in the lecture. Clicking on any text cues the audio player to begin playing at the time that stroke was generated. Above the slide are two navigation bars. The topmost bar is a timeline for the entire lecture and enables the user to jump to various slides and see how much time in the class was spent on that slide. Underneath that timeline bar is an expanded view of the current slide. This navigation bar provides one-minute indexes into the audio stream and also shows when the slide was written upon.

used very much and subtracted from the all-important screen real estate teachers wanted for a writing surface.

Our electronic whiteboards provide two features that were lacking in commercial counterparts we investigated. First, the artifacts that are produced are easily distributed via the Web. Second, our electronic whiteboards keep information about when various activities occur. For example, we know when a lecture began, when slides were displayed and when every single penstroke was created. This information is critical for the integration of the teacher's lecture material with the audio or other streams of information that are recorded during class.

The teachers we supported had lecturing styles that required two different presentation styles. Teachers with prepared slides wanted to have ZenPad move slide by slide through the lecture with the ability to display a slide and annotate on top of the slide. Other teachers simply wanted ZenPad to provide a continuous scrollable blank writing surface upon which the entire lecture could be handwritten.

The audio track for the lecture is recorded both to a high fidelity DAT tape for later analysis and backup and to a lower fidelity digital streaming format for later delivery over the Web.

Post-production or integration

Once class is complete, there is some work necessary to provide for the integration between the captured electronic whiteboard activity and the audio stream of the class. One of the critical concerns here is the granularity of integration between handwritten notes and the audio stream, which we discuss later. There is also some post-production work necessary to produce a Web-based interface that makes it easy for the students to access the augmented notes from a class home page. This Web-based interface is the subject of the access phase.

Access

In the access phase, students and teachers are provided a Web interface to browse past lectures. As we mentioned before, the ZenPad system provides a browse-only mode that is suitable for this purpose, but we have also produced a number of HTML interfaces. Figure 2 shows two examples of interfaces we have used. In all cases, there is the ability to jump from the displayed lecture material to the audio for that lecture. Different prototypes provided different indexing capabilities. For example, the interface on the left of Figure 2 allowed the student to index into the audio at time points defined by when slides were visited. In browse mode, ZenPad allows indexing down to every penstroke. The interface on the right side of Figure 2 provides a granularity roughly at the word level.

SUMMARIZING OUR EXPERIENCE

One of our major goals is to demonstrate by example that applications research in ubiquitous computing must proceed by putting large-scale systems into everyday use so that their impact can be observed. This section will summarize our observations on the use and impact of Classroom 2000.

The observations discussed in this section are the result of a number of different evaluation techniques. Student reactions to Classroom 2000 have been obtained through

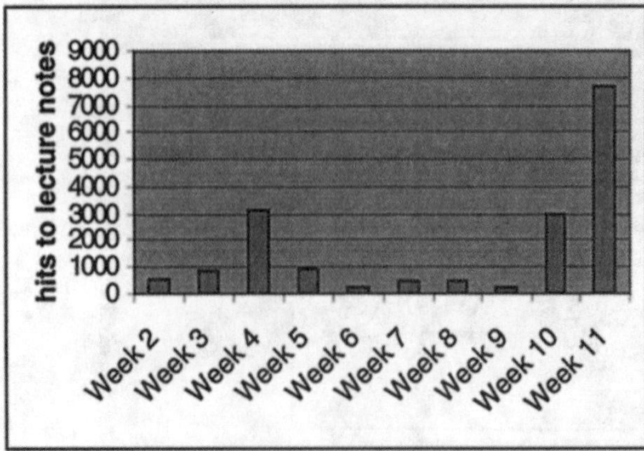

Figure 3 Student requests for lecture notes. Data covers 5 courses taught in Spring 1997.

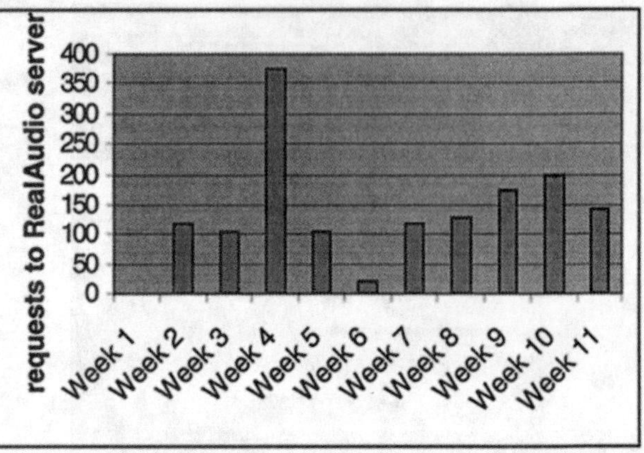

Figure 4 Student requests for audio integrated with lecture notes for the same 5 courses.

post-course questionnaires, videotaped interviews, and access logs to course material. Teacher reactions were obtained via interviews, questionnaires and analysis of videotaped lectures. All of the data we present was taken from students and instructors for the Spring Quarter, 1997.

Student usage and reactions

Analysis of Web logs to class material is somewhat tricky, since course notes were usually publicly available. To provide better quality data without sacrificing anonymity of the students, we restricted our analysis to IP addresses within our university sub-domain and eliminated obvious non-student addresses. We were interested in seeing how often students accessed the lecture notes. Five courses were supported in the Spring Quarter of 1997. Three undergraduate courses in Calculus, Artificial Intelligence, and Software Engineering had average enrollment of 45 students and 2 graduate courses in Computer Vision and Machine Learning had average enrollment of 15. 89% of all students attempted to access the on-line lecture materials, with 78% reporting that they were successful in accessing the notes and 49% reporting success in accessing audio. One entire class received inadequate training for accessing notes, so our results are negatively skewed. As we had suspected, access to lecture notes showed dramatic peaks in the few days preceding exams (usually a midterm in the fourth week of term and/or a final exam during week 10 or 11). Figure 3 shows the number of requests for lecture material by week for all five classes over the quarter.

Figure 4 shows student requests for audio. The profile is similar to the general Web access, but we observe that audio requests are approximately an order of magnitude less frequent. When asked for reasons why they accessed the on-line lecture notes, student responses were (out of 165 respondents):

- 27% to catch up on a missed lecture
- 14% to answer questions from own written notes
- 14% to help in doing homework assignments
- 36% to study for exams
- 9% other

70% of the students did not feel that the availability of captured lecture materials encouraged them to miss class. 78% felt that the technology in Classroom 2000 made the classroom experience more engaging or interesting. 58% responded that their note-taking practices changed during the quarter. 17 students explicitly stated that they stopped taking notes because of the availability of the notes after class and 30 stated that they could spend more time listening to and understanding the lecture instead of writing down notes. When asked if their study habits changed, 18 students said they had stopped relying on their own notes in favor of the captured notes. Despite this favorable reaction to the availability of captured lecture notes, 70% of the students did not feel strongly that their performance in the class improved as a result.

Usage patterns by lecturers

65% of the students felt that the technology in the classroom did change the way the instructor taught and only 8% thought that this change was for the worse. But how did the teachers react to the automatic capture of their lectures? We observed videotapes of 5 different teachers and surveyed the teachers to get some of their general impressions.

The teachers had one of two lecturing styles when using the electronic whiteboard. Two lectured with prepared slides and three simply used a blank whiteboard. One of the teachers would have liked to use prepared slides on occasion, but felt that the process of creating slides in PowerPoint involved too much effort.

All of the lecturers felt that the capture of their lecture materials was a valuable service that outweighed the negative features of the ZenPad system, described below.

All of the teachers agree that the size of the whiteboard was too small. The electronic whiteboard has a 67-inch diagonal screen that is suitable for use in a small conference room but at least one-third the size of a traditional whiteboard in a classroom that seats 50 students. Teachers felt unable to write as much on the electronic whiteboard as desired in an effort to conserve screen real estate. Several of the lecturers were tied to the electronic whiteboard and very much limited their movement and student interaction to a small portion of the classroom. A larger surface might remove that tendency.

Other negative reactions were to the overall speed and lack of naturalness to the electronic whiteboard. Loading pages would take anywhere from 2-5 seconds. This caused awkward pauses during a lecture and discouraged navigation back and forth through the lecture. Erasing was clumsy enough that most teachers preferred instead to cross out mistakes. Some of the teachers felt that a larger electronic whiteboard that displayed the recent history of a lecture would alleviate some of their frustration with navigation. Despite this overall clumsiness of the interface, we only noticed one teacher actually falling back to the regular whiteboard in the room. The confinement of the teacher coupled with the inability to easily navigate within the lecture could help explain why some students thought that the technology worsened the way the instructor taught.

Three of the teachers regularly used the electronic whiteboard to run programs other than ZenPad. The most common use was to pull up a Web browser. Though they were pleased to be able to do this, they were disappointed when that part of the class was not captured for students to see later.

We were interested in the relationship between what a lecturer said and what was written on the electronic whiteboard. Since timestamps on the penstrokes were the basis for integrating the notes and audio, it matters how synchronized those two streams actually are. There was no general trend to report across all teachers, but individuals were fairly consistent across lectures in how their writing synchronized with what they said. Two of the teachers (both teaching mathematical subjects) would speak as they wrote, so individual penstrokes were fairly closely aligned with the audio stream. One lecturer consistently verbalized an idea and then summarized it on the electronic whiteboard, usually without saying a word. Others would write something and then talk about it afterwards. The middle strategy will cause an index to overshoot the relevant audio, causing possible confusion for the listener.

The most experienced user of ZenPad was also the one whose lecturing style was most modified. This teacher said that he felt much more like a scribe on behalf of the class, and would frequently write marks on the board to assist students during the access phase. He even told the students that he was doing this to assist them. This teacher also had the practice of writing down student questions on the board, a practice he admitted he never did before using ZenPad.

Teachers said they were conscious that they were being recorded. While they did not feel this changed the way they taught, two noted that they were more reserved with their language.

ISSUES WITH CAPTURE, INTEGRATION AND ACCESS

In addition to gaining a better insight into how students and teachers have come to use our technology, we have identified some important issues for further consideration.

Capture

The electronic whiteboard must provide a larger interactive surface. As a result, we have built a prototype system that partners the highly interactive surface of the electronic whiteboard with a number of additional projected displays. We are using this system now to determine if it alleviates any of the problems of the smaller system. Though our solution provides a larger persistent display of lecture notes, the lack of interactivity may still be a source of frustration for some instructors.

We have spent a lot of time automating post-production activities at the expense of attending to the start-up activities for a class. Our solution has been to provide human support at the beginning of lectures. This problem is exacerbated by our desire to record more and more streams of information in the class, all with appropriate backup. Every new stream of information captured (e.g., video, other programs) requires another human to kick-start the recording to ensure that all streams are properly synchronized. There must be a better way!

Despite this synchronization problem, it is very desirable to capture additional streams of activity in the classroom. One immediate goal is to use video in addition to audio. Teachers quickly started to take advantage of the large screen networked computer to pull up information on the Web during class or to demonstrate other software. We have modified the system now to capture Web browsing activity and it is being used to great advantage in current courses.

Integration

There are three issues with integration. The first issue has to do with the granularity of time-based integration. What kind of control should we provide for linking lecture material to the audio stream? Our initial prototype, shown on the left side of Figure 2, offered resolution to an individual slide. If a teacher visited a slide repeatedly during a lecture, each visit would create another index into the audio stream. We felt this was too coarse because an instructor can spend many minutes on a slide. Having the ability to link only to the beginning of a slide forces the student to guess when ink was written. In ZenPad a link to the audio stream is created for every penstroke (defined as a pen down to pen up sequence). Our experience has shown that this strategy is too fine- students have to click on the first stroke of a sentence (as opposed to anywhere in the sentence or word) to hear the audio for that sentence. The interface shown on the right of Figure 2 uses a simple time and space clustering heuristic to group related penstrokes together. In addition, we have provided an interactive timeline that allows access to the audio without relying on a penstroke. This latter strategy is especially useful for lecturers who don't write that much.

Our integration scheme has been driven by a single stream, the teacher's writing. Other streams of information can also be used to provide more content-based integration. For example, we would like to use keywords to search the audio stream. We have built a prototype system that converts a high-quality audio stream to a searchable sequence of phonemes. We will use this to decorate a lecture timeline with occurrences of teacher-supplied keywords. We can also provide arbitrary, student-generated keyword searches within and across lectures.

Other streams can also be analyzed to support content-based integration. We can analyze video to detect gestures that associate what is going on in the class with some material being presented. It is often important to know what the focus of the class is at any point in time. The behavior of the teacher can be analyzed to determine which of a number of streams is the focus of discussion. Students themselves can produce actions which index into the classroom experience. Imagine a simple switch that a student controls that would indicate important points during the lecture. We have built such a "switch" using a Pilot PDA as the input device. We intend to experiment with these alternative integration strategies in the near future and report on their effectiveness.

Access

One of the most important requirements of Classroom 2000 is that it produces universally accessible lecture material. An elaborate integration mechanism to facilitate content-based search is useless if students cannot execute it when and where they study. If students don't use a feature because they cannot get it to work, then our observations on use are tainted. Many of our system design compromises directly reflect this requirement. For example, all multimedia playback facilities must be cross-platform with reasonable performance over a 28.8 Kbaud modem connection.

This same requirement has caused compromises in the programming language we use to present information to the student reviewer. We use the Web as the delivery infrastructure, and we want to use Java as a cross-platform language to develop highly interactive access capabilities. Unfortunately, commercial browsers that support Java do not do a very good job yet, so we have had to relax our desire to use Java exclusively. Our most reliable access interface consists of inline GIF images with client-side image maps written in HTML. Our long-term strategy lies beyond the capabilities of HTML, as we will demonstrate.

Several students requested a playback feature in which the audio actually drives an animation of the lecturer's notes. This feature would make it easier to follow a lecture while listening to the audio. In general, we need to provide better ways to visualize the entire contents of a stream to facilitate searching. Being able to quickly scroll through thumbnail images can help to locate a section of the lecture of interest.

We have experimented with students taking their own personal notes with a tablet-sized electronic notebook. Some simple controlled experiments reported in [1] indicated that the individual notebooks were ineffective, so we stopped. It is still a goal, however, to allow students to produce private notes that are integrated with the public notes created by the lecturer. We want to provide a way to protect a student's privacy while also allowing them to share their personal notes with others as they see fit.

It is a serious restriction that captured notes are immutable. Students often want to review a lecture and write summaries or otherwise modify their notes taken during class. For one class, we provided an interface that allowed students to edit their own private copy of notes from a lecture. We sacrificed this feature when scaling up to support multiple classes, but we will soon re-introduce it.

Other issues

We are well on our way to satisfying the research goal of demonstrating how to do applications research in ubiquitous computing. There are further issues of scale that we must still address. As Classroom 2000 expands from a single room to an entire campus and from isolated classes to an entire curriculum, we will face grand challenges in system design and information retrieval.

As our understanding of the actual use of capture, integration and access in education increases, we will be able to address our other goal related to assessing the impact on teaching and learning practices. In the coming years, we will be able to conduct long-term studies to measure the effectiveness of our approach and observe how teaching and learning practices evolve to suit the capabilities of ubiquitous computing technology.

CONCLUSION

We have defined the general problem of capture, integration and access for ubiquitous computing and demonstrated its application in a large-scale educational application to support university lecturing. The goal of Classroom 2000 is to determine what positive impact ubiquitous computing can have on teaching and learning. Before we can make any solid assessment of the new technology, however, we must first understand how it is used in large-scale, everyday practice. This presents significant engineering challenges that any ubiquitous computing researcher must face.

We have succeeded in implementing an environment that provides a reasonable amount of automation to record a classroom experience. Eighteen months of everyday use has fed an iterative development cycle. Our observations show that students have come to depend on captured lecture material and have reduced their in-class note-taking and increased the effort to listen and participate in the classroom experience. With this favorable result, we are encouraged to begin deeper assessment studies of the impact of capture, integration and access on teaching and learning objectives.

ACKNOWLEDGMENTS

Johan LeMon and Tommy Enqvist are visiting students to the GVU Center from the Royal Institute of Technology in Stockholm, Sweden. The authors would like to thank the many members of the Future Computing Environments Group at Georgia Tech for their support. Dr. Abowd's work on Classroom 2000 is supported by a National Science Foundation CAREER grant #IRI-9703384. More information about Classroom 2000 can be found at http://www.cc.gatech.edu/fce/c2000.

REFERENCES

1. Abowd, G.D., et al. Teaching and learning as multimedia authoring: The Classroom 2000 project. In the proceedings of *Multimedia'96*, November, 1996.
2. Abowd, G.D.. Ubiquitous computing: Research themes and open issues in from an applications perspective. Georgia Institute of Technology, GVU Center Technical Report GIT-GVU-96-24. September 1996.
3. Degen, L., R. Mander and G. Salomon. Working with audio: Integrating personal tape recorders and desktop computers. In the proceedings of *CHI'92,* pp. 413-418, May 1992.
4. Elrod, S. et al. Liveboard: A large interactive display supporting group meetings, presentations and remote collaboration. In the proceedings of *CHI'92*, pp. 599-607, May 1992.
5. Fowler, J., D. Baker, R. Dargahi, V. Kouranajian, H. Gilson, K. Brook Long, C. Petermann and G. Gorry. Experience with the virtual notebook system: Abstraction in hypertext. In the proceedings of *CWCW'94*, pp. 133-143, November 1994.
6. Hadwin, A. F., J. R. Kirby and R. A. Woodhouse. Individual differences in note-taking summarization and learning from lectures. To appear in the *Journal of Contemporary Educational Psychology*, 1997.
7. Hindus, D and C. Schmandt. Ubiquitous audio: Capturing spontaneous collaboration. In the proceedings of *CSCW'92*, pp. 210-217, November 1992.
8. Kiewra, K. A. Investigating note taking and review: A depth of processing alternative. *Education Psychologist*, **20**:23-32, 1985.
9. Kiewra, K. A. et al. Effects of repetition on recall and note-taking: Strategies for learning from lectures. *Journal of Educational Psychology*, **83**:120-123, 1991.
10. Lai, M.-C., B.-H. Chen and S.-M. Yuan. Toward a new educational environment. In the proceedings of *The International World Wide Web Conference WWW'4*, December 1995.
11. Minneman, S. et al. A confederation of tools for capturing and accessing collaborative activity. In proceedings of *Multimedia'95*, pp. 523-534, November 1995.
12. Moran, T. et al. Evolutionary engagement in an ongoing collaborative work process: A case study. In proceedings of *CWCW'96*, November 1996.
13. Moran, T. et al. I'll get that off the audio: A case study of salvaging multimedia meeting records. In the proceedings of *CHI'97*, pp. 202-9, March 1997.
14. Schroeder, U., B Tritsch and A. Knierriem-Jasnoch. A modular training system for education in the WWW environment. In the proceedings of *The International World Wide Web Conference WWW'4*, December 1995..
15. Stifelman, L.J. Augmenting real-world objects: A paper-based audio notebook. In proceedings of *CHI'96*. Short paper, pp. 199-200, April 1996.
16. Weber, K. and A. Poon. A tool for real-time video logging. In the proceedings of *CHI'94*, pp. 58-64, April 1994.
17. Weiser, M. The computer of the 21st century. *Scientific American*, **265**(3):66-75, September 1991.
18. Weiser, M. Some computer science issues in ubiquitous computing. *Communications of the ACM*, **36**(7):75-84, July 1993.
19. Whittaker, S., P. Hyland and M. Wiley. Filochat: Handwritten notes provided access to recorded conversations. In the proceedings of *CHI'94*, pp. 271-7, April 1994.
20. Wilcox, L., B. Schilit and N. Sawhney. Dynomite: A dynamically organized ink and audio notebook. In the proceedings of *CHI'97*, pp. 186-193, March 1997.

Finding and Visualizing Inter-site Clan Graphs

Loren Terveen and Will Hill

AT&T Labs - Research
180 Park Avenue, P.O. Box 971
Florham Park, NJ 07932-0971 USA
+1 973 360 {8343, 8342}
{terveen, willhill}@research.att.com

ABSTRACT

For many purposes, the Web page is too small a unit of interaction. Users often want to interact with larger-scale entities, particularly collections of topically related items. We report three innovations that address this user need.

- We replaced the web page with the web *site* as the basic unit of interaction and analysis.
- We defined a new information structure, the *clan graph*, that groups together sets of related sites.
- We invented a new graph visualization, the *auditorium visualization*, that reveals important structural and content properties of sites within a clan graph.

We have discovered interesting information that can be extracted from the structure of a clan graph. We can identify structurally important sites with many incoming or outgoing links. Links between sites serve important functions: they often identify "front door" pages of sites, sometimes identify especially significant pages within a site, and occasionally contain informative anchor text.

KEYWORDS

Social filtering, collaborative filtering, information access, information retrieval, information visualization, human-computer interaction, computer supported cooperative work, social network analysis, co-citation analysis.

INTRODUCTION

Web search and navigation are two difficult problems that have received much attention, with search engines and indices like Yahoo being the most widespread solution attempts. However, users have larger and longer term information needs, in particular, how to manage lasting interest in a broad topic and to comprehend collections of multimedia documents pertaining to the topic.

CHI 98 Los Angeles CA USA
Copyright 1998 0-89791-975-0/98/ 4..$5.00

Our goal is to address these user needs. We replaced the Web page with the *site* — a structured collection of pages, a multimedia document — as the basic unit of interaction. A site is more appropriate for several reasons. (1) A site usually contains a coherent body of content on a given topic (e.g., song lyrics, episode guides for a TV show, current weather conditions), divided into pages to ease navigation and download time. Thus, users want to know what's available at a given site, not a single page. (2) Most hyperlinks *to* a site point to the "front door" page, while most links *from* a site come from the index page. Thus to analyze inter-site structure appropriately (which is our goal), we must correctly group pages into sites.

Second, we defined a new information structure, the *clan graph*, to represent collections of densely connected sites. The clan graph has clear intuitive motivation based on concepts from social network analysis, social filtering, and co-citation analysis. A clan graph is defined in terms of a user specified set of seed (example) sites and is constructed by following hypertext links from the seeds. It is easy for users to specify seeds, e.g., they may get them from their bookmarks file, from an index page they found on the web, or from a search engine. And the clan graph construction algorithm is tolerant of "noise" in the seeds: a few off-topic seeds will not affect the quality of the graph.

Third, to enable users to comprehend and manage the information we extract, we have developed the *auditorium visualization*, which communicates key information such as whether a site is structurally central or peripheral, whether a site is more of a content provider or index, important internal structure of a site, and how sites link together. Figure 4 (which we discuss in a later section) shows an example auditorium visualization.

Our system is implemented in Java. We have built and analyzed clan graphs for dozens of topics, performed some experiments to evaluate our algorithms, and iterated our interface design significantly in response to user feedback.

RELATED WORK: EXTRACTING AND VISUALIZING HIGH LEVEL STRUCTURES FROM THE WEB

Our work is most closely related to research that aims to raise the level of abstraction at which users interact with the

Web. Researchers have sought to define useful, higher-level structures that can be extracted from hypertext collections, such as "collections" [19], "localities" [17], "patches" or "books"[3]. This approach opens up four major avenues of innovation: definitions of new structures, algorithms to extract the structures, visualization techniques that enable users to comprehend the structures, and interface techniques that create a workspace in which it is easy to specify, modify, and experiment with the structures. We survey some leading projects in this area, then compare and contrast our approach.

Kleinberg [11] defines algorithms that identify *authoritative* and *hub* pages within a hypertext. Authorities and hubs are mutually dependent: a good authority is a page that is linked to by many hubs, and a good hub is one that links to many authorities. An equilibrium algorithm is used to identify hubs and authorities in a hypertext collection. For both Kleinberg and WebQuery [4], a collection consists of the results of a search query augmented with all pages that link to or are linked to by any page in the original set of results. WebQuery sorts pages into equivalence classes based on their total degree (number of other pages in the collection they are connected with), and displays the pages in a "bullseye" layout, a series of concentric circles each containing pages of equal degree. WebCutter [14] builds a collection of URLs based on text similarity metrics, then presents the results in tree, star, and fisheye views. twURL [22] organizes URLs into outlines based on properties such as server, domain, and number of incoming links.

Pitkow and Pirolli [19] report cluster algorithms based on co-citation analysis[7]. The intuition is that if two documents, say A and B, are both cited by a third document, this is evidence that A and B are related. The more often a pair of documents is co-cited, the stronger the relationship. They applied two algorithms to Georgia Tech's Graphic Visualization and Usability Center web site and were able to identify interesting clusters.

Card, Robertson, and York [3] describe the WebBook, which uses a book metaphor to group a collection of related web pages for viewing and interaction, and the WebForager, an interface that lets users view and manage multiple WebBooks. They also present a set of automatic methods for generating collections (WebBooks) of related pages, such as recursively following all relative links from a specified web page, following all (absolute) links from a page one level, extracting "book-like" structures by following "next" and "previous", and grouping pages returned from a search query.

Pirolli, Pitkow, and Rao [17] defined a set of functional roles that web pages can play, such as "head" (roughly the "front door" of a group of related pages), "index", and "content". They then developed an algorithm that used hyperlink structure, text similarity, and user access data to categorize pages into the various roles. They applied these algorithms to the Xerox web site and were able to categorize pages with good accuracy.

Mackinlay, Rao, and Card [13] developed a novel interface for accessing articles from a citation database. The central UI object is a "Butterfly", which represents one article, its references, and its citers. The interface makes it easy for users to browse from one article to a related one, group articles, and generate queries to retrieve articles that stand in a particular relationship to the current article.

Mukherjea et al [16] and Botafogo et al [2] report on algorithms for analyzing arbitrary networks, splitting them into structures (such as "pre-trees" or hierarchies) that are easier for users to visualize and navigate.

Other efforts propose novel ways to view and navigate information structures. The Navigational View Builder [15] combines structural and content analysis to support four viewing strategies: binding, clustering, filtering and hierarchization. Through the extensive use of single user operations on multiple windows, the Elastic Windows browser [10] provides efficient overview and sense of current location in information structures. Lamping et al [12] explored hyperbolic tree visualization of information structures. Furnas [6] presents a theory of how to create structures that are easy for users to navigate.

Somewhat less directly related are the SenseMaker [1] and Scatter/Gather [18] systems. SenseMaker supports users in the contextual evolution of their interest in a topic. The focus is on making it easy for users to view and manage the results of a query and to create new queries based on the existing context. Scatter/Gather supports the browsing of large collections of text, allowing users to iteratively reveal topic structure and locate desirable documents.

There are some similarities between these research efforts and ours. We are experimenting with a purely structural analysis, like [2, 4, 13, 19], although we concentrate on links between sites, not pages. We are interested in the functional roles a web page can play, like [11, 17]. As in [3], seed sites in our system serve as "growth sites" that form the basis for a particular type of "related reference query" [1] that retrieves a structure of related sites. Finally, like [3] we are interested in citations between documents.

Our work also has important differences. Most significantly, we must induce both the basic units, the sites, and the collections into which they are structured. Previous efforts either took the collection as a given (e.g., all the web pages rooted at a particular URL like www.xerox.com), offered methods for supporting users in creating collections, or defined the collection as an augmentation of the results of a search engine query. Card et al [3] do offer some automated techniques for creating collections, but the basic unit out of which their collections are built is a single web page. Thus, the resulting collections are more local than our clan graphs; in particular, some of them are more or less a single site. Through the use of multiple seed sites, our system benefits from a kind of "triangulation" effect when identifying new sites of interest. Another important difference is that the web consists of many ecologies of dynamic, evolving documents. Thus, mutual concurrent citation is possible, even normative, unlike with paper articles where lengthy publishing cycles makes it rare. (Note, however that if journals rather than articles are taken as the units for co-citation analysis, then by-year concurrent citation also is possible [7]). The clan graph is a new structure that generalizes the co-citation relationship, takes mutual citation and transitivity of citation into account, and draws on social filtering insights [5, 8, 21].

CLAN GRAPHS: CONCEPTS AND ALGORITHMS

A clan graph is a directed graph, where nodes represent content objects (such as documents) and edges represent a citation of or reference to the contents of the target node by the source node. Before we can describe how we construct and visualize clan graphs, we define our terms precisely.

Terminology

Universal Graph — the graph of all inter-document (e.g., inter-site) links in the information structure.

Topic Graph — A subgraph of the universal graph that contains sites on the same or similar topics. This is an ideal construct that can only be approximated, e.g., through analysis of structure or similarity of content.

Local Clan Graph — For a specified set of seed sites, this is the subgraph of the universal graph whose nodes are the seed sites or are "closely connected" to the seeds.

Observed Clan Graph — It is practically impossible to construct the entire local clan graph because:

- the web is huge: trying to fetch all the pages on a site and to follow all the links off a site takes a long time;
- the web is unreliable: some sites always are down.
- the web is constantly changing, so the universal and local graphs are moving targets.

Thus, the observed graph is the subgraph of the local graph that we observe when we attempt to construct the graph.

Local clan graph: a formal definition

Our goal is to find the local clan graph for a set of seed sites. Precisely what does it mean to be "closely connected" to the seeds in the local clan graph? We experimented with several definitions, but converged on a simple, appealing definition building on concepts from social network analysis [9, 20], co-citation analysis [7], and social filtering [5, 8, 21]:

- the NK local clan graph for a seed set S is {(v,e) | v is in an N-clan with at least K members of S}.

An N-clan[20] is a graph where (1) every node is connected to every other node by a path of length N or less, and (2) all of the connecting paths only go through nodes in the clan. We are interested primarily in 2-clans, that is, the 2K local clan graph. The clan graph is a key construct for us; we

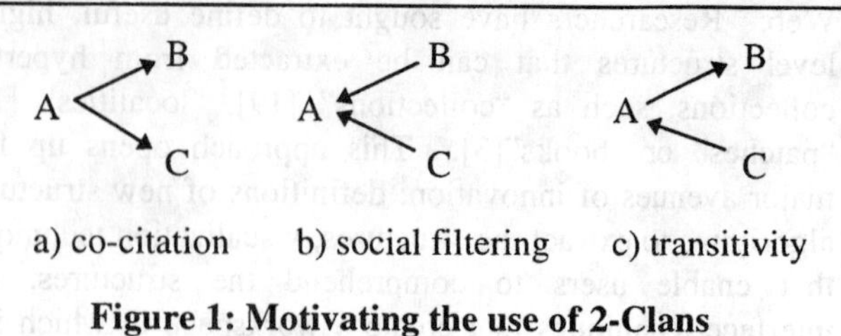

Figure 1: Motivating the use of 2-Clans

believe it productively formalizes notions like "collection" and "locality". We now attempt to justify this belief.

Why 2-clans? Figure 1 graphically depicts three types of inter-document relationships. In each case, an interesting relationship between two of the documents can be inferred based on a known relationship between the other two. Co-citation analysis (1a) says that documents B and C are related if A cites them both. Social filtering (1b) says that if documents B and C both refer to A, then B and C may be link to similar sorts of items in general, and thus deal with similar topics. Figure 1c shows a limited (2-edge) transitivity; we could interpret this as "if C is on a particular topic, and cites A, then A is likely to be on topic; and if A cites B, then B is likely (though somewhat less so) to be on the same topic."

These three relationships are the minimal 2-clans. They show why 2-clans are appropriate to represent topically related subgraphs of items in a larger graph. 2-clans are necessary because no smaller structures allow us to make inferences about document relatedness, and they are sufficient because no larger structure enables other simple inferences.

Notice that 2-clans are defined over undirected graphs: in other words, we take A and B as connected whether A links to B or vice versa. Again, we think this is appropriate. We have observed many sites that are topically central but that have only in-links (content sites) or out-links (index sites). A measure that required bi-directional paths between nodes would underrate some important sites. Therefore we first establish connectivity; subsequent analysis takes directionality into account in order to identify important structures like sinks and sources.

Finally, the 2-clan definition avoids the use of an arbitrary graph density parameter (density is the proportion of actual links in a graph to the maximum possible number of links): is a graph dense enough if its density is 0.2? 0.4? 0.5? ... ?

Why K seeds? By requiring that sites be related to a certain number of seeds, we ensure that we find not just dense graphs, but graphs in which a certain number of the seeds participate. Since we assume that the seeds (at least most of them) deal with a specific topic, this is a way to stay on topic. This is how we operationalize the "triangulation" effect we mentioned earlier. And making K larger is a simple way to get smaller, more tightly connected graphs. This usually means that the sites in the graph are more likely to be both on-topic and central to the topic. Of course, the optimal value of K depends in part on the number of seeds. For example, one almost certainly would want to pick a larger value of K for a seed set of size 20 than for one of size 5.

Constructing the observed clan graph

We designed a heuristic algorithm for constructing the observed graph. The algorithm is not guaranteed to produce the complete NK local clan graph; however, what it does produce always is a subgraph of the NK clan graph. In the next subsections, we discuss the role of the seed sites, sketch the algorithm and describe the scoring function for site selection, and discuss how sites are defined.

Input: the seed

The observed graph we obtain depends on the properties of the seed sites we start with. Our experience is that users are able to choose good seeds. Good seeds have three properties. First, the seed set must cohere: if the seed sites have few outgoing links or link to few of the same sites, the observed clan graph will be small or even empty (i.e., there is no N-clan that contains at least K seeds). This implies that the seeds do not participate in a significant dense subgraph within the universal graph. Second, the seeds must cover the topic: a poorly chosen seed set may lead to an observed graph that is a small subset of the topic subgraph. This can be the case if there are too few seeds, or the seeds are not well distributed across components in the topic graph. Finally, the seeds must be accurate: if some of the seeds are off-topic, then the clan graph may contain off-topic sites. However, if most of the seeds are on-topic, this is not a problem in practice. The parameter K plays an important role here: because any site added to the graph must be in a 2-clan with at least K seeds, as long as fewer than K off-topic sites are themselves related, sites they link to will not make it above this threshold.

The algorithm

We needed a type of web crawler, which fetches html pages, follows (some of the) links found on the pages and induces sites from pages. Sites that are linked-to are stored on a queue and become candidates for expansion (fetching and analysis). The major decision the algorithm must make is which sites from the queue to expand. Here is a sketch of the algorithm:

queue ← seed sites
while there is a queue element with a score above threshold **do**
  get the highest scored site from the queue
  expand this site
  add the expanded site to the observed graph
  merge new sites and links from the expanded site into the queue
  re-organize and re-score the sites on the queue
end

Scoring sites on the queue

We need a scoring metric that estimates the likelihood that a site on the queue is in the local graph with the seed sites, i.e., that it is in a 2-clan with at least K seeds. The metric must be efficient to compute, since it must be applied to each site on the queue, and the queue typically contains hundreds or thousands of sites.

We currently use the following scoring metric:

- score of site S = the number of seed sites that are linked to S by paths of length 2 or less.

This metric is cheap to compute. It also is a reasonable heuristic, since 2-clans are composed of 1 and 2-paths. Thus, if a site has a score of (say) 5, then it already is known to be in a 2-clan with 5 seeds. We are in the process of experimenting with and evaluating this heuristic and considering other heuristics at different points along the accuracy/efficiency continuum.

Sites

A site (multimedia document) is an organized collection of pages on a specific topic maintained by a single person or group. Sites have structure, with pages that play certain roles (front-door, table-of-contents, index). A site is not the same thing as a domain: for example, thousands of sites are hosted on www.geocities.com. And what counts as a site may be context dependent. For example, if one is taking a survey of research labs, www.media.mit.edu might well be considered a site, while if one is investigating social filtering projects, individual researchers' sites hosted on www.media.mit.edu are probably the proper units.

The last observation suggested a way to operationalize the definition of a site that suits our needs. When building a clan graph, the relevant known context is the set of URLs that have been linked to by the expanded sites. The intuition is that if sites in the clan graph link to two URLs, one of which is in a directory that contains the other, then they are likely to be from the same site[1]. More precisely:

- if url A has been linked to and url A/B has been linked to, then assume that A is the root page of the site and that A/B is an internal url.

This rule applies recursively, so the urls A/B/C, A/B, and A would be merged into a site with root page A and internal pages A/B and A/B/C.

This rule can fail — two URLs that belong to the same site will not be merged if no common ancestor in the directory structure (the "real" root page) has been linked to, and two URLs from distinct sites can be merged, (e.g., if there are links to two distinct sites hosted on www.geocities.com and to www.geocities.com itself). We are refining this rule with

[1] Notice that our notions of site and clan graph are interdependent: a site is defined in terms of links from within the graph, and the graph is constructed by following links from sites.

site-splitting heuristics based on the idea that when some "internal" pages are linked to significantly more often than is the (supposed) root page, then the heavily linked-to internal pages may be separate sites. And we are considering site-merging heuristics based on the idea that if (supposedly) distinct sites point to many of the same pages in the same domain, they may be part of the same site.

We also must decide whether a link from a page is within the site or to another site. We classify links based on their relationship to the root page of the site. If a link is contained within the directory that contains the root page, then we classify it as internal; otherwise, we classify it as a link to an external site. Internal links are added to a site-internal queue of candidate pages to be fetched.

Finally, we must specify how many pages to fetch from a site, i.e., what it means to expand the site,. The primary reason for fetching pages is to find links to other sites, which are the building blocks of the clan graph. For this purpose, finding a site's index page presumably would yield most or all such links, so we could stop expanding the site then. Indeed, we try to find index pages first by sorting pages on the site-internal queue by name, preferring pages whose names contain words like "links", "pages", "sites", "web", and "internet".

However, there is another reason to fetch pages, namely to build a profile that can be used to evaluate a site. Factors like site size (in pages) and amount of content (text, images, audio files) are important. The more pages we fetch, the more accurate a site profile we can create. Therefore, to serve both goals, we introduce a parameter P (default = 25) that controls how many pages to fetch from a site.

ANALYZING CLAN GRAPHS

After constructing a clan graph, we analyze it to extract additional structure to aid user comprehension. We first compute structural properties of sites; for each site, we tally the number of 2-clans it is a member of and the number of in and out links. Combining this structural information with site profile data like size (in pages) and the amount and type (text, audio files, images) of content makes it possible to distinguish "official" sites (for a TV show, for example), which tend to have lots of content and in-links and few or no out-links, from index sites, which tend to have little content and lots of out-links. Thus, users don't get stuck following links from one index site to another, never getting to the content that they really want.

We also identify internal pages of a site that multiple external sites have linked to. By providing direct access to these pages, we create "shortcuts" to places the topic community found worth endorsing. These can be considerable aids to navigation.

Finally, we analyze the text associated with the hyperlinks to each site. Much of the time the text is either the site title or a close variation. However, sometimes it is a useful alternative description of what the site is good for. We are experimenting with techniques to identify useful descriptions and use them in the interface.

VISUALIZING CLAN GRAPHS

The structure of clan graphs that we have observed in the web is complicated and not easy to visualize or understand. For example, figure 2 is a direct node/edge representation of the clan graph for the Television show "Roar" observed in August of 1997. The drawing was produced by a sophisticated graph layout tool, *dot*, which minimizes edge crossings, yet the drawing still is complicated. The clutter of edge crossings, edge angles and local node constellations divert visual attention to non-significant graphic elements. A viewer can identify some nodes of high and low degree, but the layout reveals no overall pattern. It is virtually impossible to visually discern central and peripheral sites.

Figure 2: Graph view with least edge crossings

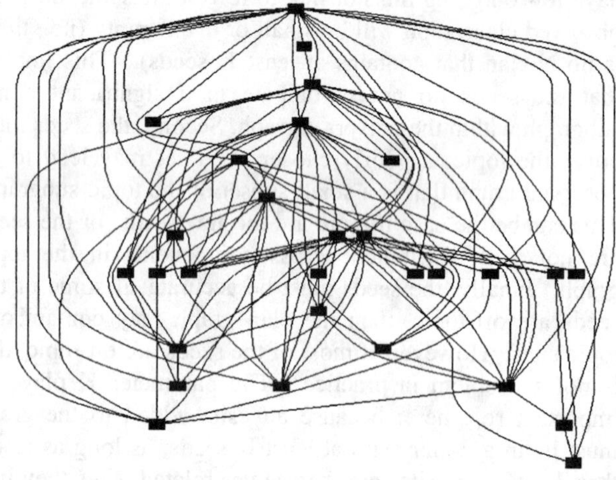

For the purpose of revealing node degree, simply collapsing the graph structure into a list of nodes ordered by degree is a better interface. The ordered list form of figure 3 makes it easy for users to compare node degree and check quantities. Note that the eighth site in the list ("Universal Studios") contains substructure, i.e., an internal page that was linked to by multiple sites. The list view is quick and easy to produce but still hides many important properties of sites and the graph. The list view is linear, so it easily communicates only one dimension. It is textual, so it cannot exploit graphical display properties, either images from the sites or the use of color, position, shape, etc. to communicate site properties. It is static, so there is no dynamic focusing, no hiding and revealing of structure.

We wanted users to see the results of our clan graph analysis in terms of the graph itself. These results include site centrality/peripherality, in-link to out-link ratio, patterns of inter-site links, and how sites rank in terms of properties such as size, number of images, audio and download files.

Figure 3: HTML view of clan graph

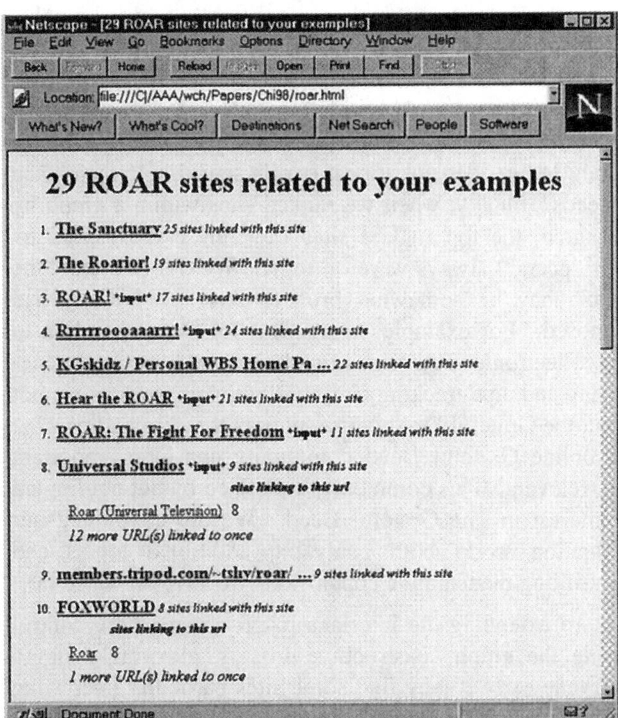

Figure 4: Auditorium view of clan graph

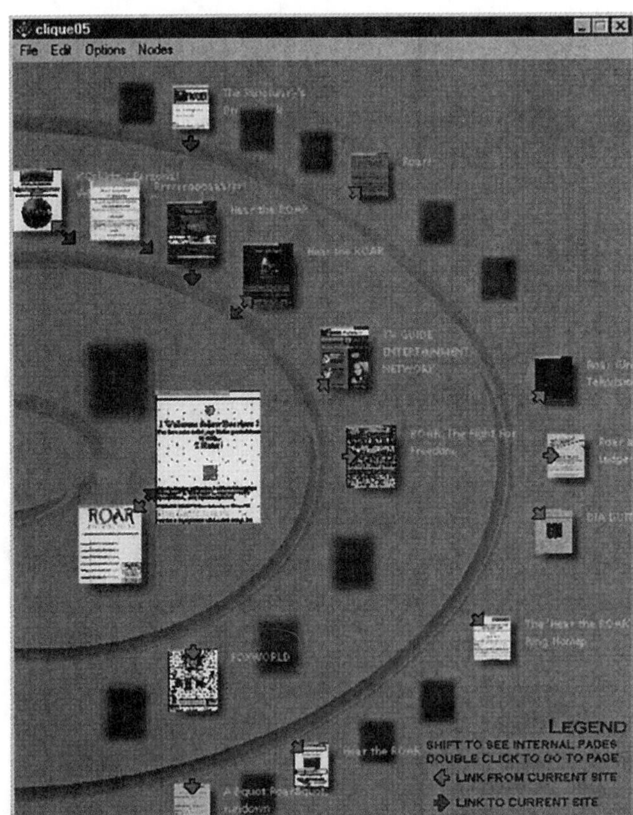

The Auditorium view: how it satisfies our design goals

To meet these goals, we have iterated cycles of design and usability testing, arriving at a design that we call the *auditorium seating visualization.* The metaphor is to the arrangement of seating in an auditorium: row upon row curved around a center stage. Figure 4 and color plate 1 show the auditorium seating visualization of the clan graph for the television show "Roar!". Thumbnails of site "front door" pages serve as iconic representations of sites. The auditorium seating visualization is dynamic. By moving the mouse over a site thumbnail, users switch from a general view of the graph to a view focused around the indicated site. Figure 4 shows the visualization in the site-focused mode. The thumbnail of the focused site is enlarged, and green "in" arrows and red "out" arrows appear on sites that the focused site is linked with. Other unlinked sites are blanked, but their drop shadows are left to note their positions. As the result of user experience with many design versions, we came to use a large number of techniques to communicate information necessary to satisfy user needs. We now discuss these in detail. Please refer to figure 4 or color plate 1 to identify the graphic elements discussed.

- *Concentric semi-circles* of sites group sites into equivalence classes from most to least important on some user-settable property. By default, sites are assigned to rows based on the number of in-links, so the closer to the center a site is, the more of its "peer sites" have linked to it.

- *Dynamic ordering within semi-circles.* Our original design used concentric circles instead of semi-circles. However, user feedback showed the desirability of ordering sites within each row, and while circles "wrap around", the properties important for ordering (such as number of in or out links and amount of content) do not. Semi-circles, on the other hand, with their definite end points, were suitable for our purpose.

  An important distinction users made was between index sites and content sites. Allowing dynamic ordering of sites within a row by properties like number and proportion of in and out links, and amount of content (audio files, images, or all types of content) makes these distinctions apparent. By default, we order sites within rows by the amount of content, so sites with lots of content appear at the top of each row.

- *Graded colored bands* aid in interpreting the values of the within-row ordering property of sites. Bands are graded from bright red to bright green, with the color break occurring at the median value of the ordering property. For example, if sites are ordered by the proportion of in links to out links, the break point is a visual cutoff between sites that serve more as indices and sites that serve more as content repositories.

- *Hiding graph spaghetti* — We wanted to reveal the fine structure of inter-site links without producing visual spaghetti as in figure 2. Users typically focused either on all the links from or to a single site or traced the edge between two sites. We designed to support those two visual tasks while removing as many distracting visual elements as possible. We did this with "one-site at a time" dynamic presentation of graph structure. Users move the mouse cursor over a site to focus on it, and only links from or to the focused site are shown. To further reduce clutter, we do not draw complete links between sites, since they draw too much user attention to uninformative crossings and edge angles. Instead, we represent links with small in and out arrows.

- *Linked views* The auditorium view is linked to a web browser; clicking on a thumbnail drives the browser to that web site.
- *Progressive revelation* of greater detail. While a site is in focus, holding down the shift key reveals any internal pages of that site that are linked to by other sites. These are pages that the author of the linking site found worthy of special attention. The link text often is more informative in these cases
- *Thumbnail representations* reveal quite a bit of information about sites. Overall design and color scheme can be seen. Ratio of text to graphics on the front door page tells users something about what to expect from a site. Saturated color, positioning and shape of banner ads reveal their presence in thumbnails. If a user has browsed a site previously, a thumbnail usually is sufficient to identify the site.

Early user testing highlighted for us the necessity of relevance feedback, leading to construction of a new observed clan graph. Users can judge sites as on-topic (good) or off-topic (bad). On-topic sites are added to the original seed set, and off-topic sites are added to a stop list. Thus, users can nudge the graph into a somewhat different area, moving it closer to the ideal topic they have in mind.

FUTURE WORK: EVALUATION AND DEPLOYMENT

We must verify experimentally that the NK local clan graph is a useful construct. A graph should contain mostly on-topic sites, and the quality of the graph should not be too dependent on precisely which sites are selected as seeds. Our informal inspections of dozens of graphs show these conditions to be satisfied, but clearly we need more systematic evaluation. To that end, we did a pilot study on the topic of the rock group The Grateful Dead. We used 63 URLs obtained from Yahoo as a starting point for our experiment. We randomly divided these URLs into sets of size 5, 10, and 20. We used these as seed sets for our clan graph construction algorithm, also experimenting with different values of K. Analysis of the results so far has confirmed some of our intuitions. First, larger seed sets (size 10 or 20) tend to result in graphs that better cover a topic than do smaller seed sets (size 5). Since the Web contains many index pages, it is easy to obtain a sufficient number of seeds on many topics. Second, increasing the parameter K results in smaller, more tightly focused graphs, while decreasing K leads to larger, but perhaps not as accurate graphs. Third, sites with large numbers of in-links almost always are discovered by the clan construction algorithm regardless of the sites in the seed set. Therefore, the algorithm does not appear overly sensitive to the choice of seeds. Finally, when we ranked sites within a graph by in-degree, the top ranked sites (i.e., those most cited by their "peers") always were on-topic. We did find that "the topic" may be somewhat broader than we initially had supposed. For example, many Grateful Dead sites link to The Electronic Frontier Foundation and various tape-trading and tape-tracking sites. Although these sites are not about the Grateful Dead per se, clearly they are part of what the online Grateful Dead community considers important and relevant. This community is defined by but not limited to interest in The Grateful Dead. We are continuing our evaluation work, both analyzing additional topics and quantifying the tentative conclusions we have drawn so far.

We are extending the interface to give users more control during the graph construction process, allowing them to intervene early if they find some sites particular interesting (or not), thus influencing subsequent sites that are added to the graph. We also are considering methods to scale our visualization. Currently, it can handle around 35-40 sites. We would like to scale it up to at least 100 sites and are confident that techniques like fisheye views and zooming will get us there. Finally, one of our colleagues, Brian Amento, is preparing to carry out formal user studies of the auditorium visualization and a dynamic text-table interface to the same data (i.e., a clan graph). We are seeking experimental evidence of the utility of the clan graph information structure and the relative utility and usability of the auditorium visualization and the best dynamic textual interface we can design.

Finally, we are making our system robust enough for widespread use. We will first open it up for use within our laboratory. After any fixes and enhancements this leads to, we intend to distribute the system freely, thus enabling anyone to create collections of online documents on topics they are interested in. We will put up a server where people can publish and retrieve collections. It is our hypothesis that relatively few people will choose to build collections, but many will want to view and interact with collections someone else has built. By distributing our software and maintaining a server, we will be able to test this hypothesis, and, in general, to investigate the social nature and social roles of communities that organize their interests around online information resources.

CONCLUSIONS

The goal of the work reported here is to help people find and manage collections of documents related to topics they care about. We offer a novel information structure, the clan graph, to formalize the notion of a topically related collection of interlinked documents. We present an algorithm to construct a clan graph from a set of seed documents. The algorithm also tackles the hard problem "what is an online document?": it aggregates individual web pages (URLs) into sites (multimedia documents) based on the context of links from other documents. Finally, we introduce and illustrate the auditorium visualization. It gives a graphical overview of the most important several dozen sites for a topic, lets users explore structural relationships between sites and the internal structure of individual sites, and allows dynamic sorting to aid users in understanding the structural role a site plays within the community of related sites. We are moving from informal to formal evaluations of both our algorithms and interface and are making our implementation robust enough to be freely distributed and used.

ACKNOWLEDGMENTS

We thank Brian Amento, Josh Creter and Peter Ju for their system implementation work. We also thank Harley Manning, Steve Whittaker, Lynn Cherny, and Julia Hirschberg for many useful design discussions.

REFERENCES

1. Baldonado, M.Q.W., and Winograd, T. An Information-Exploration Interface Supporting the Contextual Evolution of a User's Interests, in *Proceedings of CHI'97* (Atlanta GA, March 1997), ACM Press, 11-18.
2. Botafogo, R.A., Rivlin, E., and Shneiderman, B. Structural Analysis of Hypertexts: Identifying Hierarchies and Useful Metrics. *ACM Transactions on Information Systems 10, 2*, 142-180.
3. Card, S.K., Robertson, G.C., and York, W. The WebBook and the Web Forager: An Information Workspace for the World-Wide Web, in *Proceedings of CHI'96* (Vancouver BC, April 1996), ACM Press, 111-117.
4. Carrière, J., and Kazman R. WebQuery: Searching and Visualizing the Web through Connectivity, in *Proceedings of WWW6* (Santa Clara CA, April 1997).
5. *Communications of the ACM,* Special issue on Recommender Systems, 40, 3 (March 1997). Resnick, P., and Varian, H.R., guest editors.
6. Furnas, G.W. Effective View Navigation, in *Proceedings of CHI'97* (Atlanta GA, March 1997), ACM Press, 367-374.
7. Garfield, E. *Citation Indexing*. ISI Press, Philadelphia, PA, 1979.
8. Hill, W.C., Stead, L., Rosenstein, M. and Furnas, G. Recommending and Evaluating Choices in a Virtual Community of Use, in *Proceedings of CHI'95* (Denver CO, May 1995), ACM Press, 194-201.
9. Jackson, M.H. Assessing the Structure of Communication on the World Wide Web. *Journal of Computer-Mediated Communication , 3, 1*, June 1997
10. Kandogan, E., and Shneiderman, B. Elastic Windows: A Hierarchical Multi-Window World-Wide Web Browser, in *Proceedings of UIST'97* (forthcoming), preprint at http://www.cs.umd.edu/users/kandogan/papers/uist97/paper.html
11. Kleinberg, J.M. Authoritative Sources in a Hyperlinked Environment, in *Proceedings of 1998 ACM-SIAM Symposium on Discrete Algorithms* (forthcoming).
12. Lamping, J., Rao, R., and Pirolli, P. A Focus + Context Technique Based on Hyperbolic Geometry for Visualizing Large Hierarchies, in *Proceedings of CHI'95* (Denver CO, May 1995), ACM Press, 401-408.
13. Mackinlay, J.D., Rao, R., and Card, S.K. An Organic User Interface for Searching Citation Links, in *Proceedings of CHI'95* (Denver CO, May 1995), ACM Press, 67-73.
14. Maarek Y.S., Jacovi, M., Shtalhaim, M., Ur, S., Zernik, D., and Ben Shaul, I.Z. WebCutter: A System for Dynamic and Tailorable Site Mapping, in *Proceedings of WWW6* (Santa Clara CA, April 1997).
15. Mukherjea, S., and Foley, J. D. Visualizing the World-Wide Web with the navigational view finder. *Computer Networks and ISDN Systems 27, 1*, (1995), 1075-1087.
16. Mukherjea, S., Foley, J.D., and Hudson, S. Visualizing Complex Hypermedia Networks through Multiple Hierarchical Views, in *Proceedings of CHI'95* (Denver CO, May 1995), ACM Press, 331-337.
17. Pirolli, P., Pitkow, J., and Rao, R. Silk from a Sow's Ear: Extracting Usable Structures from the Web, in *Proceedings of CHI'96* (Vancouver BC, April 1996), ACM Press, 118-125.
18. Pirolli, P., Schank, P., Hearst, M., and Diehl, Scatter/Gather Browsing Communicates the Topic Structure of a Very Large Text Collection, in *Proceedings of CHI'96* (Vancouver BC, April 1996), ACM Press, 213-220.
19. Pitkow, J., and Pirolli, P. Life, Death, and Lawfulness on the Electronic Frontier, in *Proceedings of CHI'97* (Atlanta GA, March 1997), ACM Press, 383-390.
20. Scott, J. *Social Network Analysis: A Handbook.* SAGE Publications, London, 1991.
21. Terveen, L.G., Hill, W.C., Amento, B., McDonald, D., and Creter, J. Building Task-Specific Interfaces to High Volume Conversational Data, in *Proceedings of CHI'97* (Atlanta GA, March 1997), ACM Press, 226-233.
22. *What is twUrl?* http://www.roir.com/whatis.htm

Effects of Interfaces for Annotation on Communication in a Collaborative Task

Patricia G. Wojahn
Robert Morris College
Coraopolis, PA 15108 USA
+1 412 262 8666
pw1u+@andrew.cmu.edu

Christine M. Neuwirth
Carnegie Mellon University
Pittsburgh, PA 15213 USA
+1 412 268 8702
cmn@andrew.cmu.edu

Barbara Bullock
Wright State University
Fairborn, OH 45435 USA
+1 512 767 2036
bbullock@desire.wright.edu

ABSTRACT

Various interfaces exist for annotations. Little is known, however, about how such interface variations affect communication. We designed an annotation interface intended to facilitate annotation and undertook a study to compare this interface to two commonly used alternatives. Results support the hypothesis that annotation interfaces affect the number and types of problems about which collaborators communicate. Results also suggest the need for more research on interface effects within other communicative contexts.

Keywords

Annotations, display format, interface design, computer-mediated communication, computer-supported cooperative work, collaborative writing

INTRODUCTION

When people attempt to arrive at a "common understanding of what they want to say and how they want to say it" [12], communication difficulties seem inevitable--especially when these attempts occur at a distance and on-line. In the latter case, human-computer interaction can influence human-human interaction, particularly in group efforts involving the creation of shared documents and other artifacts [7]. Difficulties can occur as group members attempt to coordinate disparate and sometimes conflicting ideas and actions; share distributed knowledge; guide distributed work toward a shared goal; or represent and use "knowledge about beliefs, actions, plans [and] goals" [1]. Overcoming these difficulties is in large part contingent upon effective communication, which, in turn, depends on the technology affordances of the communication medium. Affordances, or "properties of the world that are compatible with and relevant for people's interactions" [8], affect communication outcomes.

An important area in computer support for cooperative work concerns affordances for communication about collaboratively produced artifacts such as documents, graphics, and other objects. A common communication practice is to make "annotations"--critical or explanatory notes added to the artifact. Despite the fact that practices such as passing drafts and annotating them are widespread, even among those who work in the same office building or department [6, 12], little is known about the effects of the interfaces that are being used to support such work. Previous research that has been done, however, demonstrates that interfaces can have marked effects on the amount and nature of communication in work groups. For instance, the use of voice annotations vs. keyboarded annotations affects both production and reception in the annotation process [15]. The study reported here focuses on interfaces that are either widely used or intended to support keyboarded communication about shared documents, and explores their effects on annotation production.

CHI 98 Los Angeles CA USA
Copyright 1998 0-89791-975-0/98/ 4..$5.00

THEORETICAL FRAMEWORK & HYPOTHESES

Previous research examining the affordances of interfaces has demonstrated that perceptual characteristics of displays can affect human problem-solving behavior for complex cognitive tasks. Brooke & Duncan [2], for instance, found that display format affected the ability of a fault-finding diagnostician to perceive what was relevant and what was not.

In analyzing the Brooke & Duncan study and others, Woods [23] offers the concept of "visual momentum," defined as the affordance a display provides in supporting users' needs for finding and fixating important areas. According to this analysis, displays affording low visual momentum, in which users must work relatively hard to find and fixate important areas, increase the user's mental workload because demands are increased on limited capacity processing systems and because additional, irrelevant mental tasks are imposed on the user [19]. Such effects are likely to be found for annotation interfaces, since detecting problems in a document and communicating about those problems is a complex cognitive task. Thus, our first hypothesis is

H1: Annotation interfaces will affect the cognitive problem-solving of users.

In addition, we hypothesized that negative effects would be greater when the problems being communicated about were more difficult–just when the need for effective communication is presumably most critical.

Difficulty of Problems. Writers working together often communicate about two types of problems: problems in the text itself and problems in other reviewers' annotations about the text. Both types of problems can have different degrees of difficulty.

Problems in the Text Itself. Studies have indicated that preferences for media are influenced by the type of communication required, in particular, whether the communication involves an equivocal, or ambiguous, task for which many solutions or interpretations are possible, as opposed to an unequivocal task that does not require "hunches, discussion, or social support" [3]. Moreover, studies have indicated that media vary in their ability to support communication involving equivocality, particularly with respect to issues of time and distance (such as synchronous vs. asynchronous interactions and face-to-face vs. remote interactions) [13].

Problems in texts vary in equivocality, with some problems, such as a grammatical errors, lower in equivocality and some, such as "the tone of a piece," higher in equivocality. Although problems that are high in equivocality presumably are more in need of discussion, difficulties in communicating about such problems (ironically) results in their sometimes receiving less communication, not more, especially under conditions where the costs of communication are relatively high [13, 15].

H2: Effects of annotation interfaces will be most pronounced when the problems are high in equivocality.

Problems with Other Reviewers' Annotations on the Text. A number of studies of computer-mediated communication have found that users discuss more issues, take longer to reach consensus, and experience more difficulty in achieving consensus than do their counterparts not working on-line [11, 14, 20, 21]. Similar findings have been reported for those using computer support as opposed to more traditional tools (such as pen and paper) even in face-to-face meetings [18].

In the task of communicating about problems in a text, different reviewers sometimes disagree with one another and consider others' annotations as "invalid." These points of disagreement presumably need more communication than points of agreement, especially when the points of disagreement revolve around problems high in equivocality.

H3: There will be more communication about annotations perceived to be invalid than annotations perceived to be valid.

H4: Effects of annotation interfaces will be most pronounced when the problems are most difficult: high equivocal problems in the text with annotations that are perceived to be invalid.

METHOD

Subjects. Subjects, 30 second-year MBA students at Carnegie Mellon University's Graduate School of Industrial Administration, were recruited via calls for participation on electronic mail and bulletin boards. Each was given a small remuneration for participation, with a potential twenty-five dollar bonus for the four people subsequently judged to have written the best sets of comments. Of the 29 subjects for whom information was available, all listed Microsoft Word as the word processor they had used most frequently throughout the past year; one mentioned frequently using WordPerfect as well. Eight of these subjects reported experience in annotating on-line by using font differentiation (via color, bold-facing, brackets, etc.) to distinguish annotations from the text; none reported having used an annotation feature of Word or other software designed for annotations.

Interfaces. Participants in our study used one of three types of interfaces to annotate texts: "Split-Screen," "Interlinear," or "Aligned." The first two are interfaces commonly used for annotating texts. The third is an interface we designed specifically for annotating documents. We have previously proposed a set of requirements [17] for annotation interfaces, which we will draw upon to discuss aspects of the user interfaces under study:

- *There is a minimum of motion required to make an annotation.* Annotation interfaces vary considerably in how many actions the user must take to create an annotation. Human-computer interaction research has argued that minimizing the mapping of actions to frequent tasks is crucial to the learnability and usability of designs [9].
- *The primary text is easily distinguishable from the annotation text.* This requirement allows readers, who may not have seen either the original text or the annotations, to orient themselves to the texts quickly.
- *The annotations are visible "at a glance" while reading the primary text.* This requirement minimizes the problems readers have in accessing annotations.
- *The relationship between the primary text and the annotations is easy to see.* This requirement insures that readers will be able to see which annotations refer to particular portions of text.
- *Different annotators are readily distinguishable.* This requirement aids readers in interpreting annotations by different commentators.

The Split-Screen Interface. A recent version (6.0) of the widely used word processor Microsoft Word presents the main text and the annotations in separate panes, in a split-screen format similar to the formats common to footnote presentation (Figure 1). We hypothesized that this display format has the highest workload: it requires annotators to direct eye fixations across a relatively wide area on the screen in a vertical direction, and annotators wishing to communicate about problems in the text must move between the top and the bottom frames.[1]

***Figure 1.* Split-Screen Interface**

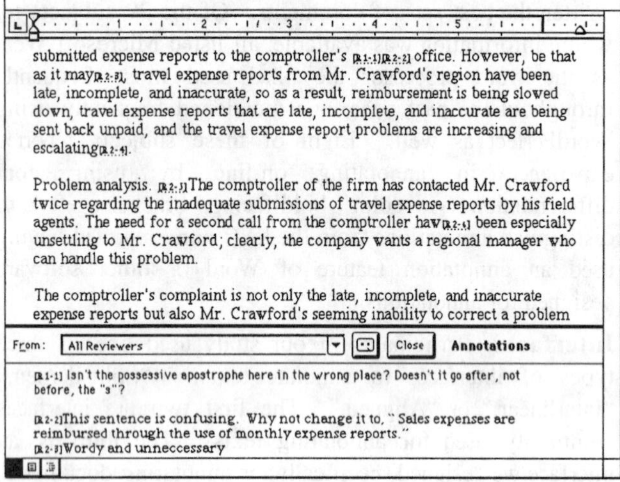

The Interlinear Interface. Despite the increasing number of programs specifically designed to support annotation, interlinear annotations are still widely used for making on-line annotations, either within a standard word processed text or in an electronic mail message. In this approach, embedded, or "interlinear," comments are differentiated from the text through formatting features--brackets, capitalization, bold-face, italics, and the like (Figure 2). We hypothesized that the Interlinear display format requires less work than the Interlinear but more than the Aligned. The person wishing to make a comment does not need to direct eye fixations across as wide a distance as in the Split-Screen interface, but those fixations do have to move, for the most part, in a vertical direction rather than from left-to-right. Perhaps more importantly, because annotations are actually embedded within the text, the interlinear annotations can interfere with reading/re-reading the base document itself.[2] Making an annotation typically requires the user either to select the target text and format it in a different typeface or to add characters, such as brackets, to distinguish it from the primary text.

***Figure 2.* Interlinear Interface**

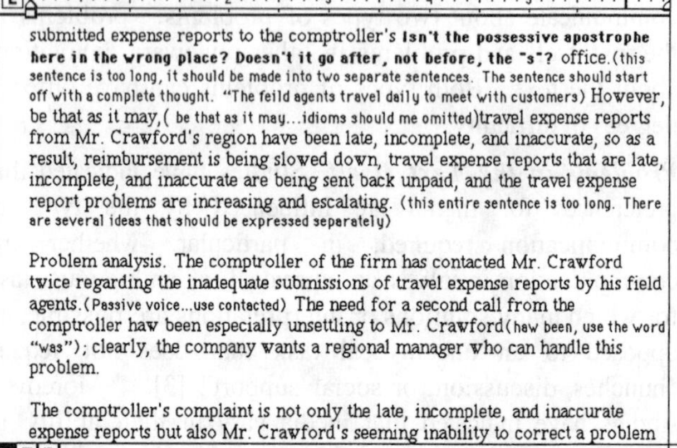

The Aligned Interface. Figure 3 depicts the Aligned interface of the PREP Editor, a prototype application intended to support annotations of linear texts and embedded graphics [17]. The default, larger font size and greater width of the primary text helps to distinguish it from the annotation texts. Annotations are visible "at-a-glance," horizontally aligned to the primary text with which they are associated, but in a visually distinct space in the margin. Annotations remain associated with the text to which they are linked, even under most editing operations. The scope of the annotation is indicated in the primary text by a selection box that is highlighted either when the user clicks in the corresponding annotation (the default) or "upon coming into view" (selectable by a menu item). Different annotators can be assigned different marginal spaces. To make an annotation, the user selects the text to be annotated and clicks in the right margin.[3] We hypothesized that this interface would require less work than the other two.

Text Materials. Materials in the study consisted of a draft manuscript and a reviewer's comments on that draft. To rule out the possibility that particular topics interact with the predicted results, we used two drafts written in response to two different business cases [4]. The manuscripts were based on MBA students' rough drafts.

---

[1] Space precludes a more formal analysis of the workload of the interfaces [22].

[2] Depending on how the interlinear annotations are formatted, it can also be difficult to differentiate the text from comments about the text. In the study reported here, care was taken to make the interlinear annotations clearly distinguishable. The base document was formatted in 14-pt. Times; annotations from a reviewer were in 10-pt. Geneva bold; the subjects' annotations were in 10-pt. Geneva.

[3] Our description of the annotation features of the PREP Editor prototype focus on those that are relevant to the study reported here. The prototype, however, has other features, such as the ability to hide all the annotations from a particular reviewer, to merge annotations from multiple reviewers who were sent copies of the same base document, etc. [cf. 16, 17].

***Figure 3.* Aligned Interface**

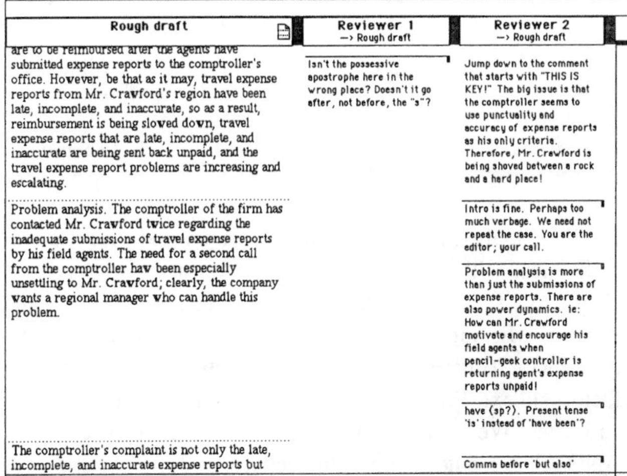

The manuscripts. The draft manuscripts were manipulated as follows: four types of problems lower in equivocality (problems in spelling, punctuation, wordiness due to redundancies or empty phrases, and physical presentation/format) and four types of problems higher in equivocality (problems in organization, development, audience/purpose, and genre) were identified. Two or three cases of each problem (such as punctuation or organization) were planted in the text. (Planted problems were drawn, to the extent possible, from similar problems in MBA students' drafts.) As much as possible, other problems were eliminated from the manuscripts.

To test the manipulations, two independent raters trained in writing read the manuscripts to identify problems. Any time different people review a document, they are likely to identify and/or comment on different errors, so it was not assumed that the raters would point out each of the planted problems. However, it was expected that the raters would identify the majority of the problems and that they would do so at a similar rate for each of the two documents. This proved to be the case. Both identified the majority of the planted problems in each document (62% for Document A; 52% for Document B). In approximately one-third of the other cases in each document, one of the raters identified the planted problem. Five percent of the planted problems in Document A and seventeen percent of the problems in Document B were not identified by either of the two raters. A third rater, a first-year MBA student familiar with the subject matter domain was asked to read the manuscripts. At this point, all problems were acknowledged to exist by at least one of the three readers.

Next, trained raters independently coded each planted problem (but with the problem *identified* as a problem) for its equivocality: high or low. The inter-rater reliability of the two coders as indicated by Cohen's Kappa was .83 for Document A and .84 for Document B.

The reviewer's comments on the manuscripts. As with the problem manipulations, the annotations were based on actual work of first-year MBA students. In this case, the MBA students annotated the manuscripts with comments about the problems. The annotations were then manipulated. For each problem (such as punctuation), the following types of annotations were added (or retained):

- Valid Annotation (Hit): Correct identification of the problem and/or appropriate suggestion for improvement.
- Missing Annotation (Miss): No annotation provided about the problem.
- Invalid Annotation (False Alarm): Identification of a problem where none existed, or mis-identification of either the problem or its solution.

One case of each planted problem type was randomly designated to serve as a "hit," or valid annotation. One case of each problem was designated to serve as a "miss," with no initial annotation. Where three cases of a problem existed, the third annotation was designated to be a false alarm due to incorrect identification of the problem or an incorrect solution to the problem. Where just two cases of a problem existed, a false alarm incorrectly suggested the existence of the given problem where the problem did not exist. (For a visual representation of the planted problem and annotation combinations, see Table 1.)

***Table 1.* Problem Manipulations**

	Valid Annotation	Missing Annotation	Invalid Annotation
Higher Equivocal Problem	"Solutions are not presented in an effective order."	[No annotation, despite the existence of an organizational problem.]	"The organization of problems & solutions works well."
Lower Equivocal Problem	"Semi-colon rather than comma before 'however.'"	[No annotation despite existence of punctuation error.]	"Semi-colon rather than comma after 'however.'"

To test this manipulation, two independent raters classified each annotation as either "valid" or "invalid." The inter-rater reliability of the two independent coders was .86 for Document A and .88 for Document B by Cohen's Kappa. With one (inadvertant) "high miss" problem, the total number of planted problems was 25.

Design. The study employed a 3 (Interface) x 2 (Text Problem) x 3 (Annotation Problem) mixed factorial design, with 30 subjects randomly assigned to one of the three interface conditions: Split-Screen, Interlinear, or Aligned. The screen display size was the same for all conditions. In all interface conditions, subjects viewed a document containing problems. Text problem equivocality was varied within subjects: half of the planted text problems were rated as high in equivocality; half were rated as low. Subjects also viewed another collaborator's annotations about problems in the text. Annotation validity was also varied within subjects: annotations were valid, invalid or missing.

Procedures. Subjects read a one-page explanation of the collaborative task (to create two brief case analysis reports) and their role as a collaborator within a collaborative group of three students enrolled in an organizational behavior class. Subjects were to assume that their case analysis report, drafted by one collaborating student and initially annotated by a second member of the collaborative team, was due to a professor in less than two days. Subjects were to assume that they were, by necessity, writing their annotations from a conference hotel in a city distant from the collaborators. Subjects were told that one member of the collaborative group had offered to revise the documents based on comments from both an initial reviewer and the subject. Subjects were also told that the voluntary reviser desired comments only--they were to make no actual revisions to the text or to the initial reviewer's comments. Subjects were asked to comment both on the draft and on the initial set of annotations that had been created by a collaborator.

Next, subjects were given training on the software. The training in all conditions consisted of a brief introduction to and practice with those procedures commonly used for annotating (such as searching the text or creating comments).

In addition to being provided on-line versions of the annotated manuscripts, subjects were given hardcopies of the instructions from the professor and hardcopies of the two business case scenarios that had prompted the drafts. Subjects were also given a written document explaining their task and role in the group, a brief user guide for the software (with the same procedures explained for each software program), and hardcopies of the group's initial rough drafts.

Following the introduction and a brief software training session, subjects worked on the cases alone in a room. Subjects were instructed to work until they were satisfied that their annotations "would help a collaborative partner do the best possible job of revising each document."

Measures. We operationalized "amount of communication" as the number of annotations subjects made on planted problems in the documents. Two independent raters coded all subjects' annotations from Document A to judge whether or not they addressed any of the planted text and annotation problems. Inter-rater reliability on a randomly selected 15% of the data was .82 by Cohen's Kappa. (Subjects' annotations not addressing the planted problems were put aside for future analysis, as were data related to Document B.) We also measured the time subjects worked on the documents.

RESULTS

Time on task did not vary significantly across conditions and did not interact with dependent measures and so was dropped from further analyses (Table 2).

***Table 2.* Mean (S.D.) Time on Task by Interface**

	Interface		
	Split-Screen	Interlinear	Aligned
Time in minutes	60 (19.75)	66 (19.19)	62 (18.77)

In the analyses reported here, we tested for overall differences with a 3 (Split-Screen, Interlinear, Aligned) x 2 (High vs. Low Text Problem Equivocality) x 3 (Valid, Invalid, Missing Annotation Problem) ANOVA with the first factor (Interface) between subjects and the last two factors (Text Problem and Annotation Problem) within subjects. We used a least-significant difference (LSD) ANOVA to locate specific differences.

Overall Rate of Communication about Problems

As can be seen on Table 3, across all problem types, subjects using different annotation interfaces communicated about problems at different rates, $F(2, 27) = 6.30$; $p < .01$. An LSD ANOVA indicated that those in the Interlinear and Aligned conditions communicated about significantly more problems (M=10.9 and 11.4 respectively) than those in the Split-Screen condition (M=6.5).

Overall, subjects commented, on average, to 38% of the planted problems, with those in the Interlinear and Aligned conditions responding, on average, to 44% and 46% respectively, compared to responses to 26% of the planted problems on average among those in the Split-Screen condition.

Contrary to our hypothesis, subjects responded on average to 36% of the higher equivocal problems and 41% of lower equivocal problems. Subjects using the Interlinear and Aligned interfaces communicated about high and low equivocal problems at about equal rates (M=5.1 vs. 5.8 in the Interlinear condition; M=5.4 vs. 6.0 in the Aligned condition); subjects using the Split-Screen interface were somewhat more likely to communicate about high (M=3.7) as opposed to low (M=2.8) equivocal problems.

Although subjects using the Interlinear and Aligned interfaces appear to have communicated about more text problems rated high in equivocality (M=5.1 and 5.4 respectively) than those using the Split-Screen interface (M=3.7), this difference is not significant. The amount of communication about low equivocal problems by interface, however, was significant, $F(2,27) = 6.06$, $p < .01$. Subjects in the Interlinear (M= 5.8) and Aligned (M=6.0) conditions communicated about more low equivocal problems than subjects in the Split-Screen condition (M=2.8).

Table 3. **Mean (S.D.) Number of Communications about Text and Annotation Problems by Interface for Document A**

Problem		Interface			
Text Problem Equivocality	**Annotation Validity**	Split-Screen N=10	Interlinear N=10	Aligned N=10	*Means*
Higher	Valid	1.5 (1.1)	2.2 (1.3)	2.1 (1.3)	*1.9*
	Invalid	1.5 (1.0)	1.9 (1.0)	1.9 (0.9)	*1.8*
	Missing	0.7 (0.8)°	1.0 (0.7)°	1.4 (1.4)°	*1.0*
	Means	*3.7*	*5.1*	*5.4*	*4.7* [13]
Lower	Valid	1.0 (0.8)	1.8 (1.3)	2.1 (1.4)	*1.6*
	Invalid	0.9 (0.9)	2.4 (1.2)	2.4 (1.2)	*1.9*
	Missing	0.9 (0.7)	1.5 (0.7)	1.6 (0.8)	*1.3*
	Means	*2.8*	*5.8*	*6.0*	*4.9* [12]
Overall Means		*6.5*	*10.9*	*11.4*	*9.6* [25]

Note: For cells with °, the number of planted problems = 5; cells not marked reflect responses to 4 total planted problems; [n] = total number of problems.

These results are contrary to our hypothesis that interface effects would be greatest when problems are most difficult. One possible explanation for these results can be found in the computer-mediated communication literature: subjects appear to compensate for greater production difficulty, not by sacrificing the production of important ideas, but by communicating those ideas more tersely [13, 14, 15, 20].

Subjects communicated about far fewer problems when an annotation was "Missing," that is, when a problem was not identified by an annotation from an initial reviewer, $F(2,27) = 8.11$, $p < .01$. Across the board, subjects responded on average to 45% of the valid annotations, 46% of the invalid annotations, and 26% of problems in the text for which no annotation had been made by an initial reviewer.

Somewhat interestingly, the Aligned interface approached significance in affecting the amount of communication about planted problems that had no corresponding annotations ("Missing" annotations), $F(2,27) = 3.0$, $p < .07$. Subjects in the Aligned condition communicated about more problems for which there was no annotation (M=3.0) than subjects in the Split-Screen condition (M=1.6); the amount of communication by subjects in the Interlinear condition (M=2.5) did not differ significantly from the Aligned or Split-Screen conditions. Although only approaching significance, this is consonant with the idea that side-by-side alignment makes it easier to scan the original text for problems, an aspect of annotating (and revising) that is worth investigating further. It is possible that initial annotations may be drawing attention away from unidentified problems in a text presented in some types of interfaces more so than in others.

Subjects using different interfaces communicated about invalid annotations at different rates, $F(2,27) = 4.03$, $p < .05$. In both the Interlinear and Aligned conditions, subjects communicated more frequently about invalid annotations (M=4.3 for both) than subjects in the Split-Screen condition (M=2.4). Subjects in both the Interlinear and Aligned conditions (M=2.4 for both) communicated more frequently about invalid annotations concerning low equivocal problems, $F(2,27) = 6.39$, $p < .01$, than subjects in the Split-Screen condition (M=0.9).

We had expected a higher rate of response to annotations that subjects considered invalid as opposed valid. After all, the subject was to assume that the reviser would follow both the first reviewer's annotations and the subject's, so not negating the first reviewer's invalid annotations could have serious consequences for the success of the product. One reason for these results may be that the participants communicated mainly about problems about which they felt most certain--typically, problems lower in equivocality. Another reason may be that the subject did not know and had not met the collaborative partner who had provided the first set of annotations. Prior research has shown that longer standing groups–in which members have a history and a future--perform differently than ad hoc groups in which members, who may or may not know one another, come together for a single, terminal project [5]. It could be the case that subjects were, for instance, hesitant to criticize or contradict a partner whom they had not met and with whom they had no history when the topic was "open" to interpretation, that is, high in equivocality. While at this point we cannot say why subjects did not respond at a higher rate to problems which had Invalid annotations, future analysis of supplemental think-alouds we took from six additional subjects (whose data is not reported here) should help provide some insights.

CONCLUSIONS

The interface affected both the number and types of problems writers discussed. The fact that subjects communicated about more problems in the Interlinear and Aligned conditions, without a significant difference in time on task, than subjects in the Split-Screen condition is consonant with our hypothesis that differences in annotation interfaces can affect the cognitive problem-solving of users. Other main findings were as follows:

- The interface used did not affect time on task.
- Differences in amount of communication about low equivocal problems varied significantly by interface, with those in the Interlinear and Aligned conditions responding at a higher rate than those in the Split-Screen condition.
- Differences in amount of communication about invalid annotations varied significantly by interface, with those in the Interlinear and Aligned conditions responding at a higher rate than those in the Split-Screen condition.
- Subjects were more likely to comment on problems which had been discussed by an initial reviewer than they were to comment on text problems which had not been discussed by an initial reviewer.
- Those in the Aligned condition were more likely than those in the Split-Screen condition to comment on "misses," text problems that had not been discussed by an initial reviewer.
- Overall, subjects did not comment at significantly higher rates to problems higher as opposed to lower in equivocality.
- Overall, subjects did not comment at significantly higher rates to invalid as opposed to valid annotations from an initial reviewer.

The theoretical framework developed for this study, namely equivocality of problems in the text and the validity of annotations, also appeared to be useful in discriminating interfaces for communicating about shared artifacts. More theoretical work is needed in order to have a fuller understanding of possible effects of interfaces on communication.

In this study, we were interested in establishing overall differences in amount of communication and the nature of that communication. We did not set out to investigate the underlying reasons for differences yet to be established. One possibility, though, is that the Split-Screen interface does, indeed, make it more difficult to find and fixate relevant areas on the screen. Another is that it is more difficult to create annotations with the Split-Screen system. Future research should explore how different components of these interfaces (and others such as displays with movable post-it notes) contribute to the effects this study established.

Communication frequency and types were quite similar for those in the Interlinear and Aligned conditions (though failure to see a difference does not mean one is not there). Moreover, this study only examined the production of annotations, not the use of those annotations in the subsequent task of revision. Future research should also examine how differences in annotation interfaces affect the full context of making, receiving, *and* using annotations. Of course, differences in the amount of problems and types of problems that are annotated are likely to affect revision. But holding those constant, we expect that the Interlinear condition will require revisers to engage in more work than the Split-Screen as well as the Aligned conditions, both of which present communications surrounding a text separate from the text itself.

Here we have shown variations in interface displays to affect communication in the annotation task, a task common to most collaborative work, including problem-solving and decision-making, as well as creating artifacts such as written documents and software products. Much more work is needed so we can better understand (1) the ways that different communication technologies may afford particular support as well as impose particular constraints for various types of communications, (2) the ways that particular types of communication may affect the outcomes of collaboration, and (3) the ways that people's manner or patterns of use of different technologies for communication in various contexts in turn contribute to shaping a technology's effects and significance in collaborative on-line work.

The need for more such information about human-computer interaction and its specific effects on the nature and role of communication within collaborative work groups continues to grow as the need for more effective collaboration technologies continues to expand [10].

ACKNOWLEDGMENTS

This work was supported by a grant from the National Science Foundation (Grant Number IRI-8902891). Other members of the PREP Editor project group (Rob Chandhok, David Kaufer, Jim Morris, Paul Erion, & Dale Wiggins) contributed user interface ideas for the PREP Editor. The PREP Editor prototype is available for download at http://eng.hss.cmu.edu/software/prep/.

REFERENCES

1. Bond, A.H., & Gasser, L., Eds. (1988). *Readings in distributed artificial intelligence*. San Mateo, CA: Morgan Kaufmann.
2. Brooke, J. B. & Duncan, K. D. (1981). Effects of system display format on performance in a fault location task. *Ergonomics, 24* , 174-189.

3. Daft, R.L., Lengel, R.H., Trevino, L.K. (1987). Message equivocality, media selection, and manager performance: Implications for information systems. *MIS Quarterly,* 355-366.

4. Deitzer, B.A., and Shilliff, K.A. (1977). *Contemporary Management Incidents.* Columbus: Grid Inc.

5. Finholt, T., Sproull, L., & Kiesler, S. (1990). Communication and performance in ad hoc task groups. In J. Galegher, R. Kraut, and C. Egido (Eds.), *Intellectual teamwork: Social and technological foundations of cooperative work* (pp. 291-325). Hillsdale, NJ: Erlbaum.

6. Fleming, D., Werner, M., Sinsheimer-Weeks, A., & Kaufer, D.S. (forthcoming). Conflict in collaborative design: A framework for analysis with three case studies. In Burnett, R.E., & Duin, A.H. (Eds.) *Collaboration in technical communication: Research perspectives.* Hillsdale, NJ: Lawrence Erlbaum.

7. Galegher, J., & Kraut, R.E. (1990). Technology for intellectual teamwork: Perspectives on research and design. In J. Galegher, R.E. Kraut, & C. Egido (Eds.) *Intellectual teamwork: The social and technological bases of cooperative work* (pp. 1-20). Hillsdale, NJ: Lawrence Erlbaum Associates.

8. Gaver, D.D. (1991). Technology affordances. *Proceedings of the ACM CHI '91 Conference on Human Factors in Computing Systems* (pp. 29-84). New York: The Association for Computing Machinery.

9. Howes, A, & Young, R. M. (1991). Predicting the learnability of task-action mappings. In Scott Robertson P., Gary M. Olson and Judith S. Olson (Eds.), *CHI'91 Conference Proceedings* (pp. 113-118). New Orleans, Louisiana: The Association for Computing Machinery.

10. Kaufer, D.S., & Carley, K.M. (1993). *Communication at a distance: The influence of print on sociocultural organization and change.* Hillsdale, NJ: Lawrence Erlbaum Associates.

11. Kraemer, K.K., & Pinsonneault (1990). *Technology and groups: Assessment of the empirical research.* In J. Galegher, R.E. Kraut, & C. Egido (Eds.) *Intellectual teamwork: The social and technological bases of cooperative work* (pp. 375-405). Hillsdale, NJ: Lawrence Erlbaum Associates.

12. Kraut, R.E., Galegher, J., & Egido, C. (1987-88). Relationships and tasks in scientific research collaborations. *Human-Computer Interaction, 3,* 31-58.

13. Kraut, R.E., Galegher, J., Fish, R., & Chalfonte, B. (1992). Task requirements and media choice in collaborative writing. *Human-Computer Interaction, 7,* 375-407.

14. McGuire, T., Kiesler, S., & Siegel, J. (1987). Group and computer-mediated discussion effects in risk decision making. *Journal of Personality and Social Psychology, 52,* 917-930.

15. Neuwirth, C.M., Chandhok, R., Charney, D., Wojahn, P., & Kim, L. (1994). Distributed collaborative writing: A comparison of spoken and written modalities for reviewing and revising documents. In *Human Factors in Computing Systems: CHI '94 Conference Proceedings* (pp. 51-57). New York: The Association for Computing Machinery Press.

16. Neuwirth, C.M., Chandhok, R., Kaufer, D.S., Erion, P., Morris, J., & Miller, D. (1992). Flexible diff-ing in a collaborative writing system. In *Proceedings of the Fourth Conference on Computer-Supported Cooperative Work (CSCW '92)* (pp. 147-154). New York: The Association for Computing Machinery Press.

17. Neuwirth, Christine M., Kaufer, D. S., Chandhok, R. & Morris, J.H. (1990). Issues in the design of computer support for co-authoring and commenting. In *Proceedings of the Third Conference on Computer Supported Cooperative Work (CSCW'90)* (pp. 183-195). Baltimore, MD: Association for Computing Machinery Press.

18. Olson, J., Olson, J.S., Carter, M.R., and Storrosten, M. (1992). Small group design meetings: An analysis of collaboration. *Human-Computer Interaction, 7,* 347-374.

19. Rasmussen, J. (1980). The human as a system component. In Smith, R.H., & Green, T.R.G. (Eds.) *Human interaction with computers.* London: Academic Press.

20. Siegel, J., Dubrovsky, V., Kiesler, S., and McGuire, T. (1986). Group processes in computer-mediated communication. *Organizational Behavior and Human Decision Processes, 37,* 157-187.

21. Sproull, L., & Kiesler, S. (1991). *Connections: New ways of working in the networked organization.* Cambridge: MIT Press.

22. Wojahn, P. (thesis in preparation). Collaborative writing at a distance: The effects of computer screen displays on peer review interactions.

23. Woods, D. D. (1984). Visual momentum: a concept to improve the cognitive coupling of person and computer. *Int. J. Man-Machine Studies, 21,* 229-244.

Awareness Driven Video Quality of Service in Collaborative Virtual Environments

Gail Reynard, Steve Benford, Chris Greenhalgh and Christian Heath
The University of Nottingham
Nottingham NG7 2RD, UK.
+44 115 951 4203
{gtr, sdb, cmg}@cs.nott.ac.uk

ABSTRACT

We extend previous work on texture mapping video streams into virtual environments by introducing awareness driven video QoS. This uses movements within a shared virtual world to activate different video services. In turn, these services have different settings for underlying QoS parameters such as frame-rate, resolution and compression. We demonstrate this technique through a combined conferencing/ mediaspace application which uses awareness driven video for facial expressions and for views into remote physical environments. We reflect on the issues of spatial consistency, privacy, seamless shifts in mutual involvement and making underlying QoS mechanisms more visible, malleable and flexible.

Keywords

Video, CSCW, CVEs, Multimedia, Networks

INTRODUCTION

Recent years have seen a growing interest in the integration of video into collaborative virtual environments (CVEs). Several systems have demonstrated the approach of displaying live video windows as dynamically updated texture maps within a virtual world (e.g., *Freewalk* [12] and *CU-SeeMe VR* [9]). We extend this work with the technique of "awareness driven video quality of service (QoS)" where spatial actions in a virtual world drive the underlying QoS of textured video streams. We demonstrate this technique through a combined conferencing/mediaspace application which uses awareness driven video for facial expressions and for views into remote physical environments. There are three general motivations for this work: addressing problems of spatial consistency in video applications; providing information about the physical world in CVEs; and extending underlying video QoS mechanisms to be more visible, malleable and flexible. We now consider each of these in turn.

Spatial consistency in video applications

In part, the integration of video with CVEs has emerged in the light of a growing dissatisfaction with more conventional video conferencing and media space technologies and their (in)ability to support mutual awareness and flexible collaborative work. For example, it has been found that the absence of a mutually available, or common, video space has engendered certain communicative asymmetries, undermining the participants' abilities both to produce action and draw the appropriate inferences from the conduct of others [10]. We anticipate that the integration of video and CVEs may ease some of these problems by situating video views of local physical domains within a consistent spatial environment. This approach also builds on previous attempts to support gaze direction in video conferencing (e.g., the Hydra [13] and Majic [11] systems). In contrast to these previous approaches which require the careful configuration of cameras and monitors into a mutually consistent spatial arrangement, the more software oriented approach of displaying video within CVEs may afford more dynamic configurability.

Providing information about the physical world in CVEs

From the perspective of CVEs, video can provide information about physical world artefacts and locations. An obvious role for video is adding facial expressions to embodiments. A second role is to provide awareness of the real world context within which participants are located. Drawing on studies of social interaction within the MASSIVE-1 CVE [2], activities in the physical world have an impact on those within the virtual world (e.g., the problems that arise when participants become distracted by physical world events but remain visibly embodied as being present within the virtual world). Video views into a local physical context may assist other users in coping with such problems.

Making QoS mechanisms visible, malleable and flexible

Supporting guaranteed end-to-end video QoS has become a major focus for multimedia research. Indeed, the next generation of Internet protocols (the so-called Integrated Services Architecture [3]), will provide this facility. However, in spite of considerable advances in the underlying QoS mechanisms, it has been noted that there has been little consideration of how to make QoS visible at the user interface [14]. Furthermore, current approaches to QoS have been strongly driven by the relatively static requirements of applications such as video on demand. In contrast, human communication can be highly fluid, involving the negotiation of social interaction among dynamically changing groups of participants. Awareness driven video QoS is intended to make QoS issues more visible to end-users, more easily controlled and also more suited to the dynamic requirements of human social interaction.

We return to these motivations in detail at the end of this paper. Before that, the following sections introduce the technique of awareness driven video QoS and demonstrate its use in our conferencing/mediaspace application.

INTRODUCING AWARENESS DRIVEN VIDEO QOS

Awareness driven video QoS involves the application of the previously defined spatial model of interaction [8] to the medium of video. The inhabitants of a CVE move about a shared virtual world. These movements are used to calculate different levels of mutual awareness through the spatial model mechanisms of aura, focus, nimbus and third party objects. The underlying system (i.e., the processors and network concerned with video transmission) uses the awareness level associated with each video source to switch between different video services. These services are defined with different levels of video QoS using parameters such as frame-rate, resolution and compression. Users' spatial movements therefore provide a high level, medium independent way of dynamically managing the QoS of multiple video streams which can then be displayed within the virtual world. As necessary background we now very briefly summarise the spatial model.

A review of the spatial model of interaction

The spatial model of interaction allows the inhabitants of virtual spaces to negotiate social interaction in terms of levels of mutual awareness. In turn, these levels of awareness drive the exchange of information across different communication media. The key concepts of the model are:

- **Aura** - a region of space which scopes an object's presence. When auras collide, communication becomes possible (e.g. network connections are established).
- **Awareness** - a measure of mutual interest between an observing and an observed object that can be influenced by both using focus and nimbus. **Focus** represents an observer's region of interest. **Nimbus** is an observed's region of influence or projection (a key aspect of the model is that an object can use nimbus to try to interrupt or influence another). The awareness that an object, A, has of another, B, is a function of A's focus on B and B's nimbus on A. Aura, focus and nimbus are defined on a *per medium basis* as general spatial fields. They can therefore be multi-valued (not just simple containment regions). They can also dynamically change shape and extent.
- **Third party objects** - introduce various contextual effects into awareness negotiation, such as the effects of spatial boundaries around regions or the creation of dynamic groupings of objects such as crowds of participants [1]. They have two general kinds of effects: *adaptation* of existing awareness relationships and the generation *of secondary source* views of groups of other objects.

An overview of awareness driven video QoS

Awareness driven video QoS involves establishing a mapping between the high-level, medium independent spatial model mechanisms and lower-level video specific QoS parameters. This is shown in figure 1.

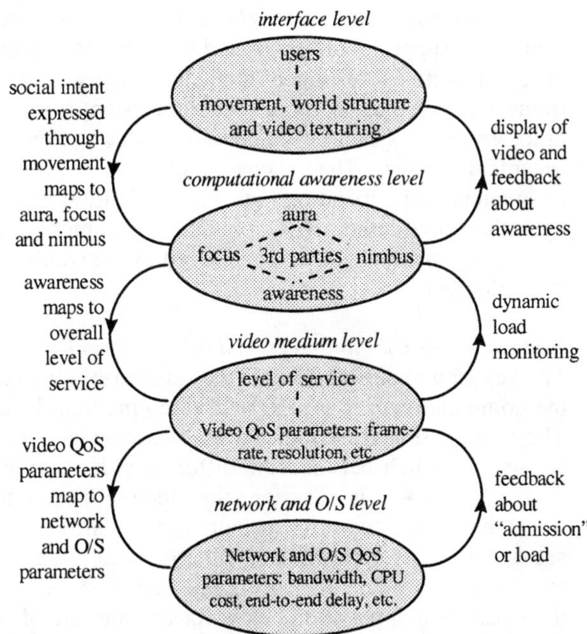

Figure 1: Awareness driven video QoS

The interface level

The top-most level of the mapping is the interface level where users express their communication requirements through spatial movements. Their communication is further influenced by spatial structures and objects within the world (e.g. boundaries and regions). The resulting video information is displayed as dynamic texture maps within the 3-D graphical environment.

The computational awareness level

The next level down is the computational awareness level. Spatial actions from the interface level are mapped onto manipulations of video aura, video focus, video nimbus and third party objects in the video medium. For example, a movement may cause new objects to come into video aura range; may alter levels of the user's video focus on current objects; may alter the level of these objects' video nimbi on the user; or may activate various third party objects. These manipulations result in the ongoing re-calculation of the awareness level associated with each video stream. In some circumstances aura, focus and nimbus may be made explicitly visible at the user interface, providing feedback about current awareness levels or allowing users to explicitly manipulate them by choosing different settings or changing shape and extent.

The video medium level

The video medium level is concerned with providing both generic and application specific video services. For example, a conferencing tool might define two levels of service, a high resolution service to be associated with the most active or interesting speakers and a low resolution service to be associated with passive or more peripherally interesting speakers. As a second example, a mediaspace might support a low frame-rate *porthole* service and higher frame-rate *glance, v-phone* and *office-share* services. As these examples suggest, different video services involve different settings of video QoS parameters such as frame-rate, resolution, colour, compression type and ratio, level of synchronisation with audio, price and acceptable jitter. The choice and combination of parameters will depend on both the application and the operating environment (i.e., on which parameters can be directly manipulated or guaranteed by a given set of technologies).

Mapping between the awareness and video medium levels

The key step in our mapping is the relationship between the computational awareness and video medium levels. The awareness level associated with each video stream is used to switch between the different video services. A simple mapping is to arrange the video services into a linear ordering according to increasing quality and to set awareness thresholds which determine the transitions between the different services (see our demonstration application below for an example of this approach). A more sophisticated mapping is to compare awareness values across all available video streams and to allocate the highest levels of service to a restricted number of streams with the current highest awareness values. This would ensure that only a limited number of high quality streams had to be processed at a time, but would dynamically reallocate these between different sources.

In some circumstances, information about the specific levels of focus and nimbus which are contributing to a given level of awareness might provide additional support for controlling video QoS. Whereas awareness can be interpreted as an overall expression of desired QoS for a given video stream, focus and nimbus can be interpreted as the extent to which the sink and source associated with that stream wish to be responsible for that level of QoS. For example, if A is peripherally aware of B, this may be because A is strongly interested in receiving from B (high focus) but B is not very interested in transmitting to A (low nimbus) or vice versa. In the former case, we might expect A to bear most of the responsibility for the communication and in the latter case, we might expect B to. This has a particular bearing on the QoS parameters of price and compression. If the overall awareness level is mapped onto the price paid for a given stream as part of a billing mechanism, then focus and nimbus levels might determine the relative financial contributions of the sink and source. Similarly, the choice of compression technique will have different impacts on the source and sink. For example, MPEG-2 places much higher load on the source than on the sink whereas JPEG requires a more evenly balanced distribution of effort. Given a video stream where the source had a high nimbus and the sink a low focus, this might suggest the use of MPEG-2, whereas a more even balance between focus and nimbus might suggest the use of JPEG.

Finally, we use dynamic load monitoring to provide feedback from the video medium level to the computational awareness level. The underlying system can monitor the load on the network and the processors that are connected to it. If this exceeds an acceptable level, then aura, focus and nimbus can be automatically adjusted. For example, a consequence of increasing load might be to automatically retract video aura, focus and nimbus in order to reduce the number of video connections or to reduce the quality of existing connections so as to bring the load back under control.

The network and O/S level

The lowest level of our mapping is the network and operating system level. This level is concerned with general (i.e., video independent) low-level QoS parameters such as bandwidth, error-rate, end-to-end delay and CPU time. The settings chosen for the video specific parameters in the video medium level map to the settings of these network and O/S parameters (e.g., the choice of frame-rate for a video stream will impact on underlying bandwidth). Where only best-effort QoS is supported (e.g., current Internet protocols), network congestion and overloaded CPUs may mean that the desired video QoS cannot be obtained and feedback may be provided to higher levels through load monitoring. Where guaranteed QoS is supported, then there will be a negotiation between the video and network and O/S levels as to whether the desired QoS can be provided and feedback will be provided in terms of acceptance or rejection of a given request (termed call admission or non-admission).

This concludes our introduction to awareness driven video QoS. In order to utilise this approach, an application developer has to take a number of key decisions. How is video information to be presented in the virtual world? What kinds of actions will be made available at the user interface in order to manipulate awareness (e.g. what kinds of movement are possible and is the spatial model directly visible)? What are appropriate functions for aura, focus and nimbus and how should the world be structured in terms of third party objects so as to yield appropriate awareness levels? What classes of video service are required by this application, how are they defined in terms of video QoS parameters and how do they relate to awareness levels? Is guaranteed or best effort QoS available and what feedback can be obtained about network and system load? and how can this feedback be used to adjust aura, focus and nimbus? The following section presents a demonstration of awareness driven video QoS which addresses these questions.

DEMONSTRATION - A COMBINED CONFERENCING AND MEDIASPACE APPLICATION

Our demonstration application combines the functions of traditional conferencing tools with those of mediaspaces. The result is an integrated environment which supports personal communication between multiple participants as well as general awareness of the presence and activities of others in both the virtual environment and in local physical environments. Our design has three key properties: a navigable 3-D interface which uses textured video windows for facial expressions and for views into physical offices; the use of spatial awareness to trigger three levels of video service: *portholes*, *glances* and *communication*, each with a different underlying video frame-rate; and the visible embodiment of those who are browsing the environment so as to promote mutuality of awareness.

An overview of the application

We begin with an overview of the application before considering its use of awareness driven video QoS.

The structure of the virtual environment

Our application involves a shared virtual world within which participants can establish a personal territory, referred to as a "virtual office". These virtual offices are arranged into a navigable 3-D structure, such as our current circular configuration as shown in figure 2. Two video windows, each showing the same overview of its owner's physical office (i.e., an "in context" video view), are texture mapped onto each virtual office. One is located on the roof and this offers what is termed a *porthole* style service - a low frame-rate video image at one frame every five minutes (see below for a more formal discussion of services). A user who levitates above the virtual offices and looks down (to obtain the viewpoint in figure 2) will therefore see the equivalent of a 2-D portholes style interface to a mediaspace [5]. The second video window is located on the front of the virtual office. Most of the time this will also offer a porthole service which can be seen from ground level. However, when someone who is browsing the environment stands directly in front of this window and looks in this is upgraded to what is termed a *glance* service - a medium frame-rate video window at one frame a second. Thus, users can browse through the environment to obtain a general awareness of who is present in their physical offices or can approach a specific office for a detailed look inside.

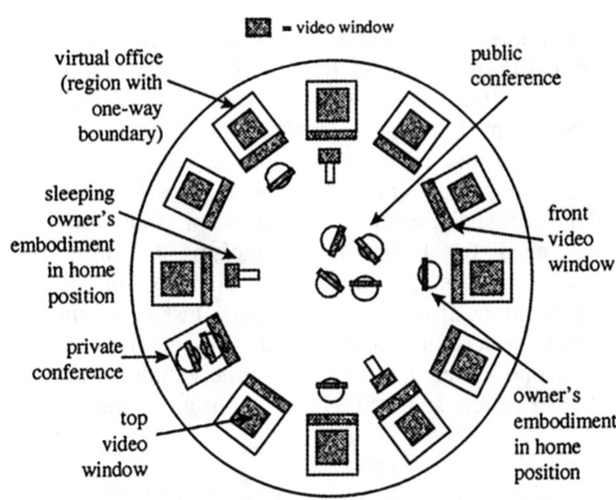

Figure 2: The structure of the virtual environment

Using third party objects from the spatial model of interaction, we have defined each virtual office as an independent sub-region of the virtual world. The boundary of a virtual office operates so that those outside cannot see or hear what is happening inside, but those inside can still see and hear what is happening outside (the video textures are one-sided polygons so as not to obscure the view from inside). The inside of a virtual office therefore provides a private meeting space, but one where its occupants can still see and hear who is approaching from the public space outside.

The embodiment of those who are browsing

A key aspect of our design is the visible embodiment of those who are active within the application. Each user is given a graphical embodiment which they move through the virtual world in order to look into different virtual offices or to meet other users (either by chance or by design). This embodiment features a video face to display their facial expression as captured by a camera on their workstation. When directly face-to-face with their embodiment, this offers what is termed the *communication* service - a high frame-rate video view of roughly twenty frames a second. Note that our design requires two cameras in each physical office, one to provide an in context view to be displayed on the user's virtual office and the other to provide a close-up facial view to be displayed on their embodiment. Through the use of a microphone and speakers or headphones, users are also able to speak to one another via their embodiments (this audio is controlled through a separate audio aura, focus and nimbus). Each embodiment is also assigned a home position, directly in front of its owner's virtual office. Home positions are the default resting place for an embodiment when its owner is not actively browsing the media space or engaged in a private conversation inside their virtual office. When its owner is not even logged on to the application, the embodiment assumes a sleeping position to explicitly show their absence and all video views associated with that user can be switched off.

An important aspect of embodiments is that they enable mutuality of awareness. In particular, in order to glance into an office, a user must position their embodiment directly in front of it, making their action directly visible to the occupants of the office and to other passers by. We anticipate that this will result in a degree of social control over the use of glances, without the need for technical mechanisms to limit their availability (e.g. time-limited glancing or explicit notifications from the system [6]). Just as in the real world, where it could be impolite to hang around someone's open door for a long time without taking any further action, so it could be in the virtual world.

Available awareness information

As table 1 shows, the combination of video windows on virtual offices and the embodiment of browsers provides rich awareness information about the presence and activities of users in the real and virtual worlds.

Awareness provided	Mechanism
User present/available in physical environment?	Appear in the video view of physical office
User not logged on?	Is embodiment sleeping?
User logged on remotely?	Active embodiment but not visible in video view
Engaged with visitors	Embodiment of visitors
Currently browsing or in a private meeting	Embodiment not visible near virtual office

Table 1: Available awareness information

Figures 3 and 4 are screenshots from our application. Figure 3 shows four virtual offices, embodiments and associated video windows. Note the two sleeping embodiments, one whose owner is not logged in (in front of the unoccupied office) and the other whose owner is logged in but is not currently active. Figure 4 shows an embodiment glancing into a virtual office (note - we are looking at the back of their head) with another nearby embodiment facing us. Crossing the "glance line" on the floor activates the glance service.

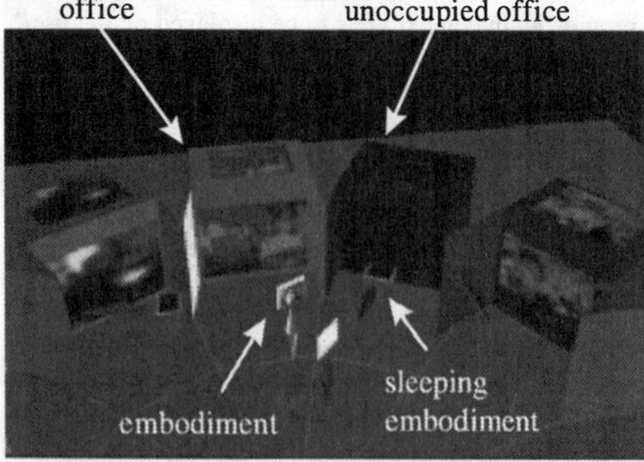

Figure3: Four virtual offices and embodiments

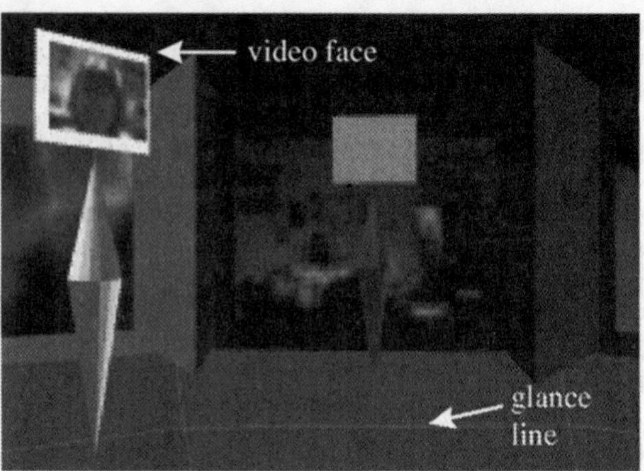

Figure 4: Glancing into a virtual office

The use of awareness driven video QoS

We now describe how our application makes use of awareness driven video QoS. Previous mediaspace research has proposed the idea of the *service* as the basic unit of interaction. For example, the Goddard interface to the RAVE media space introduced four main services: the *glance*, a time limited one way view into a physical office; the *v-phone*, a two way video phone call; an *office-share*, a long term connection between offices; and *background*, the equivalent of the view out of an office door or window [6]. To these can be added the *porthole*s service which provided slowly updated frame-grabs from a camera in an office so as to promote background awareness of availability [5].

Our design builds on this approach. We define three distinct levels of service: *porthole*, *glance*, and *communication*, which can be triggered by actions within the virtual world. In our interpretation, a porthole provides background awareness of activity; a glance provides a moderately detailed view of this activity; and communication is used for facial expressions. In terms of QoS, these services are distinguished by their frame-rate. A porthole corresponds to one frame every five minutes; a glance to one frame a second; and communication to twenty or more frames a second. We have chosen frame-rate because it is relatively easy to manipulate, it has a major impact on underlying bandwidth and hence scaleability; and it reflects privacy requirements in that a low-frame rate view provides some awareness of presence but without details of specific activities.

As described above, three video textures are associated with each occupant of the virtual world: the face on their embodiment and the front and roof of their virtual office. Spatial awareness is configured so that the roof can only ever display the porthole service and the front of the office can display the porthole or the glance service, with the latter only being enabled when the observer is standing directly in front of the office looking in. Faces, on the other hand, can be associated with all three video services: portholes for distant views, glances for close-up and communication for very close-up and face-to-face (so that an observer could only ever access one communication service at a time).

Table 2 summarises the different video services that are defined by our application, their uses, their relation to awareness and their associated frame-rates.

	use	awareness	QoS
porthole	offices and faces	low	1 frame in 5 mins
glance	offices and faces	peripheral	1 frame a second
commun-ication	faces only	high	20 frames a second

Table 2: Conferencing/mediaspace video services

Although not implemented at present, it would also be possible to introduce an *office share* style of service by extending focus and nimbus sideways from a virtual office so as to open up a permanent porthole, glance or communication service with one or more neighbours. Additional video textures could be placed on the inside of each virtual office to display these views. Each user could enter into multiple office-shares (i.e., someone inside a virtual office might see video views of several neighbours). Unlike traditional mediaspaces, our office-share wouldn't be so much a new service, as the long term use of an existing one caused by an appropriate spatial arrangement within the virtual world. Thus, we make a clear separation between different levels of service corresponding to different underlying QoS and the various ways in which these can be activated within a virtual world so as to enable different styles of communication.

Implementation and network architecture

Although full details of the implementation of our application are beyond the scope of this paper, we do offer a brief glimpse of how awareness driven video QoS is realised in the network before passing on to the discussion of general issues raised by this work.

Our application has been implemented using MASSIVE-2, a CVE application development platform which realises the spatial model of interaction [1]. Like other recent CVEs, MASSIVE-2 utilises network multicasting to enhance scaleability. Multicasting is a technique which allows a single message to be efficiently sent to any number of recipients such that the message never crosses any network link more than once [4]. The video medium in MASSIVE-2 exploits network multicasting as follows. Each source of video is associated with its own separate multicast group for each level of video service that is offered for this particular application (three in our case). The source continually transmits video via all of these groups. A recipient of video (a sink) *automatically* joins the appropriate multicast group according to its current level of awareness of the source. Figure 5 shows how this operates between a single source and a single sink.

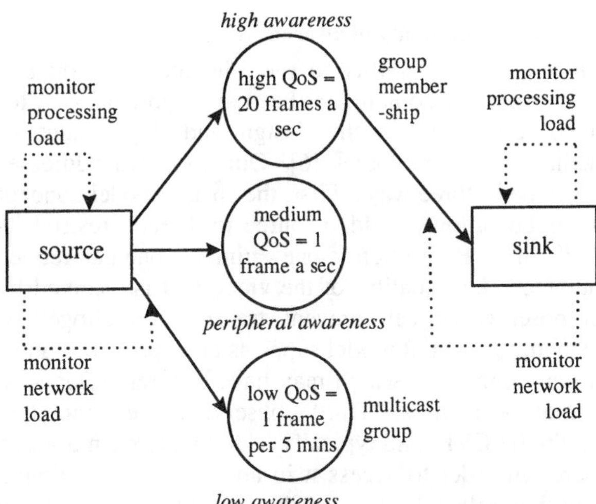

Figure 5: Multicast groups and different levels of QoS

The source is transmitting video to three multicast groups corresponding to our three levels of service. The sink currently has full awareness of the source and so has joined the highest QoS group in order to receive video at the highest frame-rate. We can also see that both the source and sink monitor local processing load and the volume of network traffic and are able to adjust awareness accordingly

DISCUSSION

We conclude by drawing out some more general issues arising from the integration of video in CVEs and from the specific technique of awareness driven video QoS.

Spatial consistency

As noted in the introduction, the use of video can give rise to various environmental incongruities, especially the creation of dislocated spaces within which participants find it hard to establish mutual reference to one another or to shared resources. Moreover, conventional video-conferencing and mediaspace has undermined participants' abilities to engage in more complex forms of collaborative work by principally focusing on the provision of face-to-face views to the exclusion of an individual's local physical environment [7]. The approach of situating video displays within a shared virtual environment may alleviate these problems. The virtual environment is itself spatially consistent so that participants can establish mutual reference from the position and orientation of their embodiments. Each local physical domain is then linked to this environment through a boundary which allows the inhabitants of each to see into the other. Spatial consistency is also preserved across this boundary so that distance and orientation have a consistent meaning between the physical and virtual worlds (as is the case with two party video conferencing). Finally, multiple video views (e.g. faces, in-context views and document views) might be integrated within a common spatial frame of reference.

Privacy and mutuality of awareness

Privacy, and the ability to see who looks at you and your respective domain, has been an important issue for video, especially in the design and deployment of mediaspace technologies [6]. Our approach addresses this issue in three ways. First, the spatial model concept of nimbus allows a video source to directly restrict its availability. By retracting one's nimbus, one can reduce the detail (i.e., quality) of the video that is received by an observer or can prevent transmission altogether. Second, the spatial model supports an explicit notion of virtual boundaries which may have different effects on mutual awareness. Third, observers are embodied within the CVE, and typically have to approach a video source in order to access it in any detail. In so doing, they themselves become visible to both the source and to other observers. We argue that this provides the stimulus for the social negotiation of privacy.

Seamless shifts in mutual involvement and access

A further issue concerns how participants adjust their visual and spatial access with regard to changing demands of particular activities. Some video-conferencing and mediaspace systems have begun to provide participants with access views other than the faces of the co-participants. In many cases this simply consists of a document view, but may include access to the other's environment. With almost all these systems, participants have to *deliberately* select the alternative view. The problem which arises is that, in the course of an activity, the participants have to shift their involvement from the activity in which they are engaged, in order to select the appropriate views they require for engaging in that activity. Shifts in alignment emporally rupture the task and interaction. Our own approach is designed to facilitate significant changes in mutual access as an integral part of the ways in which the participants behave. For example, simply moving from the overview of the environment towards a particular individual or domain, transforms your video access to the other, and of course the other's access to you. In this way shifts in mutual access become a feature of the ways in which you organise your interaction and activity at hand, without requiring participants to temporarily suspend their involvement, in order to explicitly change the ways in which they are aligned to each other.

Related to these various social concerns is the corresponding technical issue of providing appropriate control over underlying video QoS so as to meet dynamically changing communication requirements. We focus on four aspects of this problem: making QoS visible at the user interface; dynamically negotiating QoS; managing multiple video streams; and expressing QoS trade-offs between communications media.

Making video QoS visible at the interface

As noted earlier, in spite of many developments in the underlying technology, relatively little attention has been paid as to how to make QoS visible at the user interface [14]. We argue that current QoS mechanisms are limited by being too low level and by being medium specific. Participants should not be expected to reason about video frame-rates, resolutions, compression, bandwidth, delay and the complex inter-dependencies between them. Our approach addresses this problem by allowing participants to employ familiar spatial behaviours in order to control underlying QoS. At the highest level participants are concerned with spatial actions such as movement or with the use of spatial structures such as boundaries. Even if aura, focus and nimbus are made visible, we argue that they are relatively intuitive, being concerned with extent of presence, focus of attention and projection of information. They are also medium independent so that users do not have to learn the mechanics of QoS in each available communication.

Dynamic (re)negotiation of QoS

Current approaches to QoS are based on a relatively static model of communication. Even where QoS re-negotiation is possible, it is seen as an exceptional event. In contrast many social situations are highly fluid, involving dynamic groups of participants and rapidly changing communication requirements. At the heart of awareness driven video QoS is the idea of an on-going negotiation of mutual awareness and hence QoS. Rapid spatial movements such as re-orientation can have a dramatic effect on communication (e.g. turning away from one set of video sources to face another) and so very dynamic changes are possible. Furthermore, the separation of focus from nimbus in the spatial model directly reflects the idea of negotiating QoS between a video source and sink and the intervening network.

Simultaneous management of multiple video streams

Another limitation of current approaches is that they focus on managing the QoS of a single video stream at a time. Although this may be sufficient for services such as video on demand, collaborative applications will require users to allocate resources across a number of participants. The problem then becomes how to achieve the best allocation. The mechanisms defined at the user interface level (i.e., spatial movement and structures) and the computational awareness of our framework are inherently multi-stream. A single action in the virtual world or a single adjustment to the shape of an aura, focus or nimbus will affect the QoS settings for potentially many video streams.

Cross medium trade-offs

Beyond the synchronisation of video and audio from a single source, cross-medium QoS issues have received little attention to date. We argue that human communication involves a number of important trade-offs between media. Our senses are such that we can often see objects that we cannot hear (e.g. distant objects) or vice versa (e.g. objects that are behind us or are occluded by a nearby object). We believe that these differences are highly significant to social interaction because they establish key distinctions between direct and peripheral awareness. Thus, one can listen to someone talking while watching out for others who are approaching or can study an object while overhearing a peripheral conversation. Under our approach, the spatial model mechanisms can be configured differently for each medium of interaction (e.g. one could have a spherical audio focus and a directed visual focus) but can be jointly manipulated through the same spatial actions. Thus, spatial movement may re-configure QoS across different objects in different media, but will maintain the overall balance between what is directed and what is peripheral in each.

SUMMARY

We have extended previous work on texturing video streams into CVEs through the introduction of awareness driven video QoS. Movements in a shared virtual environment are mapped onto different levels of mutual awareness via the spatial model of interaction. In turn, awareness levels map onto different video services corresponding to different QoS parameters. We have demonstrated this approach through an integrated conferencing and mediaspace application which uses textured video streams to display facial expressions and to provide views into local physical environments. This uses awareness driven QoS to seamlessly move between three different video services (*porthole*, *glance* and *communication*) according to a user's movements.

We argue that the general approach of situating video displays within a 3-D virtual world offers three main advantages: it may help establish a degree of spatial consistency between different video views; it allows a direct representation of the viewpoints of those who are accessing video images (essentially, the third dimension allows the representation of a viewpoint that is separate from and looking at a 2-D plane); and it uses natural movements to switch between different video views without disrupting the activity at hand. Given these observations, our technique of awareness driven video QoS then introduces greater flexibility into the way that such video displays are managed within a virtual world. Specifically, it allows users to establish an optimal allocation of limited resources (processing and network) across multiple video streams and contains explicit support for privacy. However, perhaps the most important feature of this work is that it forges a direct link between social concerns and lower level technical concerns (i.e., emerging network QoS mechanisms).

Of course, a number of important issues require further consideration. The overall communication space is still fragmented into multiple physical spaces connected by a shared virtual space - will users be able to reconcile these different spaces? Will the increased overhead of rendering 3-D video textures as compared to 2-D video windows be outweighed by the benefits of this approach? The answers to these questions await deployment and experimentation. However, even given these potential reservations, we believe that the technique of awareness driven QoS represents a potentially powerful extension to previous work on video texturing in virtual environments and video communications in general.

ACKNOWLEDGMENTS

We are grateful to EPSRC, BT Laboratories and the EU's ESPRIT I[3] programme for supporting this work.

REFERENCES

1. Benford, S. D., Greenhalgh, C. M. and Lloyd, D., Crowded Collaborative Environments, *Proc CHI'97*, Atlanta, pp. 59-66, USA, March 1997, ACM Press.
2. Bowers, J., Pycock, J. and O'Brien, J., Talk and Embodiment in Collaborative Virtual Environments, *Proc CHI'96*, ACM Press, 1996.
3. Braden, R., Clark, D., Shenker, S., Integrated Services in the Internet Architecture: An Overview, *IETF RFC 1663*, July 1994.
4. Deering, S., Host Extensions for IP Multicasting, *IETF RFC 1112*, August 1989.
5. Dourish, P. and Bly, S., Portholes: Supporting Awareness in Distributed Workgroups, *Proc CHI'92*, May 1992.
6. Dourish, P., Culture and Control in a Media Space, *Proc. ECSCW'93*, Milano, September 1993, Kluwer.
7. Gaver, W., Sellen, A., Heath, C. And Luff, P., One is not enough: multiple views in a media space, *Computer Human Interaction*, Amsterdam,pp 220-240.
8. Greenhalgh, C. and Benford, S., MASSIVE: A Virtual Reality System for Tele-conferencing, *ACM TOCHI, 2 (3)*, pp. 239-261, ACM Press, 1995.
9. Han, J. and Smith, B., CU-SeeMe VR Immersive Desktop Teleconferencing, *Proc. Multimedia'96*, Nov 18-22, Boston, USA, pp199-208, ACM Press.
10. Heath, C. And Luff, P., Disembodied Conduct: Communication through Video in a Multi-media Environment, *Proc. CHI'91*, ACM Press, pp 99-103.
11. Ichikawa, Y., Okada, K., Jeong, G., Tanaka, S. and Matushita, Y., MAJIC Videoconferencing System: Experiments, Evaluation and Improvement, *Proc ECSCW'95*, Stockholm, Sweden, 1995, Kluwer.
12. Nakanishi, H., Yoshida, C., Nishimura, T. and Ishida, T., Freewalk: Supporting Causal Meetings in a Network, *Proc. CSCW'96*, pp. 308-314, ACM Press.
13. Sellen, S. and Buxton, B., Using Spatial Cues to Improve Videoconferencing, *Proc. CHI'92*, May 3-9, 1992, pp 651-652, ACM Press.
14. Vogel, A., Kerhervé, B., von Bochmann, G., and Gecsei, J., Distributed Multimedia and QOS: A Survey, *IEEE Multimedia*, Summer 1995, pp 10-19.

Supporting Situated Actions in High Volume Conversational Data Situations

Christopher Lueg
AI-Lab, Department of Computer Science
University of Zurich
Winterthurerstrasse 190, CH-8057 Zurich, Switzerland
Tel. +41 1 63 54577 Fax +41 1 63 56809
lueg@ifi.unizh.ch

ABSTRACT

The global conferencing system Usenet news offers an amount of articles per day that exceeds human cognitive capabilities by far although the articles are already organized in hierarchically structured discussion groups covering distinct topics. We report here on a situated information filtering system that significantly reduces the burden by supporting the user in acting situated. Interpreting the user's actions as situated actions, the approach complements current filtering and recommender approaches by completely avoiding the modeling of user interests; the user is the only instance for assigning (un-)interestingness to Usenet discussions.

Keywords

Situated cognition, situated actions, Usenet news, information filtering

INTRODUCTION

The huge and increasing amount of information available in the information age suggests to investigate new ways to support humans in gathering information that might be interesting, helpful, or necessary for them. Since the overall amount of information exceeds human cognitive capabilities by far, computers are increasingly used to help users to find the information they are looking for. One of the central questions is how to provide adequate support for the information seeking process. From a cognitive science and situated cognition perspective, the goal is not to automate but to support this process in order to allow for situatedness and the peculiarities of human cognition.

In this paper, we present a situated information filtering approach to support users in coping with high volume conversational data. This approach is based on the perspective that human behavior is inherently situated (see below) and complements other approaches by avoiding to automatically find information that might be interesting to the user. Support is given by a potentially significant reduction of the amount of new Usenet articles that are to be investigated by the user. In addition, the user is supported in becoming aware of his or her interests. Data gained by monitoring the user's browsing behavior is used to find out about discussions that are likely to be *uninteresting* (instead of trying to determine the interesting discussions, since this would involve modeling of the user's interests). In order to avoid misinterpretations, the situated information filtering approach uses a high degree of interactivity. The augmented newsreader interface always allows the user to accept or to reject indicated consequences of his or her actions.

We will proceed as follows. First, we give a brief overview about several approaches currently used to support users in coping with high volume conversational data situations and other so-called "information overload" [18] situations. Then, we introduce the notion of situatedness and discuss some implications of this view for the design of human-computer interfaces. Based on these considerations, we discuss the benefits of the situated information filtering approach and describe how the state-of-the-art newsreader `Knews` has been modified to support situated information filtering in the Usenet news domain. The paper concludes with a discussion of first user experiences with the augmented newsreader which we call `spynews` because of the additional spying behavior.

CURRENT SUPPORT FOR INFORMATION SEEKING PROCESSES

Objects that are potentially interesting to users may vary from virtual entities, such as World Wide Web (WWW) pages or Usenet articles, to real-world entities, such as books, CDs, or movies. The former are accessible to computers while the latter typically are inaccessible to computers. Concerning the way objects are dealt with, basically two distinct approaches can

CHI 98 Los Angeles CA USA
Copyright 1998 0-89791-975-0/98/ 4..$5.00

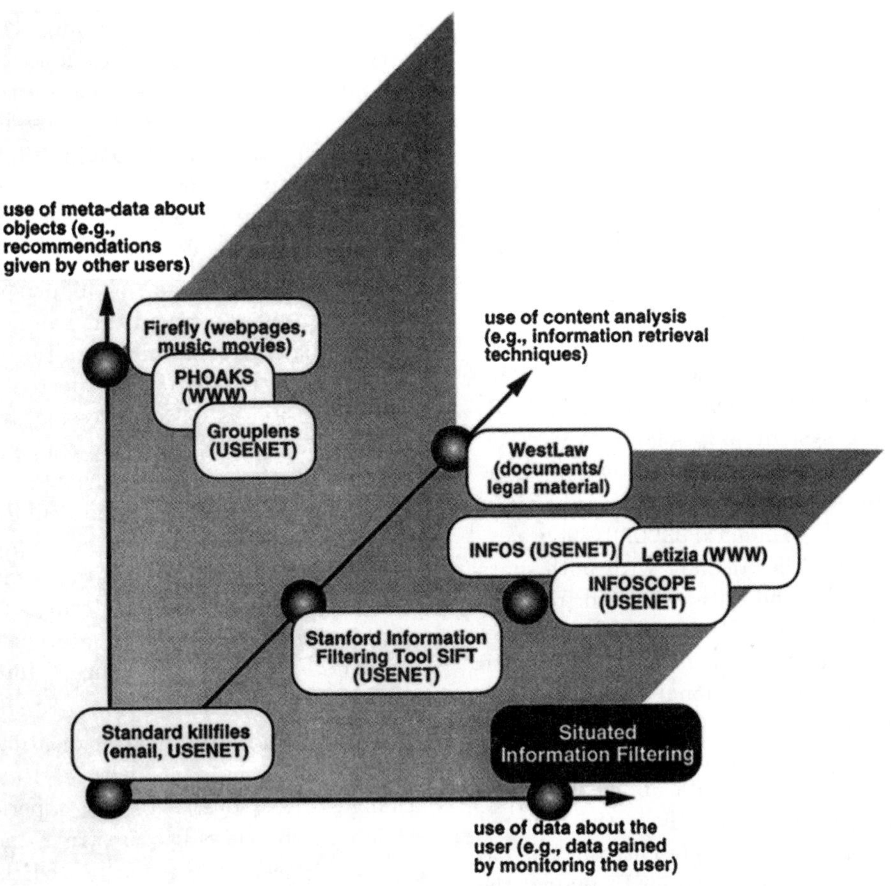

Figure 1: Classification of several systems according to the way they deal with the objects under investigation and the extent with which they rely upon monitoring user behavior (see text).

currently be distinguished (see figure 1).

On the one hand, traditional *information filtering systems* [23] directly deal with potentially interesting objects by analyzing these objects and extracting certain features indicating "interestingness". Commonly, these systems deal only with textual objects (i.e., documents), such as most WWW pages or Usenet articles, and incorporate information-retrieval techniques, which can be applied to information filtering [4]. Documents are dealt with by conversion into surrogates more amenable to automatic processing. Boolean, vector space, and probabilistic retrieval models are the main techniques in order to match models of user interests, commonly referred to as profiles, and models of documents [8]. The best matching documents are considered most promising and are presented to the user. Adaptive filtering systems use characteristic features of documents actually selected by the user to adapt the model of the user's interests to changes in these interests. Most current information-retrieval techniques are actually limited to textual representations although techniques for multimedia information retrieval are subject to research [19].

On the other hand, *recommender systems* [25], also referred to as social filtering systems or collaborative filtering systems, mimic the social process of giving recommendations to friends and colleagues in situations, when the information at hand is insufficient to make a good choice. Recommender systems collect and aggregate recommendations given by other users in order to give advice upon request. One of the main advantages of this automation of the "word of mouth" [26] is that the recommendation approach is completely independent from the actual topic and the representation of the objects to be recommended. Therefore, recommender systems can deal with both virtual objects and real-world objects. Indeed, recommender systems exist for topics as different as movies, music, and documents, such as Usenet articles and most WWW pages. As in adaptive filtering systems, requests for advice and feedback on user satisfaction are used to construct a model of the user's interests.

Figure 1 classifies several major approaches according to the way they deal with the objects under investigation and the extend with which the approaches rely upon monitoring user behavior. Examples for systems that directly deal with textual objects without additional user data are standard "killfiles" incorporating simple keyword-matching algorithms in order to hide or highlight certain emails or Usenet articles. Examples for systems incorporating this kind of filtering are the newsreaders `Gnus`[1] and `Knews`[2]. A prime example for an advanced filtering system directly dealing with documents is the Stanford information filtering tool `SIFT` [34] doing brute-force filtering.

Examples for systems that do not directly access the objects under consideration but deal with (meta-)data about these objects are the `GroupLens`[3] [24, 12] collaborative filtering system for Usenet news, the `PHOAKS`[4] collaborative filtering system [32, 33] for WWW resources, the `Firefly`[5] recommender system, and the `MORSE`[6] movie recommendation system.

`Letizia` [15], `INFOS` [21], and `INFOSCOPE` [29] are examples for hybrid approaches dealing with both, data about the user's behavior and data extracted from the documents (WWW pages and Usenet articles, respectively). The `GroupLens` researchers are also investigating the incorporation of additional data about the user's reading behavior [20]. The situated information filtering approach shares a lot of similarities with these systems in that it incorporates data about the user's information seeking behavior. However, the situated information filtering approach [16] presented in this paper is different, since it completely avoids to analyze the potentially interesting objects and it does not incorporate modeling of the user's interests (see below).

ABSTRACTIONS AND SITUATEDNESS

Both, the recommender approach and the information-retrieval-based filtering approach, abstract away from the objects they are dealing with (e.g., pictures or documents). In the case of recommender systems, the abstraction is done when humans express their likes and dislikes in terms of numerical ratings and when these ratings are aggregated to preference profiles. Regarding the recommendations, the social context of a recommendation is abstracted away from its social embedding; the recommendation is de-contextualized [17]. In the case of information-retrieval-based filtering systems, the abstraction is done implicitly, since most information retrieval techniques deal only with representations and not with the pragmatic meaning the text has to the users.

It is a prerequisite of these approaches that they construct an abstract representation of the user's interests, commonly referred to as profile. The profile is necessary -within the chosen rationalistic approach [18]- to automatically match assumed user interests with documents potentially satisfying these interests. However, apart from its computational advantages, such as efficient matching of profiles with objects, the use of abstraction implies a gap between actual user interests and their abstract descriptions.

From a situated cognition [6] perspective, it would be best to completely avoid this gap in order to allow for the peculiarities of human cognition. In contrast to the so-called "rationalistic" perspective, which views human cognition as data-processing and behavior as being largely predetermined by plans, the situated cognition perspective suggests to view cognition, knowledge, and behavior as being fundamentally *situated*: cognition and knowledge are emergent properties of the interaction of an individual with its environment, i.e., its current situation (thus, the term "situatedness"). Cognition cannot be reduced to internal "data-processing", it cannot be "de-contextualized" into a set of abstract descriptions [31, 6].

One important implication of situatedness is that the way a human interacts with a situation continuously changes based on his or her experience. Knowledge should not be viewed as substrate that can be extracted but as something that is located in physical interaction and social participation [6]. Accordingly, "interest" should be viewed as something that is dynamically generated, i.e., an emergent property of the interaction of an individual with an "information situation" [17]. This perspective, however, does not necessarily question the existence of so-called long-term interests which is a basic assumption in traditional information filtering [23]. The situated perspective demands new tools that support the user in acting situated in "information overload" situations instead of imposing restrictions or constraints on the user and his or her interests.

INFORMATION SEEKING AND SITUATED ACTIONS

Traditional adaptive information filtering is based on the assumption that certain human actions, such as selecting a particular document or spending a sufficient amount of time reading a document, can be reasonably interpreted as indicators for "interest" in the corresponding document. However, even supposedly clear "expressions of interest" are always subject to the frame-of-reference-problem [5]. The frame-of-reference problem states that things might appear different from the user's and observer's perspective. In other words, the observer must be careful not to mix up observable behaviors with the user's internal mechanisms causing these behaviors. In case of information seeking behavior, the interest or information need is generated in the

[1] `http://www.gnus.org/`
[2] `http://www.student.nada.kth.se/~su95-kjo/knews.html`
[3] `http://www.cs.umn.edu/Research/GroupLens/`
[4] `http://www.phoaks.com/`
[5] `http://www.firefly.com/`
[6] `http://www.labs.bt.com/innovate/multimed/morse/morse.htm`

head of the observer, rather than in the head of the observed subject. Also, the information need is not so much "inside the user's head" [4], but a result of the interaction of the user with a continuously changing situation.

Results from research on the notion of interest indicate that it is hard to determine *why* a specific document has actually been selected. Experiments revealed that explanations of why a document was chosen for reading, or why it was found to be interesting varied and changed over time. The same result was obtained when the subjects were asked about their initial information need [14, 21, 11]. Now, if the selection of a document is interpreted as a "situated action" some of the putative "inconsistencies" and "irregularities" in the observations reported in the literature can be explained.

From the situated cognition perspective it can be explained why it is so hard to describe an information need. Information-need situations are dynamic and constantly changing [3]. Information needs cannot be reduced to internal information processes alone, but require interaction with the current information situation. This cognitive science perspective is in line with results from research on relevance also indicating that situational factors other than just the topical content of a selected document influence relevance judgments. Factors influencing the judgments are any factors that users bring into the situation, such as experience, background, knowledge level, beliefs, and personal preferences [3]. Also, the user judgments are influenced by the purposes, expectations, the relevance of references, and future time savings [30].

SITUATED INFORMATION FILTERING

We have investigated new ways to support humans in high volume conversational data situations. Our situated information filtering approach focuses on supporting the user in acting situated rather than doing the information filtering for him or her. Avoiding to model the user's interests, our approach helps the user focus on what *might* be interesting by filtering what has shown to be uninteresting (see below).

A prime example for high volume conversational data situations is participating in the global conferencing system Usenet news. Due to its high data volume and its global availability, Usenet is frequently used for information filtering experiments (e.g., [10, 27, 13, 21]). Usenet offers more than 300000 articles per day[7] and the amount is still increasing. Although the articles are already organized within a hierarchy of more than 15.000 newsgroups (groups of articles sharing a particular topic, e.g., the newsgroup `comp.ai` has the topic computers and artificial intelligence), it is not uncommon that high volume newsgroups still offer more than 1000 articles per day.

Most Usenet users participate in several newsgroups covering different topics. It is not uncommon to scan 20-30 newsgroups for interesting articles. Typically, only a minor part of all articles in a newsgroup is actually read.

From the observer's perspective, the main problem *seems* to be to detect the "interesting" articles among the uninteresting ones. Accordingly, most approaches to help users in coping with high volume conversational data or other "information overload" situations try to partly automate the information seeking process by matching models of user interests with potentially interesting documents (e.g., [10, 27, 13, 21, 15]).

However, considering the frame-of-reference problem and the inherent dynamic of interests suggests to make as few assumptions as possible about the user's motivation and his or her actual interests. Consequently, the main difference between the situated information filtering approach and more traditional information filtering approaches how the data about the user's behavior is interpreted and how the data is exploited for filtering. The situated information filtering approach does neither consider assumed interests of the users nor the content of selected documents. Instead, situated information filtering helps the user to focus on potentially interesting articles by reducing (filtering) the amount of uninteresting data. The following design guidelines [18] helped to ensure that our approach appropriately accounts for situatedness:

1. Not too much value should be attributed to (single) user actions; they should not be interpreted as clear indicators of interest (sometimes, humans make faults, or they are under the influence of events that do not directly relate to the document search; documents may turn out to be uninteresting after having selected them).

2. Selection of a document should not be interpreted as necessarily indicating an information need.

3. Not too much importance should be attributed to author, title, etc.

4. Information needs depend on the actual situation: they are dynamic, not static.

For our Usenet experiments, the state-of-the-art **Knews**[8] newsreader has been augmented in order to provide support for situated information filtering. The resulting **spynews** newsreader [16] monitors most user actions, such as selecting a newsgroup, selecting a discussion (commonly referred to as thread) within a news-

[7] Usenet traffic statistics are published by UUNet in `de.admin.lists` and other newsgroups.

[8] `http://www.student.nada.kth.se/~su95-kjo/knews.html`

group, saving or printing an article, posting a follow-up, etc. Also, implicit data about the user's behavior is collected, such as the delay between the selection of a particular document and the selection of the next document (i.e., time *supposedly* spent to read the document) and whether the user has read a discussion partly or completely (i.e., whether all previously unread articles in the discussion have been read). Also, the user's basic browsing behavior is monitored. In order to inspect a particular discussion the user has to move a bar up or down to select the discussion among other discussions that are displayed in the main discussion window. Moving the bar can be accomplished by either using the arrow keys on the keyboard or pointing and clicking with the mouse. However, the data about the basic browsing behavior is not used for finding out about user interests but for gaining insights into the user's newsreading behavior, such as the detection of varying browsing habits in distinct newsgroups. First results indicate that the newsreading habits vary significantly between newsgroups and range from selecting only a few discussions to sequentially reading all available discussions.

The situated information filtering approach is a *discussion-oriented* approach and differs in this respect from most traditional filtering approaches focusing on single articles. Moreover, the situated information filtering approach focuses on the discussions the user is *not* interested in since evidence for *not* being interested in a discussion is much stronger than evidence for being interested in a discussion.

The detection of uninteresting discussions can be accomplished by monitoring whether the user repeatedly *ignores* a discussion while browsing a newsgroup. While the user is moving the selection bar towards a discussion he or she is interested in, the bar will be be moved across other discussions. This does not necessarily mean that the user is not interested in these discussions at all but it is at least an indicator that the user is less interested in the discussion. Ignoring a discussion does not cause the discussion to vanish immediately but to fade out gradually according to the overall "attention" paid to this discussion.

The "behavioral" status of a discussion is visualized as an augmentation to the representation of a discussion (in `Knews` a text line containing the subject of the discussion, the number of unread articles, and the author of the first article). A little mark changes its shape according to the user's actions. Ignoring a discussion causes the mark (and the newsgroup, accordingly) to migrate towards its final "uninteresting" state. Only if a discussion status reaches one of these states, the discussion will be marked as read or marked for filtering for a user-defined period of time. These actions are executed automatically when the user leaves the newsgroup. However, the user always has the opportunity to abandon the indicated consequences by clicking the third mouse button on a discussion which immediately resets the status of the discussion. Also, entering a discussion decreases the status since entering is interpreted as weak "interest". The complete advanced newsreader behavior can be controlled via user-definable parameters. These parameters do not only determine how often, for example, a subject has to be ignored in order to be filtered, but also allow an adaptation of the advanced newsreader behavior to different newsgroups since browsing varies significantly between different Usenet newsgroups. Put in a nutshell, the markers always indicate the consequences of the user's actions to ensure a comprehensible, predictable, and controllable user interfaces [28].

Leaving a newsgroup still containing unread discussions is interpreted as being less interested in the remaining discussions. Accordingly, the status of the discussions is slightly increased towards "uninteresting". However, if the user leaves the newsgroup by marking all unread discussions as read (the so-called `catchup` command) this is interpreted as stronger indicator for not being interested in the remaining discussions. Accordingly, the status of the discussions is more seriously increased compared to just leaving the newsgroup.

The final status of all discussions in the newsgroup is preserved in a database for further newsreading sessions. When the user (re-)enters the newsgroup, the status of the discussions is restored in order to reorder the discussions according to their supposed interestingness. Since no "interestingness" information about new discussions is available, these discussions are assumed potentially interesting and are located at the top. Below new discussions, the discussions that are already known are listed according to their status. Since no model of user interests is used to infer a degree of interestingness, the ordering of the discussions is decreasing, so that the less interesting discussions are located at the bottom of the window. This reordering of newsgroups between different sessions causes discussions behave like bubbles floating up and down according to the user's attention (in terms of actions) paid to the discussions. It is important to note that the status of a discussion is not determined on the basis of the content of the corresponding articles but the status is a result of the interaction of the user with the discussion.

The situated information filtering approach exploits the dynamic nature of Usenet and its technical constraints [9]. Two different methods to relate incoming articles to discussions are available. On the one hand, articles can be grouped to discussions by comparing the `Subject:` entries since all articles with the same `Subject:` entry are assumed to belong to the same discussion. This pattern-matching approach has some severe technical drawbacks, such as problems with entries that were not modified strictly according to the general Usenet rules in case of follow-ups or topical changes. On the other hand, considering a special `References:` entry allows to relate newly arriving articles to discussions (commonly referred to as threading). `Knews` and other state-of-the-art newsreaders already use references to organize articles to discussions. `spynews` as a discussion-oriented approach filters on the basis of both the subject and the references. `spynews` detects that the user ignores discussions on the basis of the subject but the actual filtering is done based on `Knews`'s threading of the corresponding articles. The filtering of the subsequent articles is based on the assumption that follow-ups to uninteresting articles are also uninteresting [22].

However, technically "belonging to the same discussion" does not necessarily mean that follow-up articles still have the same topic as the original article since it is a peculiarity of Usenet discussions to keep a discussion title while the topic of the discussion has already shifted to another topic. According to the situated perspective, the decision whether this new topic under the old subject is still interesting should be completely left to the user. Therefore, filtering of discussions is limited in time. Also, it is left to the user whether split-off discussions (commonly referred to as subthreads) are to be filtered if the original discussion is already filtered.

DISCUSSION

In this paper, we have presented a situated information filtering approach to support users in coping with high volume conversational data situations in the Usenet domain. The approach accounts for situatedness by avoiding to model the user's interests or to interpret his or her actions as clear indicators of interest. Instead, help is provided to focus the user's attention on potentially interesting articles by gradually fading out, deleting, and reordering subjects that have shown to be less interesting. Depending on the actual newsgroup, this significantly reduces the amount of potentially interesting subjects the user has to browse.

For our Usenet experiments, the state-of-the-art `Knews`[9] newsreader has been augmented in order to provide support for situated information filtering. Experiences with the resulting `spynews` newsreader prototype have shown that it is indeed possible to provide an encouraging level of support without automating the information seeking process by matching models of user interests with documents. Experienced Usenet users find this more situated approach useful. However, further experiments have to be conducted to clarify whether this also holds true for less experienced or even novel users.

[9] `http://www.student.nada.kth.se/~su95-kjo/knews.html`

Users like the high degree of interactivity and the permanent visual feedback provided by the `spynews` interface since this feedback guarantees that the filtering is predictable and controllable. However, these results are preliminary since they only reflect the opinions of experienced Usenet users which were familiar with the standard `Knews` newsreader. Long-term user tests involving less experienced users and users preferring other newsreaders than `Knews` are under preparation and are scheduled for the next few months.

The efficiency of this discussion-oriented approach, however, depends on the average length (i.e., number of unread articles) of the uninteresting discussions. The length of Usenet discussions varies significantly between newsgroups. For example, "discussions" in announcement newsgroups are typically quite short, while discussions in newsgroups dealing with recreational topics or with topics related to computer security or Usenet administration may comprise hundreds of articles. It is one of the strengths of this discussion-oriented approach to release the user from long-lasting discussions that have shown to be uninteresting.

Running `spynews` on low-end Sun workstations under SunOS and Solaris, experiences have shown that the additional database accesses at the beginning and at the end of browsing a newsgroup do not significantly influence the runtime behavior of the *spynews* newsreader. Also, the size of such a database (currently one database per newsgroup the user is subscribed to) is still less than 100 kilobytes after several weeks of usage. The expire time (i.e., how long subjects are kept in the `spynews` database) has been set to one month.

Although first results are encouraging, they should not be interpreted as if this purely situated approach is an *alternative* to traditional filtering and recommendation approaches. Instead, the more situated approach should be regarded as a *complement* to traditional approaches. The golden mean is probably somewhere between a more rationalistic approach and this purely situated approach. Extended user experiments are under preparation to find out about the extent to which the situated filtering perspective can be reasonably exploited.

Currently, our focus is on Usenet only but we believe that the situated perspective is also valuable for other domains with "information overload" situations, such as email or the WWW. Also, the notion of situatedness introduces an important perspective into the technology-driven, largely rationalistic, Internet culture.

RELATED WORK

Although based on a different perspective, which is strongly influenced by results from research on situated cognition, the situated filtering approach shares similarities with traditional recommender or information filtering approaches.

Similar to most advanced filtering and recommending approaches in the Usenet domain [7, 22, 21] or in the WWW domain [1, 15, 2], the situated information filtering system spynews exploits data gained "for free" [15] by monitoring the user's behavior. However, based on the user's actions, these approaches try to infer what the user is interested in. spynews is different in that it avoids to infer user interests. To the contrary, it supports the user in focusing on potentially interesting discussions by filtering discussions that have shown to be uninteresting.

As in recommender systems, spynews does not directly deal with the objects under consideration. However, recommender systems abstract ratings to profiles while spynews avoids this abstraction step. The "interestingness" of discussions is solely based on the interaction of the user with the available discussions. Of course, user actions are interpreted in spynews, i.e., meaning is projected onto the actions, but the interpretations are not used to infer what the user is interested in. Also, the consequences of the interpretations are weak and interactivity ensures allows the user to accept or reject the indicated consequences.

In particular, spynews shares basic assumptions with two of the above mentioned systems, INFOSCOPE [7] and Letizia [15]. Both systems aim at supporting the user instead of completely automating the task at hand. Both systems try to make the best use of the most limited resource of the user, which is the user's attention. Also, both systems try to keep the context of their recommendations: Letizia provides on-line support while the user is browsing the WWW and INFOSCOPE regroups Usenet articles to artificial special-interest newsgroups. However, spynews completely avoids the modeling of interests.

ACKNOWLEDGMENTS

The author would like to thank Ralf Salomon and Elke Siemon for their help and is grateful to Rolf Pfeifer for a stimulating research environment. Special thanks go to Karl-Johan Johnsson for the permission to use and to modify his Knews newsreader for the Usenet experiments.

References

[1] Robert Armstrong, Dayne Freitag, Thorsten Joachims, and Tom Mitchell. Webwatcher: A learning apprentice for the world wide web. In *Information gathering from heterogeneous, distributed environments : Papers from the 1995 AAAI Spring Symposium*, Menlo Park, California, 1995. AAAI Press.

[2] Marko Balabanović. An adaptive web page recommendation service. In *Proceedings of the First International Conference on Autonomous Agents*, 1997.

[3] Carol L. Barry. User-defined relevance criteria: An exploratory study. *Journal of the American Society for Information Science (JASIS)*, 45(3):149–159, 1994.

[4] Nicholas J. Belkin and W. Bruce Croft. Information filtering and information retrieval: Two sides of the same coin? *Communications of the ACM*, 35(12):29–38, December 1992.

[5] William J. Clancey. The frame of reference problem in the design of intelligent machines. In K. van Lehn, editor, *Architectures for Intelligence. The 22nd Carnegie Mellon Symposium on Cognition*, pages 257–423. 1991.

[6] William J. Clancey. *Situated Cognition. On Human Knowledge and Computer Representations.* Cambridge University Press, 1997.

[7] Gerhard Fischer and Curt Stevens. Information access in complex, poorly structured information spaces. In *Proceedings of the Annual ACM SIGCHI Conference on Human Factors in Computing Systems (CHI'91)*, pages 63–70. ACM Press, April 1991.

[8] Peter W. Foltz and Susan T. Dumais. Personalized information delivery: An analysis of information filtering methods. *Communications of the ACM*, 35(12):51–60, December 1992.

[9] M. Horton and R. Adams. RFC-1036 (request for comments), December 1987.

[10] Andrew Jennings and Hideyuki Higuchi. A personal news service based on a user model neural network. *IE-ICE Transactions on Information Systems*, March 1992.

[11] Fredrik Kilander, Eva Fåhræus, and Jacob Palme. Intelligent information filtering. Technical report, Department of Computer and Systems Science, Stockholm University, February 1997.

[12] Joseph A. Konstan, Bradley N. Miller, David Maltz, Jonathan L. Herlocker, Lee R. Gordon, and John Riedl. Applying collaborative filtering to Usenet news. *Communications of the ACM*, 40(3):77–87, March 1997.

[13] Ken Lang. Newsweeder: Learning to filter netnews. In *Proceedings of the Twelth International Conference on Machine Learning*. Morgan Kaufmann, 1995.

[14] Ann Lantz. How do experienced users of the system Usenet news select their information? Technical report, Department of Computer and Systems Science, University of Stockholm, 1993.

[15] Henry Lieberman. Autonomous interface agents. In *Proceedings of the Annual ACM SIGCHI Conference on Human Factors in Computing Systems (CHI'97)*, pages 67–74. ACM Press, March 1997.

[16] Christopher Lueg. An adaptive Usenet interface supporting situated actions. In *Proceedings of the 3rd ERCIM Workshop on User Interfaces for All*, 1997.

[17] Christopher Lueg. Social filtering and social reality. In *Proceedings of the 5th DELOS Workshop on Filtering and Collaborative Filtering*, 1997.

[18] Christopher Lueg and Rolf Pfeifer. Cognition, situatedness, and situated design. In Jonathan P. Marsh, Chrystopher L. Nehaniv, and Barbara Gorayska, editors, *Proceedings of the Second International Conference on Cognitive Technology*, pages 124–135. IEEE Computer Society, 1997.

[19] Mark T. Maybury, editor. *Intelligent Multimedia Information Retrieval*. MIT Press, 1997.

[20] Bradley N. Miller, John T. Riedl, and Joseph A. Konstan. Experiments with GroupLens: Making Usenet useful again. In *Proceedings of the 1997 USENIX Winter Technical Conference*, January 1997.

[21] Kenrick J. Mock. Hybrid hill-climbing and knowledge-based techniques for intelligent news filtering. In *Proceedings of the National Conference on Artificial Intelligence (AAAI'96)*, Menlo Park, California, 1996. AAAI Press.

[22] Masahiro Morita and Yoichi Shinoda. Information filtering based on user behavior analysis and best match text retrieval. In *Proceedings of the ACM-SIGIR Conference on Research and Development in Information Retrieval (SIGIR'94)*. Springer-Verlag London, 1994.

[23] Douglas W. Oard and Gary Marchionini. A conceptual framework for text filtering. Technical Report CS-TR-3643, University of Maryland, May 1996.

[24] Paul Resnick, Neophytos Iacovou, Mitesh Suchak, Peter Berstrom, and John Riedl. GroupLens: An open architecture for collaborative filtering of netnews. In Richard Furuta and Christine Neuwirth, editors, *Proceedings of the International Conference on Computer Supported Cooperative Work (CSCW'94)*, pages 175–186. ACM Press, October 1994.

[25] Paul Resnick and Hal R. Varian. Recommender systems. *Communications of the ACM*, 40(3):56–58, March 1997.

[26] Upendra Shardanand and Pattie Maes. Social information filtering: Algorithms for automating "word of the mouth". In Irvin Katz et al., editor, *Proceedings of the Annual ACM SIGCHI Conference on Human Factors in Computing Systems (CHI'95)*, pages 210–217. ACM Press, May 1995.

[27] Beerud Sheth and Pattie Maes. Evolving agents for personalized information filtering. In *Ninth International Conference on Artificial Intelligence for Applications*, pages 345–352. IEEE Computer Society Press, March 1993.

[28] Ben Shneiderman. Direct manipulation for comprehensible, predictable, and controllable user interfaces. In *Proceedings of the International Conference on Intelligent User Interfaces (IUI'97)*, pages 33–39, January 1997.

[29] Curt Stevens. Automating the creation of information filters. *Communications of the ACM*, 35(12), December 1992.

[30] Louise T. Su. The relevance of recall and precision in user evaluation. *Journal of the American Society for Information Science (JASIS)*, 45(3):207–217, 1994.

[31] Lucy Suchman. *Plans and situated actions - The Problem of Human-Machine Communication*. Cambridge University Press, 1987.

[32] Loren Terveen, Will Hill, Brian Amento, David McDonald, and Josh Creter. PHOAKS: A system for sharing recommendations. *Communications of the ACM*, 40(3):59–62, March 1997.

[33] Loren Terveen, William C. Hill, Brian Amento, David McDonald, and Josh Creter. Building task-specific interfaces to high volume conversational data. In *Proceedings of the Annual ACM SIGCHI Conference on Human Factors in Computing Systems (CHI'97) Conference Proceedings*, pages 226–233. ACM Press, 1997.

[34] Tak W. Yan and Hector Garcia-Molina. SIFT - a tool for wide-area information dissimination. In *1995 USENIX technical conference*, pages 177–186, 1995.

Heart Rate Variability: Indicator of User State as an Aid to Human-Computer Interaction

Dennis W. Rowe
The MITRE Corporation
1820 Dolly Madison Boulevard
McLean, VA 22101 USA
+1 703 883 5883
drowe@mitre.org

John Sibert
The George Washington University
Washington, D.C. 20052 USA
+1 202 994 4953
sibert@seas.gwu.edu

Don Irwin
MAJ USAF HQ USAF/TEP
1530 Air Force Pentagon
Washington, D.C. 20330 USA
+1 703 695 0900
irwind@seas.gwu.edu

ABSTRACT

This preliminary study explores the use of Heart Rate Variability (HRV) as an indicator of user state. In the study, a visual display is used to vary the levels of a complexity factor to assess the impact on user mental effort in a monitoring task. Mental effort is measured both subjectively and physiologically. Two findings indicate the potential value of HRV. First, user HRV showed significant discriminatory sensitivity to the manipulation of the independent variable on the basis of domain experience. Second, HRV appeared to indicate the point at which user capacity to process targets was exceeded. Results warrant further investigation but suggest the use of HRV as a tool for design and analysis of user interfaces, and as a research basis for use as component of an adaptive interface.

Keywords

Heart rate variability, mental effort, user state, air traffic management, airspace complexity, free flight

INTRODUCTION

Over the past three decades, human monitoring of visual displays has become relatively commonplace. During this same timeframe however, the information to be monitored has become increasingly more complex, often in both pattern and in sheer volume of information displayed. Because of this increased complexity, situations requiring human monitoring are apt to create cognitive loads on users that can adversely affect their performance. Errors resulting from cognitively burdened users may have disastrous consequences in terms of monetary losses, or worse, the loss of human lives [1].

We believe that having a computer monitor the state of the user via physiological measures can alleviate challenges brought about by the complexity of information on the visual display. Evolving computer technology should enable interfaces to be developed that possess a special sensitivity to the states of attention and intentions of users as suggested by Velichkovsky and Hansen [19]. Computer knowledge of user state should not only be useful in designing effective interfaces, but also in adapting interfaces to accommodate individual user differences.

It is widely recognized that perceptions of complexity vary from individual to individual. Differences among individuals such as age, experience, and training, to name a few, account for some of the variation in these perceptions [11]. The important role that individual differences play in the way humans perceive the visual display information highlights the need for designing future human-computer interfaces that are sensitive to the capabilities and limitations of individual users. Computer system designs that account for individual differences will be of value, as they will foster a human-machine synergy allowing both the human and computer system to operate at peak efficiency. Given their unique "signatures" and often high correlation with perceived workload, physiological measures of mental effort are perhaps the most likely areas to draw from in order to provide a foundation for the analysis and design of future user interfaces [17].

Advantages of Physiological Measures in Determining Mental Effort

The advantages of using physiological measures to determine mental effort are manifold. First, they are relatively unobtrusive; assuming of course that users adapt to the few transducers that are affixed to their bodies. Secondly, they provide measures which do not require overt performance; that is, most physiological measures can be recorded in the absence of overt behavior. It should be noted, however, that it is often advantageous to obtain measures of both performance and physiology in order to infer changes in user strategies and workload with variations in system demands. Third, physiological measures are inherently multi-dimensional and can provide a number of 'views' of user mental workload.

CHI 98 Los Angeles CA USA
Copyright 1998 0-89791-975-0/98/ 4..$5.00

Lastly, since most physiological signals are recorded continuously, they offer the potential for providing measures that respond relatively quickly to phasic shifts in mental effort and workload [8].

Several physiological measures have been used as an index of user mental effort and mental workload. Included are two general classes of physiological measures: central nervous system and peripheral nervous system measures. Central nervous system measures include electroencephalographic (EEG) activity, event-related brain potentials (ERP), magnetoencephlographic activity (MEG), measures of brain metabolism such as positron emission tomography (PET), and measures of electro-oculographic (EOG) activity. Peripheral nervous system measures include cardiovascular measures, measures of pupil diameter, respiratory measures, and measures of electrodermal activity (EDA) [8]. Each of these measures has its strengths and weaknesses in terms of the relative difficulty in collecting, analyzing, and interpreting their meaning; each also differs along the lines of sensitivity, diagnosticity, intrusiveness, reliability, and generality of application.

The most popular physiological techniques employed in the assessment of mental effort and mental workload in the last 30 years have been measures of cardiac activity [21]. Sensitivity of a number of different cardiac measures to variations in workload have been examined. These techniques include: the electrocardiogram (ECG), blood pressure measures, and measures of blood volume. Of these three, measures of electrocardiographic activity have shown the most promise [8].

In the current study, we examined several possible measures for assessing user state [21]. Based upon the criteria of sensitivity, diagnosticity, ease of data collection, and nonintrusiveness, we decided to use a measure of electrocardiographic activity; specifically, Heart rate variability (HRV).

This study examines the efficacy of using HRV under conditions of varying complexity to provide feedback to a computer on the state of the human user. We envision that the computer system can use this feedback to form the basis for adapting to individual user differences, thus creating a human-computer system synergy for ensuring acceptable levels of human performance.

The study seeks to answer the following broad question: To what extent can HRV be used as an indicator of user effort under conditions of varying workload? This question has the following sub-components:

- How do changes in the complexity factor affect subjective measures of user mental effort and user workload?
- How sensitive is HRV to changes in the complexity factor? What is the nature of this sensitivity?
- What is the relationship between HRV and the subjective measure of user mental effort? To what extent, and under what conditions do these measures correlate?

We believe that answers to these questions can support the use of HRV as a means of identifying problem areas of user interfaces. We also think that answers to these questions may point to the use of HRV as real-time mechanism for adapting visual displays to the needs of individual users.

Background

Acceptance of HRV as a Measure of Mental Effort

Since the early 1980s, Heart rate variability (HRV), or sinus arrhythmia, has gained widespread acceptance as a measure of mental effort. HRV is a measure of the oscillation of the interval between consecutive heartbeats. The literature is replete with references to this measure that are expressed in terms of consecutive cardiac cycles. Such terms include: cycle length variability, heart period variability, R-R interval variability (referring to the beat-to-beat interval formed by consecutive R-waves of the cardiac signal), and the R-R interval tachogram [6, 7].

The use of HRV in both laboratory and field settings is valued not only because of its nonintrusiveness, but also because of its utility where continuous recording is required [17]. In laboratory studies, HRV has consistently responded to changes from rest to task conditions and to a range of between-task manipulations [1,13,16]. In operational contexts, HRV has seen increased use as an indicator of the extent of task engagement in information processing requiring significant mental effort, particularly in flight-related studies [8, 16, 17, 22, 23]. HRV has also responded rapidly to changes in user workload and strategies, usually within seconds [1, 2]. Thus, HRV has been able to detect rapid transient shifts in mental workload [8].

Spectral Analysis of Sinus Arrhythmia

Spectral analysis methods have been applied to the cardiac interval tachogram. Power spectral density analysis provides information on how power (or variance) distributes as a function of frequency. With the cardiac interval tachogram, the power spectral density analysis yields a measure of how the heart fluctuates as a result of changes in the autonomic nervous system [7].

Spectral components of the cardiac interval signal for short-term changes in HRV fall into three frequency ranges: the Very Low Frequency (VLF) range, the Low Frequency (LF) range, and the High Frequency (HF) range. For long-term changes in HRV, e.g. 24 hour recordings, the Ultra Low Frequency (ULF) range is also examined [6].

The LF component, known as the baroreflex band, is of chief interest as an indicator of cognitive workload. This component, commonly referred to as the 0.10 Hz component, reflects short-term changes in blood pressure and spans a range from 0.04-0.15 Hz. That is, there are approximately 6 fluctuations of the heart per minute due to changes in blood pressure. A peak in this component is indicative of lower cognitive workload conditions. A flattening of this component reflects conditions of greater mental workload [7].

Sparse Discrete Fourier Transform (SDFT)

A method of computing Fourier transforms on the cardiac interval signal which requires relatively few data points for computation is known as the Sparse Discrete Fourier Transform (SDFT) [12]. This method is ideal for recordings of short duration where 300 to 500 data points exist for computing spectral values. With SDFT, the times between successive R-peak signals from selected overlapping groups of R-peak waves are used to compute spectral values for the 0.10 Hz component of the cardiac interval signal. Thus, SDFT computations provide a trace of the change in the 0.10 Hz component of the cardiac interval signal over time so that changes in mental effort can be recorded throughout the entire period of a trial.

Use of HRV in Determining Mental Effort

In a recent study involving the level of user control and changes in HRV during simulated flight maintenance, the demands of dynamic monitoring and fault diagnosis for 11 trainee flight engineers were examined in relation to changes in HRV [17]. HRV was found to be sensitive to the different phases of the work environment. In particular, the frequency 0.07-0.14 Hz range was suppressed during the mentally demanding problem solving mode. The findings of this study support both the use of HRV as a physiological index of mental effort and its value in operational contexts.

In a 1987 study, Aasman, Mulder, and Mulder found HRV to be associated with the changing levels of user effort. In this study, participants were given a simple (non-counting) and complex (counting) condition of a task. In the simple condition, participants were required to indicate the presence or absence of a target by pressing one of two buttons. In the complex condition, participants were required to keep a running mental count of each memory set item. In the complex condition, the operations of updating the counters and rehearsing them had to be time shared with other operations. Participants rated this task as one requiring great mental effort.

The 1987 study showed that the amplitude of the 0.10 Hz component of the cardiac interval signal was particularly affected in the complex task condition, as long as the subjects were working within the limits of working memory. When the limits of working memory were exceeded, most subjects were unable to cope with the demands of the task as evidenced by a performance decrement and an increase in HRV. Thus, when working memory was exceeded, participants gave up, indicating that less effort was invested.

Mental effort expended by a user has not necessarily been found to be related to task load [20]. The amount of effort invested by a user is determined by internal goals and criteria they choose to adopt. Situations have been observed in which an increase in task demands resulted in a decrease in mental effort [18]. The explanation for this seemingly paradoxical result is that the task became so difficult that performance could not be maintained at an acceptable level so users settled for lower performance and reduced the amount of mental effort they were investing in the task.

In our recent informal study, which provided the foundation for the current study, the sensitivity of HRV to the cognitive demands of playing different versions of a computer game was examined. Participants included 2 males and 4 females who ranged in age from 11 to 19 years. The game was an abstraction of an air traffic control scenario in which some objects moved across the screen following fixed routes, while others moved in "off route" patterns. Participants were asked to keep "like" objects from colliding as they moved across the screen.

The primary goal of this experiment was to answer the following question: How is HRV affected by the presence of certain combinations of intersecting routes and "off route" objects, both in the time and frequency domains. Results of this experiment indicated that there was no statistically significant effect of the number of intersecting routes on HRV, $F(2, 10) = 0.22$, $p=0.81$. With the number of "off route" objects, however, there was an effect at the 0.15 level, $F(2, 10) = 2.31$, $p= 0.15$.

A taxonomy of display monitoring tasks

Display monitoring tasks fall into two broad categories: those involving monitoring of relatively static displays and those involving monitoring displays with movement. Static monitoring tasks include those where information appears in the same relative position, but values are subject to change. Examples include digital readout displays and displays with dials, knobs or scales whose indicators change value in order to reflect changes in system status.

Monitoring tasks involving movement offer a variety of combinations of different parameters. In general, tasks with movement may be classified as those with constrained movement and those with unconstrained movement. In tasks with unconstrained movement, objects may move on the display in any direction and at varying speeds In addition, there may also be encoding associated with objects which indicates movement in more than one direction. Classic examples include 3-D and 4-D air-to-air and air-to-ground intercept applications, as well as many air traffic management applications.

Monitoring tasks involving constrained movement are those in which an object's location, direction, or speed is moderated or bounded in some fashion. That is, objects may be confined to movement along predetermined paths, or with a specified velocity or a limited range of velocities. As with unconstrained movement tasks, there may also be encoding which indicates movement in more than one dimension.

Within the overall task space of display monitoring, we chose a task for the current study which required monitoring of moving, relatively constrained objects. In particular, this task approximated that employed in air traffic management using an air traffic management visual display. We believe that that the air traffic management visual display offers a rich environment for examining the applicability of HRV as an index of mental effort, in that multiple moving objects are displayed whose parameters can be varied to create different cognitive demands on human monitors.

Air Traffic Management: Decision Making Model

A simple decision making model documented in an air traffic management training manual and used in the work by Mogford, et al., assumes that a user makes decisions in four phases: scanning, projecting, planning, and acting [9].

In the ***scanning*** phase, user attention is continuously switched between different stimulus sources. The research team in [9] assumed that the purpose of scanning is to update the mental representation of the visual display and attendant communications systems as the basis for detecting potential problems. As a potential conflict is detected, a user then ***projects*** the future positions of objects and assesses the likelihood of a conflict. During the ***planning*** phase, the user reviews possible solutions to the problem. Finally, during the ***acting*** phase, the user selects and implements a solution. This Scan-Project-Plan-Act paradigm, matched air traffic controller's reports of their decision making processes and was sufficient to guide preliminary research [9].

Air Traffic Management: Complexity factors

Grossberg defined airspace complexity as, "a construct referring to the characteristics, dynamic and static, affecting the rate at which workload increases", and also defined 12 "complexity factors" which could be used to describe an airspace [11]. Based on the research of Grossberg and Mogford [9, 10, 11], together with a consideration for the most salient factors affecting airspace complexity in the future air traffic management system, we chose two factors for use in the current study: the number of intersecting flight paths formed by fixed routes of flight, and the number of complex aircraft routings. Based on the results of a pilot study, the number of intersecting flight paths formed by fixed routes of flight was set at 3 as a condition of the experiment. The number of complex aircraft routings, or "Free Flyers", was varied at levels of 0, 4, 8, 12, and 16.

METHOD

Participants

Thirteen people (age 21 to 60 years) participated in the experiment. All participants had a college degree, were adept at using a mouse, and used a computer daily. Three participants were female. Five participants had Air Traffic Control experience. Each participant was paid for participating in the study.

Apparatus

The experimental task was performed using a Compaq laptop computer with a 120 MHz Pentium processor running Windows 95. The laptop's keyboard was used for text input on the demographic survey, but a mouse was used for all other inputs. A 17" color SVGA monitor was used for display during the game with a resolution of 640x480 and 256 colors.

Electrocardiogram (ECG) equipment consisted of Dataq's WinDaq/200 hardware and software used in conjunction with a Windows 3.1 based 80386 PC [3]. Delphi Developer 2.0 was used to develop the computer game used in the experimental task. CARSPAN and SAS software packages were used for data reduction and analysis.

Task

Participants were required to play a series of five games while connected via three leads to ECG recording equipment. (One lead was positioned near the heart, another on the left wrist, and the third above the right ankle). The games were abstractions of an air traffic management environment designed to simulate a future "Free Flight" paradigm; that is, some aircraft targets moved across the screen following fixed routes, while others followed off-route or "Free Flight" paths. Task difficulty was manipulated by varying the number of free flight aircraft targets. Five games were played, a control game with no free flyers and four games with treatments of 4, 8, 12, and 16 free flyers. A view of the screen with the 16 Free Flyer treatment is shown in Figure 1.

During each game, participants were required to keep objects at the same altitude from colliding as they moved across the screen. Aircraft targets had one of two altitudes: Flight Level 350 (35,000 feet), or Flight Level 330 (33,000 feet). Participants could change altitudes of an aircraft target by using the mouse to click on either the aircraft target symbol "X", or its altitude "350" or "330". Clicking on the 350 altitude changed it to a 330 altitude, and clicking on the 330 altitude changed it to a 350 altitude.

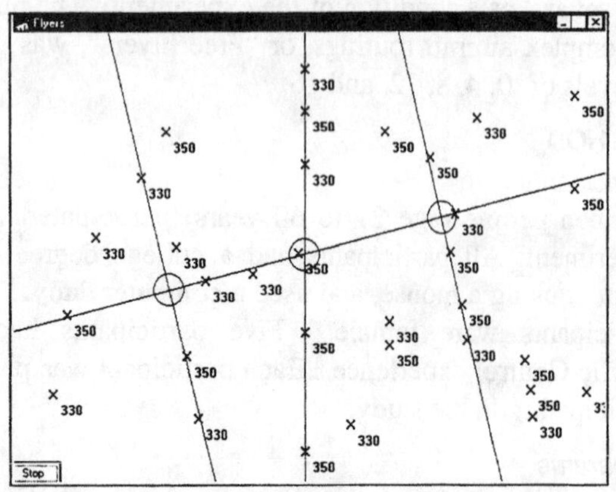

Figure 1
Game Display with 16 Fixed Flyers and 16 Free Flyers

A condition of the current experiment established four fixed routes with three intersections formed by these routes. This condition was based on the results of a previous experiment in which the number of the number of intersections formed by fixed routes and the number of objects not on fixed routes were manipulated in a 3 x 3 factorial repeated measures design. An additional condition of the current experiment was 16 aircraft were flying on the fixed routes of the display throughout each game.

Procedure
The experiment was divided into four phases: a welcome phase, an observation and training phase, a game phase, and a debriefing phase. During the welcome phase, participants completed a consent form, which provided a high-level description of the experiment, its duration, and its research benefits, and then a demographic survey was given to each participant. At the conclusion of this phase, a five minute resting baseline ECG was recorded for each participant.

At the outset of the observation and training phase, experiment instructions were read to each individual. These instructions provided a description of the object of the game, as well as a brief tutorial on how to change the altitudes of the aircraft targets. Participants were then allowed to observe a sample game for approximately 2 minutes. During this observation period, an explanation of the nature of the movement of the targets was provided so as to aid participants in reducing the number of false detections during the course of the upcoming games.

During the game phase, each participant played 5 games. Based on techniques used in previous studies, games alternated in relative difficulty between easy and hard [1]. The fixed route/Free Flyer configuration for each game is shown in Table 1.

	Game 1	Game 2	Game 3	Game 4	Game 5
Fixed Route Aircraft	16	16	16	16	16
Free Flight Aircraft	4	12	0	16	8

Table 1
The Fixed Route/Free Flyer Configuration

Performance statistics were compiled for each participant on the number and time of each aircraft collision per game, as well as the number and time of altitude changes. At the completion of each game, participants completed a subjective workload assessment based on NASA's Task Load Index (TLX) multi-dimensional rating procedure [5]. Participants provided responses to scales which ranged from very low to very high in six different workload areas: mental demand, physical demand, time pressure, performance, effort, and frustration.

At the conclusion of the experiment, participants were debriefed on their impressions of the experiment.

RESULTS

Subjective Measure of Mental Effort
NASA's TLX sub-scale for Mental Demand was used to validate participants' perceived mental effort across trials. A repeated measures Analysis of Variance (ANOVA) on the responses of all participants to the NASA TLX Mental Demand sub-scale demonstrated that free flyers had a significant effect on the subjective measure of mental effort ($F(4,48) = 5.92$, $p=0.001$) (see Figure 2).

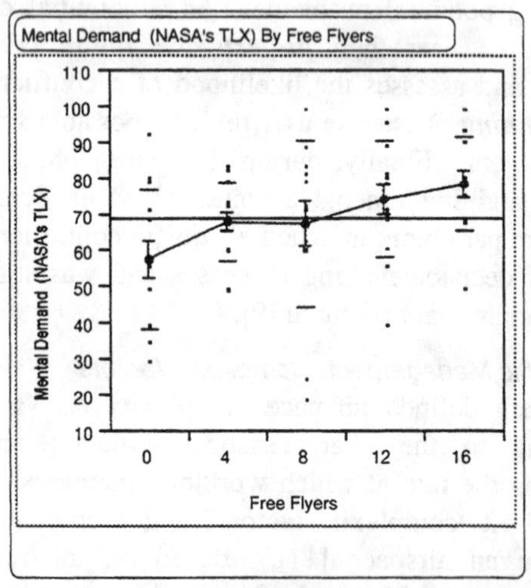

Figure 2
Mental Demand Sub-Scale Scores on NASA's TLX for All Participants (by Number of Free Flyers).

Subjective responses on the Mental Demand sub-scale for each of the free flyer treatments were tested against the control (no free flyer treatment) for significant differences using a *t* test for non-independent samples. Contrasts between the control and the 4, 8, 12 and 16 free flyer treatments were significant for the 12 Free Flyer treatment using Dunnett's test (|d|=2.99).

It should also be noted that the complexity factor (free flyers) had a significant effect on the subjective measure of Overall Workload, F(4, 48) = 7.33, p<0.001. (The NASA TLX Overall Workload score is a composite of six sub-scale scores, of which Mental Effort is one).

Physiological Measure of Mental Effort

Results of HRV for the participants were obtained across all trials. While there was a marginally significant effect of HRV across trials for all participants (F(4, 48) = 2.49, p=0.06), the Group with ATC experience showed significant sensitivity to the manipulation of the independent variable, F(4, 16) = 4.75, p=0.01. Figure 3 shows a consistent decrease in HRV for those with ATC experience as free flyers were increased from 0 to 12 (an indication of an increase in mental effort). The increase from 12 to 16 free flyers, however, resulted in an increase in HRV. An ANOVA comparison between the 12 free flyer and 16 free flyer trials yielded a marginally significant result, F(1, 4) =4.21, p=0.11.

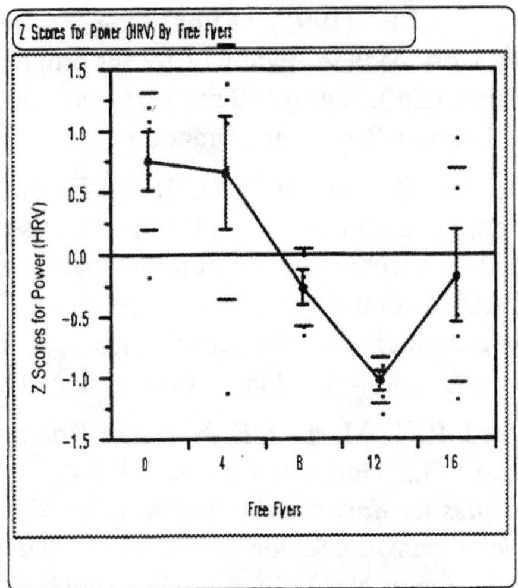

Figure 3
HRV Scores for Participants with ATC Experience (by Number of Free Flyers).

DISCUSSION

While the results of this study are preliminary and warrant further experimental investigation, there are two findings that indicate the potential value of HRV. The first is that HRV showed sensitivity to the manipulation of the independent variable. For the group with ATC experience, there was significant sensitivity; for all participants there was marginal sensitivity.

A second finding is that while HRV of the ATC experienced population appeared to decrease consistently with increases in the number of free flyers in the environment (an indication of an increase in mental effort), the increase from 12 to 16 free flyers resulted in an increase in HRV. This points to the potential use of HRV as an indicator of the point at which the capacity of human resources to process the increased number of free flying targets is being exceeded. It has been found that when tasks become too difficult there is a tendency for humans to disengage from the task, resulting in an increase in HRV [1]. Thus, the increase in HRV between the 12 and 16 free flyer condition may provide an indication that the user is "losing the mental picture" of the visual display -- a condition which suggests increased safety risk for the free flying and surrounding aircraft.

While not conclusive, there is evidence that suggests that the increase from 12 to 16 free flyers marks the point at which users move from what Norman and Bobrow refer to as a resource-limited condition to a data-limited condition [14]. As free flyers are increased from 0 to 12, users appear to be resource-limited as evidenced by the increase in mental effort. That is, users attempt to maintain acceptable levels of performance by increasing the amount of effort expended in keeping the aircraft targets from colliding. This increase in mental effort is supported by a corresponding decrease in HRV. As free flyers are increased from 12 to 16, users are presented with more data than they can handle with acceptable performance. This is what Norman and Bobrow call a data-limited condition; that is, more effort expended will not necessarily result in improved performance [14]. In fact, the overall increase in HRV provides an indication of a decrease of expenditure of effort and a willingness to settle for lesser performance. This phenomenon may explain the marginally significant effect for HRV obtained for all 13 participants. In other words, for those individuals not previously experienced in performing ATC tasks, even the tasks with 12 or fewer free flyers in this experiment were too difficult to be able to use HRV as a reliable discriminator for the expenditure of mental effort.

Another possible explanation for the increase in HRV between the 12 and 16 free flyer trials for the ATC experienced group is that the 16 free flyer trial did not require as much workload or mental demand as the 12 free flyer trial. NASA's TLX Overall Workload ratings and Mental Demand sub-scales scores did not support this explanation, however. Both showed an increase in the perceived workload and mental demand as free flyers were increased from 12 to 16.

FUTURE RESEARCH

We believe that if the level of mental effort exerted by a user while interacting with an interface is reflected in HRV, then exploratory research in using HRV for interface design and analysis, as well as a component of an adaptive interface design would be logical follow-ons to the current study.

Used in conjunction with other design tools, HRV may be an aid in both forecasting and diagnosing problematic interfaces. Perhaps HRV may even be discriminating enough to identify the types of individuals who would be most troubled by certain aspects of an interface. Given the "unique" signature of an individual's HRV, the tailoring of an interface to meet the specific needs of individual users may be possible.

Assuming that HRV can be established as a reliable indicator of user state, it may also provide a research basis for its use as a component of an adaptive interface. Within the framework of current interface design methodologies, it is often known that some designs are more effective than others. However, the reason for their effectiveness may not be known. The inclusion of a physiological measure such as HRV as a part of an adaptive interface design methodology may provide useful additional insight as to what will and what will not work in the context of adaptive interface development.

Results of this study suggest conducting a more carefully designed study in which HRV is used as the basis for altering an interface. Overall task performance would be measured; correlations between HRV and performance, and between HRV and a complexity measure would also be examined. Profiles for each participant would be developed in which HRV is plotted against performance for varying measures of complexity to determine the presence of main effects and interactions. Also important, will be to ensure that the experiment design controls for order effects and other threats to internal and external validity. Finally, ensuring a sufficient a number of participants is needed to increase the power of statistical tests of significance.

ACKNOWLEDGMENTS

We thank the MITRE Corporation for providing the funding for the ECG and data analysis software used in the study. Thanks are due also to the members of the HCI group at the George Washington University for their helpful suggestions on drafts of this document. Finally, we would like to thank the referees for their valuable insights and comments that were incorporated in the final version of this paper.

REFERENCES

1. Aasman, J., Mulder, G., and Mulder L.J.M (1987). Operator effort and the measurement of heart-rate variability. *Human Factors*, 29, 161-170.

2. Coles, M.G.H., and Sirevaag, E. (1987). Heart rate and sinus arrhythmia. In Gale, A. and Christie, B. (Eds), *Psychophysiology and the Electronic Workplace*, Chichester, UK: Wiley.

3. *Dataq Instruments WinDaq/200 User's Manual*, software release level 1, Akron, Ohio (1996).

4. Federal Aviation Administration (1995). *FAA Aviation Forecasts -- Fiscal Years 1995-2006* (FAA-APO-95-1). Washington, DC: Federal Aviation Administration.

5. Hart, S.G., and Staveland, L.E. (1988). Development of NASA-TLX (Task Load Index): Results of empirical and theoretical research. In P.A. Hancock and N. Meshkati (Eds.), *Human Mental Workload* (pp. 139-178). North-Holland: Elsevier Science Publishers B.V.

6. Heart Rate Variability: Standards of Measurement, Physiological Interpretation, and Clinical Use (1996). Task Force of the European Society of Cardiology and the North American Society of Pacing and Electrophysiology. *Circulation*, 93, No. 5, 1043-1065.

7. Hopman, J. C. W., Kollee, L. A. A., Stoelinga, G. B. A., van Geijn, H. P., and van Ravenswaaij-Arts, C. M. A. (1993). Heart Rate Variability. *Annals of Internal Medicine*, 118, 436-447.

8. Kramer, A. F. (1991). Physiological metrics of mental workload: A review of recent progress. In D. L. Damos (Ed.), *Multiple-Task performance* (pp. 279-328). London: Taylor and Francis.

9. Mogford, R.H., Murphy, E.D., Raske-Hofstrand, R.J., Yastrop, G., Guttman, J. A. (1993). The use of direct and indirect techniques to study airspace complexity in air traffic control. In *Proceedings of the First Mid-Atlantic Human Factors Conference* (pp. 196-202). Virginia Beach, VA.: Human Factors Society.

10. Mogford, R.H., Murphy, E.D., Raske-Hofstrand, R.J., Yastrop, G., Guttman, J. A. (1994). *Research techniques for documenting cognitive processes in Air Traffic Control: Sector complexity and decision making* (Report No. DOT/FAA/CT-TN94/3). Atlantic City International Airport, N.J.: FAA Technical Center.

11. Mogford, R.H., Guttman, J. A., Morrow, S. L., and Kopardekar, P. (1995). *The complexity construct in air traffic control* (Report No. DOT/FAA/CT-TN95/22). Atlantic City International Airport, N.J.: FAA Technical Center.

12. Mulder, L. J. M., Van Roon, A. M., and Schweizer, D. A.. *Cardiovascular Data Analysis Environment*

(CARSPAN) User's Manual, Groeningen, The Netherlands (1995).

13. Mulder, L. J. M., and Mulder, G. (1987). Cardiovavscular reactivity and mental workload. In O. Rompelman and R. I. Kitney (Eds.), *The beat-by-beat investigation of cardiovascular function* (pp. 216-253). Oxford, UK: Oxford University Press.
14. Norman and Bobrow (1975). Data and resource processing limits. *Cognitive Psychology* (7), 44-64.
15. RTCA (1995, October). Final Report of RTCA Task *Force 3 Free Flight Implementation.* Washington, D.C.: RTCA Task Force 3.
16. Sirevaag, E. J., Kramer, A. F., Wickens, C. D., Reisweber, M., Strayer, D. L., and Grenell, J. F. (1993). Assessment of pilot performance and mental workload in rotary wing aircraft. *Ergonomics*, 36, 1121-1140.
17. Tattersall, A., and Hockey, G. (1995). Level of Operator Control and Changes in Heart Rate Variability during Simulated Flight Maintenance. *Human Factors*, 1995, 37(4), 682-698.
18. Tulga, M.K., and Sheridan, T.B. (1980). Dynamic decisions and workload in multitask supervisory control. *IEEE Transactions on Systems, Man, and Cybernetics*, 1980, 10, 217-232.
19. Velichkovsky, B. M., and Hansen, J. P. (1996). New technological windows into mind: There is more in eyes and brains for human-computer interaction. In *CHI 96 Proceedings* (pp. 496-503). Vancouver, BC Canada.
20. Vicente, K.J., Thornton, D. C., and Moray, N. (1987). Spectral Analysis of Sinus Arrhythmia: A Measure of Mental Effort. *Human Factors*, 1987, 29(2), 171-182.
21. Wierwille, W. W., and Eggemeier, F. T. (1993). Recomendations for mental workload measurement in a test and evaluation environment. *Human Factors*, 35(2), 263-281.
22. Wilson, G. F. (1993). Air-to-Ground training missions: A psychophysiological workload analysis. *Ergonomics*, 36, 1071-1087.
23. Wilson, G.F., and Eggemeier, F. T. (1991). Psychophysiological assessment of workload in multi-task environments. In D. L. Damos (Ed.), *Multiple-task-performance* (pp. 329-360). London: Taylor and Francis.

Evolution of the Conversation Machine: A Case Study of Bringing Advanced Technology to the Marketplace

Catherine G. Wolf and Wlodek Zadrozny
IBM T.J. Watson Research Center
30 Saw Mill River Road
Hawthorne, NY 10532 USA
+1 914 784-7728, 7835
{cwolf, wlodz}@watson.ibm.com

ABSTRACT

This paper describes the evolution of the Conversation Machine, a conversational speech system which allows users to carry out common banking transactions over the telephone using a conversational-style interface. The discussion is organized according to three phases of the project—the demonstration, laboratory, and customer phases. The different phases of the project had different goals and brought different design issues to the forefront. In particular, the realities of working with a customer partner have affected the design of the user interface and functionality of the system in ways not anticipated at earlier stages of the project.

Keywords

speech recognition, natural language, design rationale, requirements, business transformation,

INTRODUCTION

Technologists often present a vision of the future in which information systems are seamlessly integrated and machines understand and intelligently anticipate their users' intentions (cf. Apple's famous Knowledge Navigator video). In the area of conversational interfaces, we are beginning to see convincing demonstrations of this vision of the future for limited domains. These laboratory systems employ speech recognition, natural language understanding, and agent technology to allow users to converse with a computer system (usually over the phone) about a limited range of topics. MailCall [4], for example, is a conversational interface to email over the telephone which uses information from the user's calendar and other computer desktop sources to prioritize email. Prototype conversational interfaces have also been applied to calendar functions, weather reports, stock quotes [9], and banking [7].

Much of the work reported in the human-computer interaction literature has focused on the description of innovative conversational systems [3,4], understanding how people behave when conversing with machines through the use of simulations and laboratory experiments [5,6] and designing user interfaces which compensate for the less than perfect technologies [8,9]. In order to develop useful, useable systems, the issues with which this work deals must be addressed. However, the goal of bringing conversational interfaces out of the laboratory and into the world presents additional challenges. In our experience, these additional challenges have to do with the characteristics and constraints of legacy systems with which the new conversational interfaces must be integrated, differing needs of the various shareholders in a project, and the complexity and scope required of a system for real people attempting to accomplish real goals.

This paper presents a review of the experience of bringing the Conversation Machine from a demonstration prototype to a functional system used by real users. The Conversation Machine is a conversational speech system which allows users to carry out common banking transactions over the telephone using a conversational-style interface. As of this writing, the experience is still ongoing; we will begin a field trial with users in several months.

The reader should note that the paper is about moving conversational technology from the lab to the customer in a systematic, replicable way, and is not about the technology innovations per se, or about making new technology successful in the market.

With these caveats, we can start discussing a number of the issues that we have faced at different stages of the project and the activities we have undertaken in order to develop a useful, useable system. The different phases of the project had different goals and brought different design issues to the forefront. In particular, the realities of working with a customer partner have affected the design of the user interface and functionality of the system in ways not anticipated at earlier stages of the project.

The paper is organized as follows. First, a brief description of the Conversation Machine is given. Next, the experience of developing the Conversation Machine will be discussed in terms of three phases of the project, demonstration phase, laboratory phase, and customer phase. The name of a phase reflects the focus of activity during that time period, although, for example, demonstrations were conducted during the laboratory and customer phase as well as the demonstration phase. The paper concludes with a reflection on the contributions of the different phases to designing a useful and useable system.

THE CONVERSATION MACHINE: WHAT IT IS

The Conversation Machine allows users to carry out a number of common banking transactions using a conversational-style interface over the telephone. Some examples of dialogs from a version of the Conversation Machine tested in the laboratory phase are shown in Figure 1.

User: What's my checking balance?
CM: Your checking balance is $925.00. What else can I do for you?
User: Tell me about my bills.
CM: Which bills do you want to know about?
User: Mastercard and phone.
CM: Your Mastercard balance is $325.50. Your phone balance is $45.00. What else can I do for you?
User: Pay them.

Figure 1. Sample Dialog from Laboratory Phase (CM stands for Conversation Machine)

The command structure was flat, and the top-level prompt, "What else can I do for you?" simply signaled that the system was ready to accept another request. Some dialogs required additional information from the user for completion. In these sub-dialogs, the users were asked for the additional information and only responses appropriate to the dialog were accepted. For operations which changed the balance of an account, the user was asked to confirm the transaction before it was executed.

When a recognition failure occurred at a top-level dialog, the user was asked to rephrase the request. When an acceptable response was not given within a sub-dialog, several levels of prompting were used, giving progressively more explicit instructions.

The Conversation Machine makes use of the following user interface technologies:

- Continuous speech recognition—to recognize the words in the user's speech
- Natural language/dialog processing—which uses semantic, syntactic and pragmatic information to determine which action to perform [10,11]
- Speech output—to present information in response to the user's requests (the system's side of the conversation)

GOALS AND PHASES OF THE PROJECT

The ultimate goal of the project is to take the conversational technology to the market. However, our customer partner was interested in something more: our vision how this new technology would change their business.

Given these goals, and recognizing that no activity can ignore time and resource constraints, we arrive at the three necessary phases of the project:

- Demonstration phase—to show that ours is (one of) the best among competing visions, resulting in allocation of resources (by both IBM and a customer).
- Laboratory phase--using allocated resources, to address known and unknown shortcomings of the system and prepare for the customer phase.
- Customer phase--to learn how much of the original vision can actually be accomplished, to better understand the customer's needs and how the technology must evolve to meet these needs, and to gauge the cost and conditions under which similar solutions can be replicated with other customers.

THE DEMONSTRATION PHASE

The demonstration is a tangible statement of the possibilities of the new technology. A goal of the demonstration is to persuade a potential partner that the technology can meet their business needs. As such, the demo is crafted to show off the strengths of the technology, rather than to address specific issues in its application to a business environment. The demonstration of the Conversation Machine featured the ability to perform compound actions (e.g. " Please tell me my checking and savings balances."), the use of reference (e.g. "pay them" to pay previously named bills), the ability to accomplish goals in far fewer steps than a conventional keypad interface, and a natural, flexible, conversational style. We believed that features such as these offered a number of advantages over keypad input (the conventional alternative) for telephone-based services such as home banking.

The demonstration embodied assumptions about the back-end system capabilities and consumer banking habits that made for a successful demonstration. For example, the demonstration assumed that the user had one checking account and one savings account, rather than multiple accounts of a particular type. This made it possible for the Conversation Machine and user to refer to the accounts simply as "your (my) checking account" and "your (my) savings account" rather than describe them in some more cumbersome way.

The user-system dialog was based on observations of customer interactions with Call Center personnel, experience with other prototype conversational systems we had designed, and the human-computer interaction literature. The user interface design efforts were focused on making the demonstration look good. During this phase, human speech recorded by an actress was substituted for synthetic text-to-speech prompts. The dialogs were honed so that the tone of the prompts was consistently first person and conversational Numerous changes were made to the dialogs to make them consistent and to provide adequate feedback for system actions. Given the "success orientation" of the user interface design efforts at this stage, we did not devote much effort to error recovery dialogs.

While the "success orientation" of the demonstration phase selectively ignored some issues of functionality and user interface design, this was not necessarily a bad thing. It effectively conveyed the benefits of the new interaction style to people who were not technologists. It succeeded in gaining a customer partner. This meant access to opportunities to understand both consumer needs and bank needs, to observe how customers interacted with available telephone banking channels (voice response unit (VRU) and customer service representative), and to understand the infrastructure into which the Conversation Machine would have to be integrated. During the customer phase when the constraints of working in the real world required design tradeoffs and compromises, the demonstration system served as a reminder of the original vision. The danger at the demonstration phase is that potential customers and other non-technical people involved in the project may assume that the technology is more mature than it is, given the polish of the demonstration. This can lead to unrealistic expectations concerning what can be delivered in the customer phase and the resources required to do it.

THE LABORATORY PHASE

Two important goals of the laboratory phase were to better understand how people would interact with the Conversation Machine and improve the system based on this understanding. In contrast to the demonstration phase, the laboratory phase took a "problem orientation"--a focus of the laboratory phase was to find shortcomings of the system. The laboratory phase occurred in preparation for working with a customer partner. One of the major usability activities of this phase was an empirical laboratory study of the Conversation Machine [7]. The study took as its starting point the version of the system that had been developed during the demonstration phase. We will summarize the study and how what we learned helped us improve the system.

The study had several purposes:

•To understand how people interact with the system in order to improve the usability of the system. In particular, we wanted to know what strategies people used when the system made an error.

•To collect data about the way people spoke to the system in order to more adequately cover the variety of utterances people use.

•To assess the system's accuracy in recognizing users' utterances, and users' success in accomplishing their goals with the system.

The Study Procedure

Since one of the goals of the study was to collect information on how people spoke to the system, we did not want to "put words in their mouths" by presenting the tasks they were to do in words they might use to accomplish these tasks. Accordingly, we created scenarios that either described a situation the study participants were to resolve or required the participants to fill in missing information in a table, without using phrases they might employ to accomplish the goal. An example of the first kind of scenario is: "You are at the airport leaving for a two-week vacation. You have an uneasy feeling that you forgot the electricity bill. Check to see if it needs attention, and if so, take care of it."

Twenty-two people participated in the study. Sixteen were recruited from a temporary employment agency and were paid for their services; six were internal employees who volunteered for the study.

Study Results

Accuracy and Goal Success

One measure of accuracy was based on whether the system performed the correct action in response to a participant's utterance. Because many different recognized results may be mapped to the same system action, it is possible for the appropriate response to be given to the user, even if the system does not recognize the user's utterance exactly on a word-for-word basis. The average utterance accuracy according to this measure was 58%.

The participants, however, perceived the accuracy of the Conversation Machine to be much greater. Figure 2 shows the participants' estimate of the percentage of time the system correctly understood their request and the estimate of the percentage of time it misunderstood their request (collected in independent questions), as well as the actual accuracy and error rates.

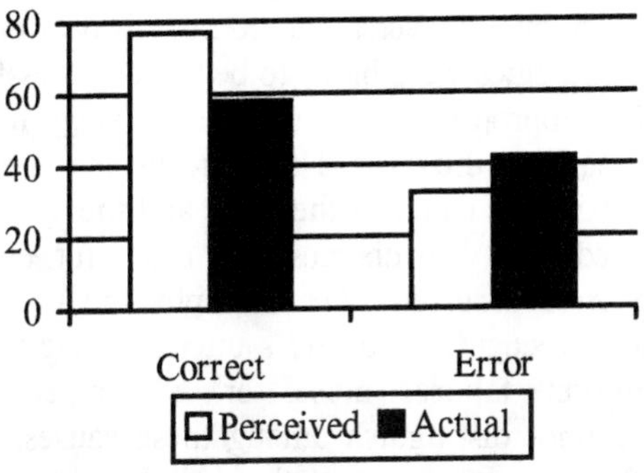

Figure 2. Perceived and Actual Accuracy

Some insight into the cause of the overestimation of accuracy came from a measure of whether or not the study participants were able to accomplish their goals (such as transferring money or paying a bill), regardless of the number of consecutive attempts it took. On the average, participants were able to accomplish 92% of the goals they attempted. In addition, this measure was significantly correlated with the participants' ratings of ease of use and sense of control over the system, whereas the utterance accuracy measure was not. Taken together, these findings suggested that the ability to accomplish one's goals may be a more important factor in satisfaction than utterance level accuracy, and may affect the perception of accuracy. The implications for system design were that in addition to working on improving accuracy, it was very important to work on ways to help users easily recover from errors and thus, accomplish their intended goals.

Specific insight on how to facilitate error recovery and improve accuracy came from an analysis of sources of errors and participants' strategies in responding to errors.

Categories of Error

Errors were classified into a number of categories as shown in Figure 3. The largest proportion of errors (26%) were misrecognition errors, in which the system recognized the user's utterance as a different request. About 20% of the errors were recognition failures, in which the system was unable to produce a match for the user's utterance. For both these categories, the utterance should have been correctly recognized in principle. The problem resulted from an error of speech recognition and the utterance would have been handled correctly by the natural language component.

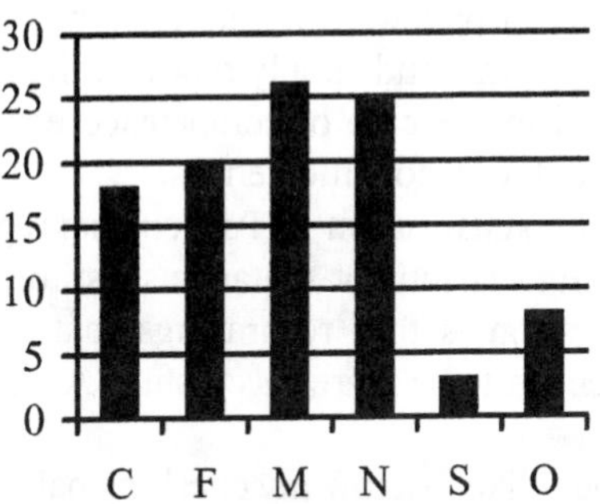

Figure 3. Percentage of Errors due to Competence (C) , Recognition Failure (F), Misrecognition (M), Noise (N), Sub-dialog (S) and Other (O)

About 25% of the errors were due to noise, in which the system picked up background noise or breathing noises when nothing was spoken, or speech intended for the experimenter. These errors are due to the combined effects of the sensitivity of the telephone microphone to background sounds, the speech recognizer's ability to distinguish signal from noise, and the fact that the system as tested could not be put on pause or mute. To deal with the noise problem, we added a pause function to the Conversation Machine to give the user some control over when the system was listening for speech; also, the current Conversation Machine uses a version of speech recognition which does a better job of distinguishing noise from intentional speech.

About 18% of the errors were competence errors, in which the user made a request which was outside the system's competence. For example, one user made the request, "If I write a check for $200, will it bounce?" Some of the requests in this category were for information or actions which the system could handle if phrased in a different way, such as this example. Other requests were beyond the system's capabilities, such as providing a history of bill payments.

Sub-dialog errors were errors in which the participant was in a sub-dialog but made a top level dialog request. In many of these cases, the participant had gotten into the sub-dialog as a result of an earlier recognition error and essentially repeated the original request.

How People Respond to Errors

As a starting point in designing user interfaces that help people recover from errors, we did a qualitative analysis of the strategies participants used in dealing with errors and the effectiveness of these strategies. The analysis revealed the following strategies in dealing with errors.

Repetition — Often people were at a loss to rephrase their request in a different way and simply repeated the request. This never worked in the case of competence errors, but occasionally worked for recognition errors.

Semantic/syntactic substitution — Participants rephrased a request by making semantic or syntactic substitutions (or both). Our impression is that rephrasings that involved larger changes tended to be more successful. An example follows:

Original: I would like to know my checking balance.

Follow-up: How much is in my checking account?

Elaboration – Participants elaborated on a failed request, adding redundant or new information. In the few cases where a very brief original request was expanded, this strategy worked. Although elaboration often works with human conversation partners, in most cases, the elaboration strategy produced a long request which failed. The following example comes from the participant with the highest utterance error rate.

Original: Uhm, how much would my electric company bill be this month?

Follow-up (1): My electric bill for the month, uh, just wondering how much would come out to this month?

Follow-up (2): My electricity bill, I want to know, uhm, what the amount will be at the end of the month, how much will I owe?

Simplification – Participants simplified a request, resulting in a briefer request. This sometimes also involved breaking a compound request into parts. This strategy often worked. For example,

Original: I would like to take care of my bills, and I would like to know the checking account balance.

Follow-up: What is my checking account balance?

Ignore sub-dialog prompt – When participants found themselves in a sub-dialog due to a recognition error, they sometimes ignored the prompt because it did not offer them acceptable alternatives. Because the system was designed to handle responses to the prompt only, this strategy failed. For example,

Original: I want a transfer...

CM: Which bills should I pay?

Follow-up (1): I want a transfer, of a hundred dollars...

CM: Which bill? Phone, insurance, Mastercard, or electricity?

Follow-up (2): No, no bills {pause}. I just want to transfer money from my savings account into the checking...

Goal shift – On occasion, participants changed their goal when faced with an error. There are at least three situations when this happened: 1. The system responded with information or began a transaction that was relevant to the scenario (although not the correct response to the user's request), and the participant changed his/her goal to match the response. 2. The participant had attempted a request that was beyond the application's competence (such as providing bill payment history), and then changed his/her goal to one within the system's abilities. 3. The user gave up on the goal and tried something else.

Our analyses of error categories and participants' strategies in dealing with errors suggested that strategies based on human-human conversation did not always work, although some strategies were likely to be more successful than others. The appropriate error recovery strategy may depend on the source of the error. However, the user is not likely to understand the cause of the error and the system may have limited ability to diagnose the cause (or even detect that an error occurred). For example, the system may be unable to recognize the user's utterance due to a speech recognition failure, noise, or a competence problem, and cannot distinguish among these causes. In addition to making improvements to the underlying speech technology, these findings caused us to focus on user interface approaches for dealing with errors that were largely independent of the source of the error.

One approach is to suggest a generally useful strategy when the system is unable to recognize an utterance. The original prompt when the system was unable to recognize an utterance asked the user to rephrase the request (encouraging the semantic/syntactic substitution strategy). However, users sometimes are at a loss for how to make the request in a different way. Based on the observation that simplification tends to be a successful strategy, we enhanced the prompting so that if a second attempt was also unsuccessful the prompt suggested the use of "short, simple requests." User studies in the customer phase have indicated that this prompt often results in a successful request. If the user was still not successful, examples of acceptable requests are given. This third prompt was intended to provide more guidance for semantic/syntactic substitutions and also encourage users to try a goal shift if appropriate. Yankelovich [8] has reported that the use of progressive assistance when the system cannot recognize the utterance make users less frustrated. The hope here is that by encouraging some of the more successful strategies that people use, goal success might be increased.

A design principle we implemented to deal with sub-dialog errors and misrecognition errors which put the user in an unexpected state, is to always give the user explicit feedback for state in each prompt, even if that feedback has just been given in the preceding prompt. The goal is to make it easier for the user to detect the occurrence of an error.

In the course of the laboratory phase, we developed the guideline that the Conversation Machine should always suggest an appropriate next step. However, the demonstration system that we started with generally did this only for cases when the user was in the intended state (for example, the user had asked to transfer money and the system requested that the user enter the amount). In the case of an error which gets the user into an unintended sub-dialog, the appropriate next step is to get out of that sub-dialog. To provide guidance in such instances, the prompts were modified so that the user was reminded how to get out of a sub-dialog, using either a touch-tone key or the word "cancel".

Observations on the Laboratory Phase

During the laboratory phase, the Conversation Machine was improved based on a detailed analysis of sources of errors and users' strategies for coping with errors. We expanded and made explicit the guidelines for user interface design. By taking a "problem orientation" rather than a "success orientation" we made changes to the user interface which facilitated error recovery and error avoidance. Our focus was on the end user and we had not yet begun to consider the demands and constraints of working with customers in a real world environment.

CUSTOMER PHASE

In the customer phase, we began working with a forward-looking bank partner. Our contract with the bank committed us to build a version of the Conversation Machine for a limited pilot study in which a small number of users would conduct actual banking transactions with the system. The usability activities leading up to the pilot study included an early reaction study to better understand how potential users might react to a conversational interface to telephone banking and to gather data on how they might talk to such a system, observations in the bank Call Center of customer interactions with service representatives, assessments of versions of the working system, and user interface design. Throughout this phase, we worked closely with our bank partner, who was very cooperative in giving us access to customers, service representatives, and other bank personnel. Although the design principles developed on the basis of the laboratory study continued to guide the work, we were now driven by the need to develop a system which worked for the functions offered by our partner's keypad-based VRU. This was a larger and somewhat different set of functions than the set our demonstration and laboratory phase systems covered. In addition, we found that a number of requirements and constraints which we had not anticipated caused us to change some aspects of the system and user interface design. Several examples are given here.

Legacy System Constraints and Characteristics

Our demonstration and laboratory systems had implicitly taken a customer-centric approach; that is, our dialogs assumed that once the customer had been identified, information about all the customer's accounts was available for use by the Conversation Machine. In fact, the bank's systems took an account-centric approach. The bank's system required the customer to enter the account number for each account involved in a transaction or information request. Since entering account numbers is a cumbersome and error-prone task, this requirement could make dialogs less efficient than with the demonstration/laboratory system.

Our solution was to store account numbers entered in a session so if a customer had entered his/her savings account number, for example, in a previous transaction, it was not necessary to enter the number again. However, some customers had multiple accounts of the same type (e.g. two savings accounts) and the account-centric system did not know when this was the case. Consequently, it was possible (although perhaps not likely) that a customer's second reference to a particular type of account was intended to apply to a different account. To accommodate this possibility without requiring users to always enter account numbers, we modified the dialogs so that the last four digits of the presumed account were given as part of the transaction feedback (e.g. "I'm about to transfer $100 from savings account 5678 to . . ."). Since users were always given an opportunity to cancel a transaction that changed account balances before it was carried out, this feedback reduced the probability of executing unintended transactions due to confusion about the accounts involved.

Some functions from the demonstration and laboratory systems, such as getting a summary of all accounts, were too complicated to attempt to implement given the legacy system constraints, since it would require the Conversation Machine to query the user for each account type and number.

Differing Needs of Various Shareholders

A somewhat different example of customer phase impact resulted from the combined effects of legacy system design and the different perspectives of the various shareholders in the project. The VRU allowed users to get a history of transactions on their checking accounts. Users were often interested in only one type of transaction, such as cleared checks. This transaction history, however, included all types of transactions, e.g. cleared checks, deposits, ATM withdrawals, fees, etc. The VRU presumably had been designed this way to keep the number of options in the menu down to a reasonable size. The VRU prompt made it clear that the option provided all types of transactions and users seemed to understand this. With the conversational interface, users could and did express their goals in their own words, such as, " I want to know about cleared checks." However, the legacy system functionality still returned all types of transactions. This mismatch between the user's expressed goal and the system's capabilities could make for some awkward, non-human-like conversations.

In this case, it would have been possible to filter the list of transactions returned by the legacy system and present only the cleared checks. The designers favored this alternative in the interests of creating a system which matched users' needs. However, the bank personnel were wary of any "enhancements" to the system; they wanted to maintain control of the banking functionality and viewed the Conversation Machine as an alternative front-end to the existing VRU functionality. From the software engineering and maintenance perspective, it made sense to them not to mix code for banking functions with code for the user interface. The interim solution has been to provide all types of transactions in response to any transaction history request, and provide feedback which is intended to make it clear that all transactions are included. We expect that this decision may be revisited based on the reactions of users in assessments underway and in the future.

The Complexity and Scope of a System for Real People Trying to Accomplish Real Goals

It came as no surprise that the range of goals and complexity of situations for which people call a bank are far greater than the set we accommodated in our laboratory and demonstration systems. Two consequences of this greater scope and complexity are discussed here — the challenge of achieving high goal success for a larger set of functions, and the challenge of providing guidance for the range of functions and utterances which the system accommodates [8].

The first problem is that as the number of functions and, thus, potential utterances which the system attempts to handle increase, the probability of a misrecognition increases. We are taking a pragmatic approach to this problem. Since some functions, such as checking a balance, are used much more frequently than others, we are concentrating our efforts on accommodating the variety of utterances people might used for these functions, at the expense of less frequently used functions. We expect that this approach will result in higher overall goal success, greater customer satisfaction, and fewer calls handled by customer service representatives than attempting to handle the full range of utterances consumers might employ for less frequent functions.

A second approach is to attempt to anticipate a user's next request based on the current state and present that anticipated request as an option. For example, customers often call with the goal of verifying their checking balance. If the balance does not match their records, they frequently ask for checking transaction history in order to determine the cause of the mismatch. When a customer's initial request is for a checking balance, our system asks if the user wants his/her checking transaction history, thus reducing speech recognition to a simple yes/no distinction. This example is part of an overall strategy of moving towards a system based on user goals as opposed to banking transactions.

The issue of providing guidance for conversation results from the fact that in practice there are limitations on what can be requested and the ways in which the spoken requests can be made. Since the user initiates the request (rather than the system presenting a menu of options), the user sometimes does not know what he/she can say. During the laboratory phase, we focused on ways to provide guidance to the user through the use of dialogs and prompts. This remains an important approach to the problem. In the customer phase, we have found that an old-fashioned device, the performance aid, was welcomed by many users. The performance aid lists the main functions provided by the system using language which the Conversation Machine can handle (many other phrases are also acceptable). Its contents could easily fit on a wallet-sized card. When the performance aid was introduced during user testing, recognition accuracy and goal success increased. Our hope is that even if users do not refer to the card when interacting with the Conversation Machine, they will recall enough of the style and vocabulary to facilitate use. Although this low-tech solution might never make it into a visionary video like the Knowledge Navigator, it works!

Contributing to the challenge of creating a useable system of considerable scope and complexity was the fact that we did not have a complete specification of the functionality to be delivered to the customer. Late in the development cycle a number of new requirements surfaced with potentially pervasive effects on the design of the natural language and speech grammar components. To avoid the risk of making large changes late in the development cycle, we quickly evaluated several design alternatives with users and picked an acceptable alternative that minimized the need for changes to these components.

Observations on the Customer Phase

The customer phase presented us with new challenges and requirements that we had to meet with limited time and resources. Several characteristics of our mode of operation helped us respond to these challenges. 1. We relied on user interface design guidelines that had been explicitly articulated in the laboratory phase in making new design decisions. Consequently, changes and new dialogs were consistent with the existing interface and based on knowledge acquired over the course of the project. 2. The evolving Conversation Machine was available almost continuously for use in trying out new user interface ideas. Because of this we were able to conduct many quick rounds of user testing to drive design decisions. 3. When confronted with the need to make tradeoffs, we looked at the potential impact of each alternative on overall user and customer satisfaction. 4. We had weekly conference call meetings with the customer and much informal communication through email and follow-up calls. This helped us understand the rationale for various constraints on design due to the bank's legacy systems and practices, allowed us to get feedback on the acceptability of different design alternatives, and helped the customer understand why certain requirements were difficult to meet within the time frame of our engagement.

CONCLUSION AND SUMMARY

As observed by Carroll [1], different design activities bring different requirements into focus. In the present case, the three phases discussed had different goals and served different purposes in the evolution of the Conversation Machine. The system in the demonstration phase was a tangible statement of the possibilities of conversational interfaces as applied to telephone banking. It presented our vision of how the banking business could be transformed by creating easy access to banking data, and the replacement of cumbersome keypad interfaces by conversational interfaces. It was also a sales tool for attracting the customer necessary to bring the new interface to the marketplace. However, the system in the demonstration phase was not so much a guiding vision *for design*, but a starting point in the design process.

The laboratory phase had the goals of understanding user-system interaction and improving the system based on this understanding. The study and detailed analyses conducted in this phase helped us develop approaches for error recovery and avoidance based on an understanding of the causes of error and the strategies people use for dealing with errors. The insight gained in this phase also resulted in user interface guidelines that served us well when new requirements emerged in the customer phase.

The customer phase revealed new requirements and caused re-design. We found that the scope of the application, characteristics of legacy systems, and customer practices and values shaped our design in ways that had not been anticipated in the previous stages. Understanding and coping with these factors was critical to the success of the project. Several aspects of our work practices helped us deal with the challenges of the customer phase: fast, frequent user testing, design based on user interface guidelines developed in the laboratory phase, good communication with the customer, pragmatic evaluation of the impact of design changes on customer satisfaction.

While the details of this story are specific to this case, the general theme is not. As a project moves through different stages, different design issues will come to the foreground. When introducing novel HCI technology, much of the challenge of designing a useful and useable system is motivated by the customer context of use.

REFERENCES

1. Carroll, J. M., Rosson, M. B. Chin, G. and Koenemann, J. Requirements development: Stages of opportunity for collaborative needs discovery. In G. van der Veer, A. Henderson, S. Coles (Eds.) *DIS 97 Conference Proceeding,* 1997, 55-63.

2. Clark, H. H. and Brennan, S. E. Grounding in communication. In J. Levine, L. B. Resnick, and S. D. Behrand (Eds.), *Shared Cognition: Thinking as Social Practice*. APA Books, Washington, 1991.

3. Ly, E. and Schmandt, C. Chatter: A conversational learning speech interface. *AAAI Spring Symposium on Intelligent Multi-Media Multi-Modal Systems*, 1994.

4. Marx, M. and Schmandt, C. MailCall: Message presentation and navigation in a nonvisual environment. *CHI '96 Conference Proceedings*, 1996, 165-172.

5. Oviatt, S. Predicting spoken disfluencies during human-computer interaction. *Computer Speech and Language, 9*, 1995, 19-35.

6. Oviatt, S. L Multimodal interfaces for dynamic interactive maps. *CHI '96 Conference Proceedings*, 1996, 95-102.

7. Wolf, C. G., Kassler, M., Zadrozny, W., Opyrchal, L. Talking to the Conversation Machine: An empirical study. *Interact 97 Conference Proceedings,* 1997, 461-468.

8. Yankelovich, N. How do users know what to say? *interactions, 3.6*, 1996, 32-43.

9. Yankelovich, N., Levow, G. A., and Marx, M. Designing SpeechActs: Issues in speech user interfaces. *CHI '95 Conference Proceedings*, 1995, 369-376.

10. Zadrozny, W. From utterances to situations: Parsing with constructions in small domains. *Language, Logic and Computation: The 1994 Moraga Proceedings,* 1995.

11. Zadrozny, W. Natural language processing: Structure and complexity. *Proceedings of the Eight International Conference on Software Engineering and Knowledge Engineering*, 1996, 595-602.

Trust Breaks Down in Electronic Contexts but Can Be Repaired by Some Initial Face-to-Face Contact

Elena Rocco
Collaboratory for Research on Electronic Work (CREW)
The School of Information
University of Michigan
701 Tappan Street
Ann Arbor MI 48109-1234 USA
+1 313 7646715
rakele@umich.edu

ABSTRACT

Trust is the prerequisite for success when a collaborative task involves risk of individualistic or deceitful behaviors of others. Can trust emerge in electronic contexts? This issue is explored in an experiment in which trust emergence is measured in both face-to-face (F-t-F) and electronic contexts. In this experiment trust is revealed by the degree of cooperation the group is able to reach in solving a social dilemma, i.e. a situation in which advantages for individualistic behavior make group cooperation highly vulnerable. The experiment consists of two stages. The first stage analyzes the effects of F-t-F and electronic communication on trust. Trust succeeds only with F-t-F communication. The second stage investigates whether a pre-meeting F-t-F can promote trust in electronic contexts. Results are positive. Examination of how people converse in these two contexts sheds some light on the effects of technical characteristics and social circumstances on the emergence of trust.

Keywords

CSCW, trust, cooperation and conflict, teamwork

INTRODUCTION

Groupware technologies turn out to be not fully appropriate when the prerequisite for action is the establishment of trust. An action demonstrates trust if it "*increases one's vulnerability to another whose behavior is not under control*" [1]. Field evidence shows that people engaged in such activities are reluctant to use computer-based media of communication because the lack of face-to-face (F-t-F) contact reduces trust and commitment [2]. Others report need for a prior F-t-F meeting before accepting electronic mail or video-conference as an alternative to F-t-F communication [3]. Sensible as these conclusions are, these studies are based on observations not backed by controlled comparisons.

Reluctance toward electronic media of communication appears to be particularly strong when vulnerability derives from the risk of individualistic or deceitful behaviors. When no standardized procedures or hierarchy guarantee control on individual behaviors, uncertainty and therefore vulnerability increase. In this situation, mutual adjustment and trust are the only coordination mechanisms able to make an organization survive. However, mutual adjustment and trust are very delicate resources rooted in the flow of informal F-t-F relations [4]. This would explain reluctance toward CSCW technologies. As Nohria and Eccles argue, "*effectiveness of electronic network will depend on an underlying network of social relationships, based on face-to-face relationships.*" [5]

A goal of this study is to achieve a better understanding of the requirements for trust, by disentangling causes of vulnerability depending on the task, the characteristics of the groupware technology, and the social circumstances in which the technology is used by a group. The communication technology employed in this study is an electronic mailing list used in a synchronous way. It approached a chat box in terms of speed, but users had to open and close messages like in regular electronic mail. Group members were assigned electronic mail accounts from which they could send messages to the whole group through a group alias. Messages were not anonymous and everyone could read messages posted by everybody else. Messages were accessed like usual electronic mail messages. No private or sub-group exchange of electronic mail was permitted in this experiment. The experiment took place in a laboratory, where six-person groups were engaged in an iterative task involving investment of personal funds and receiving a payment dependent on what others invested. The task embodied a dilemma, known in the literature as "social dilemma" [6]. In a social dilemma individuals face the temptation to defect rather than cooperate to achieve a common goal. Since there is no superior control and the incentive to defect is higher than the incentive to cooperate (no matter whether the individual cooperates, she benefits from the outcome of others' cooperation), everybody should theoretically defect, either to take advantage of the situation or to avoid the risk of being the victim of others' opportunism. The moral of a social dilemma is that overall defection leads to miserable results for the group.

But empirical and experimental evidence shows that people naturally ignore the pessimistic moral, in particular when individuals can communicate F-t-F to establish trust within the group [8, 9]. Positive impact of F-t-F communication in social dilemmas motivates this investigation into whether similar results occur when people communicate electronically by a mailing list.

The study is organized in two stages. The first stage analyzes the effects of F-t-F and electronic communication in groups consisting of strangers. Expectations are that the existence of effects associated with computer-mediated communication will make it difficult for trust to emerge [10]. For instance, de-personalization, lack of contextual presence and non-verbal cues might fail to signal a desire for teamwork and goodwill. The second stage of the study looks at the effect of different social circumstances. In this stage each group meets the day before the experiment to play a game intended to promote group socialization. The day after, the same groups face the usual social dilemma experiment with electronic communication. We expect more cooperation. F-t-F socialization may overcome reluctance toward computer-based technologies of communication when collaborative tasks require trust. On the other hand, it is also possible that future groupware technologies could be designed to include features that are revealed in this study to be necessary to establish trust.

THE EXPERIMENT

Method

Experimental groups were composed of six subjects who met for about 3.5 hours to serve in the experiment. Subjects were physically located in the same room; everybody sat in front of a networked computer. Subjects were undergraduate students at the University of Venice (Italy), with experience in the use of electronic mail. Individuals were grouped in such a way that friendship or acquaintance relationships within the group are minimum. Quantitative methods are used to describe groups' performance, participation in the discussion and communication patterns. Qualitative data sources include participant observation, post-experiment questionnaires, analysis of communication transcripts. The experiment is drawn upon a previous experiment for the study of F-t-F communication on the emergence of cooperation [9].

Experimental Task

The individual task consisted of an investment in a market. The same task was repeated for about 28 rounds. In each round, once everybody invested, the group payoff was

Amount given to an individual to invest per round	13 tokens
Number of subjects	6
group investment at *social optimum* (cooperation)	36 tokens
group investment at *naïve social optimum* (cooperation)	46 tokens
group investment at *individualistic optimum* (non cooperation)	60 tokens
Individual payoff at *social optimum*	119 cents
Individual payoff at *individualistic optimum*	95 cents
Individual payoff for 1 non cooperator when only 5 subjects respect the *social optimum*	159 cents

Table 1. Some values of the experiment

calculated in correspondence to the sum of individual investments. Then each subject received her individual payoff as a share of the group payoff. Subjects had a table with complete information about the market payoff in correspondence of each possible investment. At the beginning of each round each subject received the same number of tokens to invest. She also received an updated record of her past individual investments and payoffs, and a record of the total group investment in each round of the game (investments are measured in tokens, payoffs are calculated in cents). But she was not given information about how much each person invested. Thus a subject could monitor group behavior but not individual ones.

At the end of the experiment everybody received a monetary payoff proportional to the individual payoff accumulated in the game.

The main problem faced by the subjects was that the market hid a trap: after a certain level of group investment, the bigger the group investment, the *lower* the group payoff. In other words, the market payoff had a parabolic profile: if subjects made large investments everybody was worse off. People however wanted to make large investments because the way in which the individual share of group payoff was calculated in the game. This share was proportional to the individual investment of the group investment. For instance, if a subject invested 10 tokens and the group had invested 40 tokens, then this subject got 10/40 of the group payoff. Thus, this rule encouraged everybody to make large individual investments. The dilemma was: should I make small investments to avoid the trap built in the market or large investments to earn as much as possible? Cooperation or defection? When a subject chose a small investment he was aware of being vulnerable, since there was no guarantee that others would have done the same. Total group investment was the only signal every participant received at the end of each round to measure group cooperation.

Two group investments are particularly relevant: the *social optimum* indicating the optimal amount a cooperative group as a whole should invest, and *individualistic optimum* indicating the optimal amount for a group of non-cooperative people. Social optimum provides higher payoff to everybody but is more risky, since a single defector can earn a lot exploiting the small investment of the others (Table 1). Subjects had all the necessary information to calculate these solutions. Miscalculation of the social optimum brings to a result called *naïve social optimum.* It indicates that subjects are cooperating but without perfectly optimizing how much they can earn from the market.

In this study, after the 10th, 15th and 20th rounds of this game, the group members participated in a round table-like discussion. The purpose of the discussion was to reach an agreement to establish cooperation. Agreements were not enforceable. Indicating with X a round of the task and with C a communication period, the experiment has the following structure:

XXXXXXXXX C XXXXX C XXXXX C XXXX....

Communication conditions

Twelve groups participated in the experiment. Different communication conditions were designed for them in the 3 communication periods. In the first stage of the study 3 groups communicated F-t-F and 6 groups used a non anonymous electronic mailing list. In the second stage 3 groups played a F-t-F game the day before the experiment and then participated in the experiment with communication supported by a non-anonymous electronic mailing list.

Condition I: Face-to-Face

Subjects had the possibility to discuss for 10 minutes in each communication period. They left the computer and met around a table in another room. A hidden camera recorded groups' behavior for the analysis of communication and patterns of actions.

Condition II: Electronic Mailing List

Subjects had the possibility to discuss for 30 minutes in each communication period. Communication was supported by an electronic mailing list resembling important features of a traditional F-t-F round table: messages were not anonymous and everybody could read everybody else's messages. Messages were recorded in a file for the analysis of communication protocols.

Condition III: Face-to-Face socialization before using the electronic mailing list

This condition differed from the previous one to the extent that subjects were exposed to a special treatment the day before the experiment. The treatment consisted of playing a 45-minute game aimed to elicit socialization through in-group collaboration. In this game the three groups competed against each other to build the best tower out of paper according to some pre-defined criteria. The day after the same groups played the usual experiment with communication supported by a mailing list.

FIRST STAGE OF THE STUDY

In the first stage, conditions I and II are analyzed. The study aimed to see if trust breaks down when electronic communication replaces F-t-F communication and individuals face a task characterized by high degree of vulnerability.

Results

Some recurring aspects describe groups' behavior in condition I. First, after the first communication period stable cooperation emerged. Second, at the end of each communication period groups reached a unanimous agreement even if some subjects show skepticism about the optimality of the decision. Third, groups got always locked in a naïve social optimum during the first communication period. Only two groups were capable of finding the social optimum and implemented the right strategy after the second communication period. On average group investment coalesced at a low level (Fig. 1). This indicates that subjects had overcome the vulnerability intrinsic in the task and had instead established trust-based cooperation.

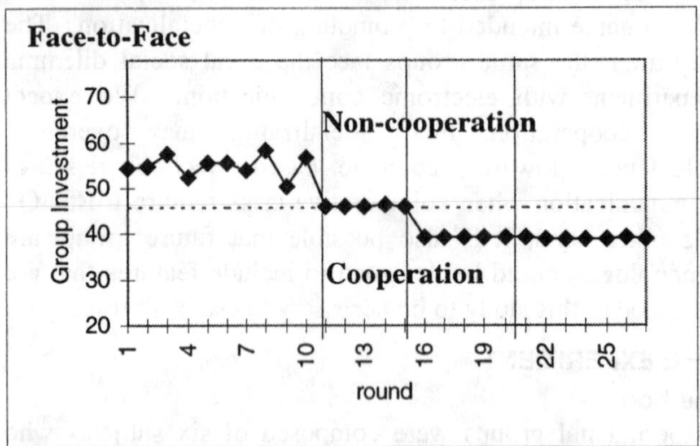

Fig 1.

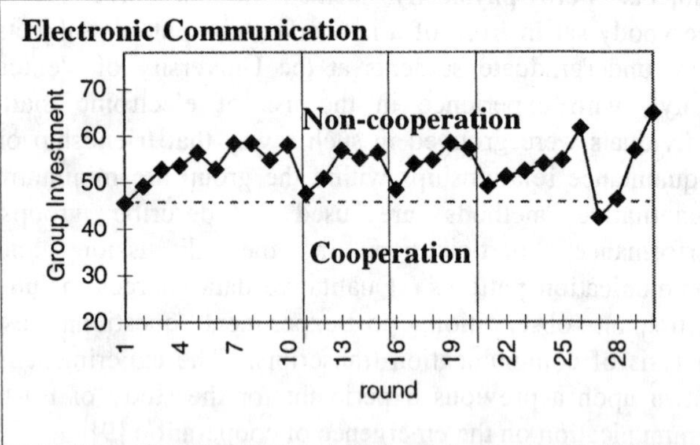

Fig. 2. Average group investment in the rounds of the experiment. Vertical lines represent the communication periods. The horizontal line indicates the threshold for cooperation: above 46 (naïve social optimum) non cooperation occurs.

In condition II individuals showed less stable and highly individualistic behavior than in condition I, reflected in the profile of the group investment (Fig. 2). Also in this condition some recurring aspects characterize group behavior. First, cooperation never succeeded despite of several attempts to define an agreement during the communication periods (15 out of 18 communication periods end up with a verbal agreement). Agreements were rarely unanimous (5 out of 15 agreements reach unanimity). However every agreement was systematically disregarded: immediately after communication, a few subjects broke the covenant, triggering a snowball-like defection of the rest of the group. In Fig. 2 notice that group investment always gradually rose after a communication period. The deceitful behavior of early defectors is a concrete example of opportunism, here referred to as "electronic opportunism" to emphasize that interactions occurred electronically. Electronic opportunism was highly profitable for early defectors who made large investments taking advantage of smaller investors.

The second commonality is that communication had a decreasing impact on eliciting cooperation because individuals experienced disenchantment and frustration about the group's trustworthiness. Frustration increased also because the flow of communication got very chaotic as time passed.

Third, groups were better in problem solving than in condition I in terms of number and quality of solutions generated. In fact groups communicating by mailing list generated and explored more solutions (5 in condition II versus 3.4 in condition I on average, per communication period). Also, 4 out of 6 groups did not get locked in the naive social optimum during the first communication period. However, in condition II only 2 groups were able to deploy the social optimum solution in a non unanimous agreement. Lack of trust and skepticism weakened individual intentions to respect any agreement. On average group investment was much higher than in condition I, indicating the breakdown of trust in the groups.

Interpretation

Analysis of video tapes and communication protocols revealed some factors that could be responsible for the differences observed between the two communication conditions.

Intelligible communication as a prerequisite for cooperation.

Participation in the communication periods was very different when subjects used an electronic mailing list. This technology does not provide support for rules of sequentiality and turn taking that govern F-t-F communication [11]. Sequentiality permits the discussion to gain coherence. In the mailing list participants received a multitude of messages whose topics were rarely in sequence. In contrast to F-t-F communication in which speakers govern the sequence of the discussion, in the mailing list sequence depends on the recipient of the messages who decides what to read first. The lack of need to take turns permits several threads to be discussed at the same time, causing the focus of the discussion to be lost. But it also meant that one can avoid responding to questions and ignore messages because of the lack of physical presence which usually compels responses. The breakdown of traditional rules of communication makes discussion nearly unintelligible. The argument here is that absence of cooperation in achieving an intelligible discussion fed skepticism about the possibility of achieving cooperation on the task.

"Cheap" coordination facilitates cooperation.

Cheap coordination refers to mechanisms such as informal division of labor and leadership that often takes place in F-t-F settings. In condition I a cheap division of labor characterized group problem solving. Analysis of video tapes revealed that different sub-groups were engaged in different activities: some did calculations, others explored alternative solutions, others explained the current strategy to those who showed skepticism or doubts about the strategy to adopt. The decomposition into sub-groups emerged by evolution rather than by design [12]. In condition II this coordination never emerged. This explains why subjects came up with the solution individually, exploring solutions and doing calculations alone. Ultimately, individual problem solving made it harder to reach an agreement because everybody wanted to impose her or his own solution onto the others.

Moreover, informal leadership of one or two subjects emerged in condition I. Leadership is related to the effect known as "first advocacy effect" [13]. First advocacy effect says that the first advocate is likely to gain leadership attribution by group members. That person's proposal is more likely to be implemented as group solution. Analysis of communication protocols shows that in condition I the first solution was indeed generally deployed in a group agreement. In condition II first advocacy effect was almost absent. Many solutions were simultaneously discussed until the end of the communication period. Then subjects engaged in a confused last minute voting that made it very hard to define the agreement.

Early establishment of social norms shapes cooperative attitudes.

Norms and conventions represent a crucial aspect of the groups' life. In both conditions I and II subjects engaged in the definition of norms. However, norms assumed very different connotations. In condition I groups stressed from the early minutes of the first communication period the need to respect cooperation, even in the face of possible defection. Conversely, in condition II groups postponed the discussion of norms to the end of the first communication period. Bad timing of social norms establishment might have increased the sense of vulnerability. At the end of the communication period subjects experienced high anxiety because they wanted to reach some agreement. The need for cooperation was enforced by threats of defection as a deterrence to punish possible opportunism (a variation of the famous tit-for-tat). In condition I the subjects never threatened. After the first communication period they did not need to reassert social norms once cooperation emerged. In condition II, the existence of electronic opportunism enhanced the need to establish norms. Aggressive expressions of disappointment (flaming), mistrust and blame dominated the second and third communication periods. The norm of cooperation was not the only norm to be violated.

SECOND STAGE OF THE STUDY

The previous results indicate that F-t-F communication elicits trust when the group is engaged in a task characterized by high degrees of vulnerability. However, when the group's relationships already carry a sort of group identity we could expect that cooperation might more easily emerge even if communication occurs electronically. Group identity, common values and history are recognized as prerequisites for long lasting trust-based cooperation [8]. Thus social circumstances might have a large impact on the use of a computer-based medium of communication. The second stage of the study investigated this hypothesis by introducing F-t-F socialization before groups engaged in electronic communication.

Results

In condition III, subjects demonstrated firm willingness to come to an agreement from the first communication period in marked contrast to subjects in condition II. But cooperation initially fell as indicated by the group investment that increased between the first and second communication periods (Fig. 3). Analysis of communication protocols suggests that cooperation fell not because of electronic opportunism, but because the groups experienced difficulties in understanding the final agreement. In one case, for instance, the group split in two sub-groups, each cooperating, but using different agreements. After the second communication period all groups overcame communication problems and reached stable cooperation. On average, the second and third communication periods lasted respectively 18 and 5 minutes, in spite of having 30 minutes available, since participants quickly converged to the agreement and asked the experimenter to continue with more investment rounds.

A post-experiment questionnaire confirmed that the F-t-F treatment had successfully achieved some degree of socialization. On average 4.3 subjects/group reported that it stimulated group identity and 3.6 of them thought the rest of the group experienced the same feeling. Also 4.6 subjects/group reported that prior F-t-F positively affected cooperation during the experiment.

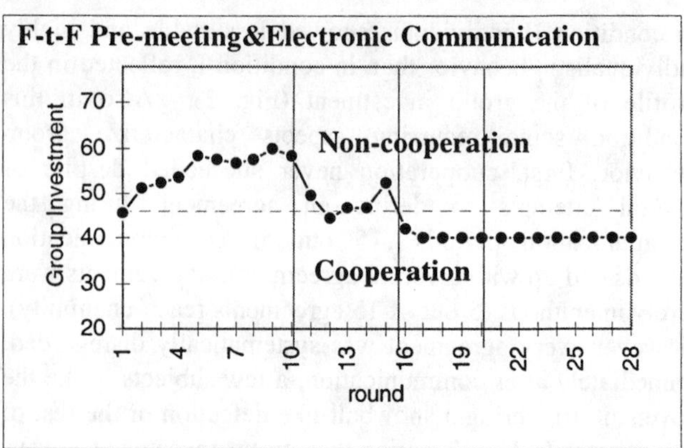

Fig. 3. Average group investment in the rounds of the experiment. Vertical lines represent the communication periods. The horizontal line indicates the threshold for cooperation: above 46 (naïve social optimum) non cooperation occurs.

Interpretation

Results are highly informative about the possible effects of F-t-F socialization before a text-based technology, like an electronic mailing list, is used for communication. Groups that had established socialization and perhaps trust were able and willing to overcome difficulties due to the communication technology. Some observations can be made about factors that make trust successful in condition III.

Group identity affects task's interpretation.

The content analysis of messages exchanged by the mailing list indicated that groups recognized a sort of group identity. Behaviors such as answering each others' questions, frequent use of the pronoun "*us*" rather than "*anyone*" or "*you*", and emphasis given to the concept of "*our interest*" were very common. This finding contrasts what was noticed in condition II, where subjects' behaviors resembled that of competitors in a market rather than that of members of a group. Frequent use of "*anyone*" and "*you*", emphasis on "*my payoff*" versus "*your payoff*" and statements such as "*loyalty is not a requirement*" conveyed the absence of group identity in condition II. The argument here is that the existence of group identity affects the task's interpretation to the extent that the same task can assume different natures according to the social circumstances. In condition III subjects stated that "*the game's goal is to maximize group payoff*" and "*our task is to figure out how to reach even individual payoffs*". Conversely, in condition II individuals framed the task in individualistic terms, trying to maximize their own payoff, with the awareness that "*a cartel will be difficult to sustain.*"

Cooperation revealed by styles of use of the technology.

Groups in condition III appropriated the technology differently from groups in setting II. In setting II discussion was dominated by many parallel threads, causing chaos and ambiguity. As a consequence, everybody was discouraged to read and understand the discussion. Many threads were alive until the last minute of the communication period. This boosted disagreement rather than convergence toward a consensus. Some threads invoked cooperation. But others seriously undermined cooperation proposing sabotages and stating the impossibility of reaching consensus. Conversely, a lower number of threads that decreased over time characterized communication in condition III. Individuals cooperated to make the discussion more intelligible. This facilitated the convergence toward the agreement.

Respect of social norms signals trustworthiness.
Like in condition I, subjects showed the need to establish social norms from the first minute of communication. They sent messages like "*the group must cooperate*". Then cooperation was taken for granted once the agreement was reached. There was no need to enforce the agreement by threats. Also, in condition III subjects never showed disappointment or frustration about the difficulties in using an electronic mailing list, nor expressed anger for the initial failure of cooperation. This behavior contributed to diffusing confidence about cooperation. Subjects showed concerns for the norm of fairness, especially after the initial breakdown of cooperation. This behavior preserved the group from dissolution. Instead, in condition II breakdown of cooperation and electronic opportunism created the breakdown of social norms, provoking threats, flaming and bluffs (misrepresentation of the purpose of past investments, phony declarations of honesty, etc).

CONCLUSION

A potential source of teamwork's failure is the perception of vulnerability due to the risk of individualistic or deceitful behaviors of team members. In these cases establishment of trust is the prerequisite for action. The greater the risk, the greater the need for trusting relationships because people do not take great risks with those they do not trust. Communication plays a central role in forging trusting relationships. However, when communication occurs electronically, in particular in text-based formats, the perception of vulnerability can increase. As a consequence, team members fail to develop trust.

This study sheds some light on the impact of electronic versus F-t-F communication on trust development, with a specific focus on the issue of trust in teams of strangers. Two main conclusions can be drawn. The first stage of the study reveals that factors such as intelligible communication, cheap coordination and early establishment of collaborative norms are mainly responsible for the successful emergence of trust in F-t-F context. When communication is supported by an electronic mailing list these factors appear fragile or even absent. This causes the breakdown of trust and, ultimately, of cooperation. Therefore, a first conclusion is that electronic communication might turn out to be inappropriate to support teamwork when trustworthiness is a prerequisite for action and members cannot rely on past experiences shared with the others. The need to verify whether the technology is the only cause responsible for the breakdown of trust led to the second stage of the study in which F-t-F socialization is introduced before individuals use the electronic mailing list. The study shows that trust can be achieved when team members have an initial F-t-F contact. Various elements signal that trust is in place: existence of group identity, style of use of the technology, respect of social norms.

Several research avenues could follow up these results. From the technical standpoint, design of future communication technologies should take into account the role of the factors revealed to be necessary for the development of trust. For instance, the study emphasizes the importance of intelligibility of electronic communication. Intelligible communication reduces risks of misunderstandings and encourages participation. Applications more advanced and more structured than mailing lists could support better intelligibility. Other tools could be developed to increase intelligibility by visual aids (e.g. visualization of communication threads, with messages displayed along the line in chronological order and situated at different levels to indicate the relative importance). Visualization of the communication threads might improve intelligibility and reduce the rigidity implicit in text-based forms of communication. Other features could be added depending on the possible causes of vulnerability intrinsic in the task (e.g. need for visual contact).

A different question regards the appropriate use of actual group technologies when a team's members need to establish trust before engaging in collaborative activities. It might be that reluctance toward groupware could indicate lack in the group trustworthiness or reliability. Although collaborative activities do not always imply risks of opportunistic or deceitful behavior like in a social dilemma described above, social norms play a crucial role in coordinating group behavior. For instance, a group coping with time pressure may need social norms to deal with exceptional events (occasional delays, unavailability of a team member, ...). To avoid risks of delays, uncertainties or internal conflicts, social norms should be discussed beforehand.

Socialization facilitates definition of social norms in many ways. After establishing personal relationships, individuals are usually more comfortable in revealing personal opinions, preferences and concerns [7]. Such disclosure brings to the surface potential obstacles, making it easier to foresee difficulties and negotiate appropriate social norms. Moreover, socialization supports the establishment of the group identity and the existence of group identity enhances the respect of norms [9]. As a consequence computer-supported collaboration could be improved by planning ahead one or more face-to-face meetings to support socialization. In general, this study suggests the need to explore further the issue of socialization in electronic environments. We need to analyze what the impediments to socialization are when people rely on computer-based media of communication. Also, we need to investigate whether a different or more intensive use of these media could overcome these impediments. The success of CSCW and design of future applications rely on our understanding of the transient and permanent effects of technology on teamwork.

ACKNOWLEDGMENTS

I am grateful to Judy Olson for her comments on and support with this research. I also would like to thank the members of the Collaboratory for Research on Electronic Work for their insightful feedback on a previous draft of this paper.

REFERENCES

1. Zand, D. E. Trust and Managerial Problem Soving. *Administrative Science Quarterly,* 1972, 17, 229-239.
2. Olson, J. S. and Teasley, S. Groupware in the Wild. Lessons Learned from a Year of Virtual Collocation. In *Proceedings of CSCW 96* (Boston, Nov. 1996), ACM Press, 419-427.
3. O'Hare-Devereaux, M. and Johansen, R. *Globalwork: bridging distances, culture and time.* San Francisco, Jossey-Bass Publisher, 1994.
4. Mintzberg, H. *The Structuring of Organizations.* Prentice Hall, Englewood Cliffs, 1979.

5. Nohria, N and Eccles, R. Face-to-Face Making Network Organization Work. Nohria, N. and Eccles, R. (eds.) *Networks and Organizations.* Cambridge, MA, HBS Press, 228-308, 1992.
6. Dawes, R. M. Social Dilemmas. *Annual Review of Psychology,* 1980, 31, 169-193.
7. Pruitt, D.G. *Negotiation Behavior.* New York: Academic Press, 1981.
8. Sally, D. Conversation and Cooperation in Social Dilemma. *Rationality and Society,* 1995, 7(1), 58-92.
9. Ostrom, E., Walker, J. and Gardner, R. Covenants with and without a Sword: Self-Governance is Possible. *American Political Science Review,* 1992, 86, 404-417.
10. Garton, L. and Wellman, B. Social Impacts of Electronic Mail in Organizations: A Review of the Research Literature. Brant R. Burleson (Ed) *Communication Yearbook* (18), Thousand Oaks, CA: Sage, 1995.
11. Suchman, L. A. *Plans and Situated Action. The problem of human machine communication.* Cambridge University Press, NY, 1987.
12. Hutchins, E. Organizing Work by Adaptation. *Organization Science,* 1991, 2(1), 14-39.
13. Weisband, S. P. Group Discussion and First Advocacy Effect in Computer-Medited and Face-to-Face Decision Making Groups. *Organizational Behavior and Human Decision Processes,* 1992, 53, 352-380.

Expertise, Collaboration and Bandwidth

Alonso H. Vera
Dept. of Psychology
vera@hkucc.hku.hk

Thomas Kvan
Dept. of Architecture
tkvan@arch.hku.hk

Robert L. West
Dept. of Psychology
rwest@hku.hk

Simon Lai
Dept. of Psychology
h9408159@hkusub.hku.hk

The University of Hong Kong
Pokfulam Road, Hong Kong

ABSTRACT

This paper describes the results of a study evaluating the effects of computer mediation on collaboratively solving architectural design problems. Pairs of graduate design students were asked to work on a landscape architecture design problem via computer terminals. In one condition they were allowed to communicate with an electronic whiteboard and a chat-line while in the other, the chat-line was substituted with video-conferencing (real-time video and audio). The protocols were evaluated according to two models. First, they were coded according to the pattern of collaboration, distinguishing meta-planning, negotiation, evaluation, and individual work. No differences were found between the two groups when coded this way. The protocols were also coded in terms of the problem-solving content, distinguishing task-related exchanges, interface-related exchanges, low-level design exchanges, and high-level design exchanges. The results showed that in the bandwidth-limited chat-line condition, participants cut down task and interface-related as well as low-level design exchanges but attempted to maintain the same amount of high-level design exchanges. When the final designs were evaluated by professional architects, no differences were found between two conditions indicating that chat-line participants implicitly compensate for the narrower bandwidth interface.

Keywords

Cognitive Models, Expertise, Collaboration, CSCW

INTRODUCTION

There is a long history of research into the role and application of computers to communication and collaboration from which have arisen a variety of tools to facilitate work done in groups (see [7] for a historical overview). It is not necessary here to review the various directions and conclusions of this research but it is important to note that computer mediation has been found to impact the collaborative process in significant ways. For example: Process structure benefits (e.g., [14]); greater participation (e.g., [8]); and better results (e.g., [9]).

In addition, some researchers have suggested that social processes play a critical role. For example, Harrison and Minneman [5] argue that Xerox PARC research on collaborative work reaches a common conclusion:

> "that social processes are crucial; that these social factors are significantly affected by being physically distributed; and that design participant's social actions are altered by the technologies that connect remote locations." (p. 687)

This belief that social processes play a critical role is often unquestioned, to the extent that some CSCW research [4] *assumes* that collaborative activities, especially remote collaboration, can only be understood in terms of its context. By assuming that situated actions, for example, are "givens" ([4], p. 334), the studies have reinforced the assumption that replication of physical spaces are necessary for virtual spaces to succeed. This automatically leads to the assumption that video and audio communication at a high bandwidth are *a priori* tools for successful collaborative distal design. Hollan and Stornetta [6] have highlighted the difficulties in this assumption and the failures of attempting such replication.

It is also important to note, however, that the question of whether computer tools actually influence how experts use their task specific *knowledge* in the performance of complex collaborative tasks has not been addressed by researchers in this area. Similar to Harrison and Minneman, we examined the process of collaborative architectural design but reached very different conclusions. If our findings are correct, then approaches to designing computer support for these tasks need to be fundamentally re-thought.

Our central research question concerned the effect of bandwidth limitations on collaboration and the consequent interface implications. Since this question was raised in the context of computer mediation for collaborative work, the relative effects of different modalities of communication were explored in terms of how they impacted on the collaborative process in terms of activities such as task planning, interactive negotiation and individual effort. We also evaluated how different forms of computer mediation affected the level of discussion in the problem-solving process. Specifically, we wanted to determine whether low-level and high-level design concerns are consistently present in design discussions regardless of the nature of the interface. Finally, we also wanted to know whether any such differences that might arise have an effect on the quality of the completed architectural design.

ARCHITECTURAL COLLABORATION

Collaborative architectural design requires that participants work together to solve a series of problems and arrive at one result. In going through the steps to solve the design problem, the designers must organize their activities around two facets: *when* to carry out particular tasks and *what* tasks to undertake [16]. We have distinguished between these two dimensions of their problem solving by identifying one as a *collaborative process* model of problem solving – deciding when work is done – and one as a *design process* model – deciding what work is done.

Collaboration Process Model

We began by constructing a traditional cognitive model of collaboration based on the hypothesis that expert collaborative problem-solving is structured very much like individual expert problem-solving. In collaboration, each participant can be considered as an individual agent working in parallel with other agents to achieve a common goal. We modelled collaborators as agents with sets of problem-solving skills and sets of goals.

When attending to design, experienced architects working collaboratively on a problem should behave like typical experts in any other area of expertise. They should have large chunks of knowledge which they can apply quickly and in a fairly error free way. They should also be able to work forward from the initial state of the problem (novices tend to use strategies such as working backwards from the goal). Furthermore, they should be able to reason by analogy from a large base of well cross-referenced knowledge about the field. Experts also plan better and monitor their progress more carefully than novices (see [1] for an extensive account of expert/novice differences).

The sort of cognitive processing demonstrated by experts on well-learned tasks allows us to predict the process of problem-solving with a reasonable degree of detail. The model of collaboration which will be evaluated in these studies is shown in Figure 1. The first step involves a process of planning how to execute the task in a coordinated way. It is a *meta-planning* process in the sense that it is about how to break down the problem into individually manageable units as well as about how and when the collaborators should come together to integrate their individual efforts. This process is followed by another collaborative step, *negotiation*, regarding specific aspects of the design problem. Following an initial negotiation, each participant separately engages in well-learned routine expert problem-solving guided by the meta-plan that was agreed upon and constrained by the jointly-made, task-specific negotiated decisions.

When the participants have completed their agreed upon components, they interactively *evaluate* the outcome and are then either finished or they iterate through the steps again. Additional meta-planning may or may not be required and the process may begin again following further task-specific negotiation. That the best architectural practitioners place great emphasis on the initiation of design exercises has been documented in earlier work on the process of design (e.g., [2]; [3]).

It is clear that, in addition to the problem-solving process, collaboration will also involve personality, emotion, culture, and many other social psychological factors. We suggest that these do not play an important role in shaping (or reshaping) the combined expert knowledge or the measurable product of the collaboration. As in Olson et al. [15], our focus is on the cognitive aspects of collaboration. We argue that the skills and expertise of the participants - i.e., the knowledge component of the collaboration rather than social or situational ones - primarily shape this. Therefore, although context effects, socio-cultural variables, and other non-knowledge level individual differences will influence many aspects of the collaboration (e.g., as suggested by Harrison and Minneman, [5]), they should not alter the process implicit in the knowledge level of the participants.

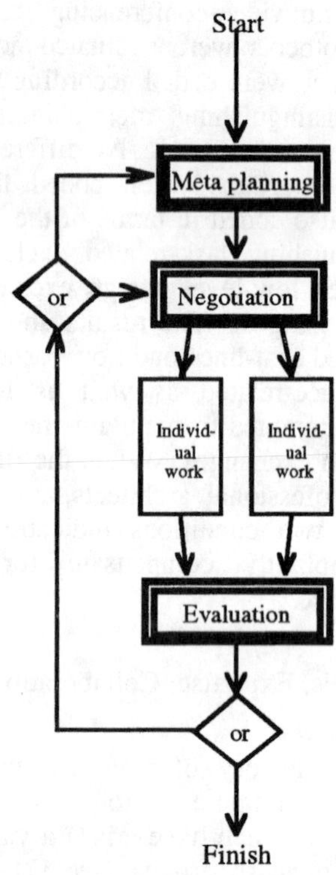

Figure 1. Model of Collaborative Design

Social/psychological variables, which are unrelated to the task-specific knowledge of each participant may affect things, such as the degree to which the collaboration is enjoyed or disliked. However, the real result of the collaboration, in this case, an architectural design, will be largely the consequence of the knowledge and experience of each collaborator. A long history of research in cognitive science supports this view (see Newell & Simon, [13], for an account of this perspective).

If our model is correct then the tools used to support collaborative work should focus on facilitating the meta-planning, negotiation and evaluation components of the process. Otherwise, the tools should be no different than those used for individual work, except for requiring a means to share the results.

Design Process Model

The task given to our participants can be seen as having two aspects: the collaborative process, as discussed above, and an architectural *design* process. Design consists of a large number of activities which can be considered to fall into four broad categories. Initially, designers digest the information given, gathering and reading facts and determining the data at hand. These we called *task-focused* activities. Next the designer strategizes solutions, making broad decisions which will affect significant aspects of their later decisions. These we call *high-level design* (HLD) activities. These activities include planning the site, laying out major components and identifying primary routes. Once these have been completed, *low-level design* (LLD) activities can be expected to start, such as placing individual elements such as trees, benches and parking places into the framework set by the high-level design actions, resolving issues of drafting (e.g. line type) and drafting actions. Thus, a prototypical design flow by someone exhibiting expert behaviors will have more HLD at the beginning of a design session and more LLD later in the session. Among all of these activities we can expect the designer to need to deal with the particular medium within which they are working. If they work in pencil and paper, it would include things such as sharpening the pencil. In our context, these *interface-specific* activities address issues of menus, commands, and connections.

Predicted Outcomes

Performance was measured in terms of the quality of the final output. The quality of the final output is contingent on the ability of the designers to accommodate the particular computer-mediated interface's information-sharing characteristics to their expert task. We therefore examined collaborations using video conferencing (high band-width) and chat-line (low band-width) with the expectation that subjects would create more efficient meta-plans under the low band-width condition.

In addition, the method of communication was expected to influence the distribution of types of design communication exchanges. We expected to see fewer exchanges with low band-width channels, of which a greater proportion would be HLD exchanges since the burden of the interface makes it impractical for low value exchanges. Inversely, higher band-width communication would be more profligately used.

METHOD

The subjects were twenty two graduate students from the University of Hong Kong. Fourteen were peers from the Department of Architecture and eight were peers from the Department of Landscape Architecture.

Two adjoining rooms were each equipped with Pentium computers. Both computers were equipped for video conferencing and were connected by a local network. For software we used Microsoft's NetMeeting which supports remote audio and video as well as a shared electronic white board and a chat line. For the audio we used head sets with a connected microphone so that subject's hands would be free. For the video we used Connectrix's Color QuickCam for Windows. However, even with the computers directly connected we found that the audio and video were of poor quality. To remedy this we used a phone line for the audio and a direct feed for the video (i.e., the video cameras sat on one computer but were actually connected to the computer in the other room). All connections passed through the wall so that, with the door between the rooms shut, subjects were cut off from any direct communication. This allowed us to simulate a high band width communication between remote hosts.

The Task

The participants were presented with site plans (see Figure 2) and a written problem definition as follows.

Objectives: *To resolve site access problems using basic rules of site design.*

You are to work as a pair together to design a rest area and car parking with pedestrian access within a sloped site as described in the attached site plan. The site consists of an evenly sloping site with a 13 meter difference in height from a hospital entrance at the top to a bus stop at the bottom. A car park for six cars is to placed on the site half way up the slope with access from Middle Road.

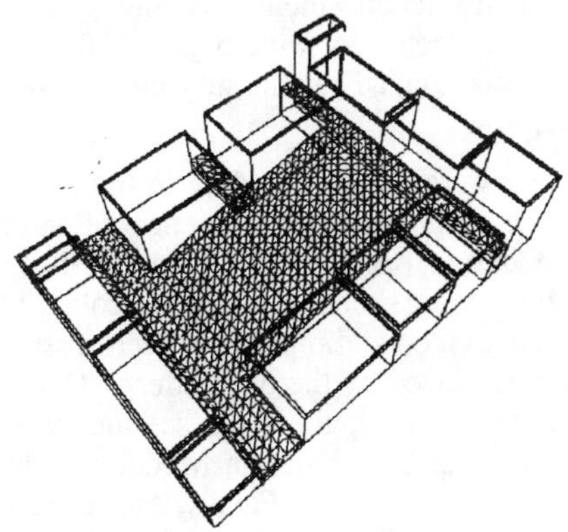

Figure 2. Design Site

The design challenge is to provide

1. *access from the bus stop to the hospital*
2. *access from the car park to the bus stop and the hospital*
3. *a seating area for up to six people and perhaps a play ground for children at an appropriate point on the site*
4. *routes which are not too steep*
5. *appropriate vegetation and landscaping to complete the design concept*
6. *a sense of arrival at each site access point*

While achieving these goals, you should try to:

- *minimize cut and fill*
- *minimize contour changes*
- *drain the site appropriately*

Useful information

During this exercise, use the following guidelines:

Maximum angles for slopes should be:

1:2 50% slopes for unmowed landscapes

1:3	*33%*	*for mowed grass surfaces*
1:6.7	*15%*	*maximum slope for cars*
1:12	*8.33%*	*handicap access ramps*
1:20	*5%*	*parking area surface (drain water off parking area)*
1:1.5	*66%*	*stair*

Minimum angles for slopes should be:

1:67	*1.5%*	*minimum slope for drainage*
1:3	*33%*	*minimum slope for stair*

Procedure

There were two conditions, one in which subjects could communicate using audio and video (i.e., they could see and hear each other), and one in which subjects used only a chat-line (i.e., they could send written messages to each other). In both conditions subjects could also use the electronic white board. Subjects were run in pairs. The video conferencing condition had five pairs and the chat-line condition had six pairs. Each pair of subjects was instructed in how to operate the conferencing technology and told that they would have one hour to solve a well defined architectural problem using the shared space of the electronic white board. They were then given the problem and separated into the two rooms. Each room contained an experimenter to directly observe the subject's actions, and a video camera to record them. A site plan was already present on the electronic white board. After one hour the experiment was stopped and the subjects were debriefed.

RESULTS

The protocols were coded according to the two models, one to extract the *collaborative* process engaged and the other to extract the *design* process employed by the participants. Two of the authors coded the protocols. A chat-line protocol and a video/audio protocol were first selected and extensively reviewed by the two coders. Once the coding schemes were finalized, all of the sessions were coded by one coder for the Collaboration Model and by the other coder for the Design Model. Finally, each cross-checked the reliability of the other coder by independently coding one protocol under the other's model. For the Collaboration Model, the interrater reliability was 86% with a Cohen's kappa = 0.768 while it was 62% with a Cohen's kappa = 0.52 for the Design Model. Finally, all design products were graded by teaching staff in the Department of Architecture to determine their design value.

Design Evaluation

We will report first on the evaluation of the finished designs since this is, perhaps, the most surprising result. In order to evaluate the quality of the finished designs, we had the designs independently graded by two lecturers from the University of Hong Kong's Architecture Department. Agreement between the two markers was high (80% overlap in the rank order of the grades). The disagreements were minor and were resolved through discussion. Subjects were graded according to the percentage of the required design tasks they completed, the degree to which they satisfied the technical requirements of the tasks which they did complete, and the overall quality of their design. A reliability analysis revealed an Alpha coefficient of 0.877 indicating that all three measures were tapping the same construct, which we assumed to be a general competency for the task. Taking an average of the three measures to create an overall score, the two groups (video/audio versus chat-line) showed no difference, both producing a mean overall score of 6 out of 10. Although the number of subject pairs was too low to rule out any effect for the conferencing technology we could rule out the existence of any large systematic effects. This, despite the very real limitations imposed by the bandwidth in the chat-line condition (i.e., in the video/audio condition, subjects could talk and draw at the same time whereas in the chat-line condition they could only do one at a time). Figure 3 shows an example of a completed design.

It should also be noted that there was considerable variability in the final design products and the ways in which they were created. For example, some subject pairs worked together on each design element while others worked in parallel on different elements. Also, some subject pairs worked in a very egalitarian, democratic manner while other pairs were dominated by a single authoritarian subject.

Collaborative Process Encoding

Overall, the protocols of participant pairs in the video/audio condition had approximately twice as many exchanges as those of participant pairs in the chat-line condition. Given that the final performance on the task was the same between the two conditions, one has to wonder how the participants in the chat-line condition made up for the overall decrease in communication.

Figure 3 Sample of a completed design.

Our initial hypothesis was that the chat-line participants achieved this by increasing the relative amount of meta-planning they did during the task. Meta-Planning, includes dividing-up the task (e.g., "So maybe we can have a division of labor: I deal with the access and you deal with the car park, OK?"), planning the order of task execution (e.g., "I suggest that we identify the plan first before we start to do anything."), and strategies for completing the task (e.g., "So we have to do the sketch design first before any calculation."). The other communicative activities participants demonstrated were Negotiation (e.g., "I intend to erase some of the seating, what do you think?") and Evaluation (e.g., "The car park is too small, I think.") The fourth element included in the Collaborative Process Model

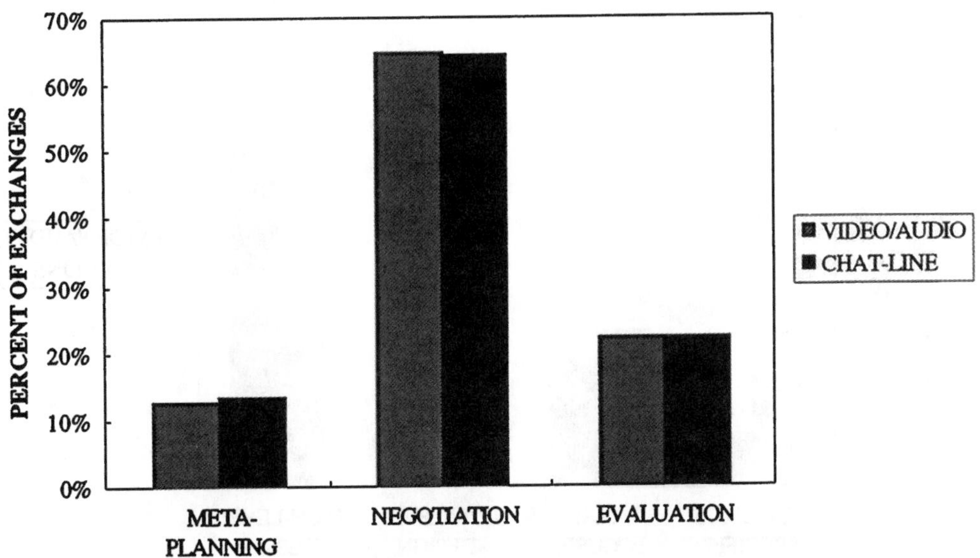

Figure 4. Results of coding the protocols with the Collaborative Process Model.

was *Individual Work.* Although there was some verbal evidence of it in the protocols (e.g., "OK, I'm drawing trees now."), the videotapes of the sessions indicated that it was going on continually though out the design process.

As stated, we expected that the amount of Meta-Planning would increase while Negotiation and Evaluation would decrease in the chat-line condition, thereby accounting for the lack of difference in the quality of the finished designs. This was not the case, however, as Figure 4 shows. The total amount of each type of interaction decreased *proportionately* from the video/audio condition to the chat-line condition. Although the number of participants was relatively low, it is important to note that the aggregate pattern shown in Figure 4 was demonstrated by *all* the collaborator pairs. The correlations among the patterns of communication shown by subject pairs were all above .7 and significant at the .05 level.

This extremely consistent pattern along the three categories indicates that the collaborative process was undisturbed by the two very different communicative conditions. It also suggests that this approach to breaking down the collaboration captures something essential about the process. Given two different channels of communication, participants in both conditions maintain a very similar pattern of collaboration (a ratio of Meta-Planning to Negotiation to Evaluation of 1:5:2). The Collaborative Process Model therefore successfully describes the way in which people engage in collaborative work by strategizing, dividing-up the task and temporally ordering the activities, regardless of the nature of the communication channel.

These findings are similar to those of Olson et al. [16] who categorized protocols from meetings using a coding scheme much like ours. They coded interactions into three clusters of categories: Coordination/Management Activities similar to our Meta-Planning category, Direct Design Activities similar to our Negotiation category, and Summary/Walkthrough Activities similar to our Evaluation category. The relative percentages of these three clusters were 27%, 43%, and 30% respectively. Although, different to our results in terms of the magnitude of the differences between the three categories, the relative pattern was similar. The magnitude difference may be the consequence of the fact that *coordination* and *design* activities were not distinguished in their coding scheme. The two models proposed here pull apart these two kinds of activities. The Collaboration Model focuses exclusively on the collaboration (i.e., coordination) aspects of the interaction while the Design Model captures the other side. We would therefore argue that the larger differences between the categories found in our study are the consequence of using two separate models to code the protocols, resulting in a more sensitive instrument to evaluate the content of the interactions.

Given that there was a 60% decrease in the total number of exchanges in the chat-line condition (distributed evenly over Meta-Planning, Negotiation, and Evaluation), one would expect to find a significant negative impact on the design outcomes. Since the Collaborative Process Model does not provide an explanation for why the design outcomes were equivalent in the two conditions, another explanation is necessary. As indicated above, we expected that the relative amount of Meta-Planning would increase in the chat-line condition, counterbalancing the effect of fewer exchanges. The results from the Collaborative Process analysis could not be clearer, however -- there was no change in the ratio of the types of exchanges. Something else must have been at work, something not captured by the model, that allowed subjects in the chat-line condition to produce equally good designs. Our next hypothesis was that it was related to *what* work was carried out collaboratively as opposed to the allocation of the work between the participants.

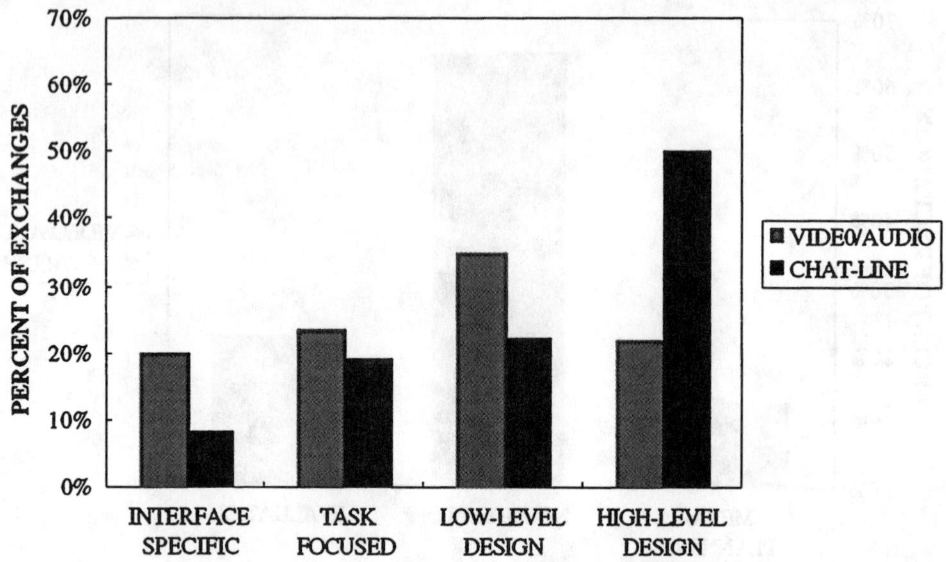

Figure 5. Results of coding the protocols with the Design Process Model.

Design Process Encoding

It would appear that more restricted channels of communication require more selective exchanges of communications and that the communication sacrificed would be low content-level exchanges. Thus, the differences between communication channels might appear in the Design Process Model but not in the Collaborative Process Model.

In order to evaluate the nature of design communication, all exchanges for the sessions were reviewed and encoded as one of the four following types: *Task Focused*: (e.g., reading the instruction), *Interface specific* (e.g. "Sorry, can you speak louder."), *High-Level Design* (HLD) (e.g. "I propose a zigzag route from here to here"), and *Low-Level Design* (LLD), (e.g., "what color do you like for the seating?").

Coding the protocols this way showed a clear difference in the content of the chat-line condition to that found in the video/audio condition. Chat-line communication contained a notably higher percentage of HLD content, 50% of all exchanges, compared to video/audio, where only 22% of all exchanges were HLDs. *The ratio of LLD to HLD was inverted,* with chat-line showing proportionately more HLDs than LLDs while video/audio showed the opposite effect. (see Figure 5). Basically, participants in the chat-line conditions made up for having a narrower communication channel by decreasing the amount of LLD in order to maintain a high number of HLDs. The participants also sacrificed the other two types of communicative exchanges to achieve the high proportion of HLD exchanges in the chat-line: Task-Focused was 19% for chat-line and 24% for video/audio; Interface Specific was 8% for chat-line and 20% for video/audio. Participants in the video/audio condition, on the other hand spent a much greater proportion of their time discussing Low-Level Design issues as well as Task and Interface issues. As in the Collaboration Model, the pattern of results found for each pair of subjects was very consistent with the aggregate data. For the chat-line condition all pairs except one showed the pattern in Figure 5. The same was true for the video/audio condition.

The fact that the chat-line collaborators did just as well on their designs as the video/audio collaborators suggests that it is the High-Level Design exchanges that play the most significant role in determining the quality of the outcome. Most importantly, the nature of the communicative channel would seem to have little effect on this aspect of collaborative work as participants appear to implicitly adapt to communicative constraints by either increasing or decreasing the amount of low-level discussion.

DISCUSSION

Building from research that suggests collaborative interfaces must involve a high throughput of information (e.g., tonal inflections, gestures, voice, and so on), we started with the assumption that designers faced with limitations in communication bandwidth would adjust their collaborative strategy to compensate for the restrictions in communication. Instead, we found the collaborative strategies to be the same. Compensation obviously had to occur since there was a marked reduction in the amount of communication.

We found compensation occurred in the *content* of the communications, not in the *strategy* of collaboration. As band-width was reduced, subjects shifted the content of their exchanges from discussing low-level issues to engaging in much more high level discussion. We also found a marked reduction in the number of task-related exchanges and comments on the interface during chat-line communication. This suggests that the chat-line subjects worked more independently, collaborating primarily when strategizing. While not the expected compensation mechanism, the outcome is not surprising. It is interesting that this shift in balance between HLD and LLD occurs without any explicit discussion between the subjects; there was no evidence that participants were even aware of the shift.

The research described here challenges assumptions evident in much previous research in the field of computer-mediated collaborative design. Typically, previous work has been driven by the need to recreate a "design space" in all its properties, without critically evaluating the contribution of these properties to design outcomes. An example of such work is that found in Tang [12]. Here, the author identifies actions of "writing, freehand drawing and gesturing activities that occur when three or four people work around whiteboards or large sheets of paper," (p. 143) noting that

> "Collaborative drawing tools should not be based only on what features computer technology offers...the design of collaborative technology needs to be guided by an understanding of how collaborative work is accomplished. By understanding what resources the collaborators use and what hindrances they encounter in their work, tools can be designed to augment resources while removing obstacles." ([20], p. 143)

While we agree with this point that the design of tools for collaboration should be based on a good understanding of the process, the author goes on to conclude that gestures are as important as any other communication and that

> "design of tools to support collaborative drawing activity should consider:
> - conveying gestures, maintaining their relationship to the drawing space;
> - conveying the process of creating and using drawings, with minimal time delay;
> - providing concurrent access to the drawing space;
> - allowing intermixing among drawing space actions and functions; and
> - enabling all participants to share a common view of the drawing space." ([20], p. 156)

We have found that the context is not an over-riding factor in successful collaboration. While it cannot be denied that the context within which an activity is carried out will affect the outcome, it is clear that we are, as humans, adaptive to our environment (we learn to shut out the noises which interrupt us as we design) and adaptive of it (we find that shutting a window helps to control the noise). That users adapt successfully to the quality and capabilities of the tools at hand is widely noted in studies of the application of computer tools [e.g. 11]. Although we exist in an environment with infinite levels of complexity, we solve each problem and make each decision in a much more restricted informational context [19]. So it is in any collaborative communication - we adapt to it and we adapt it to our needs. Since our individual cognitive systems are not built to cope with the full complexity of the environment at any one time, we pick out what is relevant and necessary in order to proceed.

The pattern of problem-solving found in this study reflects the knowledge the subjects had (from their classes) regarding how to solve this kind of problem. More importantly, it reflects a collaborative mechanism whereby the nature of the communication itself is implicitly shaped to the nature of the communicative channel without any loss in the quality of the collaborative outcome. The consistent allocation of time or effort in different stages of collaborative process found across our different bandwidth conditions mirrors the consistency found by Olson [16, 17] in their analysis of design meetings. As with the chaotic activities which constitute a face-to-face meeting, the messy data recorded during our design studies shrouded consistent patterns of work. So, although the collaboration *looks* very situated, it is in reality shaped and guided by the collaborators' individual knowledge of the task and their tacit ability to adapt to communicative situations.

Much has been said recently about the special nature of collaborative work, especially on open-ended, creative problem-solving tasks such as architectural design (e.g., [20]; [5]). Our findings, however, paint a simpler picture: experts in a particular area of knowledge solve problems in consistent and regular ways. Moreover, the process of collaboration is remarkably consistent along certain dimensions and remarkably adaptive along others.

CONCLUSION

The results of this study suggests that there is negligible influence of communication channels on the collaborative execution of expert tasks. The participants in this project carried out their collaborative tasks using the same collaborative process (Meta-Planning, Negotiating and Evaluation) regardless of the communication channel. Changing the communication channel did have an effect; the profile of communication content changed (i.e. the ratio of HLD to LLD) but, importantly, the change in communication channels did not influence the design outcome. Thus, we conclude that designers adapt the nature of their communication to the bandwidth of the channel available without compromising their collaborative strategy or expert contributions. That the communication bandwidth or technology had no effect on the outcomes of the task is resonant with the findings by Kraut et al. [10] "We found no evidence that differences in communication technology influenced success in collaboration" (p. 64). This finding is also consistent with Olson [18], although they note that a significant deterioration in design quality was found when comparing face-to-face to non-video (audio only) communication.

The findings presented are not intended to be interpreted as suggesting that the nature of the comunication channel never makes a difference in collaboration. We view these results as one data point in a space of possible combinations between *task* (i.e., design, meeting, conflict resolution, social, etc.), *types of collaborators* (i.e., relative knowledge, social/hierarchical relationship, etc.) and *outcome measures* (i.e., quality of output, solution of problem, individual satisfaction, etc.), as shown in Figure 6. Each box in the space needs to be filled in with the tools necessary to achieve the specific goals of the collaboration. It may be valuable to view one goal of CSCW research as filling in the different boxes in this collaboration space.

We have filled in one box with a well-defined design task, two knowledgeable collaborators with similar backgrounds, and quality of design as an outcome measure. Nevertheless, these findings, especially the implicit shift in the level of communicative exchanges, beg an explanation. We expect that this explanation will be better framed, not within situated descriptions of activity, but rather at the *knowledge-level* as postulated by Newell [12].

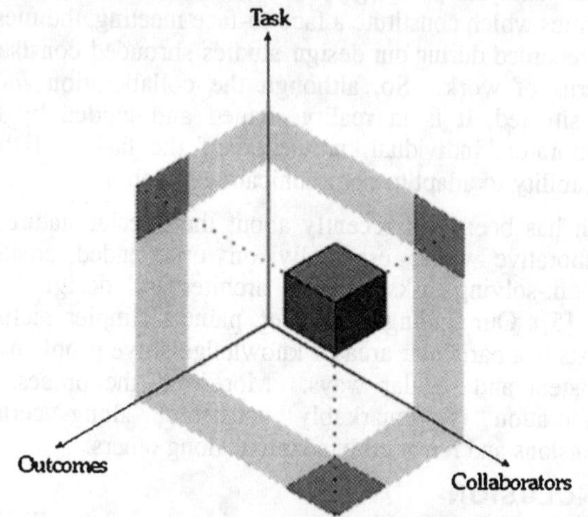

Figure 6. Space of collaboration characteristics requiring different computer-support solutions.

There are also implications for interface design - if collaborative work is much like individual work within this model, then a collaborative interface need not be different. Furthermore, if the designers can adjust to their level of communication and achieve the same outcomes, there is no need to compromise an interface by providing excess communicative information.

ACKNOWLEDGEMENTS

This research was supported by the University of Hong Kong under a grant from the CRCG. The authors are grateful for the assistance and support provided by the Departments of Architecture and Psychology and to Ms. N. Y. W. Cheng for use of her design problem as a basis for the task used in this research. The comments of eight CHI reviewers where invaluable in helping us prepare the final version of this paper.

REFERENCES

1. Bedard, J. and Chi, M.. Expertise. *Directions in Psychological Science,* Vol. 1, 1992, 135-139.
2. Coxe, W. Role models of excellence. *In Search of Design Excellence* American Institute of Architects, Washington DC, 1989.
3. Cuff, D. *Architecture: the story of practice.* Cambridge, MA: MIT Press, 1991.
4. Fitzpatrick G., Kaplan, S. and Mansfield, T. Physical spaces, virtual places and social worlds: A study of work in the virtual. *Proceeding of CSCW '96,* Cambridge MA, ACM Press, 1996 334-343.
5. Harrison, S. and Minneman, S. Studying collaborative design to build design tools. *The Global Design Studio,* M. Tan and R Teh (Eds.), Centre for Advanced Studies in Architecture, National University of Singapore, Singapore, 1995.
6. Hollan, J. and Stornetta, S. Beyond being there. *Proceeding of CHI'92,* Monterey, CA, 1992.
7. Holtham, C. Groupware: Its past and future. *Groupware in the 21st Century,* P. Lloyd (Ed.), Westport, CT: Praeger, 1994.
8. Kiesler, S. and Sproull. L. Group decision making and communication technology. *Organizational Behavior and Human Decision Process,* Vol. 52, 1992, 96–123.
9. Kraemer, K. L. and Pinsonneault, A. Technology and groups: Assessment of the empirical research. *Intellectual Teamwork* J. Galegher, R. E. Kraut and C. Egido (Eds.), Hillsdale, NJ: Lawrence Erlbaum Associates, 1990.
10. Kraut, R. E., Miller, M. D. and Siegel, J. Collaboration in performance of physical tasks: Effects on Outcomes and Communication. *Proceeding of CSCW '96,* Cambridge MA, ACM Press, 1996, 57-66.
11. Moran, T. P., Chiu, P., Harrison, S., Kurtenbach, G., Minneman, S., and van Melle, W. Evolutionary engagement in an ongoing collaborative work process. *Proceeding of CSCW '96,* Cambridge MA, ACM Press, 1996, 150-159.
12. Newell, A. The knowledge level. *AI Magazine,* Vol. 2, 1981.
13. Newell, A. and Simon, H. A. *Human problem solving.* Englewood Cliffs, NJ: Prentice-Hall, 1972.
14. Nunamaker, J. F., Briggs, R. O. and Mittleman, D. D. Electronic meeting systems: Ten years of lessons learned. *Groupware: Technology and Applications,* D. Coleman and R. Khanna (Eds.), New York, NY: Prentice-Hall, 1995.
15. Olson, G. M. and Olson, J. S. User-centered design of collaboration technology. *Journal of Organizational Computing,* Vol. 1, 1991, 61-83.
16. Olson, G. M., Olson, J. S., Carter M. R., and Storrøsten, M. Small group design meetings: An analysis of collaboration. *Human Computer Interaction,* Vol. 7, 1992, 347-374.
17. Olson, G. M., Olson, J. S., Storrøsten, M., Carter, M., Herbsleb J., and Rueter, H. Structure of activity during design meetings. *Design Rationale: Concepts, Techniques and Use,* P. T. Moran and J. M. Carroll (Eds.), Hillsdale, NJ: Lawrence Erlbaum Associates, 1996.
18. Olson J. S., Olson, G. M. and Meader, D. Face-to-face group work compared to remote group work with and without video. *Video-Mediated Communication,* K. E. Finn, A. J. Sellen and S. B. Wilbur (Eds.), Hillsdale, NJ: Lawrence Erlbaum Associates, 1997.
19. Simon, H. A. *Sciences of the artificial.* Cambridge, MA: MIT Press, 1969.
20. Tang, J. C. Findings from observational studies of collaborative work. *International Journal of Man-Machine Studies,* Vol. 34, 1991, 143–160.

Effects of Awareness Support on Groupware Usability

Carl Gutwin
Department of Computer Science
University of Saskatchewan
Saskatoon, SK, S7N 5A9, Canada
+1 306 966-4886
gutwin@cs.usask.ca
www.cs.usask.ca/faculty/gutwin

Saul Greenberg
Department of Computer Science
University of Calgary
Calgary, AB, T2N 1N4, Canada
+1 403 220-6087
saul@cpsc.ucalgary.ca
www.cpsc.ucalgary.ca/~saul

ABSTRACT

Collaboration in current real-time groupware systems is often an awkward and clumsy process. We hypothesize that better support for workspace awareness can improve the usability of these shared computational workspaces. We conducted an experiment that compared people's performance on two versions of a groupware interface. The interfaces used workspace miniatures to provide different levels of support for workspace awareness. The basic miniature showed information only about the local user, and the enhanced miniature showed the location and activity of others in the workspace as well. In two of three task types tested, completion times were lower with increased awareness support, and in one task type, communication was more efficient. Participants also greatly preferred the awareness-enhanced system. The study provides empirical evidence of, and underlying reasons for, the value of supporting workspace awareness in groupware.

Keywords

workspace awareness, groupware, usability

INTRODUCTION

Real-time distributed groupware allows people to work together at the same time from different places. Many of these systems provide shared computational workspaces—two-dimensional areas akin to whiteboards or tabletops—where people can create and manipulate task artifacts. Although many of the technical problems of constructing these systems have been solved, their usability problems have not yet been eliminated. Collaboration in groupware workspaces is often awkward, stilted, and frustrating compared to face-to-face settings. The difficulty is particularly acute when the workspace is larger than the screen and people navigate independently through the workspace (called relaxed-WYSIWIS view sharing [12]).

Part of the problem with current systems is that they don't provide much information about other participants in the session. When people work together in a face-to-face setting, a wide variety of perceptual cues help them keep track of what others are doing. This awareness of others in the workspace is *workspace awareness*, the up-to-the-moment understanding of another person's interaction with the shared space [7,8]. At a simple level, it involves knowledge of who is present, where they are working, and what they are doing. Workspace awareness is used in collaboration to coordinate activity, to simplify verbal communication, to provide appropriate assistance, and to manage movement between individual and shared work. Current groupware systems provide only a fraction of the information needed to maintain workspace awareness. They lack many of the natural affordances that exist in face-to-face settings, and they rarely provide artificial support.

We believe that increased support for workspace awareness will improve the usability of groupware. A previous study provided qualitative evidence that awareness support is valuable [5]. It also showed that *workspace miniatures*—miniature representations of the entire workspace—are useful vehicles for this information. In this experiment we are interested in the quantitative effects of awareness support on groupware usability. We compare two groupware interfaces that provide different amounts of awareness information through their workspace miniatures. In particular, we compare a basic miniature to one that adds three kinds of information:

- the location of others' viewports in the workspace;
- the location and motion of people's cursors; and
- the motion of workspace objects as they are moved.

The awareness-enhanced version of the miniature is called the *radar view* [6]. The experiment measures three aspects of groupware usability: how well groups perform with each interface, the efficiency of their collaboration, and the group's satisfaction with the system.

The adaptability and resourcefulness of groups makes groupware difficult to evaluate [4,10]. Nevertheless, we believe that support for awareness will make substantial differences to usability, because of the importance of the workspace in collaborative interaction. The workspace is an external representation of a joint activity, and a stage on which the collaboration is acted out. Previous investigations have recognized that a shared workspace and the artifacts in it change the way people communicate through actions, speech, and gesture [1,3,14,15]. Workspace awareness is one of the keys that allows people to interact in and through the shared workspace. This study takes initial steps towards an empirical understanding of the role played by workspace awareness, and how to support it in groupware.

METHODS AND PROCEDURE

The study's basic question asks whether information about another person's location and activity in the visual workspace will help groups complete tasks. In particular, we compared people's performance, perception of effort, and verbal efficiency for two interfaces that provided different levels of awareness support. Both interfaces used workspace miniatures, but the basic overview only showed information about the local participant, whereas the enhanced radar view added information about the location and activity of others in the workspace. Groups completed three kinds of tasks to give us a broad perspective on awareness in collaborative situations. Groups also worked with both interfaces, and were asked which they preferred.

Groupware System and Interface Conditions

A direct-manipulation groupware application was built for the experiment, using the GroupKit groupware toolkit [11]. The application is a pipeline construction kit that allows the assembly and manipulation of simple pipeline networks in a shared two-dimensional workspace (Figure 1). Users can create, move, and rotate sections of pipe, and can join or split sections using a welding tool. The workspace is rectangular, and four times larger than the computer screen in each direction. Users scroll around the workspace by dragging their cursor past the window border.

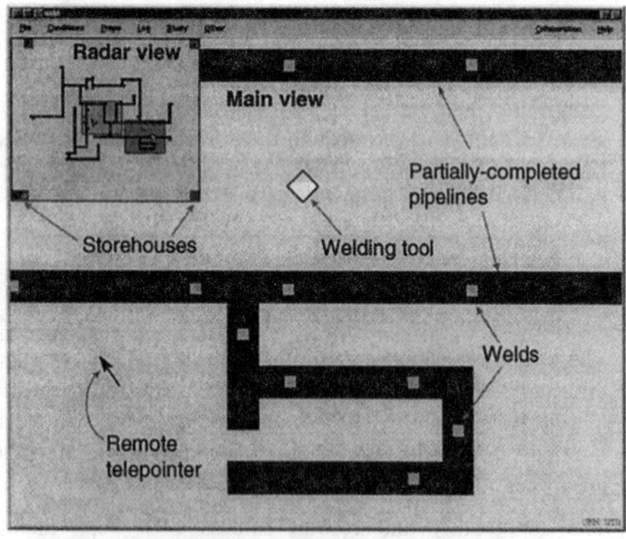

Figure 1. The pipeline system (radar view version)

The pipeline system's interface consists of two windows. The *main view* takes up most of the screen and shows objects in full size and detail. The main view allows users to manipulate objects and to scroll to other areas of the workspace. People create pipelines by dragging pipe sections from storehouses in the corners of the workspace, aligning the sections, and then welding them together by dropping a diamond-shaped welding tool onto the joint. Welds are marked by a yellow square, and once pieces are welded, they move as a unit.

The second window is one of two miniature views, the *radar view* or the *overview*. This view is inset into the top left corner of the main view, and shows the entire workspace in miniature. The radar view and the overview differed in three ways, as compared in Figure 2.

1. The radar showed workspace objects as they moved; the overview was only updated after the move was complete.
2. The radar showed people's viewports (the area of the workspace visible in each person's main view) and the overview showed only the local user's viewport.
3. The radar showed miniature telepointers for both users, and the overview did not show any telepointers.

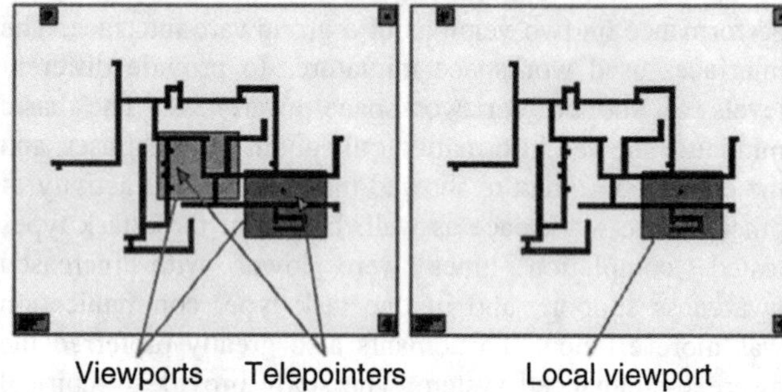

Figure 2. Radar view (left) and Overview (right).

In sum, the two conditions differed only in the awareness information presented in the miniature. The overview only showed information about the local user, and the radar showed where the other person was located, showed their pointer, and showed moves as they occurred.

Tasks

Participants completed three kinds of tasks. Tasks were designed to mimic episodes and activities that we observed in face-to-face collaboration, but were constrained to meet three criteria. First, we wanted tasks that required people to move independently around the workspace. Second, we wanted tasks that used location or activity information. Third, we wanted realistic tasks that were likely to occur in a wide variety of workspace activities. Division of responsibility in the tasks was similar to Chapanis' communication studies, where the *source* has information that the *seeker* needs to do their part of the task [2].

The **follow** task asked participants to make ten specific welds on an existing pipe network. One person, the joiner, was given a paper map showing the locations to be welded, and had to prepare the pipe sections at each place. The other person was the welder, and would follow the joiner to each location and weld the pipe. Since the welder had no map, the joiner was also responsible for ensuring that the welder went to the correct location.

The **copy** task asked participants to construct two identical structures from two existing stockpiles of pipe sections. The stockpiles were located at opposite ends of the workspace. One person, the leader, had a paper picture of what was to be built, and used this to find the next piece in their stockpile. The other person, the copier, did not have the picture, and so had to copy the leader's actions. The leader was responsible for making sure that the copier knew which piece to take next and where to place it.

The **direct** task asked one participant to verbally guide the other through adding six specific pipe sections to an existing network. The director had a map showing which pieces were to be added, and where they were to be added, but was not allowed to move around in the workspace. The actor did the work, following the director's instructions. The director did not see their main view during this task, so the only visual feedback that they received of the actor's progress was from the miniature view.

Study Design

The study combines two independent variables in a two-way mixed factorial design: View is a between-subjects factor; Task is a repeated-measures factor. Our hypothesis is that additional awareness information will improve people's speed, efficiency, and satisfaction with a groupware system. The hypothesis is tested by looking for effects of View in interaction with Task. Differences between tasks are expected, since the different task types are not related. Three dependent variables—completion time, perceived effort, and communication efficiency—are measured within each cell of the diagram in Table 1.

		Task:		
		Follow	Copy	Direct
View:	Radar view	G 1-10	G 1-10	G 1-10
	Overview	G 11-20	G 11-20	G 11-20

Table 1. Diagram of study design (G = Group).

In addition to the between-subjects comparison, we wanted to gather preference data; therefore, participants used both the radar and overview interfaces. After finishing the first three tasks, groups were asked to complete a second set of tasks using the other interface. They then chose which interface they preferred. The same three measures were taken for the second set of tasks, so that exploratory within-subjects analyses could be carried out as well.

Participants

Undergraduate and graduate students experienced with mouse-and-window-based applications were recruited from the University of Calgary, and were paid $10 for taking part. Forty people participated in the study, 30 men and 10 women. Participants were assigned a partner for the study, either choosing one themselves or by random assignment. Sex pairings were equalized across the two conditions.

Procedure

The experiment was carried out in several stages. Participants were first asked to sign consent forms and fill out a short demographic questionnaire, and then were introduced to the situation and the system's functions using standardized instructions. Pairs were randomly assigned to either the radar or the overview condition, and the specifics of their miniature view were explained. Participants were then allowed to practice with the system until they could each perform a basic set of simple operations such as scrolling, drąg-scrolling, welding, and unwelding. They then completed a practice task.

Pairs then completed six test tasks: three with one kind of view (radar or overview), and then three with the other. The order of the tasks was counterbalanced across groups. For each task, the experimenter gave standard instructions, then started the pair on the task. After each task, the pair filled out a questionnaire. At the end of the session, participants were asked which system they preferred. A short interview was then conducted to follow up episodes observed during the session or particular questionnaire responses.

Physical setup

Participants worked at two workstations, angled so that they could not see each others' screens, but so that they could see and talk to one another.

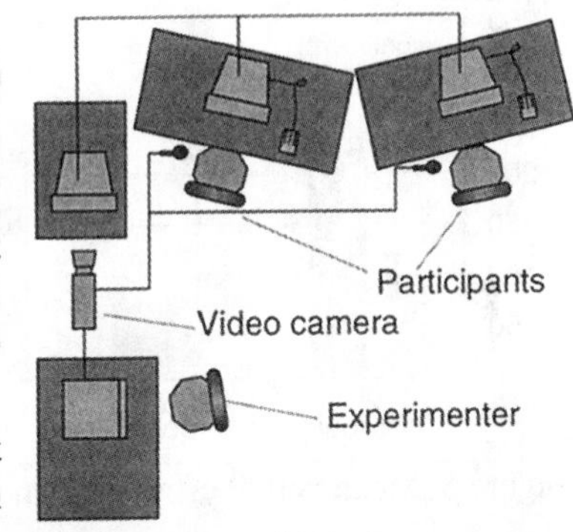

Figure 3. Experiment room setup

The experimenter sat at a recording station at the back of the room. The actions of both participants were transmitted to a third computer that showed a composite of the workspace. This computer's screen and both voices were recorded on videotape.

RESULTS

Completion Time

Our hypothesis predicts that people will be able to complete tasks more quickly with more awareness information. Completion times for the first three tasks are summarized in Figure 4; error bars represent standard deviation.

We compared the independent variables Task and View using two-way analysis of variance (ANOVA). There was

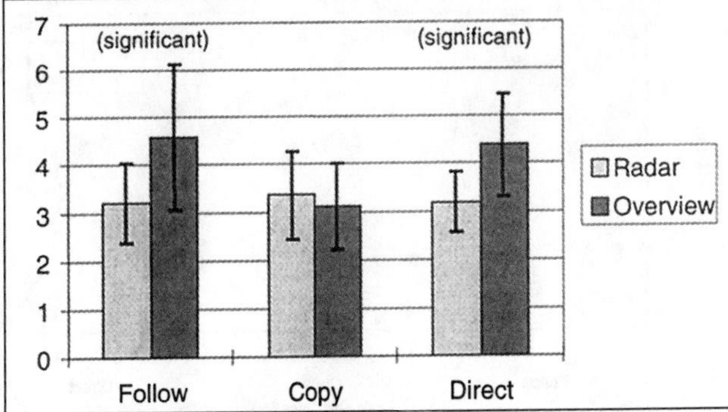

Figure 4. Mean completion times for tasks 1-3 (in minutes)

an interaction between Task and View (F = 7.772, $p < 0.05$). Posthoc comparisons of radar and overview completion times were carried out for each task type using one-tailed t-tests. To maintain alpha below 0.05, only those effects with $p < 0.0167$ were considered significant. Of the three tasks, differences in Follow ($t = 2.48$, $p<0.0167$) and Direct ($t = 3.05$, $p<0.0167$) were significant.

Communication Efficiency

Verbal interaction was recorded and transcribed. Communication efficiency was measured by counting the number of words used to give directions to the other person (in the Follow and Direct tasks), and the number of words used to indicate pieces (in the Copy task). Two assistants each coded half the transcripts and counted the direction and indication words. On a test set of four transcripts, inter-rater agreement between the two coder's counts (using Pearson's *r*) was above 80% for all three tasks.

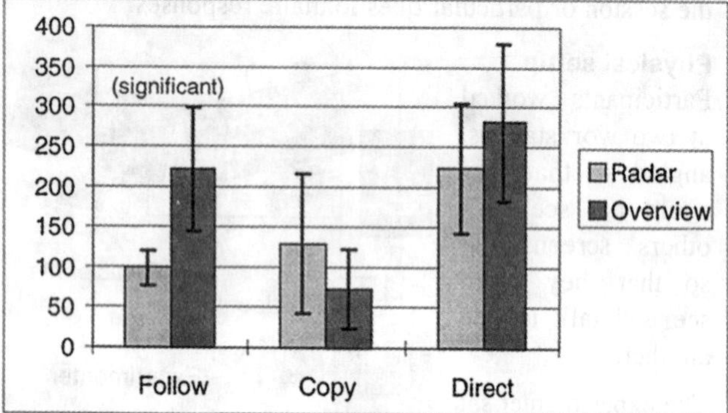

Figure 5. Mean verbal efficiency (in number of words)

Posthoc t-tests showed a significant difference for the Follow task ($t = 4.34$, $p < 0.0167$); no differences were found for the Copy or Direct tasks.

Perceived Effort

Perception of effort was measured by a repeated questionnaire given after each task. The questionnaire looked at four aspects of how hard a task was: (1) overall difficulty, (2) effort required, (3) concentration required, and (4) difficulty discussing the task. Questions used five-point scales with semantic anchors. Responses were translated to interval scores, using 1 to represent least effort and 5 to represent most effort. Figure 6 summarizes mean responses for each question in each task. Lines connecting

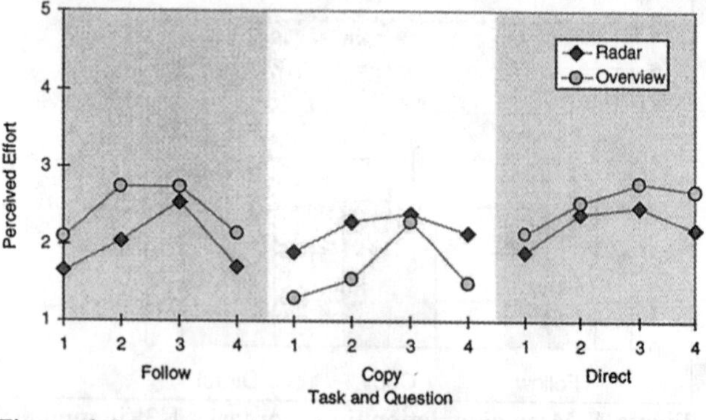

Figure 6. Mean questionnaire responses for Tasks 1-3

the points are intended only to visually differentiate the two conditions, not to imply connections between questions.

Posthoc one-tailed t-tests were used to compare radar to overview on each question, this time dividing alpha of 0.05 between the 12 tests. None of the analyses showed significant differences.

Within-Subjects Exploratory Results

Completion times and questionnaire results were also gathered for the second trio of tasks, those completed with the group's alternate interface. These measures allowed us to consider the question of what happens when a group moves from one view type to the other. We assume that all groups will perform better in the second set of tasks because of practice, but we wondered whether the improvement would be greater when going from the radar view to the overview, or when going from the overview to the radar view.

Figure 7 shows changes in completion time between the first and second attempts at each task. For all task types, groups were faster if they used the overview and then the radar; if they used the radar and then the overview, only the Copy task was faster in the second attempt.

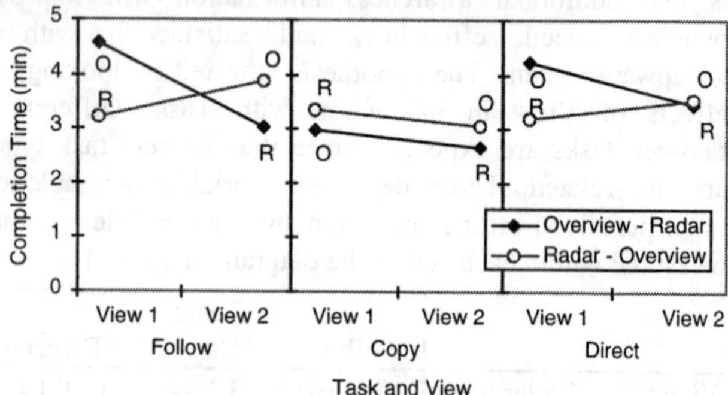

Figure 7. Mean changes in completion time between first and second attempts at a task.

A similar analysis was done with questionnaire responses. Figure 8 shows differentials in perceived effort—that is, the second response to a question minus the first response. When groups used the radar and then the overview, they felt that the second task was more difficult than the first; when they used the overview and then the radar, they felt that the

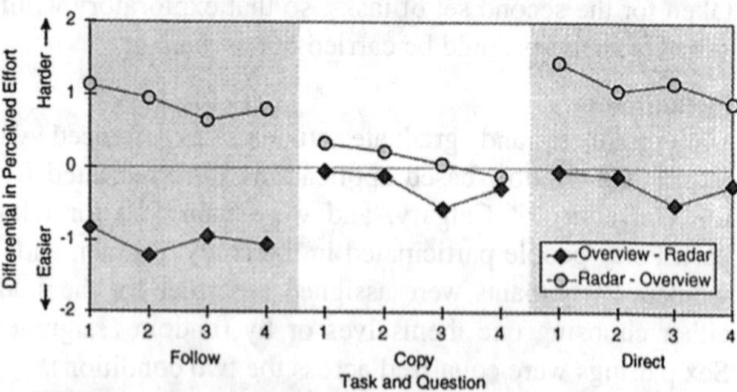

Figure 8. Perceived effort differentials between first and second attempts at a task. Points below the line indicate that the second task was perceived to be easier than the first.

second task was easier. Again, the lines in Figure 8 are intended only to differentiate the two conditions.

Overall Preference

After all tasks were completed and pairs had used both interfaces, participants were asked three questions about which system they preferred. The questions asked which system better supported collaborative work, which system was easier to use for group tasks, and which system the participant preferred overall. Almost all of the participants who responded chose the radar view, as shown in Table 2.

Which system:	Radar	Overview
1. ...better supported collaboration	35	3
2. ...was easier for group work	38	0
3. ...did you prefer overall	38	0

Table 2. Number of participants preferring each interface

Chi-square analysis showed in each case that the number of participants choosing the radar view was significantly higher than the expected number: for question 1, $\chi^2 = 26.95$, $p<0.0167$; for question 2, $\chi^2 = 38.0$, $p<0.0167$; for question 3, $\chi^2 = 38.0$, $p<0.0167$.

Summary of Results

A variety of results were obtained, some showing improvement when there was additional awareness information, and some showing no difference between the two displays. When using the radar view, groups finished the Follow and Direct tasks significantly faster, and used significantly fewer words in the Follow task. The within-subjects measures appear to reinforce these findings, and participants overwhelmingly preferred the radar view when they had seen both interfaces. However, no differences were found in perceived effort for any of the tasks, and no differences were found on any measure for the Copy task.

DISCUSSION

The two versions of the interface differed only in that the radar view provided visual indications of the other person's location, the location of their cursor, and the motion of objects that they moved. The significant differences between these two very similar interfaces clearly suggests that the additional awareness information helped people complete some tasks more quickly and more efficiently. We interpret and explain our findings below. First, we consider two reasons why the additions to the radar view were successful: that they allow visual communication, and that they provide continuous feedback. Second, we examine the measures of perceived effort, and consider why the Copy task was not affected by the view type.

Visual vs. Verbal Communication

Visual indication of the other person's location and activity in the radar view helped people to complete the Weld and Direct tasks more quickly. One way that it did so was by allowing people to use different and more effective strategies to carry out the task. Although we did not specifically analyze strategy, the video record clearly shows that different strategies were prevalent in each condition.

In the Follow task, there were two main strategies used. When pairs used the overview, they generally used a "describe" strategy. The joiner (the person with the map) had to describe the workspace location to the welder (who had no map) and verbally guide them to the right place. Since the structures in the workspace were not particularly easy to describe, the joiner had to be careful in planning and delivering her utterances. Even so, the descriptions were often fairly complicated:

J: The second weld is near the bottom in the middle section, there's two pieces of pipe, ok, there's two longer pieces of pipe, ok, there's, umm, right in the middle, right on top of the lowermost piece of pipe, in the middle there, there's two welds that need to be done.

F: Uh, ok...

With the radar view, people could use a "follow-me" strategy: the welder could find the right location simply by following the joiner's view rectangle. The visual indication of the joiner's location transformed the task from a series of complicated verbal exchanges to a relatively simple perceptual task of aligning rectangles on the screen.

This transformation also explains why groups used fewer words in the Follow task when they used the radar view. Groups using the "follow-me" strategy had the necessary location information available in the radar, and so they did not need to communicate locations verbally. Joiners would often make general statements about the location of the next weld, but they would let the radar supply the specifics:

J: ok, we're going over to the left...that's getting welded
J: OK, now, way over here...ok, that needs to be welded
J: OK, and just over left, same height, weld this together...

The overview did actually show the other person's location whenever they dropped a piece of pipe or the welding tool, and so did allow a limited kind of visual communication (the "here-I-am" strategy). However, this technique was hard to detect in the overview and clumsy for the welder, and only a few groups were able to use it effectively.

In the Direct task, the director was not active in the workspace, so radar users could not employ the "follow-me" strategy. Even though the director in both conditions had to provide verbal descriptions of location, the information in the radar view allowed them to use different kinds of descriptions. With the overview, directors had to describe a specific destination to the actor, and like the Follow task, these descriptions were not easy to construct:

D: ok, near the very bottom you'll notice that there's a vertical line right in the middle in the bottom of the pipeline, ok there is a T, a T, under that corner piece...

With the radar view, however, directors could see where the actor was located, and could give them relative directions (up, down, right, left) that were much easier to construct and much less prone to misinterpretation. For example:

D: ok, move to the left, stop, stop. Move up, move straight up, move straight up, stop. Go a little bit to the left, stop, stop. Ok, now you see there are two T sections…

The use of descriptive or relative directions can also partly explain why the radar did *not* lead to fewer words spoken in the Direct task (see Figure 5). Even though these two methods of giving directions differ greatly, nothing about giving relative directions implies that fewer words will be needed. For example, the first of the two utterances above might be harder to plan and to understand, but the utterances contain the same number of words. Therefore, word counts may be an insufficient measure of verbal efficiency; other metrics like utterance length or vocabulary size may have been more appropriate.

In summary, the location information presented in the radar view allowed people to communicate required information visually in the Follow and Direct tasks. The visual information allowed different strategies for carrying out the tasks, and allowed simplification of verbal utterances.

Continuous Feedback

The radar view provided continuous feedback about location and piece position, feedback that allowed groups to complete the Follow and Direct tasks more quickly. In particular, this feedback gave people visual evidence of understanding [1], which was more effective and less error-prone than verbal evidence.

In the Direct task, the director guides the actor's movement by giving her an instruction. With each instruction, the director requires evidence that he has succeeded in conveying the correct meaning to the actor, and that the actor has successfully moved where she is supposed to go. In addition, the director cannot give the next instruction until he knows that the actor has successfully completed the current one. The information differences between the radar view and the overview provide different kinds of evidence, and afford different means for establishing that instructions have been understood and carried out.

The overview lets the actor give evidence in two ways: verbal acknowledgment (e.g. "ok, I'm there") or the "here-I-am" strategy of dropping an object to indicate their location (e.g. "ok, can you see my piece?"). In both of these methods, the evidence is given at the end of an action: that is, the director gives the instruction, and the actor carries it out to the best of their ability before acknowledging. The problem with this form of interaction is that the director may give poor descriptions and the actor may go the wrong way. Providing evidence only at the end of the action means that time is wasted when the actor makes a mistake:

D: …go up to that part that's jetting across the middle…
A: <moves>
A: <drops piece> this part right here?
D: Uh, on the left side actually, on the left side…

In addition, both the verbal and the "here-I-am" methods of acknowledgment have other drawbacks. If the actor believes that they have followed the instruction correctly, but really haven't, they will mislead the director with their acknowledgment. The director has little chance to detect the error, and so may continue, piling error upon error. The "here-I-am" strategy at least gives the director concrete information about the actor's location, but this information can be out of date. We observed actors drop objects, then pick them up and keep moving. The director, however, saw only the out-of-date picture of the dropped piece. If they assumed that the location of the piece was also the location of the actor, errors could ensue.

The awareness information in the radar provided different kinds of evidence. Verbal acknowledgment was still possible, but the radar also showed up-to-date object movement and viewport location. In the Direct task, these representations could be used as immediate visual evidence of the actor's understanding and intentions. If the actor started moving the wrong way, the director would see the misunderstanding immediately:

D: ok, just above where you were working before…
A: <begins moving>
D: oh, not too far…yep, right…nope, up, up, up, higher, yeah, right there.

The availability of continuous evidence also made it possible for people to give continuous instructions. This is a strategy with far fewer verbal turns, and where the actor acknowledges implicitly through their actions. Clark summarizes the difference between verbal and visual acknowledgment for on-going "installment" utterances like instructions: "in installment utterances, speakers seek acknowledgments of understanding (e.g. 'yeah') after each installment and formulate the next installment contingent on that acknowledgment. With visual evidence, [the speaker] gets confirmation or disconfirmation while he is producing the current installment" ([3], p. 326).

Evidence of understanding and action in the radar was accurate, easy to get, and timely. The director was able to determine more quickly whether the instruction was going to succeed, and could reduce the cost of errors.

Perceived Effort

Measures of perceived effort in the between-subjects analysis showed no differences between the two conditions for any task. This runs contrary to both our expectations and our observations. We observed groups having more difficulty discussing the task, and making more errors, when they used the overview. It is possible that the questionnaire was a poor measure of effort. The main problem was that people had nothing to compare their experience to, and may have been unable to accurately indicate their effort on the scales given. This problem seems more likely considering that once participants had seen both interfaces, questionnaire responses showed greater differences (see Figure 8). The overwhelming preference for the interface with the added awareness information (see Table 2) also suggests that there were real differences in the experience of using the system, but that our measures were insensitive to these differences.

Explaining the Copy Task

The Copy task showed no effects of View on any measure. There are several reasons why the additional awareness information did not improve performance or efficiency, and the most important of these again concerns strategy. Participants typically used one of two strategies to indicate the next piece to their partners: they could describe the piece verbally (describe-piece), or they could show it to them through the radar by dragging it (show-by-drag) or through the overview by dropping it (show-by-drop). Describing pieces was certainly the wordier strategy and was also slower.

One underlying reason for the lack of effect is that there were equivalent strategies in both the radar and overview conditions. The show-by-drag and show-by-drop strategies provide almost the same information to the person doing the copying. However, since show-by-drop is a less obvious strategy than show-by-drag, we had expected describe strategies to be more prevalent in the overview condition. However, this was not the case. Even though the radar view allowed people to point out pieces quite easily, the video record suggests that more groups used the describe-piece strategy in the radar condition than in the overview condition. In a few cases, choosing to describe rather than show pieces seemed to be the result of inexperience: during one session, the leader said "oh right—I keep forgetting that we can both see the same radar view," whereupon she switched from a describe to a show strategy.

The combination of an equivalent strategy in the overview condition and a greater use of description in the radar condition account for the lack of speed or efficiency differences between the two conditions for the Copy task.

LESSONS FOR GROUPWARE DESIGNERS

There are several lessons that groupware designers can take from this study. First, the findings reiterate the value of workspace miniatures, as suggested in our previous study [5]. In the present experiment, we regularly observed people using both the radar and the overview to orient themselves in the workspace, to navigate, to keep track of the current global state of the activity, and to carry out individual work that did not fit inside the main view. All shared-workspace groupware systems will benefit from a workspace miniature.

Second, the main finding of the study is that adding workspace awareness information to the miniature—visual indications of viewport location, cursor movement, and object movement—can significantly improve speed, efficiency, and satisfaction. These awareness components should be included in shared-workspace applications.

The tasks we examined are common to many kinds of collaboration, and we believe that support for workspace awareness will also benefit more realistic tasks. Specifically, in tasks where information about locations and activities is used, and where that information is difficult to provide verbally, the radar view will have a positive effect. However, the size of the effect on real-world tasks depends upon what portion of the task can benefit from visual information and continuous feedback. In Follow and Direct, the radar condition was faster by about 25%, a substantial margin. However, these controlled tasks constrained the activity. More realistic tasks will likely include a mix of different activities, some that will benefit from the awareness information, and some that will not. Although the information will still be useful for part of the task, differences will be harder to measure.

Third, the experience of the Copy task provides a cautionary note, and suggests that the benefits of the radar view do not automatically improve performance. Potential improvements are dependent upon the information requirements of the activity and on the ways that groups choose to carry out the task. Designers should carefully consider what information is available and consider the strategies that will be used to carry out the task.

CONCLUSION

In this paper, we considered the problem of groupware usability, and the hypothesis that interface support for workspace awareness can improve usability. We carried out an experiment to look at the effects of showing viewports, cursors, and object motion in a workspace miniature. For tasks that use information about location and activity, and where constructing verbal descriptions is difficult, the workspace awareness information in the radar can reduce completion time, improve communicative efficiency, and increase satisfaction.

The study adds quantitative evidence to the qualitative findings of the prior study [5], and begins to put intuitions about awareness onto an empirical footing. Our further research in this area will move in two directions. First, we will continue work on quantitative evaluations of groupware usability. Some of the questions that we were unable to explore in this experiment include the effects of awareness support in other kinds of tasks such as organization or creation, and how well the radar view works when there are more than two people in the group.

Second, we want to look more closely at the links between shared workspaces, communication, and collaborative interaction. Work in this direction will look more carefully at naturalistic situations and use methods like conversation analysis and interaction analysis [13]. We believe that the connection between communication and the environment can tell us a great deal about groupware usability and about the information requirements of the next generation of groupware systems.

Appendix: Measuring Groupware Usability

One of our broader research goals is to find effective methods and measures for evaluating groupware usability. Groupware systems are difficult to evaluate because groups are more variable and adaptable than individuals.

Performance measures are particularly problematic. Several previous studies have manipulated the interaction facilities available to a distributed group (e.g. [3,10]). These studies show that performance measures are "only sensitive to gross changes in the facilities available for communication" ([10], p. 125). The present study showed that awareness information can be one of these major changes. However, to detect differences between the conditions we still had to carefully constrain the tasks.

Questionnaire and transcript measures are less affected by adaptability, but have other problems. Questionnaires, as discussed earlier, may be more appropriate in situations where people are comparing interfaces or experiences rather than making absolute judgments. The transcript measures were extremely useful in showing us some of the subtleties of interaction during the tasks. However, transcribing and coding conversations is time-consuming and difficult. The fragmentary nature of dialogue in a shared workspace often makes categorization problematic. Furthermore, counting words is too broad a metric to detect some aspects of communicative complexity and efficiency.

Finally, our decision to explore multiple tasks and take multiple measures considerably enriched the study, although it complicated the analysis. Our intention was to look at the hypothesis from several different angles, and offset the drawbacks of individual methods [9]. Although this approach requires careful planning, it is a valuable way to look at the complex interactions in shared workspaces.

ACKNOWLEDGMENTS

Thanks to Krista McIntosh and Jase Chugh for assistance in running the study and analyzing the results; to Ted O'Grady, Donald Cox, and Mark Roseman for comments; and to NSERC and Intel Corporation for financial support.

Software Availability

GroupKit and the pipeline system used in the study are freely available at www.cpsc.ucalgary.ca/projects/grouplab.

REFERENCES

1. Brennan, S. *Seeking and Providing Evidence for Mutual Understanding*, Unpublished Ph.D. thesis, Stanford University, Stanford, CA, 1990.
2. Chapanis, A. Interactive Human Communication, *Scientific American, 232*, 1975, 36-42.
3. Clark, H. *Using Language*. Cambridge: Cambridge University Press, 1996.
4. Grudin, J. Groupware and Cooperative Work: Problems and Prospects, in *The Art of Human-Computer Interface Design*, B. Laurel ed., Addison-Wesley, Reading, Mass., 1990, 171-185.
5. Gutwin, C., Roseman, M., and Greenberg, S. A Usability Study of Awareness Widgets in a Shared Workspace Groupware System. *Proceedings of the Conference on Computer-Supported Cooperative Work (CSCW'96)*, Boston, 1996, 258-267.
6. Gutwin, C. and Greenberg, S. Workspace Awareness Support with Radar Views. *Conference companion of the Conference on Human Factors in Computing Systems (CHI'96)*, Vancouver, 1996, 210-211.
7. Gutwin, C. and Greenberg, S. Workspace Awareness for Groupware. *Conference companion of the Conference on Human Factors in Computing Systems (CHI'96)*, Vancouver, 1996, 208-209.
8. Gutwin, C. *Workspace Awareness in Real-Time Distributed Groupware*. Unpublished Ph.D. dissertation, University of Calgary, Calgary, AB, 1997. Available at: www.cpsc.ucalgary.ca/~gutwin/dissertation/
9. McGrath, J. Methodology Matters: Doing Research in the Behavioral and Social Sciences. Reprinted in R. Baecker, J. Grudin, W. Buxton, and S. Greenberg (eds.), *Human-Computer Interaction: Towards the Year 2000*, San Francisco, Morgan Kaufmann, 1995, 152-169.
10. Monk, A., J. McCarthy, L. Watts, and O. Daly-Jones. Measures of Process, in *CSCW Requirements and Evaluation*, P. Thomas ed., Springer-Verlag, London, 1996, 125-139.
11. Roseman, M. and Greenberg, S. (1996). Building Real Time Groupware with GroupKit, A Groupware Toolkit. *Transactions on Computer-Human Interaction*, 3(1), 66-106.
12. Stefik, M., D. Bobrow, G. Foster, S. Lanning, and D. Tatar, WYSIWIS Revised: Early Experiences with Multiuser Interfaces, *ACM Transactions on Office Information Systems,* 5(2), 147-167, 1987.
13. Suchman, L., and Trigg, R. Understanding Practice: Video as a Medium for Reflection and Design. In J Greenbaum and M. Kyng (eds.), *Design at Work: Cooperative Design of Computer Systems*, Hillsdale NJ, Lawrence Erlbaum, 1991, 65-89.
14. Tang, J. Findings from Observational Studies of Collaborative Work, *International Journal of Man-Machine Studies,* 34(2), 1991, 143-160.
15. Tatar, D., G. Foster, and D. Bobrow. Design for Conversation: Lessons from Cognoter, *International Journal of Man-Machine Studies*, 34(2), 1991, 185-210.

Composing Magic Lenses

David Fox
NYU Media Research Lab
719 Broadway, New York, NY 10003
dsf@acm.org

ABSTRACT

Since the publication of the first paper on Magic Lenses, various methods have been proposed for implementing lenses which filter the objects seen through them. However, all the methods proposed suffer from various flaws. In particular, none of these methods solve the problem of composing lenses in a general way. A method which solves all these problems is described here. By substituting *delegation* for the more conventional *class inheritance*, a simple and elegant solution emerges. We have implemented delegation-based Magic Lenses in the *Tabula Rasa* zooming user interface (ZUI) system, using an object system related to CLOS.

Keywords: Magic Lens, Pad, filter, portal, lens, transparent, work-through interface, delegation, inheritance, object-oriented, CLOS, Scheme

INTRODUCTION

This work began with the desire to make modular applications using the Magic Lens metaphor, and to be able to create lenses that would compose in a natural way with a minimum of effort. We had success in certain domains where the interaction of different lenses is straightforward, such as lenses that implement database selections that can be composed using set theory, or the filtering of an image to produce another image. However, other types of applications presented difficulties. In particular, it was not clear how interactive applications should be filtered.

We made some unsuccessful attempts to solve this problem using conventional object oriented programming methods. We noticed that while these methods allow re-use of the structure of an object and the code associated with an object, they do not support building additional structure onto an existing object. For this, a less conventional type of inheritance known as delegation was found to solve the problem.

Once we adopted delegation style inheritance, the solution to the problem of generalized composable Magic Lenses emerged naturally. This result suggests that programming structures can be an important element in the design of a graphical user interface system. It also suggests that new styles of interaction can require new types of programming language support. This paper presents a technique for using delegation style inheritance to implement Magic Lenses which compose in a natural way, and which are simple to implement and amenable to reuse.

PRIOR WORK

The notion of the Magic Lens was introduced in *Toolglass and Magic Lenses* by Eric Bier *et. al.* [6], and a similar idea was presented as the *Portal Filter* in Perlin and Fox's paper from the same conference [21]. A Magic Lens is a transparent or semi-transparent user interface element which can be placed over objects to change their appearance and/or their interactive behavior.

The promise of Magic Lenses has not been fully realized due to the lack of a suitable theoretical basis for characterizing the types of transformations these lenses perform, especially one which allows the composition of two or more lenses placed on top of one another to perform more complex operations.

Since the Bier and Perlin papers were published in 1993, a number papers have built on that work, including subsequent papers from Bier, Stone, and the Xerox group [5] [22] and Bederson and Hollan's Pad++ papers [2] [3]. Other groups have extended the idea in various directions, including the three dimensional filters in [24] by Viega *et. al.* and specific applications, such as the paper on debugging filters by Scott Hudson *et. al.* [15].

Three techniques for implementing filtering are presented in [5] . The first, *Recursive Ambush*, obtains from each object a procedural description of itself (for example, a PostScript program) and interprets that description using modified primitives which results in a modified appearance. For example, the `draw-line` primitive might be modified to always draw red lines. The authors mention three disadvantages of this approach: the need to re-implement numerous graphics primitives in order to implement a given filter is onerous; the results of composition can be mystifying; and the performance of composed filters deteriorates rapidly because the entire computation must be re-done for each pair of filters that see one other. Furthermore, because filters are placed by hand, each one usually gets at least a peek at each of the filters below it, causing a doubling of computation time per added filter.

The second technique is called *Model-In Model-Out* (MIMO). Here a modified copy of the original object, or a new object of a different type is created. This new object is what the user sees and interacts with through the filter. This approach trades storage space for a substantial performance advantage. It also frees the filter from the domain of the graphics language – filters can now be designed to operate in the application domain. Other advantages mentioned include performance and relative ease of authoring and debugging. Disadvantages include the high storage requirements of making complete copies of all the filtered objects, and problems associated with propagating changes made to the model back to the original object.

The third technique presented in [5] is called *Reparameterize and Clip*, where the filter doesn't perform the drawing itself, but instead alters the parameters and clip area of another renderer and thus directs its output. The performance of this approach is similar to the MIMO approach.

Enhanced Dynamic Queries via Movable Filters by Fishkin and Stone [12] presents a mechanism for composing filters, but because these filters are tools for making database queries the results are less general than what we seek. The lenses are simply selecting or omitting objects, not altering them, so composition is done according to boolean set operations.

Two methods for implementing filters are mentioned by Bederson and Meyer in [4]: *layers* and *procedural objects*. Layers simply reveal a different set of objects when the filter is present. The procedural object approach lets a single object implement two rendering methods, and the renderer is queried about which one is to be invoked. These techniques have the benefit of speed, but they don't provide a real framework for the composition of lenses.

DELEGATION

It is possible to devise a mechanism which has all the advantages and none of the drawbacks of the various approaches to filtering presented in the previous section. To allow composition without an undue performance penalty, we need to maintain information about the state of the objects being filtered. The mechanism should not be limited to the domain of graphics primitives, instead it should operate in the domain of the objects which are being modelled. We want to avoid the high storage requirements of the MIMO approach. We want the filtered object to have extended capabilities over the original, but we also want to perform our operations on the original object, not a copy. And finally, we want composed filters to behave in a natural way, without the need to consider the implications of every possible filter combination.

The solution to these problems proposed here is a limited form of the object inheritance mechanism called *delegation*. Delegation means that instead of an object owning newly allocated storage for each slot of its super class, it contains a reference to a pre-existing instance. This pre-existing instance is known as the *delegate*, and in this relationship the new object is known as the *principal* - the principal instance delegates certain requests to the delegate super class instance. This terminology captures the working relationship between the objects well, but it does not express the ephemeral quality of the principal objects in this paper – principal instances are created as the lens is passed over an object which it considers a suitable delegate instance.

Operations on the slots inherited from the delegate super class are transparently converted to operations on the delegate instance. Cardelli and Wegner discuss type systems that allow delegation in their 1985 paper [9], and the terminological distinction between delegation and inheritance was finally established in a panel at OOPSLA 1987 known as the "Treaty of Orlando" [18]. This technique is not present in today's most popular programming languages but has been used in some research systems such as Self (Ungar and Smith [23]). It also turns out to be a simple matter to implement a limited form of delegation sufficient for our purposes within CLOS [7] style object oriented programming systems. It should also be noted that the "Decorator" design pattern described on page 175 of the book by Erich Gamma *et. al.* [14] uses delegation techniques, though without formal language support. The technique can also be referred to as a "wrapper pattern".

This object filtering technique described below has been implemented in the author's *Tabula Rasa* (or simply *Tab*) zoomable user interface system. In the object system *Taboo* which is used to implement Tab, normal classes are created using a macro named `define-class`. This macro is passed a list of slots and a list of super classes, and the resulting class has an inheritance relationship with each super class. The limited form of delegation required here is implemented as a macro named `define-principal` which is used in exactly the same way as `define-class`, except for the additional delegate-class argument. We will refer to the class that results from a call to `define-principal` as a *principal class*, and an instance of a principal class is a *principal instance* or simply *principal*. The principal class has zero or more super classes, plus one delegate class. This delegate class is also a super class of the principal class. An instance of a delegate class is a *delegate instance* or *delegate*.

When a principal instance is created, the slots that it inherits from the delegate class are not newly allocated, but instead refer to the slots of an existing delegate instance as shown in figure 1. When the delegate's slot values change, so do the values of those slots in the principal, and vice versa – they are actually the same slot. This behavior is implemented using a "virtual slot" mechanism which is available in the object system whereby references to the slot are transparently

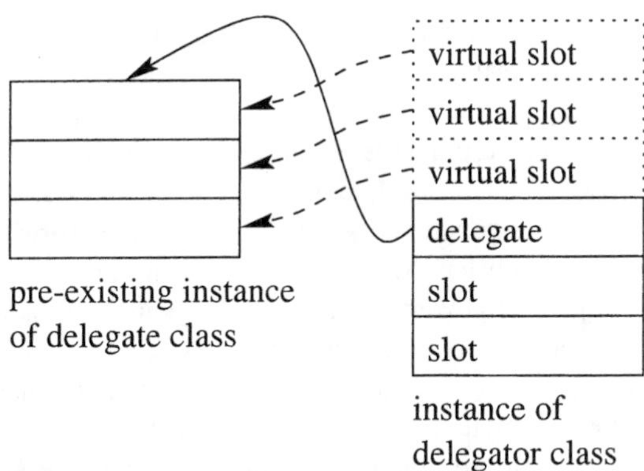

Figure 1: A principal and its delegate. The virtual slots in the principal class are not allocated, instead references to them are converted into references to those slots in the delegate class.

converted into calls to *getter* and *setter* functions. Because the principal class is a subclass of the delegate class, all the methods of the delegate class will be invoked in the usual way when passed a principal instance, and can be overridden by new methods in the usual way.

DELEGATION-BASED MAGIC LENSES

To implement Magic Lenses using delegation we assign to the lens a delegate class and a principal class. When the lens is placed over an instance of its delegate class, it generates a corresponding instance of its principal class. A new principal is created for each delegate that becomes visible through the lens. These principal instances, with their extended functionality, are what the user sees and interacts with when working through the lens.

Figure 2 shows *Tab* propagating an event, either an input event or a drawing event. The system saves each lens the event passes through into a list. After the event hits an object the resulting list of lenses is searched to find a lens that considers the object to be a delegate – that is, it looks for a lens whose delegate class is a super class of the object's class. If such a lens is found the system requests from it the principal instance associated with the object. The lens looks for the principal in a dictionary keyed on the delegates and returns it, creating it if necessary. If no lens with a suitable delegate class can be found the event is sent directly to the object – no filtering will be performed.

As an example, consider a class `text`, representing a text buffer with no interactive features, but with primitive methods to modify and display the buffer's content. We can derive from the `text` class a principal class `text-being-edited` which adds slots for the row and column position of the cursor and overrides the delegate's `draw` method so the cursor is drawn after the delegate draws the text. In figure 2 the principal object is shown with a cursor box around the "s" in "sentence" to indicate this. The principal class would also add event handling methods which would respond to keyboard input, translating them into cursor motion and calls to the text modification primitives of the underlying `text` class. Figure 3 shows the resulting screen output.

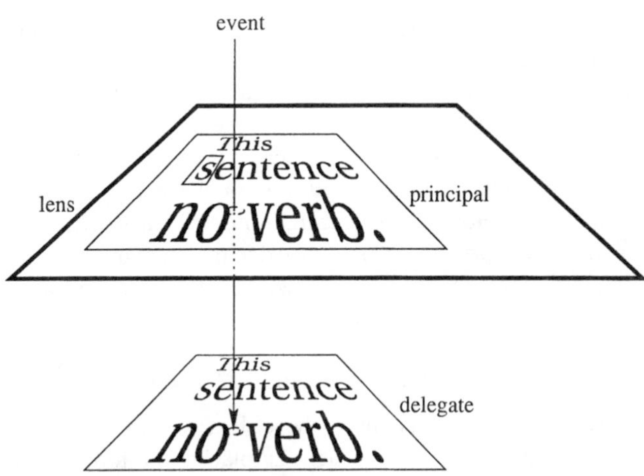

Figure 2: A lens which has created a principal for a text object (marked "delegate"). The principal actually has the same location as the delegate, but it is shown here at the level of the lens to emphasize the fact that the lens owns and manages it. After the event hits the delegate, the system searches the lens stack for the principal and re-directs the event there.

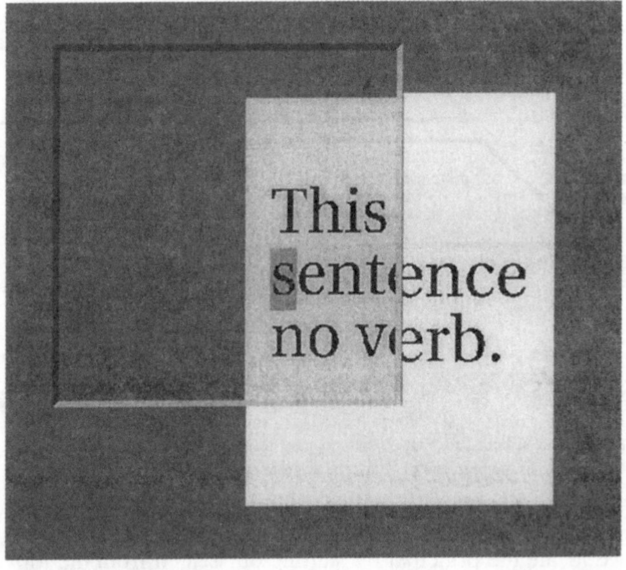

Figure 3: The user's view of the text editor lens. Because the cursor is part of the principal created by the lens, it is only visible when the lens is in place.

Note that the class is called `text-being-edited`, rather than `text-editor`. It is the lens that is the `text-editor`, and the `text-being-edited` objects are created by the lens. If the lens sits over several `text` objects, it will create one `text-being-edited` object for each.

Lenses affect the appearance of objects by creating principals which override the delegate's `draw` method. For example, the `draw` method of the `text` object might simply draw black text on a white background. The `draw` method of the text-being-edited object first fills the background with light gray and cursor area with orange. It then invokes a text method which draws the text but doesn't fill in the background. In this way not only is the cursor added but a distinctive background color indicates that the object is being edited. One might then put a spell checker lens on top of the text editor lens to highlight misspelled words. The spell checker principal would override the draw method and directly invoke the primitive drawing methods of the text class.

COMPOSITION OF MAGIC LENSES

Now let us consider how these lenses will compose. We would like a lens which is placed on top of the text-editor lens to use the text-being-edited objects as delegates for its own principal type (if it knows how.) Lenses you would place over a text editor lens might implement various input methods for international character sets, or otherwise augment the text editor.

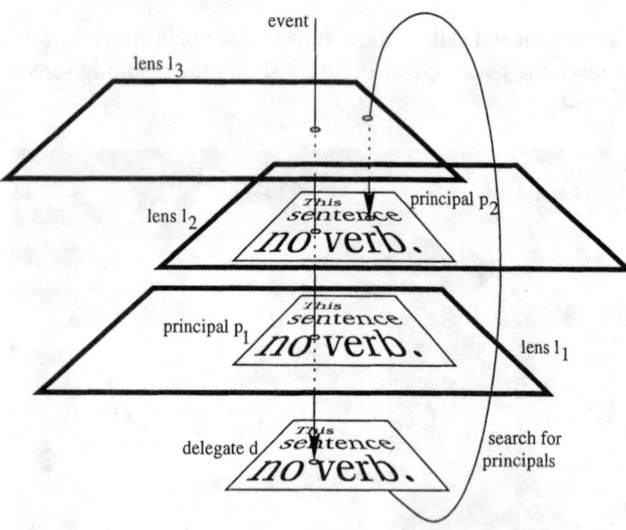

Figure 4: An event passes through lenses l_3, l_2 and l_1 and hits an object. Then the lens stack is searched for that object's topmost principal, p_2, which is found in l_2. Note that p_1 is the principal of d, and the delegate of p_2.

For composition to work correctly, it is important that we locate the principal by starting our search from the topmost lens, which is also the first lens the event encountered. In this way we will locate the em most derived principal, which includes the most functionality. If we describe figure 4 in terms of our example, the delegate object d is a text object, and the principal p_1 created by lens l_1 is a text-being-edited object, while l_2 has built a principal p_2 that extends p_1 (which is a delegate in this context.) Lens l_3 does not participate, as it does not recognize any superclass of p_2 as a delegate class.

There is one final bit of complexity to be noted here – how principals are created. If an event arrives before either of the principal objects in figure 4 have been created, the lower principal p_1 must be created *before* p_2, so that p_2 can use p_1 as its delegate. This is accomplished by a recursive call to the principal creation procedure.

Now suppose we place one text-editor lens on top of another. The topmost lens will see the principals of class text-being-edited, but it will treat them as text principals and generate its own text-being-edited principals. Each lens will manage its own cursor for each text object, and events sent to each principal will perform modifications on the underlying text object. The two editors can co-exist and modify the text as long as the methods in the underlying text object are called atomically.

It should also be noted that composed filters are able to build on the results of other filters, but also co-exist peacefully if they lack knowledge of one another. This technique has all the advantages of the MIMO (Model In - Model Out) approach without the drawbacks of wasted storage and the difficulties of propagating changes back to the original object. The delegation technique also subsumes the Recursive Ambush technique, which is equivalent to overriding the render method in the principal class.

IMPLEMENTATION

Tab is implemented primarily in the Scheme programming language, and uses an object system named *Taboo*, which was derived by the author from Erick Gallesio's STklos.[13][1] The Taboo object system differs from STklos primarily in the fact that it is not tied to any particular implementation of Scheme, and in particular can be used with some of the non-proprietary Scheme compilers which are now available.[1][11]

The implementation of delegation style inheritance in Taboo is shown in figure 5. Except for the added delegate argument the define-principal macro is used just as the define-class macro, but it generates some additional code. It starts by calling define-class to create a new class object with no super class, but with an extended slot list. In addition to the slots passed to the macro, a slot to hold a pointer to the delegate instance is added. Also, a virtual slot is created for each of the slots found in the delegate class.

First, the slot list is constructed and the class is defined. Before the delegate class is added to the list of super classes, an initialize method is created so that initialization will not re-initialize the pre-existing delegate instance – it must be created using the original class precedence list. Next, the delegate class is added to the class object's list of direct super classes and the class precedence list (CPL) is re-computed and stored in the CPL slot. Now the new class is a subclass of the delegate class with respect to method dispatch, but it does not change the way instances are allocated.

[1]STklos, in turn, was derived from Kiczales' TinyCLOS [16], which was intended as a pedagogical Scheme implementation of CLOS, the Common Lisp Object System [7]. All these object systems include a Meta Object Protocol (MOP) [17], which means in part that classes are themselves instances of the class <class>, and can be manipulated like other instances in the system

```
(define-macro (define-principal name delegate supers slots)
  `(begin
     (define-class ,name ,supers
       (,@slots
        (delegate :init-keyword :delegate)
        ,@(map (lambda (slot)
                 `(,(car slot)
                   :allocation :virtual
                   :slot-ref
                   (lambda (self)
                     (slot-ref (slot-ref self 'delegate) ',(car slot)))
                   :slot-set!
                   (lambda (self v)
                     (slot-set! (slot-ref self 'delegate) ',(car slot) v))))
               (slot-ref (eval delegate) 'slots))))
     (define-method initialize ((self ,name) args) (next-method))
     (slot-set! ,name 'direct-supers
       (cons ,delegate (slot-ref ,name 'direct-supers)))
     (slot-set! ,name 'cpl (compute-cpl ,name))))
```

Figure 5: Scheme macro to create a principal class.

One deficiency of the implementation shown is that any attempt to replace the `initialize` method and call `next-method` will produce a method that *does* re-initialize the delegate instance, with unfortunate results. One workaround is to derive another class from the principal class and override *its* `initialize` method. It should also be possible to perform this second class creation transparently.

DYNAMIC PRINCIPAL CLASS CREATION

There is still a problem with the way that lens composition will behave using the implementation described above. Suppose we have two lenses with the same delegate class but different principal classes, for example, a text editor lens and a spell checker lens. If we put the spell checker lens on top of the text editor lens the resulting principals will have the spell checker behavior but not the text editor behavior. This is because the `text-being-spell-checked` principal class is a subclass of `text` rather than `text-being-edited`. If we swap the lenses we will be able to edit the text but we won't see the spell checker's output. It may seem surprising that we don't see the result of the lowest lens that encountered the object, but although the lowest lens is filtering the object, its efforts are obscured by the lenses above it which are filtering it in different ways.

In abstract terms, the problem is that the principal class of the top lens is not a subclass of the principal class of the lens below it. Instead, it is a subclass of the delegates at the bottom level. We need the delegate class of the top lens to be a subclass of the principal class of the lens below it, so it can then further extend the functionality of the principals the lower lens produces.

This problem can be solved by using the ability of a CLOS-style object systems to create new classes at run time. Instead of creating a single principal class for a lens, we create a new one whenever we see an object which is of an unfamiliar subclass of the delegate class. These *(delegate-class, principal-class)* pairs can be stored in a hash table associated with the class of the lens. Now a new class will be created to represent a `text-being-edited` object which has a spell checker lens over it, a "text being edited being spell checked" class. The render method of this new class will invoke the `text-being-edited` render method before making its annotations.

The dynamic creation of principal classes allows lenses which were not specifically designed to work with each other to cooperatively produce combined views. The performance considerations of this approach are discussed in the Performance section below.

EXAMPLES

As presented above, lens composition is essentially object inheritance made visible, and interesting examples can be constructed by applying the same techniques as those used in object oriented design. In the Tab system, a `file` object can be created to represent a file, and this object simply displays a rectangular background and the file's name. It also provides versions of the standard input/output functions to access the file's content.

Various lenses can then be applied to a `file`. For example, an image viewing lens would examine the file's content, decide whether it was an image file and of what format, and then construct and display a visual representation of that image. Besides providing the image rendering method, the principal class for this lens would also provide methods to access the pixels and dimensions of the image.

Lenses could then be placed on top of this basic image display lens to allow interactive manipulation of the image. Note that these lenses need have no knowledge of the format of the image file – the underlying image display lens hides the details of the JPEG or TIFF format and provides a uniform set of methods for accessing the image data. Some image formats carry a text annotation field along with the image information. Replacing the image lens with a text lens would display the file as text, and provide methods for text access and manipulation. An editing lens could then be applied to alter the text. Thus, lens composition can be used as a type of layered design discipline.

PERFORMANCE

Good performance is crucial to the practicality of this system. There are several areas of concern which can be identified and addressed:

- Use of a dynamically typed language such as Lisp rather than the more common statically typed languages such as C, C++ or Java,
- slot access in a multiple inheritance object system, and method dispatch in a multiple dispatch object system,
- the virtual slot mechanism used in delegation,
- searching the lens stack for principals,
- dynamically creating principal classes,
- using instances of a dynamically created class.

The first three items are issues which have been addressed by language and compiler designers. Current Scheme compilers such as Marc Feeley's *Gambit* [11] approach the performance of C compilers within a factor of two, and the best Lisp compilers come even closer. The implementation of multiple inheritance and multiple dispatch have benefitted from similar attention. A good presentation of some techniques which can be used to reduce these operations to a few machine instructions is presented in [19].

The cost of using the virtual slot mechanism is more specific to this system. To access such a slot requires evaluating a Scheme function. The cost of this will vary from implementation to implementation, but theoretically it should compile to an array access and a slot reference. Finally, there is also a cost associated with searching the lens stack for principals, which involves a dictionary search of each lens based on the delegate. While this is a more complex operation than those above, it is only done once per event processed or per redraw, and because there is no practical use for huge stacks of lenses, it may not have a great impact. However, the best way to assess these problems is to gain more experience building and using this type of Magic Lens.

Dynamic creation of principal classes is even less frequent, and thus less likely to degrade performance. It is only done when a the standard search for a principal class fails, which is only once per new delegate subclass encountered. The final point, using instances of such classes, is more of a concern, and we envision several approaches to solving this problem. These include (1) identifying and precompiling common combinations, (2) "just in time" compilation, and (3) exploiting the similarities of the new class with the classes from which it is generated. Because all that is new about the dynamically generated class is the class precedence list, only the method dispatch and the implementation of `next-method` need to be different.

FUTURE WORK

The most important goal of our future research is to gain experience implementing different types of delegation based Magic Lenses. Issues of performance and portability will also be addressed. Several improvements to the object system need to be implemented, including a perfect hashing technique for slot lookup and caching for method dispatch. The performance of various Scheme implementations should be evaluated; while the `Scheme->C` compiler [1] currently used is much faster than a Scheme interpreter, there are newer Scheme compilers which incorporate features which might benefit Tab's performance.

Portability is also important, so that users of non-Unix platforms (notably Microsoft Windows 95 and Windows NT) can have convenient access to this software. The `Scheme->C` compiler does run on the Windows platforms, but the underlying graphics libraries are based on the X Windows library. Work is underway to devise a compatibility library for Tab which is similar to that used in the Tk system.[20]

CONCLUSION

There is a well worn saying that if the only tool you have is a hammer, every problem will start to look like a nail. Once the delegation mechanism is added to our toolbox, the problem of implementing Magic Lenses that compose naturally becomes fairly simple. Without it, the problem remains quite difficult. This indicates how much programming language constructs can influence the programs written.

The lens metaphor presented here provides an application-level analogue to the code-reuse benefits conferred by object-oriented programming techniques, and encourages the creation of software systems with a smaller granularity. By providing a way for applications to cooperate, and a visual metaphor to help users intuit how to make them do so, the tendency towards monolithic applications we see in today's software market can be reduced. However, the technique is dependent on programming language constructs which are not present in the most common languages of the day.

In [10] Brooks Conner describes in general terms how delegation and multi-methods can be used to produce simpler and more general implementations of interactive computer graphics systems, and presents specific cases of how the lack of these features leads to unnecessary complexity in several real-world cases. In addition to delegation and multi-methods, we believe that multiple inheritance confers similar benefits, such as allowing the easy mixing and matching of the various features of a lens. The popularity of Java's "Interface" mechanism, which can be seen as a limited form of multiple inheritance where the classes are not allowed to have slots, supports our claim of this feature's importance.

There are many factors that affect one's choice of language for implementing a system, including the stability of the language's definition and the quality and quantity of its implementations. The developer's personal familiarity with the language can also be important. If the language will also be used as the system's extension language, the acceptability of its syntax to end users also becomes a factor. Often, the actual features the language provides comes relatively low on an implementor's list of considerations. This paper has presented a technique which solves some of the problems which have plagued the implementors of Magic Lenses and work-through interfaces. Although the solution uses language features which are not present in the most popular programming languages of today, they are present in languages for which implementations are available on nearly every computing platform.[8] Perhaps in the future these language features will begin to rise towards the top of the list of implementor's considerations.

ACKNOWLEDGEMENTS

My appreciation to Ken Perlin, Cliff Beshers, Jon Meyer, and Matthew Fuchs, who helped in many ways.

REFERENCES

1. Joel F. Bartlett. SCHEME->C: a Portable Scheme to C Compiler. Technical Report 89.1, Digital Equipment Corporation, January 1989. http://www.research.digital.com/wrl/techreports/abstracts/89.1.html.
2. Benjamin B. Bederson and James D. Hollan. Pad++: A Zooming Graphical Interface for Exploring Alternate Interface Physics. In *UIST Symposium Proceedings*, pages 17–26, 1994. http://www.acm.org/pubs/citations/proceedings/uist/192426/p17-bederson/%.
3. Benjamin B. Bederson and James D. Hollan. Pad++: A Zoomable Graphical Interface. In *CHI Conference Proceedings*, pages 23–24, 1995. http://www.acm.org/pubs/citations/proceedings/chi/223355/p23-bederson/.
4. Benjamin B. Bederson and Jon Meyer. Implementation of Pad++. Submitted to *Software Practice and Experience*, 1997.
5. Eric A. Bier, Maureen C. Stone, Ken Fishkin, William Buxton, and Thomas Baudel. A Taxonomy of See-Through Tools. In *CHI Conference Proceedings*, page 358, 1994. http://www.acm.org/pubs/citations/proceedings/chi/223904/p415-fishkin/.
6. Eric A. Bier, Maureen C. Stone, Ken Pier, William Buxton, and Tony D. DeRose. Toolglass and Magic Lenses: The See-Through Interface. In *SIGGRAPH Conference Proceedings*, pages 73–80, 1993. http://www.acm.org/pubs/citations/proceedings/graph/166117/p73-bier/.
7. D. G. Bobrow, L. G. DeMichiel, R. P. Gabriel, S. E. Keene, G. Kiczales, and D. A. Moon. Common Lisp Object System Specification X3J13. *SIGPLAN Notices Special Issue*, 23, September 1988.
8. Per Bothner. Kawa, the Java-based Scheme system, 1996. http://www.cygnus.com/~bothner/kawa.html.
9. Luca Cardelli and Peter Wegner. On understanding types, data abstraction, and polymorphism. *ACM Computing Surveys*, 17, December 1985.
10. D. Brookshire Conner. Supporting Graphics Using Delegation and Multi-Methods. Technical Report CS-93-33, Brown University, September 1993. http://www.cs.brown.edu/publications/techreports/reports/CS-93-33.html.
11. Marc Feeley. *Gambit Scheme System*. http://www.iro.umontreal.ca/~gambit/.
12. Ken Fishkin and Maureen C. Stone. Enhanced Dynamic Queries via Movable Filters. In *CHI Conference Proceedings*, pages 415–420, 1995.
13. Erick Gallesio. Embedding a Scheme Interpreter in the Tk Toolkit. In *First Tcl/Tk Workshop*, pages 103–109, Berkeley, CA, 1993. http://kaolin.unice.fr/STk.html.
14. Erich Gamma, Richard Helm, Ralph Johnson, and John Vlissides. *Design Patterns: Elements of Reusable Object-Oriented Software*. Addison-Wesley, 1995.
15. Scott E. Hudson, Roy Rodenstein, and Ian Smith. Debugging Lenses: A New Class of Transparent Tools for User Interface Debugging. In *UIST Symposium Proceedings*, 1997.
16. Gregor Kiczales. TinyCLOS, 1992. ftp://parcftp.xerox.com/pub/openimpls/tiny/.
17. Gregor Kiczales and Daniel Bobrow. *The Art of the Meta-Object Protocol*. MIT Press, 1992.
18. Henry Lieberman, Lynn Andrea Stein, and David Ungar. Of Types and Prototypes: The Treaty of Orlando. In *OOPSLA Conference Proceedings Addendum*, 1987.
19. Kelly E. Murray. Under the Hood: CLOS. *Journal of Object-Oriented Programming*, pages 82–86, September 1996.
20. John K. Ousterhout. *Tcl and the Tk toolkit*. Addison-Wesley, 1994.
21. Ken Perlin and David Fox. Pad: An Alternative Approach to the Computer Interface. In *SIGGRAPH Conference Proceedings*, 1993. http://www.acm.org/pubs/citations/proceedings/graph/166117/p57-perlin/.
22. Maureen C. Stone, Ken Fishkin, and Eric A. Bier. The Movable Filter as a User Interface Tool. In *CHI Conference Proceedings*, page 306, 1994. http://www.acm.org/pubs/citations/proceedings/chi/191666/p306-stone/.
23. David Ungar and Randall B. Smith. Self: The Power of Simplicity. In *OOPSLA Conference Proceedings*, pages 227–241, Orlando, FL, October 1987.
24. John Viega, Matthew W. Conway, George Williams, and Randy Pausch. 3D Magic Lenses. In *UIST Symposium Proceedings*, 1996. http://www.acm.org/pubs/citations/proceedings/uist/237091/p51-viega/.

Generalized Pointing: Enabling Multiagent Interaction

Dan R. Olsen Jr., Daniel Boyarski, Thom Verratti, Matthew Phelps, Jack L. Moffett, Edson L. Lo
Human-Computer Interaction Institute, Carnegie-Mellon University
Pittsburgh, PA 15213, dolsen@cs.cmu.edu

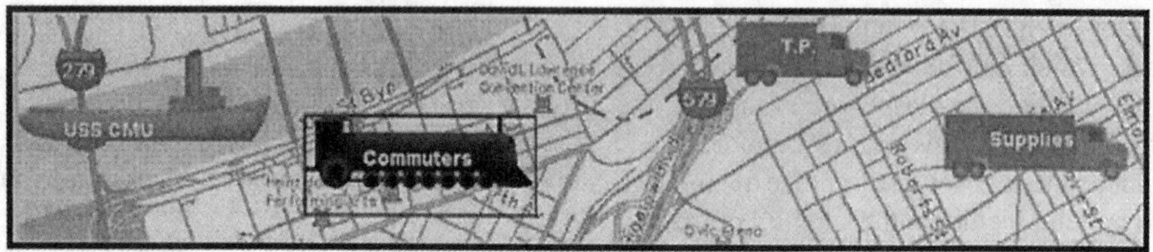

ABSTRACT

We describe an architecture which allows any external agent (human or software) to point into the visual space of an interactive application. We describe the visual design of a scheme for highlighting any information in any application. This architecture requires the application to provide information about its semantic structure as part of its redraw algorithms. Based on this semantic map generalized pointer descriptions are defined and used to reference objects to be highlighted. The architecture is demonstrated using a multibookmark agent framework and several example applications.

THE MULTIAGENT POINTING PROBLEM

This work takes as its fundamental assumption the importance of transforming the single-user interactive environment into one where multiple agents interact with the user in the same work context. We use the term agents to refer to any human or process that acts independently in the same work context as the primary user. Agents may be other people, spell checkers, design critics [3], grammar checkers, assistance wizards, scripting by example or other tools that can offer assistance in the interactive workspace.

A second basic assumption of our work is that multiagent activity must be pervasive throughout the interactive environment and not confined to specific applications. This is true because 1)users will need assistance (human or software) in all aspects of their endeavors not just special "cooperative places," and 2) the mechanisms for conversing with other agents need to be uniform across the environment so that the burden of cooperation does not become so high that it is worthless.

Achieving a multiagent interactive environment is too large a challenge for this paper. A fundamental stepping stone towards this goal, however, is the ability for agents to point into a visual space without interfering with the user's ability to interact in that space. Whenever two people discuss anything that has a physical manifestation, whether document, image, automobile part, or dog, they regularly gesture and point. The ability to draw visual attention to the particular aspect being discussed is fundamental. It is this ability of a software-based agent to point (draw the user's attention) into the visual space of any application in the environment that is the key contribution of this paper.

This pointing problem manifests itself in many forms in existing software. It occurs when a spreadsheet wants to show all cells on which some formula is dependent, when a search agent shows all instances of the word "foo" in a drawing, when Widgets By Example [7] needs to show the objects referenced in an inferred constraint, when a design critic must indicate all objects violating design rules, or when a change management tool must show recently modified objects.

An important design assumption in our work is that pointing by other agents needs to attract attention rather than coerce it. The behavior of tools such as Find or Spell Check, which commandeer the user's selection mechanism as a means of drawing the user's attention, is unacceptable. The user must be in control of how much attention other agents can demand.

Our approach

Our attack on this problem has two aspects. The first is the visual design task of developing a highlighting or pointing mechanism that will visually attract a user's attention without interfering with the user's work, and without requiring any application to change the design of its information display. The second problem is to algorithmically modify an application's display so as to present the highlight to the user without forcing application programmers to embed the highlighting scheme into the code of every application. The pointing or highlighting scheme must also support multiple agents working simultaneously in consort with the user.

VISUAL DESIGN OF HIGHLIGHTING

The problem with designing a highlighting scheme that works across all applications is that any visual cue that one might choose could conflict with visual cues coded into a given application. We were very unwilling to restrict the visual design space of applications in order to accommodate the highlighting. The problem is to draw the user's attention to an area without obscuring the application information already there and without having the highlight be mistaken for application content.

A second requirement is that the user must be able to control the strength of a highlighting scheme. Unlike spell checkers, which function by dominating the interaction, we wanted the user to be aware or ignore the activities of independent agents as desired. This means that highlighted as well as unhighlighted portions of the display must be visible and usable at the user's discretion.

A third requirement is that multiple simultaneous agents must be supported. If there is a grammar checker, a spell checker, and a change management tool active in the environment, it must be possible for each to draw the user's attention and the user must be able to discriminate among them visually.

The last requirement is that the highlighting must involve a simple direct algorithm that is easily implemented as part of the application drawing architecture. The drawing of the highlight cannot impede the performance of the application.

The process

Our approach to this design problem was to take screen dumps of as many existing application as we could find. For each screen dump we devised a set of possible objects to be highlighted. This formed our visual test-bed against which we could test the effectiveness of our ideas. We tested and discarded a number of ideas:

- *Bolding or thickening of selected objects.* This distorts the nature of the selected objects.
- *Blurring of unselected information.* This is quite effective in visually highlighting but reduced clarity.
- *Make the selected objects wiggle.* Motion is very difficult to ignore and therefore too demanding for our purposes.

Basic highlight

We concluded that there was no acceptable highlighting that would be visually orthogonal to every application's information display. We instead focused on "bending the color space" of unhighlighted items so that they would visually recede relative to the highlighted objects. Our approach is a simple blending of all unhighlighted colors with some neutral color. Blending unhighlighted items with a neutral color reduces their contrast and detail, making the highlighted items more visually prominent and unchanged.

Choice of the neutral blending color is somewhat application-dependent. For most applications a light gray is very effective. For applications which are monochrome, a pastel color is effective because the unselected items assume a hue that contrasts with gray levels of the selected items.

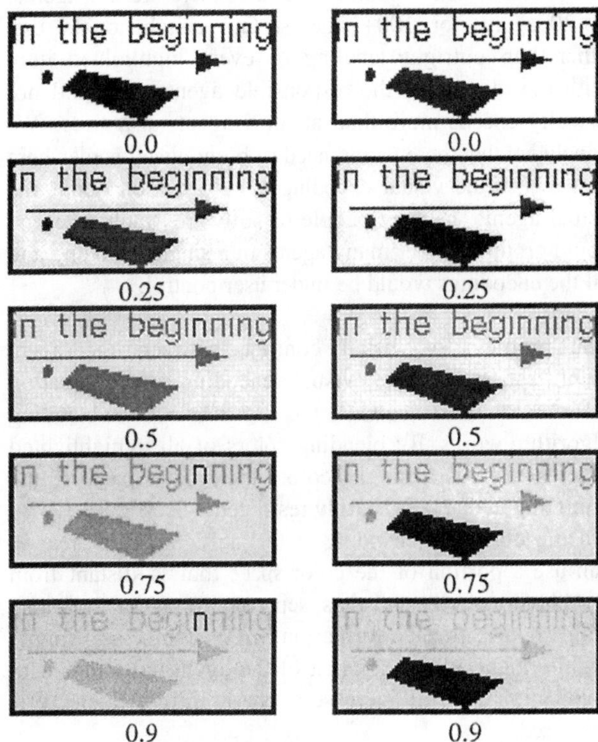

Figure 1 - Varying the highlight intensity

The parameters to our function are the *blending color* and the *highlight intensity*. Highlight intensity is a user controlled parameter ranging from 0.0 (no highlighting) to 1.0 (only selected objects can be seen). Our experiments showed that users must have control of the highlighting. First, because user goals may vary, and secondly, because various application objects have different levels of visual strength. Compare the highlighting intensities in the right column of figure 1 to those in the left. Note that the polygon on the right stands out as a highlight much sooner than the "n" on the left.

The effect of the highlighted polygon is much more striking on a large display than in the small images of figure 1. The "n" in a large image must show very high highlight intensity before it is visible at all. Note, however, that high highlighting intensity makes the unhighlighted objects much harder to work with. The intensity parameter gives the user the necessary control to adjust to the task at hand.

Given the two parameters (BC and HI) and a color for an unhighlighted object(OC) the formula for the blended color is BC•HI + OC•(1-HI).

Multiagent highlight

The blending method serves to bring highlighted objects into the foreground. This does not deal with the problem of discriminating among multiple agents. Solutions to this problem will depend on whether there are 2-3 agents, 10-20 agents, or 100+ agents. Our conclusion is that other than outright labeling of every highlighted item with the identity of the responsible agent, we could not visually encode more than about 5 agents at a time. We concluded that there would need to be a legend somewhere that related the visual encoding to information about the actual agents, be they people or software. Such a legend could group together many agents in a single encoding and all the encodings would be under user control.

The problem of visual conflict between the agent identification and the visual encoding of application information is mitigated by the way in which the blending algorithm works. By blending colors of all unhighlighted objects towards a single color, the color space of the unhighlighted area is sharply restricted. (See figure 1.) By placing our agent encoding in the unhighlighted area we can use a portion of the color space that is distant from the blending color and thus separate the agent indicators from application information. As with the simple highlight the visual contrast of the agent indicators with application data will increase as the highlight intensity is increased.

Our agent encoding technique computes a rectilinear region for the selected area of each agent, expands that region by a small number of pixels, and then draws that region's border using the color associated with the agent. By expanding the region before drawing it, we push the agent encoding away from the highlighted objects so that it does not interfere with them and out into the blended areas where the visual contrast will be better. If the blending color is a gray (which we have found effective in most cases), encoding agents with color that have above average saturation works very well.

One of the problems with multiagent pointing is that more than one agent may point at the same object. The agent indicators (in our case the borders) may overlap and obscure each other. We have accommodated this by expanding each agent's region by a different number of pixels. This prevents the overlap and preserves the encoding information. The end result is shown in figure 2.

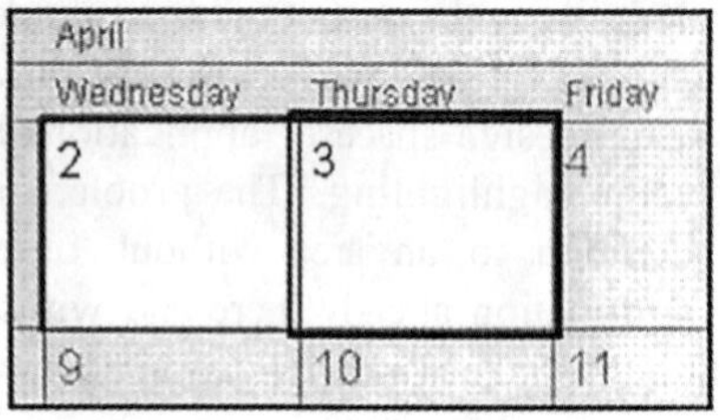

Figure 2 - Multiagent Selection

THE NATURE OF POINTING

The purpose of this work is to allow multiple agents to draw a user's attention to various items in the workspace. In most real applications this has both a local and a global aspect, due to the fact that real applications typically occupy a visual space much larger than is available on a computer screen. Local pointing involves highlighting those currently visible objects to which the agents want to draw attention. The highlighting techniques described above deal with the local pointing problem.

The global pointing problem involves drawing the user's attention to objects that are not currently visible. Global pointing depends on the organizational model for the information and how the user will navigate the information space. The simplest of these is the infinite 2D surface with scrolling as the navigation technique. Techniques for pointing in this model have already been developed including scroll-bar variants [5,6] and radar views [4]. A software architecture for integrating these techniques with any application is discussed later in this paper.

Other information organizations include the zooming model of Pad++ [1]. Hierarchic or linked organizations are also used as in the Macintosh Finder or the workbook sheets in the new versions of Microsoft Excel. The zooming model shares most of the features of the scrolling model with the exception of objects that are "zoomed" to smaller than a pixel. Zoomed objects that are outside the currently visible range can be dealt with just as with other "scrolled-away" objects. By assigning any selected object a minimum region of 1 pixel and then expanding that region by several pixels, even objects that are zoomed into invisibility can be highlighted.

In hierarchic organizations, there is always a visible object that serves as a surrogate for a group of hidden objects. In the Finder, for example, the surrogate for a hidden directory is the folder icon. In the Excel workbook there is a tab across the bottom for each hidden sheet. If objects inside of a hidden group are selected by an agent, the surrogate object can be highlighted using the techniques already described. For example, a directory folder can be highlighted if any of its contents are being referenced by an agent. The user thus has sufficient information to locate the highlighted material.

All of the above models for information can use the blended highlight with other global pointing widgets to provide a complete pointing mechanism for multiple agents. The one exception to this is the searchable space. This is a space such as a database that has no visual organization. Queries are created and results are returned but there never is any global geometry assigned to the entire space of information. No pointing technique is useful in this case. In such cases agents must describe possible queries that would return the selected information. Such techniques are important but outside the scope of this work.

A notable hybrid is the World Wide Web. For the web as a whole, there is no global visualization. The WWW in a global sense is a searchable rather than a navigable space. On the other hand, once a page is selected a local traversal tree of direct and indirect links from that page can then be treated using the techniques described above. Agents will then have an organization into which they can point and techniques for doing the pointing.

IMPLEMENTATION OF POINTING

There are several problems in actually implementing these pointing techniques on top of any application in the interactive environment. Our goal is to require only minimal changes to the applications and that these simple changes suffice for a wide range of agents and interactive services.

The first and most important problem is to actually define what a pointer is. For pointers to have any real meaning they must be defined in terms of the semantic structure of the application. For our highlighting techniques to work this semantic structure must be mapped onto the objects drawn on the screen by the application. Having defined the nature of a pointer we need algorithms to implement the highlighting without requiring a rewrite of all applications. Lastly we need to extract geometry information about the highlighted regions so that agent indicators and other global pointing widgets can be implemented.

Semantic / Surface Mapping

Every interactive application has some form of the architecture shown in figure 3. In most such applications this architecture is replicated for each independent view of the model, or views of different models.

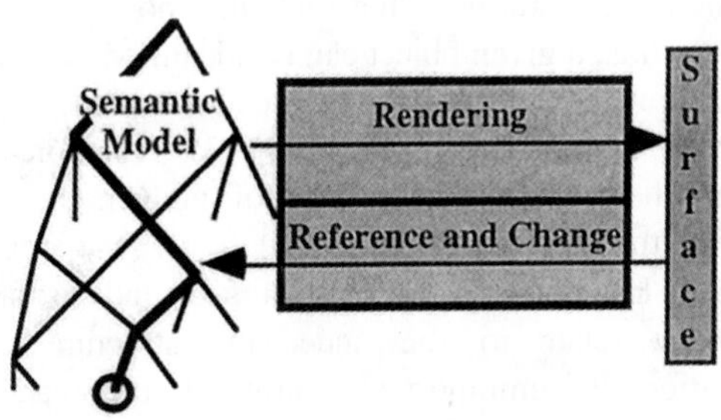

Figure 3 - Application Architecture

The goal of the application is to present and manipulate the information in the semantic model. For a given view, there is code that renders some portion of the semantic model onto an infinite 2D surface. Scrolling or other navigation techniques are used to present this surface on the limited screen space available to the application. As part of this rendering operation, the application usually traverses the semantic model in a semirecursive fashion, extracting information from the model and transforming it into drawing primitives on the surface.

The user in turn generates inputs in terms of the images presented on the surface. The application must translate these surface-based inputs into references to objects in the semantic model and changes to that model. Frequently such manipulations are defined in terms of a selected object or objects (as indicated by the circle in figure 3). These selected objects are the raw material for our pointers.

The problem is to define application-independent references to such selected objects so that external agents can save, manipulate and highlight the referenced objects. When the rendering code traverses the semantic model, it generates a tree traversal of the information regardless of the actual structure of the model. Different views will take different traversals and thus generate different trees. Our approach is to capture the structure of this traversal tree during the rendering process so as to create a map between this traversal tree and geometric objects on the surface.

As the model is being traversed, the rendering software moves from object to object by following links of various sorts. Each such link can be identified by a textual name or an integer index. Such identifiers need only have meaning to the application itself.

Defining pointers

Note that pointing, highlighting and selecting operations are all defined at the surface where the user can perceive them. Because of this surface orientation we use the renderer's traversal tree as our model description rather than the full generality of the semantic model's structure. Based on this, a given object can be identified by the path from the root of the traversal tree to the desired object (as shown by the darkened line in figure 3). A simple object pointer, therefore, is a sequence of integers or strings defining the links between objects in the rendering traversal. Exactly what these strings or indices are and how they relate to the underlying structure of the application is unimportant, provided they are used consistently by the application. This approach for defining pointers is similar to our earlier work on semantic telepointers [8].

In many cases an agent will need to reference more than one object. A spell checker, for example, must reference all misspelled words. We extended our referencing mechanism to combine the paths of all selected objects into a single tree by combining paths with common prefixes into the same subtree. Some nodes in the tree can also represent ranges of indices rather than individual nodes for each index. This would be appropriate for the 3 consecutive days highlighted in the calendar application in figure 2.

Capturing drawing calls

Having a representation for pointers that is application-independent, our general tools need access to the drawing behavior of the application. We exploit a technique pioneered in [2] of using specialized drawing classes. In most modern windowing systems, the actual mechanisms for drawing into a window are isolated from the application by an abstract interface. This may be object-oriented as in the case of Java's `Graphics` class or SubArctic's `drawable` class, or it may be pseudo-object-oriented as in the Microsoft Windows device context.

By substituting our own class for the standard drawing class, we capture all of the calls that the application's rendering code may generate. This provides us with complete control over the application's drawing behavior without interfering with the application's normal implementation. We must, however, impose our first requirement on the application - it must be capable of rendering its entire 2D surface rather than just the portion in the visible window. We need access to the entire surface so that we can extract the global pointing information for showing where scrolled-away items can be found. The inefficiencies of requiring an application to render everything rather than just the portion visible in the window can be mitigated by visible bounds techniques. If the application will interrogate the clipping rectangle, it can optimize what sections of the surface should be drawn. By setting the clipping rectangle to the size of the whole surface we can capture the entire drawing area. By invoking an application's Redraw or Paint method with one of our specialized drawing classes, we can capture any information about the application's visual presentation while imposing minimal changes on the application's architecture.

Capturing the semantic map

Simply capturing drawing calls is not sufficient to implement the highlighting techniques because they contain no information about which drawn objects are mapped to which semantic objects in the rendering traversal tree.

To accommodate this need we have added three calls to the `drawable` class. They are:

```
GroupStart(String Name, String Type)
GroupStart(int Index, String Type)
GroupEnd()
```

As part of its rendering algorithm, an application is expected to call `GroupStart` before drawing information from a particular object. The object can be identified by a string name or by an index depending on the `GroupStart` method used. In addition to identifying the object, a string type for the object can also be supplied. The type information is not used by the highlighting mechanism but is helpful for other surface-based techniques that we are developing. After an object is drawn, `GroupEnd` is called. The calls to `GroupStart` and `GroupEnd` can be nested to any depth. Example pseudo-code for drawing the calendar application on a surface S is shown in figure 5.

```
For each month M
{  S.GroupStart(M.name,"Month");
   S.draw the month name
   S.draw the days of the week
   For each day D in M
   {  S.GroupStart(D.date,"Day");
      S.draw day rectangle
      S.draw day border
      S.draw the date
      S.GroupEnd();
   }
   S.GroupEnd();
}
```

Figure 5 - Example Calendar Rendering Code

These calls provide all of the information necessary to capture the rendering traversal tree. Including `GroupStart` and `GroupEnd` calls in the rendering code is the second major implementation requirement that we impose on an application. We do not consider this excessive, however, because such calls are relatively straightforward to add to existing rendering code with reasonable structure. It is far easier, for example, to include the `GroupStart/GroupEnd` calls than to implement Cut/Copy/Paste or OLE objects. These calls provide a link between surface geometry and the underlying model structure. A major part of our future research will leverage this surface/model mapping to support more powerful agent behavior than simple pointing.

Implementing highlighting

Based on the machinery described above, we can define a special `HighlightSurface` class which is a subclass of `drawable`. (We are using SubArctic. Similar techniques will work in most other object-oriented windowing systems.) The `HighlightSurface` class passes all drawing routines on to `drawable` with the exception of the calls to set colors and the `GroupStart` and `GroupEnd` calls. The purpose of `HighlightSurface` is to draw the application information using blended highlights. The global pointing widgets and the agent identifiers are handled separately. In order to draw correctly, the `HighlightSurface` class must have a reference to all objects being highlighted, a blending color, and a highlight intensity.

Whenever the application redraws itself as part of its interactive behavior, it is given a `HighlightSurface` instead of a `drawable`. At each `GroupStart` call the surface will compare the name or index to the reference tree to determine if this group is selected or not. The selected state and position in the reference tree before `GroupStart` was called are pushed onto a stack. If the group is selected, then the current draw color, as requested by the application, is passed on to the `drawable`. If the group is not selected the draw color is blended with the blend color as described above. The resulting blended color is passed to the `drawable` instead of the application's requested color. When `GroupEnd` is called the stack is popped and the color settings restored to what they should be given the selected state of the enclosing group. The application rendering code never knows that highlighting has been done. This technique produces the drawings in figure 1. This blended highlight technique has very minimal impact on the drawing speed of the application.

Capturing the selected region

In order to draw the agent identifiers and to implement the global pointing widgets, we need to compute a geometric region on the surface for all selected objects identified by a given reference. Note that a reference may point at multiple objects, and that a given object may appear on the surface in multiple places.

As with blended highlights, we create a subclass of `drawable` called `SelectedRegion`. The `SelectedRegion` class does not pass any of its calls on to `drawable`. As with `HighlightSurface`, the `SelectedRegion` must be given a reference tree. To compute the region geometry corresponding to the reference tree, the Paint or Redraw method on the application is called with a `SelectedRegion` for its `drawable`. The clipping rectangle associated with `SelectedRegion` is the size of the whole surface. The `SelectedRegion` initializes a `Region` object to empty. The `Region` object collects the bounding region for all selected groups. Each `GroupStart` is compared with the reference tree to determine selectedness. Whenever a drawing call is encountered within a selected group, that drawing primitive's bounding region is unioned into the `Region` object. Any drawing call encountered in an unselected group is ignored. At the end of this process the `Region` object contains the bounding region for all selected groups.

Executing the redraw code for an entire surface just to compute the bounding region for a single object can be very inefficient. For this reason the `GroupStart` method returns `true` if the named or indexed group is of interest and `false` otherwise. When drawing into the `HighlightSurface`, `GroupStart` always returns `true` because all groups need to be drawn. The `SelectedRegion`, however, returns `false` for any group that does not contain selected objects. The pseudo-code of figure 5 can be optimized to that shown in figure 6. This structure will minimize the cost of computing regions.

```
For each month M
{ if (S.GroupStart(M.name,
        "Month"))
    {
      S.draw the month name
      S.draw the days of the week
      For each day D in M
      {  if(S.GroupStart(D.date,
              "Day"))
         {
           S.draw day rectangle
           S.draw day border
           S.draw the date
         }
         S.GroupEnd();
      }
    }
    S.GroupEnd();
}
```

Figure 6 - Optimized Rendering Code

One problem with computed highlight regions is that they may move as the application's data is changed. We can track such changes in the same way that display changes are handled. When application data changes, the rendering system will damage the changed area causing the windowing system to request that those areas be repainted. Similarly such damage information can be used to recompute reference regions so that they are up to date.

Once a region has been computed for a given agent, the region is expanded by a specified number of pixels and its border drawn in the agent's color to produce the agent indicator. This is done for all agents after the highlight drawing has been done. Again the application knows nothing about any of this being done other than the successive calls to its drawing routine.

BOOKMARKS FRAME DEMO

In order to test the efficacy of our architecture we assigned students in our lab to implement 4 different applications using the standard SubArctic toolkit. They were: a drawing application, an appointment calendar, a tabular data presentation and editing tool, and a map-based planning application. Those implementing the applications did not know about the highlighting algorithms.

We then built a simple framework that supports multiple bookmarks, shown in figure 7. The essence of the framework is that any object selected by any application embedded in the framework can be saved as a bookmark or added to an existing bookmark. The multiple bookmarks serve as surrogates for multiple agents, which we did not implement.

The test was to take the existing applications and embed them in the bookmark framework, thus adding the multibookmark pointing feature to any application. Because we require some modifications to application code, we wanted to test how long it took to modify an application to work within the framework. Once the framework itself was debugged, each application took less than one man-day to embedding in the framework. The last application took less than 30 minutes to convert.

The framework required that the application implement four new methods:

```
interactor getSurfaceInteractor();
Rectangle getViewableArea();
TRef getModelRef();
void scrollSurfaceInteractor
        (int x, int y);
```

Because we were embedding arbitrary applications into the framework, the first two methods are required so that the framework can separate controls and buttons from the working surface of the application. We decided that applications would use their own selection mechanisms which the bookmark facility exploits by requesting a reference to the currently selected object. The fourth method allows global pointing widgets to force the application to scroll to a particular area in response to user inputs. Such coercion only occurs at the user's request.

The bookmark framework provides controls for the blend color and highlight intensity. The user has direct control over the highlight intensity using a scroll bar. The bookmark framework substitutes a `HighlightSurface` whenever the application is drawn and uses the blend color and intensity to provide the highlighting. When necessary, a `SelectedRegion` is used to compute the region for each bookmark. Each bookmark border is then drawn clipped to the viewable area rectangle. This implement the highlighting required for the bookmarks.

In addition the bookmark frame provides three global pointing widgets. By projecting the bookmark regions along X and Y, we can define widgets that provide highlights along the vertical and horizontal axis. Greenberg reports that these are not very effective for collaborative use; however, the vertical version can implement the "wear marks" techniques of Hill and Hollan [5]. We find that when the total surface is very narrow in one dimension, the global pointing widget of the other dimension is very effective. In addition to these projected widgets there is a rectangular "radar view" [4] which represents the entire surface area in miniature with the highlight regions drawn in their agent identification colors. Clicking on any of the global pointing widgets will force the application to scroll so as to make the indicated area visible. This supports navigating directly to highlighted areas. All of these global pointing widgets use the selected regions calculated from the drawing surface. These widgets are also independent of bookmarks and can be used by any agent needing global pointing.

SUMMARY

We have defined a mechanism for visually highlighting any object or objects in any application using our blended highlight technique. We also identify the responsible agent using our colored region borders. Selected regions calculated from the drawn images also drive the global pointing widgets. The heart of our algorithms are in the model/surface mapping information provided by the `GroupStart` and `GroupEnd` calls. These deliver semantic information to the surface where external agents can support the end user's work.

REFERENCES

1. Bederson, B. and Hollan, J. Pad++ A Zooming Graphical Interface For Exploring Alternate Interface Physics. *UIST '94,* (Nov 1994), 17-26.
2. Edwards, W. K., Hudson, S. E., Marinacci, J., Rodenstein, R., Rodriguez, T., and Smith, I. Systematic Output Modification in a 2D User Interface Toolkit. *UIST '97,* (Oct 1997).
3. Fischer, G., McCall, R., and Morch, A., Design Environments for Constructive and Argumentative Design. *CHI '89,* (May 1989), 269-279
4. Gutwin, C., Roseman, M., and Greenberg, S. A Usability Study of Awareness Widgets in a Shared Workspace Groupware System. *CSCW '96,* (Nov 1996), 258-267).
5. Hill, W. C., and Hollan, J. D. Edit Wear and Read Wear. *Human Factors in Computing Systems (CHI '92),*(May 1992), 3-9.
6. Olsen, D. R., Bookmarks: An Enhanced Scroll Bar. *ACM Transactions on Graphics.* (July 1992).
7. Olsen, D. R., Ahlstrom, B., Kohlert, D., Building Geometry-based Widgets by Example. *CHI '95,* (May 1995).
8. Olsen, D. R., and Rodham, K. Smart Telepointers: Maintaining Telepointer Consistency in the Presence of User Customization. *ACM Transactions on Graphics* (July 1994)

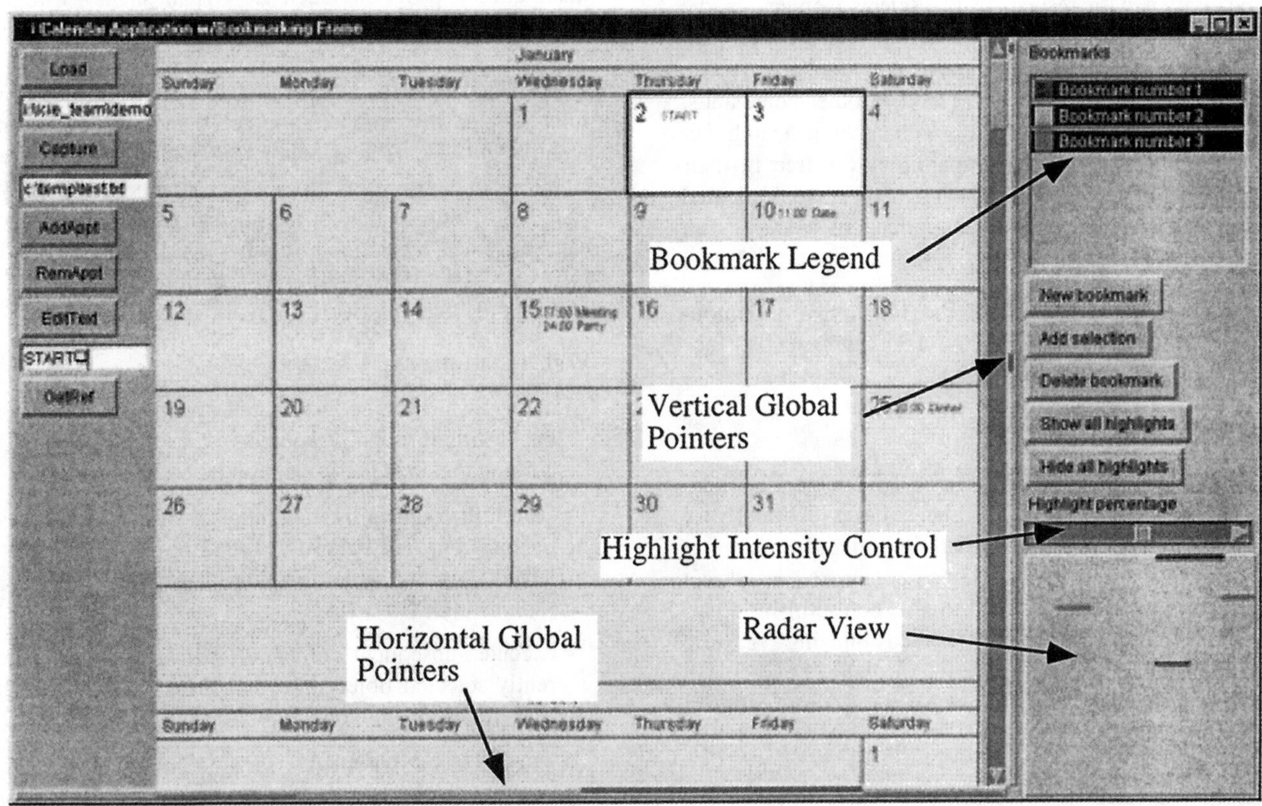

Figure 7 - Bookmark Framework

Scripting Graphical Applications by Demonstration

Brad A. Myers
Human Computer Interaction Institute
Carnegie Mellon University
Pittsburgh, PA 15213
bam@cs.cmu.edu http://www.cs.cmu.edu/~bam

ABSTRACT

Writing scripts (often called "macros") can be helpful for automating repetitive tasks. Scripting facilities for text editors like Emacs and Microsoft Word have been widely used and available. However, for graphical applications, scripting has been tried many times but has never been successful. This is mainly due to the data description problem of determining how to generalize the particular objects selected at demonstration time. Previous systems have mostly tried to solve this using inferencing, but this has a number of problems, including guessing wrong and providing appropriate feedback and control to users. Therefore, the Topaz framework does not use inferencing and instead allows the user to specify how the appropriate objects should be found. This is achieved by recording changes to which objects are selected and searches for objects, so that scripts can be written with respect to the selected object, in the same way as Emacs keyboard macros. Furthermore, all values can be explicitly generalized in a number of ways, and scripts can be invoked as a result of other commands. By leveraging off of Amulet's command object architecture, programmers get these capabilities for free in their applications. The result is that much more sophisticated scripting capabilities available in applications with no extra work for programmers.

Keywords: Scripting, Macros, Programming by Demonstration (PBD), Command Objects, Toolkits, User Interface Development Environments, Amulet.

INTRODUCTION

Creating scripts (also called "macros") for textual applications like text editors and spreadsheets has a long and very successful history. These scripts are important for automating repetitive tasks that are so common in direct manipulation interfaces. They can also be useful for creating new commands and for customizing generic applications to be more effective for specialized tasks (such as making a drawing program like MacDraw more efficient for creating charts).

CHI 98 Los Angeles CA USA

To create a script, the user typically goes into record mode, then performs some commands, which operate normally in addition to being recorded. The recorded script can then be re-executed later in different contexts. For example, the keyboard macro facility of the Emacs text editor [13] is easy to use and extremely useful for manipulating the text. Many Emacs users claim that such facilities are essential to use the editor efficiently, especially when making repetitive changes. Scripting facility also exist in Microsoft Word using Visual Basic, and spreadsheets have a long history of creating scripts by example.

However, for graphical applications, such scripting facilities have mostly been unsuccessful. Graphical applications here refers to programs such as drawing editors, CAD programs, graphical programming languages, and iconic manipulation programs such as "visual shells" which are graphical interfaces to the file system (like the Macintosh Finder or the Windows Desktop). We have analyzed the fundamental features that allow text editors to be successfully scripted by demonstration and then incorporated these features into a graphical editor framework called "Topaz." Topaz stands for transcripts of programs activated with zeal. The result is that powerful and sophisticated scripts can be created by example in any graphical program. This is in contrast to special-purpose scripting languages like Chimera [3] that only work for a drawing editor.

With Topaz, the user is able to:

- change which object is selected by moving forwards and backwards through the objects in a variety of ways, recording the change of selection in a script,
- search for objects by matching on various properties or by location, and cause the found object to become selected (this is a generalization of *graphical search and replace* [4]),
- execute subsequent commands with respect to the currently selected objects, so that the next time the script runs, it will operate on newly selected objects,
- generalize the parameters of the operations (colors, locations, numbers, strings, etc.) in a variety of ways, so the values can be computed at run-time,
- execute the script a specified number of times or continuously until an error occurs (such as a search failing),
- specify that the script should be automatically invoked before or after other commands are executed.

Figure 1. A drawing program created using Topaz showing the result of a script which subdivides a triangle into 3 smaller triangles, applied 13 times. This is called a "Sierpinski Gasket." Figure 6 shows the code of the script.

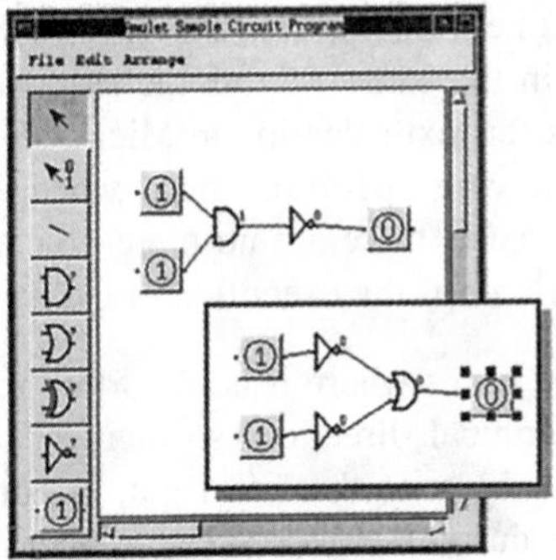

Figure 2. A sample circuit design program created using Topaz showing a circuit. The inset picture is the result of a script that converts an And gate and a Not gate into two Not gates and an Or gate and reconnects the wires.

The result is that users can create scripts *by demonstration* that perform such actions as replacing objects with patterns, performing repetitive edits, and creating graphical abbreviations. Specific examples of scripts created with Topaz are to:

- Build interesting patterns like the "Sierpinski Gasket" of Figure 1.
- Replace an And gate and a Not gate with the equivalent circuit according to DeMorgan's law, connecting all the wires appropriately, as shown in Figure 2.
- Put a drop-shadow beneath any type of selected object.
- Put an arch inside each rectangle as in Mondrian [6]. The user has full control over the whether the width of the side pieces and the height of the top is proportional to the size of the rectangle or constant.
- Insert a new node in a row of nodes and move all of the nodes that are on the right of the insert point further to the right to make room.
- Create a bar chart by making a row of rectangles whose heights depend on a given a list of numbers.
- Whenever a string is created, create a rectangle that is 10 pixels bigger than the string and center the rectangle behind the string.
- Perform the same edits to a set of graphics files, for example to replace all uses of an old logo picture with a new picture, and move all of the other objects a few pixels to the right and down to make room.
- And many more....

Of course, a particular application might have some of these commands built-in, but the goal here is to allow end users, who will not necessarily know how to program, to construct these kinds of scripts by demonstration when the application does *not* have the built-in command that they need.

We have implemented the Topaz framework using the Amulet toolkit [12], leveraging off of Amulet's command object architecture [11]. The result is that graphical applications get these sophisticated scripting facilities without any extra code in their applications. At this point, these facilities have been tested with a drawing program and a circuit editor, and we are working on a visual shell.

WHY ARE TEXT EDITORS EASIER TO SCRIPT THAN GRAPHICAL APPLICATIONS?

In a text editor like Emacs and Microsoft Word, most operations are performed with respect to the cursor, and there are a wide variety of ways to move the cursor using the keyboard and the mouse. These include moving the cursor forward and backward by characters, by words, by lines, or by sentences. The movement operations work in text documents because the content is an ordered sequence of characters, so forward and backwards are meaningful. Furthermore, for text with any kind of structure (including program code, content lists, etc.) moving forward by a line or by a certain number of words will correspond to moving by a *semantically* meaningful unit.

Scripts for repetitive actions take advantage of this ordering. A very common idiom used in Emacs keyboard macros is to move or search to the next occurrence of a pattern, and then perform operations on it. This script can then be repeated until all occurrences are processed. It is interesting to note that many powerful scripts can be written in this way without using conditionals or iterations, other than repeating the entire script until a search or move fails.

There are no equivalent operations in graphical programs. Just recording the low-level input events, which works well for keyboard events, does not work for mouse events since the specific location of the mouse is recorded when the buttons are clicked, and when the script is replayed, often the wrong object is at that location. Indeed Microsoft Word turns off the use of the mouse to move the cursor while recording a script. Many attempts to provide scripting in graphical programs therefore try to infer the *meaning* of the mouse locations (that is, what is at this mouse location, and why was that object clicked on?). Other programs try to match the objects that were used in different executions of the script to try to create generalizations. These programs must use heuristics which means that the system can guess incorrectly, and often will not infer the correct program.

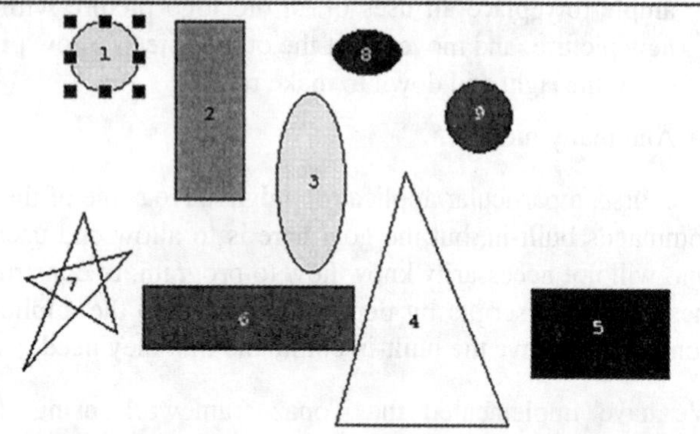

Figure 3. Circle 1 is selected. Moving the selection to the right will select rectangle 2, but then should oval 3 or 8 be selected? Currently, when moving to the right, Topaz selects objects in the order 1, 2, 3, 4, 5. But then moving the selection left from 5 selects 5, 4, 6, 7.

The approach taken in Topaz is to allow the user to specify how to find the correct objects using capabilities similar to those found in text editors, rather than trying to infer the generalizations. In graphics programs, the *selection* (often shown by black squares around objects as in Figure 3) corresponds to the cursor in text editors, and most commands operate on the selected set of objects. The innovation in Topaz is that users can change which objects are selected in graphical applications in a variety of ways, and have these recorded in a script.

Other innovations in Topaz are that there are various ways that the user can explicitly generalize a script so it will work in new contexts, and the ability to invoke a script automatically before or after other commands execute, as proposed in [2].

MOVING THE GRAPHICAL SELECTION

Text has a natural order, so commands like "forward" and "backward" are meaningful. However, in a graphical application, it is not so obvious what the order for all objects would be. The requirements for the ordering is that it have a well-defined first and last object, moving forward from the first object should go through every object exactly once, and moving backwards from the last object should select all the objects in the reverse order as forwards. It would also be good if the order made sense to users. However, in many cases, the particular order does not matter—it is often only important that each object be visited exactly once.

Our first idea was to go top-to-bottom, left-to-right, but this is not well-defined for some layouts of objects, and the backwards order is often not the reverse of the forwards order (see Figure 3).

Therefore, we decided to make the primary order for traversing objects be the display "Z" order from back to front. This has a number of advantages: it is well defined, reversible, and usually corresponds to the chronological order in which objects were created (older objects are further back unless the user has explicitly changed the order with a `To-Top` or `To-Bottom` command). A sophisticated user can also take advantage of this order in scripts. For example, to make sure that a script that creates arch inside of rectangles does not create arches inside the arches themselves, the script might start at the *end* of the list and move backwards. Since new rectangles are always created after the current end of the list, the selection will never get to the rectangles of the arch.

The current user interface for moving the selection is that the HOME key on the keyboard selects the first object, the END key selects the last object, and the left and right arrow keys select the next and previous objects in the Z order. If the shift key is held down, then the new object is added to the selection, in the same way as the shift key works with the arrow keys for text selection in Microsoft Word. All of the selection moving operations beep when a movement is not possible because there are no more objects on which to operate, and this stops the execution of the script.

There are some cases where it is important to find the next object in a graphical direction, so there are commands to select the next object to the left, right, up, down, inside or outside of the current object. These operations find the nearest object in that direction to the selected object that overlaps in the other dimension, so the reverse direction does not necessarily choose the same objects, as shown in Figure 3. These operations are available as buttons at the bottom of the search window (Figure 4).

SEARCHING FOR OBJECTS

Often it is important for scripts to only execute on specific objects. Previous demonstrational graphical systems have often tried to infer the properties from one or more examples, which is error-prone. Instead, Topaz allows the user to *search* for the appropriate object. This graphical search was introduced in 1988 [4] but still is not available even in sophisticated graphics editors like Adobe Illustrator, although it is provided by some CAD programs.

Topaz extends this searching to make it work in any graphical application, not just a drawing program. All objects in Amulet have a well-defined protocol for querying their properties. Topaz uses this to find what types of objects can be created and what parameters are available for each type. This does not require any new code in the application. Topaz automatically constructs a dialog box that allows the user to choose which properties should be used for a search, as shown in Figure 4. Of course, this dialog box could be made to look much nicer if it was designed by hand, but we wanted to minimize the amount of custom code needed in each application, so we used a straightforward automatic mechanism to generate the search dialog. This is why it uses internal names (like FILL_STYLE) and a naïve layout.

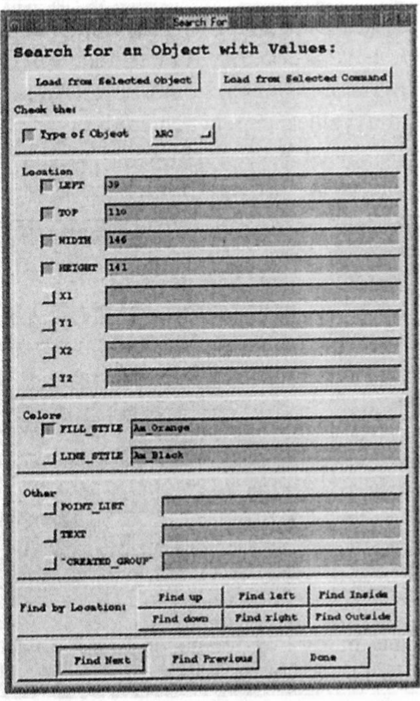

Figure 4. The search (find) dialog box automatically created by Topaz for the graphical editor of Figure 1. The values from an arc (oval) have been loaded.

To perform a search, the user can type in a value, or load the values from an existing object. There are eight ways to search for the next object, using the buttons at the bottom of the window. `Find Next` and `Previous` search in the "Z" order, and the others find in graphical layout order. All searches start from the current selection, or if nothing is selected, then from the first item in that order. For example, when searching to the `Right`, the first item is the left-most. "`Find Inside`" finds the back-most (in Z order) object on top of the selected object that is entirely inside it. This is useful for finding enclosed objects, like the label inside a box. "`Find Outside`" finds the front-most object behind the selection and completely surrounding it, and is useful for going from a label to its box. If nothing is selected, `Find Inside` starts from the back-most object, and `Find Outside` starts from the front-most.

When searching, Topaz only matches on the properties that have their checkboxes selected, so if nothing is checked, the search is through all objects. Selecting various properties supports more complex searches, such as "find the wire which is down from the selected object" which was needed for the script for Figure 2.

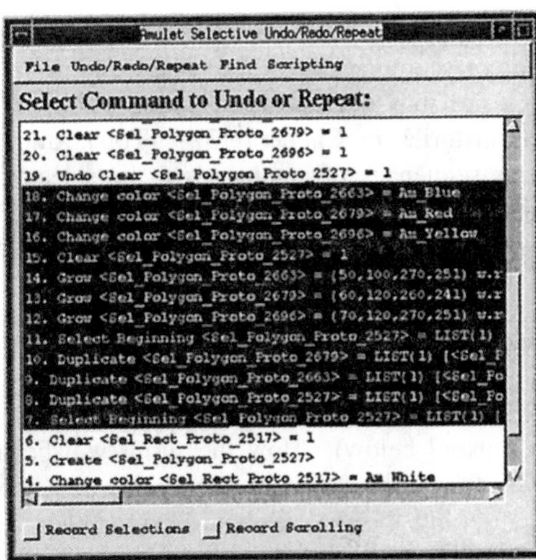

Figure 5. The undo history dialog box, in which previous commands can be selected for undo, repeat or scripting. Recording of selections and scrolling can also be turned on and off. Here, the commands for the script to create the triangles of Figure 1 are selected.

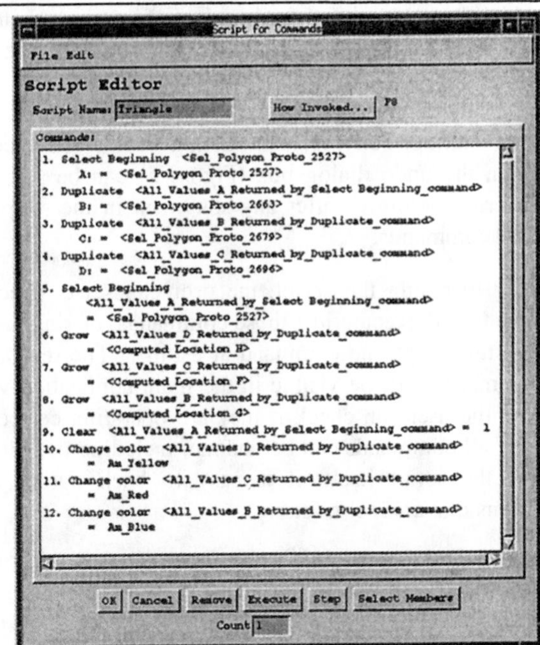

Figure 6. The commands of Figure 5 displayed in the scripting window, with some of the parameters already generalized into placeholders.

USER INTERFACE FOR SCRIPTING

Unlike most other demonstrational scripting facilities where the user has to think ahead that the next operations should be in a script, Topaz allows scripts to be created by selecting the desired commands from the list of commands displayed in the undo dialog box (see Figure 5). This list shows all the previous commands that have been executed. As reported earlier [11], the user can select any command in this list for selective undo or selective repeat.

The new feature added by Topaz is the ability to select a sequence of commands to be included in a script. (Selecting previous commands also was available for the graphical histories in Chimera [3].) Topaz allows non-contiguous sequences of commands to be selected (using the standard shift- and control- clicking), so that unlike other systems, the sequence of commands for the script do not have to be executed flawlessly without errors.

Once selected, the commands are expanded to show all their parameters, and are displayed in the scripting window (Figure 6). Now, the user can edit the script in various ways (discussed below). How the script will be invoked can be specified (the script of Figure 6 will be executed when the user hits the "F8" keyboard key). When the script is ready, it can be executed, saved, or removed (deleted).

EDITING AND DEBUGGING SCRIPTS

Many previous programming-by-demonstration systems seem to have assumed that all scripts would work the first time and never need to be changed, since there was no way to edit the recorded script (a notable exception was Chimera [3], which had nice editing facilities). In fact, some systems do not even have a reasonable representation of the recorded script that can be viewed. Topaz provides full editing of the script, including selecting the commands and deleting, cutting, copying, and pasting them. Also, commands in the undo dialog box (Figure 5) can be selected and inserted before or after any statement in the script to add new commands.

In order to debug the script, the user can select specific commands and execute just those commands, or single step through the script one command at a time. The results of the commands will be visible in the main application window, so the user can check if they are operating correctly. Because all commands can be undone, including the execution of the script itself, it is easy to back out of any operations that are incorrect.

An important capability not available in other systems that is this editing makes possible, is the ability to *demonstrate* new commands to be added to the middle of a script. The user can single step the script to the appropriate point, then execute the desired new commands, which will appear in the undo dialog box. These commands can be selected and inserted into the script at the current point. Then the user can continue single stepping the script to make sure that the subsequent script commands still work correctly.

GENERALIZATION OF PARAMETERS

An important feature of Topaz is the ability to *generalize* the parameters of operations. This is important to have a different object, position, or value used when the script is run, rather than the specific constant object used when the script was demonstrated. The user can select any value displayed in the script window and double-click (or use the "generalize" menu item in the Edit menu) to bring up a dialog box. After generalizing, the value displayed in the script is replaced with a descriptive placeholder. Bringing up the dialog box for a placeholder will allow it to be edited, or changed back into a constant. This is related to the "data description" property sheets in the SmallStar visual shell [1], but here they are domain independent. If an application has a special type of value, the programmer can add a new dialog box to handle it, but the built-in dialog boxes seem sufficient for many applications. Also, the dialog boxes have a "custom" option that will in the future link to a programming subsystem where any expression for computing the values can be entered in a language like JavaScript or Visual Basic. However, we have found the built-in options to be sufficient for most scripts.

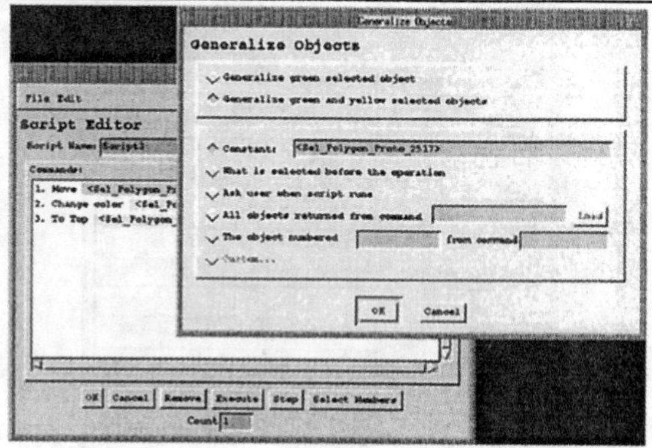

Figure 7. The dialog box for generalizing objects, with the script window in the background.

There are three built-in dialog boxes: one for generalizing objects, one for positions, and one for all other values. The dialog box for generalizing objects (see Figure 7) lets the user pick how to get the object when the script runs:

- Use a constant object (which defaults to the original object, but the user can type a new value).
- Use whatever objects are selected at that point in the script. Often the user will arrange for the appropriate object to be selected before executing an operation.
- Pause the script and ask the user to select some objects.
- Use the object or objects that are returned or operated on by a previous operation in the script. For example, a resize operation might be generalized to operate on the object returned by a previous create command. The user specifies which previous command to use by selecting the command in Figure 6 and clicking the "Load" button in Figure 7. There are two options for this, because many commands return a variable number of objects (e.g., paste, duplicate or select-all) and there must be a way to specify that subsequent commands operate on *all* of the objects, no matter how many, or on a particular object (e.g., the first one) from the set.

Figure 7 shows that the clicked on object is used in three places in this script. The one the user actually clicked on is shown in green, and all other uses are shown in yellow.

The top of the generalizing dialog box allows all of these uses to be replaced at the same time, or just the specific one that the user clicked on.

Topaz performs one generalization automatically. When a set of commands is brought into the script window, Topaz first checks to see if any of the commands are the kind that create a new set of objects. This includes create commands (including Paste and Duplicate) as well as selection commands that define a set of objects. Topaz searches for any subsequent uses of these objects, and if found, replaces the occurrences with placeholders that refer to the results of the create commands. This replacement is made automatically because in almost every script, if an object is created and then manipulated, when the script is run, the manipulation should operate on the newly created object and not on the original constant object. For example, all of the object generalizations for the script of Figure 6 were automatically performed by this mechanism. If the user really wants to use the original, constant object, the automatically generated placeholder can be edited using the standard dialog box (Figure 7) back to the constant value, but this has never been necessary so far.

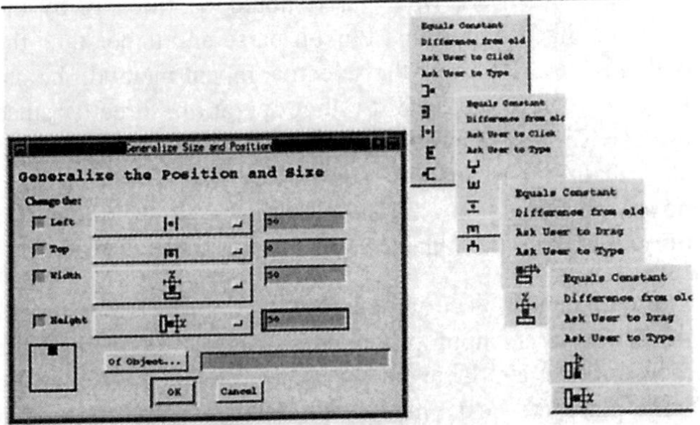

Figure 8. The dialog box for generalizing locations, along with the pop-up menus for setting the left, top, width and height. The picture in the lower left of the dialog box shows the result of the Left and Top selections.

Figure 8 shows the dialog box for generalizing locations. The user can click on the check boxes at the left of the dialog box to choose which parameters of the location to generalize. The options for the left coordinate are to be constant, a difference from the old value, a value specified by the user at run time either by clicking in the picture or typing, or a value computed with respect to a different object either by being to the right outside, right inside, center, left inside or left outside. If the center is selected, then the text input field is for the percent of the way across (the default is 50% which is in the center, but the user could type another value such as 33% to make the object be 1/3 of the way across). For all other relationships, the text box is the offset from the other object. The top properties are similar. For the width and height, the bottom two icons are to make it depend on another object by offset (e.g., my width is the other object's width + 10) or percent (my width is 50% of the other's width). When an option is chosen that depends on another object, the user can select which object to use. The normal choice is whatever is selected when this command runs.

All other types of values use a dialog box which allows the value to be constant, the current value from the palette if there is a palette registered for this type of value (like the color palette), a value chosen from a list, a value that the user types, or the value computed by a previous command.

One use for the list of values is to create a script that will process a number of files. The file `Open` and `Save-As` commands have the filename as their parameter, so the user can record a script with open and save in them, and then generalize the filename parameter to either be a list of filenames or to ask the user for the filenames.

Generalizing the values integrates well with the Search dialog box, since the search command uses as its parameters the values that were searched for. The user can therefore generalize parameters for a search in the same way as any other command, for example to search for the next object whose color is the same as the selected object, rather than some constant color.

INVOCATION OF SCRIPTS

Topaz supports a variety of ways to invoke a script. First, the `Execute` button on the script window (bottom of Figure 6) can be used. Second, Topaz supports the conventional ways to invoke scripts, using a keyboard accelerator or by putting the script into a menu of the application. In the future, scripts will be able to be executed at a certain time (for example to cleanup a disk every night).

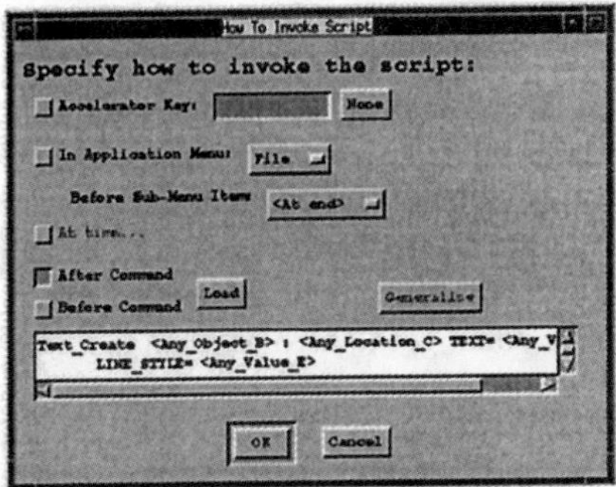

Figure 9. The dialog box for specifying how to invoke scripts. The `Text_Create` command description was automatically entered when the user clicked on the `Load` button.

Topaz also supports a novel way to invoke scripts: before or after any other command is executed. This idea was proposed earlier [2], but it has never previously been implemented in any system. The idea is that the user not only can demonstrate the script to be executed, but also which commands the script should run after or before. For example, after demonstrating a script to surround an object with a rectangle, the user brings up the invocation dialog box of Figure 9. Next, the user selects the "After" option, then demonstrates a `Text_Create` operation and selects it in the main undo dialog box (Figure 5) (or else the user can just select any previously executed `Text_Create` operation). Finally, the user hits the "`Load`" button in Figure 9 which loads the command description into the field. By default, all the parameters to the command are generalized so the script will be invoked whenever any `Text_Create` command is executed. This will put a rectangle behind any strings created. Alternatively, the user can select any parameter and use the original value of the example or any of the other generalizations discussed in the previous sections.

This provides the ability to create many intriguing scripts. For example, graphical abbreviations can be defined such as "whenever the text 'logo' is created, delete it and put in the logo picture read from a file." Since scrolling operations can be recorded, a script to scroll down after a search could be created.

To further the analogy with Emacs, scripts can be executed a specified number of times (using the count field at the bottom of Figure 6). The user can type a value or, like in Emacs, ^U will multiply the current count value by 4. For many scripts, the user will pick some really large number of times to execute, because, also like Emacs, all scripts are stopped if anything causes a beep (the low-level beep function was modified to set a global flag if a beep happens, and Topaz clears the flag before executing any script and checks the flag before each operation). Error dialogs always beep, and searches and movements of the selection causes a beep if they fail, and nothing beeps when everything is OK, so this is a good heuristic for stopping script execution.

Scripts are represented as a command like any other command, and are listed in the undo dialog box, so the execution of a script can be undone, repeated, or even included in other scripts. The count of the number of times to execute is the parameter for a script (which can be generalized), so a recursive script could even be written that would stop when the count got to zero or when there was a beep.

IMPLEMENTATION

An important feature of Topaz is that it requires almost no work from the application developer to use scripting, if the application is created using the Amulet framework. Amulet requires that all operations be encoded into the methods and data values of a *command object* [11]. Due to the way that these command objects are designed, they already provide Topaz with most of the information it needs. Command objects have a "Do" method that performs the operation, and an "Undo" method for undoing. They also contain methods to support *selective-repeat* and *selective-undo* which are when the user selects the command in the list of Figure 5 and asks for it to be repeated or undone in the current context. The scripting mechanism uses this selective-repeat to execute each command of the list. Selective-undo is used when the script itself is undone—it just undoes each of the component commands in the script. The selective-repeat has a companion method that tests whether the command can be executed in the current context, and this is used by the script before each command is executed to verify that it can be executed, and if not, an appropriate error message is provided. This makes it safe for Topaz to allow the user to insert or delete arbitrary commands in the script, since at run-time there will be a check to make sure that each command can execute. Command objects also adhere to a standard protocol for describing their parameters and generated values, so Topaz can inspect, display and generalize the values of any command.

Using the selective repeat mechanism, instead of just invoking the original Do method again, has a number of advantages. The Do method does not take any parameters, since the values to be used come from the selected object, the palette, and pop-up dialog boxes that ask the user. This is a very annoying feature of the scripts in Microsoft Word—they keep popping up the dialog boxes when the script is run. Pursuit [9] used "meta-dialog boxes" to allow the user to specify whether the dialog box should appear at run time, and if so, what parts should be filled in by the user, but this required that Pursuit parse and understand the dialog boxes. By using the selective repeat method, the parameters can be passed to the operation directly since usually Topaz computes the values. Of course, it would also be useful to let the user pop up the original dialog boxes when desirable, by using the original Do method of the command rather than the selective-repeat.

The command object architecture also helps Topaz record the scripts at the appropriate level. Scripts recorded at the mouse-movement-level fail because objects are not at the same place the next time. Applications written in Amulet must already encode the semantics of their operations into command objects, so recording at this level allows Topaz to create robust, repeatable and generalizable scripts without requiring Topaz to try to infer the "meaning" of the operations or of mouse events. Also, users can invoke commands in any way that is convenient (from the mouse, menus or keyboard accelerators) and these are recorded the same way in scripts, since they all use the same command object.

Amulet's built-in save and load mechanism allows applications to save and load their files with a minimum of code. All that is necessary is to register each of the main types that the user can create, and the important parameters of those types. Topaz takes advantage of this information to automatically construct the Search window, so again no extra work is required of the programmer.

Most graphical applications use Amulet's selection handles widget, and so the selection moving operations and searching come for free when this widget is used. Note that a Replace operation as in [4] could *not* be added without new code in the application, because Topaz would not know how to create new objects. In the current design, Topaz can *inspect* all of the graphical objects, but it can only *change* the objects by re-executing commands that have already been demonstrated by the user.

All extra code in the application is optional. The programmer should register the palettes in the application, so that the value generalization can tell if the selected value can be computed from a palette. Also, the main menubars should be registered with Topaz so it will know how to add scripts to the menus if requested by the user (Figure 9).

STATUS AND FUTURE WORK

Topaz is mostly working, and has been integrated with a drawing program and a small circuit design program. The main hole is the lack of a general-purpose programming language for the "custom" generalization options. We would also like to investigate writing scripts that work across multiple applications. As we get more experience with users and test Topaz with a wider variety of applications, we will continuously refine the interface.

RELATED WORK

The main influence on Topaz is Emacs [13], and we have tried to provide the key features of Emacs to graphical editors, which has not been done previously. Vmacs [5] was an early attempt to apply Emacs ideas to graphics, but it did not support any scripting by example, and instead concentrated on parsing of freehand drawings. The idea of dialog boxes to generalize parameters in scripts was used in the SmallStar [1] visual shell, and Topaz provides this capability for any graphical application. Graphical search was introduced in [4] for a graphics editor, and Topaz allows it to be used in scripts and for multiple types of applications. Topaz is also the first to allow the generalization of the parameters of the search. Chimera [3] supported graphical histories of operations in a graphics editor, and allowed commands to be selected for scripts, but supported only rudimentary generalizations.

There are many previous examples of scripting by demonstration in graphical applications, including Peridot [10], MetaMouse [7], Mondrian [6], Pursuit [9], Gamut [8], etc., but most of these concentrated on inferencing algorithms rather than providing sophisticated controls to users.

CONCLUSIONS

Topaz allows the user to construct sophisticated scripts by demonstrating the desired commands and then explicitly generalizing the parameters, usually without the need for conditionals and embedded iterations. This is achieved by generalizing the cursor movement capabilities from Emacs to a graphical domain. Topaz also allows scripts to be executed before or after other commands. These capabilities are provided to users with almost no effort on the part of the application developer. We hope that these capabilities will be generally useful, and that they will appear in many more kinds of applications.

ACKNOWLEDGMENTS

For help with this paper, I would like to thank Bernita Myers, Rob Miller, Rich McDaniel, and Bruce Kyle. This research was partially sponsored by NCCOSC under Contract No. N66001-94-C-6037, Arpa Order No. B326, and partially by NSF under grant number IRI-9319969. The views and conclusions contained in this document are those of the authors and should not be interpreted as representing the official policies, either expressed or implied, of the U.S. Government.

REFERENCES

1. Halbert, D.C. "SmallStar: Programming by Demonstration in the Desktop Metaphor," in *Watch What I Do: Programming by Demonstration.* 1993. Cambridge, MA: MIT Press. pp. 102-123.

2. Kosbie, D.S. and Myers, B.A., "PBD Invocation Techniques: A Review and Proposal," in *Watch What I Do: Programming by Demonstration*, A. Cypher, Editor 1993, MIT Press. Cambridge, MA. pp. 423-431.

3. Kurlander, D. "Chimera: Example-Based Graphical Editing," in *Watch What I Do: Programming by Demonstration.* 1993. Cambridge, MA: MIT Press. pp. 271-290.

4. Kurlander, D. and Bier, E.A. "Graphical Search and Replace," in *Proceedings SIGGRAPH'88: Computer Graphics.* 1988. Atlanta, GA: **22**. pp. 113-120.

5. Lakin, F., *et al.*, "The Electronic Design Notebook: Performing Medium And Processing Medium." *Visual Computer: International Journal of Computer Graphics*, 1989. **5**(4): pp. 214-226.

6. Lieberman, H. "Dominos and Storyboards: Beyond Icons on Strings," in *IEEE Computer Society: 1992 IEEE Workshop on Visual Languages.* 1992. Seattle, WA: pp. 65-71.

7. Maulsby, D.L. and Witten, I.H. "Inducing Procedures in a Direct-Manipulation Environment," in *Proceedings SIGCHI'89: Human Factors in Computing Systems.* 1989. Austin, TX: pp. 57-62.

8. McDaniel, R.G. and Myers, B.A. "Building Applications Using Only Demonstration," in *1998 International Conference On Intelligent User Interfaces.* 1998. San Francisco, CA: To appear.

9. Modugno, F., Corbett, A.T., and Myers, B.A., "Graphical Representation of Programs in a Demonstrational Visual Shell -- An Empirical Evaluation." *ACM Transactions on Computer-Human Interaction*, 1997. **4**(3): pp. 276-308.

10. Myers, B.A., "Creating User Interfaces Using Programming-by-Example, Visual Programming, and Constraints." *ACM Transactions on Programming Languages and Systems*, 1990. **12**(2): pp. 143-177.

11. Myers, B.A. and Kosbie, D. "Reusable Hierarchical Command Objects," in *Proceedings CHI'96: Human Factors in Computing Systems.* 1996. Vancouver, BC, Canada: pp. 260-267.

12. Myers, B.A., *et al.*, "The Amulet Environment: New Models for Effective User Interface Software Development." *IEEE Transactions on Software Engineering*, 1997. **23**(6): pp. 347-365.

13. Stallman, R.M., *Emacs: The Extensible, Customizable, Self-Documenting Display Editor.* MIT Artificial Intelligence Lab, 1979.

Illuminating Light: An Optical Design Tool with a Luminous-Tangible Interface

John Underkoffler and Hiroshi Ishii
MIT Media Laboratory
Cambridge, MA
{jh,ishii}@media.mit.edu

ABSTRACT
We describe a novel system for rapid prototyping of laser-based optical and holographic layouts. Users of this optical prototyping tool – called the *Illuminating Light* system – move physical representations of various optical elements about a workspace, while the system tracks these components and projects back onto the workspace surface the simulated propagation of laser light through the evolving layout. This application is built atop the *Luminous Room* infrastructure, an aggregate of interlinked, computer-controlled projector-camera units called *I/O Bulbs*. Philosophically, the work embodies the emerging ideas of the *Luminous Room* and builds on the notions of 'graspable media'.

We briefly introduce the *I/O Bulb* and *Luminous Room* concepts and discuss their current implementations. After an overview of the optical domain that the *Illuminating Light* system is designed to address, we present the overall system design and implementation, including that of an intermediary toolkit called *voodoo* which provides a general facility for object identification and tracking.

Keywords
engineering simulation, optics, holography, luminous interface, tangible interface, augmented reality, prototyping tool, interactive projection, tangible bits

SCENARIO
Two optical engineering students stand at an ordinary table. One pulls from a box a stylized plastic object – it looks a bit like a laser – and places it on the table. Immediately a luminous beam, projected from above onto the table's surface, appears to shoot forward from the laser model's aperture. The student moves the laser from the center to the corner of the table, and the beam tracks along with it, always originating from same point on the laser's front surface. The second student places a small aluminum representation of an optical-grade mirror on the table, and then moves an additional model representing a beamsplitter into the path of the existing laser beam. At this point of intersection a second, weaker beam is generated, reflecting off the splitter's surface. The student rotates the beamsplitter model in place (the partially-reflected beam sweeping across the table in response to the changing orientation of the splitter) until the reflected beam strikes the mirror set out earlier. The first student, meanwhile, is grasping this faux mirror and swivels it until the beam now also reflected from it runs the length of the table, parallel to the part of the original laser beam that continues through the beamsplitter.

During these and subsequent manipulations, the various optical components – though simple inert representations (unwired and sensor-free) – behave very much as their real counterparts would, directing and modifying the light that passes through them; and these physically accurate 'beams' of light are wholly simulated and projected down in careful registration with the optics. The students continue adding and adjusting components until a complete hologram-recording setup has been constructed. As they work, a continuously updated display at the far end of the table shows the layout's relative optical pathlengths as well as a rendered simulation of how the object would appear in a real, analogously recorded hologram.

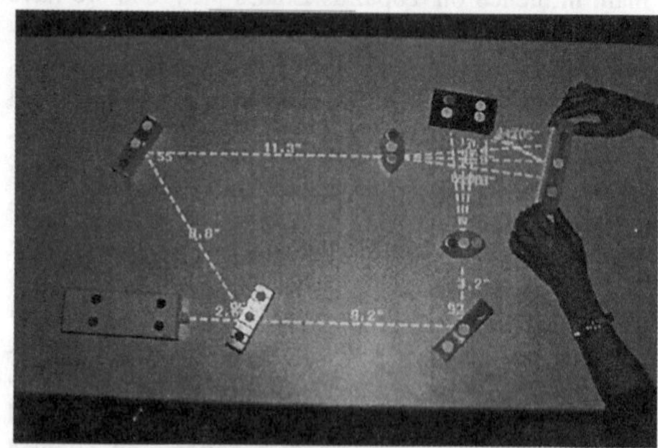

FIGURE 1: THE ILLUMINATING LIGHT SYSTEM IN USE

INTRODUCTION
The scenario described above is *Illuminating Light*, a working application of the *Luminous Room* infrastructure and the central topic of this paper. It is built atop *voodoo*, a toolkit for constructing layout-based interactive simulations, and employs a Medium-Scale *I/O Bulb* for display and scene capture. Its half-physical interaction style also extends *Tangible Interface* ideas explored elsewhere.

I/O Bulb
We offer a conceptual generalization of the familiar lightbulb, as follows: from a slightly unconventional point of view, we can see an ordinary incandescent bulb as a projector – albeit an especially low resolution one. Indeed, such a projector has a resolution of 1x1 pixels; this single, large pixel originates at the position of the bulb and is overlaid on the entire surrounding room. The information stream that drives this 'projector' happens also to be its power feed. From here, however, it is easy to imagine increasing the bulb's resolution, so that the intensity and color of the emitted light is directionally dependent. Now the lightbulb is capable of projecting images into the space around it. At the same time, we imagine incorporating a video camera into this device, so that there is a mechanism not only for

output but for input as well; this new kind of lightbulb is always 'looking where it's going'. To this novel bulb's power feed we must now add a two-way information stream.

In the context of this paper, the *I/O Bulb* is the atomic unit of required physical mechanism, i.e. a single, compact device that performs coincident (or near-coincident) projection and video acquisition. For most of what follows we

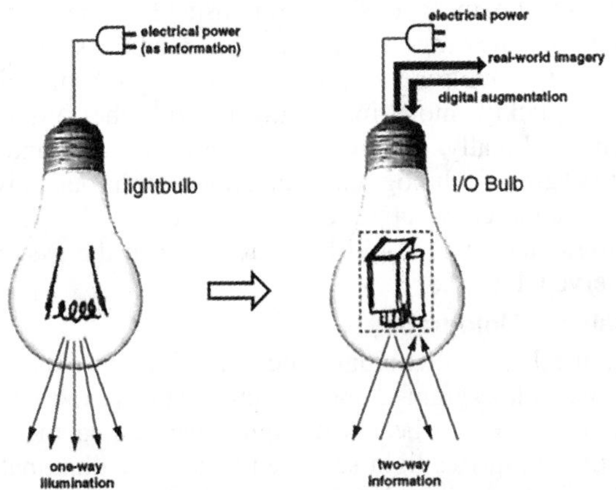

FIGURE 2: FROM LIGHTBULB TO I/O BULB

will simply presume that such a facility is available, although we briefly describe below three different experimental *I/O Bulb* apparati, all constructed using commercially available projectors and cameras optically bound together. (A separate, parallel line of research, not discussed here, is the development of a 'true' *I/O Bulb* – a single glass housing containing an optically and electronically integrated miniature projector and tiny camera.)

Luminous Room

The notion of a *Luminous Room* infrastructure involves extrapolating from just one to a collection of many *I/O Bulbs*, interlinked and distributed throughout some architectural space. The resulting aggregate of two-way optical nodes – exhibiting various levels of resolution, some nodes positioned to provide overlapping 'regions of influence' – acts to extend the meaning of architectural space, making every surface a potential site for digital interaction, display, and manipulation [9].

Implementation Scales

An idealistic vision would see the *Luminous Room* structure implemented by supplanting every extant lighting fixture in a room with an *I/O Bulb* of appropriate size; in the exploratory meantime we have built three contrasting but complementary prototypes of such an apparatus, each addressing a different 'scale' of detail, extent of addressable space, and motility.

Large Scale (ceiling-mounted gimbal system)

This prototype *I/O Bulb* consists of a high-resolution video projector mounted in a computer-controlled gimbal; it is designed to be suspended just below the ceiling of a room. Through a combination of mechanical and optical degrees of freedom its projection can reach every unoccluded part of the surrounding space, including the ceiling itself. Its associated video camera is subject to these same optomechanical rotations and thus is constantly aimed to view the portion of the room currently projected onto. This gimbal-based apparatus is designed to enable 'room-scale' interactions: this means both interactions with mobile access to the entire room (e.g. manipulable information that tracks a user around the space) and interactions of significant spatial extent (e.g. fixed, reactive architectural annotations along an entire wall).

FIGURE 3: LARGE-SCALE I/O BULB APPARATUS

Small Scale ('Luxo' desk lamp configuration)

The Luxo-style prototype comprises a very small video projector and coaxially-aligned miniature video camera mounted on an articulated arm. The camera-projector mount and the arm's joints are outfitted with high-resolution encoders that report the instantaneous angular disposition of the device's five degrees of freedom; forward kinematic calculations then provide the exact three-space position and orientation of the active elements.

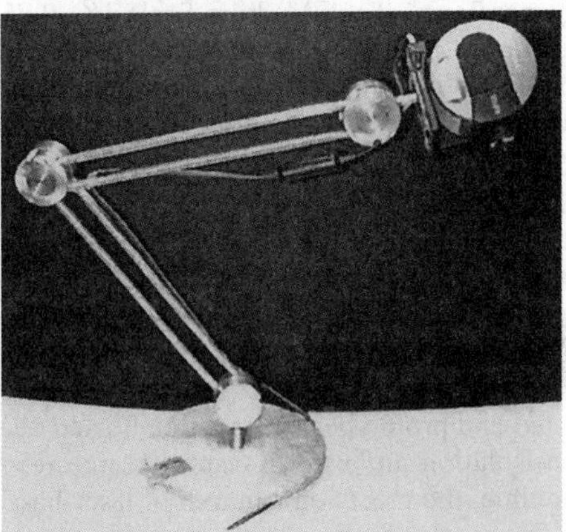

FIGURE 4: SMALL-SCALE I/O BULB APPARATUS

In many respects, this apparatus acts in a manner complementary to that of its large-scale counterpart: where the gimbal system moves autonomously, the small-scale version is moved volitionally by the user; where the large-scale system is intended for broad, room-scale tasks, the small-scale apparatus is intended for spatially constrained, high-detail work; and where the gimbal rotates from a central position to operate 'radially outward', the Luxo-style device typically moves about the boundary of the interaction space it addresses, looking 'radially inward'.

Indeed, we intend that its use should be suggested by that of an analogous desk lamp: just as such a lamp can be moved within a small volume to shed more light on some particular region or object, so the small-scale *I/O Bulb* can be moved around its working space to 'shed more information' at a desired point.

Medium Scale (fixed conference table system)

The Medium Scale *I/O Bulb* prototype is intended as a 'dedicated' fixture: an immobile ceiling-mounted projector-and-coincident-camera apparatus that serves some restricted area, like a conference table or a workbench. Being fixed allows the system to make stronger assumptions about the space below it; in particular, certain machine vision problems become simpler, since users' hands and arms will in general be the 'largest portion of human' that will occlude the table's surface. At the same time, such a system is able to provide higher resolution to its target area than would the gimbal-mounted version.

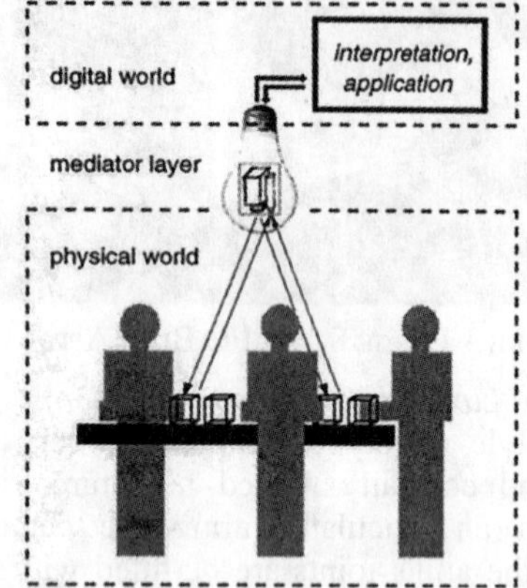

FIGURE 5: MEDIUM-SCALE I/O BULB SCHEMATIC

This paper describes an application that was implemented as a 'proof of concept' of the *Luminous Room* infrastructure in general and of the Medium Scale *I/O Bulb* concept in particular; a proper proof required identification of a domain in which a genuinely useful system could be built and evaluated.

APPLICATION DOMAIN: HOLOGRAPHY

For a variety of reasons, holographic engineering emerged as an ideal first field for our attentions. High-quality optical elements are simultaneously expensive and notoriously susceptible to damage: a single fingerprint can destroy a two-hundred-dollar front-surface mirror instantly and permanently. The breadboarding tables on which experiments are constructed and prototypes built – often floated on sensitive vibration-isolation air pistons – are a scarce resource. At the same time, the precision required of laser-based optical systems frequently results in setup and iterative refinement times that greatly exceed the time spent running the actual experiment. All of this suggests that a well-designed 'simulated optics workbench' could be a valuable tool. Such a workbench should permit the optical engineer to tinker with a setup, interactively manipulating an accurate simulation of the evolving layout and its operation. Having eventually arrived at an optimal configuration 'offline', the engineer could then rapidly reproduce the setup on the real table to perform the end experiment.

Several powerful mouse-and-CRT-based optical layout and analysis packages exist (LightTools, ACCOS, ZEMAX, OptiCAD, etc.). However, intuition both for the behavior of optical systems and for their proper design comes principally through physical interaction with real-world components; for many of the field's students, theory does not gel until the effects promised in textbooks are observed and manipulated firsthand in the laboratory. Thus, a simulator whose input and output were arranged to emulate the real thing – not just visually, but haptically and spatially as well – could both foster and exploit such geometric understanding skills. In short, we set out to provide a virtual optical workbench with which experimenters can physically manipulate three-dimensional stand-ins of different optical components and directly observe the results.

Additionally, in applied holography 'correct' design solutions are unambiguously distinguishable from 'incorrect' solutions, allowing us to evaluate the usefulness of our system: can practitioners build optical design X more easily, more quickly, more imaginatively with the system than without? Finally, the presence of an established and ongoing program in holographic imaging within our university promised a ready supply of holographers, both student and professional, who could be invited to use the system and observed doing so.

Basics of Holography

The mechanics of holographic recording are conceptually simple. A fine-grained photographic plate is exposed simultaneously to two beams of light: one, called the 'object beam', comprises light scattered from laser illumination of the object or scene being recorded; the other, called the 'reference beam', is uniform, unmodulated laser light [4]. In order for a stable (and thus photographically recordable) interference pattern to result from the overlap of these two beams, they must originate from the same laser. This is accomplished with a beamsplitter – often a partially silvered mirror – which allows some of the laser's light to pass undiverted through it while reflectively redirecting the remainder into a second beam. Moreover, because of the limited coherence provided by prevalent Helium-Neon lasers, it is a typical constraint of holographic setups that the length of the object path and that of the reference path (as measured from the beamsplitter, where these two paths become distinct) must be equal. Additional geometric

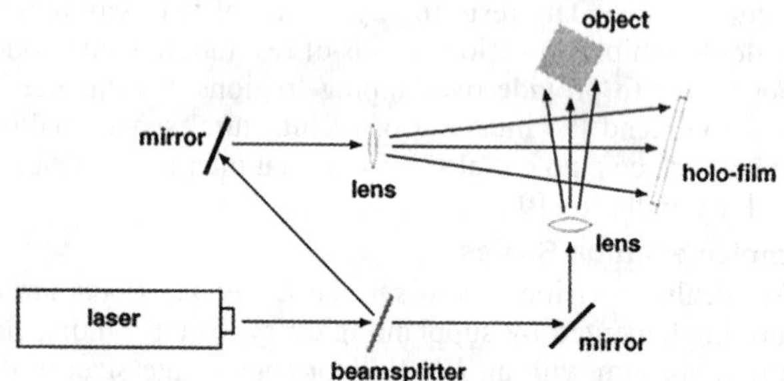

FIGURE 6: TYPICAL HOLOGRAM-RECORDING LAYOUT

requirements are often imposed on the setup, such as the desirability of some particular angle of incidence of the reference beam on the recording plate. Finally, the distance from and angle at which the object is illuminated are inevitably of great import, as these factors directly control the eventual appearance and aesthetics of the three-dimensional image produced by the finished hologram. Thus the principal challenge of designing a working holographic layout is the simultaneous satisfaction of various geometric requisites with a single configuration of optical components. An example of such a layout is shown in Figure 6.

SYSTEM DESIGN REQUIREMENTS

Our intent was to build, using the facilities of an *I/O Bulb*, a prototyping tool for holographic recording setups that would accurately simulate the interaction of laser light with various optical elements. These elements would be represented by physical models, while the 'beams of laser light' would be projected from above in careful alignment with the models. Although the optical elements and the laser beams – the former moved volitionally by human users, the latter computationally generated and projectively inserted into the real space – would be *implementationally* decoupled, the application would convincingly cause them to *appear* causally coupled.

Direct manipulation of the optics models would be close enough to working with the 'real thing' to be at once instructive to students and helpfully familiar to professionals. The system would furnish a selection of fairly standard optical components and allow their arrangement in arbitrary ways, but would also provide certain additional information (like relative optical pathlengths) of particular relevance and necessity to the construction of holographic recording layouts. The system would also be able to detect when a 'successful' holographic setup had been constructed.

We required that the system reject the standard 'one object at a time' restriction of mouse-and-keyboard input. Instead, users must be allowed to manipulate as many objects concurrently as necessary or convenient. The comparative efficiency of two-handed or simultaneous-translation-and-rotation handling has been clearly established [3]; we also demand of our application that it accommodate collaborative work, with two or more participants making simultaneous adjustments to many optical components.

Finally, the system should provide a memory feature, so that the instantaneous state of an optical layout could be recorded pictorially and then, later, projectively overlaid at proper scale on the empty workspace – either for purposes of subsequent 'off-line' review or so that users could rapidly and accurately replicate an earlier setup.

From this checklist we constructed the holographic workbench simulator called *Illuminating Light.*

BACKGROUND

The full concept of a *Luminous Room* infrastructure is related in a variety of ways to many recent and emerging strands of research that are often loosely collected under the tag 'Computer Augmented Environments' [8]. *Illuminating Light* considered as an individual application, however, is related a few particularly relevant works.

We find Pierre Wellner's *Digital Desk* research inspirational [10]; the extensive mixing of physical and digital artifacts through the use of video projection is a powerful notion. However, where Wellner proposed a migration of the virtual desktop off the CRT and back onto the real desktop, we are interested in enhancing or assisting the execution of real, physical activities – here, optical engineering – that are ordinarily outside the realm of 'computing'.

The *Illuminating Light* application represents an approach that is complementary to the usual methods of *Augmented Reality* systems, such as Steven Feiner's *KARMA* [2]; the unwieldy nature of head-mounted displays and the difficulties of ensuring real-world alignment and calibration make the prospect of 'untethered' interaction attractive. Further, the difficulty of providing a common reference when *physically personal* equipment is used to provide augmentation (a problem shared also by *Wearable Computing* rigs, as in [7]) can similarly be addressed with reality-aligned direct projection. Work at Stanford (the *Two-User Responsive Workbench* [1]) has shown one way to address the issue of 'shareable' virtual space – two independently head-tracked users equipped with stereo goggles are able to refer without spatial confusion to the same three-dimensional virtual objects, thanks to a four-processor, two-Infinite-Reality-pipeline SGI Onyx that generates two stereo image pairs for each timestep. We are following a contrasting path in which a single, external projection into the common, real-world workspace instantly offers shareability to an arbitrary number of users without requiring the proliferation of tracking, rendering, and viewing hardware.

The *Tangible Bits* work at the MIT Media Laboratory has provided a strong direction, prompting thought on seamless couplings of the digital and physical worlds [5]. The idea of 'phicons' – physical, functional icons – is of particular relevance to our optical simulation system. But where much of the Tangible Bits research has made use of phicons with various *symbolic correspondences* between digital meanings and physical manifestations, the objects in our application will have a *direct correspondence* to other physical objects (real optics) with definite, distinct uses and significance.

IMPLEMENTATION

The *Illuminating Light* system is built as a hierarchy of hardware and software systems. The physical apparatus on which it is dependent – a 'Medium Scale' *I/O Bulb* – is assumed for the duration of this paper. The software portions and application-specific physical components of the system and its supporting hierarchy are detailed here.

Overview

Users of *Illuminating Light* manipulate models of optical elements on which are affixed unique patterns of small colored dots. Visual input of the workspace is passed from an overhead *I/O Bulb* to a succession of vision analysis systems (*glimpser* and *voodoo*) that parse the dot patterns into recognized objects with attendant positions and orientations. The spatial configuration of objects thus identified is then used by a ray-based optical simulator to determine the resultant path of laser light; this path is visually rendered and, together with ancillary numerical and graphical information, accurately projected via the same *I/O Bulb* back into the workspace.

Vision

Machine vision is not yet reliable as a *general* input mechanism; however, under certain constrained circumstances it can be made to function reasonably well. In the case of the *Illuminating Light* system, vision analysis of a live video stream comprises the principal input.

For reasons both of reliability and of computational speed and efficiency, we decided to build upon a very modest 'raw vision' model: the *glimpser* program, generalized from an earlier version built by the authors and already in use in several projects around our laboratory, simply identifies colored dots in its visual input. Built as a client-server facility, *glimpser* accepts commands over a network connection to define, create, destroy, and condition 'finders'.

Each finder is an independent directive to locate within the input frame a specific-sized region of some particular color. Finders, once created, can be restricted to a certain subregion of the input field, can be temporarily deactivated and reactivated, and can be 'de-emphasized' to be evaluated less frequently in order to streamline the search when input movements are known to be slow or very sporadic. Finally, each finder may be instructed to report only one color-spot location per frame, to report up to some fixed number of spot locations per frame, or to report fully as many spot locations as may be found per frame.

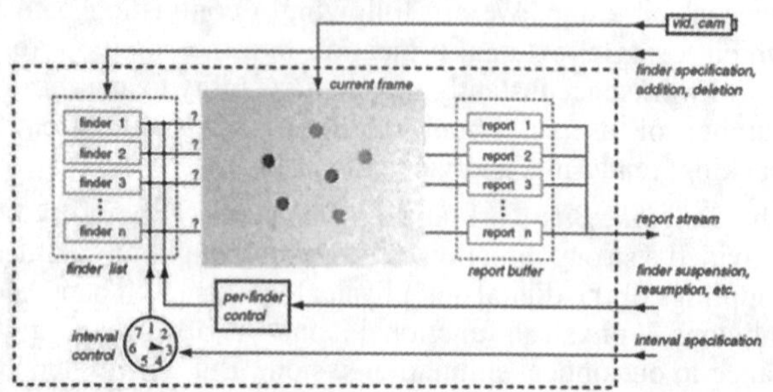

FIGURE 7: SIMPLE VISION ANALYSIS: GLIMPSER

Simulation Toolkit (voodoo)

An application-independent geometric parsing toolkit called *voodoo* interprets the simple colored-dot-location output of the *glimpser* program. *voodoo* analyzes each unorganized per-frame collection of found color dots into a list of unique patterns that have been registered with it by the application it serves. These patterns specify a sequence of colors; associated with each pair of adjacent color dots in a pattern is a required distance, and with each contiguous triplet of dots a required angle. Every pattern is defined by a unique disposition of these parameters.

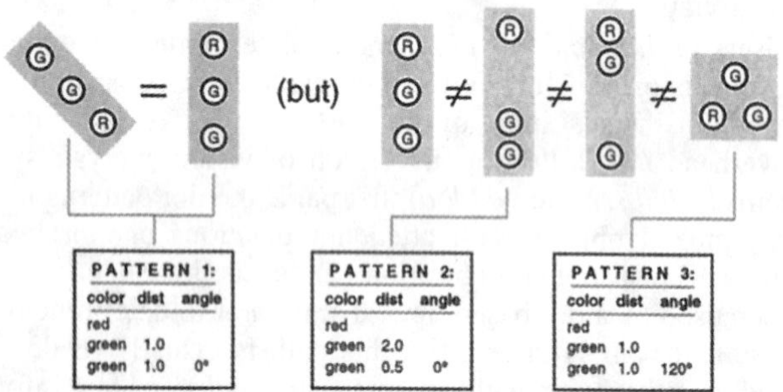

FIGURE 8: PATTERN PARSING WITH VOODOO

Further, each distance or angle specification has associated with it an individual tolerance within which range a 'match' may still be recognized. The intent of this provision is twofold. First, such a measure permits *voodoo* to absorb the inevitable inaccuracies and occasional single-pixel indecisions of machine vision algorithms – without this kind of allowance, vision-based pattern matches would simply fail most of the time. Second, the tolerance specification makes possible the definition of unique but 'parametric' patterns: for example, a lens in the *Illuminating Light* system is identified as the sequence 'red, blue, green' with a certain distance and a minimal tolerance specified for the red-blue pair, but with a 180° turn required between the red-blue and blue-green segments and a large tolerance for the blue-green distance. This means that a lens will be identified wherever a red and a blue dot are appropriately spaced and have a green dot *somewhere* along the line between them; but the application then uses the relative position of this intermediate green dot to define the power of the lens (10x, 20x, 40x, etc.). Thus, definable distance and angular precisions can provide a kind of end-user-adjustable degree of freedom – a way to build simple sliders and dials.

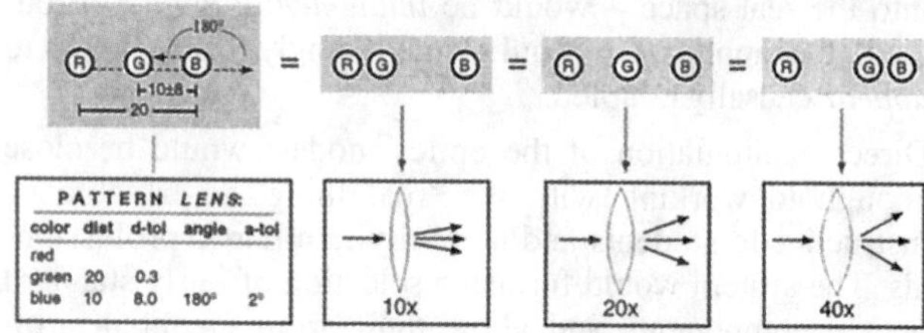

FIGURE 9: VARIABLE SINGLE OBJECT RECOGNITION WITH VOODOO

voodoo also provides an 'object persistence' mechanism: it is wise to assume that low-level vision will occasionally fail (for a frame or two) to report the presence of extant color dots, and – more critically – that users' hands will periodically occlude dots. In these cases, we would like the object-representing patterns identified in previous frames to exhibit a bit of 'temporal inertia'. The persistence mechanism, then, allows objects to continue to exist for a short while even in the absence of positive visual data, and is implemented as a coherence algorithm that attempts to produce a one-to-one match between the patterns detected in the current frame and the patterns from the previous frame. The algorithm allows for a certain amount of translation and rotation frame to frame; the parameters specifying these amounts may be adaptively adjusted to reflect changing frame rates and expected user-induced object velocities.

voodoo, as an independent toolkit, implies and makes easy a whole range of *Luminous-Room*-based simulation applications that use evolving layouts or distributions as a primary input. For example, we are currently constructing an urban planning system in which city engineers can continuously arrange *voodoo*-tagged architectural models and observe resultant simulations of traffic and pedestrian flow projected in perfect alignment back into the miniature urban space. Indeed, nearly any simulation that proceeds from the instantaneous and evolving arrangement of physical models, be they purely symbolic or more literally representational, will find *voodoo* a sturdy and convenient backbone.

Physical Representations of Optical Components

The holography setups to be executed with the *Illuminating Light* system require six basic optical elements: a laser, mirrors, beamsplitters, lenses, a 'holo-object' (the physical thing being visually recorded; in the present case, a small car), and the holographic film plate itself. From the point of view of the system's strictly technical implementation, these elements could be perfectly well represented with nothing more than their individual arrangements of colored dots, perhaps pasted onto cardboard strips. With regard for actual human users, however, we felt that carefully designed physical representations of these components would be an important element in the finished system.

Clearly, the objects have to be easily graspable; so a certain amount of corporeality is in order. The size of the workspace and the demand for a given spatial resolution from the *glimpser* dot-finder dictate an approximate scale. Each object needs to have its identifying dot pattern affixed to a top plane parallel to the workspace surface, and needs also to rest reliably on this surface – thus 'extruded' shapes with flat tops and bottoms are required. In the current implementation, all are about 1.25 inches tall and most about four inches long. The model mirrors, beamsplitters, lenses, and holographic plate are roughly an inch wide.

We require of the objects that they be simultaneously evocative and aesthetic (visually *and* haptically), balanced between direct representation and suggestive visual abstraction, and appropriate for the technical requirements of the vision system. We considered ourselves on the right design path when passers-by would more often than not stop to touch, pick up, or manipulate the object prototypes left on our work table even when the system was not turned on; the six current incarnations are shown in Figure 9.

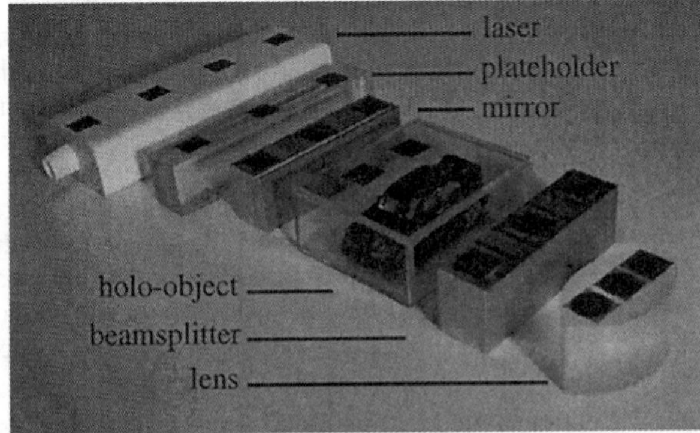

FIGURE 9: ILLUMINATING LIGHT'S SIX OPTICAL COMPONENTS

Optical Simulation

The outward, user-level function of the *Illuminating Light* application is holographic-optical simulation. The underlying simulator is heavily ray-based, both in its implicit treatment of optical behavior and in its implementation. Its three principal software objects are the *Ray*, the *OptElement*, and the *OptSystem*. Each *Ray* specifies an origin and a direction, and may also name a terminus – the downstream point at which the ray intersects an optical element and is transformed by it in one way or another. Each *OptElement*, meanwhile, represents some optical element and is defined by two essential functions: the first calculates, for any ray, whether the ray and the element intersect and (if so) the distance from the ray's origin to that point of intersection. The second generates a list (possibly empty) of new rays generated by the effect of the optical element on an intersecting ray. Each distinct kind of optical element is represented by an *OptElement* with different versions of these two functions, whose particular specification is alone enough to describe every possible sort of ray-based optical behavior.

Thus, for example, a beamsplitter is a kind of *OptElement* that generates two new rays for each one that intersects it: one continues forward undiverted and the other emerges from the intersection point at the calculated 'mirror-bounce' angle.

An *OptSystem*, finally, is a 'bookkeeping' object that contains a list of *Rays* and a list of all participating *OptElements*. Each simulation cycle involves first allowing every generator element – i.e. every element that, as does the laser, spontaneously generates output rays without first being intersected by an incoming ray – to produce its initial ray. Each of these initial rays is then made to terminate at the closest intersecting optical element (if any), and that element is allowed to 'process' the ray and transform it into zero or more output rays, according to the element's individual behavior. This same process is repeated for each of these secondary rays, and so on.

Miscellany

Display

The visual output of *Illuminating Light* is simple; its principal component is the rendered path of laser light. An initial implementation of this path as a set of static, unbroken lines projected in careful alignment between the model optical elements proved not entirely satisfactory: so long as components were being moved, the path of the beams would of course constantly evolve, and thus remain visually prominent; but when the setup was allowed to remain untouched, even for a short while, the beams tended to 'disappear' perceptually. The current implementation shows each beam as a dashed line whose segments move slowly forward (though the line's endpoints are fixed). This modest dynamism not only causes the beams to remain permanently in perceptual view, but also imparts a subtle and inviting 'life' to the system. Of course, it also serves conveniently to make the direction of beam propagation clear.

Numbers indicating the lengths of individual beam segments and various angles throughout the evolving optical layout are projected at appropriate locations. To these visual elements we also impart a small smooth sinusoidal motion that lends them unobtrusive visibility and assures that in regions of high graphical density each number is periodically moved 'out of the clutter'.

Finally, a real-time computer graphics rendering of the setup's holo-object, shown beside the active area of the workspace, simulates the visual output of a real hologram recorded according to the current optical configuration. This rendering shows only a silhouette if the setup is incomplete or improperly realized, but is shown fully shaded once a valid arrangement has been constructed.

All display elements are projected in grayscale; this is a precaution that acknowledges our colored-dot-based machine vision algorithm: introducing sufficiently saturated colors into the workspace can cause *glimpser* to report 'input' where there is none.

Memory Feature

The application automatically saves a frame of its host *I/O Bulb*'s video at regular intervals (every twenty seconds seems to work well). Additionally, a user may 'cheat' with a keystroke that causes the current visual state of the workspace to be immediately stored. These frames may be subsequently 'played back' into the workspace, either singly or as a sequence.

Hardware

glimpser and the *Illuminating Light* application work as a client server pair; however, they currently both run on one machine, a single R5000-processor Silicon Graphics O_2. An InFocus LitePro 620 provides projection onto a table surface from sixty-five inches overhead; a Panasonic KS-

152 miniature video camera is used for visual input.

RESULTS

Quantifiable

Even with both processes running on the same CPU, the application executes from thirty-two to forty complete simulation-cycle and output-frame-rendering iterations per second, while *glimpser* performs its work on input video frames at eight to twelve Hz. The comparative slowness of the input portion of the system (i.e. *glimpser* plus *voodoo* only managing an update of objects' positional and angular changes at 8-12 Hz) is made less noticeable by the high update rate of the animated laser beams and measurement displays – the 'world' always seems to continue running smoothly.

User Testing & Experience

A group of eight holographers and holography students has worked with the *Illuminating Light* application singly, in twos, and in threes; an additional unknown number of passers-by has also experimented freely with the system.

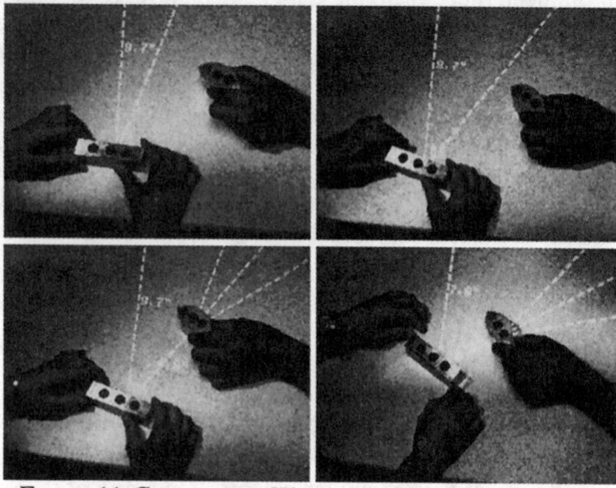

FIGURE 11: COOPERATIVE WORK WITH ILLUMINATING LIGHT

The immediately apparent advantage of using the *Illuminating Light* application is that it permits much faster prototyping than would be usual with real optics deployed on a breadboard or vibration-isolation table. The principal reasons for this are the evident durability and inexpensiveness of the model components and the comparative ease of their manipulation. Users were able to abandon the slow, deliberate care that is mandatory when handling real optical elements. Indeed, most of the holographers and holography students who helped test the system evinced a certain delight in being able to simply grab components and move them very quickly, not worrying about getting fingerprints on expensive optical surfaces or having to loosen and retighten magnetic bases. During collaborative use, a typical working suggestion like "let's move the laser and then swap the mirror and the beamsplitter" would usually be carried out in little more than twenty seconds. The same operation in a 'real' lab setting would require at least five minutes of a seasoned optical engineer and twenty or more minutes of an average team of holography students.

At the same time, the coupling between the physical optics models and the projected laser-path simulation was tight enough so that users tended to dismiss the distinction as irrelevant. Users indicated that they quickly came to "believe" the non-substantive laser beam (after the novelty of manipulating physical objects and seeing collocated projections respond had worn off).

The test subjects felt that the floating component-to-component distance measurements and the ray-to-ray angular measurements were helpful – in a real setup these quantities have to be measured carefully by hand and recorded in a lab notebook. They also responded favorably to the pathlength matching information presented outside the boundary of the 'active holography workspace', although several commented that it was a little strange to find these numbers in a separate 'display' area – that it would be more convenient if the information were incorporated into the evolving setup. Finally, users were unsure about the effectiveness of the rendered 'finished hologram' view presented in the side display area.

DISCUSSION & FUTURE WORK

The comments of test users suggest that we might do well to explore alternatives to the separate 'display' region on the table's surface, folding its functionality into the active optics region. The pathlength matching information could receive straightforward treatment as additional, appropriately positioned textual and numerical annotation throughout the setup. The 'finished hologram' view is a bit more difficult to incorporate into the workspace, particularly as the system can only project onto the '*x-y*' plane while most of a hologram's relevant visual information resides in the inaccessible '*y-z*' plane. This would be an opportunity, however, to demonstrate the profitable overlap of two separate *I/O Bulb* instances: the Small-Scale 'Luxo-style' prototype could be placed in the workspace to project such 'orthogonal' details into the setup.

We have demonstrated that under certain circumstances use of *Illuminating Light* permits much faster prototyping than is possible on a real optical table with real optics. However, as this application is poised somewhere between physical optical system layout and a software tool (like ZEMAX) intended for highly precise optical design and analysis, its comparison against this latter class of tool will be of clear importance. We intend therefore to perform a series of tests (again with real holographers and holography students) to establish the relative merits of these two approaches, both in the context of education and of professional engineering.

There is an ongoing issue, endemic to such physical interface systems, regarding control of parameters beyond the narrow bounds of the simulation. For example: how, other than via the keyboard or mouse, should a user of *Illuminating Light* be able to switch the display of automatic angle and distance measurements on and off? What is an appropriate way to trigger the capture and storage of memory frames, and then later select among various saved frames for retrieval and display? Such manipulations are ordinarily handled quite adequately (if somewhat inelegantly) by screen-based GUI elements. But to introduce additional 'control objects' that are tracked throughout the workspace in the same manner as the optical elements would not only dilute the purity and directness of the interface to the simulation but would also likely necessitate cordoning off a portion of the workspace as a distinct 'control zone'. Finding a solution to this dilemma is important.

While *voodoo* is an efficient and reliable means of performing object tracking, the colored dots that it employs do somewhat compromise the aesthetic design of the objects themselves. An alternative is the use of a template-matching vision algorithm – such as the one reported in [6] – that can be 'trained' on the appearances of the objects themselves. Although there are predictable tradeoffs (e.g. partial occlusion of an object by a grasping hand is more likely to confuse template recognition than *voodoo* recognition, and redesign of an existing object or addition of a new object requires a full retraining instead of the simple application of new colored dots) we intend to build a version of *Illuminating Light* that uses such a vision system.

Illuminating Light has helped to prove the effectiveness of its hardware platform (i.e. the Medium-Scale *I/O Bulb* apparatus) and of *voodoo* in rapid construction of simulation systems. We are already at work on several new, contrasting systems. In addition to the urban planning scenario detailed earlier, we are exploring a less physically literal application: a signal-processing tool that allows designers to manipulate physical representations of digital elements (i.e. delays, adders, gain elements, etc.) and view intermediate versions of the signal shown along the connections between elements.

A larger issue concerns the projective philosophy of the *Luminous Room* and *I/O Bulb* structures. While active-surface systems (e.g. the *MetaDesk* system in [5]) never suffer from occlusion problems, a projective system has certain other advantages: it is possible to place information not only *around* but also *on* objects in the workspace. Further, it is possible to projectively address objects that may be located away from a supporting surface. Indeed, the large-scale *I/O Bulb* can address an entire room; a similarly ambitious active-panel approach would require quite a few panels.

CONCLUSION

We have described a system that, in accordance with the aims of the *Luminous Room* architecture, uses real-world surfaces as an arena both for display and for direct-manipulation input. The application, called *Illuminating Light*, succeeds through its mimicking of an optical workbench in marrying light and physicality: although its user-handled physical optics models and the computer-simulated path of laser light are in reality very distinct (at least from the point of view of the system), their close cognitive cause-and-effect coupling tends to mitigate the perception of the one as an *input* channel and the other as an *output* channel.

The system heavily exploits the advantages of control via graspable implements (as explored in other tangible interface work), but the additional strength of this particular application domain is that the system's components act not just as physically instantiated abstractions but as direct representations of the 'real thing'. This allows *Illuminating Light* to provide constant visual feedback in a form that is already intrinsic to the simulation's real-world counterpart – and so the 'virtual' part of the application does not seem distracting or glaringly distinct from its 'real' part. We may note that we do not perceive our interactions with normal, non-digital reality as characterized by *input* and *output*, but rather as a participation in a kind of continuous *causality*. In natural consonance with this interaction approach, the system cleanly permits two-handed and collaborative use.

Even though machine vision is not yet a reasonable general-purpose input mechanism, in controlled circumstances like the ones detailed here it can be acceptably effective (and even efficient: the entire *Illuminating Light* system, comprising one process for low-level vision and another for visual input parsing and the actual optical simulation with attendant rendering and display, runs on a single low-end SGI machine). We have found the *voodoo* toolkit, together with the *glimpser* vision software, useful for rapidly assembling such layout-based simulation systems; construction of the portions of the *Illuminating Light* application hierarchically above *voodoo* took roughly one week.

As one test-subject holographer noted, the 'in-plane' restrictions resulting from our projective architecture reduce what is in general a three-dimensional task to two dimensions. Indeed, while the beam path in most real holography setups is actually purely planar, running parallel to the table's surface and elevated some eight inches above it, a few setups require vertical inclination of the beam. Thus, while *Illuminating Light* accommodates perhaps ninety percent of typical holographic layouts, there remains a number of layouts that fundamentally cannot be addressed using a projection-based system.

ACKNOWLEDGEMENTS

We thank David Kung and Kevin Parent for early formulating discussions of reagent grade; Matt Slayter for dogged & relentless fabrication of several *I/O Bulb* prototypes; Andy Dahley and Paul Yarin for indefatigable help with optics model design & construction and for clarifying camaraderie, early and late; and Wendy Plesniak and Rob Poor for countless lambent insights at every step.

REFERENCES

[1] Agrawala, M., Beers, A., Fröhlich, B., et. al. The Two-User Responsive Workbench: Support for Collaboration Through Individual Views of a Shared Space, in *Proceedings of SIGGRAPH '97*: 327-332, August 1997.

[2] Feiner S, MacIntyre B, Seligmann D. Knowledge-Based Augmented Reality. *Communications of the ACM*, Vol. 36, No. 7, July 1993

[3] Fitzmaurice, G. W., Ishii, H. and Buxton, W. Bricks: Laying the Foundations for Graspable User Interfaces, in *Proceedings of CHI '95*,: 442-449, 1995.

[4] Hariharan, P. *Optical Holography: Principles, Techniques and Applications*. Cambridge University Press, 1984.

[5] Ishii, H. and Ullmer, B. Tangible Bits: Towards Seamless Interfaces between People, Bits and Atoms, in *Proceedings of CHI '97*: 234-241, March 1997.

[6] Niyogi, S. and Freeman, W.T. Example-based Head Tracking, in *Proc. 2nd International Conference on Automatic Face and Gesture Recognition*: 374-378, 1996.

[7] Starner, T., Mann, S., Rhodes, B., et. al. Augmented Reality Through Wearable Computing, to appear in *Presence* Special Issue on Augmented Reality, 1997.

[8] Underkoffler, J. Antisedentary Beigeless Computing. *Personal Technologies*, Vol. 1, No. 1, March 1997.

[9] Underkoffler, J. A View From The Luminous Room. *Personal Technologies*, Vol. 1, No. 2, June 1997.

[10] Wellner, P. Interacting with Paper on the DigitalDesk. *Comm'ns of the ACM*. Vol. 36, No. 7: 87-96, July 1993

Insight Lab: An Immersive Team Environment Linking Paper, Displays, and Data

Beth M. Lange, Mark A. Jones, James L. Meyers
Andersen Consulting
Center for Strategic Technology Research
3773 Willow Road
Northbrook, IL 60062-6212 USA
+1 847 714 2418
lange@cstar.ac.com, mark.a.jones@ac.com, jlmeyers@cstar.ac.com

ABSTRACT
The Insight Lab is an immersive environment designed to support teams who create design requirements documents. Requirements emerge from a deep understanding of a problem domain, which is achieved through in-depth analysis of large amounts of qualitative data. The goal of the Lab is to facilitate the data analysis process through the seamless interaction of computer-based technologies with objects in the environment. Team members can use paper and whiteboards to sketch, annotate, and display their analysis work. Barcodes are used to link papers and whiteboard printouts to the multimedia data stored in the computer.

Keywords
Interaction design, collaboration, analysis methods, video analysis, hybrid paper electronic interfaces, digital documents, group memory, barcode technology

INTRODUCTION
Identifying and developing the design requirements for a new system, service or product is a complex problem. Designers need to understand and organize vast amounts of qualitative data collected about the work and environment in which the system will be used. By analyzing data about an environment, its work practices, and the technology in use, the designers can base the requirements on evidence of the current practices. Achieving a full understanding of a problem domain may involve an in-depth review of audio and video recordings, photos, interview notes, and other materials. A team needs to find the important content and organize it in meaningful ways. A successful design document organizes the volumes of data into manageable units such as the key dimensions of a problem, the interdependence among contributing factors of a problem, and the major shifts expected from implementing a new system.

The Insight Lab was built to improve how teams create requirements documents by supporting the process of transforming data into insights. In the spirit of Video Mosaic [10], we attempt to support an iterative process that relies on sketching ideas, viewing and displaying a lot of material at one time, and utilizing the spatial relationships between materials to provide meaning for the work being done. It is important to enable a team to manipulate, record, and review its work, in any format used, throughout the entire design process. Enabling a team to effectively create requirements documents is based on three separate, but interdependent elements that are highlighted in the paper:

1. *Analysis Framework*
   An analysis framework and a structured process are necessary to facilitate the analysis of enormous amounts of qualitative data [7], [20]. Without an agreed-upon process, the team spends valuable time negotiating a process; and lack of an analysis framework can lead to ad-hoc and possibly incomplete analysis.
2. *Managing and Displaying the Data*
   Software tools to digitize, store, index, and access large amounts of multimedia data enable a team to easily work with any of the data by following established links [3], [19].
3. *Connecting Paper to the Computer*
   It is important to create a working environment that facilitates team interaction as well as the capture of design rationales through the innovative, integrated use of paper, whiteboards, and computers [16], [21], [20], [1], [10].

The Insight Lab is an immersive team environment. It consists of software tools to manage multimedia data, numerous display devices and writing surfaces, and the use of barcodes to link paper, displays, and data. This paper presents the key features of the Insight Lab: the Analysis Framework, Managing the Data, Displaying the Data, and Connecting Paper to the Computer. Examples of use are presented throughout the paper. The paper closes with reflections on our experiences using the Insight Lab.

BACKGROUND

Our own experiences transforming data into requirements documents led to the creation of the Insight Lab. Over the past few years we have participated in projects to develop knowledge management systems, collaborative tools for multi-site project teams, mobile computing applications, and interactive multimedia applications. For example, in late 1996, we completed an extensive project to develop a knowledge management vision for an organization. The resultant documents – a Vision Report, and the supporting Human-Centered Design Analysis Report – were based on data collected at 17 sites in seven countries, where a team of four people observed and interviewed more than 150 people over a three month period.

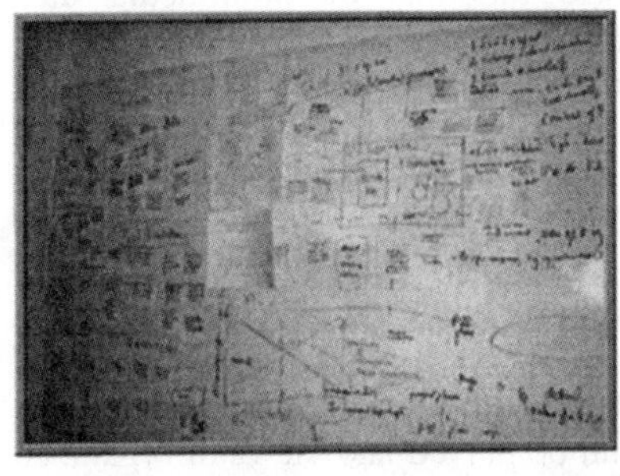

Figure 1: Working with PostIts™, electronic whiteboard printouts, and whiteboards during data analysis.

During the knowledge management project, we used a simple, custom-built data structuring software application to catalogue the data and begin the analysis. However, the in-depth analysis was done without the benefit of computerized tools. Using well-known knowledge management frameworks to structure the analysis, we used an electronic whiteboard to sketch scenarios and PostIts™ placed on a whiteboard to create diagrams, matrices, and tables. The PostIts and electronic whiteboard printouts helped us display key issues and the problems to address. While this process worked, it was cumbersome, inefficient and time-consuming. In the end we had a scattered pile of PostIts and much of the project history was not preserved.

DESIGN RATIONALE

During the knowledge management project we documented all of our activities by recording our work as digital images and 35mm slides. Using these materials, we reviewed and reflected upon our experiences to identify the key factors that influenced the way we conducted our design sessions. The outcome was a set of goals for the Insight Lab: to support team-based analysis, facilitate informal interaction, utilize technology to improve the process, and enable teams to use common objects including pen and paper.

A basic premise of the Insight Lab design is that the analysis and synthesis of observational data into requirements documents should be accomplished by teams, since teams bring in multiple perspectives to minimize the influence of individual biases. A typical team may consist of experts in a company or industry, social scientists experienced in describing and identifying social and cultural factors, designers, and perhaps the people who are expected to use the resultant technological system [7], [9].

Moran and his colleagues demonstrate the importance of supporting informal collaborative work [11], [12]. Their research focuses on using technology to augment intensive discussion-based teamwork. They supported groups reviewing and rating many documents in short meetings. We are supporting a team working together over a period of weeks to "make sense" of multimedia data. In both cases the social interaction involved in building consensus is crucial. A team working on complex problems establishes a common context regarding the meaning of data by discussing, analyzing, and repeatedly reviewing it together.

Researchers examining the use of technologies for group work point out the importance of natural interactions between team members, especially when using computers to assist or support the team's activities [15], [12]. Issues involve shared displays, turn-taking, recording activities and modes of interaction with objects.

ANALYSIS FRAMEWORK

At Andersen Consulting, we employ data collection methods such as video ethnography and contextual inquiry to observe everyday work practices, organizations' activities, and consumer behaviors. The practical benefits of these methods are well-documented [5], [6], [17]. They ensure a rich understanding of an environment, situation, or activity, which is to be supported by a new or changing technology solution.

Analysis is typically done by looking for patterns in the data. For example, Suchman and Trigg utilized utterance-based transcriptions to understand air-traffic controllers [18]; Xerox and IRL pioneered the use of Interaction Analysis [7]; and Conklin championed the use of IBIS to structure the issues and decision points identified during data analysis [4].

Building on these approaches, we created a simple analysis framework, which structures the data and allows for the use of numerous clustering and brainstorming techniques throughout the analysis, synthesis and design phases of a project. This simple structuring provides for a bottom-up approach for reaching the highest levels of data abstraction, going from data to requirements. At the same time, hypotheses are used for a top-down approach to ensure full coverage of a problem domain.

Elements of the Analysis Framework

Figure 2 diagrams the elements of the Analysis Framework, which are described below, while Figure 3 presents an example for each element.

Evidence is the basic unit of analysis. A piece of evidence is a significant action, quote, or description taken directly from the multimedia data gathered during observation. A project usually has hundreds to thousands of pieces of evidence, each of which is tagged to a piece of media.

Keywords are important concepts that are used to assemble the evidence into meaningful subsets during the initial stages of analysis. A piece of evidence is usually tagged to multiple keywords. In our experience, a project may have fifty keywords.

Figure 2: Analysis Framework

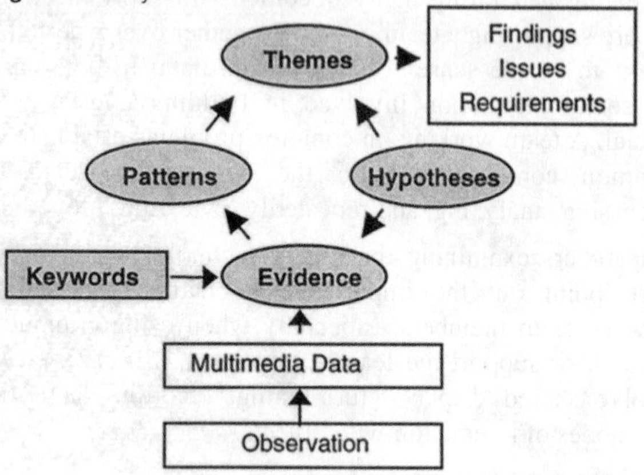

Themes → Findings Issues Requirements
Patterns
Hypotheses
Keywords → Evidence
Multimedia Data
Observation

Patterns are meaningful groupings of evidence derived from a bottom-up clustering of evidence. Our projects typically result in fifty to one hundred patterns.

Hypotheses are a special type of Pattern. They are key questions the team needs to address when gathering data. Evidence is gathered to confirm or disconfirm hypotheses.

Themes are the important dimensions of a problem domain that emerge during the analysis process. A project typically results in less than a dozen themes.

Figure 3: Examples of the Analysis Elements: Knowledge Management

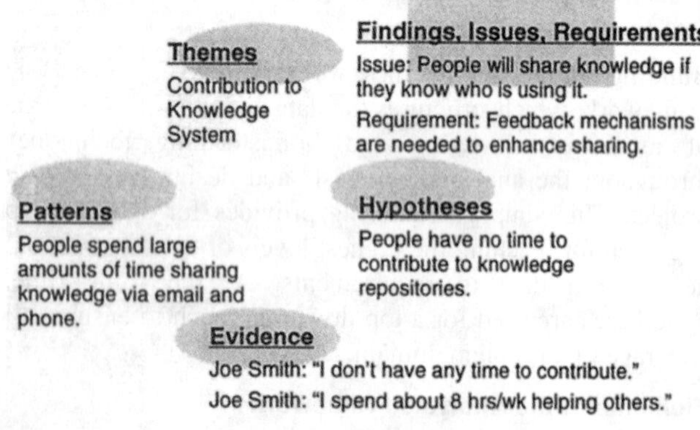

Flexibility of the Analysis Framework

Experience showed us that every project would have varying needs with regard to the data to be captured and analyzed. Our analysis framework is simple, yet flexible, providing the freedom to assign specific types of labels to data instead of creating an overly structured, and therefore inflexible analysis framework. For example, in a current project we have "suggested solutions" and "surprises" keywords to organize subsets of evidence that may not directly relate to the bottom-up approach of identifying themes and patterns from evidence.

Following the approach of others who found that new tools need to work in concert with many other team activities [12], [20] the Insight Lab allows a team to use any number of techniques or tools to transform evidence into patterns, and patterns into themes. For example, cluster analysis was useful in a project in which we were interested in the intersection of evidence across many keywords. Similarly, affinity diagramming is used to identify themes from patterns.

MANAGING THE DATA

The Insight Lab utilizes software tools to digitize, store, index, and access large amounts of multimedia data including the video, audio, and photographic data gathered during data collection. All of the elements of the analysis framework just described are also captured and stored.

Insight MAST (Multimedia Analysis Software Tool)

We developed Insight MAST (Multimedia Analysis Software Tool) for use throughout the entire analysis and synthesis process. Insight MAST supports data capture and storage, data entry, and searching and display capabilities. Digitized media clips can be played and views of organized subsets of the analysis data can be displayed. All of the interactions between the Insight Lab's objects, devices, equipment, and displays are managed by Insight MAST.

The best way to quickly and easily view data is to digitize it [3], [13]. Providing easy, non-linear access to the original source data is essential. For example, during analysis a team views media clips to create consensus about the meaning of pieces of evidence and to clarify their interpretations of events that transpire in a particular media segment.

Figure 4: Design of the Insight Lab

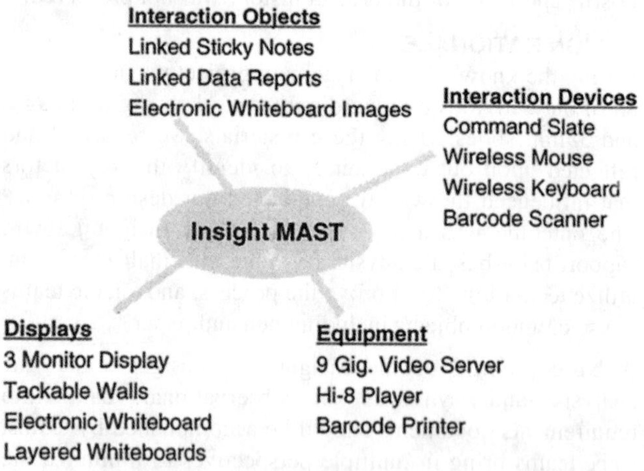

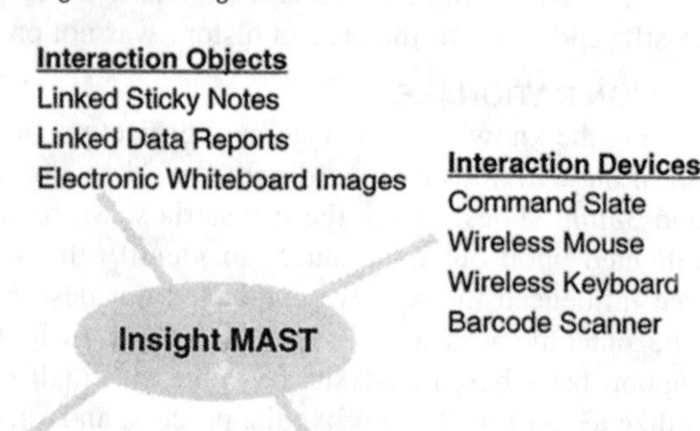

Insight MAST, as shown in Figure 4 above, is the glue that holds all of the elements of the Insight Lab together. In the Lab, team members can work with Interaction Objects, use

the Interaction Devices to input, save, and retrieve data, view materials on the Display surfaces, and write on the whiteboards. The use of these objects and devices are detailed in the sections that follow.

Traceability: Preserving a Project's History

Insight MAST maintains the links between multimedia data and evidence, and links between the various analysis elements as well as storing electronic whiteboard drawings. Providing this automatic "traceability" of the analysis and design process is a key feature of MAST. Preserving the history of the team's activities provides a rich design rationale. There have been numerous efforts to capture design histories such as [2], [4], and [20] often requiring the team to take extra steps to document their work. Our approach to this challenging problem is to make it an easy, almost invisible part of the analysis process.

The value of the captured history is apparent during the analysis process. It allows teams to easily review their work when there are questions about how they arrived at particular conclusions. In creating the final project documents accessing the captured history provides linkages between the underlying empirical data and the findings and issues which shape the final outcomes.

DISPLAYING THE DATA

The ability to manipulate and view large amounts of data at one time is critical throughout data analysis. The Insight Lab supports the use of a multi-monitor computer display, as well as using the Lab's walls as displays.

High-Resolution Computer Displays

Three 800x600 resolution displays provide a large surface for groups to view the Insight MAST information and see several levels of data detail simultaneously. Our decision to utilize a large display was based on the experiences of Swaminathan and Sato [19], who take advantage of a large surface to display several domain contexts simultaneously. The Lab's long and narrow, 9 feet by 27 feet space prevented us from using three contiguously displayed high-resolution projectors on the long wall because a projector's focal length is more than nine feet. Therefore we place the displays on the nine-foot wall using a projector in the center and thirty-one-inch color monitors on the left and right, as shown in Figure 5. The different sizes of the displays creates a discontinuity causing some problems when moving the mouse between screens [19].

The different sizes of the displays also presents a challenge regarding readability. We determined that the content of each display should be legible from twelve feet away, since teams sitting around a table are likely to be seated at that distance. To achieve the perception that text displayed on each screen is approximately the same size, the smaller monitors use a larger font size than the center projector. A 10pt. font is used on the center display and an 18pt. font on the two side monitors. As can be seen from the picture in Figure 5, the relative sizes of the fonts in the windows appear comparable. The use of varying font sizes constrains the movement of windows from one monitor to the other.

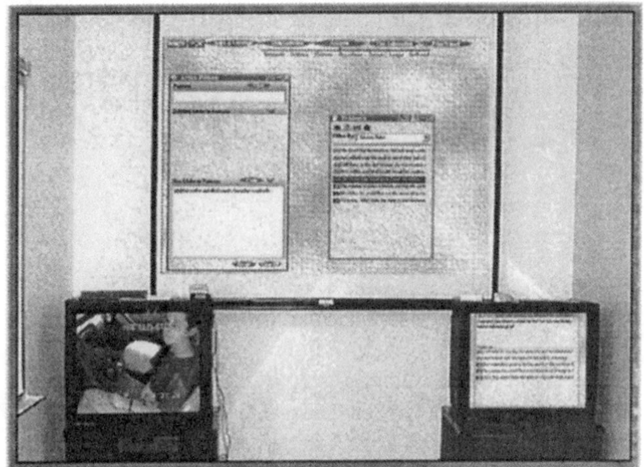

Figure 5: The Insight Lab's three screen display.

Interaction Windows in Insight MAST

The Insight MAST application consists of a combination of interaction windows and windows that are used for display only. Windows that require user interaction are placed on the center screen, whereas video clips are played on the left monitor, and additional details of data is viewed on the right monitor. The interaction windows on the center screen are used to create and maintain links among different levels of data. Example windows are shown below in Figures 6, 7, and 8.

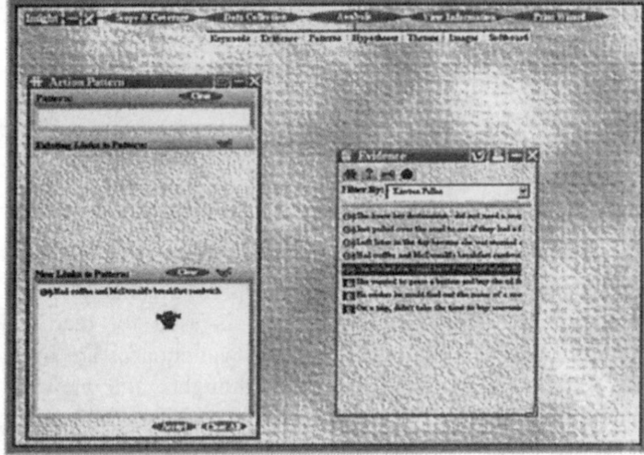

Figure 6: The user is creating a pattern by dragging evidence from one window into another. These windows are displayed on the large projection screen in the middle.

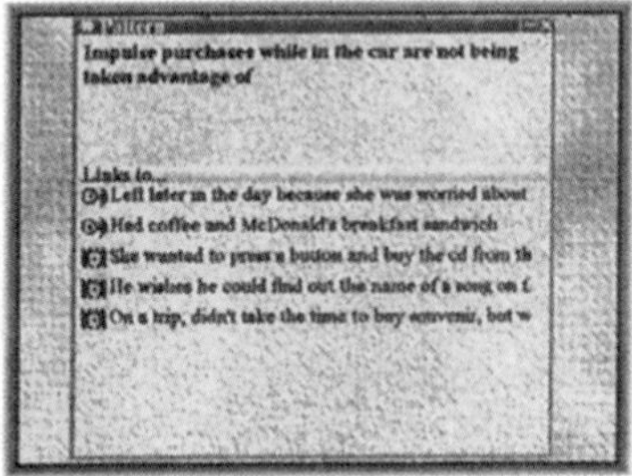

Figure 7: The right monitor displays additional details about a particular item highlighted on the center screen. This example shows all the evidence associated with a pattern.

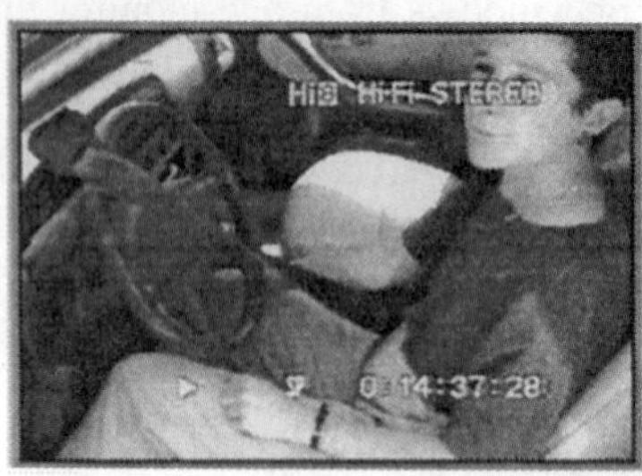

Figure 8: Video clips are displayed on the left monitor. This frame is from a series of video clips associated with the pattern displayed in Figure 7.

Walls as Displays

During our knowledge management project we covered all of the Lab's walls with diagrams, notes, matrices, drawings, and affinity diagrams. We found it very useful to have easy access to the materials. This was important for comparing different ideas at one time, as well as quickly and easily moving items around to make new groupings of information. Even the use of three high-resolution displays does not provide sufficient display space so we continue to rely on walls to provide additional display surface. Thus, in designing the Insight Lab we wanted to preserve this capability, while also creating connections between the papers and sketches with the materials stored in the computer. When the walls are covered with paper linked to the computer via barcodes, the entire room, in essence, becomes a huge computer display.

Figure 9: Using walls as display spaces for information.

CONNECTING PAPER TO THE COMPUTER

The uses of paper and whiteboards by teams is well understood [12], [15]. [17]. Paper is used for reading, sketching, and annotating. Similarly, whiteboards are used for sketching, capturing emerging thoughts and viewing materials. The use of whiteboards in the Insight Lab is discussed in the section on Linked Images on the following page.

Sellen and O'Hara's research shows how individuals annotate paper to gain an understanding of what they are reading. Paper is also used to spatially display a lot of material at one time, and to easily move between documents or sections of documents [14].

The key to the Insight Lab success is the creation of a seamless interaction between the computer and these other forms, namely paper and whiteboard. We utilize a barcode reader, a custom designed barcode command slate, and barcode enabled paper forms, which we call "Linked Sticky Notes" and "Linked Data Reports," to facilitate this interaction between paper objects outside of the computer and the data stored in the computer.

Just as Video Mosaic [10] connects paper-based storyboard elements, digital elements and video clips through the use of scanners and barcodes, we connect the basic components of a design project using barcodes. DigitalDesk [21] supports activities that utilize pre-existing paper documents. For example, the calculator tool retrieves numbers from a printed page using image processing technology eliminating the need to punch the numbers into a calculator before they can be manipulated. These two systems provide important evidence of the ways in which paper usage is an integral part of many activities.

In accounting for the use of the paper, sticky notes, and whiteboards, we made a concerted effort to understand where a team's focus is at any given point in the analysis process and what activity they are doing. When team members are working individually we support the use of personalized printouts. When they are discussing items we support the use of the personal printouts, as well as the computer displays and whiteboards to create a shared workspace. The following sections provide examples of how the team uses paper during different points in the analysis process.

Linked Data Reports

Insight MAST can generate any number of customized data reports filtered or sorted using various criteria. The example below shows a report of evidence sorted by keywords. Associated with every item on a report is a barcode identifier that can be scanned to display details about the item. Scanning the barcode for a piece of evidence plays its digitized video or audio clip.

Figure 10: Reviewing a list of evidence to identify patterns in the data.

The first step of data analysis is to create patterns from evidence. The team begins by reviewing all of the evidence using linked evidence reports. The team members spend time individually reviewing the evidence and making annotations on their own printed reports, which is followed by a discussion about the pieces of evidence. When hundreds to thousands of pieces of evidence are collected by multiple people, individuals may need additional information to understand evidence they have not seen before. To gain context, they can view a corresponding video clip for any piece of evidence by scanning the barcode associated with a piece of evidence listed on a report. Scanning a barcode to review a media clip is simpler and faster than using the computer to search for the particular clip to play. Similarly, when the team is already using the printed reports, it is far simpler to scan barcodes to link a piece of evidence to a pattern than it is to turn attention to the computer to open windows, search for an item in a window and drag-and-drop it to a pattern window.

Linked Sticky Notes

As a team conducts analysis and creates patterns and themes, Insight MAST is used to create associations of evidence into patterns and themes. New patterns or themes are printed on 2"x3" magnetic cards, as shown below. A "Linked Sticky Note" can be placed on a magnetic whiteboard.

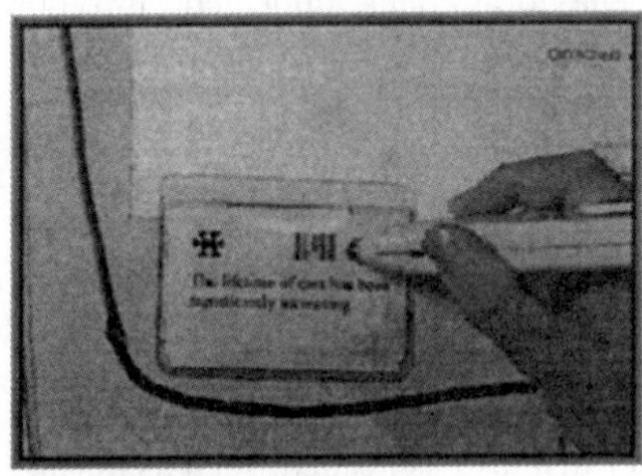

Figure 11: This person is scanning a Linked Sticky Note to view the information associated with a pattern.

Scanning the barcode identifier on a pattern's Linked Sticky Note displays its underlying information on the computer monitor. There is a natural fluidity in the way that one can point to an object and scan it to view its underlying information, rather than turning attention from the object to the computer to search for the item. This retains the person's focus on the object they are already using.

Enabling a team member to easily trace the history of the pattern by viewing all of the underlying data ensures that the team is referencing the actual data, not working from memory. It is common for team members to review all of the evidence linked to a pattern; it helps the team maintain a common understanding of the meaning of the pattern.

Linked Images

When the team is developing conclusions, extensive discussions are captured using the electronic whiteboard. Team members sketch ideas, diagram relationships between interesting elements of the domain, and articulate key points. As they are working at the whiteobard the team does not want to think about which drawings will be important. Thus, every image is automatically saved and stored. All of the electronic whiteboard images created by the team are digitally stored in the Insight MAST database. These images, tagged with barcode identifiers, are printed and displayed on a tackable fabric wall. We call these "Linked Images". Figure 12 shows numerous Linked Images created using the electronic whiteboard.

Figure 12: The electronic whiteboard surrounded by Linked Images tacked to the wall.

As themes begin emerging, Linked Images of previous analysis sessions are moved around the room and placed with images of related discussions. These images are easily associated with themes. They can be displayed on the large projection screen for easy viewing by the entire team, and can be retrieved for editing using Adobe Photoshop™ or other image editing programs.

Barcode Command Slate

The Barcode Command Slate provides shortcuts to initiate the actions most commonly used during analysis. It is a printed list of barcoded commands for invoking specific actions. The use of the Slate enables the team to maintain focus on their work by providing a better mapping between what they want to do and how they start it.

Figure 13: A barcode command slate in use.

To "Create a Pattern" they scan the "Create a Pattern" barcode rather than using a series of mouse moves and mouse clicks to find and open a series of windows that are needed to create patterns. The Barcode Command Slate has three different types of commands:

1) Direct Action Commands

← When this type of command barcode is scanned, an action occurs. "Start Electronic Whiteboard" is an example.

2) Commands on Objects

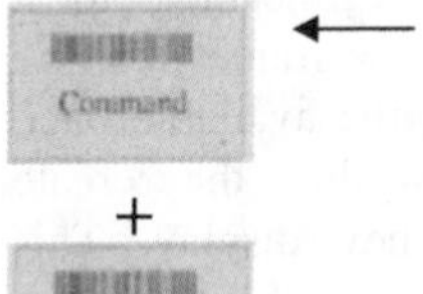

← Command barcodes perform an action on a specific object. Using the command "View Media For..." and scanning a pattern plays the media associated with each of the pattern's pieces of evidence.

3) MultiObject Commands

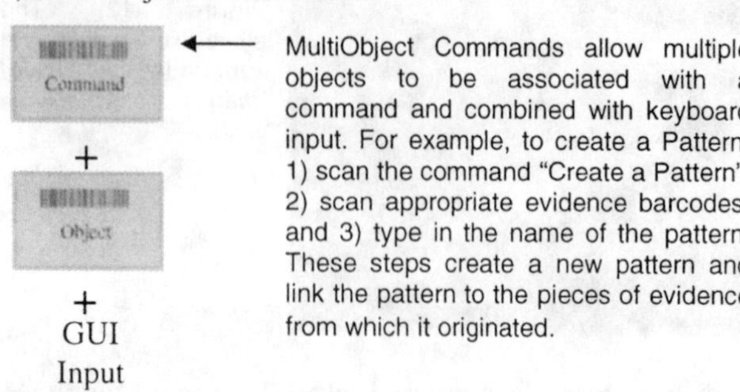

The Barcode Command Slate works in conjunction with the MAST interface. When a command is invoked the appropriate windows are opened and displayed, providing feedback that the Barcode Command Slate actions are working properly. For example, when the "Create a Pattern" barcode is scanned, the "Action Pattern" window is opened and displayed. As pieces of evidence are scanned to add them to the pattern, the evidence is displayed in the Action Pattern Window.

The use of the Command Slate and wireless keyboard extends the reach of the computer application, saves time, and makes complex actions simple. The Command Slate is particularly valuable when creating patterns from evidence reports and creating themes from pattern Linked Sticky Notes.

BARCODE OBJECTS IN USE

The interplay between paper, sticky notes, and computer occurs throughout the analysis process. Using the Linked Interaction Objects together – Linked Sticky Notes, Linked Data Reports, and Linked Images – dramatically enhances the analysis process. The team can focus on the content of their work because the use of these objects minimizes the amount of effort required to access, manipulate, view, and create data.

Figure 14: An analysis session in progress. Linked Sticky Notes and Linked Images are organized into a matrix. The underlying details of any Linked Sticky Note can be viewed by scanning the barcode.

The challenging part of analysis is developing the higher-level frameworks that explain or give meaning to a particular problem. A team arrives at these frameworks by repeatedly organizing and reorganizing the available data. People attach meaning to spatial relationships they create between the objects and materials they display. This improves how they interpret and remember the data. The use of Linked Sticky Notes allow the team members to easily move the content around on the whiteboard. For example, they can group the Notes into an affinity diagram. They can create themes, which associate all of the Linked Sticky Notes included in the diagram. The group can then either retain the diagram or move the Sticky Notes knowing that they have recorded the theme, which is also represented by a Linked Sticky Note.

REFLECTIONS

While we continue to develop and enhance the Insight Lab, we learn about its strengths and limitations by using the Lab. We recently completed a project to describe information needs surrounding the use of a car; this will be used to identify new services that could be delivered to people with in-car computing and GPS (Global Positioning System.) Three researchers used the Insight Lab for over a month to analyze behavioral data collected through numerous observational techniques, resulting in activity logs, video, audio, and photographic data.

Our experience reinforced the design decisions we made with regard to team attention and focus. The team spent numerous days reviewing the evidence reports to create patterns. Using the Lab has dramatically improved the speed and effectiveness of creating these patterns. We also found that all team members would only direct their attention to the computer displays as needed, such as during discussions about precise wording of a pattern. During later stages of analysis, the Linked Sticky Notes were effective in allowing the team to fluidly move back-and-forth between high-level issues and underlying data in a unified manner.

There are some limitations to the Insight Lab in its current form. The Lab is the result of a research project and to date has only been used by its creators. Usability testing would be necessary before making the Lab widely available. The MAST application in its current form is not robust and the facilities for digitizing the multimedia data are incomplete.

Some additional capabilities would enhance the use of the Lab. For example, we use the Linked Sticky Notes placed on the Whiteboard to manually carry out affinity diagramming. To create a theme and associate patterns and images with it, the team members must use the command slate, barcode scanner, and keyboard. Instead, we would like to pursue the ideas presented in SILK [8] for using screen (Whiteboard) gestures to make the association between patterns. By circling a group of clustered patterns and images, a theme would be created. We are also considering the use of audio interface components to enhance how data can be manipulated by teams in a way that increases their focus on the data, not interaction with the computer.

We are currently extending the use of the Lab into other aspects of the design and development process. We are investigating the use of the Lab for design teams who are reviewing the Requirements documents. As such, we have developed hybrid paper documents that take advantage of the Insight Lab capabilities by utilizing the best of paper, the media server, three-screen display, and the barcode scanner. The document enables team members to create electronic annotations, bookmarks, and keywords, which link back to a paper-based document [1].

ACKNOWLEDGMENTS

Our conceptual thinking about the goals and designs of the Insight Lab benefited from the advice of our colleague Kishore Swaminathan. We thank Kelly Dempski for his contributions to the technical design and implementation.

REFERENCES

1.Arai, T., Aust, D., and Hudson, S. E. PaperLink: A Technique for Hyperlinking from Real Paper to Electronic Content, in *Proceedings of CHI '97* (Atlanta GA, March 1997), ACM Press, 327-334.

2.Bellotti, V., Integrating Theoreticians' and Practioners' Perspectives with Design Rationale, in *Proceedings of InterCHI '93* (Amsterdam, April 1993), ACM Press, 101-106.

3.Carroll, J., Alpert, S., Karat, J., Van Dusen, M., and Rosson, M. Raison d'Etre: Capturing design history and rationale in multimedia narratives, *in Proceedings of CHI '94* (Boston MA, April 1994), ACM Press, 192-197.

4.Conklin, J. and Begeman, M.L. gIBIS: A Hypertext Tool for Exploratory Policy Discussion, *in Proceedings of CSCW '88* (Portland OR, September 1988), ACM Press, 140-152.

5.Holtzblatt, K. and Jones, S., Conducting and Analyzing a Contextual Interview, in Namioka and Schuler (Eds.) *Participatory Design: Principles and Practice,*. Lawrence Erlbaum Associates, Hillsdale, NJ, 1993.

6.Hughes, J., King, V, Rodden, T., and Andersen, H. The Role of Ethnography in Interactive Systems Design. *Interactions*, 2, 2 (April 1995), 57-65.

7.Jordan, B., and Henderson, A. Interaction Analysis: Foundations and Practice. *The Journal of the Learning Sciences* 4, 1 (1995), 39-103.

8.Landay, J. A., and Myers, B. A. Interactive Sketching for the Early Stages of User Interface Design, *in Proceedings of CHI '95* (Denver CO, May 1995), ACM Press, 43–50.

9.Lewis, S., Mateas, M., Palmiter, S., and Lynch, G. Ethnographic Data for Product Development: A Collaborative Process. *Interactions*, 3, 6 (November/December 1996), 53-69.

10.Mackay, W.E., and Pagani, D.S. Video Mosaic: Laying Out Time in a Physical Space, in *Proceedings of Multimedia '94* (San Francisco, CA, October 1994), ACM Press, 165-172.

11.Moran, T. P. and Anderson, R. J., The Workaday World as a Paradigm for CSCW Design, in *Proceedings of CSCW '90* (Los Angeles CA, October 1990), ACM Press, 381-393.

12.Moran, T. P., Chiu, P., Harrison, S., Kurtenbach, G., Minneman, S., and van Melle, W. Evolutionary Engagement in an Ongoing Collaborative Work Process: A Case Study, in *Proceedings of CSCW '96* (Cambridge MA, November 1996), ACM Press, 150-159.

13.Moran, T. P., Palen, L., Harrison, S., Chiu, P., Kimber, D., Minneman, S., van Melle, W., and Zellweger, P. "I'll Get That Off the Audio": A Case Study of Salvaging Multimedia Meeting Records, in *Proceedings of CHI '97* (Atlanta GA, March 1997), ACM Press, 202-209.

14.O'Hara, K., and Sellen, A. A Comparison of Reading Paper and On-Line Documents, in *Proceedings of CHI '97* (Atlanta GA, March 1997), ACM Press, 335-342.

15.Pedersen, E., McCall, K., Moran, T., and Halasz, F. Tivoli: an Electronic Whiteboard for Informal Workgroup Meetings, in *Proceedings of InterCHI '93* (Amsterdam, May 1993), ACM Press, 391-398.

16.Sellen, A., and Harper, R. Paper as an Analytic Resource for the Design of New Technologies, *in Proceedings of CHI '97* (Atlanta GA, March 1997), ACM Press, 319-326.

17.Suchman, L. Representations of Work. *Communications of the ACM* 38, 9 (entire issue).

18.Suchman, L. A., and Trigg, R. H. Understanding Practice: Video as a Medium for Reflection and Design, in Greenbaum and Kyng (Eds.) *Design at Work: Cooperative Design of Computer Systems.* Lawrence Erlbaum Associates, Hillsdale, NJ, 1993.

19.Swaminathan, K., and Sato, S. Interaction Design for Large Displays. *Interactions* 4, 1(Jan-Feb. 1997), 15-24.

20.Wall, P., and Mosher, A. Representations of Work: Bringing Designers and Users Together, in *Proceedings of PDC '94* (Chapel Hill NC, October 1994), ACM Press, 87-98.

21. Wellner, P. Interacting with Paper on the DigitalDesk. *Communications of the ACM* 36, 7 (1993), 97-96.

Reinventing the Familiar: Exploring an Augmented Reality Design Space for Air Traffic Control

Wendy E. Mackay, Anne-Laure Fayard, Laurent Frobert and Lionel Médini
Centre d'Études de la Navigation Aérienne
Orly Sud 205
94542 ORLY AÉROGARES FRANCE
mackay@lri.fr

ABSTRACT

This paper describes our exploration of a design space for an augmented reality prototype. We began by observing air traffic controllers and their interactions with paper flight strips. We then worked with a multi-disciplinary team of researchers and controllers over a period of a year to brainstorm and prototype ideas for enhancing paper flight strips. We argue that augmented reality is more promising (and simpler to implement) than the current strategies that seek to replace flight strips with keyboard/monitor interfaces. We also argue that an exploration of the design space, with active participation from the controllers, is essential not only for designing particular artifacts, but also for understanding the strengths and limitations of augmented reality in general.

Keywords: Augmented Reality, Design Space, Interactive Paper, Participatory Design, Video Prototyping

INTRODUCTION

Air traffic control is a complex, collaborative activity, with well-established and successful work practices. The work is highly situated, requiring rapid responses to constantly-changing conditions. The work is also risky: a controller holds the fates of thousands people in the course of an hour. Mistakes that result in crashes are simply not acceptable.

The tools and procedures used by controllers were initially developed over forty years ago. Although the details have evolved continuously as traffic and other conditions have changed, the basic tools have not. Controllers use radio and telephone for communication, RADAR to see a two-dimensional representation of the planes, and paper flight strips to track and modify information about planes and flight plans (see Hopkin, 1995, for an excellent summary).

Despite the success of the current system, mounting levels of traffic and aging equipment make it imperative that the system be improved. This is an interesting design challenge: The existing system is already extremely safe: No fatalities have ever been attributed to French civilian controllers. Any new tool must enable controllers to effectively manage the compromise between the safety of the planes and the smooth flow of traffic, enhancing the controllers' judgment without decreasing their vigilance and effectiveness. Unfortunately, the history of automation is filled with examples of expensive new computer systems that reduced user productivity or were completely discarded as unusable (Zuboff, 1988, Dertouzous, 1990). Air traffic control is no exception: numerous research projects have been ultimately rejected as unusable by the controllers.

Many air traffic controllers are investigating new tools that either replace flight strips with electronic versions (Leroux, 1993, Bressolle et al., 1995) or get rid of them entirely (Vortac et al., 1990, Bentley et al., 1992). Although these projects acknowledge the importance of flight strips, they generally concentrate on the information they contain, rather than the controllers' interactions with them. The problem with these approaches is that they force an abrupt change in the controllers' familiar styles of interaction. Controllers must learn to use new input and output devices that work perfectly from the first day, are immune to equipment failures, and can be easily adopted even by controllers with many years of experience with flight strips.

We propose an alternative solution, based on a radical change of assumption: Automation need *not* require getting rid of paper strips. We suggest keeping the existing paper flight strips as physical objects, with all their subtlety and flexibility, and augmenting them directly by capturing and displaying information to the controllers. Enhancing the flight strip separates issues of input and output from the content of the flight tools themselves, emphasizing the controllers' interactions with the strips as much as the information they contain. Augmented strips may also provide a more modern input/output solution than the old mouse and keyboard designed for office automation.

Augmented flight strips have several advantages: We can take advantage of the highly successful work practices that already exist. We can introduce changes incrementally and give controllers a more active role in the design. We can develop new kinds of interaction with the system and among controllers that were never before possible. Note that this approach does not preclude eventually replacing strips. Rather, it provides an evolutionary path to any of a number of new methods of flight control. Our work has

CHI 98 Los Angeles CA USA
Copyright 1998 0-89791-975-0/98/ 4..$5.00

two main components: investigation of the existing work practices of air traffic controllers and exploration of a range of possibilities for augmenting flight strips. Our goal is to ground our design explorations in the real-world activities of air traffic controllers and to understand the advantages and disadvantages of different technical solutions.

This article describes the participatory design project that accompanied our ethnographic study of a team of air traffic controllers (Mackay & Fayard, 1997a). We first describe paper flight strips and our design approach. We then explain why augmenting existing flight strips may prove a better path to automating air traffic control than replacing them with electronic strips. We describe our exploration of the design space of augmented flight strips, using a series of prototypes developed in collaboration with the air traffic controllers. We conclude by arguing that exploring a design space is essential, not only for the particular problem of air traffic control, but for the more general problem of understanding augmented reality and its relation to new forms of human-computer interaction.

Flight strips and air traffic control

We observed controllers from team 9W in the Paris en route control center (Fig. 1), arguably the most complex in Europe. They handle air traffic traveling in all directions over approximately one-fifth of France, including traffic going to and from the two main Paris airports, Roissy Charles de Gaulle and Orly. The air space is divided into "sectors", complex three-dimensional airspaces crossed with various routes. Controllers work in teams and are qualified to handle either "east" or "west" traffic. West consists of 11 sectors, which may be merged in different configurations and managed from as little as one position (late at night). Controllers rely on flight plans, requests by pilots, requests from other sectors, current weather and traffic conditions to manage the air traffic, judging the safest and most efficient ways for planes to proceed through the air space.

Figure 1 : Controllers working with flight strips at the Paris en route control center in Athis Mons, France.

Unlike airport control centers that handle take-off and landing, Athis Mons has no control tower. Controllers "see" the airplanes via the RADAR screen. Each plane is represented by a point of light, accompanied by the flight identifier, current speed, flight level and a tail showing recent positions. Some but not all routes and beacons are indicated in background. The two-dimensional RADAR image represents a dynamic, three-dimensional space.

The other key tool for tracking planes is the flight strip, shown in Figure 2. Flight strips are similar from control room to control room: They consist of a band of paper printed with flight information, including airline, flight number and type of aircraft, as well as the requested and authorized flight plan (speed, level and route, with expected times for particular cross-points). Preux (1994) provides a detailed description of flight strips used in Athis Mons.

Figure 2: Two flight strips in strip holders.

Unlike airport control towers that pass (or throw!) strips from sector to sector, en route control centers print a new strip for each sector. Figure 3 shows a set of annotated strips, indicating changes in flight level, routing, and speed.

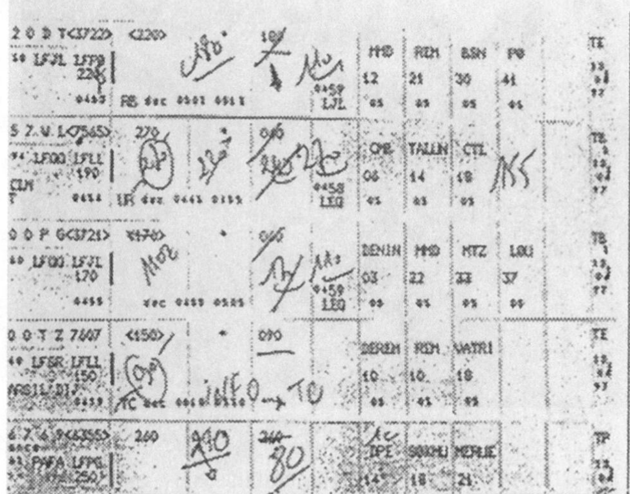

Figure 3 : Annotations on a set of flight strips

Like most en route centers, Paris controllers place paper strips into plastic stripholders. Figure 4 shows how the strip holders fit into metal rails (the stripboard), making it easy to slide and rearrange the strips. Some control centers, as in Bordeaux, do not use strip holders but instead lay the strips on a "stepped" table located between controllers.

Figure 4 : Fight strips in a strip board at Athis Mons

The importance of flight strips

Many researchers have emphasized the importance of flight strips (Harper et al., 1991, Preux, 1994, Hopkin, 1993). Our own observations confirm that they are extremely flexible, taking advantage of both visual and tactile memory. Controllers often take strips in their hands as a reminder to do something. They slide them left or right to highlight different conditions, such as two planes in conflict. Even the act of writing is important: controllers find it easier to remember something they wrote than an item from a menu. Controllers have a dynamic, physical relationship to the strips and with each other (Figure 5).

Figure 5: Controllers communicate physically, via strips

Two controllers may work simultaneously on different strips on the same stripboard, using body language to indicate the importance of different annotations or actions (e.g., by sliding or rearranging). Stressful situations can be identified not only by the number of strips; but by how the controllers collectively interact with them and each other.

Our studies have led us to challenge two widely-held assumptions. The first is that controllers resist new systems because they are "conservative" and dislike new technology. In fact, we found many computer enthusiasts in team 9W; they enjoy discussing the latest software and debating the merits of Macs vs. pc's. They do not fear computers; on the contrary, they look forward to using more 'modern' tools. They do, however, resist systems that slow them down with a mouse or keyboard to enter data.

It is also a mistake to assume that air traffic control systems are static simply because they rely on non-computer tools. Over the past year and a half, we have seen numerous changes, from adding a new sector to changing the controllers' schedules. Even senior controllers being requalified struggle to relearn details. Air traffic control is understandably conservative, since no one wants to reduce safety. On the other hand, it is organized to constantly evolve, flexibly handling ever-increasing levels of traffic.

Thus the "conservatism" we see with respect to new computer interfaces is not due to a general resistance to computers, nor to a general resistance to change. It appears to be , in fact, a rational response. Software designers tend to focus on the added functionality a new system will provide. Controllers must also consider the functionality they will lose with a new system. French controllers have a powerful voice; they can afford to wait until something arrives that adds new functionality without interfering with their existing, highly-functional work practices.

PARTICIPATORY DESIGN APPROACH

Our research approach involves "triangulating" (Mackay & Fayard, 1997b) across scientific and design disciplines (Figure 6). As in the English air traffic control studies (Hughes et al., 1992, Bentley et al., 1992), we use a combination of ethnography and design. However, we emphasize keeping rather than replacing flight strips. These design activities let controllers innovate, not just evaluate. The goal is to create an environment that controllers can co-

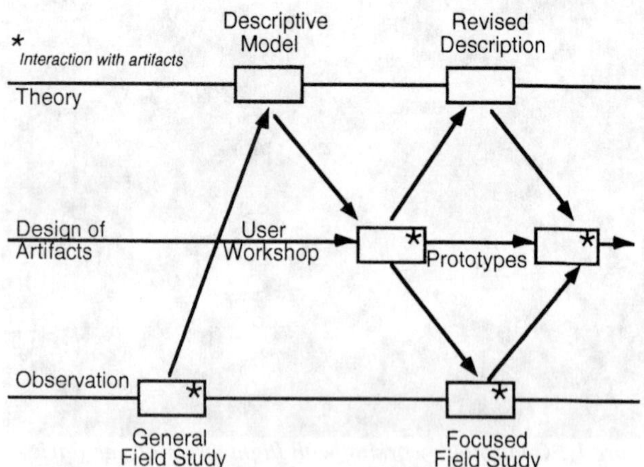

Figure 6: The project involves traditional inductive and deductive methods, observing behavior in real world settings and generating theoretical frameworks, in conjunctive with participatory design to create and evaluate prototypes.

adapt, simultaneously evolving the technology and their work practices to meet their continuously-changing needs.

Ethnographic Study

We studied team 9-West from the Paris en route control center, following their schedule for four months, including nights and weekends, in order to experience a full range of traffic conditions. They welcomed us and spent many hours explaining their work and patiently answering questions.

The Paris center is organized around self-managed teams of 12-15 people. Team 9W had five students, six qualified controllers and four senior controllers, plus various guests, such as controllers being requalified. Students are generally given as many hours as possible, making it difficult to find situations in which the traffic was being controlled exclusively by senior controllers. The Paris center has a reputation for being particularly informal, perhaps because they deal with the most complex traffic conditions. Controllers who are not currently needed generally congregate near team members who are working, chatting with each other until some subtle cue tells them they are needed. They then can stop, mid-sentence, and turn to help the controllers. They never ask what needs to be done: all the information they need is available via strips, RADAR and the peripheral cues that tell them what is going on.

We made detailed, timed notes of over 100 hours of observation, including 50 hours of video over a full range of air traffic situations. We paid particular attention to their communication patterns and their use of tools, especially paper flight strips, RADAR, Digitatron, radio and telephone. We selected ten sessions for more in-depth coding and quantitative and qualitative and analysis. A complete report on the results is beyond the scope of this article. However, the following observations from this analysis directly affected our design explorations:

1. *Air traffic control is mostly routine*: Controllers engage in a constantly-repeated cycle of systematically looking at each plane on the RADAR and the corresponding paper flight strip. This routine is important, not only when things are hectic, but also when things are slow. During emergencies, this routine enables controllers to handle all the other simultaneous jobs that do not go away. In slow periods, the routine enables controllers to stay vigilant. Computer tools that successfully reduce the controllers' work in high-stress situations by eliminating routine activities risk creating dangerous situations under low-traffic conditions, since controllers can become bored and stop paying attention.
2. *Strips form part of a controller's mental representation of the traffic.* Controllers maintain an active picture of the traffic in their heads, letting them look away and handle interruptions. Strips also provide a focal point for updating mental images of the traffic and allow controllers to instantly communicate the current state of the traffic to each other. The physical nature of strips, the ability to hold them and write on them, contributes to this shared mental representation.
3. *Controllers often communicate physically rather than verbally*, taking advantage of each other's peripheral awareness. For example, a controller who points to or writes on a strip is making an implicit statement about the urgency of dealing with that particular situation.
4. *In busy situations, controllers hold new strips in their hands* prior to integrating them into the strip board. This tactile memory is very difficult to replace.
5. *The very act of writing serves as a reminder and helps clarify thoughts.* We observed that even controllers in centers without flight strips (e.g. Maastsricht and Amsterdam approach) write notes to themselves. One controller admitted that she did not always re-read what she wrote; it was just important to be able to write it.
6. *Controllers operate in a highly interrupt-driven environment.* Most controllers dislike the noise and the urgency of the telephone, particularly when it is used for non-urgent situations. New tools should give controllers the communication flexibility they use when next to each other, even at a distance, letting them easily distinguish between urgent and less urgent problems.
7. *Controllers sometimes create hand-written strips to deal with unusual situations.* For example, planes carrying parachute jumpers stay in a particular sector for several hours without a flight plan. Controllers must track the plane in conjunction with all the other planes, giving permission when it is safe for parachutists to jump.

Design activities

We invited members of team 9-West to participate in a 9-month participatory design project, using results from the ethnographic study. We ran a series of workshops with controllers and researchers, using a combination of brainstorming, prototyping and scenario-building exercises to explore ways of augmenting flight strips. We began by showing controllers video of our other augmented reality work and a summary of their interactions with strips (drawn from our video data). Subsequent workshops were more interactive, letting controllers and researchers brainstorm new ideas and experience different prototypes. Rather than simply writing brainstormed ideas, we encouraged people to "act out" their ideas with cardboard mockups and Wizard of OZ techniques. Videotapig these ideas help us visualize the interactions and served as useful reminders as the prototypes changed over time. Video was a useful Wizard of Oz technique: the "wizard' would observe the user's interactions with real paper strips and "project" feedback using a projector above or a monitor below. This style of prototyping allowed us and the controllers to experience a variety of different augmented strips, long before any physical prototypes were operational.

We also developed scenarios, drawing from both routine and unusual activities that occurred during the ethnographic studies. Once validated by the controllers, they served as a design tool to ground our explorations of user functionality and later helped us test our prototypes with controllers.

DESIGN SPACE EXPLORATION

Rather than developing a single solution, we were interested in exploring the design space of ways to augment paper flight strips. Our exploration involved developing and comparing various prototypes and identifying a range of user functions and styles of interaction. These activities are orthogonal and complementary: we implemented each user function with at least two technical solutions and applied each technology to multiple user functions.

For example, controllers wanted a link between the paper strips and the RADAR. We implemented the idea with a graphics tablet prototype, in which the user taps the pen or writes on the paper strip to see the relevant plane change color on the RADAR. For the touch screen prototype, the user points to the desired strip with a finger in order to see the plane on the RADAR. One controller who tried it suggested that we highlight the plane's route as well. The implemented version turned out to be controversial: while several controllers liked it, others argued that it would encourage students to avoid memorizing the routes. In the subsequent implementation, one tap or point highlighted the plane and two such interactions highlighted the route.

Prototype development was accompanied by on-going observations in the control room, guided by questions raised during the workshops. One of the most important issues was the role of writing on the strips. A key insight was that annotations not only serve different functions, but also are intended for different *audiences*:

1. *For themselves: memorization and anticipation*
   - reminders (talk to pilot about change in flight level)
   - highlight (circle all the planes landing at Orly)
   - reinforce (arrow to show plane is descending)
   - warning (potential conflict)
   - not in the system (hand-written for parachute planes)
2. *For each other: communication*
   - between the radar and planning controller
   - between the current and the incoming relief controller
   - between one sector and another (or the chef de salle)
   - between groups during a regroupment or degroupment
3. *For posterity*
   - to provide a legal record
   - to provide an economic record

A forth audience appears for automated systems:

4. *For the computer*
   - to update automated tools like Erato (Leroux, 1993)

This insight helped us greatly, both to identify useful functions for the controllers and to reduce technical problems: Instead of trying to interpret everything the controllers write, we need only interpret what is necessary.

When controllers write for themselves, the system need not capture or interpret the information at all. Often the very act of writing is sufficient. When controllers use annotations to communicate with each other, the writing must be interpretable by another person, but not necessarily the computer. We need only capture the image, preferably in context, but not decipher the meaning. The 9-West controllers made it very clear they would not write solely for the "system", even if it generated useful information. On the other hand, writing to communicate with other controllers was considered both acceptable and important.

The few remaining situations in which the computer must both capture and interpret the writing can often be dealt with by taking advantage of the context. For example, a number located in a particular box on a flight strip must be one of only five or six possible flight levels.

Our prototypes emphasize communication among controllers, since writing for themselves is already handled admirably with ordinary paper and others have studied how to interpret hand-written marks by computer (Chatty and Lecoanet, 1996). Also, the 9-West controllers were most interested in support for communication, especially if it did not involve adding new, more complex interactions. The prototypes were designed to be evolvable by the controllersm with minor changes in writing conventions facilitating interpretation of certain annotations, providing interesting new features and access to new tools, and generally encouraging the use of the system.

Technology prototypes

The technology prototypes addressed three basic design problems: how to *capture* information from strips, how to *track* the location of the strips and how to *present* information onto strips. Future technologies, such as electronic paper by N. Sheridon at Xerox PARC and electronic ink by J.Jacobson at MIT (Negroponte, 1996), especially combined with small pen-based computers, will make augmented flight strips both light-weight and practical. Since these are not yet available, we used existing, somewhat less-convenient technology in order to experience different styles of interaction and experiment with ways of integrating augmented flight strips into current work practices. Our exploration of the design space helped us to evaluate the trade-offs generated by the technology in the context of the real work environment of air traffic control.

Capturing information

The choice of technology to capture information is tied to the intended use of the information: passing it on to another human being is quite different from evaluating it as numeric computer data. We limited our choices to information that could be captured directly from flight strips, eliminating devices such as the mouse or keyboard, to avoid forcing controllers to enter the same information twice. We experimented with three basic input devices:

1. Graphics tablet with pen input (several sizes)
2. Touch-sensitive screen
3. Video camera (still or moving images)

The graphics tablet allowed us to use ordinary flight strips in ordinary stripholders, allowing us to capture whatever controllers write with a pen. The touch-screen also permitted controllers to write with a pen, but restricted their movements, since they could not rest their hands on the screen. The video camera could capture anything written, as long as it was not obscured by the controller's hand or body, but had problems with resolution and being trained on the appropriate image. We experimented with software developed by Elissaoui (1997) that offers a solution: it zooms automatically when it detects a particular color (say the cap of a red pen) and grabs an image from the correct position on the strip. The graphics tablet is best at capturing precise data, whereas the video is the best at capturing information in context. The touch-screen is less precise than the graphics tablet, but permits information to be presented directly onto the strips.

Presenting information

We experimented with three projection approaches:

1. Video projector (for computer images or video)
2. Computer monitor or LCD screen
3. Touch-sensitive screen

We had already experimented with projection onto paper in Video Mosaic (Mackay & Pagani, 1994) and Ariel (Mackay, 1996). Projecting information onto flight strips is less feasible, since controllers must be able to immediately see the information and not worry about blocking the light source. Computer monitors provide high-quality images, but can only present information next to, not directly onto, the strips. The touch-screen, when used with transparent strips, can project high-quality information (from below) onto any part of the strip.

Figure 7: Transparent strip holder with diodes and contacts.

Tracking information

We experimented with two tracking approaches:

1. Video camera
2. Stripboard that detects resistance in strip holders

We tried placing information on the strips that could be detected by the video camera. However we concentrated on a second approach, Médini (1997) to track the position of stripholders in a stripboard. We embedded resistors into stripholders with metal contacts at either end (Figure 7).

A special stripboard (Figure 8) measures the resistance in the strip holders and can determine precisely which stripholder is located in which position. Solid-color strip holders were created to hold ordinary paper strips and were placed over the graphics tablet. Transparent strip holders held transparent strips and were placed over the touch screen. This prototype solved the problem of linking the relevant strips to the writing detected via the graphics tablet or touch screen.

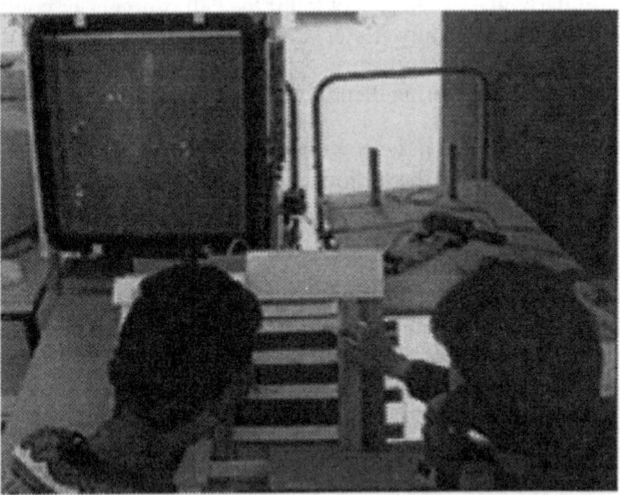

Figure 8: Stripboard that tracks position of strip holders, linked to RADAR with simulated air traffic

User functionality: The media space

The best user functions are often the most invisible: controllers value simplicity over functionality. Ideas popular with visitors and management, such as correcting flight plan information from the strip, were generally rejected as too complex by the controllers. They pointed out that the current Digitatron (a touch-screen) lets the planning controller make updates when it is convenient, rather than forcing the RADAR controller to do it. The most successful user functions were the linking of the strips to the RADAR (described earlier) and using the strips to communicate with controllers at other sectors via a modified media space (Bly et al., 1994).

We were struck by how controllers working next to each other communicate. In stressful situations, especially when the RADAR controller talks continuously to the pilots, they avoid speaking and communicate with body language and placement of strips. If the planning controller places a strip in the normal spot next to the RADAR controller, she knows that the RADAR controller is peripherally aware of it and will deal with it when he is ready. If she places it on top of the stripboard, she is placing it within his focus. If she stands up, slides several strips down, inserts the strip and writes on it, she is demanding that he look at it NOW. Similarly, the RADAR controller can wait for the planning controller's actions or actively shift his focus and integrate the strip into his working set. Others have described peripheral awareness (Heath and Luff, 1991) and situational awareness (Endsley, 1988) in various settings. We noted that controllers decide to actively or passively slide between peripheral and focused awareness, pushing information at each other or pulling information in. This subtle, but effective behavior works extremely well for controllers who are sitting next to each other, but breaks down completely for controllers at a distance. This rich interplay is reduced to a telephone call; a noisy interruption of a potentially busy person. The caller has no way of knowing if the other controller is dealing with three critical conflicts or relaxing. Similarly, the callee cannot tell if the call is urgent or could be handled at any time. Controllers complain about telephone interruptions, particularly from student controllers reassuring themselves.

We experimented with a common type of cross-sector communication, the negotiation of transfer flight levels. Before handing off a plane, two controllers must agree on a particular flight level. Each flight strip has a section with the next sector and the requested and authorized flight levels. When a controller writes a flight level in this box, other controllers immediately know that that's the proposed transfer level. When the flight level is underlined, they know the pilot has agreed and the next sector will accept the flight at that level.

If we capture what the controller writes on this section of the flight strip and make it available to the controller at the next sector, we can begin to simulate the light-weight interaction that exists when controllers are next to each other. Since this information is captured for another human being, not the computer, we need only send it, not interpret it. We experimented with several interfaces. For example, one controller writes the new flight level. The writing is captured and displayed on the appropriate section of the other controller's strip. If she underlines the flight level, everyone knows that the negotiation is done. If she writes a new level, the original controller may accept it or call to discuss it. We experimented with different ways of "sending" the information, such as having a tiny image appear and get successively bigger over time, to simulate the controller pushing the information deeper and deeper into the other controller's awareness. We are still exploring the range of possibilities suggested by this approach.

Evaluation

Throughout the project, we invited controllers to come to our laboratory and see or try out various technologies and experiment with different user functions. Our last workshop presented the most developed prototype, linked to a working simulation of real air traffic. The resulting system can now take advantage of any of the on-line tools developed by CENA (or externally). We also introduced an "Interaction Browser" that lets controllers try different ways of interacting with the strips and associating those interactions with any of the functionality available on-line. For example, a controller might specify that making an underline mark in the identification section of the strip causes information about the flight plan to appear next to the relevant plane on the RADAR. The same underline mark located in the flight transfer section of the strip is interpreted as an agreement that a particular flight level has been accepted. Controllers can save their profiles and try out the interactions on a scenario based on real traffic. The goal is to provide controllers with a system that is explicitly designed to be evolved, to take advantage of new on-line tools as they appear and to let controllers decide together on their preferred styles of interaction. (Note that the goal is not to have an individual profile for every controller, but to let controllers experiment with a range of possibilites and then collectively agree on a limited set of annotations that can be interpreted in a consistent way, just as they do now with writing conventions on paper.)

Technology: We were somewhat surprised that controllers liked the transparent strips: they could easily see why having external information displayed on the strips would be useful. (However, they were even more intrigued by future technologies such as electronic paper/ink, which promise the same advantages without the drawbacks.) Presenting information next to the strips was acceptable, particularly for functions like linking the strips and the RADAR. They did not like projection very much, since they are most likely to block the light source when they most need the information. The system for tracking the position of the strip holders made it possible to experience the flexibility of future augmented strips.

User functions: Some of the user functions were controversial, with some controllers liking a particular function and others rejecting it. Sometimes it was possible to reach a compromise, as in the two-step linking of strips and RADAR. Controllers were most likely to reject functionality that was too complex (particularly software displays or interaction techniques that required multiple steps). They were also wary of functionality that replaced part of their mental representation of the traffic: they wanted to be sure they could handle the traffic even without the RADAR and strips in case of a massive failure. Finally, they were most positive about functions that reduced annoyances, such as too many telephone interruptions.

CONCLUSIONS AND FUTURE DIRECTIONS

After conducting a four-month ethnographic study, we embarked on a nine-month participatory design effort to explore the idea of augmenting paper flight strips. We ran a series of workshops with researchers and controllers, using brainstorming, prototyping and scenario-building techniques to explore the design space. We returned often to the control room for further observations and discussions and incorporated the controllers' reactions and ideas at each stage of the prototyping process. The final workshop involved a working prototype connected to a training simulator, with access to RADAR with simulated traffic and a range of on-line tools. Our 'interaction browser' let controllers experiment with different types of annotations and link them to different on-line tools. We presented at least two different ways of handling each type of interaction, enabling us to compare both technology ideas and user interactions. A full report of the design space exploration and our data will be presented as a CENA technical report.

We began this work with a particular bias: Physical objects play an important role in cooperative work and automation efforts that get rid of them risk losing important aspects of the interface. Our observations in the Paris control center convinced us that paper flight strips play a complex role in air traffic control, beyond their information content. We argue that designers of new air traffic control systems should consider separating the problem of input/output from the content of the tools and experiment with augmenting paper flight strips. Perhaps then we can take full advantage of their rich, existing role in air traffic control, without losing the other benefits of automation.

ACKNOWLEDGMENTS

A special thanks to the members of équipe 9-West for their warm welcome and participation in our work. Special thanks to Christophe Mertz and the Paris CENA team and Stéphane Chatty and the Toulouse team for their participation in prototyping and workshops. Thanks to Michel Beaudouin-Lafon, Nicolas Roussel, Stéphane Conversy, and Paul Dourish for discussions of prototypes.

REFERENCES

Bentley, R., Hughes, J.A., Randall, D., Rodden, T., Sawyer, P., Shapiro, D. & Somerville, I. (1992) Ethnographically-informed systems design for air traffic control. In *Proceedings of CSCW '92, ACM Conference on Computer-Supported Cooperative Work.* (pp. 122-129) Toronto, Ontario: ACM Press.

Bly, S., Minneman, S. and Harrison, S. (1994) Media Spaces. Special issue of *Communications of the ACM*, 37 (1).

Bressolle, M.C., Pavard, B., & Leroux, M. (1995) The role of multimodal communicaton in cooperaton and intention recognition: The case of Air Traffic Control. In *CMC'95, The International Conference on Cooperative and Multimodal Communication: Theory and Applications.* Eindhoven, The Netherlands.

Chatty, S. & Lecoanet, P. (1996) Pen Computing and Air Traffic Control. In *Proceedings of CHI'96 ACM Conference on Human Factors in Computing*, (pp. 87-94) Vancouver, British Columbia: ACM Press.

Dertouzous, M. (1990) *Computers and Productivity.* Cambridge, MA: MIT Lab for Computer Science.

Elissaoui, A. (1997) Utilisation de la vision artificielle pour l'interaction avec un médiaspace. Rapport de stage de DEA, Université de Paris-Sud.

Endsley, M.R. (1988) Design and Evaluation for Situation Awareness Enhancement. In *Proceedings of the Human Factors Society 32nd Annual Meeting*, 32(1), pp. 97-101. Anaheim, CA: The Human Factors Society.

Harper, R., Hughes, J., & Shapiro, D. (1991) Harmonious working and CSCW: Computer Technology and Air Traffic Control. In *Studies in CSCW: Theory, Practice and Design.* Bowers, J. & Bedford, S., Eds. North Holland: Amsterdam. pp. 225-235.

Heath, C. & Luff, P. (1991) Collaborative Activity and Technological Design: Task Coordination in the London Underground Control Rooms. In *Proceedings of ECSCW'91, The European Conference on Computer-Supported Cooperative Work.* Kluwer Press.

Hopkin, V.D. (1995) *Human Factors in Air Traffic Control.* London: Taylor & Francis.

Hopkin, V.D. (1993) Human factors implications of air traffic control automation. In *Proceedings of the 5th International Conference on HCI.* Orlando, FL. pp. 145-150.

Hughes, J.A., Randall, D. & Shapiro, D. (October, 1992) Faltering from Ethnography to Design. In *Proceedings of CSCW '92, ACM Conference on Computer-Supported Cooperative Work.* (pp. 115-122) Toronto, Ontario: ACM Press.

Leroux, M. (1993) The role of expert systems in future cooperative tools for air traffic controllers. In *Proceedings of the 7th International Symposium on Aviation Psychology.* (pp. 26-29). Columbus, OH.

Mackay, W.E. & Pagani, D. (1994). Video Mosaic: Laying out time in a physical space. *Proceedings of Multimedia '94* . San Francisco, CA: ACM.

Mackay, W. (March 1996). Réalité Augmentée : le meilleur des deux mondes. *La Recherche*, numéro spécial (No. 285) L'ordinateur au doigt et à l'œil.

Mackay, W. & Fayard, A.L (1997a) HCI, Natural Science and Design : A Framework for Triangulation Across Disciplines, *DIS'97 : Designing Interactive Systems.* Amsterdam, Holland.

Mackay, W. & Fayard, A.L. (1997b) Radicalement nouveau et néanmoins familier : les strips papiers revus par la réalité augmentée. In Proceedings of IHM'97, Interaction-Homme-Machine, Poitiers, France.

Médini, L. (1997) Prototype d'interfaces en réalité augmentée pour le contrôle de la navigation aérienne. Rapport de stage de DEA, Université de Paris-Sud.

Negroponte, N. (1997) Surfaces and Displays. *Wired*, January issue, pp. 212.

Norman, D.A. (1988) *The Design of Everyday Things.* New York, NY: Basic Books.

Preux, F. (1994) Rôle des strips dans l'activité des contrôleurs. *Sélection Professionnelle* IEEAC. CENA.

Vortac, O. & Gettys, C. (1990) Cognitive Factors in the use of flight progress stripts: Implications for automation. Norman: Univ. of Oklahoma, Cognitive Processes Laboratory.

Wellner, P., Mackay, W. & Gold, R. (1993) Computer-Augmented Environments: Back to the Real World. Special issue of *Communications of the ACM*, 36 (7).

Zuboff, S. (1988). *In the Age of the Smart Machine.* New York: Basic Books.

Designing Audio Aura

Elizabeth D. Mynatt, Maribeth Back, Roy Want
Xerox Palo Alto Research Center
[mynatt,back,want]@parc.xerox.com

Michael Baer
Stanford University
calbaer@stanford.edu

Jason B. Ellis
Georgia Institute of Technology
jellis@cc.gatech.edu

ABSTRACT
In this paper, we describe the process behind the design of Audio Aura. The goal of Audio Aura is to provide serendipitous information, via background auditory cues, that is tied to people's physical actions in the workplace. We used scenarios to explore issues in serendipitous information such as privacy and work practice. Our sound design was guided by a number of strategies for creating peripheral sounds grouped in cohesive ecologies. Faced with an physical and software infrastructure under development in a laboratory distant from our sound studio, we prototyped different sonic landscapes in VRML worlds. In our infrastructure design, we made a number of trade-offs in our use of legacy systems and our client-server design.

Keywords: Audio, Augmented Reality, Auditory Icons, Active Badge, VRML, Earcons, Awareness, Periphery

INTRODUCTION

In this work we explore using audio to connect a person's activities in the physical world with information culled from the virtual world[1]. Given the richness and variety of activities in typical offices, interaction with computers is generally limited and explicit. It is primarily limited to our typing and mousing into a box seated on our desk. Our dialogue is explicit; we enter in commands and the computer responds. The purpose of Audio Aura is to create implicit dialogues with our computers that occur away from our desk. There are three targeted constraints in our design. First, we use audio to create peripheral cues. Second, we provide serendipitous information, useful but not required. Third, we tie the delivery of information to physical actions in the workplace such as stopping by someone's office.

In Audio Aura, we use audio to provide information that lies on the edge of background awareness. We naturally use our ears to monitor our environment; when we hear someone approaching, when we hear someone say our name, when we hear that our computer's disk drive is spinning. While in the midst of some conscious action, our ears are gathering information that we may or may not need to comprehend. Audio, primarily nonspeech audio, is a natural medium to create a peripheral display. Our goal is to leverage these natural abilities and create an interface that enriches the physical world without being distracting.

The information we provide via Audio Aura is designed to be serendipitous. You appreciate it when you hear it, but you do not rely on it in the same way that you rely on receiving an email message or a message reminder. The reason for this distinction should be clear. Information that you rely on must invade your periphery to ensure that it has been perceived. This limitation does not imply that serendipitous information is not of value. Conversely, many of our actions are guided by the wealth of background information in our environment. Whether we are reminded of something to do, warned of difficulty along a potential path or simply provided the spark of a new idea, our opportunistic use of serendipitous information makes our lives more efficient and rich. Our goal is to provide useful, serendipitous information in our workplace.

Computers are not particularly well designed to match the variety of activities that are part of being a physical human being. We walk around. We get coffee, the mail, our lunch. We go to conference rooms. We drop by people's offices. Although some computers are now small enough to go with us, they don't take advantage of our physical actions. In Audio Aura, our goal is to leverage everyday physical activities. One opportune time to provide serendipitous information on the periphery is when a person is walking down the hallway. If the person is concentrating on their current task, they will likely not notice or attend to the display. If, however, they are less focused, they should naturally notice and perhaps decide to attend to information on the periphery. Additionally, physical actions can guide the information content. A pause at someone's empty office is an opportune time to hear whether they have been in the office earlier that day.

In summary, the goal of Audio Aura is to provide serendipitous information, via background auditory cues, that is tied to people's physical actions in the workplace. Our current system combines three known technologies: active badges, distributed systems and digital audio delivered via portable, wireless headphones. An active badge [10] is a small electronic tag designed to be worn by a person. It repeatedly emits a unique infrared signal that is detected by a low-cost network of IR sensors placed around a building. The information from the IR sensors is collected and combined with other data sources such as online

1. Virtual world refers to cyberspace, information in networked computer systems.

CHI 98 Los Angeles CA USA
Copyright 1998 0-89791-975-0/98/ 4..$5.00

calendars and email queues. Audio cues are triggered by changes in this Audio Aura database and sent to the user's wireless headphones.

System goals are, first, to be able to provide multiple sources of information content as well as multiple means for triggering the delivery of the information. Second, the system should be easily configurable by end users because information needs and interface preferences will vary between users. Third, services using Audio Aura should be easy to author and lightweight to run.

The Design Process

In this paper, we describe the process behind the design of Audio Aura. During the course of this design we attempted to address the kinds of information that could be presented via Audio Aura, the expressiveness and aesthetics of the auditory cues and the utility and flexibility of the underlying infrastructure. In the following section, we describe three sample scenarios of serendipitous information that have guided our design. These scenarios highlight issues in the responsiveness of the system, privacy and the complexity of the information sources. We then turn to the design of the individual auditory cues and strategies for presenting these sounds. During this design we have explored the use of different types of sounds: speech, musical and sound effects.

Designing for a distributed physical environment where the underlying Audio Aura infrastructure was still under development presented several challenges. We decided to use a virtual reality environment to prototype and explore different designs. Although this virtual representation has been useful for a number of reasons, we've learned some lessons regarding transitioning designs from the virtual prototype to the physical world.

The computational and hardware infrastructure for Audio Aura is based on a legacy system for ubiquitous computing [11]. Our initial plans for building directly on top of this infrastructure were overly optimistic. Although sufficient for the visually-oriented, non-interactive applications that were created with the original system, the infrastructure for detecting the location and movements of the users as well as scripting complex responses to those actions needed to be adapted to our requirements. We describe the modifications that we made to the hardware components and the creation of software infrastructure for programming Audio Aura services. These services can easily gather and store sources of data used to trigger the display of auditory cues.

Related Work

The design of Audio Aura has been inspired by several related efforts. Most work in augmented reality systems [2][4] has focused on augmenting visual information by overlaying a visual image of the environment with additional information usually presented as text. A common configuration of these systems is a hand-held device that can be pointed at objects in the environment. The video image with overlays is displayed in a small window. These handheld systems require the user to actively probe the environment as well as indirectly view a representation of the environment on the video screen. Our system offers two primary distinctions. First, users do not have to actively probe the environment. Their everyday pattern of walking throughout an office environment triggers the delivery of aural information. Second, users do not view a representation of the physical world, but continue to interact with the physical world that includes additional real-world auditory cues. This lack of indirection changes the experience from analyzing the physical world to participating in the physical world.

Providing auditory cues based on people's motion in the physical environment has also been explored by researchers and artists, and is currently used for gallery and museum tours. The systems that most closely approach ours include one described by Bedersen [2], where a linear, usually cassette-based audio tour is replaced by a non-linear, sensor-based digital audio tour allowing the visitor to choose their own path through a museum. Several differences between our systems are apparent. First, in Bedersen's system users must carry the digital audio data with them, imposing an obvious constraint on the range and generation of audio cues that can be presented. Second, Bedersen's system is unidirectional. It does not send information from the user to the environment such as the identity, location, or history of the particular user.

Other investigations into audio awareness include Hudson [7] who demonstrated providing iconic auditory summaries of newly arrived email when a user flashed a colored card while walking by a sensor. This system still required active input from the user and only explored one use of audio in contrast to creating an additional auditory environment that does not require user input.

Explorations in providing awareness data and other forms of serendipitous information illustrate other possible scenarios in this design space. Ishii's Tangible Bits [8] focuses on surrounding people in their office with a wealth of background awareness cues using light, sound and touch. Our work follows the user outside of their office where their activities trigger different awareness cues. Gaver et al [6] explored using auditory cues in monitoring the state of a mock bottling plant. Pederson [9] has also explored using awareness cues to support awareness of other people.

SERENDIPITOUS INFORMATION

Based on informal observation of our colleagues we devised three scenarios of use for Audio Aura that guided our design. These scenarios touched on issues in system responsiveness, privacy, and the complexity and abstractness of the information presented. Each scenario grew out of a need for different types of serendipitous information. First, we are an email-oriented culture[1]. Whether we have newly-arrived email, who it is from, and what it concerns is often important. People will run by their offices between meetings to check on this important communication pipeline. Another common between-meeting activity is dropping by the bistro to get a cup of coffee or tea. One obvious tension is whether to linger with your coffee and chat with colleagues or to go check on the latest email messages. We decided to tie these activities

1. The main exception is managers who shift to using voice mail.

together. When you enter the bistro, you will hear a cue that conveys approximately how many new email messages you have and indicates messages from particular people and groups.

Second, people tend to opportunistically drop by people's offices. This practice supports communication when an email message or phone call might be inappropriate or too time consuming. When an opportunistic visitor is faced with an empty office, they may quickly survey the office trying to determine if the desired person has been in that day. In Audio Aura, the visitor now hears an auditory cue conveying whether the person has been in that day, whether they've been gone for some time, or whether you just missed them. It is important to note that these cues are *qualitative*. They do not report that "Mr. X has been out of the office for two hours and 45 minutes." The cue gives a sense akin to seeing their light on and their briefcase against the desk or hearing a passing colleague report that the person was just seen walking toward a conference room.

Third, many people are not co-located with their collaborators. These people often do not create and share a palpable sense of their group's activity analogous to one shared by a co-located group. In this scenario, various bits of information about individuals in a group become the basis for an abstract representation of a "group pulse." Whether people are in the office that day, if they are working with shared artifacts, or if a subset of them are collaborating in a face-to-face meeting triggers changes in this auditory cue. As a continuous sound, the group pulse becomes the backdrop for other Audio Aura cues.

SOUND DESIGN

In this section we discuss the design issues related to constructing sounds for Audio Aura. We created several sets, or ecologies, of auditory cues for each of the three scenarios. Each sound was crafted with attention to its frequency content, structure and interaction with other sounds. To explore a range of use and preference, we created four sound environments composed of one or more sound ecologies. The sound selections for email quantity and the group pulse are summarized in Tables 1 and 2.

Design intent: sonic ecologies

Because we intend this system for background interaction, the design of the auditory cues must avoid the "alarm" paradigm so frequently found in computational environments. Alarm sounds tend to have sharp attacks, high volume levels, and substantial frequency content in the same general range as the human voice (200 - 2,000 Hz). Most sound used in computer interfaces has (sometimes inadvertently) fit into this model. We are deliberately aiming for the auditory periphery, and our sounds and sound environments are designed to avoid triggering alarm responses in listeners.

One aspect of our design approach is the construction of sonic ecologies, where the changing behavior of the Audio Aura system is interpreted through the semantic roles sounds play. For example, particular sets of functionalities can be mapped to various beach sounds. In our current sound effects design, the amount of email is mapped to seagull cries, email from particular people or groups is mapped to various beach birds and seals, group activity level is mapped to surf, wave volume and activity, and audio footprints are mapped to the number of buoy bells.

Another idea we are exploring in these sonic ecologies is imbedding cues into a running, low-level soundtrack, so that the user is not startled by the sudden impingement of a sound. The running track itself carries information about global levels of activity within the building, within a work group, or on the network. This "group pulse" sound forms a bed within which other auditory information can lie.

Structure of individual sounds

One useful aspect of the ecological approach to sound design is considering frequency bandwidth and human perception as limited resources. Given this design perspective we must build the sounds with attention to the perceptual niche in which each sound resides.

Within each design model, we have tried several different types of sounds, varying the harmonic content, the pitch, the attack and decay, and the rhythms caused by simultaneously looping sounds of different lengths. For example, by looping three long, low-pitched sounds without much high harmonic content and with long, gentle attacks and decays, we create a sonic background in which we leave room for other sounds to be effectively heard. In the music environment this sound is a low, clear vibe sound; in the sound effects environment, it is distant surf. These sounds share the sonic attributes described above.

Types of aural environments

The Audio Aura system offers a range of sound designs: voice only, music only, sound effects only, and a rich sound environment using all three types of sound. These different types of auditory cues, though mapped to the same type of events, afford different levels of specificity and required awareness. Vocal labels, for example, provide familiar auditory feedback; at the same time they usually demand more attention than a non-speech sound. Because speech tends to carry foreground information, it may not be appropriate unless the user lingers in a location for more than a few seconds. For a user who is simply walking through an area, the sounds remain at a peripheral level, both in volume and in semantic content.

MODELING SONIC BEHAVIORS IN VRML 2.0

The Audio Aura augmented reality system is tied to the physical infrastructure of the Computer Science Lab (CSL) where the IR sensors are installed. However the sound studio where the auditory cues are designed is several halls away. This arrangement presented a logistical problem for hearing our developing sound designs. Additionally, we wanted a design environment that allowed us to hear our sonic ecologies in development. Our requirements for such an environment were:

- Ability to play multiple high-quality sounds at once, with differing behaviors
- Ability to mimic the behavior of the Audio Aura system
- Ease of translation to real system.

TABLE 1. Example of sound design variations between types for email quantity

	Sound Effects	Music	Voice	Rich
Nothing new	a single gull cry	high, short bell melody, rising pitch at end	"You have no email."	Same as SFX: a single gull cry
A little (1 - 5 new)	a gull calling a few times	high, somewhat longer melody, falling at end	"You have *n* new messages."	a gull calling a few times
Some (5 - 15 new)	a few gulls calling	lower, longer melody	"You have *n* new messages."	a few gulls calling
A lot (more than 15 new)	gulls squabbling, making a racket	longest melody, falling at end	"You have *n* new messages."	gulls squabbling, making a racket

TABLE 2. Example of sound design variation for group pulse

	Sound Effects	Music	Voice	Rich
Low activity	distant surf	vibe	none	combination of surf and vibe
Medium activity	closer waves	same vibe, with added sample at lower pitch	none (we tried breathing, but it was obnoxious)	combination of closer waves and vibe
High activity	closer more active waves	as above, three vibes at three pitches and rhythms	none	combination of waves and vibe, more active

We chose to use VRML 2.0 [1], a data protocol that allows realtime interaction with 3D graphics and audio in Web browsers. Mapping Audio Aura's matrix of system behaviors to a multi-layered sound design has been greatly aided by these prototyping efforts. By moving through a 3D graphical representation of the CSL offices and triggering audio cues either through proximity or touch, the sound designer gets a sense of how well the sounds map to the functionality of the Audio Aura system, and how well the sounds work together.

Four sound designs in VRML prototype

We used the same 3D model and sensor set to realize four different sound designs in our VRML prototypes:

- **Voice world:** Vocal labels on the doorway of each office and area give the room's name or number, e.g., "CSL Library" or "2101." These labels are designed as defaults and are meant to be changed by the room's current occupant, e.g., "Joe Smith." This environment was useful for testing how the proximity sensors and sound fields overlapped (see Figure 1) as well as exploring using Audio Aura as a navigational aid.
- **Sound effects world:** This design makes use of the "auditory icon" [6] model of auditory display where meaning is carried through sound sources. This soundscape is a beach, where group activity is mapped to wave activity, email amount is mapped to amount of seagull calls, particular email senders are mapped to various beach animals such as different birds and seals, and office-occupancy history (audio footprints) is mapped to buoy bells.
- **Music world:** This design makes extended use of the "earcon" [3] model of auditory display, where meaning is carried through short melodic phrases or musical treatments. Here, the amount of email is indicated by the changing melodies, pitches, and rhythms of a set of related short phrases. The "family" of email-quantity sounds consisted of differing sets of fast arpeggios on vibes. A different family of short phrases, this time simple, related melodies on bells, are mapped to audio footprints. Again, though the short melodies are clearly related to each other, the qualitative information about office occupancy is carried in each phrase's individual shifts in melody, rhythm, and length. Finally, a single low vibe sound played at different pitches portrays the group activity level. One aspect of the use of earcons is that they do require some learning; both of which family of sounds is mapped to what kind of data, and within each family, what the differences mean. In general, we opted for the simplest mappings, e.g., more (notes) means more (mail).
- **Rich world:** The rich environment combines sound effects, music, and voice into a rich, multi-layered environment. This combination is the most powerful because it allows wide variation in the sound palette while maintaining a consistent feel. However, this environment also requires the most careful design work, to avoid stacking too many sounds within the same frequency range or rhythmic structure.

Replicating sensor and system behavior

The design of the sensor arrays in the VRML prototype worlds does not exactly replicate the IR sensor network in

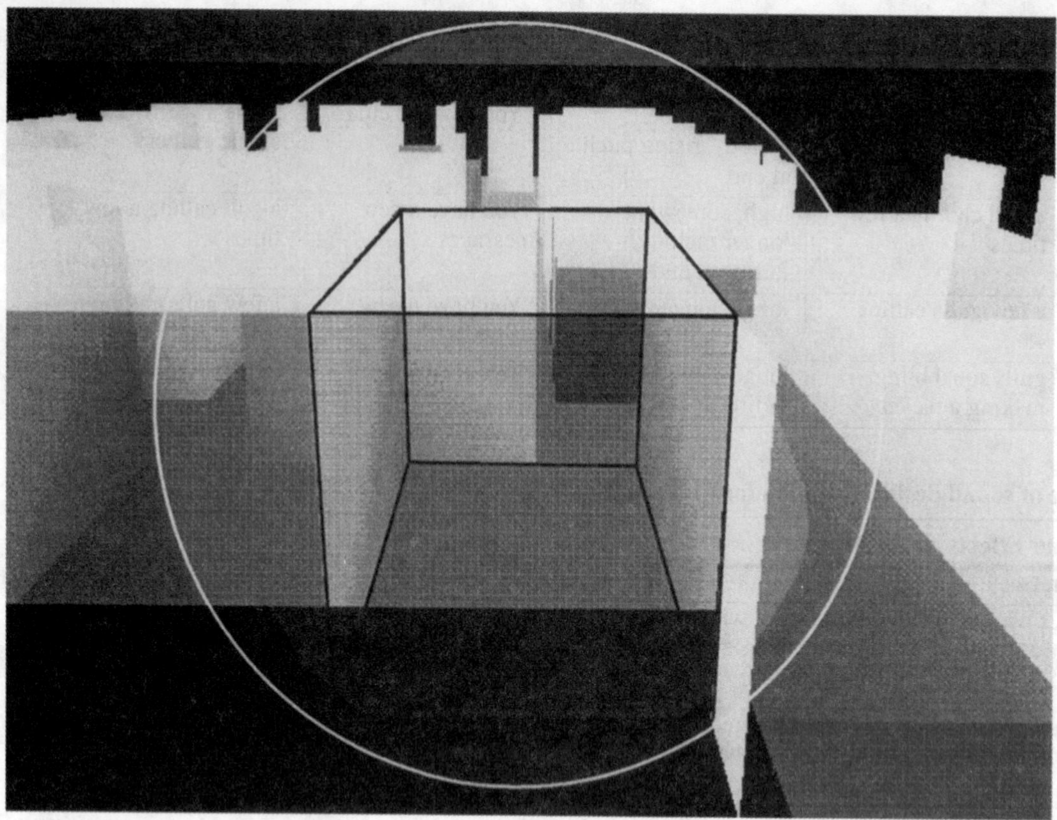

Figure 1: VRML sensor and sound geometry. The box shows the proximity sensor for the inside of this office model; the sphere shows the accompanying sound ellipse.

Each office has such a system both for its interior and for its door into the hallway.

the CSL office space. We first considered noting the physical location of each real-world IR sensor and then creating an equivalent sensor in the VRML world. However, the characteristics of the VRML sensors as well as the characteristics of VRML sound playback were not compatible with this design model. For example, the real IR sensors often require line-of sight input and the wireless headphones do not have a built-in volume mapping to proximity[1]. Because our intent in building these VRML prototypes was to understand the sonic behavior of the system, we aimed to build a set of VRML sensors and actuators that would reasonably approximate rather than replicate the behavior of the IR sensors and the Audio Aura servers. We needed to know who the user was, where the user was and at what time, within a granularity of a few feet; and we needed to be able to play sounds based on that information. We found that VRML 2.0 performed this function well.

Transition from virtual system to real system

The same sets of sounds that we use in the VRML prototypes were loaded directly into the Audio Aura services. Some performance parameters differed, like lag time before sound playback and accurate sensing of position. However we had anticipated these differences in the systems and the sounds were designed to allow a certain amount of "play."

AUDIO AURA INFRASTRUCTURE

The infrastructure for Audio Aura is comprised of legacy systems taken as is, modified legacy systems and new infrastructure built for Audio Aura. The legacy systems, as described in the following section, are the active badge system for determining people's locations in the building and the location server that collates this location information into one centralized data store. The active badge network was modified to make it more responsive fulfilling Audio Aura's need for quasi-realtime interaction. The location server, written in Modula-3 was taken as is, but new infrastructure was built to create a richer data store that supports more complex queries. This new piece, the Audio Aura server, is used by multiple Audio Aura services. For example, one of these thin clients is used for implementing each of the three scenarios. We have created a service base class in Java that facilitates the easy authoring of Audio Aura services.

Active Badges

The active badge system [10] was designed to track the locations of people in a large office building. The system operates on the premise that a person wishing to be located wears a tag called an active badge. The badge emits a

1. If you're walking away from a sound's location, it doesn't automatically diminish in volume, as it typically does in VRML.

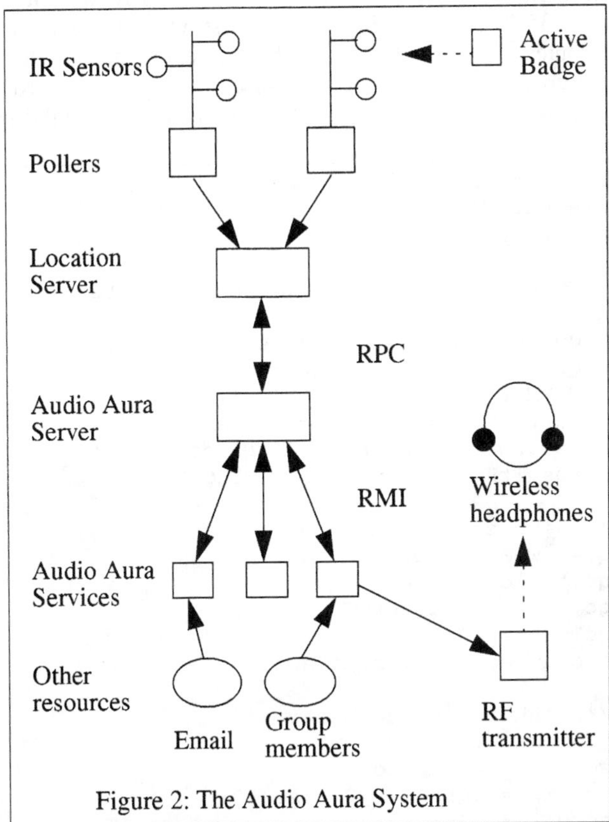

Figure 2: The Audio Aura System

unique digitally-coded infrared signal that is detected by a network of sensors, approximately once every 15 seconds. Each sensor monitors a room and detects badges up to 25 feet away. Larger rooms contain multiple sensors to ensure good coverage. Badge signals that are received by a sensor are stored in a local FIFO memory. A sensor has a unique network ID and is connected to a 9600 baud wired network that is polled by a master station (called the Poller). When a sensor is read by the Poller it returns the oldest badge sighting contained in its FIFO and then deletes it. This process continues for all subsequent reads until the sensor indicates its FIFO is empty, at which point the poller begins interrogating a new sensor. A poller collects information that associates locations with badge IDs and the time when they were read.

In our system a poller is a computer that is connected to an office LAN. A large building may contain several networks of sensors and therefore several pollers. To provide a useful network service that can be accessed by clients, the Poller information is centralized in another entity we call the location server. The location server processes and aggregates the low-level badge-ID/location-ID data and resolves the information as human understandable text. Queries can be made on the location server in order to match a person, or a location, and return the associated data. The location server also exports a network interface that allows other network clients, such as the Audio Aura system, to use the information

A design assumption implicit in the original set of active badge applications is that people generally spend much more time stationary than in motion and when they do move, it is not at any great speed. Specifically, none of the originally envisioned applications required interaction that would quickly follow a change in location. The relatively slow badge beacon rate and the use of a polled network are both a direct result of this assumption and supported trade-offs in various engineering issues such as power consumption and signal contention.

However, for Audio Aura applications a more responsive system is required. The timely delivery of audio signals to a user at a specific location is essential to the operation of Audio Aura. In order to extend the system so that Audio Aura could make use of the active badge system, we modified some of the system components. First, we decreased the beacon period of the active badges to about 5 seconds. This increased frequency results in badge locations being revealed on a more regular basis but increases the likelihood of signal collision. At this stage of Audio Aura's development with a few users of the prototype system the increased collision probability has not been problematic. Second, we increased the speed of the polling cycle removing any wait states in the polling loop. In fact, a more critical factor than the self-imposed delays were delays caused by the polling computer sharing its cycles with other processes and tasks. We have recently dedicated a whole computer to the sole task of polling.

The active badge system has been used to provide the main source of data that triggers audio delivery in the Audio Aura system. Another legacy system that forwards keyboard activity to the location server is also used. Users permitting this keyboard information to be propagated are identified to be in their office when they are typing. As the system progresses and provides more utility we plan to combine many sources of location and activity information making use of the strengths that each system brings, thus optimizing the responsiveness and generality of Audio Aura.

Server and Services

The new pieces of infrastructure built for Audio Aura are:

- **Audio Aura Server** - This is the nerve center for Audio Aura. Written in Java it communicates to the location server via RPC. In contrast to the location server, it can store data over time and respond to general queries.
- **Audio Aura Services** - Written in Java, these services tell the server (via RMI) what data to collect and provide queries to run on that data. When queries get hits, the server returns results to the appropriate service. The services use this information as well as data from other sources to trigger the presentation of auditory cues.

The system is fully client/server with relatively thin clients. Most of the computation occurs within the Audio Aura Server. This centralization reduces network bandwidth as the server need not update multiple data repositories each time it gets new data. The server only sends data over the network when queries produce results. This technique also reduces the load on client machines. So far, the delay between the clients and the server has been negligible compared to delays in the legacy system.

Audio Aura Server The Audio Aura Server provides two fundamental extensions to the existing infrastructure at PARC — the ability to store data over time and the ability to easily run complex queries over that data. When the Audio Aura Server starts, it creates a baseline table ("csight") that is known to exist at all times. This table stores the most recent sighting for each user.

When an Audio Aura Service registers with the Audio Aura Server, it provides two things:

- **Data collection specifications:** Each of these specifications creates a table in the server. The specification includes a superkey for the table as well as a lifetime for data in that table. When the server receives new data, this specification is used to decide if the data is valid for the table and if it replaces other data.
- **Queries to run against the tables:** These queries are defined in the form of a query object. This query language provides the subset of SQL relevant to our task domain. It supports cross products and subsets as well as optimizations such as short-circuit evaluation.

After the server has updated each table with the new positioning data, it executes all the queries for services. If any of the queries have hits, it notifies the appropriate service and feeds it the results.

Services can also request an ad hoc query to be executed immediately. This type of query is not installed and is executed only once.

Audio Aura Services Audio Aura Services are relatively easy to author client processes that rely on data gathered by the server. Each service specifies the data it is interested in tracking and queries that will match interesting patterns in that data. When a service starts the data specification and queries are uploaded in the server. The service is then notified when a query gets a result.

As Java applications, these services can also maintain their own state as well as gather information from other sources. A returned query from the server may result in the service playing an auditory cue, gathering other data, invoking another program and/or sending another query to the server.

To author a service, the first step is to inherit from the service base class and override a few methods; two methods defining the data specification tables and queries, and two methods awaiting results from the server. More experienced programmers may define special initialization routines, provide a new user interface, and take advantage of some of the more complicated features of the query language.

Query Language The query language in Audio Aura is heavily influenced by the Intermezzo's database system [5]. This language is the subset of SQL most relevant to our task domain, supporting our dual goals of speed and ease of authoring. A query involves two objects:

- **AuraQuery:** The root node of the query that contains general information about the query as a whole.
- **AuraQueryClause:** The basic clause tests one of the fields in a table against a user-provided value. All clauses are connected by the boolean AND operator.

The following query returns results when "John" enters room 35-2107, the CSL Bistro. First we set the query attributes such as its ID, what table it refers to, and whether it returns the matching records or a count of the records. Next, we describes the clauses in the query by specifying field-value pairs.

```
auraQuery aq;
auraQueryClause aqc;
aq=new auraQuery();

/* ID we use to identify query results */
aq.queryId = 0;
/* current sightings table */
aq.queryTable = "csight";
/* NORMAL or CROSS_PRODUCT */
aq.queryType = auraQuery.NORMAL;
/* return RECORDS or a COUNT of them */
aq.resultForm = auraQuery.RECORDS;

/* we've seen John */
aqc=new auraQueryClause();
aqc.field = "user";
aqc.cmp = auraQueryClause.EQ;
aqc.val = "John";
aq.clauses.addElement(aqc);

 /* John is in the bistro */
aqc=new auraQueryClause();
aqc.field = "locId";
aqc.cmp = auraQueryClause.EQ;
aqc.val = "35-2107";
aq.clauses.addElement(aqc);

/* John just arrived in the bistro */
aqc=new auraQueryClause();
aqc.field = "newLocation";
aqc.cmp = auraQueryClause.EQ;
aqc.val = new Boolean(true);
aq.clauses.addElement(aqc);
```

Sound Generation

Although we are eagerly awaiting the planned additions to support sound playback in Java, we are currently not using the current Java facilities for playing sounds as it is limited to 8-bit, u-law sounds. Services currently invoke an external program to play CD-quality sounds.

CONCLUDING REMARKS

This paper summarizes the steps we have taken in designing and building the Audio Aura system. Lessons learned at each phase of the process influenced our evolving design. While we were working on scenarios, we explored other uses of Audio Aura such as delivering reminders and supporting tours and other visitors. Our discussions helped clarify the intent behind serendipitous information. We used the scenarios to constrain our sound design as well as inform our system requirements.

Our sound design was guided by a number of design strategies for creating peripheral sounds grouped in cohesive ecologies. Faced with an physical and software infrastructure under development in a laboratory distant from our sound studio, we decided to prototype different sonic landscapes in VRML worlds. As a tool for "sketching" sound collections this tool was incredibly useful. By adjusting the behavior of proximity sensors and sound fields, we were able to minimize difficulties in transitioning our sounds to the "real world."

We faced a number of tradeoffs in our infrastructure design. We first needed to uncover and understand the original design assumptions behind the implementation of the active badge system. The remaining delays in the system influenced our design scenarios. For example, the auditory footprints service is for users who linger briefly in someone's office as opposed to users who glance in as they walk by. We would also like to move previously installed sensors to be closer to the entryway. Traditionally they are located near the center of the office. We also discussed trade-offs in various client-server designs for the Audio Aura server and services. By using a centralized data store and uploaded queries, we were able to minimize network traffic as well as complexities in writing services.

Initial User Reactions

Methods for evaluating a system designed to deliver serendipitous information in the periphery are difficult to design. How cues in the periphery are perceived and the overall value of serendipitous information is difficult to quantify. We recently demonstrated Audio Aura to nine volunteer subjects. The process involved a brief introduction followed by a set of self-paced tasks such as going to the CSL bistro, and ended with a questionnaire. Comments and questions were encouraged throughout as we were more interested in getting user feedback than performance numbers. We used the SFX (beach landscape) sound ecology. The three services (email, footprints, and group pulse) used static data so that all of the users heard the same sound cues.

Overall reactions were positive. Users found the sound choice to be good in general. They felt sounds remained in the periphery nicely although some found the meaning of sounds difficult to remember. Users thought services were well chosen and most found sound quality good. Not surprisingly, users said the time to play sounds was too long as the dedicated poller system was not available. We hope to be able to report on the long-term use of Audio Aura in the future.

Future Work

There is always a danger when computer systems are used to collect and store information on people's activities. We are currently designing mechanisms so that users can specify how data about them may be accessed. Although the existing services rely on accumulated data, the life of the data is still quite short (no more than one day). By using qualitative cues, we have also attempted to illustrate how information regarding people's activities should be presented.

We plan to create more Audio Aura services including tie-ins to voice mail and refinements on email and group activity data. We are committed to using high-quality sound in Audio Aura. We plan to integrate the high-quality Java audio engine when it becomes available late in 1997.

We are now designing an on-line user interface that allows personalization of system using the VRML prototype worlds. With this system, mapping of sounds to Audio Aura's functionalities be done either by a system designer or by the end user. The user can select sounds from a database or create their own, load them, and then test them via the VRML prototype. These VRML prototypes help users decide what pattern of sounds work best for them. The act of choosing VRML sounds will also select the sounds for the user's real Audio Aura services.

We are trying different methods of delivering wireless audio, including different types of wireless headsets and tiny in-ear monitors. Ideally, we would like to combine the IR badge and a wireless audio system into a single lightweight, non-intrusive, comfortable unit that will allow real-world sound as well as Audio Aura's sound into the ear.

ACKNOWLEDGMENTS

We would like to thank Keith Edwards and Ron Frederick for their help and advice.

The VRML prototypes are available on the WWW at:: **http://www.parc.xerox.com/back/AudioAura/csl.wrl.** We recommend CosmoPlayer 2.0 or WorldView browser plugins for the PC and CosmoPlayer for the SGI.

REFERENCES

[1] Ames, A., Nadeau, D., Moreland, J. *The VRML 2.0 Sourcebook.* Wiley, 1996. See also the VRML Repository at http://sdsc.edu/vrml.

[2] Bederson, B.B and Druin, (In press) A. Computer Augmented Environments: New Places to Learn, Work and Play, ed. Jakob Nielsen, in *Advances in Human Computer Interaction*, Vol. 5, Ablex Press.

[3] Blattner, M. M., Sumikawa, D. A, & Greenberg, R. M. (1991). Earcons and Icons: Their Structure and Common Design Principles. *Human-Computer Interaction* 4(1), 11-44.

[4] *Communications of the ACM*, (1993) Special Issue on Augmented Environments, 36 (7).

[5] Edwards, W.K. (1995) *Coordination Infrastructure in Collaborative Systems.* Unpublished doctoral dissertation. Georgia Institute of Technology.

[6] Gaver, W., Smith, R. and O'Shea, T. (1991), Effective Sound in Complex Systems: The ARKola Simulation. *Proc. CHI'91*, pp 85-90, ACM Press.

[7] Hudson, Scott E. and Smith, Ian, (1996) Electronic Mail Previews Using Non-Speech Audio, *CHI '96 Conference Companion*, ACM, pp. 237-238.

[8] Ishii, H. and Ullmer, B., (1997) "Tangible Bits: Towards Seamless Interfaces between People, Bits, and Atoms," in Proceedings of CHI'97, ACM, March 1997.

[9] Pederson, E.R. and Sokoloer, T. (1997), AROMA: Abstract Representation of Presence Supporting Mutual Awareness. *Proc. CHI'97*, pp 51-58, ACM Press.

[10] Want, R., Hopper, A., Falcao, V. and Gibbons, J., (1992) The Active Badge Location System, *ACM Transactions on Information Systems*. Vol. 10 (1), pp. 91-102.

[11] Weiser, M. (1991) The Computer of the 21st Century. Scientific American 265(3):94-104.

Communicating Graphical Information to Blind Users Using Music: The Role of Context

James L. Alty
LUTCHI Research Centre
Dept. of Computer Science
Loughborough University
Loughborough,
Leicestershire
LE11 3TU, UK
+1509 222648
j.l.alty@lboro.ac.uk

Dimitrios I. Rigas
School. of Computing and Mathematics
University of Huddersfield
Huddersfield,
HD1 3DH, UK
+151 231 2268
d.rigas@hud.ac.uk

ABSTRACT
We describe the design and use of AUDIOGRAPH - a tool for investigating the use of music in the communication of graphical information to blind and partially sighted users. This paper examines the use of the system to communicate complex diagrams and gives some examples of user output. Performance is not as good as expected and it is postulated that context will play an important part in the perception of diagrams communicated using music. A set of experiments are reported which indicate that context does indeed seem to play an important role in assisting meaningful understanding of the diagrams communicated. The implications for using music in auditory interface design are discussed.

Keywords
Blind Users, Music, Graphics, Interface Design, Empirical.

INTRODUCTION

Graphical user interfaces (GUIs) have now become the dominant technique used for interaction between users and computer applications. Such interfaces are said to offer a user-friendly approach with a high utility. One important reason why it is thought that they have been successful is their use of Direct Manipulation techniques, a term first coined by Shneiderman [1] to describe the emphasis on continuous representation of objects, physical actions rather than complex syntax, and rapid incremental reversible actions with instant feedback. There is no doubt that such interfaces have had a beneficial effect to users in general, but they represent a serious step backwards for blind or visually impaired users.

The emphasis on graphical representations has rendered devices such as Screen Readers (on which many blind and visually impaired users have traditionally relied) much less effective. Screen Readers are based on a speech representation of the content of the screen. Because of the intensely serial nature of speech, graphic-intensive screens can be difficult to describe using this medium.

We have been interested in exploring the use of auditory interfaces for some time, both for visually impaired users and for those with normal visual abilities. Indeed, we are particularly interested in creating what we have termed "equal opportunity interfaces" - that is, interfaces which do not make prior judgments about the media capabilities of the user population but offer a variety of communication media, from which the user can select an appropriate mix to match their capabilities and limitations. Such interfaces would not only be capable of adaptation to match users with significant hearing or visual difficulties, they would also allow trade-offs to be made between vision and audio for common applications. The work in this paper explores an extremum of this spectrum (audio only) in contrast to most interface work which is located at the other extremum (visual only).

In comparison with visual media, which have been extensively explored, non-speech use of the auditory medium has been largely ignored. The use of audio in human computer interfaces was first reported by Bly. Gaver has proposed the idea of Auditory Icons [3] and used them in the SonicFinder [4] to assist visually impaired users with editing. Such auditory icons are short bursts of familiar sounds. Edwards has developed the Soundtrack system [5] to assist blind users in editing. Blattner an co-workers has proposed the use of musical phrases called Earcons [6] - short musical melodies which shared a common structure such as rhythm. However, apart from suggesting the idea of sharing a common rhythm, no other musical techniques were suggested. Blattner has also used some properties of musical structures to communicate the flow in a turbulent liquid. During the last few years, some research workers have attempted to use music in interfaces. Brown and Hershberger [7] employed music and sound in supporting the visualisation of sorting algorithms but carried out no experimentation to see how valid their approach was. Alty [8] has developed purely musical mappings for the Bubble Sort and the Minimum Path Algorithms. Recently some progress has been made in assisting program debugging using music, for example, the work of Bock [9] , and Vickers and Alty [10]

There are very few recorded experiments which systematically evaluate the use of music in human computer interaction. Brewster [11] has used music to a limited extent in designing Earcons for Telephone based interfaces and has combined Earcons with graphical output to assist users when making slips in using menus [12]. In both cases some empirical investigations were carried out. Mynatt has investigated the [13] mapping of visual icons into auditory Earcons. She comments on the importance of metaphorical qualities of everyday sounds and how these can be used in designing good Earcons.

This paper reports continuation of our previously published work on exploring the usefulness of auditory media (particularly music) in interface design. Some of our work has concentrated on the audiolisation of algorithms (Alty, 1995) [8] , and program debugging ([10] and [14]). The work reported here is a continuation of our investigation into the use of music to communicate diagrams to blind users (Rigas and Alty, 1997) [15]. This work has already shown that the highly structured nature of music can be used successfully to convey graphical information in diagrams to visually challenged users. The only other related work of which we are aware is the AUDIOGRAF system of Kennel [17]. This system use touch to concentrate upon particular areas of the diagram. Output is by speech or a set of individual notes.

THE RATIONALE BEHIND THE INVESTIGATIONS

The main objective behind the set of experiments reported in this paper is to see if music alone can be used to transfer meaningful information to users on the computer interface. We decided to use an extreme case - to determine if blind users could, by the use of music alone, appreciate the spatial layout of objects in a graphical area using musical feedback alone. Because of this emphasis on music, and the fact that there has been little previous work on the use and evaluation of musical representations, music alone was used both to communicate all information about the interface and for all input control commands. We appreciate that in a real interface, such as a commercial computer application, it would be sensible to use speech in addition to music (particularly for conveying exact information), but we felt that the inclusion of other auditory modes of interaction would risk confusion in the interpretation of the experimental results.

THE AUDIOGRAPH SYSTEM

We therefore constructed the AUDIOGRAPH system, which we employ in our experiments with music for blind users, some of this work has already been described in an earlier paper (Rigas and Alty , 1997) [15] so only a brief

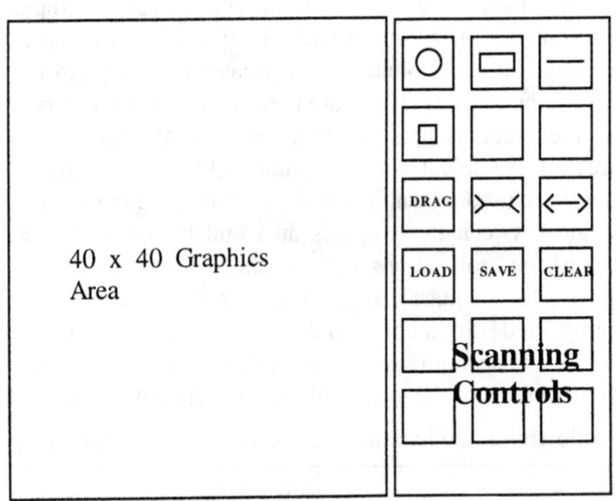

Figure 1 The AUDIOGRAPH System

description of the system will be given here. The AUDIOGRAPH system has both a visual interface (for the experimenter) and a completely auditory interface for blind users. All musical output is produced by MIDI output from Visual Basic, communicated to a stereo sound system using a Creative Labs Soundblaster 16-bit card. The actual sounds are created using a Roland MT32 Multi-timbre output device. All output information and input feedback are communicated using music alone. It is important to note that the AUDIOGRAPH tool is aimed at users with an

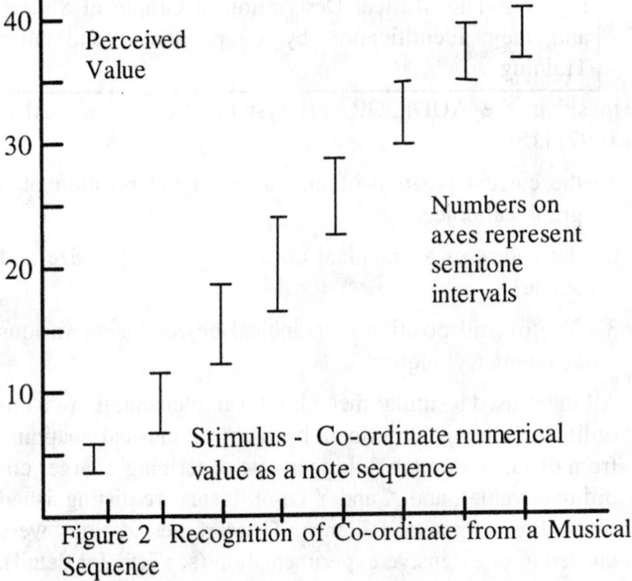

Figure 2 Recognition of Co-ordinate from a Musical Sequence

average musical ability. No special musical ability or training was expected for any of the experiments performed. A musical questionnaire was given to all participants, prior to experimentation, to check their musical experience and knowledge.

The interface (as seen by the experimenter) is shown in figure 1. There are two major areas - the grid on which diagrams are drawn and perceived, and the control area, where buttons are used to select and control actions. Input interaction with the system is exclusively via the arrow keys on the keyboard (our blind users indicated that they did not like using the mouse). These are used for moving the cursor round the graphics area (a 40x40 grid on the left of the Figure) and to select control actions. Other keys (usually any key) are used to confirm actions. The space bar is used to toggle between the graphics area and the control area. The main control actions include shape selection (circle, rectangle, line, square), shape expansion and contraction, dragging, and file loading and saving. There are also a selection of scanning controls which communicate the current contents of the graphical area in different ways.

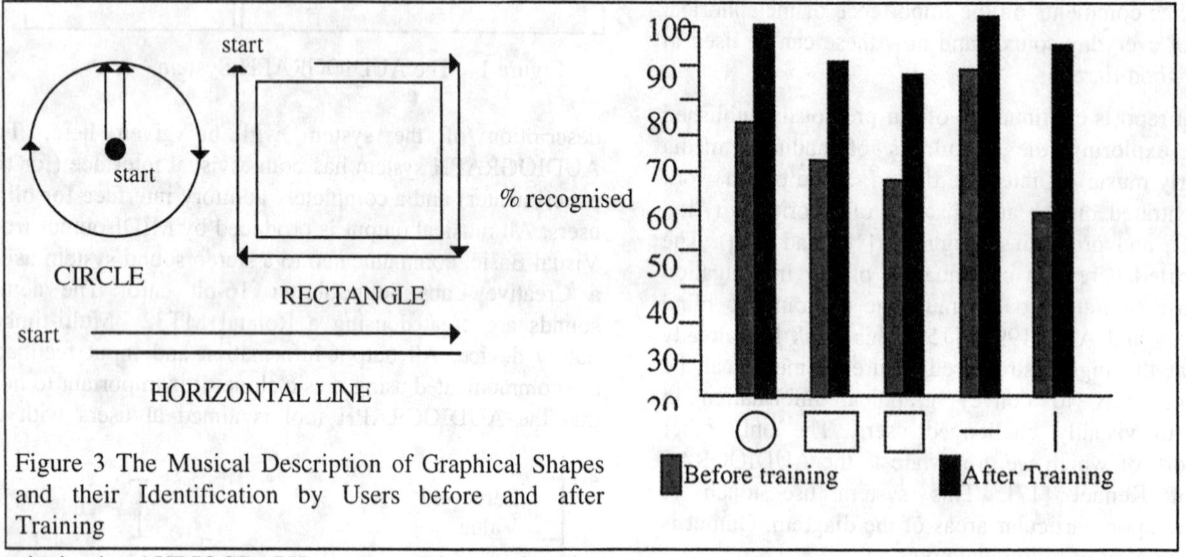

Figure 3 The Musical Description of Graphical Shapes and their Identification by Users before and after Training

The following graphical information is communicated using music in the AUDIOGRAPH system (Rigas and Alty, 1997) [15]:

1. the current position of the cursor or the position of a graphical object
2. the nature of a graphical object (e.g. its type, size and shape)
3. The overall position of graphical objects using various scanning techniques

All these used a similar metaphor for implementation - a co-ordinate point is described by using a musical mapping from distance to pitch (a higher note describing a larger co-ordinate value), and X and Y co-ordinates are distinguished by timbre (Organ and Piano). These representations were chosen after extensive experimentation (see [15] for detail). For interest we reproduce the results for pitch interval recognition in figure 2. Subjects were played the sequence of notes from the same lower note (the origin) to the note representing the co-ordinate value, and asked to determine that value.

The different timbres used to represent the X and Y axes (Piano and Organ) were chosen also after extensive experimentation on timbre perception (again see Rigas and Alty). Graphical shapes were described musically by tracing out the shape in sound using this metaphor.

Examples are given in Figure 3. Even before training most users recognized the Circle and the two lines. The training session only involved the presentation of 5 examples of each shape. The results from [15] are given in figure 3

Experiments were also carried out to see if users could estimate the size of graphical objects as well as their overall shape. The results indicated that users could estimate size to an accuracy within 10%

Control actions were communicated using meaningful Earcons (many previous Earcons have not had meaningful shapes).

For example, EXPAND used the following sequence:

and CONTRACT was represented by the inverse of this pattern. Users found these completely intuitive and no training was required. The UNDO command was represented by the playing of a tune with a "fault" in it followed by the "correct" tune. At first hearing users were baffled by this, but on hearing the explanation they understood it immediately and had no further trouble recognizing it. This is an example of the importance of context which will be examined shortly. File names were represented as simple tunes.

Three different scanning techniques were provided to enable users to obtain an overall appreciation of the graphical space and to enable them to build up a mental model of the space.

Top-Down Scanning - reads the area musically starting at the top left hand corner and scanning progressively down the area left to right.

Centre Scanning - starts at the centre of the screen and musically scans the area in increasing circles

Ascending Scanning -This scan was provided after user comments. It scanned the objects in the space in ascending order of size.

Figure 4. The two stimuli Used in the Arbitrary Graphics Set

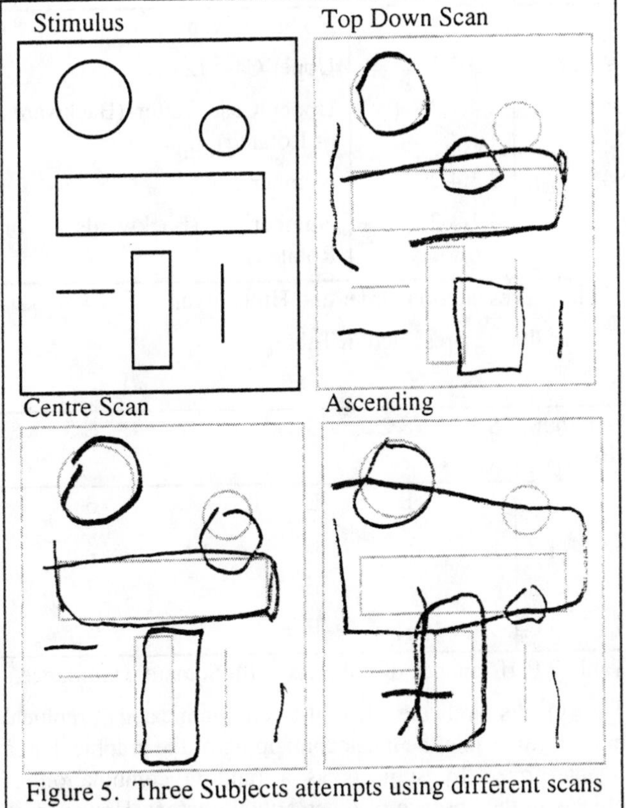

Figure 5. Three Subjects attempts using different scans

RECOGNITION OF AN ARBITRARY SET OF OBJECTS

An experiment was performed to investigate the perception and interpretation of subjects who were presented with a set of arbitrary objects from our display set (lines, circles, squares, rectangles). The two stimuli are shown in Figure 4.

Six subjects took part, three using the first stimulus and three using the second stimulus. Each subject heard the diagram three times and was then asked to draw the diagram. Drawing was carried out using paper with a raised grid on it. This in itself caused drawing problems as when the pencil crossed over a grid, the drawing necessarily became more uneven, and errors in the diagram are a combination of perception errors and drawing errors. It is impossible to devise a scoring mechanism for the output, but the success (or failure) achieved by subjects can be appreciated by examining some actual output. These are shown in Figures 5 and 6 for one subject from each group. It can be seen that subjects have obtained a broad picture of the diagrams, the first subject performing qualitatively rather better than the other.

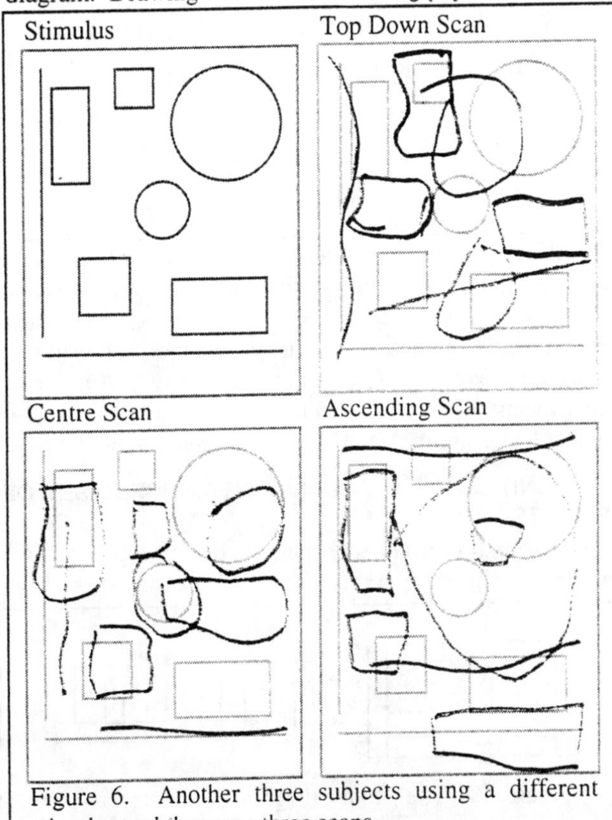

Figure 6. Another three subjects using a different stimulus and the same three scans

Whilst the diagrams generally have captured correct number of objects in the space and the distributions are broadly in agreement, the perception of size is disappointing. For example, in figure 5, Ascending Scan, the subject has realized that one circle is bigger than the other but both have been drawn incorrectly. Our previous experiments in perception and size led us to expect better performance.

The difference between our earlier experiments on individual objects and the experiments on arbitrary sets is the complexity of the latter stimuli. Users need some

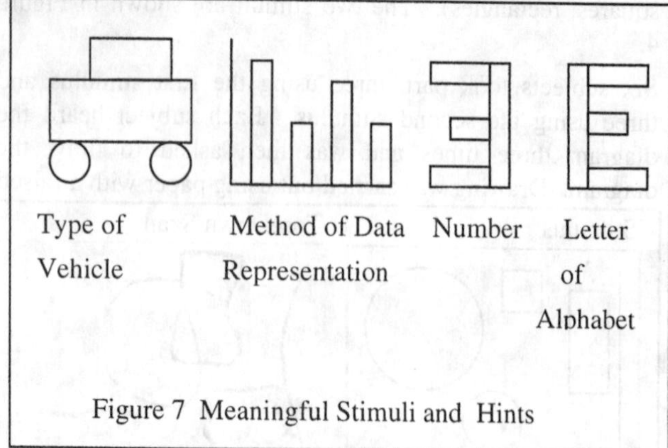

Figure 7 Meaningful Stimuli and Hints

organising principle to assist them in coping with the more complex diagrams. In reality, users rarely have to comprehend meaningless sets of shapes, and their perception is guided by their expectation of what is presented. We therefore decided to carry out a set of experiments with meaningful sets of objects to see if context had a significant effect on comprehension.

RECOGNITION OF A VISUALLY MEANINGFUL SET OF OBJECTS

Twelve blind subjects took part in the experiment. Two different groups of six subjects were constructed from these. The first group (the control group) listened to four different diagrams and were not given any guidance as to the nature of the diagrams. The second group (the experimental group) listened to the same diagrams and were given a hint or semantic guidance as to their nature. Thus, they might be told that the diagram was "a type of vehicle", "a number", "a letter of the alphabet", or "a method of data representation". Both groups knew that the diagram represented some real world concept (i.e. it was not a random collection of shapes). The four diagrams, together with the hints given are shown in figure 7.

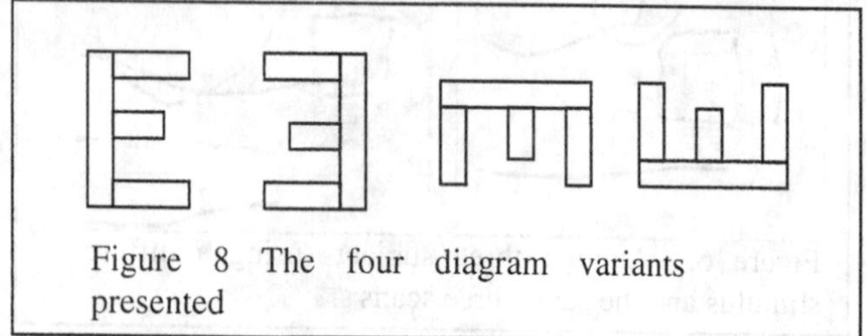

Figure 8 The four diagram variants presented

The diagrams were presented aurally using AUDIOGRAPH in a different order to each subject in each group. All subjects used the Centre-Scanning technique to explore the graphical space.

In those groups given no semantic guidance, no subjects assigned any meaning to the first two diagrams. Two subjects (33%) interpreted the third figure as a "three" and three subjects (50%) interpreted the fourth figure as the letter "E".

In contrast, in the semantic group, all subjects recognized the Car, the Number "3" and the Letter "E", and four subjects (66%) recognized the Data Set. In most cases , for either group, subjects were able to identify the individual components even if they did not get the overall meaning. It is possible that the "Car" was the most representative object in the vehicle set and might well have been guessed, in contrast to "E" and "3" which are not special items of their sets.

The presence of a narrow perceptual context therefore appeared to assist subjects in assigning meaning to the set of graphical objects by using their expectations to bridge perceptual gaps (i.e. distances between objects not properly interpreted). If this is the case, would a shift of perceptual context cause subjects to interpret the same stimulus in a different way ?

Five blind subjects (who were in the control group in the previous experiment) were presented with four diagrams as shown in figure 8 below.

The subjects were presented aurally with these four diagrams in the following order with the following hints (as in Table 1)

Subject	Presentation Order	Semantic Guidance
S1	1,2,3,4	No hint Given
S2	4,3,2,1	Upper Case Letter
S3	2,4,1,3	Upper Case Letter (Backwards or Rotated)
S4	3.1.4.2	Number
S5	4.1.3.2	Number (Backwards or Rotated)

Table 1. Presentation Order and Hints given

The results are presented in Table 2.

Diagram No.	S 1	S 2	S 3	S 4	S 5
1	-	E	E	-	3
2	-	-	E	3	3
3	-	-	E	-	3
4	-	-	E	-	3

Table 2 Performance of Subjects with Semantic Guidance

The results indicate that the communicated graphical information using the musical mapping of the graphical area is interpreted by subjects as a random combination of objects in the absence of a perceptual context. However, in the presence of an expectation, the graphical information communicated is interpreted as a meaningful shape. This implies that the perceptual context has a direct and contributing role in the interpretation of the music used to communicate the graphical objects. Thus although the musical mapping is one variable which contributes to the user's perception and interpretation simultaneously, the creation of an appropriate context in the listener is another important variable. Furthermore, the absence of a meaningful context will often result in a lack of a meaningful interpretation even though the individual elements are perceived. This finding, which has parallels in the use of other perceptual channels (for example the importance of context in visual understanding) has important implications for auditory interface design.

DISCUSSION - IMPLICATIONS FOR THE DESIGN OF AUDITORY INTERFACES

The use of music in an auditory interface to communicate graphical shapes has shown promising results. Users were able to identify shapes and their approximate size, use the tool to move them around the area, and adjust their size. They were able to use the musical controls to expand and contract shapes, file and retrieve them and drag them. Although an actual tool would have used speech output in certain operations in preference to music, the insistence of a full music interface has tested the idea quite thoroughly. User feedback was quite positive (reported in Rigas and Alty [15] but there were some adverse comments, not surprisingly on the length of the musical messages and the effort involved in interpreting them. Such comments would have to be investigated and the implications explored, in the design of any realistic tool. We believe, for example, that much more use of musical abstraction could be used to reduce the length of messages.

However, it is in the experiments on the role of context where we see some interesting lessons being drawn. Firstly, there is much more to auditory interface design than simply producing unique and identifiable mappings. This is a necessary, but not sufficient, condition for a successful design. We call this level the *DETECTABLE MUSICAL MAPPING*. At this level, the designer must allocate the musical structures (e.g. pitch, rhythm, timbre etc..) to domain structures. The target here is to produce a recognizable and distinguishable musical message, to the listener which can be understood in the presence of other musical structures in the application. This level provides a detectable mapping. There are clearly many possible detectable mappings for any problem domain.

The second level we *call CREATING PERCEPTUAL CONTEXT.*. At this level, given a detectable mapping, the designer must create the perceptual context or expectation in the listener because interpretation of the music will depend on the expectation of the listener. At this level, the individual structures are interpreted by the listener in domain terms (music being regarded as a metaphor). Listeners can now assign meaning to individual messages but cannot necessarily reason about the global interaction.

Our results also lead us to suggest the existence of a third level *THE REASONING AND SEMANTIC LEVEL.*. At this level, the listener develops higher level structures to understand the domain from a higher level viewpoint. This level allows users to assign meaning to musical messages without further training or instruction. The very act of mental activity at this level also is likely to increase memorability of the interface.

These ideas can be illustrated with examples taken from the AUDIOGRAPH. The Detectable Musical Mapping is used to identify the important characteristics of the domain which MUST be distinguishable. In the case of the AUDIOGRAPH system, the listener certainly needs to distinguish the following

1. the size of a coordinate
2. an X coordinate from a Y coordinate
3. the different graphical shapes
4. the different control actions

There may be other domain events which need to be communicated depending upon user task, but the above list is certainly the minimum required for basic understanding.

The actual mappings used were:

1. The size of a coordinate is mapped into pitch in the Chromatic Scale (higher numbers having higher note values). Additionally, the notes are grouped into 10s and the longer the sequence, the higher the coordinate value. Thus we provide three basic handles for determining a coordinate value.
2. The X and Y coordinates are distinguished by Timbre (Organ and Piano) and in Time (Y always comes after X). Additionally, we provide a distinctive drum note to prepare the listener for the start of the coordinate sequence.
3. The shapes are derived from geometrical traces of the objects which are shown by experiment to be distinguishable.
4. Control Actions are short distinct Earcons

The required domain differences under these mapping are detectable. We have already shown in [15] that users with average musical ability can distinguish between instruments in the different classes of the orchestra and map pitch (approximately) to numeric difference.

The Perceptual Context is created by use of a common mapping for coordinates, shapes, and cursor movement. The audio versions of the shapes are directly related to their geometric counterpart, in a similar manner to the coordinate description of the space. Thus they are not only detectable, but also can be understood in terms of the metaphor relating pitch to length. The control action Earcons, likewise, are underpinned using a metaphoric interpretation. The EXPAND Earcon is detectable but also does "expand" numerically and is the opposite to CONTRACT. UNDO can be heard to correct a tune and is not just a unique Earcon.

Finally we have observed users employing the third level once they become familiar with the auditory mappings. When one begins to communicate diagrams which have an underlying structure, users are rapidly able to exploit this. For example, if users knows that the graphical scene is a row of houses, and they find windows in the first house, they immediately assume that windows are likely to exist in the others. This aspect is not explicitly presented in the detectable mapping nor in the perceptual support level.

The importance of the perceptual level has been stated in other work. When Mynatt [13] initially designed the auditory icons for Mercator, she had assumed that the use of auditory icons was limited to concrete representations (e.g. sound of a typewriter). Later she was able to represent more abstract actions utilizing the metaphorical qualities of everyday sounds. She then began using sounds for which she did not want the user to identify the original source of the sound. In this respect, this is moving closer to our work in music, where the source of the sound (Clarinet, Trumpet, etc..) is not related to the use of the sound in the representation scheme for the domain. She then critically examines claims about users preferring musical to natural sounds in interface design and points out that this is not because the music somehow sounded "better" but because the musical sounds had been carefully constructed to reflect metaphorically what they were representing (like our EXPAND and CONTRACT Earcons in AUDIOGRAPH or the jagged list in the Bubble Sort). For example, her musical sequence for representing termination of a phone call ended abruptly and sounded as if the phone was being replaced on the hook.

Other musical mappings (particularly Earcons) used in a number of recent studies have relied to some extent on perceptual support. For example Brewster and Crease [12] report the use of auditory Earcons in an experiment investigating user errors when employing menus. Relationships in the menus are reflected in the auditory design (a similar set of timbres are used for items in the same menu). However other mappings were not so perceptually obvious. Moving from one menu item to another was signalled by alternating notes (B2 to E3 in the scale), whereas one might have thought gradually decreasing notes (representing the descent into the hierarchy, might have been closer, perceptually. Also rhythm was used to signal selection and slips. Although such events will be readily detectable, they are not related perceptually to the actions being described. Perhaps a glissando might have been better to describe a slip, for example. We are not suggesting that Brewster and Crease would necessarily have obtained improved results using these mappings, but are simply using the example to illustrate how the perceptual level might be applied.

We have been impressed with the capabilities offered by music in interface design particularly for those who are blind or who are visually impaired. Much more work is required at two of the levels identified in our work - the detectable level and the perceptual level.

At the detection level we need to know more about the capabilities of human beings with an average musical capability. There certainly is a basic musical capability in most people (the existence of the popular music industry is a testament to that). We need to know better how to exploit it, by finding out what people can and cannot perceive musically. Secondly, we need to explore how to support this basic detectability with perceptual support. It is possible that we could learn much here from those who write jingles for commercial television or composers of film music. We also need to know more about possible cultural differences in the ways in which human beings interpret music.

We opened this paper with a plea for the development of "equal opportunity " interfaces, interfaces in which users could decide for themselves, the distribution of information presented between the visual and audio channels and this paper has investigated the audio extremum. A full understanding of this idea will require an appreciation not only of the perceptual support which can be offered in visual and aural interfaces but also how the two interact.

ACKNOWLEDGMENTS

We would like to thank all those subjects from the Royal National Institute for the Blind who spent many hours taking part in the experiments and provided many helpful comments, and to the management of the Institute for their readiness to cooperate.

REFERENCES

[1] Shneiderman, B., "Direct Manipulation: A Step beyond Programming Languages", IEEE Computer, August, 1983, 57 - 62.

[2] Bly, S.A., Communicating with Sound, Proc. of CHI'82, ACM Press, Addison-Wesley, New York, 371-375.

[3] Gaver, W., Using Sound in Computer Interfaces, Human Computer Interaction, Vol. 2, No. 2, (1986), 167-177.

[4] Gaver, W., The SonicFinder: An Interface that Uses Auditory Icons, Human Computer Interaction, Vol. 4, No.1, (1989), 87-94.

[5] Edwards. A.D.N, (1989), Soundtrack: An Auditory Interface for Blind Users, Human Computer Interaction, Vol. 4, No. 1, (1989), 45-66.

[6] Blattner, M.M., Sumikawa, D., and Greenberg, R., Earcons and Icons: Their Structure and Common Design Principles, In Human Computer Interaction, Vol. 4, (1989), 11-44

[7] Brown, M., and Hershberger, J., Colour and Sound in Algorithm Animation, IEEE Computer Vol. 25, No. 12, , (1992), 52-63.

[8] Alty, J.L., Can we Use Music in Human Computer Interaction ?, Proc. HCI'95, People and Computers X,

Kirby, M.A, Dix, A.J., and Finlay, J.E., (eds.), ,Cambridge University Press, 409 - 423.

[9] Bock, D.S., Auditory Software diagnosis Using a Sound Domain Specification Language, Ph.D. Thesis, Syracuse University, Syracuse, (1995).

[10] Vickers, P., and Alty, J.L., CAITLIN: A Musical Program Auralisation Tool to Assist Novice Programmers with Debugging, in Proc. of ICAD'96, (1996), Santa Fe Institute.

[11] Brewster, S., Navigating Telephone-based Interfaces with Earcons, Proc. HCI'87, (Bristol, 1997), People and computers XII, (Thimbleby, H., O'Conaill, B., and Thomas, P., eds.), Springer, Berlin, 39-56.

[12] Brewster, S., and Crease, M., Making Menus Musical, Proc. INTERACT'97, (Howard, S., Hammond, J., and Lingaard, G., eds.), Chapman and Hall, London, 389-396.

[13] Mynatt, E.D., Designing Auditory Cues for Mercator, Proc. INTERACT'97, (Howard, S., Hammond, J., and Lingaard, G., eds.), Chapman and Hall, London, 236-243

[14] Vickers, P., and Alty, J.L., The CAITLIN Auralisation system: Hierarchical Leitmotif Design as a clue to Program Comprehension, in Proc. ICAD'97, (1997), Santa Fe Institute.

[15] Rigas, D., and Alty, J.L., The Use of Music in a Graphical Interface for the Visually Impaired, Proc. of INTERACT'97 (Howard., S., Hammond, J., and Lindegaard, G., (eds.)), Sydney, 1997, 228-235.

[16] Fernstrom, M., and Bannon, L., Explorations in Sonic Browsing, Proc. HCI'87, (Bristol, 1997), People and computers XII, (Thimbleby, H., O'Conaill, B., and Thomas, P., eds.), Springer, Berlin, 117-132.

[17] Kennel, A.R., AUDIOGRAF: A Diagram-Reader for the Blind. In Proc. ASSETS'96, Vancouver, ACM Press, (1996), 51 - 56.

What Can I Say?: Evaluating a Spoken Language Interface to Email

Marilyn A. Walker, Jeanne Fromer Giuseppe Di Fabbrizio, Craig Mestel, Don Hindle
ATT Labs Research
180 Park Ave., D188
Florham Park, N.J. USA
+1 973 360 8956
{walker, pino,hindle}@research.att.com , jeannie@ai.mit.edu, cmestel@leland.stanford.edu

ABSTRACT
This paper presents experimental results comparing two different designs for a spoken language interface to email. We compare a mixed-initiative dialogue style, in which users can flexibly control the dialogue, to a system-initiative dialogue style, in which the system controls the dialogue. Our results show that even though the mixed-initiative system is more efficient, as measured by number of turns, or elapsed time to complete a set of email tasks, users prefer the system-initiative interface. We posit that these preferences arise from the fact that the system initiative interface is easier to learn and more predictable.

Keywords
Spoken Language Interfaces, Initiative, Email Interfaces

INTRODUCTION
Debate about the utility of spoken language interfaces (SLIs) vs. graphical user interfaces (GUIs) has been on-going for many years. It is widely agreed that GUIs provide immediate feedback, reversible operations, and incrementality, that they support rapid scanning and browsing of information, and that they are easy for novices to use because visual information indicates the currently available options. In contrast, SLIs have been criticized for the inherent limitations of a sequential channel (speech) for delivering information, for requiring the user to learn the language the system can understand, for hiding available command options, and for leading to unrealistic expectations as to their capabilities.

Yet changes in both work practice and technology in the last ten years has greatly increased the potential benefits of SLIs. Workers are much more mobile, making remote access to information stored on a desktop computer highly desirable. The telephone is a lightweight and ubiquitous form of access, and automatic speech recognition (ASR) used in SLIs has vastly improved. These changes mean that many interface designers now believe that SLIs for remote access to a range of personal and public (often web-based) information are both practical and desirable.

However, because it has only been recently possible to build real-time SLIs, very little is known about how to design them to mitigate current limitations in component technologies, such as automatic speech recognition (ASR) and text to speech synthesis (TTS), as well as inherent limitations with SLIs [1,2,3,4,7]. The single most important design choice is the selection of dialogue strategies that the SLI uses in conversations with the user. One key factor is whether the dialogue strategy is system-initiative (SI) or mixed-initiative (MI) [7]. These strategies are illustrated in D1 and D2 for ELVIS (EmaiL Voice Interactive System), an SLI for accessing email by phone:

(D1: System Initiative Strategy)
A: Hi, Elvis here. You have 5 new and 0 unread messages in your inbox. Say Read, or Summarize, or say Help for more options.
U: Read.
A: Select by Content or Position?
U: Content.
A: Select by Sender or Subject?
U: Sender
A: Which Sender?
U: Kim.
A: The message from Kim is about Meeting Tomorrow. The meeting tomorrow is at 10:30 in 2D-516.

(D2: Mixed Initiative Strategy)
A: Hi, Elvis here. I've got your mail.
U: Read me my messages from Kim.
A: The message from Kim is about Meeting Tomorrow. The meeting tomorrow is at 10:30 in 2D-516.

The SI strategy prompts users what to say at each stage of the dialogue with directive prompts [2]. Since prompts must be short, the SI strategy typically executes actions by small increments at each turn. The MI strategy assumes that users know what to say, and never volunteers information. The MI SLI is designed so that users can specify a system function and all of its arguments in a single utterance if they desire. While it might appear obvious that users would prefer the more flexible interaction style of the MI interface, there are several complicating factors. First, MI requires more knowledge on the part of the users about what they can say, while the SI strategy directs the user. Second, because SI users are directed to produce very short utterances, the ASR performance of SI may be much better. If more error recovery and correction dialogues are necessary for MI, users may find this onerous. Too many spoken language understanding errors may also make it difficult for users to acquire a model of the system's behavior. Without knowing the effect of these factors, it is impossible to predict whether the SI strategy or the MI strategy is better.

This paper discusses the design and evaluation of ELVIS, a research prototype SLI that supports voice access to email by phone. We report experimental results from testing users with both an SI and an MI version of ELVIS. Our experimental data consists of 144 dialogues with 48 users, consisting of a total of 6481 turns. Our results show that even though the MI system is more efficient, as measured by either number of turns, or elapsed time to complete a set of email tasks, users prefer the SI interface.

DESIGNING A SPOKEN LANGUAGE INTERFACE FOR EMAIL

In addition to the dialogue strategy design, a second key aspect of SLI design is deciding what options should be available to the user at each point in the dialogue. Previous work has demonstrated the utility of Wizard of Oz studies [1,4,8,9], so we began our design process with a Wizard of Oz (WOZ) study where a person played the part of an SLI for accessing email. We collected, recorded and transcribed 15 extended conversations (1200 utterances) with 6 different prototypical users, mobile professionals accessing their email while away from their office.

We then categorized each utterance in these dialogues in terms of its use of key email access functions. Categories were based on the underlying application, as well as on language-based functionality, such as *reference* to messages by their properties, such as the sender or the subject of the message (e.g. *the message from Kim*), or in context (e.g. as *them, it, that*), Table 1 summarizes the functions used most frequently in the WOZ study. This study suggests that the SLI should minimally support: (1) reading the body of a message and the header information; (2) summarization of the contents of an email folder by content-related attributes such as the sender or subject; (3) selection of individual messages by content fields such as the sender or subject; and (4) request for clarifying help, repetition of something that was said, and undoing of previous actions.

Table 1: Email functions used in Wizard of Oz study

EMAIL ACCESS FUNCTION	N
Summarization	20
Reference	101
Folder Action	10
Read Message	67
Search for a Message	8
Message Field Access	5
Repeat	4
Clarifications	37
Help	3

Reading the message and header information requires the use of text-to-speech (TTS) since it is impossible to pre-record messages with a human voice. Reading the body of the message also requires filtering the message body for things that are unpronounceable by TTS, and recognizing attachments in the message body.

In the WOZ study, users typically requested summaries on entering a folder and referred to messages by attributes such as sender or subject in order to randomly select messages of interest in that folder. We hypothesized that summarization and selection capabilities could provide a way to scan and browse information in SLIs. In other words, one way to obviate the limitations of a sequential speech channel is to give users the ability to overview the data (with summarization) and then select the subset of items that they are interested in (with reference). Summarization and selection of messages by content attributes required reproducing searching and sorting functionality available in many email GUI interfaces. For folder summaries, the list of messages had to be converted into a coherent summary that was appropriate to the context, i.e. whether the folder had been created by selecting by sender or by subject.

Even though our WOZ subjects did not typically attempt to access to messages in the sequence in which they were received (or reverse chronological order), we felt that it was necessary to provide this as an additional option because other voice and touch-tone interfaces to voice and email messages provide this option [2,3,9]. Thus both the SI and the MI system support access to messages by relative position within a folder: users can select messages by saying *First, Next, Previous* and *Last*.

The WOZ study also confirms that the system should provide help so that users can learn its capabilities. We were particularly concerned about the design of help messages for the MI system. The SLI platform that we used to build both versions of ELVIS included a facility for specifying help messages associated with each state of the dialogue. These context-sensitive help messages indicate to the user what command options are available at each point in the dialogue, and provide a verbal analog to the visible icons in GUIs that indicate the available command options.

Context-sensitive help was available to the user in two ways: at the user's initiative if the user says *Help*, and at the system's initiative with **timeout messages**. The system plays timeout messages when the user doesn't say anything, i.e. after some expected response delay has timed out. The system keeps track of how many times a timeout occurs in each state, so that timeout messages can be modified to be more informative after each timeout.

Because help messages (and email messages) can be long, users must be able to interrupt the system to take control of the interaction at any point, while the system is talking or carrying out a command. This is called **Barge-In.** Supporting barge-in requires that a speech recognizer is always listening, even when the system is currently busy recognizing something the user said previously. Barge-In also involves the ability to abort common procedures in midstream, e.g the system needs to be able to send TTS instructions to stop talking in midstream.

Finally, the SLI must provide some way of undoing a previous command. This is useful in two cases: (1) if the user simply decides they would rather do something different; and (2) if the SLI misunderstand the user. ELVIS supports reversibility by providing an always available *cancel* command that returns the user to the dialogue state before the previous interaction.

EXPERIMENTAL DESIGN

The experiment required users, randomly assigned to either the MI or the SI version of ELVIS, to complete three tasks involving telephone access to email. All of the users regularly used computers in the course of their everyday work and were familiar with email. In one study, the 12 users were administrative assistants or researchers whose area of research was not related to SLIs. We reported results from this study elsewhere [5]. Subsequently, we noticed that response delay was longer than we wanted and that there was a different way of communicating with the email application layer that would significantly reduce it. After implementing the improved version, we then tested another 36 users in both versions of ELVIS. These subjects were summer interns, with little exposure to SLIs, many of whom were not native speakers of English. Below we discuss results from these 36 users.

Experimental instructions were given on three web pages, one for each experimental task. Each web page consisted of a brief general description of Elvis, a list of hints for using Elvis, a task description, and information on calling ELVIS. Subjects read the instructions in their offices before calling ELVIS from their office phone.

Each user performed three tasks in sequence, and each task consisted of two subtasks. Thus the results consisted of 108 dialogues representing 216 attempted subtasks. The task scenarios that the subjects were given were as follows, where subtasks 1.1 and 1.2 were done in the same conversation, similarly for 2.1 and 2.2, and 3.1 and 3.2.

- 1.1: You are working at home in the morning and plan to go directly to a meeting when you go into work. Kim said she would send you a message telling you where and when the meeting is. Find out the Meeting Time and the Meeting Place.
- 1.2: The second task involves finding information in a different message. Yesterday evening, you had told Lee you might want to call him this morning. Lee said he would send you a message telling you where to reach him. Find out Lee's Phone Number.
- 2.1: When you got into work, you went directly to a meeting. Since some people were late, you've decided to call Elvis to check your mail to see what other meetings may have been scheduled. Find out the day, place and time of any scheduled meetings.
- 2.2: The second task involves finding information in a different message. Find out if you need to call anyone. If so, find out the number to call.
- 3.1: You are expecting a message telling you when the Discourse Discussion Group can meet. Find out the place and time of the meeting.
- 3.2: The second task involves finding information in a different message. Your secretary has taken a phone call for you and left you a message. Find out who called and where you can reach them.

These tasks were based on representative tasks from the WOZ study, involving the use of summarization and reference as in Table 1. Each subtask specified the information about criteria for selecting messages, and information within the message body, that the user and the system had to exchange. For example, in scenario 1.1, the user is expecting email from Kim about a meeting and needs to find out the time and place of that meeting (as in Dialogue D1 and D2). Following [6], this scenario is represented in terms of the attribute value matrix (AVM) in Table 2. The AVM representation for all six subtasks is similar to Table 2. Note that the task's information exchange requirement represented in the AVM is independent of the dialogue strategy used to accomplish the task. The use of the AVM to calculate task success is discussed below.

We designed the experimental email folders so that for each task, the desired messages were not among the first two messages (as ordered chronologically). Thus users who accessed messages by chronological order would often have to listen to all five messages in order to complete the task, while users who accessed messages using selection by content could complete the task by listening to two messages. Thus accessing messages by relative position should have led to inefficient dialogues, while the instructions specified that users should be as efficient as possible and avoid listening to messages unnecessarily.

Table 2: Attribute Value Matrix: Email Scenario Key for Dialogues D1 and D2

ATTRIBUTE	VALUE
Selection Criteria	Kim or Meeting
Email.att1	10:30
Email.att2	2D 516

The general description and the hints on the web page for each task were identical. The subjects were asked to impersonate a different user for each task and were told that they needed to talk to ELVIS to find out some information that had been sent to them in an email message. We decided not to include any specific examples of what users could say in the hints for using ELVIS for three reasons: (1) we wanted the instructions to be identical for both SI and MI; (2) users could get information as to what they could say from the context-sensitive help messages; (3) we wanted to be able to quantify the frequency with which users accessed information on what they could say, and would not have been able to do so if this information had been presented visually. The hints were:

- Anytime you need help with what to say or with what Elvis is doing, you can say *Help*.
- If Elvis misunderstands you and does the wrong thing, you can undo it by saying *Cancel*.
- If you wait too long to tell Elvis what to do, Elvis will tell you what you can do.
- When you are finished with a task, you can go back to the previous context by saying *I'm done here*.
- You don't have to wait for Elvis to finish talking if you've heard enough or you know what you want to do; you can interrupt at any time.

We collected four types of data and extracted a number of variables. First, all dialogues were recorded. The recording supports utterance transcription and measuring aspects of the timing of the interaction, such as whether there were long system response delays, and whether users barged-in on system utterances (the variable named **BargeIn**). BargeIn may reflect learning; as users learn what they can say, they can barge in over the system's utterances. In addition, the recording was used to calculate the total time of the interaction (the variable named **Elapsed Time**).

Second, the system logged its dialogue behavior on the basis of entering and exiting each state in the state transition table for the dialogue. For each state, the system logged the number of timeout prompts (**Timeout Prompts**), the number of times the confidence level for ASR was too low and the system played a special rejection messages, e.g. *Sorry, I didn't understand you* (**ASR Rejections**), and the times the user said *Help* (**Help Requests**). The number of **System Turns** and the number of **User Turns** were calculated on the basis of this data. In addition, the results of ASR for the user's utterance was logged. A measure of the system's understanding (concept accuracy) was calculated from the recordings in combination with the logged ASR result for each utterance. Mean concept accuracy was then calculated over the whole dialogue to provide a **Mean Recognition Score** (MRS) for the dialogue.

Third, users were required to fill out the web page forms after each task specifying whether they had completed the task and the information they had acquired from the agent (Task Success), e.g. the values for Email.att1 and Email.att2 in Table 2. This supported the use of the Kappa statistic to measure Task Success [6], where Kappa is defined as:

$$K = P(A) - P(E) / 1 - P(E)$$

P(A) is the proportion of times that the AVM for the dialogue agrees with the AVM for the scenario key, and P(E) is the proportion of times we would expect the AVMs for the dialogues and keys to agree by chance. When agreement is perfect (all task information items are successfully exchanged), then Kappa=1. When agreement is only at chance, then Kappa=0.

Finally, users responded to a survey on their subjective evaluation of their performance and their satisfaction with the system's performance with the following questions:

- Did you complete the task? (**Comp**)
- Was Elvis easy to understand in this conversation? (**TTS Performance**)
- In this conversation, did Elvis understand what you said? (**ASR Performance**)
- In this conversation, was it easy to find the message you wanted? (**Task Ease**)
- Was the pace of interaction with Elvis appropriate in this conversation? (**Interaction Pace**)

- In this conversation, did you know what you could say at each point of the dialogue? **(User Expertise)**
- How often was Elvis sluggish and slow to reply to you in this conversation? **(System Response)**
- Did Elvis work the way you expected him to in this conversation? **(Expected Behavior)**
- In this conversation, how did Elvis's voice interface compare to the touch-tone interface to voice mail? **(Comparable Interface)**
- From your current experience with using Elvis to get your email, do you think you'd use Elvis regularly to access your mail when you are away from your desk? **(Future Use)**.

The user satisfaction survey was multiple choice, and the possible responses to most questions ranged over values such as (*almost never, rarely, sometimes, often, almost always*), or an equivalent range. Each of these responses was mapped to an integer between 1 and 5. Some questions had (*yes, no, maybe*) responses. Each question emphasized the user's experience with the system in the current conversation, with the hope that satisfaction measures would indicate perceptions specific to each conversation, rather than reflecting an overall evaluation of the system over the three tasks. A Cumulative Satisfaction (CSAT) score for each dialogue was calculated by summing the scores for each question. The survey also included a free text field where users were encouraged to enter any comments they might have.

The goal of the experiment was to evaluate the usability of an SLI for accessing email by phone and to compare the MI dialogue design to the SI dialogue design when the task is held constant. We wished to investigate how users would adapt to the version of the system they were using as they performed a sequence of three similar tasks. Our primary experimental variable was dialogue strategy: whether the user interacted with the SI or the MI version of ELVIS. However, we were also interested in whether the availability of summarization and selection by content increased the functionality of the system. Our hypotheses were:

- H1: The MI strategy is potentially much more efficient than the SI strategy, but its efficiency depends on ASR performance, and the lower the ASR performance the less efficient it will be.
- H2: Users will have trouble knowing what they can say to the MI SLI and this will reduce ASR performance.
- H3: Users' knowledge of what they can say to the MI SLI will improve over the three tasks.
- H4: Because of H1, H2, and H3, Cumulative Satisfaction for the system initiative SLI will be greater for the first task, but Cumulative Satisfaction for the MI SLI will be greater by the third task.
- H5: Use of summarization will increase Cumulative Satisfaction and improve efficiency.
- H6: Use of selection by content will increase Cumulative Satisfaction and improve efficiency.

These hypotheses concern the relation between dialogue strategy, Mean Recognition Score, the utilization of the summarization and selection by content options, and the users' ability to learn what options are available at each point of the dialogue and to acquire a model of the system.

EXPERIMENTAL RESULTS

Our experimental design consisted of two factors; strategy and task. Each of our result measures were analyzed using a two-way ANOVA for these factors. For each result, we report F and p values indicating its statistical significance. Effects that are significant as a function of strategy (SI vs. MI) indicate differences between the two strategies. Effects that are significant as a function of task are potential indicators of learning. We discuss results for each of these factors as they relate to our hypotheses.

We first calculated Task Success in terms of Kappa to see whether task completion rates and scores were affected by dialogue strategy [7]. The average Kappa value over all subjects and tasks was .82, indicating that the task was almost always completed successfully. An ANOVA with Kappa as the dependent variable revealed no significant differences for Kappa as a function of task or strategy.

Hypothesis H1 focuses on the relation between Mean Recognition Score (MRS) and efficiency. We examined efficiency with three efficiency measures: User Turns, System Turns and Elapsed Time. An ANOVA for each of the measures as a function of strategy and task showed that strategy was a significant predictor of efficiency in each case, and that MI was more efficient than SI: User Turns ($F(1,34)=31.9$, $p<.0001$), System Turns ($F(1,34)=14.3$, $p=.0006$) and Elapsed Time ($F(1,34)=3.92$, $p=.05$). Means for these measures are given in Table 3.

Table 3: Efficiency measures for SI versus MI

	SYSTEM (SI)	MIXED (MI)
User Turns	25.94	17.59
System Turns	28.18	21.74
Elapsed Time	328.59 s	289.43 s

Hypothesis H2 concerns the relation between MRS and efficiency. MRS was significantly lower for the MI strategy ($F(1,34)= 27.2$, $p<.0001$), with a mean of .72 for MI as compared with .88 for the SI strategy. The correlation between MRS and Elapsed Time is -.25.

Hypothesis H3 concerned the effect of learning on MRS for the MI interface, and on efficiency as a result. As we hypothesized, MRS did improve as users learned the system (F (1,70)=6.37, p<.01). The MRS of the MI strategy was .68 for task 1, .74 for task 2 and .76 for task 3, while MRS for the SI strategy was .88 for task 1, .87 for task 2 and .92 for task 3. Furthermore, efficiency was also directly affected by users' learning of the system. There was an interaction between strategy and task for both Elapsed Time (F(1,70)=4.85, p=.03) and System Turns (F(1,70)=5.23, p=.03). For the SI system, the mean Elapsed time for task 1 was 321.7s, for task 2 was 345.9s, and for task 3 was 318.2s. In contrast, the MI system started out taking more time on average (task 1=332.6s), but Elapsed Time was reduced significantly over the subsequent tasks, with task 2 taking 302.8s on average and task 3 taking 232.8s. System Turns showed a similar pattern: for the SI system, System Turns for task 1 averaged 26.7, 29.7 for task 2 and 28.1 for task 3. System Turns were reduced for each task for the MI system: task 1 took an average of 25.4 turns, task 2 averaged 22.3 turns and task 3 averaged 17.5 turns.

Hypothesis H4 posited that users' Cumulative Satisfaction (CSAT) for the SI system would be greater for task 1, but that as users learned the MI system over the three tasks, that the flexibility of the interface and the gains in efficiency would cause MI to be preferred. CSAT was greater for SI for task 1: mean CSAT for task 1 for SI was 27.2 while mean CSAT for MI for task 1 was 23.8. However, despite the fact that the MI strategy was clearly more efficient than the SI strategy by the third task, there was no interaction between strategy and task. There was a significant difference in CSAT as a function of strategy (F(1,34)= 23.59, p=.02), with mean CSAT being higher for SI (26.6) as compared with MI (23.7). The increases in CSAT for the MI strategy were not significant: mean CSAT for task 1 was 23.7, for task 2 was 22.7 and for task 3 as 24.4. Thus even with the effects of learning, CSAT for MI by the third task was still lower than CSAT for SI on the first task. (See Table 4). Thus Hypothesis H4 is disconfirmed. It appears that, contrary to H4, users' preferences are not determined by efficiency per se, as has been commonly assumed. One interpretation of our results is that users are more attuned to qualitative aspects of the interaction.

To explore this idea further, we first analyzed the relationship between CSAT and our other measures, drawing on the PARADISE framework [6], and its use of multivariate linear regression. We first normalized all measures to their Z scores to ensure that the magnitude of the coefficients in the regression equation would reflect the magnitude of the contribution of that factor to CSAT. An initial regression over a range of measures suggested that Users' perception of task completion (Comp), Mean Recognition Score (MRS) and Elapsed Time (ET) were the only significant contributors to CSAT. A second regression including only these factors resulted in the following equation:

$$CSAT = .21*Comp + .47 * MRS - .15 * ET$$

with Comp (t=2.58, p =.01), MRS (t =5.75, p =.0001) and ET(t=-1.8, p=.07) significant predictors, accounting for 38% of the variance in R-Squared (F (3,104)=21.2, p<.0001). This equation demonstrates that while efficiency and task completion are both factors in predicting CSAT, that they are not as significant as MRS. It is plausible that the qualitative behaviors that are correlated with poor MRS have a greater effect on CSAT.

Table 4: Qualitative measures for SI versus MI

	SYSTEM (SI)	MIXED (MI)
MeanRecog (MRS)	.88	.72
Time Outs	2.24	4.15
Barge Ins	5.2	3.5
ASR Rejects	.98	1.67
CSAT	26.6	23.7

This interpretation is supported by measures that more directly reflect the quality of the interaction. See Table 4. First, as discussed above, there were significant differences in Mean Recognition Score (MRS) as a function of strategy. Furthermore, even though users of the MI system were not more likely to ask for help using the always available *Help* command (F(1,34)=1.47, NS), they were much more likely to trigger Timeout Prompts (F(1,34)=10.87, p=.002). Remember that Timeout Prompts are system turns that suggest to the user what they can say, which are triggered by occasions in which the user says nothing after a system utterance. This may happen because the user does not know what they **can** say, or because the user is confused by what the system just did. The mean number of timeouts was 4.15 per dialogue for users of the MI system as opposed to 2.24 for the SI users. Another qualitative aspect of the interaction is the system's production of diagnostic error messages. In our study, it was much more common for the system to reject the utterances of users of the MI system (ASR Rejects), because of low ASR confidence scores (F(1,34)=4.38, p=.04), leading the system to produce a diagnostic error message asking the user to repeat himself or telling him what he could say. Finally, there was an interaction in the use of BargeIn between strategy and task (F (1,70)=14.18, p=.0003). Remember that BargeIn may reflect learning; as users learn what they can say, they can barge in over the system's utterances. SI users increased their use of BargeIn over the three tasks, with the number of BargeIns for task 1 at 3.55, task 2 at 4.61 and task3 at 7.33, suggesting that they were learning the interface and becoming more confident. In contrast, users of the MI system started out using BargeIn more (task 1=4.17) but the use of BargeIn decreases with task 2 at 3.89 and task 3 at 2.6. One explanation for the decrease in BargeIns is that users lost confidence in knowing what to say to the MI system.

Other evidence suggests that it was difficult for users to acquire a model of how the MI system worked. Even though the MI system made more errors, users of the SI system were much more likely to use the *Cancel* command (F(1,70)=18.41, p=.0001), which undoes the effects of the previous command. One plausible explanation of this difference is that SI users acquired a model of the dialogue flow, making it possible for them to use the cancel command effectively, while MI users did not.

Further insight into the factors that affect CSAT can be found by examining the individual satisfaction measures that CSAT is composed of. Users perceive it to be easier to find a message (Task Ease) in the SI condition (F(1,34)=9.11, p=.005. This is probably because MI users perceived that ELVIS was much less likely to understand what they said (ASR Performance) (F(1,34)=6.56, p=.02). SI users perceived that the system *often* or *almost always* understood them, while MI users thought the system only *sometimes* understood them. As we hypothesized, MI users were more confused about what they could say (User Expertise) (F(1,34=4.02), p=.04). MI users were much more likely to say that they only *rarely* or *sometimes* knew what to say, whereas SI users *often* knew what they could say. MI users were also much less likely to say that ELVIS worked the way they expected him to (Expected Behavior) (X^2=4.6, p<.05). In only 26 out of 54 dialogues did the MI users say that ELVIS behaved as they expected, in comparison with 37 out of 54 for the SI users. This resulted in many fewer MI users saying they would be willing to use ELVIS regularly to access their mail when they are away from their desk (X^2=4.97, p<.05): in 30 out of 54 MI dialogues users responded *yes* or *maybe* to this question, while the SI users responded *yes* or *maybe* in 41 dialogues out of 54.

Hypotheses H5 and H6 were that users who made use of the summarization and selection by content options provided in both the SI and the MI interfaces would have greater Cumulative Satisfaction (CSAT) and be more efficient than those who chose to listen to their messages in chronological order. In order to test hypotheses H5 and H6, we analyzed the experimental logs and transcriptions for summary use (Suse), next use (Nuse), and content-selection use (Csuse).

Both SI and MI users utilized one of the summarization options that were provided in the system, averaging 1.4 summaries per dialogue. While some users did not use summarization at all, other users summarized up to 5 times in a single dialogue. However, contrary to H5, Suse did not lead to higher CSAT, nor did it lead to greater dialogue efficiency. In fact, our results demonstrate an opposite pattern. An ANOVA with CSAT as the independent variable and Suse as a dependent variable showed Suse a significant predictor of CSAT (F(5,67)=3.45, p=.008). However CSAT goes down as Suse goes up as shown in Table 5. Furthermore, Suse is highly correlated with Elapsed Time: the correlation coefficient is .49. Thus the more subjects summarized, the less efficient their dialogues were. Analysis of the dialogue transcripts for users who requested the most summaries shows that summaries were used as an error recovery strategy. Users would summarize when the system misunderstood one of the sender or subject values that they had specified when attempting to select by content. Since the sender and subject values were provided in the summary, users would listen to the summary again to make sure that they had specified the values correctly. Thus an increase in the use of summarization indicates a user who was having recognition problems.

Table 5: Cumulative Satisfaction as a function of Summary Use

	SUSE=0	SUSE=2	SUSE=4	SUSE=5
CSAT	26.0	24.97	22.17	18.5

To test Hypothesis H6, we examined the relationship between Nuse (use of the Next command), Cuse (use of the content selection options), and both Cumulative Satisfaction (CSAT) and Elapsed Time (ET). Nuse is not a significant predictor of CSAT (F(1,106)=3.45,NS). There was also no effect for Cuse, the use of selection by content options. Further investigation reveals that the main reason for this is likely to arise from the poor performance of ASR for selection by content in the MI condition. In the MI condition, the probability of being correctly understood when using the Read option was only .63. Half of the time if the user specified a selection criteria for reading, e.g. *Read my messages from Owen*, the system misunderstood: sender values were misunderstood 43% of the time. In contrast, MI users who selected messages in chronological or reverse chronological order were correctly understood 81% of the time. Thus there was a great incentive for MI users to **not use** the selection by content options.

On the other hand, if a user chose to access messages by content rather than by order in the SI condition, it took at least three interchanges to say so (see D1). However the overall probability of correct understanding when specifying selection by sender was .76, and for selection by subject was .78. The probability of success for selection by position was .82. Thus there was little difference in the SI condition between system performance for selection by content versus by order.

Table 6: Relationship of Cumulative Satisfaction to use of the selection by Content options in the SI SLI.

	CUSE=0	CUSE=2	CUSE=4	CUSE>5
CSAT	21.0	28.2	26.0	20.0

In order to see whether selection by content is useful when ASR performs appropriately, we analyzed Cuse for the SI strategy alone. An ANOVA of CSAT as a function of Cuse shows Cuse to be highly predictive of CSAT ($F(6,47)=3.89$, $p=.003$). Table 6 shows that CSAT is greatest when Cuse matches optimal performance on the task, i.e. since each task required access to only 2 messages, when Cuse is 2. Thus H6 is disconfirmed for the MI condition, but confirmed for the SI condition.

CONCLUSIONS

This paper evaluates a mixed-initiative (MI) dialogue design in comparison with a system-initiative (SI) dialogue design in ELVIS, a spoken language interface for accessing email by phone. It has been commonly assumed that spoken language interfaces that constrain the user will be less preferred than unconstrained interfaces. Our hypotheses were that users would initially prefer the SI system, which controls the interaction so that the options available to the user are obvious at each point of the dialogue, and that ASR (automatic speech recognition) would perform better with the SI grammars. However, we hypothesized that as users performed successive tasks, they would learn how to use the MI system, which does not constrain the user, and which is more efficient. We hypothesized that as users learned how to use the MI system, their confidence with the system would increase, and that ASR performance would also increase. Thus, by the end of three tasks, we hypothesized that the satisfaction of MI users would be greater than that of the SI users.

Our results show that the additional flexibility of the MI interface leads to user confusion about their available options and poor performance by ASR. While user expertise and ASR performance did increase for MI over three tasks, these increases did not result in a preference for the MI interface. Despite the fact that the MI interface is more efficient in terms of both turns and elapsed time, the SI users report higher user satisfaction. A multivariate linear regression with user satisfaction as the dependent variable shows that ASR performance, user perception of task completion, and elapsed time are significant contributors to user satisfaction, but that ASR performance is the greatest contributor. We interpret these results to mean that the qualitative behaviors associated with poor ASR performance, the predictability of the system, and the ability of users to acquire a model of system performance, are more important than the commonly assumed performance factors of efficiency and task success.

A user preference for SI style interfaces are also suggested by the results of other work. Previous work has found that directive prompts, and dialogue strategies that structure the interaction with the user, in a similar way to our system initiative interface, are more successful and preferred by users [2,4]. However, in all of these studies, ASR performed worse in the less constrained interface. Future work should examine the role of learnability and predictability with improved ASR performance. In addition, future work should include a longer term study of daily users in the field to determine whether MI interfaces might be preferred by some (expert) users.

REFERENCES

1. Brennan S., and Hulteen E., Interaction and Feedback in a Spoken Language System. *Knowledge-Based Systems,* **8**, (2,3). 1995.

2. Kamm C., User Interfaces for Voice Applications, *Voice Communication Between Humans and Machines.* D. Roe and J. Wilpon Eds. National Academy Press, 1994.

3. Marx, M., *Toward Effective Conversational Messaging,,* MIT Media Lab Masters Thesis, 1995.

4. Oviatt S., Cohen P. and Wang M., Toward interface design for human language technology: Modality and structure as determinants of linguistic complexity. *Speech Communication*, 15, (3,4). 1994

5. Walker M., Hindle D., Fromer J., Di Fabbrizio G, and Mestel C. Evaluating competing agent strategies for a voice email agent. In *Proceedings of the European Conference on Speech Communication and Technology,* EUROSPEECH97. 1997

6. Walker M., Litman D., Kamm C. and Abella A. PARADISE: A Framework for evaluating Spoken Dialogue Agents, in *Proceedings of ACL '97* (Madrid, Spain, July 1997), MIT Press.

7. Walker M. and Whittaker S. Mixed initiative in dialogue: An investigation into discourse segmentation. *In Proc. 28th Annual Meeting of the ACL*, pages 70-79. 1990

8. Whittaker S.J. and Stenton S.P., User Studies and the design of Natural Language Systems, *Proceedings of EACL '89, p. 116-123.* 1989.

9. Yankelovich N., Levow G. and Marx M. Designing Speech Acts: Issues in Speech User Interfaces. In *Proceedings of CHI '95* (Denver CO, May 1995), ACM Press.

Device Design Methodology for Trauma Applications

Diane S. Brown
Human Factors and User Interface Design
ATL Ultrasound
22100 Bothell Everett Highway
Bothell, WA 98041-3003 USA
+1 425 487-7662
dbrown@corp.atl.com

Susan Motte
Breeze Design
6315 Greenwood Ave. N.
Seattle, WA 98103 USA
+1 206 781-8454
susanmotte@aol.com

ABSTRACT

In this paper, we describe the unique characteristics of medical environments, particularly trauma. We describe how those characteristics challenge traditional human factors methods, and the enhanced methods that work well for each development phase of medical product design.

Keywords

Trauma, medical domain, healthcare, field studies, design methodology, human factors

INTRODUCTION

A fundamental principle of designing usable products is to first begin by understanding the user's work practice well [1, 2, 5, 9]. Traditional field studies and contextual inquiry methodology dictate that work practice is best understood when the work is observed as it is happening in the user's real environment [5]. But because of such factors as doctor-patient confidentiality, time-critical work, and human drama in hospitals and clinics, traditional field study and contextual inquiry methodologies alone are not sufficient for collecting the detailed data necessary for the generation of design requirements. Other factors such as a doctor's availability and simulating realistic work scenarios stretch usability testing techniques. Human factors methods need to be combined in using a "top down" and "bottom up" approach when designing medical products used in hospital environments. Although most medical environments pose the same challenges to varying degrees, the trauma environment, in particular, pushes human factors methods to their limits. We begin by describing some of the unique characteristics of the trauma environment that challenge different human factors methods in each phase of the user-centered design process. We then describe how to combine the different methods in the process to capture the information needed for design.

CHI 98 Los Angeles CA USA
Copyright 1998 0-89791-975-0/98/ 4..$5.00

The Trauma Environment

The trauma environment can be characterized by several medical personnel undertaking time-critical tasks under physical and emotional stress with patients who have life-threatening illnesses. The clinician's attention is on the patient and task. Personnel wear protective clothing such as gloves, gowns, and masks that may interfere with using the equipment. We've seen up to seventeen people at one time working in a small room, often assuming awkward positions to accomplish their tasks. The human emotions of fear and pain are common, as are long hours and shift work for the workers [10].

EXPERIENCE APPLYING HUMAN FACTORS METHODS TO TRAUMA CASES

Figure 1 summarizes the traditional development process and problems or unique situations we faced in the trauma environment when trying to apply stand-alone methods sequentialy in each development phase. We describe the issues below in more detail, and in the typical order we use the methods in our product development process.

Field Studies

From a logistical perspective, it was difficult to find sites that would allow us to observe their trauma cases. When we did find sites, much of the trauma occurred at night and on weekends which was inconvenient for us to observe. As with all medical domains, there is a great deal of domain knowledge required by an observer to sufficiently interpret work practice [4]. Acquiring this knowledge takes time, effort, and interest.

There are few environments that pose greater challenges to the observer than trauma sites. When observing work flow, we found it difficult to focus on the work when so many people were involved, work was so rapid, and human tragedy unfolds. We could rarely videotape the work for later review since the patients were often unconscious or unable to give consent, and also taping made the doctors uncomfortable. It was difficult to find a place where we were out of the way and could still observe. Sterile fields strictly prohibited entry. Large pieces of equipment wheeled into the rooms, placed in precarious positions also limited access. Not surprisingly, there was no way we could interrupt the work to determine goals, intentions, or expectations that typical "talk aloud" contextual inquiry methods employ. In the trauma rooms, we were exposed to potentially contagious diseases from body fluids. The smell of various fluids and illnesses could be overwhelming. We fought a constant battle to focus on work rather than the distractions of the "adrenaline rush" of trauma. Many situations were stressful to us emotionally. At times we were left alone with patients. These situations required considerable interpersonal skill. As in every medical domain, there was patient confidentiality to consider. A patient's comfort may be compromised by the presence of outside observers; this limited the work we could observe. We noticed that gender makes a difference in what we were allowed to observe - small females seemed less threatening to patients and doctors than large males. Even with these challenges field studies are crucial to the design effort. No other methods provide an understanding of the true context of work, vital to product design.

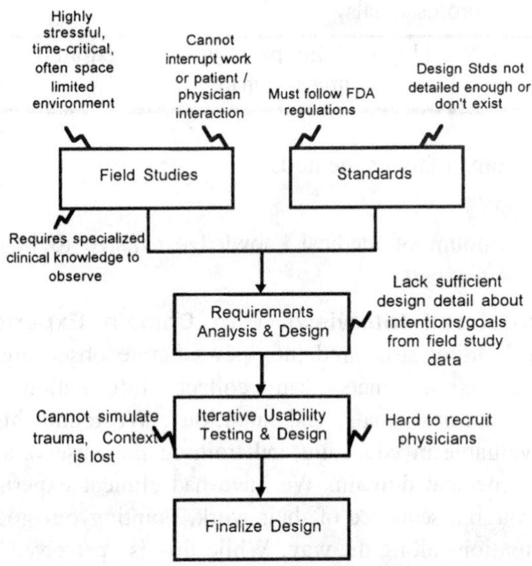

Figure 1. Overview of the development process and the problems applying human factors methods in trauma.

Design Standards

The products we design are not "desktop" software products to which traditional GUI standards apply. Our products are both hardware and software based and support hundreds of functions. The end-user's tasks are different than the desktop domain, and there are no agreed upon platform standards like computers and operating systems. Consequently, few design standards exist for this type of product. The design guidelines that do exist (ANSI, Military, FDA) are often too general to apply, or so specific they constrain the designs. Attempts by various groups at standardizing things like graphical medical icons have been usually unsuccessful. Consequently, there is no design precedence from which to critique or standardize new product designs. Even competitive products often do not use the same terminology or physical locations for similar features and functions.

Analysis and Design

A key in the accurate analysis of field data, requirements generation, and product design is understanding domain knowledge. Domain knowledge is mandatory in prioritizing the product and design requirements as well as understanding how and when to make tradeoffs. Because we cannot probe adequately, the field studies alone rarely give enough information about user intentions, expectations, and goals from which to design. The field studies give "top down" information of sequential work flow, physical environment, the users and their interactions - all of which is important. But "bottom up" information about low level goals, intentions, and expectations is also crucial. We need detailed data for design such as understanding logical groupings of functions, detailed sequences of use, and prioritized functions. Other significant challenges to design methods are the many breakpoints we observed caused by the poor integration of different manufacturers' equipment. These incompatabilities are usually not possible to remedy with a single product design.

The FDA requires that medical products are compliant with their standards and guidelines. Knowing where to find the right standards and guidelines, and understanding when and how to apply them presents a challenge to the medical product designers. The information is not centralized and does not state exact specifications for many situations.

Iterative Usability Testing and Design

Effective usability testing of our designs has always been a challenge for us, but now even more so for trauma scenarios. We continually face the dilemma of trying to simulate realistic situations in which to test our equipment, but from past experience we find that without the interruptions, real patients and illness, we lose the context of the real medical environment. Our test subjects pay more attention to the product or "tool" than they normally would in their everyday environments. This results in performances significantly better in our usability tests than when they actually use the equipment on a daily basis. This makes it difficult to predict the real usability of equipment. We found we lost the context of certain complex tasks if our prototype was low fidelity since real time physiological and anatomical data was necessary for realistic performance measures [7]. Even with these difficulties, we found important problems early with our testing and were able to change the design before the product was released.

Recruiting subjects is another problem we face [1]. Getting a doctor's time is difficult. Even when they are available, their erratic schedules cause last minute cancellations. We pay the doctors for their time, which can be expensive. The doctors are often tired when we run our tests which affects their performance and our results.

HF Method	Benefit	Shortcoming
Structured Interviews with Experts	Overview and detailed information about goals, protocol, and intentions	Perceived information, incomplete workflow and lacks contextual realism
Field Studies	Detailed, factual data, rich in contextual realism	Missing details for design because cannot probe goals, intentions in trauma situation
Standards	Provide precedents	Very few exist that influence design
Heuristic Evaluation	Detailed information collected quickly & benefit from HF, clinical expert team evaluations	Lacks contextual realism, and often does not involve actual users
Usability Testing (Investigative)	Detailed information about controlled taskflow	Lacks contextual realism
Requirements, Analysis, and Design	Leads to usable designs when have detailed design data	Need to use a variety of HF methods to collect detailed data needed for designing trauma applications
Iterative Usability Tests & Design	Provides fast, detailed design information	Lacks contextual realism of trauma situation, both difficult and expensive to recruit trauma professionals
Final Field Study	Provides contextual realism and detailed design feedback for iteration	Need high fidelity prototypes to accurately simulate trauma scenarios

Figure 2. Benefits and shortcomings of human factors methods

RECOMMENDED METHODOLOGY

Even though we face many problems using the methodology outlined in Figure 1 in hospital environments, we emphasize that no other techniques can replace these methods. However, a particular combination of human factors methods is critical for designing usable products in trauma and other medical applications. Each method contributes a crucial piece to the design puzzle, but no technique alone gives the complete picture. Several methods used together create a rich base of data that describes the user. The table in Figure 2 shows the benefits and shortcomings with the different human factors methods. Figure 3 shows how we enhanced our methodology by combining several methods which filled the gaps left by stand-alone methods.

Field Studies

Field studies form a solid foundation of data for design. They also show where product and design tradeoffs can be made. Field studies provide an in-depth understanding of work practice, environment, and interactions. Prior to site visits, observers should be trained in relevant terminology, anatomy, physiology, and protocols. This is time consuming. Including clinical experts on observation teams is an excellent way to augment the limited domain knowledge of many designers until they can come up to speed. Even experienced, trained observers rarely acquire the amount of medical knowledge required to be a true domain expert.

Structured Interviews with Domain Experts

By holding structured interviews before observing work practice, designers can collect information about expectations, goals, and intentions. We found this step invaluable in educating and training the observers about the medical domain. We have had clinical experts walk through a sequence of their work, pointing out goals and intentions along the way. While this is "perceived" rather than "actual" work flow, it gives the observers a starting point, and allows them to see deviations from the perceived work flow.

Heuristic Evaluation

Heuristic evaluation [7] is effective for existing products where domain experts have experience using the product. In this situation, forming double domain expert teams of a human factors expert and a clinical expert codiscovering problems provide additional "bottom up" details we cannot probe for during field studies. This method provides detailed information quickly.

Early Investigative Usability Testing

Usability evaluation of grouping tasks, controls, and functions have also provided important "bottom up" details useful for design. Our experience with evaluating competitors' product designs for usability data has not been fruitful. In retrospect, the data produced from these competitive evalutions did not really improve or benefit our designs. Therefore, we focus these tests on our own products.

Design Standards

The FDA has a web site to download standards and guidelines [3]. These documents provide an excellent start but, in general, truly helpful and meaningful guidelines and standards have yet to be developed and adopted in medical device design.

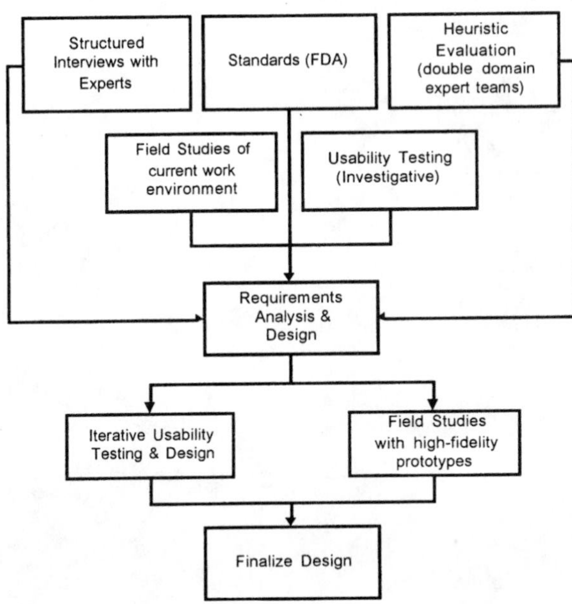

Figure 3. Human Factors Process and Methods for Trauma

Requirements Analysis and Design

Synthesizing the "top down" and "bottom up" data to create accurate work models begins the magic process of design. One technique we use often during requirements analysis is to have the doctors or domain experts review and prioritize the list of design requirements. We generate a questionnaire much like the one written by Coble, et al. [2], which works remarkably well. The prioritization helps with making tradeoffs, locating primary functions, and keeping the users involved in the design process. Methods such as QOC (questions, options, criteria) [6] are being refined but seem promising in making the design step explicit and concrete. These methods encourage us to think of several design alternatives. This "outside the box" thinking leads to more innovation designs.

Iterative Usability Testing and Design

We recommend iteratively usability testing both low and high fidelity prototypes [8]. Low fidelity prototypes work well for general screen layout and functional groupings. However, the benefits of testing navigation for our designs are limited with low fidelity prototypes. Because of the diagnostic decision making, which is highly cognitive, and the attention division due to the patient, high fidelity prototypes provide the most realism. High fidelity prototypes are better at predicting usability errors. We still face the dilemma of simulating realistic work scenarios quickly within our time and cost constraints. The military and certain disaster planning centers occasionally simulate elaborate trauma scenarios for testing procedures and equipment, but this is not feasible in most private industries. It is critical to take the high fidelity prototypes into the actual work environments.

Summary

The application of human factors methods to medical product design is not as widely adopted as it is in certain industries such as retail software. Because of the unique and demanding characteristics of the medical domain, designers face distinctive challenges in applying methods to the different phases of product development. More extensive application of human factors design needs to take place for us to make significant advances in designing usable medical products. The first step is promoting awareness about the obstacles we face in the medical environment. Designers need to reveal their real world experiences. We can learn from their successes and failures. The opportunities for usability advancements in healthcare are many. We are just beginning to scratch the surface in our efforts to improve the usability of medical products and ultimately the quality of patient care.

ACKNOWLEDGMENTS

We thank Kevin Goodwin, Jens Quistgaard, Lauren Pflugrath, and Howard Holman from ATL for supporting us in this work. Also Dr. Evelyn Cardenas who so graciously took the time to teach us about the trauma environment, and Greg Wimmenaur for his time, patience, and invaluable comments about this paper.

REFERENCES

1. Brown, D.S. The Challenges of User Based Design in a Medical Equipment Market. *Field Methods Casebook for Software Design*, Wixon and Ramey, Eds., John Wiley and Sons, 1996, 157-175.
2. Coble, J., Maffit, J.S., Orland, M.J., Kahn, M.G., Using Contextual Inquiry to Discover Physicians' True Needs. *Field Methods Casebook for Software Design*, Wixon and Ramey, Eds., John Wiley and Sons, 1996, 229-247.
3. FDA web site http://www.fda.gov/cdrh/humfac.
4. Gosbee, J., Ritchie, E. Human-Computer Interaction and Medical Software Development. *Interactions,* Vol. 4., July-August, 1997, 13-18.
5. Holtzblatt, K., Beyer, H.R., Apprenticing with the Customer, *Communications of the ACM,* Vol. 38, No. 5, May 1995, 45-52.
6. Moran, T.P., Carroll, J. M., *Design Rationale,* Lawrence Erlbaum Associates, 1997.

7. Nielsen, J., Mack, R.L., *Usability Inspection Methods.* John Wiley and Sons, 1994.

8. Rettig, M., Prototyping for Tiny Fingers. *Communications of the ACM,* Vol. 37, No. 4, April 1994, 21-27.

9. Wixon, D., Ramey, J., *Field Methods Casebook for Software Design*, Wixon and Ramey, Eds., John Wiley and Sons, 1996.

10. Xiao, Y., Hunter, W.A., MacKenzie, C.F., Jefferies, N.J. Task Complexity in Emergency Medical Care and Its Implications for Team Coordination. *Human Factors*, Vol. 38, No. 4, 1996, 636-645.

Voice-Enabled Structured Medical Reporting

Mary-Marshall Teel
Rachael Sokolowski
David Rosenthal
Lernout & Hauspie Speech Products
54 Third Avenue
Burlington, MA 01803
+1 781 893-5151
mteel@lhs.com, rsokolowski@lhs.com

Matt Belge
Vision & Logic
8 Mill St. Extension
Lincoln, MA 01773
+1 781 259 9498
mbelge@visionlogic.com

ABSTRACT
A paradox exists in applications that generate Electronic Health Records (EHRs) -- how can data be captured from health care professionals speaking in a natural manner and in a computer readable form? This paradox is historical. Physicians are accustomed to dictating to a tape recorder and the speech is transcribed to a paper-based report. This format makes electronic access difficult and is of low value to the health care institution's needs for research and analysis.

There is considerable interest in applying speech recognition to address this paradox. Users, many of whom are uncomfortable with computers, are attracted to a system that promises to simulate a transcriptionist. Institutional requirements are fulfilled as the data is created in an electronic form.

However, conflicting goals arise. Doctors have very little time, want to create reports quickly and wish to use natural narration. Health care institutions, on the other hand, want to capture information in a controlled and predictable structure. This paper describes the design of a system, currently under construction, which we have named OSSIM (*Open Systems Structured Information Manager*). OSSIM attempts to achieve a balance between difficult ease of use goals and demanding institutional goals for computer readable structured information.

Keywords
Speech Interface Design, Voice Recognition, Dictation, Clinical Reporting, Structured Reporting, SGML, EHR

INTRODUCTION
The most significant challenge to the realization of the Electronic Health Record (EHR) is the efficient acquisition of clinical findings generated by health care professionals, such as physicians and nurses.

Changes in the health care system with the advent of managed care and legislation are increasing the burden on health care professionals to see more patients and document encounter notes in less time. These changes are also mandating that institutions maintain clinical data in a format that facilitates research and analysis. For the EHR to become a reality, technology must be developed that will enable health care professionals to use personal computers to enter clinical information and create the EHR that meets the needs of the institution, without increasing the amount of time they spend on documentation.

As Lai and Vergo[1] point out, to be successful in this environment, a system must be very fast, very easy to use, and very accurate. In fact, they note that there is low tolerance for anything less than 100% accuracy.

Kurzweil A.I. (now a division of Lernout & Hauspie Speech Products) received a research grant to develop a new system that addresses the dual problems of the usability of a reporting system and the usefulness of the generated reports. OSSIM (*Open Systems Structured Information Manager)* is a voice-enabled, structured reporting application and is multi-modal, allowing for input from voice, mouse, and keyboard.

Designing a user interface that allows the clinician to create reports quickly and easily while preserving the benefits of report creation and storage, comprises the major research of the project. Our work is ongoing.

SYSTEM ARCHITECTURE
In OSSIM, the clinician speaks to a microphone connected to laptop or desktop computer, which, responds to the clinician's utterances by producing a clinical report. The system diagram is shown in Figure 1. The reports are

structured according to two widely adopted, open structuring schemes: 1) SGML and 2) CORBA. SGML *(Standard Generalized Markup Language)* is a standard means of defining document structures. Employing the use of SGML technology to health care data solves one part of the access problem; however, data that is in a structured, highly recognizable and accessible format is useful only if it can be readily exchanged between heterogeneous systems. Distributed computing technology is one solution that networks diverse information systems together to share data. CORBA *(Common Object Request Broker Architecture)* is a distributed computing industry standard for providing location and language independent method invocation for objects. By using CORBA technology, applications create interfaces to one another for data exchange. For example, a system using COBOL on an IBM mainframe can use CORBA interfaces to communicate with a system using C++ on a Windows NT workstation.

By combining SGML and CORBA technologies the document integrity is maintained and there is a means to distribute the data within that document. This combination supports the two documentation requirements for clinical data: 1) to maintain the integrity of the recordings and observation 2) to have the ability to access the data later for distribution and analysis.

WHAT IS STRUCTURED REPORTING?

In the process of creating clinical documentation, clinicians and the designers of applications that create medical documents have agreed upon a particular method and structure for reporting. For primary care, a report concerning a patient's visit with the physician has a particular format known as "SOAP", which describes the report's main sections: Subjective, Objective, Assessment and Plan. Other medical specialties have structures specific to their domains. Structured reporting presents the user with a form or template to follow that conforms to the agreed upon format.

In order to understand the benefits and outputs of structured reporting, consider the following scenario of two options for leaving a message. The first option is to leave the message by voice on an answering machine. The second option is to record the message on a pink "While You Were Out" note. The first method allows for speech to occur in a natural manner; however, it is a large and difficult task for a computer system to discern from the voice recording at what time you left the message or who called. The second option of using a structured message in the format of "While You Were Out" indicates who called, when and where the body of the message can be found. Additionally it indicates some actions to take upon receiving the message such as "Respond ASAP".

The options described above can be applied to documenting medical reports. Clinicians prefer to speak continuously or dictate reports to a recording device. Institutions, managed care companies and researchers prefer the "While You Were Out" scenario in order to gain better access to the clinical data. Computers are showing promising results of analyzing clinical data [2] in narrative text and applying structure but still are unable to accurately interpret unconstrained text.

Using the OSSIM system, the physician dictates the report to a voice-enabled personal computer. The system constructs the report in real time, according to the physician's utterances. To the primary care physician, the report looks like a traditional clinical report. All of the physician's interactions with the system are mediated by an object-oriented knowledge base of clinical information.

The system always knows what section of the report the

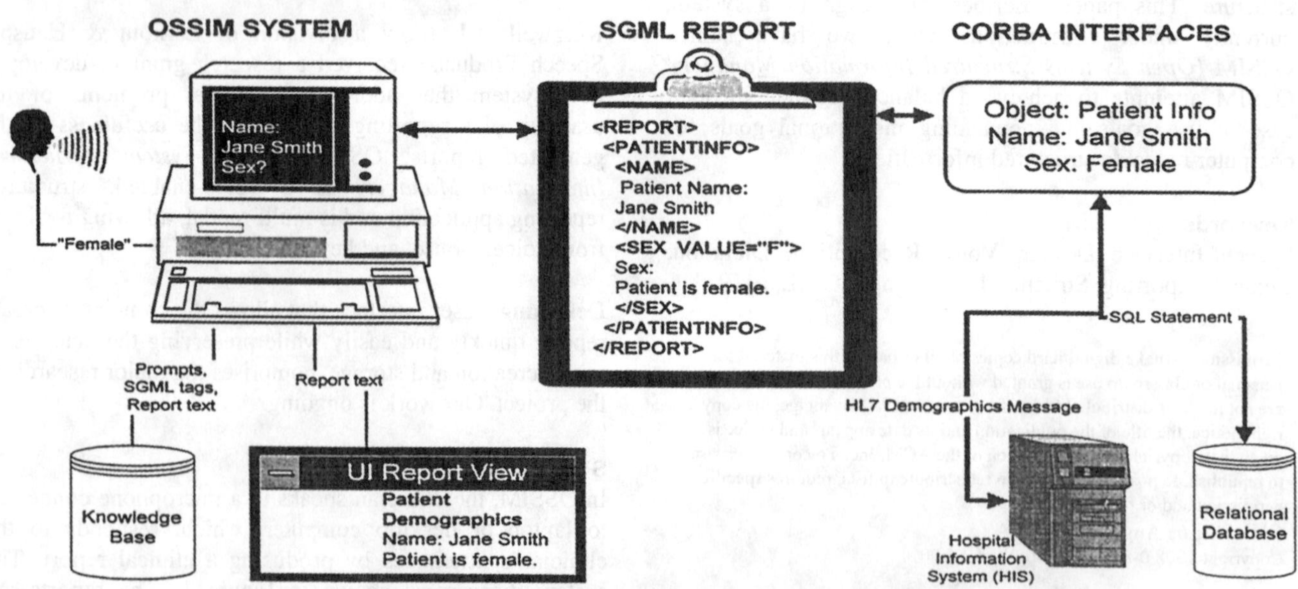

Figure 1. The System Diagram Illustrates the Flow from Input to Storage in a Database

physician is currently dictating, and as much as possible, the range of things that the physician is likely to say. In appropriate cases, the semantic content of the previously dictated parts of the report is used to aid recognition and present a convenient set of choices to the user. If, for example, the patient has complained of "earache," the system assigns special importance to words that relate to the anatomy of the ear.

We plan to extend the system to use large vocabulary continuous speech recognition (LVCSR) in the near future, which will accommodate more natural speaking style for dictation.

RELATED PRODUCTS/ EFFORTS

To date, medical reporting systems have favored either the needs of the institution by imposing highly structured templates on the clinician, or the needs of the clinicians by doing away with structured input altogether and increasing expressiveness. Table 1 lists of the major needs of both clinicians and institutions. It is a commonly held view, however, that structured data input is needed to make the EHR a reality that benefits the health care industry. [3]. Here is the dilemma for clinical reporting products: how to be sufficiently usable to be accepted by the clinician, and yet still contain the functionality that the administration/ enterprise requires. The design of the user interface for these systems requires balancing these conflicting goals.

Constituent	Primary Documentation Needs	Secondary Documentation Needs
Clinicians	Speed Ease of use Ease of learning Expressiveness Completeness	Lower malpractice risks Legible report Usefulness to EHR Increased revenue Lower costs Quality improvement
Institutions	Usefulness to EHR Increased revenue Lower costs Quality improvement Legible report	Speed Ease of learning Ease of use

Table 1: Documentation Needs for Clinicians and Institutions

The majority of medical reporting products have used a structured approach to clinical data. These systems typically provide templates for the clinician to follow. Oceania, HBOC, and Healthpoint ACS have all developed systems with templates to prompt the user, but these are not voice enabled. Kurzweil A.I. developed a voice-enabled structured reporting product. This product, Kurzweil Clinical Reporter (and its predecessor, Kurzweil Voice Report) has the advantage of structured input, but the output is stored in a flat, unstructured ASCII text file. Clinical Reporter uses discrete recognition, requiring the user to pause between words. Even though the system is voice enabled, the user interface is sometimes found to be cumbersome, controlling, and burdensome to the user. The addition of a structure, although designed in accordance with typical medical practice, is considered an imposition to the normal narrative thought processes.

Most recently, some reporting products have used continuous speech recognition for the input mode. IBM's MedSpeak/Radiology[1] in particular has an interface that allows for continuous speech input. This is a more natural interface for the user -- they can speak without pausing between words and without breaking their train of thought and is most similar to using a Dictaphone. There is no structured template that the clinician must follow. Dragon Systems also markets a dictation product for the medical market. [4] Neither the IBM nor the Dragon system outputs the information in a structured form such as SGML.

BACKGROUND FOR THE UI DESIGN

Our initial efforts were concentrated in four areas: 1) We researched the existing technologies for medical reporting. 2) We interviewed application specialists, who install the existing systems and train new users, as well as the director of the medical product managers. 3) We conducted field visits to hospitals to observe doctors under actual working conditions, and watched them use the existing system in their daily activities. For our field visits, we concentrated on two domains: primary care and pathology, which exhibit different reporting styles and techniques. We taped these visits so we could review the information. 4) We consulted with recognized experts for input on the design, including Nicole Yankelovich, a speech application expert, and Dr. Bryan Bergeron, a medical doctor who specializes in medical electronic record keeping/ informatics.

Our review of clinical reporting products included HBOC Pathways Smart Medical Record, Berdy Medical Systems' SmartClinic, and Oceania. These products covered a larger piece of the hospital information system. None of these products used voice input.

Results of Interviews

Based on our interviews with physicians, we found that many spend 25% of their time, or more, generating reports. We saw a mix of Windows expertise. Some clinicians were not at all familiar with Windows and some had limited computer experience.

The importance of being able to create a report quickly was very apparent from all of our interviews. One of our interviews was with a primary care physician, who has a small, private office practice. He said he had "two precious minutes" between patients, in which he had to capture all the information from the patient visit. He typically sees five to six patients an hour.

We interviewed one physician who exemplified the conflict of needing structure for the EHR, but wanting to have complete freedom in describing the patient visit. He was a primary care physician at a clinic for women's health in a Veteran's Hospital. He was also the Chief Information Architect for the hospital, so he was acutely aware of the overall needs for getting clinical information in the hospital information system as efficiently as possible. He stated that "physicians will do or try anything that will allow them to spend more time with patients." His statement emphasized the need for fast and easy report creation.

In our interviews, we also consistently heard the concern that the user did not know where s/he could input a specific piece of information. We had heard that the prompting was not adequate in the Kurzweil Clinical Reporter; the user wasn't sure what they could say. One story we heard was that a physician did not know how to report that an ace bandage was applied for an ankle sprain. In some cases, the users actually requested more flexibility in allowing for input that is not in the current active template; in others, just to supply a clear road map would tell them how to input the information. We think that both of these solutions are needed to solve this problem. The Director of the Pathology lab and the Director of Product Management echoed the need for a more random access to different points within the report.

Another issue we heard about consistently was the issue of reimbursement. The usefulness of a system for assisting in the reimbursement process was clearly important to all clinicians, in hospitals as well as private offices. Templates that prompt for all the information required for a specific level of Medicare reimbursement were considered useful, as well as any automatic generating of billing codes. Also, ensuring a complete report, by prompts, was important for reducing malpractice insurance costs as well.

When we discussed problems with the Kurzweil Clinical Reporter product, we consistently heard that there were too many windows. Users were confused and distracted by the number of windows. And the purposes of the windows were not obvious, as the user did not know where to go to accomplish certain functions.

The need for customization was also expressed in all our interviews. There are several types of customizations that were requested. The most complex, in terms of adapting to a structured form, was the individuality of reporting styles. We heard many examples of this issue, but one example regarded the primary care SOAP format. Some physicians did not want to strictly observe the SOAP format, especially where there were multiple complaints. Another level of customization is editing the text that is generated from an utterance, or keyboard selection. In particular, physicians whose main work product is producing a report, such as radiologists and pathologists, want o use their own words.

We visited a Pathology department in a large urban hospital. Here we saw that the pathologists, doing the microscopic examination of a specimen, had to look up from the microscope, and re-adjust their visual focus, to dictate the microscopic findings. (They were using Kurzweil Voice Report (the DOS version of Kurzweil Clinical Reporter). Each of the three pathologists who worked in the lab expressed discomfort with the requirement to re-adjust their visual focus, and noted that with the previous Dictaphone-style system was easier to create reports.

From the interviews we realized that the report structures in health care, although they may vary by domain, are quite standard; physicians learn well-understood procedures for producing reports in medical school. Physicians main interactions are with humans and the appearance of the interface should reflect this; i.e. the colors and appearance of the UI should be soft and flesh toned. Workflow must be integrated into the UI; e.g., users who are physically far from the computer should be able to read the prompts and those who do not wish to see the report text should not be forced to do so.

Goals of the Interface

From our interviews with doctors, health technicians, and others, we derived the following goals:

1. To create reports as quickly as possible, with a goal of creating a primary care report in two minutes or less.
2. To improve navigation, making it easy to find the right place to provide a given input, and to clarify and make it easier to understand what goes where.
3. To support editing of the generated report, while preserving the tagged report text.
4. To capture the information in a way that it can be tagged and used by typical EHRs.
5. To shorten the learning curve for the wide range of users including those who are not very familiar with Windows based systems.

EVOLUTION OF THE UI DESIGN

We began designing a user interface for OSSIM after we were about half way though the process of interviewing users. As we learned more about customer needs, and as our ideas matured, the UI evolved over time.

Specifying Input Focus

One of the issues we wanted to tackle right away was to eliminate confusion about input focus with multiple windows. When a user clicks with a mouse in a conventional GUI, they know where the result of their action will end up. When a user speaks to a collection of windows, it may not be clear which window is responding to their input.

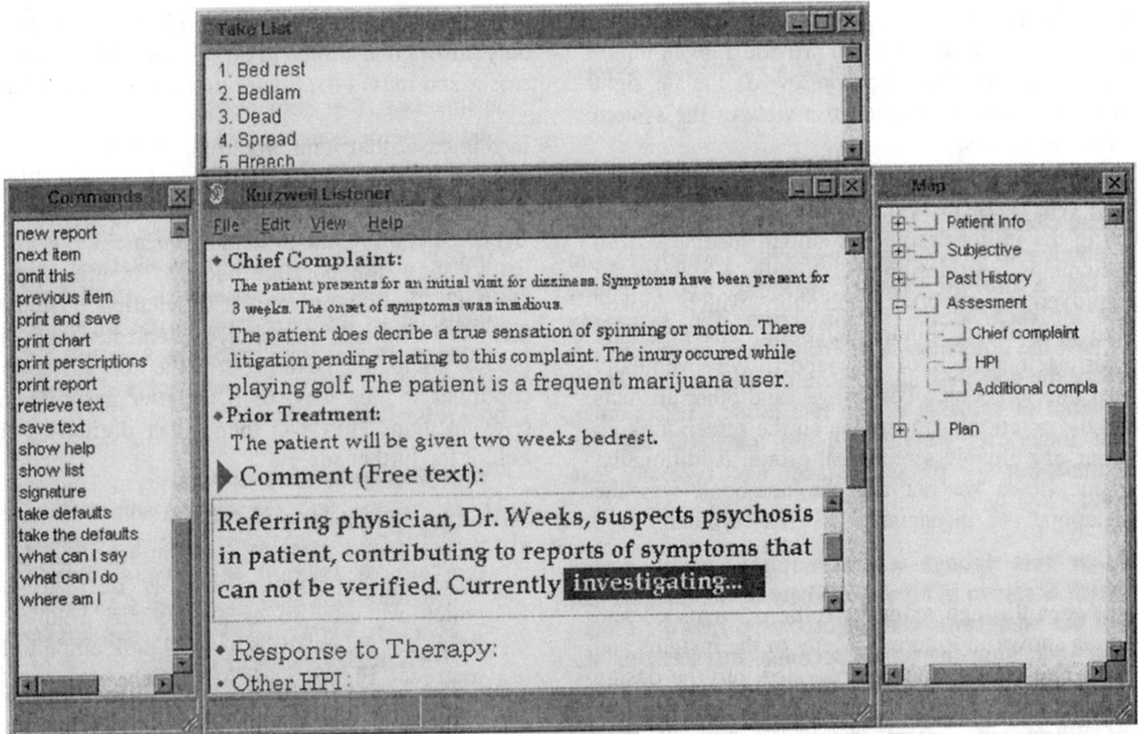

Figure 2 The First UI Design Resulting from Interviews

For example, a user can ask for a list of voice commands. This brings up a separate window listing all the commands that can be spoken by voice. At this point in time, input focus has shifted to the commands window. Users become confused when they state one of those commands, expecting it to be applied to whichever part of the system responds to that command. Instead, what actually happens is the commands window captures the input, does not recognize that particular command, and instead does nothing. We attempted to eliminate this problem in OSSIM in two ways. We recognized that the user's mental model is one in which the user does not see each window as a separate system but sees the collection as a whole. We made use of "pass through" windows, which, if they do not recognize a given command, will pass the words on to other windows to see if they know what to do with the user's command. To visually reinforce this idea, each "window" is anchored to the others so that they form one unified group. Figure 2 shows our first attempt at this design approach.

Helping Users Know What To Say

As Figure 2 shows, other design goals were first attempted. We wanted to help users know what to say at any given point in the report, and to show them the report that would be generated from their utterances. In the center window is the report itself. The user is interacting with a form, which contains prompts for various inputs. Under the section titled "Chief Complaint", we see the text of the report that has been generated in response to user input.

When the user first encountered the prompt, it appeared as a drop down scrolling list of choices. When the user said "Chief Complaint", (this is the medical term for the principal problem a patient has presented to the doctor), the list opens up to show all the possible choices. When a doctor chooses an item by saying it, the list disappears and is replaced by the text that will go in the report. The text is generated from our Knowledge Base, which "knows" what text to provide in response to a given user input. In our example, this text is "The patient presents for an initial visit for dizziness".

The Knowledge Base also contains follow-up questions to be asked if a given condition exists. For example, if a patient complains of a headache, the user will also be prompted for information regarding how long the patient has had headaches, and how severe they are.

Freeing Users from Physical Proximity to the Display

The initial design shown in Figure 2 also employed a Fish-Eye Lens [5] to attempt to make the system more legible from a distance and for doctors who switch between viewing a microscope and a computer screen. The fish eye lens makes the information in the center of the screen the largest, and information gets progressively smaller the further from the center one goes. In Figure 2, the center of the fish eye is positioned about the words "Comment (Free Text)".

The design in Figure 2 also attempted to solve a problem of helping the user know where to go to provide a given input. In our first new design, the Map window on the far right handled this. This window employed a view of the system as a collection of folders.

IMPROVING THE DESIGN - ITERATE!

After creating the initial design, we sought feedback from doctors and changed our design accordingly. A subsequent design employed a notebook metaphor, which looked literally like a three ring binder notebook. The notebook had tabs for each section of the report. We eventually evolved past the notebook. The "rings" and other artifacts that created the notebook appearance on the screen took up a fair amount of valuable screen real estate. Additionally, from our interviews we realized the notebook was the wrong metaphor -- physicians do not typically use notebooks.

The design went through several iterations, to its current state, which is shown in Figure 3. Many of the insights and results of the interviews were incorporated into the design including: indicating the report sections, emphasizing the process of filling out a form, displaying and allowing editing of the report text, including a magnifier window and improving navigation.

Report Sections

As Figure 3 shows, the improved design denotes sections of the report by using a column of icons on the far left of the screen. Typically, the doctor will simply take the sections in the order they are presented, in which case they do not have to do anything - the system will automatically move them through each section in order. The icons visually represent the content of each section and help the doctors remember the sections so that they can do them in whatever order they like simply by speaking their name. The middle section of the window, which we have called the dictation window, changes to reflect the selected report section. The icons are easier to locate and identify than the hierarchical tree representation on the right side of Figure 2. The icons are a significant improvement over the notebook design, which animated the flipping of pages when a new section was selected and suffered from a serious performance problem -- the user had to wait and watch each page turn.

Using the System

The dictation window in the center of the screen is the form the doctor must fill out. On the far right is the text of the report that will be generated in response to the doctor's utterances.

To fill out the form in Figure 3, the doctor says the word "Chief complaint" and the input focus moves to this part of the form. The item is a scrolling list, which automatically drops down to show the doctor the possible choices. The doctor chooses a choice by saying its name; in this case they said "Pediatric earache". Since this particular item only allows one choice to be selected, the list automatically closes and moves the doctor to the next item in the form.

In this case, that item would be "HPI". HPI is a standard medical term meaning "History of Present Illness". The system moves to the first item under HPI, which is "Visit Type". As before, the system automatically drops down the list to show the possible choices. In this case, they are "Initial", "Follow up" and "Consultation". The doctor says the word "Initial", the choice is selected and the system moves on to the next item in the form. Report creation continues in this way, until the user has filled in all the relevant data. They can then either digitally "sign it", or hold it for further review.

The form serves three purposes.

1) It ensures that the correct information is captured, including information that is deemed mandatory, which we refer to as a "required field". Required fields are indicated by a small pink circle to left of the item (see Figure 3.) When a field has been filled in a check mark appears next to it.
2) The labels of the form serves as a memory aid - to speak to that section of the report the doctor simply says the words of the label.
3) It ensures that the information is recorded in the proper places. Each field in the form is tagged and stored in the database accordingly.

Seeing the Report Created

The primary product that the doctor is trying to create is the actual written report itself. Doctors typically value their words, are sometimes legally held to the content of the report text and want to be sure the system is creating the correct report. In Figure 3, the window on the far right of the screen facilitated this. As the user dictates information to the form in the center window, the window on the right displays the report text that is being generated as a result.

The doctor only says the words "pediatric earache" "Initial", "4 days" and "gradual". Using this information, the system then generates a report sentence, which says, "The patient presents for an initial visit for pediatric ear ache, duration 4 days, onset gradual". The doctor spoke a total of six words; the system created a sentence with 16 words, which saves the doctor time.

Editing structured text

Doctors often want to edit the text in the final report. However, a conflict arises with the need to capture structured information. For example, if the doctor were to change the words "earache" to "heart murmur", the report needs to reflect this. To make matters more complicated, a change of this sort would cause a ripple down effect - there are different follow up questions, such as what symptoms

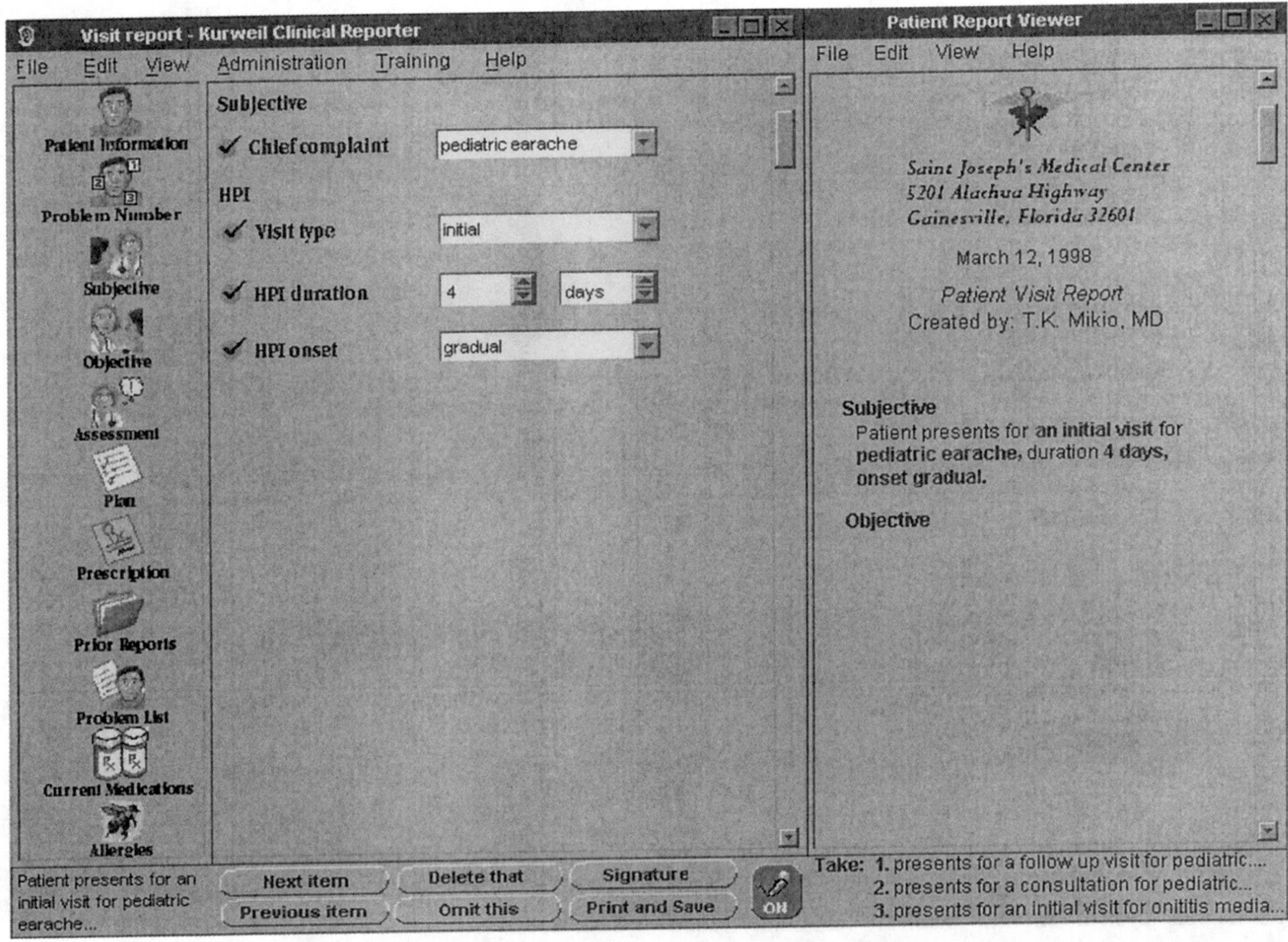

Figure 3 User Interface with Design Improvements

and the types of physical exams, that must be answered about "heart murmur" than there are about "earache". OSSIM allows doctors to directly type in words in the report window (on the far right of Figure 3). However, words that are "tagged" in SGML can not be changed in this window. If a doctor attempts to change a tagged word, a dialog box appears stating "To change this word(s) you must go back and dictate this part of the report again". If they indicate that they wish to do so, the system then brings up the appropriate form to fill out, and they can voice dictate to it.

To help doctors know what words are tagged and which ones are not, tagged words are presented in bold face, and they are colored a dark crimson.

While the ideal solution might seem to be to allow users to make changes in either place, an earlier version of our product did just that, with little success. Users had a difficult time picking out the report text in between the prompts and labels. Early feedback that we have from the field indicates that our new approach shows promise.

Magnifier window

In our earlier design, we described a Fish Eye lens technique that was designed to make it easier to read the screen. We revised the Fish Eye approach after concerns arose that the spatial orientation in a fish eye lens is difficult to follow. In its place, we are now implementing a magnifier lens window.

This magnifier will be a separate window superimposed on the center window of Figure 3, the part of the system that shows the form that is it be filled in. The magnifier will show the contents of approximately 4 lines worth of the form, magnified up by a factor of approximately 3 to 1.

The Find It Window

From the feedback we received regarding our early designs we learned that named sections alone will not completely solve the problem of not knowing where is the proper place to provide a given input. We introduced a new concept, called *Find it*, to help with this problem. Figure 4 shows the Find it window, which can be brought up by simply saying the words "Find It", or by choosing it from a menu.

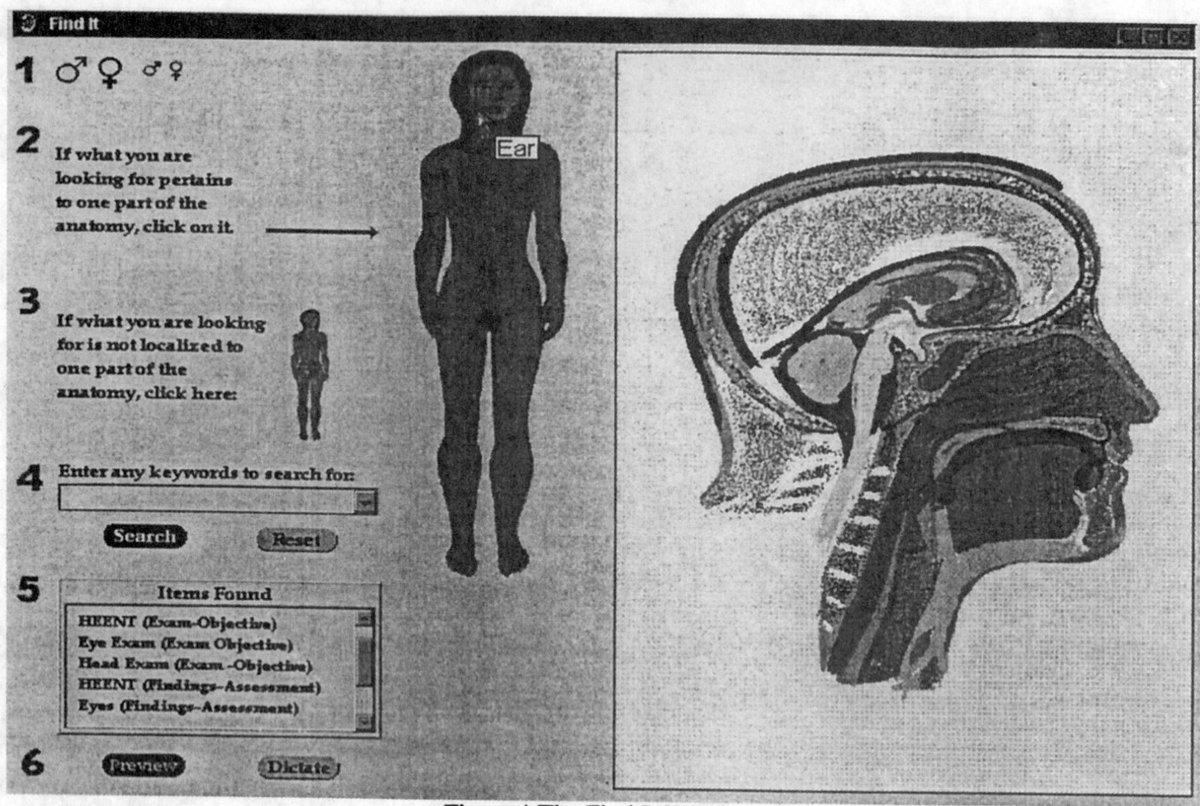

Figure 4 The Find It Window

This window stems from an idea provided by Dr. Bryan Bergeron, who told us that there is no universally accepted classification system in the medical community for organizing report information. The one universally understood hierarchy in the medical community is the human body itself.

A doctor has conducted an eye exam and wants to report on the results. After bringing up the Find It window, the doctor clicks on a part of the anatomy s/he is interested in, the full human figure shown on the left part of the screen. The right part of the screen shows a close up of that part of the anatomy. Beneath this drawing, a "Results List" shows report items that are relevant to this part of the body. In our example, HEENT (Head, Eyes, Ears, Nose, and Throat) is one of the choices in the list. The user may select this item from the list, and the anatomy drawing will replace the form for inputting an HEENT exam. The window also provides, on the left side of the screen, a place for typing in keywords. This is useful if the item the user is looking for is not localized to one part of the body (such as chicken pox, or a fever). After typing in the keywords, the results list on the right will display any report which contains those keywords.

CONCLUSIONS AND FUTURE WORK

We will perform usability tests on our current design at a local Veteran's Administration hospital. We will address any performance considerations. In conclusion, although we have not completely solved the paradox between user convenience and institutional requirements, we believe that we have made major progress in addressing the issues in both areas.

ACKNOWLEDGMENTS

This project was funded by a grant from the Advanced Technology Program of the National Institute of Standards and Technology (NIST ATP).

We thank Russ Brami for the graphic design of OSSIM, and Nicole Yankelovich for help editing this paper.

REFERENCES

1. Lai, J. and Vergo, J. Medspeak: Report Creation with Continous Speech Recognition. Proceedings of CHI'97 (Atlanta, GA, April 1997) pp. 431-438
2. Hripsack G., Friedman C., Alderson P.O., DuMouchel W., Johnson S.B., Clayton P.D., Unlocking Clinical Data from Narrative Reports: a Study of Natural Language Processing. Ann. Intern Med 122: 681-8.
3. Benet, Bernard. Dictation Systems for Windows: Dragon, IBM, Kurzweil. Seybold Report on Desktop Publishing, n10 v9, June 1995 pp 12-19.
4. Patient Care Information Systems: Successful Design and Implementation. Drazen EL, Metzger JB, Ritter JL, Schneider MK. New York: Springer-Verlag, 1995. p.91.
5. G. Furnas. Generalized fisheye views. In Proceedings of CHI '86, Conference on Human Factors in Computing Systems, pages 12-16, Boston, MA, Apr. 1986. ACM

Interactive Storytelling Environments: Coping with Cardiac Illness at Boston's Children's Hospital

Marina Umaschi Bers[†], **Edith Ackermann**[††], **Justine Cassell**[†], **Beth Donegan**[†††], **Joseph Gonzalez-Heydrich**[†††], **David Ray DeMaso**[†††], **Carol Strohecker**[††], **Sarah Lualdi**[†††], **Dennis Bromley**[††], **Judith Karlin**[†††]

[†]**MIT Media Laboratory**
20 Ames Street, E15-320
Cambridge MA 02139
USA
1 617 253 0379
marinau@media.mit.edu
justine@media.mit.edu

[††]**MERL - A Mistubishi Electric Research Laboratory**
201 Broadway, 8th floor
Cambridge MA 02139
USA
1 617 621 7500
edith@merl.com
stro@merl.com
bromley@merl.com

[†††]**Children's Hospital**
300 Longwood Avenue
Boston MA 02115 USA
1 617 355 6724
doneganb@a1.tch.harvard.edu
heydrich@a1.tch.harvard.edu
demaso@a1.tch.harvard.edu
lualdi@a1.tch.harvard.edu
judithc@tiac.net

ABSTRACT

This paper describes exploration of uses of a computational storytelling environment on the Cardiology Unit of the Children's Hospital in Boston during the summer of 1997. Young cardiac patients ranging from age 7 to 16 used the SAGE environment to tell personal stories and create interactive characters, as a way of coping with cardiac illness, hospitalizations, and invasive medical procedures. This pilot study is part of a larger collaborative effort between Children's Hospital and MERL - A Mitsubishi Electric Research Laboratory to develop a web-based application, the Experience Journal, to assist patients and their families in dealing with serious medical illness. The focus of the paper is on young patients' uses of SAGE, on SAGE's affordances in the context of the hospital, and on design recommendations for the development of future computational play kits. Preliminary analysis of children's stories indicates that children used different modes of interaction—direct, mediated, and differed—depending upon what personae the narrator chooses to take on. These modes seem to vary with the mindset and health condition of the child.

Keywords

Interactive storytelling, authoring environments, cardiology illness, coping strategies, computational play kits, soft interfaces

INTRODUCTION

The work presented here was conducted in the Cardiology Unit of Boston's Children's Hospital with cardiac patients ranging from 7 to 16 years old. Its main purposes were: 1) to gather stories and pictures to be incorporated in the Experience Journal [1], an intranet site developed at MERL to help patients, hospital professionals, and families to contribute and link narratives related to cardiac illness and medical interventions; 2) to explore the uses and limitations of SAGE [2,], a storytelling construction kit that supports children's creations of their own interactive storytellers and engages them in expressing their feelings in a playful context; and 3) to form design recommendations for future play kits that address emotional needs of young patients and their families, as well as overall design considerations for work with computational tools in hospital environments.

BACKGROUND WORK

Improvements in the management of cardiac disease have enabled children to survive who in the past would have died, however, many of these youngsters continue to experience chronic illness with repeated hospitalizations and opeartions. While existing research addresses the emotional burdens on young patients facing chronic illness [3] and stresses the crucial role of adaptive parent-child relations as a predictor in their well-being, much remains to be done in order to understand the complex relations between life-threatening heart diseases and psychological outcomes [4].

Many interventions have been developed at Children's Hospital to address the needs of patients and their families (e.g. pre-admission hospital preparatory programs, individual physician meetings, books for different ages, psychiatric consulting, etc.). The cornerstone of these interventions has been to provide children and their parents with important education regarding their illness while allowing their expression of negative emotions. We wanted to explore ways in which the affected patients and their families could develop and maintain a significant role in their own recovery process. Discussion of relevant literature and existing software, on-site hospital observations, and interviews with patients, families, and medical professionals have allowed us to identify a few areas where current interventions could be augmented. Two of these areas will be addressed here:

- The need to provide a forum where families and children can exchange experiences and learn from one another.
- The need to encourage young patients to express and share their feelings through story telling and other forms of symbolic enactment [5].

Narrative or "the story a person tells about her life" can be a helpful therapeutic tool in that it provides a means of dealing with fears and fantasies. For example, myths [6] show us how to live a meaningful life and fairy tales [7] help us develop our inner resources in order to cope with issues in growing up. Research has been done in using narrative with young patients to treat traumatic experiences [8, 9, 10]. Stories serve not only emotional and social functions, but also a cognitive one. Narratives allow us to understand past experiences and organize them in terms of future ones [11].

Work has been done to create interactive storytelling tools that explore: personal family narratives [12], theatrical approaches to human-computer interaction [13], traditional literary problems such as point of view and suspension of disbelief [14], emotionally believable agent-based systems [15], and emergent, dynamic, adaptive story creation [16]. However there have been few attempts to use computational narrative environments for therapeutic purposes.

DESCRIPTION OF THE SAGE ENVIRONMENT

SAGE (Storytelling Agent Generation Environment) is a construction kit that supports children's creation of their own wise storytellers to play with. This environment was developed at the MIT Media Laboratory to address the need for technological environments designed to encourage children's exploration of their inner worlds through the use of personal storytelling [2, 2A].

SAGE was conceived to help children "play out" what is happening in their lives by telling and listening to stories. In order to encourage children's emotional engagement, the assistant of the sage storytellers is embodied in an interactive stuffed animal — a *soft interface*. With SAGE, children become the designers as well as users of their creations. Thus, SAGE supports two modes of interaction. In the first mode, children share their personal stories with a wise sage, and its rabbit assistant, who "listen" and then offer a relevant tale in response. In the second mode, children can add to the collection of wise sages by designing their own storyteller for themselves and others to interact with.

In order to support children in creating their own characters, a visual programming language was developed to design and program: (1) the scripts that are used by the storyteller, (2) the conversational structure or flow of the interaction, (3) the body behaviors of the interactive toy, which behaves as the pet assistant of the storyteller, and (4) the database of tales that are offered in response by the character. SAGE also has multimedia capabilities allowing children to record their own stories and to draw their own characters.

Development of SAGE was guided by the educational philosophy of constructionism [17, 18], according to which people learn best when engaged in creating some tangible object that they can reflect upon and share with others. In light of this approach, SAGE focuses on creating stories and storytellers as "evocative objects" [19] that invite reflection about the child's inner world.

SAGE seeks cognitive and emotional engagement. Hence, the decision to embed the assistant of the sage storytellers in a programmable interactive stuffed animal — a soft interface [21] (see figure 1). Winnicott [20] introduced the term "transitional object" to refer to the first "not-me" object perceived by infants to give warmth, have texture, or move about "as if" endowed with a life of its own — while remaining resilient and responsive. Quintessential examples are the blanket, stuffed doll or teddy bear that many young children like to carry around. In SAGE the rabbit assistant plays the role of a transitional object.

The stuffed animal is capable of some of the types of nonverbal behaviors that humans use to indicate engagement and which are commonly found in conversational narratives between people [22]. In interaction mode, children can watch the stuffed rabbit move as they converse with it. In design mode, children can decide on the toy's communicative behaviors as well as the different personalities it might have.

Figure 1: Interactive programmable stuffed rabbit

Previous work showed that children engaged readily with SAGE [2, 21]. Children created storytellers as projections of fears, feelings, interests, and role-models. Their experiences were supported by an iterative design process that enabled children to *decenter* [23] and *debug* their characters after observing other people's interactions with them.

Our current effort aims to observe how patients with serious cardiac illness might appropriate the tool. Erich Lindemann, former Chief of Psychiatry at Massachusetts General Hospital, describes such patients as "young people who suddenly have become quite a bit older; they are facing possible death, or serious limitations in their lives; and they will naturally stop and think about life, rather than just live it from day to day" [24]. We wanted to offer SAGE to young patients in life-threatening situations as a means for exploring issues that worry them.

SETTING THE STAGE AT THE HOSPITAL

We hoped that eventually a culture would develop around the SAGE technology involving nurses, doctors, parents, and patients. We also saw possibilities for adapting SAGE to the Experience Journal and future efforts to develop software play kits. With these ideas in mind, we agreed on a work procedure that would not interfere with medical routines and adjusted the technology to fit the needs of the hospital setting. Preparations were guided by DeMaso and Gonzalez-Heydrich (psychiatrists), Donegan (child life specialist), and Lualdi (social worker). We mounted the computer and rabbit onto a wheeled cart so the setup would be mobile, safe, and properly wired. Later, we conducted sessions with SAGE at each child's bedside.

To engage the young patients, we created a character who could tell stories relevant to the medical environment. As a first example, we made "Mrs. Needle". This cartoon-type character allows for symbolic enactment of fears children have of needles. She uses humor as a way to break the ice and engage children in an interaction. Later, different children created new characters, such as "Sadly Alone" and "Mr. Tape", and hospital professionals built their own, such as "Mr. Squeeze".

SESSIONS WITH SAGE

We wanted to deepen our understandings of how young cardiac patients might work with SAGE and how SAGE could fit into a very different environment from the one it was conceived for originally. We worked with eight children ranging from 7 to 16. We explained the project to all children and their parents. Written consent was obtained from the parents to use their children's contributions.

Here we describe children's uses of SAGE and propose a framework for interpreting their stories. (The children's names have been changed in order to ensure privacy.) We then discuss SAGE's affordances for the hospital environment and make design recommendations for evolving SAGE, the Experience Journal, and play kits that may be developed in the future.

Some stories

Lisa (16) created a character (herself) called "Sadly Alone." The character asks the user, "Are you feeling sad?" and then tells a story. Lisa worked on her story with a close family member. Lisa was gravely ill when working with SAGE.

```
My name is Lisa, and I have a problem. I'm 16 years old and I have a real bad heart problem and I am getting ready to have a heart transplant really soon but the hardest thing is my mother [is very sick] And I have a little brother, so it's so hard to leave them alone  so I just stay strong and do what I have to do  and if you ever have this kind of problem just stay strong for your family and think of me. (*) Lisa *
```

Samuel (13) is an outpatient who visits the hospital regularly in order to receive treatments. He wrote three stories and then put them together under the same title.

```
The heart transplant dictionary

At first I felt very sick and I had to go into the Emergency room. First I had an IV which I never had before which I was pretty scared about and then I had a blood test on my arm and I never had one of those either which I was very scared about too but the IV was much scarier because I didn't know how much it was going to hurt. And another scary part was a lot of different doctors coming in all the time and that made me nervous because it made me think that there was something very wrong with me [...] but then I got better and I got to go home and I thought that everything will be OK but then I got sick again and I had to go back to the hospital and then they realized that I had to have a heart transplant.

After my heart transplant I was very sick because my body was rejecting my heart and it made me feel very sick and I had to go in for medicine and get biopsies twice a week where they go through a vein in your neck with a needle and they thread a catheter through and then they scrape a little piece of the heart tissue to see if you have any rejection. Rejection is when your white blood cells do not recognize your heart and think it is some bad virus or disease because it is not your original heart and your white blood cells try to attack your heart. So I kept having rejection [...] so they sent me to [another hospital] to go on a experimental drug [...] and felt better and the new drug is working very well
```

and now I have no heart rejection at all [...]

The following examples are from saved logs of interactions that patients had with different characters, some already existing and others created by the children. Interaction between CHILD and SAGE happens through the keyboard: typing input and text-to-speech or recorded output.

This is a log of an interaction between Damian (16) and the rabbit, best friend of "Mrs. Needle."

SAGE: Hi, what is your name?
CHILD: Damian
SAGE: Welcome, Damian. I am Bunny, the best friend of Mrs. Needle. She hides in the computer because she is a little shy. She thinks that all the kids hate her. So she asked me to talk on her behalf. Is that OK with you?
CHILD: yes
SAGE: Wonderful, wonderful, Damian! Mrs. Needle is worried because kids scream when they see her. But, have you met Mrs. Needle before?
CHILD: I guess yes
SAGE: Well, Mrs. Needle is my best friend and she hides in the computer. Tell me, Damian, how old are you?
CHILD: 16
SAGE: Wauh, Damian, you are older than me. I wonder if you are you scared of needles as I am ? I hate them, all except my friend Mrs. Needle. What about you?
CHILD: They are all right
SAGE: As I was telling you, Damian, I am Mrs. Needle's best friend and she asked me to find out why children hate her so much. She thinks that it is because she stings, but she is not sure. What do you think?
CHILD: yes no kid is excited to get any needles
SAGE: I see Damian ... what else can you tell me about this?
CHILD: the kids are afraid of it because it hurts and they don't like it to hurt and I guess that is it
SAGE: Well, Damian, let me see if I understand. I am sure that Mrs. Needle is very happy to hear what you have to say. Yes no kid is excited to get any needles the kids am afraid of it because it hurts and they don't like it to hurt and you guess that is it. Am I right?
CHILD: yes
SAGE: Guess what, Damian? Mrs. Needle has a story for you. She is shy but she loves to tell stories. She always says that they have power...Listen to her...
SAGE: They built me to sting, but that is not all I do. If you were a flower I could water you without hurting you. But you are not, and I am not a water pot. My nose is like a hose or like a straw and my belly has goodies than can help you to heal. When my belly is empty, the goodies are yours and you can feel better. But sometimes it is the other way around. My belly starts completely empty, and then it becomes full with your goodies. You can think of me as a someone that only stings, but I also do good. The problem is that this is not always immediately obvious.
SAGE: I loved Mrs. Needle's story, but how about you? Does it somehow relate to what you told me before, Damian?
CHILD: yes it does
SAGE: I see, Damian, please explain me the connection. I don't get it.
CHILD: the children don't realize that the stuff can help them, the medicine
SAGE: I see, Damian, you got the power of the story. I am sure my friend Mrs. Needle will be very happy. I wish that you will always have the courage to keep telling and listening to stories. I hope to see you soon....Bye !

After playing with "Mrs. Needle", Damian decided to create his own character called "Mr. Tape." He created the conversational structure[1], the scripts that "Mr. Tape" says, and also the stories that he tells. After, he interacted with the character and invited other people in the Cardiac Unit to play with him. This is a saved log of Damian's interaction.

SAGE: Hi my name is Mr. Tape. What is yours?
CHILD: Damian
SAGE: Well hello, Damian, my name is Mr. Tape. I am very sticky, as you probably may know, a lot of children don't like tape because when you have to take it off it hurts. Some kids like me to put me anywhere, like the face, hands, just for fun. Do you like tape?
CHILD: no
SAGE: I am sorry, why don't you like me. Does it hurt you?
CHILD: sometimes, yes
SAGE: Well, I am good for taping things up that are broken and I come in different kinds. I try to do the best I can with making things back to normal. So, Damian, how old are you ?
CHILD: 16

[1] A diagram of the conversational structure is displayed in a window area where children can design the flow of the conversation between the storyteller (computer or toy) and subsequent users [2, 21].

SAGE: You are lucky to be able to live that long. My life expectancy is only two to three years. Some people use me up fast and sometimes I am forgotten in the junk drawer. I get pretty lonely in there. Would you like to hear my story?
CHILD: yes
SAGE: When I am used as medical tape I am the number 1 user for nurses and doctors. I go on IVs and wrap things up. I am good to write on for the nurses to put on IV medication. You can use me just about everything in the hospital but I am not very sticky for heavier objects. I could be colored on and used for decorations for kids that are very bored. Some people just throw me around and drop me which hurts my feelings, I can't pick them up and drop them, but I thank them for using me as their number one choice. Well it was nice talking to you, maybe you will talk to me again and listen to my story. Bye

Interpretative framework

As a means of understanding the coherence in children's interactions with SAGE, we drafted an interpretative framework that groups the creations (stories and storytellers) into three categories according to narrative function. These modes correspond to ways of using SAGE. We call them "direct," "mediated," and "differed." We used some classic questions from literary studies to guide our reading: "Who is saying what to whom?" and "What persona does the narrator choose to take on?". Answering these questions led us to focus on interesting characteristics of the children's creations, such as: the role of the child as a designer (as expressed through the chosen narrative voice), the audience for whom the message (story or storyteller) is intended, and the persona used in the narrative. These characteristics seem to vary with the mindset and health condition of the child.

Some of the children employed the **direct mode**, using the first-person voice and telling stories from personal experience or creating storytellers who are clear representations of themselves. The narrator chooses to behave as an author or spokesperson and sends a message to an audience which is the world. Within this mode we identified two different approaches, which we call "expressive" and "informational." In the expressive approach, children who need or want to tell their own personal life stories open up to others about their inner feelings. In the informational approach, children give factual accounts of their illnesses and medical interventions. For example, Lisa's approach was expressive; she called her storyteller "Sadly alone" and told a very personal and sad story. Samuel used SAGE in a strictly informational way. He called his story "The heart transplant dictionary" and frequently used medical names and facts. Both children had serious health problems. However, by the time he worked with SAGE, Samuel had already overcome the worst of his illness and was an outpatient visiting the hospital periodically, while Lisa was an inpatient in very serious condition.

Some of the children employed the **mediated mode**, using SAGE to express their feelings indirectly. They may choose to interact with an already existing character who does not ask direct personal questions, or to add stories to this character's database. Children may behave as actors or performers and may use the second-person voice in their stories. The children we worked with who adopted this mode were sick but their condition was not, at the time, life-threatening. They were willing to enter into a fantasy world that allowed them to play with different aspects of their illness, without approaching the issues directly.

Some of the children employed the **differed mode**, using SAGE to its maximum potential by situating themselves in the role of a playwright or choreographer of the interaction. They created a character who may have represented themselves in a symbolic way. The audience was the whole world and the children were conscious of how audiences might react to their storytellers. The children we worked with who adopted this mode were about to go home and often chose to give a humorous profile to their characters.

Ong [25] quotes Henry James in saying that "an author makes his reader very much as he makes his character." This describes what children did using SAGE. They made characters as well as stories, but they also made their own imagined audiences. For example, Damian was very concerned, during the creation of Mr. Tape, about what "the other kids" would think while playing with the character. He was worried that they would get afraid of real tape or get ideas about things that might not really happen to them. He would carefully edit his story and dialogs — not from a literary perspective, but from an awareness of the implications and effects that his character might engender in the recipient of the message. In this context, the digital domain can offer more than printed media. Although there is a long literary tradition, as shown by Ong, in fictionalizing audience, interactive media offer the possibility, after one has created a character (and audience), to try it out. As previous work with SAGE suggested [2], the fact of actually trying out the character with the audience, in an iterative design process, helps children *decenter*, put themselves in someone else's place, and get a little closer to the audience.

SAGE'S AFFORDANCES

A few features would need further consideration if the tool were to be developed for use in hospital environments. Here we are especially concerned with young children as users.

- **Support different styles of storytelling**: The children were able to use SAGE in many different ways. They moved with ease between modalities (draw the character, record stories, write stories, create conversations, create stories, interact with the characters, have other people interact with the characters). Children need to be able to choose from a set of computer-based storytelling experiences based on the desired level of personal engagement (from personal stories to fictional stories), as well as on readiness for self-reflection.

- **The importance of voice:** Children generally liked to hear their stories read by the different text-to-speech voices in the computer. Moreso than in previous work with SAGE, young patients in the hospital enjoyed recording the stories in their own voice. Children engaged in the direct mode wanted human voices, while children engaged in the differed mode tended to prefer "funny computer voices." The recording and replay of a child's own voice needs to be better integrated in future versions of SAGE.
- **Software limitations:** The conversational structure of the tool, while important, is too complex for the current use. In order to create a conversational structure, the child needs to know some basic programming, which may require a lengthy learning curve. In the hospital, time for play is unpredictable, so it is impossible to plan a session in which a child would have some time to learn the tool and some time to actually use it in a meaningful way. To solve this problem without taking the possibility for children to design their own storyteller dialogs, we created a conversational template that children could easily change without worrying about the underlying programming.
- **A steep learning curve**: At the moment, SAGE's interface is not intuitive. It requires a knowledgeable person to first work with the children and show them what they can do and how. At the hospital, is not easy to establish times for learning a new tool. However, what we saw at first as a problem — the need for a human mediator as part of the interface — turned out to be a positive aspect of the interactions.
- **Hardware limitations**: SAGE's big computer and rabbit (with its delicate devices that must be plugged in at all times) proved too cumbersome to be easily moved around the unit to different patients' rooms. The tool setup required for each session consumed part of the time available for working with the children.

In summary, while SAGE enabled children to express emotions in different ways, it is still a prototype that requires future work on both the hardware and software.

LESSONS ABOUT THE HOSPITAL SETTING

In this section, we address issues affecting the use of technological / educational tools in hospital settings.

- **Researchers' emotional shock**: Interdisciplinary teams are needed in order to produce computational multimedia environments. Team members necessarily have different backgrounds and skills, and in our case varying exposure to severely ill children. Adjusting to the grave realities of some of the children's' situations required support from all involved.
- **Scheduling complexities**: So many interdependent procedures occur during a hospital stay that it is hard to find or guarantee time for an extra activity such as working with a computational tool like SAGE. Sessions can be very short or very long, and often there is no opportunity for follow-up. Visitors and medical professionals may arrive at the bedside at any time, and children may go home earlier than expected.
- **Children as design partners**: The children we worked with often knew a lot about their illnesses and needs. They told us about their situations and decided when or when not to engage in and sustain SAGE activities. We hope to include children, as well as their caregivers, in making decisions about future play kits.
- **Computers in public spaces:** When we were not using the computer it stayed in the unit's playroom, where patients and families spend free time. Most of these people are naive computer users. They inadvertently found ways of messing up the organization of system files, the SAGE application, and children's creations. We didn't want to lock or isolate the computer, since we want to create a culture around the technology. However some sort of protected system is needed — ideally, one that does not require people to remember a password.

RECOMMENDATIONS FOR FUTURE PLAY KITS

Severely ill children have different emotional and physical needs than healthy kids. They often get tired easily and may feel uncomfortable, helpless, or anxious. Some children, especially those in a recovery stage, need to walk, practice good posture, and do breathing exercises. Play kits should help in the physical and emotional recovery processes by empowering children, entertaining and relaxing them. The technology needs to be secure and flexible enough to allow children who are distracted and sick to play in fantasy worlds. Here we outline some recommendations for future play kits and other computer-based environments, such as our Experience Journal, for use in a hospital setting.

- **Mobility / portability**: In a hospital, ubiquitous computing becomes a must. Technologies must be portable and mobile, perhaps even wearable. This is essential to the success of a long-term project.
- **Mediation of a trained person**: At the hospital, a good computational interface may not suffice on its own. A person may need to guide and often type for patient/users (it is hard to type while wearing an IV). Both the Experience Journal and SAGE require a human gate-keeper to ensure that children will not encounter stressful contents that they may not be prepared to deal with.
- **Leaving traces and being heard**: Technological environments can help sick children to leave their trace and their signature in the world. Play kits are places for them to say "I did this" and for others to recognize and appreciate their creations. This can be very empowering in hospital environments, where children often feel disempowered. It is equally important for them to know that people who are import to them will listen and respond.
- **The potential healing power of narrative:** Although sick children are often provided with entertainment software, it is important to design play kits that allow children to explore their inner worlds. In

a hospital environment, work with play kits can complement the work of psychiatrists, psychologists, and child life specialists.

- **Collaborative play**: Play kits can encourage the participation of visiting friends and family members. Through shared creative activity, participants can learn to cope with long stays at the hospital and build trust.
- **Supporting interruptions:** Play kits need to support activity in both small and large chunks of time, and should have an automatic saving function. Such a feature ensures that children's work is safely kept, but also prevents felt "tragedies" when interruptions occur.
- **Flexible input modalities**: Children in the hospital sometimes need to exercise their bodies as well as their minds and emotions. Furthermore, children may have health limitations that impinge on their abilities to use common interface devices such as keyboard-and-mouse. Experiments with multimodal interface technologies, such as pen-based input and speech and gesture recognition, may yield useful combinations for sick children.

ETHICAL QUESTIONS IN THE WORK

The dictionary defines deontology as "the theory or study of moral obligation." It is a word that we do not use very often. However, it is always present when thinking about uses of technology in a real-world environment. Especially in a place like a hospital, where we constantly deal with life and death issues, we need to think about how our interventions affect a situation.

Often, when developing new technologies, we create prototypes and test them in the real world. These prototypes often crash and are not yet ready to be used in a reliable way. This is well known by the first users of the prototype, and if work gets erased or ill-saved, that is part of the "contract." There is always a second chance for the user to re-do his or her work and, in testing situations, there is no major emotional involvement.

However, working with a prototype with children who are sick presents a very different challenge. These users may not have a second chance, either because it is not always sure how long they will stay in the hospital or because they may die. They understand that they are working with a prototype, but nevertheless their stories and contributions are deeply meaningful for them. In many cases, testing the tool is their unique last chance to leave a trace of their existence in the world. Designers and facilitators of the technology need to take extra care in making sure that things done once will remain. The deontological question should always be in mind.

FUTURE WORK

It takes time to create a culture around a technology. We hope to keep the effort going, to ensure a smooth transition until the Experience Journal and other play kits are ready to be used at the hospital. At the present time, we are designing a transition period, the purpose of which it is to provide the hospital community with different options to keep alive the culture around narratives from personal experience that we started with SAGE. For example, Donegan and Lualdi are creating an extensive library of hospital-oriented characters for children to interact with. We are also using "low-tech" avenues to compensate for the lack of mobility / flexibility of our existing prototypes. We created special envelopes that families can take home with them and use in case they do not have Internet connection but still want to contribute to the Experience Journal.

Concurrently, we have started evolving the SAGE environment into a marionette-style play kit, anchored in puppet shows often used in health-care settings. This scenario assumes that the tool has a "low threshold" for kids who do not feel up to working with the computer and the keyboard, and a "high ceiling" for those who want to use all the computer's potential and may want to enter the world of programming.

ACKNOWLEDGMENTS

We would like to thank the children and staff of the Boston Children's Hospital for their help, engagement, insights, and kindness. We thank Prof. Brian Smith for his thoughtful comments on our draft. Sarah Gibson, Joe Marks, amd Chia Shen from MERL participated in an early phase of the project, which led to the development of the Experience Journal and laid the ground for our work with SAGE.We thank the MIT Media Laboratory Gesture & Narrative Language Group, and the Epistemology and Learning Group, as well as the wonderful team of undergraduate research assistants who worked on the SAGE implementation. We are grateful to Interval Research Corporation, for supporting part of this research, and to Lee Felsenstein, for building the rabbit. Finally, the current effort is supported by MERL - A Mitsubishi Electric Research Laboratory and Children's Hospital, Boston.

REFERENCES

1. Ackermann, E., Bromley, D., DeMaso, D., Gibson, S., Gonzalez-Heydrich, J., Marks, J., Shen, C., Strohecker, C., Umaschi, M. (1997)*Experience Journals: Using Computers to Share Personal Stories About Illness and Medical Intervention.* Paper accepted by MedInfo'98, 9th World Congress on Medical Informatics.

2. Umaschi, M. & Cassell, J. (1997) *Storytelling Systems: Constructing the Innerface of the Interface,* Proceedings of The Second International Conference on Cognitive Technology, IEEE, 98-107.

2A. Cassell, J .(in press) *Storytelling as a Nexus of Change in the Relationship between Gender and Technology: A Feminist Approach to Software Design* in Cassell, J. & Jenkins, From Barbie to Mortal Kombat: Gender and Computer Games. Cambridge MA: MIT Press.

3. Ely, E. (1992) *The Experience of Pain for School-Age Children: Blood, Band-Aids*, and Feelings. In: Children's Health Care, vol. 21, no. 3, 169-175.

4. DeMaso, D., Beardslee, W., Silbert, A., & Flyer, D. (1990) *Psychological Functioning in Children with Cyanotic Heart Defects.* In: Developmental and Behavioural Pediatrics, 1990, vol. 11, no. 6, 289-294.

5. Ackermann, E. (In Press) *Enactive Representations in Learning: Pretrense, Models, Machines*. In: Bliss, J., Light, P., & Saljo, R., Eds. Learning Sites: Social and Technological Contexts for Learning.

6. Campbell, J. (1988) The Power of Myth. NY: Doubleday.

7. Bettelheim, B. (1976) The Uses of Enchantment : The Meaning and Importance of Fairy Tales. NY: Knopf.

8. Wigren, J. (1994) *Narrative Completion in the Treatment of Trauma*, Psychotherapy, vol. 31, no. 3.

9. Freeman, M. (1991) *Therapeutic Use of Storytelling for Older Children Who Are Critically Ill*. In: Children's Health Care, vol. 20, no. 4, 209-215.

10. Gaynard, L., Goldberger, J., & Laidsley, L. (1991) *The Use of Stuffed, Body-Outline Dolls With Hospitalized Children and Adolecents*. In: Children's Health Care, vol. 20, no. 4, 216-246.

11. Schank, R. & Abelson R. (1995) *Knowledge and Memory: The Real Story*. Advances in Social Cognition, vol. VIII, 1-85. NJ: Lawrence Elbaum.

12. Don, A. (1990) *Narrative and the Interface*. In: The Art of Human-Computer Interface Design. Reading: Addison-Wesley.

13. Laurel, B. (1991) Computers as Theater. Reading: Addison-Wesley.

14. Murray, J. (1991) *Anatomy of a New Medium: Literary and Pedagogic Uses of Advanced Linguistic Computer Structures, Computers and the Humanities* 25:1-14. Netherlands: Kluwer Academic Publishers.

15. Bates, J., Maes, P., and Hayes-Roth, B., Eds. (1995) AAAI Spring Symposium, Working Notes: Interactive Story Systems, Plot and Character.

16. Davenport, G. (1994) *"Seeking Dynamic, Adaptive Story Environments."* Visions and Views, IEEE Multimedia, vol. 1, no. 3, pp. 9-13.

17. Papert, S. (1980) *Mindstorms: Children, Computers, and Powerful Ideas*. NY: Basic Books.

18. Resnick, M., Bruckman A., & Martin, A. (1996) "Pianos Not Stereos: Creating Computational Construction Kits." *Interactions* 41-49.

19. Turkle, S. (1984) The Second Self. NY: Basic Books.20. Winnicott, D. W. (1971) *Playing and Reality*. London: Tavistock Publications.

20. Winnicott D.W. (1971).Playing and Reality . London: Tavistock Publications.

21. Umaschi, M. (1997) "Soft Toys with Computer Hearts: Personal Storytelling Environments." Proceedings of ACM SIGCHI, 22-27.

22. Cassell, J. (1995) "The Role of Gestures in Stories as Multiple Participant Frameworks." AAAI Spring Symposium, Working Notes: Interactive Story Systems, Plot and Character, 23-26.

23. Piaget, J. (1962) *Play, Dreams and Imitation in Childhood*. NY: W.W. Norton.

24. Coles, R. (1990) *The Spiritual Lives of Children*. Boston: Houghton Miflin Company.

25. Ong, Walter J. (1977) *Interfaces of the Word: Studies in the Evolution of Consciousness and Culture*. N.Y.: Cornell University Press.

Progressive Design: Staged Evolution of Scenarios in the Design of a Collaborative Science Learning Environment

George Chin, Jr. and Mary Beth Rosson
Computer Science Department
Virginia Polytechnic Institute and State University
Blacksburg, VA 24061-0106 USA
+1 540 231 6931
chin@csgrad.cs.vt.edu; rosson@vt.edu

ABSTRACT

Scenario-based design techniques are increasingly popular in HCI design. Although many techniques exist, we see a growing demand for more structured and systematic methods of scenario generation and development. This paper describes a case study in which a collaborative science learning environment was designed using an evolutionary scenario-based design approach. The case study has attempted to make consistent use of scenarios and claims as design representations, to integrate the design of both the system and the activities that incorporate it, and to evolve design in an organized and principled manner. We have termed this approach *progressive design*.

Keywords

Scenarios, Task-Artifact Framework, claims, participatory design, computer-supported collaborative learning.

INTRODUCTION

The use of scenarios in HCI design has become pervasive [1, 11]. Scenarios are accepted as an effective way to capture, analyze, and communicate users' needs. At the same time, even the advocates of scenario use voice concerns about the lack of systematic methods for scenario generation and development [2, 11]. The present work describes our efforts to use scenarios in a more systematic way in the context of a participatory design project.

The work reported here is part of an educational technology project funded by the National Science Foundation's Networked Infrastructure for Education (NIE) program. The project, Learning in Networked Communities (LiNC), is a collaboration between Virginia Tech and Montgomery County (VA) Public Schools. The project is developing and evaluating networked collaborative learning tools in support of middle and high school science education. Participants include teachers and students from four Montgomery County schools and computer science and education technology researchers from Virginia Tech.

PARTICIPATORY SCENARIO-BASED DESIGN

LiNC is a participatory design (PD) project: students and teachers participate directly in the design of new educational systems. Like other PD advocates [8, 10] we believe LiNC will benefit in several ways from broad participation:

- students, teachers, and designers mutually learn about each others' fields
- the envisionment of future learning situations allow students and teachers to experience how an emerging design may impact their learning and teaching
- the design process is grounded in the actual context and practice of the classroom

In addition, we expect PD to instill greater ownership of a design among students and teachers, which in turn should increase commitment to the system and desire to see the system incorporated into classroom activities.

The LiNC team has used scenarios as its central design representation. Usage scenarios are ideal shared representations for users and developers—they are informal, evocative, work-oriented, can be sketchy or highly detailed, and are equally accessible to diverse stakeholders [1].

The LiNC project has also used scenarios as a source of analysis during the design of collaborative education tools. Carroll and Rosson [4] describe how usage scenarios can be analyzed for their usage implications using *claims*—specific features of a scenario that are associated with a set of possible positive and negative consequences (e.g., giving students a structured worksheet to record data organizes and standardizes the data collection process, but may reduce the thought students give to what they are measuring, and may reduce their feelings of control). These claims can then be used to drive design reasoning, with effort made to mitigate possible negative consequences while capitalizing or enhancing possible positive consequences [5]. In LiNC, the analysis of scenarios, their claims, and subsequent design reasoning has been shared among teachers, students, HCI designers, and software developers [7].

PROGRESSIVE DESIGN

In the LiNC project we are exploring an approach we call *progressive design*, a framework that structures our PD work, helping to ensure an orderly progression to a successful final design. In progressive design we seek to

- employ consistent design representations throughout analysis and design;
- consider the design of both the target system and the learning activity that will exercise it; and
- evolve the underlying usage context in an organized and principled fashion.

CHI 98 Los Angeles CA USA
Copyright 1998 0-89791-975-0/98/ 4..$5.00

Scenarios and Claims

Progressive design uses scenarios and claims as the main design representations. At each point in the process, we use a set of observed or hypothetical usage scenarios to document and share the team's current understanding of the design problem and possible solutions.

Following the Task-Artifact Framework [5], we elaborate, revise, or replace design scenarios by iteratively applying claims analysis (i.e., addressing both positive and negative consequences of analyzed claims). This iterative process allows us to integrate analysis and design: analysis occurs in the identification of features and claims in a scenario; design occurs in the generation or evolution of new features from existing claims and the incorporation of those features into new scenarios. Thus, scenarios and claims are mutually-generative.

Alternating System and Activity Focus

System design typically begins with an analysis of existing activities—an activity is both the general work performed by participants and the surrounding work context. One problem with this is that once we have designed a system to support a specific activity, system deployment often modifies the work and its context to a point where the original analysis is no longer applicable [3].

How should one accommodate and manage this tension between the design of systems and the evolution of users' activities? We might bring all stakeholders together, to perform simultaneous analysis and design of activities and of systems. However we have found this to be problematic, because we cannot maintain an equal emphasis on both the system and underlying activity. In most cases, the design discussion drifts into technical system details and away from the activity. Stakeholders who are not technically-oriented are "backgrounded" in these discussions and their level of participation decreases. These participants are often the users most familiar with the activity and least familiar with technology and system development.

Instead we have adopted a strategy of revolving emphasis: we alternate the focus of our design efforts, to incrementally develop both activities and the system that supports them. We design the activities based on our current vision of the system and the system on our current understanding of the activities. This iterative "bricklayer" approach helps to integrate requirements arising from activity innovations and opportunities arising from system innovations.

Staged Design Evolution

A concern for any iterative and incremental design approach is that the evolutionary path has been a "good" one, that the final result has considered all (or at least many) of the important options and not merely optimized for local concerns along the way. Elsewhere we have argued that claims analysis addresses these concerns to some extent, in that it encourages "what if" reasoning throughout the process, guiding attention to a design space rather than a single path (see also [9]).

Our progressive design framework goes a step further. Not only do we develop and evolve scenarios throughout the process, but also we move through identifiable phases in our analysis of requirements [6]. Each phase revolves around a set of scenarios and claims, but these design artifacts are constructed to examine and flesh out different dimensions of the evolving design.

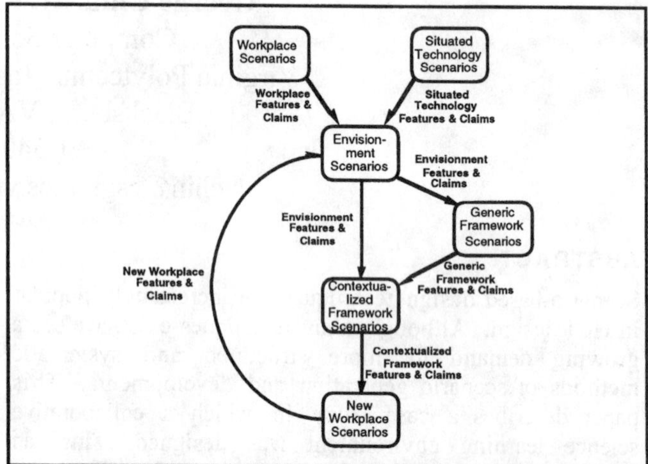

Figure 1. Evolution of Scenarios and Claims in Progressive Design

Figure 1 provides an overview of the different design phases we have explored in the LiNC project. We start with scenarios from the workplace and that explore specific technologies. These contribute to an initial envisionment, which is then refined through software design and further workplace context. The final set of new workplace scenarios, features, and claims specify both the designed activity and the system that is to support it. The iterative cycle then begins again, as the new system and activities are evaluated in the workplace.

The figure summarizes the general structure of LiNC design activities—however we do not see progressive design as a rigid process. The scenarios and claims at each phase serve as different contexts for design. Typically scenarios and claims at one phase are extensions, elaborations, or transformations of scenarios and claims produced earlier in the design process. Thus at any given point, designers will be attending to many different design requirements; progressive design simply suggests a general order in which to address these diverse requirements.

PROGRESSIVE DESIGN IN THE LINC PROJECT

Our view of progressive design has emerged through our use of scenario-based participatory techniques in the LiNC design context and we will use this project to illustrate the components we have introduced above. We do not have space to provide a complete design case but have selected representative design activities to describe in this paper.

We focus on scenarios and claims emanating from one design path through the LiNC design process. The example scenarios and claims were generated by students, teachers, HCI designers, and software developers during participatory analysis and design sessions, where stakeholders were guided in application of the Task-Artifact Framework [5,7].

Classroom Scenarios and Claims

The classroom is the workplace of the LiNC project. Thus we began with an analysis of existing classroom activities and the current classroom environment. Our initial objective was to support and enhance the collaborative activities that students performed in science classes. We found that the main form of collaboration involved execution and analysis of physical experiments. This finding was not surprising given that the experiment is the traditional medium for the scientific discovery and learning.

We observed and documented episodes of collaboration as students performed experiments. Collaboration occurred in various forms as group members worked together to assemble equipment, execute the experiment, apply scientific formulas, interpret results, and generate lab reports. Figure 2 outlines one such *workplace scenario* from a high school physics lab on inelastic collisions.

-Matilda, Dexter, Hildegarde, and Godfrey carry out a physics lab on inelastic collisions, in which two miniature cars collide and the resulting car velocities are measured using photogates.

-The students collaborate to set up the experiment: Hildegarde collects and positions the cars, Dexter and Godfrey construct the apparatus.

-The group executes the experiment collaboratively: Dexter collides the two cars together, Matilda reports the photogate results, and Godfrey catches the cars after they collide.

-As data accrues, the students discuss how to interpret their findings. They collectively perform calculations and document their results on worksheets provided by their teacher.

Figure 2. Scenario for Inelastic Collision Lab

Figure 3 documents several claims analyzed for this particular classroom scenario, for example the tradeoffs in carrying out physical experiments. We also analyzed features of the collaboration that took place among the students. Even though we had begun the project with the assumption that we would support and encourage *cross-school* collaboration, this analysis prompted us to examine and document the benefits of *co-located* real world interaction among the students. The "upsides" that we recognized in these concrete interactions became important considerations in our subsequent design of technology-enhanced collaborative work.

The classroom scenarios and claims were initial design products that were re-applied and re-evaluated in subsequent design stages. The early introduction of classroom scenarios and claims grounded the overall design process in the context and practice of the classroom.

Situated Technology Scenarios and Claims

In the situated technology design phase, we brought a range of technology into the classroom to evaluate its impact—computer-based simulations, Internet tools, and computer-mediated communications mechanisms such as video teleconferencing, text chat, e-mail, and shared electronic whiteboards. Note that the design context was quite different at this point: although the teachers worked to define learning activities that used the existing technology, our main goal was to see what would happen when the technology was introduced into the classroom–we produced *situated technology scenarios* and claims to analyze and evaluate the current designs of existing computer-based tools in the classroom context.

Feature: Physical inelastic collision experiment
Pros: practices collaborative skills; practices negotiation of tasks and roles; provides concrete, hands-on experience; resembles real-world situations
Cons: but experiment apparatus may not be available; but conditions may be hard to test; but students at different sites cannot work together

Feature: Joint execution of experiment
Pros: practices collaborative skills; allows students to take on more complex and rewarding experiments; involves students in peer learning
Cons: but students at different sites cannot work together

Feature: Joint interpretation and analysis of data
Pros: practices collaborative skills; may improve analysis results by pooling ideas; involves students in peer learning
Cons: but students at different sites cannot work together

Figure 3. Claims for Inelastic Collision Lab

Figure 4 outlines a situated technology scenario involving the use of a block and plane simulation, an electronic whiteboard, and a video conferencing package. Note that in contrast to the scenario in Figure 2, this is a *design* scenario specifying how we intended the technology to be used (in fact, we did observe use episodes of this sort). The narrative summarizes a remote collaboration exercise in which a high school physics student guides a group of middle school students in the use and analysis of a computer-based block and plane simulation.

-Mertyl, Ethel, and Sandy—middle school students in Ms. Snodgrass' science class—have elected to work together on a force and motion assignment in which the group is to execute a computer-based block and plane simulation and graph the simulation results. Terri—a high school physics student—has been assigned to mentor them for this assignment.

-Each group completes the assignment over a two-day period, with. mentoring occurring in the thirty minutes of overlap time between the middle and high school classes. Different groups of middle school students rotate through three computers over several days.

-Mertyl, Ethel, and Sandy meet Terri over the computer, using a video conferencing package.

-Terri guides the middle school students through the block-and-plane simulation. She steps through the simulation on her computer, describing the process as she proceeds. She occasionally picks up the camera and aims it towards her screen to show the middle schoolers the state of the simulation on her screen. Sometimes Terri takes a snapshot of her screen and copies it onto an electronic whiteboard, annotating or highlighting specific features of interest.

Figure 4. Scenario for Block and Plane Mentoring

Our experience with this situated technology scenario raised a number of design issues, some of which are captured by the claims of Figure 5. Some of these claims were anticipated in advance of fielding the technology (e.g., that simulations support more rapid data collection), others were realized by observations of the activities in progress (e.g., the inability to import other relevant content to the whiteboard we had provided).

Feature: Block and plane simulation
Pros: allows multiple, concurrent executions; allows testing of boundary conditions; supports rapid data collection
Cons: but concurrent execution may be distracting; but mapping to real-world phenomenon may not be obvious or clear

Feature: Electronic whiteboard
Pros: offers a salient space for collaboration; supports sharing of text and images; may increase awareness of non-local collaborators' activities (via telepointers)
Cons: but students may erase or overwrite each other's work; but may support limited media or imports from other useful applications; but may distract students from other activity

Feature: Video conferencing
Pros: increases remote presence; makes learning experience more vivid, engaging; is natural to students
Cons: but may provide poor sound; but students may be especially frustrated when technical problems occur

Feature: Small number of computers in classroom
Pros: makes the technology less physically intrusive
Cons: requires students to time-share computers; prohibits class-wide activities

Feature: Short, overlapping class periods
Pros: reflects typical scheduling of classes
Cons: but restricts synchronous collaboration with remote sites

Figure 5. Claims for Block and Plane Mentoring

This scenario also raised more pragmatic issues. Each classroom was equipped with only three computers. Thus, it was difficult to construct a class-wide learning activity. Another issue was the non-alignment of class periods at different schools. This meant that remote synchronous collaboration had to take place within the typically very short time intervals of overlap. These issues had very important consequences for our evolving design, for example prompting us to reconsider the project's emphasis on synchronous collaboration. We believe that pragmatic issues such as these are not specific to our project, but rather identify general limitations to the introduction of collaborative technologies into the classroom.

Envisionment Scenarios and Claims

Our greater understanding of classroom activities and technology acquired during the first two design stages put us in a better position to develop *envisionment scenarios* depicting computer-enhanced learning activities. Our goal was to design activities that were responsive to our analysis of both classroom and situated technology scenarios and claims. For example, an important concern was the identification of pedagogically-sound learning activities that require remote collaboration. We re-focused our attention on the activity, with the technology taking on more of a supporting role.

A key design move at this point was the envisionment of a project-based science activity. Projects were seen as a way to address some of the positive and negative consequences analyzed for both the classroom and situated technology scenarios. For example, because a project takes place over an extended period of time, students' collaboration may be supported with a range of technology, including asynchronous interaction. This minimizes the downsides associated with non-overlapping schedules and relatively few computers in each classroom. At the same time, a collaborative research project can be relatively complex and extended in time, can foster long-term collaboration, and thus can be a realistic scientific experience, much as we had observed for physical experimentation. Indeed many of the positive effects arising from collaboration on real-time physical experiments can also be realized through a long-term collaborative research project.

Figure 6 outlines an envisionment scenario in which a group of students collaborate in an investigation of the Mars Pathfinder mission. The scenario develops general notions of collaborative work areas and project-based research. These features along with possible positive and negative consequences appear in Figure 7.

-Maynard and Ethel (middle schoolers from Auburn) form a project group with Felicity and Mertyl (middle schoolers from Blacksburg) to study the Mars Pathfinder Mission. They meet using video conferencing when both classes are in session.

-They first brainstorm questions to address. As questions emerge group members add them to the shared work area. They negotiate a final set of questions, then divide the questions among individuals.

-Maynard volunteers to research "What is the Pathfinder lunar vehicle and how does it work?" He searches the Web and finds text passages and images describing Pathfinder at the main NASA website. He copies these onto the work area.

-Maynard also looks for simulations in the Virtual School. He finds a Mars landing simulation, copies it into the work area and executes it. The simulation allows students to land the NASA Lander spacecraft and to navigate Pathfinder off its dock and onto Martian terrain.

-To organize his findings, Maynard marks the original question as a "question" and the resources he has found as "answers". He draws lines from the question to each answer to identify relationships among the research resources he has collected. He notifies his group of his findings with an e-mail message and proceeds to another research question.

-Later the group meets over the computer to review each other's findings in detail and to negotiate which research items should go into the final project report. Maynard describes his Pathfinder findings, using a telepointer to point at and discuss the items he has placed in the work area. He also demonstrates the Pathfinder simulation. Felicity and Mertyl provide and attach comments and notes on the various research items and try out the simulation themselves.

Figure 6. Scenario for Project-Based Research

Feature: Project-based collaboration **Pros:** illustrates the scientific process; resembles the experience of real-world scientists; encourages long-term collaboration; invites complex research topics **Cons:** but may increase the demands on class time; but may be difficult to organize and schedule during school year
Feature: Collaborative work area **Pros:** allows sharing and annotation of research findings; allows storage, demo and reuse of computer simulations **Cons:** but students may erase or overwrite each other's work; but varying kinds and sources of work may lead to a complex display that is difficult to interpret; but students may compete for control

Figure 7. Claims for Project-Based Research

Note that the students use a special place for collaborative work. This work area is a sort of "descendent" of the electronic whiteboard in the block and plane scenario. However the activity design has addressed a limitation of the prior technology, namely the variety of media that can be shared (e.g., simulations can be added to the work area). At the same time, a greater range of media may increase display complexity, and this is captured as a possible "downside" for consideration in subsequent design work.

In the project-based research scenario, we have shown how the scenario and its features and claims are driven from the analysis and claims of previous design stages (e.g., projects, collaborative work areas). We have also shown how the emerging envisionment scenario establishes claims of its own (e.g., media support, complex display). These dual functions exemplify the evolutionary nature of our design process as we continually evolve and create scenarios and claims to address new contexts.

Generic Framework Scenarios and Claims

Following activity envisionment, we again shifted our focus to technology, this time to the design of components that might comprise a collaborative science learning environment we call the "Virtual School". Whereas activity envisionment was a relatively unfettered exploration of ideas about collaborative learning, our design of the *generic framework scenarios* aimed to extract, make concrete, and organize the proposed functionality.

The envisionment scenarios produced in the previous design stage may be viewed as representative examples of use of an ideal system. Our goal during this stage is to support and extrapolate beyond the envisionment scenarios to design specific system features that are generally applicable to a variety of different learning situations. These derived system features become the components of a generic framework that define and organizes the capabilities of the Virtual School.

Figure 8 refines the Mars Pathfinder envisionment scenario with specific, concrete system features such as a collaborative electronic workbench and a search tool. These concrete features and their associated claims are described in Figure 9.

-Group members meet over the computer using video conferencing, audio, or text chat channel. -They begin by brainstorming research questions, documenting possible questions with electronic notes on the workbench. Through negotiation, the group chooses a final set of questions to address and partitions the questions among individuals. - Maynard volunteers to research "What is the Pathfinder lunar vehicle and how does it work?". Using the Virtual School search mechanism, Maynard searches for information on "Pathfinder". The search function returns a number of resources including a URL to the NASA website and a Pathfinder simulation. -From the NASA website, Maynard finds some relevant text passages and images that describe the Pathfinder vehicle. He copies these text passages and images onto the workbench. Next, Maynard copies the simulation onto a collaborative electronic workbench and executes it. To organize his findings on the Pathfinder vehicle, Maynard draws lines from the original note containing the research question to each collected research item.

Figure 8. Scenario for Generic Virtual School

Feature: Search Mechanism **Pros:** provides an internal search mechanism for locating local resources; structures and supports the research process **Cons:** but may be confusing to some students; but may not always locate useful resources
Feature: Collaborative electronic workbench **Pros:** offers a salient space for collaboration; supports awareness of synchronous activities of remote users; offers place for students to store, demonstrate, and reuse simulations; supports sharing and annotation of individual findings; allows access to shared material; provides map view of work area **Cons:** but the variety in sharing may lead to complex displays that are difficult to interpret and organize

Figure 9. Claims for Generic Virtual School

In some cases, the framework components are straightforward mappings of features in the envisionment scenario. For example, we operationalized the collaborative work area as a synchronous, shared electronic workbench that supports storage and sharing of a variety of media. In response to the earlier concerns about display complexity, the workbench was designed to include a map view for overall coordination, and control policies to manage access to individual contributions.

In other cases, a framework component extends the envisioned activities. The scenario in Figure 6 assumes that Maynard uses a Web-based search mechanism to locate information about Pathfinder. This general activity notion was refined during Virtual School framework design: an effort was made to specify a search mechanism that was generic enough to retrieve many different kinds of objects (e.g., people, Web pages, simulations, images, data sets). This resulted in a specialized search and browse facility in the Virtual School and a protocol for identifying searchable resources. The upside is that more powerful and general support is provided for retrieval; one downside is that it adds to the complexity of the overall system.

These two examples again emphasize the constant interplay between activity and system design: the Virtual School design responded to the activity requirement for a shared work area, while at the same time raising a new opportunity for more extensive resource retrieval.

Contextualized Framework Scenarios and Claims

Once a generic framework had been designed, the LiNC team shifted back to activity design, refining and evaluating the activities envisioned earlier within the system context now provided by the Virtual School framework. In contrast to earlier stages where we used scenarios and claims as support for brainstorming, the generic framework scenarios and claims were applied as constraints. We produced *contextualized framework scenarios,* mapping learning activities to functions of the generic framework. In so doing, we both identified areas of mismatch or weaknesses in system design and refined the classroom activities to leverage the organization of the system. This reflects a shift in design reasoning from envisionment to constraint application—due to both the increasing structure of our design and the need to integrate explicitly the learning activities with the system.

We refined the project-based learning activities to address claims analyzed for the envisionment and generic framework scenarios. For example, in the original Mars Pathfinder envisionment scenario, Maynard shared his research findings directly with his group in a shared collaborative work area. When this kind of research sharing was applied to the workbench component of the generic framework, additional design issues emerged concerning how group members share research findings and items. These sorts of design issues could have surfaced during the design of the envisionment scenarios, but did not in our case—the envisionment scenarios encouraged us to brainstorm general concepts, features, and attributes of an idealized learning activity, while applying the concepts, features, and attributes to a possible system forced us to think in specific, concrete details.

To understand how students share research findings, we revisited our classroom scenarios and claims. We found that in extended assignments, students often partitioned research work amongst themselves. Students would perform research and collect data individually, then meet to integrate findings. Thus we extended the scenario to include this notion of "personal pockets" of research.

Note that this personalization of individual contributions also addresses the display complexity downside associated with the unconstrained sharing of multiple media types in a shared workbench. Thus by adding a personal folder feature, we were able to accommodate the research habits of students *and* add structure to electronic collaboration.

Another framework component that underwent design evolution was the search mechanism. Activity designers felt that a sophisticated search mechanism would be too complicated for middle school students to use. The solution was to add the concept of science labs as a secondary retrieval mechanism. A science lab is a pre-organized set of resources available for students working on a particular science topic.

The contextualized Virtual School scenario in Figure 10 summarizes the refinements to the original Pathfinder scenario. Minor changes such as multiple workbench folders and predefined science labs containing teacher-defined research resources contextualized the generic framework against the project-based research activities. These refined features and their associated claims are presented in Figure 11.

-Maynard volunteers to research "What is the Pathfinder lunar vehicle and how does it work?" He begins by visiting various on-line science labs in the Virtual School. A science lab is a collection of resources organized along a specific science topic and populated by the teacher.

-Maynard discovers the "Space Lab," which contains resources on astronomy and the solar system, including the URL to the NASA website and the Pathfinder simulation.

-Maynard finds useful text passages and images at the NASA website, and he executes and explores the Pathfinder simulation in the Space Lab.

-To organize and share his findings, Maynard creates a folder "Pathfinder Vehicle (Maynard) on the shared workbench, and copies the collected text passages, images, and simulations into this folder.

Figure 10. Scenario for Contextualized Virtual School

Feature: Science Labs
Pros: allows teachers to predefine research resources; organizes the resource retrieval process
Cons: but students may be less likely to carry out comprehensive research

Feature: Personal, subgroup, and group folders on workbench
Pros: allows students to partition research work; supports both individual and group research
Cons: but adds a level of indirection to sharing of work

Figure 11. Claims for Contextualized Virtual School

New Classroom Scenarios and Claims

The final stage provides the last opportunity to rectify discrepancies between the activity and system design. The goal of this stage is to "tweak" the current system and activity designs in ways that are acceptable to all stakeholders. Furthermore, design at this stage must accommodate the resource and scheduling issues associated with software development. Scenarios and claims produced during this design stage reflect the final integration of classroom and technology contexts into a unified version. We denote the design results as new classroom scenarios and claims to signify one complete pass through the progressive design process.

As the claims in Figure 13 suggest, version 1.0 of the Virtual School again reflect accommodation of activity to system and vice versa. For example, the science labs, which were now conceived as the result of an "implicit search" can be seen as a compromise between the general-purpose flexibility provided by the Virtual School search component, and a more pre-organized view of resources provided by teachers for specific projects.

Similarly, concerns about the complexity and personal organization of a shared workbench had prompted the folder concept. But because this would have been difficult to weave into the Virtual School software development plan, a related concept of multiple workbenches was adopted.

New classroom scenarios and claims are produced through the evaluation of constraints. Unlike contextualized scenarios and claims, however, constraints are imposed by external factors such as development costs, manpower, and scheduling. This inserts a practical context for the generation of scenarios and claims in the final design stage.

In Figure 12, the Mars Pathfinder scenario is further refined to reflect the above compromises between the learning activity and the system. The features of the scenario and their associated claims are presented in Figure 13.

-Maynard volunteers to research "What is the Pathfinder lunar vehicle and how does it work?" He begins by visiting various on-line science labs in the Virtual School.

-Science labs are made available to students from a spatial room layout view. Each room contains icons representing the various resources available for the specific science topic. A science lab is essentially a search of the Virtual School for all resources associated with the particular science topic. When entering a science lab, a student implicitly performs a search with predefined search criteria.

-Maynard discovers the "Space Lab," which contains resources on astronomy and the solar system.

-To organize his findings on the Pathfinder vehicle, Maynard creates a new workbench and entitles it, "Pathfinder Vehicle (Maynard)." As he researches, he copies collected text passages, images, and simulations into this workbench.

Figure 12. Scenario for Project-Based Virtual School 1.0

Feature: Implicit search criteria
Pros: supports multi-level searching; supports both beginning and advanced users; employs existing features of Virtual School without additional development
Cons: but students may not realize that they are searching and attempt more complex queries

Feature: Multiple workbenches
Pros: allows students to partition research work; supports both individual and group research; employs existing features of Virtual School without additional development
Cons: but it may be difficult to merge or compare work saved in different workbenches

Figure 13. Claims for Project-Based Virtual School 1.0

DISCUSSION

We have described elements from a PD project in which we attempted to use scenarios and claims analysis in a more systematic fashion to guide the design process. We alternated focus between activity and technology, to continually infuse concerns from one domain into the other; we moved in a progressive fashion from initial studies of existing activities and technologies to an integrated view of new activities supported by new technology. However, while this initial study took place in the context of a specific design project, we believe that the concept of progressive design is a general one.

Through the LiNC project case study, we attempted to illustrate the evolving contexts associated with the stages of progressive design. Table 1 summarizes the set of progressive design contexts we have demonstrated.

Design Stage	Design Focus	Design Action	Design Context
Workplace	Activity	Evaluation	Analysis of existing workplace environment
Situated Technology	System	Evaluation	Analysis of existing technology in current workplace context
Envision-ment	Activity	Envision-ment	Design of ideal computer-based workplace activity
Generic Framework	System	Envision-ment	Design of general software framework
Contextual-ized Framework	Activity	Constraint Applica-tion	Workplace activity constrained by general software architecture
New Workplace	Activity + System	Constraint Applica-tion	Workplace activity and general software architecture constrained by schedule and resources

Table 1. Stages of Software Design

As illustrated in Table 1, design contexts in our model is shaped by two factors. The most notable factor is the alternating design focus between activity and system design. We have demonstrated that these two kinds of design efforts are distinctly different.

The second factor influencing the context is the design action which identifies the general design activity occurring at any one stage. Implicit in our model is a three-phased design cycle in which we evaluate, envision, and apply constraints. This three-phased design cycle underscores how we work with our design representations to achieve specific design results and to progress towards a target design. Figure 14 depicts this general design cycle.

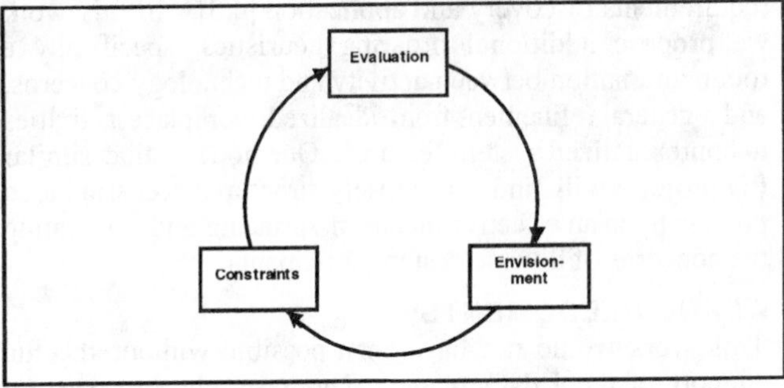

Figure 14. Three-phase cycle of progressive design

Recall how these design actions were realized in the design of the Virtual School. During the evaluation phase, we analyzed workplace and situated technology scenarios to reflect on current designs of activity and technology. During the envisionment phase, we constructed envisionment and generic framework scenarios to design new activities and technologies. During the constraint application phase, we tempered our envisioned designs by considering practical and technical constraints to produce contextualized framework and new workplace scenarios.

In this section, we have shown that the stages of progressive design are distinct, logically-oriented, and have a progressive quality to them.

Participation in Progressive Design

Progressive design partitions the design process into the incremental design of activities and system, which leads in turn to a separation of design roles. In our project, teachers felt responsible and compelled to take on the role of activity designers because designing learning activities is an intrinsic part of their job. Similarly, the technologists took on their traditional role of system designers.

These complementary roles suggest an interesting alternative to full participation by users in all aspects of design. Although we believe broad-based user involvement may possible in some situations, we found that teachers and technologists were naturally drawn to the design domains with which they were most familiar and comfortable. The progressive alternation between activity and system allowed both groups to feel empowered in the design of what they knew best. This is not to suggest that teachers and technologists design in isolation, rather that they design in groups with an alternation of leadership from one participatory session to another.

CONCLUSIONS

We have summarized some of the phases of design explored in the LiNC educational technology, phases that took us from initial analyses of the classroom and of technology opportunities, through the envisionment and refinement of new classroom scenarios. Throughout we have relied on scenarios and claims as design representations, which has convinced us that teachers, students and developers are able to understand and apply these basic analysis techniques.

Earlier work has documented how principled reasoning from claims to produce enhanced or revised scenarios adds order to what otherwise may seem a chaotic process of requirements discovery and application [4,5]. In this work we propose additional ordering heuristics, specifically a rough alternation between activity and technology concerns, and a general refinement from idealized workplace activities to contextualized system features. Our hope is that similar PD projects will find this loosely-structured scenario-based process to be an effective means of surfacing and integrating the concerns of diverse design participants.

ACKNOWLEDGMENTS

This work would not have been possible without the full support of the LiNC team. The research was partially supported by the National Science Foundation, under awards RED-9454803 and REC-9554206, and by Apple Computer.

REFERENCES

1. Carroll, J.M. (1995). Introduction: The Scenario Perspective on System Development. In Carroll, J.M. (Ed.), *Scenario-Based Design: Envisioning Work and Technology in System Development*, J. Wiley, NY, pp. 1-17.

2. Carroll, J.M. (1994). Making Use a Design Representation. *Communications of the ACM*, 37(12), pp. 29-35.

3. Carroll, J.M. and Campbell, R.L. (1989). Artifacts as Psychological Theories: The Case of Human-Computer Interaction. *Behavior and Information Technology,* 8, pp. 247-259.

4. Carroll, J.M. and Rosson, M.B. (1991). Deliberated Evolution: Stalking the View Matcher in Design Space. *Human-Computer Interaction,* 6, pp. 281-318.

5. Carroll, J.M. and Rosson, M.B. (1992). Getting around the task-artifact cycle: How to make claims and design by scenario. *ACM Transactions on Information Systems,* 10(2), pp. 181-212.

6. Carroll, J.M., Rosson M.B., Chin, G., and Koenemann, J. Requirements Development: Stages of Opportunity for Collaborative Needs. In *Proceedings of the Designing Interactive System: Processes, Methods and Techniques Conference (ACM-DIS '97).* (August 18-20, Amsterdam, The Netherlands), pp. 55-64.

7. Chin, G., Rosson, M.B., and Carroll, J.M. (1997). Participatory Analysis: Shared Development of Requirements from Scenarios. In *Proceedings of CHI'97 Conference.* (March 22-27, Atlanta, Ga.). ACM, New York, pp. 162-169.

8. Greenbaum, J. and Kyng M. (1991). Introduction: Situated Design. In Greenbaum, J. and Kyng M. (Eds.), *Design at Work: Cooperative Design of Computer Systems*, Lawrence Erlbaum Associates, Hillsdale, NJ, pp. 1-24.

9. MacLean A. and McKerlie D. (1995). Design Space Analysis and Use Representations. In Carroll, J.M. (Ed.), *Scenario-Based Design: Envisioning Work and Technology in System Development*, J. Wiley, NY, pp. 183-207.

10. Muller, M.J and Kuhn, S. (1993). Participatory Design. *Communications of the ACM*, 36(4), pp. 25-28.

11. Wolf, C.G. and Karat J. Capturing What is Needed in Multi-User System Design: Observations from the Design of Three Healthcare Systems. In *Proceedings of the Designing Interactive System: Processes, Methods and Techniques Conference (ACM-DIS '97).* (August 18-20, Amsterdam, The Netherlands).

Adapting User Interface Design Methods to the Design of Educational Activities

Clayton Lewis, Cathy Brand, Gina Cherry, and Cyndi Rader

Department of Computer Science
and Institute of Cognitive Science
University of Colorado, Boulder CO 80309
{clayton, brand, gina, crader}@cs.colorado.edu

ABSTRACT
We have adapted the programming walkthrough technique to help design computer-supported educational activities in elementary school science. We present examples from a case study which illustrate ways in which design of an educational activity is similar to and different from design of a user interface. We have found that the walkthrough approach is useful in this new setting, and that it sheds new light on the general task-centered orientation to design.

KEYWORDS: analysis methods, children, design techniques, educational applications, end user programming, task analysis.

INTRODUCTION

The central challenge in traditional user interface design is to create a computer system that supports some collection of potential user tasks in such a way that user productivity is enhanced. Productivity can be enhanced by permitting faster correct performance, by reducing the incidence of errors, or by some combination. The task-centered design approach [9], addresses this challenge by using specific example tasks to evaluate and compare design alternatives. In the early stages of task-centered design, walkthrough methods are used to generate and critique *scenarios*, which are generated by spelling out how a given example task would be performed given a particular system design.

In our work on educational software we have encountered a somewhat different design challenge. Our problem is to design not just a computer system, but also a collection of activities with that system, such that learners engaging in those activities will achieve given educational goals. Thus, the design challenge for computer-supported educational activities includes the design of tasks as well as of the system, and the measure of success is not productivity, considered simply, but a more complex evaluation of the effects of performing the tasks. For example, an educational activity that learners complete quickly and accurately is of no value if they learn nothing from it.

Despite these differences in design problems, we hypothesized that the core logic of task-centered user interface design, and of the associated walkthrough methods, could be adapted to the design of educational activities. We present the results of our exploration of this possibility by describing a case study in which we adapted the programming walkthrough technique [2, 9] to the design of a suite of educational activities about plants for an elementary school science unit.

THE CASE STUDY

The sTc project

Science Theater/Teatro de Ciencias (sTc) is a research project exploring the educational value of model creation by elementary school science students [14]. Children participating in sTc use software to create animated, graphical models of processes and mechanisms they are studying. Like other researchers in educational technology, we quickly found that simply making software available and encouraging its use did little to support learning. We have found that our design and implementation efforts have been more and more directed to the design of activities supported by the software, rather than to the design of the software itself.

The pedagogical objectives of these sTc activities fall into four major categories:

Science content. A primary goal is to deepen students' understanding of their science topics by using models to focus on "how" and "why" questions. This approach contrasts with most existing elementary science curricula, which tend to focus more on observation and the use of experiments to show, but not explain, interesting phenomena. We are also interested in addressing common science misconceptions.

Science as inquiry. In accordance with current science education reform, modeling activities are used within a framework of scientific inquiry in which students are encouraged to ask questions, speculate about possible answers, and test and revise their ideas [22, 23]. This inquiry cycle promotes a view of science as a process, rather than as a body of facts, and encourages students to bring their own experiences and conjectures into the science classroom.

Model-based reasoning and epistemology of models. A number of research efforts have focused on the potential benefits of modeling [3, 7, 8, 13, 15]. Grosslight et al. [7] have identified three levels of understanding about models. At level 1, models are viewed as simple copies of reality. At level 2, students understand that models often highlight and/or simplify some aspects of the phenomenon being modeled, rather than matching reality exactly. At level 3, students display a more sophisticated understanding of models, which includes three factors: the use of models to develop and test ideas, rather than to copy reality; the consideration of alternative models to explain the same phenomenon; and the manipulation and testing of models in order to inform and revise ideas. In sTc, our goal is to help students gain a level 3 understanding of models, with particular emphasis on the use of models to demonstrate and test ideas, and on the importance of revising models when initial ideas are found to be incorrect, or to incorporate new information.

Software mastery. A well-conceived activity will pave the way for subsequent activities by enhancing the child's knowledge of and skill in using the modeling software. By the time the students complete an introductory series of activities which includes the two in this case study, they should understand and program well enough to create their own models. In our case study, the modeling software is Visual AgentTalk [16, 17, 18], a rule-based visual programming system.

The Software

Models in Visual AgentTalk consist of a collection of software agents whose behavior is specified by a set of rules, and a worksheet in which the agents are arranged. The visual appearance of an agent is a small picture called a depiction. An agent's rules can cause it to move around on the worksheet, to change its depiction (so that it looks different), and to interact with other agents. For example, one agent can cause a nearby agent to disappear, a behavior which might represent something being eaten, or a reagent being consumed in a chemical reaction.

Models can be built from scratch, with all rules and depictions for the agents created by the user, or they can be built using agents already provided. This flexibility makes it possible to devise modeling activities that differ greatly in the sophistication required of the learner, from models in which all behavior must be specified by the learner, to ones in which the learner has only to arrange a collection of agents whose behavior is already provided.

Sample Activities

In our case study, we used a walkthrough technique to refine the design of two educational activities from a unit on plant science for fourth and fifth graders. In the *Extend-Sugar-Production* activity, the children would be given a simple model in which water was transported from the roots to the leaves. In the leaves, the water would trigger the creation of sugars, which would then be transported back to the roots. In this simple model, carbon dioxide and light, both of which are necessary for sugar production, would be present at the surface of the leaf, but the carbon dioxide would not be consumed when sugar is produced. Also, only sugar, and not oxygen, would be produced in the simple model. The learner's task would be to elaborate this model so that carbon dioxide would be consumed and oxygen produced when sugar is created.

This activity has three pedagogical objectives. The science content objective is for learners to see how plants create their own food, a difficult concept for elementary-age science students [19]. In Extend-Sugar-Production, students deal with this concept explicitly by viewing and modifying the rule in which the leaf creates food. The model epistemology objective is to show how simple models can be extended to show phenomena at deeper levels of detail. The software mastery objective is to develop skill in modifying rules, as a step towards being able to create one's own rules.

The initial conception of the *Build-A-Flower* activity was that children would build two model flowers using a set of flower parts provided for them. If the parts of their flowers were properly arranged, a model bee (also provided) would carry pollen from one flower to the other, and seeds would be produced.

Build-a-Flower has two pedagogical objectives. The science content objective is for students to solidify their understanding of flower anatomy, following up an activity in which they dissect real flowers and make labeled drawings of their parts. At the same time, Build-a-Flower should help learners link flower anatomy to flower function by demonstrating the phases of pollination and seed production. The software mastery objective of this activity is to help learners understand the relationship between the behavior of an agent in a model and the rules that specify its behavior.

The Walkthrough Method

The core logic of walkthrough methods is that a scenario is developed to represent what will happen when some complex system is deployed, and this scenario is then critiqued. In code walkthroughs in software development, the scenario is an imagined execution trace of a program, and the trace is examined to detect such faults as uninitialized data. In a cognitive walkthrough in user interface design (10, 20, 21), the scenario represents the actions a user must perform to carry out an example task using a particular interface design. The scenario is critiqued for poorly-motivated actions, actions inadequately cued by the interface, and the like.

The programming walkthrough [1, 2, 9] is a somewhat more complex technique in which a scenario consists of a series of steps, including hypothetical mental steps, through which the programmer would progress to accomplish some goal using a given programming environment. Key points in the critique include identifying choices not supported by adequate knowledge, and choices which require difficult problem solving.

The programming walkthrough includes the specification of *guiding knowledge* - knowledge which is needed by the user to make programming decisions, and which might be provided as part of the documentation or training for the programming environment. The inclusion of guiding knowledge makes it possible to apply this technique to situations in which specific background knowledge not cued by the system under evaluation is needed, while the cognitive walkthrough is more appropriate for highly-cued situations, such as arise in typical end-user applications.

We used the programming walkthrough as the starting point for our work because our tasks require programming-like operations that are not directly cued. For example, modifying a rule is done by dragging new elements from a palette into a rule, not by (say) choosing "modify rule" from a menu and interacting with a dialog box.

We held a series of walkthrough sessions for each of the two educational activities in the case study. We began by sketching our original conception of the activity, including the instructions to the learner and the initial software configuration. We then outlined the main steps learners would need to take to carry out the activity. We used "progressive deepening" in each series of sessions; that is, in each series of sessions we started with a high-level list of steps, which we progressively broke down into more and more detailed substeps in later sessions.

For example, an early step list for Extend-Sugar-Production was as follows:

1. Find the leaf rule [the rule that makes sugar is attached to the leaf agent]
2. Understand the leaf rule [that is, understand how the rule specifies what is produced and what is consumed]
3. Find the action(s) to be added to the rule [to consume carbon dioxide and/or produce oxygen]
4. Drag the action(s) into the rule box [this is how components are added to rules]
5. Edit the action as needed for this particular situation [a generic "consume" or "produce" action has to be adjusted to consume or produce a specific thing]

In a later session we expanded some of these steps; for example, we identified substeps of "Understand the leaf rule" and "Edit the action". We also debated whether "Understand the leaf rule" was necessary to accomplish the task.

All but one of the walkthrough sessions were done at a whiteboard without looking at the actual computer implementation. In the final session for the Extend-Sugar-Production activity, we did examine the actual computer implementation, in part to see whether this would suggest issues that we missed in our less detailed analyses earlier.

In each session, we critiqued the step lists, looking for steps that required knowledge learners would lack, or that would otherwise be difficult to carry out. We also examined each step list as a whole to judge whether it was likely to support the pedagogical objectives for the activity. When difficulties were found, we considered how to modify the task or the supporting system to deal with those difficulties, as illustrated below.

These discussions were time consuming. We spent about four hours analyzing Make-Sugar-Better and about eight hours analyzing Build-A-Flower.

We found that the basic mechanics of the programming walkthrough could be applied without change to educational activity design. For example, the development of the scenarios was no different. But significant differences did emerge in the specifics of the process. We describe and illustrate these differences in the following section, and at the same time illustrate the value of the process for our design problem.

RESULTS OF ADAPTING THE PROGRAMMING WALKTHROUGH TO EDUCATIONAL ACTIVITY DESIGN

Shape the task, not the system. When evaluating a programming environment or an end user application, the user tasks are givens. One cannot respond to a potential problem in an interface by changing what the user is trying to accomplish; rather, the system has to be adapted to support whatever the users' goals are thought to be.

In educational activity design, by contrast, one has the freedom to redefine the learner's task if that enhances the educational value of the activity. For example, for reasons described below, we changed the Build-a-Flower task from its original form, in which the learner's objective was simply to make pollination happen, to one in which learners also had to explain why one pollinator pollinated their flowers and another did not. Such changes are sensible in educational activity design, and not in interface or environment design, because the tasks are part of the design space and not simply benchmarks.

The fact that tasks change during the design processes does alter the character of the walkthrough process somewhat. Each time a change to a task is contemplated, at least some part of the walkthrough must be redone. This is not different in principle from what happens in a programming walkthrough or a cognitive walkthrough when a change in the system design is contemplated.

The progressive deepening approach we used for the walkthroughs seemed to work well. Many of the modifications we made to the activities were made on the basis of only a high-level look at the steps of the activities, so that we did not find ourselves revisiting the details of the activity over and over again as the activity changed.

Incorporate guiding knowledge into the task specification, not just into background information. As mentioned earlier, guiding knowledge in a programming walkthrough is normally general orienting information that is made available to users in the form of training or documentation. For example, the canons of object-oriented design form part of the guiding knowledge needed to effectively use an object-oriented programming language like C++ or Java. In our walkthroughs, we exposed some of this kind of general guiding knowledge - for example, the knowledge needed to discriminate the roles of conditions and actions in rules.

However, we also frequently encountered the need for guiding knowledge that was specific to a particular task, and not general to the modeling environment. For example, in Build-a-Flower, our walkthrough suggested that learners would not be sure in what order to assemble their flower parts, and that an unfortunate choice of order of assembly would make the task quite difficult. Our response was to identify guiding knowledge that we could incorporate into the description of the Build-a-Flower task that learners would be given: "It's a good idea to build your flowers by building up from the stem."

In common interface or environment design the analogous move is hardly possible. At best one can provide special support for common *classes* of tasks, as is done using "wizard" facilities. Thus one can provide advice about how to create charts, but not how to create some specific chart, since one does not know what specific chart the user wants to create. In designing an educational activity one often *does* know what the specific task will be, and one has the freedom to attach very specific guiding knowledge to it.

Design in failure. In user interface design, the aim is to maximize the likelihood that users will find an efficient way to perform the task. In pedagogical task design, it may be necessary to *minimize* this likelihood, so that learners will be forced to learn how to solve some kind of problem, which they would not encounter if the task were too easy.

One of the pedagogical goals of Build-a-Flower was for learners to examine the rules of the model, and to relate the content of the rules to the behavior of the model. One possible occasion for this experience was the need to determine what color flower petals would attract a pollinator. To create this occasion, it would be necessary to design the overall task in such a way that learners would be highly likely to choose the wrong petal color for their flowers: if they chose the correct color for their task, the pollinator would behave as desired, and there would be no need to examine the rules. The walkthrough suggested that our initial version of the task would yield a failure likelihood of only about 50%, too low to be effective.

As a remedy, we first considered modifying the task by providing a wide variety of petals that would not attract the pollinator, and only one that would. Further analysis showed that this approach had the serious difficulty that learners would have to change their incorrect petals to complete the task, an operation likely to be quite tedious and without any pedagogical value. This observation led to a further modification of the task, in which learners would be given two different pollinators and only one color petal. Only one of the pollinators would visit the flowers, since the only petals available would attract only one of the pollinators. The learner would be asked to observe that only one of the pollinators would visit their flowers, and to explain why this was. Looking at the pollinators' rules would help learners figure out the correct explanation.

For this version of the task, the likelihood of failure has been raised to 100%, in the sense that one of the pollinators will necessarily fail to function. On the other hand, there is no need for the learner to modify their flowers in order to observe successful pollination, since one of the two pollinators will function properly.

The fact that designing in failure sometimes makes sense in educational activity design, and not in ordinary systems design, is just one outcropping of a more general difference that we pointed to earlier. The critique applied to the scenario in activity design is different from that used in the programming or cognitive walkthroughs, in that considerations other than productivity must be included. The whole range of pedagogical objectives must be reflected in the critique, resulting in a considerably more complex evaluation.

Design for creative scope. In user interface design, while one may aim to support a wide variety of tasks, one usually tries to limit the options available to users in performing any one task. The idea is to reduce the need for costly and error-prone decision processes [11, 12]. In pedagogical task design one may wish to expand the options, at the cost of more decisions, as a way of engaging the creative efforts of the learner.

In our analysis of the flower-building task, it became clear that it is possible to build flowers with a small fixed number of parts; however, if this were enforced by the system, learners could create only a narrow range of flowers. By including parts that could be used multiple times, the range of possible flowers can be expanded. For example, if learners are allowed to insert one or more filament parts to support the anthers, learners can create flowers whose anthers are at different heights. Similarly, if petals can be built up from varying numbers of petal parts, many different petal sizes, shapes, and arrangements are possible.

Note that these variations do not increase the range of tasks learners can perform: they are still limited to building flowers that will or will not be pollinated successfully by the model pollinators provided, and the allowed variations have no influence on this. The only effect of the variations is to change the appearance of the flowers, while leaving their function unchanged. The variations permit the learners to approach the same task in different ways, corresponding to their differing conceptions of what a flower should look like. If we did not provide these variations, it is likely that the children would be less interested in the activity, and it would be more difficult for the children to connect their ideas of flowers with the models they create. These pedagogical benefits outweigh the cost of the decisions learners must make in creating flowers with a less constrained collection of flower parts.

This departure from normal interface design practice is just another reflection of the richer set of evaluation criteria appropriate to designing an educational activity. As with designing in failure, it arises from the replacement of simple productivity criteria by pedagogical criteria in the critiquing phase of the walkthrough.

Draw support from other activities. We noted earlier that one of the problems identified in the walkthrough for Build-a-Flower was the likelihood of problems in assembling a flower with its parts in the correct relative positions. We dealt with some of this problem by adding the suggestion to build the flower from the stem up. However, we still anticipated that students could place parts in the wrong arrangement - for example, placing an anther (a male part) directly on top of the ovary (a female part), blocking the pollen's access to the ovary.

We considered various ways in which the behavior of an incorrectly constructed flower might call attention to the problem. Our initial idea was that an incorrectly constructed flower would not get pollinated, and that this would indicate that the learner should revise the flower. This idea was discarded because it did not give the learner enough information about where the problem was. We then considered having the flower parts fall to the ground if incorrectly placed. This approach would let the learner know that something was wrong with a particular part, but would not help the learner figure out how to correct the problem.

To help the student correct the problem, we decided to link the Build-a-Flower activity explicitly to an earlier class activity: flower dissection. In order to support the computer activity, we decided to recommend to the teacher that the children create labeled drawings of flower parts as part of this activity. We then revised the instructions for Build-a-Flower to ask the children to refer to these drawings. These drawings should help resolve some of the possible positional uncertainties within the Build-a-Flower activity. There is, of course, the chance that some children will not be able to relate the parts in their flower drawings with the corresponding parts as represented in the software for Build-a-Flower but we think working on these connections has pedagogical value in itself.

Here again, we have a kind of design initiative that is not often possible in user interface design. We can do it here because we can rely on a set sequence of learner activities which we created with the teacher. Not only did we draw support from related hands-on activities but to some degree we changed the nature of these activities.

Motivate software mastery by links to content domain. One of the pedagogical objectives of Extend-Sugar-Production is to help learners understand how to modify rules. In our initial thinking about the activity, we had not identified consuming carbon dioxide and producing oxygen as the specific modifications for learners to make; rather, we had a general idea that the initial, unelaborated sugar model would be a good base for learners to work from. The specific activity involving carbon dioxide and water arose from the walkthrough analysis as we tried to envision what activity goals would induce learners to examine and modify one or more rules in the base model.

Our choice of activity was influenced by our desire not to give learners explicit instructions to examine and modify rules. Rather, we wanted to present an activity that was well-defined and well-motivated by its science content, in this case creating a more accurate model, and that would require learners to deal with the software features we wanted them to learn about. This preference derives from our previous experience with more traditional ways of introducing software concepts which did not interest many of the children and consequently were not effective in teaching them enough programming skills to create conceptually rich models.

Analogous considerations could be brought into ordinary interface design, but seldom are, except implicitly. Implicitly, it is content concerns that presumably drive most learning of applications, at least by discretionary users. But might not interfaces be explicitly designed to "show off" the content possibilities that their features support? The idea of a catalog of application examples as part of an interface [6] is one approach to this issue.

Design to avoid generating misconceptions. Some of the design choices which arose from our walkthroughs were influenced by the need to avoid presenting misleading models to the learners. Unfortunately, using simple modeling tools and methods that are accessible to children, many important physical processes cannot be represented faithfully.

The treatment of light in Extend-Sugar-Production illustrates this point. We considered asking the children to elaborate the base sugar model so as to show photons being consumed when sugar is produced, rather than just showing that light must be present. Unfortunately, making photons move on a two dimensional surface that is also populated by (for example) carbon dioxide molecules, is complex. Simple approaches result in photons being stopped by air molecules. Other approaches would result in complex rules which would be difficult for learners to understand or revise. The walkthrough allowed us to anticipate this problem and redesign the activity to avoid it.

Familiar walkthrough results

In this presentation, we have stressed ways in which the use of walkthroughs in activity design differs from their use in environment or interface design. But in fact, some of our results are just as would be expected from an ordinary interface critique. For example, when we examined the details of Extend-Sugar-Production we found that identifying the portion of a rule that consumes something is potentially quite tricky. The relevant part of the rule does not actually describe the thing being consumed but refers to it by its location relative to the agent to which the rule is attached. To find out what is going to be consumed one has to look at the condition of the rule to see what kind of thing will be in the position where the consumption will take place.

There is a further difficulty here. In the condition of a rule, the agents that must be present are represented only by their depictions - small diagrammatic pictures. This means that the learner must be able to identify these depictions, without the aid of (for example) names. This consideration led to one suggestion for the design of the Visual AgentTalk software itself which came out of our walkthroughs: that conditions be redesigned to contain both an agent's name and its depiction.

Incidentally, these detailed criticisms only emerged when we examined the actual software. We had not anticipated them in our whiteboard discussions.

DISCUSSION

We found the walkthrough process to be of great value in developing the activities in the case study. The examples we have presented are illustrative of a large number of changes we were led to make in the activities, some of them quite profound. These results have been very important for a project that needs to have educational activities developed on a tight schedule that is coordinated with children's ongoing science curriculum.

Given our schedule, it may not be practical for us to analyze every activity we plan in such detail. We did find that we learned enough from the case study that we can make some changes to other related activities without performing walkthroughs on them at the same level of detail as we did in the case study.

One of the factors that made our walkthrough process time consuming was that we were simultaneously redesigning the software and the task; thus, a large number of options were available to us at every decision point. This would not be the case if the walkthrough technique were applied to educational activities using commercially available software.

The balance of costs and benefits for the method is hard to assess very accurately. It is easy to argue that the method is cheap at the rate of a few hours per activity designed, if one imagines large numbers of children and teachers working with the resulting activities. We suspect that we, and many other designers, are guilty of under-budgeting for analysis and evaluation in our development work, and that that contributes to a feeling that the method is expensive.

Besides the time required, another reservation we have about the method is that it would not work as well for less well defined activities. The sTc project includes more open opportunities for children to create models of processes or phenomena of their own choosing, and it is clear that it would be much harder to anticipate the difficulties they might face in doing this, and to come up with ways to get around these difficulties, than it was for the better-defined activities we worked on in the case study.

Stepping back, we also found our exploration to be of considerable methodological interest. The central notion of task-centered design is revealed to be more subtle, and more flexible, than we thought. The simple notion of a task as being defined simply by a user's goals and a context, which suffices for common interface work, can be extended to include not only the user's goals but also those of other parties to the design - in our case, our various pedagogical goals.

An earlier effort to pushing task-centered design into a new domain (an unpublished student project [4] for the first author) anticipated some of our findings in another domain. They worked with an artist on the design of a robotic drawing facility, and found that there as the simple notion of task needs to be broadened. Their artist collaborator found it very uncomfortable to imagine an artistic "task" separate from the tools that support it, so in that study as in this one the tasks used in the design process were in flux well into the process.

Returning to standard interface design, it appears that some of the considerations that we have had to deal with in our pedagogical setting might usefully be imported. We can look beyond simple speed and accuracy goals to create interfaces that promote learning and creativity.

An example of the possibilities could be developed from DiGiano's work on self-disclosing systems [5]. These systems display information about how to make more sophisticated use of their facilities while the user is at work; for example, when a user performs an operation by direct manipulation the system shows how commands in a script could accomplish the same result. One can argue that a rational designer would accept some short-run usability penalty for such a facility that would be repaid in the long run by more effective advanced usage. Thus, as in our work, the design evaluation should consider not only usability characteristics of the user's tasks but also their pedagogical implications.

ACKNOWLEDGMENTS

This work was supported by a grant from the Applications of Advanced Technologies program of the National Science Foundation. We thank the other members of the sTc group, Erika Arias, Cory Buxton, Heidi Carlone, Carlos Garcia, Teresa Garcia, Linda Hagen, Page Pulver, Steve Guberman and Mary Lou Salazar, the students at University Hill Elementary School in Boulder, and Alex Repenning, the creator of Visual AgentTalk, for their assistance and contributions.

REFERENCES

1. Bell, B., Citrin, W., Lewis, C., Rieman, J., Weaver, R., Wilde, N. and Zorn, B. Using the programming walkthrough to aid in programming language design. *Software Practice and Experience 24*, 1 (1994), pp. 1-25.
2. Bell, B, Rieman, J, and Lewis, C. Usability testing of a graphical programming system: Things we missed in a programming walkthrough. In Proc. *CHI'91 Conference on Human Factors in Computing Systems* (New Orleans, April 28-May 2, 1991), ACM New York, pp. 7-12.
3. Bliss, J. From Mental Models to Modeling, in H. Mellar, J. Bliss, R. Boohan, J. Ogborn and C. Tompsett, Eds., *Learning with Artificial Worlds: Computer Based Modeling in the Curriculum*, The Falmer Press, Washington, DC, 1994.
4. Clark, C., Justus, S. and Santiago, C. Mapping the LEGO Brick to Fine Arts Applications. Course project report, Department of Computer Science, University of Colorado, 1995.
5. DiGiano, Chris, and Michael Eisenberg. Supporting the end-user programmer as a lifelong learner . Department of Computer Science Technical Report CU-CS-761-95, University of Colorado at Boulder, 1991.
6. Fischer, G). Domain-Oriented Design Environments, in L. Johnson and A. Finkelstein, Eds., *Automated Software Engineering*, Kluwer, 1994.
7. Grosslight, L., Unger, C., Jay, E., and Smith, C. Understanding Models and their Use in Science: Conceptions of Middle and High School Students and

Experts. *Journal of Research in Science Teaching 28*, 9 (1991), 799-822.

8. Jackson, S. The ScienceWare Modeler: A Learner-Centered Tool for Students Building Models. *Human Factors in Computing Systems: CHI'95 Conference Proceedings*, ACM, New York, 1995, pp. 7-8.
9. Lewis, C, Rieman, J, and Bell, B. Problem-centered design for expressiveness and facility in a graphical programming system. *Human-Computer Interaction 6*, 1991, pp. 319-355.
10. Lewis, C. and Wharton, C. (in press) Cognitive walkthroughs. In Helander, M., Landauer, T., and Prabhu, P. (Eds.) *Handbook of Human-Computer Interaction, 2d Edition*. Amsterdam:Elsevier Science.
11. Olson, J.R., and Nilsen, E. Analysis of the cognition involved in spreadsheet software interaction. *Human-Computer Interaction 3*, 1988, 309-350.
12. Olson, J.R. and Olson, G.M. The Growth of Cognitive Modeling in Human-Computer Interaction Since GOMS. *Human-Computer Interaction 5*, 1990, Lawrence Erlbaum Associates, Inc.
13. Penner, D. E., Giles, N. D., Lehrer, R. and Schauble, L. (1997). Building Functional Models: Designing an Elbow. *Journal of Research in Science Teaching 34*, 2, 125-143.
14. Rader, C., Brand, C. and Lewis, C. Degrees of Comprehension: Children's Mental Models of a Visual Programming Environment, *Human Factors in Computing Systems: CHI'97 Conference Proceedings*, ACM, New York, 1997.
15. Raghavan, K. and Glaser, R. Model-Based Analysis and Reasoning in Science: The MARS Curriculum, *Science Education 79*, 1 (1995), 37-61.
16. Repenning, A. and Ambach, J. Tactile Programming: A Unified Manipulation Paradigm Supporting Program Comprehension, Composition and Sharing. *Proceedings of the Visual Languages Conference*, Boulder, CO, 1996.
17. Repenning, A. and Ioannidou, A. Behavior Processors: Layers between End-Users and Java Virtual Machines. *Proceedings of the Visual Languages Conference*, Capri, Italy, 1997.
18. Repenning, A. and Smith, J.T. II, Perrone, C. Agentsheets Common Ground: Shared Visual AgenTalk. *Proceedings of COOP*, Juan-les-Pins, France, June 1996.
19. Smith, E.L. and Anderson, C.W. Plants as Producers: A Case Study of Elementary Science Teaching. *Journal of Research in Science Teaching 21*, 1984, pp. 685-698.
20. Wharton, C., Rieman, J., Lewis, C. and Polson, P. The cognitive walkthrough method: A practitioner's guide. In J. Nielsen and R. Mack (Eds.), *Usability Inspection Methods*. Wiley, New York, NY, 1994.
21. Wharton, C. and Lewis, C. The role of psychological theory in usability inspection methods. In J. Nielsen and R. Mack (Eds.) *Usability Inspection Methods*. Wiley, New York, NY, 1994.
22. White, B. and Frederiksen, J. (1994), Using Assessment to Foster A Classroom Research Community, *Educator 1994*, 19-26.
23. Wong, E.D. Students' Scientific Explanations and the Contexts in Which They Occur. *The Elementary School Journal 96*, 5(1996), 495-509.

The Progress Portfolio: Designing Reflective Tools for a Classroom Context

Ben Loh, Josh Radinsky, Eric Russell, Louis M. Gomez, Brian J. Reiser, Daniel C. Edelson
School of Education and Social Policy
Northwestern University
2115 N Campus Drive
Evanston, IL 60208 USA
+1 847 467 2815
{bloh, j-radinsky, eric-r, l-gomez, reiser, d-edelson}@nwu.edu

ABSTRACT
A great deal of effort has gone into developing open-ended inquiry activities for science education as well as complex computer tools for accessing scientific data to help students learn science. To be successful with these tools and activities, students need to learn a set of inquiry skills and to develop a new mode of classroom work: *reflective inquiry*. In this paper we describe the design of the Progress Portfolio, a software environment to promote reflective inquiry, and we examine the influences of the unique practices and features of classroom contexts on our design process.

Keywords
Children, collaborative learning, education applications, learner-centered design, inquiry support tools

THE NEED FOR REFLECTIVE INQUIRY
There is increasing effort in science education to engage K12 students in more active and authentic learning in which students take responsibility for conducting sustained inquiries [11]. Students are being asked to formulate researchable questions, design their own investigations, gather and interpret data, and communicate their results [7]. To this end, curriculum and technology developers have designed a variety of software tools and learning activities that immerse students in data-rich environments with complex tools to conduct authentic scientific inquiry, such as digital libraries, simulations, and data visualizers.

While these complex tools provide new learning opportunities, they also place new demands on students. Students need to learn new skills to manage complex investigations so that they can avoid the potential overload of rich collections of information. They need to coordinate data and interpretations gathered from several environments, such as images from a visualizer and images or text from information resources like the world wide web. When students use tools like the web, they often visit many sites without a clear goal or sense of how these resources are relevant to their investigations [5]. As students explore they lose track of the inquiry, failing to realize possible connections and leaving important questions unresolved. Students are often overwhelmed by the number of analyses they generate, which may be unwieldy to keep in mind or reconstruct. Yet they are unlikely to record data and results whose immediate relevance is not clear. Even when relevant results are recorded, students often do not record how they generated the analyses or what they found important about the results.

CHI 98 Los Angeles CA USA

Students must do more than pursue questions in undirected exploration. Being successful in these new learning contexts requires a new set of skills: students must develop the practices of *reflective inquiry*. They need to organize, evaluate, and monitor the progress of an investigation. They need to keep inquiry plans and candidate explanations in mind, systematically interpreting their collected data, periodically reflecting, evaluating their progress, and replanning. They must focus their attention not only on the products and results of their work, but also on their inquiry processes. These practices of reflective inquiry can help students to be more successful in their investigations.

Students need to be reflective inquirers not only in order to successfully complete an investigation, but also because they need to *learn the process* of doing inquiry itself. Students need to learn a style of work and thinking in which they make visible and tangible the reasoning behind their decisions, so that they can evaluate their process with the goal of improving it and learning from it. Students can learn to be better inquirers by reflecting on their mistakes in understanding and dead-ends in their investigative paths. In this sense, the inquiry process itself is a designed artifact, and the need for reflective inquiry is akin to the need for design rationale (cf. [10]). Like designers, students conducting classroom investigations must be able to make explicit their reasoning and tradeoffs, to justify the decisions they have made in the course of their project. Students need to be thinking and talking about the process of their investigation activities, generating a rationale for their inquiry in order to learn from their experiences.

To help students become reflective inquirers with complex tools, we are engaged in design research to develop an inquiry support software environment, and explore its application in a classroom context.

KEY CHALLENGES OF THIS WORK

The two key challenges in this design work are:

1. What kinds of software tools are needed to help students develop reflective inquiry skills?
2. What are the features of the social and activity structures of classrooms that should inform this design?

These challenges form the two foci of our design research, as described below.

Progress Portfolio: A Reflective Inquiry Support Tool

We are designing and implementing a software environment, called the *Progress Portfolio*, to promote the development of reflective inquiry skills and habits in students. We use the term *portfolio* to convey the sense in which students use our software to document their work by collecting artifacts representing their investigations. But unlike traditional educational uses of portfolios that only document final products, the Progress Portfolio is meant to document the *progress* that students are making as they work through their investigations, capturing records of both processes and products.

The Progress Portfolio works in conjunction with a wide range of "off-the-shelf" software-based *investigation environments*, such as data visualization software, simulations, and digital libraries [9]. These investigation environments provide tools for students to generate and analyze data. The Progress Portfolio augments these investigation environments by providing a workspace in which to document, manage, and communicate about the investigation — a workspace for reflection. It is intended to be used throughout the investigative process, helping learners to document their questions and understandings, their data gathering, analyses, revisions, and presentations. The essential elements of the Progress Portfolio are a set of tools that make the normally invisible aspects of inquiry — i.e. processes, understandings, and reflections — into tangible, concrete objects to be worked with, discussed, presented, and revised, allowing students to tell the story of their investigation and reflect on their inquiry process.

A Classroom-Centered Design Approach

Designing such tools for classrooms poses some unique challenges. Classrooms are environments in which learning necessitates designs that go beyond supporting existing task needs, to foster the learning of new tasks and understandings. Soloway et al [18] have proposed a Learner-Centered Design approach to developing software environments to address three special needs of users by reconceptualizing them as learners [19]: growth, or the need for change in skills and knowledge; motivation, or the need for support in maintaining focus on work; and diversity, or the need to support a wide range of abilities and styles. This shift in focus from *user* to *learner* is consonant with our design considerations for developing reflective inquiry software for classrooms. While it is useful to think of classrooms as being composed of individual user-learners, they are also complex socio-cultural contexts in which teachers and students interact in highly specialized and ever-changing roles and activities [1]. The design of tools for these contexts needs to embody the values of the community in which they are being used [2]. This understanding of context can and should shape software design [20].

Software for schools needs to be informed by a *classroom-centered design* approach [17]. We see four characteristics of inquiry-oriented classrooms that need special attention:

• Collaboration is the norm

Inquiry-oriented classrooms are collaborative spaces where students work with each other in groups to accomplish complex tasks, reflecting more authentic real world work as well as building group social skills [6; 16].

• Communication is a primary mode of learning

Activity in the classroom is heavily mediated by language. In inquiry-oriented classrooms, student-student communication is a mode of interaction that can encourage the exchange of ideas as well as peer scaffolding. Also, student-teacher communication is an important mode for assessing students' emerging understandings.

• Teachers facilitate and guide student work

Teachers participate in various ways in students' learning activities: motivating, facilitating, and guiding students in their construction of knowledge and their social interactions with other students. Teachers need to gauge student understanding and progress, and to provide direction and feedback about their work [12].

• Curricular activity structures shape tool use

The use of any software is always situated in the broader context of a task. With computer-based activities in particular, the ways in which software tools are used or not used are determined by the activity structures of the classroom, and the values assigned within these structures to different kinds of work.

DESIGN ELEMENTS FOR REFLECTIVE INQUIRY

Tools for Promoting Reflective Inquiry

Learning the reflective mode of inquiry required for open-ended investigations in complex environments means students must become effective story-tellers, or historians, of their work. They must learn to describe important features of their inquiry experiences to peers and teachers in order to explore conceptual issues and make informed decisions during their investigations. This kind of activity requires at least three key skill sets:

1. Documenting inquiry actions and understandings while working;
2. Organizing and making sense of these documented elements of inquiry;
3. Describing inquiry processes and products.

In this section we describe the role that each of these skills plays in reflective inquiry, the design features of the Progress Portfolio that support their acquisition, and the ways that these software tools are designed to work in the classroom environment.

1. Documenting inquiry actions and understandings

The processes of inquiry — e.g. decisions made during inquiry, changes in understandings, and data-gathering strategies — are normally invisible aspects of investigations. To tell the story of their investigation and reflect on their reasoning, students need something concrete and visible to refer to. Students must learn to work like scientists, computer programmers, writers, and other reflective professionals who need to document their own work and thinking [15]. This documentation includes *records of intermediate work products* and *records of the thinking* around these products.

The Progress Portfolio provides students with a data collection tool called the *Data Camera* for documenting their work products. The Data Camera "floats" on top of the screen and is always accessible while working in other applications (see Figure 1). Students document their work by using the Data Camera to capture screen images of their activity from an investigation environment. These captured images are then stored in the Progress Portfolio. In this way, students begin the process of accumulating *investigation artifacts* that provide a record of their intermediate work products to document the progress of their investigations.

Figure 1. The Data Camera being used to capture a temperature map from an earth sciences visualization environment (WorldWatcher).

In addition to collecting records of their work products as they proceed in their investigations, students also need to record a history of their thinking around these items. Once students have captured an image, they can attach a record of their thinking directly to it by using the Progress Portfolio's *note tool* to attach colored "sticky" notes to the images. These notes also have arrows to point out key features of an image (see Figure 2, where students are using notes and arrows to describe the similarities of two fingerprints), and can be labeled to serve different documentation purposes. For example, yellow notes might be labeled "Questions" and blue notes "Evidence of..." Alternatively, note labels can be used to denote authorship when working collaboratively (e.g. Javier might use purple "Javier" notes, and Tanisha blue "Tanisha" notes).

The Progress Portfolio also provides *drawing tools* that give students the ability to visually describe their thinking by drawing directly on top of images. For example, students can draw a thick red line on a map to indicate where they believe a tectonic plate boundary is located an earthquake investigation map.

With the note and drawing tools students can begin to document what they were doing and thinking about as they conducted their investigation. Combined with the raw investigation artifacts collected by the Data Camera, these captured images and annotations of reasoning provide students with a tangible representation of their inquiry process — they provide students with objects to reflect on and work with.

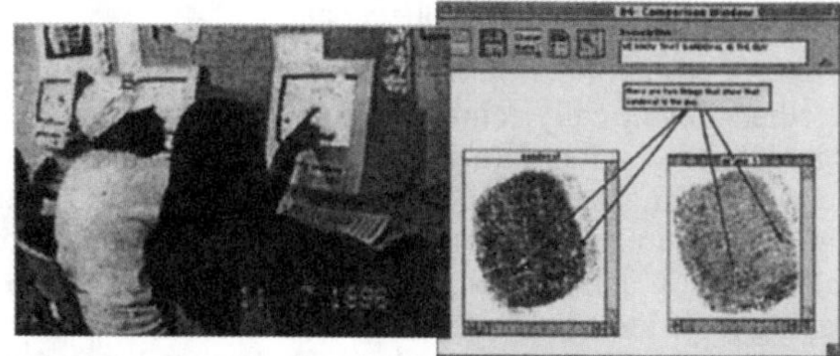

Figure 2. Students comparing and annotating fingerprint images in a "Crime Scene" investigation. The arrows are pointing to features that provide evidence that the two fingerprints belong to the same person.

2. Organizing and making sense of the elements of inquiry

In addition to documenting, reflective inquiry demands that students must also organize and make sense of their investigation artifacts. The act of organizing and reorganizing work artifacts is a step towards the goal of constructing an investigation history. This process provides important opportunities for reflection. Making decisions (e.g. how to group data items, what relation a particular artifact has to an investigation, and how to name or where to store an item) requires students to step back from their immediate work and reflect on their purpose. Negotiating these management decisions with collaborators requires additional reflection on the relative merit of a variety of ideas about managing information.

The Progress Portfolio provides three main structures for reflective management of information: *pages*, *templates*, and *clusters*.

Pages are the basic structural unit of the Progress Portfolio. A page is a container for a set of captured data images, annotations (notes and drawings) on and around these images, and text entry fields. Annotations are suited for shorter text that can be moved around on a page, while text fields provide a more permanent area for recording lengthier descriptions and other information.

Templates are predesigned page types, which structure the items arranged on a given page to help students focus on important aspects of their data collection and analysis. Various types of templates can be created by activity designers, teachers, or students to enable users to quickly construct a page with specific items on it (e.g. a "compare trials" page, such as Figure 3, designed by students to ease the task of comparing of 3 sound waves). The text entry fields on templates can be used to structure students' documentation strategies by designating names for particular fields to prompt students to record their thinking and observations (e.g., a "Next steps" field, or an "Amplitude of wave" field). These text entry fields can also be used by the teacher to prompt specific reflections and observations from students, such as "How does this relate to your research question?" or more specifically "What can you predict about this animal's offspring from its genotype?" The flexibility of the templates allows teachers and designers to tailor templates so that they target specific inquiry skills in specific investigation environments, e.g. data collecting strategies with WorldWatcher. Page templates prompt students to consistently consider elements of an investigation as they collect data.

Clusters are collections of pages that students group together thematically, chronologically, or by some other organizational scheme (e.g. students can put all "temperature data" maps into one cluster, and "elevation data" maps into another). As students capture more and more images, their collections may contain dozens of pages, making it difficult to locate things and make sense of them. Grouping pages into clusters allows students to break down the collection into more manageable subgroups. These groups are essentially collections of pages that represent significant events in their investigative process.

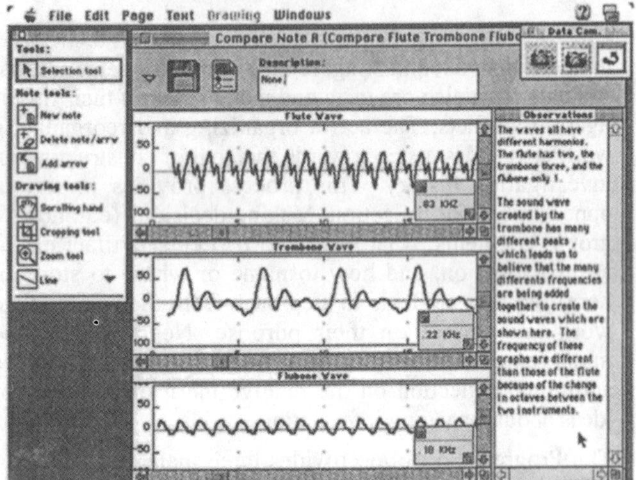

Figure 3. A page from a Progress Portfolio investigation displaying three captured data images from a visualization environment (Sound 3.0.1), annotations recording sound frequencies, and a customized "Observations" text entry field with student comments.

As students work through an investigation, pages provide the basic repository for individual investigation artifacts and documentation of reasoning. Templates provide a way for both teachers and students to structure pages and target reasoning and inquiry strategies around work with pages. Clusters allow students to organize their collections of pages to manage large collections of data, and to review and deconstruct their investigation. Together with the documentation tools of the Progress Portfolio, these organization tools provide students with tangible, manipulable artifacts to help them reflect on and compose a story of their investigation.

3. Describing inquiry processes and products

In order for students to learn reflective inquiry practices, they need to engage in discussions with the teacher and with each other about the process of inquiry. Presenting the story of one's inquiry is one way to promote this interaction. The Progress Portfolio provides a *presentation tool* that allows students to easily create a "slide-show" presentation from the pages and clusters of their collections. The presentation tool provides a simple interface to allow students to quickly create presentation slides from their collected pages, fine tune their presentation, and easily page through the slides as they present their report. The process of creating such a presentation prompts students to reflect as they revisit the history of their investigation, making decisions about which aspects of their investigation tell the best story. The process of preparing a report becomes the process of organizing a history of their investigation, promoting reflection on inquiry processes.

Together, the various tools of the Progress Portfolio help students to document and tell the story of their investigation, and reflect on their activities and thinking as they work. In this way, the Progress Portfolio not only helps students to be successful in their investigations, but also helps them learn to be reflective inquirers.

Integration of the Progress Portfolio Design with the Classroom Context

How does the design of the Progress Portfolio promote reflective inquiry in the context of classroom activities? The value of the Progress Portfolio in promoting reflective inquiry does not come from any particular tool provided by the software, but rather from the mode of student work that the suite of tools affords in the classroom context. We discuss these affordances below, in terms of the four characteristics of classroom-centered design outlined earlier: collaboration, communication, teacher facilitation, and classroom activity structures.

Supporting Collaboration in the Classroom

Reflection is not a solitary process [4; 14]. As students proceed through their inquiry investigations, their work in the Progress Portfolio promotes collaborative reflection. Constructing a representative history of their investigation can be a highly collaborative process. Students take on different roles as they collaborate around the computer, some doing the data gathering, others concentrating on documenting and presenting their results. The "off-the-shelf" investigation tools encourage students to think about and work with the low-level details of their investigation, and the Progress Portfolio tools encourage students to think about and work with more meta-level aspects of their investigation. Invisible group processes are transformed into tangible records of shared work as group members manipulate and document their thinking. The Progress Portfolio encourages a collaborative mode of work by providing tools and artifacts that can capture the collaborative process and focus the activity of group members on various key aspects of the investigation.

Supporting Communication in the Classroom

The construction of this public work record, or public knowledge base, can serve as the catalyst for conversations about reflective practice, instigating discussions of meaning, interpretation, and investigation plans with peers and teachers [13]. As students construct artifacts that represent the history of their investigation, they must negotiate an agreed-upon articulation of their story, e.g. "What should we write down for this set of data?" "How should we organize this?" "Should we present this part of our investigation?"

The tangible products of their work and thinking provide the basis for communication about the process of inquiry. While there is a language for talking about work *products* in schools (e.g. final reports, worksheets, correct and incorrect answers), students are much less accustomed to describing their ephemeral work *processes*. The Progress Portfolio provides students and teachers with artifacts that can be used as referents in classroom discourse, to help students to describe their thinking and inquiry actions clearly and to illustrate their descriptions in detail using their collected artifacts. Teachers can also use these artifacts to prompt students to share their thinking, and to target problem areas in student work — "What were you thinking here? And then what did that show you?"

Supporting Teacher Facilitation and Guidance

The Progress Portfolio is not just a tool for students: it is also a tool that addresses the needs of teachers to guide and assess student work. The teacher is responsible for setting an atmosphere of reflective inquiry in the classroom. By facilitating and guiding student activities, the teacher instills reflective practices in students. The tools of the Progress Portfolio support teachers in their task of facilitation by helping them structure students' activities in investigation environments. Organizing structures like pages, templates, and clusters help to decompose the task of information management into understandable subtasks for students, scaffolding the activities of reconsidering and sorting sets of information. Through the use of various customized templates, teachers can emphasize different project tasks and knowledge work. For example, a template might ask students to simply record data that they have generated, or to draw generalizations from data.

In classrooms, teachers also need to gauge student work. Teachers can use the results of student work with documentation tools for assessing student understanding, assessing effort, and evaluating their own teaching. The documentation tools of the Progress Portfolio provide teachers with opportunities for new forms of assessment that value the process as well as the products of an investigation. By providing images and annotations showing the interim states of students' project work, the Progress Portfolio can encourage teachers to emphasize aspects of the practice of reflective inquiry that are ordinarily difficult to make clear to students, or that might even be absent from prior classroom instruction.

Supporting Classroom Activity Structures

As new kinds of products and processes are valued in the science classroom — such as explanations of inquiry processes, including mistakes and dead-ends — the Progress Portfolio makes these products and processes tangible to students and teachers as objects of reflection. In this way the Progress Portfolio can support the instructional goals of new inquiry-based curricula and standards, affording the kinds of actions with data that students are expected to master to be effective inquirers.

The flexibility and customizability of the Progress Portfolio allows teachers to use it with different inquiry projects over the course of the school year. Ideally, inquiry investigations in classrooms should not be a one-time activity, but rather something that teachers build up to and revisit. The Progress Portfolio provides a consistent set of tools and activities for working with and talking about inquiry across these diverse inquiry projects. In this way, teachers can help students to learn the skills of reflective inquiry, and revisit these skills over time. Teachers can also integrate the use of the Progress Portfolio into the larger patterns of classroom activity throughout a school year to support student inquiry.

EARLY EXPERIENCE: EXPLORING STRUCTURE

We have had a number of different populations use the Progress Portfolio in order to test the usability of the software, ensure its appropriateness for different contexts, and identify new functionality required by these contexts. In this section we describe the evolution of the Progress Portfolio through these early experiences with middle school students, high school students, and teachers. In particular, we describe how the demands of the classroom highlighted the need to structure student work using the software, and the tradeoffs involved in designing the constaints and affordances of the tools for this purpose.

Middle School: The Need to Structure

Our first trial with an early prototype of the software involved 6 middle school students over six one-hour after-school sessions [8]. The primary goal of this trial was to see whether students could understand the functionality of the tools and use them effectively. We designed a series of activities to engage students in the process of capturing and annotating images from different sources, e.g. a data visualizer (WorldWatcher) and a web browser (Netscape).

As a result of these activities, we noticed that students needed help with the process of capturing and annotating. In the activities we set up, we wanted students to reflect as they were working with image-based data. For example, students constructed their own reviews of web sites. We wanted them to document why they thought a site was a good or bad, e.g. rating the quality of the information, the quality of the graphics, etc. But students tended to be very action-oriented, flitting from page to page and occasionally capturing information, but leaving no record of their thoughts about each page. We had to constantly remind them to write down what they found interesting and why. The tool needed to scaffold students in their capturing and annotation work.

The main way in which this early prototype Progress Portfolio structured activity was with named sticky-note types. Labeling a note as a "Question" or "Observation" note could encourage students to think about recording their questions and observations on the page, but we realized that students needed more explicit structuring, and there needed to be a more permanent repository of annotations. We also realized that students were being distracted by the need to arrange the elements on a page every time an image was captured (e.g. the captured images and notes). To address these issues, we added the functionality of templates, which structure student work via text prompts that remind them to document particular aspects of their investigation (e.g.

"Why do you think this web site is good?"), text-entry fields for students to enter more extended and permanent annotations, and a fixed page layout of the image and text fields to ease the burden of arranging the page elements.

Another realization that came out of the middle school studies was the need for a final product of the inquiry that could be created in the Progress Portfolio to help students communicate about their investigation. Having completed an investigation, students had difficulty with the process of telling a story about their work without getting bogged down in the activity of opening and closing pages and recounting every detail of their investigation. So we designed presentation tools to structure an activity where students needed to review and reflect on the details of their investigation, then construct presentation slides from their pages to communicate a coherent story about their investigation. From the insights gained with the middle school students, we redesigned the Progress Portfolio to add more structure to student activities using templates and presentation tools.

High School: Too Much Structure and the Role of Teachers in Structuring

We used this new more structured version of the Progress Portfolio with high school students in a regular classroom setting. The goal of this trial was to see if the mode of work and the kinds of interactions supported by the Progress Portfolio were amenable to an in-school activity directed by a teacher rather than researchers. Two small groups of students in high school physics classes used the Progress Portfolio over a period of 6 weeks as part of a long-term physics inquiry project. This included a literature search, a computer-based physics experiment, an oral presentation, a final written report, and interim milestones.

One of the two groups (2 seniors and 1 junior) used the Progress Portfolio in conjunction with a simulation environment, Interactive Physics, to investigate the nature of Pluto's chaotic orbit around the sun. The other group (2 seniors and 2 juniors) used the Progress Portfolio with a sound wave visualizer, Sound 3.0.1, to investigate relationships between the sound waves of notes played on two instruments, and to support the design of a novel instrument.

Both groups successfully used the Progress Portfolio to document their literature search of online resources, document their investigations in their respective investigation environments by capturing and annotating data, and create presentations describing the history of their investigation, showing artifacts they collected along the way [8]. The process of creating a presentation relating their investigation prompted the students to review the history of their investigation and reflect on how to tell the best story about their process. This process facilitated reflective conversations with the teacher about the significance and interpretations of their investigative process and findings.

We found that templates in particular were effective in structuring the documentation process and supporting reflection. The teacher-designed page templates prompted students to record information such as data sources (e.g. "sound wave generated by a flute, playing the note A, using the following fingering"), and specific measurements made in the investigation environment (e.g. "The frequency of this flute A is .83 KHZ, the wavelength is 1.2 ms, and the amplitude is 40."). Additionally, students used the templates to structure their own analytic process. The "Music Group" (using Sound 3.0.1) wanted to compare the similarities and differences of the sound waves generated by their three instruments. To that end, they designed a page template that allowed them to easily construct comparisons across the three waves (see Figure 3). The process of creating the template itself also prompted them to reflect on their data collection strategies as they negotiated within their group about how to design this page template and how to gather their data.

While templates helped structure the documentation process, the students often found them to be too restrictive. We designed the templates to "lock-down" what could and could not be on a page (e.g. number, size and position of images and text boxes). We did not want students to waste time playing with the layout of the page nor arbitrarily deleting teachers' prompts that they did not want to deal with. Instead, we wanted them to focus on the task at hand, documenting and reflecting on their work. But this design also meant that students could not easily add additional text or images to a page beyond those provided by the template, short of creating a whole new template. The students we worked with found that they needed more flexibility in changing the structure of pages on-the-fly (e.g. needing to add an extra text box to describe the physical construction of the flute) without having to change the basic design of that page template. Thus, while structuring student work with templates was helpful, having too much structure could also hinder student work. We are now engaged in the process of redesigning the tools to provide both flexibility and structure.

As we observed students interacting with the software and the teacher, it became clear that teachers structured student work much more than the software did. The mode of use of the software is greatly shaped by the teacher, and the teacher plays a crucial role in guiding students to be reflective with the tools provided. The ways in which students use the Progress Portfolio are intimately tied to the value system that the teacher establishes for the classroom.

For example, we find that students are masters of efficiency — unless there is a tangible benefit to a task, they won't do it. It needs to be made clear to the student that capturing the process of their work has a payoff, e.g. it will make it easier to create their presentation, which will in turn help their performance and grade in the class. This payoff needs to be designed into the activity structure, to instill a sense of the real value of reflection in generating worthwhile products and understandings. For instance, students can be instructed to capture data at certain set intervals when they first begin using the Progress Portfolio; this artificial constraint on their use of the tool can then be lifted as they become familiar with what kinds of captured data are more and less helpful to them and they begin to construct their own sense of what is valuable to capture.

The next logical step in our exploration of structuring was to involve teachers in design discussions to see how they would structure student work: how they could fit the Progress Portfolio into their existing classroom practices, how the software could potentially evolve their classroom practices to be more reflective, and how their insights could inform our redesign of the software.

Teachers: Structuring Progress Portfolio Activities

We conducted a teacher workshop with six elementary, middle, and high school teachers to explore how the design of curriculum activities and the Progress Portfolio software could structure student work. Groups of teachers were engaged in a day-long session of exploration and design of curricular activities for their classrooms, ranging from reworking existing curricula for use with the Progress Portfolio, to generating completely new curriculum ideas.

Teachers saw benefits and applicability of the software

All of the teachers we worked with saw clear advantages to using the software, and how it fit into or extended their curricular activities. They talked about the ability of the tool to bring attention from "lower order thinking" to "higher order thinking" as students create, manipulate, document, and reflect with the Progress Portfolio.

The teachers reported that while collaborative inquiry work gave them a sense of the general level of understanding in the class, assessing the understanding level of individuals was much more difficult because of the invisibility of individual student work. They felt that the Progress Portfolio could provide a way for individuals to leave a record of their work, even while working in groups, thus providing an assessment mechanism that can tap into individual student understanding in a manner that is otherwise difficult in project-oriented classrooms.

Teachers' approaches to using the tool for structuring

The teachers also designed activities to use the Progress Portfolio tools to structure student work. One group of teachers in particular thought about how they could teach the students to use the software and to be reflective as they worked. The teachers designed an activity that started with two visualization images already captured in the Progress Portfolio for the students, allowing students to focus on the knowledge activities around these images — i.e. comparing and contrasting, documenting observations and interpretations — to begin to learn how to use the Progress Portfolio tools. The activity would then lead students into capturing their own images and conducting their own investigations. The teachers also designed templates and pages that encouraged students to compare and contrast two different data visualizations, with prompts like "What do you see?" "How are they different?" and "Why?" These pages were designed not only to help students think about data, but also to help them learn the mode of work of the Progress Portfolio (see Figure 4). In this way, teachers could structure classroom activities that both introduce the tools and teach an appropriate mode of work.

Teachers mapping the tool to their classroom practices

The teachers also drew from their own toolkit of learning activities, suggesting ways in which the Progress Portfolio might be made to take advantage of both the reflective tools it provides and the learning activities that the teachers currently enact in their classrooms. Two teachers talked about their use of graphic organizers to help students think about the relationships between objects and ideas. Graphic organizers are essentially epistemic forms [3] such as lists, tables, trees, cycles, timelines, flowcharts, etc., that people use to organize and look for relationships in information. The clusters, or lists, provided by the Progress Portfolio offer a primitive epistemic form for organizing data. Adding more graphic organizers to the Progress Portfolio could structure activities by giving students different ways for manipulating the records that they collect, as well as to represent their understanding in alternative ways, e.g. exploring visual and spatial relationships.

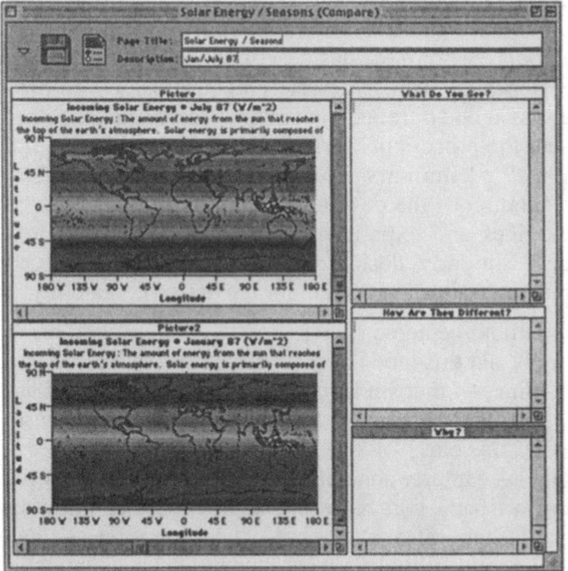

Figure 4. A page template designed by teachers to introduce students to the Progress Portfolio and structure student work using images captured from WorldWatcher.

This takes an existing classroom practice and replicates it on the computer, extending it by taking advantage of the power offered by the computer to access and manipulate large amounts of information. For example, students could build concept maps of the data they collect to represent how items are related to each other, or they could use a table to construct a series of comparisons across data points. The addition of such graphic organizers to the Progress Portfolio would offer students and teachers a new way to think about the concepts and processes of investigations.

Designing supports for the classroom context requires attention to the issue of structuring classroom activities. As discussed above, this structuring can take place in the software, in the activities set in motion by teachers, or under the direction of the teachers themselves. Finding the right level of structuring in the software remains a challenge. It requires an exploration of the tradeoffs between maintaining enough flexibility to support different modes of work, yet remaining structured enough to successfully guide students to be reflective in their work. It also requires attention to the structuring influences outside the software, in particular, the structure provided by the existing classroom practices of teachers and the affordances of the software to support these contexts.

DISCUSSION

Our approach to designing reflective supports for classroom inquiry, embodied in the Progress Portfolio, has shown promise in early implementation trials. Both students and teachers demonstrated that they were able to understand the purpose of the tools and to use them effectively. These trials have suggested a number of possible directions for us to pursue in redesigning the tools to better promote reflective inquiry in classrooms.

In addition to its utility for students and teachers, this basic toolkit for reflection also has potential beyond the classroom. The need to be reflective inquirers is not limited to just schools. Schön [14] has described reflective practices in the workplace across a variety of professions. In particular, this mode of reflection centered around artifacts that represent the process of work is widespread. For example, architects' preliminary sketches and drafts provide a documentation of the development of ideas around which both novices and experts discuss issues of designs and tradeoffs. Similarly, design rationale research is concerned with making rationale apparent for the design community.

Our classroom-centered design process is intended to bring these tools and this mode of work effectively into the world of schooling, so that students may acquire these important skills, and apply them in the classroom and elsewhere. However, the class of tools provided by the Progress Portfolio — capture, annotation and organization tools for creating artifacts that represent a process, and imbuing them with the rationale behind their creation — has potential applicability to a wide range of work contexts in which the intermediate products of work are unavailable for inspection. We believe that the design described here suggests promising directions for future work.

ACKNOWLEDGMENTS

We are grateful to our teacher-collaborators: Laura Walhoff, Jennifer Mundt, Judy Whitcomb, Marilyn Havlik, Kim Alamar, Albert Delgado, and John Leary; and to Diana Joseph, Brian K. Smith, and Iris Tabak for comments. This work is funded by DARPA/CAETI No. N66001-95-C-8630 and NSF Grant Nos. 9720377 and 9454155.

REFERENCES

1. Brown, J. S., Collins, A., & Duguid, P. (1989). Situated cognition and the culture of learning. *Educational Researcher*, *18*, 32-42.
2. Brown, J. S., & Duguid, P. (1990). Enacting Design for the Workplace. Paper presented at *Technology and the Future of Work*, Stanford University.
3. Collins, A. M., & Ferguson, W. (1993). Epistemic forms and epistemic games: Structures and strategies to guide inquiry. *Educational Psychologist*, *28*, 25-42.
4. Dunbar, K. (1995). How scientists really reason: Scientific reasoning in real-world laboratories. In R. J. Sternberg & J. E. Davidson (Eds.), *The nature of insight* (pp. 365-395). Cambridge, MA: MIT Press.
5. Gomez, L. M., Gordin, D. N., & Carlson, P. (1995). A case study of open-ended scientific inquiry in a technology supported classroom. In J. Greer (Ed.), *AI-Ed '95, Seventh World Conference on Artificial Intelligence in Education*, (pp. 17-24). Charlottesvile, VA: Association for the Advancement of Computing in Education.
6. Johnson, D. W., Johnson, R. T., Johnson-Holubec, E., & Roy, P. (1984). *Circles of learning: Cooperation in the classroom*. Alexandria, VA: Association for Supervision and Curriculum Development.
7. Linn, M. C., Songer, N. B., & Eylon, B. S. (1996). Shifts and convergences in science learning and instruction. In D. C. Berliner & R. C. Calfee (Eds.), *Handbook of Educational Psychology* (pp. 438-490). New York: Macmillan.
8. Loh, B., Radinsky, J., Reiser, B. J., Gomez, L. M., Edelson, D. C., & Russell, E. (1997). The Progress Portfolio: Promoting reflective inquiry in complex investigation environments. In R. Hall, N. Miyake, & N. Enyedy (Eds.), *Proceedings of Computer Supported Collaborative Learning '97*. Ontario, Canada:
9. McArthur, D., Lewis, M., & Bishay, M. (1990). *ESSCOTS for Learning: Transforming Commercial Software into Powerful Educational Tools* Report No. DRU-625-NSF. Santa Monica, CA: RAND Corporation.
10. Moran, T. P., & Carroll, J. M. (Eds.). (1996). *Design Rationale: Concepts, Techniques, and Use*. Mahwah, New Jersey: Lawrence Erlbaum Associates.
11. NRC (1996). *National science education standards*. Washington, DC: National Research Council.
12. Polman, J. L. (1997). *Guiding Science Expeditions: The Design of a Learning Environment for Project-Based Science*. Unpublished doctoral dissertation, Northwestern University.
13. Scardamalia, M., & Bereiter, C. (1994). Computer support for knowledge-building communities. *The Journal of the Learning Sciences*, *3*, 265-283.
14. Schön, D. (1983). *The Reflective Practictioner: How Professionals Think in Action*. New York: Basic Books.
15. Schön, D. A. (1987). *Educating the reflective practitioner*. San Francisco, CA: Jossey-Bass.
16. Slavin, R. E. (1983). *Cooperative learning*. NY: Longman.
17. Smith, B. K., & Reiser, B. J. (1998). National Geographic Unplugged: Designing Interactive Nature Films for Classrooms. In *Proceedings of CHI 98*. Los Angeles, CA: ACM Press.
18. Soloway, E., Guzdial, M., & Hay, K. E. (1994). Learner-Centered Design: The Challenge for HCI in the 21st Century. *Interactions*, *1*(2), 36-48.
19. Soloway, E., Jackson, S. L., Klein, J., Quintana, C., Reed, J., Spitulnik, J., Stratford, S. J., Studer, S., Eng, J., & Scala, N. (1996). Learning Theory in Practice: Case studies of Learner-Centered Design. In *Proceedings of CHI 96*, (pp. 189-196). Vancouver, British Columbia, Canada: Addison-Wesley.
20. Suchman, L. (1983). Office procedures as practical actions: Models of work and system design. *ACM Transactions on Office Information Systems*, *1*(4), 320-328.

CHI 98 Video Program

The CHI 98 Video Program includes the following technical videos:

ambientROOM: Integrating Ambient Media with Architectural Space
Hiroshi Ishii, Craig Wisneski, Scott Brave, Andrew Dahley, Matt Gorbet, Brygg Ullmer, Paul Yarin, *MIT Media Laboratory*

Digital Ink: A Familiar Idea with Technological Might!
Chris Kasabach, Chris Pacione, John Stivoric, Francine Gemperle, Dan Siewiorek, *Carnegie Mellon University*

BUILD-IT: A Planning Tool for Construction and Design
Mathias Rauterberg, Morten Fjeld, Helmut Krueger, Martin Bichsel, Uwe Leonhardt, Markus Meier, *Swiss Federal Institute of Technology*

The Information Periscope 'I-Steer'
Junko Misawa, Junichi Osada, *NEC Design*

Digital Fukuwari: New Game Concept Using Live Videos
Hiroshi Matoba, *NEC*

OLGA - A Multimodal Interactive Information Assistant
Olle Sundblad and Yngve Sundblad, *KTH*

WebTOC: A Tool to Visualize and Quantify Web Sites Using a Hierarchical Table of Contents Browser
David A. Nation, *University of Maryland*

Bringing Treasures to the Surface: Previews and Overviews in a Prototype for the Library of Congress National Digital Library
Catherine Plaisant, Gary Marchionini, Anita Komlodi, *University of Maryland*

Using Elastic Windows for World-Wide Web Browsing
Eser Kandogan, Ben Shneiderman, *University of Maryland*

Semantic Highlighting
Ali Hussam, Brian Ford, Jack Hyde, Ali Merayyan, Bill Plummer, *University of Missouri-Columbia*
Terry Anderson, *University of Ulster*

Developing a Community Internet
Rachel Bellamy, Eileen Genevro, Stephanie Houde, Lori Leahy, Gary Young, *Apple Computer*

Video Figures

The following papers of the CHI 98 Conference Proceedings have video figures which can be found at the end of the CHI 98 Video Program:

An Efficient Text Input Method for Pen-based Computers
Toshiyuki Masui, *Sony Computer Science Lab*

Triangles: Tangible Interface for Manipulation and Exploration of Digital Information Topography
Matt Gorbet, Maggie Orth, Hiroshi Ishii, *MIT Media Lab*

Insight Lab: An Immersive Environment Utilizing Barcodes to Link Paper, Displays and Data
Beth M. Lange, Mark A. Jones, James L. Meyers, *Anderson Consulting*

Scripting Graphical Applications by Demonstration
Brad Myers, *Carnegie Mellon University*

NaviPoint: An Input Device for Mobile Information Browsing
Kiyokuni Kawachiya, Hiroshi Ishikawa, *IBM Tokyo Research Laboratory*

PRoP: Personal Roving Presence
Eric Paulos, John Canny, *University of California, Berkeley*

Copies of the CHI 98 Video are available in VHS (PAL or NTSC) and may be ordered prepaid from:

ACM Member Services
1515 Broadway
New York, NY 10036, USA
Telephone: +1 212 626 0500
Fax: +1 212 944 1318
Email: acmorder@acm.org

NTSC Video
ACM Order Number: 608984
ISBN Number: 1-58113-031-7

PAL Video
ACM Order Number: 608983
ISBN Number: 1-58113-032-5

Visual Task Characterization for Automated Visual Discourse Synthesis

Michelle X. Zhou, Steven K. Feiner

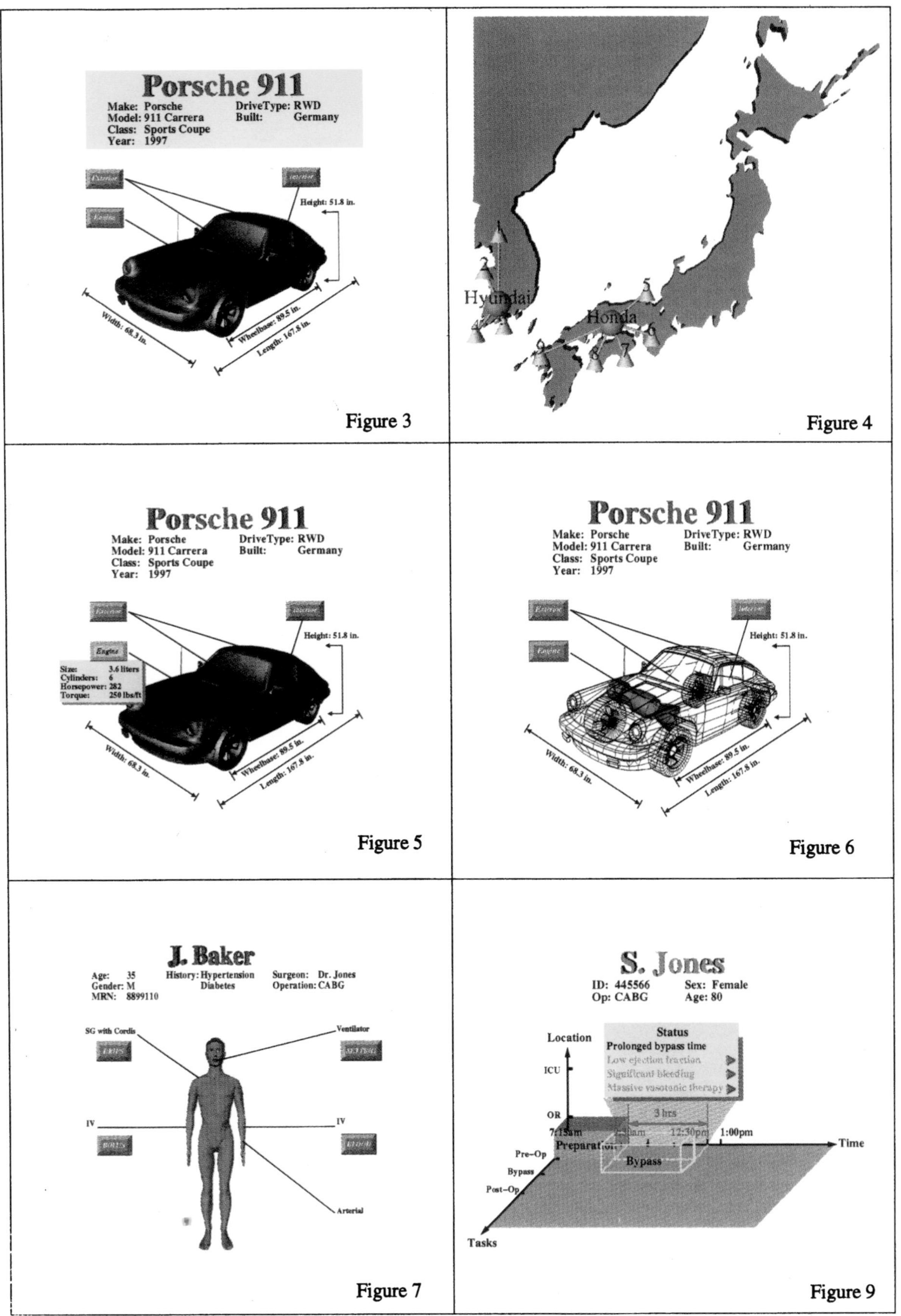

Figure 3 Figure 4 Figure 5 Figure 6 Figure 7 Figure 9

Color images for "Visual Task Characterization for Automated Visual Discourse Synthesis"

Visualizing the Evolution of Web Ecologies

Ed H. Chi, James Pitkow, Jock Mackinlay, Peter Pirolli, Rich Gossweiler, Stuart K. Card

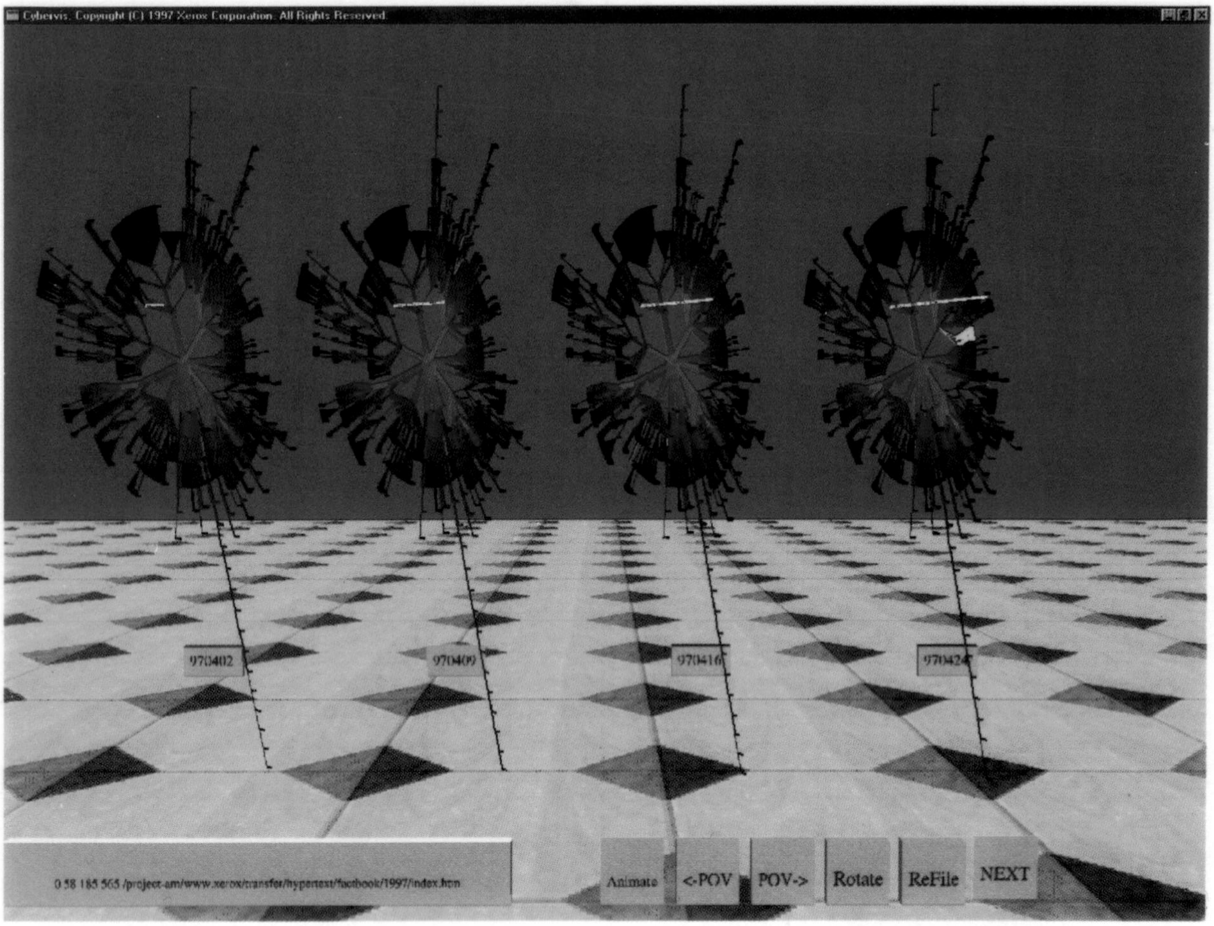

Figure 1: Time Tube shows the evolution of a time-extended document ecology (www.xerox.com during April 1997). This Time Tube is composed of four Disk Trees, each representing one week of April.

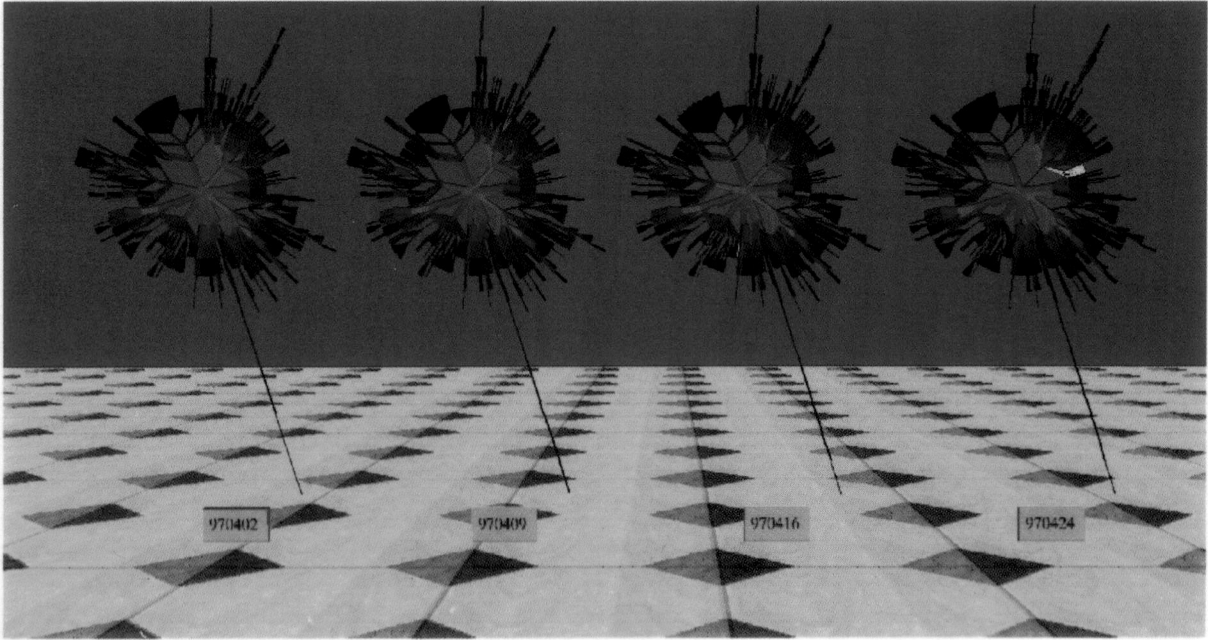

Figure 2: Each of the four **Disk Tree** shows a discrete time slice of a Web ecology (www.xerox.com , April, 1997).

Visualizing the Evolution of Web Ecologies

Ed H. Chi, James Pitkow, Jock Mackinlay, Peter Pirolli, Rich Gossweiler, Stuart K. Card

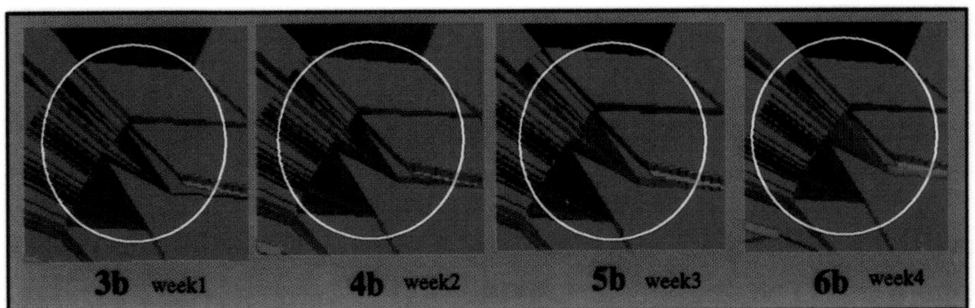

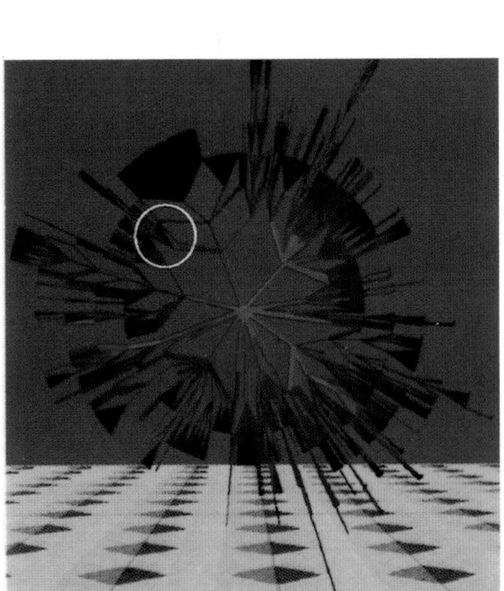

Figure 3: Week 1, April 1997

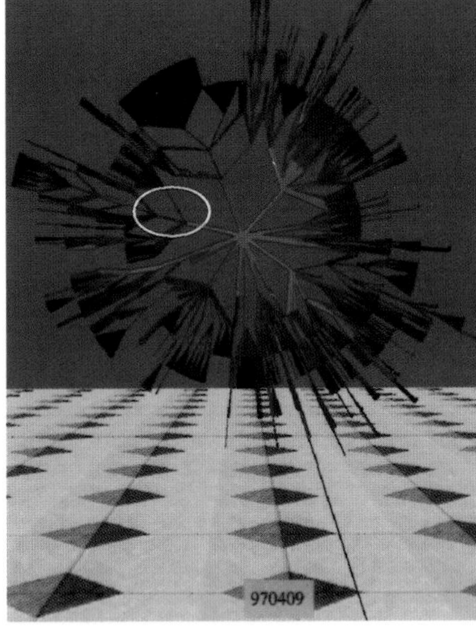

Figure 4: Week 2, April 1997

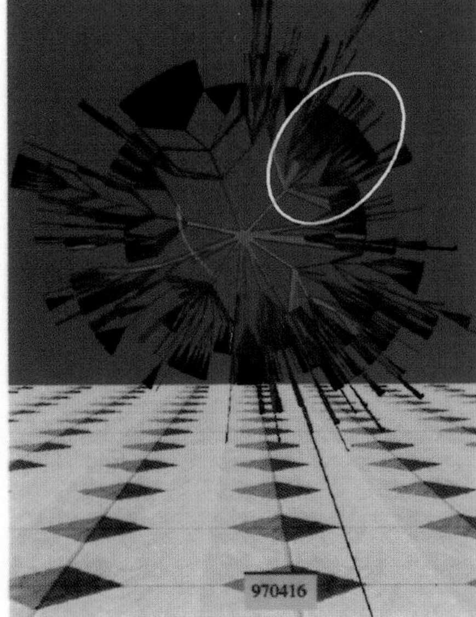

Figure 5: Week 3, April 1997

Figure 6: Week 4, April 1997

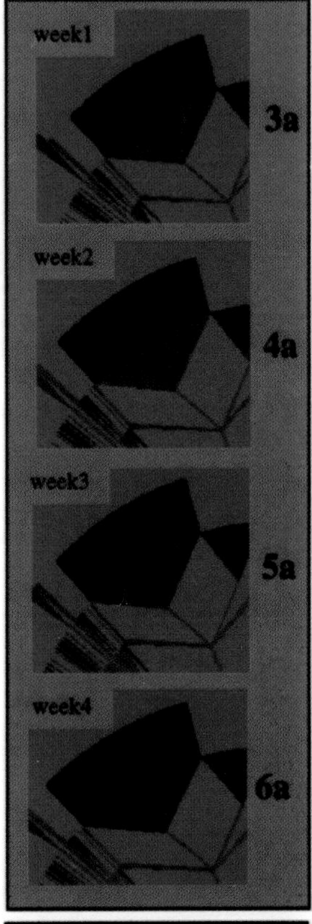

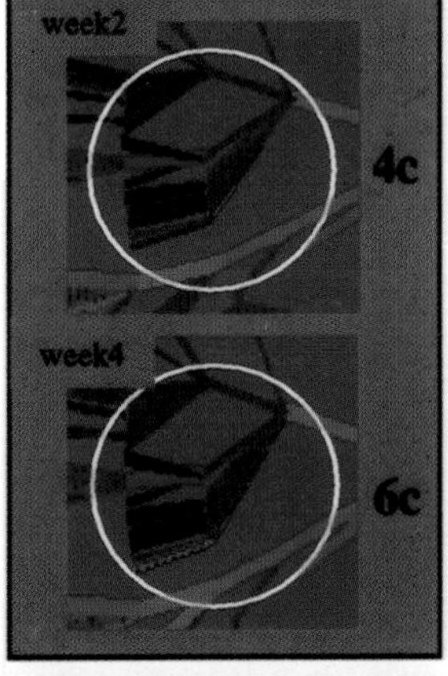

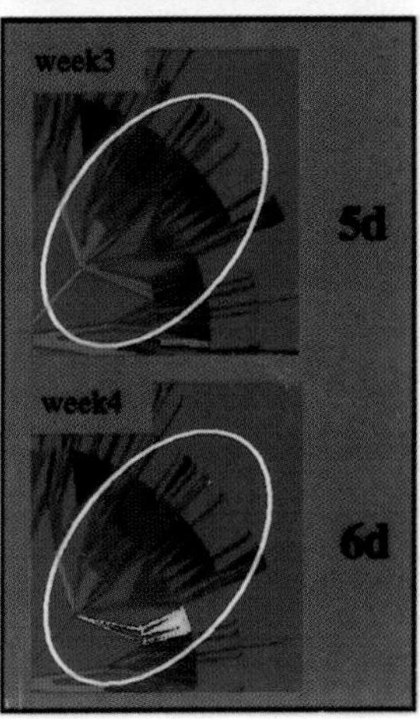

Finding and Visualizing Inter-site Clan Graphs

Loren Terveen, Will Hill

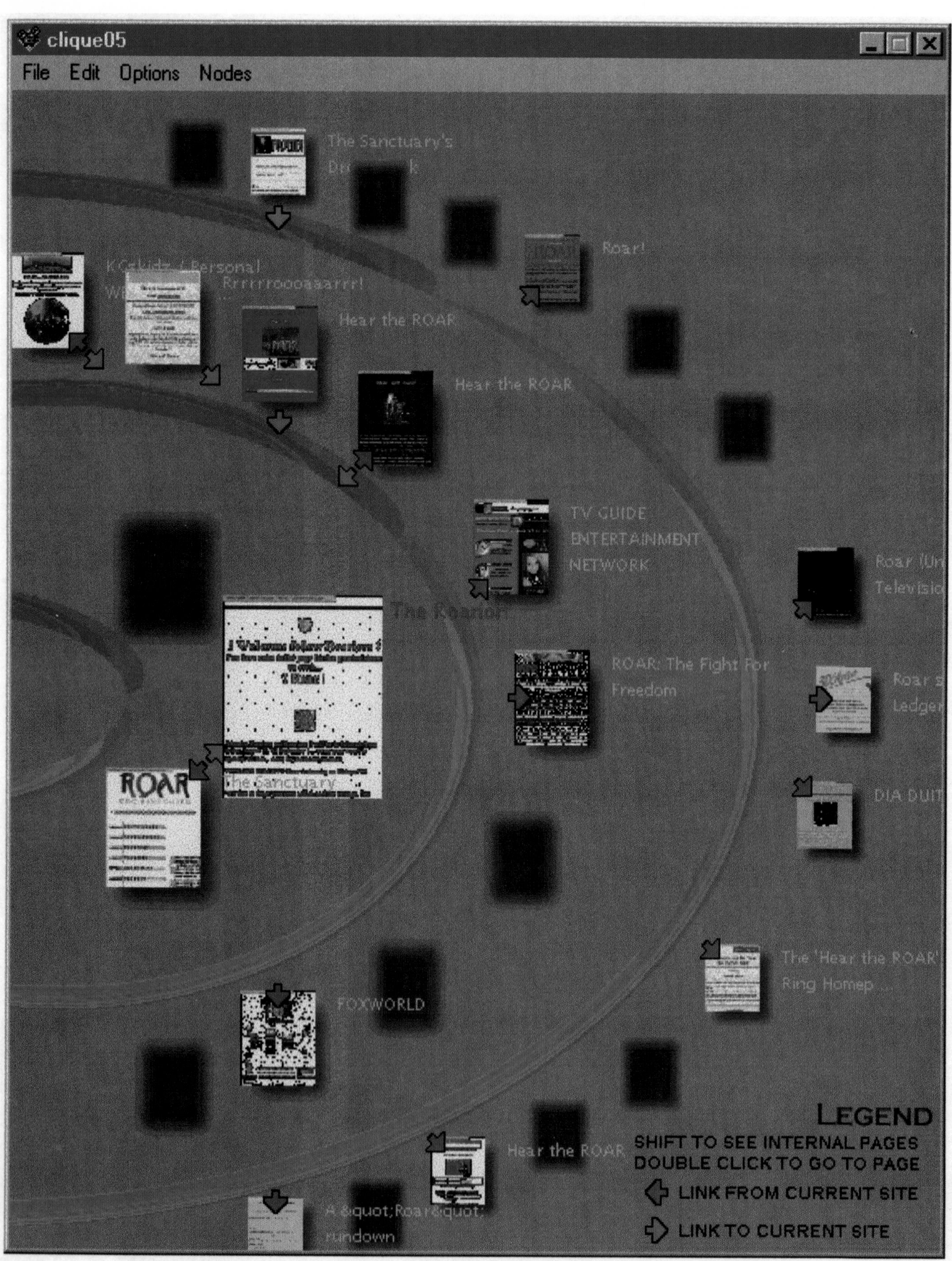